THE AFRICAN EXPERIENCE
Volume IIIA:
Bibliography

THE
AFRICAN
EXPERIENCE

Volume IIIA:
Bibliography

compiled and edited by
JOHN N. PADEN
and
EDWARD W. SOJA

Northwestern University Press
Evanston 1970

Library of Congress Catalog Card Number: 70–98466
ISBN 0–8101–0312–5
Copyright © 1970 by Northwestern University Press
All rights reserved
Manufactured in the United States of America

JOHN N. PADEN is Assistant Professor of Political
Science at Northwestern University.
EDWARD W. SOJA is Associate Professor of Geography
at Northwestern University.

Book design by Elizabeth G. Stout.
Cover design by Edward Hughes.
Photograph by Russell Kay.
Chi-Wara antelope headdress, worn by Bambara (Mali) dance society,
from the collection of Robert Plant Armstrong.

Contents

Acknowledgments

WE ARE GRATEFUL to Mrs. Diana Cohen and Mrs. Ruth Graf for administrative assistance on all aspects of this volume; to Mr. Hans Panofsky, Curator of Africana, Northwestern University Library, for his advice and cooperation; to Kevin Sherman, Richard Cunningham, Betty Goetz, and Debbie Pellow for keypunching; to Anne Potter and Pat Miller for typing; and to Donald Dillaman, Gene Larimore, and Dr. Kenneth Janda for advice and assistance on the computerization aspects of the bibliography. We would also like to thank the staff of Northwestern University Press for their support and advice on this experimental project. Finally, this volume could not have been completed without the continuing support of the Program of African Studies, Northwestern University.

Certain of the bibliographic references in this volume were contained in a volume we prepared for the U.S. Office of Education in August, 1968. As mentioned in the preface to that volume, "projects under Government sponsorship are encouraged to express freely their professional judgment in the conduct of the project. Points of view or opinions stated do not, therefore, necessarily represent official Office of Education position or policy."

Introduction

The African Experience, Volume III, is divided into two parts, the first (IIIA) consisting of selected bibliographic references to accompany the volume of *Essays* and the *Syllabus*. This will henceforth be referred to as the *Bibliography*. Volume IIIB, *Guide to Resources*, contains a set of articles dealing with various aspects of the organization and use of available published resources in African studies.

The *Bibliography* is divided into three sections. The first contains references arranged to follow the topic summaries or modules of the *Syllabus*. Section II is composed of references arranged by country for the forty-two independent states of Africa and its surrounding islands, plus Rhodesia and the remaining colonial territories. These references supply materials for a case-study approach to African studies which can either supplement or be an alternative to the modular structure of the *Syllabus*. Section III is an alphabetical index to authors whose works are cited in either of the two previous sections.

REFERENCES FOR THE *SYLLABUS* MODULES

The major purpose of the *Bibliography* is to provide an organized and annotated set of references to accompany the *Syllabus*. We have retained the 100 module categories, and full references to works cited in the *Syllabus* are found here. Although over 4,000 references are thus keyed into the *Syllabus*, we regard this as a *selected* bibliography in two senses: first, it has been drawn from a reference reservoir of well over 100,000 items; second, within each of the 100 categories, five classes of references have been indicated. These include (1) *introductory* references (those which are considered to be major and important sources for a broad understanding of the particular topic and which are fully annotated); (2) further *references* (for supplemental use by teachers or students with a special interest in the topic); (3) *general theory* references (which may not deal directly with Africa but which provide insight into the general problems or theory of a particular subject); (4) *less accessible* sources (including references in French, in journals with limited circulation, or, in a few cases, in unpublished form); and (5) *case-study* references (which may illustrate the more general points through examination of a particular case, country, or group of people). Within a category, each of these five types of entries contains references arranged alphabetically by author.

For introductory references, the annotation usually consists of a summary of the contents of the volume. In some cases, however, we have inserted our comments as to whether the reference is "dated," "controversial," "excellent," or "weak in certain areas," or whether it is written from a particular point of view (e.g., "colonial" or "nationalist"). It is important to stress that we have not selected references to represent one particular point of view or another. Thus we have included works by Kwame Nkrumah, former president of Ghana, as well as works by Sir Charles Arden-Clarke, former colonial governor of the Gold Coast (Ghana). We have not, as a rule, identified authors by race or ideology, although in some cases we mention nationality. We do not assume that these criteria are unimportant to a teacher, particularly those who may be engaged in Black Studies or who may personally wish to present a radical, moderate, or conservative point of view; we do assume that each teacher is in a position to judge the teaching-material needs of his own classroom and that he is capable of selecting from the broader range of literature to suit those needs.

References in French have been included, as French is the official language (and the language of scholarship) in more than half of the African states. While many of the writings of French-speaking Africans have been translated into English (e.g., Léopold Senghor, Mamadou Dia, Cheikh Anta Diop, Cheikh Hamidou Kane, Ferdinand Oyono), nonetheless, most of the literature, social thought, and scholarship of French-speaking Africa is available only in the French language.

Because of the rapid increase in numbers of references on all aspects of the African experience, we recognize that bibliographies tend to become outdated very quickly. The *Bibliography* includes references through 1969, and to facilitate periodic updating, we have put the entire bibliography on computer tape, as this would seem the best way to quickly generate revised editions of the bibliography (see the article in Volume IIIB, *Guide to Resources*, by Larimore and Dillaman). Those colleges and universities with computer facilities may wish to obtain a magnetic tape of the bibliography, insert their own new references directly, and then print-out "revised" bibliographies.

The Selection of Syllabus References

The *Bibliography*, like the *Syllabus*, is essentially experimental. Our experience in the selection of bibliographic references, therefore, is probably less a model than a pilot effort from which lessons may be learned. There have been six distinct stages in the generation of this bibliography.

The first stage entailed selection of the topic categories that we would use as a substantive guide to the selection of references. Two major conferences were held at Northwestern University (in 1967 and 1968), which were attended by specialists in various aspects of African studies. Together we tried to design a balanced, introductory, interdisciplinary "one-year college course" in African studies. This basic framework, or outline, provided us with the five-part structure for the *Essays, Syllabus,* and *Bibliography* volumes.

The second stage in the preparation of the *Bibliography* involved correspondence with college teachers throughout the country who had offered courses in those aspects of African studies which were relevant to our overall framework. We requested lists of books which were being used in their classrooms. We collated replies to our queries and prepared a master list of works which were being used in the classroom (making special note of those works which were most widely used.)

The third stage entailed working with the twenty-six consultants who were writing the *Essays.* We incorporated into our master list those references which were stressed in the *Essays,* as well as additional works recommended by the consultants. In some cases, the consultants provided annotations. (We have also included, at our own discretion, a somewhat disproportionate number of references by the contributors to the *Essays,* since students and teachers may wish to consult other works by these contributors.)

The fourth stage entailed supplementing the master list. We contacted major publishers in the African field and requested literature and/or review copies of their most recent books. In addition, we worked in the Northwestern University Library (Africana section), selecting references which seemed relevant. Although we were well aware of our limitations in making the selections, we felt it necessary that the master list be amplified and balanced with a supplementary list of additional sources. At this point we made our final selections, completed the annotations, and supervised the keypunching and computer print-out of the references.

The fifth stage was the circulation of our final selections. The final print-out was photographically reduced and compiled into a 200-page volume. More than 200 copies were circulated to a broad cross-section of teachers and librarians throughout the country (as well as to the consultants), and their suggestions and criticisms were solicited. Circulation of this volume was begun in September, 1968, and continued until September, 1969. Files were kept of comments and suggestions.

The sixth stage was the incorporation of newly suggested references into the master list and the selection by the co-authors of relevant books and journal articles that appeared from mid-1968 through the end of 1969.

At this point, topic categories from the *Bibliography* were again circulated to scholars in the· appropriate fields for comment. Because of the publisher's deadline for corrections (February, 1970) we were not able to distribute the final print-out to all the consultants (especially those in Africa). The co-authors gratefully acknowledge the assistance and advice of many specialists in the preparation of the bibliography but take full responsibility for the final selection of references and for the annotations.

An Evaluation of the Syllabus References

The quality of the *Syllabus* references varies in accordance with the topic under consideration. Some topics which we feel are important to the *Syllabus* have yet to be systematically studied; other topics are well researched, and such research is available in published form. We have not tried to compile a bibliography of the best works in African studies but rather of the best works within each of the categories we have set. We hope that the obvious gaps will be an incentive to future research and writing. African studies is at present undergoing dramatic changes in the quality, quantity, and priorities of research, and these changes too will have a direct effect on the nature of materials available in the Africana libraries of tomorrow.

The relationship between research priorities and Africana resources is clear: research priorities affect what research is undertaken; the research undertaken determines to a large degree the publications which result; and publications determine the types of materials which are available in libraries. Thus, for example, while studies of African resistance to colonialism are now appearing, there is still little research being done in Africa on problems of injustice or corruption within the new African regimes, or on emerging patterns of neo-colonialism. The reasons for selection of research priorities vary, but clearly the new African states are increasingly determining these priorities themselves (see Module 100 in the *Syllabus*). Such priorities are being set by politicians and civil servants as well as by African universities. Many of the research priorities being established by African social scientists in independent African universities, however, often have difficulties in financing. For example, the major barrier to an understanding of early African history, especially the possible migration of peoples from the Upper Nile Valley to West Africa, is probably lack of finances for archaeological work. Such work is long-range and expensive. It appears that major digs are frequently emergency efforts undertaken primarily in areas about to be flooded by dams (e.g., note the illuminating archaeological work associated with the construction of the Kainji dam in Nigeria, the Volta River dam in Ghana, and the Aswan dam in the U.A.R.).

There is usually a lag time of at least five years between the establishment of research priorities and the final publication of research. That is, once priorities have been established, it may take two years to complete the research, eighteen months to write it up, and another eighteen months to publish it in book form. The publications of 1970 probably reflect the priorities of 1965; and the priorities of 1970 will probably determine the publications of 1975.

Following the outline of the 100 *Syllabus* categories, perhaps the greatest lack of *published* research, at present, is in the following fields: the dynamics of ethnicity (especially in relationship to emergent class formation), patterns of multilingualism and language contact, traditional conceptual systems, early state formation, early trade and migration, African interpretations of Western contact, cultural aspects of African personality, the development of urban social networks and interurban linkages, specific mechanisms of national integration, and the impact of Africa on Afro-American identity and social change (and vice versa). Within the above categories, and even in other categories where major work has been done, there is seldom the breadth of study which allows even rudimentary comparative statements to be made about Africa. For this reason, many teachers will probably prefer to approach module topics by means of case studies.

CASE-STUDY REFERENCES

Although the *Syllabus* is in part a response to the demand for generalization about Africa as a whole, it is clear that, in a real sense, attempts at generalization are premature. In the process of generalization, however, case studies are usually the first step. Although "general" patterns are too often inferred from too few case studies, many of the best general works at present on various aspects of Africa are anthologies which may consist of a set of case studies by different authors, and a set of conclusions by the editor(s). The number of major works on the various module topics which are based on anthologies is clear from Appendix I to the *Syllabus* (key works per module) in which such volumes are marked by a double asterisk. Included among these volumes are those by Ajayi and Espie (1965), Anene and Brown (1966), Carter (1966), Cohen and Middleton (1970), Coleman and Rosberg (1964), Forde and Kaberry (1967), Fortes and Dieterlen (1965), Gibbs (1965), Hazelwood (1967), Legum (1966), I. M. Lewis (1966), Lloyd (1966), and Miner (1967). In addition to the anthologies, however, there are two major sources of case-study materials in this volume: (1) within each of the module categories there is a section of case-study references; (2) in Section II, case-study references are provided for each of the 42 independent countries plus 4 additional zones of European domination in Africa.

Selection and Use of Country Case Studies

Within each of the African states there exist patterns of culture, history, social change, nation-building, and participation in world affairs. In the future, the context for such patterns may be enlarged from the new states to the entire continent. Yet the decade of the 1970s is likely to see the idea of national sovereignty even more firmly implanted in Africa. It is primarily within national contexts that combinations of cultural traditions and language patterns are relevant, that urban migration is occurring, that economic development is progressing (or not progressing), and that political decisions are being made which affect fundamentally the lives of the citizens of that country.

Without making a fetish of the national state, or even presuming that it is more than a temporary phase in African history, it may be useful for teaching purposes to examine many of the topics contained in the *Syllabus* by looking at them within the context of country case studies. In situations where the classroom focus is on broad patterns, students may wish to immerse themselves in individual research projects which deal with particular countries of special interest. Within such country case studies it would be possible to examine, for example, the relationship of ethinic, historical, and social change patterns to contemporary literature or foreign policy.

Country case studies may be a useful means of focusing on or exploring the Study Questions which appear at the end of each part in the *Syllabus*. They may also be used in the preparation of lectures. For example, a teacher may wish to select a few countries as continuing case studies throughout the entire *Syllabus*, or he may wish to select the countries most relevant to the particular modules.

Students and teachers may choose a particular country for further study either for reasons of country interest or topic interest. With regard to country interest, many people are interested in Nigeria, Ethiopia, and Congo because of their large populations and international significance. On the other hand, it is more likely that interest in a particular country may emerge from the relevance of that country to some substantive concern on the part of the student or teacher.

Thus, if one were interested in traditional, religious-based states, the examples of Morocco, Ethiopia, and the Somali Republic would perhaps be most relevant. If the interest were in black-white confrontation, the examples of Kenya, Algeria, Rhodesia, and South Africa would be most appropriate. If the concern were for the "buffer zone" between Black Africa and white-controlled Africa, the small states of Malawi, Botswana, Swaziland, and Lesotho, along with South-West Africa and the Portuguese territories of Angola and Mozambique, would be paramount. If the interest were in internal Arab-Black African relations, one would look at the examples of Mauritania, Chad, and Sudan. If the interest were in "revolutionary" states, the examples of Ghana (under Nkrumah), Guinea, Congo-Brazzaville (under Bokassa), Mali (under Keita), or Tanzania would be most apt. If the interest were in states exhibiting the most rapid economic development, the examples of Ivory Coast and Zambia might be germane. Those with an interest in the historical relationship between Afro-Americans and West Africa might focus on Liberia and Sierra Leone (or on countries with Yoruba, Fon, and Ashanti populations). For those with an interest in literature, Senegal and Nigeria have probably produced as much modern literature as the rest of Africa combined. If the interest is in traditional art, certain parts of southern Nigeria, Cameroon, Mali, Ivory Coast, and Congo would probably be of most significance.

Although each of the African states probably illustrates some important theoretical topic, it is our experience that college teachers in the United States usually select four countries from which most examples are drawn: Nigeria, Ghana, Kenya, and Tanzania. All are English-speaking, and there is a wealth of published literature available on each. Insofar as French-speaking countries are selected for study, they tend to be Congo-Kinshasa, Senegal, Ivory Coast, or Guinea. The reasons for this pattern are not particularly obscure. Nigeria is the largest state on Africa, and nearly one in four black Africans is Nigerian. With the civil war now ended, Nigeria will probably emerge as the single most important state in Africa. It is one of the most economically advanced states in Africa (despite the apparent backwardness of the north), has a long tradition of written literature (Hausa), and the Yoruba people of western Nigeria have especially close cultural links with many of the black communities in the Americas. More recently, the civil war between Nigeria and Biafra has received extensive newspaper coverage.

The origin of American interest in Ghana probably predates that of any other African state. Ghana was the first wholly black African state to break the bonds of colonialism. Under the charismatic leadership of President Nkrumah, Ghana became a symbol to many people of the "New Africa." The heavy construction program in Ghana (whatever the difficulties in financing) was perhaps the most impressive in Africa, and the ideology of Pan-Africanism seemed to be centered in Accra. Even with the fall of Nkrumah in 1966, Ghana has remained a leader in African economic development and political sophistication.

The interest in Kenya is probably threefold. First, the violent aspects of the nationalist movement (Mau Mau) attracted the attention of the world in the 1950s. Second, close economic and educational ties were established with the United States in the 1960s (partly the result of efforts by the late Tom Mboya, who arranged for hundreds of Kenyan students to study in the United States). Third, Kenya has become a center of tourism in Africa.

Tanzania has more recently eclipsed Kenya, Nigeria, and Ghana as an experiment in African socioeconomic and political development. As a result of the personal charisma and leadership of President Nyerere, the egalitarian approach to economic development and political participation epitomized in the Arusha Declaration, and the presence of many southern African nationalist groups in exile in Dar es Salaam, Tanzania has replaced Ghana as a symbol of Pan-Africanism and creative innovation in African economic and political development.

Two of the most widely spoken languages in sub-Saharan Africa—Hausa and Swahili—are heavily represented in Ghana/Nigeria and Kenya/Tanzania, respectively. The balance between East Africa and West Africa is also attractive to many teachers.

As mentioned earlier, the most common case-study countries in French-speaking Africa are probably Congo-Kinshasa, Senegal, Ivory Coast, and Guinea. Congo, because of its size, complexity, and civil war (1960–65) has become almost a symbol of the problems of nation-building in Africa. The other three states seem to be noted, respectively, in the popular mind for a rich literary heritage, an advanced stage of economic development, and an ardent anticolonialism.

Selection and Quality of Country References

Section II of this volume contains references arranged by each of the 42 independent (i.e., U.N. members) countries in Africa, plus 4 areas of continued colonial rule. Within each country we have divided the references into twelve categories, which reflect the five parts of the *Syllabus*: society and culture, history, social change, nation-building, and participation in the modern world. We have selected twelve categories of references because within several of the five major segments there are important subdivisions which have their own literature. Also, we have added references to general materials and bibliographies. Thus, the references for each country are arranged in the following manner.

I.   *African Society and Culture*
    1. Ethnic groups and culture

II.   *Perspectives on the Past*
    2. History

III.   *Social Change*
    3. Social change—general
    4. Elite development (including writings
      by political leaders)
    5. Urbanization

IV.   *Consolidation of Nation-States*
    6. National integration
    7. Politics
    8. Economics

V.   *Africa and the Modern World*
    9. International relations
    10. Literature (and intellectual thought)

VI.   *General*
11. General materials
12. Bibliographies

For reasons to do with the computerized retrieval system, we have identified each country with a number (from 101 to 142 for independent states and 143 to 146 for colonial territories). We have subnumbered the topics within each country from 1 to 12. Thus, urbanization in Mali would be 123–05; elites in Ivory Coast would be 116–04; and international relations of Somali would be 133–09.

The primary means of selecting references for the country case-study categories has been the cross-referencing of items in the *Syllabus* reference section. Since these references were initially selected to illustrate particular topics, they may not represent the best available literature on a particular country. In order to deal with that problem, we have added several hundred references to the country case-study section which do not appear in the *Syllabus* reference section. We have not, however, tried to find references for all twelve categories within each country. A number of countries, such as Equatorial Guinea, have very few appropriate references in French or English (or, indeed, Spanish).

The balance of references within the country case-study section is more in accordance with our assessment as to which countries are most often used by teachers as case studies (i.e., Nigeria, Ghana, Kenya, Tanzania, plus Congo, Senegal, Ivory Coast, Guinea) than in accordance with any strict parity of representation.

We do recognize our relative lack of references on North Africa, and especially Egypt (United Arab Republic), which by any standards, including size, is one of the most important African states. It is our feeling, however, that references to the Middle East, including U.A.R., are readily available. For example, a project at the University of Wisconsin, under the direction of Professor Menahem Mansoor, has computerized an index to more than 35,000 documents on the Middle East.

The quality of the references in the country case studies varies considerably. The eight major case-study countries all have a wealth of good literature available, with the possible exception of Guinea. The location of major research universities at Ibadan (Nigeria), Legon (Ghana), Dakar (Senegal), Louvanium (Congo), Dar es Salaam (Tanzania), and Nairobi (Kenya) has resulted in an increasing supply of good materials. The university and IFAN center at Abidjan (Ivory Coast) is beginning to do more in the way of published research.

For other countries, there is an uneven quality to the materials available in English. Sometimes a single scholar has carried nearly the entire burden of interpreting a country or culture. For some countries, such as Gambia, there are few works, and they are of uneven quality, although some specific works on Gabon and Sierra Leone are models of excellence. Some of the smaller African states, however, have not been extensively researched: Niger Republic, Togo,

Dahomey, Swaziland, Rwanda, Burundi, Equatorial Guinea, Chad, and Central African Republic. It should be mentioned that the Pall Mall Press series of country studies in Africa is quite useful. Also, Cornell University Press is bringing out a series of country studies, edited by G. M. Carter, in monograph form.

AUTHOR INDEX

Finally, we have included an alphabetical listing by author of all the works mentioned in the *Syllabus* references and in the case-study section. This listing does not include the annotations, but it is cross-referenced to the complete listings in the first two sections.

J.N.P.
E.W.S.

I

References
for Syllabus Modules

PROLOGUE
The African Experience

1. AFRICAN SOCIETY, HISTORY, AND SOCIAL CHANGE

001

AJAYI J F ADE   ESPIE IAN   EDS
A THOUSAND YEARS OF WEST AFRICAN HISTORY-- A HANDBOOK FOR
TEACHERS AND STUDENTS.
IBADAN, IBADAN UNIVERSITY PRESS; ALSO LONDON, THOMAS NELSON
AND SONS, 1965
001,036,
> MAJOR THEMES IN WEST AFRICAN HISTORY INTERPRETED BY
> SCHOLARS CURRENTLY WORKING IN THE FIELD. LIKE ANENE
> AND BROWN. A PRODUCT OF WORKSHOP ON TEACHING AFRICAN
> HISTORY HELD AT IBADAN, 1965. EMPHASIS ON AFRICAN-
> NESS AND AVOIDANCE OF EUROPEAN ETHNOCENTRISM. NEARLY
> HALF OF CONTRIBUTORS WEST AFRICAN. COVERS PERIOD FROM
> A.D. 1000 TO THE PRESENT. FOREWARD BY K. O. DIKE.

ANENE JOSEPH C   BROWN GODFREY N   EDS
AFRICA IN THE NINETEENTH AND TWENTIETH CENTURIES-- A HAND-
BOOK FOR TEACHERS AND STUDENTS.
IBADAN, IBADAN UNIVERSITY PRESS; ALSO LONDON, THOMAS NELSON AND
SONS 1966
001,
> INCLUDES MANY PAPERS PRESENTED AT WORKSHOP ON THE
> TEACHING OF AFRICAN HISTORY HELD BY INSTITUTE OF EDU-
> CATION AND DEPARTMENT OF HISTORY, UNIVERSITY OF IBA-
> DAN, 1965. TWENTY REGIONAL PAPERS PRECEDED BY PRO-

LOGUE ON TEACHING APPROACHES AND FOLLOWED BY EPILOGUE
ON PAN-AFRICANISM AND NATIONALISM BY LEGUM. FOREWARD
BY K. O. DIKE, HISTORIAN AND FORMER VICE-CHANCELLOR,
UNIVERSITY OF IBADAN.

001
    BOHANNAN PAUL
    AFRICA AND AFRICANS
    NEW YORK, NATURAL HISTORY PRESS, 1964
    001,003,010,016,
        SUCCESSFUL ATTEMPT TO PUT AFRICAN CULTURE IN MODERN
        PERSPECTIVE. INFORMAL, PERSONAL STATEMENT BY OUT-
        STANDING ANTHROPOLOGIST, WHICH IS CHALLENGING AND
        OFTEN CONTROVERSIAL. COVERS WIDE RANGE FROM EARLY
        PEOPLING OF CONTINENT, TO NATIONALISM AND
        INDEPENDENCE. EXAMINES EARLY STATE FORMATION, THE
        SLAVE TRADE, COLONIALISM, THE ARTS, FAMILY LIFE,
        ECONOMY, RELIGION. BASIC INTRODUCTORY READING.

    DAVIDSON BASIL
    AFRICA-- HISTORY OF A CONTINENT.
    LONDON, WEIDENFELD AND NICOLSON, 1966; ALSO NEW YORK, MCMILLAN,
    1966
    001,
        TWENTY-FIVE DOLLAR VOLUME, MAGNIFICENTLY ILLUSTRATED,
        PROVIDES FINEST POPULAR YET ACCURATE INTRODUCTION TO
        AFRICAN HISTORY. COVERS EARLY DEVELOPMENT OF MAN,
        EARLY MIGRATIONS, EGYPT, ETHIOPIA AND NORTH AFRICA,
        SUDANIC STATES, PENETRATION OF ISLAM, OTHER AFRICAN
        KINGDOMS, THE SLAVE TRADE, COLONIALISM AND NATIONAL-
        ISM. PHOTOGRAPHS BY WERNER FORMAN.

    DAVIDSON BASIL
    AFRICA IN HISTORY.
    NEW YORK, MACMILLAN, 1968
    001,028,036,
        A MUCH EXPANDED AND UPDATED EDITION OF 'AFRICA--HISTORY
        OF A CONTINENT' (WITHOUT THE PHOTOGRAPHS). VERY WELL
        WRITTEN CHRONOLOGICAL SYNTHESIS FOR THE ENTIRE CONTI-
        NENT AND PARTICULARLY HELPFUL IN IDENTIFYING BROAD
        THEMES AND OUTLINES. A MUCH MORE EFFECTIVE WRITTEN
        INTRODUCTION TO AFRICAN HISTORY THAN THE 1966 VOLUME.

    GIBSON GORDON D
    A BIBLIOGRAPHY OF ANTHROPOLOGICAL BIBLIOGRAPHIES-AFRICA
    CURRENT ANTHROPOLOGY 10 1969 PP 527-566
    001,098,
        RECENT SPECIALIZED LIST OF OVER 870 BIBLIOGRAPHIC
        REFERENCES ON AFRICA DEALING PRIMARILY WITH ANTHROPO-
        LOGY AND HISTORY. AN EXCELLENT SOURCE FOR COUNTRY
        CASE STUDIES. SPECIAL SECTIONS ON GENERAL SOURCES,
        LIBRARY COLLECTIONS, PERIODICALS, ARCHEOLOGY, PREHIS-
        TORY, THE ARTS, HISTORY, LINGUISTICS, RELIGION, SOCIAL
        SCIENCES. SHOULD BE REFERRED TO FOR CASE STUDY REFER-
        ENCE.

    HERSKOVITS MELVILLE J
    THE HUMAN FACTOR IN CHANGING AFRICA.
    NEW YORK, ALFRED A KNOPF, 1962
    001,038,045,047,

MAJOR WORK OF SYNTHESIS ON THE PATTERNS AND PROBLEMS
PRIMARILY DURING THE COLONIAL PERIOD. EXCELLENT
SUMMARY CHAPTERS ON AFRICA IN THE WORLD SETTING, CUL-
TURE AREAS, AGRICULTURAL AND INDUSTRIAL GROWTH, LAW,
EDUCATION, URBANIZATION, NATIONALISM, AND MORE RECENT
PROBLEMS OF ECONOMIC AND POLITICAL CHANGE, RELIGION
AND THE ARTS, AND THE SEARCH FOR VALUES.

001

LLOYD PETER C
AFRICA IN SOCIAL CHANGE-- CHANGING TRADITIONAL SOCIETIES
IN THE MODERN WORLD.
BALTIMORE, PENGUIN, 1967
001,038,053,
COMPREHENSIVE AND PENETRATING ANALYSIS OF SOCIAL
CHANGE IN WEST AFRICA, FOCUSING PRIMARILY ON GROWTH
AND PRESENT ROLE OF EDUCATED ELITE. EXAMINES
TRADITIONAL BACKGROUND, IMPACT OF WEST, CHANGING
INSTITUTIONS (FAMILY, URBAN ASSOCIATIONS, POLITICAL
PARTIES), AND CONTEMPORARY PROBLEMS OF IDEOLOGY,
TRIBALISM, AND POLITICAL INSTABILITY. AUTHOR TAUGHT
15 YEARS IN NIGERIA, NOW TEACHES SOCIAL ANTHROPOLOGY
AT SUSSEX. BIBLIOGRAPHY AND STATISTICAL APPENDIX.

MCEWAN PETER J   ED
AFRICA FROM EARLY TIMES TO 1800.
LONDON, OXFORD UNIVERSITY PRESS, 1968
001,036,
FIRST OF THREE VOLUMES OF REPRINTS OF MAJOR ARTICLES
IN AFRICAN HISTORY. INCLUDES WORKS BY J. D. CLARK, C.
WRIGLEY, VANSINA, MAUNY, THOMAS, FAGE, URVOY, ROUCH,
HODGKIN, MURDOCK, BRIGGS, B. LEWIS, POSNANSKY, MATHEW,
BATES, SCHAPERA, BOVILL, DIKE, OLIVER, BOXER, BLAKE,
PERHAM, JONES, I. M. LEWIS, TRIMINGHAM, ADLOFF,THOMP-
SON, AJAYI, FERNANDEZ, CHRONOLOGICAL TABLE. BEST
COLLECTION OF SUPPLEMENTARY READINGS ON THIS PERIOD.

OGOT BETHWELL A   KIERAN J A
ZAMANI: A SURVEY OF EAST AFRICAN HISTORY
NAIROBI, EAST AFRICAN PUBLISHING HOUSE, 1968
ALSO AVAILABLE THROUGH NORTHWESTERN UNIVERSITY PRESS.
001,036,
MOST RECENT CONTRIBUTION BY RESEARCH SCHOLARS IN THE
FIELD SURVEYING MAJOR THEMES IN EAST AFRICAN HISTORY.
COVERS PERIOD FROM EARLY COASTAL TRADE TO CONTEMPORARY
NATIONALIST MOVEMENTS. OGOT   IS PROFESSOR OF HISTORY
AT UNIVERSITY OF EAST AFRICA, NAIROBI, AND DIRECTOR OF
THE EAST AFRICAN ACADEMY.

OLIVER ROLAND   FAGE JOHN D
A SHORT HISTORY OF AFRICA.
BALTIMORE, PENGUIN BOOKS, 1962
001,036,
LANDMARK INTRODUCTION BY EDITORS OF JOURNAL OF AFRI-
CAN HISTORY. EXCEPTIONALLY READABLE SYNTHESIS OF EXI-
STING RESEARCH AND DISCOVERIES AND PERCEPTIVE PRESEN-
TATION OF STILL EXISTING QUESTIONS AND PROBLEMS.
RANGES FROM EARLY MAN TO INDEPENDENT AFRICA. EXCELL-
ENT MAPS, EVALUATORY BIBLIOGRAPHY. NOW

SLIGHTY DATED.

001
ROTBERG ROBERT I
A POLITICAL HISTORY OF TROPICAL AFRICA.
NEW YORK, HARCOURT BRACE AND WORLD, 1965
001,036,
WELL DOCUMENTED THEMATIC HISTORY OF AFRICAN POLITICAL
DEVELOPMENT FROM ANCIENT TIMES TO EMPIRES AND CITY-
STATES (800-1500), EARLY EUROPEAN EXPANSION (1400-
1700), SAVANNA AND FOREST KINGDOMS (1500-1800), SLAVE
TRADE (1600-1800), INTERIOR DEVELOPMENTS (1800-1880),
AFRICA AND EUROPE (1788-1884), COLONIAL PARTITION
(1885-1902), CONSOLIDATION (1891-1918), ADMINISTRATION
(1919-39) AND NATIONALISM (1940-65). 48 PAGE BIBLIO-
GRAPHY.

2. AFRICAN NATION-BUILDING AND THE MODERN WORLD

002
ANDERSON CHARLES   VON DER MEHDEN FRED YOUNG CRAWFORD
ISSUES OF POLITICAL DEVELOPMENT.
ENGLEWOOD CLIFFS, N. J., PRENTICE-HALL, 1967
002,
THE THREE AUTHORS REPRESENT RESEARCH IN LATIN AMERICA,
ASIA, AND AFRICA, RESPECTIVELY, AND SYNTHESIZE GENERAL
INSIGHTS ON POLITICAL DEVELOPMENT IN NEW NATIONS.
EXCELLENT COVERAGE ON NATURE OF ETHNICITY, PLURALISM,
SOCIAL CHANGE, CULTURAL CONFLICT, AND NATION-BUILDING.
PART II DEALS WITH POLITICAL ORDER AND VIOLENCE, WITH
CASE STUDY ON CONGO. PART III DEALS WITH CONCEPTS OF
REVOLUTION, SOCIALISM, AND IDEOLOGY. AUTHORS FROM
UNIVERSITY OF WISCONSIN.

CARTER GWENDOLEN M   PADEN ANN   EDS
EXPANDING HORIZONS IN AFRICAN STUDIES.
EVANSTON, NORTHWESTERN UNIVERSITY PRESS, 1969
002,100,
TWENTIETH ANNIVERSARY CONFERENCE AT PROGRAM OF AFRICAN
STUDIES, NORTHWESTERN UNIVERSITY. SCHOLARS FROM ALL
FIELDS PARTICIPATED AND GAVE THEIR VIEWS AS TO RESEARCH
PRIORITIES IN AFRICA IN THE NEXT TWENTY YEARS.

COLEMAN JAMES S   ROSBERG CARL G   EDS
POLITICAL PARTIES AND NATIONAL INTEGRATION IN TROPICAL
AFRICA.
BERKELEY, CALIFORNIA, UNIVERSITY OF CALIFORNIA PRESS, 1964
002,061,
ADAPTS CONCEPTS OF SOCIAL SCIENCE (ESPECIALLY STRUC-
TURAL/FUNCTIONALISM) TO AFRICAN CONTEXT. EDITORS MAKE
DISTINCTIONS BETWEEN SINGLE PARTY SYSTEMS IN AFRICA--
1) PRAGMATIC-PLURALISTIC-- 2) REVOLUTIONARY-CENTRALI-
ZING. SUBSEQUENT MILITARY REGIMES NOW DATE SOME OF
THE TWELVE COUNTRY CASE STUDIES. EXCELLENT CHAPTERS
ON VOLUNTARY ASSOCIATIONS, TRADE UNIONS, TRADITIONAL

RULERS, AND STUDENTS.

002

COWAN L GRAY
THE DILEMMAS OF AFRICAN INDEPENDENCE.
NEW YORK, WALKER, 1968
002,076,

COMPLETELY REVISED EDITION OF EARLIER WORK. AUTHOR
HAS FOUR SECTIONS-- NATIONALISM AND AFTER, PROSPECT
FOR POLITICAL DEVELOPMENT, AFRICA S ECONOMIC FUTURE,
AND FOREIGN POLICIES OF THE AFRICAN STATES. AUTHOR IS
PROFESSOR OF GOVERNMENT AT COLUMBIA UNIVERSITY.
SECOND HALF OF BOOK IS REFERENCE DATA ON AFRICA COM-
PILED BY A. E. STIEFBOLD AND S. MCNAMARA, WHICH
INCLUDES MAPS, VITAL STATISTICS, AND CAPSULE DESCRIP-
TIONS OF STATE/REGIONAL ORGANIZATIONS.

DAVIDSON BASIL
WHICH WAY AFRICA-- THE SEARCH FOR A NEW SOCIETY.
HARMONSWORTH, MIDDLESEX, PENGUIN BOOKS, 1964
002,

AUTHOR PROVIDES POPULAR OVERVIEW OF CONTEMPORARY
ISSUES IN AFRICAN DEVELOPMENT, ALTHOUGH DOES NOT ANTI-
CIPATE MILITARY SOLUTIONS WHICH HAVE EMERGED SINCE
1963. DISCUSSES RELATIONSHIP OF AFRICA TO EXTERNAL
CONTEXT, IDEAS OF AFRICAN NATIONALISM, PAN-AFRICANISM,
AND AFRICAN PERSONALITY, THE PROBLEMS OF FORGING A NEW
SOCIETY (ONE-PARTY STATES, AFRICAN SOCIALISM, NEUTRAL-
ISM, NEO-COLONIALISM, NEW MODELS).

JEUNE AFRIQUE   EDS
AFRICA 1969-70:A REFERENCE VOLUME ON THE AFRICAN CONTINENT
NEW YORK, AFRICANA PUBLISHING CORPORATION, 1969
002,

ANNUAL COMPILED BY EDITORIAL BOARD OF WEEKLY FRENCH
INTERNATIONAL NEWSMAGAZINE CONTAINS ENCYCLOPEDIC
COVERAGE OF ALL AFRICAN COUNTRIES. GOOD SOURCE FOR
DETAILED STATISTICAL DATA AND BASIC FACTUAL
INFORMATION.MANY MAPS AND ILLUSTRATIONS. NOT AIMED AT
SCHOLARLY AUDIENCE. CONTAINS SHORT WHO'S WHO.

LEGUM COLIN   DRYSDALE JOHN
AFRICA CONTEMPORARY RECORD.
LONDON, AFRICA RESEARCH LIMITED, 1969
002,062,080,081,087,

BEST EXISTING GENERAL REFERENCE FOR DETAILS OF EACH
AFRICAN COUNTRY IN THE FIELDS OF FOREIGN RELATIONS,
GOVERNMENT AND ECONOMICS. IT IS WRITTEN FOR THE SPE-
CIALIST, BUT CAN BE USED BY THE TEACHER AS WELL.

MAZRUI ALI A
ON HEROES AND UHURU-WORSHIP
LONDON, LONGMANS, 1967
002,097,

ESSAYS ON INDEPENDENT AFRICA BY PROFESSOR AND HEAD OF
DEPARTMENT OF POLITICAL SCIENCE,MAKERERE UNIVERSITY
COLLEGE,UGANDA.SEPARATELY NOTED CHAPTERS GROUPED INTO
4 SECTIONS-THE TRIALS OF SELF DETERMINATION,PROBLEMS
OF UNITY,IDEOLOGY AND DEVELOPMENT,AFRICA AND WORLD
POLITICS.READABLE,WELL-WRITTEN AND VERY THOUGHT

PROVOKING.

002

MCEWAN PETER J   ED
TWENTIETH CENTURY AFRICA.
LONDON, OXFORD UNIVERSITY PRESS, 1968
002,076,
     REPRINTS OF MAJOR ARTICLES BY WELL-KNOWN SCHOLARS.
     ARRANGED REGIONALLY-- WEST AFRICA, NORTH AFRICA,
     EGYPT, ETHIOPIA, EAST AFRICA, SOUTH AFRICA, SOUTHERN
     RHODESIA, ZAMBIA AND MALAWI. CONCLUDED WITH SECTION
     ON NATIONALISM AND PAN-AFRICANISM. CHRONOLOGICAL
     TABLE. BOOK IS INTENDED FOR TEXTBOOK USE AT
     UNIVERSITY LEVEL. EXTREMELY USEFUL FOR INTRODUCTION
     TO CASE STUDIES. LAST OF THREE VOLUME SERIES ON
     AFRICAN HISTORY.

MCEWAN PETER J   SUTCLIFFE ROBERT B   EDS
MODERN AFRICA.
NEW YORK, THOMAS CROWELL, 1965
002,076,097,
     EXCELLENT SELECTION OF REPRINTS, ARRANGED THEMATICALLY
     AS AN INTRODUCTION TO AFRICAN STUDIES. TWO MAJOR SEC-
     TIONS TO THE BOOK-- THE TRADITIONAL BACKGROUND, AND
     THE CONTEMPORARY SCENE. FORMER DEALS WITH TRADITIONAL
     SOCIAL STRUCTURE, VALUE SYSTEMS, TRIBAL GOVERNMENT,
     AND TRADITIONAL ECONOMIC SYSTEMS. SECOND PART DEALS
     WITH RISE OF NATIONS, POLITICS, ECONOMIC AND SOCIAL
     CHANGE, AND ROLE OF AFRICA IN WORLD AFFAIRS.

MORRISON DONALD G   ET AL
BLACK AFRICA- A HANDBOOK FOR COMPARATIVE ANALYSIS
NEW YORK, FREE PRESS, 1970
002,058,064,098,
     CO-EDITED BY R.C.MITCHELL,H.M.STEVENSON AND J.N.PADEN.
     COMPREHENSIVE DATA SOURCE BOOK FOR 32 SUB-SAHARAN
     STATES.PART 1-DETAILED DATA FOR OVER 200 VARIABLES
     INCLUDING ANALYSIS OF BASIC PATTERNS.PART 2- COUNTRY
     PROFILES OF BASIC INFORMATION ON URBAN,ECONOMIC AND
     POLITICAL PATTERNS.PART 3-ESSAYS ON DATA RELIABILITY,
     BASES OF ETHNIC CLASSIFICATION,PATTERNS AND PROCESSES
     OF NATURAL INTEGRATION.

ROBINSON ARMSTEAD   FOSTER CRAIG   OGILVIE DONALD
BLACK STUDIES IN THE UNIVERSITY--A SYMPOSIUM.
NEW HAVEN, YALE UNIVERSITY PRESS, 1969
002,094,095,
     VOLUME PRESENTS A VARIETY OF VIEWPOINTS, YET ALL BY
     PERSONS WITH EXPERIENCE IN BLACK STUDIES. RECORD OF
     SYMPOSIUM BY BLACK STUDENT ALLIANCE AT YALE IN MAY
     1968 CONCERNED WITH THE INADEQUACIES WHICH HAVE TYPI-
     FIED THE INTELLECTUAL TREATMENT OF THE AFRO-AMERICAN
     EXPERIENCE.

WALLERSTEIN I M
AFRICA-- THE POLITICS OF UNITY.
NEW YORK, RANDOM HOUSE, 1967
002,079,080,097,
     SEQUEL TO AUTHOR'S PREVIOUS BOOK ON POLITICS OF
     INDEPENDENCE. IS INTERPRETATION OF MAJOR POLITICAL

DEVELOPMENTS IN AFRICA FROM 1957 TO 1965, SEEN IN PER-
SPECTIVE OF SOCIAL CHANGE. DISTINGUISHES BETWEEN
MOVEMENTS AND ALLIANCES IN THE EFFORTS OF AFRICAN
STATES TO ACHIEVE WIDER UNITY. INTERPRETS FIRST AND
SECOND CONGO CRISES, ORGANIZATION OF AFRICAN UNITY,
RHODESIA AND SOUTH AFRICAN PROBLEMS, AND REGIONAL
UNITY PATTERNS.

PART I
African Society
and Culture

3. THE AFRICAN ETHNIC MOSAIC

003
      BOHANNAN PAUL
      AFRICA AND AFRICANS
      NEW YORK, NATURAL HISTORY PRESS, 1964
      001,003,010,016,
            SUCCESSFUL ATTEMPT TO PUT AFRICAN CULTURE IN MODERN
            PERSPECTIVE. INFORMAL, PERSONAL STATEMENT BY OUT-
            STANDING ANTHROPOLOGIST, WHICH IS CHALLENGING AND
            OFTEN CONTROVERSIAL. COVERS WIDE RANGE FROM EARLY
            PEOPLING OF CONTINENT, TO NATIONALISM AND
            INDEPENDENCE. EXAMINES EARLY STATE FORMATION, THE
            SLAVE TRADE, COLONIALISM, THE ARTS, FAMILY LIFE,
            ECONOMY, RELIGION. BASIC INTRODUCTORY READING.

      GREENBERG JOSEPH H
      STUDIES IN AFRICAN LINGUISTIC CLASSIFICATION.
      NEW YORK, VIKING PRESS, COMPASS BOOKS, 1955
      003,011,
            LANDMARK IN AFRICAN LINGUISTICS. SYNTHESIZES PRE-
            VIOUS WORK INTO A NEW CLASSIFICATION OF AFRICAN LAN-
            GUAGES. FIRST TO USE PURELY LINGUISTIC CRITERIA VS.
            RACIAL STEREOTYPES, ETC. DESTROYS HAMITIC MYTH,
            DEVELOPS AFRO-ASIATIC FAMILY AND LAYS BASIS FOR MANY
            PREVALENT EXPLANATIONS OF BANTU MIGRATIONS. MAP
            BECOMES STANDARD REFERENCE UNTIL GREENBERG'S NEW

CLASSIFICATION IN 1963.

003
GREENBERG JOSEPH H
THE LANGUAGES OF AFRICA.
BLOOMINGTON, INDIANA UNIVERSITY PRESS, 1963
003,011,
RECLASSIFICATION OF AFRICAN LANGUAGES DONE IN 1963.
GREATLY SIMPLIFIES 1955 CLASSIFICATION. MUCH MORE
CONTROVERSIAL. STILL BEING DEBATED BY LINGUISTS.
MAJOR LANGUAGE FAMILIES NOW INCLUDE CONGO-KORDOFANIAN
NILO-SAHARAN, AFRO-ASIATIC AND KHOISAN.

HERSKOVITS MELVILLE J
THE BASELINE OF CHANGE.
IN M J HERSKOVITS, THE HUMAN FACTOR IN CHANGING AFRICA, KNOPF,
NEW YORK, 1962, CHAP 3, 4
003,
CONTAINS MOST RECENT ANALYSIS OF AFRICAN CULTURE
AREAS BY LATE AMERICAN ANTHROPOLOGIST WHO INTRODUCED
THE CONCEPT OF CULTURE AREAS TO AFRICAN STUDIES. DI-
VIDED INTO TWO SECTION-- FOOD GATHERING AND HERDING
PEOPLES, AND AGRICULTURAL PEOPLES. MAP INCLUDED.

MURDOCK GEORGE P
AFRICA--ITS PEOPLES AND THEIR CULTURE HISTORY.
NEW YORK, MCGRAW HILL, 1959
003,
HIGHLY CONTROVERSIAL, MAJOR WORK OF AFRICAN ETHNO-
GRAPHIC SYNTHESIS. DETAILED DESCRIPTION OF CULTURAL
CHARACTERISTICS OF SEVERAL HUNDRED ETHNIC GROUPS.
CONTAINS MANY HYPOTHESES WHICH HAVE STIMULATED NEW RE-
SEARCH. EXCELLENT THEMATIC INTRODUCTION ON GEOGRAPHY,
RACE, LANGUAGE, ECONOMY, SOCIETY, GOVERNMENT, HISTORY.
SUPPLEMENTARY TRIBAL MAP IS STILL STANDARD REFERENCE,
DESPITE SOME INCONSISTENCIES IN GROUPING PEOPLES AND
BOUNDARIES.

OTTENBERG SIMON   OTTENBERG PHOEBE
CULTURES AND SOCIETIES OF AFRICA.
NEW YORK, RANDOM HOUSE, 1960
003,012,016,
EXCELLENT COLLECTION OF CASE STUDIES, ETHNIC AND THE-
MATIC. SECTIONS COVER PEOPLE AND ENVIRONMENT (BUSH-
MEN, FULANI, BEMBA), SOCIAL GROUPINGS (UNILINEAL DES-
CENT GROUPS, SECRET SOCIETIES, AGE SETS, URBANIZATION,
MARRIAGE), AUTHORITY AND GOVERNMENT (TUTSI, TIV, KON-
KOMBA, ASHANTI), VALUE, RELIGION AND AESTHETICS (ROLE
OF CATTLE, WITCHCRAFT, INITIATION, FOLKLORE, ART),
CULTURE CONTACT AND CHANGE (ISLAM, CHRISTIANITY),
URBANISM). INTRODUCTION SUPERB.

VANSINA JAN
INTRODUCTION A L'ETHNOGRAPHE DU CONGO.
BRUXELLES, EDITIONS UNIVERSITAIRES DU CONGO, NO. 1, 1966
003,108-01,
ONE OF THE BEST ILLUSTRATIONS OF CLASSIFICATIONS
OF AFRICAN ETHNIC GROUPS WITHIN A COUNTRY.
AUTHOR USES MULTIPLE CRITEREA.

BOHANNAN PAUL
THE PEOPLES OF AFRICA CHP 5.
IN AFRICA AND AFRICANS, NEW YORK, THE NATURAL HISTORY PRESS,
1964
003,
        REFERENCE

003
DRAKE ST CLAIR
THE RESPONSIBILITY OF MEN OF CULTURE FOR DESTROYING THE
HAMITIC MYTH.
PRESENCE AFRICAINE 1 1959 PP 228-243
003,
        REFERENCE

FAGE JOHN D
REVIEW OF MURDOCK-- AFRICA, ITS PEOPLE AND THEIR CULTURE
HISTORY.
THE JOURNAL OF AFRICAN HISTORY VOL 2 NO 2 1961 PP 299-309
003,
        REFERENCE

GREENBERG JOSEPH H
LANGUAGES AND HISTORY IN AFRICA.
PRESENCE AFRICAINE 17 JANUARY 1963 PP 114-122
003,
        REFERENCE

GREENBERG JOSEPH H
AFRICA AS A LINGUISTIC AREA, CHAPTER 2.
IN WILLIAM BASCOM AND MELVILLE HERSKOVITS, CONTINUTY AND
CHANGE IN AFRICAN CULTURES, CHICAGO, UNIVERSITY OF CHICAGO
PRESS, 1962, PP 15-27
003,011,
        REFERENCE

GULLIVER P H
REVIEW OF MURDOCK-- AFRICA, ITS PEOPLES AND THEIR CULTURE
HISTORY.
AMERICAN ANTHROPOLOGIST VOL 62 1960 PP 900-903
003,
        REFERENCE

GUTHRIE MALCOLM
REVIEW OF GREENBERG'S LANGUAGES OF AFRICA.
JOURNAL OF AFRICAN HISTORY 5 1 1964
003,
        REFERENCE

HERSKOVITS MELVILLE J
PEOPLES AND CULTURES OF SUB-SAHARAN AFRICA.
IN PETER J MCEWAN AND ROBERT B SUTCLIFFE (EDS), MODERN AFRICA
NEW YORK, THOMAS CROWELL, 1965, PP 15-25
003,
        REFERENCE

MURDOCK GEORGE P
ETHNOGRAPHIC ATLAS.
PITTSBURGH, UNIVERSITY OF PITTSBURGH PRESS, 1967
003,

REFERENCE

003
OTTENBERG SIMON   OTTENBERG PHEOBE
SOCIAL GROUPINGS.
IN PETER J MCEWAN AND ROBERT B SUTCLIFFE (EDS) MODERN AFRICA
NEW YORK, THOMAS CROWELL, 1965, PP 26-44
003,
      REFERENCE

SANDERS EDITH R
THE HAMITIC HYPOTHESIS ITS ORIGINS AND FUNCTIONS IN TIME
PERSPECTIVE.
IN JOURNAL OF AFRICAN HISTORY VOL 10 1969 P 521
003,
      REFERENCE

BAUMANN H   WESTERMANN D
LES PEUPLES LES CIVILISATIONS DE L'AFRIQUE NOIRE (THE
PEOPLES AND THE CIVILIZATIONS OF BLACK AFRICA).
PARIS, PAYOT, 1962
003,
      LESS ACCESSIBLE

MFOULOU JEAN
SCIENCE ET PSEUDO-SCIENCE DES LANGUES AFRICAINES (SCIENCE
AND PSEUDO-SCIENCE OF AFRICAN LANGUAGES).
PRESENCE AFRICAINE, NO. 70, 2ND QUARTER, 1969, PP. 147-161
011,003,
      LESS ACCESSIBLE

MEAD MARGARET   ED
SCIENCE AND THE CONCEPT OF RACE.
NEW YORK (COLUMBIA), MCGILL-QUEEN'S,1969
003,
      GENERAL THEORY

HERSKOVITS MELVILLE J
THE CULTURE AREAS OF AFRICA.
AFRICA 3 JAN 1930 PP 59-77
003,
      REFERENCE

4. THE NATURE OF ETHNICITY

004
COHEN RONALD   MIDDLETON JOHN   EDS
FROM TRIBE TO NATION IN AFRICA.
SAN FRANCISCO CHANDLER 1970
004,006,057,
      ORIGINAL CASE STUDIES BY WELL-KNOWN ANTHROPOLOGISTS ON
      THE PROCESSES BY WHICH ETHNIC SOCIETIES INCORPORATE
      NEIGHBORING GROUPS INTO A LARGER, AND SOMETIMES NEW,
      ETHNIC FRAMEWORK. THEORETICAL INTRODUCTION SYNTHE-
      SIZES THESE STUDIES INTO FUNDAMENTAL PROPOSITIONS

ABOUT THE NATURE OF ETHNICITY UNDER MODERN CIRCUM-
STANCES.

004

FRIED MORTON H
THE EVOLUTION OF POLITICAL SOCIETY
NEW YORK, RANDOM HOUSE, 1967
004, 009,
    PROVOCATIVE ANALYSIS BY PROMINENT EVOLUTIONARY
    ANTHROPOLOGIST. POLITICAL EVOLUTION VIEWED WITH
    RESPECT TO SEQUENTIAL DEVELOPMENT OF SHARING, RANKING,
    AND STRATIFICATION. CONTAINS EXCELLENT DISCUSSION
    ON THE CONCEPT OF TRIBE AND CHAPTERS ON HUNTING BANDS
    AND EARLY STATE FORMATION. GLOBAL IN SCOPE BUT WITH
    MANY AFRICAN EXAMPLES.

GIBBS JAMES JR   ED
PEOPLES OF AFRICA.
NEW YORK, HOLT, RINEHART AND WINSTON, 1965
004,016,
    CULTURE PROFILES OF 15 SOCIETIES IN SUB-SAHARAN AFRICA
    CHOSEN TO REPRESENT A CROSS SECTION OF ECOLOGY,
    CULTURE AREAS, SUBSISTENCE ECONOMIES, AND LANGUAGES.
    GROUPS INCLUDE IBO, HAUSA, YORUBA, FULANI, TIV, GANDA,
    BUSHMEN, PYGMIES, SOMALI, JIE, SWAZI, SUKU, RWANDA,
    TIRIKI, KPELLE. EACH DONE BY EXPERIENCED ANTHROPOLO-
    GIST. AUTHOR PROFILES AND BRIEF PRONUNCIATION GUIDE
    FOR AFRICAN WORDS.

MERCIER PAUL
ON THE MEANING OF TRIBALISM IN BLACK AFRICA.
IN PIERRE VAN DEN BERGHE (ED), AFRICA-- SOCIAL PROBLEMS OF
CHANGE AND CONFLICT, SAN FRANCISCO, CHANDLER, 1965, PP 483-501
004,
    AUTHOR IS A LEADING FRENCH SOCIOLOGIST WITH LONG EX-
    PERIENCE IN AFRICA. OUTSTANDING EARLY ATTEMPT TO DE-
    FINE CONCEPT OF ETHNICITY IN TERMS OF SELF-ASCRIPTIVE
    GROUP DEFINITIONS. GIVES EXAMPLES OF ETHNIC BOUNDARY
    REDEFINITIONS IN AFRICAN CONTEXT.

MURDOCK GEORGE P
SOCIAL STRUCTURE.
NEW YORK,   MACMILLAN CO, 1956
004,008,
    STANDARD REFERENCE WORK ON KINSHIP TERMINOLOGY AND
    CONCEPTS. INCLUDES SECTIONS ON THE NUCLEAR FAMILY,
    CONSANGUINAL KIN GROUPS, THE CLAN, THE COMMUNITY, EVO-
    LUTION OF SOCIAL ORGANIZATION AND GENERAL THEORETICAL
    APPROACHES TO THE STUDY OF KINSHIP. CONTAINS DEFINI-
    TIONS OF NEARLY ALL MAJOR TERMS REFERRING TO DESCENT,
    GENEALOGY AND MARRIAGE.

SHIBUTANI TAMOTSU   KWAN KIAN
ETHNIC STRATIFICATION-- A COMPARATIVE APPROACH.
NEW YORK, MACMILLAN COMPANY, 1965
004,057,
    AUTHORS DEAL WITH MAJOR ISSUES OF ETHNIC IDENTITY AND
    CHANGING IDENTITY IN COMPARATIVE FRAMEWORK. SOME CASE
    STUDY MATERIAL ON AFRICA. CHAPTERS INCLUDE FOCUS ON
    ETHNIC DIFFERENCES, ETHNIC SYMBOLS, ASSIMILATION, AND

ETHNIC INTEGRATION.

004

WALLERSTEIN I M
ETHNICITY AND NATIONAL INTEGRATION IN WEST AFRICA
CAHIERS D'ETUDES AFRICAINES 3 OCTOBER 1960 PP 129-139
004,007,057,
       BASIC INTRODUCTION TO CONCEPT OF ETHNICITY AND TO
       ENDURING ROLE OF ETHNICITY IN URBAN ENVIRONMENTS.
       ACCORDING TO AUTHOR,MEMBERSHIP IN AN ETHNIC GROUP IS A
       MATTER OF SOCIAL DEFINITION,THE INTERPLAY OF THE SELF
       DEFINITION OF MEMBERS AND THE DEFINITION OF OTHER
       GROUPS.

MAZRUI ALI A
POLITICAL SCIENCE AND THE DECLINE OF AFRICAN NATIONALISM.
IN CARTER, GWENDOLEN M. AND ANN PADEN (EDS) EXPANDING
HORIZONS IN AFRICAN STUDIES, EVANSTON, NORTHWESTERN
UNIVERSITY PRESS, 1969, PP. 147-156
004,100,
       REFERENCE

MERRIAM ALAN P
THE CONCEPT OF CULTURE CLUSTERS APPLIED TO THE BELGIAN
CONGO.
SOUTHWESTERN JOURNAL OF ANTHROPOLOGY VOL 15 1959 PP 373-395
004,108-01,
       REFERENCE

MIDDLETON JOHN   ED
BLACK AFRICA- ITS PEOPLES AND THEIR CULTURES TODAY
LONDON, MACMILLAN, 1970
004,016,053,
       REFERENCE

SKINNER ELLIOTT P
GROUP DYNAMICS IN THE POLITICS OF CHANGING SOCIETIES-- THE
PROBLEM OF TRIBAL POLITICS IN AFRICA.
IN JUNE HELM (ED), ESSAYS ON THE PROBLEM OF TRIBE, AMERICAN
ETHNOLOGICAL SOCIETY,1968,PP 170-185
004,005,006,007,
       REFERENCE

COULT ALLAN D
LINEAGE SOLIDARITY, TRANSFORMATIONAL ANALYSIS AND THE MEAN-
ING OF KINSHIP TERMINOLOGIES.
MAN VOL 2 NO 1 MARCH 1967 PP 26-47
004,
       GENERAL THEORY

5. ON THE CONCEPT OF "TRIBE"

005

FRIED MORTON H
ON THE CONCEPTS OF TRIBE AND TRIBAL SOCIETY.

IN HELM (ED), ESSAYS ON THE PROBLEM OF TRIBE AMERICAN
ETHNOLOGICAL SOCIETY, 1968
   005,
      SEMINAL ARTICLE CHALLENGING PREVAILING CONCEPTS OF
      TRIBE. EXAMINES VARIETY OF CURRENT USAGES RELATION-
      SHIP WITH LANGUAGE AND OTHER UNITS ROLES IN THEORIES
      OF POLITICAL EVOLUTION. VIEW TRIBES AS REACTION FORM-
      ATIONS STIMULATED BY THE APPEARANCE OF RELATIVELY
      HIGHLY ORGANIZED SOCIETIES AMIDST OTHER SOCIETIES
      WHICH ARE ORGANIZED MORE SIMPLY. BASIS FOR SYMPOSIUM
      OF AMERICAN ETHNOLOGICAL ASSOCIATION. SEE HELM, 1967

005
   HELM JUNE ED.
   ESSAYS ON THE PROBLEM OF TRIBE-- PROCEEDINGS OF THE
   ANNUAL SPRING MEETINGS OF THE AMERICAN ETHNOLOGICAL
   SOCIETY SAN FRANCISCO 1967.
   SEATTLE UNIVERSITY OF WASHINGTON PRESS 1968
   005,
      REPORT OF SYMPOSIUM OF AMERICAN ETHNOLOGICAL SOCIETY
      DEALING WITH QUESTIONS RAISED IN ARTICLE BY M H FRIED
      REPRINTED IN PROCEEDINGS ON CONCEPTS OF TRIBE AND
      TRIBAL SOCIETY. COVERS TRIBE AS CULTUNIT AS A STAGE
      IN POLITICAL EVOLUTION, AS A PROBLEM IN CONTEMPORARY
      SOCIOPOLITICAL CONTEXTS. THREE ARTICLES DEAL MAINLY
      WITH AFRICA, NEARLY ALL ARE RELEVANT. EXCELLENT
      BIBLIOGRAPHIES.

   COHEN RONALD
   THE JUST-SO SO-- A SPURIOUS TRIBAL GROUP IN WESTERN SUDANIC
   HISTORY.
   MAN 62 1962 PP 153-154
   005,
      REFERENCE

   DOLE GERTRUDE E
   TRIBE AS THE AUTONOMOUS UNIT
   IN HELM(ED), ESSAYS ON THE PROBLEM OF TRIBE, AMERICAN
   ETHNOLOGICAL SOCIETY 1968 PP 83-100
   005,
      REFERENCE

   LEE RICHARD B   DEVORE IRVEN   EDS
   MAN THE HUNTER
   CHICAGO, ALDINE, 1968
   005, 009,
      REFERENCE

   SAHLINS MARSHALL D
   TRIBESMEN.
   ENGLEWOOD CLIFFS, NEW JERSEY, PRENTICE-HALL, 1968
   005,006,010,
      REFERENCE

   SKINNER ELLIOTT P
   GROUP DYNAMICS IN THE POLITICS OF CHANGING SOCIETIES-- THE
   PROBLEM OF TRIBAL POLITICS IN AFRICA.
   IN JUNE HELM (ED), ESSAYS ON THE PROBLEM OF TRIBE, AMERICAN
   ETHNOLOGICAL SOCIETY, 1968, PP 170-185
   004,005,006,007,

REFERENCE

005

CHAPELLE JEAN
REGARDS SUR LE PASSE (A LOOK AT THE PAST) CHAPTER 1.
NOMADES NOIRS DU SAHARA,PARIS,LIBRARIE PLON,1957
005,
        LESS ACCESSIBLE

COHEN RONALD   SCHLEGEL A
THE TRIBE AS A SOCIO-POLITICAL UNIT-- A CROSS CULTURAL
EXAMINATION.
IN HELM (ED), ESSAYS ON THE PROBLEM OF TRIBE, AMERICAN
ETHNOLOGICAL SOCIETY, 1968,PP 120-149
005,
        GENERAL THEORY

NAROLL RAOUL R
ON ETHNIC UNIT CLASSIFICATION.
CURRENT ANTHROPOLOGY 5 OCTOBER 1964 PP 283-312
005,
        GENERAL THEORY

SAHLINS MARSHALL D
THE SEGMENTARY   LINEAGE--AN ORGANIZATION OF PREDATORY
EXPANSION.
AMERICAN ANTHROPOLOGIST, VOL. 63, 1961, PP. 322-345
005,
        GENERAL THEORY

SAHLINS MARSHALL D SERVICE ELMAN R   EDS
EVOLUTION AND CULTURE.
ANN ARBOR, UNIVERSITY OF MICHIGAN, 1960
005,
        GENERAL THEORY

SERVICE ELMAN R
PRIMITIVE SOCIAL ORGANIZATION.
NEW YORK,RANDOM HOUSE,1962
005,009,
        GENERAL THEORY

6. THE CHANGING NATURE OF ETHNIC BOUNDARIES

006

COHEN RONALD   MIDDLETON JOHN   EDS
FROM TRIBE TO NATION IN AFRICA.
SAN FRANCISCO,CHANDLER,1970
004,006,057,
        ORIGINAL CASE STUDIES BY WELL-KNOWN ANTHROPOLOGISTS ON
        THE PROCESSES BY WHICH ETHNIC SOCIETIES INCORPORATE
        NEIGHBORING GROUPS INTO A LARGER, AND SOMETIMES NEW,
        ETHNIC FRAMEWORK. THEORETICAL INTRODUCTION SYNTHE-
        SIZES THESE STUDIES INTO FUNDAMENTAL PROPOSITIONS
        ABOUT THE NATURE OF ETHNICITY UNDER MODERN CIRCUM-

STANCES.

006

KUPER LEO   SMITH M G   EDS
PLURALISM IN AFRICA.
BERKELEY AND LOS ANGELES, UNIVERSITY OF CALIFORNIA PRESS,
1969
006,007,016,057,
     WORK OF MAJOR THEORETICAL SIGNIFICANCE, AS WELL AS IM-
     PORTANT CASE STUDIES BY VAN DEN BERGHE, ALEXANDRE, DA-
     VIDSON, LOFCHIE, MAZRUI, THOMPSON, GLUCKMAN AND HILDA
     KUPER. FOCUS IS ON PLURAL SOCIETY-I.E. RACIAL, TRIBAL,
     RELIGIOUS, OR REGIONAL GROUPS HELD TOGETHER BY FORCE
     RATHER THAN PLURALISTIC SOCIETY BASED ON CROSS-CUTTING
     CLEAVAGES.

MELSON ROBERT   WOLPE HOWARD   EDS
NIGERIA-MODERNIZATION AND THE POLITICS OF COMMUNALISM.
EAST LANSING, MICHIGAN STATE UNIVERSITY PRESS, 1970
006,065,128-03,
     BASIC THEORETICAL ARGUMENT IS THAT COMMUNALISM DEVELOPS
     IN RESPONSE TO COMPETITION IN MODERN SPHERE. CONTRIBU-
     TORS, WHO HAVE WORKED IN ALL PARTS OF NIGERIA, EXPLORE
     CASE STUDY SITUATIONS OF MODERN COMMUNALISM AND ETHNI-
     CITY, INCLUDING THE WAY IN WHICH HAUSA AND IBO IDENTI-
     TIES HAVE EMERGED IN RECENT TIMES.

TURNBULL COLIN M
TRIBALISM AND SOCIAL EVOLUTION IN AFRICA.
THE ANNALS OF THE AMERICAN ACADEMY OF POLITICAL AND SOCIAL
SCIENCE VOL 354 JULY 1964 PP 22-31
006,013,
     AUTHOR IS ASSISTANT CURATOR OF AFRICAN ETHNOLOGY AT
     AMERICAN MUSEUM OF NATURAL HISTORY. IN ARTICLE AUTHOR
     SUGGESTS THAT AFRICAN TRIBAL SYSTEMS HAVE BASIC SIMI-
     LARITIES. STRESSES THE IMPORTANCE OF RELIGIOUS ASPECT
     OF ETHNIC COMMUNITY, AND THE FLEXIBILITY OF ETHNIC
     GROUPS IN MEETING NEW SITUATIONS.

GELLNER ERNEST
TRIBALISM AND SOCIAL CHANGE IN NORTH AFRICA.
IN WILLIAM H LEWIS (ED), FRENCH-SPEAKING AFRICA, THE SEARCH
FOR IDENTITY, NEW YORK, WALKER AND CO, 1965, PP 107-118
006,126-03,
     REFERENCE

KRADER LAWRENCE
THE FORMATION OF THE STATE.
ENGLEWOOD CLIFFS, NEW JERSEY, PRENTICE-HALL, 1968
006,009,
     REFERENCE

PADEN JOHN N
URBAN PLURALISM, INTEGRATION, AND ADAPTATION OF COMMUNAL
IDENTITY IN KANO, NIGERIA.
IN RONALD COHEN AND JOHN MIDDLETON (EDS), FROM TRIBE TO NA-
TION IN AFRICA, SAN FRANCISCO, CHANDLER, 1970
006,128-05,
     REFERENCE

SAHLINS MARSHALL D
TRIBESMEN.
ENGLEWOOD CLIFFS, NEW JERSEY, PRENTICE-HALL, 1968
005,006,010,
       REFERENCE

006

SKINNER ELLIOTT P
GROUP DYNAMICS IN THE POLITICS OF CHANGING SOCIETIES-- THE
PROBLEM OF TRIBAL POLITICS IN AFRICA.
IN JUNE HELM (ED), ESSAYS ON THE PROBLEM OF TRIBE, AMERICAN
ETHNOLOGICAL SOCIETY, 1968, PP 170-185
004,005,006,007,
       REFERENCE

SMITH M G
SOCIAL AND CULTURAL PLURALISM.
ANNALS OF THE NEW YORK ACADEMY OF SCIENCES 83 JANUARY 1960
006,
       REFERENCE

WOLFF HANS
LANGUAGE, ETHNIC IDENTITY, AND SOCIAL CHANGE IN SOUTHERN
NIGERIA.
ANTHROPOLOGICAL LINGUISTICS JANUARY 1967
006,128-03,
       REFERENCE

BANTON MICHAEL P
RACE RELATIONS.
LONDON, TAVISTOCK, 1968
006,030,089,
       GENERAL THEORY

MORRIS H S
SOME ASPECTS OF THE CONCEPT PLURAL SOCIETY.
MAN VOL 2 NO 2 JUNE 1967 PP 169-184
006,
       GENERAL THEORY

PARENTI MICHAEL
ETHNIC POLITICS AND THE PERSISTENCE OF ETHNIC IDENTIFICA-
TION.
AMERICAN POLITICAL SCIENCE REVIEW VOL LXI NO 3 SEPTEMBER
1967 PP 717-726
006,
       GENERAL THEORY

REX JOHN
THE PLURAL SOCIETY IN SOCIOLOGICAL THEORY.
BRITISH JOURNAL OF SOCIOLOGY VOL X NO 2 JUNE 1959 PP 114-124
006,
       GENERAL THEORY

7. MODERN VARIANTS OF ETHNICITY

007

COHEN ABNER
CUSTOM AND POLITICS IN URBAN AFRICA--A STUDY OF HAUSA
MIGRANTS IN YORUBA TOWNS.
BERKELEY, UNIVERSITY OF CALIFORNIA PRESS, 1969
007,128-05,

> AMONG OTHER THINGS, DISCUSSES THE WAY IN WHICH MIGRANTS
> FROM VARIOUS NORTHERN TOWNS TAKE ON BROADER HAUSA ID-
> ENTITY WITHIN A YORUBA CONTEXT, (PRIMARILY IBADAN).
> ALSO DISCUSSES ETHNICITY PATTERNS OF YORUBA BUTCHERS
> VIS-A-VIS HAUSA CATTLE TRADERS.

EPSTEIN ARNOLD L
URBANIZATION AND SOCIAL CHANGE IN AFRICA.
CURRENT ANTHROPOLOGY 8 NO 4 OCTOBER 1967 PP 275-283
007,046,

> OUTSTANDING SURVEY ARTICLE, WHICH INCLUDES CRITIQUES
> BY LEADING URBAN ANTHROPOLOGISTS. DESCRIBES THREE DE-
> TERMINANTS OF URBAN SOCIAL STRUCTURE-- INDUSTRIAL,
> CIVIC, AND DEMOGRAPHIC. USING THESE CATEGORIES,
> AUTHOR EXAMINES INTRA-URBAN RELATIONSHIPS (NETWORK
> RELATIONS-- CATEGORICAL RELATIONS, OR TRIBALISM --
> AND FORMAL, OR ASSOCIATIONAL RELATIONS).

GREENBERG JOSEPH H
URBANISM,MIGRATION AND LANGUAGE
CHAPTER 4 IN HILDA KUPER (ED), URBANIZATION AND MIGRATION IN
WEST AFRICA,BERKELEY,UNIVERSITY OF CALIFORNIA PRESS,1965
007,046,

> ASSESSES THE SHIFT OF RURAL ETHNIC MEMBERS TO URBAN
> SETTING IN TERMS OF IMPACT ON ETHNIC IDENTITY AND ON
> ETHNIC CULTURE TRAITS. SUGGESTS THAT EVERY AFRICAN IS
> DETRIBALIZED AS SOON AS HE LEAVES HIS TRIBAL AREA.
> HOWEVER HE SUGGESTS THAT URBAN ETHNICITY HAS IMPORTANT
> DIMENSIONS ESPECIALLY IN VOLUNTARY ASSOCIATIONS. BEST
> INTRODUCTION TO LINGUISTIC ASPECTS OF URBANIZATION AND
> MIGRATION-ONLY REASONABLE SURVEY.

KUPER LEO   SMITH M G   EDS
PLURALISM IN AFRICA.
BERKELEY AND LOS ANGELES, UNIVERSITY OF CALIFORNIA PRESS,
1969
006,007,016,057,

> WORK OF MAJOR THEORETICAL SIGNIFICANCE, AS WELL AS IM-
> PORTANT CASE STUDIES BY VAN DEN BERGHE, ALEXANDRE, DA-
> VIDSON, LOFCHIE, MAZRUI, THOMPSON, GLUCKMAN AND HILDA
> KUPER. FOCUS IS ON PLURAL SOCIETY-I.E. RACIAL, TRIBAL,
> RELIGIOUS, OR REGIONAL GROUPS HELD TOGETHER BY FORCE
> RATHER THAN PLURALISTIC SOCIETY BASED ON CROSS-CUTTING
> CLEAVAGES.

WALLERSTEIN I M
ETHNICITY AND NATIONAL INTEGRATION IN WEST AFRICA
CAHIERS D'ETUDES AFRICAINES 3 OCTOBER 1960 PP 129-139

004,007,057,
        BASIC INTRODUCTION TO CONCEPT OF ETHNICITY AND TO
        ENDURING ROLE OF ETHNICITY IN URBAN ENVIRONMENTS.
        ACCORDING TO AUTHOR,MEMBERSHIP IN AN ETHNIC GROUP IS A
        MATTER OF SOCIAL DEFINITION.THE INTERPLAY OF THE SELF-
        DEFINITION OF MEMBERS AND THE DEFINITION OF OTHER
        GROUPS.

007
    BRAUSCH GEORGES
    AFRICAN ETHNOCRACIES-- SOME SOCIOLOGICAL IMPLICATIONS OF
    CONSTITUTIONAL CHANGE IN EMERGENT TERRITORIES OF AFRICA.
    CIVILISATIONS VOL XIII NO 1-2 1963 PP 82-95
    007,
        REFERENCE

    DOOB LEONARD W
    FROM TRIBALISM TO NATIONALISM IN AFRICA.
    JOURNAL OF INTERNATIONAL AFFAIRS 16 1962 PP 144-155
    007,
        REFERENCE

    GLUCKMAN MAX
    TRIBALISM IN MODERN BRITISH CENTRAL AFRICA.
    IN IMMANUEL WALLERSTEIN, SOCIAL CHANGE, THE COLONIAL
    SITUATION, NEW YORK, JOHN WILEY AND SONS, 1966, PP 251-264
    007,
        REFERENCE

    GULLIVER P H   ED
    TRADITION AND TRANSITION IN EAST AFRICA--STUDIES OF THE
    TRIBAL FACTOR IN THE MODERN ERA.
    BERKELEY, UNIVERSITY OF CALIFORNIA PRESS, 1969
    007,117-03,136-03,139-03,
        REFERENCE

    HYMES DELL
    LINGUISTIC PROBLEMS IN DEFINING THE CONCEPT OF TRIBE
    IN HELMS (ED),ESSAYS ON THE PROBLEM OF TRIBE,AMERICAN
    ETHNOLOGICAL SOCIETY,1968,PP 23-48
    007,
        REFERENCE

    SKINNER ELLIOTT P
    GROUP DYNAMICS IN THE POLITICS OF CHANGING SOCIETIES-- THE
    PROBLEM OF TRIBAL POLITICS IN AFRICA.
    IN JUNE HELM (ED),ESSAYS ON THE PROBLEM OF TRIBE, AMERICAN
    ETHNOLOGICAL SOCIETY,1968,PP 170-185
    004,005,006,007,
        REFERENCE

    WOLFF HANS
    INTELLIGIBILITY AND INTER-ETHNIC ATTITUDES.
    ANTHROPOLOGICAL LINGUISTICS MARCH 1959
    007,
        REFERENCE

    CROWLEY DANIEL J
    POLITICS AND TRIBALISM IN THE KATANGA.
    WESTERN POLITICAL QUARTERLY 16 MAY 1963 PP 68-78

007,108-06,
    CASE STUDY

007
  EPSTEIN ARNOLD L
  POLITICS IN AN URBAN AFRICAN COMMUNITY.
  MANCHESTER,MANCHESTER UNIVERSITY PRESS,1958
  007,046,142-05,
      CASE STUDY

  SMOCK AUDREY CHAPMAN
  THE N.C.N.C. AND ETHNIC UNIONS IN BIAFRA.
  THE JOURNAL OF MODERN AFRICAN STUDIES, 7, 1, 1969
  007,128-07,
      CASE STUDY

8. FAMILY AND KINSHIP

008
  GOODY JACK
  COMPARATIVE STUDIES IN KINSHIP.
  PALO ALTO, STANFORD UNIVERSITY PRESS, 1969
  008,
      AUTHOR, WHO IS DIRECTOR OF AFRICAN STUDIES CENTER AT
      CAMBRIDGE UNIVERSITY, DRAWS HEAVILY ON HIS OWN FIELD
      WORK IN GHANA, BUT STRESSES COMPARATIVE APPROACH. HE
      DISCUSSES ASPECTS OF INCEST, ADULTERY, MOTHER-BROTHER
      RELATIONS, SISTER-SON RELATIONS, DOUBLE DESCENT, INHER-
      ITANCE, MARRIAGE, CHILD REARING AND FOSTERING.

  MURDOCK GEORGE P
  SOCIAL STRUCTURE.
  NEW YORK, MACMILLAN CO. 1956
  004,008,
      STANDARD REFERENCE WORK ON KINSHIP TERMINOLOGY AND
      CONCEPTS. INCLUDES SECTIONS ON THE NUCLEAR FAMILY,
      CONSANGUINAL KIN GROUPS, THE CLAN, THE COMMUNITY, EVO-
      LUTION OF SOCIAL ORGANIZATION AND GENERAL THEORETICAL
      APPROACHES TO THE STUDY OF KINSHIP. CONTAINS DEFINI-
      TIONS OF NEARLY ALL MAJOR TERMS REFERRING TO DESCENT,
      GENEALOGY AND MARRIAGE.

  RADCLIFFE-BROWN A R,FORDE C DARYLL   EDS
  AFRICAN SYSTEMS OF KINSHIP AND MARRIAGE.
  LONDON, OXFORD UNIVERSITY PRESS, 1950
  008,
      CLASSIC EARLY WORK ON KINSHIP AND MARRIAGE IN AFRICA.
      SOME OF THE MATERIAL IS NOW DATED.

  SMITH MARY
  BABA OF KARO--A WOMAN OF THE MOSLEM HAUSA.
  NEW YORK, PRAEGER, 1964
  008,128-01,
      CLASSIC STUDY OF AN OLD WOMAN IN ZARIA WHO RECOUNTS THE
      COURSE OF HER LIFE, WITH DETAILED INSIGHTS INTO HAUSA

FAMILY STRUCTURE AND CUSTOMS.   AUTHOR IS WIFE OF M.G. SMITH.

008

FORTES MEYER
THE STRUCTURE OF UNILINEAL DECENT GROUPS.
IN SIMON AND PHOEBE OTTENBERG(EDS), CULTURES AND SOCIETIES
OF AFRICA, NEW YORK, RANDOM HOUSE, 1960, PP 163-190
008,
        REFERENCE

PAULME DENISE   ED
WOMEN OF TROPICAL AFRICA.
LONDON, ROUTLEDGE AND KEGAN PAUL, 1963
008,
        REFERENCE

BARRINGTON KAYE
BRINGING UP CHILDREN IN GHANA.
LONDON, GEORGE ALLEN AND UNWIN, 1962
008,114-01,
        CASE STUDY

COCKER G B A
FAMILY PROPERTY AMONG THE YORUBAS.
LAGOS, AFRICAN UNIVERSITIES PRESS, 1966
008,128-01,
        CASE STUDY

COHEN RONALD
FAMILY LIFE IN BORNU.
ANTHROPOLOGICA 9 NO. 1 1967 PP 21-42
008,128-01,
        CASE STUDY

COHEN RONALD
MARRIAGE INSTABILITY AMONG THE KANURI OF NORTHERN NIGERIA.
AMERICAN ANTHROPOLOGIST 63 1961 PP 1231-1249
008,128-01,
        CASE STUDY

COHEN RONALD
SOCIAL STRATIFICATION IN BORNU.
IN A TUDEN AND L PLOTNICOV (EDS), CLASS AND STATUS IN SUB-
SAHARAN AFRICA, NEW YORK, FREE PRESS, 1968
008,128-01,
        CASE STUDY

COHEN RONALD
THE KANURI OF BORNU.
NEW YORK, HOLT, RINEHART AND WINSTON, 1967
008,024,128-01,
        CASE STUDY

EVANS-PRITCHARD E E
KINSHIP AND MARRIAGE AMONG THE NUER.
LONDON, OXFORD UNIVERSITY PRESS, 1953
008,134-01,
        CASE STUDY

FORDE C DARYLL
YAKU STUDIES.
LONDON, OXFORD UNIVERSITY PRESS, 1964
008,
        CASE STUDY

008

FORTES MEYER
THE WEB OF KINSHIP AMONG THE TALLENSI.
LONDON, OXFORD UNIVERSITY PRESS, 1949
008,114-01,
        CASE STUDY

LEITH-ROSS SYLVIA
AFRICAN WOMEN-- A STUDY OF THE IBO OF NIGERIA.
LONDON, ROUTLEDGE AND KEGAN PAUL, 1963
008,128-01,
        CASE STUDY

LEVINE ROBERT A
GUSII SEX OFFENCES-- A STUDY IN SOCIAL CONTROL.
AMERICAN ANTHROPOLOGIST 61 1959 PP 965-990
008,117-01,
        CASE STUDY

LEWIS WILLIAM H
FEUDING AND SOCIAL CHANGE IN MOROCCO.
JOURNAL OF CONFLICT RESOLUTION 5 1961 PP 43-54
008,126-03,
        CASE STUDY

LIJEMBE JOSEPH A   APOKO ANNA   MUTUKU NZIOKI J
AN EAST AFRICAN CHILDHOOD--THREE VERSIONS.
LONDON, OXFORD UNIVERSITY PRESS, 1967
008,
        CASE STUDY

LYSTAD ROBERT A
MARRIAGE AND KINSHIP AMONG THE ASHANTI AND THE AGNI--
A STUDY OF DIFFERENTIAL ACCULTURATION CHAPTER 10.
IN WILLIAM BASCOM AND MELVILLE HERSKOVITS, CONTINUTY AND
CHANGE IN AFRICAN CULTURES, CHICAGO, UNIVERSITY OF CHICAGO
PRESS, 1962, PP 187-204
008,114-01,
        CASE STUDY

OTTENBERG SIMON
DOUBLE DESCENT IN AN AFRICAN SOCIETY--THE AFIKPO VILLAGE-
GROUP.
SEATTLE, UNIVERSITY OF WASHINGTON PRESS, 1968
008,128-01,
        CASE STUDY

RIGBY P J A
CATTLE AND KINSHIP AMONG THE GOGO--A SEMIPASTORAL SOCIETY OF
CENTRAL TANZANIA.
ITHACA, CORNELL UNIVERSITY PRESS, 1969
008,136-01,
        CASE STUDY

CHAPELLE JEAN
L'ORGANISATION CLANIQUE (CLAN ORGANIZATION)   CHAPTER 8.
IN NOMADES NOIRS DU SAHARA. PARIS, LIBRARIE PLON, 1957
008,009,
         LESS ACCESSIBLE

008
   CHAPELLE JEAN
   LA VIE EN SOCIETE (SOCIAL LIFE) CHAPTER 7.
   IN NOMADES NOIRS DU SAHARA, PARIS, LIBRARIE PLON, 1957
   008,
         LESS ACCESSIBLE

   CHAPELLE JEAN
   DE LA NAISSANCE A LA MORT (LIFE-CYCLE) CHAPTER 6.
   IN NOMADES NOIRS DU SAHARA, PARIS, LIBRARIE PLON, 1957
   008,
         LESS ACCESSIBLE

   FORTES MEYER
   THE DYNAMICS OF CLANSHIP AMONG THE TALLENSI.
   LONDON, OXFORD UNIVERSITY PRESS, 1945
   008, 114-01,
         LESS ACCESSIBLE

   PAULME DENISE
   STRUCTURES SOCIALES TRADITIONNELLES EN AFRIQUE NOIRE,
   (TRADITIONAL SOCIAL STRUCTURES OF BLACK AFRICA).
   CAHIERS D'ETUDES AFRICAINES 1 1960 PP 15-27
   008,
         LESS ACCESSIBLE

   BOHANNAN PAUL   MIDDLETON JOHN   EDS
   MARRIAGE, FAMILY AND RESIDENCE.
   GARDEN CITY, NEW YORK, INTERNATIONAL UNIVERSITY BOOKSELLERS,
   INC., 1968
   008,
         GENERAL THEORY

   ERIKSON ERIK H
   CHILDHOOD AND SOCIETY.
   NEW YORK, NORTON, 1964 (REVISED EDITION) CHAPTERS 8-10
   008,
         GENERAL THEORY

   EVANS-PRITCHARD E E
   THE POSITION OF WOMEN IN PRIMITIVE SOCIETIES AND OTHER
   ESSAYS IN SOCIAL ANTHROPOLOGY.
   NEW YORK, FREE PRESS, 1965
   008,
         GENERAL THEORY

   FALLERS LLOYD A   LEVY MARION J
   THE FAMILY-- SOME COMPARATIVE CONSIDERATIONS.
   IN PETER HAMMOND (ED), CULTURAL AND SOCIAL ANTHROPOLOGY
   NEW YORK, MACMILLAN CO, 1964, PP 163-166
   008,
         GENERAL THEORY

   FORTES MEYER

INTRODUCTION.
IN J GOODY (ED), THE DEVELOPMENT CYCLE IN DOMESTIC GROUPS,
CAMBRIDGE PAPERS IN SOCIAL ANTHROPOLOGY, NO. 1, CAMBRIDGE,
CAMBRIDGE UNIVERSITY PRESS, 1961
008,
    GENERAL THEORY

008
  LEVINE ROBERT A
  ROLE OF FAMILY IN AUTHORITY SYSTEMS.
  BEHAVIORAL SCIENCE 5 1960 PP 291-296
  008,
    GENERAL THEORY

9. TRADITIONAL POLITICAL SYSTEMS

009
  COHEN RONALD   MIDDLETON JOHN   EDS
  COMPARATIVE POLITICAL SYSTEMS-- A READER IN POLITICAL
  ANTHROPOLOGY.
  NEW YORK, NATURAL HISTORY PRESS, 1967
  009,
    COLLECTION OF REPRINTED STUDIES ON THE POLITICS OF
    PRE-INDUSTRIAL SOCIETIES. ARTICLES ON THE SEGMENTARY
    LINEAGE (SAHLINS), YAKO GOVERNMENT (FORDE), YORUBA
    POLITICAL SYSTEMS (LLOYD), NUPE STATE (NADEL), AND
    MODERNIZATION OF TRADITIONAL POLITICAL SYSTEMS (EISEN-
    STADT). EXCELLENT THIRTY PAGE BIBLIOGRAPHY.

  COLLINS ROBERT O   ED
  PROBLEMS IN AFRICAN HISTORY.
  ENGLEWOOD CLIFFS, NEW JERSEY, PRENTICE-HALL, INC., 1968
  009,019,020,036,
    EDITOR HAS ARRANGED ARTICLES BY MAJOR SCHOLARS INTO
    SEVEN PARTS--AFRICA ANC EGYPT, BANTU ORIGINS AND MIGRA-
    TIONS, NILOTIC ORIGINS AND MIGRATIONS, THE HISTORIAN
    AND STATELESS SOCIETIES, AFRICAN STATES, TRADE IN PRE-
    COLONIAL AFRICA, AND THE AFRICAN SLAVE TRADE. THIS
    VOLUME IS INTENDED FOR TEACHING PURPOSES AND IS AVAIL-
    ABLE IN PAPERBACK.

  CROWDER MICHAEL   IKIME OBARO   EDS
  WEST AFRICAN CHIEFS--THEIR CHANGING STATUS UNDER COLONIAL
  RULE AND INDEPENDENCE.
  NEW YORK, AFRICANA PUBLISHING CORPORATION, FORTHCOMING
  009,013,035,
    CASE STUDIES FROM WEST AFRICA--PRIMARILY NIGERIA--ON
    CHANGING ROLE OF CHIEFS. CONTAINS CASE STUDIES OF PAT-
    TERNS WHICH PROVIDE INSIGHT INTO DISTINCTION BETWEEN
    'DIRECT' AND 'INDIRECT' RULE. TO LESSER EXTENT, DEALS
    WITH CONTEMPORARY ISSUES ON MODERN ROLE OF CHIEFS.

  FORTES MEYER   EVANS-PRITCHARD E E EDS
  AFRICAN POLITICAL SYSTEMS.
  LONDON, OXFORD UNIVERSITY PRESS, 1940 (1962)

009,099,
> FIRST COMPREHENSIVE CLASSIFICATION OF TRADITIONAL
> AFRICAN POLITICAL SYSTEMS. CATEGORIES INCLUDE HUNTING
> BANDS, SEGMENTARY LINEAGE SOCIETIES, AND CENTRALIZED
> STATES. COUNTERACTS STEREOTYPE OF SMALL-SCALE SOCIE-
> TIES NOT HAVING GOVERNMENT BY DESCRIBING HOW POLITICAL
> FUNCTIONS ARE PERFORMED WITHOUT NECESSITY OF CENTRAL-
> IZED AUTHORITY. SUPPORTED BY CASE STUDIES FROM LEAD-
> ING ANTHROPOLOGISTS.

009
FRIED MORTON H
THE EVOLUTION OF POLITICAL SOCIETY
NEW YORK, RANDOM HOUSE, 1967
004, 009,
> PROVOCATIVE ANALYSIS BY PROMINENT EVOLUTIONARY
> ANTHROPOLOGIST. POLITICAL EVOLUTION VIEWED WITH
> RESPECT TO SEQUENTIAL DEVELOPMENT OF SHARING, RANKING,
> AND STRATIFICATION. CONTAINS EXCELLENT DISCUSSION
> ON THE CONCEPT OF TRIBE AND CHAPTERS ON HUNTING BANDS
> AND EARLY STATE FORMATION. GLOBAL IN SCOPE BUT WITH
> MANY AFRICAN EXAMPLES.

GLUCKMAN MAX
POLITICS LAW AND RITUAL IN TRIBAL SOCIETY.
CHICAGO, ALDINE PUBLISHING COMPANY, 1965
009,
> INTRODUCTION TO TRADITIONAL POLITICAL SYSTEMS THROUGH-
> OUT THE WORLD. ANALYZES THE SCIENCE OF SOCIAL ANTHRO-
> POLOGY, AND ITS CHANGING APPROACHES TO TRADITIONAL
> SOCIETY AND CULTURE. EXAMINES POLITICAL COMPETITION
> AND ORDER, AUTHORITY STRUCTURES, MODES OF SETTLING
> DISPUTES, RITUAL ACTION AND DIVINATION, AND TRADITION-
> AL CONCEPTS OF TIME, HISTORY AND CHANGE, PRIMARILY
> AFRICAN EXAMPLES. SHORT GLOSSARY OF TECHNICAL TERMS.

LLOYD PETER C
THE POLITICAL STRUCTURE OF AFRICAN KINGDOMS-- AN EXPLORATORY
MODEL.
IN POLITICAL SYSTEMS AND THE DISTRIBUTION OF POWER, ED BY
MICHAEL BANTON, ASSOCIATION OF SOCIAL ANTHROPOLOGISTS
MONOGRAPH NO 2, LONDON, TAVISTOCK PUBLICATIONS LTD, 1965
PP 63-112
009,
> OUTLINES EXISTING CLASSIFICATIONS OF AFRICAN KINGDOMS.
> DESCRIBES PROBLEMS ARISING FROM COMPLEXITY OF AFRICAN
> KINGDOMS. DESCRIBES POLICY MAKING PROCESSES. IN-
> TRODUCES CONCEPT OF POLITICAL CONFLICT AND COMPETI-
> TION. BUILDS MODEL BASED ON RECRUITMENT TO POLITICAL
> ELITE USED TO IDENTIFY THREE TYPES OF POLITICAL SYS-
> TEMS-- OPEN (REPRESENTATIVE)-- OPEN (BY POLITICAL
> ASSOCIATION)-- CLOSED (ROYAL ARISTOCRACY).

LLOYD PETER C
TRADITIONAL RULERS.
IN JAMES S COLEMAN AND CARL G ROSBERG JR. (EDS), POLITICAL
PARTIES AND NATIONAL INTEGRATION IN TROPICAL AFRICA, BERKE-
LY, UNIVERSITY OF CALIFORNIA PRESS, 1964, PP 382-412
009,
> AUTHOR SUMMARIZES BASIC POLITICAL CHARACTERISTICS OF

THREE MAJOR ETHNIC GROUPS-- ASHANTI, YORUBA, AND
HAUSA-FULANI. DESCRIBES EACH IN TERMS OF PRE-COLONIAL
CONTACT PATTERNS OF AUTHORITY, SUCCESSION, AND LEGITI-
MACY-- ASSESSES IMPACT OF COLONIAL PERIOD ON EACH
GROUP.

009
   MIDDLETON JOHN   TAIT D   EDS
   TRIBES WITHOUT RULERS.
   LONDON, ROUTLEDGE AND   KEGAN PAUL, 1958
   009,
         SERIES OF STUDIES ON AFRICAN SEGMENTARY (NON-CENTRAL-
         IZED) POLITICAL SYSTEMS. CASES INCLUDE TIV, MANDARI,
         DINKA, BWAMBA, KONKOMBA, AND LUGBARA. INTRODUCTORY
         SECTION LINKS THE CONCEPT OF LINEAGE WITH ALL ASPECTS
         OF THE POLITICAL SYSTEM, INCLUDING ROLE OF VIOLENCE,
         RELIGION, AND INTEGRATION. GOOD DEFINITIONS OF EX-
         TENDED FAMILY, LINEAGE, AND CLAN.

   TUDEN ARTHUR   PLOTNICOV LEONARD   EDS
   SOCIAL STRATIFICATION IN AFRICA
   NEW YORK, FREE PRESS, 1970
   009,
         11 ORIGINAL CASE STUDIES OF STRATIFICATION PATTERNS,
         CASTE SYSTEMS, AND CLASS STRUCTURE IN OR AMONG THE ALUR
         (SOUTHALL), ILA(TUDEN), GROUPS IN THE WESTERN SUDAN
         (VAUGHAN), RWANDA(MAQUET), GANDA AND NYORO(PERLMAN),
         GALLA(H.LEWIS), AMHARA(HOBEN), BORNU(COHEN), THE PEOPLE
         OF JOS IN NIGERIA(PLOTNICOV), SOUTH CENTRAL AFRICA
         (J.C.MITCHELL) AND SOUTH AFRICA (VAN DER BERGHE).

   BEATTIE J H M
   CHECKS ON THE ABUSE OF POLITICAL POWER IN SOME AFRICAN
   STATES-- A PRELIMINARY FRAMEWORK FOR ANALYSIS.
   SOCIOLOGUS 9 1959 PP 97-115
   009,
         REFERENCE

   CARLSTON KENNETH S
   SOCIAL THEORY AND AFRICAN TRIBAL ORGANIZATION.
   URBANA, UNIVERSITY OF ILLINOIS PRESS, 1968
   009,
         REFERENCE

   EISENSTADT S N
   FROM GENERATION TO GENERATION-AGE GROUPS AND SOCIAL
   STRUCTURE
   NEW YORK, FREE PRESS, 1964; ORIGINALLY PUBLISHED 1956
   009,
         REFERENCE

   GLUCKMAN MAX
   CUSTOM AND CONFLICT IN AFRICA.
   OXFORD, BLACKWELL, 1955
   009,
         REFERENCE

   KABERRY PHYLLIS M
   PRIMITIVE STATES.
   BRITISH JOURNAL OF SOCIOLOGY 8 SEPTEMBER 1957 PP 224-234

009,
       REFERENCE

009
    KRADER LAWRENCE
    THE FORMATION OF THE STATE.
    ENGLEWOOD CLIFFS, NEW JERSEY, PRENTICE-HALL, 1968
    006,009,
          REFERENCE

    LEE RICHARD B   DEVORE IRVEN   EDS
    MAN THE HUNTER
    CHICAGO, ALDINE, 1968
    005, 009,
          REFERENCE

    LEVINE ROBERT A
    THE INTERNALIZATION OF POLITICAL VALUES IN STATELESS
    SOCIETIES.
    HUMAN ORGANIZATION 19 1960 PP 51-58
    009,
          REFERENCE

    LEWIS I M
    THE CLASSIFICATION OF AFRICAN POLITICAL SYSTEMS.
    RHODES-LIVINGSTONE JOURNAL 25 MARCH 1959 PP 59-69
    009,133-06,
          REFERENCE

    MAIR LUCY P
    PRIMITIVE GOVERNMENT.
    BALTIMORE, PENGUIN, 1962
    009,
          REFERENCE

    RICHARDS AUDREY I
    EAST AFRICAN CHIEFS.
    LONDON, FABER AND FABER, 1960
    009,
          REFERENCE

    SCHAPERA ISAAC
    GOVERNMENT AND POLITICS IN TRIBAL SOCIETIES.
    LONDON, WATTS, 1956
    009,
          REFERENCE

    STEVENSON ROBERT F
    POPULATION AND POLITICAL SYSTEMS IN TROPICAL AFRICA.
    NEW YORK, COLUMBIA UNIVERSITY PRESS, 1968
    009,
          REFERENCE

    SWARTZ MARC   TURNER VICTOR W   TUDEN ARTHUR
    POLITICAL ANTHROPOLOGY
    CHICAGO, ALDINE, 1966
    009,
          REFERENCE

    VANSINA JAN

A COMPARISON OF AFRICAN KINGDOMS.
AFRICA 32 1962 PP 324-335
009,
        REFERENCE

009
    ABRAHAMS R G
    THE POLITICAL ORGANIZATION OF UNYAMWEZI.
    LONDON AND NEW YORK, CAMBRIDGE MONOGRAPHS IN SOCIAL ANTHRO-
    POLOGY, 1967
    009,136-01,
        CASE STUDY

    COHEN RONALD
    POWER, AUTHORITY, AND PERSONAL SUCCESS IN ISLAM AND BORNU.
    IN M SWARTZ,   V TURNER, AND A TUDEN (EDS), POLITICAL
    ANTHROPOLOGY, CHICAGO, ALDINE, 1966, PP 129-139
    009,128-01,
        CASE STUDY

    EVANS-PRITCHARD E E
    THE ZANDE STATE.
    JOURNAL OF THE ROYAL ANTHROPOLOGICAL INSTITUTE 93 1963
    PP 134-154
    009,134-01,
        CASE STUDY

    FALLERS LLOYD A
    BANTU BUREAUCRACY.
    CHICAGO, UNIVERSITY OF CHICAGO PRESS, 1965
    009,
        CASE STUDY

    ISICHEI ELIZABETH
    HISTORICAL CHANGE IN AN IBO POLITY ASABA TO 1885.
    IN JOURNAL OF AFRICAN HISTORY VOL 10 1969 P 421
    009,128-01,
        CASE STUDY

    KUPER HILDA
    AN AFRICAN ARISTOCRACY.
    LONDON, OXFORD UNIVERSITY PRESS, 1961
    009,135-01,
        CASE STUDY

    LEWIS HERBERT S
    A GALLA MONARCHY-- JIMMA ABBA JIFAR, ETHIOPIA, 1830-1932.
    MADISON, UNIVERSITY OF WISCONSIN PRESS, 1965
    009,110-02,
        CASE STUDY

    LEWIS I M
    A PASTORAL DEMOCRACY.
    LONDON, OXFORD UNIVERSITY PRESS, 1961
    009,133-01,
        CASE STUDY

    LLOYD PETER C
    SACRED KINGSHIP AND GOVERNMENT AMONG THE YORUBA.
    AFRICA 30 1960 PP 221-237

009,128-01,
      CASE STUDY

009

NADEL S F
A BLACK BYZANTIUM, THE KINGDOM OF NUPE IN NIGERIA.
OXFORD, OXFORD UNIVERSITY PRESS, 1942
009,010,128-01,
      CASE STUDY

OGOT BETHWELL A
KINGSHIP AND STATELESSNESS AMONG THE NILOTS
IN VANSINA, ROGEN, MAUNY (EDS), THE HISTORIAN IN TROPICAL
AFRICA, LONDON, OXFORD UNIVERSITY PRESS, 1964, PP 284-301
009,025,
      CASE STUDY

PETERS E L
SOME STRUCTURAL ASPECTS OF THE FEUDS AMONG THE CAMEL-HERDING
BEDQUIN OF CYRENAICA.
AFRICA 37 1967 PP 260-282
009,120-01,
      CASE STUDY

SKINNER ELLIOTT P
TRADITIONAL AND MODERN PATTERNS OF SUCCESSION TO POLITICAL
OFFICE AMONG THE MOSSI OF THE VOLTAIC REPUBLIC.
JOURNAL OF HUMAN RELATIONS 8 1960 PP 394-406
009,141-01,
      CASE STUDY

SOUTHALL AIDAN
ALUR SOCIETY-- A STUDY IN PROCESSES AND TYPES OF
DOMINATIONS.
CAMBRIDGE, HEFFER, 1956
009,
      CASE STUDY

WILSON MONICA
GOOD COMPANY-A STUDY OF NYAKYUSU AGE VILLAGES
LONDON, OXFORD UNIVERSITY PRESS, 1951
009,136-01,
      CASE STUDY

CHAPELLE JEAN
L'ORGANISATION CLANIQUE (CLAN ORGANIZATION) CHAPTER 8.
IN NOMADES NOIRS DU SAHARA, PARIS, LIBRARIE PLON, 1957
008,009,
      LESS ACCESSIBLE

NICOLAISEN JOHANNES
STRUCTURES POLITIQUES ET SOCIALES DES TOUAREG DE L AIR ET
DE L AHAGGAR. (POLITICAL AND SOCIAL STRUCTURES OF THE TUAREG)
ETUDES NIGERIENNES 7 (NIAMEY, INSTITUT FRANCAIS D AFRIQUE
NOIRE, 1963)
009,127-01,
      LESS ACCESSIBLE

SMITH M G
CO-OPERATION IN HAUSA SOCIETY.

INFORMATION VOL 11 1957 PP 2-20
009,128-01,
        LESS ACCESSIBLE

009
   WHITE C M N
   SOME PROBLEMS OF THE CLASSIFICATION OF TRIBAL STRUCTURES.
   IN R J APTHORPE,ED., FROM TRIBAL RULE TO MODERN GOVERNMENT,
   LUSAKA, RHODES-LIVINGSTONE INSTITUTE, 1959, PP 181-186
   009,
        LESS ACCESSIBLE

   BOHANNAN PAUL   ED
   LAW AND WARFARE-- STUDIES IN THE ANTHROPOLOGY OF CONFLICT.
   GARDEN CITY, NEW YORK, NATURAL HISTORY PRESS, 1967
   009,
        GENERAL THEORY

   COHEN ABNER
   POLITICAL ANTHROPOLOGY--THE ANALYSIS OF THE SYMBOLISM OF
   POWER RELATIONS.
   MAN, VOL. 4, NO. 2, JUNE, 1969, PP. 215-235
   009,
        GENERAL THEORY

   EISENSTADT S N
   PRIMITIVE POLITICAL SYSTEMS-- A PRELIMINARY COMPARATIVE
   ANALYSIS.
   AMERICAN ANTHROPOLOGIST 61 1959 PP 200-220. REPRINTED
   IN WILLIAM J HANNA (ED), INDEPENDENT BLACK AFRICA, CHICAGO,
   RAND MCNALLY, 1964, PP 60-85
   009,
        GENERAL THEORY

   SERVICE ELMAN R
   PRIMITIVE SOCIAL ORGANIZATION.
   NEW YORK, RANDOM HOUSE, 1962
   005,009,
        GENERAL THEORY

   SWARTZ MARC   ED
   LOCAL-LEVEL POLITICS
   CHICAGO, ALDINE, 1968
   009,047,
        GENERAL THEORY

   WISEMAN HERBERT V
   POLITICAL SYSTEMS--SOME SOCIOLOGICAL APPROACHES.
   NEW YORK, PRAEGER, 1966
   009,061,
        GENERAL THEORY

   COHEN RONALD
   POLITICAL ANTHROPOLOGY--- THE FUTURE OF A PIONEER.
   ANTHROPOLOGICAL QUARTERLY 38 1965 PP 117-131, NORTHWESTERN
   UNIVERSITY PROGRAM OF AFRICAN STUDIES REPRINT SERIES 4
   009,098,100,
        REFERENCE
        CASE STUDY

SOUTHALL AIDAN
A CRITIQUE OF THE TYPOLOGY OF STATES AND POLITICAL SYSTEMS.
IN POLITICAL SYSTEMS AND THE DISTRIBUTION OF POWER, MICHAEL
BANTON (ED), ASSOCIATION OF SOCIAL ANTHROPOLOGISTS MONOGRAPH
NO 2; LONDON, TAVISTOCK PUBLICATIONS LTD, 1965, PP 113-140
009,
    REFERENCE

10. TRADITIONAL ECONOMIC SYSTEMS

010
  ALLAN WILLIAM H
  THE AFRICAN HUSBANDMAN.
  EDINBURGH, OLIVER AND BOYD, 1965
  010, 070,
      BEST WORK ON AGRICULTURE, ECOLOGY, AND TECHNOLOGY. IS
      ESSENTIALLY A REFERENCE WORK RATHER THAN INTRODUCTION.
      CONCLUSION DEALS WITH RECENT DEVELOPMENTS IN AGRICUL-
      TURAL CHANGE.

  BOHANNAN PAUL
  AFRICA AND AFRICANS
  NEW YORK, NATURAL HISTORY PRESS, 1964
  001, 003, 010, 016,
      SUCCESSFUL ATTEMPT TO PUT AFRICAN CULTURE IN MODERN
      PERSPECTIVE. INFORMAL, PERSONAL STATEMENT BY OUT-
      STANDING ANTHROPOLOGIST, WHICH IS CHALLENGING AND
      OFTEN CONTROVERSIAL. COVERS WIDE RANGE FROM EARLY
      PEOPLING OF CONTINENT TO NATIONALISM AND
      INDEPENDENCE. EXAMINES EARLY STATE FORMATION, THE
      SLAVE TRADE, COLONIALISM, THE ARTS, FAMILY LIFE,
      ECONOMY, RELIGION. BASIC INTRODUCTORY READING.

  BOHANNAN PAUL   DALTON GEORGE   ED
  MARKETS IN AFRICA.
  EVANSTON, NORTHWESTERN UNIVERSITY PRESS, 1965
  010,
      THIS COLLECTION OF PAPERS FOCUSES ON THE EXCHANGE OF
      GOODS AND SERVICES IN TRADITIONAL AFRICAN ECONOMIC
      SYSTEMS. EXCELLENT COVERAGE OF THE CONTINENT, INCLU-
      DING WORKS ON WOLOF, YORUBA, AFIKPO, BULU, BUSHONG,
      MOSSI, HAUSA, FULANI, SOMALI, IRAQW, KIPSIGIS, GUSII,
      ZANDE, LUGBARA, TONGA AND HERERO. ABRIDGED EDITION
      AVAILABLE IN PAPERBACK.

  DALTON GEORGE
  THEORETICAL ISSUES IN ECONOMIC ANTHROPOLOGY.
  CURRENT ANTHROPOLOGY VOL 10 NO 1 JANUARY 1969
  010,
      SURVEY OF CONCEPTUAL FRAMEWORK USED IN ANALYZING PRI-
      MITIVE AND PEASANT ECONOMIES. CONTAINS OUTLINE OF
      VARIOUS TOPICS CONSIDERED IN ECONOMIC ANTHROPOLOGY AND
      CONCLUDES WITH SUMMARY OF CURRENT WORK ON SOCIO-ECONO-
      MIC ASPECTS OF DEVELOPMENT.

KENYATTA JOMO
FACING MT KENYA--THE RURAL LIFE OF THE KIKUYU.
NEW YORK, VINTAGE BOOKS, 1964
010,060,098,117-01,
    A MAJOR ANTHROPOLOGICAL CASE STUDY OF KIKUYU LIFE BY
    THE PRESIDENT OF THE REPUBLIC OF KENYA. STILL A STAN-
    DARD REFERENCE WORK, IT DERIVES FROM RESEARCH IN THE
    1930?S AT THE LONDON SCHOOL OF ECONOMICS UNDER THE
    FAMOUS ANTHROPOLOGIST, BRONISLAW MALINOWSKI (WHO WROTE
    THE INTRODUCTION). FASCINATING READING FOR ITS INSIGHTS
    NOT ONLY INTO THE KIKUYU BUT ALSO INTO THE THOUGHTS
    AND EXPERIENCES OF THE AUTHOR.

010

WHARTON CLIFTON R   ED
SUBSISTENCE AGRICULTURE AND ECONOMIC DEVELOPMENT
CHICAGO, ALDINE, 1969
010,070,
    EXCELLENT SERIES OF ARTICLES AND COMMENTARY BY 40
    SOCIAL SCIENTISTS ON SUBSISTENCE AGRICULTURE
    THROUGHOUT THE WORLD.PARTS COVER THE SUBSISTENCE
    FARMER,AGRARIAN CULTURES,AND PEASANT SOCIETIES-THE
    ECONOMIC BEHAVIOR OF SUBSISTENCE FARMERS-THEORIES OF
    CHANGE AND GROWTH-DEVELOPING SUBSISTENCE AGRICULTURE-
    RESEARCH PRIORITIES.

BIEBUYCK DANIEL
AFRICAN AGRARIAN SYSTEMS.
LONDON, OXFORD UNIVERSITY PRESS, 1963
010,070,
    REFERENCE

BOHANNAN PAUL
THE IMPACT OF MONEY ON AN AFRICAN SUBSISTENCE ECONOMY.
JOURNAL OF ECONOMIC HISTORY 19 DECEMBER 1959 PP 481-503
010,
    REFERENCE

BOHANNAN PAUL
LAND USE,LAND TENURE AND LAND REFORM
IN HERSKOVITS AND HARWITZ (EDS), ECONOMIC TRANSITION IN
AFRICA,EVANSTON,NORTHWESTERN UNIVERSITY PRESS, 1964
PP 133-150
010,
    REFERENCE

COHEN RONALD
SLAVERY IN AFRICA.
TRANS-ACTION (SPECIAL SUPPLEMENT) 4 1967 PP 44-56
010,028,
    REFERENCE

DALTON GEORGE   ED
TRIBAL AND PEASANT ECONOMIES-- READINGS IN ECONOMIC
ANTHROPOLOGY.
GARDEN CITY, NEW YORK,NATURAL HISTORY PRESS, 1967
010,
    REFERENCE

DALTON GEORGE   ED

PRIMITIVE, ARCHAIC, AND MODERN ECONOMIES-- ESSAYS OF KARL
POLANYI.
NEW YORK, DOUBLEDAY, 1968
010,
        REFERENCE

010
    DESHLER W
    CATTLE IN AFRICA DISTRIBUTION TYPES AND PROBLEMS.
    THE GEOGRAPHICAL REVIEW AMERICAN GEOGRAPHICAL SOCIETY 53
    JANUARY 1963 PP 52-58
    010,069,070,
        REFERENCE

    FORDE C DARYLL   DOUGLAS M
    PRIMITIVE ECONOMICS.
    IN H L SHAPIRO (ED.), MAN, CULTURE, AND SOCIETY, OXFORD
    UNIVERSITY PRESS, 1956 ALSO G DALTON (ED.), TRIBAL AND
    PEASANT ECONOMIES, DOUBLEDAY, 1967
    010,
        REFERENCE

    HERSKOVITS MELVILLE J   HARWITZ MITCHELL EDS
    ECONOMIC TRANSITION IN AFRICA
    EVANSTON, NORTHWESTERN UNIVERSITY PRESS, 1964
    010,073,
        REFERENCE

    HODDER B W   UKWU U I
    MARKETS IN WEST AFRICA
    IBADAN UNIVERSITY PRESS, 1969
    010,
        REFERENCE

    JONES W O
    FOOD AND AFRICULTURAL ECONOMICS OF TROPICAL AFRICA-- A
    SUMMARY VIEW.
    FOOD RESEARCH INSTITUTE BULLETIN(STANFORD UNIVERSITY) VOL.II
    NO. 1 1961
    010,
        REFERENCE

    MEEK CHARLES K
    LAND LAW AND CUSTOM IN THE COLONIES.
    LONDON, OXFORD UNIVERSITY PRESS, 1949
    010,066,070,
        REFERENCE

    MURDOCK GEORGE P
    STAPLE SUBSISTENCE CROPS OF AFRICA.
    THE GEOGRAPHICAL REVIEW AMERICAN GEOGRAPHICAL SOCIETY 50
    NO 3 OCTOBER 1960 PP 523-540
    010,069,
        REFERENCE

    READER D H
    A SURVEY OF CATEGORIES OF ECONOMIC ACTIVITIES AMONG THE
    PEOPLES OF AFRICA.
    AFRICA LONDON 34 1964 PP 28-45
    010,069,

REFERENCE

010

SAHLINS MARSHALL D
TRIBESMEN.
ENGLEWOOD CLIFFS, NEW JERSEY, PRENTICE-HALL, 1968
005,006,010,
       REFERENCE

SCHNEIDER HAROLD K
A FORMALIST VIEW OF AFRICAN ECONOMIC ANTHROPOLOGY.
IN CARTER, GWENDOLEN M. AND ANN PADEN (EDS), EXPANDING
HORIZONS IN AFRICAN STUDIES, EVANSTON, NORTHWESTERN
UNIVERSITY PRESS, 1969, PP. 243-255
010,100,
       REFERENCE

WATTERS R F
THE NATURE OF SHIFTING CULTIVATION--A REVIEW OF RECENT
RESEARCH.
PACIFIC VIEWPOINT 1 MARCH 1960 PP 59-99
010,070,
       REFERENCE

YUDELMAN M
SOME ASPECTS OF AFRICAN AGRICULTURAL DEVELOPMENT.
IN E A G ROBINSON (ED.) ECONOMIC DEVELOPMENT FOR AFRICA
SOUTH OF THE SAHARA, 1964.
010,070,
       REFERENCE

AMES DAVID W
WOLOF CO-OPERATIVE WORK GROUPS CHAPTER 12.
IN WILLIAM BASCOM AND MELVILLE HERSKOVITS, CONTINUTY AND
CHANGE IN AFRICAN CULTURES, CHICAGO, UNIVERSITY OF CHICAGO
PRESS, 1962, PP 224-237
010,130-01,
       CASE STUDY

ARNOLD ROSEMARY
A PORT OF TRADE-- WHYDAH ON THE GUINEA COAST.
IN K POLANYI, C M ARENSBERG AND H W PEARSON (EDS.), TRADE AND
MARKET IN THE EARLY EMPIRES, GLENCOE, ILLINOIS, THE FREE
PRESS, 1957
010,
       CASE STUDY

BENTSI-ENCHILL K
GHANA LAND LAW.
LONDON, SWEET AND MAXWELL, 1964
010, 066, 114-08,
       CASE STUDY

BOHANNAN PAUL
AFRICA S LAND.
IN G DALTON (ED.), TRIBAL AND PEASANT SOCIETIES, DOUBLEDAY,
1967
010,
       CASE STUDY

BOHANNAN PAUL   BOHANNAN LAURA
TIV ECONOMY.
EVANSTON, NORTHWESTERN UNIVERSITY PRESS, 1968
010,128-01,
        CASE STUDY

010
    COHEN RONALD
    SOME ASPECTS OF INSTITUTIONALIZED EXCHANGE-- A KANURI
    EXAMPLE.
    CAHIERS D'ETUDES AFRICAINES 5 1965 PP 353-369
    010,128-01,
        CASE STUDY

    COLSON ELIZABETH
    TRADE AND WEALTH AMONG THE TONGA.
    IN P J BOHANNAN AND GEORGE DALTON, EDS., MARKETS IN
    AFRICA, EVANSTON, NORTHWESTERN UNIVERSITY PRESS, 1962,
    PP 606-616
    010,142-01,
        CASE STUDY

    DOUGLAS MARY
    THE LELE--RESISTANCE TO CHANGE.
    IN BOHANNAN AND DALTON (EDS), MARKETS IN AFRICA, DOUBLEDAY,
    1965
    010,108-03,
        CASE STUDY

    FORDE C DARYLL   SCOTT R
    THE NATIVE ECONOMIES OF NIGERIA.
    LONDON, FABER, 1946
    010,128-01,
        CASE STUDY

    GULLIVER P H
    THE ARUSHA--ECONOMIC AND SOCIAL CHANGE.
    IN BOHANNAN AND DALTON (EDS), MARKETS IN AFRICA, DOUBLEDAY,
    1965
    010,136-06,
        CASE STUDY

    GULLIVER P H
    THE FAMILY HERDS-- A STUDY OF TWO PASTORAL TRIBES.
    LONDON, RUTLEDGE, 1955
    010,
        CASE STUDY

    HAMMOND PETER B
    YATENGA,TECHNOLOGY IN THE CULTURE OF A WEST AFRICAN KINGDOM
    GLENCOE, ILL, FREE PRESS, 1966
    010,141-08,
        CASE STUDY

    HODDER B W
    RURAL PERIODIC DAY MARKETS IN PART OF YORUBALAND, WESTERN
    NIGERIA.
    INSTITUTE OF BRITISH GEOGRAPHERS, PAPERS AND TRANSACTIONS
    29 1961 PP 149-159
    010,128-01,

CASE STUDY

010

KOBBEN A J F
LAND AS AN OBJECT OF GAIN IN A NON-LITERATE SOCIETY--
LAND TENURE AMONG THE BETE AND DIDA (IVORY COAST).
IN D BIEBUYCK (ED.), AFRICAN AGRARIAN SYSTEMS, LONDON,
OXFORD UNIVERSITY PRESS, 1963, PP 245-266
010,070,116-01,
    CASE STUDY

LEVINE ROBERT A
WEALTH AND POWER IN GUSIILAND.
IN PAUL BOHANNAN AND GEORGE DALTON (EDS.), MARKETS IN
AFRICA, EVANSTON, NORTHWESTERN UNIVERSITY PRESS, 1962, PP
520-536
010,117-01,
    CASE STUDY

LLOYD PETER C
CRAFT ORGANIZATIONS IN YORUBA TOWNS.
AFRICA, VOL. XXIII, 1953
010,128-01,
    CASE STUDY

MAIR LUCY P
STUDIES IN APPLIED ANTHROPOLOGY.
LONDON THE ATHLOVE PRESS 1957
010,
    CASE STUDY

MEEK CHARLES K
LAND TENURE AND LAND ADMINISTRATION IN NIGERIA AND THE
CAMEROONS.
LONDON, HER MAJESTY'S STATIONERY OFFICE, 1957
010,070,104-08,128-08,
    CASE STUDY

MIKESELL M W
THE ROLE OF TRIBAL MARKETS IN MOROCCO--EXAMPLES FROM THE
'NORTHERN ZONE'.
GEOGRAPHICAL REVIEW 48 OCTOBER 1958 PP 494-511
010,126-01,
    CASE STUDY

NADEL S F
A BLACK BYZANTIUM, THE KINGDOM OF NUPE IN NIGERIA.
OXFORD, OXFORD UNIVERSITY PRESS, 1942
009,010,128-01,
    CASE STUDY

NICOLAISEN JOHANNES
ECOLOGY AND CULTURE OF THE PASTORAL TUAREG-- WITH SPECIAL
REFERENCE TO THE TUAREG OF AHAGGAR AND AIR.
COPENHAGEN,THE NATIONAL MUSEUM OF COPENHAGEN
ETHNOGRAPHICAL SERIES 9 1963
010,127-01,
    CASE STUDY

POLANYI KARL   ROSTEIN ABRAHAM

DAHOMEY AND THE SLAVE TRADE-ANALYSIS OF AN ARCHAIC ECONOMY
SEATTLE,UNIVERSITY OF WASHINGTON PRESS,1966
010,028,
          CASE STUDY

010
    RICHARDS AUDREY I
    LAND, LABOUR AND DIET IN NORTHERN RHODESIA-- AN ECONOMIC
    STUDY OF THE BEMBA TRIBE.
    LONDON,ROUTLEDGE AND KEGAN PAUL,1939
    010,142-01,
          CASE STUDY

    SCHAPERA ISAAC
    ECONOMIC CHANGES IN SOUTH AFRICAN NATIVE LIFE.
    AFRICA,1928.ALSO G DALTON (ED.),TRIBAL AND PEASANT SOCIETIES,
    DOUBLEDAY,1967
    010,132-03,
          CASE STUDY

    SCHAPERA ISAAC   GOODWIN A J H
    WORK AND WEALTH.
    IN I SCHAPERA (ED.) THE BANTU-SPEAKING TRIBES OF SOUTH
    AFRICA, LONDON, ROUTLEDGE, 1937
    010,
          CASE STUDY

    SCUDDER T
    THE ECOLOGY OF THE GWEMBE TONGA.
    MANCHESTER,MANCHESTER UNIVERSITY PRESS,1962
    010,142-01,
          CASE STUDY

    SMET G
    COMMERCE, MARCHE ET SPECULATION CHEZ LES BARUNDI, COMMERCE
    MARKETING AND SPECULATION AMONG THE BARUNDI,.
    REVUE DE L,INSTITUT DE SOCIOLOGIE SOLVAY 18 1938 PP 53-57
    010,129-01,
          CASE STUDY

    SMITH M G
    THE HAUSA--MARKETS IN A PEASANT ECONOMY.
    IN BOHANNAN AND DALTON (EDS), MARKETS IN AFRICA, DOUBLEDAY,
    1965.
    010,128-01,
          CASE STUDY

    WATSON WILLIAM
    TRIBAL COHESION IN A MONEY ECONOMY.
    MANCHESTER,UNIVERSITY OF MANCHESTER PRESS,1958
    010,
          CASE STUDY

    DAAKU K YEBOA
    PRE-EUROPEAN CURRENCIES OF WEST AFRICA AND WESTERN SUDAN.
    GHANA NOTES AND QUERIES 2 1961 PP 12-14
    010,
          LESS ACCESSIBLE

    DURKHEIM EMILE

THE DIVISION OF LABOR IN SOCIETY.
GLENCOE, ILLINOIS, FREE PRESS, 1964, PP 70-110, 111-132, 200-232
010,
        GENERAL THEORY

010
    POLANYI KARL
    THE ECONOMY AS INSTITUTED PROCESS.
    IN K POLANYI, M ARENSBERG AND H W PEARSON (EDS), TRADE AND
    MARKET IN THE EARLY EMPIRES, GLENCOE, FREE PRESS, 1957. ALSO
    G DALTON (ED.), PRIMITIVE, ARCHAIC. AND MODERN ECONOMIES--
    ESSAYA OF KARL POLANYI, NEW YORK, DOUBLEDAY, 1968
    010,
        GENERAL THEORY

    WHEN PERCY
    THE AFRICAN HUSBANDMAN.
    IN R FIRTH, THEMES IN ECONOMIC ANTHROPOLOGY, LONDON,
    TAVISTOCK, 1967
    010,070,
        GENERAL THEORY

    DALTON GEORGE
    TRADITIONAL PRODUCTION IN PRIMITIVE AFRICAN ECONOMIES.
    QUARTERLY JOURNAL OF ECONOMICS AUGUST 1962. ALSO G DALTON,
    TRIBAL AND PEASANT ECONOMIES, DOUBLEDAY, 1967
    010,

11. LANGUAGE AND LINGUISTIC SYSTEMS

011
    FISHMAN JOSHUA   ET AL   EDS
    LANGUAGE PROBLEMS OF DEVELOPING NATIONS.
    NEW YORK, JOHN WILEY AND SONS, 1968
    011,049,
        CONTAINS BOTH THEORETICAL ARTICLES ON LANGUAGE DIVERSI-
        TY AND NATIONAL DEVELOPMENT, AND A NUMBER OF CASE STU-
        DIES FROM AFRICA--SWAHILI IN MODERN EAST AFRICA AND IN
        TANZANIA, HAUSA IN WEST AFRICA, AND IN NIGERIA--NORTH
        AFRICAN LANGUAGE PROBLEMS--LANGUAGE AND NATIONALISM IN
        SOUTH AFRICA--ENGLISH LITERATURE IN AFRICA--LANGUAGE
        POLICY IN CONGO-KINSHASA AND SUCAN--LANGUAGE POLICY IN
        WEST AFRICA--AND LINGUISTIC PROBLEMS OF NATION-BUILDING
        IN AFRICA. CO EDITED BY C FERGUSON AND J DAS GUPTA.

    GREENBERG JOSEPH H
    STUDIES IN AFRICAN LINGUISTIC CLASSIFICATION.
    NEW YORK, VIKING PRESS, COMPASS BOOKS, 1955
    003,011,
        LANDMARK IN AFRICAN LINGUISTICS. SYNTHESIZES PRE-
        VIOUS WORK INTO A NEW CLASSIFICATION OF AFRICAN LAN-
        GUAGES. FIRST TO USE PURELY LINGUISTIC CRITERIA VS.
        RACIAL STEREOTYPES, ETC. DESTROYS HAMITIC MYTH,
        DEVELOPS AFRO-ASIATIC FAMILY AND LAYS BASIS FOR MANY
        PREVALENT EXPLANATIONS OF BANTU MIGRATIONS. MAP

BECOMES STANDARD REFERENCE UNTIL GREENBERG S NEW
CLASSIFICATION IN 1963.

011
GREENBERG JOSEPH H
THE LANGUAGES OF AFRICA.
BLOOMINGTON, INDIANA UNIVERSITY PRESS, 1963
003,011,
        RECLASSIFICATION OF AFRICAN LANGUAGES DONE IN 1963.
        GREATLY SIMPLIFIES 1955 CLASSIFICATION. MUCH MORE
        CONTROVERSIAL. STILL BEING DEBATED BY LINGUISTS.
        MAJOR LANGUAGE FAMILIES NOW INCLUDE CONGO-KORDOFANIAN
        NILO-SAHARAN, AFRO-ASIATIC AND KHOISAN.

GUTHRIE MALCOLM
COMPARATIVE BANTU--AN INTRODUCTION TO THE COMPARATIVE
LINGUISTICS AND PREHISTORY OF THE BANTU LANGUAGE.
HANTS, ENGLAND, GREGG PRESS LTD., 1969
011,019,
        THIS FOUR-VOLUME SET IS THE PRODUCT OF A LIFETIME OF
        RESEARCH BY THE WORLD'S FOREMOST SPECIALIST ON BANTU
        LANGUAGES. THE VOLUMES CONTAIN MANY MAPS AND ABUN-
        DANT STATISTICAL INFORMATION, WORD LISTS, ETC. THE
        FULL SET COSTS 120 DOLLARS.

KNAPPERT JAN
LANGUAGE PROBLEMS OF THE NEW NATIONS OF AFRICA.
AFRICA QUARTERLY, JULY-SEPT., 1965, VOL. V, NO. 2
011,
        ALTHOUGH THE ARTICLE FOCUSES MAINLY ON CONTEMPORARY
        PROBLEMS OF LANGUAGE POLICY IN AFRICAN STATES, IT DOES
        DISCUSS MAJOR VERNACULAR LANGUAGES WITHIN THE AFRICAN
        COUNTRIES. AUTHOR, WHOSE EXPERIENCE IS PRIMARILY IN E.
        AFRICA, IS CONCERNED WITH ESTIMATES AS TO PEOPLE WHO
        CAN UNDERSTAND A LANGUAGE, NOT WITH NUMBER OF NATIVE
        SPEAKERS. HIS ESTIMATES OF LANGUAGES PER COUNTRY ARE
        PROBABLY LOW.

VOEGELIN C F   VOEGELIN F M
LANGUAGES OF THE WORLD--AFRICA FACSIMILE ONE
ANTHROPOLOGICAL LINGUISTICS, VOL. 6, NO. 5, MAY, 1964, PP.
1-339
011,
        USEFUL COMPILATION OF LANGUAGE PATTERNS IN AFRICA,
        USING MODIFIED GREENBERG CLASSIFICATION. ALSO SUMMARI-
        ZES IN READIBLE FORM THE EARLIER EFFORTS AT LANGUAGE
        CLASSIFICATION. VOLUME IS ONE PRODUCT OF LARGER
        U.S.O.E. PROJECT.

WESTERMANN D   BRYAN M A
LANGUAGES OF WEST AFRICA.
LONDON, OXFORD UNIVERSITY PRESS, 1952
011,
        EXCELLENT USE OF HISTORICAL APPROACH TO LANGUAGE FAM-
        ILY GROUPINGS, (HENCE DIFFERENT FROM GREENBERG'S USE OF
        LANGUAGE SIMILARITY AS CRITERIA FOR GROUPING). SLIGHTLY
        DATED.

DAMMANN E
THE INFLUENCE OF RELIGION ON AFRICAN LANGUAGES.

IN LALAGE BOWN AND MICHAEL CROWDER (EDS.), PROCEEDINGS OF
THE FIRST INTERNATIONAL CONGRESS OF AFRICANISTS, ACCRA,
1962, LONDON, LONGMANS, 1964, PP 115-123
011,
          REFERENCE

011
    FORTUNE GEORGE
    THE CONTRIBUTIONS OF LINGUISTICS TO ETHNOHISTORY.
    HISTORIANS IN TROPICAL AFRICA, PROCEEDINGS, SALISBURY,
    SOUTHERN RHODESIA, UNIVERSITY COLLEGE OF RHODESIA AND
    NYASALAND , 1962, PP 17-30
    011,
          REFERENCE

    GREENBERG JOSEPH H
    LINGUISTICS CHAPTER 15.
    IN ROBERT A LYSTAD (ED), THE AFRICAN WORLD, NEW YORK,
    PRAEGER,1965,PP 416-441
    011,
          REFERENCE

    GREENBERG JOSEPH H
    AFRICA AS A LINGUISTIC AREA CHAPTER 2.
    IN WILLIAM BASCOM AND MELVILLE HERSKOVITS, CONTINUTY AND
    CHANGE IN AFRICAN CULTURES, CHICAGO, UNIVERSITY OF CHICAGO
    PRESS, 1962, PP 15-27
    003,011,
          REFERENCE

    GREENBERG JOSEPH H
    THE HISTORY AND PRESENT STATUS OF AFRICAN LINGUISTIC
    STUDIES.
    IN LALAGE BOWN AND MICHAEL CROWDER (EDS.), PROCEEDINGS OF
    THE FIRST INTERNATIONAL CONGRESS OF AFRICANISTS, ACCRA,
    1962, LONDON, LONGMANS, 1964, PP 83-96
    011,
          REFERENCE

    GREENBERG JOSEPH H
    HISTORICAL INFERENCES FROM LINGUISTIC RESEARCH IN SUB-SAHA-
    RAN AFRICA.
    IN JEFFREY BUTLER (ED), BOSTON UNIVERSITY PAPERS IN AFRICAN
    HISTORY VOL I, BOSTON, BOSTON UNIVERSITY PRESS,1964,PP 1-16
    011,
          REFERENCE

    MEINHOF CARL   TRANSLATED BY   WARMELO N J V
    INTRODUCTION TO THE PHONOLOGY OF BANTU LANGUAGES.
    BERLIN, DIETRICH REINER/ ERNST VOHSEN,1932
    011,
          REFERENCE SOURCE

    SPENCER JOHN   ED
    LANGUAGE IN AFRICA.
    LONDON, CAMBRIDGE UNIVERSITY PRESS, 1963
    011,049,
          REFERENCE

    TUCKER A N

PHILOLOGY AND AFRICA.
BULLETIN OF THE SCHOOL OF ORIENTAL AND AFRICAN STUDIES   20
1957
011,
      REFERENCE

011
  WINSTON F D D
  GREENBERG'S CLASSIFICATION OF AFRICAN LANGUAGES.
  AFRICAN LANGUAGE STUDIES 7 PP 160-170 1966
  011,
      REFERENCE

  BIRNIE J R   ANSRE GILBERT   EDS
  PROCEEDINGS OF THE CONFERENCE ON THE STUDY OF GHANAIAN
  LANGUAGES.
  ACCRA, INTERNATIONAL UNIVERSITY BOOKSELLERS,INC., 1968
  011,
      CASE STUDY

  CHESSWAS J D
  THE ESSENTIALS OF LUGANDA.
  NAIROBI,   OXFORD UNIVERSITY PRESS, 1968
  011,139-01,
      CASE STUDY

  DUSTAN ELIZABETH   ED
  TWELVE NIGERIAN LANGUAGES.
  NEW YORK, INTERNATIONAL BOOKSELLERS, INC., 1969
  011,
      CASE STUDY

  GREEN MARGARET
  A DESCRIPTIVE GRAMMAR OF IGBO.
  BERLIN, AKADEMIE-VERLAG, 1963
  011,128-01,
      CASE STUDY

  LASEBIKAN E L
  LEARNING YORUBA.
  LONDON, OXFORD UNIVERSITY PRESS, 1958
  011,128-01,
      CASE STUDY

  TAYLOR F W
  A PRACTICAL HAUSA GRAMMAR.
  LONDON, OXFORD UNIVERSITY PRESS, 1959
  011,128-01,
      CASE STUDY

  WHITELEY W H   MULI M G
  PRACTICAL INTRODUCTION TO KAMBA.
  LONDON, OXFORD UNIVERSITY PRESS, 1962
  011,117-01,
      CASE STUDY

  ANONYMOUS
  TABLE RONDE SUR LES LANGUES AFRICAINES (ROUND TABLE ON
  AFRICAN LANGUAGES).
  PRESENCE AFRICAINE, NO. 67, 3RD QUARTER, 1968, PP. 53-156

011,
    LESS ACCESSIBLE

011
  FODOR ISTVAN
  LA CLASSIFICATION DES LANGUES NEGRO-AFRICAINES ET LA THEORIE
  DE J H GREENBERG (THE CLASSIFICATION OF THE BLACK AFRICAN
  LANGUAGES AND THE THEORY OF J H GREENBERG).
  CAHIER D'ETUDES AFRICAINES, VOL. VIII, NO. 32, 1968, PP.
  617-31
  011,
      LESS ACCESSIBLE

  MFOULOU JEAN
  SCIENCE ET PSEUDO-SCIENCE DES LANGUES AFRICAINES (SCIENCE
  AND PSEUDO-SCIENCE OF AFRICAN LANGUAGES).
  PRESENCE AFRICAINE, NO. 70, 2ND QUARTER, 1969, PP. 147-161
  011,003,
      LESS ACCESSIBLE

  WESTERMANN D
  DIE WESTLICHEN SUDANSPRACHEN (THE LANGUAGES OF THE WESTERN
  SUDAN).
  BERLIN, IN KOMMISSION BEI W. DE GRUYTER AND CO, 1927
  011,
      LESS ACCESSIBLE

  WESTERMANN D
  DIE SUDANSPRACHEN (LANGUAGES OF THE SUDAN).
  HAMBURG, L FRIEDERICSEN AND CO, 1911
  011,
      LESS ACCESSIBLE

  COMMISSION DE COOPERATION TECHNIQUE EN AFRIQUE
  REPORT OF THE SYMPOSIUM ON MULTILINGUALISM (BRAZZAVILLE).
  LONDON COMMISSION DE COOPERATION TECHNIQUE EN AFRIQUE 87
  1962
  011,
      LESS ACCESSIBLE

  FODOR ISTVAN
  THE PROBLEMS IN THE CLASSIFICATION OF THE AFRICAN LANGUAGES.
  BUDAPEST CENTER FOR AFRO-ASIAN RESEARCH OF THE HUNGARIAN
  ACADEMY OF SCIENCES NO 5 1966
  011,
      LESS ACCESSIBLE

12. LITERATURE AND ORAL TRADITION

012
  FELDMAN SUSAN   ED
  AFRICAN MYTHS AND TALES
  NEW YORK DELL PUBLISHING COMPANY 1963
  012,
      GOOD ANTHOLOGY IN PAPERBACK, WITH INTRODUCTION BY THE

EDITOR.INCLUDES OVER 100 ITEMS COVERING MYTHS OF
PRIMEVAL TIMES-THE BEGINNING OF THINGS, AND THE ORIGIN
OF DEATH,TRICKSTER TALES,EXPLANATORY TALES,DILEMMA
STORIES AND MORAL TALES,TALES OF HUMAN ADVENTURE AND
A SHORT BIBLIOGRAPHY

012

OTTENBERG SIMON   OTTENBERG PHOEBE
CULTURES AND SOCIETIES OF AFRICA.
NEW YORK,RANDOM HOUSE,1960
003,012,016,
EXCELLENT COLLECTION OF CASE STUDIES, ETHNIC AND THE-
MATIC.   SECTIONS COVER PEOPLE AND ENVIRONMENT (BUSH-
MEN, FULANI, BEMBA), SOCIAL GROUPINGS (UNILINEAL DES-
CENT GROUPS, SECRET SOCIETIES, AGE SETS, URBANIZATION,
MARRIAGE), AUTHORITY AND GOVERNMENT (TUTSI, TIV, KON-
KOMBA, ASHANTI), VALUE, RELIGION AND AESTHETICS (ROLE
OF CATTLE, WITCHCRAFT, INITIATION, FOLKLORE, ART),
CULTURE CONTACT AND CHANGE (ISLAM, CHRISTIANITY),
URBANISM).   INTRODUCTION SUPERB.

VANSINA JAN
ORAL TRADITION, A STUDY OF HISTORICAL METHODOLOGY.
CHICAGO,ALDINE,1961
012,090,
PIONEER EXPLORATION OF METHODS NECESSARY TO PROCESS
ORAL TESTIMONY.   MUCH OF TECHNIQUE BASED ON AUTHOR'S
FIELD RESEARCH IN CONGO AREA.   DEALS WITH TRADITION AS
A CHAIN OF TESTIMONIES, PROBLEMS OF UNDERSTANDING TES-
TIMONY, EVALUATION OF TESTIMONY, AND THE DIFFERENT
TYPES OF TESTIMONY RELATED TO HISTORICAL KNOWLEDGE
(POETRY, FORMULAE, LISTS, TALES, COMMENTARIES).   AU-
THOR IS PROFESSOR OF AFRICAN HISTORY AT WISCONSIN.

ABRAHAMSSON H
THE ORIGIN OF DEATH-STUDIES IN AFRICAN MYTHOLOGY
UPPSALA,ALQUIST AND WIKSELL,1951
012,
REFERENCE

BASCOM WILLIAM R
FOLKLORE AND LITERATURE.
IN ROBERT A LYSTAD (ED), THE AFRICAN WORLD, NEW YORK,
PREAGER 1965 PP 469-492
012,
REFERENCE

COHEN RONALD   VANSINA JAN   ZOLBERG ARISTIDE R
ORAL HISTORY IN AFRICA.
EVANSTON,ILLINOIS, NORTHWESTERN UNIVERSITY, PROGRAM OF
AFRICAN STUDIES, REPRINT SERIES, 2, NO.1 SEPTEMBER 1965
012,099,
REFERENCE

DADIE BERNARD
FOLKLORE AND LITERATURE.
IN LALAGE BOWN AND MICHAEL CROWDER (EDS.), PROCEEDINGS OF
THE FIRST INTERNATIONAL CONGRESS OF AFRICANISTS, ACCRA,
1962, LONDON, LONGMANS, 1964, PP 199-219
012,

REFERENCE

012

DOOB LEONARD W
ANTS WILL NOT EAT YOUR FINGERS- A SELECTION OF TRADITIONAL
AFRICAN POEMS
NEW YORK WALKER 1966
012,
      REFERENCE

DOOB LEONARD W   ED
A CROCODILE HAS ME BY THE LEG-- AFRICAN POEMS.
NEW YORK WALKER 1967
012,
      REFERENCE

JORDAN A C
TALE, TELLER, AND AUDIENCE IN AFRICAN SPOKEN NARRATIVE.
IN PROCEEDINGS OF THE CONFERENCE ON AFRICAN LANGUAGES AND
LITERATURES, NORTHWESTERN UNIVERSITY, 1966, UNITED STATES
OFFICE OF EDUCATION, NO. OE-6-14-018, PP 33-43
012,
      REFERENCE

RADIN PAUL   SWEENEY JAMES J
AFRICAN FOLKTALES AND SCULPTURE.
PRINCETON, NEW JERSEY, PRINCETON UNIVERSITY PRESS, 1969
012,014,
      REFERENCE

ROUGET GILBERT
AFRICAN TRADITIONAL NON-PROSE FORMS-- RECITING, DECLAIMING,
SINGING, AND STROPHIC STRUCTURE.
IN PROCEEDINGS OF THE CONFERENCE ON AFRICAN LANGUAGES
AND LITERATURES, NORTHWESTERN UNIVERSITY, 1966, UNITED
STATES OFFICE OF EDUCATION, NO. OE-6-14-018, PP 45-58
012,
      REFERENCE

SMITH E W
AFRICAN IDEAS OF GOD.
IN PETER J MCEWAN AND ROBERT B SUTCLIFFE (EDS), MODERN AFRICA
NEW YORK, THOMAS CROWELL, 1965, PP 6L74
013,
012,
      REFERENCE

SMITH E W
AFRICAN IDEAS OF GOD
LONDON, EDINBURGH HOUSE PRESS, 1950
012,013,
      REFERENCE

ANDRZEJEWSKI B W   LEWIS I M
SOMALI POETRY.
LONDON, OXFORD UNIVERSITY PRESS, 1964
012,133-01,
      CASE STUDY

BABALOLA S A

THE CONTENT AND FORM OF YORUBA IJALA.
LONDON, OXFORD UNIVERSITY PRESS, 1966
012,128-01,
    CASE STUDY

012

CARDINALL ALLAN W   ED
TALES TOLD IN TOGOLAND-- TO WHICH IS ADDED THE MYTHICAL AND
TRADITIONAL HISTORY OF DAGOMBA BY E F TAMAKLOE.
LONDON, OXFORD UNIVERSITY PRESS, 1931
012,137-01,
    CASE STUDY
    REFERENCE

COUPEZ A   KAMANZI THOMAS   EDS
LITTERATURE COURTOISE DU RWANDA (COURT LITERATURE OF
RWANDA).
LONDON AND NEW YORK, INTERNATIONAL UNIVERSITY BOOKSELLERS,
INC., 1969
012,129-01,
    CASE STUDY

DIOP BIRAGO
TALES OF AMADOU KOUMBA.
LONDON, OXFORD UNIVERSITY PRESS, 1966
012,130-01,
    CASE STUDY

EVANS-PRITCHARD E E
THE ZANDE TRICKSTER.
LONDON, OXFORD UNIVERSITY PRESS, 1967
012,134-01,
    CASE STUDY

FINNEGAN RUTH   ED
LIMBA STORIES AND STORY-TELLING.
LONDON, OXFORD UNIVERSITY PRESS, 1967
012,131-01,
    CASE STUDY

HAIR P E H
NOTES ON THE DISCOVERY OF THE VAI SCRIPT WITH A
BIBLIOGRAPHY.
SIERRA LEONE LANGUAGE REVIEW 2 1963 PP 36-49
012,119-01,
    CASE STUDY

HARRIES LYNDON
SWAHILI POETRY.
OXFORD, CLARENDON PRESS, 1962
012,023,
    CASE STUDY

HARRIES LYNDON
POEMS FROM KENYA--GNOMIC VERSES IN SWAHILI BY AHMAD NASSIR
BIN JUMA BHALO.
MADISON, UNIVERSITY OF WISCONSIN PRESS, 1966
012,117-01,
    CASE STUDY

HERSKOVITS MELVILLE J   HERSKOVITS FRANCES S
DAHOMEAN NARRATIVE-A CROSS CULTURAL ANALYSIS
EVANSTON, NORTHWESTERN UNIVERSITY PRESS, 1958
012,109-01,
          CASE STUDY

012

JOHNSTON H A S   ED
A SELECTION OF HAUSA STORIES.
LONDON, OXFORD UNIVERSITY PRESS, 1966
012,128-01,
          CASE STUDY

KIRK-GREENE A H M
HAUSA BA DABO BANE--A COLLECTION OF 500 PROVERBS.
IBADAN, OXFORD UNIVERSITY PRESS, 1966
012,128-01,
          CASE STUDY

MBITI JOHN S
AKAMBA STORIES.
OXFORD, CLARENDON PRESS, 1966
012,
          CASE STUDY

MORRIS HENRY F
THE HEROIC RECITATIONS OF THE BAHIMA OF ANKOLE.
LONDON, OXFORD UNIVERSITY PRESS, 1964
012,015,139-01,
          CASE STUDY

PAEZ PERO
THE GLORIOS VICTORIES OF AMDA SEYON, KING OF ETHIOPIA,
TOGETHER WITH THE HISTORY OF THE EMPEROR ADN CEON OTHERWISE
CALLED GABRA MAZCAL.
LONDON, OXFORD UNIVERSITY PRESS, 1965
012,110-02,
          CASE STUDY

PANKHURST RICHARD   ED
THE ETHIOPIAN ROYAL CHRONICLES.
LONDON, OXFORD UNIVERSITY PRESS, 1967
012,110-02,
          CASE STUDY

RATTRAY ROBERT S
AKAN-ASHANTI FOLK TALES.
OXFORD, THE CLARENDON PRESS, 1930
012,
          CASE STUDY

RATTRAY ROBERT S
ASHANTI PROVERBS
OXFORD, CLARENDON PRESS, 1916
012,
          CASE STUDY

SCHAPERA ISAAC   ED
PRAISE PEOMS OF TSWANA CHIEFS.
OXFORD, CLARENDON PRESS, 1965

012,102-01,
     CASE STUDY

012
   SKINNER NEIL
   HAUSA READINGS--SELECTIONS FROM EDGAR'S TATSUNIYOYI.
   MADISON, UNIVERSITY OF WISCONSIN PRESS, 1968
   012,128-01,
       CASE STUDY

   SKINNER NEIL   TRANS AND ED
   HAUSA TALES AND TRADITIONS.
   NEW YORK, AFRICANA PUBLISHING CORPORATION, 1969
   012,128-01,
       CASE STUDY

   SKINNER NEIL   TRANS   ED
   HAUSA TALES AND TRADITIONS-AN ENGLISH TRANSLATION OF EDGAR'S
   TATSUNIYOYI NA HAUSA,3 VOLUMES
   NEW YORK, AFRICANA PUBLISHING CORPORATION,1969
   012,
       CASE STUDY

   SOW ALFA IBRAHIM
   CHRONIQUES ET RECITS DU FOUTA DJALON (CHRONICLES AND
   RECITATIONS OF FUTA JALLON).
   PARIS, KLINCKSIECK; NEW YORK, INTERNATIONAL UNIVERSITY BOOK-
   SELLERS, 1968
   012,115-01,
       CASE STUDY

   STUART JAMES   ED
   IZIBONGO, ZULU PRAISE-POEMS.
   OXFORD, CLARENDON PRESS, 1968
   012,132-01,
       CASE STUDY

   UMEASIEGBU REMS NNA
   THE WAY WE LIVED--IBO CUSTOMS AND STORIES.
   NEW YORK, HUMANITIES PRESS INC., 1969 (LONDON, HEINEMANN
   EDUCATIONAL BOOKS)
   012,128-01,
       CASE STUDY

   WALKER BARBARA K   WALKER WARREN S   EDS
   NIGERIAN FOLK TALES.
   NEW BRUNSWICK,RUTGERS UNIVERSITY PRESS,1961
   012,
       CASE STUDY

   BEIER ULLI
   THE HISTORICAL AND PSYCHOLOGICAL SIGNIFICANCE OF YORUBA
   MYTHS.
   ODU, A JOURNAL OF YORUBA AND RELATED STUDIES 1 N C PP 17-25
   012,128-01,
       LESS ACCESSIBLE

   PADEN JOHN N
   KANO HAUSA POETRY.
   KANO STUDIES 1 SEPTEMBER 1965 PP 33-39

012,128-01,
     LESS ACCESSIBLE

012

TRAUTMANN RENE
LA LITTERATURE POPULAIRE A LA COTE DES ESCLAVES-- CONTES,
PROVERBS, DEVINETTES (POPULAR LITERATURE OF THE SLAVE COAST
-- TALES, PROVERBS, RIDDLES).
PARIS, INSTITUT D'ETHNOLOGIE, TRAVEAUX ET MEMOIRES 4, 1927
012,
     LESS ACCESSIBLE

MIDDLETON JOHN   ED
MYTH AND COSMOS.
GARDEN CITY, NEW YORK, THE NATURAL HISTORY PRESS, 1967
012,013,099,
     GENERAL THEORY

13. CONCEPTUAL SYSTEMS AND RELIGION

013

CROWDER MICHAEL   IKIME OBARO   EDS
WEST AFRICAN CHIEFS--THEIR CHANGING STATUS UNDER COLONIAL
RULE AND INDEPENDENCE.
NEW YORK, AFRICANA PUBLISHING CORPORATION, FORTHCOMING
009,013,035,
     CASE STUDIES FROM WEST AFRICA--PRIMARILY NIGERIA--ON
     CHANGING ROLE OF CHIEFS. CONTAINS CASE STUDIES OF PAT-
     TERNS WHICH PROVIDE INSIGHT INTO DISTINCTION BETWEEN
     'DIRECT' AND 'INDIRECT' RULE. TO LESSER EXTENT, DEALS
     WITH CONTEMPORARY ISSUES ON MODERN ROLE OF CHIEFS.

FORDE C DARYLL
AFRICAN WORLDS--STUDIES IN THE COSMOLOGICAL IDEAS AND
SOCIAL VALUES OF AFRICAN PEOPLES.
LONDON, OXFORD UNIVERSITY PRESS, 1965
013,
     EXCELLENT INTRODUCTION TO THE CONCEPTS AND CATEGORIES
     OF AFRICAN TRADITIONAL THOUGHT. CASE STUDIES BY LEAD-
     ING SCHOLARS ON VARIOUS ETHNIC GROUP COSMOLOGIES.

FORTES MEYER   DIETERLEN GERMAINE EDS
AFRICAN SYSTEMS OF THOUGHT
LONDON, OXFORD UNIVERSITY PRESS, 1965, INTERNATIONAL AFRICAN
INSTITUTE
013,
     FIRST PART EXCELLENT INTRODUCTION TO MAJOR THEMES-
     INDIGENOUS RELIGIOUS SYSTEMS,RITUAL AND SYMBOLISM,
     CHRISTIANITY IN AFRICA.SECOND PART IS CASE STUDIES BY
     LEADING SCHOLARS DEALING WITH ETHNIC GROUPS-SONJO,
     BORAN,NDEMBU,EDO,YAKOMA,MONGO,SOMALI,ANLCOLE,BWA,
     FULANI,FALI,SHONA AND DIOLA.ALSO THEMATIC CASE STUDIES
     DEALING WITH CONCEPT OF MISFORTUNE,SORCERY,ANCESTOR
     WORSHIP.

HORTON ROBIN
AFRICAN TRADITIONAL THOUGHT AND WESTERN SCIENCE PART 1-FROM
TRADITION TO SCIENCE, PART 2- THE CLOSED AND OPEN
PREDICAMENT
AFRICA 37 1967 PP 50-71 AND 155-187
013,040,098,
EXCELLENT ARTICLES. FIRST DEVELOPS AN APPROACH TO
TRADITIONAL AFRICAN THOUGHT WHICH STRESSES ITS CROSS-
CULTURAL SIMILARITIES,PARTICULARLY WITH WESTERN
THOUGHT AND ESPECIALLY IN RELIGION. SECOND EXAMINES
DIFFERENCES BETWEEN TRADITIONAL AND SCIENTIFIC
THOUGHT,FOCUSING ON AWARENESS OF ALTERNATIVES TO THE
ESTABLISHED BODY OF THEORETICAL TENETS.

013

TURNBULL COLIN M
TRIBALISM AND SOCIAL EVOLUTION IN AFRICA.
THE ANNALS OF THE AMERICAN ACADEMY OF POLITICAL AND SOCIAL
SCIENCE VOL 354 JULY 1964 PP 22-31
006,013,
AUTHOR IS ASSISTANT CURATOR OF AFRICAN ETHNOLOGY AT
AMERICAN MUSEUM OF NATURAL HISTORY. IN ARTICLE AUTHOR
SUGGESTS THAT AFRICAN TRIBAL SYSTEMS HAVE BASIC SIMI-
LARITIES. STRESSES THE IMPORTANCE OF RELIGIOUS ASPECT
OF ETHNIC COMMUNITY, AND THE FLEXIBILITY OF ETHNIC
GROUPS IN MEETING NEW SITUATIONS.

BEATTIE J H M   MIDDLETON JOHN   EDS
SPIRIT MEDIUMSHIP AND SOCIETY IN AFRICA
NEW YORK,AFRICANA PUBLISHING CORPORATION,1969
013,
REFERENCE

FERNANDEZ JAMES W
CONTEMPORARY AFRICAN RELIGION--CONFLUENTS OF INQUIRY.
IN CARTER, GWENDOLEN M. AND ANN PADEN (EDS), EXPANDING
HORIZONS IN AFRICAN STUDIES, EVANSTON, NORTHWESTERN
UNIVERSITY PRESS, 1969, PP. 27-46
013,050,100,
REFERENCE

FORDE C DARYLL
AFRICAN MODES OF THINKING.
IN PETER J MCEWAN AND ROBERT B SUTCLIFFE (EDS), MODERN AFRICA,
NEW YORK,THOMAS CROWELL,1965,PP 58-62
013,
REFERENCE

FORTES MEYER
THE NOTION OF FATE IN WEST AFRICA.
IN PETER J MCEWAN AND ROBERT B SUTCLIFFE (EDS),MODERN AFRICA,
NEW YORK,THOMAS CROWELL,1965,PP 75-78
013,
REFERENCE

FORTES MEYER
OEDIPUS AND JOB IN WEST AFRICA.
CAMBRIDGE, CAMBRIDGE UNIVERSITY PRESS, 1959
013,
REFERENCE

013

FORTES MEYER   EVANS-PRITCHARD E
VALUES IN AFRICAN TRIBAL LIFE.
IN PETER J MCEWAN AND ROBERT B SUTCLIFFE (EDS), MODERN AFRICA,
NEW YORK, THOMAS CROWELL, 1965, PP 55-57
013,
        REFERENCE

GLUCKMAN MAX
THE LOGIC OF WITCHCRAFT.
IN PETER J MCEWAN AND ROBERT B SUTCLIFFE (EDS), MODERN AFRICA,
NEW YORK, THOMAS CROWELL, 1965, PP 79-92
013,
        REFERENCE

GRIAULE MARCEL
CONVERSATION WITH OGOTEMMELI
NEW YORK, OXFORD, 1965
013,
        REFERENCE

HANSBERRY W L
INDIGENOUS AFRICAN RELIGIONS.
IN AMSAC, AFRICA SEEN BY AMERICAN NEGROES, PARIS,
PRESENCE AFRICAINE, 1958, PP 83-100
013,
        REFERENCE

HORTON ROBIN
RITUAL MAN IN AFRICA
AFRICA 34 1964 PP 85-104
013,
        REFERENCE

MALINOWSKI B
MAGIC, SCIENCE AND RELIGION
GARDEN CITY, DOUBLEDAY ANCHOR BOOKS, 1948
013,
        REFERENCE

MBITI JOHN S
AFRICAN RELIGIONS AND PHILOSOPHY.
NEW YORK, PRAEGER, 1969   (LONDON, HEINEMANN
EDUCATIONAL BOOKS)
013,
        REFERENCE

MBITI JOHN S
CONCEPTS OF GOD IN AFRICA.
NEW YORK, PRAEGER, 1970
013,
        REFERENCE

MENDELSOHN JACK
GOD, ALLAH AND JU JU, RELIGION IN AFRICA TODAY
NEW YORK, NELSON, 1962
013,
        REFERENCE

MIDDLETON JOHN   WINTER E H   EDS
WITCHCRAFT AND SORCERY IN EAST AFRICA
NEW YORK,PRAEGER,1963
013,
        REFERENCE

013

RICHARDS AUDREY I
AFRICAN SYSTEMS OF THOUGHT--AN ANGLO-FRENCH DIALOGUE.
MAN, VOL. 2, NO. 2, JUNE, 1967, PP. 286-298
013,
        REFERENCE

SMITH E W
AFRICAN IDEAS OF GOD.
IN PETER J MCEWAN AND ROBERT B SUTCLIFFE (EDS), MODERN AFRICA,
NEW YORK,THOMAS CROWELL, 1965,PP 6L74
013,
012,
        REFERENCE

SMITH E W
AFRICAN IDEAS OF GOD
LONDON,EDINBURGH HOUSE PRESS,1950
012,013,
        REFERENCE

SOYINKA WOLE
DANCE OF THE FORESTS.
LONDON,OXFORD UNIVERSITY PRESS,1963
013,090,
        REFERENCE

TEMPELS RES PLACID   TRANSLATED BY   KING COLIN
LA PHILOSOPHIE BANTOUE (BANTU PHILOSOPHY).
PARIS, PRESENCE AFRICAINE, 2ND ED., 1961
013,
        REFERENCE

THOMAS L V
THE STUDY OF DEATH IN NEGRO AFRICA.
IN LALAGE BOWN AND MICHAEL CROWDER (EDS.), PROCEEDINGS OF
THE FIRST INTERNATIONAL CONGRESS OF AFRICANISTS, ACCRA,
1962, LONDON, LONGMANS, 1964, PP 146-168
013,
        REFERENCE

BA AMADOU HAMPATE
THE FULBE OR FULANI OF MALI AND THEIR CULTURE
ABBIA, JULY-DECEMBER 1966, NO. 14-15, PP. 55-87
013,
        CASE STUDY

CHAPELLE JEAN
LA RELIGION DES TOUBOUS (TUBU RELIGION) CHAPTER 9.
IN NOMADES NOIRS DU SAHARA, PARIS, LIBRARIE PLON, 1957
013,106-01,
        CASE STUDY

EVANS-PRITCHARD E E

WITCHCRAFT, ORACLES, AND MAGIC AMONG THE AZANDE.
LONDON, OXFORD UNIVERSITY PRESS, 1951
013,134-01,
     CASE STUDY

013
EVANS-PRITCHARD E E
NUER RELIGION
LONDON,OXFORD UNIVERSITY PRESS,1956
013,134-01,
     CASE STUDY

GOODY JACK
DEATH, PROPERTY AND THE ANCESTORS--A STUDY OF THE MORTUARY
CUSTOMS OF THE LODAGAA OF WEST AFRICA.
STANFORD, STANFORD UNIVERSITY PRESS, 1962
013,
     CASE STUDY

GREENBERG JOSEPH H
THE INFLUENCE OF ISLAM ON A SUDANESE RELIGION.
SEATTLE, UNIVERSITY OF WASHINGTON PRESS, 1969
013,128-01,
     CASE STUDY

HARRIS W T   SAWYER HARRY
THE SPRINGS OF MENDE BELIEF AND CONDUCT.
FREETOWN, SIERRA LEONE UNIVERSITY PRESS, 1968
013,131-01,
     CASE STUDY

HERSKOVITS MELVILLE J
DAHOMEY-- AN ANCIENT WEST AFRICAN KINGDOM.
EVANSTON,NORTHWESTERN UNIVERSITY PRESS,1967
013,026,109-02,
     CASE STUDY

HOLAS B
L'IMAGE DU MONDE BETE (THE BETE IMAGE OF THE WORLD).
PARIS, PRESSES UNIVERSITAIRE DE FRANCE, NEW YORK,
INTERNATIONAL UNIVERSITY BOOKSELLERS, 1968
013,116-01,
     CASE STUDY

HORTON ROBIN
GOD,MAN AND THE LAND IN A NORTHERN IBO VILLAGE GROUP
AFRICA 26 1956 PP 17-28
013,
     CASE STUDY

HORTON ROBIN
THE KALABARI WORLD-VIEW- AN OUTLINE AND INTERPRETATION
AFRICA 32 1962 PP 197-220
013,
     CASE STUDY

LIENHARDT GODFREY
DIVINITY AND EXPERIENCE--THE RELIGION OF THE DINKA.
LONDON, OXFORD UNIVERSITY PRESS, 1961
013,134-01,

CASE STUDY

013

LLOYD PETER C
YORUBA MYTHS-- A SOCIOLOGIST'S INTERPRETATION.
ODU 2 1956 PP 20-28
013,128-01,
        CASE STUDY

MEYEROWITZ EVA L
THE AKAN OF GHANA-- THEIR ANCIENT BELIEFS.
LONDON,FABER,1958
013,114-01,
        CASE STUDY

MIDDLETON JOHN
LUGBARA RELIGION-RITUAL AND AUTHORITY AMONG AN EAST AFRICAN
PEOPLE
LONDON,OXFORD, FOR INTERNATIONAL AFRICAN INSTITUTE,1960
013,139-01,
        CASE STUDY

NADEL S F
NUPE RELIGION.
LONDON,ROUTLEDGE AND KEGAN PAUL LTD,1954
013,128-01,
        CASE STUDY

NKRUMAH KWAME
CONSCIENCISM-- PHILOSOPHY AND IDEOLOGY FOR DECOLONIZATION
AND DEVELOPMENT WITH PARTICULAR REFERENCE TO THE AFRICAN
REVOLUTION.
LONDON,HEINEMANN,1964
013,060,114-04,
        CASE STUDY

PARSONS ROBERT T
RELIGION IN AN AFRICAN SOCIETY.
LEIDEN, E.J. BRILL, 1964
013,
        CASE STUDY

RATTRAY ROBERT S
RELIGION AND ART IN ASHANTI.
LONDON,OXFORD UNIVERSITY PRESS,1959
013,114-01,
        CASE STUDY

SENGHOR LEOPOLD S
ON AFRICAN SOCIALISM.
NEW YORK,PRAEGER,1964
013,054,060,130-04,
        CASE STUDY

STENNING DERRICK J
CATTLE VALUES AND ISLAMIC VALUES IN A PASTORAL POPULATION.
IN LEWIS, ISLAM IN TROPICAL AFRICA, LONDON, OXFORD UNIVERSITY
PRESS, 1966, PP. 387-400
013,
        CASE STUDY

013

TURNER VICTOR W
THE FOREST OF SYMBOLS--ASPECTS OF NDEMBU RITUAL.
ITHACA, CORNELL UNIVERSITY PRESS, 1969
013,
        CASE STUDY

TURNER VICTOR W
THE DRUMS OF AFFLICTION.
LONDON, OXFORD UNIVERSITY PRESS, 1968
013,
        CASE STUDY

ALBERT ETHEL M
UNE ETUDE DE VALEURS EN URUNDI-A STUDY OF VALUES IN URUNDI
CAHIERS D'ETUDES AFRICAINES 2 1960 PP 148-160
013,103-01,
        LESS ACCESSIBLE

BA AMADOU HAMPATE
ANIMISME EN SAVANE AFRICAINE (ANIMISM IN THE AFRICAN
SAVANAH).
IN RENCONTRES INTERNATIONALES DE BOUAKE, LES RELIGIONS
AFRICAINES TRADITIONNELLES, PARIS, EDITIONS DU SEUIL, 1965,
PP 33-55
013,
        LESS ACCESSIBLE

BAHOKEN JEAN CALVIN
LA CONTRIBUTION DES RELIGIONS A L'EXPRESSION CULTURELLE DE
LA PERSONNALITE AFRICAINE (THE CONTRIBUTION OF RELIGION TO
THE CULTURAL EXPRESSION OF THE AFRICAN PERSONALITY).
IN COLLOQUE SUR LES RELIGIONS, ABIDJAN, APRIL, 1961, PARIS,
PRESENCE AFRICAINE, 1962, PP 155-168
013,039,
        LESS ACCESSIBLE

BASTIDE ROGER
RELIGIONS AFRICAINES ET STRUCTURES DE CIVILISATION (AFRICAN
RELIGIONS AND STRUCTURES OF CIVILIZATION).
PRESENCE AFRICAINE, NO. 66, 2ND QUARTER, 1968, PP. 98-111
013,
        LESS ACCESSIBLE

DICKSON KWESI
BASES ETHIQUES ET SPIRITUELLES DE L'HUMANISME ANIMISTE
(ETHICAL AND SPIRITUAL BASES OF ANIMISTIC HUMANISM).
IN COLLOQUE SUR LES RELIGIONS, ABIDJAN, APRIL, 1961, PARIS,
PRESENCE AFRICAINE, 1962, PP 81-86
013,
        LESS ACCESSIBLE

FOTE H MEMEL
RAPPORT SUR LA CIVILISATION ANIMISTE (A REPORT ON THE
ANIMIST CIVILIZATION).
IN COLLOQUE SUR LES RELIGIONS, ABIDJAN, 5-12 APRIL, 1961,
PARIS, PRESENCE AFRICAINE, 1962
013,
        LESS ACCESSIBLE

013

GRAVAND R P
LA DIGNITE SERERE (SERERE DIGNITY).
IN COLLOQUE SUR LES RELIGIONS, ABIDJAN, APRIL, 1961, PARIS,
PRESENCE AFRICAINE, 1962, PP 87-90
013,130-01,
     LESS ACCESSIBLE

HERSKOVITS MELVILLE J
LA STRUCTURE DES RELIGIONS AFRICAINES (THE STRUCTURE OF
AFRICAN RELIGIONS).
IN COLLOQUE SUR LES RELIGIONS, ABIDJAN, APRIL, 1961, PARIS,
PRESENCE AFRICAINE, 1962, PP 71-80
013,
     LESS ACCESSIBLE

HIMMELHEBER HANS
LE SYSTEME DE LA RELIGION DES DAN (THE RELIGIOUS SYSTEM OF
THE DAN).
IN RENCONTRES INTERNATIONALES DE BOUAKE, LES RELIGIONS
AFRICAINES TRADITIONNELLES, PARIS, EDITIONS DU SEUIL, 1965,
PP 75-96
013,109-01,
     LESS ACCESSIBLE

MAQUET JACQUES J
CONNAISSANCE DES RELIGIONS TRADITIONELLES (KNOWLEDGE OF
TRADITIONAL RELIGIONS).
IN RENCONTRES INTERNATIONALES DE BOUAKE, LES RELIGIONS
AFRICAINES TRADITIONNELLES, PARIS, EDITIONS DU SEUIL, 1965,
PP 57-74
013,
     LESS ACCESSIBLE

PAULME DENISE
QUE SAVONS-NOUS DES RELIGIONS AFRICAINES (WHAT DO WE KNOW
ABOUT AFRICAN RELIGIONS).
IN RENCONTRES INTERNATIONALES DE BOUAKE, LES RELIGIONS
AFRICAINES TRADITIONNELLES, PARIS, EDITIONS DU SEUIL, 1965,
PP 13-32
013,
     LESS ACCESSIBLE

PRESENCE AFRICAINE ED
COLLOQUE SUR LES RELIGIONS. (COLLOQUIUM ON RELIGIONS).
ABIDJAN 5/12 APRIL 1961, PARIS, PRESENCE AFRICAINE, 1962
013,050,
     LESS ACCESSIBLE

ROUCH JEAN
LA RELIGION ET LA MAGIE SONGHAY (RELIGION AND MAGIC OF
SONGHAY).
PARIS, PRESSES UNIVERSITAIRES DE FRANCE, 1960
013,127-01,
     LESS ACCESSIBLE

THOMAS L V
ETAT ACTUEL ET AVENIR DE L'ANIMISME (THE ACTUAL STATE AND
FUTURE OF ANIMISM).

IN COLLOQUE SUR LES RELIGIONS, ABIDJAN, 5-12 APRIL, 1961,
PARIS PRESENCE AFRICAINE, 1962, PP 59-70
013,
        LESS ACCESSIBLE

013
    VERGER PIERRE
    LES RELIGIONS TRADITIONNELLES AFRICAINES, SONT ELLES
    COMPATABLE AVEC LES FORMES ACTUELLES DE L'EXISTENCE
    (TRADITIONAL AFRICAN RELIGIONS, ARE THEY COMPATABLE WITH
    ACTUAL FORMS OF DAILY LIFE).
    IN RENCONTRES INTERNATIONALES DE BOUAKE, LES RELIGIONS
    AFRICAINES TRADITIONELLES, PARIS, AUX EDITIONS DU SEUIL,
    1965, PP 97-118
    013,
        LESS ACCESSIBLE

    BANTON MICHAEL P   ED
    ANTHROPOLOGICAL APPROACHES TO THE STUDY OF RELIGION.
    ASSOCIATION OF SOCIAL ANTHROPOLOGISTS MONOGRAPHS 3
    LONDON TAVISTOCK PUBLICATION
    NEW YORK, PRAEGER, 1966
    013,
        GENERAL THEORY

    BELLAH ROBERT
    RELIGIOUS SYSTEMS.
    IN EVON Z. VOGT AND ETHEL M. ALBERT (EDS), PEOPLE OF RIMROCK
    --A STUDY OF VALUES IN FIVE CULTURES, CAMBRIDGE, HARVARD
    UNIVERSITY PRESS, 1966, P. 227
    013,
        GENERAL THEORY

    DURKHEIM EMILE
    THE ELEMENTARY FORMS OF RELIGIOUS LIFE.
    NEW YORK, MACMILLAN, 1965, PP 1-33
    013,
        GENERAL THEORY

    GLOCK CHARLES Y   STARK RODNEY
    RELIGION AND SOCIETY IN TENSION.
    CHICAGO, RAND MCNALLY, 1965
    013,
        GENERAL THEORY

    LEVI-STRAUSS CLAUDE
    STRUCTURAL ANTHROPOLOGY
    NEW YORK, BASIC BOOKS, 1963; AND ANCHOR BOOKS 1967
    013,
        GENERAL THEORY

    MAIR LUCY P
    WITCHCRAFT.
    NEW YORK, INTERNATIONAL UNIVERSITY BOOKSELLERS, INC., 1969
    013,
        GENERAL THEORY

    MIDDLETON JOHN   ED
    MYTH AND COSMOS.
    GARDEN CITY, NEW YORK, THE NATURAL HISTORY PRESS, 1967

012,013,099,
        GENERAL THEORY

013
    WALLACE ANTHONY F
    RELIGION-AN ANTHROPOLOGICAL VIEW
    NEW YORK, RANDOM HOUSE, 1966
    013,
        GENERAL THEORY

    WEBER MAX
    THE SOCIOLOGY OF RELIGION.
    BOSTON, BEACON PRESS, 1963
    013,
        GENERAL THEORY

    ALBERT ETHEL M
    SOCIO-ECONOMIC ORGANIZATION AND RECEPTIVITY TO CHANGE-SOME
    DIFFERENCES BETWEEN RUANDA AND URUNDI
    SOUTHWESTERN JOURNAL OF ANTHROPOLOGY 16 1960 PP 46-74
    013, 038, 103-03, 129-03,

        CASE STUDY

    HORTON ROBIN
    DESTINY AND THE UNCONSCIOUS IN WEST AFRICA.
    AFRICA 31 1961 PP 110-116
    013,
        REFERENCE

14. VISUAL ARTS

014
    ARMSTRONG ROBERT P
    GUINEAISM.
    TRI-QUARTERLY 5 1966 PP 137-146
    014,015,
        ATTEMPT TO FORMULATE A GENERAL CONCEPT OF AESTHETICS
        WHICH ENCOMPASSES ALL OF THE ARTS (MUSIC, DANCE,
        SCULPTURE) WITHIN THE WEST AFRICAN CONTEXT.

    BIEBUYCK DANIEL   ED
    TRADITION AND CREATIVITY IN TRIBAL ART.
    BERKELEY, UNIVERSITY OF CALIFORNIA PRESS, 1969
    014,
        CASE STUDIES OF SEVERAL SOCIETIES, MAINLY AFRICAN,
        WHICH EMPHASIZE THE ROLE OF THE INDIVIDUAL ARTIST.
        FOLLOWING INTRODUCTORY ESSAY BY BIEBUYCK ARE ARTICLES
        BY GOLDWATER ON JUDGEMENT OF PRIMITIVE ART, FAGG ON
        THE AFRICAN ARTIST (FOCUSING ON BEININ AND IFE BRONZE)
        GERBRANDS ON THE CONCEPT OF STYLE, BASCOM ON CREATIV
        ITY AND STYLE IN AFRICAN ART, THOMPSON ON A MASTER
        YOURBA POTTER, AND COMMENTARY BY OTHER SPECIALISTS.

    BOHANNAN LAURA   BOHANNAN PAUL

THE TIV OF CENTRAL NIGERIA.
LONDON, INTERNATIONAL AFRICAN INSTITUTE, 1953
014,128-01,
> ALTHOUGH THIS WORK IS DIFFICULT TO ACQUIRE AT
> PRESENT, IT REMAINS OF MAJOR IMPORTANCE IN
> PROVIDING AN INTRODUCTION TO AFRICAN ART. THE
> AUTHOR DISCUSSES THE RELIGIOUS CONTEXT OF MOST
> AFRICAN ART, AND TRIES TO ASSESS THE FUNCTION
> OF ART WITHIN TRADITIONAL SOCIETY.

014

CARROLL KEVIN
YORUBA RELIGIOUS SCULPTURE-- PAGAN AND CHRISTIAN SCULPTURE
IN NIGERIA AND DAHOMEY.
NEW YORK, PRAEGER, 1967
014,109-01,128-01,
> DESCRIBES TRADITIONAL YORUBA SCULPTURE AND ATTEMPTS TO
> KEEP IT ALIVE BY PROVIDING A CHRISTIAN RELIGIOUS
> BASIS. EXCELLENT ON THE METHODS OF THE CARVER.
> AUTHOR IS MISSIONARY WHO HAS WORKED WITH THREE GENERA-
> TIONS OF YORUBA CARVERS.

ELISOFON ELIOT   FAGG WILLIAM
THE SCULPTURE OF AFRICA.
NEW YORK, PRAEGER, 1958
014,
> STILL ONE OF THE BEST SURVEYS OF THE ART OF AFRICA,
> ALTHOUGH THE COVERAGE IS UNEVEN. NOW OUT OF PRINT.

FAGG WILLIAM
THE ART OF WESTERN AFRICA-- SCULPTURE AND TRIBAL MASKS.
NEW YORK AND TORONTO, MENTOR UNESCO ART BOOK MQ 772, 1967
014,
> THIS AND FAGG'S VOLUME ON THE ART OF CENTRAL AFRICA
> PROVIDE A CONVENIENT AND INEXPENSIVE SOURCE OF ILLUS-
> TRATIONS FOR THE STUDENT. EXCELLENT COLOR PLATES AND
> GOOD, BRIEF DISCUSSION.

GERBRANDS A
ART AS AN ELEMENT OF CULTURE, ESPECIALLY IN NEGRO AFRICA.
LEIDEN, E J BRILL, 1957
014,
> A CLASSIC STUDY OF AFRICAN ART AND THE ARTISTS WHO
> PRODUCE IT, BASED ON A SERIES OF CASE STUDIES.

WILLETT FRANK
IFE IN THE HISTORY OF WEST AFRICAN SCULPTURE.
NEW YORK, MCGRAW-HILL, 1967
014,128-01,
> EXCELLENT DISCUSSION ON THE DATING OF IFE ART, THE
> TECHNIQUE OF LOST-WAX METAL CASTING. DISCUSSION OF
> ARCHAEOLOGICAL ART FINDS BY SITE. TRACES ELEMENTS OF
> STYLISTIC CONTINUITY FROM ANCIENT NOK TIMES TO THE
> PRESENT DAY. FULL SET OF PHOTOGRAPHIC REPRODUCTIONS.
> THIS VOLUME WOULD SERVE AS AN INTRODUCTION TO AFRICAN
> ART BY EXPLORING ALL ASPECTS OF THE YORUBA ART OF IFE,
> WHICH IS SOME OF THE WORLD'S FINEST.

ALLISON PHILIP
AFRICAN STONE SCULPTURE.

NEW YORK, PRAEGER, 1968
014,
     REFERENCE

014

AMERICAN SOCIETY OF AFRICAN CULTURE
COLLOQUIUM ON NEGRO ART--THE FUNCTION AND SIGNIFICANCE OF
NEGRO AFRICAN ART IN THE LIFE OF THE PEOPLE AND FOR THE
PEOPLE.
PARIS, INTERNATIONAL UNIVERSITY BOOKSELLERS, INC., 1969
014,
     REFERENCE

BANDI HANS G   ET-AL
THE ART OF THE STONE AGE.   (TRANS BY ANN E KEEP)
LONDON, METHUEN; NEW YORK, ART OF THE WORLD SERIES, 1961
014,
     REFERENCE

BASCOM WILLIAM R
AFRICAN ARTS EXHIBITION CATALOGUE
BERKELEY, UNIVERSITY OF CALIFORNIA PRESS, 1967
014,
     REFERENCE

BRENTJES BURCHARD
AFRICAN ROCK ART.
LONDON, INTERNATIONAL UNIVERSITY BOOKSELLERS, INC., 1969
014,
     REFERENCE

COOKE C K
THE ROCK PAINTINGS AND ENGRAVINGS OF AFRICA.
TARIKH 1 1966 PP 45-66
014,018,
     REFERENCE

CORDWELL JUSTINE M
THE PROBLEM OF PROCESS AND FORM IN WEST AFRICAN ART.
PROCEEDINGS OF THE THIRD INTERNATIONAL WEST AFRICAN
CONFERENCE 1949 LAGOS 1956 PP 53-60
014,
     REFERENCE

CROWLEY DANIEL J
TRADITIONAL AND CONTEMPORARY ART IN AFRICA.
IN CARTER, GWENDOLEN M. AND ANN PADEN (EDS), EXPANDING
HORIZONS IN AFRICAN STUDIES, EVANSTON, NORTHWESTERN
UNIVERSITY PRESS, 1969
014,093,100,
     REFERENCE

FAGG WILLIAM
TRIBES AND FORMS IN AFRICAN ART.
LONDON, METHUEN, 1965
014,
     REFERENCE

FAGG WILLIAM
THE ART OF CENTRAL AFRICA-- SCULPTURE AND TRIBAL MASKS.

NEW YORK AND TORONTO, MENTOR UNESCO ART BOOK, MQ773, 1967
014,
        REFERENCE

014
    FAGG WILLIAM
    ON THE NATURE OF AFRICAN ART.
    MEMOIRS AND PROCEEDING OF THE MANCHESTER LITERATURE AND
    PHILOSOPHICAL SOCIETY, 94, PP 93-104, 1953
    REPRINTED IN COLIN LEGUM, AFRICA, A HANDBOOK TO THE
    CONTINENT, LONDON, A BLOND, 1961, PP 414-424
    014,
        REFERENCE

    FAGG WILLIAM
    THE STUDY OF AFRICAN ART.
    BULLETIN OF THE ALLEN MEMORIAL ART MUSEUM 12 1955-56
    PP 44-61 OBERLIN COLLEGE
    014,
        REFERENCE

    FAGG WILLIAM
    AFRICAN TRIBAL IMAGES
    CLEVELAND,CASE WESTERN RESERVE,1968
    014,
        REFERENCE

    GASKIN L J P
    A BIBLIOGRAPHY OF AFRICAN ART.
    LONDON,INTERNATIONAL AFRICAN INSTITUTE,1965
    014,
        REFERENCE

    GRIAULE MARCEL
    FOLK ARTS OF BLACK AFRICA
    NEW YORK,TUDOR,1950
    014,
        REFERENCE

    HARTWIG GERALD W
    EAST AFRICAN PLASTIC ART TRADITION-A DISCUSSION OF THE
    LITERATURE
    GENEVE-AFRIQUE 7 1968 PP 31-52
    014,
        REFERENCE

    HERSKOVITS MELVILLE J
    BACKGROUND OF AFRICAN ART.
    DENVER,DENVER ART MUSEUM,1945
    014,
        REFERENCE

    HOLY L
    MASKS AND FIGURES FROM EASTERN AND SOUTHERN AFRICA
    LONDON,HAMLYN,1967
    014,
        REFERENCE

    LEIRIS MICHEL   DELANGE JACQUELINE
    AFRICAN ART

LONDON, THAMES AND HUDSON, 1968
014,
        REFERENCE

014

LEUZINGER ELSY
AFRICA-THE ART OF THE NEGRO PEOPLES
LONDON, METHUEN, 1960
014,
        REFERENCE

MUSEUM OF PRIMITIVE ART
TRADITIONAL ART OF THE AFRICAN NATIONS.
NEW YORK, UNIVERSITY PUBLISHERS, 1961
014,
        REFERENCE

PAULME DENISE
AFRICAN SCULPTURE.
LONDON, ELEK BOOKS, 1962
014,
        REFERENCE

RADIN PAUL   SWEENEY JAMES J
AFRICAN FOLKTALES AND SCULPTURE.
PRINCETON, NEW JERSEY, PRINCETON UNIVERSITY PRESS, 1969
012,014,
        REFERENCE

ROBBINS WARREN
AFRICAN ART IN AMERICAN COLLECTIONS.
NEW YORK, PRAEGER, ND
014,
        REFERENCE

SEGY LADISLAS
AFRICAN SCULPTURE SPEAKS.
NEW YORK, INTERNATIONAL UNIVERSITY BOOKSELLERS, INC., 1969
014,
        REFERENCE

SIEBER ROY
THE VISUAL ARTS.
IN ROBERT A LYSTAD (ED), THE AFRICAN WORLD, NEW YORK,
PRAEGER, 1966, PP 442-451
014,093,
        REFERENCE

SMITH MARIAN W   ED
THE ARTIST IN TRIBAL SOCIETY. PROCEEDINGS HELD AT THE
ROYAL ANTHROPOLOGICAL INSTITUTE SYMPOSIUM ON THE ARTIST
IN TRIBAL SOCIETY.
NEW YORK, FREE PRESS; AND LONDON, ROUTLEDGE AND KEGAN PAUL,
1961
014,
        REFERENCE

TROWELL MARGARET
AFRICAN DESIGN.
LONDON, FABER AND FABER, 1960; ALSO 1965, 2ND EDITION

014,
     REFERENCE

014
  TROWELL MARGARET
  CLASSICAL AFRICAN SCULPTURE.
  NEW YORK, PRAEGER, 1964, 2ND. EDITION
  014,
     REFERENCE

  UNDERWOOD LEON
  MASKS OF WEST AFRICA.
  LONDON, A TIRANTI, 1948
  014,
     REFERENCE

  UNDERWOOD LEON
  BRONZES OF WEST AFRICA.
  LONDON, A TIRANTI, 1949
  014,
     REFERENCE

  UNDERWOOD LEON
  FIGURES IN WOOD IN WEST AFRICA
  LONDON, A TARANTE, 1947
  014,
     REFERENCE

  WASSING R S
  AFRICAN ART--ITS BACKGROUND AND TRADITIONS
  NEW YORK, HARRY N ABRAMS, 1968
  014,
     REFERENCE

  WINGERT PAUL S
  THE SCULPTURE OF NEGRO AFRICA.
  NEW YORK, COLUMBIA UNIVERSITY PRESS, 1950
  014,
     REFERENCE

  BEIER ULLI
  NIGERIAN MUD SCULPTURE.
  CAMBRIDGE, CAMBRIDGE UNIVERSITY PRESS, 1963
  014,128-01,
     CASE STUDY

  BEIER ULLI
  ART IN NIGERIA 1960.
  CAMBRIDGE, CAMBRIDGE UNIVERSITY PRESS, 1960
  014,093,128-01,
     CASE STUDY

  BEN AMOS PAULA
  BIBLIOGRAPHY OF BENIN ART.
  NEW YORK, INTERNATIONAL UNIVERSITY BOOKSELLERS, INC., 1968
  014,128-01,
     CASE STUDY

  CORDWELL JUSTINE M
  NATURALISM AND STYLIZATION IN YORUBA ART.

MAGAZINE OF ART 46 1953 PP 220-226
014,128-01,
     CASE STUDY

014
   FAGG WILLIAM
   NIGERIAN IMAGES.
   NEW YORK,PRAEGER,1963
   014,020,128-01,
        CASE STUDY

   FORMAN W   FORMAN B   DARK PHILIP J C
   BENIN ART
   LONDON,PAUL HAMLYN,1960
   014,
        CASE STUDY

   GOLDWATER ROBERT
   SENUFO SCULPTURE FROM WEST AFRICA.
   GREENWHICH,CONNECTICUT,THE MUSEUM OF PRIMITIVE ART,1964
   014,114-01,
        CASE STUDY

   HIMMELHEBER HANS
   SCULPTORS AND SCULPTURES OF THE DAN.
   IN LALAGE BOWN AND MICHAEL CROWDER (EDS.), PROCEEDINGS OF
   THE FIRST INTERNATIONAL CONGRESS OF AFRICANISTS, ACCRA,
   1962, LONDON , LONGMANS, 1964, PP 243-255
   014,109-01,
        CASE STUDY

   HORTON ROBIN
   KALABARI SCULPTURE.
   LAGOS,NIGERIA,DEPARTMENT OF ANTIQUITIES,1965
   014,128-01,
        CASE STUDY

   HOTTOT R
   TEKE FETISHES.
   JOURNAL OF THE ROYAL ANTHROPOLOGICAL INSTITUTE 86
   1956 PP 25-36
   014,108-01,
        CASE STUDY

   LAJOUX JEAN D
   THE ROCK PAINTINGS OF TASSILI. (TRANS BY G D LIVERSAGE)
   CLEVELAND,WORLD PUBLISHING COMPANY,1963
   014,101-01,
        CASE STUDY

   LEM F H
   SUDANESE SCULPTURE.
   PARIS,ARTS ET METIERS GRAPHIQUES,1948
   014,
        CASE STUDY

   LEROY JULES
   ETHIOPIAN PAINTING--IN THE LATE MIDDLE AGES AND DURING THE
   GONDAR DYNASTY.
   NEW YORK, PRAEGER, 1967

014,110-02,
        CASE STUDY

014
    MUSEUM OF PRIMITIVE ART
    SCULPTURE FROM THREE AFRICAN TRIBES-- SENUFO, BAGA, DOGON.
    NEW YORK, UNIVERSITY PUBLISHERS, 1959
    014,
        CASE STUDY

    PLASS MARGARET
    AFRICAN MINIATURES-- THE GOLDWEIGHTS OF THE ASHANTI.
    LONDON, LUND HUMPHRIES, 1967; AND NEW YORK, PRAEGER, 1967
    014,
        CASE STUDY

    SIEBER ROY
    SCULPTURE OF NORTHERN NIGERIA.
    NEW YORK, MUSEUM OF PRIMITIVE ART, 1961
    014,128-01,
        CASE STUDY

    TROWELL MARGARET   WACHSMANN KLAUS
    TRIBAL CRAFTS OF UGANDA
    LONDON, OXFORD UNIVERSITY PRESS, 1953
    014,139-01,
        CASE STUDY

    WILLETT FRANK
    IFE AND ITS ARCHAEOLOGY.
    THE JOURNAL OF AFRICAN HISTORY 1 1960 PP 231-248
    014,020,026,128-01,
        CASE STUDY

    WILLETT FRANK   PICTON J
    ON THE IDENTIFICATION OF INDIVIDUAL CARVERS, A STUDY OF
    ANCESTOR SHRINE CARVINGS FROM OWO, NIGERIA.
    MAN 2 1967
    014,128-01,
        CASE STUDY

    ALTMAN RALPH C   ED
    MASTERPIECES FROM THE SIR HENRY WELLCOME COLLECTION AT UCLA.
    LOS ANGELES, MUSEUM AND LABORATORIES OF ETHNIC ARTS AND TECH-
    NOLOGY, UCLA, 1966
    014,
        LESS ACCESSIBLE

    BASTIN MARIE-LOUISE
    ART DECORATIF TSHOKWE.   (CHOKWE DECORATIVE ART).
    LISBON, COMPANHIA DE DIAMANTES DE ANGOLA, 1961, 2 VOLUMES
    014,
        LESS ACCESSIBLE

    FAGG WILLIAM
    DE L'ART DES YORUBA (ON THE ART OF YORUBA).
    L, ART NEGRE, PRESENCE AFRICAINE 10-11 PARIS 1951 PP 103-135
    014,128-01,
        LESS ACCESSIBLE

HIMMELHEBER HANS
NEGERKUNST AND NEGERKUNSTLER (NEGRO ART AND NEGRO ARTISTS).
BRUNSWICK,KLINCKHARDT AND BIERMANN,1960
014,
         LESS ACCESSIBLE

014
HOLAS B
CULTURES MATERIELLES DE LA COTE D'IVOIRE (MATERIAL CULTURE
OF THE IVORY COAST).
PARIS,PRESSES UNIVERSITAIRE DE FRANCE,1960
014,116-01,
         LESS ACCESSIBLE

KJERSMEIER CARL
CENTRES DE STYLE DE LA SCULPTURE NEGRE AFRICAINE
(STYLE CENTERS OF NEGRO AFRICAN SCULPTURE)
PARIS,A MORANCE,1935-8;AND NEW YORK,HACKER,1967
014,
         LESS ACCESSIBLE

LEUZINGER ELSY
AFRICAN SCULPTURE, A DESCRIPTIVE CATALOGUE.
ZURICH,ATLANTIS RIETBERG MUSEUM,1963
014,
         LESS ACCESSIBLE

MAESEN ALBERT
UMBANGU, ART DU CONGO AU MUSEE ROYAL DU CONGO BELGE
(UMBANGU, CONGO ART IN THE ROYAL MUSEUM OF THE BELGIAN
CONGO).
BRUXELLES,MUSEE ROYAL DE L'AFRIQUE CENTRALE,1960
014,108-01,
         LESS ACCESSIBLE

OLBRECHTS FRANS M
LES ARTS PLASTIQUES DU CONGO BELGE (SCULPTURE OF THE BELGIAN
CONGO).
BRUSSELS,EDITIONS ERASME,1959
014,
         LESS ACCESSIBLE

PRESENCE AFRICAINE
L'ART NEGRE (NEGRO ART).
PARIS,PRESENCE AFRICAINE,1966,VOLS 10-11
014,
         LESS ACCESSIBLE

VON SYDOW ECKART
AFRIKANISCHE PLASTIK (AFRICAN SCULPTURE).
BERLIN MANN VERLAG 1954
014,
         LESS ACCESSIBLE

BOAS FRANZ
PRIMITIVE ART.
NEW YORK,DOVER,1955
014,
         GENERAL THEORY

```
REDFIELD ROBERT      ET AL
ASPECTS OF PRIMITIVE ART.
NEW YORK, UNIVERSITY PUBLISHERS, 1959
014,
      GENERAL THEORY
```

014

```
   SIEBER ROY
   THE ARTS AND THEIR CHANGING SOCIAL FUNCTION.
   ANNALS OF THE NEW YORK ACADEMY OF SCIENCES
   46 1962 PP 653-658
   014,
         GENERAL THEORY
```

```
   WINGERT PAUL S
   PRIMITIVE ART-- ITS TRADITIONS AND STYLES.
   NEW YORK, OXFORD UNIVERSITY PRESS, 1962
   014,
         GENERAL THEORY
```

15. TRADITIONAL MUSIC

015

```
   ARMSTRONG ROBERT P
   GUINEAISM.
   TRI-QUARTERLY 5 1966 PP 137-146
   014,015,
         ATTEMPT TO FORMULATE A GENERAL CONCEPT OF AESTHETICS
         WHICH ENCOMPASSES ALL OF THE ARTS (MUSIC, DANCE,
         SCULPTURE) WITHIN THE WEST AFRICAN CONTEXT.
```

```
   GASKIN L J P          ED
   A SELECT BIBLIOGRAPHY OF MUSIC IN AFRICA.
   LONDON INTERNATIONAL AFRICAN INSTITUTE 1965 AFRICAN
   BIBLIOGRAPHY SERIES B
   015,
         UNSURPASSED.  MONUMENTAL WORK OF REFERENCES ON AFRICAN
         MUSIC.  DIVIDED BY GEOGRAPHIC AREA  AND BY TYPE OF
         INSTRUMENT.  AUTHOR INDEX APPENDED AND SUITABLE CROSS
         REFERENCING.  PREPARED BY THE STAFF OF THE INTER-
         NATIONAL AFRICAN INSTITUTE, LONDON.
```

```
   MERRIAM ALAN P
   MUSIC AND THE DANCE.
   IN ROBERT A LYSTAD (ED), THE AFRICAN WORLD, NEW YORK,
   PRAEGER, 1966, CHP 17
   015,
         PRIMARILY AN ESSAY ON AFRICAN MUSIC, WITH SUPPORTING
         COMMENTS ON DANCE OR ETHNO-CHOREOGRAPHY.  AUTHOR
         STRESSES POINT THAT MUSIC AND DANCE ARE LEARNED SOCIAL
         BEHAVIOR, RATHER THAN BIOLOGICALLY DETERMINED PHENOM-
         ENA.  AESTHETIC ASPECTS OF MUSIC NOT SEPARABLE FROM
         BEHAVIORAL ASPECTS.
```

```
   MERRIAM ALAN P
```

AFRICAN MUSIC CHAPTER 4.
IN WILLIAM BASCOM AND MELVILLE HERSKOVITS, CONTINUTY AND
CHANGE IN AFRICAN CULTURES, CHICAGO, UNIVERSITY OF CHICAGO
PRESS, 1962, PP 49-86
015,

> EXCELLENT OVERVIEW OF THE WAY IN WHICH AN ETHNO-MUSI-
> COLOGIST APPROACHES HIS MATERIAL. DIVIDED INTO THREE
> MAJOR SECTIONS-- 1) MAJOR ELEMENTS OF MUSICAL STRUC-
> TURE (MELODY, FORM, SCALE, HARMONY)-- 2) PROBLEM OF
> THE FUNCTION OF AFRICAN MUSIC (INSTRUMENTS, RHYTHM)--
> 3) THEORETICAL PROBLEMS (E.G., DIVIDING AFRICA INTO MU-
> SICAL AREAS, PROBLEMS OF MUSICAL CHANGE). IN AUTHOR'S
> LATER WORK (ETHNOMUSICOLOGY OF FLATHEAD INDIANS) LINKS
> SOCIAL FUNCTION AND MUSIC FORM.

015

MERRIAM ALAN P
AFRICAN MUSIC ON LP-AN ANNOTATED **DISC**OGRAPHY
EVANSTON, NORTHWESTERN UNIVERSITY PRESS, 1970
015,093,

> A LISTING OF COMMERCIALLY AVAILABLE RECORDINGS OF
> AFRICAN MUSIC UP THROUGH 1965. INFORMATION IS GIVEN
> ON THE ARTISTS FOR EACH RECORDING AND THERE ARE 18
> INDEXES LISTING THE RECORDINGS BY COUNTRY,ETHNIC GROUP
> LANGUAGE,PERFORMERS,MUSICAL INSTRUMENTS,TYPES OF
> MUSIC AND SONGS,ETC.

NKETIA J H KWABENA
UNITY AND DIVERSITY IN AFRICAN MUSIC-- A PROBLEM OF
SYNTHESIS.
IN LALAGE BOWN AND MICHAEL CROWDER (EDS.), PROCEEDINGS OF
THE FIRST INTERNATIONAL CONGRESS OF AFRICANISTS, ACCRA,
1962, LONDON, LONGMANS, 1964, PP 256-263
015,

> BROAD AND GENERAL ESSAY ON MUSICAL DIVERSITY IN AFRICA
> (INSTRUMENTS, SCALE). UNLIKE MERRIAM, AUTHOR REINFOR-
> CES DISTINCTION BETWEEN MUSICAL AND NON-MUSICAL BEHA-
> VIOR, AND FOCUSES ON FORMAL MUSICAL ANALYSIS. AUTHOR
> IS MAJOR AFRICAN ETHNOMUSICOLOGIST, CURRENTLY PROFES-
> SOR AT UNIVERSITY OF GHANA.

CARRINGTON JOHN F
TALKING DRUMS OF AFRICA
LONDON, CAREY KINGSGATE PRESS, 1949
015,
> REFERENCE

DIETZ BETTY W   OLATUNJI
MUSICAL INSTRUMENTS OF AFRICA, THEIR NATURE, USE, AND
PLACE IN THE LIFE OF A DEEPLY MUSICAL PEOPLE.
NEW YORK, JOHN DAY, 1965
015,
> REFERENCE

JONES A M
STUDIES IN AFRICAN MUSIC-2 VOLS
LONDON AND NEW YORK, OXFORD UNIVERSITY PRESS, 1959
015,
> REFERENCE

JONES A M
AFRICAN RHYTHM
AFRICA 24 1954 PP 26-47
015,
        REFERENCE

015
    LIBRARY OF CONGRESS
    AFRICAN MUSIC-A BRIEFLY ANNOTATED BIBLIOGRAPHY
    WASHINGTON,GENERAL REFERENCE AND BIBLIOGRAPHY DIVISION,
    AFRICAN SECTION,1964
    015,
        REFERENCE

    NKETIA J H KWABENA
    DRUMS,DANCE AND SONG
    ATLANTIC MONTHLY 230 1959 PP 69-72
    015,
        REFERENCE

    NKETIA J H KWABENA
    ARTISTIC VALUES IN AFRICAN MUSIC
    COMPOSER JOURNAL OF THE COMPOSERS GUILD OF GREAT BRITAIN
    19 1966 PP16-19
    015,093,
        REFERENCE

    PRIMUS PEARL E
    AFRICAN DANCE.
    IN AMSAC, AFRICA SEEN BY AMERICAN NEGROES, PARIS,
    PRESENCE AFRICAINE, 1958, PP 163-173
    015,
        REFERENCE

    VON HORNBOSTEL ERICH
    AFRICAN NEGRO MUSIC
    AFRICA 1 1928 PP 30-62
    015,
        REFERENCE

    WACHSMANN KLAUS
    ETHNOMUSICOLOGY IN AFRICAN STUDIES--THE NEXT TWENTY YEARS.
    IN CARTER, GWENDOLEN M. AND ANN PADEN (EDS),EXPANDING
    HORIZONS IN AFRICAN STUDIES, EVANSTON, NORTHWESTERN
    UNIVERSITY PRESS, 1969, PP. 131-142
    015,100,
        REFERENCE

    WACHSMANN KLAUS
    INTERNATIONAL CATALOGUE OF PUBLISHED RECORDS OF FOLK MUSIC
    LONDON,INTERNATIONAL FOLK MUSIC COUNCIL,1960
    015,
        REFERENCE

    WATERMAN RICHARD A
    AFRICAN INFLUENCE ON THE MUSIC OF THE AMERICAS
    IN SOL TAX(ED),ACCULTURATION IN THE AMERICAS,CHICAGO,
    UNIVERSITY OF CHICAGO PRESS 1952
    015,030,
        REFERENCE

015

AMES DAVID W
PROFESSIONALS AND AMATEURS-- THE MUSICIANS OF ZARIA AND
OBIMO.
AFRICAN ARTS 1 2 WINTER 1968 PP 41-45, 80-84
015,128-01,
        CASE STUDY

MORRIS HENRY F
THE HEROIC RECITATIONS OF THE BAHIMA OF ANKOLE.
LONDON, OXFORD UNIVERSITY PRESS, 1964
012,015,139-01,
        CASE STUDY

NKETIA J H KWABENA
AFRICAN MUSIC IN GHANA
EVANSTON, NORTHWESTERN UNIVERSITY PRESS, 1963
015,
        CASE STUDY

POWNE MICHAEL
ETHIOPIAN MUSIC--AN INTRODUCTION.
LONDON, OXFORD UNIVERSITY PRESS, 1968
015,110-01,
        CASE STUDY

SOWANDE FELA
OYIGIYIGI-INTRODUCTION,THEME AND VARIATIONS ON A YORUBA FOLK
THEME FOR ORGAN
NEW YORK, RICORDI, 1958
015,093,
        CASE STUDY

TRACEY H
THE DEVELOPMENT OF MUSIC IN EAST AFRICA
TANGANYIKA NOTES AND RECORDS 63 1964 PP 213-221
015,
        CASE STUDY

BEBEY F
MUSIQUE DE L'AFRIQUE--UN DISQUE D'ACCOMPAGNEMENT (MUSIC OF
AFRICA--WITH AN ACCOMPANYING RECORD).
PARIS, HORIZONS DE FRANCE, NEW YORK, INTERNATIONAL
UNIVERSITY BOOKSELLERS. 1969
015,
        LESS ACCESSIBLE

SCHAEFFNER ANDRE
LA MUSIQUE D'AFRIQUE NOIRE
IN NORBERT DUFOURQ LA MUSIQUE DES ORIGINES A NOS JOURS,
PARIS, LAROUSSE, 1946, PP 460-465
015,
        LESS ACCESSIBLE

MERRIAM ALAN P
THE ANTHROPOLOGY OF MUSIC.
EVANSTON, NORTHWESTERN UNIVERSITY PRESS, 1964
015,
        GENERAL THEORY

16. STUDY QUESTIONS: AFRICAN SOCIETY AND CULTURE

016

BOHANNAN PAUL
AFRICA AND AFRICANS
NEW YORK, NATURAL HISTORY PRESS, 1964
001,003,010,016,
> SUCCESSFUL ATTEMPT TO PUT AFRICAN CULTURE IN MODERN
> PERSPECTIVE. INFORMAL, PERSONAL STATEMENT BY OUT-
> STANDING ANTHROPOLOGIST, WHICH IS CHALLENGING AND
> OFTEN CONTROVERSIAL. COVERS WIDE RANGE FROM EARLY
> PEOPLING OF CONTINENT, TO NATIONALISM AND
> INDEPENDENCE. EXAMINES EARLY STATE FORMATION, THE
> SLAVE TRADE, COLONIALISM, THE ARTS, FAMILY LIFE,
> ECONOMY, RELIGION. BASIC INTRODUCTORY READING.

DIOP CHEIKH ANTA
THE CULTURAL UNITY OF NEGRO-AFRICA.
PARIS, PRESENCE AFRICAINE. 1962
016,039,054,099,
> AUTHOR IS SENEGALESE SCHOLAR WHO HAS UNDERTAKEN
> RESEARCH ON THE HISTORY OF THE AFRICAN CONTINENT WITH
> A VIEW TO STRESSING SIMILARITIES RATHER THAN
> DIFFERENCES AMONG THE VARIOUS ETHNIC SOCIETIES. FROM
> THESE SMILARITIES HE PROPOSES CERTAIN CULTURE-PERSON-
> ALITY PATTERNS WHICH HE FEELS DISTINGUISH AFRICANS
> FROM EUROPEANS.

GIBBS JAMES JR   ED
PEOPLES OF AFRICA.
NEW YORK, HOLT, RINEHART AND WINSTON, 1965
004,016,
> CULTURE PROFILES OF 15 SOCIETIES IN SUB-SAHARAN AFRICA
> CHOSEN TO REPRESENT A CROSS SECTION OF ECOLOGY,
> CULTURE AREAS, SUBSISTENCE ECONOMIES, AND LANGUAGES.
> GROUPS INCLUDE IBO, HAUSA, YORUBA, FULANI, TIV, GANDA,
> BUSHMEN, PYGMIES, SOMALI, JIE, SWAZI, SUKU, RWANDA,
> TIRIKI, KPELLE. EACH DONE BY EXPERIENCED ANTHROPOLO-
> GIST. AUTHOR PROFILES AND BRIEF PRONUNCIATION GUIDE
> FOR AFRICAN WORDS.

KUPER LEO   SMITH M G   EDS
PLURALISM IN AFRICA.
BERKELEY AND LOS ANGELES, UNIVERSITY OF CALIFORNIA PRESS,
1969
006,007,016,057,
> WORK OF MAJOR THEORETICAL SIGNIFICANCE, AS WELL AS IM-
> PORTANT CASE STUDIES BY VAN DEN BERGHE, ALEXANDRE, DA-
> VIDSON, LOFCHIE, MAZRUI, THOMPSON, GLUCKMAN AND HILDA
> KUPER. FOCUS IS ON PLURAL SOCIETY-I.E. RACIAL, TRIBAL,
> RELIGIOUS, OR REGIONAL GROUPS HELD TOGETHER BY FORCE
> RATHER THAN PLURALISTIC SOCIETY BASED ON CROSS-CUTTING
> CLEAVAGES.

OTTENBERG SIMON   OTTENBERG PHOEBE
CULTURES AND SOCIETIES OF AFRICA.
NEW YORK, RANDOM HOUSE, 1960
003,012,016,
        EXCELLENT COLLECTION OF CASE STUDIES, ETHNIC AND THE-
        MATIC. SECTIONS COVER PEOPLE AND ENVIRONMENT (BUSH-
        MEN, FULANI, BEMBA), SOCIAL GROUPINGS (UNILINEAL DES-
        CENT GROUPS, SECRET SOCIETIES, AGE SETS, URBANIZATION,
        MARRIAGE), AUTHORITY AND GOVERNMENT (TUTSI, TIV, KON-
        KOMBA, ASHANTI), VALUE, RELIGION AND AESTHETICS (ROLE
        OF CATTLE, WITCHCRAFT, INITIATION, FOLKLORE, ART),
        CULTURE CONTACT AND CHANGE (ISLAM, CHRISTIANITY),
        URBANISM). INTRODUCTION SUPERB.

016

DAVIDSON BASIL
THE AFRICAN GENIUS--AN INTRODUCTION TO AFRICAN AND CULTURAL
HISTORY.
BOSTON, LITTLE, BROWN, 1969
016,
     REFERENCE

MIDDLETON JOHN   ED
BLACK AFRICA- ITS PEOPLES AND THEIR CULTURES TODAY
LONDON, MACMILLAN, 1970
004,016,053,
     REFERENCE

SAWYER JACK   LEVINE ROBERT A
CULTURAL DIMENSIONS-- A FACTOR ANALYSIS OF THE WORLD ETHNO-
GRAPHIC SAMPLE.
AMERICAN ANTHROPOLOGIST VOL 68 NO 3 JUNE 1966 PP 708-731
016,040,
     REFERENCE

UCHENDU VICTOR C
PRIORITY ISSUES FOR SOCIAL ANTHROPOLOGICAL RESEARCH IN
AFRICA IN THE NEXT TWO DECADES.
IN CARTER, GWENDOLEN M. AND ANN PADEN (EDS), EXPANDING
HORIZONS IN AFRICAN STUDIES, EVANSTON, NORTHWESTERN
UNIVERSITY PRESS, 1969, PP. 3-23
016,100,
     REFERENCE

PART II
Perspectives
on the Past

17. CONTINENTAL ORIGINS AND PHYSICAL CHARACTER

017

DE BLIJ HARM J
A GEOGRAPHY OF SUB-SAHARAN AFRICA.
CHICAGO, RAND MCNALLY, 1964, CH. 1
017,
      SHORT DESCRIPTION OF AFRICAN PHYSICAL FEATURES EXPLI-
      CITLY PLACED WITHIN A FRAMEWORK CONSIDERING THE THE-
      ORY OF CONTINENTAL DRIFT. ONE OF INTRODUCTORY SEC-
      TIONS TO A REGIONAL GEOGRAPHY OF AFRICA WHICH FOCUSES
      ON IMPORTANT THEMES FOR EACH REGION.

GROVE A T
AFRICA SOUTH OF THE SAHARA
LONDON, OXFORD UNIVERSITY PRESS, 1967
017,069,
      A GOOD STANDARD GEOGRAPHY TEXT, STRONGER ON PHYSICAL
      GEOGRAPHY THAN HANCE. MANY AND GOOD MAPS IN TEXT
      SUPPLEMENTED BY 16 COLORED MAPS FROM OXFORD REGIONAL
      ECONOMIC ATLAS OF AFRICA.

ALLARD G O   HURST VERNON J
BRAZIL-GABON GEOLOGIC LINK SUPPORTS CONTINENTAL DRIFT-NEWLY
DISCOVERED TECTONIC PROVINCE IN BRAZIL MATCHES PROVINCE IN
GABON
SCIENCE 163 1969 PP 528-532

017,
     REFERENCE

017

DIXEY FRANK
THE EAST AFRICAN RIFT SYSTEM.
LONDON, HER MAJESTY'S STATIONERY OFFICE, 1956
017,
     REFERENCE

DU TOIT A L
OUR WANDERING CONTINENTS
LONDON, OLIVER AND BOYD, 1937
017,
     REFERENCE

FURON R
GEOLOGY OF AFRICA TRANSLATED BY A HALLAN AND L A STEVENS
NEW YORK, HAFNER, 1963
017,069,
     REFERENCE

GREGORY J W
THE GREAT RIFT VALLEY
LONDON, JOHN MURRAY, 1896
017,
     REFERENCE

GROVE A T   WARREN A
QUATERNARY LANDFORMS AND THE CLIMATE ON THE SOUTH SIDE OF
THE SAHARA
GEOGRAPHICAL JOURNAL 134 1968 PP 194-208
017,
     REFERENCE

HURLEY PATRICK M
THE CONFIRMATION OF CONTINENTAL DRIFT.
SCIENTIFIC AMERICAN 218 NO. 4 1968 PP 52-68
017,
     REFERENCE

HURLEY PATRICK M   ET AL
TEST OF CONTINENTAL DRIFT BY COMPARISON OF RADIOMETRIC AGES.
SCIENCE, VOL. 157, NO. 3788, AUGUST 4, 1967
017,
     REFERENCE

SULLIVAN WALTER
A FORCE THAT PUSHES CONTINENTS APART.
NEW YORK TIMES, JULY 9, 1967
017,
     REFERENCE

WAYLAND E J
THE AFRICAN BULGE
GEOGRAPHICAL JOURNAL 75 1930 PP 381-383
017,
     REFERENCE

BUTZER KARL W   HANSEN CARL L

DESERT AND RIVER IN NUBIA-GEOMORPHOLOGY AND PREHISTORIC
ENVIRONMENTS AT THE ASWAN RESERVOIR
MADISON,UNIVERSITY OF WISCONSIN PRESS, 1968
017,018,020,
   CASE STUDY

017
 HIERTZLER J R
 SEA FLOOR SPREADING
 SCIENTIFIC AMERICAN 219 1968 PP 60-70
 017,
   GENERAL THEORY

 KING LESTER C
 MORPHOLOGY OF THE EARTH.
 NEW YORK,HAFNER,1967, 2ND. ED.
 017,
   GENERAL THEORY

 KURTEN BJORN
 CONTINENTAL DRIFT AND EVOLUTION
 SCIENTIFIC AMERICAN 220 1969 PP 54-64
 017,
   GENERAL THEORY

 MAXWELL JOHN C
 CONTINENTAL DRIFT AND A DYNAMIC EARTH
 AMERICAN SCIENTIST 56 1968 PP 35-51
 017,
   GENERAL THEORY

 WEGENER ALFRED
 THE ORIGIN OF CONTINENTS AND OCEANS(TRANS BY JOHN BIRAM)
 NEW YORK,DOVER,1966 (ORIGINALLY PUBLISHED IN GERMAN IN 1929)
 017,
   GENERAL THEORY

 WILSON J TUZO
 CONTINENTAL DRIFT.
 SCIENTIFIC AMERICAN 208 NO 4 APRIL 1963 PP 86-100
 017,
   GENERAL THEORY

18. THE EVOLUTION OF MAN IN AFRICA

018
 CLARK W E LE-GROS
 MAN-APES OR APE MEN:THE STORY OF DISCOVERIES IN AFRICA
 NEW YORK,HOLT,RINEHART AND WINSTON,1967
 018,
   PERHAPS THE BEST AND MOST COMPREHENSIVE SURVEY OF
   AUSTRALOPITHECUS AND ITS PLACE IN HUMAN EVOLUTION BY
   OUTSTANDING ARCHEOLOGIST. VARIOUS CHAPTERS CHART THE
   MAJOR DISCOVERIES(DART,LEAKEY),STRUCTURAL FEATURES,
   WAY OF LIFE,AND EVOLUTIONARY ORIGINS OF

AUSTRALOPITHECUS. WELL WRITTEN AND SUITABLE FOR THE
NON-SPECIALIST AND SPECIALIST ALIKE.

018

COLE SONIA
THE PREHISTORY OF EAST AFRICA.
NEW YORK, MACMILLAN, 1963
018,
     REVISED VERSION OF EARLIER WORK, INCORPORATES MANY
     OUTSTANDING RECENT DISCOVERIES DEALING WITH THE EVOLU-
     TION OF MAN IN EAST AFRICA, INCLUDING DR. LEAKEY S
     DISCOVERIES OF EARLIEST HOMINIDS AT OLDUVAI GORGE.

HOWELL F CLARK   BOURLIERE FRANCOIS EDS
AFRICAN ECOLOGY AND HUMAN EVOLUTION.
CHICAGO, ALDINE, 1966
018,019,
     PRODUCT OF 1961 CONFERENCE OF PHYSICAL ANTHROPOLOGISTS
     ZOOLOGISTS, GEOLOGISTS, PALEOGEOGRAPHERS, PALEONTOL-
     OGISTS, AND PREHISTORIANS. CONTAINS RESEARCH REPORTS
     ON PLEISTOCENE ENVIRONMENTS AND BIOLOGICAL EVOLUTION
     OF MAN IN AFRICA INCLUDING CLIMATIC CHANGE, ECOLOGY,
     DATING METHODS, AND LEAKEY ON OLDUVAI GORGE. TRAN-
     SCRIPTS OF CONFERENCE DISCUSSIONS, OVER 100 MAPS AND
     FIGURES, AND DETAILED BIBLIOGRAPHY.

LEAKEY L S B
THE PROGRESS AND EVOLUTION OF MAN IN AFRICA.
LONDON, OXFORD UNIVERSITY PRESS, 1961
018,
     EVALUATION OF FINDINGS AT OLDUVAI GORGE, BY THE ARCH-
     AEOLOGIST WHO HAS BEEN MOST RESPONSIBLE FOR THESE EX-
     CAVATIONS. TRACES HUMAN DEVELOPMENT IN POPULAR TERMS
     FROM EARLIEST TIMES.

LEAKEY L S B   VANNE MORRIS-GOODALL
UNVEILING MAN'S ORIGINS-TEN DECADES OF THOUGHT ABOUT HUMAN
EVOLUTION
CAMBRIDGE MASS. SCHENKMAN 1969
018,
     A SHORT BUT DETAILED CHRONOLOGICAL SUMMARY OF
     RESEARCH ON HUMAN EVOLUTION WRITTEN BY TWO OUTSTANDING
     CONTRIBUTORS TO THESE DEVELOPMENTS,LEAKEY THE
     ARCHEOLOGIST AND THE FORMER JANE GOODALL,A SPECIALIST
     ON PRIMATE EVOLUTION AND BEHAVIOR.

OLIVER ROLAND   FAGE JOHN D
THIRD CONFERENCE ON AFRICAN HISTORY AND ARCHAEOLOGY-- 1961.
THE JOURNAL OF AFRICAN HISTORY VOL III NO 2 1962 (ENTIRE
VOLUME)
018,019,
     INCLUDES REPORT OF CONFERENCE, AND PAPERS ON HISTORY
     OF FOOD CROPS, LANGUAGE AND HISTORY, AND SEROLOGY AND
     HISTORY, FEUDALISM, ISLAM IN WEST AFRICA, AND TRADE
     ROUTES.

ALIMEN HENRIETTA
THE PREHISTORY OF AFRICA.
LONDON, HUTCHINSON PRESS, 1957
018,

REFERENCE

018

BISHOP WALTER W
THE LATER TERTIARY AND PLEISTOCENE IN EASTERN EQUATORIAL
AFRICA.
IN F CLARK HOWELL AND FRANCOIS BOURLIERE (EDS.), AFRICAN
ECOLOGY AND HUMAN EVOLUTION, CHICAGO, ALDINE, 1966,
PP 246-275
018,
        REFERENCE

BISHOP WALTER W   CLARK J DESMOND
BACKGROUND TO EVOLUTION IN AFRICA
CHICAGO, UNIVERSITY OF CHICAGO PRESS, 1966
018,
        REFERENCE

CLARK J DESMOND
PREHISTORY.
IN ROBERT A LYSTAD (ED), THE AFRICAN WORLD, NEW YORK,
PREAGER, 1966, PP 11-39
018,
        REFERENCE

CLARK J DESMOND
THE PREHISTORIC ORIGINS OF AFRICAN CULTURE.
JOURNAL OF AFRICAN HISTORY VOL 5 NO 2 1964 PP 161-183
018,
        REFERENCE

CLARK J DESMOND
ATLAS OF AFRICAN PREHISTORY.
CHICAGO, UNIVERSITY OF CHICAGO, 1967
018,
        REFERENCE

CLARK J DESMOND
AFRICA SOUTH OF THE SAHARA
IN BRAIDWOOD AND WILLEY,COURSES TOWARD URBAN LIFE,VIKING
FUND PUBLICATIONS IN ANTHROPOLOGY, CHICAGO, ALDINE, 1962
018,
        REFERENCE

CLARK J DESMOND
THE PREHISTORY OF SOUTHERN AFRICA
HARMONDSWORTH, PENGUIN, 1959, REVISED 1970
018,
        REFERENCE

COOKE C K
THE ROCK PAINTINGS AND ENGRAVINGS OF AFRICA.
TARIKH 1 1966 PP 45-66
014,018,
        REFERENCE

DANIELS S G H
THE LATER STONE AGE.
TARIKH 1 1966 PP 20-32
018,

REFERENCE

018
DAVIES OLIVER
LIFE AND DEVELOPMENT AMONG THE EARLIEST HUMANS IN AFRICA.
TARIKH 1 1966 PP 12-19
018,
       REFERENCE

DE HEINZELIN J
OBSERVATIONS ON THE ABSOLUTE CHRONOLOGY OF THE UPPER
PLEISTOCENE.
IN F CLARK HOWELL AND FRANCOIS BOURLIERE (EDS.), AFRICAN
ECOLOGY AND HUMAN EVOLUTION, CHICAGO, ALDINE, 1966,
PP 285-303
018,
       REFERENCE

DEVORE IRVEN   WASHBURN S L
BABOON ECOLOGY AND HUMAN EVOLUTION.
IN F CLARK HOWELL AND FRANCOIS BOURLIERE (EDS.), AFRICAN
ECOLOGY AND HUMAN EVOLUTION, CHICAGO, ALDINE, 1966,
PP 335-367
018,
       REFERENCE

GROVE A T   PULLAN R A
SOME ASPECTS OF THE PLEISTOCENE PALEOGEOGRAPHY OF THE
CHAD BASIN.
IN F CLARK HOWELL AND FRANCOIS BOURLIERE (EDS.), AFRICAN
ECOLOGY AND HUMAN EVOLUTION, CHICAGO, ALDINE, 1966,
PP 230-245
018,
       REFERENCE

HIERNAUX J
SOME ECOLOGICAL FACTORS EFFECTING HUMAN POPULATIONS
IN SUB-SAHARAN AFRICA.
IN F CLARK HOWELL AND FRANCOIS BOURLIERE (EDS.), AFRICAN
ECOLOGY AND HUMAN EVOLUTION, CHICAGO, ALDINE, 1966,
PP 534-546
018,
       REFERENCE

HOWELL F CLARK   CLARK J DESMOND
ACHEULIAN HUNTER-GATHERERS OF SUB-SAHARAN AFRICA.
IN F CLARK HOWELL AND FRANCOIS BOURLIERE (EDS.), AFRICAN
ECOLOGY AND HUMAN EVOLUTION, CHICAGO, ALDINE, 1966,
PP 458-533
018,
       REFERENCE

HOWELL F CLARK
EARLY MAN
NEW YORK, TIME INC, LIFE NATURE LIBRARY, 1965
018,
       REFERENCE

JUNKER HERMANN
THE FIRST APPEARANCE OF THE NEGROES IN HISTORY.

THE JOURNAL OF EGYPTIAN ARCHAEOLOGY 7 1921 PP 121-132
018,
        REFERENCE

018
    LEAKEY L S B
    VERY EARLY EAST AFRICAN HOMINIDAE, AND THEIR ECOLOGICAL
    SETTING.
    IN F CLARK HOWELL AND FRANCOIS BOURLIERE (EDS.), AFRICAN
    ECOLOGY AND HUMAN EVOLUTION, CHICAGO, ALDINE, 1966,
    PP 448-457
    018,
        REFERENCE

    LEAKEY L S B
    THE EVOLUTION OF MAN IN THE AFRICAN CONTINENT.
    TARIKH 1 1966 PP 1-11
    018,
        REFERENCE

    LEAKEY L S B
    MAN'S AFRICAN ORIGIN.
    ANNALS OF THE NEW YORK ACADEMY OF SCIENCES VOL 96 1962 PP
    495-503
    018,
        REFERENCE

    LEAKEY L S B
    OLDUVAI GORGE.
    LONDON, CAMBRIDGE UNIVERSITY PRESS, 1951
    018,
        REFERENCE

    ROBINSON J T
    ADAPTIVE RADIATION IN THE AUSTRALOPITHECINES AND THE
    ORIGIN OF MAN.
    IN F CLARK HOWELL AND FRANCOIS BOURLIERE (EDS.), AFRICAN
    ECOLOGY AND HUMAN EVOLUTION, CHICAGO, ALDINE, 1966,
    PP 385-416
    018,
        REFERENCE

    BIBERSON P
    HUMAN EVOLUTION IN MOROCCO, IN THE FRAMEWORK OF THE
    PALEOCLIMATIC VARIATIONS OF THE ATLANTIC PLEISTOCENE.
    IN F CLARK HOWELL AND FRANCOIS BOURLIERE (EDS.), AFRICAN
    ECOLOGY AND HUMAN EVOLUTION, CHICAGO, ALDINE, 1966,
    PP 417-447
    018,
        CASE STUDY

    BUTZER KARL W   HANSEN CARL L
    DESERT AND RIVER IN NUBIA-GEOMORPHOLOGY AND PREHISTORIC
    ENVIRONMENTS AT THE ASWAN RESERVOIR
    MADISON, UNIVERSITY OF WISCONSIN PRESS, 1968
    017,018,020,
        CASE STUDY

    MULVEY MINA WHITE
    DIGGING UP ADAM-- THE STORY OF L.S.B. LEAKEY.

NEW YORK, MCKAY, 1969
018,
     CASE STUDY

018
   HIERNAUX J
   LA DIVERSITE HUMAINE EN AFRIQUE SUBSAHARIENNE
   UNIVERSITE LIBRE DE BRUXELLES, EDITIONS DE L'INSTITUT DE
   SOCIOLOGIE, 1968
   018,
     LESS ACCESSIBLE

   CHILDE V GORDON
   A SHORT INTRODUCTION TO ARCHAEOLOGY.
   NEW YORK, MACMILLAN, 1958
   018,
     GENERAL THEORY

   CLARK GRAHAM D
   ARCHAEOLOGY AND SOCIETY
   NEW YORK, BARNES AND NOBLE, 1965
   018,
     GENERAL THEORY

   GARN STANLEY M
   HUMAN RACES
   SPRINGFIELD, ILLINOIS, CHARLES C THOMAS, 1965
   018,
     GENERAL THEORY

   WASHBURN S L
   THE STUDY OF RACE
   AMERICAN ANTHROPOLOGIST 65 1963 PP 521-531
   018,
     GENERAL THEORY

   WHEELER ROBERT E
   ARCHAEOLOGY FROM THE EARTH.
   LONDON, OXFORD UNIVERSITY PRESS, 1954
   018,
     GENERAL THEORY

19. ECOLOGICAL ADAPTATION AND DIFFUSION OF AGRICULTURE

019
   CLARK J DESMOND
   THE SPREAD OF FOOD PRODUCTION IN SUB-SAHARAN AFRICA.
   JOURNAL OF AFRICAN HISTORY 3 1962 PP 211-228
   019,
     OUTSTANDING DESCRIPTION OF THE SPREAD OF PLANT AND
     ANIMAL DOMESTICATION IN AFRICA. INCLUDES SEVERAL EX-
     CELLENT MAPS.

   COLLINS ROBERT O   ED
   PROBLEMS IN AFRICAN HISTORY.

ENGLEWOOD CLIFFS, NEW JERSEY, PRENTICE-HALL, INC., 1968
009,019,020,036,
EDITOR HAS ARRANGED ARTICLES BY MAJOR SCHOLARS INTO
SEVEN PARTS--AFRICA AND EGYPT, BANTU ORIGINS AND MIGRA-
TIONS, NILOTIC ORIGINS AND MIGRATIONS, THE HISTORIAN
AND STATELESS SOCIETIES, AFRICAN STATES, TRADE IN PRE-
COLONIAL AFRICA, AND THE AFRICAN SLAVE TRADE. THIS
VOLUME IS INTENDED FOR TEACHING PURPOSES AND IS AVAIL-
ABLE IN PAPERBACK.

019
GUTHRIE MALCOLM
COMPARATIVE BANTU--AN INTRODUCTION TO THE COMPARATIVE
LINGUISTICS AND PREHISTORY OF THE BANTU LANGUAGE.
HANTS, ENGLAND, GREGG PRESS LTD., 1969
011,019,
THIS FOUR-VOLUME SET IS THE PRODUCT OF A LIFETIME OF
RESEARCH BY THE WORLDS FOREMOST SPECIALIST ON BANTU
LANGUAGES. THE VOLUMES CONTAIN MANY MAPS AND ABUN-
DANT STATISTICAL INFORMATION, WORD LISTS, ETC. THE
FULL SET COSTS 120 DOLLARS.

HOWELL F CLARK   BOURLIERE FRANCOIS   EDS
AFRICAN ECOLOGY AND HUMAN EVOLUTION.
CHICAGO, ALDINE, 1966
018,019,
PRODUCT OF 1961 CONFERENCE OF PHYSICAL ANTHROPOLOGISTS
ZOOLOGISTS, GEOLOGISTS, PALEOGEOGRAPHERS, PALEONTOL-
OGISTS, AND PREHISTORIANS. CONTAINS RESEARCH REPORTS
ON PLEISTOCENE ENVIRONMENTS AND BIOLOGICAL EVOLUTION
OF MAN IN AFRICA INCLUDING CLIMATIC CHANGE, ECOLOGY,
DATING METHODS, AND LEAKEY ON OLDUVAI GORGE. TRAN-
SCRIPTS OF CONFERENCE DISCUSSIONS, OVER 100 MAPS AND
FIGURES, AND DETAILED BIBLIOGRAPHY.

OLIVER ROLAND   FAGE JOHN D
THIRD CONFERENCE ON AFRICAN HISTORY AND ARCHAEOLOGY-- 1961.
THE JOURNAL OF AFRICAN HISTORY VOL III NO 2 1962 (ENTIRE
VOLUME)
018,019,
INCLUDES REPORT OF CONFERENCE, AND PAPERS ON HISTORY
OF FOOD CROPS, LANGUAGE AND HISTORY, AND SEROLOGY AND
HISTORY, FEUDALISM, ISLAM IN WEST AFRICA, AND TRADE
ROUTES.

OLIVER ROLAND
THE PROBLEM OF BANTU EXPANSION.
THE JOURNAL OF AFRICAN HISTORY VII 3 1966 PP 361-366
019,
OUTSTANDING SUMMARY ARTICLE ON THEORIES OF BANTU EX-
PANSION BASED HEAVILY ON THE WORK OF MALCOLM GUTHRIE,
AND JOSEPH GREENBERG. DESCRIBES THE SUCCESSIVE STAGES
IN THE SPREAD OF BANTU-SPEAKING PEOPLES, AND POSES
SERIES OF STIMULATING QUESTIONS FOR FUTURE RESEARCH.

POSNANSKY MERRICK
BANTU GENESIS--ARCHAEOLOGICAL REFLEXIONS.
THE JOURNAL OF AFRICAN HISTORY VOL IX NO 1 1968 PP 1-12
019,
SUGGESTS THAT WEST AFRICAN ORIGINS OF BANTU ARE MORE

IMPORTANT THAN OLIVER (BASED ON GUTHRIE) INDICATES.
THIS ARTICLE IS A REASSESSMENT OF THE ARCHAEOLOGICAL
BACKGROUND FOR THE PRE-HISTORY OF BANTU MIGRATIONS,
AND SUGGESTS THAT THE MIGRATIONS ANTEDATE THE 2000
YEAR TIMESCALE PREVIOUSLY ACCEPTED.

019

CLARK J DESMOND
CULTURE AND ECOLOGY IN PREHISTORIC AFRICA.
IN DAVID BROKENSHA (ED.), ECOLOGY AND ECONOMIC DEVELOPMENT
IN TROPICAL AFRICA, BERKELEY, UNIVERSITY OF CALIFORNIA,
1965, PP 13-28
019,
        REFERENCE

DAVIES OLIVER
THE NEOLITHIC REVOLUTION IN TROPICAL AFRICA.
TRANSACTIONS OF THE HISTORICAL SOCIETY OF GHANA 4 1960
PP 14-20
019,
        REFERENCE

DAVIES OLIVER
WEST AFRICA BEFORE THE EUROPEANS
LONDON, METHUEN, 1967
019,022,026,
        REFERENCE

FAGAN BRIAN M
RADIOCARBON DATES FOR SUB-SAHARAN AFRICA VI.
JOURNAL OF AFRICAN HISTORY, X, 1, 1969, PP. 149-169
019,
        REFERENCE

GUTHRIE MALCOLM
BANTU ORIGINS-- A TENTATIVE NEW HYPOTHESIS.
THE JOURNAL OF AFRICAN LANGUAGES 1 1962 PP 9-21
019,
        REFERENCE

GUTHRIE MALCOLM
A TWO-STAGE METHOD OF COMPARATIVE BANTU STUDY.
AFRICAN LANGUAGE STUDIES 3 1962 PP 1-24
019,
        REFERENCE

HIERNAUX J
BANTU EXPANSION-THE EVIDENCE FROM PHYSICAL ANTHROPOLOGY
CONFRONTED WITH LINGUISTIC AND ARCHAEOLOGICAL EVIDENCE
JOURNAL OF AFRICAN HISTORY 4 1968 PP 505-515
019,
        REFERENCE

JONES A M
AFRICA AND INDONESIA
LEIDEN, BRILL, 1964
019,
        REFERENCE

MCMASTER D N

SPECULATIONS ON THE COMING OF THE BANANA TO UGANDA.
JOURNAL OF TROPICAL GEOGRAPHY, SINGAPORE, KUALA LUMPUR 16
OCTOBER 1962 PP 57-69
019,
        REFERENCE

019

OLIVER ROLAND
BANTU GENESIS-AN INQUIRY INTO SOME PROBLEMS OF EARLY BANTU
HISTORY
AFRICAN AFFAIRS 65 1966 PP 245-258
019,
        REFERENCE

PHILLIPSON D W
THE CHANGE FROM HUNTING AND GATHERING TO PASTORALISM AND
AGRICULTURE IN AFRICA.
TARIKH(NEW YORK,HUMANITIES PRESS)1 NO 3 1966 PP 33-44
019,
        REFERENCE

SEDDON D
THE ORIGINS AND DEVELOPMENT OF AGRICULTURE IN EAST AND
SOUTHERN AFRICA
CURRENT ANTHROPOLOGY 9 1968 PP 489-509
019,
        REFERENCE

WRIGLEY C.C.
SPECULATIONS ON THE ECONOMIC PREHISTORY OF AFRICA.
JOURNAL OF AFRICAN HISTORY 2 1960 PP 189-203
019,
        REFERENCE

FAGAN BRIAN M
PRE-EUROPEAN IRON WORKING IN CENTRAL AFRICA WITH SPECIAL
REFERENCE TO NORTHERN RHODESIA.
JOURNAL OF AFRICAN HISTORY 2 1961 PP 199-210
019,
        CASE STUDY

FAGAN BRIAN M
THE IRON AGE SEQUENCE IN THE SOUTHERN PROVINCE OF NORTHERN
RHODESIA.
JOURNAL OF AFRICAN HISTORY 4 1963 PP 157-177
019,
        CASE STUDY

FAGAN BRIAN M
SOUTHERN AFRICA IN THE IRON AGE.
LONDON THAMES AND HUDSON 1965
019,025,
        CASE STUDY

FAGAN BRIAN M
EARLY TRADE AND RAW MATERIALS IN SOUTH CENTRAL AFRICA
JOURNAL OF AFRICAN HISTORY, X, 1, 1969, PP. 1-13
019,
        CASE STUDY

FAGAN BRIAN M
IRON AGE CULTURES IN ZAMBIA--TWO VOLUMES
LONDON, 1967-69
019,142-02,
    CASE STUDY

019
  JONES A M
  INDONESIA AND AFRICA-- THE XYLOPHONE AS CULTURE-INDICATOR.
  JOURNAL OF THE ROYAL ANTHROPOLOGICAL INSTITUTE 89 1959
  PP 155-168
  019,
    CASE STUDY

20. EARLY CULTURE AND STATE FORMATION

020
  COLLINS ROBERT O   ED
  PROBLEMS IN AFRICAN HISTORY.
  ENGLEWOOD CLIFFS, NEW JERSEY, PRENTICE-HALL, INC., 1968
  009,019,020,036,
    EDITOR HAS ARRANGED ARTICLES BY MAJOR SCHOLARS INTO
    SEVEN PARTS--AFRICA AND EGYPT, BANTU ORIGINS AND MIGRA-
    TIONS, NILOTIC ORIGINS AND MIGRATIONS, THE HISTORIAN
    AND STATELESS SOCIETIES, AFRICAN STATES, TRADE IN PRE-
    COLONIAL AFRICA, AND THE AFRICAN SLAVE TRADE. THIS
    VOLUME IS INTENDED FOR TEACHING PURPOSES AND IS AVAIL-
    ABLE IN PAPERBACK.

  ROTBERG ROBERT I
  AFRICA IN ANCIENT TIMES CHAPTER 1.
  IN A POLITICAL HISTORY OF TROPICAL AFRICA, NEW YORK,
  HARCOURT, BRACE AND WORLD, 1965, PP 3-33
  020,
    INTRODUCTORY CHAPTER COVERS THE RISE AND FALL OF KUSH,
    TROPICAL AFRICA AND THE MEDITERRANEAN WORLD, THE FIRST
    AGE OF EXPLORATION, AND THE KINGDOM OF AXUM. BIBLIO-
    GRAPHY APPENDED.

  ALDRED CYRIL
  THE EGYPTIANS-- ANCIENT PEOPLE AND PLACES.
  NEW YORK, PRAEGER, 1961
  020,140-02,
    REFERENCE

  ARKELL A J
  A HISTORY OF THE SUDAN FROM THE EARLIEST TIMES TO 1821
  LONDON, ATHLONE PRESS, 1955
  020,
    REFERENCE

  CARPENTER RHYS
  A TRANS-SAHARAN CARAVAN ROUTE IN HERODOTUS.
  AMERICAN JOURNAL OF ARCHAEOLOGY 60 1956 PP 231-242
  020,

REFERENCE

020

DUNHAM DOWS
NOTES ON THE HISTORY OF KUSH 850 BC - AD 350.
AMERICAN JOURNAL OF ARCHAEOLOGY 50 1946 PP 378-388
020,
        REFERENCE

EMERY W B
ARCHAIC EGYPT
BALTIMORE, PENGUIN, 1963
020,
        REFERENCE

FAIRSERVIS WALTER
THE ANCIENT KINGDOMS OF THE NILE AND THE DOOMED MONUMENTS
OF NUBIA.
NEW YORK, THOMAS CROWELL, 1962
020,
        REFERENCE

GARDINER A
EGYPT OF THE PHAROAHS
OXFORD, CLARENDON PRESS, 1961
020,
        REFERENCE

HANSBERRY W L
ANCIENT KUSH, OLD AETHEOPIA AND THE BILAD ES SUDAN.
JOURNAL OF HUMAN RELATIONS 8 1960 PP 357-387
020,
        REFERENCE

HAYCOCK B G
THE KINGSHIP OF CUSH IN THE SUDAN
COMPARATIVE STUDIES IN SOCIETY AND HISTORY 7 1965 PP 461-80
020,
        REFERENCE

MURPHEY R
THE DECLINE OF NORTH AFRICA SINCE THE ROMAN OCCUPATION--
CLIMATIC OR HUMAN.
ANNALS OF THE ASSOCIATION OF AMERICAN GEOGRAPHERS 41
JUNE 1951 PP 116-132
020,
        REFERENCE

PERHAM MARGERY
THE KINGDOM OF AKSUM.
IN P J M MCEWAN (ED), AFRICA FROM EARLY TIMES TO 1800, LONDON
020,
        REFERENCE

SELIGMAN CHARLES G
RACES OF AFRICA.
LONDON, OXFORD UNIVERSITY PRESS, 1957
020,
        REFERENCE

SHINNIE P L
MEROE, A CIVILIZATION OF THE SUDAN.
LONDON, THAMES AND HUDSON, 1967
020,134-02,
        REFERENCE

020
    SHINNIE P L   SHINNIE M
    NEW LIGHT ON MEDIEVAL NUBIA
    JOURNAL OF AFRICAN HISTORY 6 1965 PP 263-273
    020,
            REFERENCE

    SNOWDEN FRANCK M JR
    BLACKS IN ANTIQUITY--ETHIOPIANS IN THE GRECO-ROMAN
    EXPERIENCE.
    CAMBRIDGE, HARVARD UNIVERSITY PRESS, 1969
    020,027,
            REFERENCE

    THABIT T H
    INTERNATIONAL RELATIONS OF THE SUDAN IN NAPATAN TIMES.
    SUDAN NOTES AND RECORDS 40 1959 PP 19-22
    020,
            REFERENCE

    WESCOTT R W
    ANCIENT EGYPT AND MODERN AFRICA
    JOURNAL OF AFRICAN HISTORY 2 1961 PP 311-321
    020,
            REFERENCE

    BUTZER KARL W   HANSEN CARL L
    DESERT AND RIVER IN NUBIA-GEOMORPHOLOGY AND PREHISTORIC
    ENVIRONMENTS AT THE ASWAN RESERVOIR
    MADISON, UNIVERSITY OF WISCONSIN PRESS, 1968
    017,018,020,
            CASE STUDY

    FAGG BERNARD
    THE NOK CULTURE IN PREHISTORY.
    JOURNAL OF THE HISTORICAL SOCIETY OF NIGERIA 1 1959
    PP 288-293
    020,128-02,
            CASE STUDY

    FAGG WILLIAM
    NIGERIAN IMAGES.
    NEW YORK, PRAEGER, 1963
    014,020,128-01,
            CASE STUDY

    MONTET PIERRE
    ETERNAL EGYPT.
    NEW YORK, PRAEGER PUBLISHERS, 1969
    020,140-02,
            CASE STUDY

    SHAW C T
    IGBO-UKWU-AN ACCOUNT OF ARCHEOLOGICAL DISCOVERIES IN

EASTERN NIGERIA
LONDON,FABER AND FABER;AND EVANSTON,NORTHWESTERN UNIVERSITY
PRESS,1970
020,026,128-02,
        CASE STUDY

020
    WENDORF FRED   ED
    THE PREHISTORY OF NUBIA.
    DALLAS,SMU,1968
    020,
        CASE STUDY

    WILLETT FRANK
    IFE AND ITS ARCHAEOLOGY.
    THE JOURNAL OF AFRICAN HISTORY 1 1960 PP 231-248
    014,020,026,128-01,
        CASE STUDY

21. THE IMPACT OF ISLAM IN AFRICA

021
    FROELICH JEAN C
    LES MUSULMANS D'AFRIQUE NOIRE (THE MUSLIMS OF BLACK
    AFRICA).
    PARIS,EDITIONS DE L'ORANTE,1962
    021,052,
        EXCELLENT OVERVIEW OF MODERN AFRICAN ISLAM BY DIR-
        ECTOR OF UNIVERSITY OF PARIS CENTER FOR HIGHER
        ADMINISTRATIVE STUDIES ON MODERN AFRICA AND ASIA.
        DATA DRAWN FROM UNPUBLISHED FILES, ORGANIZED INTO
        THREE PARTS-- ISLAMIZATION OF BLACK AFRICA, CHARACTER-
        ISTICS OF ISLAM IN BLACK AFRICA, AND MODERN TENDENCIES
        IN ISLAM IN BLACK AFRICA. GOOD DISCUSSION OF BROTHER-
        HOODS, AND ISLAMIC REFORMISM.

    GOUILLY ALPHONSE
    L'ISLAM DANS L'AFRIQUE OCCIDENTALE FRANCAISE (ISLAM IN
    FRENCH WEST AFRICA).
    PARIS,EDITIONS LAROSE,1952
    021,052,
        HAS BEEN THE MAJOR REFERENCE WORK ON WEST AFRICAN
        ISLAM SINCE ITS PUBLICATION IN 1952. NOW PARTLY SUPER
        CEDED BY FROELICH AND MONTEIL, YET REMAINS USEFUL ON
        THE HISTORY OF ISLAMIZATION IN WEST AFRICA INCLUDING
        BERBER, MANDINGO, SONGHAY, AND FULANI EMPIRES, ON THE
        RELIGIOUS BROTHERHOODS QADIRIYYA, TIJANIYYA, MOURID-
        IYYA, HAMALLIYYA, AHMADIYYA, SANUSIYYA, AND ON EFFECTS
        OF ISLAMIZATION LAW, PRAYER, PILGRIMMAGE, ETC.

    KRITZECK JAMES   LEWIS WILLIAM H   EDS
    ISLAM IN AFRICA
    NEW YORK, VAN NOSTRAND-REINHOLD COMPANY,1969
    021,052,
        MAJOR WORK COVERING HISTORICAL PERSPECTIVES,CULTURAL

AND DEMOGRAPHIC ASPECTS OF AFRICAN ISLAM,AND REGIONAL
DEVELOPMENTS IN ALL AREAS OF AFRICA. ORIGINAL CASE
STUDY SUMMARIES BY WELL KNOWN SCHOLARS MAKE UP THE
BULK OF THE VOLUME

021

LEWIS I M   ED
ISLAM IN TROPICAL AFRICA
LONDON,OXFORD UNIVERSITY PRESS,1966
021,052,
        COLLECTION OF STUDIES AND DISCUSSIONS FROM FIFTH
        INTERNATIONAL AFRICAN SEMINAR,ZARIA,NIGERIA,1964.
        INTRODUCTION BY EDITOR COVERS REGIONAL REVIEW AND
        DISTRIBUTION OF ISLAM,AGENTS OF ISLAMIZATION,ISLAM AND
        TRIBAL POLITICS,ISLAMIC LAW AND CUSTOMARY PRACTICE,
        ISLAM AND TRADITIONAL BELIEF AND RITUAL,ISLAM AND THE
        MODERN WORLD. SPECIAL STUDIES REFERRED TO SEPARATELY.

TRIMINGHAM J S
ISLAM IN WEST AFRICA.
OXFORD,OXFORD UNIVERSITY PRESS,1959
021,
        DESCRIBES MAJOR ASPECTS OF ISLAM-- RITUAL, BELIEF SYS-
        TEM, SOCIO-POLITICAL IMPLICATIONS, LEADERSHIP PAT-
        TERNS. FOCUS ON ISLAMIC BROTHERHOODS IN WEST AFRICA.
        IN COMPANION VOLUME, THE HISTORY OF ISLAM IN WEST
        AFRICA, THE AUTHOR TRACES DEVELOPMENT OF WEST AFRICAN
        ISLAM FROM EARLIEST TIMES. BOTH BOOKS CONTROVERSIAL
        BECAUSE AUTHOR IS FORMER MISSIONARY.

TRIMINGHAM J S
THE INFLUENCE OF ISLAM UPON AFRICA.
LONDON, LONGMANS, GREEN AND CO. LTD., 1968
021,052,
        FIVE CHAPTERS--ISLAMIC CULTURE ZONES WITH HISTORY AND
        CHARACTERISTICS (MEDITERRANEAN, WESTERN SUDAN, CENT.
        SUDAN, EAST. SUDAN, ETHIOPIC ZONE, AND E. AFRICA), PRO-
        CESSES OF RELIGIOUS AND CULTURE CHANGE (ASSIMILATION,
        ADOPITON OF ISLAM, EFFECT ON AFRICAN SOCIETY), THE REL-
        IGIOUS LIFE OF AFRICAN MUSLIMS (UNITY OF BELIEF, INSTI-
        TUTIONS, SAINT CULTS), INFLUENCE OF ISLAM ON SOCIAL
        LIFE, THE AFRICAN MUSLIM IN AN ERA OF CHANGE (SECULAR-
        ISM, NATIONALISM).

ABD AL-MAGID A
SOME GENERAL ASPECTS OF THE ARABIZATION OF THE SUDAN.
SUDAN NOTES AND RECORDS 40 1959 PP 48-74
021,134-02,
        REFERENCE

ANDERSON J N D
THE LEGAL TRADITION
IN KRITZECK AND LEWIS PP 35-53
021,
        REFERENCE

GIBB H A R
STUDIES ON THE CIVILIZATION OF ISLAM-EDITED BY S.J.SHAW AND
W.R.POLK
BOSTON,BEACON PRESS,1962

021,
     REFERENCE

021

HASAN YUSUF F
THE PENETRATION OF ISLAM IN THE EASTERN SUDAN.
IN LEWIS, ISLAM IN TROPICAL AFRICA, LONDON, OXFORD
UNIVERSITY PRESS, 1966, PP 144-159
021,
     REFERENCE

HASAN YUSUF F
THE ARABS AND THE SUDAN FROM THE SEVENTH TO THE EARLY
SIXTEENTH CENTURY.
EDINBURGH, THE UNIVERSITY PRESS, 1967
021,134-02,
     REFERENCE

KHALIL SIDI   TRANS BY   RUXTON
MALIKI LAW
LONDON, LUZAC AND CO., 1916
021,066,
     REFERENCE

LE TOURNEAU
ALMOHAD MOVEMENT IN NORTH AFRICA IN THE 12TH AND 13TH
CENTURIES.
PRINCETON, NEW JERSEY, PRINCETON UNIVERSITY PRESS, 1969
021,
     REFERENCE

MONTEIL VINCENT
MARABOUTS
IN KRITZECK AND LEWIS PP 88-109
021,
     REFERENCE

TAPIERO NORBERT
EVOLVING SOCIAL PATTERNS
IN KRITZECK AND LEWIS PP 54-87
021,
     REFERENCE

TRIMINGHAM J S
ISLAM IN EAST AFRICA.
OXFORD, CLARENDON PRESS, 1964
021,
     REFERENCE

TRIMINGHAM J S
A HISTORY OF ISLAM IN WEST AFRICA.
OXFORD, CLARENDON PRESS, 1962
021,
     REFERENCE

TRIMINGHAM J S
THE PHASES OF ISLAMIC EXOANSION AND ISLAMIC CULTURE ZONES
IN AFRICA.
IN LEWIS, ISLAM IN TROPICAL AFRICA, LONDON, OXFORD UNIVERSITY
PRESS, 1966, P. 127-143

021,
    REFERENCE

021

TRIMINGHAM J S
THE EXPANSION OF ISLAM
IN KRITZECK AND LEWIS PP 13-34
021,
    REFERENCE

WILLIS JOHN R   ED
STUDIES ON THE HISTORY OF ISLAM IN WEST AFRICA,(3 VOLS)
I--THE CULTIVATORS OF ISLAM
II--THE EVOLUTION OF ISLAMIC INSTITUTIONS
III--THE GROWTH OF ARABIC LITERATURE.
NEW YORK, INTERNATIONAL UNIVERSITY BOOKSELLERS (FORTHCOMING)
021,
    REFERENCE

WILLIS JOHN R
JIHAD FI SABIL ALLAH-ITS DOCTRINAL BASIS IN ISLAM AND SOME
ASPECTS OF ITS EVOLUTION IN NINETEENTH CENTURY WEST AFRICA
JOURNAL OF AFRICAN HISTORY 8 1967 PP 383-394
021,
    REFERENCE

BIVAR A D H   HISKETT MERVIN
THE ARABIC LITERATURE OF NIGERIA TO 1804-- A PROVISIONAL
ACCOUNT.
BULLETIN OF THE SCHOOL OF ORIENTAL AND AFRICAN STUDIES 25
1962 PP 104-148
021,060,128-02,
    CASE STUDY

BOVILL EDWARD W
THE MOORISH INVASION OF THE SUDAN.
JOURNAL OF THE AFRICAN SOCIETY 26 1926 PP 245-262 AND
27 1927 PP 47-56
021,
    CASE STUDY

PARSONS J J
THE MOORISH IMPRINT ON THE IBERIAN PENINSULA.
GEOGRAPHICAL REVIEW 52 JANUARY 1962 PP 120-122
021,
    CASE STUDY

TRIMINGHAM J S
ISLAM IN THE SUDAN.
LONDON, FRANK CASS LTD, 1965
021,134-03,
    CASE STUDY

MARTY PAUL
ETUDES SUR L ISLAM AU SENEGAL-- LES DOCTRINES ET LES
INSTITUTIONS (STUDIES ON ISLAM IN SENEGAL-- THE DOCTRINES
AND THE INSTITUTIONS).
COLLECTIONS DE LA REVUE DU MONDE,PARIS,MAISON ERNEST
LEROUX,1917
021,130-03,

LESS ACCESSIBLE

021

MARTY PAUL
ETUDES SUR L'ISLAM ET LES TRIBUS DU SOUDAN (STUDIES ON
ISLAM AND THE SUDANIC TRIBES).
PARIS, EDITIONS ERNEST LEROUX, 1920
021,123-03,
        LESS ACCESSIBLE

MARTY PAUL
LA REGION DE KAYES, LE PAYS BAMBARA, LE SAHEL DE NIORO VOL4
(THE KAYES REGION, BAMBARA COUNTRY, THE NIORO SAVANNAH).
IN ETUDES SUR L'ISLAM ET LES TRIBUS DU SOUDAN, PARIS,
EDITIONS ERNEST LEROUX, 1920
021,123-03,
        LESS ACCESSIBLE

MARTY PAUL
ETUDES SUR L'ISLAM ET LES TRIBUS MAURES-- LES BRAKNA
(STUDIES ON ISLAM AND THE MAURITANIAN TRIBES-- THE BRAKNA.
PARIS, EDITIONS ERNEST LEROUX, 1921
021,124-03,
        LESS ACCESSIBLE

MARTY PAUL
L'ISLAM ET LES TRIBUS DANS LA COLONIE DU NIGER-- EXTRAIT
DE LA REVUE DES ETUDES ISLAMIQUES (ISLAM AND THE TRIBES
OF NIGER COLONY-- EXTRACT FROM THE REVIEW OF ISLAMIC
STUDIES).
PARIS, LIBRARIE ORIENTALISTE PAUL GEUTHNER, 1931
021,127-03,
        LESS ACCESSIBLE

MARTY PAUL
ETUDES SUR L'ISLAM EN COTE D IVOIRE (STUDIES ON ISLAM IN
THE IVORY COAST).
PARIS EDITIONS ERNEST LEROUX 1922
021, 116-03,
        LESS ACCESSIBLE

MARTY PAUL
L'ISLAM EN GUINNEE-- FOUTA DJALLON (ISLAM IN GUINEA-- FOUTA
DJALON).
PARIS, EDITIONS ERNEST LEROUX, 1921
021,115-03,
        LESS ACCESSIBLE

ARBERRY A J
SUFISM, AN ACCOUNT OF THE MYSTICS OF ISLAM.
LONDON, GEORGE ALLEN AND UNWIN, 1950
021,
        GENERAL THEORY

22. EMPIRES OF THE WESTERN SUDAN

022
    BOVILL EDWARD W
    THE GOLDEN TRADE OF THE MOORS.
    LONDON,OXFORD UNIVERSITY PRESS,1958;SECOND EDITION,1968
    022,
        PIONEERING STUDY FIRST PUBLISHED IN 1933. NOW BEING
        SUPERSEDED BY RECENT RESEARCH BUT STILL AN EXCELLENT
        AND COHERENT ACCOUNT OF THE TRADE AND RELATIONS BE-
        TWEEN STATES AT BOTH ENDS OF THE CROSS-SAHARAN ROUTES.
        PARTICULARLY USEFUL ON ARAB TRAVELLERS WHO VISITED
        WESTERN SUDANIC KINGDOMS.

    DAVIDSON BASIL
    THE GROWTH OF AFRICAN CIVILIZATION-A HISTORY OF WEST AFRICA
    1000-1800
    GARDEN CITY,NEW YORK,DOUBLEDAY ANCHOR BOOKS,1969
    022,026,
        AN EXCELLENT PAPERBACK INTRODUCTION AND SURVEY OF WEST
        AFRICAN HISTORY.WELL ARRANGED AND EASY TO READ. UP-
        TO-DATE REVIEW OF CURRENT RESEARCH FINDINGS AND
        EXCELLENT CHRONOLOGY AND MAPS.

    FAGE JOHN D
    A HISTORY OF WEST AFRICA
    NEW YORK,CAMBRIDGE UNIVERSITY RRESS,1969
    022, 026, 036,
        FOURTH EDITION OF CLASSIC INTRODUCTION TO WEST
        AFRICAN HISTORY. REWRITTEN AND REVISED TO INCLUDE TWO
        NEW CHAPTERS ON POLITICAL DEVELOPMENTS IN LOWER
        GUINEA AND ON DEVELOPMENTS IN THE INTERIOR OF WEST
        AFRICA IN THE NINETEENTH CENTURY. MANY EXCELLENT MAPS

    ROUCH JEAN
    SONGHAY.
    IN P J M MCEWAN (ED),AFRICA FROM EARLY TIMES TO 1800, LONDON,
    OXFORD UNIVERSITY PRESS,1968,PP 59-89
    022,123-02,
        EXCELLENT INTRODUCTION, TRANSLATED FROM FRENCH, ON
        RISE OF SONGHAY AT BEGINNING OF 15TH CENTURY AT EX-
        PENSE OF MALI. DISCUSSES EARLY LEADER, SONNI ALI, THE
        MOROCCAN CONQUEST, AND THE COLLAPSE OF SONGHAY IN
        1591. DEALS WITH SUCCESSOR STATES TO SONGHAY, AND
        ASSESSES IMPACT OF ISLAM.

    DAVIES OLIVER
    WEST AFRICA BEFORE THE EUROPEANS
    LONDON,METHUEN,1967
    019,022,026,
        REFERENCE

    DECRAENE PHILIPPE
    LE MALI MEDIEVAL (MEDIEVAL MALI).
    CIVILISATIONS 12 1962 PP 250-258
    022,123-02,

REFERENCE

022

FAGE JOHN D
ANCIENT GHANA-- A REVIEW OF THE EVIDENCE.
TRANSACTIONS OF THE HISTORICAL SOCIETY OF GHANA 3 1957
PP 77-98
022,
　　　REFERENCE

FAGE JOHN D
SOME THOUGHTS ON STATE FORMATION IN THE WESTERN SUDAN BEFORE
THE SEVENTEENTH CENTURY.
IN JEFFREY BUTLER (ED) BOSTON UNIVERSITY PAPERS IN AFRICAN
HISTORY VOL I, BOSTON BOSTON UNIVERSITY PRESS 1964 PP 17-34
022,
　　　REFERENCE

HUNWICK JOHN
RELIGION AND STATE IN THE SONGHAY EMPIRE, 1464-1591.
IN LEWIS, ISLAM IN TROPICAL AFRICA, LONDON, OXFORD UNIVERSITY
PRESS, 1966, PP. 296-317
022,038,
　　　REFERENCE

IBN BATTUTA
THE TRAVELS OF IBN BATTUTA.
TRANS. H A R GIBB, CAMBRIDGE, CAMBRIDGE UNIVERSITY PRESS,
1962
022,
　　　REFERENCE

MAUNY RAYMOND
THE QUESTION OF GHANA.
AFRICA 24 1954 PP 200-213
022,
　　　REFERENCE

MAUNY RAYMOND
TABLEAU GEOGRAPHIQUE DE L'OUEST AFRICAIN AU MOYEN AGE
D'APRES LES SOURCES ECRITES, LA TRADITION, ET L'ARCHEOLOGIE
(GEOGRAPHIC TABLEAU OF WEST AFRICA IN THE MIDDLE AGES BASED
ON WRITTEN SOURCES TRADITIONS AND ARCHEOLOGICAL FINDINGS).
DAKAR, INSTITUT FRANCAIS D'AFRIQUE NOIRE, MEMOIRES 61 1961
022,
　　　REFERENCE

ROTBERG ROBERT I
THE ERA OF EMPIRES AND CITY-STATES, 800-1500 CHAPTER 2.
IN A POLITICAL HISTORY OF TROPICAL AFRICA, NEW YORK,
HARCOURT, BRACE AND WORLD, 1965, PP 34-66
022,023,025,
　　　REFERENCE

HAMA BOUBOU
HISTOIRE DES SONGHAY (HISTORY OF THE SONGHAY).
PARIS, PRESENCE AFRICAINE, 1968
022,123-02,
　　　CASE STUDY

NIANE DJUBRIL T
SUNDIATA--AN EPIC OF OLD MALI (TRANSLATED BY G D PICKETT)
LONDON, LONGMANS, 1965
022,123-02,
    CASE STUDY

022
    MAUNY RAYMOND
    UNE ROUTE PREHISTORIQUE A TRAVERS LE SAHARA OCCIDENTAL (A
    PREHISTORIC ROUTE ACROSS THE WESTERN SAHARA).
    BULLETIN DE L'INSTITUT FRANCAIS D'AFRIQUE NOIRE 19 1947
    PP 341-357
    022,
        LESS ACCESSIBLE

    MONTEIL CHARLES
    LES EMPIRES DU MALI (THE EMPIRES OF MALI).
    BULLETIN DU COMITE D'ETUDES HISTORIQUES ET SCIENTIFIQUES DE
    L'AFRIQUE OCCIDENTALE FRANCAISE 12 1929 PP 191-447
    022,123-02,
        LESS ACCESSIBLE

    MONTEIL CHARLES
    UNE CITE SOUDANAISE-- DJENNE METROPOLE DU DELTA CENTRAL
    DU NIGER (A SUDANESE CITY-- JENNE, METROPOLIS OF THE
    CENTRAL NIGER DELTA).
    SOCIETE D'EDITIONS DE GEOGRAPHIE MARITIME ET COLONIALE, PARIS,
    1932
    022,123-02,
        LESS ACCESSIBLE

    NIANE DJUBRIL T
    RECHERCHES SUR L'EMPIRE DU MALI AU MOYEN AGE (RESEARCH
    ON THE MALI EMPIRE IN THE MIDDLE AGES).
    RECHERCHES AFRICAINES 2 1961 PP 31-51
    022,123-02,
        LESS ACCESSIBLE

    ROUCH JEAN
    CONTRIBUTION A L'HISTOIRE DES SONGHAY (A CONTRIBUTION TO
    THE HISTORY OF SONGHAI).
    DAKAR, INSTITUT FRANCAIS D'AFRIQUE NOIRE MEMOIRE 29 1953
    022,123-02,
        LESS ACCESSIBLE

23. COASTAL STATES OF EAST AFRICA

023
    ALPERS EDWARD A
    THE EAST AFRICAN SLAVE TRADE.
    NAIROBI, EAST AFRICAN PUBLISHING HOUSE, 1967
    023,028,
        THIS SHORT BUT INCISIVE ANALYSIS CHALLENGES MANY
        WIDELY ACCEPTED VIEWS ON THE EAST AFRICAN SLAVE TRADE,
        PARTICULARLY WITH RESPECT TO ITS IMPACT ON AFRICAN

SOCIETIES, ITS SIZE AND SCOPE, AND THE ROLE OF EURO-
PEANS. LIKE OTHER PUBLICATIONS OF EAST AFRICAN PUB-
LISHING HOUSE, THIS BOOK IS DISTRIBUTED IN THE UNITED
STATES BY NORTHWESTERN UNIVERSITY PRESS.

023

COUPLAND REGINALD
EAST AFRICA AND ITS INVADERS FROM THE EARLIEST TIMES TO THE
DEATH OF SEYYID SAID IN 1856.
OXFORD,1938
023,

> AUTHOR WAS PROFESSOR IMPERIAL HISTORY AT OXFORD AND
> PRIMARILY INTERESTED IN RESEARCH ON THE ABOLITION OF
> THE SLAVE TRADE. THIS VOLUME, NOW REPRINTED, IS OUT
> OF DATE, BUT IS STILL USEFUL ON THE ARAB ASPECTS OF
> EAST AFRICAN HISTORY. HE TENDED TO DE-EMPHASIZE BLACK
> AFRICAN ASPECTS OF COASTAL HISTORY.

DAVIDSON BASIL
A HISTORY OF EAST AND CENTRAL AFRICA-TO THE LATE
NINETEENTH CENTURY
GARDEN CITY, NEW YORK, DOUBLEDAY ANCHOR, 1969
023,025,

> ANOTHER EXCELLENT INTRODUCTORY TEXT BY ONE OF THE
> MOST PROLIFIC WRITERS ON AFRICAN HISTORY. A REVISED
> VERSION OF EARLIER WORK(THE GROWTH OF AFRICAN
> CIVILIZATION,LONGMANS,GREEN,1967),THIS PAPERBACK
> SURVEYS EARLY IRON AGE DEVELOPMENTS, GROWTH AND
> EXPANSION AFTER 1000 AND DEVELOPMENTS AFTER 1500.
> USEFUL MAPS AND TIME CHARTS.

FREEMAN-GRENVILLE G S P
THE COAST-- 1498-1840.
IN ROLAND OLIVER AND GERVASE MATHEW (EDS), HISTORY OF EAST
AFRICA VOLUME ONE, OXFORD, CLARENDON PRESS, 1963, PP 129-168
023,

> ANALYSIS OF THE PERIOD BOUNDED BY FIRST INCURSION OF
> EUROPEANS INTO THE INDIAN OCEAN (PORTUGUESE) AND THE
> FINAL REMOVAL OF THE COURT OF OMAN TO ZANZIBAR. DUR-
> ING THIS PERIOD THE SWAHILI GREW AND FLOURISHED.

KIMAMBO ISARIA N
A POLITICAL HISTORY OF THE PARE KINGDOM
NAIROBI, EAST AFRICAN PUBLISHING HOUSE, 1969
023,136-02,

> DETAILED RECONSTRUCTION OF TRADE AND STATE-BUILDING
> EFFORTS AMONG A SERIES OF COMMUNITIES IN THE PARE
> HIGHLANDS NEAR THE EAST AFRICAN COAST IN TANZANIA.
> UTILIZED LOCAL TRADITIONS OF CLANS AND OCCUPATIONAL
> GROUPS TO SHOW THAT EFFORTS AT CENTRALIZATION WERE
> INDEPENDENTLY INITIATED RATHER THAN BORROWED BY DIF-
> FUSION FROM PRE-EXISTING STATE.

MATHEW GERVASE
THE EAST AFRICAN COAST UNTIL THE COMING OF THE PORTUGUESE.
IN ROLAND OLIVER AND GERVASE MATHEW (EDS), HISTORY OF EAST
AFRICA VOLUME ONE, OXFORD, CLARENDON PRESS, 1963, PP 94-128
023,

> DISCUSSION OF THE EAST AFRICAN COAST FROM APPROXIMATE-
> LY A.D. 100 TO 1498, PARTICULARLY WITHIN CONTEXT OF

INDIAN OCEAN TRADING SYSTEM. AUTHOR EMPHASIZES BLACK
AFRICAN CONTRIBUTION TO COASTAL SOCIETY.

023
  OLIVER ROLAND   MATHEW GERVASE   EDS
  HISTORY OF EAST AFRICA. VOLUME ONE.
  OXFORD,CLARENDON PRESS,1963
  023,036,
            FIRST ATTEMPT TO DRAW TOGETHER A COMPREHENSIVE HISTORY
            OF EAST AFRICA, BY THE OUTSTANDING SCHOLARS OF THE
            LATE 1950'S. IS NOW SLIGHTLY DATED, BUT REMAINS THE
            CORE WORK ON EAST AFRICA.

  SUTTON J E G
  THE EAST AFRICAN COAST-- AN HISTORICAL AND ARCHAEOLOGICAL
  REVIEW.
  NAIROBI,EAST AFRICAN PUBLISHING HOUSE,1966
  023,
            FIRST PUBLISHED PAPER OF THE HISTORICAL ASSOCIATION OF
            TANZANIA, WRITTEN BY PROFESSOR AT UNIVERSITY COLLEGE,
            DAR ES SALAAM. OUTSTANDING BRIEF (27 PAGES) HISTORY
            OF EAST AFRICAN COAST UP TO THE BEGINNING OF THE NINE-
            TEENTH CENTURY.

  WHITELEY W H
  SWAHILI-THE RISE OF A NATIONAL LANGUAGE
  NEW YORK,BARNES AND NOBLE,1969
  023,049,
            BRIEF AND IMPORTANT DISCUSSION TRACING THE DEVELOP-
            MENT OF THE SWAHILI LANGUAGE AND CULTURE AND ITS DIF-
            FUSION INTO EAST AND CENTRAL AFRICA DURING THE PRECO-
            LONIAL AND COLONICAL PERIODS.

  BOXER CHARLES RALPH DE AZEVEDO CARLOS
  FORT JESUS AND THE PORTUGESE IN MOMBASA 1593-1729
  LONDON,HOLLIS AND CARTER,1960
  023,027,
            REFERENCE

  CHITTICK H NEVILLE
  THE SHIRAZI COLONIZATION OF EAST AFRICA
  JOURNAL OF AFRICAN HISTORY 6 1965 PP 275-294
  023,
            REFERENCE

  DORMAN M H
  THE KILWA CIVILIZATION AND THE KILWA RUINS.
  TANGANYIKA NOTES AND RECORDS 6 1938 PP 61-71
  023,136-02,
            REFERENCE

  FREEMAN-GRENVILLE G S P
  EAST AFRICAN COIN FINDS AND THEIR HISTORICAL SIGNIFICANCE.
  JOURNAL OF AFRICAN HISTORY 1 1960 PP 31-43
  023,
            REFERENCE

  FREEMAN-GRENVILLE G S
  THE EAST AFRICAN COAST-SELECT DOCUMENTS FROM THE FIRST TO
  THE EARLIER NINETEENTH CENTURY

LONDON, OXFORD UNIVERSITY PRESS, 1962
023,
       REFERENCE

023
   FREEMAN-GRENVILLE G S
   THE MEDIEVAL HISTORY OF THE COAST OF TANGANYIKA
   LONDON, OXFORD UNIVERSITY PRESS, 1962
   023,
       REFERENCE

   GRAY JOHN M
   EARLY PORTUGUESE VISITORS OF KILWA.
   TANGANYIKA NOTES AND RECORDS 52 1959 PP 117-128
   023,136-02,
       REFERENCE

   GRAY JOHN M
   HISTORY OF ZANZIBAR FROM THE MIDDLE AGES TO 1856
   LONDON, OXFORD UNIVERSITY PRESS, 1962
   023,
       REFERENCE

   KIRKMAN JAMES S
   MEN AND MONUMENTS ON THE EAST AFRICAN COAST.
   LONDON LUTTERWORTH PRESS 1964
   023,
       REFERENCE

   MATHEW GERVASE
   RECENT DISCOVERIES IN EAST AFRICAN ARCHAEOLOGY.
   ANTIQUITY 27 1953 PP 212-218
   023,
       REFERENCE

   MATHEW GERVASE
   THE CULTURE OF THE EAST AFRICAN COAST IN THE 17TH AND 18TH
   CENTURIES IN THE LIGHT OF RECENT ARCHAEOLOGICAL STUDIES.
   MAN 56 1956 PP 65-68
   023,
       REFERENCE

   POSNANSKY MERRICK   ED
   PRELUDE TO EAST AFRICAN HISTORY.
   LONDON, OXFORD UNIVERSITY PRESS, 1966
   023,
       REFERENCE

   ROTBERG ROBERT I
   THE ERA OF EMPIRES AND CITY-STATES, 800-1500 CHAPTER 2.
   IN A POLITICAL HISTORY OF TROPICAL AFRICA, NEW YORK,
   HARCOURT, BRACE AND WORLD, 1965 PP 34-66
   022,023,025,
       REFERENCE

   WHEATLEY PAUL
   THE LAND OF ZANJ-- EXEGETICAL NOTES ON CHINESE KNOWLEDGE OF
   EAST AFRICA PRIOR TO AD 1500.
   IN ROBERT W STEEL AND R MANSELL PROTHERO (EDS), GEOGRAPHERS
   AND THE TROPICS-- LIVERPOOL ESSAYS, LONDON, LONGMANS,

1964, PP 139-188
023,
        REFERENCE

023
    BERG F J
    THE SWAHILI COMMUNITY OF MOMBASA, 1500-1900
    JOURNAL OF AFRICAN HISTORY 9 1968 PP 35-56
    023,
        CASE STUDY

    CHITTICK H NEVILLE
    KILWA AND THE ARAB SETTLEMENT OF THE EAST AFRICAN COAST.
    THE JOURNAL OF AFRICAN HISTORY 4 1963 PP 179-190
    023,136-02,
        CASE STUDY

    FEIERMAN S
    THE SHAMBAA
    IN A ROBERTS (ED), TANZANIA BEFORE 1900, NAIROBI, 1968, PP 1-15
    023,
        CASE STUDY

    HARRIES LYNDON
    SWAHILI POETRY.
    OXFORD, CLARENDON PRESS, 1962
    012,023,
        CASE STUDY

    CHITTICK H NEVILLE
    NOTES ON KILWA.
    TANGANYIKA NOTES AND RECORDS 53 1959 PP 179-203
    023,136-02,
        LESS ACCESSIBLE

    FREEMAN-GRENVILLE G S P
    SWAHILI LITERATURE AND THE HISTORY AND ARCHAEOLOGY OF THE
    EAST AFRICAN COAST.
    JOURNAL OF THE EAST AFRICAN SWAHILI COMMITTEE 28/2 1958
    PP 7-25
    023,
        LESS ACCESSIBLE

    HARRIES LYNDON
    THE FOUNDING OF RABAI-- A SWAHILI CHRONICLE BY MIDANI BIN
    MWIDAD.
    SWAHILI 31 1960 PP 140-149
    023,
        LESS ACCESSIBLE

24. STATES OF THE CENTRAL SUDAN

024
    JOHNSTON H A S
    THE FULANI EMPIRE OF SOKOTO.

LONDON, OXFORD UNIVERSITY PRESS, 1967
024,052,128-02,
    VERY READABLE ACCOUNT BY FORMER ADMINISTRATIVE OFFICER.
    FOR FULLER REVIEW, SEE M.G. SMITH (AFRICA, JAN. 1969),
    WHO SAYS, 'I DOUBT THIS SPLENDID WORK IS LIKELY TO BE
    SUPERSEDED.'

024
    LAST MURRAY
    THE SOKOTO CALIPHATE.
    LONDON, LONGMANS, GREEN AND COMPANY LTD., 1967
    024,128-02,
        ALTHOUGH THIS IS A DETAILED AND SCHOLARLY WORK, IT DOES
        MAKE AVAILABLE TO THE STUDENT FOR THE FIRST TIME A HIS-
        TORY OF 19TH CENTURY SOKOTO DERIVED FROM THE ARABIC
        TEXTS AND THE ORAL TRADITIONS OF THE PERSONS INVOLVED.
        DISCUSSES THE ISLAMIC CONCEPT OF JIHAD AND COMMUNITY,
        THE ESTABLISHMENT OF DAR-AL-ISLAM IN SOKOTO, AND THE
        SPECIAL ROLE OF THE WAZIRI (VIZIER).

    SMITH M G
    GOVERNMENT IN ZAZZAU, 1800-1950.
    LONDON, OXFORD UNIVERSITY PRESS, 1960
    024,128-01,
        EXCELLENT INTRODUCTION TO THE PRE-COLONIAL HAUSA AND
        FULANI CITY-STATE OF ZARIA IN NORTHERN NIGERIA. PRO-
        VIDES INSIGHT INTO THE STRUCTURE AND PROCESSES OF CEN-
        TRAL SUDANIC STATE SYSTEMS. FOCUSES ON THE OFFICES
        OF STATE AS A MEANS OF DETERMINING FUNCTIONAL DIFFER-
        ENTIATION. AUTHOR IS WEST INDIAN SOCIAL ANTHROPOLO-
        GIST AT UCLA.

    BOAHEN A ADU
    BRITAIN, THE SAHARA, AND THE WESTERN SUDAN, 1788-1861.
    OXFORD, CLARENDON PRESS, 1964
    024,
        REFERENCE

    COOLEY WILLIAM D
    THE NEGRO LAND OF THE ARABS EXAMINED AND EXPLAINED OR
    AN INQUIRY INTO THE EARLY HISTORY AND GEOGRAPHY OF CENTRAL
    AFRICA.
    NEW YORK, BARNES AND NOBLE, 1966
    024,
        REFERENCE

    GREENBERG JOSEPH H
    THE NEGRO KINGDOMS OF THE SUDAN.
    TRANSACTIONS OF THE NEW YORK ACADEMY OF SCIENCES 11 1949
    PP 126-135
    024,
        REFERENCE

    HISKETT MERVIN
    KITAB AL-FARQ-- A WORK ON THE HABE KINGDOMS ATTRIBUTED TO
    UTHMAN DAN FODIO.
    BULLETIN OF THE SCHOOL OF ORIENTAL AND AFRICAN STUDIES 23
    1960 PP 558-579
    024,128-02,
        REFERENCE

024

  HOGBEN S J   KIRK-GREENE A H M
  THE EMIRATES OF NORTHERN NIGERIA-- A PRELIMINARY SURVEY OF
  HISTORICAL TRADITIONS.
  LONDON,OXFORD UNIVERSITY PRESS, 1966
  024,128-02,
        REFERENCE

  LEVTZION NEHEMIA
  MUSLIMS AND CHIEFS IN WEST AFRICA.
  OXFORD, CLARENDON PRESS, 1968
  024,141-03,
        REFERENCE

  PROTHERO R MANSELL
  HEINRICH BARTH AND THE WESTERN SUDAN.
  THE GEOGRAPHICAL JOURNAL CXXIV 1958 PP 326-339
  024,
        REFERENCE

  ROTBERG ROBERT I
  KINGDOMS OF THE SAVANNAH AND FOREST, 1500-1800 CHAPTER 4.
  IN A POLITICAL HISTORY OF TROPICAL AFRICA, NEW YORK,
  HARCOURT, BRACE AND WORLD, 1965, PP 95-132
  024,025,026,
        REFERENCE

  SMITH H F C
  THE ISLAMIC REVOLUTIONS OF THE 19TH CENTURY.
  JOURNAL OF THE HISTORICAL SOCIETY OF NIGERIA 2 DECEMBER
  1961 PP 169-185
  024,
        REFERENCE

  ABDULLAHI IBN M
  TAZYIN AL WARAQAT.
  IBADAN,UNIVERSITY OF IBADAN PRESS,1964 (TRANSLATED AND
  EDITED, MERVYN HISKETT)
  024,128-02,
        CASE STUDY

  ARKELL A J
  THE HISTORY OF DARFUR 1200-1700 A D.
  SUDAN NOTES AND RECORDS 32 1951 PP 37-70, PP 207-238
  ALSO 33 1952 PP 129-155, PP 244-275
  024,106-02,
        CASE STUDY

  ARKELL A J
  THE MEDIEVAL HISTORY OF DARFUR IN ITS RELATION TO OTHER
  CULTURES AND TO THE NILOTIC SUDAN.
  SUDAN NOTES AND RECORDS 40 1959 PP 44-47
  024,106-02,
        CASE STUDY

  BIVAR A D H
  THE WATHIQAT AHL AL-SUDAN-- A MANIFESTO OF THE FULANI JIHAD.
  JOURNAL OF AFRICAN HISTORY 2 1961 PP 235-243
  024,128-02,

CASE STUDY

024

BIVAR A D H   SHINNIE P L
OLD KANURI CAPITALS.
JOURNAL OF AFRICAN HISTORY 3 1962 PP 1-10
024,128-02,
      CASE STUDY

BROWN WILLIAM A
TOWARD A CHRONOLOGY FOR THE CALIPHATE OF HAMDULLAHI (MASINA)
CAHIERS D'ETUDES AFRICAINE, VOL. VIII, NO. 31, 1968, PP. 428
434
024,123-02,
      CASE STUDY

COHEN RONALD
CONFLICT AND CHANGE IN A NORTHERN NIGERIAN EMIRATE.
IN G ZOLLSCHAN AND D HIRSCH (EDS), EXPLORATIONS IN SOCIAL
CHANGE,BOSTON, HOUGHTON MIFFLIN, 1964
024,128-03,
      CASE STUDY

COHEN RONALD
THE BORNU KING LISTS.
IN J BUTLER (ED), BOSTON UNIVERSITY PUBLICATIONS IN AFRICAN
HISTORY VOL 2, BOSTON, BOSTON UNIVERSITY PRESS, 1966,
PP 41-83
024,128-02,
      CASE STUDY

COHEN RONALD
THE DYNAMICS OF FEUDALISM IN BORNU.
IN J BUTLER (ED), BOSTON UNIVERSITY PUBLICATIONS IN AFRICAN
HISTORY VOL 2, BOSTON, BOSTON UNIVERSITY PRESS, 1966
PP 87-105
024,128-01,
      CASE STUDY

COHEN RONALD   BRENNER LOUIS
BORNU IN THE 19TH CENTURY.
IN A AJAYI AND MICHAEL CROWDER (EDS), THE HISTORY OF WEST
AFRICA, OXFORD, CLARENDON PRESS, 1968
024,128-02,
      CASE STUDY

COHEN RONALD
THE KANURI OF BORNU.
NEW YORK, HOLT, RINEHART AND WINSTON, 1967
008,024,128-01,
      CASE STUDY

MARTIN B G
KANEM, BORNU, AND THE FAZZAN--NOTES ON THE POLITICAL HISTORY
OF A TRADE SOURCE.
JOURNAL OF AFRICAN HISTORY, X, 1, 1969, PP. 15-27
024,106-02,
      CASE STUDY

ROBINSON ARTHUR E

THE ARAB DYNASTY OF DAR FOR (DARFUR),AD   1448–1874 OR
AH 852–1201.
JOURNAL OF THE AFRICAN SOCIETY 27 1927 PP 353–363
28 1928 PP 55–67, 274–280, 379–384 AND
29 1929 PP 53–70, 164–180
024,106–02,
        CASE STUDY

024
    SMITH M G
    THE JIHAD OF SHEHU DAN FODIO – SOME PROBLEMS.
    IN LEWIS, ISLAM IN TROPICAL AFRICA, LONDON, OXFORD UNIVERSITY
    PRESS, 1966, P. 408–424
    024,
        CASE STUDY

    BA AMADOU HAMPATE   DAGET JACQUES
    L'EMPIRE PEUL DE MACINA 1818–1853 (THE FULANI EMPIRE OF
    MACINA 1818–1853).
    BAMAKO, INSTITUT FRANCAIS D'AFRIQUE NOIRE CENTRE DU SOUDAN
    ETUDES SOUDANAISES 3 1962
    024,123–02,
        LESS ACCESSIBLE

    EL MASRI F H
    THE LIFE OF SHEHU USUMAN DAN FODIO BEFORE THE JIHAD.
    JOURNAL OF THE HISTORICAL SOCIETY OF NIGERIA 2 DECEMBER
    1963 PP 435–448
    024,128–02,
        LESS ACCESSIBLE

    ELLISON R E
    THREE FORGOTTEN EXPLORERS OF THE LATTER HALF OF THE
    NINETEENTH CENTURY, WITH SPECIAL REFERENCE TO THEIR
    JOURNEYS TO BORNU.
    JOURNAL OF THE HISTORICAL SOCIETY OF NIGERIA I 1959 PP
    322–330
    024,
        LESS ACCESSIBLE

    URVOY YVES
    HISTOIRE DE L'EMPIRE DU BORNU (HISTORY OF THE EMPIRE OF
    BORNU).
    PARIS LAROSE 1949,(IFAN MEMOIRES 7)
    024,128–02,
        LESS ACCESSIBLE

25. INDIGENOUS KINGDOMS OF EAST
AND CENTRAL AFRICA

025
    ALPERS EDWARD A
    MUTAPA AND MALAWI POLITICAL SYSTEMS.
    IN TERENCE RANGER (ED), ASPECTS OF CENTRAL AFRICAN HISTORY,
    EVANSTON, NORTHWESTERN UNIVERSITY PRESS, 1968, PP 1–28
    025,

A CONCISE AND BALANCED OUTLINE OF ZIMLABWE AND MALAWI
STATE BULDING FROM ORAL, ARCHEOLOGICAL AND SECONDARY
SOURCES. EXCELLENT INTRODUCTION TO A COMPLEX HISTORY.

025

DAVIDSON BASIL
A HISTORY OF EAST AND CENTRAL AFRICA-TO THE LATE
NINETEENTH CENTURY
GARDEN CITY, NEW YORK, DOUBLEDAY ANCHOR, 1969
023,025,

> ANOTHER EXCELLENT INTRODUCTORY TEXT BY ONE OF THE
> MOST PROLIFIC WRITERS ON AFRICAN HISTORY. A REVISED
> VERSION OF EARLIER WORK(THE GROWTH OF AFRICAN
> CIVILIZATION,LONGMANS,GREEN,1967),THIS PAPERBACK
> SURVEYS EARLY IRON AGE DEVELOPMENTS, GROWTH AND
> EXPANSION AFTER 1000 AND DEVELOPMENTS AFTER 1500.
> USEFUL MAPS AND TIME CHARTS.

OGOT BETHWELL A
HISTORY OF THE SOUTHERN LUO- VOLUME ONE,MIGRATION AND
SETTLEMENT
NAIROBI, EAST AFRICAN PUBLISHING HOUSE, 1967
025,

> GROUNDBREAKING HISTORY OF SOUTHERN LUO,A GROUP WHICH
> INCLUDES THE LUO OF KENYA,PADHOLA,ACHOLI,ALUR AND THE
> MIGRANT GROUPS WHICH PLAYED SO IMPORTANT A ROLE IN
> STATE FORMATION IN THE GREAT LAKES REGION. THE LARGER
> THEME OF NILOTIC MIGRATIONS IS NOW RECEIVING
> ATTENTION COMPARABLE TO THAT GIVEN BANTU MIGRATIONS-
> SEE THE SELECTIONS IN COLLINS, 1968.

OLIVER ROLAND
DISCERNIBLE DEVELOPMENTS IN THE INTERIOR C. 1500-1840.
IN ROLAND OLIVER AND GERVASE MATHEW (EDS), HISTORY OF EAST
AFRICA VOLUME ONE, OXFORD, CLARENDON PRESS, 1963, PP 169-211
025,

> ANALYSIS OF STATE FORMATION IN THE GREAT LAKES REGION,
> INCLUDING A DESCRIPTION OF THE MIGRATIONS OF THE LWO.
> GREAT WORK OF SYNTHESIS AND FOUNDATION ON WHICH SUB-
> SEQUENT RESEARCH HAS BEEN BUILT. DISCUSSES SPREAD OF
> NTEMI CHIEFS, AND IMPACT OF THE NGUNI INVASIONS.

RANGER TERENCE D   ED
ASPECTS OF CENTRAL AFRICAN HISTORY.
EVANSTON, NORTHWESTERN UNIVERSITY PRESS, 1968   (LONDON,
HEINEMANN EDUCATIONAL BOOKS)
025,036,

> OUTSTANDING RECENT SURVEY OF CENTRAL AFRICAN HISTORY.
> BEGINS WITH ZIMBABWE AND CONTINUES UNTIL NATIONALIST
> PERIOD. LARGELY WRITTEN BY YOUNG RESEARCH SCHOLARS
> WORKING IN THE FIELD, HENCE REPRESENTS MOST RECENT
> DATA.

SMITH ALISON
THE SOUTHERN SECTION OF THE INTERIOR, 1840-84.
IN ROLAND OLIVER AND GERVASE MATHEW (EDS) HISTORY OF EAST
AFRICA VOLUME ONE, OXFORD, CLARENDON PRESS, 1963, PP 253-96
025,

> EXAMINES PATTERNS OF SETTLEMENT AND TRADE IN THE SOU-
> THERN SECTIONS OF EAST AFRICA. PARTICULAR EMPHASIS ON

COASTAL TRADE AND ROLE OF AFRICAN MIDDLEMEN, SUCH AS
THE YAO AND NYAMWEZI. DE-EMPHASIZES IMPORTANCE OF
SLAVERY IN TRADE WITH THE COAST.

025

SUMMERS ROGER
ZIMBABWE-- A RHODESIAN MYSTERY.
CAPE TOWN,THOMAS NELSON AND SONS,1963
025,145-02,
        EXCELLENT AND HIGHLY READABLE DISCUSSION OF SUCCESSFUL
        ARCHEOLOGICAL ATTEMPTS TO SOLVE THE MYSTERY OF
        ZIMBABWE. INCLUDES A HISTORY OF EUROPEAN ATTITUDES
        TOWARD THE RUINS--KING SOLOMON'S MINES--AND A FASCINA-
        TING DESCRIPTION OF ARCHEOLOGICAL METHODS OPERATING IN
        THE FACE OF APPALLING DIFFICULTIES.

VANSINA JAN
KINGDOMS OF THE SAVANNA.
MADISON UNIVERSITY OF WISCONSIN 1968
025,108-02,
        OUTSTANDING RECONSTRUCTION OF THE POLITICAL HISTORY
        OF CENTRAL AFRICA BY BELGIAN-BORN HISTORIAN. CLASSIC
        IN THE USE OF ORAL TRADITIONS-- ALSO INCORPORATES
        ARCHEOLOGICAL, LINGUISTIC, ANTHROPOLOGICAL EVIDENCE
        AND DOCUMENTARY SOURCES. CONCENTRATES MAINLY ON KING-
        DOMS OF KONGO, LUBA, LUNDA, KAZEMBE, AND LOZI, AND OF
        THE COLONY OF ANGOLA BUT COVERS WHOLE AREA NORTH OF
        ZAMBEZI AND SOUTH OF CONGO RAINFOREST.

HUNTINGFORD G W B
THE PEOPLING OF THE INTERIOR BY ITS MODERN INHABITANTS
IN ROLAND OLIVER AND GERVASE MATHEW (EDS) HISTORY OF EAST
AFRICA VOLUME ONE,OXFORD,CLARENDON PRESS,1963,PP 58-93
025,
        REFERENCE

LOW DAVID A
THE NORTHERN INTERIOR 1840-1884
IN OLIVER AND MATHEW,HISTORY OF EAST AFRICA,LONDON,OXFORD
1963,PP 297-351
025,
        REFERENCE

ROTBERG ROBERT I
THE ERA OF EMPIRES AND CITY-STATES, 800-1500 CHAPTER 2.
IN A POLITICAL HISTORY OF TROPICAL AFRICA, NEW YORK,
HARCOURT, BRACE AND WORLD, 1965 PP,34-66
022,023,025,
        REFERENCE

ROTBERG ROBERT I
KINGDOMS OF THE SAVANNAH AND FOREST, 1500-1800 CHAPTER 4.
IN A POLITICAL HISTORY OF TROPICAL AFRICA, NEW YORK,
HARCOURT, BRACE AND WORLD, 1965,PP 95-132
024,025,026,
        REFERENCE

STOKES E   BROWN RICHARD   EDS
THE ZAMBESIAN PAST-STUDIES IN CENTRAL AFRICAN HISTORY
MANCHESTER,MANCHESTER UNIVERSITY PRESS,1966

025,122-02,142-02,145-02,
        REFERENCE

025
    VANSINA JAN
    LONG-DISTANCE TRADE-ROUTE IN CENTRAL AFRICA.
    JOURNAL OF AFRICAN HISTORY 3 1962 PP 375-390
    025,
        REFERENCE

    WHITE C M N
    THE ETHNO-HISTORY OF THE UPPER ZAMBEZI.
    AFRICAN STUDIES 21 1962 PP 10-27
    025,
        REFERENCE

    ABRAHAM D P
    THE EARLY POLITICAL HISTORY OF THE KINGDOMS OF MWENE MUTAPA
    850-1589.
    HISTORIANS IN TROPICAL AFRICA-- PROCEEDINGS,SALISBURY,
    SOUTHERN RHODESIA, UNIVERSITY COLLEGE OF RHODESIA AND
    NAYASALAND, 1962, PP 61-92
    025,145-02,
        CASE STUDY

    FAGAN BRIAN M
    SOUTHERN AFRICA IN THE IRON AGE.
    LONDON,THAMES AND HUDSON,1965
    019,025,
        CASE STUDY

    FAGAN BRIAN M
    ZIMBABWE--A CENTURY OF DISCOVERY.
    AFRICAN ARTS, SPRING 1969, VOL II, NO. 3, PP. 20-24, CONT.
    85-86
    025,145-02,
        CASE STUDY

    KIWANUKA M S
    THE EMPIRE OF BUNYORO KITARA
    CANADIAN JOURNAL OF AFRICAN STUDIES 2 1968 PP 27-48
    025,
        CASE STUDY

    LYE WILLIAM F
    THE NDEBELE KINGDOM SOUTH OF THE LIMPOPO RIVER.
    JOURNAL OF AFRICAN HISTORY, X, 1, 1969, PP. 87-104
    025,
        CASE STUDY

    OGOT BETHWELL A
    KINGSHIP AND STATELESSNESS AMONG THE NILOTS
    IN VANSINA,ROGEN,MAUNY(EDS), THE HISTORIAN IN TROPICAL
    AFRICA,LONDON,OXFORD UNIVERSITY PRESS,1964,PP 284-301
    009,025,
        CASE STUDY

    OLIVER ROLAND
    ANCIENT CAPITAL SITES OF ANKOLE.
    THE UGANDA JOURNAL 23 1959 PP 51-63

025,139-02,
        CASE STUDY

025
    ROBERTS A   ED
    TANZANIA BEFORE 1900
    NAIROBI, EAST AFRICAN PUBLISHING HOUSE, 1968
    025,136-02,
        CASE STUDY

    ROSCOE J
    THE BAGANDA
    LONDON, FRANK CASS, SECOND EDITION, 1965
    025,139-01,
        CASE STUDY

    VANSINA JAN
    L'EVOLUTION DU ROYAUME RWANDA DES ORIGINES A 1900   (EV-
    OLUTION OF THE KINGDOM OF RWANDA FROM ITS ORIGINS TO 1900.
    BRUXELLES, ACADEMIE ROYALE DE SCIENCES D'OUTRE MER, 1962
    025,129-02,
        LESS ACCESSIBLE

    VANSINA JAN
    LA FONDATION DU ROYAUME DE KASANJE (THE FOUNDATION OF THE
    KINGDOM OF KASANJE) .
    AEQUATORIA 25 1962 PP 45-62
    025,
        LESS ACCESSIBLE

    VANSINA JAN
    NOTES SUR L'ORIGINE DU ROYAUME DE KONGO (NOTES ON THE
    ORIGIN OF THE KINGDOM OF KONGO).
    JOURNAL OF AFRICAN HISTORY 4 1963 PP 33-38
    025,108-02,
        LESS ACCESSIBLE

26. FOREST STATES OF WEST AFRICA

026
    DAVIDSON BASIL
    THE GROWTH OF AFRICAN CIVILIZATION-A HISTORY OF WEST AFRICA
    1000-1800
    GARDEN CITY, NEW YORK, DOUBLEDAY ANCHOR BOOKS, 1969
    022,026,
        AN EXCELLENT PAPERBACK INTRODUCTION AND SURVEY OF WEST
        AFRICAN HISTORY.WELL ARRANGED AND EASY TO READ. UP-
        TO-DATE REVIEW OF CURRENT RESEARCH FINDINGS AND
        EXCELLENT CHRONOLOGY AND MAPS.

    FAGE JOHN D
    A HISTORY OF WEST AFRICA
    NEW YORK, CAMBRIDGE UNIVERSITY PRESS, 1969
    022, 026, 036,
        FOURTH EDITION OF CLASSIC INTRODUCTION TO WEST

AFRICAN HISTORY. REWRITTEN AND REVISED TO INCLUDE TWO
NEW CHAPTERS ON POLITICAL DEVELOPMENTS IN LOWER
GUINEA AND ON DEVELOPMENTS IN THE INTERIOR OF WEST
AFRICA IN THE NINETEENTH CENTURY. MANY EXCELLENT MAPS

026

FORDE C DARYLL   KABERRY PHYLLIS M   EDS
WEST AFRICAN KINGDOMS IN THE NINETEENTH CENTURY.
LONDON, OXFORD UNIVERSITY PRESS, 1967
026,036,
        OUTSTANDING COLLECTION OF ORIGINAL ESSAYS ON WEST AF-
        RICAN KINGDOMS. ESSAYS ALL BY SCHOLARS WHO HAVE DONE
        INTENSIVE FIELD RESEARCH, YET ALL IN THIS VOLUME TRY
        TO SYNTHESIZE DATA AND PATTERNS RATHER THAN PRESENT
        SPECIFIC RESEARCH. ESSAY BY IVOR WILKS ON ORGANIZA-
        TION OF ASHANTI BUREAUCRACY IS PARTICULARLY INSIGHT-
        FUL.

LLOYD PETER C   MABOGUNJE AKIN L   AWE B
THE CITY OF IBADAN-- A SYMPOSIUM ON ITS STRUCTURE AND
DEVELOPMENT.
CAMBRIDGE, CAMBRIDGE UNIVERSITY PRESS, 1967
026,045,128-05,
        REPORT OF SYMPOSIUM AT UNIVERSITY OF IBADAN. PROVIDES
        COMPREHENSIVE SURVEY OF THE HISTORY, GEOGRAPHY, SOC-
        IOLOGY, AND POLITICAL STRUCTURE, OF THE LARGEST TRADI-
        TIONAL BLACK AFRICAN CITY. PIONEER WORK IN INTER-
        DISCIPLINARY URBAN STUDIES, AND PERHAPS THE BEST
        SINGLE VOLUME TO DATE ON AN AFRICAN URBAN CENTER.

WILKS IVOR
ASHANTI GOVERNMENT, IN DARYLL FORDE AND P M KABERRY (EDS),
WEST AFRICAN KINGDOMS IN THE NINETEENTH CENTURY.
LONDON, OXFORD UNIVERSITY PRESS, 1967
026,038,114-01,
        DISCUSSES CENTRALIZED ASPECTS OF PRE-COLONIAL ASHANTI
        GOVERNMENT, ESPECIALLY ROLE OF ASANTEHENE, AND COUNTER-
        BALANCES RATTRAY VIEW OF DECENTRALIZED CONFEDERATION.

DAVIES OLIVER
WEST AFRICA BEFORE THE EUROPEANS
LONDON, METHUEN, 1967
019,022,026,
        REFERENCE

GOODY JACK
ETHNOHISTORY AND THE AKAN OF GHANA.
AFRICA 29 1959 PP 67-81
026,114-02,
        REFERENCE

OLIVER ROLAND   ATMORE ANTHONY
WEST AFRICA BEFORE THE COLONIAL PERIOD, 1800-1875.
IN AFRICA SINCE 1800, CAMBRIDGE, CAMBRIDGE UNIVERSITY PRESS,
1967, PP 29-42
026,
        REFERENCE

ROTBERG ROBERT I
KINGDOMS OF THE SAVANNAH AND FOREST, 1500-1800 CHAPTER 4.

IN A POLITICAL HISTORY OF TROPICAL AFRICA, NEW YORK,
HARCOURT, BRACE AND WORLD, 1965, PP 95-132
024,025,026,
        REFERENCE

026
    AGYEMAN-DUAH J
    MAMPONG ASHANTI-- A TRADITIONAL HISTORY TO THE REIGN OF NANA
    SAFO KANTANKA.
    TRANSACTIONS OF THE HISTORICAL SOCIETY OF GHANA 4 1960
    PP 21-25
    026,114-02,
        CASE STUDY

    AJAYI J F ADE   SMITH ROBERT
    YORUBA WARFARE IN THE 19TH CENTURY.
    CAMBRIDGE ENGLAND CAMBRIDGE UNIVERSITY PRESS 1964
    026,128-02,
        CASE STUDY

    AKINJOGBIN I A
    DAHOMEY AND ITS NEIGHBORS, 1708-1818.
    NEW YORK AND LONDON, CAMBRIDGE UNIVERSITY PRESS, 1967
    026,109-02,
        CASE STUDY

    ALAGOA EBIEGBERI J
    THE SMALL BRAVE CITY STATE-- A HISTORY OF NEMBRE-BRASS IN
    THE NIGER DELTA.
    MADISON, UNIVERSITY OF WISCONSIN PRESS, 1964
    026,128-02,
        CASE STUDY

    ARGYLE W J
    THE FON OF DAHOMEY-- A HISTORY AND ETHNOGRAPHY OF
    OF THE OLD KINGDOM.
    OXFORD, CLARENDON PRESS, 1966
    026,109-01,
        CASE STUDY

    BOWDICH THOMAS E
    MISSION FROM CAPE COAST CASTLE TO ASHANTEE WITH A
    STATISTICAL ACCOUNT OF THE KINGDOM AND GEOGRAPHICAL NOTICES
    OF OTHER PARTS OF THE INTERIOR OF AFRICA.
    LONDON, CASS, 1967
    026,114-02,
        CASE STUDY

    BRADBURY R E
    THE BENIN KINGDOM AND THE EDO-SPEAKING PEOPLES OF SOUTH-
    WESTERN NIGERIA.
    LONDON, OXFORD UNIVERSITY PRESS, 1957
    026,128-01,
        CASE STUDY

    BRADBURY R E
    CHRONOLOGICAL PROBLEMS IN THE STUDY OF BENIN HISTORY.
    JOURNAL OF THE HISTORICAL SOCIETY OF NIGERIA 1 1959
    PP 263-287
    026,128-01,

CASE STUDY

026

BRAIMAH J A　　　　　GOODY J R
SALAGA--THE STRUGGLE FOR POWER.
LONDON, LONGMANS, GREEN AND COMPANY LIMITED, 1967
026,114-02,
　　　CASE STUDY

CLARIDGE W WALTON
A HISTORY OF THE GOLD COAST AND ASHANTI.
LONDON, CASS, 1964
026,114-02,
　　　CASE STUDY

DIKE K O
BENIN-- A GREAT FOREST KINGDOM OF MEDIEVAL NIGERIA.
PRACTICAL ANTHROPOLOGY 8 1961 PP 31-35
026,128-02,
　　　CASE STUDY

DUPUIS JOSEPH
JOURNAL OF A RESIDENCE IN ASHANTEE.
LONDON, CASS, 1967
026,114-02,
　　　CASE STUDY

EGHAREVBA JACOB
A SHORT HISTORY OF BENIN.
IBADAN UNIVERSITY PRESS, 1960
026,128-02,
　　　CASE STUDY

HERSKOVITS MELVILLE J
DAHOMEY-- AN ANCIENT WEST AFRICAN KINGDOM.
EVANSTON, NORTHWESTERN UNIVERSITY PRESS, 1967
013,026,109-02,
　　　CASE STUDY

JOHNSON SAMUEL
THE HISTORY OF THE YORUBAS FROM THE EARLIEST TIMES TO THE
BEGINNING OF THE BRITISH PROTECTORATE.
LONDON, ROUTLEDGE AND KEGAN PAUL, 1966　　　(O JOHNSON, ED.)
026,128-02,
　　　CASE STUDY

LLOYD ALAN
THE DRUMS OF KUMASI-- THE STORY OF THE ASHANTI WARS.
LONDON, LONGMANS, 1964
026,114-02,
　　　CASE STUDY

OJO G J AFOLABI
YORUBA CULTURE- A GEOGRAPHICAL ANALYSIS
IFE AND LONDON, UNIVERSITY OF LONDON PRESS, 1966
026,
　　　CASE STUDY

PHILLIPS EARL
THE EGBA AT ABEOKUTA--ACCULTURATION AND POLITICAL CHANGE,

1830-1870.
JOURNAL OF AFRICAN HISTORY, X, 1, 1969, PP. 117-131
026,128-02,
    CASE STUDY

026
  PRIESTLEY MARGARET WILKS IVOR
  THE ASHANTI KINGS IN THE EIGHTEENTH CENTURY-- A REVISED
  CHRONOLOGY.
  THE JOURNAL OF AFRICAN HISTORY 1 1960 PP 83-92
  026,114-02,
    CASE STUDY

  RATTRAY ROBERT S
  ASHANTI LAW AND CONSTITUTION.
  OXFORD, CLARENDON PRESS, 1929
  026,066,099,114-01,
    CASE STUDY

  SHAW C T
  NIGERIA'S PAST UNEARTHED.
  WEST AFRICAN REVIEW DECEMBER 1960 PP 30-37
  026,128-02,
    CASE STUDY

  SHAW C T
  IGBO-UKWU-AN ACCOUNT OF ARCHEOLOGICAL DISCOVERIES IN
  EASTERN NIGERIA
  LONDON, FABER AND FABER; AND EVANSTON, NORTHWESTERN UNIVERSITY
  PRESS, 1970
  020,026,128-02,
    CASE STUDY

  SMITH ROBERT
  KINGDOMS OF THE YORUBA
  LONDON, METHUEN, 1969
  026,128-01,
    CASE STUDY

  TORDOFF WILLIAM
  THE ASHANTI CONFEDERACY.
  JOURNAL OF AFRICAN HISTORY 3 1962 PP 399-417
  026,114-02,
    CASE STUDY

  TORDOFF WILLIAM
  THE EXILE AND THE REPATRIATION OF NANA PREMPEH 1 OF ASHANTI
  1896-1924.
  TRANSACTIONS OF THE HISTORICAL SOCIETY OF GHANA 4 1960
  PP 33-58
  026,114-02,
    CASE STUDY

  TORDOFF WILLIAM
  ASHANTI UNDER THE PREMPEHS. 1888-1935.
  LONDON, OXFORD UNIVERSITY PRESS, 1965
  026,114-02,
    CASE STUDY

  WILKS IVOR

THE RISE OF THE AKWAMU EMPIRE 1650-1710.
TRANSACTIONS OF THE HISTORICAL SOCIETY OF GHANA 3 1957
PP 99-136
026,114-02,
        CASE STUDY

026
    WILKS IVOR
    AKAMU AND OTUBLOHUM-- AN EIGHTEENTH CENTURY AKAN
    MARRIAGE ARRANGEMENT.
    AFRICA 29 1959 PP 391-404
    026,114-01,
        CASE STUDY

    WILKS IVOR
    A NOTE ON THE TRADITIONAL HISTORY OF MAMPONG.
    TRANSACTIONS OF THE HISTORICAL SOCIETY OF GHANA 4 1960
    PP 26-29
    026,114-02,
        CASE STUDY

    WILKS IVOR
    THE NORTHERN FACTOR IN ASHANTI HISTORY.
    LEGON, INSTITUTE OF AFRICAN STUDIES, UNIVERSITY COLLEGE OF
    GHANA, 1961
    026,114-02,
        CASE STUDY

    WILLETT FRANK
    INVESTIGATIONS AT OLD OYO, 1956-1957-- AN INTERIM REPORT.
    JOURNAL OF THE HISTORICAL SOCIETY OF NIGERIA 2 1960 PP 57-77
    026,128-02,
        CASE STUDY

    WILLETT FRANK
    IFE AND ITS ARCHAEOLOGY.
    THE JOURNAL OF AFRICAN HISTORY 1 1960 PP 231-248
    014,020,026,128-01,
        CASE STUDY

    GEAY J
    ORIGINE, FORMATION ET HISTOIRE DU ROYAUME DE PORTO-NOVO
    (THE ORIGIN, FORMATION AND HISTORY OF THE KINGDOM OF
    PORTO-NOVO).
    BULLETIN DU COMITE D'ETUDES HISTORIQUES ET SCIENTIFIQUES DE
    L'AFRIQUE OCCIDENTALE FRANCAISE 7 1924 PP 619-634
    026,109-02,
        LESS ACCESSIBLE

    PALAU MARTI M
    LE ROI-DIEU AU BENIN (THE GOD-KING OF BENIN).
    PARIS,BERGER-LEVRAULT,1964
    026,128-01,
        LESS ACCESSIBLE

27. EARLY WESTERN CONTACT

027

CURTIN PHILIP D
THE IMAGE OF AFRICA-- BRITISH IDEAS AND ACTION, 1780-1850.
MADISON, UNIVERSITY OF WISCONSIN PRESS, 1964
027,029,

> EXAMINES EUROPEAN, PARTICULARLY BRITISH, ATTITUDES AND
> IMAGES OF AFRICA FROM LATE EIGHTEENTH CENTURY UNTIL
> MID-NINETEENTH CENTURY. ATTEMPTS TO UNDERSTAND MIS-
> CONCEPTIONS ABOUT AFRICA THAT PARTLY MOTIVATED EXPLOR-
> ATION AND COLONIZATION MOVEMENTS, AND FREED SLAVE
> SETTLEMENT SCHEMES.

DUFFY JAMES
PORTUGUESE AFRICA.
CAMBRIDGE, HARVARD UNIVERSITY PRESS, 1959
027,087,088,144-06,

> DEALS PRIMARILY WITH ANGOLA AND MOZAMBIQUE. FIRST
> SCHOLARLY HISTORY OF PORTUGUESE CONTACT WITH AFRICA
> FROM EARLIEST TIME (FIFTEENTH CENTURY) TO MID-TWENTI-
> ETH CENTURY. DEALS WITH THE REALITY, OFTEN HARSH, OF
> PORTUGUESE CONTACT RATHER THAN WITH THE OFFICIAL POLI-
> CY AND COLONIAL IDEALS ESPOUSED BY LISBON.

PRIESTLEY MARGARET
WEST AFRICAN TRADE AND COAST SOCIETY-A FAMILY STUDY
NEW YORK, OXFORD UNIVERSITY PRESS, 1969
027,

> CASE STUDY OF THE BREW FAMILY OF THE FANTI AREA IN
> SOUTHERN GHANA. THROUGH THIS FAMILY HISTORY, THE BROADER
> ISSUES OF AFRO-EUROPEAN CONTACT ARE EXPLORED AND ELITE
> DEVELOPMENT AND SOCIAL CHANGE ARE ILLUMINATED.

ARELSON E
THE PORTUGESE IN SOUTHEAST AFRICA 1600-1700
JOHANNESBURG, WITWATERSRAND UNIVERSITY PRESS, 1960
027,

> REFERENCE

AXELSON E   ED
SOUTH AFRICAN EXPLORERS
LONDON, OXFORD UNIVERSITY PRESS, 1954
027,

> REFERENCE

BIRMINGHAM DAVID
THE PORTUGUESE CONQUEST OF ANGOLA.
LONDON, OXFORD UNIVERSITY PRESS, 1965
027, 144-02,

> REFERENCE

BLAKE JOHN W
EUROPEAN BEGINNINGS IN WEST AFRICA 1454-1578.
LONDON, LONGMANS, GREEN, 1937
027,

REFERENCE

027
BLAKE JOHN W
EUROPEANS IN WEST AFRICA 1450-1560.
LONDON, HAKLUYT SOCIETY, 1942, 2 VOLUMES
(TRANSLATED AND EDITED, JOHN W BLAKE)
027,
        REFERENCE

BOXER CHARLES RALPH
PORTUGUESE SOCIETY IN THE TROPICS--THE MUNICIPAL COUNCILS
OF GOA, MACAO, BAHIA AND LUANDA 1510-1800.
MADISON, UNIVERSITY OF WISCONSIN PRESS, 1965
027, 144-07,
        REFERENCE

BOXER CHARLES RALPH DE AZEVEDO CARLOS
FORT JESUS AND THE PORTUGESE IN MOMBASA 1593-1729
LONDON, HOLLIS AND CARTER, 1960
023,027,
        REFERENCE

BURTON RICHARD
THE LAKE REGIONS OF CENTRAL AFRICA.
TWO VOLUMES, NEW YORK, HORIZON PRESS, 1961 (REPRINT)
027,
        REFERENCE

COUPLAND REGINALD
THE EXPLOITATION OF EAST AFRICA 1856-1890.
LONDON, 1939; REPRINTED 1968 BY NORTHWESTERN UNIVERSITY PRESS
027,
        REFERENCE

DELCOURT ANDRE
LA FRANCE ET LES ETABLISSEMENTS FRANCAIS AU SENEGAL ENTRE
1713 ET 1763 (FRANCE AND FRENCH SETTLEMENTS IN SENEGAL
BETWEEN 1713 AND 1763).
DAKAR, INSTITUT FRANCAIS D'AFRIQUE NOIRE 1952
027,
        REFERENCE

DIFFIE BAILEY W
PRELUDE TO EMPIRE-- PORTUGAL OVERSEAS BEFORE HENRY THE
NAVIGATOR.
LINCOLN, UNIVERSITY OF NEBRASKA PRESS, 1960
027,
        REFERENCE

HALLETT ROBIN   ED
THE NIGER JOURNAL OF RICHARD AND JOHN LANDER.
LONDON, ROUTLEDGE AND KEGAN PAUL, 1965
027,
        REFERENCE

HOWARD C
WEST AFRICAN EXPLORERS
LONDON, OXFORD UNIVERSITY PRESS, 1951
027,

REFERENCE

027

LAWRENCE ARNOLD W
TRADE CASTLES AND FORTS OF WEST AFRICA.
LONDON, JONATHAN CAPE, 1963
027,
        REFERENCE

MAZRUI ALI A
EUROPEAN EXPLORATION AND AFRICAS SELF DISCOVERY
JOURNAL OF MODERN AFRICAN STUDIES 7 1969 PP 661-676
027,038,100,
        REFERENCE

NORREGARD GEORG
DANISH SETTLEMENTS IN WEST AFRICA.
BOSTON, BOSTON UNIVERSITY PRESS, 1966
027,
        REFERENCE

PERHAM MARGERY   SIMMONS J
AFRICAN DISCOVERY
EVANSTON, NORTHWESTERN UNIVERSITY PRESS, 1963 (NEW EDITION)
027,
        REFERENCE

RICHARDS C   PLACE J   EDS
EAST AFRICAN EXPLORERS
LONDON, OXFORD UNIVERSITY PRESS, 1960
027,
        REFERENCE

ROTBERG ROBERT I
AFRICA AND THE FIRST WAVE OF EUROPEAN EXPANSION,
1400-1700 CHAPTER 3.
IN A POLITICAL HISTORY OF TROPICAL AFRICA, NEW YORK,
HARCOURT, BRACE AND WORLD, 1965 PP 67-94
027,
        REFERENCE

SNOWDEN FRANCK M JR
BLACKS IN ANTIQUITY--ETHIOPIANS IN THE GRECO-ROMAN
EXPERIENCE.
CAMBRIDGE, HARVARD UNIVERSITY PRESS, 1969
020,027,
        REFERENCE

SPEKE J H
JOURNAL OF DISCOVERY OF THE SOURCE OF THE NILE.
LONDON, WILLIAM BLACKWOOD AND SONS, 1863
027,
        REFERENCE

STANLEY H M
THROUGH THE DARK CONTINENT.
LONDON, 1878, TWO VOLUMES
027,
        REFERENCE

STRANDES J
THE PORTUGESE PERIOD IN EAST AFRICA
TRANSACTIONS OF THE KENYA HISTORICAL SOCIETY VOLUME 11
NAIROBI, EAST AFRICAN LITERATURE BUREAU, 1961
027,
     REFERENCE

027

BARTH HEINRICH
TRAVELS AND DISCOVERIES IN NORTH AND CENTRAL AFRICA 1849-
1855
LONDON, CASS, 1968, 3 VOLUMES
027,099,
     CASE STUDY

BECKINGHAM C F   HUNTINGFORD G W B
PRESTER JOHN OF THE INDIES.
LONDON, 1961
027,
     CASE STUDY

BIRMINGHAM DAVID
TRADE AND CONFLICT IN ANGOLA-- THE MBUNDU AND THEIR
NEIGHBOURS UNDER THE INFLUENCE OF THE PORTUGUESE 1483-1790.
LONDON, OXFORD UNIVERSITY PRESS, 1966
027, 144-02,
     CASE STUDY

BOVILL EDWARD W   ED
MISSIONS TO THE NIGER-- THE JOURNAL OF FRIEDRICH
HORNEMANN'S TRAVELS-- (AND) THE LETTERS OF MAJOR ALEXANDER
GORDON LAING.
CAMBRIDGE, ENGLAND, UNIVERSITY PRESS, 1964
027,
     CASE STUDY

CAILLIE RENE
TRAVELS THROUGH CENTRAL AFRICA TO TIMBUCTOO AND ACROSS THE
GREAT DESERT TO MOROCCO PERFORMED IN THE YEARS 1824-1828.
LONDON, 1830, 2V.
027,
     CASE STUDY

CLAPPERTON HUGH
JOURNAL OF A SECOND EXPEDITION INTO THE INTERIOR OF AFRICA
FROM THE BIGHT OF BENIN TO SOCCATOO.
LONDON, CASS, 1966
027,
     CASE STUDY

DENHAM DIXON   CLAPPERTON HUGH   OUDNEY WALTER
NARRATIVE OF TRAVELS AND DISCOVERIES IN NORTHERN AND CENTRAL
AFRICA IN THE YEARS 1822, 1823 AND 1824.
LONDON, CAMBRIDGE UNIVERSITY PRESS, 1966, 3 VOLUMES
E W BOVILL. (ED.)
027,099,
     CASE STUDY

DIKE K O
TRADE AND POLITICS IN THE NIGER DELTA 1830-1885.

OXFORD, CLARENDON PRESS, 1956
027, 128-02,
          CASE STUDY

027
    DUFFY JAMES
    PORTUGAL IN AFRICA
    BALTIMORE, PENGUIN, 1962
    027, 087, 088, 144-06,
          CASE STUDY

    JONES GWILYN I
    THE TRADING STATES OF THE OIL RIVERS-- A STUDY OF
    POLITICAL DEVELOPMENT IN EASTERN NIGERIA.
    LONDON, OXFORD UNIVERSITY PRESS, 1963
    027, 035, 128-02,
          CASE STUDY

    LAIRD MACGREGOR   OLDFIELD RICHARD
    NARRATIVE OF AN EXPEDITION INTO THE INTERIOR OF AFRICA BY
    THE RIVER NIGER IN THE STEAM VESSELS QUORRA AND ALBURKAH IN
    1832, 1833, AND 1834.
    LONDON, CASS, 1966
    027,
          CASE STUDY

    LANDER RICHARD   ED
    RECORDS OF CAPTAIN CLAPPERTON'S LAST EXPEDITION TO AFRICA.
    LONDON, CASS, 1967, 2 VOLUMES
    027,
          CASE STUDY

    LANDER RICHARD   LANDER J
    JOURNAL OF AN EXPEDITION TO EXPLORE THE COURSE AND
    TERMINATION OF THE NIGER.
    NEW YORK, HARPER AND BROTHERS, 1837
    027, 099,
          CASE STUDY

    LIVINGSTONE DAVID
    MISSIONARY TRAVELS AND RESEARCHES IN SOUTH AFRICA.
    LONDON, J MURRAY, 1865
    027,
          CASE STUDY

    LIVINGSTONE DAVID   LIVINGSTONE C
    NARRATIVE OF AN EXPEDITION TO THE ZAMBESI AND ITS
    TRIBUTARIES AND THE DISCOVERY OF THE LAKES SHIRWA AND
    NYASSA 1858-1865.
    LONDON, J MURRAY, 1965
    027,
          CASE STUDY

    LIVINGSTONE DAVID   WALLER HORACE   EDS
    THE LAST JOURNALS OF DAVID LIVINGSTONE IN CENTRAL AFRICA.
    LONDON, J MURRAY, 1874, 2 VOLUMES
    027,
          CASE STUDY

    NATHAN MATHEW

THE GOLD COAST AT THE END OF THE SEVENTEENTH CENTURY UNDER
THE DANES AND THE DUTCH.
JOURNAL OF THE AFRICAN SOCIETY IV 1904 PP 1-32
027,114-02,
        CASE STUDY

027
NEWITT M D D
THE PORTUGUESE ON THE ZAMBEZI--AN HISTORICAL INTERPRETATION
OF THE PRAZO SYSTEM.
JOURNAL OF AFRICAN HISTORY, X, 1, 1969, PP. 67-85
027, 144-02,
        CASE STUDY

RYDER A F C
THE RE-ESTABLISHMENT OF PORTUGUESE FACTORIES ON THE COSTA
DA MINA TO THE MID-EIGHTEENTH CENTURY.
JOURNAL OF THE HISTORICAL SOCIETY OF NIGERIA I 1958 PP 157-
183
027,
        CASE STUDY

RYDER A F C
AN EARLY PORTUGUESE TRADING VOYAGE TO THE FORCADOS RIVER.
JOURNAL OF THE HISTORICAL SOCIETY OF NIGERIA I 1959 PP 294
-321
027,
        CASE STUDY

RYDER A F C
MISSIONARY ACTIVITY IN THE KINGDOM OF WARRI TO THE EARLY
NINETEENTH CENTURY.
JOURNAL OF THE HISTORICAL SOCIETY OF NIGERIA 22 1960 PP 2-
27
027,128-02,
        CASE STUDY

BRUNSCHWIG HENRI
L'EXPANSION ALLEMANDE OUTRE-MER DU XV SIECLE A NOS JOURS
(GERMAN EXPANSION IN AFRICA FROM THE FIFTEENTH CENTURY TO
MODERN TIMES).
PARIS, PRESSES UNIVERSITAIRES DE FRANCE, 1957
027,033,
        LESS ACCESSIBLE

FAIDHERBE LOUIS L
LE SENEGAL-- LA FRANCE DANS L'AFRIQUE OCCIDENTAL
(SENEGAL-- FRANCE IN WEST AFRICA).
PARIS, HACHETTE, 1889
027,130-02,
        LESS ACCESSIBLE

KUP A P
EARLY PORTUGESE TRADE IN THE SIERRA LEONE AND GREAT
SCARCIES RIVERS.
BOLETIM CULTURAL DA GUINE PORTUGUESA XVIII 1963 PP 107-124
027,131-02,
        LESS ACCESSIBLE

COOMBS DOUGLAS

THE GOLD COAST BRITAIN AND THE NETHERLANDS 1850–1874.
LONDON, OXFORD UNIVERSITY PRESS, 1963
027,114-02,

027
HALLETT ROBIN
THE EUROPEAN APPROACH TO THE INTERIOR OF AFRICA IN THE
EIGHTEENTH CENTURY.
THE JOURNAL OF AFRICAN HISTORY IV 1963 PP 191-206
027,
        REFERENCE

28. ORIGINS AND GROWTH
OF THE SLAVE TRADE

028
ALPERS EDWARD A
THE EAST AFRICAN SLAVE TRADE.
NAIROBI, EAST AFRICAN PUBLISHING HOUSE, 1967
023,028,
        THIS SHORT BUT INCISIVE ANALYSIS CHALLENGES MANY
        WIDELY ACCEPTED VIEWS ON THE EAST AFRICAN SLAVE TRADE,
        PARTICULARLY WITH RESPECT TO ITS IMPACT ON AFRICAN
        SOCIETIES, ITS SIZE AND SCOPE, AND THE ROLE OF EURO-
        PEANS. LIKE OTHER PUBLICATIONS OF EAST AFRICAN PUB-
        LISHING HOUSE, THIS BOOK IS DISTRIBUTED IN THE UNITED
        STATES BY NORTHWESTERN UNIVERSITY PRESS.

CURTIN PHILIP D
THE ATLANTIC SLAVE TRADE--A CENSUS.
MADISON, UNIVERSITY OF WISCONSIN, 1969
028,
        A MAJOR COMPREHENSIVE ANALYSIS OF THE ATLANTIC TRADE
        FROM THE 19TH CENTURY.   AUTHOR'S ESTIMATES OF NUMBER
        OF SLAVES SHIPPED, THEIR ORIGINS AND DESTINATIONS
        CHALLENGE MOST EXISTING STUDIES AND FORCE A MAJOR RE-
        THINKING OF THE SCOPE AND SIGNIFICANCE OF THE TRADE.

DAVIDSON BASIL
THE AFRICAN SLAVE TRADE.
BOSTON, ATLANTIC-LITTLE, BROWN, 1961
028,
        ORIGINALLY PUBLISHED AS BLACK MOTHER. A REASSESSMENT
        OF AFRICAN-EUROPEAN INTERACTION FROM 1450 TO 1850.
        EXAMINES NATURE OF CONTACT, ITS IMPACT ON AFRICA AND
        THE BACKGROUND TO COLONIAL INVASION AND CONQUEST. A
        BASIC REFERENCE ON AFRICAN SLAVE TRADE BY OUTSTANDING
        POPULARIZER OF AFRICAN HISTORY. EXAMINES BACKGROUND,
        NUMBERS INVOLVED, SOURCE REGIONS AND THE IMPACT OF
        SLAVERY IN WEST AFRICA, THE CONGO BASIN AND EAST
        AFRICA. GOOD BIBLIOGRAPHY.

DAVIDSON BASIL
AFRICA IN HISTORY.
NEW YORK, MACMILLAN, 1968
001,028,036,

A MUCH EXPANDED AND UPDATED EDITION OF 'AFRICA--HISTORY
OF A CONTINENT' (WITHOUT THE PHOTOGRAPHS). VERY WELL
WRITTEN CHRONOLOGICAL SYNTHESIS FOR THE ENTIRE CONTI-
NENT AND PARTICULARLY HELPFUL IN IDENTIFYING BROAD
THEMES AND OUTLINES. A MUCH MORE EFFECTIVE WRITTEN
INTRODUCTION TO AFRICAN HISTORY THAN THE 1966 VOLUME.

028

MANNIX DANIEL   COWLEY MALCOLM
BLACK CARGOES-- A HISTORY OF THE ATLANTIC SLAVE TRADE 1518-
1865.
NEW YORK,VIKING PRESS,1962
028,
        WELL-WRITTEN DESCRIPTIVE ACCOUNT DEALING WITH THE AT-
        MOSPHERE AND CONDITIONS OF THE SLAVE TRADE. DOES NOT
        CONTRIBUTE NEW HISTORICAL DATA OR ANALYSIS, BUT IS EX-
        CELLENT ON POPULAR LEVEL.

COHEN RONALD
SLAVERY IN AFRICA.
TRANS-ACTION (SPECIAL SUPPLEMENT) 4 1967 PP 44-56
010,028,
        REFERENCE

COUPLAND REGINALD
THE EXPLOITATION OF EAST AFRICA, 1856-1890.
EVANSTON, NORTHWESTERN UNIVERSITY PRESS, 1939, 1967
028,
        REFERENCE

CURTIN PHILIP D   VANSINA JAN
SOURCES OF THE 19TH CENTURY ATLANTIC SLAVE TRADE.
JOURNAL OF AFRICAN HISTORY 5 1964 PP 185-208
028,
        REFERENCE

CURTIN PHILIP D
AFRICA REMEMBERED-- NARRATIVES BY WEST AFRICANS FROM THE
ERA OF THE SLAVE TRADE.
MADISON,UNIVERSITY OF WISCONSIN PRESS,1967
028,030,
        REFERENCE

DONNAN ELIZABETH   ED
DOCUMENTS ILLUSTRATIVE OF THE HISTORY OF THE SLAVE TRADE
TO AMERICA.
NEW YORK,OCTAGON,1965
028,
        REFERENCE

DOWD JEROME
THE AFRICAN SLAVE TRADE.
JOURNAL OF NEGRO HISTORY 2 1917 PP 1-20
028,
        REFERENCE

DRAKE RICHARD
OF RICHARD DRAKE.
NEW YORK,DEWITT,1960
028,

REFERENCE

028
   EDINBURGH UNIVERSITY
   THE TRANSATLANTIC SLAVE TRADE FROM WEST AFRICA
   CENTRE OF AFRICAN STUDIES,PAPERS AND DISCUSSION REPORTS
   CONTRIBUTED TO A SEMINAR HELD JUNE 4-5,1965
   028,
         REFERENCE

   FAGE JOHN D
   SLAVERY AND THE SLAVE TRADE IN THE CONTEXT OF WEST AFRICAN
   HISTORY.
   IN JOURNAL OF AFRICAN HISTORY VOL 10 1969 P 393
   028,
         REFERENCE

   MCPHERSON   JAMES M
   THE WORLD THE SLAVEHOLDERS MADE
   NEW YORK, PANTHEON BOOKS, 1969
   028,
         REFERENCE

   RODNEY WALTER
   WEST AFRICA AND THE ATLANTIC SLAVE-TRADE.
   NAIROBI, EAST AFRICAN PUBLISHING HOUSE, 1967
   028,
         REFERENCE

   RODNEY WALTER
   AFRICAN SLAVERY AND OTHER FORMS OF SOCIAL OPPRESSION ON THE
   UPPER GUINEA COAST IN THE CONTEXT OF THE AFRICAN SLAVE TRADE
   JOURNAL OF AFRICAN HISTORY 3 1966 PP 431-433
   028,
         REFERENCE

   ROTBERG ROBERT I
   TROPICAL AFRICA AND THE WIDER WORLD-- COMMERCIAL CONNECTIONS
   AND THE GROWTH OF THE SLAVE TRADE, 1600-1800 CHAPTER 5.
   IN A POLITICAL HISTORY OF TROPICAL AFRICA, NEW YORK,
   HARCOURT, BRACE AND WORLD, 1965, PP 133-164
   028,
         REFERENCE

   STAMPP KENNETH
   THE PECULIAR INSTITUTION.
   NEW YORK, ALFRED A KNOPF, 1956
   028,030,
         REFERENCE

   WILLIAMS E
   CAPITALISM AND SLAVERY
   CHAPEL HILL, UNIVERSITY OF NORTH CAROLINA PRESS,1944
   028,
         REFERENCE

   WYNDHAM H A
   THE ATLANTIC AND SLAVERY
   LONDON, OXFORD UNIVERSITY PRESS, 1935
   028,

REFERENCE

028

BALANDIER GEORGES
DAILY LIFE IN THE KINGDOM OF THE CONGO- TRANS FROM THE
FRENCH BY H WEAVER
NEW YORK,PANTHEON BOOKS,1968
028,
        CASE STUDY

COHEN RONALD
SLAVERY AMONG THE KANURI.
TRANS ACTION, 1967
028,128-01,
        CASE STUDY

GRAHAM J
THE SLAVE TRADE,DEPOPULATION AND HUMAN SACRIFICE IN BENIN
HISTORY
CAHIERS D'ETUDES AFRICAINES 5 1965 PP 317-324
028,
        CASE STUDY

KLEIN HERBERT S
THE TRADE IN AFRICAN SLAVES TO RIO DE JANEIRO 1795-1811
ESTIMATES OF MORTALITY AND PATTERNS OF VOYAGES.
IN JOURNAL OF AFRICAN HISTORY VOL 10 1969 P 533
028,
        CASE STUDY

KUP A P
A HISTORY OF SIERRA LEONE 1400-1787
NEW YORK,CAMBRIDGE UNIVERSITY PRESS,1961
028,
        CASE STUDY

MASON MICHAEL
POPULATION DENSITY AND SLAVE RAIDING-THE CASE OF THE
MIDDLE BELT OF NIGERIA
JOURNAL OF AFRICAN HISTORY 10 1969 PP 551-564
028,
        CASE STUDY

MCCALL DANIEL F
SLAVERY IN ASHANTI.
TRANS-ACTION, 1967
028,114-01,
        CASE STUDY

MIDDLETON JOHN
SLAVERY IN ZANZIBAR.
TRANS-ACTION, 1967
028,136-02,
        CASE STUDY

NEWBURY COLIN W
AN EARLY ENQUIRY INTO SLAVERY AND CAPTIVITY IN DAHOMEY.
ZAIRE 14 1960 PP 53-67
028,109-02,
        CASE STUDY

028

NEWTON JOHN
THE JOURNAL OF A SLAVE TRADER 1750-1754.
LONDON, EPWORTH PRESS, 1962 (BERNARD MARTIN AND MARK SPURRELL
EDS.)
028,
        CASE STUDY

POLANYI KARL   ROSTEIN ABRAHAM
DAHOMEY AND THE SLAVE TRADE-ANALYSIS OF AN ARCHAIC ECONOMY
SEATTLE, UNIVERSITY OF WASHINGTON PRESS, 1966
010,028,
        CASE STUDY

SULLIVAN CAPT G L
DHOW CHASING IN ZANZIBAR WATERS (1873).
NEW YORK, HUMANITIES PRESS, INC., 1967 (NEW INTRODUCTION)
028,136-02,
        CASE STUDY

TUDEN ARTHUR
ILA SLAVERY (ZAMBIA).
TRANS-ACTION, 1967
028,142-01,
        CASE STUDY

UCHENDU VICTOR C
SLAVERY IN SOUTHEAST NIGERIA.
TRANS-ACTION, 1967
028,128-01,
        CASE STUDY

BANDINEL JAMES
SOME ACCOUNT OF THE TRADE IN SLAVES FROM AFRICA AS
CONNECTED WITH EUROPE AND AMERICA.
LONDON, LONGMAN, BROWN, 1842
028,
        LESS ACCESSIBLE

BENEZET ANTHONY
SOME HISTORICAL ACCOUNT OF GUINEA, ITS SITUATION, PRODUCE
AND THE GENERAL DISPOSITION OF ITS INHABITANTS, WITH AN
INQUIRY INTO THE RISE AND PROGRESS OF THE SLAVE TRADE.
PHILADELPHIA, J CRUKSHANK, 1771
028,
        LESS ACCESSIBLE

BUXTON THOMAS F
THE AFRICAN SLAVE TRADE.
LONDON, J MURRAY, 1839
028,
        LESS ACCESSIBLE

CLARKSON THOMAS
THE SUBSTANCE OF THE EVIDENCE OF SUNDRY PERSONS ON THE SLAVE
TRADE COLLECTED IN THE COURSE OF A TOUR MADE IN THE AUTUMN
OF THE YEAR 1788.
LONDON, 1789
028,

LESS ACCESSIBLE

028
   DOW GEORGE F   ED
   SLAVE SHIPS AND SLAVING.
   SALEM, MARINE RESEARCH SOCIETY, 1927
   028,
          LESS ACCESSIBLE

   FALCONBRIDGE A
   AN ACCOUNT OF THE SLAVE TRADE ON THE COAST OF AFRICA.
   LONDON, J PHILLIPS, 1788
   028,
          LESS ACCESSIBLE

   GENOVESE EUGENE D
   THE POLITICAL ECONOMY OF SLAVERY.
   NEW YORK, PANTHEON BOOKS, 1956
   028,
          GENERAL THEORY

   RUBIN VERA   ED
   PLANTATION SYSTEMS OF THE NEW WORLD.
   WASHINGTON, 1959
   028,
          GENERAL THEORY

29. ABOLITION AND STATES FOR FREED SLAVES

029
   CURTIN PHILIP D
   THE IMAGE OF AFRICA-- BRITISH IDEAS AND ACTION, 1780-1850.
   MADISON, UNIVERSITY OF WISCONSIN PRESS, 1964
   027,029,
          EXAMINES EUROPEAN, PARTICULARLY BRITISH, ATTITUDES AND
          IMAGES OF AFRICA FROM LATE EIGHTEENTH CENTURY UNTIL
          MID-NINETEENTH CENTURY. ATTEMPTS TO UNDERSTAND MIS-
          CONCEPTIONS ABOUT AFRICA THAT PARTLY MOTIVATED EXPLOR-
          ATION AND COLONIZATION MOVEMENTS, AND FREED SLAVE
          SETTLEMENT SCHEMES.

   HARGREAVES JOHN D
   AFRICAN COLONIZATION IN THE NINETEENTH CENTURY-- LIBERIA AND
   SIERRA LEONE.
   IN JEFFREY BUTLER (ED), BOSTON UNIVERSITY PAPERS IN AFRICAN
   HISTORY VOLUME I. BOSTON, BOSTON UNIVERSITY PRESS, 1964, PP 55-
   76
   029,119-02,131-02,
          SIERRA LEONE AND LIBERIA WERE TWO MAJOR ATTEMPTS TO
          FOUND SETTLEMENTS FOR FREED SLAVES. AMERICA WAS PRI-
          MARILY RESPONSIBLE FOR LIBERIA, GREAT BRITAIN FOR
          SIERRA LEONE. AUTHOR PROVIDES GOOD INTRODUCTION TO
          THE POLICIES OF THESE TWO POWERS WITH RESPECT TO EMI-
          GRATION, THE PATTERNS OF TRANSPORTATION BACK TO AFRI-
          CA, SOURCES OF EXTERNAL FINANCIAL SUPPORT, AND LI-

BERIA'S EXTERNAL RELATIONS WITH OTHER AFRICAN AREAS.

029
   LIEBENOW J GUS
   LIBERIA--THE EVOLUTION OF PRIVILEGE.
   ITHACA, CORNELL UNIVERSITY PRESS, 1969
   029,058,119-07,
        FIRST OF SERIES OF COUNTRY CASE STUDIES ON AFRICA IN
        THE MODERN WORLD. AUTHOR REVIEWS THE HISTORY OF
        LIBERIA AND ITS MAJOR SOCIAL AND ECONOMIC PATTERNS,
        THE EVOLUTION OF CONTEMPORARY POLICIES PRIMARILY AMONG
        THE AMERICO-LIBERIANS AND ASSESSES THE INFLUENTIAL
        ROLE OF PRESIDENT TUBMAN BOTH IN LIBERIA AND THROUGH-
        OUT AFRICA.

   PETERSON JOHN
   PROVINCE OF FREEDOM--A HISTORY OF SIERRA LEONE 1787-1870.
   EVANSTON, NORTHWESTERN UNIVERSITY PRESS, 1969
   029,131-02,
        AUTHOR IS AMERICAN CHAIRMAN OF HISTORY AT UNIVERSITY
        OF SIERRA LEONE. TRACES ORIGINS OF THE COLONY, ITS
        EARLY PROBLEMS, THE MERCANTILE ACTIVITIES OF THE
        SIERRA LEONE COMPANY AND THE COLONY GOVERNMENT, THE
        ROLE OF THE CHURCH MISSIONARY SOCIETY AND THE PATTERNS
        OF LIBERATED AFRICAN SOCIETY. ENDS WITH GENERAL ASSE-
        SSMENT OF CULTURAL DIVERSITY AND UNITY IN FREETOWN.

   AZIKIWE NNAMDI
   IN DEFENCE OF LIBERIA.
   JOURNAL OF NEGRO HISTORY 17 JANUARY 1932 PP 30-49
   029,119-02,128-04,
        REFERENCE

   BETHELL LESLIE
   THE MIXED COMMISSIONS FOR THE SUPPRESSION OF THE TRANS-
   ATLANTIC SLAVE TRADE IN THE NINETEENTH CENTURY
   JOURNAL OF AFRICAN HISTORY 7 1966 PP 79-93
   029,
        REFERENCE

   BOOTH ALAN R
   THE UNITED STATES AFRICAN SQUADRON 1843-1861.
   IN JEFFREY BUTLER (ED), BOSTON UNIVERSITY PAPERS IN AFRICAN
   HISTORY VOL I. BOSTON, BOSTON UNIVERSITY PRESS, 1964, PP 77-118
   029,
        REFERENCE

   COUPLAND REGINALD
   THE BRITISH ANTI-SLAVERY MOVEMENT.
   LONDON, CASS, 1964
   029,
        REFERENCE

   DUFFY JAMES
   A QUESTION OF SLAVERY-LABOUR POLICIES IN PORTUGESE AFRICA
   AND THE BRITISH PROTEST,1850-1920
   CAMBRIDGE, HARVARD UNIVERSITY PRESS, 1967
   029,
        REFERENCE

DUIGNAN PETER   CLENDENEN CLARENCE
THE UNITED STATES AND THE AFRICAN SLAVE TRADE 1619-1862.
STANFORD, HOOVER INSTITUTE, 1963
029,
     REFERENCE

029
  ELKINS STANLEY
  SLAVERY A PROBLEM IN AMERICAN INSTITUTIONAL AND
  INTELLECTUAL LIFE.
  CHICAGO, UNIVERSITY OF CHICAGO PRESS, 1959
  029,030,
       REFERENCE

  HARGREAVES JOHN D
  PRELUDE TO THE PARTITION OF WEST AFRICA.
  NEW YORK, ST MARTIN'S, 1963
  029,033,
       REFERENCE

  LYNCH HOLLIS R
  PAN-NEGRO NATIONALISM IN THE NEW WORLD.
  IN JEFFREY BUTLER (ED), BOSTON UNIVERSITY PAPERS ON AFRICAN
  HISTORY VOLUME 2, BOSTON, BOSTON UNIVERSITY PRESS, 1966, PP
  147-180
  029,030,
       REFERENCE

  STANDENRAUS P J
  THE AFRICAN COLONIZATION MOVEMENT 1816-1865.
  NEW YORK, COLUMBIA UNIVERSITY PRESS, 1961
  029,
       REFERENCE

  WYNDHAM H A
  THE ATLANTIC AND EMANCIPATION
  LONDON, OXFORD UNIVERSITY PRESS, 1937
  029,
       REFERENCE

  BUELL RAYMOND L
  LIBERIA-- A CENTURY OF SURVIVAL 1847-1947.
  PHILADELPHIA, UNIVERSITY OF PENNSYLVANIA PRESS, 1947
  029,
       CASE STUDY

  DU BOIS W E B
  LIBERIA THE LEAGUE AND THE UNITED STATES.
  IN AFRICA SEEN BY AMERICAN NEGROES, NEW YORK, AMERICAN
  SOCIETY OF AFRICAN CULTURE, 1963, PP 329-344
  029,
       CASE STUDY

  FYFE CHRISTOPHER
  A HISTORY OF SIERRA LEONE.
  LONDON, OXFORD UNIVERSITY PRESS, 1962
  029,131-02,
       CASE STUDY

  HARGREAVES JOHN D

THE ESTABLISHMENT OF THE SIERRA LEONE PROTECTORATE AND THE
INSURRECTION OF 1898.
THE CAMBRIDGE HISTORICAL JOURNAL 12 1956 PP 56-80
029,
        CASE STUDY

029
    HOLDEN E
    BLYDEN OF LIBERIA-AN ACCOUNT OF THE LIFE AND LABOUR OF
    EDWARD WILMOT BLYDEN
    NEW YORK, VANTAGE PRESS, 1966
    029,030,
        CASE STUDY

    LYNCH HOLLIS R
    EDWARD WILMOT BLYDEN--PAN-NEGRO PATRIOT 1832-1912.
    LONDON, OXFORD UNIVERSITY PRESS, 1967
    029,030,119-02,
        CASE STUDY

    MOWER J H
    THE REPUBLIC OF LIBERIA.
    THE JOURNAL OF NEGRO HISTORY XXXII 1947 PP 265-306
    029,119-02,
        CASE STUDY

    STAUDENRAUS P J
    THE AFRICAN COLONIZATION MOVEMENT,1816-1865
    NEW YORK, COLUMBIA UNIVERSITY PRESS,1961
    029,119-02,
        CASE STUDY

    WESLEY CHARLES H
    THE STRUGGLE FOR THE RECOGNITION OF HAITI AND LIBERIA AS
    INDEPENDENT REPUBLICS.
    THE JOURNAL OF NEGRO HISTORY II 1917 PP 369-383
    029,119-02,
        CASE STUDY

    CLARKSON THOMAS
    AN ESSAY ON THE COMPARATIVE EFFICIENCY OF REGULATION OR
    ABOLITION AS APPLIED TO THE SLAVE TRADE.
    LONDON, J PHILLIPS, 1789
    029,
        LESS ACCESSIBLE

    AZIKIWE NNAMDI
    LIBERIA IN WORLD POLITICS.
    LONDON, A H STOCKWELL, 1934
    029,119-02,128-04,
        CASE STUDY

    SHERWOOD HENRY N
    THE FORMATION OF THE AMERICAN COLONIZATION SOCIETY.
    THE JOURNAL OF NEGRO HISTORY II 1917 PP 209-228
    029,
        REFERENCE

30. THE AFRICAN LEGACY IN THE NEW WORLD

030
    REDDING SAUNDERS
    THEY CAME IN CHAINS
    PHILADELPHIA,J.B.LIPPINCOTT,1950
    030,094,
        AUTHOR IS WELL-KNOWN AFRO-AMERICAN WRITER,WHOSE
        PORTRAIT OF BLACK MEN IN THE AMERICAS IS INFORMED BY
        HIS EXTENSIVE KNOWLEDGE OF AFRICAN HISTORY,HIS
        LITERARY INSIGHTS,AND HIS KNOWLEDGE OF AMERICAN
        HISTORY.VOLUME,WHICH IS NOW SLIGHTLY DATED,COVERS
        PERIOD 1619-1950.

    VAN DEN BERGHE P
    RACE AND RACISM-- A COMPARATIVE PERSPECTIVE.
    NEW YORK,JOHN WILEY,1967
    030,088,132-06,
        AUTHOR PROVIDES THEORETICAL INTRODUCTION TO ISSUE OF
        RACE, INCLUDING CRITIQUE OF DOMINANT TRENDS IN RACE
        RELATIONS, DEFINITIONS, ORIGINS AND DISTRIBUTION OF
        RACISM, RACE AND PERSONALITY, RACE AS DIFFERENTIATION
        AND STRATIFICATION, A TYPOLOGY OF RACE RELATIONS, AND
        RACE AND THE THEORY OF PLURALISM AND CONFLICT. CASE
        STUDIES INCLUDE MEXICO, BRAZIL, THE UNITED STATES, AND
        SOUTH AFRICA. ATTEMPTS ANALYTICAL COMPARISON.

    WHITTEN NORMAN E   SZWED JOHN F   EDS
    AFRO-AMERICAN ANTHROPOLOGY
    NEW YORK,THE FREE PRESS,1970
    030,
        22 ORIGINAL ARTICLES COVER TOPICS IN URBAN
        ANTHROPOLOGY,ETHNOSCIENCE,CULTURE ECOLOGY,SOCIO-
        ECONOMIC EVOLUTION,ETHNOMUSICOLOGY,LINGUISTICS,ETHNIC
        IDENTITY AND SYNCRETIC RELIGIONS. COVERS GEOGRAPHICAL
        AREA INCLUDING THE UNITED STATES,SOUTH AMERICA,CENTRAL
        AMERICA,CARIBBEAN,AND EASTERN CANADA.

    AMERICAN SOCIETY OF AFRICAN CULTURE
    THE AMERICAN NEGRO BIBLIOGRAPHY.
    NEW YORK, AMERICAN SOCIETY OF AFRICAN CULTURE, 1967
    030,
        REFERENCE

    APTHEKER HERBERT
    A DOCUMENTARY HISTORY OF THE NEGRO PEOPLE IN THE UNITED
    STATES.
    NEW YORK,CITADEL PRESS,1951
    030,
        REFERENCE

    APTHEKER HERBERT
    NEGRO SLAVE REVOLTS IN THE U.S.
    NEW YORK,INTERNATIONAL PUBLISHERS,1939
    030,
        REFERENCE

030

ASIEGBU JOHNSON U J
SLAVERY AND THE POLITICS OF LIBERATION 1787-1861.
NEW YORK, AFRICANA PUBLISHING CORPORATION, 1970
030,
      REFERENCE

BENNETT LERONE
BEFORE THE MAYFLOWER-A HISTORY OF THE NEGRO IN AMERICA,
1619-1964
BALTIMORE, PENGUIN, REVISED EDITION, 1966
030,
      REFERENCE

BENNETT LERONE
PIONEERS IN PROTEST
BALTIMORE, PENGUIN, 1969
030,095,
      REFERENCE

BENNETT LERONE
CONFRONTATION-BLACK AND WHITE
BALTIMORE, PENGUIN, 1966; REVISED EDITION, 1968
030,094,
      REFERENCE

BENNETT LERONE
THE NEGRO MOOD.
CHICAGO, JOHNSON PUBLISHING CO, 1964
030,095,
      REFERENCE

CLARK KENNETH
DARK GHETTO, DILEMMAS OF SOCIAL POWER.
NEW YORK, HARPER AND ROW, 1965
030,
      REFERENCE

CRUM MASON
GULLAH-- NEGRO LIFE IN THE CAROLINA SEA ISLANDS.
DURHAM, DUKE UNIVERSITY PRESS, 1940
030,
      REFERENCE

CURTIN PHILIP D
AFRICA REMEMBERED-- NARRATIVES BY WEST AFRICANS FROM THE
ERA OF THE SLAVE TRADE.
MADISON, UNIVERSITY OF WISCONSIN PRESS, 1967
028,030,
      REFERENCE

DAVIS JOHN P   ED
THE AMERICAN NEGRO REFERENCE BOOK.
THE PHELPS-STOKES FUND, ENGLEWOOD CLIFFS, NEW JERSEY, 1966
030,
      REFERENCE

DU BOIS W E B
BLACK RECONSTITUTION IN AMERICA.

LONDON, FRANK CASS AND CO. LTD., 1966
030,
     REFERENCE

030
  ELKINS STANLEY
  SLAVERY A PROBLEM IN AMERICAN INSTITUTIONAL AND
  INTELLECTUAL LIFE.
  CHICAGO, UNIVERSITY OF CHICAGO PRESS, 1959
  029,030,
     REFERENCE

  FERGUSON J H
  LATIN AMERICA-- THE BALANCE OF RACE REDRESSED.
  NEW YORK, OXFORD UNIVERSITY PRESS, 1961
  030,
     REFERENCE

  FRANKLIN JOHN H
  FROM SLAVERY TO FREEDOM A HISTORY OF NEGRO AMERICANS.
  NEW YORK, ALFRED A. KNOPF, 1968
  030,
     REFERENCE

  FRANKLIN JOHN H   STARR ISADORE
  THE NEGRO IN TWENTIETH CENTURY AMERICA.
  NEW YORK, VINTAGE BOOKS, 1967
  030,
     REFERENCE

  FRAZIER E FRANKLIN
  THE NEGRO FAMILY IN THE UNITED STATES.
  NEW YORK, DRYDEN PRESS, 1948
  030,
     REFERENCE

  GENOVESE EUGENE D
  THE LEGACY OF SLAVERY AND THE ROOTS OF BLACK NATIONALISM.
  STUDIES ON THE LEFT 6 1966 PP 3-65
  030,
     REFERENCE

  GRIMSHAW ALLEN D
  URBAN RACIAL VIOLENCE IN THE UNITED STATES CHANGING
  ECOLOGICAL CONSIDERATIONS.
  THE AMERICAN JOURNAL OF SOCIOLOGY 66 SEPTEMBER 1960
  PP 109-119
  030,
     REFERENCE

  HAMMOND PETER B
  AFRO-AMERICAN INDIANS AND AFRO-ASIANS--CULTURAL CONTACTS
  BETWEEN AFRICA AND THE PEOPLES OF ASIA AND ABORIGINAL
  AMERICA.
  IN CARTER, GWENDOLEN M. AND ANN PADEN (EDS), EXPANDING
  HORIZONS IN AFRICAN STUDIES, EVANSTON, NORTHWESTERN
  UNIVERSITY PRESS, 1969, PP. 275-290
  030,094,100,
     REFERENCE

HARRIS MARVIN
PATTERNS OF RACE IN THE AMERICAS.
NEW YORK, WALKER, 1964
030,
        REFERENCE

030

HERSKOVITS MELVILLE J
ON THE PROVENIENCE OF NEW WORLD NEGROES.
SOCIAL FORCES 12 1933
030,
        REFERENCE

HERSKOVITS MELVILLE J
THE CONTRIBUTION OF AFROAMERICAN STUDIES TO AFRICANIST
RESEARCH.
AMERICAN ANTHROPOLOGIST 50 1948 PP1-10
030,
        REFERENCE

HERSKOVITS MELVILLE J
THE MYTH OF THE NEGRO PAST.
BOSTON, BEACON PRESS, 1962
030,
        REFERENCE

HERSKOVITS MELVILLE J
THE AHISTORICAL APPROACH TO AFRO-AMERICAN STUDIES-- A
CRITIQUE.
AMERICAN ANTHROPOLOGIST 62 1960 PP 559-568
030,
        REFERENCE

HERSKOVITS MELVILLE J
THE PRESENT STATUS AND NEEDS OF AFROAMERICAN RESEARCH.
JOURNAL OF NEGRO HISTORY 36 1951 PP 123-147
030,
        REFERENCE

HERSKOVITS MELVILLE J
PROBLEM METHOD AND THEORY IN AFRO-AMERICAN STUDIES.
PHYLON 7 1946 PP 337-354
030,
        REFERENCE

HERSKOVITS MELVILLE J
THE AMERICAN NEGRO.
BLOOMINGTON, INDIANA UNIVERSITY PRESS, 1964
030,
        REFERENCE

HERSKOVITS MELVILLE J
THE NEW WORLD NEGRO--SELECTED PAPERS
BLOOMINGTON, INDIANA UNIVERSITY PRESS, 1966
030,
        REFERENCE

HUGHES LANGSTON   MELTZER MILTON
A PICTORIAL HISTORY OF THE NEGRO IN AMERICA.
NEW YORK, CROWN, 1963

030,
        REFERENCE

030
    JAHN JANHEINZ
    MUNTU
    NEW YORK, GROVE PRESS, 1961
    030,
        REFERENCE

    JORDAN WINTHROP
    WHITE OVER BLACK AMERICAN ATTITUDES TOWARD THE NEGRO
    1550-1812.
    CHAPEL HILL, UNIVERSITY OF NORTH CAROLINA PRESS, 1967
    030,
        REFERENCE

    KEIL CHARLES
    URBAN BLUES.
    CHICAGO, UNIVERSITY OF CHICAGO PRESS, 1966
    030,
        REFERENCE

    KING KENNETH J
    AFRICA AND THE SOUTHERN STATES OF THE USA NOTES ON J H
    OLDHAM AND AMERICAN NEGRO EDUCATION FOR AFRICANS.
    IN JOURNAL OF AFRICAN HISTORY VOL   10 1969 P 659-677
    030,
        REFERENCE

    LOGAN RAYFORD W
    THE HISTORICAL ASPECTS OF PAN-AFRICANISM-- A PERSONAL CHRON-
    ICLE.
    AFRICAN FORUM I 1 1965 PP 90-104
    030,079,
        REFERENCE

    LYNCH HOLLIS R
    PAN-NEGRO NATIONALISM IN THE NEW WORLD.
    IN JEFFREY BUTLER (ED), BOSTON UNIVERSITY PAPERS ON AFRICAN
    HISTORY VOLUME 2, BOSTON, BOSTON UNIVERSITY PRESS, 1966, PP
    147-180
    029,030,
        REFERENCE

    LYND STAUGHTON
    RETHINKING SLAVERY AND RECONSTRUCTION.
    JOURNAL OF NEGRO HISTORY 1 JULY 1965 PP 198-209
    030,
        REFERENCE

    MELTZER MILTON   ED
    IN THEIR OWN WORDS-- A HISTORY OF THE AMERICAN NEGRO.
    NEW YORK, CROWELL, 1: 1619-1865; 2: 1865-1916; 3: 1916-1966
    030,
        REFERENCE

    MILLER ELIZABETH
    THE NEGRO IN AMERICA, A BIBLIOGRAPHY.
    CAMBRIDGE, HARVARD UNIVERSITY PRESS, 1968

030,094,
    REFERENCE

030
PARSONS TALCOTT   CLARK KENNETH   EDS
THE NEGRO AMERICAN.
BOSTON,HOUGHTON MIFFLIN,DAEDALUS LIBRARY 7,1966
030,
    REFERENCE

PHILLIPS ULRICH B
THE SLAVE ECONOMY OF THE OLD SOUTH--SELECTED ESSAYS IN
ECONOMIC AND SOCIAL HISTORY.
BATON ROUGE, LOUISIANA STATE UNIVERSITY PRESS, 1968
030,
    REFERENCE

PORTER JAMES A
THE TRANSCULTURAL AFFINITIES OF AFRICAN NEGRO ART.
IN AMSAC, AFRICA SEEN BY AMERICAN NEGROES, PARIS,
PRESENCE AFRICAINE, 1958, PP 119-130
030,
    REFERENCE

QUARLES BENJAMIN
THE NEGRO IN THE MAKING OF AMERICA
NEW YORK, MACMILLAN, 1969(REVISED EDITION)
030,
    REFERENCE

STAMPP KENNETH
THE PECULIAR INSTITUTION.
NEW YORK, ALFRED A KNOPF, 1956
028,030,
    REFERENCE

STUCKEY STERLING
AFRICAN AND AFRO-AMERICAN RELATIONSHIPS--RESEARCH POSSIBIL-
ITIES.
IN CARTER, GWENDOLEN M. AND ANN PADEN (EDS), EXPANDING
HORIZONS IN AFRICAN STUDIES, EVANSTON, NORTHWESTERN
UNIVERSITY PRESS, 1969, PP. 291-302
030,094,100,
    REFERENCE

TANNENBAUM FRANK
SLAVE AND CITIZEN THE NEGRO IN THE AMERICAS.
NEW YORK, ALFRED A KNOPF, 1947
030,
    REFERENCE

TURNER LORENZO
AFRICANISMS IN THE GULLAH DIALECT
NEW YORK, ARNO PRESS,1969;ORIGINALLY PUBLISHED IN 1949
030,
    REFERENCE

TURNER LORENZO D
AFRICAN SURVIVALS IN THE NEW WORLD WITH SPECIAL EMPHASIS ON
THE ARTS.

IN AMSAC, AFRICA SEEN BY AMERICAN NEGROES, PARIS,
PRESENCE AFRICAINE, 1958, PP 101-116
030,
        REFERENCE

030
    WARD W E F
    THE ROYAL NAVY AND THE SLAVERS.
    NEW YORK, INTERNATIONAL UNIVERSITY BOOKSELLERS, INC., 1969
    030,
        REFERENCE

    WATERMAN RICHARD A
    AFRICAN INFLUENCE ON THE MUSIC OF THE AMERICAS
    IN SOL TAX (ED) ACCULTURATION IN THE AMERICAS, CHICAGO,
    UNIVERSITY OF CHICAGO PRESS, 1952
    015,030,
        REFERENCE

    WELSCH ERWIN K
    THE NEGRO IN THE UNITED STATES-A RESEARCH GUIDE.
    BLOOMINGTON, INDIANA UNIVERSITY PRESS, 1965
    030,
        REFERENCE

    BLYDEN EDWARD W
    AFRICAN LIFE AND CUSTOMS.
    LONDON, INTERNATIONAL UNIVERSITY BOOKSELLERS, INC., 1969
    030,
        CASE STUDY

    BLYDEN EDWARD W
    CHRISTIANITY, ISLAM AND THE NEGRO RACE.
    EDINBURGH, UNIVERSITY PRESS, 1967
    030,
        CASE STUDY

    CLARKE JOHN HENRIK
    HARLEM, A COMMUNITY IN TRANSITION.
    NEW YORK, CITADEL PRESS, 1964
    030,
        CASE STUDY

    DAVIS ALLISON   GARDINER B   GARDINER M R
    DEEP SOUTH.
    CHICAGO, UNIVERSITY OF CHICAGO PRESS, 1941
    030,
        CASE STUDY

    DOUGLAS FREDERICK
    NARRATIVE OF THE LIFE OF FREDERICK DOUGLAS AN AMERICAN
    SLAVE WRITTEN BY HIMSELF.
    CAMBRIDGE, HARVARD UNIVERSITY PRESS, 1960
    030,
        CASE STUDY

    DRAKE ST CLAIR   CAYTON HORACE
    BLACK METROPOLIS.
    NEW YORK, HARCOURT BRACE, 1945
    030,

CASE STUDY

030

HOLDEN E
BLYDEN OF LIBERIA-AN ACCOUNT OF THE LIFE AND LABOUR OF
EDWARD WILMOT BLYDEN
NEW YORK, VANTAGE PRESS, 1966
029,030,
    CASE STUDY

LYNCH HOLLIS R
EDWARD WILMOT BLYDEN--PAN-NEGRO PATRIOT 1832-1912.
LONDON, OXFORD UNIVERSITY PRESS, 1967
029,030,119-02,
    CASE STUDY

NICHOLS CHARLES H
MANY THOUSAND GONE--THE EX-SLAVES ACCOUNT OF THEIR BONDAGE
AND FREEDOM.
BLOOMINGTON, INDIANA UNIVERSITY PRESS, 1969
030,
    CASE STUDY

BASTIDE ROGER
LES AMERICQUES NOIRES-- LES CIVILIZATIONS (THE BLACK AMERI-
CAS-- THE CIVILIZATIONS).
AFRICAINES DANS LE NOUVEAU MONDE, PARIS, PAYOT, 1967
030,
    LESS ACCESSIBLE

BOUCHE DENISE
LES VILLAGES DE LIBERTE EN AFRIQUE NOIRE, 1887-1910 (THE
LIBERTY SETTLEMENTS IN BLACK AFRICA, 1887-1910).
PARIS, MOUTON, 1968
030,
    LESS ACCESSIBLE

MONOD THEODORE   ED
LES AFRO-AMERICAINES (THE AFRO-AMERICANS).
DAKAR, MEMOIRES DE L'INSTITUTE FRANCAIS D'AFRIQUE NOIRE 27
1953
030,
    LESS ACCESSIBLE

BANTON MICHAEL P
RACE RELATIONS.
LONDON, TAVISTOCK, 1968
006,030,089,
    GENERAL THEORY

31. WHITE AND BLACK MIGRATIONS IN SOUTHERN AFRICA

031

WILSON MONICA   THOMPSON LEONARD   EDS
THE OXFORD HISTORY OF SOUTH AFRICA. VOL I   SOUTH AFRICA

TO 1870
LONDON, OXFORD UNIVERSITY PRESS, 1970
031,032,132-02,
        VIEWS CENTRAL THEME OF SOUTH AFRICAN HISTORY AS INTER-
        ACTION BETWEEN PEOPLES OF DIVERGENT ORIGINS, LANG-
        UAGES, TECHNOLOGIES, IDEOLOGIES AND SOCIAL SYSTEMS.
        BEGINS WITH DETAILED PRE-COLONIAL HISTORY, FOLLOWED BY
        ANALYSIS OF BLACK AND WHITE MIGRATIONS, THE STRUGGLE
        FOR LAND, RISE OF SHAKA AND MOSHWESHWE KINGDOMS, AND
        DISCOVERY OF DIAMONDS.

031
    BINNS C T
    DINIZULU-THE DEATH OF THE HOUSE OF SHAKA
    LONDON, LONGMANS, 1968
    031,
        REFERENCE

    BUNTING BRIAN
    THE RISE OF THE SOUTH AFRICAN REICH
    LONDON, PENGUIN, 1964
    031,032,
        REFERENCE

    DE KIEWIET C W
    A HISTORY OF SOUTH AFRICA--SOCIAL AND ECONOMIC
    NEW YORK, OXFORD UNIVERSITY PRESS, 1967
    031,032,
        REFERENCE

    DE KIEWIET C W
    THE IMPERIAL FACTOR IN SOUTH AFRICA-A STUDY IN POLITICS AND
    ECONOMICS
    CAMBRIDGE, UNIVERSITY PRESS, 1937
    031,032,
        REFERENCE

    GLUCKMAN MAY
    THE RISE OF A ZULU EMPIRE
    SCIENTIFIC AMERICAN 202 1960 PP 157-168
    031,
        REFERENCE

    LIESEGANG GERHARD
    DINGANES ATTACK ON LOURENCO MARQUES IN 1833
    JOURNAL OF AFRICAN HISTORY 10 1969 PP 565-580
    031,
        REFERENCE

    LYE WILLIAM F
    THE DIFAQANE-THE MFECANE IN THE SOUTHERN SOTHO AREA 1822-24
    JOURNAL OF AFRICAN HISTORY 8 1967 PP 107-131
    031,118-02,132-02,
        REFERENCE

    MORRIS DONALD R
    THE WASHING OF THE SPEARS-A HISTORY OF THE RISE OF THE ZULU
    NATION UNDER THE SHAKA AND ITS FALL IN THE ZULU WAR OF 1879
    NEW YORK, SIMON AND SCHUSTER, 1965
    031,

REFERENCE

031
    SANDERS P B
    SEKONYELA AND MOSHESHWE-FAILURE AND SUCCESS IN THE AFTERMATH
    OF THE DIFAGANE
    JOURNAL OF AFRICAN HISTORY 10 1969 PP 439-456
    031,
        REFERENCE

    THOMPSON LEONARD   ED
    AFRICAN SOCIETIES IN SOUTHERN AFRICA.
    NEW YORK, OXFORD UNIVERSITY PRESS, 1970
    031,132-01,
        REFERENCE

    BECKER PETER
    RULE OF FEAR,THE LIFE AND TIMES OF DINGANE KING OF THE ZULU
    LONDON, LONGMANS, GREEN, 1964
    031,132-02,
        CASE STUDY

    BINNS C T
    THE LAST ZULU KING
    LONDON, LONGMANS, GREEN, 1963
    031,132-02,
        CASE STUDY

    OKOYE FELIX N C
    DINGANE--A REAPPRAISAL.
    JOURNAL OF AFRICAN HISTORY, X, 2, 1969, PP. 221-235
    031,
        CASE STUDY

    SMITH EDWIN W
    GREAT LION OF BECHUANALAND
    LONDON, INDEPENDENT PRESS, 1957
    031,102-02,
        CASE STUDY

    SMITH K W
    THE FALL OF THE BAPEDI OF THE NORTH-EASTERN TRANSVAAL.
    JOURNAL OF AFRICAN HISTORY, X, 1, 1969, PP. 237-252.
    031,132-02,
        CASE STUDY

    WALKER ERIC
    A HISTORY OF SOUTHERN AFRICA.
    LONDON, LONGMANS, 1957
    031,132-02,
        CASE STUDY

32. AFRICAN REACTIONS TO EUROPEAN SETTLEMENT

LEGUM COLIN   LEGUM MARGARET
THE BITTER CHOICE--EIGHT SOUTH AFRICANS RESISTANCE TO
TYRANNY
CLEVELAND AND NEW YORK, WORLD, 1968
032, 089,
    AUTHORS--SOUTH AFRICAN EXILES BANNED FROM RETURNING
    SINCE 1964--ASSESS THE PATTERNS OF REACTION AND
    RESISTANCE TO APARTHEID OF AUTHOR ALAN PATON, NOBEL
    PRIZE WINNER ALBERT LUTULI, NELSON MANDELA, ROBERT
    SOBUKWE, C F B NAUDE, NANA SITA, DENNIS BRUTUS, AND
    MICHAEL SCOTT

032
OMER-COOPER J D
THE ZULU AFTERMATH-- A NINETEENTH-CENTURY REVOLUTION
IN BANTU AFRICA.
LONDON, LONGMANS, 1966
032, 034, 132-02,
    MAJOR COMPILATION OF DATA REGARDING CAUSES AND EFFECTS
    OF BANTU MIGRATIONS IN RELATIONSHIP TO EUROPEAN EXPAN-
    SION INTO SOUTHERN AFRICA.

SIMONS H J   SIMONS R E
CLASS AND COLOR IN SOUTH AFRICA 1850-1950
BALTIMORE, PENGUIN, 1969
032, 089,
    A RECENT SOCIAL AND HISTORICAL ANALYSIS OF THE LABOR
    AND NATIONAL MOVEMENTS IN SOUTH AFRICA. FOCUSES ON
    REACTION AND RESISTENCE OF VARIOUS AFRICAN, INDIAN,
    AND COLOURED GROUPS AND THE CLASS STRUGGLES INVOLVED
    IN SOCIALIST AND COMMUNIST PARTICIPATION IN AND
    INTERPRETATION OF SOUTH AFRICAN PROBLEMS.

WILSON MONICA   THOMPSON LEONARD   EDS
THE OXFORD HISTORY OF SOUTH AFRICA. VOL I   SOUTH AFRICA
TO 1870
LONDON, OXFORD UNIVERSITY PRESS, 1970
031, 032, 132-02,
    VIEWS CENTRAL THEME OF SOUTH AFRICAN HISTORY AS INTER-
    ACTION BETWEEN PEOPLES OF DIVERGENT ORIGINS, LANG-
    UAGES, TECHNOLOGIES, IDEOLOGIES AND SOCIAL SYSTEMS.
    BEGINS WITH DETAILED PRE-COLONIAL HISTORY, FOLLOWED BY
    ANALYSIS OF BLACK AND WHITE MIGRATIONS, THE STRUGGLE
    FOR LAND, RISE OF SHAKA AND MOSHWESHWE KINGDOMS, AND
    DISCOVERY OF DIAMONDS.

AUSTIN DENNIS
BRITAIN AND SOUTH AFRICA.
LONDON, OXFORD UNIVERSITY PRESS, 1966
032, 033, 132-09,
    REFERENCE

BUNTING BRIAN
THE RISE OF THE SOUTH AFRICAN REICH
LONDON, PENGUIN, 1964
031, 032,
    REFERENCE

CAPLAN GERALD L
BAROTSELAND'S SCRAMBLE FOR PROTECTION.

JOURNAL OF AFRICAN HISTORY, X, 2, 1969, PP. 277-294
032,142-02,
        REFERENCE

032
    COPE J
    KING OF THE HOTTENTOTS-BIOGRAPHY OF A SOUTH AFRICAN
    HOTTENTOT AT THE CAPE IN 1613
    CAPE TOWN, TIMMINS, 1967
    032,
        REFERENCE

    DE KIEWIET C W
    A HISTORY OF SOUTH AFRICA--SOCIAL AND ECONOMIC
    NEW YORK, OXFORD UNIVERSITY PRESS, 1967
    031,032,
        REFERENCE

    DE KIEWIET C W
    THE IMPERIAL FACTOR IN SOUTH AFRICA-A STUDY IN POLITICS AND
    ECONOMICS
    CAMBRIDGE, UNIVERSITY PRESS, 1937
    031,032,
        REFERENCE

    FEIT EDWARD
    AFRICAN OPPOSITION IN SOUTH AFRICA.
    PALO ALTO, CALIFORNIA, HOOVER INSTITUTION PRESS, 1967
    032,089,132-07,
        REFERENCE

    FRYE WILLIAM
    IN WHITEST AFRICA--THE DYNAMICS OF APARTHEID
    ENGLEWOOD CLIFFS, PRENTICE-HALL, 1968
    032,089,
        REFERENCE

    HAMMOND-TOOKE W D
    THE TRANSKEIAN COUNCIL SYSTEM 1895-1955-AN APPRAISAL
    JOURNAL OF AFRICAN HISTORY 9 1968 PP 455-477
    032,
        REFERENCE

    HERD NORMAN
    1922-THE REVOLT ON THE RAND
    NEW YORK, HUMANITIES PRESS, 1966
    032,
        REFERENCE

    HUNTER MONICA
    REACTION TO CONQUEST.
    LONDON, OXFORD UNIVERSITY PRESS, 1961
    032,
        REFERENCE

    KUPER LEO
    PASSIVE RESISTANCE IN SOUTH AFRICA
    NEW HAVEN, YALE UNIVERSITY PRESS, 1967
    032,
        REFERENCE

032

KUPER LEO
PASSIVE RESISTANCE IN SOUTH AFRICA
LONDON, JONATHAN CAPE, 1956
032,
     REFERENCE

LE MAY G M C
BRITISH SUPREMACY IN SOUTH AFRICA-1899-1907
LONDON, OXFORD UNIVERSITY PRESS, 1967
032,
     REFERENCE

MANSERGH NICOLAS
SOUTH AFRICA 1906-1961- THE PRICE OF MAGNANIMITY
NEW YORK, PRAEGER, 1962
032,
     REFERENCE

MBEKI GOVAN
SOUTH AFRICA- THE PEASANTS REVOLT
LONDON AND NEW YORK, PENGUIN, 1964
032,
     REFERENCE

PATON ALAN
CRY, THE BELOVED COUNTRY
NEW YORK, SCRIBNER, 1948
032,089,
     REFERENCE

PATTERSON SHEILA
THE LAST TREK
LONDON, ROUTLEDGE AND KEGAN PAUL, 1957
032,
     REFERENCE

REEVES RICHARD A
SHOOTING AT SHARPVILLE-THE AGONY OF SOUTH AFRICA
BOSTON, HOUGHTON MIFFLIN, 1961
032,
     REFERENCE

ROUX EDWARD
TIME LONGER THAN ROPE--A HISTORY OF THE BLACK MAN'S STRUGGLE
FOR FREEDOM IN SOUTH AFRICA.
MADISON, WISCONSIN, UNIVERSITY OF WISCONSIN PRESS, 1966
032,132-07,
     REFERENCE

SACKS B
SOUTH AFRICA, AN IMPERIAL DILEMMA- NON-EUROPEANS AND THE
BRITISH NATION 1902-1914
ALBUQUERQUE, UNIVERSITY OF NEW MEXICO PRESS, 1967
032,
     REFERENCE

THOMPSON LEONARD
THE UNIFICATION OF SOUTH AFRICA 1902-1910

OXFORD CLARENDON PRESS 1960
032,
        REFERENCE

032
    TRAPIDO STANLEY
    AFRICAN DIVISIONAL POLITICS IN THE CAPE COLONY,1884 TO 1910
    JOURNAL OF AFRICAN HISTORY 9 1968 PP 79-98
    032,
            REFERENCE

    VAN DEN BERGHE P
    SOUTH AFRICA- A STUDY OF CONFLICT
    MIDDLETOWN, CONNECTICUT, WESLEYAN UNIVERSITY PRESS, 1965
    032,089,
            REFERENCE

    WALKER ERIC
    THE GREAT TREK
    LONDON, ADAM AND CHARLES BLACK, 1948
    032,
            REFERENCE

    WALSHE A P
    THE ORIGIN OF AFRICAN POLITICAL CONSCIOUSNESS IN SOUTH
    AFRICA
    JOURNAL OF MODERN AFRICAN STUDIES 7 1969 PP 583-610
    032,089,
            REFERENCE

    HALPERN JACK
    SOUTH AFRICA'S HOSTAGES-- BASUTOLAND, BECHUANALAND,
    AND SWAZILAND.
    BALTIMORE, PENGUIN, 1965
    032,088,102-07,118-07,135-07,
            CASE STUDY

    GALBRAITH JOHN S
    RELUCTANT EMPIRE,BRITISH POLICY ON THE SOUTH AFRICAN
    FRONTIER,1834-1854
    BERKELEY, UNIVERSITY OF CALIFORNIA PRESS, 1963
    032,132-02,

    HANCOCK SIR WILLIAM
    SMUTS-THE SANGUINE YEARS,1870-1919 VOLUME 1
    NEW YORK, OXFORD, 1962
    032,089,132-02,

33. THE SCRAMBLE FOR AFRICA

033
    GANN LEWIS H   DUIGNAN PETER
    THE HISTORY AND POLITICS OF COLONIALISM, 1870-1914
    VOL 1--COLONIALISM IN AFRICA, 1870-1960
    CAMBRIDGE, UNIVERSITY PRESS 1969

033,
> FIRST OF FOUR VOLUMES ON HISTORY OF AFRICA DURING
> COLONIAL RULE SPONSORED BY HOOVER INSTITUTION AT
> STANFORD UNIVERSITY. ALL UNDER GENERAL EDITORSHIP OF
> DUIGNAN AND GANN.   THIS VOLUME AND NEXT COVER
> HISTORY AND POLITICS OF IMPERIALISM AND THE SCRAMBLE
> FOR AFRICA TO COLONIZATION.   VOL 3--IMPACT OF
> COLONIALISM ON AFRICAN SOCIETIES.   VOL 4--THE
> ECONOMICS OF COLONIALISM.

033

KANYA-FORSTNER A S
THE CONQUEST OF WESTERN SUDAN--A STUDY IN FRENCH MILITARY
IMPERIALISM.
CAMBRIDGE, UNIVERSITY PRESS, 1969
033,
> DEALS WITH LATE NINETEENTH CENTURY EFFORTS OF FRENCH
> MILITARY AND COLONIAL ELEMENTS TO CONQUER WESTERN
> SUDAN. DISCUSSES GENERAL IMPACT ON WESTERN SUDAN AND
> RELEVANCE TO PATTERNS OF PARTITIONING BETWEEN FRANCE
> AND OTHER COLONIAL POWERS.

ROBINSON RONALD   GALLAGHER JOHN
AFRICA AND THE VICTORIANS-- THE CLIMAX OF IMPERIALISM IN THE
DARK CONTINENT.
NEW YORK, ST MARTIN'S, 1961
033,
> AUTHORS SUGGEST THAT MAJOR REASON FOR EUROPEAN OCCU-
> PATION OF AFRICA AT END OF NINETEENTH CENTURY WAS MIL-
> ITARY STRATEGY IN INTERNATIONAL RELATIONS SYSTEM, RA-
> THER THAN SPECIFIC ECONOMIC GAINS FROM AFRICA. EX-
> TREMELY WELL DOCUMENTED EVIDENCE (MUCH FROM BRITISH
> FOREIGN OFFICE). PROVIDES DETAILS OF ACTUAL EUROPEAN
> COMPETITION IN AFRICA.

AUSTIN DENNIS
BRITAIN AND SOUTH AFRICA.
LONDON, OXFORD UNIVERSITY PRESS, 1966
032, 033, 132-09,
> REFERENCE

CAIRNS H A C
PRELUDE TO IMPERIALISM-BRITISH REACTIONS TO CENTRAL AFRICAN
SOCIETY 1840-1890
LONDON, ROUTLEDGE AND KEGAN PAUL, 1965
033,
> REFERENCE

COLLINS ROBERT O
KING LEOPOLD, ENGLAND AND THE UPPER NILE, 1899-1909.
NEW HAVEN, CONN. (YALE), MCGILL-QUEEN'S PRESS, 1969
033,134-02,
> REFERENCE

CROWE SYBIL E
THE BERLIN WEST AFRICAN CONFERENCE, 1884-1885.
LONDON, LONGMANS, 1942
033,
> REFERENCE

GIFFORD PROSSER   LOUIS WILLIAM ROGER
BRITAIN AND GERMANY IN AFRICA--IMPERIAL RIVALRY AND COLONIAL
RULE.
NEW HAVEN, CONN. (YALE), MCGILL-QUEEN'S PRESS, 1969
033,
     REFERENCE

033

GRENVILLE J A S
LORD SALISBURY AND FOREIGN POLICY-- THE CLOSE OF THE
NINETEENTH CENTURY.
LONDON, ATHLONE PRESS, 1964
033,
     REFERENCE

HAMMOND R J
PORTUGAL AND AFRICA, 1815-1910.
STANFORD, STANFORD UNIVERSITY, OXFORD UNIVERSITY PRESS, 1966
033, 144-02
     REFERENCE

HARGREAVES JOHN D
PRELUDE TO THE PARTITION OF WEST AFRICA.
NEW YORK, ST MARTIN'S, 1963
029,033,
     REFERENCE

HAYWOOD AUSTIN   CLARKE F A S
THE HISTORY OF THE ROYAL WEST AFRICAN FRONTIER FORCE.
ALDERSHOT, GALE AND POLDEN LIMITED, 1964
033,
     REFERENCE

NEWBURY COLIN W
THE DEVELOPMENT OF FRENCH POLICY ON THE LOWER AND UPPER
NIGER-- 1880-1898.
JOURNAL OF MODERN HISTORY 31 1959 PP 146-155
033,
     REFERENCE

NEWBURY COLIN W
THE FORMATION OF THE GOVERNMENT GENERAL OF FRENCH WEST
AFRICA.
JOURNAL OF AFRICAN HISTORY 1 1960 PP 111-128
033,
     REFERENCE

NEWBURY COLIN W   KANYA-FORSTNER A S
FRENCH POLICY AND THE ORIGINS OF THE SCRAMBLE FOR WEST
AFRICA.
JOURNAL OF AFRICAN HISTORY, X,2, 1969, PP. 253-276
033,
     REFERENCE

OLIVER ROLAND   ATMORE ANTHONY
COLONIAL RULE IN TROPICAL AFRICA-- POLITICAL AND ECONOMIC
DEVELOPMENTS, 1885-1914.
IN AFRICA SINCE 1800, CAMBRIDGE, CAMBRIDGE UNIVERSITY PRESS,
1967, PP 128-140
033,

REFERENCE

033

OLIVER ROLAND   ATMORE ANTHONY
THE PARTITION OF AFRICA ON THE GROUND, 1891-1901.
IN AFRICA SINCE 1800, CAMBRIDGE, CAMBRIDGE UNIVERSITY PRESS,
1967, PP 114-127
033,
        REFERENCE

OLIVER ROLAND   ATMORE ANTHONY
THE PARTITION OF AFRICA ON PAPER, 1879-1891.
IN AFRICA SINCE 1800, CAMBRIDGE, CAMBRIDGE UNIVERSITY PRESS,
1967, PP 103-114
033,
        REFERENCE

PANKHURST RICHARD
ITALIAN SETTLEMENT POLICY IN ERITREA AND ITS REPERCUSSIONS,
1889-1894.
IN JEFFREY BUTLER (ED), BOSTON UNIVERSITY PAPERS IN AFRICAN
HISTORY VOL I, BOSTON, BOSTON UNIVERSITY PRESS,1964, PP 119-
154
033,110-02,
        REFERENCE

ROBERTS STEPHEN H
HISTORY OF FRENCH COLONIAL POLICY 1870-1925.
LONDON, CASS, 1963
033,
        REFERENCE

ROTBERG ROBERT I
POLITICAL CHANGE IN THE INTERIOR, 1800-1880 CHAPTER 6.
IN A POLITICAL HISTORY OF TROPICAL AFRICA, NEW YORK,
HARCOURT, BRACE AND WORLD, 1965, PP 165-189
033,
        REFERENCE

ROTBERG ROBERT I
THE INTERACTION OF AFRICA AND EUROPE, 1788-1884 CHAPTER 7.
IN A POLITICAL HISTORY OF TROPICAL AFRICA, NEW YORK,
HARCOURT, BRACE AND WORLD, 1965, PP 190-243
033,
        REFERENCE

ROTBERG ROBERT I
THE PERIOD OF THE EUROPEAN PARTITION, 1885-1902 CHAPTER 8.
IN A POLITICAL HISTORY OF TROPICAL AFRICA, NEW YORK,
HARCOURT, BRACE AND WORLD, 1965, PP 244-285
033,
        REFERENCE

SUNDIATA I K
THE MORES OF EXPANSION--1837-1914.
PRESENCE AFRICAINE, 2ND QUARTER, 1969, NO. 70, P. 46-65
033,
        REFERENCE

TOUVAL SAADIA

TREATIES BORDERS AND THE PARTITION OF AFRICA.
JOURNAL OF AFRICAN HISTORY 7 1966 PP 279-294
033,059,
        REFERENCE

033
    WOOLF LEONARD
    EMPIRE AND COMMERCE IN AFRICA-A STUDY IN ECONOMIC
    IMPERIALISM
    LONDON, ALLEN&UNWIN, 1968
    033,
        REFERENCE

    ACHERSON NEAL
    THE KING INCORPORATED,LEOPOLD II IN THE AGE OF TRUSTS
    NEW YORK,DOUBLEDAY, 1964
    033,108-02,
        CASE STUDY

    AJAYI J F ADE
    THE BRITISH OCCUPATION OF LAGOS 1851-1861.
    NIGERIA MAGAZINE 69 1961 PP 96-105
    033,128-02,
        CASE STUDY

    ALLEN BERNARD M
    GORDON AND THE SUDAN.
    LONDON,MACMILLAN,1931
    033,134-02,
        CASE STUDY

    ANSTEY ROGER T
    BRITAIN IN THE CONGO IN THE 19TH CENTURY.
    OXFORD,CLARENDON PRESS,1962
    033,108-02,
        CASE STUDY

    ANSTEY ROGER T
    KING LEOPOLD'S LEGACY-- THE CONGO UNDER BELGIAN RULE.
    LONDON,OXFORD UNIVERSITY PRESS,1966
    033,108-02,
        CASE STUDY

    AYDELOTTE W O
    BISMARCK AND THE BRITISH COLONIAL POLICY-- THE PROBLEM OF
    SOUTHWEST AFRICA 1883-1885.
    PHILADELPHIA,UNIVERSITY OF PENNSYLVANIA PRESS,1937
    033,
        CASE STUDY

    COLLINS ROBERT O
    THE SOUTHERN SUDAN, 1883-1898-- A STRUGGLE FOR CONTROL.
    NEW HAVEN,YALE UNIVERSITY PRESS,1962
    033,134-02,
        CASE STUDY

    DAVIES KENNETH G
    THE ROYAL AFRICAN COMPANY.
    LONDON,LONGMANS,1957
    033,

CASE STUDY

033

GILLARD D R
SALISBURY S AFRICAN POLICY AND THE HELIGOLAND OFFER OF 1890.
THE ENGLISH HISTORICAL REVIEW 75 1960 PP 631-653
033,
        CASE STUDY

GORDON DAVID C
THE PASSING OF FRENCH ALGERIA.
NEW YORK, OXFORD UNIVERSITY PRESS. 1966
033,055,056,101-02,
        CASE STUDY

HENDERSON WILLIAM O
GERMAN EAST AFRICA, 1884-1918.
IN VINCENT HARLOW AND E M CHILVER (EDS), HISTORY OF EAST
AFRICA VOL II, OXFORD, CLARENDON PRESS, 1965, PP 123-162
033,
        CASE STUDY

LOUIS WILLIAM ROGER
RUANDA-URUNDI-- 1884-1919.
OXFORD, CLARENDON PRESS, 1963
033,103-02,129-02,
        CASE STUDY

LOW DAVID A
UGANDA-- THE ESTABLISHMENT OF THE PROTECTORATE, 1894-1919.
IN VINCENT HARLOW AND E M CHILVER (EDS), HISTORY OF EAST
AFRICA VOL II, OXFORD, CLARENDON PRESS, 1965, PP 57-122
033,139-02,
        CASE STUDY

LOW DAVID A
BRITISH EAST AFRICA-- THE ESTABLISHMENT OF BRITISH RULE,
1895-1912.
IN VINCENT HARLOW AND E M CHILVER (EDS), HISTORY OF EAST
AFRICA VOL II, OXFORD, CLARENDON PRESS, 1965, PP 1-56
033,
        CASE STUDY

LUGARD FREDERICK D
THE RISE OF OUR EAST AFRICAN EMPIRE.
LONDON, BLACKWOOD, 2 VOLS, 1893
033,
        CASE STUDY

LUGARD FREDERICK D
THE STORY OF THE UGANDA PROTECTORATE.
LONDON, H MARSHALL, 1901
033,139-02,
        CASE STUDY

OLIVER ROLAND
SOME FACTORS IN THE BRITISH OCCUPATION OF EAST AFRICA 1884-
1894.
THE UGANDA JOURNAL 15 1951 PP 49-64
033,

CASE STUDY

033

OLIVER ROLAND
SIR HARRY JOHNSTON AND THE SCRAMBLE FOR AFRICA.
LONDON, CHATTO AND WINDUS, 1957
033,
         CASE STUDY

PRESTAGE EDGAR
THE ASHANTI QUESTION AND THE BRITISH-- EIGHTEENTH-CENTURY
ORIGINS.
THE JOURNAL OF AFRICAN HISTORY II 1961 PP 35-60
033,114-32,
033, 114-02,

RANGER TERENCE O
TRADITIONAL AUTHORITIES AND THE RISE OF MODERN POLITICS IN
SOUTHERN RHODESIA 1898-1930.
CONFERENCE OF THE HISTORY OF CENTRAL AFRICAN PEOPLES, LUSAKA
1963, RHODES-LIVINGSTONE INSTITUTE, 1963
033, 145-02,
         CASE STUDY

RUDIN HARRY R
GERMANS IN THE CAMEROONS 1884-1914-- A STUDY IN MODERN
IMPERIALISM.
LONDON 1938
033,
         CASE STUDY

ADAMS MARGARET
THE BRITISH ATTITUDE TO GERMAN COLONIZATION 1880-1885.
BULLETIN OF THE INSTITUTE OF HISTORICAL RESEARCH 15 1937
PP 190-193
033,
         LESS ACCESSIBLE

BRUNSCHWIG HENRI
L'EXPANSION ALLEMANDE OUTRE-MER DU XV SIECLE A NOS JOURS
(GERMAN EXPANSION IN AFRICA FROM THE FIFTEENTH CENTURY TO
MODERN TIMES).
PARIS, PRESSES UNIVERSITAIRES DE FRANCE, 1957
027,033,
         LESS ACCESSIBLE

BRUNSCHWIG HENRI
MYTHES ET REALITES DE L'IMPERIALISME COLONIAL FRANCAISE
(FACTS AND FANCIES ABOUT FRENCH COLONIAL IMPERIALISM) 1871
-1914.
PARIS, A COLIN, 1960
033,
         LESS ACCESSIBLE

SCHNAPPER BERNARD
LA POLITIQUE ET LE COMMERCE FRANCAIS DANS LE GOLFE DE
GUINEE DE 1838 A 1871 (POLITICS AND FRENCH COMMERCE IN THE
GULF OF GUINEA FROM 1836-1871).
PARIS, MOUTON, 1961
033,

LESS ACCESSIBLE

34. AFRICAN RESISTANCE AND REACTION

034

MAZRUI ALI A   ROTBERG ROBERT I   EDS
THE TRADITIONS OF PROTEST IN BLACK AFRICA, 1886-1966.
CAMBRIDGE, MASSACHUSETTS, HARVARD UNIVERSITY PRESS, 1970
034,035,
    ORIGINAL ESSAYS BY WELL-KNOWN SCHOLARS. FIRST THREE
    SECTIONS OF BOOK DEAL WITH RESISTANCE TO CONQUEST (HE-
    HE WARS, SAMORY, MENELIK AT ADOWA, UMBUNDU), EARLY RE-
    BELLIONS AGAINST ALIEN RULE (MAJI MAJI, ZULU REBELLION
    IN 1906, CHILEMBWE, BAI BUREH, NYABINGI), AND RELIGI-
    OUS EXPRESSION OF DISCONTENT (NEO-CHRISTIAN FORMS AND
    NEO-ISLAMIC FORMS).

OLORUNTIMEHIN B O
RESISTANCE MOVEMENTS IN THE TUKULOR EMPIRE.
CAHIERS D'ETUDES AFRICAINES, VOL. VIII, 1968, NO. 29,
PP. 123-143
034,123-02,
    ALTHOUGH THE MAJOR FOCUS IS ON ANTI-TUKULOR MOVEMENTS,
    PRIMARILY BAMBARA, WITHIN THE TUKULOR EMPIRE, THERE IS
    REFERENCE TO THE WAY IN WHICH FRENCH FORCES UTILIZED
    THIS CLEAVAGE TO THEIR OWN ENDS IN THE 1890≠S.

OMER-COOPER J D
THE ZULU AFTERMATH-- A NINETEENTH-CENTURY REVOLUTION
IN BANTU AFRICA.
LONDON, LONGMANS; EVANSTON, NORTHWESTERN UNIVERSITY PRESS, 1966
032,034,132-02,
    MAJOR COMPILATION OF DATA REGARDING CAUSES AND EFFECTS
    OF BANTU MIGRATIONS IN RELATIONSHIP TO EUROPEAN EXPAN-
    SION INTO SOUTHERN AFRICA.

BENNETT NORMAN   ED
LEADERSHIP IN EASTERN AFRICA-- SIX POLITICAL BIOGRAPHIES.
BROOKLINE, MASS, BOSTON UNIVERSITY PRESS, 1968
034,
    REFERENCE

CROWDER MICHAEL
WEST AFRICA UNDER COLONIAL RULE.
LONDON, HUTCHINSON; EVANSTON, NORTHWESTERN UNIVERSITY PRESS,
1968
034,035,
    REFERENCE

HESS ROBERT L
THE MAD MULLAH AND NORTHERN SOMALIA.
JOURNAL OF AFRICAN HISTORY 5 1964 PP 415-433
034,133-02,
    REFERENCE

KLEIN MARTIN A
ISLAM AND IMPERIALISM IN SENEGAL-- SINE-SALOUM, 1847-1941.
STANFORD, CALIFORNIA, STANFORD UNIVERSITY PRESS, 1967
034,130-02,
      REFERENCE

034
  MARTIN B G
  MUSLIM POLITICS AND RESISTANCE TO COLONIAL RULE.
  IN JOURNAL OF AFRICAN HISTORY VOL 10 1969 P 471
  034,
      REFERENCE

  MUFFETT DAVID M J
  CONCERNING BRAVE CAPTAINS-- BEING A HISTORY OF THE BRITISH
  OCCUPATION OF KANO AND SOKOTO AND OF THE LAST STAND OF THE
  FULANI FORCES.
  LONDON, A DEUTSCH, 1964
  034,128-02,
      REFERENCE

  RANGER TERENCE O
  CONNEXIONS BETWEEN PRIMARY RESISTANCE MOVEMENTS AND
  MODERN MASS NATIONALISM IN EAST AND CENTRAL AFRICA 2 PARTS
  JOURNAL OF AFRICAN HISTORY 9 1968 PP 437-453 AND 631-642
  034,055,
      REFERENCE

  RANGER TERENCE O
  REVOLT IN SOUTHERN RHODESIA, 1896-97--A STUDY IN AFRICAN
  RESISTANCE.
  EVANSTON, NORTHWESTERN UNIVERSITY PRESS, 1967 (LONDON,
  HEINEMANN EDUCATIONAL BOOKS)
  034, 145-02,
      REFERENCE

  ROTBERG ROBERT I
  THE CONSOLIDATION OF THE COLONIAL INITIATIVE, 1891-1918
  CHAPTER 9.
  IN A POLITICAL HISTORY OF TROPICAL AFRICA, NEW YORK,
  HARCOURT, BRACE AND WORLD, 1965, PP 286-314
  034,
      REFERENCE

  BEACHEY R W
  THE ARMS TRADE IN EAST AFRICA IN THE LATE
  NINETEENTH CENTURY.
  JOURNAL OF AFRICAN HISTORY 3 1962 PP 451-467
  034,
      CASE STUDY

  BELL R M
  THE MAJI-MAJI REBELLION IN THE LIWALE DISTRICT.
  TANGANYIKA NOTES AND RECORDS 28 1950 PP 38-57
  034,136-02,
      CASE STUDY

  FALLERS LLOYD A
  THE KING'S MEN-- LEADERSHIP AND STATUS IN BUGANDA ON THE
  EVE OF INDEPENDENCE.

LONDON OXFORD UNIVERSITY PRESS 1964
034,038,139-03,
      CASE STUDY

034
   GWASSA G C K   ILIFFE JOHN   EDS
   RECORDS OF THE MAJI MAJI RISING.
   NAIROBI, EAST AFRICAN PUBLISHING HOUSE(AND EVANSTON,
   NORTHWESTERN UNIVERSITY PRESS), 1967
   034,
         CASE STUDY

   HOLT PETER M
   THE MAHDIST STATE IN THE SUDAN -- 1881-1898.
   OXFORD, CLARENDON PRESS, 1958
   034,134-02,
         CASE STUDY

   IKIME OBARO
   MERCHANT PRINCE OF THE NIGER DELTA-THE RISE AND FALL OF NANA
   OLOMU,LAST GOVERNOR OF THE BENIN RIVER
   NEW YORK, AFRICAN PUBLISHING CORPORATION, 1969
   034,
         CASE STUDY

   ILIFFE JOHN
   THE ORGANIZATION OF THE MAJI MAJI REBELLION.
   THE JOURNAL OF AFRICAN HISTORY 8 1967 PP 495-512
   034,136-02,
         CASE STUDY

   MURIUKI G
   KIKUYU REACTION TO TRADERS AND BRITISH ADMINISTRATION 1850-
   1904
   IN OGOT-ED-HADITH 1, NAIROBI, EAST AFRICAN PUBLISHING HOUSE
   1967 PP 101-118
   034,
         CASE STUDY

   MWASE GEORGE SIMEON ROTBERG ROBERT   ED
   STRIKE A BLOW AND DIE.
   CAMBRIDGE, HARVARD UNIVERSITY PRESS, 1967
   034, 122-02,
         CASE STUDY

   RANGER TERENCE O
   THE ORGANIZATION OF THE REBELLIONS OF 1896 AND 1897.
   CONFERENCE OF THE HISTORY OF CENTRAL AFRICAN PEOPLES,
   LUSAKA, RHODES-LIVINGSTONE INSTITUTE, 1963
   034,
         CASE STUDY

   RANGER TERENCE O
   REVOLT IN PORTUGUESE EAST AFRICA-- THE MAKOMBE RISING OF
   1917.
   ST ANTHONY'S PAPERS 15 1963 PP 54-80, AFRICAN AFFAIRS 2
   034,
         CASE STUDY

   REDMAYNE ALISON

MKWAWA AND THE HEHE WARS
JOURNAL OF AFRICAN HISTORY 9 1968 PP 409-436
034,
        CASE STUDY

034

    SANDERSON G N
    THE FOREIGN POLICY OF THE NEGUS MENELIK, 1896-1898.
    JOURNAL OF AFRICAN HISTORY 5 1964 PP 87-98
    034,110-02,
        CASE STUDY

    SHEPPERSON GEORGE   PRICE THOMAS
    INDEPENDENT AFRICAN-- JOHN CHILEMBWE AND THE ORIGINS SETTING
    AND SIGNIFICANCE OF THE NYASALAND RISING OF 1915.
    EDINBURGH,EDINBURGH UNIVERSITY PRESS,1958
    034,122-02,
        CASE STUDY

    THEOBALD A B
    THE MAHDIYA-- A HISTORY OF THE ANGLO-EGYPTIAN SUDAN 1881-
    1899.
    LONDON,LONGMANS,1951
    034,052,134-02,
        CASE STUDY

    WASSERMAN B
    THE ASHANTI WAR OF 1900-A STUDY OF CULTURAL CONFLICT
    AFRICA 31 1961 PP 167-179
    034,
        CASE STUDY

    ADIMOLA A B
    THE LAMOGI REBELLION 1911-1912.
    THE UGANDA JOURNAL 18 1954 PP 166-177
    034,139-02,
        LESS ACCESSIBLE

    GREENFIELD RICHARD
    ETHIOPIA--A NEW POLITICAL HISTORY.
    LONDON, PALL MALL, 1967
    034,110-07,

35. THE NATURE OF COLONIAL SYSTEMS

035
    BUELL RAYMOND L
    THE NATIVE PROBLEM IN AFRICA.
    HAMDEN,CONNECTICUT, ARCHON PRESS,1965
    035,
        AUTHOR WAS PROFESSOR AT HARVARD WHO TRAVELLED WIDELY
        IN AFRICA. BOOK IS MONUMENTAL IN SCOPE AND INSIGHT,
        COVERING COLONIAL SITUATIONS IN BRITISH, BELGIUM, AND
        FRENCH AFRICA. STILL REMAINS USEFUL SOURCE OF DATA ON
        EARLY COLONIAL PERIOD, HAS BEEN REPRINTED IN 1965.

035
CROWDER MICHAEL   IKIME OBARO   EDS
WEST AFRICAN CHIEFS--THEIR CHANGING STATUS UNDER COLONIAL
RULE AND INDEPENDENCE.
NEW YORK, AFRICANA PUBLISHING CORPORATION, FORTHCOMING
009,013,035,
          CASE STUDIES FROM WEST AFRICA--PRIMARILY NIGERIA--ON
          CHANGING ROLE OF CHIEFS. CONTAINS CASE STUDIES OF PAT-
          TERNS WHICH PROVIDE INSIGHT INTO DISTINCTION BETWEEN
          'DIRECT' AND 'INDIRECT' RULE. TO LESSER EXTENT, DEALS
          WITH CONTEMPORARY ISSUES ON MODERN ROLE OF CHIEFS.

LUGARD FREDERICK D
THE DUAL MANDATE IN BRITISH TROPICAL AFRICA.
LONDON, CASS,1965
035,
          AUTHOR WAS ONE OF MAJOR BRITISH COLONIAL GOVERNORS IN
          AFRICA, AND IS CREDITED WITH INCEPTION OF SO-CALLED
           INDIRECT RULE THEORY. THIS VOLUME OUTLINES THE
          PRINCIPLES OF INDIRECT RULE WITH REGARD TO DEALINGS
          WITH INDIGENOUS PEOPLES, TAXATION, LAW, ETC. FIRST
          PUBLISHED IN 1922, BECAME BIBLE FOR ADMINISTRATORS IN
          NIGERIA.

MANNONI DOMINIQUE O
PROSPERO AND CALIBAN-- THE PSYCHOLOGY OF COLONIZATION.
LONDON, METHUEN AND COMPANY, 1956 (NEW YORK, PRAEGER, 1964)
035,041,088,121-03,
          AUTHOR ASSESSES PSYCHOLOGICAL IMPACT OF COLONIAL RE-
          LATIONSHIP ON BOTH THE EUROPEAN IN AFRICA AND ON THE
          INDIGENOUS POPULATIONS. FOCUSED ON MADAGASCAR, BUT
          HAS BROAD INSIGHTS INTO THE NATURE OF COLONIAL SYSTEMS
          IN OTHER AREAS. SUGGESTS THAT SUPERIOR-SUBORDINATE
          RELATIONSHIP IS DAMAGING TO BOTH AFRICANS AND EUROPE-
          ANS. BOOK IS IMPRESSIONISTIC RATHER THAN BASED ON
          SPECIFIC RESEARCH.

MAZRUI ALI A   ROTBERG ROBERT I   EDS
THE TRADITIONS OF PROTEST IN BLACK AFRICA, 1886-1966.
CAMBRIDGE, MASSACHUSETTS, HARVARD UNIVERSITY PRESS, 1970
034,035,
          ORIGINAL ESSAYS BY WELL-KNOWN SCHOLARS. FIRST THREE
          SECTIONS OF BOOK DEAL WITH RESISTANCE TO CONQUEST (HE-
          HE WARS, SAMORY, MENELIK AT ADOWA, UMBUNDU), EARLY RE-
          BELLIONS AGAINST ALIEN RULE (MAJI MAJI, ZULU REBELLION
          IN 1906, CHILEMBWE, BAI BUREH, NYABINGI), AND RELIGI-
          OUS EXPRESSION OF DISCONTENT (NEO-CHRISTIAN FORMS AND
          NEO-ISLAMIC FORMS).

MOREL E D
RED RUBBER-THE STORY OF THE RUBBER SLAVE TRADE FLOURISHING
ON THE CONGO IN THE YEAR OF GRACE 1906
LONDON,FISHER UNWIN,1906
035,108-02,
          EXPOSE OF KING LEOPOLD'S SYSTEM OF EXPLOITATION IN THE
          CONGO.HAD A PROFOUND EFFECT ON SUBSEQUENT BELGIAN
          COLONIAL POLICY AND INFLUENCED THE ATTITUDES OF OTHER
          EUROPEAN POWERS

AUSTEN RALPH A
NORTHWEST TANZANIA UNDER GERMAN AND BRITISH RULE.
NEW HAVEN, CONN. (YALE), MCGILL-QUEEN'S PRESS, 1969
035,136-02,
    REFERENCE

035
  AZIKIWE NNAMDI
  ETHICS OF COLONIAL IMPERIALISM.
  JOURNAL OF NEGRO HISTORY 16 JULY 1931 PP 287-308
  035,128-04,
      REFERENCE

  BALANDIER GEORGES
  LA SITUATION COLONIALE-- APPROCHE THEORETIQUE
  (THE COLONIAL SITUATION-- THEORETICAL APPROACH).
  CAHIERS INTERNATIONAUX DE SOCIOLOGIE 11 1951 PP 44-79,
  IN PIERRE VAN DEN BERGHE, AFRICA-- SOCIAL PROBLEMS OF
  035,
      REFERENCE

  BENNETT GEORGE
  SETTLERS AND POLITICS IN KENYA UP TO 1945.
  IN VINCENT HARLOW AND E M CHILVER (EDS), HISTORY OF EAST
  AFRICA VOL II, OXFORD, CLARENDON PRESS, 1965, PP 265-332
  035,117-02,
      REFERENCE

  COHEN ANDREW
  BRITISH POLICY IN CHANGING AFRICA.
  LONDON, ROUTLEDGE AND KEGAN PAUL, 1959
  035,
      REFERENCE

  CROWDER MICHAEL
  WEST AFRICA UNDER COLONIAL RULE.
  LONDON, HUTCHINSON; EVANSTON, NORTHWESTERN UNIVERSITY PRESS,
  1968
  034,035,
      REFERENCE

  CROWDER MICHAEL
  INDIRECT RULE FRENCH AND BRITISH STYLE.
  AFRICA 34 1964 PP 197-205
  035,
      REFERENCE

  DELAVIGNETTE R L
  FREEDOM AND AUTHORITY IN FRENCH WEST AFRICA.
  LONDON, OXFORD UNIVERSITY PRESS, 1950
  035,
      REFERENCE

  DUFFY JAMES
  PORTUGAL IN AFRICA.
  IN PHILIP W QUIGG (ED.), AFRICA, NEW YORK, PRAEGER, 1964,
  PP 86-102
  035,087,144-06,
      REFERENCE

GANN LEWIS H   DUIGNAN PETER
BURDEN OF EMPIRE--AN APPRAISAL OF WESTERN COLONIALISM IN
AFRICA SOUTH OF THE SAHARA.
NEW YORK, PRAEGER, 1967
035,
     REFERENCE

035
HAILEY LORD
AN AFRICAN SURVEY-- A STUDY OF PROBLEMS ARISING IN AFRICA
SOUTH OF THE SAHARA.
LONDON, OXFORD UNIVERSITY PRESS, 1957
035,
     REFERENCE

HAILEY LORD
NATIVE ADMINISTRATION IN BRITISH AFRICAN TERRITORIES.
LONDON, HER MAJESTY'S STATIONERY OFFICE, 1950-1953, 5VOLS
035,
     REFERENCE

HENDERSON WILLIAM O
STUDIES IN GERMAN COLONIAL HISTORY.
LONDON, CASS, 1962
035,
     REFERENCE

HERSKOVITS MELVILLE J
NATIVE SELF-GOVERNMENT.
IN PHILIP W QUIGG (ED.), AFRICA, NEW YORK, PRAEGER, 1964,
PP 103-113
035,
     REFERENCE

ILIFFE JOHN
TANGANYIKA UNDER GERMAN RULE 1905-1912.
LONDON, CAMBRIDGE UNIVERSITY PRESS, 1969
035,136-02,
     REFERENCE

KIRK-GREENE A H M   ED
LUGARD AND THE AMALGAMATION OF NIGERIA--A DOCUMENTARY
RECORD.
LONDON, FRANK CASS AND COMPANY LIMITED, 1968
035,128-02,
     REFERENCE

KNIGHT M M
FRENCH COLONIAL POLICY-- THE DECLINE OF ASSOCIATION.
JOURNAL OF MODERN HISTORY 5 1933 PP 208-224
035,
     REFERENCE

LEWIS MARTIN D
ONE HUNDRED MILLION FRENCHMEN-- THE ASSIMILATION THEORY IN
FRENCH COLONIAL POLICY.
COMPARATIVE STUDIES IN SOCIETY AND HISTORY 4 1962 PP 129-153
035,
     REFERENCE

LUGARD FREDERICK D
THE WHITE MAN'S TASK IN TROPICAL AFRICA.
IN PHILIP W QUIGG (ED.), AFRICA, NEW YORK, PRAEGER, 1964,
PP 5-16
035,
        REFERENCE

035

MAIR LUCY P
NATIVE POLICIES IN AFRICA.
LONDON, G ROUTLEDGE, 1936
035,
        REFERENCE

MIDDLETON JOHN
KENYA-- CHANGES IN AFRICAN LIFE, 1912-1945.
IN VINCENT HARLOW AND E M CHILVER (EDS), HISTORY OF EAST
AFRICA VOL II, OXFORD, CLARENDON PRESS, 1965, PP 333-394
035,117-02,
        REFERENCE

NEWBURY COLIN W
THE GOVERNMENT GENERAL AND POLITICAL CHANGE IN FRENCH WEST
AFRICA.
ST ANTHONY'S PAPERS 10, SOUTHERN ILLINOIS UNIVERSITY PRESS,
1961, PP 41-59
035,
        REFERENCE

OLIVER ROLAND   ATMORE ANTHONY
THE INTER-WAR PERIOD, 1918-1938
IN AFRICA SINCE 1800, CAMBRIDGE, CAMBRIDGE UNIVERSITY PRESS,
1967, PP 160-171
035,
        REFERENCE

OLIVER ROLAND   ATMORE ANTHONY
COLONIAL RULE IN TROPICAL AFRICA-- SOCIAL AND RELIGIOUS
DEVELOPMENTS.
IN AFRICA SINCE 1800, CAMBRIDGE, CAMBRIDGE UNIVERSITY PRESS,
1967, PP 141-159
035,050,
        REFERENCE

PERHAM MARGERY
COLONIAL SEQUENCE 1930-1949.
LONDON, METHUEN AND CO, 1967
035,
        REFERENCE

PERHAM MARGERY
THE BRITISH PROBLEM IN AFRICA.
IN PHILIP W QUIGG (ED.), AFRICA, NEW YORK, PRAEGER, 1964,
PP 131-144
035,
        REFERENCE

ROBINSON KENNETH
COLONIAL ISSUES AND POLICIES WITH SPECIAL REFERENCE TO
TROPICAL AFRICA.

ANNALS OF THE AMERICAN ACADEMY OF POLITICAL AND SOCIAL
SCIENCES MARCH 1955 PP 84-94
035,
        REFERENCE

035
   ROBINSON KENNETH
   THE DILEMMAS OF TRUSTEESHIP-- ASPECTS OF BRITISH COLONIAL
   POLICY BETWEEN THE WARS.
   LONDON, OXFORD UNIVERSITY PRESS, 1965
   035,
        REFERENCE

   ROTBERG ROBERT I
   THE ADMINISTRATIVE INTERLUDE, 1919-1939 CHAPTER 10.
   IN A POLITICAL HISTORY OF TROPICAL AFRICA, NEW YORK,
   HARCOURT, BRACE AND WORLD, 1965, PP 315-347
   035,
        REFERENCE

   WHITTLESEY DERWENT
   BRITISH AND FRENCH COLONIAL TECHNIQUE IN WEST AFRICA.
   IN PHILIP W QUIGG (ED.), AFRICA, NEW YORK, PRAEGER, 1964
   PP 57-70
   035,
        REFERENCE

   AMENUMEY D E K
   GERMAN ADMINISTRATION IN SOUTHERN TOGO.
   IN JOURNAL OF AFRICAN HISTORY VOL 10 1969 P 623
   035,
        CASE STUDY

   BRAUSCH GEORGES
   BELGIAN ADMINISTRATION IN THE CONGO.
   LONDON, OXFORD UNIVERSITY PRESS, 1961
   035,108-06,
        CASE STUDY

   BURNS ALAN C
   COLONIAL CIVIL SERVANT.
   LONDON, ALLEN AND UNWIN, 1949
   035,
        CASE STUDY

   CAMERON SIR D
   MY TANGANYIKA SERVICE AND SOME NIGERIA.
   LONDON, ALLEN AND UNWIN, 1939
   035,128-02,136-02,
        CASE STUDY

   CHIDZERO BERNARD T
   TANGANYIKA AND INTERNATIONAL TRUSTEESHIP.
   LONDON, OXFORD UNIVERSITY PRESS, 1961
   035,136-02,
        CASE STUDY

   COOK ARTHUR NORTON
   BRITISH ENTERPRISE IN NIGERIA.
   PHILADELPHIA, UNIVERSITY OF PENNSYLVANIA PRESS, 1943

035,128-08,
        CASE STUDY

035

    CROWDER MICHAEL
    SENEGAL-- A STUDY IN FRENCH ASSIMILATION POLICY.
    LONDON,OXFORD UNIVERSITY,1962 (REVISED,METHUEN,1967)
    035,130-02,
        CASE STUDY

    DILLEY MARJORIE R
    BRITISH POLICY IN KENYA COLONY
    LONDON,FRANK CASS,1966,SECOND EDITION
    035,117-02,
        CASE STUDY

    EAST AFRICA ROYAL COMMISSION
    EAST AFRICA ROYAL COMMISSION 1953-1955 REPORT.
    LONDON,HER MAJESTY'S STATIONERY OFFICE,COMMAND PAPER NO 9475
    REPRINT 482 1961
    035,045,
        CASE STUDY

    FLINT J E
    ZANZIBAR, 1890-1950.
    IN VINCENT HARLOW AND E M CHILVER (EDS),HISTORY OF EAST
    AFRICA VOL II,OXFORD,CLARENDON PRESS,1965,PP 641-671
    035,136-02,
        CASE STUDY

    GORDON DAVID C
    NORTH AFRICA'S FRENCH LEGACY 1954-1962.
    CAMBRIDGE, MASS,HARVARD UNIVERSITY PRESS,1962
    035,
        CASE STUDY

    HESS ROBERT L
    ITALIAN COLONIALISM IN SOMALIA
    CHICAGO,UNIVERSITY OF CHICAGO PRESS,1966
    035,
        CASE STUDY

    HEUSSLER ROBERT
    THE BRITISH IN NORTHERN NIGERIA.
    LONDON, OXFORD UNIVERSITY PRESS, 1968
    035,128-02,
        CASE STUDY

    HUXLEY ELSPETH
    WHITE MAN'S COUNTRY-- LORD DELAMERE AND THE MAKING OF KENYA.
    LONDON,CHATTO AND WINDUS,1953
    035,117-02,
        CASE STUDY

    INGHAM KENNETH
    TANGANYIKA-- SLUMP AND SHORT-TERM GOVERNORS, 1932-1945.
    IN VINCENT HARLOW AND E M CHILVER (EDS),HISTORY OF EAST
    AFRICA VOL II,OXFORD,CLARENDON PRESS,1965, PP 594-624
    035,136-02,
        CASE STUDY

035

INGHAM KENNETH
TANGANYIKA-- THE MANDATE AND CAMEROUN, 1919-1931.
IN VINCENT HARLOW AND E M CHILVER (EDS), HISTORY OF EAST
AFRICA VOL II, OXFORD, CLARENDON PRESS, 1965, PP 543-593
035,136-02,
        CASE STUDY

JONES GWILYN I
THE TRADING STATES OF THE OIL RIVERS-- A STUDY OF
POLITICAL DEVELOPMENT IN EASTERN NIGERIA.
LONDON, OXFORD UNIVERSITY PRESS, 1963
027,035,128-02,
        CASE STUDY

KIRK-GREENE A H M
THE PRINCIPLES OF NATIVE ADMINISTRATION IN NIGERIA--
SELECTED DOCUMENTS 1900-1947.
LONDON, OXFORD UNIVERSITY PRESS, 1965
035,128-02,
        CASE STUDY

LIEBENOW J GUS
COLONIAL RULE AND POLITICAL DEVELOPMENT IN TANZANIA-THE
CASE OF THE MAKONDE
EVANSTON, NORTHWESTERN UNIVERSITY PRESS, 1970
035,055,063,136-07,
        CASE STUDY

LOW DAVID A   PRATT R CRANFORD
BUGANDA AND BRITISH OVERRULE 1900-1955.
LONDON, OXFORD UNIVERSITY PRESS, 1960
035,139-02,
        CASE STUDY

MAIR LUCY P
NATIVE ADMINISTRATION IN CENTRAL NYASALAND.
LONDON, HIS MAJESTY'S STATIONERY OFFICE, 1952
035,122-02,
        CASE STUDY

MARIE-ANDRE SISTER
TRIBAL LABOUR AND SOCIAL LEGISLATION IN FRENCH TROPICAL
AFRICA.
INTERNATIONAL LABOUR REVIEW 68 DECEMBER 1953 PP 493-508
035,
        CASE STUDY

MIDDLETON JOHN
KENYA-- ADMINISTRATION AND CHANGES IN AFRICAN LIFE
1912-45 CHAPTER 7.
IN ROLAND OLIVER AND GERVASE MATHEW, HISTORY OF EAST

AFRICA, 2, LONDON, OXFORD UNIVERSITY PRESS, 1965,
PP 333-392
035,117-03,
        CASE STUDY

035

MORGAN W T W
THE 'WHITE HIGHLANDS' OF KENYA.
GEOGRAPHICAL JOURNAL 129 JUNE 1963 PP 140-155
035,117-02,
        CASE STUDY

MUNGEAM G H
BRITISH RULE IN KENYA 1895-1912
OXFORD, CLARENDON PRESS, 1967
035,117-02,
        CASE STUDY

PADEN JOHN N
ASPECTS OF EMIRSHIP IN KANO
IN MICHAEL CROWDER AND OBARO IKIME (EDS), WEST AFRICAN CHIEFS-
THEIR CHANGING STATUS UNDER COLONIAL RULE AND INDEPENDENCE,
NEW YORK, AFRICANA PUBLISHING CORPORATION, 1970
035,
        CASE STUDY

PERHAM MARGERY
LUGARD-- THE YEARS OF ADVENTURE.
LONDON, COLLINS, 1956
035,
        CASE STUDY

PERHAM MARGERY
LUGARD-- THE YEARS OF AUTHORITY.
LONDON, COLLINS, 1960
035,
        CASE STUDY

PERHAM MARGERY
THE SYSTEM OF NATIVE ADMINISTRATION IN   TANGANYIKA.
AFRICA 2 1931 PP 302-312
035,136-02,
        CASE STUDY

PERHAM MARGERY
NATIVE ADMINISTRATION IN NIGERIA.
LONDON, OXFORD UNIVERSITY PRESS, 1961
035,128-02,
        CASE STUDY

PERHAM MARGERY   HUXLEY ELSPETH
RACE AND POLITICS IN KENYA.
LONDON, FABER, 1944
035,117-06,
        CASE STUDY

PRATT R CRANFORD
ADMINISTRATION AND POLITICS IN UGANDA, 1919-1945.
IN VINCENT HARLOW AND E M CHILVER (EDS), HISTORY OF EAST
AFRICA VOL II, OXFORD, CLARENDON PRESS, 1965, PP 476-542

035,139-02,
     CASE STUDY

035

ROTBERG ROBERT I
THE FEDERATION MOVEMENT IN BRITISH EAST AND CENTRAL AFRICA
1889-1953.
JOURNAL OF COMMONWEALTH POLITICAL STUDIES 2 1964 PP 141-160
035,
     CASE STUDY

RYCKMANS PIERRE
BELGIAN COLONIALISM .
IN PHILIP Q QUIGG (ED), AFRICA, NEW YORK, PRAEGER, 1964,
PP 71-83 ALSO FOREIGN AFFAIRS 34 1955 PP 89-101
035,108-02,
     CASE STUDY

SLADE RUTH
KING LEOPOLD S CONGO.
LONDON,OXFORD UNIVERSITY PRESS,1962
035,108-02,
     CASE STUDY

VAN VELSEN J
THE ESTABLISHMENT OF THE ADMINISTRATION IN TONGALAND.
SALISBURY, HISTORIANS IN TROPICAL AFRICA, UNIVERSITY
COLLEGE OF RHODESIA AND NYASALAND, 1962, PP 177-196
035,142-02,
     CASE STUDY

ASSOCIATION DES ANCIENS ETUDIANTS DE L'INUTOM
L'EVOLUTION POLITIQUE DU CONGO BELGE ET LES AUTORITES
INDIGENES (POLITICAL EVOLUTION OF THE BELGIAN CONGO AND THE
NATIVE AUTHORITIES).
PROBLEMS DE L'AFRIQUE CENTRALE 13 1959 PP 3-77
035,108-07,
     LESS ACCESSIBLE

DESCHAMPS HUBERT J
METHODES ET DOCTRINES COLONIALES DE LA FRANCE (FRENCH
COLONIAL DOCTRINES AND METHODS).
PARIS,LIBRARIE ARMAND COLIN,1953
035,
     LESS ACCESSIBLE

GIDE ANDRE
VOYAGE AU CONGO (VOYAGE TO THE CONGO).
PARIS,GALLIMARD,1929
035,108-02,
     LESS ACCESSIBLE

FURNIVALL JOHN S
COLONIAL POLICY AND PRACTICE.
CAMBRIDGE,ENGLAND,CAMBRIDGE UNIVERSITY PRESS,1948
035,057,
     GENERAL THEORY

PRIESTLEY HERBERT
FRANCE OVERSEAS-- A STUDY OF MODERN IMPERIALISM.

NEW YORK, APPLETON-CENTURY, 1938
035,
        GENERAL THEORY

36. STUDY QUESTIONS: PERSPECTIVES
   ON THE PAST

036
AJAYI J F ADE   ESPIE IAN   EDS
A THOUSAND YEARS OF WEST AFRICAN HISTORY-- A HANDBOOK FOR
TEACHERS AND STUDENTS.
IBADAN, IBADAN UNIVERSITY PRESS; ALSO LONDON, THOMAS NELSON
AND SONS, 1965
001,036,
        MAJOR THEMES IN WEST AFRICAN HISTORY INTERPRETED BY
        SCHOLARS CURRENTLY WORKING IN THE FIELD. LIKE ANENE
        AND BROWN, A PRODUCT OF WORKSHOP ON TEACHING AFRICAN
        HISTORY HELD AT IBADAN, 1965. EMPHASIS ON AFRICAN-
        NESS AND AVOIDANCE OF EUROPEAN ETHNOCENTRISM. NEARLY
        HALF OF CONTRIBUTORS WEST AFRICAN. COVERS PERIOD FROM
        A.D. 1000 TO THE PRESENT. FOREWARD BY K. O. DIKE.

COLLINS ROBERT O   ED
PROBLEMS IN AFRICAN HISTORY.
ENGLEWOOD CLIFFS, NEW JERSEY, PRENTICE-HALL, INC., 1968
009,019,020,036,
        EDITOR HAS ARRANGED ARTICLES BY MAJOR SCHOLARS INTO
        SEVEN PARTS--AFRICA AND EGYPT, BANTU ORIGINS AND MIGRA-
        TIONS, NILOTIC ORIGINS AND MIGRATIONS, THE HISTORIAN
        AND STATELESS SOCIETIES, AFRICAN STATES, TRADE IN PRE-
        COLONIAL AFRICA, AND THE AFRICAN SLAVE TRADE. THIS
        VOLUME IS INTENDED FOR TEACHING PURPOSES AND IS AVAIL-
        ABLE IN PAPERBACK.

CURTIN PHILIP D
AFRICAN HISTORY.
NEW YORK, MACMILLAN CO, 1964
036,
        A SHORT EXPOSITORY SYNTHESIS AND BIBLIOGRAPHIC ESSAY
        AIMED AT TEACHERS OF AFRICAN HISTORY. REMARKABLY SUC-
        CINCT AND PERCEPTIVE IN ITS TREATMENT OF MAJOR THEMES,
        CRITICISM OF BIAS IN MANY EXISTING WORKS AND SUGGES-
        TIONS OF FUTURE RESEARCH FRONTIERS. AN EXCELLENT
        STARTING POINT FOR ANY ANALYSIS OF AFRICAN HISTORY OR
        SOURCE FOR DISCUSSION QUESTIONS.

DAVIDSON BASIL   EDITORS OF TIME-LIFE
AFRICAN KINGDOMS.
NEW YORK, TIME INCORPORATED, 1966
036,
        PART OF TIME-LIFE'S POPULAR SERIES ON GREAT AGES OF
        MAN--HISTORY OF WORLD CULTURES. EIGHT SECTIONS, EACH
        WITH TEXTUAL INTRODUCTION AND PICTORIAL ESSAY CONCEN-
        TRATE ON BOTH LARGE CENTRALIZED STATES AND SMALL-SCALE
        VILLAGE SOCIETIES. STRONGLY ORIENTED TOWARD THE HERI-
        TAGE OF AFRICAN ART, SCULPTURE AND URBAN DESIGN. EX-

CELLENT MAPS AND EXTREMELY GOOD PHOTOGRAPHS.

036

DAVIDSON BASIL
THE AFRICAN PAST-- CHRONICLES FROM ANTIQUITY TO
MODERN TIMES.
BOSTON, LITTLE, BROWN, 1964; PENGUIN, 1966
036,
> OUTSTANDING ANTHOLOGY OF HISTORICAL DOCUMENTS AND
> ACADEMIC STUDIES. SOURCES COVER ANTIQUITY (KUSH,
> MEROE), EARLY WEST AFRICA (NOK, YORUBA, STATE FORMA-
> TION), EARLY EAST AFRICA (KILWA, SWAHILI), THROUGH
> EARLY WESTERN CONTACTS (SLAVE TRADE, SOUTH AFRICA),
> EXPLORATION AND COLONIALISM, TO CONTEMPORARY
> PERSPECTIVES. INTRODUCTION AND CONNECTING PIECES BY
> AUTHOR PROVIDE EXCELLENT NARRATIVE BACKGROUND.

DAVIDSON BASIL
THE LOST CITIES OF AFRICA.
BOSTON, LITTLE, BROWN AND CO., 1959
036,
> OUTSTANDING POPULAR INTRODUCTION TO PRECOLONIAL
> AFRICA. COVERS EARLY MIGRATIONS, KUSH, MEROWE AND
> AXUM, NOK, GHANA, MALI AND SONGHAY, THE WEST AFRICA
> FOREST STATES, THE EAST AFRICAN COAST, ZIMBABWE AND
> THE CENTRAL AFRICAN INTERIOR. FINAL SECTIONS OFFER
> STIMULATING PERSPECTIVE ON AFRICAN HISTORY.
> CHALLENGING, INFORMATIVE AND VERY WELL WRITTEN.

DAVIDSON BASIL
AFRICA IN HISTORY.
NEW YORK, MACMILLAN, 1968
001,028,036,
> A MUCH EXPANDED AND UPDATED EDITION OF 'AFRICA--HISTORY
> OF A CONTINENT' (WITHOUT THE PHOTOGRAPHS). VERY WELL
> WRITTEN CHRONOLOGICAL SYNTHESIS FOR THE ENTIRE CONTI-
> NENT AND PARTICULARLY HELPFUL IN IDENTIFYING BROAD
> THEMES AND OUTLINES. A MUCH MORE EFFECTIVE WRITTEN
> INTRODUCTION TO AFRICAN HISTORY THAN THE 1966 VOLUME.

DE GRAFT-JOHNSON J
AFRICAN GLORY-- THE STORY OF VANISHED NEGRO CIVILIZATIONS.
NEW YORK, WALKER, 1966
036,
> BOOK IS POPULAR ACCOUNT OF PRE-COLONIAL AFRICAN KING-
> DOMS. DISCUSSES ROMAN NORTH AFRICA, MUSLIM INVASION
> OF AFRICA, RISE OF AFRICAN EMPIRES SUCH GHANA, MALI,
> SONGHAI, EARLY PORTUGUESE CONTACT IN EAST, WEST, AND
> CENTRAL AFRICA, AND THE IMPACT OF THE SLAVE TRADE.

FAGE JOHN D
AN ATLAS OF AFRICAN HISTORY
LONDON, EDWARD ARNOLD, 1958
036,
> THE BEST EXISTING ATLAS ON AFRICAN HISTORY.COVERS
> WIDE RANGE OF SUBJECTS FROM EARLY STATE FORMATION TO
> MODERN ECONOMIC DEVELOPMENT.BECOMING DATED BUT STILL
> STANDARD WORK.

FAGE JOHN D   ED

AFRICA DISCOVERS HER PAST
NEW YORK, OXFORD UNIVERSITY PRESS, 1969
036, 100,
    VOLUME OF ESSAYS ASSESSES CURRENT METHODS AND
    FINDINGS OF RESEARCH IN AFRICAN HISTORY. ESPECIALLY
    GOOD ON COMPARATIVE ANALYSIS OF ORAL, DOCUMENTARY, AND
    ARCHEOLOGICAL SOURCES. ALSO EXAMINES THE DEVELOPMENT
    OF HISTORICAL WRITING AND RESEARCH IN THE VARIOUS
    REGIONS OF AFRICA.

036
  FAGE JOHN D
  A HISTORY OF WEST AFRICA
  NEW YORK, CAMBRIDGE UNIVERSITY PRESS, 1969
  022, 026, 036,
    FOURTH EDITION OF CLASSIC INTRODUCTION TO WEST
    AFRICAN HISTORY. REWRITTEN AND REVISED TO INCLUDE TWO
    NEW CHAPTERS ON POLITICAL DEVELOPMENTS IN LOWER
    GUINEA AND ON DEVELOPMENTS IN THE INTERIOR OF WEST
    AFRICA IN THE NINETEENTH CENTURY. MANY EXCELLENT MAPS

  FORDE C DARYLL   KABERRY PHYLLIS M   EDS
  WEST AFRICAN KINGDOMS IN THE NINETEENTH CENTURY.
  LONDON, OXFORD UNIVERSITY PRESS, 1967
  026,036,
    OUTSTANDING COLLECTION OF ORIGINAL ESSAYS ON WEST AF-
    RICAN KINGDOMS. ESSAYS ALL BY SCHOLARS WHO HAVE DONE
    INTENSIVE FIELD RESEARCH, YET ALL IN THIS VOLUME TRY
    TO SYNTHESIZE DATA AND PATTERNS RATHER THAN PRESENT
    SPECIFIC RESEARCH. ESSAY BY IVOR WILKS ON ORGANIZA-
    TION OF ASHANTI BUREAUCRACY IS PARTICULARLY INSIGHT-
    FUL.

  MCCALL DANIEL F
  AFRICA IN TIME-PERSPECTIVE--A DISCUSSION OF HISTORICAL
  RECONSTRUCTION FROM UNWRITTEN SOURCES.
  NEW YORK, OXFORD UNIVERSITY PRESS, 1969
  036,
    ORIGINALLY PUBLISHED IN 1964. THE NEW PAPERBACK VERSION
    HAS UPDATED BIBLIOGRAPHY. DEALS WITH THE NATURE OF
    HISTORICAL EVIDENCE, AND THE WAYS IN WHICH CULTURAL
    ARTIFACTS, ETHNO-BOTANY, ETHNO-ZOOLOGY, LINGUISTICS,
    ROCK PAINTINGS, ETC. CAN BE USED TO RECONSTRUCT HISTORY
    IN PRE-LITERATE SOCIETIES.

  MCEWAN PETER J   ED
  AFRICA FROM EARLY TIMES TO 1800.
  LONDON, OXFORD UNIVERSITY PRESS, 1968
  001,036,
    FIRST OF THREE VOLUMES OF REPRINTS OF MAJOR ARTICLES
    IN AFRICAN HISTORY. INCLUDES WORKS BY J. D. CLARK, C.
    WRIGLEY, VANSINA, MAUNY, THOMAS, FAGE, URVOY, ROUCH,
    HODGKIN, MURDOCK, BRIGGS, B. LEWIS, POSNANSKY, MATHEW,
    BATES, SCHAPERA, BOVILL, DIKE, OLIVER, BOXER, BLAKE,
    PERHAM, JONES, I. M. LEWIS, TRIMINGHAM, ADLOFF, THOMP-
    SON, AJAYI, FERNANDEZ, CHRONOLOGICAL TABLE. BEST
    COLLECTION OF SUPPLEMENTARY READINGS ON THIS PERIOD.

  OGOT BETHWELL A   KIERAN J A
  ZAMANI. A SURVEY OF EAST AFRICAN HISTORY

NAIROBI, EAST AFRICAN PUBLISHING HOUSE, 1968
ALSO   AVAILABLE THROUGH NORTHWESTERN UNIVERSITY PRESS.
001,036,
    MOST RECENT CONTRIBUTION BY RESEARCH SCHOLARS IN THE
    FIELD SURVEYING MAJOR THEMES IN EAST AFRICAN HISTORY.
    COVERS PERIOD FROM EARLY COASTAL TRADE TO CONTEMPORARY
    NATIONALIST MOVEMENTS. OGOT   IS PROFESSOR OF HISTORY
    AT UNIVERSITY OF EAST AFRICA, NAIROBI, AND DIRECTOR OF
    THE EAST AFRICAN ACADEMY.
    SUGGESTS THAT WEST AF

036

  OGOT BETHWELL A   ED
  HADITH 1.
  KENYA, EAST AFRICAN PUBLISHING HOUSE, 1968
  036,
    PROCEEDINGS OF THE ANNUAL CONFERENCE OF THE HISTORICAL
    ASSOCIATION OF KENYA, 1967. INCLUDES PAPERS ON APPROA-
    CHES TO AFRICAN HISTORY (OGOT), CHRONOLOGY OF PASTORAL
    MAASAI (JACOBS), WANGA KINGDOM (OSOGO), URBAN DEVELOP-
    MENT IN MOMBASA (BERG AND WALTER), KIKUYU REACTION TO
    BRITISH (MURIUKI), LINGUISTICS AN HISTORICAL TOOL
    (EHRET), HISTORY SYLLABUSES (HARDYMAN) AND ARCHAEOLOGY
    (LOWTHER).

  OLIVER ROLAND   FAGE JOHN D
  A SHORT HISTORY OF AFRICA.
  BALTIMORE, PENGUIN BOOKS, 1962
  001,036,
    LANDMARK INTRODUCTION BY EDITORS OF JOURNAL OF AFRI-
    CAN HISTORY. EXCEPTIONALLY READABLE SYNTHESIS OF EXI-
    STING RESEARCH AND DISCOVERIES AND PERCEPTIVE PRESEN-
    TATION OF STILL EXISTING QUESTIONS AND PROBLEMS.
    RANGES FROM EARLY MAN TO INDEPENDENT AFRICA. EXCELL-
    ENT MAPS, EVALUATORY BIBLIOGRAPHY. NOW
    SLIGHTY DATED.

  OLIVER ROLAND   MATHEW GERVASE   EDS
  HISTORY OF EAST AFRICA, VOLUME ONE.
  OXFORD, CLARENDON PRESS, 1963
  023,036,
    FIRST ATTEMPT TO DRAW TOGETHER A COMPREHENSIVE HISTORY
    OF EAST AFRICA, BY THE OUTSTANDING SCHOLARS OF THE
    LATE 1950 S. IS NOW SLIGHTLY DATED, BUT REMAINS THE
    CORE WORK ON EAST AFRICA.

  RANGER TERENCE D   ED
  ASPECTS OF CENTRAL AFRICAN HISTORY.
  EVANSTON, NORTHWESTERN UNIVERSITY PRESS, 1968   (LONDON,
  HEINEMANN EDUCATIONAL BOOKS)
  025,036,
    OUTSTANDING RECENT SURVEY OF CENTRAL AFRICAN HISTORY.
    BEGINS WITH ZIMBABWE AND CONTINUES UNTIL NATIONALIST
    PERIOD. LARGELY WRITTEN BY YOUNG RESEARCH SCHOLARS
    WORKING IN THE FIELD, HENCE REPRESENTS MOST RECENT
    DATA.

  RANGER TERENCE O   ED
  EMERGING THEMES OF AFRICAN HISTORY.
  KENYA, EAST AFRICAN PUBLISHING HOUSE, 1965 (LONDON,

HEINEMANN EDUCATIONAL BOOKS)
036,
>   EDITED PAPERS EXPLORING FULL RANGE OF AFRICAN HISTORI-
>   CAL ISSUES--ISLAMIC HISTORIOGRAPHY, PERIODIZATION,
>   WESTERN HISTORIOGRAPHY, ARCHAEOLOGY, ETHNOGRAPHIC DATA,
>   ROLE OF THE PASTORALIST, THE SLAVE TRADE, THE AFRICAN
>   DIASPORA, RESISTANCE AND REBELLION, CONTINUITY OF AFRI-
>   CAN INSTITUTIONS UNDER COLONIALISM, AND THE EMERGENCE
>   OF NATIONS.

036

ROTBERG ROBERT I
A POLITICAL HISTORY OF TROPICAL AFRICA.
NEW YORK, HARCOURT, BRACE AND WORLD, 1965
001,036,
>   WELL DOCUMENTED THEMATIC HISTORY OF AFRICAN POLITICAL
>   DEVELOPMENT FROM ANCIENT TIMES TO EMPIRES AND CITY-
>   STATES (800-1500), EARLY EUROPEAN EXPANSION (1400-
>   1700), SAVANNA AND FOREST KINGDOMS (1500-1800), SLAVE
>   TRADE (1600-1800), INTERIOR DEVELOPMENTS (1800-1880),
>   AFRICA AND EUROPE (1788-1884), COLONIAL PARTITION
>   (1885-1902), CONSOLIDATION (1891-1918), ADMINISTRATION
>   (1919-39) AND NATIONALISM (1940-65). 48 PAGE BIBLIO-
>   GRAPHY.

WIEDNER DONALD
A HISTORY OF AFRICA SOUTH OF THE SAHARA.
NEW YORK, RANDOM HOUSE, 1962
036,
>   ORIGINAL AND SOMEWHAT CONTROVERSIAL INTRODUCTORY TEXT,
>   WITH THREE MAJOR SECTIONS-- OLD AFRICA, REMAKING
>   AFRICA AND NEW AFRICA. HIGHLIGHTED BY EXCELLENT MAPS.

DIKE K O
THE STUDY OF AFRICAN HISTORY.
IN LALAGE BOWN AND MICHAEL CROWDER (EDS.), PROCEEDINGS OF
THE FIRST INTERNATIONAL CONGRESS OF AFRICANISTS, ACCRA,
1962, LONDON, LONGMANS, 1964, PP 55-67
036,
>   REFERENCE

GABEL CREIGHTON   NORMAN BENNETT   EDS
RECONSTRUCTING AFRICAN CULTURE HISTORY.
BROOKLINE, BOSTON UNIVERSITY PRESS, 1967
036,
>   REFERENCE

GAVIN R J
THE MAKING OF MODERN AFRICA
VOL I--THE NINETEENTH CENTURY TO THE PARTITION.
NEW YORK, HUMANITIES PRESS, 1969
036,
>   REFERENCE

HALLETT ROBIN
AFRICA TO 1875
ANN ARBOR, UNIVERSITY OF MICHIGAN PRESS, 1969
036,
>   REFERENCE

HOWE RUSSELL WARREN
BLACK AFRICA-- AFRICA SOUTH OF THE SAHARA FROM PRE-
HISTORY TO INDEPENDENCE.
CHICAGO, WALKER, 1967
036,076,
        REFERENCE

036

INGHAM KENNETH
A HISTORY OF EAST AFRICA
NEW YORK, PRAEGER, 1967
036,
        REFERENCE

LEWIS I M
HISTORY AND SOCIAL ANTHROPOLOGY
LONDON, TAVISTOCK, 1968
036,
        REFERENCE

MCCALL DANIEL F   BENNETT NORMAN   BUTLER JEFFREY
EASTERN AFRICAN HISTORY
NEW YORK, PRAEGER, 1969
036,
        REFERENCE

MCCALL DANIEL F   BENNETT NORMAN   BUTLER JEFFREY
WESTERN AFRICAN HISTORY
NEW YORK, PRAEGER, 1969
036,
        REFERENCE

SINGLETON F SETH   SHINGLER JOHN
AFRICA IN PERSPECTIVE.
NEW YORK, HAYDEN BOOK COMPANY, 1967
036,
        REFERENCE

VANSINA JAN   ET AL   EDS
THE HISTORIAN IN TROPICAL AFRICA.
LONDON, OXFORD UNIVERSITY PRESS, 1964
036,099,
        REFERENCE

WILLETT FRANK
ARCHAEOLOGY IN AFRICA.
IN CARTER, GWENDOLEN M. AND ANN PADEN (EDS) EXPANDING
HORIZONS IN AFRICAN STUDIES, EVANSTON, NORTHWESTERN
UNIVERSITY PRESS, 1969, PP. 91-110
036,100,
        REFERENCE

USSR ACAD SCIENCES INSTITUTE OF AFRICA
A HISTORY OF AFRICA 1914-1967
MOSCOW, NAUKA PUBLISHING HOUSE CENTRAL DEPARTMENT OF ORIENTAL
LITERATURE, 1968
036,
        LESS ACCESSIBLE

PART III
Processes
of Change

37. CONCEPTS OF SOCIAL CHANGE AND MODERNIZATION

037

APTER DAVID E
THE POLITICS OF MODERNIZATION.
CHICAGO, UNIVERSITY OF CHICAGO PRESS, 1965
037,061,
     INFLUENTIAL THEORETICAL WORK BY SCHOLAR WITH EXTEN-
     SIVE AFRICAN EXPERIENCE. ANALYZES POLITICAL ASPECTS
     OF CHANGE, ESPECIALLY PATTERNS OF CONSOLIDATION OF
     AUTHORITY, THE ROLE OF POLITICAL LEADERSHIP, AND
     RELEVANCE OF WESTERN LIBERAL-DEMOCRATIC MODELS TO
     DEVELOPING COUNTRIES. MANY REFERENCES TO AFRICA.

BRODE JOHN
THE PROCESS OF MODERNIZATION--AN ANNOTATED BIBLIOGRAPHY ON
THE SOCIOCULTURAL ASPECTS OF DEVELOPMENT.
CAMBRIDGE, HARVARD UNIVERSITY PRESS, 1969
037,
     REFERENCES ARE DIVIDED INTO FOUR SECTIONS--GENERAL MO-
     DERNIZATION THEORY, INDUSTRIALIZATION, URBANIZATION,
     AND RURAL MODERNIZATION. BIBLIOGRAPHY IS PART OF LAR-
     GER PROJECT--SOCIOCULTURAL ASPECTS OF DEVELOPMENT, AT
     HARVARD UNIVERSITY, DIRECTED BY PROFESSOR ALEX INKELES.

DUMONT RENE
FALSE START IN AFRICA.

NEW YORK, PRAEGER PUBLISHERS, 1969
037,053,070,
> LEADING FRENCH AGRONOMIST, WITH SYMPATHY FOR AFRICAN
> INDEPENDENCE, MAKES CRITICAL AND CONTROVERSIAL ASSESS-
> MENT OF AFRICAN SOCIO-ECONOMIC DEVELOPMENT IN THE
> POST-COLONIAL PERIOD. EMPHASIZES THE NECESSITY FOR
> AGRICULTURAL REFORM TO PROVIDE CAPITAL BASIS FOR ECO-
> NOMIC TAKE-OFF INTO A FULLY INDUSTRIALIZED SOCIETY.

037

FINKLE JASON L   GABLE RICHARD W   EDS
POLITICAL DEVELOPMENT AND SOCIAL CHANGE.
NEW YORK, JOHN WILEY, 1966
037,
> SOCIAL-SCIENCE APPROACH TO SOCIAL CHANGE. REPRINTED
> ARTICLES-- SYSTEMS APPROACH (SOCIETIES AS SYSTEMS,
> TRADITIONAL AND TRANSITIONAL SOCIETIES)-- INDIVIDUALS
> AND IDEAS (ACHIEVEMENT MOTIVATION, IDEOLOGY, COMMUNI-
> CATIONS)-- CONCOMITANTS OF POLITICAL DEVELOPMENT (IN-
> DUSTRIALIZATION, URBANIZATION, ECONOMIC DEVELOPMENT)--
> MODERNIZERS (ELITES, MILITARY, BUREAUCRACY)-- POLITI-
> CAL DEVELOPMENT (SOCIAL STRATIFICATION, PARTY SYSTEMS,
> INTEGRATION).

GEERTZ CLIFFORD   ED
OLD SOCIETIES AND NEW STATES--THE QUEST FOR MODERNITY
IN ASIA AND AFRICA.
NEW YORK, FREE PRESS, 1963
037,
> ANTHOLOGY OF ORIGINAL CONCEPTUAL ESSAYS BY FACULTY
> AT UNIVERSITY OF CHICAGO'S NEW NATIONS INSTITUTE.
> GOOD RANGE OF COVERAGE, INCLUDING COMPARATIVE THEORY
> OF NEW STATES, CULTURAL POLICY IN NEW STATES, POLIT-
> ICAL RELIGION IN NEW NATIONS, PROBLEMS OF NATIONAL
> INTEGRATION, PATTERNS OF EQUALITY/MODERNITY AND DEM-
> OCRACY IN NEW STATES, PROBLEMS OF LAW IN AFRICA, ED-
> UCATION AND DEVELOPMENT, POLITICAL SOCIALIZATION AND
> CULTURE CHANGE.

WALLERSTEIN I M   ED
SOCIAL CHANGE, THE COLONIAL SITUATION.
NEW YORK, JOHN WILEY, 1966
037,038,053,
> VOLUME CONSISTS OF REPRINTED ARTICLES BY WELL-KNOWN
> SCHOLARS, ARRANGED INTO NINE CATEGORIES-- DEFINITIONS
> OF THE COLONIAL SITUATION, MIGRATION OF LABOR AND ITS
> SOCIAL CONSEQUENCES, DECLINE AND CHANGING ROLE OF TRA-
> DITIONAL AUTHORITIES, CREATION OF URBAN ETHNICITY,
> CLASS, EDUCATION AND POWER, NEW NETWORK OF VOLUNTARY
> ASSOCIATIONS, NATIONALISM, WESTERNIZATION, RELIGIOUS
> CHANGE.

WILSON GODFREY   WILSON MONICA
THE ANALYSIS OF SOCIAL CHANGE-BASED ON OBSERVATIONS IN
CENTRAL AFRICA
CAMBRIDGE, CAMBRIDGE UNIVERSITY PRESS, 1945; NEW EDITION, 1968
037,038,048,
> BASED LARGELY ON FIELD WORK IN TANZANIA, MALAWI, AND
> ZAMBIA, THIS BOOK HAS BECOME STANDARD REFERENCE ON
> CONCEPT OF INCREASING SOCIETAL SCALE AND ITS

IMPORTANCE IN THE PROCESS OF CHANGE. SCALE IS DEFINED
AS THE NUMBER OF PEOPLE IN RELATION WITH ONE ANOTHER
AS A GROUP AND THE INTENSITY OF THESE RELATIONS.

037

BAFFOUR R P
SCIENCE AND TECHNOLOGY IN RELATION TO AFRICA'S DEVELOPMENT.
IN LALAGE BOWN AND MICHAEL CROWDER (EDS.), PROCEEDINGS OF
THE FIRST INTERNATIONAL CONGRESS OF AFRICANISTS, ACCRA,
1962, LONDON, LONGMANS, 1964, PP 301-308
037,075,
        REFERENCE

EISENSTADT S N
MODERNIZATION-PROTEST AND CHANGE
ENGLEWOOD CLIFFS, NEW JERSEY, PRENTICE-HALL, 1966
037,
        REFERENCE

EISENSTADT S N
MODERNIZATION AND CONDITIONS OF SUSTAINED GROWTH
WORLD POLITICS 16 JULY 1964 PP 576-594
037,073,
        REFERENCE

GINZBERG E   ED
TECHNOLOGY AND SOCIAL CHANGE
NEW YORK, COLUMBIA UNIVERSITY PRESS, 1964
037,075,
        REFERENCE

KILSON MARTIN L
AFRICAN POLITICAL CHANGE AND THE MODERNIZATION PROCESS.
JOURNAL OF MODERN AFRICAN STUDIES 1 DECEMBER 1963
PP 425-440
037,
        REFERENCE

BLACK CYRIL E
THE DYNAMICS OF MODERNIZATION.
NEW YORK, HARPER AND ROW, 1966
037,073,
        GENERAL THEORY

DEUTSCH KARL W
SOCIAL MOBILIZATION AND POLITICAL DEVELOPMENT CHAPTER 6.
IN JASON L FINKLE AND RICHARD W GABLE, POLITICAL
DEVELOPMENT AND SOCIAL CHANGE, NEW YORK, JOHN WILEY, 1966
037,
        GENERAL THEORY

EISENSTADT S N
BREAKDOWNS OF MODERNIZATION CHAPTER 16.
IN JASON L FINKLE AND RICHARD W GABLE, POLITICAL
DEVELOPMENT AND SOCIAL CHANGE, NEW YORK, JOHN WILEY, 1966
037,
        GENERAL THEORY

FRIEDMANN G
THE SOCIAL CONSEQUENCES OF TECHNICAL PROGRESS.

INTERNATIONAL SOCIAL SCIENCE BULLETIN 4 1952 PP 243-260
037,
        GENERAL THEORY

037
HAGEN EVERETT E
HOW ECONOMIC GROWTH BEGINS-- A THEORY OF SOCIAL CHANGE
CHAPTER 4.
IN JASON L FINKLE AND RICHARD W GABLE, POLITICAL
DEVELOPMENT AND SOCIAL CHANGE, NEW YORK, JOHN WILEY, 1966
037,073,
        GENERAL THEORY

HAGEN EVERETT E
ON THE THEORY OF SOCIAL CHANGE
HOMEWOOD, ILLINOIS, DORSEY PRESS, 1962
037,
        GENERAL THEORY

HOSELITZ BERTHOLD
ECONOMIC GROWTH AND DEVELOPMENT CHAPTER 8.
IN JASON L FINKLE AND RICHARD W GABLE, POLITICAL
DEVELOPMENT AND SOCIAL CHANGE, NEW YORK, JOHN WILEY, 1966
037,073,
        GENERAL THEORY

HUNTINGTON SAMUEL
THE POLITICAL MODERNIZATION OF TRADITIONAL MONARCHIES.
DAEDALUS 95 SUMMER 1966 PP 763-788
037,
        GENERAL THEORY

LERNER DANIEL
THE PASSING OF TRADITIONAL SOCIETY-- MODERNIZING THE MIDDLE
EAST.
NEW YORK, FREE PRESS, 1958
037,
        GENERAL THEORY

LEVY MARION J
MODERNIZATION AND THE STRUCTURE OF SOCIETIES-- A SETTING
FOR INTERNATIONAL AFFAIRS.
PRINCETON, NEW JERSEY, PRINCETON UNIVERSITY PRESS, 1966
037,
        GENERAL THEORY

MCCLELLAND DAVID
THE ACHIEVEMENT MOTIVE IN ECONOMIC GROWTH CHAPTER 4.
IN JASON L FINKLE AND RICHARD W GABLE, POLITICAL
DEVELOPMENT AND SOCIAL CHANGE, NEW YORK, JOHN WILEY, 1966
037,
        GENERAL THEORY

MCCLELLAND DAVID C
THE ACHIEVING SOCIETY.
PRINCETON, NEW JERSEY, VAN NOSTRAND, 1961
037,041,
        GENERAL THEORY

MCLUHAN H MARSHALL

THE GUTENBERG GALAXY.
TORONTO, UNIVERSITY OF TORONTO PRESS, 1962
037,043,
        GENERAL THEORY

037
    MILLIKAN MAX F   BLACKMER DONALD   EDS
    RESISTANCE AND CONFLICT IN THE MODERNIZATION PROCESS CHP 3.
    IN EMERGING NATIONS, CENTER FOR INTERNATIONAL STUDIES, MIT,
    BOSTON, LITTLE, BROWN, 1961; ALSO LEWIS P FICKETT, ED, PROBLEMS
    OF THE DEVELOPING NATIONS, NEW YORK, CROWELL, 1966, PP 12-20
    037,
        GENERAL THEORY

    MOORE WILBERT E
    SOCIAL CHANGE
    ENGLEWOOD CLIFFS, NEW JERSEY, PRENTICE-HALL, 1963
    037,
        GENERAL THEORY

    MYRDAL GUNNAR
    RICH LANDS AND POOR.
    NEW YORK, HARPER, 1957 (ESP. CHAPTERS 1-3)
    037,071,073,
        GENERAL THEORY

    NETTL J P
    POLITICAL MOBILIZATION.
    NEW YORK, BASIC BOOKS, 1967
    037,063,
        GENERAL THEORY

    RIGGS FRED W
    THE THEORY OF DEVELOPING POLITIES.
    WORLD POLITICS 16 OCTOBER 1963 PP 147-171
    037,098,
        GENERAL THEORY

    SINAI I ROBERT
    THE CHALLENGE OF MODERNIZATION-- THE WEST≠S IMPACT ON THE
    NON-WESTERN WORLD.
    LONDON, CHATTO AND WINDUS, 1964
    037,
        GENERAL THEORY

    WEINER MYRON
    POLITICAL MODERNIZATION AND EVOLUTIONARY THEORY.
    IN HR BARRINGER, GI BLANKSTEN, RW MACK, SOCIAL CHANGE IN
    DEVELOPING AREAS, CAMBRIDGE, MASS, SCHENKMAN, 1965,
    PP 102-111
    037,
        GENERAL THEORY

    WEINER MYRON   ED
    MODERNIZATION-THE DYNAMICS OF GROWTH
    NEW YORK, BASIC BOOKS, 1966
    037,
        GENERAL THEORY

    MCELRATH DENNIS

SOCIETAL SCALE AND SOCIAL DIFFERENTIATION--ACCRA, GHANA.
THE NEW URBANIZATION, ED   SCOTT GREER   ET AL., NEW YORK,
ST. MARTIN'S PRESS, 1968
037,114-05,

38. SOCIAL CHANGE AND MODERNIZATION IN AFRICA

038
BASCOM WILLIAM R   HERSKOVITS MELVILLE J
CONTINUITY AND CHANGE IN AFRICAN CULTURES.
CHICAGO, UNIVERSITY OF CHICAGO PRESS, 1962
038,

> EXAMINES PROBLEMS OF STABILITY AND CHANGE IN AFRICA,
> FOCUSED ON PROCESSES OF ACCULTURATION. INCLUDES
> ESSAYS ON LANGUAGE, ART, MUSIC, ETHNOHISTORY, MAR-
> RIAGE, KINSHIP, THE ECONOMIC ROLE OF WOMEN, AND
> RELIGION. WRITTEN BY ANTHROPOLOGISTS WHO RECEIVED
> THEIR TRAINING AT NORTHWESTERN UNIVERSITY, PRIMARILY
> UNDER THE LATE MELVILLE HERSKOVITS.

HERSKOVITS MELVILLE J
THE HUMAN FACTOR IN CHANGING AFRICA.
NEW YORK, ALFRED A KNOPF, 1962
001,038,045,047,

> MAJOR WORK OF SYNTHESIS ON THE PATTERNS AND PROBLEMS
> PRIMARILY DURING THE COLONIAL PERIOD. EXCELLENT
> SUMMARY CHAPTERS ON AFRICA IN THE WORLD SETTING, CUL-
> TURE AREAS, AGRICULTURAL AND INDUSTRIAL GROWTH, LAW,
> EDUCATION, URBANIZATION, NATIONALISM, AND MORE RECENT
> PROBLEMS OF ECONOMIC AND POLITICAL CHANGE, RELIGION
> AND THE ARTS, AND THE SEARCH FOR VALUES.

LEVINE ROBERT A
DREAMS AND DEEDS.
CHICAGO, UNIVERSITY OF CHICAGO PRESS, 1966
038,041,098,128-03,

> A SYSTEMATIC ANALYSIS OF PERSONALITY FACTORS RELATED
> TO DIFFERENCES IN MODERNIZING ATTITUDES AMONG THE
> THREE MAJOR ETHNIC GROUPS IN NIGERIA-- IBO, YORUBA,
> AND HAUSA. BASED ON ANALYSIS OF DREAM REPORTS AND
> WRITTEN ESSAYS BY NIGERIAN STUDENTS. FINDINGS INDI-
> CATE DISTINCT ETHNIC DIFFERENCES IN MOTIVATION. HIGH-
> LY CONTROVERSIAL, PARTICULARLY IN NIGERIA.

LLOYD PETER C
AFRICA IN SOCIAL CHANGE-- CHANGING TRADITIONAL SOCIETIES
IN THE MODERN WORLD.
BALTIMORE, PENGUIN, 1967
001,038,053,

> COMPREHENSIVE AND PENETRATING ANALYSIS OF SOCIAL
> CHANGE IN WEST AFRICA, FOCUSING PRIMARILY ON GROWTH
> AND PRESENT ROLE OF EDUCATED ELITE. EXAMINES
> TRADITIONAL BACKGROUND, IMPACT OF WEST, CHANGING
> INSTITUTIONS (FAMILY, URBAN ASSOCIATIONS, POLITICAL
> PARTIES), AND CONTEMPORARY PROBLEMS OF IDEOLOGY,

TRIBALISM, AND POLITICAL INSTABILITY. AUTHOR TAUGHT
15 YEARS IN NIGERIA, NOW TEACHES SOCIAL ANTHROPOLOGY
AT SUSSEX. BIBLIOGRAPHY AND STATISTICAL APPENDIX.

038

VAN DEN BERGHE P
AFRICA-- SOCIAL PROBLEMS OF CHANGE AND CONFLICT.
SAN FRANCISCO, CHANDLER, 1965
038,053,
EXCELLENT SELECTION OF REPRINTED ARTICLES, FOCUSED ON
BOTH SOCIAL CHANGE AND SOCIAL CONFLICT. CASE STUDIES
ALL ILLUSTRATE THEORETICAL POINTS. UNLIKE THE WALLER-
STEIN VOLUME OR THE FINKLE AND GABLE VOLUME, VAN DEN
BERGHE DEALS EXCLUSIVELY WITH AFRICAN MATERIAL.

WALLERSTEIN I M   ED
SOCIAL CHANGE, THE COLONIAL SITUATION.
NEW YORK, JOHN WILEY, 1966
037,038,053,
VOLUME CONSISTS OF REPRINTED ARTICLES BY WELL-KNOWN
SCHOLARS, ARRANGED INTO NINE CATEGORIES-- DEFINITIONS
OF THE COLONIAL SITUATION, MIGRATION OF LABOR AND ITS
SOCIAL CONSEQUENCES, DECLINE AND CHANGING ROLE OF TRA-
DITIONAL AUTHORITIES, CREATION OF URBAN ETHNICITY,
CLASS, EDUCATION AND POWER, NEW NETWORK OF VOLUNTARY
ASSOCIATIONS, NATIONALISM, WESTERNIZATION, RELIGIOUS
CHANGE.

WILKS IVOR
ASHANTI GOVERNMENT, IN DARYLL FORDE AND P M KABERRY (EDS),
WEST AFRICAN KINGDOMS IN THE NINETEENTH CENTURY.
LONDON, OXFORD UNIVERSITY PRESS, 1967
026,038,114-01,
DISCUSSES CENTRALIZED ASPECTS OF PRE-COLONIAL ASHANTI
GOVERNMENT, ESPECIALLY ROLE OF ASANTEHENE, AND COUNTER-
BALANCES RATTRAY VIEW OF DECENTRALIZED CONFEDERATION.

WILSON GODFREY   WILSON MONICA
THE ANALYSIS OF SOCIAL CHANGE-BASED ON OBSERVATIONS IN
CENTRAL AFRICA
CAMBRIDGE, CAMBRIDGE UNIVERSITY PRESS, 1945; NEW EDITION, 1968
037,038,048,
BASED LARGELY ON FIELD WORK IN TANZANIA, MALAWI, AND
ZAMBIA, THIS BOOK HAS BECOME STANDARD REFERENCE ON
CONCEPT OF INCREASING SOCIETAL SCALE AND ITS
IMPORTANCE IN THE PROCESS OF CHANGE. SCALE IS DEFINED
AS THE NUMBER OF PEOPLE IN RELATION WITH ONE ANOTHER
AS A GROUP AND THE INTENSITY OF THESE RELATIONS.

APTHORPE RAYMOND J
POLITICAL CHANGE, CENTRALIZATION AND ROLE DIFFERENTIATION.
CIVILISATIONS 10 1960 PP 217-224
038,
REFERENCE

BASCOM WILLIAM R   HERSKOVITS MELVILLE J
THE PROBLEM OF STABILITY AND CHANGE IN AFRICAN CULTURE
CHAPTER 1.
IN CONTINUITY AND CHANGE IN AFRICAN CULTURES, CHICAGO,
UNIVERSITY OF CHICAGO PRESS, 1962, PP 1-14

038,
      REFERENCE

038

FORDE C DARYLL
THE CONDITIONS OF SOCIAL DEVELOPMENT IN WEST AFRICA.
CIVILISATIONS 3 1953 PP 471-489
038,
      REFERENCE

FULLER CHARLES E
ETHNOHISTORY IN THE STUDY OF CULTURE CHANGE IN SOUTHEAST
AFRICA CHAPTER 6.
IN WILLIAM BASCOM AND MELVILLE HERSKOVITS, CONTINUTY AND
CHANGE IN AFRICAN CULTURES, CHICAGO, UNIVERSITY OF CHICAGO
PRESS, 1962, PP 113-129
038,
      REFERENCE

GOULD PETER   ED
AFRICA CONTINENT OF CHANGE
BELMONT, CALIFORNIA, WADSWORTH PUBLISHING COMPANY, 1961
038,
      REFERENCE

HUNTER GUY
FROM THE OLD CULTURE TO THE NEW.
IN PETER J MCEWAN AND ROBERT B SUTCLIFFE (EDS), MODERN AFRICA,
NEW YORK, THOMAS CROWELL, 1965, PP 315-325
038,
      REFERENCE

HUNWICK JOHN
RELIGION AND STATE IN THE SONGHAY EMPIRE, 1464-1591.
IN LEWIS, ISLAM IN TROPICAL AFRICA, LONDON, OXFORD UNIVERSITY
PRESS, 1966, PP 296-317
022,038,
      REFERENCE

INTERNATIONAL LABOUR OFFICE
TRANSITION FROM TRIBAL TO MODERN FORMS OF SOCIAL AND
ECONOMIC ORGANIZATION.
GENEVE INTERNATIONAL LABOR ORGANIZATION 1952
038,
      REFERENCE

KIMBLE GEORGE
SOME PROBLEMS OF SOCIAL CHANGE.
IN PETER J MCEWAN AND ROBERT B SUTCLIFFE (EDS), MODERN AFRICA,
NEW YORK, THOMAS CROWELL, 1965, PP 305-314
038,
      REFERENCE

MAIR LUCY P
SOCIAL CHANGE IN AFRICA.
INTERNATIONAL AFFAIRS 36 OCTOBER 1960 PP 447-456
038,
      REFERENCE

MAZRUI ALI A

EUROPEAN EXPLORATION AND AFRICA'S SELF DISCOVERY
JOURNAL OF MODERN AFRICAN STUDIES 7 1969 PP 661-676
027,038,100,
       REFERENCE

038
   MITCHELL J CLYDE
   LABOUR MIGRATION AND THE TRIBE.
   IN PRUDENCE SMITH (ED.), AFRICA IN TRANSITION, LONDON,
   REINHARDT, 1956, PP 54-61
   038,
       REFERENCE

   RIDDELL J BARRY
   THE SPATIAL DYNAMICS OF MODERNIZATION IN SIERRA LEONE
   EVANSTON,NORTHWESTERN UNIVERSITY PRESS,1970
   038,048,131-06,
       REFERENCE

   SOJA EDWARD W
   THE GEOGRAPHY OF MODERNIZATION IN KENYA.
   SYRACUSE, SYRACUSE UNIVERSITY PRESS, 1968
   038,047,048,117-03,
       REFERENCE

   SOUTHALL AIDAN   ED
   SOCIAL CHANGES IN MODERN AFRICA
   LONDON, OXFORD UNIVERSITY PRESS, 1961
   038,
       REFERENCE

   BARNES JAMES A
   POLITICS IN A CHANGING SOCIETY-- A POLITICAL HISTORY OF THE
   FORT JAMESON NGONI.
   NEW YORK, OXFORD UNIVERSITY PRESS, 1954
   038,142-03,
       CASE STUDY

   BROKENSHA DAVID
   SOCIAL CHANGE AT LARTEH, GHANA.
   LONDON, OXFORD UNIVERSITY PRESS, 1966
   038,114-03,
       CASE STUDY

   CHILVER E M   KABERRY PHYLLIS M
   FROM TRIBUTE TO TAX IN A TIKAR CHIEFDOM.
   AFRICA (LONDON) 30 1960 PP 1-19
   038,
       CASE STUDY

   COHEN ABNER
   POLITICS OF THE KOLA TRADE CHAPTER 14.
   IN EDITH WHETHAM AND JEAN CURRIE, (EDS.) READINGS IN THE
   APPLIED ECONOMICS OF AFRICA, LONDON, CAMBRIDGE UNIVERSITY
   PRESS, 1, 1967, PP 153-163
   038,
       CASE STUDY

   COLSON ELIZABETH
   INCORPORATION IN TONGA.

IN R COHEN AND J MIDDLETON EDS, FROM TRIBE TO NATION IN
AFRICA, SAN FRANCISCO, CHANDLER, 1968
038,142-01,
       CASE STUDY

038

    CORY HANS
    REFORM OF TRIBAL POLITICAL INSTITUTIONS IN TANGANYIKA.
    JOURNAL OF AFRICAN ADMINISTRATION 12 APRIL 1960 PP 77-84
    038,
       CASE STUDY

    DORJAHN VERNON R
    THE CHANGING POLITICAL SYSTEM OF TEMNE.
    IN IMMANUEL WALLERSTEIN (ED.) SOCIAL CHANGE-- THE
    COLONIAL SITUATION, NEW YORK, ROBERT WILEY, 1966,
    PP 171-209
    038,131-03,
       CASE STUDY

    FALLERS LLOYD A
    THE KING'S MEN-- LEADERSHIP AND STATUS IN BUGANDA ON THE
    EVE OF INDEPENDENCE.
    LONDON, OXFORD UNIVERSITY PRESS, 1964
    034,038,139-03,
       CASE STUDY

    FALLERS LLOYD A
    THE PREDICAMENT OF THE MODERN AFRICAN CHIEF-- AN
    INSTANCE FROM UGANDA.
    AMERICAN ANTHROPOLOGIST 57 1955 PP 290-305; ALSO WILLIAM J
    HANNA, ED, INDEPENDENT BLACK AFRICA, CHICAGO, RAND MCNALLY,
    1964, PP 278-296
    038,139-03,
       CASE STUDY

    GLUCKMAN MAX
    ANALYSIS OF A SOCIAL SITUATION IN MODERN ZULULAND.
    MANCHESTER, MANCHESTER UNIVERSITY PRESS, 1958
    038,132-03,
       CASE STUDY

    HALPERN MANFRED
    THE POLITICS OF SOCIAL CHANGE IN THE MIDDLE EAST AND NORTH
    AFRICA.
    PRINCETON, NEW JERSEY, PRINCETON UNIVERSITY PRESS, 1965
    038,
       CASE STUDY

    HAMMOND PETER B
    ECONOMIC CHANGE AND MOSSI ACCULTURATION CHAPTER 13.
    IN WILLIAM BASCOM AND MELVILLE HERSKOVITS, CONTINUTY AND
    CHANGE IN AFRICAN CULTURES, CHICAGO, UNIVERSITY OF CHICAGO
    PRESS, 1958, PP 238-256
    038,
       CASE STUDY

    HUNWICK JOHN
    RELIGION AND STATE.
    IN I.M. LEWIS ISLAM IN TROPICAL AFRICA, LONDON, OXFORD

UNIVERSITY PRESS, 1966
038,
        CASE STUDY

038
    LEWIS I M
    LINEAGE CONTINUITY AND MODERN COMMERCE IN NORTHERN
    SOMALILAND.
    IN PAUL BOHANNAN AND GEORGE DALTON (EDS.) MARKETS IN
    AFRICA, EVANSTON, NORTHWESTERN UNIVERSITY PRESS, 1962, PP
    365-385
    038,133-03,
        CASE STUDY

    LUCAS J OLUMIDE
    THE RELIGION OF THE YORUBAS.
    LAGOS, C.M.S. BOOKSHOP, 1948
    038,
        CASE STUDY

    MIDDLETON JOHN
    SOCIAL CHANGE AMONG THE LUGBARA OF UGANDA.
    CIVILIZATIONS 10 1960 PP 446-456
    038, 139-03,
        CASE STUDY

    OTTENBERG PHOEBE
    THE CHANGING ECONOMIC POSITION OF WOMEN AMONG THE AFIKPO
    IBO CHAPTER 11.
    IN WILLIAM BASCOM AND MELVILLE HERSKOVITS, CONTINUTY AND
    CHANGE IN AFRICAN CULTURES, CHICAGO, UNIVERSITY OF CHICAGO
    PRESS, 1962, PP 205-223
    038,128-03,
        CASE STUDY

    OTTENBERG SIMON
    IBO RECEPTIVITY TO CHANGE CHAPTER 7.
    IN WILLIAM BASCOM AND MELVILLE HERSKOVITS, CONTINUTY AND
    CHANGE IN AFRICAN CULTURES, CHICAGO, UNIVERSITY OF CHICAGO
    PRESS, 1962, PP 130-143
    038,128-03,
        CASE STUDY

    ROSMAN ABRAHAM
    SOCIAL STRUCTURE AND ACCULTURATION AMONG THE KANURI
    OF BORNU PROVINCE, NORTHERN NIGERIA.
    TRANSACTIONS OF THE NEW YORK ACADEMY OF SCIENCE 21 MAY
    1958 PP 620-630
    038,128-01,
        CASE STUDY

    SCARRITT JAMES R
    THE IMPACT OF NATIONALISM.
    IN POLITICAL CHANGE IN A TRADITIONAL AFRICAN CLAN-- A
    STRUCTURAL-FUNCTIONAL ANALYSIS OF THE NSITS OF NIGERIA
    DENVER MONOGRAPH SERIES IN WORLD AFFAIRS 3 1964-5UNIVERSITY
    OF DENVER
    038,128-03,
        CASE STUDY

SCHAPERA ISAAC
MIGRANT LABOUR AND TRIBAL LIFE-- A STUDY OF CONDITIONS
IN THE BECHUANALAND PROTECTORATE.
LONDON, OXFORD UNIVERSITY PRESS, 1947
038,102-03,
        CASE STUDY

038

SCHNEIDER HAROLD K
PAKOT RESISTANCE TO CHANGE CHAPTER 8.
IN WILLIAM BASCOM AND MELVILLE HERSKOVITS, CONTINUTY AND
CHANGE IN AFRICAN CULTURES, CHICAGO, UNIVERSITY OF CHICAGO
PRESS, 1962, PP 144-167
038,
        CASE STUDY

SKINNER ELLIOTT P
LABOUR MIGRATION AND ITS RELATIONSHIP TO SOCIOCULTURAL
CHANGE IN MOSSI SOCIETY.
AFRICA (LONDON) 30 1960 PP 375-401
038,141-03,
        CASE STUDY

VAN VELSEN J
LABOUR MIGRATION AS A POSITIVE FACTOR IN THE CONTINUITY
OF TONGA TRIBAL SOCIETY.
ECONOMIC DEVELOPMENT AND CULTURAL CHANGE 8 1960 PP 265-278
038,142-03,
        CASE STUDY

APTHORPE RAYMOND J   ED
FROM TRIBAL RULE TO MODERN GOVERNMENT-- THE 13TH
CONFERENCE OF THE RHODES-LIVINGSTONE INSTITUTE FOR SOCIAL
RESEARCH.
LUSAKA, RHODES-LIVINGSTONE INSTITUTE, 1959
038,
        LESS ACCESSIBLE

BALANDIER GEORGES
ASPECTS DE L'EVOLUTION SOCIALE CHEZ LES FANG
(ASPECTS OF SOCIAL EVOLUTION AMONG THE FANG).
CAHIERS INTERNATIONAUX DE SOCIOLOGIE 9 1950 PP 76-106
038,112-03,
        LESS ACCESSIBLE

FORTES MEYER
THE ASHANTI SOCIAL SURVEY-- A PRELIMINARY REPORT.
RHODES-LIVINGSTONE JOURNAL 6 1948 PP 1-36
038,
        LESS ACCESSIBLE

PFEFFER LEO
CHURCH, STATE AND FREEDOM.
BOSTON, BEACON PRESS, 1967
038,
        GENERAL THEORY

ALBERT ETHEL M
SOCIO-ECONOMIC ORGANIZATION AND RECEPTIVITY TO CHANGE-SOME
DIFFERENCES BETWEEN RUANDA AND URUNDI

SOUTHWESTERN JOURNAL OF ANTHROPOLOGY 16 1960 PP 46-74
013, 038, 103-03, 129-03,

      CASE STUDY

39. THE CONCEPT OF AFRICAN PERSONALITY

039
    CAROTHERS J C
    THE AFRICAN MIND IN HEALTH AND DISEASE.
    GENEVA, WORLD HEALTH ORGANIZATION, MONOGRAPH SERIES, NO 17,
    1953
    039,
        BRITISH PSYCHOLOGIST OF COLONIAL PERIOD, EPITOMIZES
        STEREOTYPED AND ETHNO-CENTRIC IMAGES OF AFRICAN PER-
        SONALITY. HIGHLY CRITICIZED AND REMAINS AS EXAMPLE OF
        COLONIAL BIAS. AUTHOR ALSO WROTE EQUALLY ETHNO-CEN-
        TRIC AND CRITICIZED ACCOUNT OF THE MAU MAU MOVEMENT IN
        KENYA.

    CLIGNET REMI   FOSTER PHILIP
    THE FORTUNATE FEW.
    EVANSTON NORTHWESTERN UNIVERSITY PRESS 1966
    039,043,116-03,
        A STUDY OF SECONDARY SCHOOLS AND STUDENTS IN THE IVORY
        COAST. INTRODUCTION DEALS WITH NATURE OF COLONIAL ED-
        UCATIONAL POLICIES, THE POST-COLONIAL PERIOD, AND THE
        CRUCIAL POSITION OF SECONDARY SCHOOLS. OTHER CHAPTERS
        DEAL WITH ETHNIC, SOCIAL AND CULTURAL ORIGINS OF STU-
        DENTS-- RECRUITMENT OF STUDENTS-- STUDENTS ATTITUDES
        AND ADJUSTMENTS-- OCCUPATIONAL ASPIRATIONS AND EXPEC-
        TATIONS.

    DIOP CHEIKH ANTA
    THE CULTURAL UNITY OF NEGRO-AFRICA.
    PARIS, PRESENCE AFRICAINE, 1962
    016,039,054,099,
        AUTHOR IS SENEGALESE SCHOLAR WHO HAS UNDERTAKEN
        RESEARCH ON THE HISTORY OF THE AFRICAN CONTINENT WITH
        A VIEW TO STRESSING SIMILARITIES RATHER THAN
        DIFFERENCES AMONG THE VARIOUS ETHNIC SOCIETIES. FROM
        THESE SIMILARITIES HE PROPOSES CERTAIN CULTURE-PERSON-
        ALITY PATTERNS WHICH HE FEELS DISTINGUISH AFRICANS
        FROM EUROPEANS.

    DOOB LEONARD W
    PSYCHOLOGY.
    IN ROBERT A LYSTAD (ED), THE AFRICAN WORLD, NEW YORK,
    PRAEGER, 1966, PP 373-415
    039,
        GOOD REVIEW AND BIBLIOGRAPHY OF PSYCHOLOGICAL RESEARCH
        IN AFRICA. DEALS WITH IMPORTANT QUESTIONS FOR FUTURE
        RESEARCH INVOLVING GENETIC DIFFERENCES, PERCEPTION,
        INTELLIGENCE AND APTITUDES, TRADITIONAL PERSONALITY
        TESTS, ABNORMALITY, SOCIALIZATION, ACCULTURATION.

CONCLUDES WITH BROAD-RANGING ANALYSIS OF PSYCHOLOGY
AND THE SOCIAL SCIENCES, STRESSING THE VALUES OF DIS-
CIPLINARY CROSS-FERTILIZATION IN IDEAS, THEORIES AND
TECHNIQUES.

039

LEVINE ROBERT A
AFRICA.
IN FRANCES K HSU, ED., PSYCHOLOGICAL ANTHROPOLOGY, HOMEWOOD
ILLINOIS, DORSEY PRESS, 1961 PP 48-92
039,099,100,
A MAJOR SURVEY OF PYCHOLOGICAL RESEARCH WHICH ATTEMPTS
TO DERIVE BROAD GENERALIZATIONS ABOUT AFRICAN PERSON-
ALITY DEVELOPMENT IN CHILDHOOD AND ADOLESCENCE, APPLI-
CATION OF TAT IN SOUTH AFRICA AND CONGO, PERSONALITY
AND ACCULTRUATION. PSYCHOCULTURAL INTERPRETATIONS OF
RITUAL, WITCHCRAFT AND DREAMS, MENTAL ILLNESS.

DIOP ALIOUNE
REMARKS ON AFRICAN PERSONALITY AND NEGRITUDE
IN AMERICAN SOCIETY OF AFRICAN CULTURE,PAN-AFRICANISM
RECONSIDERED,BERKELEY, UNIVERSITY OF CALIFORNIA PRESS,1962
PP 337-345
039,054,077,079,
REFERENCE

DRAKE ST CLAIR
PAN-AFRICANISM NEGRITUDE AND THE AFRICAN PERSONALITY.
BOSTON UNIVERSITY GRADUATE JOURNAL 10 1961 PP 38-51, IN
WILLIAM J HANNA,INDEPENDENT BLACK AFRICA,CHICAGO, RAND
MCNALLY,1964, PP 530-541
039,054,077,
REFERENCE

FRANTZ CHARLES
THE AFRICAN PERSONALITY-- MYTH AND REALITY.
JOURNAL OF HUMAN RELATIONS 8 1960 PP 455-464
039,
REFERENCE

HERSKOVITS MELVILLE J
REVIEW OF J C CAROTHERS, THE AFRICAN MIND IN HEALTH AND
DISEASE.
MAN 26 1954 PP 388-389
039,
REFERENCE

KI-ZERBO JOSEPH
THE NEGRO-AFRICAN PERSONALITY.
IN ALBERT BERRIAN AND RICHARD LONG (EDS), NEGRITUDE--
ESSAYS AND STUDIES, HAMPTON, VIRGINIA, HAMPTON INSTITUTE
PRESS, 1967, PP 56-62
039,
REFERENCE

KI-ZERBO JOSEPH
AFRICAN PERSONALITY AND THE NEW AFRICAN SOCIETY.
IN WILLIAM J HANNA (ED), INDEPENDENT BLACK AFRICA, CHICAGO,
RAND MCNALLY, 1964, PP 46-59
039,

REFERENCE

039

QUAISON-SACKEY ALEX
THE AFRICAN PERSONALITY CHAPTER 2.
IN AFRICA UNBOUND, NEW YORK, PRAEGER, 1963
PP 35-58
039,
        REFERENCE

SEGALL MARSHALL H
THE GROWTH OF PSYCHOLOGY IN AFRICAN STUDIES.
IN CARTER, GWENDOLEN M. AND ANN PADEN (EDS), EXPANDING
HORIZONS IN AFRICAN STUDIES, EVANSTON, NORTHWESTERN
UNIVERSITY PRESS, 1969, PP. 47-65
039,098,100,
        REFERENCE

SENGHOR LEOPOLD S
THE PSYCHOLOGY OF THE AFRICAN NEGRO.
IN ALBERT BERRIAN AND RICHARD LONG (EDS), NEGRITUDE--
ESSAYS AND STUDIES, HAMPTON, VIRGINIA, HAMPTON INSTITUTE
PRESS, 1967, PP 48-55
039,
        REFERENCE

WICKERT FREDERIC R   ED
READINGS IN AFRICAN PSYCHOLOGY FROM FRENCH LANGUAGE SOURCES.
EAST LANSING MICHIGAN STATE UNIVERSITY PRESS 1967
039,040,098,
        REFERENCE

BAHOKEN JEAN CALVIN
LA CONTRIBUTION DES RELIGIONS A L'EXPRESSION CULTURELLE DE
LA PERSONNALITE AFRICAINE (THE CONTRIBUTION OF RELIGION TO
THE CULTURAL EXPRESSION OF THE AFRICAN PERSONALITY).
IN COLLOQUE SUR LES RELIGIONS, ABIDJAN, APRIL, 1961, PARIS,
PRESENCE AFRICAINE, 1962, PP 155-168
013,039,
        LESS ACCESSIBLE

DANIELOU R P
CATHOLICISME ET PERSONNALITE CULTURELLE DES PEUPLES
(CATHOLICISM AND CULTURAL PERSONALITY OF PEOPLES).
IN COLLOQUE SUR LES RELIGIONS, ABIDJAN, APRIL, 1961, PARIS,
PRESENCE AFRICAINE, 1962, PP 215-218
039,
        LESS ACCESSIBLE

GRAVAND R P
CONTRIBUTION DU CHRISTIANISME A L'AFFIRMATION DE LA
PERSONNALITE AFRICAINE EN PAYS SERERE (CONTRIBUTION OF
CHRISTIANITY TO THE AFFIRMATION OF THE AFRICAN PERSONALITY
IN SERERE COUNTRY).
IN COLLOQUE SUR LES RELIGIONS, ABIDJAN, APRIL, 1961, PARIS
PRESENCE AFRICAINE, 1962, PP 209-214
039,050,130-03,
        LESS ACCESSIBLE

MBITI JOHN S

LA CONTRIBUTION PROTESTANTE A L'EXPRESSION CULTURELLE DE LA
PERSONNALITE AFRICAINE (THE PROTESTANT CONTRIBUTION TO
CULTURAL EXPRESSION OF THE AFRICAN PERSONALITY).
IN COLLOQUE SUR LES RELIGIONS, ABIDJAN, APRIL, 1961, PARIS
PRESENCE AFRICAINE, 1962, PP 137-146
039,050,
        LESS ACCESSIBLE

039
    SASTRE L'ABBE
    CONTRIBUTION DE L'EGLISE CATHOLIQUE A L'EXPRESSION
    CULTURELLE DE LA PERSONNALITE AFRICAINE (CONTRIBUTION OF
    THE CATHOLIC CHURCH TO THE CULTURAL EXPRESSION OF THE
    AFRICAN PERSONALITY).
    IN COLLOQUE SUR LES RELIGIONS, ABIDJAN, APRIL, 1961, PARIS,
    PRESENCE AFRICAINE, 1962, PP 183-194
    039,050,
        LESS ACCESSIBLE

    SHELTON AUSTIN J
    THE CYCLIC PRINCIPLE OF AFRICAN PERSONALITY.
    IN ALBERT BERRIAN AND RICHARD LONG (EDS), NEGRITUDE--
    ESSAYS AND STUDIES, HAMPTON, VIRGINIA, HAMPTON INSTITUTE
    PRESS, 1967, PP 63-68
    039,

40. CHARACTERISTICS OF AFRICAN PERSONALITY

040
    ABRAHAM W E
    THE MIND OF AFRICA.
    CHICAGO, UNIVERSITY OF CHICAGO PRESS, 1962 (LONDON,
    WEIDENFELD AND NICOLSON)
    040,060,091,099,114-01,
        AUTHOR IS GHANAIAN SCHOLAR AND PHILOSOPHER, FORMER
        VICE-CHANCELLOR OF THE UNIVERSITY OF GHANA. BOOK AS-
        SESSES THE IDEA OF LATENT IDEOLOGY, OR CULTURAL BE-
        LIEFS. DRAWS ON PARADIGM OF ASHANTI SOCIETY TO GEN-
        ERALIZE ABOUT AFRICAN PERSONALITY-CULTURE PATTERNS.
        BRILLIANT THEORETICAL ANALYSIS, AND GOOD HISTORICAL
        SURVEY OF AFRICA BEFORE, DURING AND AFTER COLONIALISM.
        WEAKEST ON EXTRAPOLATION FROM ASHANTI CASE STUDY.

    HORTON ROBIN
    AFRICAN TRADITIONAL THOUGHT AND WESTERN SCIENCE PART 1-FROM
    TRADITION TO SCIENCE, PART 2- THE CLOSED AND OPEN
    PREDICAMENT
    AFRICA 37 1967 PP 50-71 AND 155-187
    013,040,098,
        EXCELLENT ARTICLES. FIRST DEVELOPS AN APPROACH TO
        TRADITIONAL AFRICAN THOUGHT WHICH STRESSES ITS CROSS-
        CULTURAL SIMILARITIES,PARTICULARLY WITH WESTERN
        THOUGHT AND ESPECIALLY IN RELIGION. SECOND EXAMINES
        DIFFERENCES BETWEEN TRADITIONAL AND SCIENTIFIC
        THOUGHT,FOCUSING ON AWARENESS OF ALTERNATIVES TO THE

ESTABLISHED BODY OF THEORETICAL TENETS.

040

CHAPLIN J H
A NOTE ON CENTRAL AFRICAN DREAM CONCEPTS.
MAN 58 1958 PP 90-92
040,
        REFERENCE

EVANS J L
CHILDREN IN AFRICA-A REVIEW OF PSYCHOLOGICAL RESEARCH
NEW YORK, TEACHER'S COLLEGE PRESS,FORTHCOMING
040,
        REFERENCE

JAHODA GUSTAV
IMMINENT JUSTICE AMONG WEST AFRICAN CHILDREN.
JOURNAL OF SOCIAL PSYCHOLOGY 47 1958 PP 241-248
040,
        REFERENCE

KLINGELHOFER E L
A BIBLIOGRAPHY OF PSYCHOLOGICAL RESEARCH AND WRITINGS ON
AFRICA
UPPSALA,SCANDANAVIAN INSTITUTE OF AFRICAN STUDIES,1967
040,
        REFERENCE

LAMBO T ADEOYE
IMPORTANT AREAS OF IGNORANCE AND DOUBT IN THE PSYCHOLOGY OF
THE AFRICAN.
IN LALAGE BOWN AND MICHAEL CROWDER (EDS.), PROCEEDINGS OF
THE FIRST INTERNATIONAL CONGRESS OF AFRICANISTS, ACCRA,
1962, LONDON, LONGMANS, 1964, PP 337-344
040,
        REFERENCE

SAWYER JACK   LEVINE ROBERT A
CULTURAL DIMENSIONS-- A FACTOR ANALYSIS OF THE WORLD ETHNO-
GRAPHIC SAMPLE.
AMERICAN ANTHROPOLOGIST VOL 68 NO 3 JUNE 1966 PP 708-731
016,040,
        REFERENCE

SEGALL MARSHALL H   CAMPBELL DONALD T   HERSKOVITS MELVILLE
THE INFLUENCE OF CULTURE ON VISUAL PERCEPTION
INDIANAPOLIS, BOBBS-MERRILL, 1966
040,
        REFERENCE

TURNBULL COLIN M
THE LONELY AFRICAN.
NEW YORK, DOUBLEDAY, 1963
040,
        REFERENCE

WICKERT FREDERIC R   ED
READINGS IN AFRICAN PSYCHOLOGY FROM FRENCH LANGUAGE SOURCES.
EAST LANSING,MICHIGAN STATE UNIVERSITY PRESS,1967
039,040,098,

REFERENCE

040

AINSWORTH MARY D
INFANCY IN UGANDA.
BALTIMORE, JOHNS HOPKINS PRESS, 1967
040,139-01,
        CASE STUDY

ALBINO RONALD C   THOMPSON VIRGINIA
THE EFFECTS OF SUDDEN WEANING ON ZULU CHILDREN.
BRITISH JOURNAL OF MEDICAL PSYCHOLOGY 29 1956 PP 177-210
040,
        CASE STUDY

DAWSON J L M
TRADITIONAL CONCEPTS OF MENTAL HEALTH IN SIERRA LEONE.
THE JOURNAL OF THE SIERRA LEONE SOCIETY NO. 18 JANUARY 1966
PP 18-28
040,131-01,
        CASE STUDY

FIELD M J
SEARCH FOR SECURITY-- AN ETHNO-PSYCHIATRIC STUDY OF
RURAL GHANA.
EVANSTON, NORTHWESTERN UNIVERSITY PRESS, 1960; ALSO LONDON,
FABER AND FABER, 1960
040,114-01,
        CASE STUDY

FOX IRENE K   ET-AL
EAST AFRICAN CHILDHOOD-- THREE EXPERIENCES.
NEW YORK, OXFORD UNIVERSITY PRESS, 1967
040,
        CASE STUDY

JAHODA GUSTAV
BOYS' IMAGES OF MARRIAGE PARTNERS AND GIRLS' SELF IMAGES
IN GHANA.
SOCIOLOGUS 8 1958 PP 155-169
040,114-03,
        CASE STUDY

KNAPEN M TH
SOME RESULTS OF AN ENQUIRY INTO THE INFLUENCE OF CHILD-
TRAINING ON THE DEVELOPMENT OF PERSONALITY IN A BACINGO
SOCIETY (BELGIAN CONGO).
JOURNAL OF SOCIAL PSYCHOLOGY 47 1958 PP 223-229
040,108-03,
        CASE STUDY

LAMBO T ADEOYE
THE ROLE OF CULTURAL FACTORS IN PARANOID PSYCHOSES AMONG
THE YORUBA TRIBE.
JOURNAL OF MENTAL SCIENCE 101 1955 PP 239-265
040,128-03,
        CASE STUDY

LEVINE ROBERT A   KLEIN N   OWEN C
FATHER-CHILD RELATIONSHIPS AND CHANGING LIFE-STYLES IN

IBADAN, NIGERIA.
IN HORACE MINER (ED), THE CITY IN MODERN AFRICA, NEW YORK,
PRAEGER, 1967
040,128-03,
      CASE STUDY

040

LYSTAD MARY H
PAINTINGS OF GHANAIAN CHILDREN.
AFRICA 30 1960 PP 238-242
040,114-03,
      CASE STUDY

LYSTAD MARY H
TRADITIONAL VALUES OF GHANAIAN CHILDREN.
AMERICAN ANTHROPOLOGIST 42 1960 PP 454-464
040,114-01,
      CASE STUDY

SEGALL MARSHALL H   EVANS J L
LEARNING TO CLASSIFY BY COLOR AND FUNCTION-A STUDY IN
CONCEPT FORMATION BY GANDA CHILDREN
JOURNAL OF SOCIAL PSYCHOLOGY 77 1969 PP 35-53
040,
      CASE STUDY

EDGERTON R B
AN ECOLOGICAL VIEW OF WITCHCRAFT IN FOUR AFRICAN SOCIETIES.
AFRICAN STUDIES ASSOCIATION MEETINGS, PHILADELPHIA, OCTOBER
1965
040,
      LESS ACCESSIBLE

BARRY H
REGIONAL AND WORLDWIDE VARIATIONS IN CULTURE.
ETHNOLOGY 7 1968 PP 207-217
040,
      GENERAL THEORY

EDGERTON R B
CULTURAL VERSUS ECOLOGICAL FACTORS IN THE EXPRESSION OF
VALUES, ATTITUDES AND PERSONALITY CHARACTERISTICS.
AMERICAN ANTHROPOLOGIST 67 1965A PP 442-447
040,
      GENERAL THEORY

JAHODA GUSTAV
ASSESSMENT OF ABSTRACT BEHAVIOR IN A NON-WESTERN CULTURE.
JOURNAL OF ABNORMAL AND SOCIAL PSYCHOLOGY 53 1956 PP 237-243
040,
      GENERAL THEORY

LEVINE ROBERT A
SOCIALIZATION, SOCIAL STRUCTURE, AND INTERSOCIETAL IMAGES.
IN HERMAN KELMAN, ED, INTERNATIONAL BEHAVIOR-- A SOCIAL
PSYCHOLOGICAL ANALYSIS, NEW YORK, HOLT, RINEHART AND
WINSTON, 1965
040,
      GENERAL THEORY

NADEL S F
THE CONCEPT OF SOCIAL ELITES.
PARIS INTERNATIONAL SOCIAL SCIENCE BULLETIN A SUMMER
1956 PP 413-423
040,
        GENERAL THEORY

41. PERSONALITY AND SOCIAL CHANGE

041
FANON FRANTZ
BLACK SKIN, WHITE MASKS-- THE EXPERIENCES OF A BLACK
MAN IN A WHITE WORLD.
NEW YORK, GROVE PRESS, 1967
041,085,088,101-03,
        AUTHOR IS BLACK PSYCHIATRIST WHO WORKED IN ALGERIA
        DURING FRENCH-ALGERIAN WAR. BOOK BEGINS WITH FACT OF
        HIS OWN BLACKNESS, AND HOSTILITY OF WHITE WORLD.
        GIVES PSYCHOPATHOLOGICAL AND PHILOSOPHICAL ANALYSIS OF
        STATE OF BEING BLACK IN SUCH A WORLD. CRITICIZES
        MANNONI. EXPLORES LITERATURE, DREAMS, CASE HISTORIES,
        AND SPECIAL ISSUE OF BLACK MEN AND WHITE WOMEN.

LEVINE ROBERT A
DREAMS AND DEEDS.
CHICAGO, UNIVERSITY OF CHICAGO PRESS, 1966
038,041,098,128-03,
        A SYSTEMATIC ANALYSIS OF PERSONALITY FACTORS RELATED
        TO DIFFERENCES IN MODERNIZING ATTITUDES AMONG THE
        THREE MAJOR ETHNIC GROUPS IN NIGERIA-- IBO, YORUBA,
        AND HAUSA. BASED ON ANALYSIS OF DREAM REPORTS AND
        WRITTEN ESSAYS BY NIGERIAN STUDENTS. FINDINGS INDI-
        CATE DISTINCT ETHNIC DIFFERENCES IN MOTIVATION. HIGH-
        LY CONTROVERSIAL, PARTICULARLY IN NIGERIA.

MANNONI DOMINIQUE O
PROSPERO AND CALIBAN-- THE PSYCHOLOGY OF COLONIZATION.
LONDON, METHUEN AND COMPANY, 1956 (NEW YORK, PRAEGER, 1964)
035,041,088,121-03,
        AUTHOR ASSESSES PSYCHOLOGICAL IMPACT OF COLONIAL RE-
        LATIONSHIP ON BOTH THE EUROPEAN IN AFRICA AND ON THE
        INDIGENOUS POPULATIONS. FOCUSED ON MADAGASCAR, BUT
        HAS BROAD INSIGHTS INTO THE NATURE OF COLONIAL SYSTEMS
        IN OTHER AREAS. SUGGESTS THAT SUPERIOR-SUBORDINATE
        RELATIONSHIP IS DAMAGING TO BOTH AFRICANS AND EUROPE-
        ANS. BOOK IS IMPRESSIONISTIC RATHER THAN BASED ON
        SPECIFIC RESEARCH.

MEMMI ALBERT
DOMINATED MAN.
BOSTON, BEACON PRESS, 1969
041,
        ESSAYS DEAL WITH THE SUPRESSION OF THE BLACK MAN, THE
        COLONIZED, WOMEN, THE PROLETARIAT, JEWS, AND DOMESTIC
        SERVANTS.

041

AINSWORTH LEONARD   AINSWORTH MARY D
ACULTURATION IN EAST AFRICA.
JOURNAL OF SOCIAL PSYCHOLOGY 57 1962 PP 391-432
041,
       REFERENCE

BOHANNAN PAUL   ED
AFRICAN HOMICIDE AND SUICIDE.
PRINCETON, NEW JERSEY, PRINCETON UNIVERSITY PRESS, 1960
041,
       REFERENCE

DELAMATER J   ET AL
SOCIAL PSYCHOLOGICAL RESEARCH IN DEVELOPING COUNTRIES
JOURNAL OF SOCIAL ISSUES 24 1968 PP 1-298
041,099,
       REFERENCE

DOOB LEONARD W
THE PSYCHOLOGICAL PRESSURE ON MODERN AFRICANS.
IN PETER J MCEWAN AND ROBERT B SUTCLIFFE (EDS), MODERN AFRICA,
NEW YORK, THOMAS CROWELL, 1965, PP 376-392
041,
       REFERENCE

JAHODA GUSTAV
LOVE MARRIAGE AND SOCIAL CHANGE.
AFRICA 24 1959 PP 177-190
041,
       REFERENCE

PARRINDER GEOFFREY
WEST AFRICAN PSYCHOLOGY.
LONDON, BUTTERWORTH PRESS, 1951
041,
       REFERENCE

DERIDDER J C
THE PERSONALITY OF THE URBAN AFRICAN IN SOUTH AFRICA.
NEW YORK, HUMANITIES PRESS, 1961
041, 089, 132-05,
       CASE STUDY

FALLERS LLOYD A   FALLERS M C
HOMICIDE AND SUICIDE IN BUSOGA.
IN PAUL BOHANNAN   (ED), AFRICAN HOMICIDE AND SUICIDE,
PRINCETON, PRINCETON UNIVERSITY PRESS, 1960, PP 65-93
041,
       CASE STUDY

FERNANDEZ JAMES W
THE SHAKA COMPLEX
TRANSITION 29 1967 PP 11-14
041,
       CASE STUDY

FOSTER PHILIP
STATUS POWER AND EDUCATION IN A TRADITIONAL COMMUNITY.

SCHOOL REVIEW 72 1964 PP 158-172
041,
     CASE STUDY

041

GAY J   COLE M
THE NEW MATHEMATICS AND THE OLD CULTURE
NEW YORK, HOLT, RINEHART AND WINSTON, 1967
041,119-03,
     CASE STUDY

JAHODA GUSTAV
WHITE MAN-- A STUDY OF THE ATTITUDE OF AFRICANS TO EUROPEANS
IN GHANA DURING INDEPENDENCE.
LONDON, OXFORD UNIVERSITY PRESS, 1961
041,088,114-06,
     CASE STUDY

JAHODA GUSTAV
SOCIAL ASPIRATIONS, MAGIC AND WITCHCRAFT IN GHANA - A SOCIAL
PSYCHOLOGICAL INTERPRETATION.
IN LLOYD, THE NEW ELITES OF TROPICAL AFRICA, LONDON, OXFORD
UNIVERSITY PRESS, 1966, P. 199-215
041,114-04,
     CASE STUDY

LEBLANC MARIA
ACCULTURATION OF ATTITUDE AND PERSONALITY AMONG KATANGESE
WOMEN.
JOURNAL OF SOCIAL PSYCHOLOGY 47 1958 PP 257-264
041,108-03,
     CASE STUDY

LEIGHTON A H   ET-AL
PSYCHIATRIC DISORDER AMONG THE YORUBA-- A REPORT FROM THE
CORNELL ARO-MENTAL HEALTH RESEARCH PROJECT IN THE WESTERN
REGION NIGERIA.
ITHACA, CORNELL UNIVERSITY PRESS, 1963
041,128-03,
     CASE STUDY

LOUDON J B
PSYCHOGENIC DISORDER AND SOCIAL CONFLICT AMONG THE ZULU.
IN MARVIN K OPLER (ED.), CULTURE AND MENTAL HEALTH, NEW YORK,
MACMILLAN, PP 351-369
041,132-03,
     CASE STUDY

MINER HORACE M
CULTURE CHANGE UNDER PRESSURE-- A HAUSA CASE.
HUMAN ORGANIZATION 19 FALL 1960 PP 164-167
041,128-03,
     CASE STUDY

MUNSTERBERGER W   KISHNER I
HASARDS OF CULTURE CLASH-- A REPORT ON THE HISTORY AND
DYNAMICS OF A PSYCHOTIC EPISODE IN A WEST AFRICAN EXCHANGE
STUDENT.
IN W MUNSTERBERGER AND S AXERAD   EDS THE PSYCHO-
ANALYTIC STUDY OF SOCIETY 4 NEW YORK INTERNATIONAL

UNIVERSITIES PRESS, PP 99-123
041,
        CASE STUDY

041

  ROTBERG ROBERT I
  MISSIONARIES AS CHIEFS AND ENTREPRENEURS-- NORTHER RHODESIA,
  1887-1924.
  IN JEFFREY BUTLER (ED), BOSTON UNIVERSITY PAPERS IN AFRICAN
  HISTORY VOL I, BOSTON, BOSTON UNIVERSITY PRESS,1964,PP 195-
  216
  041,142-03,
        CASE STUDY

  SCOTCH NORMAN A
  A PRELIMINARY REPORT ON THE RELATION OF SOCIOCULTURAL
  FACTORS TO HYPERTENSION AMONG THE ZULU.
  ANNALS OF THE NEW YORK ACADEMY OF SCIENCES 134 1960
  PP 1000-1009
  041,132-03,
        CASE STUDY

  CLIGNET REMI
  REFLEXIONS SUR LES PROBLEMS DE PSYCHOLOGIE EN AFRIQUE
  (REFLECTIONS ON THE PROBLEMS OF PSYCHOLOGY IN AFRICA).
  BULLETIN DE L'INSTITUT NATIONAL D'ORIENTATION
  PROFESSIONNELLE 18 1962 PP 86-94
  041,
        LESS ACCESSIBLE

  RICHELLE MARC
  ASPECTS PSYCHOLOGIQUE DE L'ACCULTURATION (PSYCHOLOGICAL
  ASPECTS OF ACCULTURATION).
  ELISABETHVILLE, KATANGA CENTRE D'ETUDE DES PROBLEMS SOCIAUX
  INDIGENES VOL 6 1960
  041,
        LESS ACCESSIBLE

  AINSWORTH LEONARD
  RIGIDITY, STRESS, AND ACCULTURATION.
  JOURNAL OF SOCIAL PSYCHOLOGY 49 1959 PP 131-136
  041,
        GENERAL THEORY

  MCCLELLAND DAVID C
  THE ACHIEVING SOCIETY.
  PRINCETON, NEW JERSEY, VAN NOSTRAND, 1961
  037,041,
        GENERAL THEORY

42. EDUCATIONAL SYSTEMS IN AFRICA

042
  ABERNETHY DAVID B
  THE POLITICAL DILEMMA OF POPULAR EDUCATION--AN AFRICAN CASE.

PALO ALTO, STANFORD UNIVERSITY PRESS, 1969
042,128-03,
    AUTHOR DISCUSSES RELATIONSHIP OF EDUCATION, POLITICS
    AND MODERNIZATION WITHIN SOUTHERN NIGERIAN CONTEXT.
    PART I TRACES EDUCATIONAL EXPANSION FROM 1842-1950--
    PART II THE ERA OF UNIVERSAL PRIMARY EDUCATION, DEALS
    WITH POLITICAL DEMANDS FOR EDUCATION--PART III THE
    CONSEQUENCES OF EDUCATIONAL EXPANSION, ASSESSES IMPACT
    OF EDUCATION ON THE POLITICAL SYSTEM, AND ON TRENDS
    TOWARD EQUALITY AND INTEGRATION.

042
JOLLY RICHARD   ED
EDUCATION IN AFRICA--RESEARCH AND ACTION.
KENYA, EAST AFRICAN PUBLISHING HOUSE, 1969
042,
    PAPERS ORGANIZED INTO FIVE PARTS--AFRICAN TRENDS IN ED-
    UCATIONAL STRUCTURE (INCLUDING ADDIS ABABA CONFERENCE,
    REGIONAL TARGETS, COMPARATIVE STATISTICAL DATA, AND
    COSTS)--NEW APPROACHES AND ATTITUDES (EDUCATION FOR
    SELF RELIANCE, THE HARAMBEE SCHOOLS, SCHOOL LEAVERS,
    RURAL AND ADULT EDUCATION)--CURRICULUM AND ABILITIES
    (USE OF ENGLISH, SCIENCE, LANGUAGE)--ISLAMIC EDUCATION
    AND SUPPORTING SERVICES

SASNETT MARTENA   SEPMEYER INEZ
EDUCATIONAL SYSTEMS OF AFRICA.
BERKELY, UNIVERSITY OF CALIFORNIA PRESS, 1966
042,
    COMPILATION OF ENORMOUS SIZE WITH SUMMARY DESCRIPTIONS
    AND STATISTICAL DATA ON THE EDUCATIONAL SYSTEMS OF
    EACH AFRICAN STATE.

ASHBY ERIC
AFRICAN UNIVERSITIES AND THE WESTERN TRADITION.
CAMBRIDGE, MASSACHUSETTS, HARVARD UNIVERSITY PRESS, 1964
042,
    REFERENCE

ASHBY ERIC
UNIVERSITIES-- BRITISH, INDIAN, AFRICAN, A STUDY IN THE ECO-
LOGY OF HIGHER EDUCATION.
CAMBRIDGE, MASSACHUSETTS, HARVARD UNIVERSITY PRESS, 1966
042,
    REFERENCE

BROWN GODFREY N
BRITISH EDUCATIONAL POLICY IN WEST AND CENTRAL AFRICA.
JOURNAL OF MODERN AFRICAN STUDIES 2 1964 PP 365-377
042,
    REFERENCE

BURNS D G
AFRICAN EDUCATION.
LONDON, OXFORD UNIVERSITY PRESS, 1965
042,
    REFERENCE

BUSIA KOFI A
PURPOSEFUL EDUCATION FOR AFRICA.

THE HAGUE, MOUTON, 1964
042, 114-04,
        REFERENCE

042
    CLIGNET REMI   FOSTER PHILIP
    FRENCH AND BRITISH COLONIAL EDUCATION IN AFRICA.
    COMPARATIVE EDUCATIONAL REVIEW 8 1964 PP 191-198
    042,
        REFERENCE

    COWAN L GRAY
    BRITISH AND FRENCH EDUCATION IN AFRICA-- A CRITICAL
    APPRAISAL CHP 8.
    IN DONALD PIPER AND TAYLOR COLE ,EDS., POST PRIMARY
    EDUCATION AND POLITICAL AND ECONOMIC DEVELOPMENT, DURHAM,
    NORTH CAROLINA, DUKE UNIVERSITY PRESS, 1964
    042,
        REFERENCE

    COWAN L GRAY   O CONNELL JAMES   SCANLON DAVID G
    EDUCATION AND NATION-BUILDING IN AFRICA.
    NEW YORK, PRAEGER, 1965
    042,043,
        REFERENCE

    DILLON WILTON S
    UNIVERSITIES AND NATION-BUILDING IN AFRICA.
    JOURNAL OF MODERN AFRICAN STUDIES 1 MARCH 1963 PP 75-89
    042,058,
        REFERENCE

    DU SAUTOY PETER
    THE PLANNING AND ORGANIZATION OF ADULT LITERACY PROGRAMMES
    IN AFRICA.
    PARIS, UNESCO, 1966
    042,
        REFERENCE

    HANNA WILLIAM J
    STUDENTS.
    IN JAMES S. COLEMAN AND CARL G. ROSBERG (EDS), POLITICAL PAR-
    TIES AND NATIONAL INTEGRATION IN TROPICAL AFRICA, BERKELY,
    UNIVERSITY OF CALIFORNIA PRESS, 1964, PP 413-511
    042,
        REFERENCE

    HILLIARD F H
    A SHORT HISTORY OF EDUCATION IN BRITISH WEST AFRICA.
    LONDON, THOMAS NELSON, 1957
    042,
        REFERENCE

    HOWE C WALTER
    AFRICAN APPROACHES TO THE DEVELOPMENT OF HIGHER EDUCATION
    CHP 7.
    IN DONALD PIPER AND TAYLOR COLE ,EDS. , POST PRIMARY
    EDUCATION AND POLITICAL AND ECONOMIC DEVELOPMENT, DURHAM,
    NORTH CAROLINA, DUKE UNIVERSITY PRESS, 1964
    042,

REFERENCE

042

KIMBLE GEORGE
EDUCATIONAL PROBLEMS IN SUB-SAHARAN AFRICA.
IN PETER J MCEWAN AND ROBERT B SUTCLIFFE (EDS), MODERN AFRICA,
NEW YORK, THOMAS CROWELL, 1965, PP 354-365
042,
    REFERENCE

KITCHEN HELEN   ED
THE EDUCATED AFRICAN-- A COUNTRY BY COUNTRY SURVEY OF EDU-
CATIONAL DEVELOPMENT IN AFRICA.
NEW YORK PRAEGER 1962
042,
    REFERENCE

LOGAN RAYFORD W
EDUCATION IN FORMER FRENCH WEST AND EQUATORIAL AFRICA AND
MADAGASCAR.
JOURNAL OF NEGRO EDUCATION 30 1961 PP 277-285
042,
    REFERENCE

MOUMOUNI ABDOU
EDUCATION IN AFRICA.
NEW YORK, PRAEGER, 1968
042,
    REFERENCE

NICOL DAVIDSON
POLITICS NATIONALISM AND UNIVERSITIES IN AFRICA.
AFRICAN AFFAIRS 62 JANUARY 1963 PP 20-28
042,
    REFERENCE

SCANLON DAVID G   ED
CHURCH, STATE AND EDUCATION IN AFRICA.
NEW YORK, TEACHERS COLLEGE PRESS, COLUMBIA UNIVERSITY, 1966
042,
    REFERENCE

SCANLON DAVID G   ED
TRADITIONS OF AFRICAN EDUCATION.
NEW YORK, COLUMBIA UNIVERSITY, 1964
042,
    REFERENCE

STABLER ERNEST
EDUCATION SINCE UHURU-- THE SCHOOLS OF KENYA.
MIDDLETOWN, CONN, WESLEYAN UNIVERSITY PRESS, 1969
042,117-04,
    REFERENCE

UNESCO
THE DEVELOPMENT OF HIGHER EDUCATION IN AFRICA-- REPORT OF
THE CONFERENCE, TANANARIVE, SEPTEMBER 1962.
PARIS, UNESCO, 1963
042,
    REFERENCE

042

BESHIR MOHAMED O
EDUCATIONAL DEVELOPMENT IN THE SUDAN
NEW YORK OXFORD UNIVERSITY PRESS 1969
042,134-04,
        CASE STUDY

CLIGNET REMI   FOSTER PHILIP
THE SOCIAL, ECONOMIC AND EDUCATIONAL SCENE IN THE IVORY
COAST CHAPTER 2.
IN THE FORTUNATE FEW,EVANSTON, NORTHWESTERN UNIVERSITY
PRESS, 1966
042,116-03,
        CASE STUDY

CURLE ADAM
NATIONALISM AND HIGHER EDUCATION IN GHANA.
UNIVERSITIES QUARTERLY 16 JUNE 1962 PP 229-242
042,114-03,
        CASE STUDY

IKEJIANI OKECHUKWU   ED
EDUCATION IN NIGERIA.
NEW YORK, PRAEGER, 1965
042,128-03,
        CASE STUDY

WEILER HANS N
ERZIEHUNGSWESEN AND POLITIK IN NIGERIA, EDUCATION AND
POLITICS IN NIGERIA (BILINGUAL EDITION)
FREIBURG IM BREISGAU,   VERLAG ROMBACH, 1964
042,043,128-03,
        CASE STUDY

GAUCHER JOSEPH
LES DEBUTS DE L'ENSEIGNMENT EN AFRIQUE FRANCOPHONE--JEAN
DARD ET L'ECOLE MUTELLE DE SAINT-LOUIS DU SENEGAL (THE
BEGINNINGS OF EDUCATION IN FRENCH-SPEAKING AFRICA--JEAN
DARD AND THE MUTUAL SCHOOL AT SAINT-LOUIS IN SENEGAL).
PARIS, INTERNATIONAL UNIVERSITY BOOKSELLERS, INC., 1968
042,130-03,
        LESS ACCESSIBLE

LEWIS W ARTHUR
EDUCATION FOR SCIENTIFIC PROFESSIONS IN THE POOR COUNTRIES.
DAEDALUS 91 SPRING 1962 PP 310-318
042,075,
        GENERAL THEORY

PIPER DONALD C   COLE TAYLOR   EDS
POST PRIMARY EDUCATION AND POLITICAL AND ECONOMIC
DEVELOPMENT.
DURHAM, NORTH CAROLINA, DUKE UNIVERSITY PRESS, 1964
042,
        GENERAL THEORY

UNESCO
VERNACULAR LANGUAGES IN EDUCATION.
UNESCO, 1953

042,
    GENERAL THEORY

43. EDUCATION AND ELITE RECRUITMENT

043
    CLIGNET REMI   FOSTER PHILIP
    THE FORTUNATE FEW.
    EVANSTON, NORTHWESTERN UNIVERSITY PRESS, 1966
    039,043,116-03,
            A STUDY OF SECONDARY SCHOOLS AND STUDENTS IN THE IVORY
            COAST. INTRODUCTION DEALS WITH NATURE OF COLONIAL ED-
            UCATIONAL POLICIES, THE POST-COLONIAL PERIOD, AND THE
            CRUCIAL POSITION OF SECONDARY SCHOOLS. OTHER CHAPTERS
            DEAL WITH ETHNIC, SOCIAL AND CULTURAL ORIGINS OF STU-
            DENTS-- RECRUITMENT OF STUDENTS-- STUDENTS ATTITUDES
            AND ADJUSTMENTS-- OCCUPATIONAL ASPIRATIONS AND EXPEC-
            TATIONS.

    LLOYD PETER C   ED
    THE NEW ELITES OF TROPICAL AFRICA
    LONDON, OXFORD UNIVERSITY PRESS, 1966
    043,044,
            DEFINES ELITE AS ANY PERSON WESTERN EDUCATED WITH
            ANNUAL INCOME OF AT LEAST 700 DOLLARS. DISCUSSES
            EDUCATIONAL SYSTEMS OF AFRICAN STATES AND DEGREE TO
            WHICH CONTEMPORARY ELITE IS DRAWN FROM THE MASSES,
            PARTICIPATION OF MODERN ELITE IN TRADITIONAL
            ORGANIZATIONS AND THE CULTURAL VALUES OF ELITE AND
            ACHIEVEMENT MOTIVATION. SUPPORTED BY EXCELLENT
            ORIGINAL CASE STUDIES(SIERRA LEONE,GHANA,TOGO,YORUBA,
            TRANSKEI, UGANDA, ETHIOPIA).

    CLIGNET REMI
    ETHNICITY SOCIAL DIFFERENTIATION AND SECONDARY SCHOOLING
    IN WEST AFRICA.
    CAHIERS D'ETUDES AFRICAINES 7 1967 PP 361-378
    043,
            REFERENCE

    CLIGNET REMI   FOSTER PHILIP
    INTRODUCTION.
    IN REMI CLIGNET AND PHILIP FOSTER, THE FORTUNATE FEW,
    EVANSTON, NORTHWESTERN UNIVERSITY PRESS, 1966, PP 3-22
    043,
            REFERENCE

    COWAN L GRAY   O CONNELL JAMES   SCANLON DAVID G
    EDUCATION AND NATION-BUILDING IN AFRICA.
    NEW YORK, PRAEGER, 1965
    042,043,
            REFERENCE

    KOPF DAVID   VON DER MUHLL G
    POLITICAL SOCIALIZATION IN KENYA AND TANZANIA.

JOURNAL OF MODERN AFRICAN STUDIES 5 MAY 1967 PP 13-51
043,117-03,136-03,
        REFERENCE

043
LEVINE VICTOR T
POLITICAL ELITE RECRUITMENT AND POLITICAL STRUCTURE IN
FRENCH-SPEAKING AFRICA.
CAHIERS D'ETUDES AFRICAINES, VOL. VIII, NO. 31, 1968,
PP. 369-389
043,
        REFERENCE
REFERENCE

LEWIS WILLIAM H
FUNCTIONAL ELITES-AN EMERGENT POLITICAL FORCE
IN NEW FORCES IN AFRICA,GEORGETOWN COLLOQUIUM ON AFRICA
PAPERS,WASHINGTON,PUBLIC AFFAIRS PRESS,1962, PP 114-128
043,
        REFERENCE

TARDITS M CLAUDE
THE NOTION OF THE ELITE AND THE URBAN SOCIAL SURVEY
IN AFRICA.
INTERNATIONAL SOCIAL SCIENCE BULLETIN 8 1956 PP 492-495
043,
        REFERENCE

TAYLOR A   ED
EDUCATIONAL AND OCCUPATIONAL SELECTION IN WEST AFRICA.
LONDON, OXFORD UNIVERSITY PRESS, 1962
043,
        REFERENCE

CLIGNET REMI   FOSTER PHILIP
THE HIERARCHY OF POSTPRIMARY SCHOOLS-- ITS IMPACT ON ETHNIC
AND SOCIAL RECRUITMENT OF STUDENTS CHAPTER 4.
IN REMI CLIGNET AND PHILIP FOSTER, THE FORTUNATE FEW,
EVANSTON,NORTHWESTERN UNIVERSITY PRESS,1965
043,
        CASE STUDY

CLIGNET REMI   FOSTER PHILIP
THE ETHNIC, SOCIAL AND CULTURAL ORIGIN OF STUDENTS IN THE
POSTPRIMARY SCHOOL CHAPTER 3.
IN REMI CLIGNET AND PHILIP FOSTER, THE FORTUNATE FEW,
EVANSTON, NORTHWESTERN UNIVERSITY PRESS , 1966
043,
        CASE STUDY

CURLE ADAM
EDUCATIONAL PROBLEMS OF DEVELOPING SOCIETIES--WITH CASE
STUDIES OF GHANA AND PAKISTAN.
NEW YORK, PRAEGER PUBLISHERS, 1969
043,114-03,
        CASE STUDY

DAVIDSON S
PSYCHIATRIC WORK AMONG THE BEMBA.
RHODES-LIVINGSTONE JOURNAL 7 1949 PP 75-86

043,142-03,
     CASE STUDY

043
  DZOBO N K
  THE BRAIN CRISIS IN THE TEACHING PROFESSION IN GHANA.
  IN COLIN LEGUM AND JOHN DRYSDALE, AFRICA CONTEMPORARY
  RECORD, AFRICA RESEARCH LIMITED, LONDON, 1969, PP.875-77
  043,114-03,
     CASE STUDY

  GUTKIND PETER C W
  THE ENERGY OF DESPAIR--SOCIAL ORGANIZATION OF THE UNEMPLOYED
  IN TWO AFRICAN CITIES-- LAGOS AND NAIROBI.
  CIVILISATIONS, VOL. XVII, 1967, PP. 186-380
  043,128-05,117-05,
     CASE STUDY

  LLOYD BARBARA B
  EDUCATION AND FAMILY LIFE IN THE DEVELOPMENT OF CLASS
  IDENTIFICATION AMONG THE YORUBA.
  IN LLOYD, THE NEW ELITES OF TROPICAL AFRICA, LONDON, OXFORD
  UNIVERSITY PRESS, 1966, P. 163-183
  043,128-04,
     CASE STUDY

  MERCIER PAUL
  EVOLUTION OF SENEGALESE ELITES
  INTERNATIONAL SOCIAL SCIENCE BULLETIN 8 1956 PP 441-451
  043,130-05,
     CASE STUDY

  RESNICK IDRIAN N   ED
  TANZANIA--REVOLUTION BY EDUCATION.
  NEW YORK, HUMANITIES PRESS INC., 1968
  043,136-03,
     CASE STUDY

  SKINNER ELLIOTT P
  INTERGENERATIONAL CONFLICT AMONG THE MOSSI-- FATHER
  AND SON.
  JOURNAL OF CONFLICT RESOLUTION 5 1961 PP 55-60
  043,141-03,
     CASE STUDY

  WEILER HANS N
  ERZIEHUNGSWESEN AND POLITIK IN NIGERIA, EDUCATION AND
  POLITICS IN NIGERIA (BILINGUAL EDITION)
  FREIBURG IM BREISGAU,   VERLAG ROMBACH, 1964
  042,043,128-03,
     CASE STUDY

  CLIGNET REMI   FOSTER PHILIP
  LA PREEMINENCE DE L'ENSEIGNEMENT CLASSIQUE EN COTE D'IVOIRE
  UN EXAMPLE D'ASSIMILATION (THE PREEMINENCE OF THE CLASSICAL
  EDUCATION IN THE IVORY COAST-- AN EXAMPLE OF ASSIMILATION).
  REVUE FRANCAISE DE SOCIOLOGIE 7 1966 PP 32-47
  043,
     LESS ACCESSIBLE

NDIAYE JEAN-PIERRE
ELITES AFRICAINES ET CULTURE OCCIDENTALE--ASSIMILATION OU
RESISTANCE (AFRICAN ELITES AND WESTERN CULTURE--
ASSIMILATION OR RESISTANCE).
PARIS, PRESENCE AFRICAINE, 1969
043,
     LESS ACCESSIBLE

043

NDIAYE JEAN-PIERRE
ENQUETE SUR LES ETUDIANTS NOIRS EN FRANCE (STUDY OF BLACK
STUDENTS IN FRANCE)
PARIS, EDITIONS REALITES AFRICAINES, 1962
043,096,
     LESS ACCESSIBLE

PAUVERT J C
URBANISATION ET PLANIFICATION DE L'EDUCATION (URBANIZATION
AND PLANNING OF EDUCATION).
CIVILISATIONS, VOL. XVIII, 1967, PP. 30-44
043,
     LESS ACCESSIBLE

BELL WENDELL
SOCIAL CHANGE AND ELITES IN AN EMERGENT NATION.
IN BARRINGER GEORGE BLANKSTEN RAYMOND MACK, SOCIAL CHANGE
IN DEVELOPING AREAS, CAMBRIDGE, MASS., SCHENKMAN PUBLISHING
COMPANY, 1965, PP 155-204
043,
     GENERAL THEORY

COLEMAN JAMES S
THE EDUCATION OF MODERN ELITES IN DEVELOPING COUNTRIES PT 3.
IN JAMES S COLEMAN (ED), EDUCATION AND POLITICAL
DEVELOPMENT, PRINCETON, NEW JERSEY, PRINCETON UNIVERSITY
PRESS, 1965
043,
     GENERAL THEORY

MCLUHAN H MARSHALL
THE GUTENBERG GALAXY.
TORONTO, UNIVERSITY OF TORONTO PRESS, 1962
037,043,
     GENERAL THEORY

SELIGMAN LESTER G
ELITE RECRUITMENT AND POLITICAL DEVELOPMENT CHAPTER 10.
IN JASON L FINKLE AND RICHARD W GABLE, POLITICAL
DEVELOPMENT AND SOCIAL CHANGE, NEW YORK, JOHN WILEY, 1966
043,
     GENERAL THEORY

44. THE NEW ELITES OF AFRICA

AWOLOWO OBAFEMI
AWO--THE AUTOBIOGRAPHY OF CHIEF OBAFEMI AWOLOWO.
CAMBRIDGE, CAMBRIDGE UNIVERSITY PRESS, 1960
044,128-04,
    AUTOBIOGRAPHY OF FORMER LEADER OF ACTION GROUP PARTY IN
    NIGERIA, WHO IS NOW COMMISSIONER OF FINANCE IN NIGERIA.
    AUTHOR IS IDENTIFIED WITH NON-TRADITIONAL YORUBA POLI-
    TICAL FORCES, AND A LEADING PROPONENT OF AFRICAN SOC-
    IALISM AND DEMOCRACY. BOOK TRACES HIS CHILDHOOD, HIS
    LEGAL TRAINING IN LONDON, AND HIS ENTRY INTO NATIONAL-
    IST POLITICS IN PRE-INDEPENDENCE PERIOD.

044

GUEYE LAMINE
ITINERAIRE AFRICAIN (AFRICAN ITINERARY).
PARIS, PRESENCE AFRICAINE, 1966
044,060,130-04,
    POLITICAL AUTOBIOGRAPHY BY ONE OF EARLIEST SENEGALESE
    POLITICIANS. GIVES INTERPRETATION OF POLITICAL EVENTS
    AND PERSONALITIES IN SENEGAL FROM 1913 TO 1965.

KENYATTA JOMO
SUFFERING WITHOUT BITTERNESS--THE FOUNDING OF THE KENYA
NATION.
KENYA, EAST AFRICAN PUBLISHING HOUSE, 1968
044,117-04,
    AUTOBIOGRAPHY OF KENYAN LEADER, WITH EMPHASIS ON POLI-
    TICAL CAREER--HIS TRIAL DURING MAU MAU PERIOD, HIS
    PRISON INTERLUDE, HIS RELEASE AND DEMAND FOR KENYAN IN-
    DEPENDENCE, THE ELECTION AND POST-INDEPENDENCE PATTERN.
    FULL APPENDIX OF SPEECHES FROM 1963-67.

LLOYD PETER C   ED
THE NEW ELITES OF TROPICAL AFRICA
LONDON, OXFORD UNIVERSITY PRESS, 1966
043,044,
    DEFINES ELITE AS ANY PERSON WESTERN EDUCATED WITH
    ANNUAL INCOME OF AT LEAST 700 DOLLARS. DISCUSSES
    EDUCATIONAL SYSTEMS OF AFRICAN STATES AND DEGREE TO
    WHICH CONTEMPORARY ELITE IS DRAWN FROM THE MASSES,
    PARTICIPATION OF MODERN ELITE IN TRADITIONAL
    ORGANIZATIONS AND THE CULTURAL VALUES OF ELITE AND
    ACHIEVEMENT MOTIVATION. SUPPORTED BY EXCELLENT
    ORIGINAL CASE STUDIES(SIERRA LEONE,GHANA,TOGO,YORUBA,
    TRANSKEI, UGANDA, ETHIOPIA).

MARKOVITZ IRVING L
LEOPOLD SENGHOR AND THE POLITICS OF NEGRITUDE.
NEW YORK, ATHENEUM, 1969 (LONDON, HEINEMANN
EDUCATIONAL BOOKS)
044,054,130-04,
    DEALS WITH THE POLITICAL CONTEXT--SENEGAL--IN WHICH
    SENGHOR HAS DONE HIS WRITINGS. DISCUSSES THE FORMATIVE
    PERIODS IN THE EMERGENCE OF SENGHOR'S CONCEPTS OF NE-
    GRITUDE, AND PROVIDES A THOROUGH EVALUATION OF THE SUB-
    STANTIVE CONCEPTS OF NEGRITUDE.

MBOYA TOM
FREEDOM AND AFTER.
BOSTON, LITTLE, BROWN, AND COMPANY, 1963

044,060,117-04,
POLITICAL AUTOBIOGRAPHY OF RECENTLY ASSASSINATED LEADER
OF KENYA FEDERATION OF LABOR AND GOVERNMENT MINISTER.
DISCUSSES HIS EARLY DAYS IN SCHOOL (INCLUDING CONSIDER-
ING THE PRIESTHOOD), HIS TRAINING AS SANITARY INSPECTOR
 HIS ENTRY INTO TRADE UNIONISM, HIS ENTRY INTO NATION-
ALIST POLITICS, AND THE STRUGGLE FOR INDEPENDENCE.
FINAL CHAPTERS GIVE HIS VIEWS ON AFRICAN SOCIALISM, NEO
COLONIALISM, TRADE UNIONISM, PAN-AFRICANISM, AND AFRI-
CAN RELATIONS WITH THE WORLD.

044

MERCIER PAUL
PROBLEMS OF SOCIAL STRATIFICATION IN WEST AFRICA 1954.
IN IMMANUEL WALLERSTEIN, SOCIAL CHANGE-- THE COLONIAL
SITUATION, NEW YORK, WILEY, 1966 , PP 340-358
044,
DEALS WITH THE RISE OF AN AFRICAN ELITE WITHIN THE
COLONIAL CONTEXT-- DEFINES MEANING OF TERM SOCIAL
CLASS -- COMPARES FORMATION OF SOCIAL CLASSES WITH
OTHER GROUPS-- AND EXAMINES THE DEVELOPMENT OF TEN-
SIONS AND ANTAGONISMS. BASICALLY A STUDY OF SOCIAL
CLASSES IN GESTATION .

NKRUMAH KWAME
GHANA--THE AUTOBIOGRAPHY OF KWAME NKRUMAH.
NEW YORK, NELSON, 1957
044,114-04,
AUTOBIOGRAPHY BY FORMER PRESIDENT OF GHANA, TRACES HIS
CHILDHOOD ON COAST, HIS SCHOOLING, HIS HIGHER EDUCATION
IN AMERICA, HIS OCCUPATIONAL ENDEAVORS IN AMERICA, HIS
RETURN TO ENGLAND TO ENGAGE IN NATIONALIST ORGANIZATION
 AND HIS RETURN TO GHANA TO PARTICIPATE IN THE LIBER-
ATION STRUGGLE. A SUBSEQUENT VOLUME--I SPEAK OF FREE-
DOM--TRACES SUBSEQUENT POLITICAL CAREER IN GHANA.

REUTERS NEWS AGENCY
THE NEW AFRICANS--REUTERS GUIDE TO THE CONTEMPORARY HISTORY
OF EMERGENT AFRICA AND ITS LEADERS.
LONDON, PAUL HAMLYN, 1967
044,
BASED ON THE REPORTS OF ABOUT 50 REUTERS CORRESPON-
DENTS, COVERS IN VARYING DEGREES OF DEPTH THE BIOGRAPH-
IES OF THE MAJOR LEADERS OF ALL 33 COUNTRIES IN BLACK
AFRICA. FULLER DETAILS ARE GIVEN OF SUCH LEADERS AS
KWAME NKRUMAH, HASTINGS BANDA, JOMO KENYATTA, JOSEPH
KASAVUBU, AND JOSEPH MOBUTU.

SEGAL RONALD
POLITICAL AFRICA--A WHO'S WHO OF PERSONALITIES AND PARTIES.
NEW YORK, PRAEGER, 1961
044,
ALTHOUGH NOW SUPERSEDED BY REUTERS' DIRECTORY OF AFRI-
CAN LEADERS, THIS VOLUME REMAINS A PRIMARY REFERENCE
SOURCE FOR BIOGRAPHICAL DETAILS OF THE NEW AFRICAN POL-
ITICAL ELITE.

AJAYI J F ADE   WEBSTER J B
THE EMERGENCE OF A NEW ELITE IN AFRICA
IN CHAPTER 9 IN J C ANENE AND GODFREY BROWN,AFRICA IN THE

NINETEENTH AND TWENTIETH CENTURIES,LONDON,NELSON;AND IBADAN
UNIVERSITY PRESS,1966
044,
        REFERENCE

044
   CALLAWAY ARCHIBALD
   UNEMPLOYMENT AMONG AFRICAN SCHOOL LEAVERS
   JOURNAL OF MODERN AFRICAN STUDIES 1 1963 PP 351-371
   044,
        REFERENCE

   DAVIES IOAN
   AFRICAN TRADE UNIONS.
   BALTIMORE,PENGUIN BOOKS,1966
   044,073,
        REFERENCE

   FRIEDLAND WILLIAM H
   SOME SOURCES OF TRADITIONALISM AMONG MODERN AFRICAN ELITES.
   IN WILLIAM J HANNA (ED), INDEPENDENT BLACK AFRICA, CHICAGO,
   RAND MCNALLY, 1964, PP 363-369
   044,
        REFERENCE

   HODGKIN THOMAS
   THE AFRICAN MIDDLE CLASS
   IN WALLERSTEIN,SOCIAL CHANGE-THE COLONIAL SITUATION,NEW YORK,
   JOHN WILEY AND SONS,1966,PP 359-362;AND IN CORONA 8 1956
   PP 85-88
   044,
        REFERENCE

   MAZRUI ALI A
   ON HEROES AND UHURU-WORSHIP CHAPTER 2.
   IN ON HEROES AND UHURU-WORSHIP, LONDON, LONGMANS,
   1967, PP 19-34
   044,
        REFERENCE

   NICOL DAVIDSON
   THE FORMATION OF A WEST AFRICAN INTELLECTUAL COMMUNITY
   CHAPTER 3.
   IN THE WEST AFRICAN INTELLECTUAL COMMUNITY SEMINAR
   IBADAN, IBADAN UNIVERSITY PRESS,1962,PP 10-17
   044,
        REFERENCE

   POLK WILLIAM R
   GENERATIONS CLASSES AND POLITICS.
   IN TIBOR KEREKES (ED), THE ARAB MIDDLE EAST AND MUSLIM
   AFRICA, NEW YORK,PRAEGER,1961,PP 105-120
   044,
        REFERENCE

   SMYTHE HUGH H   SMYTHE MABEL M
   BLACK AFRICA'S NEW POWER ELITE.
   SOUTH ATLANTIC QUARTERLY 59 WINTER 1960 PP 13-23
   044,
        REFERENCE

044

SMYTHE HUGH H   SMYTHE MABEL M
AFRICA'S NEW CLASS.
QUEEN'S QUARTERLY 47 SUMMER 1960 PP 225-231
044,
        REFERENCE

ABU-LUGHOD IBRAHIM
THE TRANSFORMATION OF THE EGYPTIAN ELITE.
THE MIDDLE EAST JOURNAL, SUMMER, 1967, PP. 325-343
044,140-04,
        CASE STUDY

AZIKIWE NNAMDI
ZIK-- A SELECTION FROM THE SPEECHES OF DOCTOR NNAMDI AZIKIWE
CAMBRIDGE ENGLAND CAMBRIDGE UNIVERSITY PRESS 1961
044,060,091,096,128-04,
        CASE STUDY

BELLO AHMADU
MY LIFE.
CAMBRIDGE, ENGLAND, CAMBRIDGE UNIVERSITY PRESS, 1962
044,128-04,
        CASE STUDY

CHAGULA W K
THE ROLE OF THE ELITE, THE INTELLIGENTSIA AND EDUCATED EAST
AFRICANS, IN THE DEVELOPMENT OF UGANDA, KENYA AND TANZANIA.
KAMPALA,EAST AFRICAN ACADEMY, SECOND FOUNDATION LECTURE, 1966
044,117-03,136-03,139-03,
        CASE STUDY

FOSTER PHILIP
EDUCATION   AND SOCIAL CHANGE IN GHANA.
CHICAGO,UNIVERSITY OF CHICAGO PRESS, 1965
044,114-03,
        CASE STUDY

GARIGUE PHILIP
THE WEST AFRICAN STUDENTS UNION.
AFRICA 23 1953 PP 55-69
044,
        CASE STUDY

GOODY JACK
ANOMIE IN ASHANTI.
AFRICA 26 1957 PP 356-363
044,114-03,
        CASE STUDY

IKEOTUONYE VINCENT
ZIK OF NEW AFRICA.
LONDON, P R MACMILLAN, 1961
044,128-04,
        CASE STUDY

KAUNDA KENNETH
SOME PERSONAL REFLECTIONS CHAPTER 2.
IN AFRICA'S FREEDOM, NEW YORK, BARNES AND NOBLE, 1964,

PP 24-37
044,142-04,
     CASE STUDY

044

KILBY PETER
INDUSTRIALIZATION IN AN OPEN ECONOMY--NIGERIA 1945-1966.
CAMBRIDGE, UNIVERSITY PRESS, 1969
044,071,128-08,
     CASE STUDY

MITCHELL N C
YORUBA TOWNS.
IN K M BARBOUR AND R M PROTHERO, (EDS.), ESSAYS ON
AFRICAN POPULATION, NEW YORK, PRAEGER, 1962, PP 279-301
044,
     CASE STUDY

O'CONNELL JAMES
SENGHOR, NKRUMAH AND AZIKIWE-- UNITY AND DIVERSITY IN THE
WEST AFRICAN STATES.
NIGERIAN JOURNAL OF ECONOMIC AND SOCIAL STUDIES 5 MARCH
1963 PP 77-93
044,114-04,128-04,130-04,
     CASE STUDY

SAADALLAH BELKACEM
THE RISE OF THE ALGERIAN ELITE, 1900-24.
THE JOURNAL OF MODERN AFRICAN STUDIES 5 MAY 1967 PP 69-77
044,101-04,
     CASE STUDY

SMYTHE HUGH H
AFRICAN ELITE IN NIGERIA.
IN AMSAC, AFRICA SEEN BY AMERICAN NEGROES, PARIS,
PRESENCE AFRICAINE, 1958, PP 71-82
044,128-04,
     CASE STUDY

MILICENT ERNEST   SORDE MONIQUE
LEOPOLD SEDAR SENGHOR ET LA NAISSANCE DE L'AFRIQUE MODERNE
(LEOPOLD SEDAR SENGHOR AND THE BIRTH OF MODERN AFRICA).
PARIS, INTERNATIONAL UNIVERSITY BOOKSELLERS, INC., 1969
044,130-04,
     LESS ACCESSIBLE

BACHRACH PETER
THE THEORY OF DEMOCRATIC ELITISM.
BOSTON, LITTLE, BROWN AND COMPANY, 1966
044,
     GENERAL THEORY

BULMER-THOMAS IVOR
DEVELOPMENT OF A MIDDLE CLASS IN TROPICAL AND SUB-TROPICAL
COUNTRIES.
BRUSSELS, INTERNATIONAL INSTITUTE OF DIFFERING CIVILIZATIONS,
GENERAL REPORT, 1955, PP 356-364
044,
     GENERAL THEORY

LASSWELL HAROLD
THE COMPARATIVE STUDY OF ELITES.
STANFORD, CALIFORNIA, HOOVER INSTITUTE STUDIES, 1952
044,
        GENERAL THEORY

044
LASSWELL HAROLD   LERNER DANIEL
WORLD REVOLUTIONARY ELITES
CAMBRIDGE, MASS., MIT PRESS, 1965
044,
        GENERAL THEORY

SHILS EDWARD
THE INTELLECTUALS IN THE POLITICAL DEVELOPMENT OF NEW
STATES.
WORLD POLITICS 12 APRIL 1960 PP 329-368
044,
        GENERAL THEORY

LLOYD PETER C
CLASS CONSCIOUSNESS AMONG THE YORUBA.
IN LLOYD, THE NEW ELITES OF TROPICAL AFRICA, LONDON, OXFORD
UNIVERSITY PRESS, 1966, P. 328-341
044,128-04,

MERCIER PAUL
ELITES ET FORCES POLITIQUES.
IN LLOYD, THE NEW ELITES OF TROPICAL AFRICA, LONDON, OXFORD
UNIVERSITY PRESS, 1966, P. 367-380
044,

SOUTHALL AIDAN
THE CONCEPT OF ELITES AND THEIR FORMATION IN UGANDA.
IN LLOYD, THE NEW ELITES OF TROPICAL AFRICA, LONDON, OXFORD
UNIVERSITY PRESS, 1966, P. 342-366
044,139-04,

45. THE DEVELOPMENT OF URBAN SOCIETY

045
BREESE GERALD
URBANIZATION IN NEWLY DEVELOPING COUNTRIES.
ENGLEWOOD CLIFFS, NJ, PRENTICE-HALL, 1966
045,
        GENERAL STUDY OF URBANIZATION INTENDED FOR INTRODUC-
        TORY USE. INCLUDES SECTIONS ON THE SCALE AND PACE OF
        URBANIZATION-- THE ROLE, FORM, AND STRUCTURE OF CITIES
        (INCLUDING A COMPARATIVE ANALYSIS OF URBANIZATION)--
        THE NATURE OF URBAN INHABITANTS-- PATTERNS IN THE DE-
        VELOPING CITY-- AND AN ATTEMPT TO EVALUATE THE FUTURE
        OF URBANIZATION IN THE NEW STATES.

BREESE GERALD   ED
THE CITY IN NEWLY DEVELOPING COUNTRIES.

ENGLEWOOD CLIFFS, NJ, PRENTICE-HALL, 1969
045,
   REPRINTS OF KEY THEORETICAL AND CASE STUDY ARTICLES,
   INCLUDING SEVERAL ON AFRICA--SIZE AND GROWTH OF URBAN
   POPULATION IN AFRICA. CAPITALS OF THE NEW AFRICA. UR-
   BANIZATION AND SOCIAL CHANGE IN AFRICA. MIGRANT AD-
   JUSTMENT TO CITY LIFE IN EGYPT. AFRICAN URBANISM, MO-
   BILITY, AND SOCIAL NETWORK. COMPARISON OF LEOPOLDVILLE
   AND LAGOS.

045

HERSKOVITS MELVILLE J
THE HUMAN FACTOR IN CHANGING AFRICA.
NEW YORK ALFRED A KNOPF 1962
001,038,045,047,
   MAJOR WORK OF SYNTHESIS ON THE PATTERNS AND PROBLEMS
   PRIMARILY DURING THE COLONIAL PERIOD. EXCELLENT
   SUMMARY CHAPTERS ON AFRICA IN THE WORLD SETTING, CUL-
   TURE AREAS, AGRICULTURAL AND INDUSTRIAL GROWTH, LAW,
   EDUCATION, URBANIZATION, NATIONALISM, AND MORE RECENT
   PROBLEMS OF ECONOMIC AND POLITICAL CHANGE, RELIGION
   AND THE ARTS, AND THE SEARCH FOR VALUES.

LLOYD PETER C   MABOGUNJE AKIN L   AWE B
THE CITY OF IBADAN-- A SYMPOSIUM ON ITS STRUCTURE AND
DEVELOPMENT.
CAMBRIDGE, CAMBRIDGE UNIVERSITY PRESS, 1967
026,045,128-05,
   REPORT OF SYMPOSIUM AT UNIVERSITY OF IBADAN. PROVIDES
   COMPREHENSIVE SURVEY OF THE HISTORY, GEOGRAPHY, SOC-
   IOLOGY, AND POLITICAL STRUCTURE, OF THE LARGEST TRADI-
   TIONAL BLACK AFRICAN CITY. PIONEER WORK IN INTER-
   DISCIPLINARY URBAN STUDIES, AND PERHAPS THE BEST
   SINGLE VOLUME TO DATE ON AN AFRICAN URBAN CENTER.

MABOGUNJE AKIN L
URBANIZATION IN NIGERIA.
NEW YORK, AFRICANA PUBLISHING CORPORATION, 1969
045,047,128-05,
   ALTHOUGH PRIMARILY A CASE STUDY OF NIGERIA, INTRODUC-
   TORY SECTIONS PROVIDES EXCELLENT OVERVIEW OF THE HIST-
   ORICAL PROCESS OF URBANIZATION WHILE LAST CHAPTERS
   FOCUS ON PROBLEMS OF ECONOMIC DEVELOPMENT. UNIQUE IN
   ITS ANALYSIS OF AN ENTIRE URBAN SYSTEM, COMBINING
   HISTORICAL-DESCRIPTIVE APPROACH WITH MODERN QUANTITA-
   TIVE TECHNIQUES. ONLY DRAWBACK IS ALMOST UNAVOIDABLE
   DEPENDENCE ON 1955 CENSUS DATA. A GROUND-BREAKING
   WORK BY OUTSTANDING AFRICAN GEOGRAPHER.

HAMDAN G
CAPITALS OF THE NEW AFRICA.
ECONOMIC GEOGRAPHY 40 JULY 1964 PP 239-253
045,
   REFERENCE

MABOGUNJE AKIN L
URBANIZATION IN WEST AFRICA.
INTERNATIONAL REVIEW OF MISSIONS 55 JULY 1966
045,
   REFERENCE

045

MCCALL DANIEL F
DYNAMICS OF URBANIZATION IN AFRICA.
ANNALS OF THE AMERICAN ACADEMY OF POLITICAL AND SOCIAL
SCIENCES NO 298 1955 PP 151-160; ALSO P R GOULD, AFRICA-- CONT-
INENT OF CHANGE, WADSWORTH, 1961, PP 183-195
045,
        REFERENCE

MITCHELL J CLYDE
THEORETICAL ORIENTATIONS IN AFRICAN URBAN STUDIES.
IN MICHAEL BANTON (ED), THE SOCIAL ANTHROPOLOGY OF COMPLEX
SOCIETIES, NEW YORK, PRAEGER, 1966
045,
        REFERENCE

ORAM N
TOWNS IN AFRICA.
LONDON, OXFORD UNIVERSITY PRESS, 1965
045,
        REFERENCE

THOMAS B E
THE LOCATION AND NATURE OF WEST AFRICAN CITIES CHAPTER 2.
IN HILDA KUPER (ED), URBANIZATION AND MIGRATION IN WEST
AFRICA, BERKELEY, UNIVERSITY OF CALIFORNIA PRESS, 1965
045,
        REFERENCE

BANTON MICHAEL P
WEST AFRICAN CITY--A STUDY OF TRIBAL LIFE IN FREETOWN.
LONDON, OXFORD UNIVERSITY PRESS, 1957
045,131-05,
        CASE STUDY

BETTS   RAYMOND F
THE PROBLEM OF THE MEDINA IN THE URBAN PLANNING OF DAKAR
SENEGAL
AFRICAN URBAN NOTES, VOL IV, NO. 3, SEPT. 1969, PP. 5-15
045,092,
        CASE STUDY

BOATENG E A
THE GROWTH AND FUNCTIONS OF ACCRA.
BULLETIN OF THE GHANA GEOGRAPHICAL ASSOCIATION 4 JULY 1959
PP 4-15
045,114-05,
        CASE STUDY

CALDWELL JOHN C
AFRICAN RURAL-URBAN MIGRATION--THE MOVEMENT TO GHANA≠S
TOWNS.
NEW YORK (COLUMBIA), MCGILL-QUEEN'S UNIVERSITY PRESS, 1969
045,114-05,
        CASE STUDY

DE BLIJ HARM J
MOMBASA-- AN AFRICAN CITY.
EVANSTON, NORTHWESTERN UNIVERSITY PRESS, 1968

```
045,117-05,
     CASE STUDY
```

045

```
DE BLIJ HARM J
DAR ES SALAAM.
EVANSTON, NORTHWESTERN UNIVERSITY PRESS, 1963
045,136-05,
     CASE STUDY
```

```
EAST AFRICA ROYAL COMMISSION
EAST AFRICA ROYAL COMMISSION 1953-1955 REPORT.
LONDON, HER MAJESTY'S STATIONERY OFFICE, COMMAND PAPER NO 9475
REPRINT 482 1961
035,045,
     CASE STUDY
```

```
FYFE CHRISTOPHER     JONES ELDRED        EDS
FREETOWN--A SYMPOSIUM.
FREETOWN, SIERRA LEONE UNIVERSITY PRESS, 1968
045,131-05,
     CASE STUDY
```

```
HORVATH RONALD J
THE WANDERING CAPITALS OF ETHIOPIA.
JOURNAL OF AFRICAN HISTORY, X, 2, 1969, PP. 205-219
045,110-05,
     CASE STUDY
```

```
MABOGUNJE AKIN L
THE EVOLUTION OF RURAL SETTLEMENT IN EGBA DIVISION, NIGERIA.
JOURNAL OF TROPICAL GEOGRAPHY, SINGAPORE AND KUALA LUMPUR
13 DECEMBER 1959 PP 65-77
045,128-05,
     CASE STUDY
```

```
MINER HORACE M
THE PRIMITIVE CITY OF TIMBUCTOO
GARDEN CITY, NEW JERSEY, DOUBLEDAY, 1965
045,123-05,
     CASE STUDY
```

```
PANKHURST RICHARD
MENELIK AND THE FOUNDATION OF ADDIS ABABA.
JOURNAL OF AFRICAN HISTORY 2 1961 PP 103-117
045,110-05,
     CASE STUDY
```

```
SCHWAB WILLIAM B
OSHOGBO- AN URBAN COMMUNITY CHAPTER 6.
IN HILDA KUPER (ED), URBANIZATION AND MIGRATION IN WEST
AFRICA, BERKELEY, UNIVERSITY OF CALIFORNIA PRESS, 1965
045,
     CASE STUDY
```

```
WHITTLESEY DERWENT
KANO A SUDANESE METROPOLIS.
GEOGRAPHICAL REVIEW 27 APRIL 1937 PP 177-200
045,
     CASE STUDY
```

045

CHARPY JACQUES
LA FONDATION DE DAKAR (THE FOUNDATION OF DAKAR) 1845-1857-
1869.
PARIS,LAROSE,1958
045,130-05,
        LESS ACCESSIBLE

ROUCH JEAN
MIGRATION AU GOLD COAST (MIGRATION TO THE GOLD COAST).
JOURNAL DE LA SOCIETE DES AFRICANISTES 26 1956 PP 33-196
045,114-05,
        LESS ACCESSIBLE

SJOBERG GIDEON
FOLK AND FEUDAL SOCIETIES CHAPTER 2.
IN JASON L FINKLE AND RICHARD W GABLE, POLITICAL
DEVELOPMENT AND SOCIAL CHANGE, NEW YORK, JOHN WILEY, 1966
045,
        GENERAL THEORY

SJOBERG GIDEON
THE PREINDUSTRIAL CITY, PAST AND PRESENT.
GLENCOE, ILLINOIS,   FREE PRESS, 1960
045,
        GENERAL THEORY

46. THE NATURE OF URBAN LIFE

046

EPSTEIN ARNOLD L
URBANIZATION AND SOCIAL CHANGE IN AFRICA.
CURRENT ANTHROPOLOGY 8 NO 4 OCTOBER 1967 PP 275-283
007,046,
        OUTSTANDING SURVEY ARTICLE, WHICH INCLUDES CRITIQUES
        BY LEADING URBAN ANTHROPOLOGISTS. DESCRIBES THREE DE-
        TERMINANTS OF URBAN SOCIAL STRUCTURE-- INDUSTRIAL,
        CIVIC, AND DEMOGRAPHIC. USING THESE CATEGORIES,
        AUTHOR EXAMINES INTRA-URBAN RELATIONSHIPS (NETWORK
        RELATIONS-- CATEGORICAL RELATIONS, OR TRIBALISM --
        AND FORMAL, OR ASSOCIATIONAL RELATIONS).

GREENBERG JOSEPH H
URBANISM,MIGRATION AND LANGUAGE
CHAPTER 4 IN HILDA KUPER (ED),URBANIZATION AND MIGRATION IN
WEST AFRICA,BERKELEY,UNIVERSITY OF CALIFORNIA PRESS,1965
007,046,
        ASSESSES THE SHIFT OF RURAL ETHNIC MEMBERS TO URBAN
        SETTING IN TERMS OF IMPACT ON ETHNIC IDENTITY AND ON
        ETHNIC CULTURE TRAITS. SUGGESTS THAT EVERY AFRICAN IS
        DETRIBALIZED AS SOON AS HE LEAVES HIS TRIBAL AREA.
        HOWEVER HE SUGGESTS THAT URBAN ETHNICITY HAS IMPORTANT
        DIMENSIONS ESPECIALLY IN VOLUNTARY ASSOCIATIONS. BEST
        INTRODUCTION TO LINGUISTIC ASPECTS OF URBANIZATION AND

MIGRATION-ONLY REASONABLE SURVEY.

046

GREER SCOTT   MCELRATH DENNIS   MINAR DAVID
THE NEW URBANIZATION.
NEW YORK, ST MARTIN'S PRESS 1968
046,
    OUTSTANDING ANTHOLOGY. INCLUDES INTRODUCTORY OVERVIEW
    OF HOW URBANIZATION IN NEW NATIONS IS DIFFERENT IN
    NATURE FROM WESTERN EXPERIENCE. CASE STUDIES OF
    URBANIZATION IN NIGER BY VAN HOEY, AND SOCIETAL SCALE
    AND SOCIAL DIFFERENTIATION IN ACCRA, BY MCELRATH.

GUTKIND PETER C W
AFRICAN URBANISM, MOBILITY AND THE SOCIAL NETWORK.
INTERNATIONAL JOURNAL OF COMPARATIVE SOCIOLOGY 6 1965 PP
48-60 SPECIAL ISSUE ON KINSHIP AND GEOGRAPHICAL
MOBILITY, R PIDDINGTON, GUEST ED
046,
    DISTINGUISHES BETWEEN KIN BASED AND ASSOCIATION BASED
    NETWORKS IN URBAN CONTEXT. ALTHOUGH NOT MUTUALLY
    EXCLUSIVE, THE FORMER MEET DEMANDS OF RECIPROCAL ROLES
    WHILE THE LATTER MEET NEW SITUATIONS TO WHICH ROLE
    RESPONSES ARE NOT YET ESTABLISHED. AUTHOR IS PROFES-
    SOR AT MCGILL UNIVERSITY, AND LEADING URBAN ANTHRO-
    POLOGIST.

GUTKIND PETER C W
THE AFRICAN URBAN MILIEU-- A FORCE IN RAPID CHANGE.
CIVILISATIONS 12 1962 PP 167-195
046,
    EXCELLENT DISCUSSION OF NEW AND OLD TOWNS (WITH EMPHA-
    SIS ON REGIONAL VARIATIONS)-- OF THE GROWTH OF TOWNS--
    OF CONTEMPORARY PROBLEMS IN NEW URBAN AREAS (PHYSICAL,
    SOCIAL, ECONOMIC AND POLITICAL SETTINGS)-- EXAMINED
    WITHIN FRAMEWORK OF THE SUBSTANTIAL BREAK WITH TRADI-
    TION USUALLY SEEN IN URBAN AREAS.

LITTLE KENNETH
WEST AFRICAN URBANIZATION-A STUDY OF VOLUNTARY ASSOCIATIONS
IN SOCIAL CHANGE
CAMBRIDGE CAMBRIDGE UNIVERSITY PRESS 1965
046,
    PIONEERING WORK, DIVIDES URBAN VOLUNTARY ASSOCIATIONS
    INTO TRIBAL UNIONS AND SYNCRETIST CULTS, GROUPS
    CONCERNED WITH MUTUAL BENEFIT AND WITH RECREATION, AND
    ASSOCIATIONS BASED ON COMMON INTEREST OF MEMBERS IN
    CHRISTIAN RELIGION AND WESTERN CULTURE.

PLOTNICOV LEONARD
STRANGERS TO THE CITY-- URBAN MAN IN JOS, NIGERIA.
PITTSBURGH, UNIVERSITY OF PITTSBURGH PRESS, 1967
046,128-05,
    REASSESSES PREVIOUS STUDIES WHICH EMPHASIZE THE BREAK-
    DOWN OF THE FAMILY AND ETHNIC RELATIONSHIPS IN URBAN
    CONTEXT. INTENSIVE STUDY OF SELECTED ETHNIC REPRESEN-
    TATIVES IN JOS, A MODERN MINING TOWN IN NIGERIA. IN-
    DICATES THAT BEHAVIOR WITH RESPECT TO STRESSES OF
    URBAN LIVING, IS NOT CONFUSED AND DISORGANIZED, BUT
    REASONABLE AND PRAGMATIC.

046
WALLERSTEIN I M
VOLUNTARY ASSOCIATIONS.
IN JAMES S COLEMAN AND CARL ROSBERG (EDS) POLITICAL
PARTIES AND NATIONAL INTEGRATION IN TROPICAL AFRICA
BERKELEY UNIVERSITY OF CALIFORNIA PRESS 1964 PP 318-339
046,
     DISTINGUISHES VARIATIONS IN URBAN VOLUNTARY ASSOCIA-
     TIONS, AND GIVES HISTORICAL BACKGROUND AS TO THE DE-
     VELOPMENT OF SUCH ASSOCIATIONS DURING THE COLONIAL
     PERIOD. MANY EXAMPLES DRAWN FROM GHANA AND IVORY
     COAST WHERE AUTHOR DID FIELD RESEARCH.

BASCOM WILLIAM R
THE URBAN AFRICAN AND HIS WORLD.
CAHIERS D'ETUDES AFRICAINES 4 APRIL 1963 PP 163-185
046,
     REFERENCE

CLIGNET REMI
MANY WIVES, MANY POWERS--AUTHORITY AND POWER IN POLYGYNOUS
FAMILIES.
EVANSTON, NORTHWESTERN UNIVERSITY PRESS, 1970
046,116-03,
     REFERENCE

CLIGNET REMI   SWEEN JOYCE
SOCIAL CHANGE AND TYPE OF MARRIAGE.
AMERICAN JOURNAL OF SOCIOLOGY, VOL. 74, NO. 1, JULY 1969,
PP. 123-145
046,
     REFERENCE

FAGE JOHN D
SOME THOUGHTS ON MIGRATION AND URBAN SETTLEMENT CHAPTER 3.
IN HILDA KUPER (ED), URBANIZATION AND MIGRATION IN WEST
AFRICA, BERKELEY, UNIVERSITY OF CALIFORNIA PRESS,1965
046,
     REFERENCE

GUTKIND PETER C W
AFRICAN URBAN CHIEFS-- AGENTS OF STABILITY OR CHANGE IN
AFRICAN URBAN LIFE.
ANTHROPOLOGICA 8 1966 PP 249-268
046,
     REFERENCE

GUTKIND PETER C W
AFRICAN URBAN LIFE.
ANTHROPOLOGICA 8 1966 PP 249-268
046,
     REFERENCE

HANNA WILLIAM J   HANNA JUDITH L
THE INTEGRATIVE ROLE OF URBAN AFRICA S MIDDLEPLACES AND
MIDDLEMEN.
CIVILISATIONS, VOL. XVII, 1967, PP. 12-30
046,
     REFERENCE

046

KUPER HILDA   ED
URBANIZATION AND MIGRATION IN WEST AFRICA.
BERKELEY, UNIVERSITY OF CALIFORNIA PRESS, 1965
046,
        REFERENCE

KUPER LEO
SOCIOLOGY-- SOME ASPECTS OF URBAN PLURAL SOCIETIES.
IN ROBERT A LYSTAD (ED), THE AFRICAN WORLD, NEW YORK,
PRAEGER, 1966, PP 107-130
046,
        REFERENCE

LITTLE KENNETH
THE ORGANIZATION OF VOLUNTARY ASSOCIATIONS IN WEST AFRICA.
CIVILIZATIONS 9 1959 PP 283-300
046,
        REFERENCE

RICHARDS AUDREY I
MULTI-TRIBALISM IN AFRICAN URBAN AREAS.
CIVILISATIONS 16 1966 PP 354-364
046,
        REFERENCE

SHINAR P
NOTE ON THE SOCIO-ECONOMIC AND CULTURAL ROLE OF SUFI
BROTHERHOODS AND MARABUTISM IN THE MODERN MAGHRIB.
IN LALAGE BOWN AND MICHAEL CROWDER (EDS.), PROCEEDINGS OF
THE FIRST INTERNATIONAL CONGRESS OF AFRICANISTS, ACCRA,
1962, LONDON, LONGMANS, 1964, PP 272-285
046,
        REFERENCE

SKALNIKOVA O
ETHNOGRAPHICAL RESEARCH INTO THE PRESENT CHANGES IN THE
MODE OF LIFE OF URBAN POPULATION IN AFRICA.
IN LALAGE BOWN AND MICHAEL CROWDER (EDS.), PROCEEDINGS OF
THE FIRST INTERNATIONAL CONGRESS OF AFRICANISTS, ACCRA,
1962, LONDON, LONGMANS, 1964, PP 286-297
046,
        REFERENCE

SKINNER ELLIOTT P
STRANGERS IN WEST AFRICAN SOCIETIES.
AFRICA (LONDON) 33 1963 PP 307-320
046,
        REFERENCE

AKINOLA R A
THE INDUSTRIAL STRUCTURE OF IBADAN.
NIGERIAN GEOGRAPHICAL JOURNAL IBADAN 7 DECEMBER 1964
PP 115-130
046,128-05,
        CASE STUDY

BANTON MICHAEL P
THE ORIGINS OF TRIBAL ADMINISTRATION IN FREETOWN.

SIERRA LEONE STUDIES 2 1954 PP 109-119
046,131-05,
    CASE STUDY

046
  DE BLIJ HARM J
  THE FUNCTIONAL STRUCTURE AND CENTRAL BUSINESS DISTRICT OF
  LOURENCO MARQUES, MOZAMBIQUE.
  ECONOMIC GEOGRAPHY, 38 JANUARY 1962 PP 56-77
  046,144-05,
      CASE STUDY

  ELKAN WALTER
  MIGRANTS AND PROLETARIANS, URBAN LABOUR IN THE
  ECONOMIC DEVELOPMENT OF UGANDA.
  LONDON, OXFORD UNIVERSITY PRESS, 1960
  046,
      CASE STUDY

  EPSTEIN ARNOLD L
  POLITICS IN AN URBAN AFRICAN COMMUNITY.
  MANCHESTER, MANCHESTER UNIVERSITY PRESS, 1958
  007,046,142-05,
      CASE STUDY

  LARIMORE A E
  THE ALIEN TOWN--PATTERNS OF SETTLEMENT IN BUSOGA, UGANDA.
  UNIVERSITY OF CHICAGO, DEPT OF GEOGRAPHY RESEARCH PAPERS,
  AUGUST 1958, PP 1-210
  046,139-05,
      CASE STUDY

  MABOGUNJE AKIN L
  THE GROWTH OF RESIDENTIAL DISTRICTS IN IBADAN.
  GEOGRAPHICAL REVIEW, JANUARY 1962, PP 56-77
  046,128-05,
      CASE STUDY

  MCDONELL G
  THE DYNAMICS OF GEOGRAPHIC CHANGE--THE CASE OF KANO.
  ANNALS OF THE ASSOCIATION OF AMERICAN GEOGRAPHERS
  5J SEPTEMBER 1964 PP 355-371
  046,128-05,
      CASE STUDY

  MCLOUGHLIN P F M
  THE SUDAN'S THREE TOWNS--A DEMOGRAPHIC AND ECONOMIC PROFILE
  OF AN AFRICAN URBAN COMPLEX
  ECONOMIC DEVELOPMENT AND CULTURAL CHANGE 12 1963 AND 1964,
  PP 70-83, 158-173, 286-304
  046,074,134-05,
      CASE STUDY

  MEILLASSOUX CLAUDE
  URBANIZATION OF AN AFRICAN COMMUNITY--VOLUNTARY ASSOCIATIONS
  IN BAMAKO.
  SEATTLE, UNIVERSITY OF WASHINGTON PRESS, 1968
  046,123-05,
      CASE STUDY

NNOCHIRI ENYINNAYA
PARASITIC DISEASE AND URBANIZATION IN A DEVELOPING
COMMUNITY.
LONDON, OXFORD MEDICAL PUBLICATIONS, 1968
046,
    CASE STUDY

046
PARKIN DAVID J
NEIGHBORS AND NATIONALS IN AN AFRICAN CITY WARD.
BERKELEY, UNIVERSITY OF CALIFORNIA, 1969
046,139-05,
    CASE STUDY

PARRINDER GEOFFREY
RELIGION IN AN AFRICAN CITY.
LONDON, OXFORD UNIVERSITY PRESS, 1953
046,
    CASE STUDY

PONS VALDO
STANLEYVILLE-AN AFRICAN URBAN COMMUNITY UNDER BELGIAN
ADMINISTRATION
NEW YORK, OXFORD UNIVERSITY PRESS, 1969
046,108-05,
    CASE STUDY

ROUCH JEAN
SECOND GENERATION MIGRANTS IN GHANA AND THE IVORY COAST.
IN AIDAN SOUTHALL (ED.), SOCIAL CHANGE IN MODERN AFRICA.
LONDON, OXFORD UNIVERSITY PRESS, 1961
046,114-03,116-03,
    CASE STUDY

SIMMS RUTH P
URBANIZATION IN WEST AFRICA-- A REVIEW OF CURRENT
LITERATURE.
EVANSTON, NORTHWESTERN UNIVERSITY PRESS, 1965
046,
    CASE STUDY

SMYTHE HUGH H
URBANIZATION IN NIGERIA.
ANTHROPOLOGICAL QUARTERLY 33 JULY 1960 PP 143-148
046,
    CASE STUDY

WINDER R BAYLEY
THE LEBANESE IN WEST AFRICA.
COMPARATIVE STUDIES IN SOCIETY AND HISTORY 4 APRIL 1962
PP 296-333
046,
    CASE STUDY

VAN DER VAEREN-AGUESSY D
LES FEMMES COMMERCANTES AU DETAIL SUR LES MARCHES DAKAROIS.
IN LLOYD, THE NEW ELITES OF TROPICAL AFRICA, LONDON, OXFORD
UNIVERSITY PRESS, 1966, P. 244-255
046,130-05,
    LESS ACCESSIBLE

046

    COLEMAN JAMES S
    CONCLUSION
    IN ALMOND AND COLEMAN, THE POLITICS OF THE DEVELOPING AREAS,
    PRINCETON, PRINCETON UNIVERSITY PRESS, 1960, PP 532-576
    046,
          GENERAL THEORY

    FALLERS LLOYD A   ED
    IMMIGRANTS AND ASSOCIATIONS.
    THE HAGUE, MOUTON, 1967
    046,047,
          GENERAL THEORY

    KOMAROVSKY MIRRA
    THE VOLUNTARY ASSOCIATIONS OF URBAN DWELLERS.
    AMERICAN SOCIOLOGICAL REVIEW 11 DECEMBER 1946 PP 686-698
    (BOBBS-MERRILL REPRINT 151)
    046,
          GENERAL THEORY

    SOUTHALL AIDAN
    DETERMINANTS OF THE SOCIAL STRUCTURE OF AFRICAN URBAN
    POPULATIONS, WITH SPECIAL REFERENCE TO KAMPALA, (UGANDA)
    (1956).
    IN IMMANUEL WALLERSTEIN, SOCIAL CHANGE-- THE COLONIAL
    SITUATION, NEW YORK, WILEY, 1966, PP 321-339
    046,139-05,
          REFERENCE

47. PROBLEMS OF URBANIZATION

047

    HERSKOVITS MELVILLE J
    THE HUMAN FACTOR IN CHANGING AFRICA.
    NEW YORK, ALFRED A KNOPF, 1962
    001,038,045,047,
          MAJOR WORK OF SYNTHESIS ON THE PATTERNS AND PROBLEMS
          PRIMARILY DURING THE COLONIAL PERIOD. EXCELLENT
          SUMMARY CHAPTERS ON AFRICA IN THE WORLD SETTING, CUL-
          TURE AREAS, AGRICULTURAL AND INDUSTRIAL GROWTH, LAW,
          EDUCATION, URBANIZATION, NATIONALISM, AND MORE RECENT
          PROBLEMS OF ECONOMIC AND POLITICAL CHANGE, RELIGION
          AND THE ARTS, AND THE SEARCH FOR VALUES.

    MABOGUNJE AKIN L
    URBANIZATION IN NIGERIA.
    NEW YORK, AFRICANA PUBLISHING CORPORATION, 1969
    045,047,128-05,
          ALTHOUGH PRIMARILY A CASE STUDY OF NIGERIA, INTRODUC-
          TORY SECTIONS PROVIDES EXCELLENT OVERVIEW OF THE HIST-
          ORICAL PROCESS OF URBANIZATION WHILE LAST CHAPTERS
          FOCUS ON PROBLEMS OF ECONOMIC DEVELOPMENT. UNIQUE IN
          ITS ANALYSIS OF AN ENTIRE URBAN SYSTEM, COMBINING

HISTORICAL-DESCRIPTIVE APPROACH WITH MODERN QUANTITA-
TIVE TECHNIQUES. ONLY DRAWBACK IS ALMOST UNAVOIDABLE
DEPENDENCE ON 1955 CENSUS DATA. A GROUND-BREAKING
WORK BY OUTSTANDING AFRICAN GEOGRAPHER.

047

MINER HORACE M   ED
THE CITY IN MODERN AFRICA.
NEW YORK, PRAEGER, 1967
047,

EXCELLENT COLLECTION OF PAPERS FROM RESEARCH PRIORI-
TIES CONFERENCE ON URBANIZATION IN AFRICA. INCLUDES
ANALYSES OF THE CITY AND MODERNIZATION, URBANIZATION
AND ECONOMIC GROWTH, RACIAL PLURALISM, POLITICAL
STRUCTURE, BUREAUCRACY, FAMILY LIFE AND KINSHIP
CHANGES. SPECIFIC REFERENCE TO SUCH CITIES AS LAGOS,
KAMPALA-MENGO, IBADAN, ACCRA, AND ABIDJAN.

UNESCO
SOCIAL IMPLICATIONS OF INDUSTRIALIZATION AND URBANIZATION
IN AFRICA SOUTH OF THE SAHARA.
PARIS, UNESCO, 1956
047,071,074,
FIRST MAJOR SYMPOSIUM ON PROBLEMS OF URBANIZATION AND
INDUSTRIALIZATION IN AFRICA. INCLUDES INTRODUCTORY
ESSAY BY DARYLL FORDE, AND SECTIONS ON SOCIAL EFFECTS
ON ECONOMIC DEVELOPMENT AND URBANIZATION, INCLUDING
NUMEROUS CASE STUDIES FROM ALL PARTS OF AFRICA SOUTH
OF THE SAHARA.

FORDE C DARYLL
THE SOCIAL IMPACT OF INDUSTRIALIZATION AND URBAN CONDITIONS
IN AFRICA SOUTH OF THE SAHARA.
INTERNATIONAL SOCIAL SCIENCE BULLETIN 7 WINTER 1955
PP 114-127
047,071,
REFERENCE

FRAZIER E FRANKLIN
URBANIZATION AND ITS EFFECTS UPON THE TASK OF NATION -
BUILDING IN AFRICA SOUTH OF THE SAHARA.
JOURNAL OF NEGRO EDUCATION 30 SUMMER 1961 PP 214-222
047,
REFERENCE

HANNA WILLIAM J
THE STUDY OF URBAN AFRICA-- A REVIEW ESSAY.
JOURNAL OF LOCAL ADMINISTRATION OVERSEAS 5 APRIL 1966 PP
124-7
047,
REFERENCE

LEWIS WILLIAM H
URBAN CRUCIBLE--PARALLELS AND DIVERGENCES.
AFRICA REPORT, MAY/JUNE 1969, PP. 62-65
047,
REFERENCE

SOJA EDWARD W
THE GEOGRAPHY OF MODERNIZATION IN KENYA.

SYRACUSE, SYRACUSE UNIVERSITY PRESS, 1968
038,047,048,117-03,
REFERENCE

047

SOJA EDWARD W
RURAL-URBAN INTERACTION
CANADIAN JOURNAL OF AFRICAN STUDIES 1 1969 PP 284-290
047,
REFERENCE

SOJA EDWARD W
SPECIAL GEOGRAPHY ISSUE
AFRICAN URBAN NOTES 2 MAY 1967
047,048,
REFERENCE

WOOD ERIC W
THE IMPLICATIONS OF MIGRANT LABOUR FOR URBAN SOCIAL SYSTEMS
IN AFRICA.
CAHIERS D'ETUDES AFRICAINES, VOL. VIII, 29, 1968, PP. 5-31
047,
REFERENCE

ABIODUN JOSEPHINE O
CENTRAL PLACE STUDY IN ABEOKUTA PROVINCE,SOUTHWEST NIGERIA
JOURNAL OF REGIONAL SCIENCE 8 1968
047,048,128-05,
CASE STUDY

ARDENER EDWIN   ARDENER S   WARMINGTON W A
PLANTATION AND VILLAGE IN THE CAMEROONS.
LONDON,OXFORD UNIVERSITY PRESS,1960
047,104-01,
CASE STUDY

CALDWELL JOHN C
AFRICAN RURAL-URBAN MIGRATION THE MOVEMENT TO GHANA≠S TOWNS
NEW YORK,COLUMBIA UNIVERSITY PRESS,1969
047,
CASE STUDY

DAVIES R J
THE SOUTH AFRICAN URBAN HIERARCHY
SOUTH AFRICAN GEOGRAPHICAL JOURNAL 49 1967 PP 9-19
047,048,132-05,
CASE STUDY

GARDINIER DAVID E
URBAN POLITICS IN DOUALA, CAMEROON, 1944-1955
AFRICAN URBAN NOTES, VOL IV, NO. 3, SEPT. 1969, PP. 20-29
047,104-05,
CASE STUDY

GUTKIND PETER C W
ACCOMODATION AND CONFLICT IN AN AFRICAN PERI-URBAN AREA.
ANTHROPOLOGICA 4 1962 PP 163-174
047,
CASE STUDY

HARVEY MILTON
IMPLICATIONS OF MIGRATION TO FREETOWN-- A STUDY OF THE
RELATIONSHIP BETWEEN MIGRANTS, HOUSING AND OCCUPATION.
CIVILISATIONS, VOL. XVIII, NO. 2, 1968, PP. 247-69
047,131-05,
     CASE STUDY

047

MABOGUNJE AKIN L
URBANIZATION IN NIGERIA-A CONSTRAINT ON ECONOMIC DEVELOPMENT
ECONOMIC DEVELOPMENT AND CULTURAL CHANGE 13 1965 PP 413-438
047,128-05,
     CASE STUDY

MAYER PHILIP
TOWNSMEN OR TRIBESMEN-- CONSERVATISM AND THE PROCESS OF
URBANIZATION IN A SOUTH AFRICAN CITY.
CAPETOWN, OXFORD UNIVERSITY PRESS, 1961
047,089,132-05,
     CASE STUDY

MCNULTY MICHAEL
URBAN STRUCTURE AND DEVELOPMENT-THE URBAN SYSTEM OF GHANA
JOURNAL OF THE DEVELOPING AREAS,3 1969 PP 159-176
047,048,114-05,
     CASE STUDY

PARKIN DAVID J
TYPES OF URBAN AFRICAN MARRIAGE IN KAMPALA.
AFRICA 36 JULY 1966 PP 269-285
047,139-05,
     CASE STUDY

FORTHOME G
MARRIAGE ET INDUSTRIALISATION-- EVOLUTION DE LA MENTALITE
DANS UNE CITE DE TRAVAILLEURS D'ELISABETHVILLE (MARRIAGE
AND INDUSTRIALIZATION-- EMERGENCE OF THE MENTALITY IN A
WORKER'S DOMAIN OF ELISABETHVILLE).
LIEGE, H VALLIANT-CARMANNE, 1957
047,108-05,
     LESS ACCESSIBLE

BANFIELD EDWARD C
THE POLITICAL IMPLICATIONS OF METROPOLITAN GROWTH.
DAEDALUS, THE JOURNAL OF THE AMERICAN ACADEMY OF ARTS AND
SCIENCES 90 WINTER 1960 PP 61-78 (BOBBS-MERRILL REPRINT S-7)
047,
     GENERAL THEORY

BECKMANN MARTIN J
CITY HIERARCHIES AND DISTRIBUTION OF CITY SIZE.
ECONOMIC DEVELOPMENT AND CULTURAL CHANGE 6 APRIL 1958
B-M REPRINT S-338
047,
     GENERAL THEORY

BERRY BRIAN J L   GARRISON WILLIAM
ALTERNATE EXPLANATIONS OF URBAN RANK-SIZE RELATIONSHIPS.
ANNALS OF THE ASSOCIATION OF AMERICAN GEOGRAPHERS 48 MARCH
1958 B-M REPRINT S-341

047,
    GENERAL THEORY

047

BERRY BRIAN J L
CITY SIZE DISTRIBUTIONS AND ECONOMIC DEVELOPMENT.
IN K M BARBOUR AND R M PROTHERO, (EDS.), ESSAYS ON
ECONOMIC DEVELOPMENT AND CULTURAL CHANGE, 9 JULY 1961,
B-M REPRINT S-340
047,
    GENERAL THEORY

DICKINSON ROBERT E
CITY AND REGION-A GEOGRAPHIC INTERPRETATION
LONDON, ROUTLEDGE AND KEGAN PAUL, 1964
047,
    GENERAL THEORY

FALLERS LLOYD A   ED
IMMIGRANTS AND ASSOCIATIONS.
THE HAGUE, MOUTON, 1967
046,047,
    GENERAL THEORY

SWARTZ MARC   ED
LOCAL-LEVEL POLITICS
CHICAGO, ALDINE, 1968
009,047,
    GENERAL THEORY

TANGRI SHANTI
URBANIZATION, POLITICAL STABILITY AND ECONOMIC GROWTH
CHAPTER 9.
IN JASON L FINKLE AND RICHARD W GABLE, POLITICAL
DEVELOPMENT AND SOCIAL CHANGE, NEW YORK, JOHN WILEY, 1966
047,074,
    GENERAL THEORY

WEINER MYRON
URBANIZATION AND POLITICAL PROTEST.
CIVILISATIONS, VOL. XVII, 1967, PP. 44-53
047,
    GENERAL THEORY

48. SPATIAL ASPECTS OF TRANSPORTATION AND COMMUNICATIONS

048

GOULD PETER
TANZANIA 1920-1963-THE SPATIAL IMPRESS OF THE MODERNIZATION
PROCESS
WORLD POLITICS 22 1970 PP 149-170
048,136-03,
    AUTHOR MAPS THE MODERNIZATION SURFACE OF TANZANIA IN
    5 TIME SLICES FROM THE EARLY TWENTIES TO THE EARLY
    SIXTIES.STRIKINGLY SHOWS HOW INSIGHTFUL SPATIAL

ANALYSIS OF THE MODERNIZATION PROCESS CAN BE CONDUCTED
UNDER APPARENTLY SEVERE DATA RESTRICTIONS.

048

HANCE WILLIAM A
AFRICAN ECONOMIC DEVELOPMENT.
NEW YORK, PRAEGER, 1967 (REVISED EDITION)
048,069,072,
        EXCELLENT SURVEY WITH DETAILED CASE STUDIES OF THE
        GEZIRA SCHEME, THE VOLTA RIVER PROJECT, TRANSPORT,
        ECONOMIC INTEGRATION IN EAST AFRICA, LIBERIA, MADA-
        GASCAR AND OTHERS. FINAL CHAPTER EXAMINES DEVELOPMENT
        POTENTIALS BY COUNTRY WITH A GOOD SUMMARY TABLE.

PYE LUCIAN W   ED
COMMUNICATIONS AND POLITICAL DEVELOPMENT.
PRINCETON PRINCETON UNIVERSITY PRESS 1963
048,
        EXCELLENT INTRODUCTION TO THE ROLE OF COMMUNICATIONS
        IN POLITICAL DEVELOPMENT. EDITOR'S INTRODUCTION GIVES
        OVERVIEW OF COMMUNICATIONS APPROACH FOLLOWED BY BRIEF
        DISCUSSION OF TRADITIONAL, TRANSITIONAL, AND MODERN
        COMMUNICATIONS SYSTEMS. NOT SPECIFICALLY FOCUSED ON
        AFRICA.

TAAFFE E J   MORRILL R L   GOULD PETER
TRANSPORT EXPANSION IN UNDERDEVELOPED COUNTRIES--A
COMPARATIVE ANALYSIS.
GEOGRAPHICAL REVIEW 53 OCTOBER 1963 PP 503-529
048,
        THREE LEADING GEOGRAPHERS DISCUSS A DESCRIPTIVE MODEL
        OF TRANSPORT NETWORK GROWTH, WITH A PRIMARY EMPHASIS
        ON AFRICA, ESPECIALLY GHANA AND NIGERIA. MAJOR GROWTH
        STAGES IDENTIFIED INCLUDE HISTORICAL PERIODS OF SCAT-
        TERED COASTAL PORTS, PENETRATION AND PORT CONCENTRA-
        TION, FEEDER LINE DEVELOPMENT, INTER-URBAN CONNECTIVI-
        TY AND THE CONSTRUCTION OF HIGH PRIORITY LINKAGES.
        THEY ALSO EXAMINE FACTORS AFFECTING TRANSPORT DENSITY.

WILSON GODFREY   WILSON MONICA
THE ANALYSIS OF SOCIAL CHANGE-BASED ON OBSERVATIONS IN
CENTRAL AFRICA
CAMBRIDGE, CAMBRIDGE UNIVERSITY PRESS, 1945 NEW EDITION 1968
037,038,048,
        BASED LARGELY ON FIELD WORK IN TANZANIA, MALAWI, AND
        ZAMBIA, THIS BOOK HAS BECOME STANDARD REFERENCE ON
        CONCEPT OF INCREASING SOCIETAL SCALE AND ITS
        IMPORTANCE IN THE PROCESS OF CHANGE. SCALE IS DEFINED
        AS THE NUMBER OF PEOPLE IN RELATION WITH ONE ANOTHER
        AS A GROUP AND THE INTENSITY OF THESE RELATIONS.

CHURCH R J HARRISON
GEOGRAPHICAL FACTORS IN THE DEVELOPMENT OF TRANSPORT IN
AFRICA.
NEW YORK, UNITED NATIONS TRANSPORT AND COMMUNICATIONS REVIEW
2 NO 3 1949 PP 3-11
048,
        REFERENCE

ECONOMIC COMMISSION FOR AFRICA

TRANSPORT PROBLEMS IN RELATION TO ECONOMIC DEVELOPMENT IN
WEST AFRICA.
NEW YORK, U N DOCUMENT NO 62.11.K.2, 1963
048,
     REFERENCE

048

GOULD PETER
GEOGRAPHY, SPATIAL PLANNING, AND AFRICA--THE RESPONSIBILIT-
IES OF THE NEXT TWENTY YEARS.
IN CARTER, GWENDOLEN M. AND ANN PADEN (EDS), EXPANDING
HORIZONS IN AFRICAN STUDIES, EVANSTON, NORTHWESTERN
UNIVERSITY PRESS, 1969, PP. 181-203
048,100,
     REFERENCE

GOULD PETER
A NOTE ON RESEARCH INTO THE DIFFUSION OF DEVELOPMENT
JOURNAL OF MODERN AFRICAN STUDIES 2 1964 PP 123-125
048,
     REFERENCE

HAMILTON F E IAN
REGIONAL ECONOMIC ANALYSIS IN BRITAIN AND THE COMMONWEALTH-
A BIBLIOGRAPHIC GUIDE
NEW YORK, SCHOCKEN BOOKS, 1970
048,069,072,
     REFERENCE

RIDDELL J BARRY
THE SPATIAL DYNAMICS OF MODERNIZATION IN SIERRA LEONE
EVANSTON, NORTHWESTERN UNIVERSITY PRESS, 1970
038,048,131-06,
     REFERENCE

SOJA EDWARD W
THE GEOGRAPHY OF MODERNIZATION IN KENYA.
SYRACUSE, SYRACUSE UNIVERSITY PRESS, 1968
038,047,048,117-03,
     REFERENCE

SOJA EDWARD W
SPECIAL GEOGRAPHY ISSUE
AFRICAN URBAN NOTES 2 MAY 1967
047,048,
     REFERENCE

THOMAS B E
MODERN TRANS-SAHARAN ROUTES.
GEOGRAPHICAL REVIEW 42 APRIL 1952 PP 267-282
048,
     REFERENCE

THOMAS B E
RAILWAYS AND PORTS IN FRENCH WEST AFRICA.
ECONOMIC GEOGRAPHY 33 NO 1 JANUARY 1957 PP 1-15
048,
     REFERENCE

THOMAS B E

TRANSPORTATION AND PHYSICAL GEOGRAPHY IN WEST AFRICA.
LOS ANGELES, NATIONAL ACADEMY OF SCIENCES NATIONAL RESEARCH
COUNCIL, 1960
048,
        REFERENCE

048

VAN DONGEN I S
ROAD VERSUS RAIL IN AFRICA.
GEOGRAPHICAL REVIEW 52 1962 PP 296-298
048,
        REFERENCE

WITTHUHN BURTON O
THE SPATIAL INTEGRATION OF UGANDA AS EVIDENCED BY THE
DIFFUSION OF POSTAL AGENCIES-1900-1965
EAST LAKES GEOGRAPHER 4 1968 PP 5-20
048,
        REFERENCE

ABIODUN JOSEPHINE O
CENTRAL PLACE STUDY IN ABEOKUTA PROVINCE, SOUTHWEST NIGERIA
JOURNAL OF REGIONAL SCIENCE 8 1968
047,048,128-05,
        CASE STUDY

DAVIES R J
THE SOUTH AFRICAN URBAN HIERARCHY
SOUTH AFRICAN GEOGRAPHICAL JOURNAL 49 1967 PP 9-19
047,048,132-05,
        CASE STUDY

FAIR T J D
A REGIONAL APPROACH TO ECONOMIC DEVELOPMENT IN KENYA.
SOUTH AFRICAN GEOGRAPHICAL JOURNAL 45 DECEMBER 1963 PP 55-77
048,073,117-08,
        CASE STUDY

FORDE ENID
THE POPULATION OF GHANA-A STUDY OF THE SPATIAL RELATIONSHIPS
OF SOCIOCULTURAL AND ECONOMIC CHARACTERISTICS
EVANSTON, DEPARTMENT OF GEOGRAPHY, NORTHWESTERN UNIVERSITY
PRESS, 1968
048,
        CASE STUDY

GOULD PETER
THE DEVELOPMENT OF THE TRANSPORTATION PATTERN IN GHANA
EVANSTON, DEPARTMENT OF GEOGRAPHY, NORTHWESTERN UNIVERSITY
PRESS, 1960
048,114-05,
        CASE STUDY

GREEN L P   FAIR T J D
DEVELOPMENT IN AFRICA- A STUDY IN REGIONAL ANALYSIS WITH
SPECIAL REFERENCE TO SOUTHERN AFRICA
JOHANNESBURG, WITWATERSRAND UNIVERSITY PRESS, 1962
048,073,132-08,145-08,
        CASE STUDY

HAEFELE E T   STEINBERG E B
GOVERNMENT CONTROLS ON TRANSPORT-AN AFRICAN CASE (ZAMBIA)
WASHINGTON, BROOKINGS INSTITUTE, 1965
048,142-08,
      CASE STUDY

048

HANCE WILLIAM A
GABON AND ITS MAIN GATEWAYS-- LIBREVILLE AND PORT GENTIL.
TIJDSCHRIFT VOOR ECONOMISHE EN SOCIALE GEOGRAFIE (AMSTERDAM)
52STE JAARGANG NOVEMBER 1961 PP 286-295
048,112-08,
      CASE STUDY

HANCE WILLIAM A   VAN DONGEN I S
DAR ES SALAAM, THE PORT AND ITS TRIBUTARY.
ANNALS OF THE ASSOCIATION OF AMERICAN GEOGRAPHERS
48 DECEMBER 1958 PP 419-435
048,136-08,
      CASE STUDY

HANCE WILLIAM A   VAN DONGEN I S
LOURENCO MARQUES IN DELAGOA BAY.
ECONOMIC GEOGRAPHY 33 JULY 1957 PP 238-256
048,144-05,
      CASE STUDY

HANCE WILLIAM A   VAN DONGEN I S
THE PORT OF LOBITO AND THE BENGUELA RAILWAY.
GEOGRAPHICAL REVIEW 46 OCTOBER 1956 PP 460-487
048,
      CASE STUDY

HANCE WILLIAM A   VAN DONGEN I S
MATADI, FOCUS OF BELGIAN AFRICAN TRANSPORT.
ANNALS OF THE ASSOCIATION OF AMERICAN GEOGRAPHERS 48
MARCH 1958 PP 41-72
48 MARCH 1958 PP 41-72
048,
      CASE STUDY

MCNULTY MICHAEL
URBAN STRUCTURE AND DEVELOPMENT-THE URBAN SYSTEM OF GHANA
JOURNAL OF THE DEVELOPING AREAS,3 1969 PP 159-176
047,048,114-05,
      CASE STUDY

MUNGER EDWIN S
RELATIONAL PATTERNS OF KAMPALA, UGANDA.
UNIVERSITY OF CHICAGO, DEPT OF GEOGRAPHY RESEARCH PAPERS,
SEPTEMBER 1951, PP 1-178
048,139-05,
      CASE STUDY

PANKHURST RICHARD
TRANSPORTATION AND COMMUNICATIONS IN ETHIOPIA 1835-1935.
JOURNAL OF TRANSPORT HISTORY 5 1961 PP 69-88, 6 1962 PP166-
181, 233-254
048,110-08,
      CASE STUDY

048

SOJA EDWARD
COMMUNICATIONS AND TERRITORIAL INTEGRATION IN EAST AFRICA-
AN INTRODUCTION TO TRANSACTION FLOW ANALYSIS
EAST LAKES GEOGRAPHER 4 1968 PP 39-57
048,059,077,
        CASE STUDY

THOMAS B E
TRADE ROUTES OF ALGERIA AND THE SAHARA.
BERKELEY, UNIVERSITY OF CALIFORNIA PRESS, 1957
048,101-08,
        CASE STUDY

VAN DONGEN I S
THE BRITISH EAST AFRICA TRANSPORT COMPLEX.
UNIVERSITY OF CHICAGO, DEPARTMENT OF GEOGRAPHY, PAPER 38
1954
048,
        CASE STUDY

VAN DONGEN I S
NACALA--NEWEST MOZAMBIQUE GATEWAY TO INTERIOR AFRICA.
TIJDSCRIFT VOOR ECONOMISHE EN SOCIALE GEOGRAFIE(AMSTERDAM)
48STE JAARGANANG MARCH 1959 PP 65-73
048,
        CASE STUDY

WEINSTEIN BRIAN
GABON--NATION-BUILDING ON THE OGOOUE.
CAMBRIDGE, MASSACHUSETTS INSTITUTE OF TECHNOLOGY PRESS, 1966
048,057,112-06,
        CASE STUDY

DEUTSCH KARL W
NATIONALISM AND SOCIAL COMMUNICATIONS-- AN INQUIRY INTO
THE FOUNDATIONS OF NATIONALITY.
NEW YORK, JOHN WILEY, 1953; CAMBRIDGE, MASSACHUSETTS INSTITUTE
OF TECHNOLOGY PRESS, 1966
048,
        GENERAL THEORY

DEUTSCH KARL W
SHIFTS IN THE BALANCE OF COMMUNICATION FLOWS.
IN NELSON POLSBY, ROBERT DENTLER, AND PAUL SMITH, POLITICS
AND SOCIAL LIFE, BOSTON, HOUGHTON MIFFLIN, 1963
048,
        GENERAL THEORY

EISENSTADT S N
COMMUNICATION SYSTEMS AND SOCIAL STRUCTURE-- AN
EXPLORATORY COMPARATIVE STUDY.
PUBLIC OPINION QUARTERLY 19 SUMMER 1955 PP 153-167
048,
        GENERAL THEORY

FAGEN RICHARD R
POLITICS AND COMMUNICATION.
BOSTON, LITTLE, BROWN AND COMPANY, 1966

048,
>   GENERAL THEORY

048

FAGEN RICHARD R
RELATIONS OF COMMUNICATION GROWTH TO NATIONAL POLITICAL
SYSTEMS IN THE LESS DEVELOPED COUNTRIES.
JOURNALISM QUARTERLY 41 WINTER 1964 PP 87-94
048,
>   GENERAL THEORY

HAGGETT PETER
LOCATIONAL ANALYSIS IN HUMAN GEOGRAPHY
NEW YORK, ST. MARTIN'S PRESS, 1965
048,
>   GENERAL THEORY

JACOB PHILIP E   TOSCANO JAMES V
THE INTEGRATION OF POLITICAL COMMUNITIES.
PHILADELPHIA, LIPPINCOTT, 1964
048,057,
>   GENERAL THEORY

KATZ ELIHU
THE TWO-STEP FLOW OF COMMUNICATION.
PUBLIC OPINION QUARTERLY 21 SPRING 1957 PP 61-78
048,
>   GENERAL THEORY

LERNER DANIEL
COMMUNICATION SYSTEMS AND SOCIAL SYSTEMS-- A STATISTICAL
EXPLORATION IN HISTORY AND POLICY.
BEHAVIORAL SCIENCE 4 OCTOBER 1957 PP 266-275
IN JASON L FINKLE AND RICHARD W GABLE, POLITICAL DEVELOPMENT
AND SOCIAL CHANGE, NEW YORK, JOHN WILEY, 1966
048,
>   GENERAL THEORY

OWEN WILFRED
STRATEGY FOR MOBILITY.
WASHINGTON, THE BROOKINGS INSTITUTION, 1964
048,
>   GENERAL THEORY

PARK ROBERT E
REFLECTIONS ON COMMUNICATION AND CULTURE.
AMERICAN JOURNAL OF SOCIOLOGY 44 1939 PP 191-205
048,
>   GENERAL THEORY

PYE LUCIAN W
COMMUNICATIONS AND POLITICAL DEVELOPMENT CHAPTER 8.
IN ASPECTS OF POLITICAL DEVELOPMENT, BOSTON, LITTLE, BROWN,
1966, PP 153-171
048,
>   GENERAL THEORY

PYE LUCIAN W
COMMUNICATION PATTERNS AND THE PROBLEMS OF REPRESENATATIVE
GOVERNMENT IN NON-WESTERN SOCIETIES.

PUBLIC OPINION QUARTERLY 20 1956 PP 249-457
048,
        GENERAL THEORY

048
    ROGERS EVERETT M
    MODERNIZATION AMONG PEASANTS--THE IMPACT OF COMMUNICATION.
    NEW YORK, HOLT, RINEHART AND WINSTON, INC., 1969
    048,
        GENERAL THEORY

    SMITH BRUCE L
    COMMUNICATIONS RESEARCH ON NON-INDUSTRIAL COUNTRIES.
    PUBLIC OPINION QUARTERLY 16 WINTER 1952-1953 PP 527-538
    048,
        GENERAL THEORY

49. NEW MODES OF COMMUNICATION

049
    FISHMAN JOSHUA   ET AL   EDS
    LANGUAGE PROBLEMS OF DEVELOPING NATIONS.
    NEW YORK, JOHN WILEY AND SONS, 1968
    011,049,
        CONTAINS BOTH THEORETICAL ARTICLES ON LANGUAGE DIVERSI-
        TY AND NATIONAL DEVELOPMENT, AND A NUMBER OF CASE STU-
        DIES FROM AFRICA--SWAHILI IN MODERN EAST AFRICA AND IN
        TANZANIA, HAUSA IN WEST AFRICA, AND IN NIGERIA--NORTH
        AFRICAN LANGUAGE PROBLEMS--LANGUAGE AND NATIONALISM IN
        SOUTH AFRICA--ENGLISH LITERATURE IN AFRICA--LANGUAGE
        POLICY IN CONGO-KINSHASA AND SUCAN--LANGUAGE POLICY IN
        WEST AFRICA--AND LINGUISTIC PROBLEMS OF NATION-BUILDING
        IN AFRICA. CO EDITED BY C FERGUSON AND J DAS GUPTA.

    UNESCO
    WORLD COMMUNICATIONS-PRESS,RADIO,TELEVISION,FILM
    PARIS, UNESCO, 1966
    049,
        DETAILED COMPILATION OF STATISTICAL INFORMATION ON
        COMMUNICATIONS FACILITIES BY COUNTRY. INTRODUCTORY
        CHAPTERS INCLUDE SHORT REVIEWS OF COMMUNICATIONS
        MEDIA FOR AFRICA AS A WHOLE.

    WHITELEY W H
    SWAHILI-THE RISE OF A NATIONAL LANGUAGE
    NEW YORK, BARNES AND NOBLE, 1969
    023,049,
        BRIEF AND IMPORTANT DISCUSSION TRACING THE DEVELOP-
        MENT OF THE SWAHILI LANGUAGE AND CULTURE AND ITS DIF-
        FUSION INTO EAST AND CENTRAL AFRICA DURING THE PRECO-
        LONIAL AND COLONIAL PERIODS.

    AFRICAN STUDIES ASSOCIATION
    AFRICAN FILM BIBLIOGRAPHY 1965.
    AFRICAN STUDIES ASSOCIATION OCCASIONAL PAPERS NO. 1 1966

049,093,
    REFERENCE

049
   AINSLIE ROSALYNDE
   THE PRESS IN AFRICA-- COMMUNICATIONS PAST AND PRESENT.
   LONDON, GOLLANCZ, 1966
   049,
        REFERENCE

   BARTON FRANK.
   THE PRESS IN AFRICA
   NAIROBI, EAST AFRICA PUBLISHING HOUSE, 1966
   049,
        REFERENCE

   DOOB LEONARD W
   COMMUNICATION IN AFRICA--A SEARCH FOR BOUNDARIES.
   NEW HAVEN, YALE UNIVERSITY PRESS, 1961
   049,
        REFERENCE

   FODOR ISTVAN
   LINGUISTIC PROBLEMS AND 'LANGUAGE PLANNING' IN AFRICA.
   LINGUISTICS, 25, SEPT. 1966, PP. 18-33
   049,
        REFERENCE

   KITCHEN HELEN
   THE PRESS IN AFRICA.
   WASHINGTON, RUTH SLOAN ASS., 1956
   049,
        REFERENCE

   MORGENTHAU HENRY
   ON FILMS AND FILMMAKERS
   AFRICA REPORT 14 MAY-JUNE 1969 PP 71-75
   049,093,
        REFERENCE

   MOWLANA HAMID
   COMMUNICATIONS MEDIA IN AFRICA--A CRITIQUE IN RETROSPECT AND
   PROSPECT.
   IN CARTER, GWENDOLEN M. AND ANN PADEN (EDS), EXPANDING
   HORIZONS IN AFRICAN STUDIES, EVANSTON, NORTHWESTERN
   UNIVERSITY PRESS, 1969, PP. 259-274
   049,100,
        REFERENCE

   NKETIA J H KWABENA
   THE LANGUAGE PROBLEM AND THE AFRICAN PERSONALITY.
   PRESENCE AFRICAINE, NO. 67, 3RD QUARTER, 1968, PP. 157-171
   049,
        REFERENCE

   SINGH J   ED
   AFRICAN FILM
   NAIROBI, DRUM PUBLICATIONS, 1968
   049,093,
        REFERENCE

049

SPENCER JOHN   ED
LANGUAGE IN AFRICA.
LONDON, CAMBRIDGE UNIVERSITY PRESS, 1963
011,049,
        REFERENCE

UNESCO
DEVELOPING INFORMATION MEDIA IN AFRICA.
UNESCO, REPORTS AND PAPERS ON MASS COMMUNICATION NO. 37
049,
        REFERENCE

AFRICAN NEWSLETTER
THE PRESS OF NIGERIA.
AFRICAN NEWSLETTER 1 NUMBER 3 SUMMER 1963 PP 40-45
049,128-03,
        CASE STUDY

CHING JAMES C
MASS COMMUNICATION IN THE REPUBLIC OF CONGO.
JOURNALISM QUARTERLY 41 SPRING 1964 PP 237-244
049,
        CASE STUDY

CONDON JOHN C
NATION BUILDING AND IMAGE BUILDING IN THE TANZANIAN PRESS
JOURNAL OF MODERN AFRICAN STUDIES 5 1967 PP 335-354
049,
        CASE STUDY

HACHTEN WILLIAM A
THE PRESS IN A ONE-PARTY STATE--KENYA SINCE
INDEPENDENCE.
JOURNALISM QUARTERLY 42 SPRING 1965 PP 262-266
049,117-03,
        CASE STUDY

LAQUEUR WALTER Z
REPORTING WEST AFRICA.
NEW REPUBLIC 148 JANUARY 19 1963 PP 13-14
049,
        CASE STUDY

MACKAY IAN K
BROADCASTING IN NIGERIA.
IBADAN, IBADAN UNIVERSITY PRESS, 1964
049,128-03,
        CASE STUDY

FISHMAN JOSHUA
NATIONAL LANGUAGES AND LANGUAGES OF WIDER COMMUNICATION IN
THE DEVELOPING NATIONS.
ANTHROPOLOGICAL LINGUSITICS, VOL II, NO. 4, APRIL 1969, PP.
111-135
049,
        GENERAL THEORY

NIXON RAYMOND B

FACTORS RELATED TO FREEDOM IN NATIONAL PRESS SYSTEMS.
JOURNALISM QUARTERLY 37 WINTER 1960 PP 13-28
049,
    GENERAL THEORY

049

NIXON RAYMOND B
FREEDOM IN THE WORLD'S PRESS-- A FRESH APPRAISAL OF NEW
DATA.
JOURNALISM QUARTERLY 42 WINTER 1965 PP 3-14, 118-119
049,
    GENERAL THEORY

SCHRAMM WILBUR
THE ROLE OF INFORMATION IN NATIONAL DEVELOPMENT (ABRIDGED
VERSION OF MASS MEDIA AND NATIONAL DEVELOPMENT)
PARIS, UNESCO, 1964
049,
    GENERAL THEORY

HOPKINSON TOM
THE PRESS IN AFRICA.
IN AFRICA—A HANDBOOK TO THE CONTINENT, COLIN LEGUM, NEW YORK,
PRAEGER, 1966
049,
    CASE STUDY
    REFERENCE

50. THE IMPACT OF CHRISTIANITY

050
BAETA C G   ED
CHRISTIANITY IN TROPICAL AFRICA.
LONDON, OXFORD UNIVERSITY PRESS, 1968
050,
    ESSAYS FROM 7TH INTERNATIONAL AFRICAN SEMINAR, UNIVERS
    OF GHANA, APRIL 1965. BEST RANGE AND DEPTH OF
    MATERIALS ON CHRISTIANITY IN AFRICA. PART I ON HIS-
    TORICAL PERSPECTIVE (THE ESTABLISHMENT OF MISSIONS,
    AND EARLY CHURCH-STATE PROBLEMS). PART II ON ANALY-
    TICAL PERSPECTIVE (CONVERTS, MARTYRS, GUILT AND SHAME,
    POLYGAMY, ETHIOPIANISM, RELATIONS WITH TRADITIONAL
    RELIGION, THEOLOGY, EVANGELISM, SOCIAL CHANGE).

BEETHAM T A
CHRISTIANITY AND THE NEW AFRICA.
LONDON, PALL MALL PRESS, 1967
050,
    GOOD SUMMARY OF RECENT PATTERNS OF CHRISTIANITY IN AF-
    RICA--DEALS WITH THE COMING OG CHRISTIANITY TO AFRICA,
    THE WEAKNESS AND STRENGTH OF THE CHURCH AT THE TIME OF
    INDEPENDENCE, THE CHALLENGES FACING THE CHURCH TODAY,
    AND THE TYPE OF RESPONSES TO THESE CHALLENGES. THE
    AUTHOR IS SECRETARY OF THE MISSIONARY SOCIETIES OF GRT.
    BRITAIN AND IRELAND, AND HAS HAD LONG EXPERIENCE IN

GHANA.

050

BALANDIER GEORGES
MESSIANISMES ET NATIONALISMES EN AFRIQUE NOIRE (MESSIANIC
CULTS AND NATIONALISM IN BLACK AFRICA).
CAHIERS INTERNATIONAUX DE SOCIOLOGIE 14 1953 PP41-65(ENGLISH
TRANSLATION-- VANDENBERGHE)
050,051,
        REFERENCE

DESAI RAM   ED
CHRISTIANITY IN AFRICA AS SEEN BY THE AFRICANS
DENVER, ALAN SWALLOW, 1962
050,
        REFERENCE

DU BOIS VICTOR D
NEW STATES AND AN OLD CHURCH.
IN KALMAN SILVERT, ED, CHURCHES AND STATES-- THE RELIGIOUS IN-
STITUTION AND MODERNIZATION, NEW YORK, AMERICAN
UNIVERSITIES FIELD STAFF INC,1967, PP 51-80
050,
        REFERENCE

FERNANDEZ JAMES W
CONTEMPORARY AFRICAN RELIGION--CONFLUENTS OF INQUIRY.
IN CARTER, GWENDOLEN M. AND ANN PADEN (EDS) EXPANDING
HORIZONS IN AFRICAN STUDIES, EVANSTON, NORTHWESTERN
UNIVERSITY PRESS, 1969, PP. 27-46
013,050,100,
        REFERENCE

GROVES C P
THE PLANING OF CHRISTIANITY IN AFRICA.
LONDON, 4 VOLUMES, 1948-58.
050,
        REFERENCE

HODGKIN THOMAS
PROPHETS AND PRIESTS CHAPTER 3.
IN NATIONALISM AND COLONIAL AFRICA, NEW YORK, NEW
YORK UNIVERSITY PRESS, 1965
050,
        REFERENCE

IDOWU BOLAJI
TOWARDS AN INDIGENOUS CHURCH.
LONDON, OXFORD UNIVERSITY PRESS, 1965
050,
        REFERENCE

NORTHCOTT WILLIAM C
CHRISTIANITY IN AFRICA
PHILADELPHIA, WESTMINSTER PRESS, 1963
050,
        REFERENCE

OLIVER ROLAND   ATMORE ANTHONY
COLONIAL RULE IN TROPICAL AFRICA-- SOCIAL AND RELIGIOUS

DEVELOPMENTS.
IN AFRICA SINCE 1800, CAMBRIDGE, CAMBRIDGE UNIVERSITY PRESS,
1967, PP 141-159
035,050,
  REFERENCE

050
 PARRINDER GEOFFREY
 RELIGION IN AFRICA.
 NEW YORK, PRAEGER PUBLISHERS AND BALTIMORE, PENGUIN, 1969
 050,
   REFERENCE

 SHEPPERSON GEORGE
 ETHIOPIANISM AND AFRICAN NATIONALISM.
 PHYLON 14 1953 PP 9-18
 050,051,
   REFERENCE

 SMYKE RAYMOND
 CHRISTIANITY IN AFRICA.
 AFRICA REPORT, MAY 8, 1968
 050,
   REFERENCE

 TAYLOR J V
 CHRISTIANITY AND POLITICS IN AFRICA
 LONDON, PENGUIN BOOKS, 1957
 050,
   REFERENCE

 TODD H M
 AFRICAN MISSION-A HISTORICAL STUDY OF THE SOCIETY OF AFRICAN
 MISSIONS
 LONDON, BURNS AND GATES, 1962
 050,
   REFERENCE

 WATT W M   ED
 RELIGION IN AFRICA
 EDINBURGH, CENTRE OF AFRICAN STUDIES, UNIVERSITY OF EDINBURGH,
 1964
 050,
   REFERENCE

 WESTERMANN D
 AFRICA AND CHRISTIANITY.
 LONDON, OXFORD UNIVERSITY PRESS, 1937
 050,
   REFERENCE

 AYANDELE E A
 THE MISSIONARY IMPACT ON MODERN NIGERIA.
 LONDON, LONGMANS, 1964
 050,
   CASE STUDY

 DEBRUNNER HANS
 A CHURCH BETWEEN COLONIAL POWERS--A STUDY OF THE CHURCH IN
 TOGO.

LONDON, LUTTERWORTH PRESS, 1965
050,137-03,
     CASE STUDY

050

MARIOGHAE MICHAEL   FERGUSON JOHN
NIGERIA UNDER THE CROSS.
LONDON, THE HIGHWAY PRESS, 1965
050,128-03,
     CASE STUDY

MULLIN JOSEPH
THE CATHOLIC CHURCH IN MODERN AFRICA-- A PASTORAL THEOLOGY.
LONDON, CHAPMAN, 1965
050,
     CASE STUDY

OLIVER ROLAND
THE MISSIONARY FACTOR IN EAST AFRICA
LONDON, LONGMANS, 1952
050,
     CASE STUDY

ROTBERG ROBERT I
CHRISTIAN MISSIONARIES AND THE CREATION OF NORTHERN
RHODESIA, 1800-1924.
PRINCETON, PRINCETON UNIVERSITY PRESS, 1965
050,142-03,
     CASE STUDY

ROTBERG ROBERT I
PLYMOUTH BRETHREN AND THE OCCUPATION OF KATANGA 1886-1907.
JOURNAL OF AFRICAN HISTORY 5 1964 PP 285-297
050,108-03,
     CASE STUDY

SKINNER ELLIOTT P
CHRISTIANITY AND ISLAM AMONG THE MOSSI.
AMERICAN ANTHROPOLOGIST 60 DECEMBER 1958 PP 1102-1119
050,052,141-03,
     CASE STUDY

SLADE RUTH
ENGLISH SPEAKING MISSIONS IN THE CONGO INDEPENDENT STATE--
1878-1908.
BRUXELLES, ACADEMIE ROYALE DES SCIENCES COLONIALES, 1959
050,108-03,
     CASE STUDY

SMITH NOEL
THE PRESBYTERIAN CHURCH OF GHANA 1835-1960--A YOUNGER CHURCH
IN A CHANGING SOCIETY.
GHANA, GHANA UNIVERSITIES PRESS, 1966
050,114-03,
     CASE STUDY

TAYLOR JOHN   LEHMANN D A
CHRISTIANS OF THE COPPERBELT-- THE GROWTH OF CHURCH IN
NORTHERN RHODESIA.
LONDON, SUDAN CHRISTIAN MISSION PRESS, 1961

050,142-03,
      CASE STUDY

050
   ULLENDORFF EDWARD
   ETHIOPIA AND THE BIBLE.
   LONDON, OXFORD UNIVERSITY PRESS, 1968
   050,110-02,
      CASE STUDY

   WILLIAMSON SIDNEY G
   AKAN RELIGION AND THE CHRISTIAN FAITH.
   GHANA, GHANA UNIVERSITIES PRESS, 1965
   050,114-03,
      CASE STUDY

   BASSIR OLUMBE
   LE QUAKERISME ET LA PERSONNALITE AFRICAINE (THE QUAKER FAITH
   AND THE AFRICAN PERSONALITY).
   COLLOQUE SUR LES RELIGIONS, ABIDJAN, APRIL, 1961, PARIS,
   PRESENCE AFRICAINE, 1962, PP 173-178
   050,
      LESS ACCESSIBLE

   EKOLLO PASTEUR
   ILLUSTRATION DU GENIE AFRICAINE AU SIEN DE LA COMMUNAUTE
   PROTESTANTE EN AFRIQUE (ILLUSTRATION OF THE AFRICAN SPIRIT
   IN THE BOSOM OF THE PROTESTANT COMMUNITY IN AFRICA).
   IN COLLOQUE SUR LES RELIGIONS, ABIDJAN, APRIL, 1961, PARIS,
   PRESENCE AFRICAINE, 1962, PP 147-154
   050,
      LESS ACCESSIBLE

   GRAVAND R P
   CONTRIBUTION DU CHRISTIANISME A L'AFFIRMATION DE LA
   PERSONNALITE AFRICAINE EN PAYS SERERE (CONTRIBUTION OF
   CHRISTIANITY TO THE AFFIRMATION OF THE AFRICAN PERSONALITY
   IN SERERE COUNTRY).
   IN COLLOQUE SUR LES RELIGIONS, ABIDJAN, APRIL, 1961, PARIS,
   PRESENCE AFRICAINE, 1962, PP 209-214
   039,050,130-03,
      LESS ACCESSIBLE

   MBITI JOHN S
   LA CONTRIBUTION PROTESTANTE A L EXPRESSION CULTURELLE DE LA
   PERSONNALITE AFRICAINE (THE PROTESTANT CONTRIBUTION TO
   CULTURAL EXPRESSION OF THE AFRICAN PERSONALITY).
   IN COLLOQUE SUR LES RELIGIONS, ABIDJAN, APRIL, 1961, PARIS,
   PRESENCE AFRICAINE, 1962, PP 137-146
   039,050,
      LESS ACCESSIBLE

   NZEKWU M
   LA CONTRIBUTION CATHOLIQUE (THE CATHOLIC CONTRIBUTION).
   IN COLLOQUE SUR LES RELIGIONS, ABIDJAN, APRIL, 1961, PARIS,
   PRESENCE AFRICAINE, 1962, PP 195-198
   050,
      LESS ACCESSIBLE

   PRESENCE AFRICAINE   ED

COLLOQUE SUR LES RELIGIONS. (COLLOQUIUM ON RELIGIONS).
ABIDJAN 5/12 APRIL 1961 PARIS, PRESENCE AFRICAINE 1962
013,050,
        LESS ACCESSIBLE

050

SASTRE L'ABBE
CONTRIBUTION DE L'EGLISE CATHOLIQUE A L'EXPRESSION
CULTURELLE DE LA PERSONNALITE AFRICAINE (CONTRIBUTION OF
THE CATHOLIC CHURCH TO THE CULTURAL EXPRESSION OF THE
AFRICAN PERSONALITY).
IN COLLOQUE SUR LES RELIGIONS, ABIDJAN, APRIL, 1961, PARIS,
PRESENCE AFRICAINE, 1962, PP 183-194
039,050,
        LESS ACCESSIBLE

TEMPELS REV PLACID
L'HOMME BANTOU ET LE CHRIST (THE BANTU MAN AND CHRIST).
IN COLLOQUE SUR LES RELIGIONS, ABIDJAN, APRIL, 1961, PARIS,
PRESENCE AFRICAINE, 1962, PP 219-224
050,
        LESS ACCESSIBLE

COLEMAN JAMES S
SOCIAL CLEAVAGE AND RELIGIOUS CONFLICT.
JOURNAL OF SOCIAL ISSUES 12 1956 B-M REPRINT 47
050,
        GENERAL THEORY

AJAYI J F ADE
CHRISTIAN MISSIONS IN NIGERIA.
EVANSTON, NORTHWESTERN UNIVERSITY PRESS, 1965
050,128-03,
        CASE STUDY

CARPENTER GEORGE
THE ROLE OF CHRISTIANITY AND ISLAM IN CONTEMPORARY AFRICA.
IN CHARLES G HAINES (ED), AFRICA TODAY, BALTIMORE, THE JOHNS
HOPKINS PRESS, 1955, PP 90-112
050,
        REFERENCE

51. INNOVATION, SYNTHESIS, AND INDEPENDENCY

051

BARRETT DAVID B
SCHISM AND RENEWAL IN AFRICA--AN ANALYSIS OF SIX THOUSAND
CONTEMPORARY RELIGIOUS MOVEMENTS.
NAIROBI, OXFORD UNIVERSITY PRESS, 1968
051,
        AUTHOR , WHO HAS B.D. AS WELL AS ENGINEERING/SOCIOLOGY
        DEGREE, DEALS IN A QUANTITATIVE MANNER WITH THE PHENO-
        MENON OF INDEPENDENCY, THE CORRELATES OF INDEPENDENCY,
        AND THE FUTURE PROSPECTS FOR INDEPENDENCY. USEFUL MAP
        --RELATIONSHIP OF INDEPENDENCY TO ETHNICITY.

051

MITCHELL ROBERT C   TURNER HAROLD
A COMPREHENSIVE BIBLIOGRAPHY OF MODERN AFRICAN RELIGIOUS
MOVEMENTS.
EVANSTON, NORTHWESTERN UNIVERSITY PRESS, 1966
051,
      AN ANNOTATED BIBLIOGRAPHY OF ABOUT 1,300 REFERENCES
      TO SYNCRETISTIC, OR INDEPENDENCY CHURCHES IN ALL PARTS
      OF AFRICA. THE AUTHORS PROVIDE A THEORETICAL INTRO-
      DUCTION WHICH ASSESSES BRIEFLY THE CHARACTERISTICS OF
      RELIGIOUS SYNCRETISM IN AFRICA.

BALANDIER GEORGES
MESSIANISMES ET NATIONALISMES EN AFRIQUE NOIRE (MESSIANIC
CULTS AND NATIONALISM IN BLACK AFRICA).
CAHIERS INTERNATIONAUX DE SOCIOLOGIE 14 1953 PP41-65(ENGLISH
TRANSLATION-- VANDENBERGHE)
050,051,
      REFERENCE

BANTON MICHAEL P
AFRICAN PROPHETS.
RACE 5 OCTOBER 1963 PP 42-55
051,
      REFERENCE

BARRETT DAVID B
CHURCH GROWTH AND INDEPENDENCY AS ORGANIC PHENOMENA-- AN
ANALYSIS OF TWO HUNDRED AFRICAN TRIBES.
IN C G BAETA (ED), CHRISTIANITY IN TROPICAL AFRICA, LONDON,
OXFORD UNIVERSITY PRESS, 1968, PP 269-288
051,
      REFERENCE

KOPYTOFF IGOR
CLASSIFICATION OF RELIGIOUS MOVEMENTS-ANALYTICAL AND
SYNTHETIC
IN SYMPOSIUM ON NEW APPROACHES TO THE STUDY OF RELIGION,
PROCEEDINGS OF THE 1964 ANNUAL SPRING MEETING OF THE
AMERICAN ETHNOLOGICAL SOCIETY,SEATTLE, 1964, PP 77-90
051,
      REFERENCE

SHEPPERSON GEORGE
ETHIOPIANISM AND AFRICAN NATIONALISM.
PHYLON 14 1953 PP 9-18
050,051,
      REFERENCE

TURNER H W
A TYPOLOGY FOR AFRICAN RELIGIOUS MOVEMENTS
JOURNAL OF RELIGION IN AFRICA 1 1964 PP 1-34
051,
      REFERENCE

WELBOURN F B
EAST AFRICAN REBELS-- A STUDY OF SOME INDEPENDENT CHURCHES.
LONDON, SUDAN CHRISTIAN MISSION PRESS, 1961
051,

REFERENCE

051

ANDERSSON EFRIAM
MESSIANIC POPULAR MOVEMENTS IN THE LOWER CONGO.
UPSALA, ALMQUIST AND WIKSELL,1958
(STUDIA ETHNOGRAPHICA UPSALIENSIA, 14)
051,108-03,
    CASE STUDY

CHRISTENSEN JAMES
THE ADAPTIVE FUNCTIONS OF FANTI PRIESTHOOD CHAPTER 13.
IN WILLIAM BASCOM AND MELVILLE HERSKOVITS, CONTINUTY AND
CHANGE IN AFRICAN CULTURES, CHICAGO, UNIVERSITY OF CHICAGO
PRESS, 1962, PP 238-256
051,114-03,
    CASE STUDY

FABIAN JOHANNES
CHARISMA AND CULTURAL CHANGE-THE CASE OF THE JAMAA MOVEMENT
IN KATANGA(CONGO REPUBLIC)
COMPARATIVE STUDIES IN SOCIETY AND HISTORY 11 1969 PP155-173
051,108-03,
    CASE STUDY

FEHDERAU HAROLD W
KIMBANGUISM-- PROPHETIC CHRISTIANITY IN THE CONGO.
PRACTICAL ANTHROPOLOGY 9 1962 PP 157-178
051,108-03,
    CASE STUDY

HERSKOVITS MELVILLE J
REDISCOVERY AND INTEGRATION-- RELIGION AND THE
ARTS CHAPTER 13.
IN THE HUMAN FACTOR IN CHANGING AFRICA, NEW YORK, ALFRED
A KNOPF, 1962, PP 417-450
051,
    CASE STUDY

LONG NORMAN
SOCIAL CHANGE AND THE INDIVIDUAL--A STUDY OF THE SOCIAL AND
RELIGIOUS RESPONSES TO INNOVATION IN A ZAMBIAN RURAL
COMMUNITY.
NEW YORK, HUMANITIES PRESS, INC., 1968
051,142-03,
    CASE STUDY

MESSENGER JOHN C
REINTERPRETATIONS OF CHRISTIAN AND INDIGENOUS BELIEF IN A
NIGERIAN NATIVIST CHURCH.
AMERICAN ANTHROPOLOGIST 62 APRIL 1960 PP 268-278
051,128-03,
    CASE STUDY

MESSENGER JOHN C
RELIGIOUS ACCULTURATION AMONG THE ANANG IBIBIO CHAPTER 15.
IN WILLIAM BASCOM AND MELVILLE HERSKOVITS, CONTINUITY AND
CHANGE IN AFRICAN CULTURES, CHICAGO, UNIVERSITY OF CHICAGO
PRESS, 1962, PP 279-299
051,128-03,

CASE STUDY

051
   OGOT BETHWELL A   WELBOURN F B
   A PLACE TO FEEL AT HOME--A STUDY OF TWO INDEPENDENT CHURCHES
   IN WESTERN KENYA.
   LONDON, OXFORD UNIVERSITY PRESS, 1966
   051,117-03,
        CASE STUDY

   PARRINDER GEOFFREY
   INDIGENOUS CHURCHES IN NIGERIA.
   WEST AFRICAN REVIEW 31 SEPTEMBER 1960 PP 87-93
   LONDON, AFRICA RESEARCH LIMITED, 1969, P. 53-54
   051,128-03,
        CASE STUDY

   PEEL J D Y
   ALADURA--A RELIGIOUS MOVEMENT AMONG THE YORUBA.
   LONDON, OXFORD UNIVERSITY PRESS, 1968
   051,128-03,
        CASE STUDY

   SHEPPERSON GEORGE
   THE POLITICS OF AFRICAN CHURCH SEPARATIST MOVEMENTS IN
   BRITISH CENTRAL AFRICA 1892-1916.
   AFRICA 24 1954 PP 233-245
   051,
        CASE STUDY

   SHEPPERSON GEORGE
   NYASALAND AND THE MILLENIUM.
   IN SYLVIA L THRUPP (ED), MILLENNIAL DREAMS IN ACTION,
   THE HAGUE, MOUTON, 1962, PP 144-159
   051,122-03,
        CASE STUDY

   SUNDKLER BENGT
   BANTU PROPHETS IN SOUTH AFRICA.
   LONDON, OXFORD UNIVERSITY PRESS (2ND ED), 1961
   051,132-03,
        CASE STUDY

   TURNER HAROLD
   AFRICAN INDEPENDENT CHURCH-- THE LIFE AND FAITH OF THE
   CHURCH OF THE LORD (ALADURA).
   LONDON, OXFORD UNIVERSITY PRESS, 1967
   051,128-03,
        CASE STUDY

   WEBSTER J B
   THE AFRICAN CHURCHES AMONG THE YORUBA 1888-1922.
   OXFORD, CLARENDON PRESS, 1964
   051,128-03,
        CASE STUDY

   WISHLADE R L
   SECTARIANISM IN SOUTHERN NYASALAND.
   LONDON, OXFORD UNIVERSITY PRESS, 1965
   051,122-03,

CASE STUDY

051

ALAPINI M
LE CULTE DE VODOUN ET DE ORICHA CHEZ LES FON ET LES NAGO
DU DAHOMEY (THE CULT OF VODOUN AND ORICHA AMONG THE FON AND
THE NAGO OF DAHOMEY).
IN COLLOQUE SUR LES RELIGIONS, ABIDJAN, APRIL, 1961, PARIS,
PRESENCE AFRICAINE, 1962, PP 91-96
051,110-03,
        LESS ACCESSIBLE

CHOME JULES
LA PASSION DE SIMON KIMBANGU 1921-1951 (THE PASSION OF
SIMON KIMBANGU 1921-1951).
BRUXELLES, AMIS DE PRESENCE AFRICAINE, 1959
051,108-03,
        LESS ACCESSIBLE

HOLAS B
LE SEPARATISME RELIGIEUX EN AFRIQUE NOIRE-- L'EXAMPLE
DE LA COTE D'IVOIRE (RELIGIOUS SEPARATISM IN BLACK AFRICA--
THE EXAMPLE OF THE IVORY COAST).
PARIS, PRESSES UNIVERSITAIRES DE FRANCE, 1965
051,116-03,
        LESS ACCESSIBLE

LANTERNARI V
SYNCRETISMES, MESSIANISMES, NEOTRADITIONALISMES-- POSTFACE
A UNE ETUDE DES MOUVEMENTS RELIGIEUX DE L'AFRIQUE NOIRE
(SYNCRETISM, MESSIANISM, NEO-TRADITIONALISM-- A REVIEW OF
A STUDY OF RELIGIOUS MOVEMENTS OF BLACK AFRICA).
ARCHIVES DE SOCIOLOGIE DES RELIGIONS 19 1965 PP 99-116
051,
        LESS ACCESSIBLE

LINTON RALPH
NATIVISTIC MOVEMENTS.
AMERICAN ANTHROPOLOGIST 45 APRIL 1943 PP 230-240
051,
        GENERAL THEORY

WALLACE ANTHONY F
REVITALIZATION MOVEMENTS.
AMERICAN ANTHROPOLOGIST 58 APRIL 1956
051,
        GENERAL THEORY

52. ISLAMIC REFORMATION MOVEMENTS

052

ABUN-NASR JAMIL
THE TIJANIYYA--A SUFI ORDER IN THE MODERN WORLD.
LONDON OXFORD UNIVERSITY PRESS 1965
052,

ONLY EXISTING MAJOR STUDY IN ENGLISH OF AN ISLAMIC
BROTHERHOOD WHICH HAS ROOTS IN BOTH NORTH AND WEST
AFRICA. THE TIJANIYYA BROTHERHOOD IS THE MAJOR BRO-
THERHOOD IN WEST AFRICA. AUTHOR S FOCUS, HOWEVER,
PRIMARILY ON NORTH AFRICA. NARRATIVE IS READABLE BY
NON-SPECIALIST, ALTHOUGH FULL ARABIC REFERENCES ARE
CITED.

052

FROELICH JEAN C
LES MUSULMANS D'AFRIQUE NOIRE (THE MUSLIMS OF BLACK
AFRICA).
PARIS,EDITIONS DE L'ORANTE,1962
021,052,
EXCELLENT OVERVIEW OF MODERN AFRICAN ISLAM BY DIR-
ECTOR OF UNIVERSITY OF PARIS CENTER FOR HIGHER
ADMINISTRATIVE STUDIES ON MODERN AFRICA AND ASIA.
DATA DRAWN FROM UNPUBLISHED FILES, ORGANIZED INTO
THREE PARTS-- ISLAMIZATION OF BLACK AFRICA, CHARACTER-
ISTICS OF ISLAM IN BLACK AFRICA, AND MODERN TENDENCIES
IN ISLAM IN BLACK AFRICA. GOOD DISCUSSION OF BROTHER-
HOODS, AND ISLAMIC REFORMISM.

GOUILLY ALPHONSE
L'ISLAM DANS L'AFRIQUE OCCIDENTALE FRANCAISE (ISLAM IN
FRENCH WEST AFRICA).
PARIS,EDITIONS LAROSE,1952
021,052,
HAS BEEN THE MAJOR REFERENCE WORK ON WEST AFRICAN
ISLAM SINCE ITS PUBLICATION IN 1952. NOW PARTLY SUPER
CEDED BY FROELICH AND MONTEIL, YET REMAINS USEFUL ON
THE HISTORY OF ISLAMIZATION IN WEST AFRICA INCLUDING
BERBER, MANDINGO, SONGHAY, AND FULANI EMPIRES, ON THE
RELIGIOUS BROTHERHOODS QADIRIYYA, TIJANIYYA, MOURID-
IYYA, HAMALLIYYA, AHMADIYYA, SANUSIYYA, AND ON EFFECTS
OF ISLAMIZATION LAW, PRAYER, PILGRIMMAGE, ETC.

JOHNSTON H A S
THE FULANI EMPIRE OF SOKOTO.
LONDON, OXFORD UNIVERSITY PRESS, 1967
024,052,128-02,
VERY READABLE ACCOUNT BY FORMER ADMINISTRATIVE OFFICER.
FOR FULLER REVIEW, SEE M.G. SMITH (AFRICA, JAN. 1969),
WHO SAYS, 'I DOUBT THIS SPLENDID WORK IS LIKELY TO BE
SUPERSEDED.'

KRITZECK JAMES   LEWIS WILLIAM H   EDS
ISLAM IN AFRICA
NEW YORK, VAN NOSTRAND-REINHOLD COMPANY, 1969
021,052,
MAJOR WORK COVERING HISTORICAL PERSPECTIVES,CULTURAL
AND DEMOGRAPHIC ASPECTS OF AFRICAN ISLAM,AND REGIONAL
DEVELOPMENTS IN ALL AREAS OF AFRICA. ORIGINAL CASE
STUDY SUMMARIES BY WELL KNOWN SCHOLARS MAKE UP THE
BULK OF THE VOLUME

LEWIS I M   ED
ISLAM IN TROPICAL AFRICA
LONDON,OXFORD UNIVERSITY PRESS,1966
021,052,

COLLECTION OF STUDIES AND DISCUSSIONS FROM FIFTH
INTERNATIONAL AFRICAN SEMINAR,ZARIA,NIGERIA,1964.
INTRODUCTION BY EDITOR COVERS REGIONAL REVIEW AND
DISTRIBUTION OF ISLAM,AGENTS OF ISLAMIZATION,ISLAM AND
TRIBAL POLITICS,ISLAMIC LAW AND CUSTOMARY PRACTICE,
ISLAM AND TRADITIONAL BELIEF AND RITUAL,ISLAM AND THE
MODERN WORLD. SPECIAL STUDIES REFERRED TO SEPARATELY.

052

TRIMINGHAM J S
THE INFLUENCE OF ISLAM UPON AFRICA.
LONDON, LONGMANS, GREEN AND CO. LTD., 1968
021,052,
     FIVE CHAPTERS--ISLAMIC CULTURE ZONES WITH HISTORY AND
     CHARACTERISTICS (MEDITERRANEAN, WESTERN SUDAN, CENT.
     SUDAN, EAST. SUDAN, ETHIOPIC ZONE, AND E. AFRICA), PRO-
     CESSES OF RELIGIOUS AND CULTURE CHANGE (ASSIMILATION,
     ADOPITON OF ISLAM, EFFECT ON AFRICAN SOCIETY), THE REL-
     IGIOUS LIFE OF AFRICAN MUSLIMS (UNITY OF BELIEF, INSTI-
     TUTIONS, SAINT CULTS), INFLUENCE OF ISLAM ON SOCIAL
     LIFE, THE AFRICAN MUSLIM IN AN ERA OF CHANGE (SECULAR-
     ISM, NATIONALISM).

FISHER HUMPHREY J
SEPARATISM IN WEST AFRICA
IN KRITZECK AND LEWIS, PP 127-138
052,
     REFERENCE

HISKETT MERVIN
AN ISLAMIC TRADITION OF REFORM IN THE WESTERN SUDAN
FROM THE SIXTEENTH TO THE EIGHTEENTH CENTURY.
BULLETIN OF THE SCHOOL OF ORIENTAL AND AFRICAN STUDIES 25
1962 PP 577-596
052,
     REFERENCE

LEWIS WILLIAM H
ISLAM--A RISING TIDE IN TROPICAL AFRICA.
REVIEW OF POLITICS 19 OCTOBER 1957 PP 446-461
052,
     REFERENCE

RICHARDSON S S
SOCIAL LEGAL REFORM
IN KRITZECK AND LEWIS, PP 110-126
052,
     REFERENCE

ABUN-NASR JAMIL
THE SALAFIYYA MOVEMENT IN MOROCCO-- THE RELIGIOUS BASES
OF THE MOROCCAN NATIONALIST MOVEMENT.
IN IMMANUEL WALLERSTEIN, SOCIAL CHANGE-THE COLONIAL
SITUATION, NEW YORK, JOHN WILEY AND SONS, 1966
052,126-03,
     CASE STUDY

BEHRMAN LUCY
MUSLIM BROTHERHOODS AND POLITICS IN SENEGAL
CAMBRIDGE, HARVARD UNIVERSITY PRESS, 1970

052,130-03,
    CASE STUDY

052

COHEN ABNER
THE POLITICS OF MYSTICISM IN SOME LOCAL COMMUNITIES.
LOCAL-LEVEL POLITICS, MARC J. SWARTZ (ED.), CHICAGO, ALDINE
PUBLISHING CO., 1968, PP. 361-376
052,128-03,
    CASE STUDY

FISHER HUMPHREY J
AHMADIYYAH, A STUDY IN CONTEMPORARY ISLAM ON THE WEST
AFRICAN COAST.
LONDON, OXFORD UNIVERSITY PRESS, 1963
052,
    CASE STUDY

LEVTZION NEHEMIA
COASTAL WEST AFRICA
IN KRITZECK AND LEWIS, PP 301-318
052,
    CASE STUDY

O BRIEN DONAL CRUISE
LE TALIBE MOURIDE--ETUDE D≠UN CAS DE DEPENDANCE SOCIALE
(THE MOURIDE DISCIPLE-STUDY OF A CASE OF SOCIAL DEPENDENCE).
CAHIERS D'ETUDES AFRICANES. VOL. IX, NO. 35, 1969, PP. 502-
507
052,130-03,
    CASE STUDY

SCHACHT JOSEPH
ISLAM IN NORTHERN NIGERIA.
STUDIA ISLAMICA 8 SUMMER 1957 PP 123-146
052,128-03,
    CASE STUDY

SKINNER ELLIOTT P
CHRISTIANITY AND ISLAM AMONG THE MOSSI.
AMERICAN ANTHROPOLOGIST 60 DECEMBER 1958 PP 1102-1119
050,052,141-03,
    CASE STUDY

THEOBALD A B
THE MAHDIYA-- A HISTORY OF THE ANGLO-EGYPTIAN SUDAN 1881-
1899.
LONDON, LONGMANS, 1951
034,052,134-02,
    CASE STUDY

BA AMADOU HAMPATE
L'ISLAM ET L'AFRIQUE NOIRE (ISLAM AND BLACK AFRICA).
IN COLLOQUE SUR LES RELIGIONS, ABIDJAN, APRIL, 1961, PARIS,
PRESENCE AFRICAINE, 1962, PP 101-118
052,
    LESS ACCESSIBLE

FROELICH JEAN C
L'IMPORTANCE ET L'INFLUENCE DE L≠ISLAM DU CHRISTIANISME ET

DES SECTES EN AFRIQUE NOIRE (THE IMPORTANCE AND THE
INFLUENCE OF ISLAM, OF CHRISTIANITY AND SECTS IN BLACK
AFRICA).
EUROPE-FRANCE OUTREMER 396 1963 PP 36-40
052,
        LESS ACCESSIBLE

052

FROELICH JEAN C
ESSAI SUR LES CAUSES ET METHODES DE L'ISLAMISATION DE
L'AFRIQUE DE L'OUEST DU XI SIECLE AU XX SIECLE.
IN LEWIS, ISLAM IN TROPICAL AFRICA, LONDON, OXFORD UNIVERSITY
PRESS, 1966, P. 160-173
052,
        LESS ACCESSIBLE

MONTEIL VINCENT
UNE CONFRERIE MUSULMANE-- LES MOURIDES DU SENEGAL (A MUSLIM
BROTHERHOOD-- THE MOURIDES OF SENEGAL).
ARCHIVES DE SOCIOLOGIE DES RELIGIONS 14 JULY 1962 PP 77-102
052,130-03,
        LESS ACCESSIBLE

MONTEIL VINCENT
LAT DIOR-- DAMAL DU KAYOR (1842-1886) ET L≠ISLAMISATION DES
WOLOFS (LAT DIOR-- DAMAL OF KAYOR (1842-1886) THE
ISLAMIZATION OF THE WOLOF).
ARCHIVES DE SOCIOLOGIE DES RELIGIONS 16 JULY 1963 PP 77-104
052,130-03,
        LESS ACCESSIBLE

MONTEIL VINCENT
L'ISLAM NOIRE.   (BLACK ISLAM).
PARIS, EDITIONS DU SEUIL, 1964
052,
        LESS ACCESSIBLE

MOREAU R L
LES MARABOUTS DE DORI (THE MARABOUS OF DORI).
ARCHIVES DE SOCIOLOGIE DES RELIGIONS 17 JANUARY 1964
PP 113-134
052,123-03,
        LESS ACCESSIBLE

SY CHEIKH TIDIANE
LA CONFRERIE SENEGALAISE DES MOURIDES (THE SENEGAL
BROTHERHOOD OF MOURIDES).
PARIS, PRESENCE AFRICAINE, 1969
052,130-03,
        LESS ACCESSIBLE

BIOBAKU SABURI O   AL-HAJJ MUHAMMAD
THE SUDANESE MAHDIYYA AND THE NIGER-CHAD REGION.
IN LEWIS, ISLAM IN TROPICAL AFRICA, LONDON, OXFORD UNIVERSITY
PRESS, 1966, P. 425-441
052,134-03,

HODGKIN THOMAS
THE ISLAMIC LITERARY TRADITION IN GHANA.
IN LEWIS, ISLAM IN TROPICAL AFRICA, LONDON, OXFORD UNIVERSITY

PRESS, 1966, P. 442-462
052,114-03,

53. STUDY QUESTIONS: PROCESSES OF CHANGE

053

CALDWELL JOHN C   OKONJO C   EDS
THE POPULATION OF TROPICAL AFRICA.
LONDON, LONGMANS, 1968
053,074,076,
        RECORD OF FIRST AFRICAN POPULATION CONFERENCE AT THE
        UNIVERSITY OF IBADAN, 1966. FIRST SECTION EXAMINES
        BASIC DEMOGRAPHIC DATA, PROBLEMS OF COLLECTION, AND
        ROLE OF MIGRATION AND URBANIZATION. SECOND SECTION
        COVERS POPULATION GROWTH AND ECONOMIC DEVELOPMENT,
        PARTICULARLY WITH RESPECT TO PLANNING. TOTAL OF
        FORTY-SIX CONTRIBUTORY ARTICLES.

DUMONT RENE
FALSE START IN AFRICA.
NEW YORK, PRAEGER PUBLISHERS, 1969
037,053,070,
        LEADING FRENCH AGRONOMIST, WITH SYMPATHY FOR AFRICAN
        INDEPENDENCE, MAKES CRITICAL AND CONTROVERSIAL ASSESS-
        MENT OF AFRICAN SOCIO-ECONOMIC DEVELOPMENT IN THE
        POST-COLONIAL PERIOD. EMPHASIZES THE NECESSITY FOR
        AGRICULTURAL REFORM TO PROVIDE CAPITAL BASIS FOR ECO-
        NOMIC TAKE-OFF INTO A FULLY INDUSTRIALIZED SOCIETY.

LLOYD PETER C
AFRICA IN SOCIAL CHANGE-- CHANGING TRADITIONAL SOCIETIES
IN THE MODERN WORLD.
BALTIMORE, PENGUIN, 1967
001,038,053,
        COMPREHENSIVE AND PENETRATING ANALYSIS OF SOCIAL
        CHANGE IN WEST AFRICA, FOCUSING PRIMARILY ON GROWTH
        AND PRESENT ROLE OF EDUCATED ELITE. EXAMINES
        TRADITIONAL BACKGROUND, IMPACT OF WEST, CHANGING
        INSTITUTIONS (FAMILY, URBAN ASSOCIATIONS, POLITICAL
        PARTIES), AND CONTEMPORARY PROBLEMS OF IDEOLOGY,
        TRIBALISM, AND POLITICAL INSTABILITY. AUTHOR TAUGHT
        15 YEARS IN NIGERIA, NOW TEACHES SOCIAL ANTHROPOLOGY
        AT SUSSEX. BIBLIOGRAPHY AND STATISTICAL APPENDIX.

MIDDLETON JOHN
THE EFFECTS OF ECONOMIC DEVELOPMENT ON TRADITIONAL POLITICAL
SYSTEMS IN AFRICA SOUTH OF THE SAHARA.
THE HAGUE, MOUTON, 1966
053,073,
        EXCELLENT SURVEY, HAS CHAPTERS ON TRADITIONAL AND
        CHANGING ECONOMIC AND POLITICAL SYSTEMS OF AFRICA--
        STUDIES OF CHANGE IN RURAL AREAS-- AND STUDIES OF
        URBANISM AND URBANIZATION. AUTHOR IS PROFESSOR OF
        URBAN ANTHROPOLOGY AT NEW YORK UNIVERSITY. FORTY PAGE
        BIBLIOGRAPHY ARRANGED BY TOPIC, E.G. PEASANT COMMUNI-

TIES, ELITES AND SOCIAL CLASSES, NATIONALISM, URBANI-
ZATION, CHIEFSHIP AND GOVERNMENT.

053

VAN DEN BERGHE P
AFRICA-- SOCIAL PROBLEMS OF CHANGE AND CONFLICT.
SAN FRANCISCO, CHANDLER, 1965
038,053,
      EXCELLENT SELECTION OF REPRINTED ARTICLES, FOCUSED ON
      BOTH SOCIAL CHANGE AND SOCIAL CONFLICT. CASE STUDIES
      ALL ILLUSTRATE THEORETICAL POINTS. UNLIKE THE WALLER-
      STEIN VOLUME OR THE FINKLE AND GABLE VOLUME, VAN DEN
      BERGHE DEALS EXCLUSIVELY WITH AFRICAN MATERIAL.

WALLERSTEIN I M   ED
SOCIAL CHANGE, THE COLONIAL SITUATION.
NEW YORK, JOHN WILEY, 1966
037,038,053,
      VOLUME CONSISTS OF REPRINTED ARTICLES BY WELL-KNOWN
      SCHOLARS, ARRANGED INTO NINE CATEGORIES-- DEFINITIONS
      OF THE COLONIAL SITUATION, MIGRATION OF LABOR AND ITS
      SOCIAL CONSEQUENCES, DECLINE AND CHANGING ROLE OF TRA-
      DITIONAL AUTHORITIES, CREATION OF URBAN ETHNICITY,
      CLASS, EDUCATION AND POWER, NEW NETWORK OF VOLUNTARY
      ASSOCIATIONS, NATIONALISM, WESTERNIZATION, RELIGIOUS
      CHANGE.

MIDDLETON JOHN   ED
BLACK AFRICA- ITS PEOPLES AND THEIR CULTURES TODAY
LONDON, MACMILLAN, 1970
004,016,053,
      REFERENCE

HUNTER GUY
THE NEW SOCIETIES OF TROPICAL AFRICA.
LONDON, OXFORD UNIVERSITY PRESS, 1962
053,075,
      REFERENCE

PART IV
Consolidation of
Nation-States

54. CONCEPTS OF NATIONALISM

054
    AYANDELE E A
    NATIONALIST MOVEMENTS IN NORTH AFRICA CHP 12.
    IN JC ANENE AND GODFREY BROWN AFRICA IN THE 19TH AND 20TH
    CENTURIES, LONDON, NELSON IUP, 1966
    054,
        AN AREA STUDY OF NATIONALISM COVERING EGYPT, TUNISIA,
        MOROCCO, AND ALGERIA. COMPARES BRITISH AND FRENCH
        COLONIAL ATTITUDES AND RESISTANCE TO INDEPENDENCE
        MOVEMENTS, AND DISCUSSES THE PROCESSES BY WHICH INDE-
        PENDENCE WAS ACHIEVED. INCLUDES BRIEF REFERENCE TO
        ALGERIAN WAR (THE FIERCEST WAR IN COLONIAL AFRICA).
        CASE STUDY

    CARTER GWENDOLEN M
    AFRICAN CONCEPTS OF NATIONALISM IN SOUTH AFRICA.
    MELVILLE HERSKOVITS MEMORIAL LECTURE, EDINBURGH, EDINBURGH
    UNIVERSITY PRESS, MARCH 1965
    054,089,132-06,
        SHORT ESSAY ON THE DISTINCTIVENESS OF SOUTH AFRICAN
        NATIONALISM IN SETTING OBJECTIVES AND TACTICS.
        DISTINGUISHING FEATURES INCLUDE CONFRONTATION WITH
        LOCAL WHITE POWER STRUCTURE-- WITH A COMPETING WHITE
        (AFRIKANER) NATIONALISM-- WITH A DYNAMIC AND FAR
        REACHING INDUSTRIAL AND COMMERCIAL STRUCTURE-- AND WITH

A CONTEXT IN WHICH THE POLITICAL RIGHTS OF AFRICANS
HAVE BECOME INCREASINGLY RESTRICTED.

054
DIA MAMADOU   TRANSLATED BY   COOK MERCER
THE AFRICAN NATIONS AND WORLD SOLIDARITY.
LONDON, THAMES AND HUDSON, 1962
054,060,130-04,
    SUGGESTS BASIC DEFINITIONS OF NATIONALISM AS A COLLEC-
    TIVE VOCATION. DISTINGUISHES VARIOUS TYPES OF NATION-
    ALISM. AUTHOR IS FORMER DEPUTY PREMIER OF SENEGAL.

DIOP CHEIKH ANTA
THE CULTURAL UNITY OF NEGRO-AFRICA.
PARIS, PRESENCE AFRICAINE, 1962
016,039,054,099,
    AUTHOR IS SENEGALESE SCHOLAR WHO HAS UNDERTAKEN
    RESEARCH ON THE HISTORY OF THE AFRICAN CONTINENT WITH
    A VIEW TO STRESSING SIMILARITIES RATHER THAN
    DIFFERENCES AMONG THE VARIOUS ETHNIC SOCIETIES. FROM
    THESE SIMILARITIES HE PROPOSES CERTAIN CULTURE-PERSON-
    ALITY PATTERNS WHICH HE FEELS DISTINGUISH AFRICANS
    FROM EUROPEANS.

EMERSON RUPERT
NATIONALISM AND POLITICAL DEVELOPMENT.
JOURNAL OF POLITICS 22 FEBRUARY 1960 PP 3-28.
ALSO IN FINKLE J L AND GABLE R W,POLITICAL DEVELOPMENT AND
SOCIAL CHANGE,NEW YORK, JOHN WILEY,1966, CH 5
054,
    SUGGESTS THAT IN AFRICA THE COLONIAL REGIMES WERE
    MAJOR INSTRUMENTS IN SHAPING THE NEW NATIONS. ASSES-
    SES NATIONALISM AS AN ANTI FEELING, AND AS A FOUN-
    DATION FOR POLITICAL DEVELOPMENT. EXCELLENT BASIC
    DEFINITIONS OF TERMINOLOGY. AUTHOR IS PROFESSOR OF
    GOVERNMENT AT HARVARD UNIVERSITY WITH WIDE EXPERIENCE
    IN STUDY OF NATIONALISM IN EUROPE, ASIA, AND AFRICA.

MARKOVITZ IRVING L
LEOPOLD SENGHOR AND THE POLITICS OF NEGRITUDE.
NEW YORK, ATHENEUM, 1969 (LONDON, HEINEMANN
EDUCATIONAL BOOKS)
044,054,130-04,
    DEALS WITH THE POLITICAL CONTEXT--SENEGAL--IN WHICH
    SENGHOR HAS DONE HIS WRITINGG. DISCUSSES THE FORMATIVE
    PERIODS IN THE EMERGENCE OF SENGHOR'S CONCEPTS OF NE-
    GRITUDE, AND PROVIDES A THOROUGH EVALUATION OF THE SUB-
    STANTIVE CONCEPTS OF NEGRITUDE.

ABU-LUGHOD IBRAHIM
NATIONALISM IN A NEW PERSPECTIVE-- THE AFRICAN CASE.
IN HERBERT J SPIRO, ED, PATTERNS OF AFRICAN DEVELOPMENT,
ENGLEWOOD CLIFFS, PRENTICE-HALL, 1967, PP 35-62
054,
    REFERENCE

BASTIDE ROGER
VARIATIONS ON NEGRITUDE.
PRESENCE AFRICAINE 36 1ST TRIMESTRE 1961 PP 7-17.
ALSO ALBERT BERRIAN RICHARD LONG, EDS,NEGRITUDE-- ESSAYS AND

STUDIES, HAMPTON, VIRGINIA, HAMPTON INSTITUTE PRESS, 1967, PP
69-78
054,
     REFERENCE

054

    BUSIA KOFI A
    THE CHALLENGE OF NATIONALISM CHP 11.
    IN THE CHALLENGE OF AFRICA, NEW YORK, PRAEGER, 1962
    054,
        REFERENCE

    CESAIRE AIME
    RETURN TO MY NATIVE LAND.
    PARIS, PRESENCE AFRICAINE, 1968
    054,091,
        REFERENCE

    DEBRAH E M
    THE PSYCHOLOGY OF AFRICAN NATIONALISM.
    IN WILLIAM H LEWIS, NEW FORCES IN AFRICA, GEORGETOWN
    COLLOQUIUM ON AFRICA PAPERS, WASHINGTON, PUBLIC AFFAIRS
    PRESS, 1961, PP 51-66
    054,
        REFERENCE

    DIA MAMADOU
    TOWARDS A NEW DEFINITION OF NATION CHP 1.
    IN THE AFRICAN NATIONS AND WORLD SOLIDARITY, NEW YORK,
    PRAEGER, 1961
    054,
        REFERENCE

    DIOP ALIOUNE
    REMARKS ON AFRICAN PERSONALITY AND NEGRITUDE
    IN AMERICAN SOCIETY OF AFRICAN CULTURE, PAN-AFRICANISM
    RECONSIDERED, BERKELEY, UNIVERSITY OF CALIFORNIA PRESS, 1962
    PP 337-345
    039,054,077,079,
        REFERENCE

    DRAKE ST CLAIR
    PAN-AFRICANISM, NEGRITUDE AND THE AFRICAN PERSONALITY.
    BOSTON UNIVERSITY GRADUATE JOURNAL 10 1961 PP 38-51; IN
    WILLIAM J HANNA, INDEPENDENT BLACK AFRICA, CHICAGO, RAND
    MCNALLY, 1964, PP 530-541
    039,054,077,
        REFERENCE

    EMERSON RUPERT   KILSON MARTIN L
    IDEAS AND CONTEXT OF AFRICAN NATIONALISM CHP 2.
    IN THE POLITICAL AWAKENING OF AFRICA, ENGELWOOD CLIFFS,
    NEW JERSEY, PRENTICE-HALL, 1965
    054,
        REFERENCE

    IRELE ABIOLA
    NEGRITUDE OR BLACK CULTURAL NATIONALISM.
    JOURNAL OF MODERN AFRICAN STUDIES 3 OCTOBER 1965 PP 321-348
    054,

REFERENCE

054

LEWIS WILLIAM H
NATIONALISM AND MODERNISM
IN KRITZECK AND LEWIS, PP 185-201
054,
         REFERENCE

PERHAM MARGERY
THE PSYCHOLOGY OF AFRICAN NATIONALISM.
IN WILLIAM J HANNA (ED), INDEPENDENT BLACK AFRICA, CHICAGO,
RAND MCNALLY, 1964, PP 176-191
054,
         REFERENCE

SITHOLE NDABANINGI
AFRICAN NATIONALISM.
LONDON, OXFORD UNIVERSITY PRESS, 1968
054,091,145-04,
       REFERENCE

WELCH CLAUDE E
DREAM OF UNITY-PAN-AFRICANISM AND POLITICAL UNIFICATION IN
WEST AFRICA
ITHACA, CORNELL UNIVERSITY PRESS, 1966
054,059,079,
         REFERENCE

YOUNG CRAWFORD
POLITICS IN THE CONGO--DECOLONIZAT2ON AND INDEPENDENCE.
PRINCETON, NEW JERSEY, PRINCETON UNIVERSITY PRESS, 1965
054,061,081,108-07,
         REFERENCE

AHIDJO AHMADOU
CONTRIBUTION TO NATIONAL CONSTRUCTION.
PARIS, PRESENCE AFRICAINE, 1964
054,060,104-04,
       CASE STUDY

AHMED JAMAL M
THE INTELLECTUAL ORIGINS OF EGYPTIAN NATIONALISM.
NEW YORK, OXFORD UNIVERSITY PRESS, 1960
054,140-06,
       CASE STUDY

ARDENER EDWIN
THE NATURE OF THE REUNIFICATION OF CAMEROON CHAPTER 8.
IN ARTHUR HAZLEWOOD, AFRICAN INTEGRATION AND DISINTEGRATION,
LONDON, OXFORD UNIVERSITY PRESS, 1967, PP 285-337
054,104-06,
       CASE STUDY

AWOLOWO OBAFEMI
THOUGHTS ON NIGERIAN CONSTITUTION.
NIGERIA, OXFORD UNIVERSITY PRESS,1966
054,068,128-04,
       CASE STUDY

CESAIRE AIME
LETTER TO MAURICE THOREZ.
PARIS, PRESENCE AFRICAINE, 1956
054,
        CASE STUDY

054
KAUNDA KENNETH
ZAMBIA--INDEPENDENCE AND BEYOND.
LONDON, NELSON, 1966
054,060,142-04,
        CASE STUDY

MUTESA II
THE DESECRETION OF MY KINGDOM.
LONDON, CONSTABLE, 1967
054,064,139-04,
        CASE STUDY

POST KENNETH W J
NATIONALISM AND POLITICS IN NIGERIA-- A MARXIST APPROACH.
NIGERIAN JOURNAL OF ECONOMIC AND SOCIAL STUDIES 6 JULY
1964 PP 169-176
054,128-06,
        CASE STUDY

REPUBLIC OF KENYA
AFRICAN SOCIALISM AND ITS APPLICATION TO PLANNING IN KENYA
NAIROBI GOVERNMENT PRINTER 1965
054,072,077,117-08,
        CASE STUDY

SENGHOR LEOPOLD S
ON AFRICAN SOCIALISM.
NEW YORK, PRAEGER, 1964
013,054,060,130-04,
        CASE STUDY

SNYDER FRANCIS G
THE POLITICAL THOUGHT OF MODIBO KEITA.
JOURNAL OF MODERN AFRICAN STUDIES 5 MAY 1967 PP 79-106
054,123-04,
        CASE STUDY

TOUVAL SAADIA
SOMALI NATIONALISM-- INTERNATIONAL POLITICS AND THE DRIVE
FOR UNITY IN THE HORN OF AFRICA.
CAMBRIDGE, MASS., HARVARD UNIVERSITY PRESS, 1963
054,055,133-09,
        CASE STUDY

CESAIRE AIME
DISCOURS SUR LE COLONIALISME (DISCOURSE ON COLONIALISM).
PRESENCE AFRICAINE,
054,
        LESS ACCESSIBLE

DIOP CHEIKH ANTA
LES FONDEMENTS CULTURELS, TECHNIQUES ET INDUSTRIELS D≠UN
FUTUR, ETAT FEDERAL D'AFRIQUE NOIRE.

PARIS, PRESENCE AFRICAINE, 1960
054,
     LESS ACCESSIBLE

054

DIOP CHEIKH ANTA
L'AFRIQUE NOIRE PRE-COLONIALE (PRE-COLONIAL BLACK AFRICA).
PARIS, PRESENCE AFRICAINE, 1960
054,099,
     LESS ACCESSIBLE

DIOP CHEIKH ANTA
NATIONS NEGRES ET CULTURE (BLACK NATIONS AND CULTURE).
PARIS, EDITIONS AFRICAINES, 1955
054,
     LESS ACCESSIBLE

THIAM DOUDOU
LE NATIONALISME (NATIONALISM) CHP 1.
IN LA POLITIQUE ETRANGER DES ETATS AFRICAINES, PRESSES
UNIVERSITAIRES DE FRANCE, PARIS, 1963
054,
     LESS ACCESSIBLE

AL-RAZZAZ MUNIF
THE EVOLUTION OF THE MEANING OF NATIONALISM.
GARDEN CITY, NEW YORK, DOUBLEDAY, 1963
054,
     GENERAL THEORY

DEUTSCH KARL W
NATIONALISM AND ITS ALTERNATIVES
NEW YORK, ALFRED KNOPF, 1969
054,
     GENERAL THEORY

EMERSON RUPERT
FROM EMPIRE TO NATION.
CAMBRIDGE, MASS, HARVARD UNIVERSITY PRESS, 1960
054,
     GENERAL THEORY

GELLNER ERNEST
NATIONALISM CHP 7.
IN THOUGHT AND CHANGE, CHICAGO, UNIVERSITY OF CHICAGO
PRESS, 1965
054,
     GENERAL THEORY

HAYES CARLTON J
NATIONALISM-- A RELIGION.
NEW YORK, MACMILLAN, 1960
054,
     GENERAL THEORY

KEDOURIE ELIE
NATIONALISM.
LONDON, HUTCHISON, 1960
054,
     GENERAL THEORY

054

    KILSON MARTIN L
    THE ANALYSIS OF AFRICAN NATIONALISM.
    WORLD POLITICS APRIL 1958 PP 484-497
    054,
            GENERAL THEORY

    KOHN HANS
    THE IDEA OF NATIONALISM.
    NEW YORK, MACMILLAN, 1961
    054,
            GENERAL THEORY

    SYMMONS-SYMONOLEWICZ K
    NATIONALISM MOVEMENTS-- AN ATTEMPT AT A COMPARATIVE
    TYPOLOGY.
    COMPARATIVE STUDIES IN SOCIETY AND HISTORY 7 JANUARY 1965
    PP 221-230
    054,
            GENERAL THEORY

    TALMON JACOB L
    MESSIANIC NATIONALISM PT 2.
    IN POLITICAL MESSIANISM, NEW YORK, PRAEGER, 1960
    054,
            GENERAL THEORY

    VON GRUNEBAUM G
    PROBLEMS OF MUSLIM NATIONALISM CHP 9.
    IN MODERN ISLAM-- THE SEARCH FOR CULTURAL IDENTITY,BERKELEY
    UNIVERSITY OF CALIFORNIA PRESS, CHP 9, 1962
    054,
            GENERAL THEORY

55. PATTERNS OF AFRICAN NATIONALISM

.055

    COLEMAN JAMES S
    NATIONALISM IN TROPICAL AFRICA.
    IN WILLIAM J HANNA (ED), INDEPENDENT BLACK AFRICA, CHICAGO,
    RAND MCNALLY, 1964, PP 208-234
    055,
            EARLY ACCOUNT OF AFRICAN NATIONALISM. DISCUSSES TRA-
            DITIONALIST, SYNCRETISTIC, AND MODERNIST MOVEMENTS.
            ASSESSES ECONOMIC, SOCIOLOGICAL, RELIGIOUS, PSYCHOLO-
            GICAL AND POLITICAL FACTORS AFFECTING AFRICAN NATION-
            ALISM, PLUS SPECIAL PROBLEMS OF RESEARCH INTO AFRICAN
            NATIONALISM, AND IMPACT OF UNITED STATES ON AFRICAN
            NATIONALISM. AUTHOR FORMER PROFESSOR AT UCLA, CUR-
            RENTLY WITH ROCKEFELLER FOUNDATION IN EAST AFRICA.

    HODGKIN THOMAS
    NATIONALISM IN COLONIAL AFRICA.
    NEW YORK UNIVERSITY PRESS, 1965

055,

PUBLISHED BEFORE AFRICAN NATIONALISTS HAD ACHIEVED
INDEPENDENCE, BOOK REMAINS KEY WORK ON THE INTERACTION
OF COLONIALISM AND NATIONALISM. DEALS WITH COLONIAL
POLICIES OF THE EUROPEAN POWERS, THE IMPACT OF NEW
TOWNS, NEW ASSOCIATIONS, RELIGIOUS EXPRESSION OF
POLITICAL DISCONTENT, WORKING CLASS AND LABOR
MOVEMENTS, AND DEVELOPMENT OF POLITICAL PARTIES.
AUTHOR HAD BEEN JOURNALIST AND SCHOLAR MANY YEARS IN
AFRICA, AND IS NOW PROFESSOR AT OXFORD UNIVERSITY.

055

ITOTE WARUHIU
'MAU MAU' GENERAL.
KENYA, EAST AFRICAN PUBLISHING HOUSE, 1967
055,117-06,

AUTOBIOGRAPHY OF 'GENERAL CHINA' IN PAPERBACK, DISCUS-
SES FROM INSIDE POINT OF VIEW THE MAU MAU MOVEMENT, IN-
CLUDING TRAINING AND CARRYING OUT OF FOREST FIGHTING.
ALSO DEALS WITH THE NEGOTIATIONS FOR INDEPENDENCE, HIS
POST-INDEPENDENCE ROLE IN NATIONAL YOUTH SERVICE, AND
HIS ISRAELI MILITARY TRAINING.

POST KENNETH W J
NATIONALIST MOVEMENTS IN WEST AFRICA CHP 20.
IN JC ANENE AND GODFREY BROWN AFRICA IN THE 19TH AND 20TH
CENTURIES LONDON NELSON IUP 1966
055,

BRIEF DISCUSSION OF HISTORICAL BACKGROUND TO INDEPEN-
DENCE IN FORMER FRENCH AND BRITISH WEST AFRICA. IN-
CLUDES VALUABLE SECTION ON TEACHING PROBLEMS AND SUG-
GESTIONS, AS WELL AS QUESTIONS FOR FURTHER STUDY AND D
CUSSION.

ROSBERG CARL G   NOTTINGHAM JOHN
THE MYTH OF MAU-MAU-- NATIONALISM IN KENYA.
NEW YORK PRAEGER 1966
055,117-06,

STIMULATING AND CONTROVERSIAL ANALYSIS OF THE RISE OF
AFRICAN NATIONALISM IN KENYA. MAU MAU SEEN AS A MYTH
CREATED BY RESIDENT EUROPEAN COMMUNITY. AUTHORS AS-
SERT THAT EMERGENCY OF 1950'S WAS PART OF ONGOING PRO-
CESS OF AFRICAN POLITICAL ACTIVITY WHICH BEGAN IN THE
1920'S. PROVIDES POWERFUL COUNTERBALANCE TO COLONIAL
BIAS OF THE GOVERNMENT-SPONSORED CORFIELD REPORT OF
1960.

ROTBERG ROBERT I
THE ORIGINS OF NATIONALIST DISCONTENT IN EAST AND
CENTRAL AFRICA.
JOURNAL OF NEGRO HISTORY 48 1963 PP 130-141
055,

SUGGESTS THAT COLONIALISM GAVE RISE TO PROTEST MOVE-
MENTS WHICH PRE-DATE ORGANIZED NATIONALISM. EXAMINES
NATURE OF COLONIAL RULE AND BASIS OF AFRICAN GRIEV-
ANCES. DISCUSSES AFRICAN VOLUNTARY ASSOCIATIONS,
(TRIBAL AND NON-TRIBAL), AND THE RELIGIOUS VARIETIES
OF ANTI-COLONIALISM, (ESPECIALLY SEPARATIST CHURCHES).
DISCUSSES EARLY CONGRESSES OR PARTIES. AUTHOR IS
PROFESSOR OF HISTORY AND POLITICAL SCIENCE AT M.I.T.

055

ZOLBERG ARISTIDE R
PATTERNS OF NATIONAL INTEGRATION.
THE JOURNAL OF MODERN AFRICAN STUDIES, 5, 4, 1967, PP 449-67
055,058,116-06,123-06,
        AN EXAMINATION OF MALI AND THE IVORY COAST WHICH INDI-
        CATES HOW SOCIAL AND ECONOMIC CHANGES DURING THE COLO-
        NIAL PERIOD, AS WELL AS THE IDEOLOGIES AND ORGANIZA-
        TIONAL ACTIVITIES OF THE NEW AFRICAN ELITES HAVE CON-
        TRIBUTED TO THE FORMATION OF DISTINCT PATTERNS OF IN-
        CIPIENT NATIONAL INTEGRATION.

CHIDZERO BERNARD T
AFRICAN NATIONALISM IN EAST AND CENTRAL AFRICA.
INTERNATIONAL AFFAIRS 36 OCTOBER PP 464-475
055,
        REFERENCE

EMERSON RUPERT
CRUCIAL PROBLEMS INVOLVED IN NATION-BUILDING IN AFRICA.
JOURNAL OF NEGRO EDUCATION 30 1961 PP 193-205
055,
        REFERENCE

GUTTERIDGE WILLIAM
THE NATURE OF NATIONALISM IN BRITISH WEST AFRICA.
WESTERN POLITICAL QUARTERLY 11 1958 PP 574-582
055,
        REFERENCE

HEINTZEN HARRY
THE ROLE OF ISLAM IN THE ERA OF NATIONALISM.
IN WILLIAM H LEWIS, NEW FORCES IN AFRICA, GEORGETOWN
COLLOQUIUM ON AFRICA PAPERS, WASHINGTON, PUBLIC AFFAIRS
PRESS, 1962, PP 42-50
055,
        REFERENCE

HODGKIN THOMAS
ISLAM AND NATIONAL MOVEMENTS IN WEST AFRICA.
JOURNAL OF AFRICAN HISTORY 3 1962 PP323-327
055,
        REFERENCE

HODGKIN THOMAS
A NOTE ON THE LANGUAGE OF AFRICAN NATIONALISM.
IN WILLIAM J HANNA (ED), INDEPENDENT BLACK AFRICA, CHICAGO,
RAND MCNALLY, 1964, PP 235-252,
IN K KIRKWOOD (ED), ST ANTHONY'S PAPERS, 10, SOUTHERN
ILLINOIS UNIVERSITY PRESS, 1961, PP 22-40
055,
        REFERENCE

KILSON MARTIN L
NATIONALISM AND SOCIAL CLASSES IN BRITISH WEST AFRICA.
JOURNAL OF POLITICS 20 MAY 1958 PP 368-387
055,
        REFERENCE

KILSON MARTIN L
THE RISE OF NATIONALIST ORGANIZATIONS AND PARTIES IN
BRITISH WEST AFRICA.
IN AFRICA SEEN BY AMERICAN NEGROES, NEW YORK, AMERICAN
SOCIETY OF AFRICAN CULTURE, 1963, PP 35-69
055,
        REFERENCE

055

LEWIS WILLIAM H
ISLAM AND NATIONALISM IN AFRICA.
IN TIBOR KEREKES (ED), THE ARAB MIDDLE EAST AND MUSLIM
AFRICA, NEW YORK, PRAEGER, 1961, PP 83-84
055,
        REFERENCE

RANGER TERENCE O
CONNEXIONS BETWEEN PRIMARY RESISTANCE MOVEMENTS AND
MODERN MASS NATIONALISM IN EAST AND CENTRAL AFRICA 2 PARTS
JOURNAL OF AFRICAN HISTORY 9 1968 PP 437-453 AND 631-642
034,055,
        REFERENCE

ROBINSON KENNETH
POLITICAL DEVELOPMENT IN FRENCH WEST AFRICA.
IN CALVIN STILLMAN (ED.), AFRICA IN THE MODERN WORLD, CHICAGO
UNIVERSITY OF CHICAGO PRESS, 1955, PP 140-181
055,
        REFERENCE

ROTBERG ROBERT I
THE TRIUMPH OF NATIONALISM, 1940-1965 CHAPTER 11.
IN A POLITICAL HISTORY OF TROPICAL AFRICA, NEW YORK,
HARCOURT, BRACE AND WORLD, 1965, PP 348-372
055,
        REFERENCE

APTER DAVID E
THE POLITICAL KINGDOM IN UGANDA--A STUDY IN BUREAUCRATIC
NATIONALISM.
PRINCETON, PRINCETON UNIVERSITY PRESS, 1961; REVISED, 1967
055,139-06,
        CASE STUDY

APTER DAVID E
THE ROLE OF TRADITIONALISM IN THE POLITICAL
MODERNIZATION OF GHANA AND UGANDA.
WORLD POLITICS 13 OCT 1960 PP 45-68 ALSO WILLIAM J HANNA, ED,
INDEPENDENT BLACK AFRICA, CHICAGO, RAND MCNALLY, 1964, PP
254-277
055,114-03,139-03,
        CASE STUDY

APTER DAVID E
THE DEVELOPMENT OF GHANA NATIONALISM.
UNITED ASIA 9 1957 PP 23-30
055,114-06,
        CASE STUDY

AUSTIN DENNIS

POLITICS IN GHANA 1946-1960.
LONDON, OXFORD UNIVERSITY PRESS, 1964
055,114-07,
     CASE STUDY

055

AWOLOWO OBAFEMI
PATH TO NIGERIAN FREEDOM.
LONDON, FABER, 1966
055,128-04,
     CASE STUDY

BOAHEN A ADU
THE ROOTS OF GHANAIAN NATIONALISM.
JOURNAL OF AFRICAN HISTORY 5 1964 PP 127-132
055,114-06,
     CASE STUDY

BOURRET F M
GHANA-- THE ROAD TO INDEPENDENCE 1919-1957.
STANFORD, STANFORD UNIVERSITY PRESS, 1960
055,056,114-07,
     CASE STUDY

BURKE FRED G
POLITICAL EVOLUTION IN KENYA CHAPTER 5.
IN STANLEY DIAMOND AND FRED G BURKE (EDS.), THE
TRANSFORMATION OF EAST AFRICA, NEW YORK, BASIC BOOKS, 1966
055,117-07,
     CASE STUDY

CLARCK MICHAEL K
ALGERIA IN TURMOIL--A HISTORY OF THE REBELLION.
NEW YORK, PRAEGER, 1959
055,101-06,
     CASE STUDY

COLEMAN JAMES S
NIGERIA BACKGROUND TO NATIONALISM.
BERKELEY, UNIVERSITY OF CALIFORNIA PRESS, 1958
055,128-06,
     CASE STUDY

CORFIELD F D
HISTORICAL SURVEY OF THE ORIGINS AND GROWTH OF MAU MAU.
NAIROBI, GOVERNMENT PRINTER, 1960
055,117-06,
     CASE STUDY

FALLERS LLOYD A
POPULISM AND NATIONALISM-- A COMMENT ON D A LOW'S 'THE ADVENT
OF POPULISM IN BUGANDA?.
COMPARATIVE STUDIES IN SOCIETY AND HISTORY 6 JULY 1964
055,139-06,
PP 445-448
     CASE STUDY

GORDON DAVID C
THE PASSING OF FRENCH ALGERIA.
NEW YORK, OXFORD UNIVERSITY PRESS, 1966

033,055,056,101-02,
    CASE STUDY

055

  HALSTEAD JOHN P
  REBIRTH OF A NATION-THE ORIGINS AND RISE OF MOROCCAN
  NATIONALISM,1912-1944
  CAMBRIDGE,MASS,HARVARD UNIVERSITY PRESS, 1967
  055,126-06,
    CASE STUDY

  HOLT PETER M
  SUDANESE NATIONALISM AND SELF DETERMINATION.
  IN WALTER LAQUEUR, THE MIDDLE EAST IN TRANSITION, NEW YORK,
  PRAEGER, 1958, PP 166-182
  055,134-06,
    CASE STUDY

  JONES-QUARTEY K A
  PRESS AND NATIONALISM IN GHANA.
  UNITED ASIA 9 FEBRUARY 1957 PP 55-60
  055,114-06,
    CASE STUDY

  KILSON MARTIN L
  LAND AND POLITICS IN KENYA-- AN ANALYSIS OF AFRICAN
  POLITICS IN A PLURAL SOCIETY.
  WESTERN POLITICAL QUARTERLY 10 SEPTEMBER 1957 PP 559-581
  055,117-06,
    CASE STUDY

  KILSON MARTIN L
  BEHIND THE MAU MAU REBELLION.
  DISSENT 3 SUMMER 1956 PP 264-275
  055,117-06,
    CASE STUDY

  KIMBLE DAVID A
  A POLITICAL HISTORY OF GHANA-- THE RISE OF GOLD COAST
  NATIONALISM 1850-1958.
  OXFORD, CLARENDON PRESS, 1963
  055,114-06,
    CASE STUDY

  KOINAGE MBIYU
  THE PEOPLE OF KENYA SPEAK FOR THEMSELVES.
  DETROIT, KENYA PUBLICATION FUND, 1955
  055,117-06,
    CASE STUDY

  LEAKEY L S B
  MAU MAU AND THE KIKUYU.
  LONDON, METHUEN, 1954
  055,117-06,
    CASE STUDY

  LEMARCHAND RENE
  THE BASES OF NATIONALISM AMONG THE BAKONGO.
  AFRICA 31 OCTOBER 1961 PP 344-354
  055,108-06,

CASE STUDY

055

LEMARCHAND RENE
POLITICAL AWAKENING IN THE BELGIAN CONGO.
BERKELEY, UNIVERSITY OF CALIFORNIA PRESS, 1964
055,108-07,
     CASE STUDY

LEVINE VICTOR T
THE CAMEROONS FROM MANDATE TO INDEPENDENCE.
BERKELEY, UNIVERSITY OF CALIFORNIA PRESS, 1964
055,104-06,
     CASE STUDY

LEWIS I M
INTEGRATION IN THE SOMALI REPUBLIC CHAPTER 7.
IN ARTHUR HAZLEWOOD, AFRICAN INTEGRATION AND DISINTEGRATION.
LONDON, OXFORD UNIVERSITY PRESS, 1967, PP 251-284
055,133-06,
     CASE STUDY

LEWIS I M
THE MODERN HISTORY OF SOMALILAND-- FROM NATION TO STATE.
LONDON, WEIDENFELD AND NICOLSON, 1965
055,133-06,
     CASE STUDY

LIEBENOW J GUS
COLONIAL RULE AND POLITICAL DEVELOPMENT IN TANZANIA-THE
CASE OF THE MAKONDE
EVANSTON, NORTHWESTERN UNIVERSITY PRESS, 1970
035,055,063,136-07,
     CASE STUDY

LOFCHIE MICHAEL
ZANZIBAR-- BACKGROUND TO REVOLUTION.
PRINCETON, NEW JERSEY, PRINCETON UNIVERSITY PRESS, 1965
055,136-06,
     CASE STUDY

LOW DAVID A
THE ADVENT OF POPULISM IN BUGANDA.
COMPARATIVE STUDIES IN SOCIETY AND HISTORY 6 JULY 1964
PP 424-444
055,139-06,
     CASE STUDY

LOW DAVID A
POLITICAL PARTIES IN UGANDA 1949-1962.
LONDON, 1962
055,139-07,
     CASE STUDY

PRATT R CRANFORD
NATIONALISM IN UGANDA.
POLITICAL STUDIES   JUNE 1961 PP 157-178
055,139-06,
     CASE STUDY

ROTBERG ROBERT I
THE RISE OF NATIONALISM IN CENTRAL AFRICA-- THE MAKING
OF MALAWI AND ZAMBIA, 1873-1964.
CAMBRIDGE, HARVARD UNIVERSITY PRESS, 1966
055,122-06,142-06,
        CASE STUDY

055

    TOUVAL SAADIA
    SOMALI NATIONALISM-- INTERNATIONAL POLITICS AND THE DRIVE
    FOR UNITY IN THE HORN OF AFRICA.
    CAMBRIDGE, MASS.,HARVARD UNIVERSITY PRESS,1963
    054,055,133-09,
        CASE STUDY

    AUSTEN RALPH A
    NOTES ON THE PRE-HISTORY OF TANU.
    MAKERERE JOURNAL 9 1963 PP 1-6
    055,
        LESS ACCESSIBLE

    BALANDIER GEORGES
    CONTRIBUTION A L'ETUDE DES NATIONALISMES EN AFRIQUE NOIRE
    (CONTRIBUTIONS TO THE STUDY OF NATIONALISM IN BLACK AFRICA).
    ZAIRE 8 1954 PP 379-389
    055,
        LESS ACCESSIBLE

    BENNETT GEORGE
    AN OUTLINE OF HISTORY OF TANU.
    MAKERERE JOURNAL 7 1962 PP 15-32
    055,136-07,
        LESS ACCESSIBLE

    DE ANDRADE MARIO
    LE NATIONALISME ANGOLAIS (ANGOLAN NATIONALISM).
    PRESENCE AFRICAINE 42 1962 PP 5-24
    055,
        LESS ACCESSIBLE

    JUMEAUX R
    ESSAI D ANALYSE DU NATIONALISME MALGACHE ESSAY ANALYZING
    MALAGASY NATIONALISM.
    L'AFRIQUE ET L'ASIE 40 1957 PP 31-42
    055,121-06,
        LESS ACCESSIBLE

    SHEPPERSON GEORGE
    EXTERNAL FACTORS IN THE DEVELOPMENT OF AFRICAN NATIONALISM
    WITH PARTICULAR REFERENCE TO BRITISH CENTRAL AFRICA.
    SALISBURY, S R, HISTORIANS IN TROPICAL AFRICA, UNIVERSITY
    OF RHODESIA AND NYASALAND, 1962, PP 144-159
    055,
        LESS ACCESSIBLE

    FICKETT LEWIS P   ED
    PROBLEMS OF THE DEVELOPING NATIONS.
    NEW YORK, CROWELL, 1966
    055,
        GENERAL THEORY

055

BASCOM WILLIAM R
TRIBALISM NATIONALISM AND PAN-AFRICANISM.
ANNALS OF THE AMERICAN ACADEMY OF POLITICAL AND SOCIAL
SCIENCE PHILADELPHIA JULY 1962 PP 21-29
055,
        REFERENCE

KARIUKI JOSIAH M
MAU MAU DETAINEE--THE ACCOUNT BY A KENYA AFRICAN OF HIS
EXPERIENCES IN DETENTION CAMPS 1953-1960.
LONDON, OXFORD UNIVERSITY PRESS, 1963
055,117-06,

MORGENTHAU RUTH SCHACHTER
POLITICAL PARTIES IN FRENCH-SPEAKING WEST AFRICA.
OXFORD, OXFORD UNIVERSITY PRESS, 1964
055,058,061,109-07,123-07,130-07,

NERES PHILIP
FRENCH-SPEAKING WEST AFRICA, FROM COLONIAL STATUS TO
INDEPENDENCE.
LONDON, OXFORD UNIVERSITY PRESS, 1962
055,056,
        REFERENCE

ROTBERG ROBERT I
THE RISE OF AFRICAN NATIONALISM-- THE CASE OF EAST AND
CENTRAL AFRICA.
WORLD POLITICS, OCTOBER 1962, P 75
055,
        REFERENCE

56. INDEPENDENCE

056

CARTER GWENDOLEN M
INDEPENDENCE FOR AFRICA.
NEW YORK, PRAEGER, 1960
056,
        A SERIES OF PERSONAL IMPRESSIONS BASED ON FIRST-HAND
        EXPERIENCES OF THE FORCES FOR AFRICAN INDEPENDENCE AT
        WORK IN 1960. INCLUDES CHAPTERS ON RACIAL POLICY IN
        TANGANYIKA, BELGIAN POLICY IN CONGO, KIKUYU RESETTLE-
        MENT IN KENYA, AND APARTHEID IN SOUTH AFRICA. AUTHOR
        IS DIRECTOR OF PROGRAM OF AFRICAN STUDIES AT NORTH-
        WESTERN UNIVERSITY.

LEGUM COLIN   ED
AFRICA-- HANDBOOK TO A CONTINENT.
NEW YORK, PRAEGER, 1966
056,076,
        CAPSULE SUMMARY OF EACH AFRICAN STATE INCLUDES VITAL
        STATISTICS ON POLITICS, ECONOMICS, DEMOGRAPHY, AND

COLONIAL HISTORY.   SECOND PART IS SUMMARY OF MAJOR
TOPICS-- INTERNATIONAL RELATIONS, ART, LITERATURE,
RELIGION, ECONOMICS, EDUCATION, LAW, TRADE UNIONS,
PRESS, UNITED NATION ACTIVITIES IN AFRICA.   EDITOR
IS BRITISH JOURNALIST WITH LONG AFRICAN EXPERIENCE.

056

WALLERSTEIN I M
THE POLITICS OF INDEPENDENCE.
NEW YORK, VINTAGE, 1961
056,076,
        INTERPRETS TOTALITY OF AFRICAN HISTORICAL DEVELOPMENT
        IN CLEAR AND INSIGHTFUL PERSPECTIVE. FOCUSES ON THE
        PERIOD OF NATIONALISM AND INDEPENDENCE. AUTHOR IS
        PROFESSOR OF SOCIOLOGY AT COLUMBIA UNIVERSITY.

CROWDER MICHAEL
INDEPENDENCE AS A GOAL IN FRENCH WEST AFRICAN POLITICS, 1944
-1960.
FRENCH-SPEAKING AFRICA (LEWIS), NEW YORK, WALKER AND CO.,
1965
056,
     REFERENCE

HATCH JOHN
AFRICA THE REBIRTH OF SELF-RULE.
LONDON, OXFORD UNIVERSITY PRESS, 1967
056,
     REFERENCE

LUSIGNAN GUY DE
FRENCH-SPEAKING AFRICA SINCE INDEPENDENCE.
NEW YORK, PRAEGER PUBLISHERS, 1969
056,061,104-11,105-11,106-11,107-11,109-11,112-11,
115-11,116-11,123-11,137-11,141-11,
     REFERENCE

OLIVER ROLAND   ATMORE ANTHONY
THE LAST YEARS OF COLONIAL RULE, 1940-1960.
IN AFRICA SINCE 1800, CAMBRIDGE, CAMBRIDGE UNIVERSITY PRESS,
1967, PP 213-222
056,
     REFERENCE

PERHAM MARGERY
THE COLONIAL RECKONING.
NEW YORK, KNOPF, 1962
056,
     REFERENCE

VAN LANGENHOVE F
FACTORS OF DECOLONIZATION.
IN WILLIAM J HANNA (ED), INDEPENDENT BLACK AFRICA, CHICAGO,
RAND MCNALLY, 1964, PP 150-175
056,
     REFERENCE

APTER DAVID E
GHANA IN TRANSITION.
NEW YORK, ATHENEUM, 1963

056,058,114-07,
        CASE STUDY

056
    ARDEN-CLARKE C
    GOLD COAST INTO GHANA, SOME PROBLEMS OF TRANSITION.
    INTERNATIONAL AFFAIRS 34 1958 PP 49-56
    056,114-06,
        CASE STUDY

    BOURRET F M
    GHANA-- THE ROAD TO INDEPENDENCE 1919-1957.
    STANFORD, STANFORD UNIVERSITY PRESS 1960
    055,056,114-07,
        CASE STUDY

    GORDON DAVID C
    THE PASSING OF FRENCH ALGERIA.
    NEW YORK, OXFORD UNIVERSITY PRESS, 1966
    033,055,056,101-02,
        CASE STUDY

    HAYFORD CASELY
    GOLD COAST NATIVE INSTITUTIONS.
    LONDON, LONGMANS, 1967
    056,114-01,
        CASE STUDY

    OWIREDU P A
    PROPOSALS FOR A NATIONAL LANGUAGE FOR GHANA.
    AFRICAN AFFAIRS 63 APRIL 1964 PP 142-145
    056,114-06,
        CASE STUDY

    PRESCOTT J R V
    NIGERIA'S REGIONAL BOUNDARY PROBLEMS.
    GEOGRAPHICAL REVIEW 49 OCTOBER 1959 PP 485-505
    056,
        CASE STUDY

    RICE BERKELEY
    ENTER GAMBIA-- THE BIRTH OF AN IMPROBABLE NATION.
    BOSTON, HOUGHTON MIFFLIN, 1967
    056,113-06,
        CASE STUDY

    TAMUNO TEKENA N
    NIGERIA AND ELECTIVE REPRESENTATION 1923-1947.
    LONDON, HEINEMANN, 1966
    056,063,128-07,
        CASE STUDY

    ALEXANDRE PIERRE
    PROBLEMES LINGUISTIQUES DES ETATS NEGRO-AFRICAINES A L'HEURE
    DE L'INDEPENDANCE(LINGUISTIC PROBLEMS OF NEGRO AFRICAN
    STATES AT THE TIME OF INDEPENDENCE).
    CAHIERS D'ETUDES AFRICAINES 2 1961 PP 177-195
    056,
        LESS ACCESSIBLE

NERES PHILIP
FRENCH-SPEAKING WEST AFRICA, FROM COLONIAL STATUS TO
INDEPENDENCE.
LONDON, OXFORD UNIVERSITY PRESS, 1962
055,056,
REFERENCE

57. INTERETHNIC INTEGRATION

057

CARTER GWENDOLEN M   ED
NATIONAL UNITY AND REGIONALISM IN EIGHT AFRICAN STATES--
NIGERIA, NIGER, CONGO, GABON, CENTRAL AFRICAN REPUBLIC,
CHAD, UGANDA, ETHIOPIA.
ITHACA, CORNELL UNIVERSITY PRESS, 1966
057,076,
CASE STUDIES OF THE CONFLICTS BETWEEN REGIONALISM AND
THE DESIRE FOR NATIONAL UNITY. AUTHORS FOLLOW COMMON
OUTLINE WHICH INCLUDES HISTORICAL BACKGROUND, LAND AND
PEOPLE, THE POLITICAL PROCESS, CONTEMPORARY PROBLEMS,
EXTERNAL AFFAIRS, AND BIBLIOGRAPHY. CONCLUSION SYN-
THESIZES MAJOR POINTS OF INDIVIDUAL STUDIES.

COHEN RONALD   MIDDLETON JOHN   EDS
FROM TRIBE TO NATION IN AFRICA.
SAN FRANCISCO, CHANDLER, 1970
004,006,057,
ORIGINAL CASE STUDIES BY WELL-KNOWN ANTHROPOLOGISTS ON
THE PROCESSES BY WHICH ETHNIC SOCIETIES INCORPORATE
NEIGHBORING GROUPS INTO A LARGER, AND SOMETIMES NEW,
ETHNIC FRAMEWORK. THEORETICAL INTRODUCTION SYNTHE-
SIZES THESE STUDIES INTO FUNDAMENTAL PROPOSITIONS
ABOUT THE NATURE OF ETHNICITY UNDER MODERN CIRCUM-
STANCES.

DEUTSCH KARL W   FOLTZ WILLIAM J   EDS
NATION-BUILDING.
ATHERTON PRESS, 1966
057,076,
A MAJOR RECENT ANTHOLOGY DEALING WITH NATION-BUILDING
THROUGH-OUT THE WORLD, INCLUDING EUROPE. ESSAY BY
RUPERT EMERSON ON NATION-BUILDING IN AFRICA GIVES
CLEAR OVERVIEW OF ETHNICITY, PLURALISM, AND TRIBALISM
IN MODERN CONTEXT. ALSO ASSESSES RELIGION AND OTHER
CULTURAL PATTERNS AS THEY AFFECT NATIONAL INTEGRATION
INTRODUCTORY ESSAY BY DEUTSCH IS EXCELLENT SUMMARY OF
CONCEPTS AND DEFINITIONS. SELECT BIBLIOGRAPHY OF
RECENT WORKS ON NATION-BUILDING.

EAST AFRICAN INSTITUTE OF SOCIAL AND CULTURAL AFFAIRS
RACIAL AND COMMUNAL TENSIONS IN EAST AFRICA.
KENYA, EAST AFRICAN PUBLISHING HOUSE, 1966
057,085,
CONFERENCE ESSAYS IN PAPERBACK, GIVE WIDE RANGE OF CO-
VERAGE ON RACIAL AND ETHNIC PROBLEMS IN EAST AFRICA--

PRIMARILY BY AFRICAN SCHOLARS. TOPICS INCLUDE--ROLE
OF ASIANS IN EAST AFRICA, RACIAL CONSCIOUSNESS AMONG
AFRICANS, TRIBALISM AS A FACTOR IN INTERNATIONAL TEN-
SIONS, ECONOMIC ASPECTS OF RACE RELATIONS, AND CULTURAL
TENSIONS IN A MIXED SOCIETY.

057

KUPER LEO   SMITH M G   EDS
PLURALISM IN AFRICA.
BERKELEY AND LOS ANGELES, UNIVERSITY OF CALIFORNIA PRESS,
1969
006,007,016,057,
        WORK OF MAJOR THEORETICAL SIGNIFICANCE, AS WELL AS IM-
        PORTANT CASE STUDIES BY VAN DEN BERGHE, ALEXANDRE, DA-
        VIDSON, LOFCHIE, MAZRUI, THOMPSON, GLUCKMAN AND HILDA
        KUPER. FOCUS IS ON PLURAL SOCIETY-I.E. RACIAL, TRIBAL,
        RELIGIOUS, OR REGIONAL GROUPS HELD TOGETHER BY FORCE
        RATHER THAN PLURALISTIC SOCIETY BASED ON CROSS-CUTTING
        CLEAVAGES.

SHIBUTANI TAMOTSU   KWAN KIAN
ETHNIC STRATIFICATION-- A COMPARATIVE APPROACH.
NEW YORK, MACMILLAN COMPANY, 1965
004,057,
        AUTHORS DEAL WITH MAJOR ISSUES OF ETHNIC IDENTITY AND
        CHANGING IDENTITY IN COMPARATIVE FRAMEWORK. SOME CASE
        STUDY MATERIAL ON AFRICA. CHAPTERS INCLUDE FOCUS ON
        ETHNIC DIFFERENCES, ETHNIC SYMBOLS, ASSIMILATION, AND
        ETHNIC INTEGRATION.

WALLERSTEIN I M
ETHNICITY AND NATIONAL INTEGRATION IN WEST AFRICA
CAHIERS D'ETUDES AFRICAINES 3 OCTOBER 1960 PP 129-139
004,007,057,
        BASIC INTRODUCTION TO CONCEPT OF ETHNICITY AND TO
        ENDURING ROLE OF ETHNICITY IN URBAN ENVIRONMENTS.
        ACCORDING TO AUTHOR,MEMBERSHIP IN AN ETHNIC GROUP IS A
        MATTER OF SOCIAL DEFINITION,THE INTERPLAY OF THE SELF
        DEFINITION OF MEMBERS AND THE DEFINITION OF OTHER
        GROUPS.

COLEMAN JAMES S
THE EMERGENCE OF AFRICAN POLITICAL PARTIES.
IN CHARLES G HAINES (ED), AFRICA TODAY, BALTIMORE, JOHNS
HOPKINS PRESS, 1955, PP 225-255
057,
        REFERENCE

COLEMAN JAMES S
THE PROBLEM OF POLITICAL INTEGRATION IN EMERGENT AFRICA.
WESTERN POLITICAL QUARTERLY 8 MARCH 1955 PP 44-58
057,
        REFERENCE

EMERSON RUPERT
PARTIES AND NATIONAL INTEGRATION IN AFRICA.
IN J LAPALOMBARA AND M WEINER (EDS), POLITICAL PARTIES IN
POLITICAL DEVELOPMENT, PRINCETON, NEWJERSEY, PRINCETON
UNIVERSITY PRESS,1966, PP 267-302
057,

REFERENCE

057

FOLTZ WILLIAM J
BUILDING THE NEWEST NATIONS.
IN LEWIS P FICKETT, (ED) PROBLEMS OF THE DEVELOPING NATIONS,
NEW YORK, CROWELL, 1966   PP 124-137
057,
        REFERENCE

GEERTZ CLIFFORD
THE INTEGRATION REVOLUTION--PRIMORDIAL SENTIMENTS AND CIVIL
POLITICS IN THE NEW STATES.
IN OLD SOCIETIES AND NEW STATES, NEW YORK, FREE PRESS OF
GLENCOE, 1963, PP 105-158
057,   FROM A SYMPOSIUM ON
        COLONIAL RULE SPONSORED BY HOOVER INSTITUTION AT
        STANFORD UNIVERSITY. ALL UNDER GENERAL EDITORSHIP OF
        DUIGNAN AND GANN.   THIS VOLUME AND NEXT COVER
        HISTORY AND POLITICS OF IMPERIALISM AND THE SCRAMBLE
        FOR AFRICA TO COLONIZATION.   VOL 3--IMPACT OF
        COLONIALISM ON AFRICAN SOCIETIES.   VOL 4--THE
        ECONOMICS OF COLONIALISM.
        REFERENCE

MITCHELL J CLYDE
TRIBALISM AND THE PLURAL SOCIETY.
LONDON, OXFORD UNIVERSITY PRESS, 1960
057,
        REFERENCE

RIVKIN ARNOLD   ED
NATIONS BY DESIGN-- INSTITUTION BUILDING IN AFRICA.
NEW YORK,   1969
057,
        REFERENCE

AKIWOWO AKINSOLA
THE SOCIOLOGY OF NIGERIAN TRIBALISM.
PHYLON 25 SUMMER 1964 PP 155-163
057,128-06,
        CASE STUDY

BINDER LEONARD
EGYPT--THE INTEGRATIVE REVOLUTION.
IN LUCIEN W PYE AND S VERBA (EDS), POLITICAL CULTURE AND
POLITICAL DEVELOPMENT, PRINCETON, PRINCETON UNIVERSITY PRESS,
1965, PP 396-449
057,140-06,
        CASE STUDY

CAPLAN GERALD L
BAROTSELAND--THE SECESSIONIST CHALLENGE TO ZAMBIA.
THE JOURNAL OF MODERN AFRICAN STUDIES, VOL. 6, NO. 3, 1968,
PP. 343-360
057,142-06,
        CASE STUDY

CHIDZERO BERNARD T
THE PLURAL SOCIETY OF TANGANYIKA CHP 7.

IN TANGANYIKA AND INTERNATIONAL TRUSTEESHIP, NEW YORK,
OXFORD. UNIVERSITY PRESS, 1961
057,136-06,
     CASE STUDY

057

GHAI YASH
PROSPECTS FOR ASIANS IN EAST AFRICA.
IN LAWRENCE SAGINI (ED), RACIAL AND COMMUNAL TENSIONS IN EAST
AFRICA. NAIROBI, EAST AFRICAN PUBLISHING HOUSE, 1966, PP 9-26
057,
     CASE STUDY

GREAT BRITAIN   COLONIAL OFFICE
REPORT OF THE COMMISSION TO ENQUIRE INTO THE FEARS OF
MINORITIES AND THE MEANS OF ALLAYING THEM.
HER MAJESTY'S STATIONERY OFFICE, COMMAND 505 JULY 1958
057,128-06,
     CASE STUDY

JOHNSON WILLARD R
CAMEROON FEDERATION--POLITICAL INTEGRATION IN A FRAGMENTARY
SOCIETY.
PRINCETON, NEW JERSEY, PRINCETON UNIVERSITY PRESS, 1970
057,059,104-06,
     CASE STUDY

KOPYTOFF IGOR
EXTENSION OF CONFLICT AS A METHOD OF CONFLICT RESOLUTION
AMONG THE SUKU OF THE CONGO.
JOURNAL OF CONFLICT RESOLUTION 5 MARCH 1961, PP 61-69
057,108-01,
     CASE STUDY

LEMARCHAND RENE
REVOLUTIONARY PHENOMENA IN STRATIFIED SOCIETIES--RWANDA AND
ZANZIBAR.
CIVILISATIONS, VOL XVIII, NO. 1, 1968, PP. 16-51
057,129-06,136-06,
     CASE STUDY

LIBOIS JULES G
KATANGA SECESSION.
MADISON, UNIVERSITY OF WISCONSIN PRESS, 1966
057,059,108-06,
     CASE STUDY

LLOYD PETER C
TRIBALSIM IN NIGERIA.
IN A A DUBB (ED), THE MULTI-TRIBAL SOCIETY, 16TH RHODES-
LIVINGSTON INSTITUTE CONFERENCE PROCEEDINGS, 1962, LUSAKA,
PP 133-147
057,128-06,
     CASE STUDY

MPHAHLELE EZEKIEL
CULTURAL TENSIONS IN A MIXED SOCIETY.
IN LAWRENCE SAGINI (ED), RACIAL AND COMMUNAL TENSIONS IN EAST
AFRICA, NAIROBI, EAST AFRICAN PUBLISHING HOUSE, 1966, PP 123-
127

057,
     CASE STUDY

057
   MUSTAFA SOPHIA
   RACIAL AND COMMUNAL TENSIONS IN EAST AFRICA.
   IN LAWRENCE SAGINI (ED), RACIAL AND COMMUNAL TENSIONS IN EAST
   AFRICA. NAIROBI, EAST AFRICAN PUBLISHING HOUSE, 1966, PP 52-57
   057,
        CASE STUDY

   NAFZIGER E WAYNE
   INTER-REGIONAL ECONOMIC RELATIONS IN THE NIGERIAN FOOTWEAR
   INDUSTRY.
   THE JOURNAL OF MODERN AFRICAN STUDIES, VOL 6, NO. 4, 1968,
   PP. 531-542
   057,128-06,
        CASE STUDY

   O'CONNELL JAMES
   POLITICAL INTEGRATION-- THE NIGERIAN CASE CHAPTER 5.
   IN ARTHUR HAZLEWOOD, AFRICAN INTEGRATION AND DISINTEGRATION,
   LONDON, OXFORD UNIVERSITY PRESS, 1967, P   129-184
   057,128-06,
        CASE STUDY

   OKELLO JOHN
   REVOLUTION IN ZANZIBAR.
   KENYA, EAST AFRICAN PUBLISHING HOUSE, 1967
   057,059,136-06,
        CASE STUDY

   OKUMU W A J
   RACIALISM AND TRIBALISM AS FACTORS IN NATIONAL AND INTER-
   NATIONAL TENSIONS.
   IN LAWRENCE SAGINI (ED), RACIAL AND COMMUNAL TENSIONS IN EAST
   AFRICA, NAIROBI, EAST AFRICAN PUBLISHING HOUSE, 1966, PP 113-
   122
   057,
        CASE STUDY

   PADEN JOHN N
   LANGUAGE PROBLEMS OF NATIONAL INTEGRATION IN NIGERIA-- THE
   SPECIAL POSITION OF HAUSA.
   IN JOSHUA A FISHMAN, CHARLES FERGUSON, AND JYOTIRINDRA DAS
   GUPTA (EDS), LANGUAGE PROBLEMS IN DEVELOPING NATIONS, NEW
   YORK, JOHN WILEY, 1968, P. 199-214
   057,128-06,
        CASE STUDY

   RICHARDS AUDREY I
   THE MULTICULTURAL STATES OF EAST AFRICA.
   MONTREAL, MCGILL-QUEENS, 1969
   057,
        CASE STUDY

   ROTHCHILD DONALD S
   SAFE GUARDING NIGERIAN MINORITIES.
   INSTITUTE OF AFRICAN AFFAIRS PUBLICATION, PHILADELPHIA,
   UNIVERSITY OF PENSYLVANIA, 1964

057,128-06,
        CASE STUDY

057

ROTHCHILD DONALD S
ETHNIC INEQUALITIES IN KENYA
JOURNAL OF MODERN AFRICAN STUDIES 7 1969 PP 689-711
057,117-03,
        CASE STUDY

SAGINI LAWRENCE
SOME THOUGHTS ON RACIAL AND COMMUNAL TENSIONS IN EAST
AFRICA.
IN LAWRENCE SAGINI (ED), RACIAL AND COMMUNAL TENSIONS IN EAST
AFRICA, NAIROBI, EAST AFRICAN PUBLISHING HOUSE, 1966
057,
        CASE STUDY

SKLAR RICHARD L
THE CONTRIBUTION OF TRIBALISM TO NATIONALISM IN WESTERN
NIGERIA.
IN IMMANUEL WALLERSTEIN, SOCIAL CHANGE, THE COLONIAL
SITUATION, NEW YORK, JOHN WILEY AND SONS, 1966, PP 290-300
057,128-06,
        CASE STUDY

VARMA S N
NATIONAL UNITY AND POLITICAL STABILITY IN NIGERIA.
INTERNATIONAL STUDIES 4 JANUARY 1963 PP 265-280
057,
        CASE STUDY

WEINSTEIN BRIAN
GABON--NATION-BUILDING ON THE OGOOUE.
CAMBRIDGE, MASSACHUSETTS INSTITUTE OF TECHNOLOGY PRESS, 1966
048,057,112-06,
        CASE STUDY

ZOLBERG ARISTIDE R
MASS PARTIES AND NATIONAL INTEGRATION--THE CASE OF IVORY
COAST.
JOURNAL OF POLITICS 25 FEBRUARY 1963 PP 36-48
057,116-06,
        CASE STUDY

DEPUIS J
UN PROBLEME DE MINORITE-- LES NOMADES DANS L'ETAT SOUDANAISE
(A MINORITY PROBLEM-- NOMADS IN THE STATE OF SUDAN).
L'AFRIQUE ET L'ASIE 50 1960 PP 19-44
057,123-06,
        LESS ACCESSIBLE

TOURE SEKOU
EXPERIENCE GUINEENNE ET UNITE AFRICAINE (GUINEAN EXPERIENCE
AND AFRICAN UNITY).
PARIS, PRESENCE AFRICAINE, 1959
057,115-09,
        LESS ACCESSIBLE

AKE CLAUDE

A THEORY OF POLITICAL INTEGRATION
HOMEWOOD, ILLINOIS, THE DORSEY PRESS, 1967
057,076,
        GENERAL THEORY

057
   FRANCIS E K
   THE ETHNIC FACTOR IN NATION-BUILDING.
   SOCIAL FORCES, VOL. 46, NO. 3, MARCH, 1968, PP. 338-346
   057,
        GENERAL THEORY

   FURNIVALL JOHN S
   COLONIAL POLICY AND PRACTICE.
   CAMBRIDGE, ENGLAND, CAMBRIDGE UNIVERSITY PRESS, 1948
   035,057,
        GENERAL THEORY

   GORDON MILTON M
   ASSIMILATION IN AMERICA-- THEORY AND REALITY.
   DAEDALUS 90 SPRING 1961 (BOBBS-MERRILL REPRINT S-407)
   057,
        GENERAL THEORY

   GORDON MILTON M
   ASSIMILATION IN AMERICAN LIFE-- THE ROLE OF RACE, RELIGION
   AND NATIONAL ORIGINS.
   NEW YORK, OXFORD UNIVERSITY PRESS, 1964
   057,
        GENERAL THEORY

   JACOB PHILIP E   TOSCANO JAMES V
   THE INTEGRATION OF POLITICAL COMMUNITIES.
   PHILADELPHIA, LIPPINCOTT, 1964
   048,057,
        GENERAL THEORY

   WEINER MYRON
   POLITICAL INTEGRATION AND POLITICAL DEVELOPMENT CHAPTER 15.
   IN JASON L FINKLE AND RICHARD W GABLE, POLITICAL
   DEVELOPMENT AND SOCIAL CHANGE, NEW YORK, JOHN WILEY, 1966
   057,
        GENERAL THEORY

   DE SMITH S A
   FEDERALISM, HUMAN RIGHTS AND THE PROTECTION OF MINORITIES
   CHAPTER 11.
   IN DAVID P CURRIE, FEDERALISM AND THE NEW NATIONS OF AFRICA,
   CHICAGO, UNIVERSITY OF CHICAGO PRESS, 1964, PP 279-314
        REFERENCE
   057,
        REFERENCE

   MAQUET JACQUES J
   THE PREMISE OF INEQUALITY IN RUANDA.
   LONDON, OXFORD UNIVERSITY PRESS, 1961
   057,129-01,

   NYE JOSEPH S
   POLITICAL INTEGRATION CHAPTER 4.

IN PAN-AFRICANISM AND EAST AFRICAN INTEGRATION, CAMBRIDGE,
MASS, HARVARD UNIVERSITY PRESS, 1965
057,059,
    REFERENCE

58. MASS-ELITE INTEGRATION

058

AKE CLAUDE
POLITICAL INTEGRATION AND THE MASS-ELITE GAP
IN CLAUDE AKE, A THEORY OF POLITICAL INTEGRATION
HOMEWOOD, ILLINOIS, THE DORSEY PRESS, 1967, PP 68-81
058,
    YOUNG NIGERIAN AUTHOR DISCUSSES THEORETICAL AND
    PHILOSOPHICAL BACKGROUND TO MASS-ELITE INTEGRATION
    DRAWS HEAVILY ON SHILS AND WALLERSTEIN. EXCELLENT
    REVIEW OF THE LITERATURE ON ELITEDEVELOPMENT IN NEW
    IN NEW NATIONS, PARTICULARLY AFRICA. ARGUES FOR
    LEGITIMACY AND CONSENSUS THEORY OF INTEGRATION

HODGKIN THOMAS
AFRICAN POLITICAL PARTIES.
BALTIMORE, PENGUIN, 1961
058,061,
    FIRST MAJOR ATTEMPT TO EXAMINE SYSTEMATICALLY ALL AF-
    RICAN POLITICAL PARTIES, AND TO CLASSIFY THEM ACCORD-
    ING TO SOCIAL BASE, PARTY ORGANIZATION, PARTY ACT-
    IVITIES, AND PARTY OBJECTIVES. DISTINCTION MADE BE-
    TWEEN MASS AND PATRON PARTIES. AUTHOR IS CURRENTLY
    PROFESSOR AT OXFORD UNIVERSITY. APPENDIX OF DATA ON
    POLITICAL PARTIES BY COUNTRY.

LEVINE VICTOR T
POLITICAL LEADERSHIP IN AFRICA.
PALO ALTO. THE HOOVER INSTITUTION ON WAR, REVOLUTION AND
PEACE, STANFORD UNIVERSITY, 1967
058,
    AUTHOR DEALS WITH POST-INDEPENDENCE CONFLICT BETWEEN
    YOUNGER AND OLDER ELITES IN UPPER VOLTA, SENEGAL, NI-
    GER, DAHOMEY, AND THE CENTRAL AFRICAN REPUBLIC. GOOD
    DISCUSSION OF CONCEPT OF AFRICAN ELITES, AND THE NO-
    TION OF POLITICAL PARTICIPATION. INCLUDES METHODOLO-
    GICAL APPENDIX.

LIEBENOW J GUS
LIBERIA--THE EVOLUTION OF PRIVILEGE.
ITHACA, CORNELL UNIVERSITY PRESS, 1969
029,058,119-07,
    FIRST OF SERIES OF COUNTRY CASE STUDIES ON AFRICA IN
    THE MODERN WORLD. AUTHOR REVIEWS THE HISTORY OF
    LIBERIA AND ITS MAJOR SOCIAL AND ECONOMIC PATTERNS,
    THE EVOLUTION OF CONTEMPORARY POLICIES PRIMARILY AMONG
    THE AMERICO-LIBERIANS AND ASSESSES THE INFLUENTIAL
    ROLE OF PRESIDENT TUBMAN BOTH IN LIBERIA AND THROUGH-
    OUT AFRICA.

058

MORRISON DONALD G   ET AL
BLACK AFRICA- A HANDBOOK FOR COMPARATIVE ANALYSIS
NEW YORK,FREE PRESS,1970
002,058,064,098,
> CO-EDITED BY R.C.MITCHELL,H.M.STEVENSON AND J.N.PADEN.
> COMPREHENSIVE DATA SOURCE BOOK FOR 32 SUB-SAHARAN
> STATES PART 1-DETAILED DATA FOR OVER 200 VARIABLES
> INCLUDING ANALYSIS OF BASIC PATTERNS PART 2- COUNTRY
> PROFILES OF BASIC INFORMATION ON URBAN,ECONOMIC AND
> POLITICAL PATTERNS PART 3-ESSAYS ON DATA RELIABILITY,
> BASES OF ETHNIC CLASSIFICATION,PATTERNS AND PROCESSES
> OF NATURAL INTEGRATION.

SKLAR RICHARD L
POLITICAL SCIENCE AND NATIONAL INTEGRATION- A RADICAL
APPROACH.
JOURNAL OF MODERN AFRICAN STUDIES 5 MAY 1967 PP 1-11
058,
> AUTHOR ARGUES THAT MAJOR PROBLEM IN AFRICAN NATIONAL
> INTEGRATION IS THE INCREASING GAP BETWEEN THE POLITI-
> CAL CLASS OF ENTREPRENEURS, POLITICIANS, AND WESTERN
> ELITES, WITH THE MASSES OF COMMON PEOPLE. RELATES THE
> NOTION OF POLITICAL INTEGRATION TO THAT OF CLASS FOR-
> MATION. ARGUES AGAINST STRUCTURAL-FUNCTIONAL APPROACH
> TO NATIONAL INTEGRATION THEORY.

TANZANIA AFRICAN NATIONAL UNION
THE ARUSHA DECLARATION AND TANU'S POLICY ON SOCIALISM AND
SELF-RELIANCE.
DAR ES-SALAAM,GOVERNMENT PRINTER,1967
058,060,070,073,136-04,
> MAJOR STATEMENT OF THE POLITICAL PHILOSOPHY OF PRESI-
> DENT JULIUS NYERERE WITH RESPECT TO THE PROBLEMS OF
> MODERNIZATION AND INTERNATIONAL FINANCING OF ECONOMIC
> DEVELOPMENT. ASSERTS THAT NEW AFRICAN STATES MUST
> GENERATE THEIR OWN FINANCING, CONTROL THEIR OWN ECONO-
> MIES, AND BUILD UPON THEIR STRENGTHS IN AGRICULTURE.

ZOLBERG ARISTIDE R
PATTERNS OF NATIONAL INTEGRATION.
THE JOURNAL OF MODERN AFRICAN STUDIES, 5, 4, 1967, PP 449-67
055,058,116-06,123-06,
> AN EXAMINATION OF MALI AND THE IVORY COAST WHICH INDI-
> CATES HOW SOCIAL AND ECONOMIC CHANGES DURING THE COLO-
> NIAL PERIOD, AS WELL AS THE IDEOLOGIES AND ORGANIZA-
> TIONAL ACTIVITIES OF THE NEW AFRICAN ELITES HAVE CON-
> TRIBUTED TO THE FORMATION OF DISTINCT PATTERNS OF IN-
> CIPIENT NATIONAL INTEGRATION.

DILLON WILTON S
UNIVERSITIES AND NATION-BUILDING IN AFRICA.
JOURNAL OF MODERN AFRICAN STUDIES 1 MARCH 1963 PP 75-89
042,058,
> REFERENCE

GRUNDY KENNETH W
THE CLASS STRUGGLE IN AFRICA-- AN EXAMINATION OF
CONFLICTING THEORIES.

JOURNAL OF MODERN AFRICAN STUDIES 2 NOVEMBER 1964 PP 379-394
058,
        REFERENCE

058
    HODGKIN THOMAS
    THE RELEVANCE OF 'WESTERN' IDEAS FOR NEW AFRICAN STATES--
    THE ELITE MASSES MYTH.
    IN JR PENNOCK, SELF GOVERNMENT IN MODERNIZING NATIONS,
    NEW YORK, PRENTICE-HALL, 1964
    058,
        REFERENCE

    KILSON MARTIN L
    THE MASSES, THE ELITE, AND POST-COLONIAL POLITICS IN
    AFRICA CHAPTER 14.
    IN JASON L FINKLE AND RICHARD W GABLE, POLITICAL
    DEVELOPMENT AND SOCIAL CHANGE, NEW YORK, JOHN WILEY, 1966
    058,
        REFERENCE

    APTER DAVID E
    GHANA IN TRANSITION.
    NEW YORK, ATHENEUM, 1963
    056,058,114-07,
        CASE STUDY

    APTER DAVID E
    GHANA.
    JAMES S. COLEMAN AND CARL G. ROSBERG JR. (EDS), POLITICAL
    PARTIES AND NATIONAL INTEGRATION IN TROPICAL AFRICA,
    BERKELEY, UNIVERSITY OF CALIFORNIA PRESS, 1966
    058,062,114-07,
        CASE STUDY

    MUFFETT DAVID J M
    THE FAILURE OF ELITE-MASS COMMUNICATION--SOME PROBLEMS
    CONFRONTING THE MILITARY REGIMES AND CIVIL SERVICES OF
    NIGERIA.
    THE SOUTH ATLANTIC QUARTERLY, VOL. LXVII, NO. 1, WINTER 1968
    , PP. 125-140
    058,128-06,
        CASE STUDY

    NYE JOSEPH S
    SOCIAL INTEGRATION CHP 3.
    IN PAN-AFRICANISM AND EAST AFRICAN INTEGRATION, CAMBRIDGE,
    MASS, HARVARD UNIVERSITY PRESS, 1965
    058,
        CASE STUDY

    ZOLBERG ARISTIDE R
    ONE PARTY GOVERNMENT IN THE IVORY COAST.
    PRINCETON, PRINCETON UNIVERSITY PRESS, 1964 (AND 1969)
    058,061,116-06,
        CASE STUDY

    SZENTES TAMAS
    ECONOMIC AND SOCIAL DISINTEGRATION AND SOME QUESTIONS OF
    SELF-HELP IN THE DEVELOPING COUNTRIES.

BUDAPEST, STUDIES ON DEVELOPING COUNTRIES SERIES, 1967, 23P.
058,
     GENERAL THEORY

058
   MORGENTHAU RUTH SCHACHTER
   POLITICAL PARTIES IN FRENCH-SPEAKING WEST AFRICA.
   OXFORD, OXFORD UNIVERSITY PRESS, 1964
   055,058,061,109-07,123-07,130-07,

59. TERRITORIAL INTEGRATION AND BOUNDARIES

059
   HAZLEWOOD ARTHUR   ED
   AFRICAN INTEGRATION AND DISINTEGRATION-- POLITICAL AND
   ECONOMIC CASE STUDIES.
   LONDON OXFORD UNIVERSITY PRESS 1967
   059,078,
        EXCELLENT COLLECTION OF ORIGINAL ARTICLES. ANALYSES
        OF ECONOMIC UNIONS, ACTUAL AND PROJECTED, IN EQUATOR-
        IAL AFRICA, EAST AFRICA, SENEGAL-GAMBIA, POLITICAL
        UNIONS EXTANT AND DEFUNCT NIGERIA, CENTRAL AFRICAN
        FEDERATION, SOMALI REPUBLIC. CAMEROONS, AND WIDER
        GROUPINGS FRENCH-SPEAKING AFRICA, PAN-AFRICANISM.
        INTRODUCTORY ESSAY BY EDITOR, ECONOMIST AND SENIOR RE-
        SEARCH STATISTICIAN AT OXFORD UNIVERSITY. MAPS,
        BIBLIOGRAPHY.

   WIDSTRAND CARL   ED
   AFRICAN BOUNDARY PROBLEMS
   UPPSALA,THE SCANDANAVIAN INSTITUTE OF AFRICAN STUDIES; AND NEW
   YORK, AFRICANA PUBLISHING CORPORATION, 1969
   059,078,080,
        A COMPREHENSIVE COLLECTION OF PAPERS ON BOUNDARIES AND
        THE LAW,THE ECONOMICS OF BOUNDARIES,THE OAU AND
        AFRICAN BOUNDARIES,FOREIGN AND MILITARY POLITICS,
        STATUS QUO VERSUS IRRIDENTISM,THE SOUTHERN BORDER,
        INTER-AFRICAN ECONOMIC COOPERATION,COLONIALISM AND
        TERRITORIAL CONFLICTS.EDITOR SURVEYS AFRICAN
        BOUNDARY PROBLEMS IN FINAL CHAPTER. APPENDIXES MAP AND
        LIST BOUNDARY DISPUTES AND CHART LENGTH AND STATUS OF
        ALL.

   ZARTMAN I WILLIAM
   INTERNATIONAL RELATIONS IN THE NEW AFRICA.
   NEW JERSEY, PRENTICE-HALL, 1966
   059,078,080,
        BEST INTRODUCTION TO AFRICAN INTERNATIONAL RELATIONS
        ON POLITICAL LEVEL. DISCUSSES AFRICAN STATE ALLIANCES
        IN THE PRE-INDEPENDENCE AND POST-COLONIAL PERIODS, AS
        WELL AS REGIONAL RELATIONS WITHIN THE ORGANIZATION OF
        AFRICAN UNITY (OAU). ANALYZES CRITERIA FOR AFRICAN
        STATE POLICY (NATIONAL SECURITY, SUBNATIONAL INTERESTS
        IDEOLOGY) AND THE PATTERNS OF INTRA-AFRICAN POLICY
        (ESPECIALLY BOUNDARY PROBLEMS).

059

   CASTAGNO A A JR
   THE SOMALI-KENYA CONTROVERSY
   JOURNAL OF MODERN AFRICAN STUDIES 2 1964 PP 165-188
   059, 117-09, 133-09,
        REFERENCE

   CHURCH R J HARRISON
   AFRICAN BOUNDARIES
   CHAPTER 21 IN W G EAST AND A E MOODIE(EDS), THE CHANGING
   WORLD,LONDON 1956
   059,
        REFERENCE

   KAPIL RAVI L
   ON THE CONFLICT POTENTIAL OF INHERITED BOUNDARIES IN AFRICA.
   WORLD POLITICS 18 JULY 1966 PP 656-673
   059,
        REFERENCE

   NYE JOSEPH S
   PATTERNS AND CATALYSTS IN REGIONAL INTEGRATION.
   IN INTERNATIONAL REGIONALISM,ED BY J S NYE,JR,BOSTON,
   LITTLE,BROWN,1968,PP 333-349
   059,
        REFERENCE

   PRESCOTT J R V
   AFRICA'S MAJOR BOUNDARY PROBLEMS.
   AUSTRALIAN GEOGRAPHER 9 MARCH 1963 PP 3-12
   059,
        REFERENCE

   REYNER ANTHONY S
   CURRENT BOUNDARY PROBLEMS IN AFRICA.
   INSTITUTE OF AFRICAN AFFAIRS NO 15,DUQUESNE UNIVERSITY PRESS,
   1964
   059,
        REFERENCE

   TOUVAL SAADIA
   TREATIES BORDERS AND THE PARTITION OF AFRICA.
   JOURNAL OF AFRICAN HISTORY 7 1966 PP 279-294
   033,059,
        REFERENCE

   WELCH CLAUDE E
   DREAM OF UNITY-PAN-AFRICANISM AND POLITICAL UNIFICATION IN
   WEST AFRICA
   ITHACA,CORNELL UNIVERSITY PRESS,1966
   054,059,079,
        REFERENCE

   ZARTMAN I WILLIAM
   THE POLITICS OF BOUNDARIES IN NORTH AND WEST AFRICA.
   JOURNAL OF MODERN AFRICAN STUDIES 8 AUGUST PP 155-173
   059,
        REFERENCE

AUSTIN DENNIS
THE UNCERTAIN FRONTIER-GHANA-TOGO
JOURNAL OF MODERN AFRICAN STUDIES 1 1963 PP 139-145
059,
     CASE STUDY

059

JOHNSON WILLARD R
CAMEROON FEDERATION--POLITICAL INTEGRATION IN A FRAGMENTARY
SOCIETY.
PRINCETON, NEW JERSEY, PRINCETON UNIVERSITY PRESS, 1970
057,059,104-06,
     CASE STUDY

LEGUM COLIN
KENYA S LITTLE GUERRILLA WAR HEATS UP.
AFRICA REPORT 12 APRIL 1967 P 39
059,117-06,
     CASE STUDY

LEMARCHAND RENE
THE LIMITS OF SELF-DETERMINATION-- THE CASE OF THE KATANGA
SECESSION.
AMERICAN POLITICAL SCIENCE REVIEW 56 JUNE 1962 PP 404-416
059,108-06,
     CASE STUDY

LEWIS I M
PAN AFRICANISM AND PAN SOMALISM
JOURNAL OF MODERN AFRICAN STUDIES 1 1963 PP 147-162
059,077,133-09,
     CASE STUDY

LIBOIS JULES G
KATANGA SECESSION.
MADISON, UNIVERSITY OF WISCONSIN PRESS, 1966
057,059,108-06,
     CASE STUDY

OKELLO JOHN
REVOLUTION IN ZANZIBAR.
KENYA, EAST AFRICAN PUBLISHING HOUSE, 1967
057,059,136-06,
     CASE STUDY

PANKHURST ESTELLE
ETHIOPIA AND ERITREA-- LAST PHASE OF THE REUNION STRUGGLE
1941-1952.
WOODFORD GREEN, LALIBELA HOUSE 1953
059,110-06,
     CASE STUDY

REYNER ANTHONY S
THE REPUBLIC OF THE CONGO-- DEVELOPMENT OF ITS INTERNATIONAL
BOUNDARIES.
PITTSBURGH, DUQUESNE UNIVERSITY PRESS, 1961, AFRICAN REPRINT
SERIES, 9
059,108-06,
     CASE STUDY

REYNER ANTHONY S
MOROCCO'S INTERNATIONAL BOUNDARIES--A FACTUAL BACKGROUND.
JOURNAL OF MODERN AFRICAN STUDIES 1 SEPTEMBER 1963
PP 313-326
059,
    CASE STUDY

059
  SOJA EDWARD
  COMMUNICATIONS AND TERRITORIAL INTEGRATION IN EAST AFRICA-
  AN INTRODUCTION TO TRANSACTION FLOW ANALYSIS
  EAST LAKES GEOGRAPHER 4 1968 PP 39-57
  048,059,077,
      CASE STUDY

  PRESCOTT J R V
  THE GEOGRAPHY OF FRONTIERS AND BOUNDARIES
  CHICAGO, ALDINE, 1965
  059,
      GENERAL THEORY

  NYE JOSEPH S
  POLITICAL INTEGRATION CHAPTER 4.
  IN PAN-AFRICANISM AND EAST AFRICAN INTEGRATION, CAMBRIDGE,
  MASS, HARVARD UNIVERSITY PRESS, 1965
  057,059,
      REFERENCE

60. THE ROLE OF IDEOLOGY
IN NATION-BUILDING

060
  ABRAHAM W E
  THE MIND OF AFRICA.
  CHICAGO, UNIVERSITY OF CHICAGO PRESS, 1962 (LONDON,
  WEIDENFELD AND NICOLSON)
  040,060,091,099,114-01,
      AUTHOR IS GHANAIAN SCHOLAR AND PHILOSOPHER, FORMER
      VICE-CHANCELLOR OF THE UNIVERSITY OF GHANA. BOOK AS-
      SESSES THE IDEA OF LATENT IDEOLOGY, OR CULTURAL BE-
      LIEFS. DRAWS ON PARADIGM OF ASHANTI SOCIETY TO GEN-
      ERALIZE ABOUT AFRICAN PERSONALITY-CULTURE PATTERNS.
      BRILLIANT THEORETICAL ANALYSIS, AND GOOD HISTORICAL
      SURVEY OF AFRICA BEFORE, DURING AND AFTER COLONIALISM.
      WEAKEST ON EXTRAPOLATION FROM ASHANTI CASE STUDY.

  APTER DAVID E   ED
  IDEOLOGY AND DISCONTENT.
  NEW YORK, FREE PRESS OF GLENCOE, 1964
  060,
      EDITORS INTRODUCTION IS EXCELLENT SOURCE OF DEFINI-
      NITIONS REGARDING IDEOLOGY. SUGGESTS IDEOLOGY RELATES
      DOCTRINE WITH ACTION, AND SERVES DUAL FUNCTION OF
      BINDING COMMUNITY TOGETHER AND ORGANIZING ROLE PERSON-
      ALITIES OF INDIVIDUALS (I.E. SOLIDARITY AND IDENTITY
      FUNCTIONS). ANALYSES NATIONALISM AND SOCIALISM AS

IDEOLOGIES IN DEVELOPING AREAS. NOT SPECIFICALLLY FO-
CUSED ON AFRICA, ALTHOUGH AUTHOR HAS DONE MAJOR RE-
SEARCH IN AFRICA.

060

BUSIA KOFI A
AFRICA IN SEARCH OF DEMOCRACY.
NEW YORK PRAEGER 1967
LONDON, ROUTLEDGE AND KEGAN PAUL, 1967
060,114-04,
     PROFESSOR OF SOCIOLOGY, CURRENTLY HEAD-OF-GOVERNMENT
     IN GHANA. BOOK WRITTEN WHILE IN EXILE. IS ARGUMENT
     FOR RECOGNITION OF PLURALISM IN AFRICAN SOCIETY.
     DISCUSSES AFRICAN RELIGIOUS HERITAGE, POLITICAL
     HERITAGE, COLONIALISM, COMMUNISM, SOCIALISM,
     DEMOCRACY, TRIBALISM, ONE-PARTY SYSTEMS, WORLD
     BROTHERHOOD. STRONG ARGUMENT FOR DEMOCRACY IN AFRICA.

DIA MAMADOU   TRANSLATED BY   COOK MERCER
THE AFRICAN NATIONS AND WORLD SOLIDARITY.
LONDON, THAMES AND HUDSON, 1962
054,060,130-04,
     SUGGESTS BASIC DEFINITIONS OF NATIONALISM AS A COLLEC-
     TIVE VOCATION. DISTINGUISHES VARIOUS TYPES OF NATION-
     ALISM. AUTHOR IS FORMER DEPUTY PREMIER OF SENEGAL.

EMERSON RUPERT   KILSON MARTIN L   EDS
THE POLITICAL AWAKENING OF AFRICA.
ENGLEWOOD CLIFFS, NJ, PRENTICE-HALL, 1965
060,
     EDITORS HAVE SELECTED KEY WRITINGS BY AFRICAN LEADERS
     AND ARRANGED THEM BY THEMES-- 1) REACTIONS TO COLON-
     IALISM--SELF-IDENTITY IN AFRICAN DEVELOPMENT-- 2)
     IDEAS AND CONTEXT OF AFRICAN NATIONALISM-- 3) POLICIES
     AND METHODS OF AFRICAN POLITICAL PARTIES-- 4) INTER-
     AFRICAN PROBLEMS AND PAN-AFRICANISM. VOLUME IS EXCEL-
     LENT INTRODUCTION TO MODERN AFRICAN POLITICAL IDEOLO-
     GY.

FRIEDLAND WILLIAM H ROSBERG CARL G   EDS
AFRICAN SOCIALISM.
LONDON, OXFORD UNIVERSITY PRESS, 1965
060,077,
     MAJOR SOURCE OF WRITINGS AND ESSAYS ON AFRICAN SOCIAL-
     ISM.

GUEYE LAMINE
ITINERAIRE AFRICAIN (AFRICAN ITINERARY).
PARIS, PRESENCE AFRICAINE, 1966
044,060,130-04,
     POLITICAL AUTOBIOGRAPHY BY ONE OF EARLIEST SENEGALESE
     POLITICIANS. GIVES INTERPRETATION OF POLITICAL EVENTS
     AND PERSONALITIES IN SENEGAL FROM 1913 TO 1965.

KENYATTA JOMO
FACING MT KENYA--THE RURAL LIFE OF THE KIKUYU.
NEW YORK, VINTAGE BOOKS, 1964
010,060,098,117-01,
     A MAJOR ANTHROPOLOGICAL CASE STUDY OF KIKUYU LIFE BY
     THE PRESIDENT OF THE REPUBLIC OF KENYA. STILL A STAN-

DARD REFERENCE WORK, IT DERIVES FROM RESEARCH IN THE
1930'S AT THE LONDON SCHOOL OF ECONOMICS UNDER THE
FAMOUS ANTHROPOLOGIST, BRONISLAW MALINOWSKI (WHO WROTE
THE INTRODUCTION). FASCINATING READING FOR ITS INSIGHTS
NOT ONLY INTO THE KIKUYU BUT ALSO INTO THE THOUGHTS
AND EXPERIENCES OF THE AUTHOR.

060

MAZRUI ALI A
TOWARDS A PAX AFRICANA-- A STUDY OF IDEOLOGY AND AMBITION.
LONDON, WEIDENFELD AND NICOLSON, 1967
CHICAGO, UNIVERSITY OF CHICAGO PRESS 1967
060,077,099,
> THREE MAJOR SECTIONS-- 1) IDEOLOGY AND IDENTITY (IDI-
> OM OF SELF-DETERMINATION, PRINCIPLE OF RACIAL SOVER-
> EIGNTY, CONCEPT WE ARE ALL AFRICANS , NEO-DEPENDENCY,
> PRINCIPLE OF CONTINENTAL JURISDICTION, AND PAN-AFRICAN
> IMPLICATIONS OF SOCIALISM AND ONE-PARTY STATE)-- 2)
> DILEMNAS OF STATEHOOD (PEACE VERSUS HUMAN RIGHTS, NON-
> ALIGNMENT, PAN-AFRICANISM AND COLD WAR, CONCEPT OF
> PAX AFRICANA)-- 3) APPENDICES (CHARTER OF ORGANIZA-
> TION OF AFRICAN UNITY).

MBOYA TOM
FREEDOM AND AFTER.
BOSTON, LITTLE, BROWN, AND COMPANY, 1963
044,060,117-04,
> POLITICAL AUTOBIOGRAPHY OF RECENTLY ASSASSINATED LEADER
> OF KENYA FEDERATION OF LABOR AND GOVERNMENT MINISTER.
> DISCUSSES HIS EARLY DAYS IN SCHOOL (INCLUDING CONSIDER-
> ING THE PRIESTHOOD), HIS TRAINING AS SANITARY INSPECTOR,
>   HIS ENTRY INTO TRADE UNIONISM, HIS ENTRY INTO NATION-
> ALIST POLITICS, AND THE STRUGGLE FOR INDEPENDENCE.
> FINAL CHAPTERS GIVE HIS VIEWS ON AFRICAN SOCIALISM, NEO-
> COLONIALISM, TRADE UNIONISM, PAN-AFRICANISM, AND AFRI-
> CAN RELATIONS WITH THE WORLD.

NKRUMAH KWAME
NEO-COLONIALISM, THE LAST STAGE OF IMPERIALISM.
NEW YORK, INTERNATIONAL PUBLISHERS, 1965
060,082,114-04,
> BOOK WRITTEN WHILE AUTHOR WAS PRESIDENT OF GHANA.
> DEVELOPS CONCEPT OF NEOCOLONIALISM AS CONTINUED
> CONTROL OVER AFRICAN STATES BY EUROPEAN POWERS,
> DESPITE FORMAL INDEPENDENCE. DETAILS THE PATTERN OF
> INTERNATIONAL CAPITALISM IN AFRICA, ESPECIALLY IN THE
> CONGO AND SOUTHERN AFRICA. THE BOOK IS AN IDEOLOGICAL
> DOCUMENT, ALTHOUGH THE ECONOMIC AND FINANCIAL DATA IS
> REASONABLY ACCURATE.

NKRUMAH KWAME
HANDBOOK OF REVOLUTIONARY WARFARE.
NEW YORK, INTERNATIONAL PUBLISHERS, INC., 1969
060,091,114-04,
> DEALS WITH PRINCIPLES OF GUERRILLA WARFARE--ORGANIZA-
> TION OF PEOPLE, TECHNICAL ASPECTS OF ARMS AND HEALTH.
> WRITTEN BY FORMER PRESIDENT OF GHANA WHO IS IN EXILE IN
> GUINEA. SPECIAL FOCUS ON LIBERATION IN SOUTHERN AFRICA.

TANZANIA AFRICAN NATIONAL UNION

THE ARUSHA DECLARATION AND TANU'S POLICY ON SOCIALISM AND
SELF-RELIANCE.
DAR ES-SALAAM GOVERNMENT PRINTER 1967
058,060,070,073,136-04,
     MAJOR STATEMENT OF THE POLITICAL PHILOSOPHY OF PRESI-
     DENT JULIUS NYERERE WITH RESPECT TO THE PROBLEMS OF
     MODERNIZATION AND INTERNATIONAL FINANCING OF ECONOMIC
     DEVELOPMENT. ASSERTS THAT NEW AFRICAN STATES MUST
     GENERATE THEIR OWN FINANCING, CONTROL THEIR OWN ECONO-
     MIES, AND BUILD UPON THEIR STRENGTHS IN AGRICULTURE.

060
  ZOLBERG ARISTIDE R
  CREATING POLITICAL ORDER-- THE PARTY STATES OF WEST AFRICA.
  NEW YORK RAND-MCNALLY 1966
  060,061,
     REASSESSES THE SIGNIFICANCE OF POLITICAL PARTIES
     IN THE POLITICAL DEVELOPMENT OF WEST AFRICA, AND SUG-
     GESTS THAT STRUCTURES OR SCOPE ARE LESS IMPORTANT THAN
     HOW THEY HANDLE BASIC TASK OF MAINTAINING SOME DEGREE
     OF POLITICAL ORDER. PARTIES OF THE CONSENSUAL VA-
     RIETY, THE AUTHOR SUGGESTS ARE MORE LIKELY TO HAVE
     LEGITIMACY, AND HENCE ACHIEVE STABILITY.

  ADELAJA KOLA
  SOURCES IN AFRICAN POLITICAL THOUGHT.
  PRESENCE AFRICAINE, NO. 70, 2ND QUARTER, 1969, PP. 7-26
  060,
     REFERENCE

  BERRIAN ALBERT H   LONG RICHARD A   EDS
  NEGRITUDE--ESSAYS AND STUDIES.
  HAMPTON, VIRGINIA, HAMPTON INSTITUTE PRESS, 1967
  060,
     REFERENCE

  DUFFY JAMES   MANNERS ROBERT   EDS
  AFRICA SPEAKS.
  PRINCETON, VAN NOSTRAND, 1961
  060,
     REFERENCE

  FANON FRANTZ
  THE WRETCHED OF THE EARTH
  NEW YORK, GROVE PRESS, 1963
  060,091,101-03,
     REFERENCE

  FOLTZ WILLIAM J
  THE RADICAL LEFT IN FRENCH SPEAKING WEST AFRICA.
  IN WILLIAM H LEWIS, EMERGING AFRICA, WASHINGTON, PUBLIC
  AFFAIRS PRESS, 1963, PP 29-42
  060,
     REFERENCE

  GRUNDY KENNETH W
  POLITICAL POWER AND ECONOMIC THEORY IN RADICAL WEST
  AFRICA.
  ORBIS 8 SUMMER 1964 PP 405-424
  060,

REFERENCE

060

LEGUM COLIN
MODERN POLITICAL IDEAS.
IN PETER J MCEWAN AND ROBERT B SUTCLIFFE (EDS), MODERN AFRICA,
NEW YORK, THOMAS CROWELL, 1965 PP 239-263
060,
    REFERENCE

MAZRUI ALI A
BORROWED THEORY AND ORIGINAL PRACTICE IN AFRICAN POLITICS.
IN HERBERT SPIRO ED, PATTERNS OF AFRICAN DEVELOPMENT,
ENGLEWOOD CLIFFS, NEW JERSEY, PRENTICE HALL, 1967
060,
    REFERENCE

NYERERE JULIUS K
UJAMAA--ESSAYS ON SOCIALISM
NEW YORK, OXFORD UNIVERSITY PRESS, 1969
060,077,
    REFERENCE

ROACH PENELOPE
POLITICAL SOCIALIZATION IN THE NEW NATIONS OF AFRICA.
NEW YORK, TEACHERS COLLEGE PRESS, COLUMBIA UNIVERSITY PRESS
1967
060,
    REFERENCE

AHIDJO AHMADOU
CONTRIBUTION TO NATIONAL CONSTRUCTION.
PARIS, PRESENCE AFRICAINE, 1964
054,060,104-04,
    CASE STUDY

AZIKIWE NNAMDI
NIGERIAN POLITICAL INSTITUTIONS.
JOURNAL OF NEGRO HISTORY 14 1929 PP 328-340
060,128-04,
    CASE STUDY

AZIKIWE NNAMDI
ZIK-- A SELECTION FROM THE SPEECHES OF DOCTOR NNAMDI AZIKIWE
CAMBRIDGE ENGLAND CAMBRIDGE UNIVERSITY PRESS 1961
044,060,091,096,128-04,
    CASE STUDY

BALEWA ABUBAKAR T
NIGERIA LOOKS AHEAD.
IN PHILIP W QUIGG (ED.), AFRICA, NEW YORK, PRAEGER, 1964
PP 302-313
060,128-04,
    CASE STUDY

BIVAR A D H   HISKETT MERVIN
THE ARABIC LITERATURE OF NIGERIA TO 1804-- A PROVISIONAL
ACCOUNT.
BULLETIN OF THE SCHOOL OF ORIENTAL AND AFRICAN STUDIES 25
1962 PP 104-148

021,060,128-02,
   CASE STUDY

060

BRETTON HENRY L
CURRENT POLITICAL THOUGHT AND PRACTICE IN GHANA.
AMERICAN POLITICAL SCIENCE REVIEW 52 MARCH 1958 PP 46-63
060,114-04,
   CASE STUDY

BUSIA KOFI A
THE CHALLENGE OF AFRICA.
NEW YORK, PRAEGER, 1962
060, 114-04,
   CASE STUDY

CHISIZA D K
THE OUTLOOK FOR CONTEMPORARY AFRICA CHAPTER 3.
IN AFRICA,S FREEDOM, NEW YORK, BARNES AND NOBLE, 1964,
PP 38-54
060,122-04,
   CASE STUDY

CHISIZA D K
AFRICA-- WHAT LIES AHEAD.
NEW YORK AFRICAN AMERICAN INSTITUTE 1962
LONDON,COMMAND 1030 HER MAJESTY'S STATIONERY OFFICE,1960
060,122-04,
   CASE STUDY

FALLERS LLOYD A
IDEOLOGY AND CULTURE IN UGANDA NATIONALISM.
AMERICAN ANTHROPOLOGIST 63 1961 PP 677-686
060,139-06,
   CASE STUDY

FORTMAN BASTIAAN DE ED
AFTER MULUNGUSHI--THE ECONOMICS OF ZAMBIAN HUMANISM.
KENYA, EAST AFRICAN PUBLISHING HOUSE, 1969
060,142-08,
   CASE STUDY

KAUNDA KENNETH
ZAMBIA SHALL BE FREE.
NEW YORK,PRAEGER,1963 (LONDON, HEINEMANN EDUCATIONAL BOOKS)
060,142-04,
   CASE STUDY

KAUNDA KENNETH
ZAMBIA--INDEPENDENCE AND BEYOND.
LONDON, NELSON, 1966
054,060,142-04,
   CASE STUDY

KENYATTA JOMO
HARAMBEE--THE PRIME MINISTER OF KENYA'S SPEECHES 1963-1964.
LONDON,OXFORD UNIVERSITY PRESS,1964
060,117-04,
   CASE STUDY

LUMUMBA PATRICE
CONGO, MY COUNTRY.
NEW YORK, PRAEGER PUBLISHERS, 1962
060,108-04,
    CASE STUDY

060

MADIERA KIETA
THE SINGLE PARTY IN AFRICA.
PRESENCE AFRICAINE 30 FEBRUARY 1960 PP 3-24
060,061,065,123-04,
    CASE STUDY

MBOYA TOM
THE PARTY SYSTEM AND DEMOCRACY IN AFRICA.
IN PHILIP W QUIGG (ED.), AFRICA, NEW YORK, PRAEGER, 1964
PP 327-338
060,117-04,
    CASE STUDY

MBOYA TOM
AFRICAN SOCIALISM CHAPTER 6.
IN AFRICA'S FREEDOM, NEW YORK, BARNES AND NOBLE, 1964,
PP 78-87
060,117-04,
    CASE STUDY

MBOYA TOM
TENSIONS IN AFRICAN DEVELOPMENT CHAPTER 4.
IN AFRICA'S FREEDOM, NEW YORK, BARNES AND NOBLE, 1964,
PP 55-66
060,117-04,
    CASE STUDY

MBOYA TOM
VISION IN AFRICA.
IN WILLIAM J HANNA (ED), INDEPENDENT BLACK AFRICA, CHICAGO,
RAND MCNALLY, 1964, PP 515-520
060,117-04,
    CASE STUDY

NKRUMAH KWAME
CONSCIENCISM-- PHILOSOPHY AND IDEOLOGY FOR DECOLONIZATION
AND DEVELOPMENT WITH PARTICULAR REFERENCE TO THE AFRICAN
REVOLUTION.
LONDON, HEINEMANN, 1964
013,060,114-04,
    CASE STUDY

NKRUMAH KWAME
MOVEMENT FOR COLONIAL FREEDOM.
PHYLON 16 1955 PP 397-409
060,114-04,
    CASE STUDY

NKRUMAH KWAME
CHALLENGE OF THE CONGO-- A CASE STUDY OF FOREIGN PRESSURES
IN AN INDEPENDENT STATE.
NEW YORK, INTERNATIONAL PUBLISHERS, 1967
060,114-04,

CASE STUDY

060

NKRUMAH KWAME
I SPEAK OF FREEDOM.
NEW YORK, PRAEGER, 1961 (LONDON, HEINEMANN EDUCATIONAL BOOKS)
060,114-04,
CASE STUDY

NKRUMAH KWAME
AFRICAN PROSPECT.
IN PHILIP W QUIGG (ED.), AFRICA, NEW YORK, PRAEGER, 1964,
PP 272-282
060,114-04,
CASE STUDY

NYERERE JULIUS K
UJAMAA-- THE BASIS OF AFRICAN SOCIALISM CHAPTER 5.
IN AFRICA'S FREEDOM, NEW YORK, BARNES AND NOBLE, 1964,
PP 67-77
060, 136-04,
CASE STUDY

NYERERE JULIUS K
THE AFRICAN AND DEMOCRACY.
IN WILLIAM J HANNA (ED), INDEPENDENT BLACK AFRICA, CHICAGO,
RAND MCNALLY, 1964, PP 521-527
060, 136-04,
CASE STUDY

NYERERE JULIUS K
TANGANYIKA TODAY-- THE NATIONALIST VIEW.
INTERNATIONAL AFFAIRS 36 1960 PP43-47
060,136-04,
CASE STUDY

NYERERE JULIUS K
ESSAYS ON SOCIALISM.
LONDON AND NEW YORK, INTERNATIONAL BOOKSELLERS, INC., 1969
060,077,136-04,
CASE STUDY

OMER-COOPER J D   ET-AL
NIGERIAN MARXISM AND SOCIAL PROGRESS.
NIGERIAN JOURNAL OF ECONOMIC AND SOCIAL STUDIES 6 JULY
1964 PP 133-198 SYMPOSIUM ON NIGERIA
060,128-04,
CASE STUDY

PADMORE GEORGE
AFRICA-- BRITAIN'S THIRD EMPIRE.
LONDON, D DOBSON, 1949
060,
CASE STUDY

PADMORE GEORGE
THE GOLD COAST REVOLUTION-- THE STRUGGLE OF AN AFRICAN
PEOPLE FROM SLAVERY TO FREEDOM.
LONDON, D DOBSON, 1953
060,114-04,

CASE STUDY

060

SENGHOR LEOPOLD S
ON AFRICAN SOCIALISM.
NEW YORK, PRAEGER, 1964
013,054,060,130-04,
        CASE STUDY

SENGHOR LEOPOLD S
WEST AFRICA IN EVOLUTION.
FOREIGN AFFAIRS 39 1960-61 PP 240-246; ALSO PHILIP W QUIGG,
ED, AFRICA NEW YORK, PRAEGER, 1964, PP 283-291
060,130-04,
        CASE STUDY

SKURNIK W A E
AFRICAN POLITICAL THOUGHT--LUMUMBA, NKRUMAH, AND TOURE.
DENVER, COLORADO, INTERNATIONAL UNIVERSITY BOOKSELLERS, INC.
   1968
060,108-04,114-04,115-04,
        CASE STUDY

SNYDER FRANCIS G
POLITICAL IDEOLOGY AND PERCEPTIONS.
IN ONE-PARTY GOVERNMENT IN MALI--TRANSITION TOWARD CONTROL,
NEW HAVEN, YALE UNIVERSITY PRESS, 1965
060,
        CASE STUDY

SPARK
SOME ESSENTIAL FEATURES OF NKRUMAISM.
NEW YORK, INTERNATIONAL PUBLISHERS, 1965
THE SPARK-JOURNAL OF THE CONVENTION PEOPLE S PARTY, GHANA
BY THE EDITORS
060,114-04,
        CASE STUDY

SPARK
SOME ESSENTIAL FEATURES OF NKRUMAISM.
NEW YORK, INTERNATIONAL PUBLISHERS, 1965
060,
        CASE STUDY

THOMPSON W SCOTT
GHANA'S FOREIGN POLICY,1957-1966- DIPLOMACY,IDEOLOGY AND THE
NEW STATE
PRINCETON, PRINCETON UNIVERSITY PRESS, 1969
060,082,083,084,085,114-09,
        CASE STUDY

TIMOTHY BANKHOLE
KWAME NKRUMAH-- HIS RISE TO POWER.
LONDON, ALLEN AND UNWIN, 1963
060,114-03,
        CASE STUDY

TOURE SEKOU
AFRICA'S FUTURE AND THE WORLD.
IN PHILIP W QUIGG (ED.), AFRICA, NEW YORK, PRAEGER, 1964

PP 314-326
060,115-04,
     CASE STUDY

060
  TOWNSEND E REGINALD ED
  THE OFFICIAL PAPERS OF WILLIAM V S TUBMAN, PRESIDENT OF THE
  REPUBLIC OF LIBERIA.
  NEW YORK, HUMANITIES PRESS INC., 1968
  060,119-04,
       CASE STUDY

  WALLERSTEIN I M
  THE POLITICAL IDEOLOGY OF THE PDG.
  PRESENCE AFRICAINE 12 JANUARY 1962 PP 30-41
  060,115-04,
       CASE STUDY

  CESAIRE AIME
  LA PENSEE POLITIQUE DE SEKOU TOURE (THE POLITICAL THOUGHT
  OF SEKOU TOURE).
  PRESENCE AFRICAINE 29 JANUARY 1960
  060,115-04,
       LESS ACCESSIBLE

  DZIRASA STEPHEN
  THE POLITICAL THOUGHT OF DR KWAME NKRUMAH.
  ACCRA, GUINEA PRESS
  060,114-04,
       LESS ACCESSIBLE

  FISCHER GEORGES
  QUELQUES ASPECTS DE LA DOCTRINE POLITIQUE GUINEENE (SOME
  ASPECTS OF GUINEA POLITICAL DOCTRINE).
  CIVILIZATIONS 9 1959 PP 457-478
  060,115-04,
       LESS ACCESSIBLE

  SENGHOR LEOPOLD S
  PIERRE TEILHARD DE CHARDIN ET LA POLITIQUE AFRICAINE (PIERRE
  TEILHARD DE CHARDIN AND AFRICAN POLITICS).
  PARIS, EDITIONS DU SEUEL, 1962
  060,
     LESS ACCESSIBLE

  VAN LIERDE JEAN
  LA PENSEE POLITIQUE DE PATRICE LUMUMBA.   (THE POLITICAL
  THOUGHT OF PATRICE LUMUMBA).
  PARIS, PRESENCE AFRICAINE, 1963
  060,108-04,
       LESS ACCESSIBLE

  BELL DANIEL
  THE END OF IDEOLOGY IN THE WEST--AN EPILOGUE.
  IN THE END OF IDEOLOGY, GLENCOE ILLINOIS, FREE
  PRESS, 1962, PP 393-404
  060,
       GENERAL THEORY

  BERGER MORROE

IDEOLOGIES NATIONAL AND INTERNATIONAL CHAPTER 9.
IN THE ARAB WORLD TODAY, GARDEN CITY, NEW YORK, DOUBLEDAY,
1964, PP 322-384
060,
      GENERAL THEORY

060
    BINDER LEONARD
    THE IDEOLOGICAL REVOLUTION IN THE MIDDLE EAST.
    NEW YORK, WILEY, 1964
    060,
        GENERAL THEORY

    BIRNBAUM NORMAN
    THE SOCIOLOGICAL STUDY OF IDEOLOGY-- 1940-1960.
    CURRENT SOCIOLOGY 9 1960 PP 91-126
    060,
        GENERAL THEORY

    LIPSET SEYMOUR M
    THE END OF IDEOLOGY CHAPTER 12.
    IN POLITICAL MAN, NEW YORK, DOUBLEDAY, 1960, PP 403-417
    060,
        GENERAL THEORY

    MANNHEIM KARL
    IDEOLOGY AND UTOPIA CHAPTER 2.
    IN IDEOLOGY AND UTOPIA, NEW YORK, HARCOURT, BRACE AND
    WORLD, 1936, PP 49-96
    060,
        GENERAL THEORY

    SIGMUND PAUL
    THE IDEOLOGIES OF THE DEVELOPING NATIONS.
    NEW YORK, PRAEGER, 1963
    060,
        GENERAL THEORY

    ABRAHAM W E
    IDEOLOGY AND SOCIETY CHAPTER 1.
    IN THE MIND OF AFRICA, LONDON, WEIDENFELD AND NICOLSON,
    1962, PP 11-43
    060,
        REFERENCE

    NYERERE JULIUS K
    FREEDOM AND UNITY--UHURU NA UMOJA.
    LONDON, OXFORD UNIVERSITY PRESS, 1967
    060,077,136-04,

61. TYPES OF CIVILIAN REGIMES

061
    APTER DAVID E
    THE POLITICS OF MODERNIZATION.

CHICAGO, UNIVERSITY OF CHICAGO PRESS, 1965
037,061,
> INFLUENTIAL THEORETICAL WORK BY SCHOLAR WITH EXTEN-
> SIVE AFRICAN EXPERIENCE. ANALYZES POLITICAL ASPECTS
> OF CHANGE. ESPECIALLY PATTERNS OF CONSOLIDATION OF
> AUTHORITY, THE ROLE OF POLITICAL LEADERSHIP, AND
> RELEVANCE OF WESTERN LIBERAL-DEMOCRATIC MODELS TO
> DEVELOPING COUNTRIES. MANY REFERENCES TO AFRICA.

061
COLEMAN JAMES S
THE POLITICS OF SUB-SAHARAN AFRICA CHP 3.
IN ALMOND AND COLEMAN (EDS) THE POLITICS OF DEVELOPING
AREAS, PRINCETON, PRINCETON UNIVERSITY PRESS, 1960
061,
> PART OF FIRST MAJOR ANTHOLOGY ON POLITICS IN DEVELOP-
> ING AREAS. AUTHOR DEALS WITH BACKGROUND SETTING
> (TRADITIONS, WESTERN IMPACT), PROCESSES OF CHANGE
> (COMMERCIALIZATION, WESTERN EDUCATION, WESTERN EDUCA-
> TION, RESTRATIFICATION, SECULARIZATION), POLITICAL
> GROUPS (POLITICAL PARTIES, INTEREST GROUPS), POLITICAL
> FUNCTION (INTEREST ARTICULATION, AGGREGATION, SOCIAL-
> IZATION, COMMUNICATIONS), GOVERNMENTAL STRUCTURES AND
> FUNCTIONS, AND POLITICAL INTEGRATION.

COLEMAN JAMES S   ROSBERG CARL G   EDS
POLITICAL PARTIES AND NATIONAL INTEGRATION IN TROPICAL
AFRICA.
BERKELEY, CALIFORNIA UNIVERSITY OF CALIFORNIA PRESS, 1964
002,061,
> ADAPTS CONCEPTS OF SOCIAL SCIENCE (ESPECIALLY STRUC-
> TURAL/FUNCTIONALISM) TO AFRICAN CONTEXT. EDITORS MAKE
> DISTINCTIONS BETWEEN SINGLE PARTY SYSTEMS IN AFRICA--
> 1) PRAGMATIC-PLURALISTIC-- 2) REVOLUTIONARY-CENTRALI-
> ZING. SUBSEQUENT MILITARY REGIMES NOW DATE SOME OF
> THE TWELVE COUNTRY CASE STUDIES. EXCELLENT CHAPTERS
> ON VOLUNTARY ASSOCIATIONS, TRADE UNIONS, TRADITIONAL
> RULERS, AND STUDENTS.

HODGKIN THOMAS
AFRICAN POLITICAL PARTIES.
BALTIMORE, PENGUIN, 1961
058,061,
> FIRST MAJOR ATTEMPT TO EXAMINE SYSTEMATICALLY ALL AF-
> RICAN POLITICAL PARTIES, AND TO CLASSIFY THEM ACCORD-
> ING TO SOCIAL BASE, PARTY ORGANIZATION, PARTY ACT-
> IVITIES, AND PARTY OBJECTIVES. DISTINCTION MADE BE-
> TWEEN MASS AND PATRON PARTIES. AUTHOR IS CURRENTLY
> PROFESSOR AT OXFORD UNIVERSITY. APPENDIX OF DATA ON
> POLITICAL PARTIES BY COUNTRY.

ZOLBERG ARISTIDE R
CREATING POLITICAL ORDER-- THE PARTY STATES OF WEST AFRICA.
NEW YORK, RAND-MCNALLY, 1966
060,061,
> REASSESSES THE SIGNIFICANCE OF POLITICAL PARTIES
> IN THE POLITICAL DEVELOPMENT OF WEST AFRICA, AND SUG-
> GESTS THAT STRUCTURES OR SCOPE ARE LESS IMPORTANT THAN
> HOW THEY HANDLE BASIC TASK OF MAINTAINING SOME DEGREE
> OF POLITICAL ORDER. PARTIES OF THE CONSENSUAL VA-

RIETY, THE AUTHOR SUGGESTS ARE MORE LIKELY TO HAVE
LEGITIMACY, AND HENCE ACHIEVE STABILITY.

061

ADAM THOMAS R
GOVERNMENT AND POLITICS IN AFRICA SOUTH OF THE SAHARA.
NEW YORK, RANDOM HOUSE, 1965
061,
        REFERENCE

BURKE FRED G
AFRICA S QUEST FOR ORDER.
ENGLEWOOD CLIFFS, PRENTICE-HALL, 1964
061,
        REFERENCE

CARTER GWENDOLEN M
AFRICAN ONE-PARTY STATES.
IN PETER J MCEWAN AND ROBERT B SUTCLIFFE (EDS), MODERN AFRICA,
NEW YORK, THOMAS CROWELL, 1965, PP 201-209
061,
        REFERENCE

COLEMAN JAMES S
THE CHARACTER AND VIABILITY OF AFRICAN POLITICAL SYSTEMS
CHAPTER 2.
IN THE UNITED STATES AND AFRICA, BACKGROUND PAPERS OF THE
13TH ASSEMBLY, THE AMERICAN ASSEMBLY, COLUMBIA UNIVERSITY,
1958, PP 27-62
061,
        REFERENCE

CURRIE DAVID P
FEDERALISM AND THE NEW NATIONS OF AFRICA.
CHICAGO, UNIVERSITY OF CHICAGO PRESS, 1964
061,078,
        REFERENCE

EMERSON RUPERT
POLITICAL MODERNIZATION-- THE SINGLE-PARTY SYSTEM.
MONOGRAPH NO 1, DENVER, DENVER UNIVERSITY PRESS, 1964
061,
        REFERENCE

GRAY ROBERT F
POLITICAL PARTIES IN NEW AFRICAN NATIONS-- AN
ANTHROPOLOGICAL VIEW.
COMPARATIVE STUDIES IN SOCIETY AND HISTORY 4 JULY 1963
PP 449-465
061,
        REFERENCE

GRAY ROBERT F
POLITICAL PARTIES IN NEW AFRICAN STATES-- A REPLY TO
LUCY MAIR.
COMPARATIVE STUDIES IN SOCIETY AND HISTORY 6 JANUARY 1964
PP 230-232
061,
        REFERENCE

HODGKIN THOMAS
THE NEW WEST AFRICA STATE SYSTEM.
UNIVERSITY OF TORONTO QUARTERLY 31 OCTOBER 1961 PP 74-82
061,
        REFERENCE

061

HODGKIN THOMAS
A NOTE ON WEST AFRICAN POLITICAL PARTIES.
IN WHAT ARE THE PROBLEMS OF PARLIAMENTARY GOVERNMENT IN
WEST AFRICA, THE HANSARD SOCIETY, LONDON, CHISWICK PRESS,
1958, PP 51-62
061,
        REFERENCE

HODGKIN THOMAS
WELFARE ACTIVITIES OF AFRICAN POLITICAL PARTIES.
IN PETER J MCEWAN AND ROBERT B SUTCLIFFE (EDS), MODERN AFRICA
NEW YORK, THOMAS CROWELL, 1965, PP 194-200
061,
        REFERENCE

KILSON MARTIN L
AUTHORITARIANISM AND SINGLE PARTY TENDENCIES IN TROPICAL
AFRICA.
WORLD POLITICS JANUARY 1963 PP 262-294
061,
        REFERENCE

LEWIS W ARTHUR
POLITICS IN WEST AFRICA.
LONDON, GEORGE ALLEN AND UNWIN LTD, 1965
061,
        REFERENCE

LUSIGNAN GUY DE
FRENCH-SPEAKING AFRICA SINCE INDEPENDENCE.
NEW YORK, PRAEGER PUBLISHERS, 1969
056,061,104-11,105-11,106-11,107-11,109-11,112-11,
115-11,116-11,123-11,137-11,141-11,
        REFERENCE

MOORE CLEMENT H
MASS PARTY REGIMES IN AFRICA.
IN HERBERT J SPIRO, ED., AFRICA THE PRIMACY OF POLITICS,
NEW YORK, RANDOM HOUSE, 1966, PP 85-115
061,
        REFERENCE

MORGENTHAU RUTH SCHACHTER
SINGLE-PARTY SYSTEMS IN WEST AFRICA.
AMERICAN POLITICAL SCIENCE REVIEW 55 JUNE 1961 PP 294-307
061,
        REFERENCE

O CONNELL JAMES
THE CHANGING ROLE OF THE STATE IN WEST AFRICA.
NIGERIAN JOURNAL OF ECONOMIC AND SOCIAL STUDIES 3 NOVEMBER
1961 PP1-21
061,

REFERENCE

061

   POST KENNETH W J
   THE USE OF POWER.
   IN WILLIAM J HANNA (ED), INDEPENDENT BLACK AFRICA, CHICAGO,
   RAND MCNALLY, 1964, PP 444-453
   061,
        REFERENCE

   SPIRO HERBERT J
   THE PRIMACY OF POLITICAL DEVELOPMENT.
   IN AFRICA THE PRIMACY OF POLITICS,
   NEW YORK, RANDOM HOUSE, 1966, PP 150-169
   061,
        REFERENCE

   SPIRO HERBERT J   ED
   AFRICA, THE PRIMACY OF POLITICS.
   NEW YORK, RANDOM HOUSE, 1966
   061,
        REFERENCE

   SPIRO HERBERT J   ED
   PATTERNS OF AFRICAN DEVELOPMENT-- FIVE COMPARISONS.
   ENGLEWOOD CLIFFS, NEW JERSEY, PRENTICE-HALL (SPECTRUM), 1967
   061,
        REFERENCE

   SUTTON FRANCIS X
   AUTHORITY AND AUTHORITARIANISM IN THE NEW AFRICA.
   IN WILLIAM J HANNA (ED), INDEPENDENT BLACK AFRICA, CHICAGO,
   RAND MCNALLY, 1964, PP 407-418
   061,
        REFERENCE

   WALLERSTEIN I M
   THE DECLINE OF THE PARTY IN SINGLE-PARTY AFRICAN STATES.
   IN J LAPALOMBARA AND M WEINER, POLITICAL PARTIES AND
   POLITICAL DEVELOPMENT, PRINCETON, PRINCETON UNIVERSITY
   PRESS, 1966, PP 201-216
   061,
        REFERENCE

   YOUNG CRAWFORD
   POLITICS IN THE CONGO--DECOLONIZAT2ON AND INDEPENDENCE.
   PRINCETON, NEW JERSEY, PRINCETON UNIVERSITY PRESS, 1965
   054,061,081,108-07,
        REFERENCE

   ALUKO S A
   FEDERAL ELECTION CRISIS 1964-- AN ANALYSIS.
   ONITSHA, ETUDO LTD, 1965
   061,064,128-07,
        CASE STUDY

   ANONYMOUS
   AFRICAN POLITICAL PARTIES IN EQUATORIAL GUINEA 1968.
   AFRICA REPORT, MARCH 18, 1968
   061,111-07,

CASE STUDY

061

AWA EME O
FEDERAL GOVERNMENT IN NIGERIA.
BERKELEY, UNIVERSITY OF CALIFORNIA PRESS, 1964
061,128-07,
        CASE STUDY

AZIKIWE NNAMDI
THE DEVELOPMENT OF POLITICAL PARTIES IN NIGERIA.
LONDON 1957 (1792 OFFICE OF THE COMMISSIONER IN THE U K
FOR THE EASTERN REGION OF NIGERIA)
061,128-04,
        CASE STUDY

BARNES JAMES A
SOME ASPECTS OF POLITICAL DEVELOPMENT AMONG THE FORT
JAMESON NGONI.
AFRICAN STUDIES 7 1948 PP 99-109
061,142-07,
        CASE STUDY

BIENEN HENRY
TANZANIA-- PARTY TRANSFORMATION AND ECONOMIC DEVELOPMENT.
PRINCETON, PRINCETON UNIVERSITY PRESS, 1967
061,136-07,
        CASE STUDY

BRAND J A
THE MID-WEST STATE MOVEMENT IN NIGERIAN POLITICS-- A STUDY
IN PARTY FORMATION.
POLITICAL STUDIES 13 OCTOBER 1965 PP 346-365
061,128-07,
        CASE STUDY

BRETTON HENRY L
THE RISE AND FALL OF KWAME NKRUMAH.
NEW YORK, PRAEGER, 1966
061,114-04,
        CASE STUDY

BUSIA KOFI A
THE POSITION OF THE CHIEF IN THE MODERN POLITICAL SYSTEM OF
ASHANTI.
LONDON, OXFORD UNIVERSITY PRESS, 1951
061,099,114-01,
        CASE STUDY

CARTER GWENDOLEN M   ED
AFRICAN ONE-PARTY STATES.
ITHACA, CORNELL UNIVERSITY PRESS, 1962
061,
        CASE STUDY

CARTER GWENDOLEN M   ED
POLITICS IN AFRICA--SEVEN CASES.
NEW YORK HARCOURT BRACE AND WORLD 1966
061,
        CASE STUDY

061

COLSON ELIZABETH
MODERN POLITICAL ORGANIZATION OF THE PLATEAU TONGA.
AFRICAN STUDIES 7 1948 PP 85-98
061,142-07,
     CASE STUDY

DUDLEY B J O
PARTIES AND POLITICS IN NORTHERN NIGERIA.
LONDON, FRANK CASS AND CO. LTD., NEW YORK, HUMANITIES PRESS,
1968
061,128-07,
     CASE STUDY

GOVERNMENT OF TANZANIA
REPORT OF THE PRESIDENTIAL COMMISSION ON THE ESTABLISHMENT
OF A DEMOCRATIC ONE-PARTY STATE.
DAR ES SALAAM, 1965
061,136-04,
     CASE STUDY

HESS ROBERT L   LOEWENBERG GERHARD
THE ETHIOPIAN NO-PARTY STATE--A NOTE ON THE FUNCTIONS OF
POLITICAL PARTIES IN DEVELOPING STATES.
JASON L. FINKLE AND RICHARD W. GABLE (EDS), POLITICAL
DEVELOPMENT AND SOCIAL CHANGE, JOHN WILEY AND SONS, INC.,
NEW YORK, 1966, PP. 530-535
061,110-07,
     CASE STUDY

LEVINE DONALD N
ETHIOPIA--IDENTITY, AUTHORITY, AND REALISM.
LUCIAN W. PYE AND SIDNEY VERBA (EDS), POLITICAL CULTURE AND
POLITICAL DEVELOPMENT, PRINCETON, NEW JERSEY, PRINCETON
UNIVERSITY PRESS, 1965
061,110-07,
     CASE STUDY

LEYS COLIN
POLITICIANS AND POLICIES-- AN ESSAY IN AXCHOLI
UGANDA 1962-65.
NAIROBI, KENYA, THE EAST AFRICAN PUBLISHING HOUSE, 1967
061,139-07,
     CASE STUDY

LOFCHIE MICHAEL
PARTY CONFLICT IN ZANZIBAR.
JOURNAL OF MODERN AFRICAN STUDIES 1 1963 PP 185-207
061,136-07,
     CASE STUDY

MACKINTOSH JOHN P
FEDERALISM IN NIGERIA.
POLITICAL STUDIES 10 OCTOBER 1962 PP 223-247
061,128-07,
     CASE STUDY

MACKINTOSH JOHN P   ED
NIGERIAN GOVERNMENT AND POLITICS.

EVANSTON, NORTHWESTERN UNIVERSITY PRESS, 1966
061,128-07,
        CASE STUDY

061

    MADIERA KIETA
    THE SINGLE PARTY IN AFRICA.
    PRESENCE AFRICAINE 30 FEBRUARY 1960 PP 3-24
    060,061,065,123-04,
        CASE STUDY

    MAZRUI ALI A
    NKRUMAH-- THE LENINIST CZAR CHAPTER 8.
    IN ON HEROES AND UHURU-WORSHIP, LONDON, LONGMANS,
    1967, PP 113-134
    061,114-04,
        CASE STUDY

    MAZRUI ALI A
    ANTI-MILITARISM AND POLITICAL MILITANCY IN TANZANIA
    JOURNAL OF CONFLICT RESOLUTION 12 1968 PP269-284
    061,136-07,
        CASE STUDY

    MOORE CLEMENT H
    ONE-PARTYISM IN MAURITANIA.
    JOURNAL OF MODERN AFRICAN STUDIES 3 OCTOBER 1965 PP 409-420
    061,124-07,
        CASE STUDY

    MOORE CLEMENT H
    THE NEO-DESTOUR PARTY OF TUNISIA-- A STRUCTURE FOR
    DEMOCRACY CHAPTER 15.
    IN JASON L FINKLE AND RICHARD W GABLE, POLITICAL
    DEVELOPMENT AND SOCIAL CHANGE, NEW YORK, JOHN WILEY, 1966
    061,138-07,
        CASE STUDY

    OMARI T PETER
    KWAME NKRUMAH--THE ANATOMY OF AN AFRICAN DICTATORSHIP.
    NEW YORK, AFRICANA PUBLISHING CORPORATION, 1970
    061,114-07,
        CASE STUDY

    SKINNER ELLIOTT P
    THE MOSSI OF THE UPPER VOLTA-- THE POLITICAL DEVELOPMENT OF
    A SUDANESE PEOPLE.
    STANFORD, STANFORD UNIVERSITY PRESS, 1964
    061,141-07,
        CASE STUDY

    SKLAR RICHARD L
    NIGERIAN POLITICAL PARTIES-- POWER IN AN EMERGENT AFRICAN
    NATION.
    PRINCETON, NEW JERSEY, PRINCETON UNIVERSITY PRESS, 1963
    061, 128-07,
        CASE STUDY

    SNYDER FRANCIS G
    ONE-PARTY GOVERNMENT IN MALI-- TRANSITION TOWARD CONTROL.

NEW HAVEN, YALE UNIVERSITY PRESS, 1965
061,123-07,
        CASE STUDY

061
    WEISS HERBERT
    POLITICAL PROTEST IN THE CONGO--THE PARTI SOLIDAIRE AFRICAIN
    DURING THE INDEPENDENCE STRUGGLE.
    PRINCETON, PRINCETON UNIVERSITY PRESS, 1967
    061,108-07,
        CASE STUDY

    WHEARE JOAN
    THE NIGERIAN LEGISLATIVE COUNCIL.
    LONDON, FABER, 1950
    061,128-07,
        CASE STUDY

    WHITAKER C S
    THE POLITICS OF TRADITION-CONTINUITY AND CHANGE IN NORTHERN
    NIGERIA
    PRINCETON, NEW JERSEY, PRINCETON UNIVERSITY PRESS, 1970
    061,128-07,
        CASE STUDY

    ZOLBERG ARISTIDE R
    ONE PARTY GOVERNMENT IN THE IVORY COAST.
    PRINCETON, PRINCETON UNIVERSITY PRESS, 1964 (AND 1969)
    058,061,116-06,
        CASE STUDY

    BLANCHET ANDRE
    L'ITINERAIRE DES PARTIS AFRICAINES DEPUIS BAMAKO
    (GUIDEBOOK OF AFRICAN PARTIES SINCE BAMAKO).
    PARIS PLON 1958
    061,
        LESS ACCESSIBLE

    APTER DAVID E
    THE POLITICAL PARTY AS A MODERNIZING INSTRUMENT CHP 6.
    IN THE POLITICS OF MODERNIZATION, CHICAGO, CHICAGO
    UNIVERSITY PRESS, 1965
    061,
        GENERAL THEORY

    APTER DAVID E
    SOME REFLECTIONS ON THE ROLE OF A POLITICAL OPPOSITION IN
    NEW NATIONS.
    COMPARATIVE STUDIES IN SOCIETY AND HISTORY 4 JANUARY 1962
    PP 154-168 ALSO WILLIAM J HANNA, ED, INDEPENDENT BLACK AFRICA,
    CHICAGO, RAND MCNALLY, 1964, PP 456-471
    061,
        GENERAL THEORY

    CARNELL FG
    POLITICAL IMPLICATIONS OF FEDERALISM IN NEW STATES.
    IN FEDERALISM AND ECONOMIC GROWTH IN UNDERDEVELOPED
    COUNTRIES. SYMPOSIUM BY UK HICKS AND OTHERS, LONDON, OXFORD
    UNIVERSITY PRESS, 1961, PP 16-69
    061,

GENERAL THEORY

061

DUDLEY B J O
THE CONCEPT OF FEDERALISM.
NIGERIAN JOURNAL OF ECONOMIC AND SOCIAL STUDIES 5 MARCH
1963 PP 95-103
061,
        GENERAL THEORY

DUVERGER MAURICE
POLITICAL PARTIES-- THEIR ORGANIZATION AND ACTIVITY IN THE
MODERN STATE.
NEW YORK, JOHN WILEY AND SONS, 1962
061,
        GENERAL THEORY

SHILS EDWARD
POLITICAL DEVELOPMENT IN THE NEW STATES.
S'GRAVENHAGE, MOUTON, 1962; ALSO COMPARATIVE STUDIES IN
SOCIETY AND HISTORY 2 APRIL 1960 PP 265-292 AND JULY 1960
PP 379-411
061,
        GENERAL THEORY

SHILS EDWARD
ALTERNATIVE COURSES OF POLITICAL DEVELOPMENT CHAPTER 13.
IN JASON L FINKLE AND RICHARD W GABLE, POLITICAL
DEVELOPMENT AND SOCIAL CHANGE, NEW YORK, JOHN WILEY, 1966
061,
        GENERAL THEORY

WAHL NICHOLAS
THE FRENCH CONSTITUTION OF 1958--2, THE INITIAL DRAFT AND
ITS ORIGINS.
THE AMERICAN POLITICAL SCIENCE REVIEW 53 JUNE 1959 PP 358-82
B-M REPRINT PS-361
061,
        GENERAL THEORY

WEINER MYRON   LAPALOMBARA JOSEPH   EDS
POLITICAL PARTIES AND POLITICAL DEVELOPMENT.
PRINCETON, PRINCETON UNIVERSITY PRESS, 1966
061,
        GENERAL THEORY

WISEMAN HERBERT V
POLITICAL SYSTEMS--SOME SOCIOLOGICAL APPROACHES.
NEW YORK, PRAEGER, 1966
009,061,
        GENERAL THEORY

MORGENTHAU RUTH SCHACHTER
POLITICAL PARTIES IN FRENCH-SPEAKING WEST AFRICA.
OXFORD, OXFORD UNIVERSITY PRESS, 1964
055,058,061,109-07,123-07,130-07,

62. INSTITUTIONS AND BUREAUCRACY

062
    ADU A L
    THE CIVIL SERVICE IN NEW AFRICAN STATES.
    NEW YORK, PRAEGER, 1965
    062,
        AUTHOR DEALS ESPECIALLY WITH BRITISH SYSTEM OF CIVIL
        SERVICE AS ADAPTED IN AFRICA. MAIN EMPHASIS ON STRUC-
        TURE AND PROCESS OF BUREAUCRACY, RATHER THAN ON POLI-
        TICAL CONTEXT OF CIVIL SERVICE. DISCUSSES STAFF DE-
        VELOPMENT PROBLEMS, AND AFRICANIZATION POLICY, FINAN-
        CIAL CONTROL PROCEDURES, PUBLIC SERVICE COMMISSIONS,
        AND ASSESSES CIVIL SERVICE IN CONTEMPORARY AFRICA.

    LEGUM COLIN   DRYSDALE JOHN
    AFRICA CONTEMPORARY RECORD.
    LONDON, AFRICA RESEARCH LIMITED, 1969
    002,062,080,081,087,
        BEST EXISTING GENERAL REFERENCE FOR DETAILS OF EACH
        AFRICAN COUNTRY IN THE FIELDS OF FOREIGN RELATIONS,
        GOVERNMENT AND ECONOMICS. IT IS WRITTEN FOR THE SPE-
        CIALIST, BUT CAN BE USED BY THE TEACHER AS WELL.

    ADEDEJI ADEBAYO   ED
    PROBLEMS AND TECHNIQUES OF ADMINISTRATIVE TRAINING IN
    AFRICA.
    IFE, NIGERIA, AND NEW YORK, INTERNATIONAL UNIVERSITY BOOK-
    SELLERS, INC., 1969
    062,
        REFERENCE

    APTHORPE RAYMOND J
    THE INTRODUCTION OF BUREAUCRACY INTO AFRICAN POLITIES.
    JOURNAL OF AFRICAN ADMINISTRATION 12 JULY 1960 PP 125-134
    062,
        REFERENCE

    KIRK-GREENE A H M
    BUREAUCRATIC CADRES IN A TRADITIONAL MILIEU.
    IN JAMES S COLEMAN (ED), EDUCATION AND POLITICAL DEVELOPMENT
    PRINCETON, NEW JERSEY, PRINCETON UNIVERSITY PRESS, 1965,
    PP 372-407
    062,
        REFERENCE

    NYERERE JULIUS K
    THE RELATIONSHIP BETWEEN THE CIVIL SERVICE, POLITICAL
    PARTIES AND MEMBERS OF LEGISLATIVE COUNCIL.
    INTERNATIONAL AFFAIRS 36 JANUARY 1960 PP 43-47
    062,136-04,
        REFERENCE

    APTER DAVID E   LYSTAD ROBERT A
    BUREAUCRACY, PARTY, AND CONSTITUTIONAL DEMOCRACY-- AN EXAM-
    INATION OF POLITICAL ROLE SYSTEMS IN GHANA.

IN GWENDOLEN M CARTER AND WILLIAM O BROWN (EDS), TRANSITION
IN AFRICA-- STUDIES IN POLITICAL ADAPTATION, BOSTON, BOSTON
UNIVERSITY PRESS, 1958 PP 16-43
062,114-07,
    CASE STUDY

062
   APTER DAVID E
   GHANA.
   JAMES S. COLEMAN AND CARL G. ROSBERG JR. (EDS), POLITICAL
   PARTIES AND NATIONAL INTEGRATION IN TROPICAL AFRICA,
   BERKELEY, UNIVERSITY OF CALIFORNIA PRESS, 1966
   058,062,114-07,
       CASE STUDY

   BREUTZ P L
   TSWANA LOCAL GOVERNMENT TODAY.
   SOCIOLOGUS 8 1958 PP 140-154
   062,102-07,
       CASE STUDY

   DRYDEN STANLEY
   LOCAL ADMINISTRATION IN TANZANIA.
   KENYA, EAST AFRICAN PUBLISHING HOUSE, 1968
   062,136-07,
       CASE STUDY

   DUDBRIDGE B J   GRIFFITHS J E S
   THE DEVELOPMENT OF LOCAL GOVERNMENT IN SUKUMALAND.
   JOURNAL OF AFRICAN ADMINISTRATION 3 JULY 1951 PP 141-146
   062,136-09,
       CASE STUDY

   ENGHOLM G F
   THE WESTMINSTER MODEL IN UGANDA.
   INTERNATIONAL JOURNAL 18 AUTUMN 1963 PP 468-487
   062,139-07,
       CASE STUDY

   LEE J M
   PARLIAMENT IN REPUBLICAN GHANA.
   PARLIAMENTARY AFFAIRS 16 AUTUMN 1963 PP 376-395
   062,114-07,
       CASE STUDY

   LLOYD PETER C
   THE DEVELOPMENT OF POLITICAL PARTIES IN WESTERN NIGERIA.
   AMERICAN POLITICAL SCIENCE REVIEW 49 SEPTEMBER 1955
   PP 693-707
   062,128-07,
       CASE STUDY

   PROCTOR J H
   THE HOUSE OF CHIEFS AND THE POLITICAL DEVELOPMENT OF
   BOTSWANA
   JOURNAL OF MODERN AFRICAN STUDIES 6 1968 PP 59-79
   062, 102-07,
       CASE STUDY

   GONIDEC P F

LES INSTITUTIONS POLITIQUE DE LA REPUBLIQUE FEDERAL DU
CAMAROUN (THE POLITICAL INSTITUTIONS OF THE FEDERAL
REPUBLIC OF THE CAMAROONS).
CIVILIZATIONS 11 1961 PP 370-395 AND 12 1962 PP 13-26
062,104-07,
        LESS ACCESSIBLE

062
    DUBE S C
    BUREAUCRACY AND NATION BUILDING IN TRADITIONAL SOCIETIES
    CHAPTER 12.
    IN JASON L FINKLE AND RICHARD W GABLE, POLITICAL
    DEVELOPMENT AND SOCIAL CHANGE, NEW YORK, JOHN WILEY, 1966
    062,
        GENERAL THEORY

    EISENSTADT S N
    INITIAL INSTITUTIONAL PATTERNS OF POLITICAL MODERNIZATION--
    A COMPARATIVE STUDY.
    CIVILIZATIONS 12 1962 PP 461-473 AND 13 1963 PP 15-29
    062,
        GENERAL THEORY

    HUNTINGTON SAMUEL
    POLITICAL DEVELOPMENT AND POLITICAL DECAY.
    WORLD POLITICS 17 APRIL 1965 PP 386-430
    062,
        GENERAL THEORY

    LAPALOMBARA JOSEPH   ED
    BUREAUCRACY AND POLITICAL DEVELOPMENT.
    PRINCETON,NEW JERSEY, PRINCETON UNIVERSITY PRESS, 1963
    062,
        GENERAL THEORY

    RIGGS FRED W
    BUREAUCRATS AND POLITICAL DEVELOPMENT CHAPTER 12.
    IN JASON L FINKLE AND RICHARD W GABLE, POLITICAL
    DEVELOPMENT AND SOCIAL CHANGE, NEW YORK, JOHN WILEY, 1966
    062,
        GENERAL THEORY

    RIGGS FRED W
    ADMINISTRATION IN DEVELOPING COUNTRIES-THE THEORY OF
    PRISMATIC SOCIETY
    BOSTON,HOUGHTON MIFFLIN, 1964
    062,063,098,
        GENERAL THEORY

63. PARTICIPATION AND MOBILIZATION

063
    BENNETT GEORGE   ROSBERG CARL G
    THE KENYATTA ELECTION-- KENYA 1960-1961.
    LONDON, OXFORD UNIVERSITY PRESS, 1961

063,117-07,
>ANALYSIS OF THE ELECTION WHICH SYMBOLIZED THE ACHIEVE-
MENT OF AFRICAN POLITICAL POWER IN KENYA. ELECTION
CONSIDERED TEST AS TO WHETHER NON-AFRICAN POPULATIONS
IN KENYA (EUROPEAN, ARAB, ASIAN) COULD ADAPT TO THE
NEW AFRICAN DOMINANCE, PARTICULARLY UNDER LEADERSHIP
OF PRESUMED MAU-MAU LEADER, AND NOW PRESIDENT, JOMO
KENYATTA. FULL STATISTICAL REFERENCES.

063

CLIFFE LIONEL   ED
ONE-PARTY DEMOCRACY-- THE 1965 TANZANIA GENERAL ELECTIONS.
NAIROBI, EAST AFRICAN PUBLISHING HOUSE, 1967
063,136-07,
>COLLECTION OF PAPERS ANALYZING THE 1965 TANZANIA
ELECTION--A LANDMARK AND MODEL AFRICAN ELECTION. WITH
CAMPAIGNING FOCUSED ON LOCAL ISSUES AND RESTRICTED
FROM BECOMING INVOLVED IN RACIAL OR ETHNIC ANTAGON-
ISMS, MANY PROMINENT POLITICIANS WERE VOTED OUT OF
OFFICE. CLEAR ILLUSTRATION OF HOW DEMOCRATIC ELEC-
TIONS CAN BE HELD IN ONE-PARTY STATE.

MACKENZIE W J   ROBINSON KENNETH
FIVE ELECTIONS IN AFRICA.
OXFORD, CLARENDON PRESS, 1960
063,
>EARLIEST COLLECTION OF SYSTEMATIC ELECTORAL STUDIES IN
AFRICA. COVERS ELECTIONS IN EASTERN AND WESTERN RE-
GIONS OF NIGERIA, SIERRA LEONE, SENEGAL, AND KENYA.
CONTRIBUTORS DISCUSS ELECTORAL REGULATIONS, POLITICAL
PARTIES, ROLE OF MASS COMMUNICATIONS, MAJOR ISSUES,
POLLING PROCEDURES, AND ANALYSIS OF RESULTS. GOOD
STATISTICAL DATA. CONCLUSION BY EDITORS SYNTHESIZES
MAJOR PATTERNS OF PRE-INDEPENDENCE ELECTIONS IN
AFRICA.

BROOKS ANGIE E
POLITICAL PARTICIPATION OF WOMEN IN AFRICA SOUTH OF THE
SAHARA.
THE ANNALS OF THE AMERICAN ACADEMY OF POLITICAL AND SOCIAL
SCIENCE, JAN. 1968, PP. 82-85
063,
>REFERENCE

COWAN L GRAY
LOCAL GOVERNMENT IN WEST AFRICA.
NEW YORK, COLUMBIA UNIVERSITY PRESS, 1958
063,
>REFERENCE

KILSON MARTIN L
SOCIAL FORCES IN WEST AFRICAN POLITICAL DEVELOPMENT.
JOURNAL OF HUMAN RELATIONS 8 1960 PP 576-598
063,
>REFERENCE

POST KENNETH W J
THE INDIVIDUAL AND THE COMMUNITY AND THE COMMUNITIES AND
THE POLITICAL SYSTEM.
IN WILLIAM J HANNA (ED), INDEPENDENT BLACK AFRICA, CHICAGO,

RAND MCNALLY, 1964, PP 319-340
063,
        REFERENCE

063
    AUSTIN DENNIS
    ELECTIONS IN AN AFRICAN RURAL AREA.
    IN WILLIAM J HANNA (ED), INDEPENDENT BLACK AFRICA, CHICAGO,
    RAND MCNALLY, 1964, PP 341-362
    063,114-07,
        CASE STUDY

    BENNETT GEORGE
    THE GOLD COAST GENERAL ELECTION OF 1954.
    PARLIAMENTARY AFFAIRS 7 1954 PP 430-439
    063,114-07,
        CASE STUDY

    BENNETT GEORGE
    KENYA'S FRUSTRATED ELECTION.
    WORLD TODAY 17 1961 PP 254-261
    063,117-07,
        CASE STUDY

    BINDER LEONARD
    POLITICAL RECRUITMENT AND PARTICIPATION IN EGYPT.
    JOSEPH LA POLOMBARA AND MYRON WEINER (EDS), POLITICAL
    PARTIES AND POLITICAL DEVELOPMENT. PRINCETON, NEW JERSEY,
    PRINCETON UNIVERSITY PRESS, 1966
    063,140-07,
        CASE STUDY

    BRETTON HENRY L
    POLITICAL INFLUENCE IN SOUTHERN NIGERIA.
    IN HERBERT J SPIRO, ED., AFRICA THE PRIMACY OF POLITICS,
    NEW YORK, RANDOM HOUSE, 1966, PP 49-84
    063,128-07,
        CASE STUDY

    DENT M J
    ELECTIONS IN NORTHERN NIGERIA.
    JOURNAL OF LOCAL ADMINISTRATION OVERSEAS OCTOBER 1962
    PP 213-224
    063,128-07,
        CASE STUDY

    DUDLEY B J O
    THE NOMINATION OF PARLIAMENTARY CANDIDATES IN
    NORTHERN NIGERIA.
    JOURNAL OF COMMONWEALTH POLITICAL STUDIES, 2 NOVEMBER, 1963
    LONDON, LEICESTER UNIVERSITY PRESS, PP 45-58
    063,128-07,
        CASE STUDY

    ELECTORAL COMMISSION
    REPORT ON THE NIGERIA FEDERAL ELECTIONS, DECEMBER 1959.
    LAGOS, FEDERAL GOVERNMENT PRINTER, 1960
    063,128-07,
        CASE STUDY

ENGHOLM G F
AFRICAN ELECTIONS IN KENYA, MARCH 1957, CHAPTER 7.
IN W J MACKENZIE AND KENNETH ROBINSON, FIVE ELECTIONS IN
AFRICA, LONDON, OXFORD UNIVERSITY PRESS, 1960
063,117-07,
      CASE STUDY

063
FRIEDLAND WILLIAM H
VUTA KAMBA--THE DEVELOPMENT OF TRADE UNIONS IN TANGANYIKA.
PALO ALTO, CALIFORNIA, HOOVER INSTITUTION PRESS, 1969
063,136-08,
      CASE STUDY

LIEBENOW J GUS
COLONIAL RULE AND POLITICAL DEVELOPMENT IN TANZANIA-THE
CASE OF THE MAKONDE
EVANSTON NORTHWESTERN UNIVERSITY PRESS 1970
035,055,063,136-07,
      CASE STUDY

LLOYD PETER C
SOME COMMENTS ON THE ELECTIONS IN NIGERIA.
JOURNAL OF AFRICAN ADMINISTRATION 4 1952 PP 82-92
063,128-07,
      CASE STUDY

LONSDALE JOHN
THE TANZANIAN EXPERIMENT
AFRICAN AFFAIRS 67 1968 PP 330-344
063,070,136-11,
      CASE STUDY

MACARTNEY W A J
BOTSWANA GOES TO THE POLLS
AFRICAN REPORT DECEMBER 1969 PP 28-30
063,102-07,
      CASE STUDY

MACKINTOSH JOHN P
ELECTORAL TRENDS AND THE TENDENCY TO A ONE PARTY
SYSTEM IN NIGERIA.
JOURNAL OF COMMONWEALTH POLITICAL STUDIES 1 NOVEMBER 1962
PP 194-210
063,128-07,
      CASE STUDY

MAIR LUCY P
THE NYASALAND ELECTIONS OF 1961.
LONDON, ATHLONE PRESS, 1962
063,122-07,
      CASE STUDY

MOORE CLEMENT H   HOCHSCHILD ARLIE R
STUDENT UNIONS IN NORTH AFRICAN POLITICS.
DAEDALUS, WINTER 1968, PP. 21-50
063,138-07,
      CASE STUDY

MULFORD DAVID C

THE NORTHERN RHODESIA GENERAL ELECTION 1962.
EASTERN AFRICA, OXFORD UNIVERSITY PRESS, 1964
063,142-07,
    CASE STUDY

063
O'CONNELL JAMES
THE NORTHERN REGIONAL ELECTIONS, 1961, AN ANALYSIS.
NIGERIAN JOURNAL OF ECONOMIC AND SOCIAL STUDIES 4 JULY
JULY 1962
063,128-07,
    CASE STUDY

OLUSANYA G O
THE ROLE OF EX-SERVICEMEN IN NIGERIAN POLITICS.
THE JOURNAL OF MODERN AFRICAN STUDIES, VOL. 6, NO. 2, 1968
PP. 221-32
063,128-07,
    CASE STUDY

POST KENNETH W J
THE NIGERIAN FEDERAL ELECTION OF 1959--POLITICS AND
ADMINISTRATION IN A DEVELOPING POLITICAL SYSTEM.
LONDON, OXFORD UNIVERSITY PRESS (FOR NISER), 1963
063,128-07,
    CASE STUDY

PRICE J H
THE EASTERN REGION OF NIGERIA CHAPTER 4.
IN W J MACKENZIE AND KENNETH ROBINSON, FIVE ELECTIONS IN
AFRICA, LONDON, OXFORD UNIVERSITY PRESS, 1960
063,128-07,
    CASE STUDY

ROBINSON KENNETH
SENEGAL--THE ELECTION TO THE TERRITORIAL ASSEMBLY MARCH
1957, CHAPTER 6.
IN W J MACKENZIE AND KENNETH ROBINSON, FIVE ELECTIONS IN
AFRICA, OXFORD. CLARENDON PRESS, 1960
063,130-07,
    CASE STUDY

SANGER CLYDE   NOTTINGHAM JOHN
THE KENYA GENERAL ELECTION OF 1963.
JOURNAL OF MODERN AFRICAN STUDIES 2 1964 PP 1-40
063,117-07,
    CASE STUDY
    CASE STUDY

SCOTT D J
THE SIERRE LEONE ELECTION MAY, 1957 CHAPTER 5.
IN W J MACKENZIE AND KENNETH ROBINSON, FIVE ELECTIONS IN
AFRICA, LONDON, OXFORD UNIVERSITY PRESS, 1960
063,131-07,
    CASE STUDY

TAMUNO TEKENA N
NIGERIA AND ELECTIVE REPRESENTATION 1923-1947.
LONDON, HEINEMANN, 1966
056,063,128-07,

CASE STUDY

063

WHITAKER PHILIP
THE WESTERN REGION OF NIGERIA CHAPTER 3.
IN W J MACKENZIE AND KENNETH ROBINSON, FIVE ELECTIONS IN
AFRICA, LONDON, OXFORD UNIVERSITY PRESS, 1960
063,
        CASE STUDY

NETTL J P
POLITICAL MOBILIZATION.
NEW YORK, BASIC BOOKS, 1967
037,063,
        GENERAL THEORY

RIGGS FRED W
ADMINISTRATION IN DEVELOPING COUNTRIES-THE THEORY OF
PRISMATIC SOCIETY
BOSTON, HOUGHTON MIFFLIN, 1964
062,063,098,
        GENERAL THEORY

64. ELITE INSTABILITY AND MILITARY RULE

064

AFRIFA A A COLONEL
THE GHANA COUP, 24TH FEBRUARY, 1966.
LONDON, FRANK CASS AND COMPANY, 1966, PREFACE BY KOFI A BUSIA
INTRODUCTION BY TIBOR SZAMUELY
064,114-04,
        AUTHOR IS ONE OF MILITARY LEADERS WHO OVERTHREW THE
        GHANAIAN REGIME OF PRESIDENT NKRUMAH IN FEBRUARY 1966.
        BOOK IS AUTOBIOGRAPHICAL STATEMENT AND SEMI-OFFICIAL
        MILITARY GOVERNMENT ACCOUNT OF REASONS BEHIND THE
        COUP.

MORRISON DONALD G   ET AL
BLACK AFRICA- A HANDBOOK FOR COMPARATIVE ANALYSIS
NEW YORK, FREE PRESS, 1970
002,058,064,098,
        CO-EDITED BY R.C.MITCHELL,H.M.STEVENSON AND J.N.PADEN.
        COMPREHENSIVE DATA SOURCE BOOK FOR 32 SUB-SAHARAN
        STATES PART 1-DETAILED DATA FOR OVER 200 VARIABLES
        INCLUDING ANALYSIS OF BASIC PATTERNS PART 2- COUNTRY
        PROFILES OF BASIC INFORMATION ON URBAN,ECONOMIC AND
        POLITICAL PATTERNS PART 3-ESSAYS ON DATA RELIABILITY,
        BASES OF ETHNIC CLASSIFICATION,PATTERNS AND PROCESSES
        OF NATURAL INTEGRATION.

NKRUMAH KWAME
DARK DAYS IN GHANA.
NEW YORK, INTERNATIONAL PUBLISHERS, 1968
064,114-04,
        AUTHOR IS DEPOSED HEAD OF GHANAIAN GOVERNMENT WHO RE-

COUNTS. FROM HIS EXILE IN GUINEA, HIS VERSION OF THE
EVENTS WHICH RESULTED IN HIS OVERTHROW IN FEBRUARY
1966.

064

WELCH CLAUDE E
SOLDIER AND STATE IN AFRICA.
EVANSTON, NORTHWESTERN UNIVERSITY PRESS, 1970
064,
    CASE STUDIES OF COUPS AND MILITARY RULE IN DAHOMEY
    AND UPPER VOLTA (SKURNIK), CONGO-KINSHASA (WILLAME),
    GHANA (KRAUS), AND ALGERIA (ZARTMAN), WITH
    THEORETICAL INTRODUCTION BY EDITOR, AND ESSAY ON
    ' MILITARY AND POLITICAL CHANGE ' BY VAN DEN BERGHE

AUSTIN DENNIS
POLITICAL CONFLICT IN AFRICA.
GOVERNMENT AND OPPOSITION CLEVELAND 2 NO 4 1968 PP 487-490
064,
    REFERENCE

GRUNDY KENNETH W
CONFLICTING IMAGES OF THE MILITARY IN AFRICA
NAIROBI, EAST AFRICAN PUBLISHING HOUSE, 1968
064,
    REFERENCE

GUTTERIDGE WILLIAM
THE PLACE OF THE ARMED FORCES IN SOCIETY IN AFICAN STATES.
RACE 4 NOVEMBER 1962 PP 22-33
064,
    REFERENCE

GUTTERIDGE WILLIAM
THE POLITICAL ROLE OF AFRICAN ARMED FORCES-- THE IMPACT
OF FOREIGN MILITARY ASSISTANCE.
AFRICAN AFFAIRS 66 APRIL 1967 PP 93-103
064,
    REFERENCE

KITCHEN HELEN
THE ARMIES OF AFRICA, PART 2.
IN A HANDBOOK OF AFRICAN AFFAIRS,   PRAEGER, 1964,
PP 188-239
064,
    REFERENCE

LEE J M
AFRICAN ARMIES AND CIVIL ORDER.
NEW YORK, PRAEGER PUBLISHERS, 1969
064,
    REFERENCE

LEVINE VICTOR T
INDEPENDENT AFRICA IN TROUBLE.
TRANSACTION JULY-AUGUST 1967 PP 53-62
064,
    REFERENCE

LOUCHHEIM DONALD H

THE MILITARY'S ECONOMIC LEGACY.
AFRICA REPORT 11 MARCH 1966 P 18
064,
        REFERENCE

064

MAZRUI ALI A
EDMUND BURKE AND REFLECTIONS ON THE REVOLUTION IN THE CONGO.
IN ON HEROES AND UHURU-WORSHIP, LONDON, LONGMANS, 1967
064,108-06,
        REFERENCE

ROTHCHILD DONALD S
THE POLITICS OF AFRICAN SEPARATISM.
IN WILLIAM J HANNA (ED), INDEPENDENT BLACK AFRICA, CHICAGO,
RAND MCNALLY, 1964, PP 595-606
064,
        REFERENCE

VAN DEN BERGHE P
THE ROLE OF THE ARMY IN CONTEMPORARY AFRICA.
AFRICA REPORT 10 MARCH 1965 PP 12-17
064,
        REFERENCE

WEEKS GEORGE
THE ARMIES OF AFRICA.
AFRICA REPORT 9 JANUARY 1964 PP 4-21
064,
        REFERENCE

WELCH CLAUDE E
SOLDIER AND STATE IN AFRICA.
JOURNAL OF MODERN AFRICAN STUDIES 5 NOVEMBER 1967 PP 305-322
064,
        REFERENCE

ZOLBERG ARISTIDE R
MILITARY INTERVENTION IN THE NEW STATES OF TROPICAL AFRICA--
ELEMENTS OF COMPARATIVE ANALYSIS.
HENRY BIENEN (ED), THE MILITARY INTERVENES, NEW YORK, THE
RUSSELL SAGE FOUNDATION, 1968
064,
        REFERENCE

ZOLBERG ARISTIDE R
THE STRUCTURE OF POLITICAL CONFLICT IN THE NEW STATES OF
TROPICAL AFRICA.
THE AMERICAN POLITICAL SCIENCE REVIEW, VOL. 62, NO. 1, MARCH
1968, PP. 70-87
064,
        REFERENCE

ALUKO S A
FEDERAL ELECTION CRISIS 1964-- AN ANALYSIS.
ONITSHA,ETUDO LTD,1965
061,064,128-07,
        CASE STUDY

ANKRAH J A

100 DAYS IN GHANA.
AFRICA REPORT. JUNE, 1966, PP. 21-23
064,114-06,
      CASE STUDY

064
  ANONYMOUS
  GABON-- PUTSCH OR COUP D'ETAT.
  AFRICA REPORT 9 MARCH 1964 PP 12-15
  064,112-06,
        CASE STUDY

  ANONYMOUS
  CONVULSIONS WITHIN TOGO.
  PAN AFRICA NO. 93 JANUARY 6, 1967 P 9
  064,137-06,
        CASE STUDY

  ANONYMOUS
  COUP FOILED IN GABON.
  WEST AFRICA FEBRUARY 22 1964 P 207
  064,112-06,
        CASE STUDY

  BESHIR MOHAMED O
  THE SUDAN-- A MILITARY SURRENDER.
  AFRICA REPORT 9 DECEMBER 1964 PP 3-10
  064,134-06,
        CASE STUDY

  BROWN CHARLES E
  THE LIBYAN REVOLUTION SORTS ITSELF OUT
  AFRICA REPORT DECEMBER 1969 PP 12-15
  064,
        CASE STUDY

  BUSTIN EDOUARD
  THE QUEST FOR POLITICAL STABILITY IN THE CONGO--
  SOLDIERS, BUREAUCRATS AND POLITICIANS.
  IN HERBERT J SPIRO, ED., AFRICA THE PRIMACY OF POLITICS,
  NEW YORK, RANDOM HOUSE, 1966, PP 16-48
  064,108-06,
        CASE STUDY

  CARD EMILY
  GHANA PREPARES FOR CIVILIAN RULE.
  AFRICA REPORT, APRIL 9, 1968
  064,114-07,
        CASE STUDY

  CASTAGNO A A JR
  SOMALIA GOES MILITARY
  AFRICA REPORT 15 FEBRUARY 1970 PP 25-27
  064,133-07,
        CASE STUDY

  CLAPHAM CHRISTOPHER
  THE ETHIOPIAN COUP D≠ETAT OF DECEMBER 1960.
  THE JOURNAL OF MODERN AFRICAN STUDIES, VOL. 6, NO. 4, 1968,
  PP. 495-507

064,110-06,
     CASE STUDY

064

   DU BOIS VICTOR D
   THE ROLE OF THE ARMY IN GUINEA.
   AFRICA REPORT 8 JANUARY 1963 PP 3-5
   064,115-06,
        CASE STUDY

   KILNER PETER
   MILITARY GOVERNMENT IN SUDAN--THE PAST THREE YEARS.
   WORLD TODAY 18 JUNE 1962 PP 259-268
   064,134-06,
        CASE STUDY

   KILNER PETER
   A YEAR OF ARMY RULE IN THE SUDAN.
   THE WORLD TODAY 15 1959 PP 430-441
   064,134-06,
        CASE STUDY

   KRAUS   JON
   ARMS AND POLITICS IN GHANA
   IN CLAUDE WELCH (ED), SOLDIER AND STATE IN AFRICA, EVANSTON,
   NORTHWESTERN UNIVERSITY PRESS, 1970
   064,
        CASE STUDY

   KYLE KEITH
   COUP IN ZANZIBAR.
   AFRICA REPORT 9 FEBRUARY 1964 PP 18-20
   064,136-06,
        CASE STUDY

   LEGUM COLIN
   CONGO DISASTER.
   HARMONDSWORTH,PENGUIN,1961
   064,108-06,
        CASE STUDY

   LEMARCHAND RENE
   DAHOMEY--COUP WITHIN A COUP.
   AFRICA REPORT, JUNE, 1968, P. 46
   064,109-06,
        CASE STUDY

   MARCUM JOHN A
   THREE REVOLUTIONS.
   AFRICA REPORT 12 NOVEMBER 1967 PP 8-22
   064,
        CASE STUDY

   MUTESA II
   THE DESECRETION OF MY KINGDOM.
   LONDON, CONSTABLE, 1967
   054,064,139-04,
        CASE STUDY

   NELKIN DOROTHY

THE ECONOMIC AND SOCIAL SETTING OF MILITARY TAKEOVERS IN
AFRICA.
JOURNAL OF ASIAN AND AFRICAN STUDIES, VOL. II, NOS. 3-4,
JULY AND OCTOBER, 1967, PP. 230-244
064,
        CASE STUDY

064

   SHARMA B S
   THE SUDAN.
   THE POLITICS OF DEMILITARISATION, UNIVERSITY OF LONDON
   APRIL-MAY 1966 PP 32-40
   INSTITUTE OF COMMONWEALTH STUDIES
   064,134-06,
           CASE STUDY

   SKURNIK W A E
   THE MILITARY AND POLITICS. DAHOMEY AND UPPER VOLTA.
   IN CLAUDE WELCH (ED), SOLDIER AND STATE IN AFRICA, EVANSTON,
   NORTHWESTERN UNIVERSITY PRESS, 1970
   064,
           CASE STUDY

   SNYDER FRANCIS G
   AN ERA ENDS IN MALI.
   AFRICA REPORT, MARCH/APRIL, 1969, PP. 16-53
   064,123-06,
           CASE STUDY

   VAN DEN BERGHE P
   THE MILITARY AND POLITICAL CHANGE IN AFRICA
   IN CLAUDE WELCH (ED), SOLDIER AND STATE IN AFRICA, EVANSTON,
   NORTHWESTERN UNIVERSITY PRESS, 1970
   064,
           CASE STUDY

   VERHAEGEN BENOIT
   REBELLIONS AU CONGO. REBELLIONS OF THE CONGO.
   BRUSSELS CENTRE DE RECHERCHE ET D INFORMATION SOCIO-
   POLITIQUES 1 1966
   064,108-06,
           CASE STUDY

   WILLAME JEAN-CLAUDE
   MILITARY INTERVENTION IN THE CONGO.
   AFRICA REPORT 11 NOVEMBER 1966 PP 41-45
   064,108-06,
           CASE STUDY

   WILLAME JEAN-CLAUDE
   CONGO-KINSHASA- GENERAL MOBUTU AND TWO POLITICAL
   GENERATIONS.
   IN CLAUDE WELCH (ED), SOLDIER AND STATE IN AFRICA, EVANSTON,
   NORTHWESTERN UNIVERSITY PRESS, 1970
   064,
           CASE STUDY

   YOUNG CRAWFORD
   THE OBOTE REVOLUTION.
   AFRICA REPORT 11 JUNE 1966 PP 8-14

064,139-06,
        CASE STUDY

064

    YOUNG CRAWFORD
    THE CONGO REBELLION.
    AFRICA REPORT 10 APRIL 1965 PP 6-11
    064,081,108-06,
        CASE STUDY

    ZARTMAN I WILLIAM
    THE ALGERIAN ARMY IN POLITICS.
    IN CLAUDE WELCH (ED), SOLDIER AND STATE IN AFRICA, EVANSTON,
    NORTHWESTERN UNIVERSITY PRESS, 1970
    064,
        CASE STUDY

    FINER S E
    MILITARY DISENGAGEMENT FROM POLITICS.
    THE POLITICS OF DEMILITARISATION, UNIVERSITY OF LONDON
    APRIL-MAY 1966
    INSTITUTE OF COMMONWEALTH STUDIES
    064,
        GENERAL THEORY

    GUTTERIDGE WILLIAM
    ARMED FORCES IN NEW STATES.
    LONDON, OXFORD UNIVERSITY PRESS, 1962
    064,
        GENERAL THEORY

    HOPKINS KEITH
    CIVIL-MILITARY RELATIONS IN DEVELOPING COUNTRIES.
    BRITISH JOURNAL OF SOCIOLOGY 17 JUNE 1966 PP 165-182
    064,
        GENERAL THEORY

    HUNTINGTON SAMUEL
    POLITICAL ORDER IN CHANGING SOCIETIES.
    NEW HAVEN, CONN, YALE   UNIVERSITY PRESS, 1969
    064,
        GENERAL THEORY

    JANOWITZ MORRIS
    CHANGING PATTERNS OF ORGANIZATIONAL AUTHORITY--
    THE MILITARY ESTABLISHMENT.
    ADMINISTRATIVE SCIENCE QUARTERLY 3 MARCH 1959
    064,
        GENERAL THEORY

    JANOWITZ MORRIS
    THE MILITARY IN THE POLITICAL DEVELOPMENT OF NEW NATIONS.
    CHICAGO, UNIVERSITY OF CHICAGO PRESS, 1964, TABLES 1 AND 2
    P 52
    064,
        GENERAL THEORY

    JANOWITZ MORRIS
    MILITARY ELITES AND THE STUDY OF WAR.
    JOURNAL OF CONFLICT RESOLUTION 1 MARCH 1957 PP 9-18

(BOBBS-MERRILL REPRINT 134)
064,
    GENERAL THEORY

064
LEIGHTON RICHARD M   SANDERS RALPH
MILITARY CIVIC ACTION.
IN LEWIS P FICKETT (ED), PROBLEMS OF THE DEVELOPING NATIONS,
NEW YORK, CROWELL, 1966, PP 103-122
064,
    GENERAL THEORY

PYE LUCIAN W
ARMIES IN THE PROCESS OF POLITICAL DEVELOPMENT.
IN ASPECTS OF POLITICAL DEVELOPMENT, BOSTON, LITTLE, BROWN, 1966,
PP 172-187; ALSO   LEWIS P FICKETT, ED, PROBLEMS OF THE
DEVELOPING NATIONS, NEW YORK, CROWELL, 1966, PP 85-102; ALSO
L FINKLE AND R GABLE, POLITICAL DEVELOPMENT AND SOCIAL
CHANGE, NEW YORK, JOHN WILEY, 1966
064,
    GENERAL THEORY

RAPOPORT DAVID C
COUP D'ETAT-- THE VIEW OF THE MEN FIRING PISTOLS.
IN CARL J FRIEDRICH (ED.), REVOLUTION, NEW YORK,
ATHERTON PRESS, 1966
064,
    GENERAL THEORY

RUMMEL R J
DIMENSIONS OF CONFLICT BEHAVIOR WITHIN NATIONS, 1946-59.
JOURNAL OF CONFLICT RESOLUTION 10 1966 PP 65-73
064,
    GENERAL THEORY

65. THE IMPLICATIONS OF NIGERIA-BIAFRA

065
ADLER RENATA
LETTER FROM BIAFRA.
THE NEW YORKER, OCT. 4, 1969, PP. 47-113
065,
    JOURNALIST ACCOUNT WRITTEN IN FIRST PERSON, STRONGLY
    PRO-BIAFRAN. DETAILS CURRENT HUMANITARIAN EFFORTS AND
    PROBLEMS OF RELIEF.

LEGUM COLIN   DRYSDALE JOHN
NIGERIAN CIVIL WAR.
COLIN LEGUM AND JOHN DRYSDALE, AFRICA CONTEMPORARY RECORD,
LONDON, AFRICA RESEARCH LIMITED, 1969, PP. 645-688
065,128-06,
    IMPORTANT COLLECTION OF ACTUAL DOCUMENTS ABOUT THE CI-
    VIL WAR AS TO WHY TANZANIA RECOGNIZED BIAFRA--A STATE-
    MENT BY OJUKWU AT ADDIS ABABA--AND THE ENAHARO STATE-
    MENT IN ADDIS ABABA.

065

MELSON ROBERT   WOLPE HOWARD   EDS
NIGERIA-MODERNIZATION AND THE POLITICS OF COMMUNALISM.
EAST LANSING, MICHIGAN STATE UNIVERSITY PRESS, 1970
006,065,128-03,
> BASIC THEORETICAL ARGUMENT IS THAT COMMUNALISM DEVELOPS
> IN RESPONSE TO COMPETITION IN MODERN SPHERE. CONTRIBU-
> TORS, WHO HAVE WORKED IN ALL PARTS OF NIGERIA, EXPLORE
> CASE STUDY SITUATIONS OF MODERN COMMUNALISM AND ETHNI-
> CITY, INCLUDING THE WAY IN WHICH HAUSA AND IBO IDENTI-
> TIES HAVE EMERGED IN RECENT TIMES.

OJUKWU C ODUMEGWU
BIAFRA--SELECTED SPEECHES WITH JOURNAL OF EVENTS.
NEW YORK, HARPER AND ROW, 1969
065,128-06,
> WRITTEN FROM PARTISAN POINT OF VIEW, GIVING DIARY
> TYPE ACCOUNT OF EVENTS IN 1966 LEADING UP TO CIVIL WAR
> AND EVENTS OF THE WAR THROUGH MAY 30, 1969. AUTHOR,
> NOW IN EXILE, WAS LEADER OF BIAFRA.

ADEBANJO TIMOTHY
BEYOND THE CONFLICT.
AFRICA REPORT, FEB., 1968, P. 12
065,128-06,
> REFERENCE

DIAMOND STANLEY
THE BIAFRAN POSSIBILITY.
AFRICA REPORT, FEB., 1968, P. 16
065,128-06,
> REFERENCE

FERGUSON JOHN
THE LESSONS OF BIAFRA.
THE CHRISTIAN CENTURY, AUGUST 14, 1968, PP. 1013-1017
065,128-06,
> REFERENCE

FLOYD BARRY
EASTERN NIGERIA--A GEOGRAPHICAL REVIEW.
NEW YORK, PRAEGER PUBLISHERS, 1969
065,128-08,
> REFERENCE

FORSYTH FREDERICK
THE BIAFRA STORY.
BALTIMORE, PENGUIN, 1969
065,
> REFERENCE

HANNING HUGH
LESSONS FROM THE ARMS RACE.
AFRICA REPORT, FEB., 1968, P. 42
065,
> REFERENCE

HOARE MIKE
NO PLACE FOR MERCENARIES.

AFRICA REPORT, FEB. 1968, P. 44
065,
    REFERENCE

065
  LINDSAY KENNEDY
  HOW BIAFRA PAYS FOR THE WAR.
  VENTURE, MARCH 1969
  065,128-06,
    REFERENCE

  NYERERE JULIUS K
  WHY TANZANIA RECOGNIZED BIAFRA.
  AFRICA REPORT, JUNE 27, 1968
  065,136-09,
    REFERENCE

  O'CONNELL JAMES
  THE SCOPE OF THE TRAGEDY.
  AFRICA REPORT, FEB., 1968, P. 8
  065,128-06,
    REFERENCE

  OJUKWU C ODUMEGWU
  RANDOM THOUGHTS OF C ODUMEGWU OJUKWU, GENERAL OF THE
  PEOPLES ARMY, BIAFRA.
  NEW YORK, HARPER AND ROW, 1969
  065,128-06,
    REFERENCE

  ROUNDTABLE INTERVIEW
  SOME ASSUMPTIONS REEXAMINED.
  AFRICA REPORT, FEB., 1968, P. 20
  065,
    REFERENCE

  SCHWARZ WALTER
  FOREIGN POWERS AND THE NIGERIAN WAR
  AFRICA REPORT 15 FEBRUARY 1970 PP 12-14
  065,
    REFERENCE

  SKLAR RICHARD L
  NIGERIAN POLITICS--THE ORDEAL OF CHIEF AWOLOWO, 1960-65.
  GWENDOLEN M. CARTER (ED), POLITICS IN AFRICA--7 CASES, NEW
  YORK, HARCOURT, BRACE AND WORLD INC., 1966, PP. 119-166
  065,128-07,
    REFERENCE

  SKLAR RICHARD L
  CONTRADICTIONS IN THE NIGERIAN POLOTICAL SYSTEM.
  THE JOURNAL OF MODERN AFRICAN STUDIES, VOL. 3, NO. 2, 1965,
  PP. 201-13
  065,128-06,
    REFERENCE

  SKLAR RICHARD L
  DIALOG-THE UNITED STATES AND THE BIAFRAN WAR
  AFRICA REPORT, NOVEMBER 1969, PP 22-23
  065,

REFERENCE

065
   UWECHUE RAPH
   REFLECTIONS ON THE NIGERIAN CIVIL WAR-A CALL FOR REALISM
   NEW YORK, AFRICANA PUBLISHING CORPORATION, 1970
   065,
        REFERENCE

   WHITAKER C S
   A DYSRHYTHMIC PROCESS OF POLITICAL CHANGE.
   WORLD POLITICS, XIX, NO. 2, JANUARY 1967, PP. 190-217
   065,
        REFERENCE

   DILLON WILTON S
   NIGERIA'S TWO REVOLUTIONS.
   AFRICA REPORT 11 MARCH 1966 PP 9-14
   065,128-06,
        CASE STUDY

   JARVIS STEVEN
   NIGERIA AND BIAFRA.
   AFRICA TODAY 14 DECEMBER 1967 PP 16-18
   065,128-06,
        CASE STUDY

   KLINGHOFFER ARTHUR J
   WHY THE SOVIETS CHOSE SIDES IN THE NIGERIAN WAR.
   AFRICA REPORT, FEBRUARY, 1968, P. 48
   065,084,128-06,
        CASE STUDY

   MADIERA KIETA
   THE SINGLE PARTY IN AFRICA.
   PRESENCE AFRICAINE 30 FEBRUARY 1960 PP 3-24
   060,061,065,123-04,
        CASE STUDY

   PADEN JOHN N
   COMMUNAL COMPETITION,CONFLICT AND VIOLENCE IN KANO,
   IN ROBERT MELSON AND HOWARD WOLPE (EDS), NIGERIA-MODERNIZATION
   AND THE POLITICS OF COMMUNALISM, EAST LANSING, MICHIGAN STATE
   UNIVERSITY PRESS, 1970
   065,
        CASE STUDY

   AKIWOWO AKINSOLA
   THE SOCIOLOGICAL RELEVANCE OF TRIBALISM TO THE BUILDING OF
   THE NIGERIAN NATION.
   SIXTH WORLD CONGRESS OF SOCIOLOGY, EVIAN, FRANCE, SEPT. 4-11
     1966, 32 PAGES
   065,128-06,
      LESS ACCESSIBLE

   ASIKA U
   ENOUGH IS ENOUGH.
   FEDERAL MINISTRY OF INFORMATION, DEC., 1967, 16 PAGES
   065,
        LESS ACCESSIBLE

065
    DEBONNEVILLE FLORIS
    LA MORT DU BIAFRA (THE DEATH OF BIAFRA).
    PARIS, R. SOLAR, 1968
    065,128-06,
        LESS ACCESSIBLE

    SCHWARTZ FREDERICK A
    NIGERIA--THE TRIBES, THE NATION OT THE RACE,THE POLITICS OF
    INDEPENDENCE.
    CAMBRIDGE, MASSACHUSETTS, INSTITUTE OF TECHNOLOGY PRESS,
    1965
    065,128-06,

    WHITAKER C S   SKLAR RICHARD L
    NIGERIA.
    IN G.M. CARTER (ED) NATIONAL UNITY AND REGIONALISM IN EIGHT
    AFRICAN STATES. ITHACA, CORNELL UNIVERSITY PRESS, 1966
    065,128-06,

66. LEGAL SYSTEMS IN AFRICA

066
    ANDERSON J N D
    ISLAMIC LAW IN AFRICA.
    LONDON, HER MAJESTY'S STATIONERY OFFICE 1 1954
    066,
        REMAINS MAJOR REFERENCE WORK ON ISLAMIC LAW IN BLACK
        AFRICA, ALTHOUGH MANY CHANGES IN AFRICA SINCE BOOK
        WRITTEN. PRIMARILY DEALS WITH ENGLISH-SPEAKING
        AFRICA. GLOSSARY OF TECHNICAL ARABIC TERMS MOST USE-
        FUL. AUTHOR WAS CONSULTANT TO BRITISH GOVERNMENT ON
        ISLAMIC LAW IN AFRICA, AND TEACHES ISLAMIC LAW AT
        LONDON UNIVERSITY SCHOOL OF ORIENTAL AND AFRICAN
        STUDIES.

    KUPER HILDA   KUPER LEO   EDS
    AFRICAN LAW-- ADAPTATION AND DEVELOPMENT.
    BERKELEY UNIVERSITY OF CALIFORNIA PRESS 1965
    066,067,
        BEST SET OF ORIGINAL ARTICLES ON ALL ASPECTS OF LAW IN
        AFRICA. INCLUDES THEORETICAL INTRODUCTION REGARDING
        NATURE OF LAW-- ANALYSIS OF TRADITIONAL LEGAL SYSTEMS
        BY MAYER, FORDE, VANSINA, AND GLUCKMAN-- DISCUSSION OF
        ADAPTATION AND DIRECTED CHANGE BY ANDERSON, D ARBOUS-
        SIER, ELIAS, RUBIN AND ALLOTT. GOOD BIBLIOGRAPHY.

    ALLOTT ANTHONY
    ENGLISH LAW IN AFRICA PT 1.
    IN ESSAYS IN AFRICAN LAW, LONDON, BUTTERWORTHS, 1960
    066,
        REFERENCE

    ALLOTT ANTHONY

CUSTOMARY LAW AND ITS ADMINISTRATION PT 2.
IN ESSAYS IN AFRICAN LAW, LONDON, BUTTERWORTHS, 1960
066,
        REFERENCE

066

ALLOTT ANTHONY
THE CODIFICATION OF THE LAW OF CIVIL WRONGS IN COMMON-
LAW AFRICAN COUNTRIES.
SOCIOLOGUS NEW SERIES 16 1966 PP 101-121
066,
        REFERENCE

ALLOTT ANTHONY   READ J S
THE LEGAL STATUS OF WOMEN IN AFRICA-- IN PRACTICE,
PROCEDURE AND EVIDENCE IN THE NATIVE, AFRICAN, LOCAL
OR CUSTOMARY COURTS.
JOURNAL OF AFRICAN LAW 5 AUTUMN 1961 PP 125-138
066,
        REFERENCE

ANDERSON J N D
RELATIONSHIP BETWEEN ISLAMIC AND CUSTOMARY LAW IN AFRICA.
JOURNAL OF AFRICAN ADMINISTRATION 12 OCTOBER 1960
PP 228-234
066,
        REFERENCE

ANDERSON J N D
MUSLIM PROCEDURE AND EVIDENCE.
JOURNAL OF AFRICAN ADMINISTRATION 1 JULY 1949 PP 123-129
066,
        REFERENCE

ANDERSON J N D
HOMICIDE IN ISLAMIC LAW.
LONDON UNIVERSITY, BULLITIN OF THE SCHOOL OF ORIENTAL AND
AFRICAN STUDIES 13 1951 PP 811-828
066,
        REFERENCE

DANIELS W C EKOW
THE INFLUENCE OF EQUITY IN WEST AFRICAN LAW.
INTERNATIONAL AND COMPARATIVE LAW QUARTERLY 2 1962 PP 31-58
066,
        REFERENCE

ELIAS T O
THE FORM AND CONTENT OF COLONIAL LAW.
INTERNATIONAL AND COMPARATIVE LAW QUARTERLY 3 1954
PP 645-651
066,
        REFERENCE

ELIAS T O
THE NATURE OF AFRICAN CUSTOMARY LAW.
MANCHESTER MANCHESTER UNIVERSITY PRESS 1956
066,
        REFERENCE

EPSTEIN ARNOLD L
JUDICIAL TECHNIQUES AND THE JUDICIAL PROCESS-- A STUDY IN
AFRICAN CUSTOMARY LAW.
MANCHESTER MANCHESTER UNIVERSITY PRESS 1954
066,139-06,
        REFERENCE

066

FALLERS LLOYD A
CUSTOMARY LAW IN THE NEW AFRICAN STATES.
LAW AND CONTEMPORARY PROBLEMS 27 1962 PP 605-616
066,
        REFERENCE

FRANCK THOMAS M
SOME THOUGHTS ON LEGAL STUDIES IN AFRICA.
AMERICAN BEHAVIORAL SCIENTIST 5 APRIL 1962 PP 18-19
066,100,
        REFERENCE

GLUCKMAN MAX   ED
IDEAS AND PROCEDURES IN AFRICAN CUSTOMARY LAW.
LONDON, OXFORD UNIVERSITY PRESS, 1969
066,
        REFERENCE

KHALIL SIDI   TRANS BY   RUXTON
MALIKI LAW
LONDON, LUZAC AND CO., 1916
021,066,
        REFERENCE

MEEK CHARLES K
LAND LAW AND CUSTOM IN THE COLONIES.
LONDON,OXFORD UNIVERSITY PRESS,1949
010,066,070,
        REFERENCE

NEKAM ALEXANDER
EXPERIENCES IN AFRICAN CUSTOMARY LAW.
THIRD MELVILLE J. HERSKOVITS MEMORIAL LECTURE, FEB., 1966,
13 PAGES
066,
        REFERENCE

PHILLIPS ARTHUR
SOME ASPECTS OF LEGAL DUALISM IN BRITISH COLONIAL
TERRITORIES.
CIVILISATIONS 3 SUMMER 1953 PP 189-197
066,
        REFERENCE

REINSTEIN MAX
LAW AND SOCIAL CHANGE IN AFRICA.
WASHINGTON UNIVERSITY LAW QUARTERLY 4 DECEMBER 1962
PP 443-453
066,
        REFERENCE

ROBERT A

A COMPARATIVE STUDY OF LEGISLATION AND CUSTOMARY LAW COURTS
IN THE FRENCH, BELGIAN AND PORTUGUESE TERRITORIES IN AFRICA
JOURNAL OF AFRICAN ADMINISTRATION 11 JULY 1959 PP 124-131
066,
        REFERENCE

066
  ROBERTS-WRAY K
  THE ADAPTATION OF IMPORTED LAW IN AFRICA.
  JOURNAL OF AFRICAN LAW 4 SUMMER 1960 PP 66-78
  066,
        REFERENCE

  SAWYERR G F A   ED
  EAST AFRICAN LAW AND SOCIAL CHANGE.
  NAIROBI, EAST AFRICAN PUBLISHING HOUSE, 1967
  MIMEO FORM OF SEMINAR ON LAW AND SOCIAL CHANGE IN EAST
  AFRICA, APRIL 1966
  066,
        REFERENCE

  SCHILLER A ARTHUR
  LAW CHAPTER 6.
  IN ROBERT A LYSTAD (ED), THE AFRICAN WORLD, NEW YORK,
  PRAEGER, 1966, PP 166-198
  066,
        REFERENCE

  SEIDMAN ROBERT B
  A SOURCEBOOK OF THE CRIMINAL LAW OF AFRICA.
  LONDON, SWEET AND MAXWELL, 1966
  066,
        REFERENCE

  TWINING WILLIAM
  THE RESTATEMENT OF AFRICAN CUSTOMARY LAW-- A COMMENT.
  JOURNAL OF MODERN AFRICAN STUDIES 1 JUNE 1963 PP 221-228
  066,
        REFERENCE

  VERHELST THIERRY
  SAFEGUARDING AFRICAN CUSTOMARY LAW--JUDICIAL AND LEGISLATIVE
  PROCESSES FOR ITS ADAPTATION AND INTEGRATION.
  AFRICA, OCCASIONAL PAPER NO. 7, 1968, 32 PAGES
  066,
        REFERENCE

  ZAKE S JOSHUA L
  REVISION AND UNIFICATION OF AFRICAN LEGAL SYSTEMS--THE
  UGANDA EXPERIENCE.
  IN CARTER, GWENDOLEN M. AND ANN PADEN (EDS), EXPANDING
  HORIZONS IN AFRICAN STUDIES, EVANSTON, NORTHWESTERN
  UNIVERSITY PRESS, 1969, PP. 157-168
  066, 100, 139-06,
        REFERENCE

  BENTSI-ENCHILL K
  GHANA LAND LAW.
  LONDON, SWEET AND MAXWELL, 1964
  010, 066, 114-08,

CASE STUDY

066

BOHANNAN PAUL
JUSTICE AND JUDGMENT AMONG THE TIV.
LONDON, OXFORD UNIVERSITY PRESS, 1957
066,128-01,
    CASE STUDY

CORY HANS
SUKUMA LAW AND CUSTOM.
LONDON, OXFORD UNIVERSITY PRESS, 1953
066,136-01,
    CASE STUDY

COTRAN EUGENE
SOME RECENT DEVELOPMENTS IN THE TANGANYIKA JUDICIAL
SYSTEM.
JOURNAL OF AFRICAN LAW 6 SPRING PP 19-28
066,136-06,
    CASE STUDY

DANIELS W C EKOW
THE COMMON LAW IN WEST AFRICA.
LONDON, BUTTERWORTHS, 1964
066,
    CASE STUDY

DANQUAH JOSEPH B
GOLD COAST-- AKAN LAWS AND CUSTOMS AND THE AKIM ABUAKWA
CONSTITUTION.
LONDON, ROUTLEDGE, 1928
066,114-01,
    CASE STUDY

DERRETT DUNCAN J
STUDIES IN THE LAWS OF SUCCESSION IN NIGERIA.
LONDON, OXFORD UNIVERSITY PRESS, 1965
066,128-01,
    CASE STUDY

DUNCAN PATRICK
SOTHO LAWS AND CUSTOMS.
CAPE TOWN, OXFORD UNIVERSITY PRESS, 1960
066,118-01,
    CASE STUDY

ELIAS T O
THE IMPACT OF ENGLISH LAW ON NIGERIAN CUSTOMARY LAW.
LUGARD LECTURES, CMS, NIGERIA, 1958
066,128-03,
    CASE STUDY

ELIAS T O
THE NIGERIAN LEGAL SYSTEM.
LONDON, ROUTLEDGE AND KEGAN PAUL, 1963, 2ND REV. ED.
066,128-06,
    CASE STUDY

FALLERS LLOYD A

CHANGING CUSTOMARY LAW IN BUSOGA DISTRICT OF UGANDA.
JOUNRAL OF AFRICAN ADMINISTRATION 8 JULY 1956 PP 139-144
066,139-03,
        CASE STUDY

066
    FARRAN CHARLES
    MATRIMONIAL LAWS OF THE SUDAN.
    LONDON,BUTTERWORTHS,1963
    066,134-01,
        CASE STUDY

    GLUCKMAN MAX
    THE IDEAS OF BAROTSE JURISPRUDENCE.
    NEW HAVEN,YALE UNIVERSITY PRESS,1965
    066,142-01.
        CASE STUDY

    GLUCKMAN MAX
    THE JUDICIAL PROCESS AMONG THE BAROTSE OF NORTHERN RHODESIA.
    NEW YORK,FREE PRESS,1955
    066,142-01,
        CASE STUDY

    GLUCKMAN MAX   ED
    IDEAS AND PROCEEDURES IN AFRICAN CUSTOMARY LAW--STUDIES PRE-
    SENTED AND DISCUSSED AT THE EIGTH INTERNATIONAL AFRICAN SEM-
    INAR AT THE HAILE SELLASSIE I UNIVERSITY, ADDIS ABABA,
    JANUARY 1966.
    LONDON, OXFORD UNIVERSITY PRESS, 1969
    066,
        CASE STUDY

    HARVEY WILLIAM B
    THE EVOLUTION OF GHANA LAW SINCE INDEPENDENCE.
    LAW AND CONTEMPORARY PROBLEMS 27 1962 PP 581-604
    066,114-06,
        CASE STUDY

    HAYDON E S
    LAW AND JUSTICE IN BUGANDA.
    LONDON,BUTTERWORTHS,1960
    AFRICAN LAW SERIES NO. 2
    066,139-06,
        CASE STUDY

    HOLLEMAN J F
    SHONA CUSTOMARY LAW.
    NEW YORK, HUMANITIES PRESS INC., 1969
    066, 145-01,
        CASE STUDY

    HOWELL P P
    A MANUEL OF NUER LAW.
    LONDON,OXFORD UNIVERSITY PRESS,1954
    066,134-01,
        CASE STUDY

    KEAY ELLIOT A   RICHARDSON SAMUEL
    THE NATIVE AND CUSTOMARY COURTS OF NIGERIA.

LONDON, SWEET AND MAXWELL, 1966
066,128-03,
    CASE STUDY

066

   LLOYD PETER C
   SOME MODERN DEVELOPMENTS IN YORUBA CUSTOMARY LAW.
   JOURNAL OF AFRICAN ADMINISTRATION 12 JANUARY 1960 PP 11-20
   066,128-03,
       CASE STUDY

   LLOYD PETER C
   YORUBA LAND LAW.
   LONDON, OXFORD UNIVERSITY PRESS, 1962
   066,128-01,
       CASE STUDY

   MAINI KRISHAN M
   LAND LAW IN EAST AFRICA.
   EAST AFRICA, OXFORD UNIVERSITY PRESS, 1968
   066,
       CASE STUDY

   MOFFAT R L
   AFRICAN COURTS AND NATIVE CUSTOMARY LAW IN THE URBAN AREAS
   OF NORTHERN RHODESIA.
   JOURNAL OF AFRICAN ADMINISTRATION 9 APRIL 1957 PP 71-78
   066,142-03,
       CASE STUDY

   OLLENNU NII AMAA
   PRINCIPLES OF CUSTOMARY LAND LAW IN GHANA.
   LONDON, SWEET AND MAXWELL, 1962
   066,114-01,
       CASE STUDY

   PARK ANDREW E W
   THE SOURCES OF NIGERIAN LAW.
   LAGOS, AFRICAN UNIVERSITIES PRESS, 1963
   066,128-06,
       CASE STUDY

   PAULOS TSADUA ABBA
   FETHA NEGAST--THE LAW OF THE KINGS.
   ADDIS ABABA, INTERNATIONAL UNIVERSITY BOOKSELLERS,INC., 1968
   066,110-01,
       CASE STUDY

   RATTRAY ROBERT S
   ASHANTI LAW AND CONSTITUTION.
   OXFORD, CLARENDON PRESS, 1929
   026,066,099,114-01,
       CASE STUDY

   SARBAH JOHN MENSAH
   FANTI NATIONAL CONSTITUTION.
   NEW YORK, HUMANITIES PRESS INC., 1968
   066,114-01,
       CASE STUDY

SARBAH JOHN MENSAH
FANTI CUSTOMARY LAWS.
NEW YORK, HUMANITIES PRESS INC., 1968
066,114-01,
     CASE STUDY

066

SNELL G S
NANDI CUSTOMARY LAW.
LONDON, MACMILLAN, 1954
066,
     CASE STUDY

AFRIKA-INSTITUUT
THE FUTURE OF CUSTOMARY LAW IN AFRICA.
LEIDEN, UNIVERSITAIRE PERS LEIDEN, 1956
066,
     LESS ACCESSIBLE

BERCHER L
LA RISALA PAR IBIN ABI ZAYD AL QAYRAWANI-- TEXTE ET
TRADUCTION (THE RISALA BY IBIN ABI ZAYD AL QAYRAWANI--
TEXT AND TRANSLATION).
ALGIERS, 1945
066,
     LESS ACCESSIBLE

GOVERNMENT OF FRANCE
COUTUMIERS JURIDIQUES DE L'AFRIQUE OCCIDENTALE FRANCAISE--
MAURITANIE, NIGER, COTE D'IVOIRE, DAHOMEY, GUINEE FRANCAISE
(FRENCH WEST AFRICAN JURIDIC CUSTOMS-- MAURITANIA, NIGER
IVORY COAST, DAHOMEY, FRENCH GUINEA) .
PARIS, LIBRAIRIE LAROSE, 1939, VOL3
066,109-01,115-01,116-01,124-01,127-01,
     LESS ACCESSIBLE

GOVERNMENT OF FRANCE
COUTUMIERS JURIDIQUE DE L'AFRIQUE OCCIDENTALE FRANCAISE--
SOUDAN (FRENCH WEST AFRICAN JURIDIC CUSTOMS-- SUDAN).
PARIS, LAROSE EDITEURS, 1939, VOL 2
066,123-01,
     LESS ACCESSIBLE

GOVERNMENT OF FRANCE
COUTUMIERS JURIDIQUES DE L'AFRIQUE OCCIDENTALE FRANCAISE--
SENEGAL (FRENCH WEST AFRICAN JURIDIC CUSTOMS-- SENEGAL).
PARIS, LIBRAIRIE LAROSE, 1939, VOL1
066,130-01,
     LESS ACCESSIBLE

ANDERSON J N D
ISLAMIC LAW IN THE MODERN WORLD.
NEW YORK, NEW YORK UNIVERSITY PRESS, 1959
066,
     GENERAL THEORY

COULSON NOEL J
THE CONCEPT OF PROGRESS AND ISLAMIC LAW.
IN ROBERT BALLAH, RELIGION AND PROGRESS IN MODERN ASIA,
NEW YORK, FREE PRESS, 1965, PP 74-92

066,
      GENERAL THEORY

066
   FARUKI KEMAL A
   ISLAMIC JURISPRUDENCE.
   KARACHI 1962
   066,
      GENERAL THEORY

   FYZEE A A A
   OUTLINES OF MUHAMMADAN LAW.
   LONDON, OXFORD UNIVERSITY PRESS, 1955
   066,
      GENERAL THEORY

   HANNIGAN A ST A
   THE IMPOSITION OF WESTERN LAW FORMS UPON PRIMITIVE
   SOCIETIES.
   COMPARATIVE STUDIES IN SOCIETY AND HISTORY 4 NOVEMBER 1961
   PP 1-9
   066,
      GENERAL THEORY

   KHADDURI MAJID
   NATURE AND SOURCES OF LAW PP 9-18.
   IN THE LAW OF WAR AND PEACE IN ISLAM, BALTIMORE, JOHNS
   HOPKINS PRESS, 1955
   066,
      GENERAL THEORY

   SCHACHT JOSEPH
   ISLAMIC LAW IN CONTEMPORARY STATES.
   AMERICAN JOURNAL OF COMPARATIVE LAW 8 1959 PP 133-147
   066,
      GENERAL THEORY

   SCHACHT JOSEPH
   INTRODUCTION TO ISLAMIC LAW.
   OXFORD, CLARENDON PRESS, 1964
   066,
      GENERAL THEORY

   FALLERS LLOYD A
   LAW WITHOUT PRECEDENT--LEGAL IDEAS IN ACTION IN THE COURTS
   OF COLONIAL BUSOGA.
   CHICAGO AND LONDON, THE UNIVERSITY OF CHICAGO PRESS, 1969
   066,139-06,
      CASE STUDY

   HOEBEL E ADAMSON
   THREE STUDIES OF AFRICAN LAW.
   STANFORD LAW REVIEW 8 1961 PP 418-442
   066,
      CASE STUDY

   REDDEN KENNETH R
   THE LEGAL SYSTEM OF ETHIOPIA.
   CHARLOTTESVILLE, VIRGINIA. THE MICHIE COMPANY, 1968
   066,110-06,

CASE STUDY

066

SALACUSE JESWALD W
AN INTRODUCTION TO LAW IN FRENCH-SPEAKING AFRICA--VOL I--
AFRICA SOUTH OF THE SAHARA.
CHARLOTTESVILLE, VIRGINIA, THE MICHE CO., 1969
066,
        CASE STUDY

WEBSTER JOHN B
THE CONSTITUTIONS OF BURUNDI MALAGASY AND RWANDA.
SYRACUSE NEW YORK MAXWELL GRADUATE SCHOOL OF PUBLIC AFFAIRS
THE PROGRAM OF EASTERN STUDIES, NO. 3, FEB., 1964
066,103-07,121-07,129-07,

67. THE INTEGRATION OF LEGAL SYSTEMS

067

KUPER HILDA   KUPER LEO   EDS
AFRICAN LAW-- ADAPTATION AND DEVELOPMENT.
BERKELEY, UNIVERSITY OF CALIFORNIA PRESS, 1965
066,067,
        BEST SET OF ORIGINAL ARTICLES ON ALL ASPECTS OF LAW IN
        AFRICA. INCLUDES THEORETICAL INTRODUCTION REGARDING
        NATURE OF LAW-- ANALYSIS OF TRADITIONAL LEGAL SYSTEMS
        BY MAYER, FORDE, VANSINA, AND GLUCKMAN-- DISCUSSION OF
        ADAPTATION AND DIRECTED CHANGE BY ANDERSON, D ARBOUS-
        SIER, ELIAS, RUBIN, AND ALLOTT. GOOD BIBLIOGRAPHY.

RHEINSTEIN MAX
PROBLEMS OF LAW IN THE NEW NATIONS OF AFRICA.
IN CLIFFORD GEERTZ (ED), OLD SOCIETIES AND NEW NATIONS, NEW
YORK, THE FREE PRESS 1963 PP 220-46
067,
        AUTHOR DEALS WITH NATURE OF LAW, LEGAL PROBLEMS OF
        PLURALISM, THE EFFECT OF LEGAL REFORM ON CUSTOMARY
        LAW, THE DEVELOPMENT OF MODERN LEGAL SYSTEMS, ADMINI-
        STRATION OF JUSTICE AND RULE OF LAW. DRAWS EXAMPLES
        FROM ALL PARTS OF AFRICA.

SAWYERR G F A   ED
EAST AFRICAN LAW AND SOCIAL CUSTOM.
KENYA, EAST AFRICAN PUBLISHING HOUSE, 1967
067,
        ESSAYS ON POSITION OF CUSTOMARY CRIMINAL LAW IN AFRICAN
        COUNTRIES, THE COURT IN THE TANZANIA ONE-PARTY STATE,
        THE INDUSTRIAL COURT AND LABOR RELATIONS, THE LAW OF
        INVESTMENT GUARENTEES, INTERNAL CONFLICT OF LAWS IN
        EAST AFRICA, CONTROL OF LAND AND LAW IN KENYA AND TAN-
        ZANIA, SOCIAL JUSTICE AND THE LAW, AND THE METHODOLOGY
        OF LAW REFORM. AVAILABLE IN PAPERBACK.

ALLOTT ANTHONY
THE CHANGING LAW IN A CHANGING AFRICA.

SOCIOLOGUS 11 1961 PP 115-131
067,
        REFERENCE

067
ALLOTT ANTHONY
THE UNITY OF AFRICAN LAW.
JOURNAL OF AFRICAN ADMINISTRATION 11 APRIL 1959 PP 72-83
067,
        REFERENCE

ALLOTT ANTHONY
THE PLACE OF AFRICAN CUSTOMARY LAW IN MODERN AFRICAN LEGAL
SYSTEMS.
IN LALAGE BOWN AND MICHAEL CROWDER (EDS.), PROCEEDINGS OF
THE FIRST INTERNATIONAL CONGRESS OF AFRICANISTS, ACCRA,
1962, LONDON, LONGMANS, 1964, PP 190-196
067,
        REFERENCE

ALLOTT ANTHONY   ED
THE FUTURE OF LAW IN AFRICA.
LONDON, BUTTERWORTH, 1960
067,
        REFERENCE

ANDERSON J N D
COLONIAL LAW IN TROPICAL AFRICA-- THE CONFLICT BETWEEN
ENGLISH, ISLAMIC AND CUSTOMARY LAW.
INDIANA LAW JOURNAL 35 1960 PP 433-442
067,
        REFERENCE

DE SMITH S A
INTEGRATION OF LEGAL SYSTEMS.
IN COLIN LEYS AND P ROBSON (EDS), FEDERATION IN EAST AFRICA--
OPPORTUNITIES AND PROBLEMS NAIROBI OXFORD UNIVERSITY PRESS
1965 PP 158-171
067,
        REFERENCE

GHAI YASH
SOME LEGAL ASPECTS OF AN EAST AFRICAN FEDERATION.
IN COLIN LEYS AND P ROBSON (EDS), FEDERATION IN EAST AFRICA--
OPPORTUNITIES AND PROBLEMS, NAIROBI, OXFORD UNIVERSITY PRESS,
1965, PP 172-182
067,
        REFERENCE

GOWER L C B
INDEPENDENT AFRICA--THE CHALLENGE TO THE LEGAL PROFESSION.
CAMBRIDGE, HARVARD UNIVERSITY PRESS, 1968
067,
        REFERENCE

HARVEY WILLIAM B
LAW AND SOCIAL CHANGE IN GHANA.
PRINCETON, PRINCETON UNIVERSITY PRESS, 1966
067,114-03,
        REFERENCE

067

HUTCHINSON T W   ET AL   EDS
AFRICA AND LAW-- DEVELOPING LEGAL SYSTEMS IN AFRICAN
COMMONWEALTH NATIONS.
MADISON, UNIVERSITY OF WISCONSIN PRESS, 1968
067,
        REFERENCE

MILNER ALAN   ED
AFRICAN LAW REPORTS, 2 VOLS, COMMERCIAL LAW SERIES 1966.
DOBBS FERRY, NEW YORK, INTERNATIONAL UNIVERSITY BOOKSELLERS,
INC., 1969
067,
        REFERENCE

PEASLEE AMOS
CONSTITUTIONS OF NATIONS, VOLUME I, AFRICA.
THE HAGUE, MARTINUS NIJHOFF 1965
067,068,
        REFERENCE

RUBIN NEVILLE   COTRAN EUGENE   EDS
READINGS IN AFRICAN LAW--VOLS 1 AND 2.
NEW YORK, INTERNATIONAL UNIVERSITY BOOKSELLERS,INC., 1970
067,
        REFERENCE

RUBIN NEVILLE   COTRAN EUGENE   EDS
AN ANNUAL SURVEY OF AFRICAN LAW, VOL 1.
NEW YORK, INTERNATIONAL UNIVERSITY BOOKSELLERS,INC., 1970
067,
        REFERENCE

SALACUSE JESWALD W
DEVELOPMENTS IN AFRICAN LAW.
AFRICAN REPORT, MARCH, 1968, P. 39
067,
        REFERENCE

SALACUSE JESWALD W
EXPLORING AFRICAN LAW.
AFRICA REPORT, MAY/JUNE, 1969, PP. 60-61
067,
        REFERENCE

ANDERSON J N D
RETURN TO NIGERIA-- JUDICIAL AND LEGAL DEVELOPMENTS IN THE
NORTHERN REGION.
INTERNATIONAL AND COMPARATIVE LAW QUARTERLY JANUARY 1963
PP 282-294
067,128-06,
        CASE STUDY

COTRAN EUGENE
THE UNIFICATION OF LAWS IN EAST AFRICA.
JOURNAL OF MODERN AFRICAN STUDIES 1 JUNE 1963 PP 209-220
067,
        CASE STUDY

FARNSWORTH E A
LAW REFORM IN A DEVELOPING COUNTRY-- A NEW CODE OF
OBLIGATIONS FOR SENEGAL.
JOURNAL OF AFRICAN LAW 8 SPRING 1964 PP 6-19
067,
        CASE STUDY

067
   LOWENSTEIN STEVEN
   MATERIALS FOR THE STUDY OF THE PENAL LAW OF ETHIOPIA.
   EASTERN AFRICA, OXFORD UNIVERSITY PRESS, 1965
   067,110-06,
        CASE STUDY

   YOUNG ROLAND A   FOSBROOKE H
   SMOKE IN THE HILLS-- POLITICAL TENSION IN THE MOROGORO
   DISTRICT OF TANGANYIKA.
   EVANSTON,ILLINOIS,NORTHWESTERN UNIVERSITY PRESS, 1960
   (LAND AND POLITICS AMONG THE LUGURU OF TANGANYIKA,LONDON,
   ROUTLEDGE AND KEGAN PAUL, 1960)
   067,136-03,
        CASE STUDY

   BAADE HANS W   ED
   AFRICAN LAW-- NEW LAW FOR NEW NATIONS.
   DOBBS FERRY, NEW YORK, OCEANA PUBLICATIONS, 1963
   067,
        LESS ACCESSIBLE

   ZIVS S L
   PROBLEMS OF THE ESTABLISHMENT OF NATIONAL LEGAL SYSTEMS IN
   AFRICAN COUNTRIES.
   II INTERNATIONAL CONGRESS OF AFRICANISTS, PAPERS PRESENTED
   BY THE USSR DELEGATION, DAKAR, 10 PAGES
   067,
        LESS ACCESSIBLE

68. THE DEVELOPMENT OF CONSTITUTIONAL LAW

068
   LAVROFF D G   PEISER G
   LES CONSTITUTIONS AFRICAINES (AFRICAN CONSTITUTIONS), VOL-
   UME ONE.
   PARIS, A PEDONE, 1961
   068,
        PROVIDES TEXTS AND COMMENTARIES ON CONSTITUTIONS AND
        CONSTITUTIONAL DEVELOPMENT OF ALL FRENCH-SPEAKING
        STATES IN AFRICA. ASSESSES THEMATIC SIMILARITIES AND
        DIFFERENCES ON MATTERS OF EXECUTIVE, LEGISLATIVE AND
        JUDICIAL POWERS AND STRUCTURES.

   BENTSI-ENCHILL K
   PROBLEMS IN THE CONSTRUCTION OF VIABLE CONSTITUTIONAL
   STRUCTURES IN AFRICA.
   IN CARTER, GWENDOLEN M. AND ANN PADEN (EDS), EXPANDING

HORIZONS IN AFRICAN STUDIES, EVANSTON, NORTHWESTERN
UNIVERSITY PRESS, 1969, PP. 173-180
068,100,
     REFERENCE

068

BLONDEL J
CONSTITUTIONAL CHANGES IN FORMER FRENCH BLACK AFRICA.
PARLIAMENTARY AFFAIRS 14 1961 PP 507-517
068,
     REFERENCE

BURNS ALAN C
PARLIAMENT AS AN EXPORT.
LONDON, ALLEN AND UNWIN 1966
068,
     REFERENCE

INTERNATIONAL COMMISSION OF JURISTS
AFRICAN CONFERENCE ON THE RULE OF LAW.
LAGOS,NIGERIA,1961,INTERNATIONAL COMMISSION OF JURISTS.
068,
     REFERENCE

PEASLEE AMOS
CONSTITUTIONS OF NATIONS, VOLUME I, AFRICA.
THE HAGUE, MARTINUS NIJHOFF 1965
067,068,
     REFERENCE

ROBINSON KENNETH
CONSTITUTIONAL REFORM IN FRENCH TROPICAL AFRICA.
POLITICAL STUDIES 6 FEBRUARY 1958
068,
     REFERENCE

SPIRO HERBERT J
NEW CONSTITUTIONAL FORMS IN AFRICA.
WORLD POLITICS 8 1 OCTOBER 1960 PP 69 FF
068,
     REFERENCE

ALEXANDER A S JR
THE IVORY COAST CONSTITUTION--AN ACCELERATOR, NOT A BRAKE.
THE JOURNAL OF MODERN AFRICAN STUDIES, VOL. I, NO. 3, SEPT.
1963, PP. 293-312
068,116-06,
     CASE STUDY

AWOLOWO OBAFEMI
THE PEOPLES REPUBLIC.
NIGERIA, OXFORD UNIVERSITY PRESS, 1969
068,128-04,
     CASE STUDY

AWOLOWO OBAFEMI
THOUGHTS ON NIGERIAN CONSTITUTION.
NIGERIA, OXFORD UNIVERSITY PRESS,1966
054,068,128-04,
     CASE STUDY

068

    EZERA KALU
    CONSTITUTIONAL DEVELOPMENTS IN NIGERIA.
    CAMBRIDGE, CAMBRIDGE UNIVERSITY PRESS, 1964
    068,128-07,
           CASE STUDY

    HAZARD JOHN N
    MALI'S SOCIALISM AND THE SOVIET LEGAL MODEL.
    YALE LAW JOURNAL, LXXVII, 1967, PP. 28-69
    068,123-06,
           CASE STUDY

    RUBIN LESLIE   MURRAY PAULA
    THE CONSTITUTION AND GOVERNMENT OF GHANA.
    LONDON, SWEET AND MAXWELL, 1961
    068,114-07,
           CASE STUDY

    BAYLEY DAVID H
    PUBLIC LIBERTIES IN THE NEW STATES.
    CHICAGO, RAND MCNALLY AND COMPANY, 1964
    068,
           GENERAL THEORY

    FRANCK THOMAS M
    COMPARATIVE CONSTITUTIONAL PROCESS--CASES AND MATERIALS--
    FUNDAMENTAL RIGHTS IN THE COMMON LAW NATIONS.
    NEW YORK, PRAEGER PUBLISHING COMPANY, 1968
    068,
           GENERAL THEORY

    FRIEDRICH CARL J
    SOME REFLECTIONS ON CONSTITUTIONALISM FOR EMERGENT POLITICAL
    ORDERS.
    IN HERBERT J SPIRO (ED) PATTERNS OF AFRICAN DEVELOPMENT,
    ENGLEWOOD CLIFFS, NJ, PRENTICE-HALL, 1967, PP 9-34
    068,
           GENERAL THEORY

69. AN ASSESSMENT OF RESOURCES

069

    ADY P H
    REGIONAL ECONOMIC ATLAS OF AFRICA.
    OXFORD, CLARENDON PRESS, 1965
    069,
           BEST AVAILABLE ATLAS ON AFRICA. OVER 50 PAGES OF
           STATISTICAL DATA ON POPULATION, AGRICULTURE, INDUSTRY,
           TRANSPORT. 22 MAPS OF VARIOUS REGIONS FOLLOWED BY 35
           TOPICAL MAPS (SOILS, RAINFALL, CROPS, MINERALS, INDUS-
           TRIES, TRANSPORTATION, POPULATION, LANGUAGES, CONSER-
           VATION, DISEASES).

FORDHAM PAUL
THE GEOGRAPHY OF AFRICAN AFFAIRS
BALTIMORE, PENGUIN, 1965
069,

      HANDY AND READABLE PAPERBACK PROVIDING GOOD
      INTRODUCTION TO AFRICAN GEOGRAPHY.NEARLY HALF DEVOTED
      TO GENERAL SURVEY(ENVIRONMENT,PEOPLES,HISTORY
      RESOURCES),REMAINDER REGIONAL STUDIES OF WEST,CENTRAL,
      EAST AND SOUTH AFRICA.

069

  GROVE A T
  AFRICA SOUTH OF THE SAHARA
  LONDON, OXFORD UNIVERSITY PRESS, 1967
  017,069,

      A GOOD STANDARD GEOGRAPHY TEXT,STRONGER ON PHYSICAL
      GEOGRAPHY THAN HANCE. MANY AND GOOD MAPS IN TEXT
      SUPPLEMENTED BY 16 COLORED MAPS FROM OXFORD REGIONAL
      ECONOMIC ATLAS OF AFRICA.

  HANCE WILLIAM A
  AFRICAN ECONOMIC DEVELOPMENT.
  NEW YORK, PRAEGER, 1967 (REVISED EDITION)
  048,069,072,

      EXCELLENT SURVEY WITH DETAILED CASE STUDIES OF THE
      GEZIRA SCHEME, THE VOLTA RIVER PROJECT, TRANSPORT,
      ECONOMIC INTEGRATION IN EAST AFRICA, LIBERIA, MADA-
      GASCAR AND OTHERS. FINAL CHAPTER EXAMINES DEVELOPMENT
      POTENTIALS BY COUNTRY WITH A GOOD SUMMARY TABLE.

  HANCE WILLIAM A
  THE GEOGRAPHY OF MODERN AFRICA.
  NEW YORK, COLUMBIA UNIVERSITY PRESS, 1964
  069,

      BASIC INTRODUCTORY TEXT ON AFRICAN ECONOMIC GEOGRAPHY.
      GOOD INTRODUCTORY THEMATIC CHAPTERS FOLLOWED BY
      REGIONAL COVERAGE OF ENTIRE CONTINENT. FACTUALLY
      STRONG AND UP TO DATE, EXCELLENT MAPS AND STATISTICS.
      HANCE IS PROFESSOR OF GEOGRAPHY AT COLUMBIA UNIVER-
      SITY AND PRESIDENT OF THE AFRICAN STUDIES ASSOCIATION
      IN 1968.

  AMANN HANS
  ENERGY SUPPLY AND ECONOMIC DEVELOPMENT IN EAST AFRICA.
  NEW YORK, HUMANITIES PRESS INC., 1969
  069,
      REFERENCE

  BAKER S J K
  THE EAST AFRICAN ENVIRONMENT.
  HISTORY OF EAST AFRICA 1 CHAPTER 1 1963 PP 1-22
  069,
      REFERENCE

  BROKENSHA DAVID   ED
  ECOLOGY AND ECONOMIC DEVELOPMENT IN TROPICAL AFRICA.
  BERKELEY UNIVERSITY OF CALIFORNIA PRESS 1965
  RESEARCH SERIES NO. 9 INSTITUTE OF INTERNATIONAL STUDIES
  069,070,
      REFERENCE

069

BROWN R
HEALTH AND DISEASE IN AFRICA.
TRANSITION 6 26 1966 PP 28-33
069,075,
  REFERENCE

CHURCH R J HARRISON
WEST AFRICA A STUDY OF THE ENVIRONMENT AND OF MAN'S USE
OF IT.
LONDON, LONGMANS, GREEN, 1960 AND 1966
069,
  REFERENCE

CHURCH R J HARRISON ET AL
AFRICA AND THE ISLANDS.
NEW YORK, WILEY, 1964
069,
  REFERENCE

CHURCH R J HARRISON
ENVIRONMENT AND POLICIES IN WEST AFRICA
PRINCETON, VAN NOSTRAND, 1963
069,
  REFERENCE

CLOUDSLEY THOMPSON
TSETSE-- THE SCOURGE OF AFRICA.
LONDON, SCIENCE NEWS, PENGUIN BOOKS, 1959, PP 69-78
069,075,
  REFERENCE

COLE MONICA
SOUTH AFRICA.
LONDON, METHUEN, 1966 (REVISED EDITION)
069,132-08,
  REFERENCE

DE BLIJ HARM J
A GEOGRAPHY OF SUB-SAHARAN AFRICA
CHICAGO, RAND-MCNALLY, 1964
069,
  REFERENCE

DE KUN NICHOLAS A
THE MINERAL RESOURCES OF AFRICA.
NEW YORK, AMERICAN ELSEVIER PUBLISHING CO, 1965
069,
  REFERENCE

DESHLER W
CATTLE IN AFRICA DISTRIBUTION TYPES AND PROBLEMS.
THE GEOGRAPHICAL REVIEW AMERICAN GEOGRAPHICAL SOCIETY 53
JANUARY 1963 PP 52-58
010,069,070,
  REFERENCE

ELKAN WALTER
AN AFRICAN LABOUR FORCE CHAPTER 7.

IN EDITH WHETHAM AND JEAN CURRIE, (EDS.) READINGS IN THE
APPLIED ECONOMICS OF AFRICA, LONDON, CAMBRIDGE UNIVERSITY
PRESS, 1, 1967, PP 67-71
069,
        REFERENCE

069
    FOURNIER F
    THE SOILS OF AFRICA.
    PARIS, UNESCO, 1963, PP 221-248
    069,
        REFERENCE

    FULLARD HAROLD   ED
    MODERN COLLEGE ATLAS FOR AFRICA
    LONDON, PHILIP AND SON, 1961
    069,
        REFERENCE

    FURON R
    GEOLOGY OF AFRICA TRANSLATED BY A HALLAN AND L A STEVENS
    NEW YORK, HAFNER, 1963
    017,069,
        REFERENCE

    GOUROU PIERRE   BEAVER S H   LABORDE E D
    THE TROPICAL WORLD-- ITS SOCIAL AND ECONOMIC CONDITIONS AND
    ITS FUTURE STATUS.
    LONDON, LONGMANS, 4TH EDITION, 1966
    069,075,
        REFERENCE

    HAMILTON F E IAN
    REGIONAL ECONOMIC ANALYSIS IN BRITAIN AND THE COMMONWEALTH-
    A BIBLIOGRAPHIC GUIDE
    NEW YORK, SCHOCKEN BOOKS, 1970
    048,069,072,
        REFERENCE

    HANCE WILLIAM A   KOTSCHAP V   PETEREC RICHARD J
    SOURCE AREAS OF EXPORT PRODUCTION IN TROPICAL AFRICA.
    GEOGRAPHIC REVIEW 51 OCTOBER 1961 PP 487-499
    069,
        REFERENCE

    HODDER B W   HARRIS D R   EDS
    AFRICA IN TRANSITION-GEOGRAPHICAL ESSAYS
    LONDON, METHUEN, 1967
    069,076,
        REFERENCE

    HOYLE B S
    NEW OIL REFINERY CONSTRUCTION IN AFRICA.
    GEOGRAPHY, JOURNAL OF THE GEOGRAPHICAL ASSOCIATION 48
    APRIL 1963 PP 190-194
    069,
        REFERENCE

    KAMARCK ANDREW M
    THE ECONOMICS OF AFRICAN DEVELOPMENT.

NEW YORK, PRAEGER, 1967
069,070,071,073,
        REFERENCE

069

KENWORTHY JOAN M
RAINFALL AND WATER RESOURCES OF EAST AFRICA.
LONDON, GEOGRAPHERS AND THE TROPICS, 1964, PP 111-136
069,
        REFERENCE

KIMBLE GEORGE
TROPICAL AFRICA.
NEW YORK, TWENTIETH CENTURY FUND, 1960, TWO VOLUMES (CONDENSED
VERSION, NEW YORK, DOUBLEDAY ANCHOR, 1962)
069,
        REFERENCE

LEBEUF JEAN PAUL
RECENT RESEARCH ON MIGRATION IN WEST AFRICA.
MIGRATION NEWS 7 1958 PP 13-17
069,
        REFERENCE

LORIMER FRANK   BRASS WILLIAM   VAN DE WALLE E
DEMOGRAPHY.
IN ROBERT A LYSTAD (ED), THE AFRICAN WORLD, NEW YORK,
PRAEGER, 1966, PP 271-303
069,074,
        REFERENCE

LORIMER FRANK   KARP MARK   EDS
POPULATION IN AFRICA.
BOSTON, BOSTON UNIVERSITY PRESS, 1960
069,074,
        REFERENCE

MIRACLE MARVIN P
MAIZE IN TROPICAL AFRICA.
MADISON, UNIVERSITY OF WISCONSIN PRESS, 1966
069,
        REFERENCE

MURDOCK GEORGE P
STAPLE SUBSISTENCE CROPS OF AFRICA.
THE GEOGRAPHICAL REVIEW, AMERICAN GEOGRAPHICAL SOCIETY, 50
NO 3 OCTOBER 1960 PP 523-540
010,069,
        REFERENCE

O CONNOR A M
AN ECONOMIC GEOGRAPHY OF EAST AFRICA.
NEW YORK, PRAEGER, 1966
069,
        REFERENCE

PELLETIER R A
MINERAL RESOURCES OF SOUTH-CENTRAL AFRICA.
NEW YORK, OXFORD UNIVERSITY PRESS, 1965
069,

REFERENCE

069

PHILLIPS J F
AGRICULTURE AND ECOLOGY IN AFRICA ACTUAL AND POTENTIAL
DEVELOPMENT SOUTH OF THE SAHARA.
LONDON, FABER AND FABER, 1959
069,
        REFERENCE

PROTHERO R MANSELL
MIGRANTS AND MALARIA.
LONDON, LONGMANS, 1965
069,075,
        REFERENCE

PROTHERO R MANSELL
POPULATION MOVEMENT AND PROBLEMS OF MALARIA ERADICATION IN
AFRICA.
WORLD HEALTH ORGANIZATION BULLETIN 24 1961 PP 405-425
069,075,
        REFERENCE

PROTHERO R MANSELL   ED
A GEOGRAPHY OF AFRICA--REGIONAL ESSAYS ON FUNDAMENTAL
CHARACTERISTICS, ISSUES AND PROBLEMS.
NEW YORK, PRAEGER, 1969
069,
        REFERENCE

READER D H
A SURVEY OF CATEGORIES OF ECONOMIC ACTIVITIES AMONG THE
PEOPLES OF AFRICA.
AFRICA LONDON 34 1964 PP 28-45
010,069,
        REFERENCE

ROBINSON M E
THE FOOD POTENTIAL OF AFRICA.
CHICAGO, FOOD AND CONTAINER INSTITUTE OF THE ARMED FORCES
12 1960
069,075,
        REFERENCE

RODIER J
HYDROLOGY IN AFRICA.
NEW YORK, UNESCO, 1953
069,075,
        REFERENCE

RODIER J
THE BIBLIOGRAPHY OF AFRICAN HYDROLOGY.
PARIS, UNESCO, 1963
069,075,
        REFERENCE

RUSSELL G H   ED
THE NATURAL RESOURCES OF EAST AFRICA.
NAIROBI, D A HAWKINS LTD, 1962
069,

REFERENCE

069

SCHLIPPE P
SHIFTING CULTIVATION IN AFRICA.
LONDON, ROUTLEDGE AND KEGAN PAUL, 1956
069,134-03,
       REFERENCE

SHANTZ H L
AGRICULTURAL REGIONS OF AFRICA.
ECONOMIC GEOGRAPHY 16 1940 PP 1-47 AND 341-389, 17 1941 PP
217-249, 18 1942 PP 229-246, 19 1943 PP 77-109
069,
       REFERENCE

SOMMER JOHN W
BIBLIOGRAPHY OF AFRICAN GEOGRAPHY 1940-1964
HANOVER, GEOGRAPHY PUBLICATIONS AT DARTMOUTH NUMBER 3, 1965
069,
       REFERENCE

STAMP L D
AFRICA A STUDY IN TROPICAL DEVELOPMENT.
NEW YORK, JOHN WILEY AND SONS, 1953
069,
       REFERENCE

STEEL R W
LAND AND POPULATION IN BRITISH TROPICAL AFRICA.
GEOGRAPHY, JOURNAL OF THE GEOGRAPHICAL ASSOCIATION
SHEFFIELD 40 1955 PP 1-17
069,
       REFERENCE

STEWART I G   ORD H W   EDS
AFRICAN PRIMARY PRODUCTS AND INTERNATIONAL TRADE.
EDINBURGH, UNIVERSITY PRESS 1965
069,073,
       REFERENCE

THOMPSON B W
CLIMATE OF AFRICA.
OXFORD, OXFORD UNIVERSITY PRESS, 1965
069,
       REFERENCE

UNESCO
A REVIEW OF THE NATURAL RESOURCES OF THE AFRICAN CONTINENT.
NEW YORK, COLUMBIA   UNIVERSITY PRESS, 1969
069,
     REFERENCE

BAKER S J K
THE POPULATION GEOGRAPHY OF EAST AFRICA.
EAST AFRICAN GEOGRAPHICAL REVIEW, KAMPALA, APRIL 1963 PP 1-6
069,
       CASE STUDY

CLARKE J I

OIL IN LIBYA--SOME IMPLICATIONS.
ECONOMIC GEOGRAPHY 39 JANUARY 1963 PP 40-59
069,
        CASE STUDY

069

DESHLER W
LIVESTOCK TRYPANOSOMIASIS AND HUMAN SETTLEMENT IN
NORTHEASTERN UGANDA.
GEOGRAPHICAL REVIEW 50 OCTOBER 1960 PP 541-554
069,
        CASE STUDY

GROVE A T
POPULATION DENSITIES AND AGRICULTURE IN NORTHERN NIGERIA.
AFRICAN POPULATION, NEW YORK, PRAEGER, 1962, PP 115-136
069,
        CASE STUDY

JONES WILLIAM O
MANIOC IN AFRICA.
STANFORD UNIVERSITY FOOD RESEARCH INSTITUTE NO 2 1951
069,
        CASE STUDY

PHILLIPS J F
ECOLOGICAL INVESTIGATION IN SOUTH CENTRAL AND EAST AFRICA
OUTLINE OF A PROGRESSIVE SCHEME.
CAMBRIDGE JOURNAL OF ECOLOGY 19 NO 2 1931 PP 471-483
069,
        CASE STUDY

TREWARTHA G T   ZELINSKY W
POPULATION PATTERNS IN TROPICAL AFRICA.
ANNALS OF THE ASSOCIATION OF AMERICAN GEOGRAPHERS WASHINGTON
VOL 44 JUNE 1954 PP 135-193
069,074,
        CASE STUDY

VAN DER LAAN H L
THE SIERRA LEONE DIAMONDS.
FREETOWN, UNIVERSITY OF SIERRA LEONE, 1965
069,131-08,
        CASE STUDY

BARBOUR K M   PROTHERO P MANSELL   EDS
ESSAYS ON AFRICAN POPULATION.
LONDON, ROUTLEDGE AND KEGAN PAUL, 1961
069,074,
        REFERENCE

INTER-AFRICAN LABOUR INSTITUTE
MIGRANT LABOUR IN AFRICA SOUTH OF THE SAHARA
NEW YORK INTERNATIONAL PUBLICATIONS SERVICE 1963
6TH INTER-AFRICAN LABOUR CONFERENCE ABIDJAN 1961
SCIENTIFIC COUNCIL FOR AFRICA SOUTH OF THE SAHARA NO. 79
069,
        REFERENCE

70. AGRICULTURAL REORGANIZATION

070

ALLAN WILLIAM H
THE AFRICAN HUSBANDMAN.
EDINBURGH, OLIVER AND BOYD, 1965
010,070,
> BEST WORK ON AGRICULTURE, ECOLOGY AND TECHNOLOGY. IS
> ESSENTIALLY A REFERENCE WORK RATHER THAN INTRODUCTION.
> CONCLUSION DEALS WITH RECENT DEVELOPMENTS IN AGRICUL-
> TURAL CHANGE.

DUMONT RENE
FALSE START IN AFRICA.
NEW YORK, PRAEGER PUBLISHERS, 1969
037,053,070,
> LEADING FRENCH AGRONOMIST, WITH SYMPATHY FOR AFRICAN
> INDEPENDENCE, MAKES CRITICAL AND CONTROVERSIAL ASSESS-
> MENT OF AFRICAN SOCIO-ECONOMIC DEVELOPMENT IN THE
> POST-COLONIAL PERIOD. EMPHASIZES THE NECESSITY FOR
> AGRICULTURAL REFORM TO PROVIDE CAPITAL BASIS FOR ECO-
> NOMIC TAKE-OFF INTO A FULLY INDUSTRIALIZED SOCIETY.

JONES WILLIAM O
INCREASING AGRICULTURAL PRODUCTIVITY IN TROPICAL AFRICA.
IN E F JOULSON (ED), ECONOMIC DEVELOPMENT IN AFRICA, OXFORD
BLACKWELL, 1965
070,
> A SURVEY ARTICLE ON AFRICAN AGRICULTURE AND THE PROB-
> LEMS OF INCREASING PRODUCTIVITY, BY A LEADING AMERICAN
> AUTHORITY ON AFRICAN AGRICULTURAL PROBLEMS. AUTHOR IS
> HEAD OF THE FOOD RESEARCH INSTITUTE AT STANFORD UNI-
> VERSITY.

MILLIKAN MAX F   HAPGOOD DAVID
NO EAST HARVEST-- THE DILEMMA OF AGRICULTURE IN UNDERDEVEL-
OPED COUNTRIES.
BOSTON, LITTLE, BROWN, 1967
070,
> BASED ON WORK OF A LARGE NUMBER OF DEVELOPMENT ECONO-
> MISTS AT M.I.T. NOT SPECIFICALLY FOCUSED ON AFRICA,
> BUT MANY OF PROBLEMS RELEVANT.

TANZANIA AFRICAN NATIONAL UNION
THE ARUSHA DECLARATION AND TANU'S POLICY ON SOCIALISM AND
SELF-RELIANCE.
DAR ES-SALAAM, GOVERNMENT PRINTER, 1967
058,060,070,073,136-04,
> MAJOR STATEMENT OF THE POLITICAL PHILOSOPHY OF PRESI-
> DENT JULIUS NYERERE WITH RESPECT TO THE PROBLEMS OF
> MODERNIZATION AND INTERNATIONAL FINANCING OF ECONOMIC
> DEVELOPMENT. ASSERTS THAT NEW AFRICAN STATES MUST
> GENERATE THEIR OWN FINANCING, CONTROL THEIR OWN ECONO-
> MIES, AND BUILD UPON THEIR STRENGTHS IN AGRICULTURE.

UNITED NATIONS

AFRICAN AGRICULTURAL DEVELOPMENT.
NEW YORK, 1966, E/CN 141/342
070,
    EXCELLENT REPORT ON PROBLEMS OF AGRICULTURAL DEVELOP-
    MENT, WRITTEN BY RENE DUMONT, FRENCH AGRONOMIST. IN-
    CLUDES SECTIONS ON RELATIONSHIP OF AGRICULTURE TO
    INDUSTRIAL DEVELOPMENT, AND ECONOMIC STRATEGIES FOR
    ACCELERATING GROWTH.

070

WHARTON CLIFTON R   ED
SUBSISTENCE AGRICULTURE AND ECONOMIC DEVELOPMENT
CHICAGO, ALDINE 1969
010,070,
    EXCELLENT SERIES OF ARTICLES AND COMMENTARY BY 40
    SOCIAL SCIENTISTS ON SUBSISTENCE AGRICULTURE
    THROUGHOUT THE WORLD.PARTS COVER THE SUBSISTENCE
    FARMER,AGRARIAN CULTURES,AND PEASANT SOCIETIES-THE
    ECONOMIC BEHAVIOR OF SUBSISTENCE FARMERS-THEORIES OF
    CHANGE AND GROWTH-DEVELOPING SUBSISTENCE AGRICULTURE-
    RESEARCH PRIORITIES.

YUDELMAN M
AFRICANS ON THE LAND-- ECONOMIC PROBLEMS OF AFRICAN
AGRICULTURAL DEVELOPMENT IN SOUTHERN CENTRAL AND EAST
AFRICA.
CAMBRIDGE, HARVARD UNIVERSITY PRESS, 1964
070,
    CLEAR STUDY OF PROBLEMS OF EARLY TRANSFORMATION FROM
    SUBSISTANCE TO COMMERCIAL AGRICULTURE IN AFRICAN CON-
    TEXT. AUTHOR BORN IN SOUTH AFRICA, NOW TEACHING AT
    UNIVERSITY OF MICHIGAN.

ABERCROMBIE K C
THE TRANSITION FROM SUBSISTENCE TO MARKET AGRICULTURE IN
AFRICA SOUTH OF THE SAHARA CHAPTER 1.
IN EDITH WHETHAM AND JEAN CURRIE, (EDS.) READINGS IN THE
APPLIED ECONOMICS OF AFRICA, LONDON, CAMBRIDGE UNIVERSITY
PRESS, 1, 1967, PP 1-11
070,
    REFERENCE

AHN PETER M
WEST AFRICAN AGRICULTURE.
LONDON, OXFORD UNIVERSITY PRESS, 1969
070,
    REFERENCE

ANSCHEL KURT R   BRANNON RUSSELL H   SMITH ELSON D
AGRICULTURAL COOPERATIVES AND MARKETS IN DEVELOPING
COUNTRIES.
NEW YORK, PRAEGER PUBLISHERS, 1969
070,
    REFERENCE

BARBER WILLIAM J
THE AGRICULTURAL ECONOMY OF EAST AFRICA.
CAMBRIDGE, HARVARD UNIVERSITY PRESS, 1964
070,
    REFERENCE

070

BIEBUYCK DANIEL
AFRICAN AGRARIAN SYSTEMS.
LONDON, OXFORD UNIVERSITY PRESS, 1963
010,070,
        REFERENCE

BRANNEY L
TOWARD THE SYSTEMATIC INDIVIDUALISATION OF AFRICAN LAND
TENURE.
JOURNAL OF AFRICAN ADMINISTRATION 11 OCTOBER 1959 PP 208-14
070,
        REFERENCE

BROKENSHA DAVID   ED
ECOLOGY AND ECONOMIC DEVELOPMENT IN TROPICAL AFRICA.
BERKELEY, UNIVERSITY OF CALIFORNIA PRESS, 1965
RESEARCH SERIES NO. 9, INSTITUTE OF INTERNATIONAL STUDIES
069,070,
        REFERENCE

CHAMBERS ROBERT
SETTLEMENT SCHEMES IN TROPICAL AFRICA--A STUDY OF
ORGANIZATIONS AND DEVELOPMENTS.
NEW YORK, PRAEGER PUBLISHERS, 1969
070,
        REFERENCE

CLAYTON E S
ECONOMIC AND TECHNICAL OPTIMA IN PEASANT AGRICULTURE CHAPTER
2.
IN EDITH WHETHAM AND JEAN CURRIE, (EDS.) READINGS IN THE
APPLIED ECONOMICS OF AFRICA, LONDON, CAMBRIDGE UNIVERSITY
PRESS, 1, 1967, PP 12-24
070,
        REFERENCE

DE WILDE JOHN C   ET AL
EXPERIENCES WITH AGRICULTURAL DEVELOPMENT IN TROPICAL
AFRICA 2 VOLUMES
BALTIMORE, JOHNS HOPKINS PRESS, 1967
070,
        REFERENCE

DESHLER W
CATTLE IN AFRICA DISTRIBUTION TYPES AND PROBLEMS.
THE GEOGRAPHICAL REVIEW AMERICAN GEOGRAPHICAL SOCIETY 53
JANUARY 1963 PP 52-58
010,069,070,
        REFERENCE

FALLERS LLOYD A
ARE AFRICAN CULTIVATORS TO BE CALLED PEASANTS.
CURRENT ANTHROPOLOGY 2 1961 PP 108-110
070,
        REFERENCE

FREITAG RUTH S
AGRICULTURAL DEVELOPMENT SCHEMES IN SUB-SAHARAN AFRICA- A

BIBLIOGRAPHY
WASHINGTON LIBRARY OF CONGRESS 1963
070,
       REFERENCE

070

   GREAT BRITAIN
   BIBLIOGRAPHY OF PUBLISHED SOURCES RELATING TO
   AFRICAN LAND TENURE.
   LONDON, HER MAJESTY'S STATIONERY OFFICE, 1950
   070,
          REFERENCE

   HELLEINER G K
   AGRICULTURAL PLANNING IN EAST AFRICA.
   NAIROBI, EAST AFRICAN PUBLISHING HOUSE, 1968
   070,
          REFERENCE

   IRVINE FREDERICK R
   WEST AFRICAN AGRICULTURE.
   LONDON AND NEW YORK, INTERNATIONAL UNIVERSITY BOOKSELLERS,
   INC., 1969
   070,
          REFERENCE

   JAIN SHARAD C
   AGRICULTURAL DEVELOPMENT OF AFRICAN NATIONS.
   BOMBAY, INTERNATIONAL UNIVERSITY BOOKSELLERS,INC., 1968
   070,
          REFERENCE

   KAMARCK ANDREW M
   THE ECONOMICS OF AFRICAN DEVELOPMENT.
   NEW YORK, PRAEGER, 1967
   069,070,071,073,
          REFERENCE

   MAIR LUCY P
   MODERN DEVELOPMENTS IN AFRICAN LAND TENURE-- AN ASPECT
   OF CULTURE CHANGE.
   AFRICA 18 JULY 1948 PP 184-189
   070,
          REFERENCE

   MAKINGS S M
   AGRICULTURAL PROBLEMS OF DEVELOPING AFRICAN COUNTRIES.
   EASTERN AFRICA, OXFORD UNIVERSITY PRESS, 1967
   070,
          REFERENCE

   MEEK CHARLES K
   LAND LAW AND CUSTOM IN THE COLONIES.
   LONDON, OXFORD UNIVERSITY PRESS, 1949
   010,066,070,
          REFERENCE

   MIRACLE MARVIN P
   AGRICULTURE IN THE CONGO BASIN--TRADITION AND CHANGE IN
   AFRICAN RURAL ECONOMIES.

MADISON, UNIVERSITY OF WISCONSIN PRESS, 1967
070,108-08,
        REFERENCE

070

SVANIDZE I A
THE AFRICAN STRUGGLE FOR AGRICULTURAL PRODUCTIVITY.
THE JOURNAL OF MODERN AFRICAN STUDIES, VOL. 6,1968, PP. 311-
328
070,
        REFERENCE

UNITED NATIONS   FAO
REPORT ON THE POSSIBILITIES OF AFRICAN RURAL DEVELOPMENT
IN RELATION TO ECONOMIC AND SOCIAL GROWTH.
ROME,FAO, 1961
070,
        REFERENCE

WATTERS R F
THE NATURE OF SHIFTING CULTIVATION--A REVIEW OF RECENT
RESEARCH.
PACIFIC VIEWPOINT 1 MARCH 1960 PP 59-99
010,070,
        REFERENCE

YUDELMAN M
SOME ASPECTS OF AFRICAN AGRICULTURAL DEVELOPMENT.
IN E A G ROBINSON (ED.) ECONOMIC DEVELOPMENT FOR AFRICA
SOUTH OF THE SAHARA, 1964.
010,070,
        REFERENCE

BALDWIN K D S
THE MARKETING OF COCOA IN WESTERN NIGERIA, WITH SPECIAL
REFERENCE TO THE POSITION OF MIDDLEMEN.
LONDON,OXFORD UNIVERSITY PRESS,1954
070,128-08,
        CASE STUDY

CLAYTON E S
AGRARIAN DEVELOPMENT IN PEASANT ECONOMIES-- SOME LESSONS
FROM KENYA.
LONDON,OXFORD UNIVERSITY PRESS,1964
070,117-08,
        CASE STUDY

COHEN RONALD
THE SUCCESS THAT FAILED-- AN EXPERIMENT IN CULTURE CHANGE
IN AFRICA.
ANTHROPOLOGICA 4 1962 PP 1-15
070,
        CASE STUDY

DEAN EDWIN
THE SUPPLY RESPONSES OF AFRICAN FARMERS-- THEORY
AND MEASUREMENT IN MALAWI.
AMSTERDAM,NORTH-HOLLAND PUBLISHING CO, 1966
070,122-08,
        CASE STUDY

070

ENJALBERT H
PAYSANS NOIRS-- LES KABRE DU NORD-TOGO
(BLACK PEASANTS-- THE KABRE OF NORTHERN TOGO).
CAHIERS D' OUTRE-MER 9 APRIL JUNE 1956 PP 137-180
070,137-08,
        CASE STUDY

FALLERS LLOYD A
THE POLITICS OF LANDHOLDING IN BUSOGA.
ECONOMIC DEVELOPMENT AND CULTURAL CHANGE 3 1955 PP 260-270
070,139-08,
        CASE STUDY

FOGG C DAVIS
ECONOMIC AND SOCIAL FACTORS AFFECTING THE DEVELOPMENT OF
SMALL HOLDER AGRICULTURE IN EASTERN NIGERIA CHAPTER 3.
IN EDITH WHETHAM AND JEAN CURRIE (EDS.), READINGS IN THE
APPLIED ECONOMICS OF AFRICA, LONDON, CAMBRIDGE UNIVERSITY
PRESS, 1, 1967, PP 25-31
070,128-08,
        CASE STUDY

FUGGLES-COUCHMAN N
AGRICULTURAL CHANGE IN TANGANYIKA.
STANFORD, STANFORD UNIVERSITY FOOD RESEARCH INSTITUTE, 1964
070,136-08,
        CASE STUDY

GALLETTI R   BALDWIN K D S   DINA I O
NIGERIAN COCOA FARMERS-- AN ECONOMIC SURVEY OF YORUBA
COCOA FARMING FAMILIES.
LONDON, OXFORD UNIVERSITY PRESS, 1956
070,128-08,
        CASE STUDY

GULLIVER P H
LAND SHORTAGE, SOCIAL CHANGE AND SOCIAL CONFLICT IN EAST
AFRICA.
JOURNAL OF CONFLICT RESOLUTION 5 WINTER 1961 PP 16-26
070,
        CASE STUDY

GULLIVER P H
LABOUR MIGRATION IN A RURAL ECONOMMY CHAPTER 4.
IN EDITH WHETHAM AND JEAN CURRIE, (EDS.) READINGS IN THE
APPLIED ECONOMICS OF AFRICA, LONDON, CAMBRIDGE UNIVERSITY
PRESS, 1, 1967, PP 32-37
070,
        CASE STUDY

GULLIVER P H
LAND TENURE AND SOCIAL CHANGE AMONG THE NYAKYUSA--
AN ESSAY IN APPLIED ANTHROPOLOGY IN SOUTH-WEST TANGANYIKA.
KAMPALA, EAST AFRICAN INSTITUTE OF SOCIAL RESEARCH, 1958
070,136-08,
        CASE STUDY

HENNINGS R O

SOME TRENDS AND PROBLEMS OF AFRICAN LAND TENURE IN KENYA.
JOURNAL OF AFRICAN ADMINISTRATION 4 OCTOBER 1952 PP 122-134
070,117-08,
        CASE STUDY

070
HILL P
THREE TYPES OF SOUTHERN GHANAIAN COCOA FARMER.
IN D BIEBUYCK, ED., AFRICAN AGRARIAN SYSTEMS, LONDON,
LONDON, OXFORD UNIVERSITY PRESS, 1963, PP 203-233
070,114-08,
        CASE STUDY

HILL P
MIGRANT COCOA FARMERS OF SOUTHERN GHANA.
CAMBRIDGE, CAMBRIDGE UNIVERSITY PRESS, 1963
070,114-08,
        CASE STUDY

HILL P
THE MIGRATION OF SOUTHERN GHANAIAN COCOA FARMERS.
BULLETIN OF THE GHANA GEOGRAPHICAL ASSOCIATION 5 JULY 1960
PP 9-19
070,114-08,
        CASE STUDY

KABERRY PHYLLIS M
SOME PROBLEMS OF LAND TENURE IN NSAW, SOUTHERN CAMEROONS.
JOURNAL OF AFRICAN ADMINISTRATION 12 JANUARY 1960 PP 21-28
070,104-08,
        CASE STUDY

KHIDER MAHASSIN   SIMPSON MORAG C
CO-OPERATIVES AND AGRICULTURAL DEVELOPMENT IN THE SUDAN.
THE JOURNAL OF MODERN AFRICAN STUDIES, VOL. 6, NO. 4, 1968,
PP. 509-18
070,134-08,
        CASE STUDY

KOBBEN A J F
LAND AS AN OBJECT OF GAIN IN A NON-LITERATE SOCIETY--
LAND TENURE AMONG THE BETE AND DIDA (IVORY COAST).
IN D BIEBUYCK (ED.), AFRICAN AGRARIAN SYSTEMS, LONDON,
OXFORD UNIVERSITY PRESS, 1963, PP 245-266
010,070,116-01,
        CASE STUDY

LAWRANCE J C D
A PILOT SCHEME FOR LAND TITLES IN UGANDA.
JOURNAL OF AFRICAN ADMINISTRATION 12 JULY 1960 PP 135-143
070,139-08,
        CASE STUDY

LAWSON R M
THE MARKETS FOR FOODS IN GHANA CHAPTER 16.
IN EDITH WHETHAM AND JEAN CURRIE (EDS.), READINGS IN THE
APPLIED ECONOMICS OF AFRICA, LONDON, CAMBRIDGE UNIVERSITY
PRESS, 1, 1967, PP 173-192
070,073,114-08,
        CASE STUDY

070

LEBON J H G
LAND USE IN SUDAN.
MONOGRAPH 4, SIR DUDLEY STAMP (ED.) GEOGRAPHICAL
PUBLICATIONS, BUDE, 1965
070,134-08,
     CASE STUDY

LITTLE KENNETH
THE ORGANIZATION OF COMMUNAL FARMS IN THE GAMBIA.
JOURNAL OF AFRICAN ADMINISTRATION 1 1949 PP 76-82
070,113-08,
     CASE STUDY

LONSDALE JOHN
THE TANZANIAN EXPERIMENT
AFRICAN AFFAIRS 67 1968 PP 330-344
063,070,136-11,
     CASE STUDY

MANN H S
LAND TENURE IN CHORE.
ADDIS ABABA, INSTITUTE OF ETHIOPIAN STUDIES, HAILE
SELASSIE UNIVERSITY, WITH OXFORD UNIVERSITY PRESS, 1965
070,110-08,
     CASE STUDY

MASEFIELD G B
AGRICULTURAL CHANGE IN UGANDA, 1945-1960, CHAPTER 5.
IN EDITH WHETHAM AND JEAN CURRIE, (EDS.) READINGS IN THE
APPLIED ECONOMICS OF AFRICA, LONDON, CAMBRIDGE UNIVERSITY
PRESS, 1, 1967, PP 38-57
070,139-08,
     CASE STUDY

MCLOUGHLIN P F M
THE SUDAN S GEZIRA SCHEME-- AN ECONOMIC PROFILE.
SOCIAL AND ECONOMIC STUDIES 12 1963 PP 179-199
070,134-08,
     CASE STUDY

MEEK CHARLES K
LAND TENURE AND LAND ADMINISTRATION IN NIGERIA AND THE
CAMEROONS.
LONDON, HER MAJESTY'S STATIONERY OFFICE, 1957
010,070,104-08,128-08,
     CASE STUDY

MIDDLETON JOHN
LAND TENURE IN ZANZIBAR.
LONDON, HER MAJESTY'S STATIONERY OFFICE, 1961
070,136-08,
     CASE STUDY

NETTING ROBERT
HILL FARMERS OF NIGERIA--CULTURAL ECOLOGY OF THE KOFYAR OF
THE JOS PLATEAU.
SEATTLE, UNIVERSITY OF WASHINGTON, 1968
070,128-08,

CASE STUDY

070

NORTH A C   ET-AL
AFRICAN LAND TENURE DEVELOPMENTS IN KENYA AND UGANDA AND
THEIR APPLICATION TO NORTHERN RHODESIA.
JOURNAL OF AFRICAN ADMINISTRATION 13 OCTOBER 1961
PP 211-219
070,117-08,139-08,142-08,
        CASE STUDY

OLUWASANMI H A
AGRICULTURE IN A DEVELOPING ECONOMY CHAPTER 18.
IN EDITH WHETHAM AND JEAN CURRIE, (EDS.) READINGS IN THE
APPLIED ECONOMICS OF AFRICA, LONDON, CAMBRIDGE UNIVERSITY
PRESS, 1, 1967, PP 205-216
070,
        CASE STUDY

OLUWASANMI H A
AGRICULTURE AND NIGERIAN ECONOMIC DEVELOPMENT.
NIGERIA, OXFORD UNIVERSITY PRESS, 1966
070,128-08,
        CASE STUDY

PEDRAZA G J W
LAND CONSOLIDATION IN THE KIKUYU AREA OF KENYA CHAPTER 6.
IN EDITH WHETHAM AND JEAN CURRIE, (EDS.) READINGS IN THE
APPLIED ECONOMICS OF AFRICA, LONDON, CAMBRIDGE UNIVERSITY
PRESS, 1, 1967, PP 58-71
070,117-08,
        CASE STUDY

RANDALL D
FACTORS OF ECONOMIC DEVELOPMENT AND THE OKOVANGO DELTA.
UNIVERSITY OF CHICAGO, DEPT OF GEOGRAPHY RESEARCH PAPERS,
DECEMBER 1956 PP 1-282
070,
        CASE STUDY

REINING CONRAD C
THE ZANDE SCHEME--AN ANTHROPOLOGICAL CASE STUDY OF ECONOMIC
DEVELOPMENT IN AFRICA.
EVANSTON, NORTHWESTERN UNIVERSITY PRESS, 1966
070,134-08,
        CASE STUDY

RUTHENBERG HANS
AGRICULTURAL DEVELOPMENT IN TANGANYIKA.
BERLIN SPRINGER-VERLAG 1964
070,136-08,
        CASE STUDY

SMITH HADLEY E   ED
AGRICULTURAL DEVELOPMENT IN TANZANIA.
LONDON, OXFORD UNIVERSITY PRESS, 1965
INSTITUTE OF PUBLIC ADMINISTRATION, DAR-ES-SALAAM, STUDY 2
070,136-08,
        CASE STUDY

VAN DER KOLFT G H
THE SOCIAL ASPECTS OF THE GEZIRA SCHEME IN THE SUDAN.
AMSTERDAM, TROPENINSTITUUT, 1953
070,134-08,
        CASE STUDY

070

BALANDIER GEORGES   PAUVERT J C
LES VILLAGES GABONAIS-- ASPECTS DEMOGRAPHIQUES, ECONOMIQUES
SOCIOLOGIQUES, PROJETS DE MODERNISATION (GABON VILLAGES--
DEMOGRAPHIC, ECONOMIC AND SOCIOLOGICAL ASPECTS, PROJECTS
OF MODERNIZATION).
BRAZZAVILLE, INSTITUT DES ETUDES CONTRFICAINES, 1952
070,112-03,
        LESS ACCESSIBLE

BOUTILLIER J L
LES RAPPORTS DU SYSTEME FONCIER TOUCOULEUR ET
L'ORGANISATION SOCIALE ET ECONOMIQUE TRADITIONNELLE-- LEUR
EVOLUTION ACTUELLE (THE PRODUCTIVITY OF TOUCOULEUR FARMERS--
ITS CONTEMPORARY EVOLUTION FROM THE TRADITIONAL SOCIAL AND
ECONOMIC SYSTEM).
IN D BIEBUYCK, ED., AFRICAN AGRARIAN SYSTEMS, LONDON,
OXFORD UNIVERSITY PRESS 1963, PP 116-136
070,130-05,
        LESS ACCESSIBLE

DIOP ABDOULAYE B
SOCIETE TOUCOULEUR ET MIGRATION (TUCOLOR SOCIETY AND
MIGRATION).
DAKAR, INSTITUT FRANCAIS D'AFRIQUE NOIRE, 1965
070,130-05,
        LESS ACCESSIBLE

FOUQUET J
LA TRAITE DES ARACHIDES DANS LE PAYS DE KAOLACK, ET DES
CONSEQUENCES ECONOMIQUES, SOCIALES ET JURIDIQUES,
(THE CULTIVATION OF GROUND NUTS IN KAOLACK COUNTRY, AND THE
CONSEQUENCES, ECONOMIC, SOCIAL AND JURIDIC).
SAINT LOUIS DU SENEGAL, INSTITUT FRANCAIS D'AFRIQUE NOIRE,
1958
070,130-08,
        LESS ACCESSIBLE

ZAHAN DOMINIQUE
PROBLEMS SOCIAUX POSES PAR LA TRANSPLANTATION DES MOSSI SUR
LES TERRES IRRIGUEES DE L'OFFICE DU NIGER (SOCIAL PROBLEMS
POSED BY THE SHIFTING OF THE MOSSI TO THE IRRIGATED LANDS
OF THE NIGER OFFICE).
IN D BIEBUYCK (ED), AFRICAN AGRARIAN SYSTEMS, LONDON,
OXFORD UNIVERSITY PRESS, 1963, PP 392-403
070,
        LESS ACCESSIBLE

ENKE STEPHEN
AGRICULTURAL INNOVATIONS AND COMMUNITY DEVELOPMENT.
IN LEWIS P FICKETT (ED), PROBLEMS OF THE DEVELOPING NATIONS,
NEW YORK, CROWELL, 1966, PP 21-51
070,
        GENERAL THEORY

070
    WHEN PERCY
    THE AFRICAN HUSBANDMAN.
    IN R FIRTH,THEMES IN ECONOMIC ANTHROPOLOGY, LONDON,
    TAVISTOCK, 1967
    010,070,
            GENERAL THEORY

71. THE INDUSTRIALIZATION PROCESS

071
    BELASSA BELA
    THE THEORY OF ECONOMIC INTEGRATION
    HOMEWOOD,ILLINOIS, IRWIN PRESS, 1961
    071,078,
            DISCUSSES THEORETICAL ASPECTS OF INTER-STATE ECONOMIC
            INTEGRATION WITH SPECIAL REFERENCE TO THE TYPES OF
            ORGANIZATIONAL ARRANGEMENTS ACCOMMODATING SUCH LINKAGE
            DISTINGUISHES BETWEEN CUSTOMS UNION (TARIFF VERSUS
            OUTSIDERS) COMMON MARKET (FREE COMMODITY MOVEMENTS)
            ECONOMIC UNION (FREE FACTOR FLOW) AND TOTAL UNIFICATION—
            MONETARY,FISCAL,AND SOCIAL

    EWING A F
    INDUSTRY IN AFRICA
    LONDON, OXFORD UNNIVERSITY PRESS, 1968
    071,
            GOOD SURVEY OF THE PATTERNS AND POTENTIALS OF
            INDUSTRIALIZATION IN AFRICA.AUTHOR IS FORMER UN
            ADVISER AND ANALYST.EXAMINES AFRICAN INDUSTRIALIZATION
            IN CONTEXT OF MODERN DEVELOPMENT THEORY,THE
            INSUFFICIENCY OF IMPORT SUBSTITUTION AND THE NEED FOR
            PRODUCTION OF INTERMEDIATE AND CAPITAL GOODS.LATTER
            POINT THE BASIS FOR STRONGLY URGING REGIONAL ECONOMIC
            GROUPINGS AND COOPERATION.

    GREEN REGINALD H   SEIDMAN ANN
    UNITY OR POVERTY THE ECONOMICS OF PAN-AFRICANISM.
    BALTIMORE, PENGUIN, 1968
    071,079,
            ARGUES FOR THE NECESSITY OF ECONOMIC CO-OPERATION TO
            COUNTER SUCH PROBLEMS OF BALKANIZATION AS OVERDEPEN-
            DENCE ON EXPORTS, LIMITED MARKETS, ECONOMIC ISOLATION
            AND NEO-COLONIALISM . GREEN IS CURRENTLY ECONOMIC
            ADVISER TO THE TREASURY OF TANZANIA.

    LEWIS W ARTHUR
    DEVELOPMENT PLANNING.
    NEW YORK, HARPER AND ROW, 1966
    071,072,
            DISCUSSES PRINCIPLES AND PROCESSES OF ECONOMIC PLAN-
            NING FOR DEVELOPMENT. PRESENTED IN NON-TECHNICAL LAN-
            GUAGE, BY A PROMINENT ECONOMIST.

ROBSON PETER
ECONOMIC INTEGRATION IN AFRICA
LONDON, ALLEN & UNWIN; EVANSTON, NORTHWESTERN UNIV. PRESS, 1968
071,078,
        AUTHOR DEALS WITH FIVE MAJOR TOPICS-(1) THE ECONOMICS
        OF INTEGRATION AMONG LESS DEVELOPED COUNTRIES (2) THE
        ECONOMIC SETTING IN AFRICA AND THE PROBLEMS OF
        INTEGRATION (3) ECONOMIC INTEGRATION IN EAST AFRICA
        (4) ECONOMIC INTEGRATION IN EQUATORIAL AFRICA (5)
        OTHER INITIATIVES FOR ECONOMIC INTEGRATION IN AFRICA.
        MOST COMPREHENSIVE VOLUME AVAILABLE ON ECONOMIC
        INTEGRATION BETWEEN AFRICAN STATES.

071

UNESCO
SOCIAL IMPLICATIONS OF INDUSTRIALIZATION AND URBANIZATION
IN AFRICA SOUTH OF THE SAHARA.
PARIS, UNESCO, 1956
047,071,074,
        FIRST MAJOR SYMPOSIUM ON PROBLEMS OF URBANIZATION AND
        INDUSTRIALIZATION IN AFRICA. INCLUDES INTRODUCTORY
        ESSAY BY DARYLL FORDE, AND SECTIONS ON SOCIAL EFFECTS
        ON ECONOMIC DEVELOPMENT AND URBANIZATION, INCLUDING
        NUMEROUS CASE STUDIES FROM ALL PARTS OF AFRICA SOUTH
        OF THE SAHARA.

UNITED NATIONS
INDUSTRIAL GROWTH IN AFRICA.
NEW YORK, ECONOMIC COMMISSION FOR AFRICA 1963
E/CN-14/INR/1REV.1/
071,
        EXCELLENT GENERAL SURVEY INCLUDES SECTIONS ON THE
        ECONOMIC SETTING IN AFRICA, THE PRESENT STATE OF IN-
        DUSTRIAL GROWTH, INDUSTRIALIZATION AND ECONOMIC PLAN-
        NING, RECENT DEVELOPMENTS AND PROSPECTS FOR EXPANSION
        IN SELECTED MAJOR INDUSTRIES, PROBLEMS OF NATIONAL
        POLICY AND SUB-REGIONAL COOPERATION, AND THE ROLE OF
        THE ECONOMIC COMMISSION FOR AFRICA.

UNITED NATIONS
INDUSTRIAL DEVELOPMENT IN AFRICA
NEW YORK, UNITED NATIONS, 1967
071,104-08,110-08,117-08,127-08,134-08,140-08,142-08,
        PART 1-PROGRAM AND PROBLEMS OF INDUSTRIALIZATION,
        INCLUDING POLICY ASPECTS AND SPECIFIC STUDIES OF
        FOREST,BUILDING MATERIALS,CHEMICAL,IRON AND STEEL,
        ALUMINUM AND FOOD INDUSTRIES. ALSO ESPECIALLY GOOD
        STUDY OF INDUSTRIALIZATION,ECONOMIC COOPERATION AND
        TRANSPORT. PART 2-COUNTRY REPORTS ON CAMEROON,
        ETHIOPIA,KENYA,NIGER,SUDAN,UAR,ZAMBIA.

BERG ELLIOT J
THE ECONOMICS OF THE MIGRANT LABOR SYSTEM.
IN HILDA KUPER (ED.), URBANIZATION AND MIGRATION IN
WEST AFRICA, BERKELEY, UNIVERSITY OF CALIFORNIA PRESS, 1965,
PP 160-181
071,
        REFERENCE

BERG ELLIOT J

THE DEVELOPMENT OF A LABOR FORCE IN SUB-SAHARAN AFRICA.
ECONOMIC DEVELOPMENT AND CULTURAL CHANGE, PART I, JULY, 1965
PP. 394-412
071,
     REFERENCE

071
   FORDE C DARYLL
   THE SOCIAL IMPACT OF INDUSTRIALIZATION AND URBAN CONDITIONS
   IN AFRICA SOUTH OF THE SAHARA.
   INTERNATIONAL SOCIAL SCIENCE BULLETIN 7 WINTER 1955
   PP 114-127
   047,071,
        REFERENCE

   FRIEDLAND WILLIAM H
   UNIONS, LABOR AND INDUSTRIAL RELATIONS IN AFRICA.
   ITHACA, CORNELL UNIVERSITY PRESS, 1965, ANNOTATED BIBLIOGRAPHY
   071,
        REFERENCE

   KAMARCK ANDREW M
   THE ECONOMICS OF AFRICAN DEVELOPMENT.
   NEW YORK, PRAEGER, 1967
   069,070,071,073,
        REFERENCE

   KILBY PETER
   AFRICAN LABOUR PRODUCTIVITY RECONSIDERED.
   ECONOMIC JOURNAL 17 JUNE 1961 1961 PP 273-291
   071,
        REFERENCE

   KUMALO C
   AFRICAN ELITES IN INDUSTRIAL BUREAUCRACY.
   IN LLOYD, THE NEW ELITES OF TROPICAL AFRICA, LONDON, OXFORD
   UNIVERSITY PRESS, 1966, P. 216-229
   071,139-04,
        REFERENCE

   LEWIS ARTHUR
   A REPORT ON THE INDUSTRIALIZATION OF THE GOLD COAST.
   ACCRA, GOVERNMENT PRINTING DEPARTMENT, 1953
   071,
        REFERENCE

   MOUNTJOY A B
   INDUSTRIALIZATION OF UNDERDEVELOPED COUNTRIES
   LONDON, HUTCHINSON, 1963; AND CHICAGO, ALDINE, 1967
   071,
        REFERENCE

   SEERS DUDLEY
   THE ROLE OF INDUSTRY IN DEVELOPMENT-SOME FALLACIES
   JOURNAL OF MODERN AFRICAN STUDIES 1 1963 PP 461-465
   071,
        REFERENCE

   VAN ARKADIE B
   IMPORT SUBSTITUTION AND EXPORT PROMOTION AS AIDS TO

INDUSTRIALIZATION IN EAST AFRICA CHAPTER 28.
IN EDITH WHETHAM AND JEAN CURRIE   (EDS.), READINGS IN THE
APPLIED ECONOMICS OF AFRICA, LONDON, CAMBRIDGE UNIVERSITY
PRESS, 2, 1967, PP 149-162
071,
        REFERENCE

071

HOYLE B S
THE ECONOMIC EXPANSION OF JINJA, UGANDA.
GEOGRAPHICAL REVIEW L111 JULY 1963 PP 377-388
071,139-08,
        CASE STUDY

KILBY PETER
COMPETITION IN THE NIGERIAN BREAD INDUSTRY CHAPTER 15.
IN EDITH WHETHAM AND JEAN CURRIE   (EDS.), READINGS IN THE
APPLIED ECONOMICS OF AFRICA, LONDON, CAMBRIDGE UNIVERSITY
PRESS, 1, 1967, PP 164-172
071,128-08,
        CASE STUDY

KILBY PETER
INDUSTRIALIZATION IN AN OPEN ECONOMY--NIGERIA 1945-1966.
CAMBRIDGE, UNIVERSITY PRESS, 1969
044,071,128-08,
        CASE STUDY

ONYEMELUKWE CLEMENT
PROBLEMS OF INDUSTRIAL PLANNING AND MANAGEMENT IN NIGERIA.
NEW YORK (COLUMBIA), MCGILL-QUEENS, 1969
071,128-08,
        CASE STUDY

REPORT WORKING PARTY
WHO CONTROLS INDUSTRY IN KENYA.
KENYA, EAST AFRICAN PUBLISHING HOUSE, 1968
071,117-08,
        CASE STUDY

UGOH S U
THE NIGERIAN CEMENT INDUSTRY CHAPTER 10.
IN EDITH WHETHAM AND JEAN CURRIE, (EDS.) READINGS IN THE
APPLIED ECONOMICS OF AFRICA, LONDON, CAMBRIDGE UNIVERSITY
PRESS, 1, 1967, PP 102-113
071,128-08,
        CASE STUDY

WELLS F A   WARMINGTON W A
STUDIES IN INDUSTRIALIZATION--NIGERIA AND THE CAMEROONS.
LONDON, OXFORD UNIVERSITY PRESS, 1962
071,104-08,128-08,
        CASE STUDY

WILLIAMS S
START-UP OF A TEXTILE INDUSTRY CHAPTER 11.
IN EDITH WHETHAM AND JEAN CURRIE   (EDS.), READINGS IN THE
APPLIED ECONOMICS OF AFRICA, LONDON, CAMBRIDGE UNIVERSITY
PRESS, 1, 1967, PP 114-125
071,

CASE STUDY

071

YESUFU T M
AN INTRODUCTION TO INDUSTRIAL RELATIONS IN NIGERIA.
LONDON, OXFORD UNIVERSITY PRESS, 1962
071,128-08,
        CASE STUDY

HAUSER M A
L'EMERGENCE DE CADRES DE BASE AFRICAINS DANS L'INDUSTRIE.
IN LLOYD, THE NEW ELITES OF TROPICAL AFRICA, LONDON, OXFORD
UNIVERSITY PRESS, 1966, P. 230-243
071,
        LESS ACCESSIBLE

LACROIX J L
INDUSTRIALISATION AU CONGO-LA TRANFORMATION DES STRUCTURES
ECONOMIQUE
PARIS, EDITIONS MOUTON, 1967
071,108-08,
        LESS ACCESSIBLE

DELL SIDNEY
TRADE BLOCS AND COMMON MARKETS
NEW YORK, KNOPF, 1963
071,072,073,078,
        GENERAL THEORY

DERWENT DAVID F
GROWTH POLE AND GROWTH CENTER CONCEPTS-A REVIEW,EVALUATION,
AND BIBLIOGRAPHY
BERKELEY, CENTER FOR PLANNING AND DEVELOPMENT RESEARCH,
WORKING PAPER NUMBER 89, 1968
071,
        GENERAL THEORY

HAGEN EVERETT E
THE ECONOMICS OF DEVELOPMENT.
HOMEWOOD, ILLINOIS, IRWIN PRESS, 1968
071,073,
        GENERAL THEORY

HIRSCHMAN A O
THE STRATEGY OF ECONOMIC DEVELOPMENT
NEW HAVEN, YALE UNIVERSITY PRESS, 1968
071,073,
        GENERAL THEORY

MYINT H
THE ECONOMICS OF THE DEVELOPING COUNTRIES.
NEW YORK, PRAEGER, 1964
071,073,
        GENERAL THEORY

MYRDAL GUNNAR
RICH LANDS AND POOR.
NEW YORK, HARPER, 1957 (ESP. CHAPTERS 1-3)
037,071,073,
        GENERAL THEORY

071

RIVKIN ARNOLD
THE ROLE AND SCOPE OF INDUSTRIALIZATION IN DEVELOPMENT.
IN RONALD ROBINSON, ED, INDUSTRIALIZATION IN DEVELOPING
COUNTRIES, CAMBRIDGE, CAMBRIDGE UNIVERSITY PRESS, 1965, PP 54-
66
071,
        GENERAL THEORY

THEODORSON GEORGE
ACCEPTANCE OF INDUSTRIALIZATION AND ITS ATTENDANT
CONSEQUENCES FOR THE SOCIAL PATTERNS OF NON-WESTERN
SOCIETIES CHAPTER 9.
IN JASON L FINKLE AND RICHARD W GABLE, POLITICAL
DEVELOPMENT AND SOCIAL CHANGE, NEW YORK, JOHN WILEY, 1966
071,
        GENERAL THEORY

72. PLANNING FOR DEVELOPMENT

072

HAGEN EVERETT E
PLANNING FOR ECONOMIC DEVELOPMENT.
HOMEWOOD, ILLINOIS, IRWIN PRESS, 1963
072,
        SYMPOSIUM VOLUME DEALS WITH PLANNING STRATEGY AND IM-
        PLEMENTATION IN A VARIETY OF CAPITALIST, COMMUNIST,
        AND DEVELOPING ECONOMIES.

HANCE WILLIAM A
AFRICAN ECONOMIC DEVELOPMENT.
NEW YORK, PRAEGER, 1967 (REVISED EDITION)
048,069,072,
        EXCELLENT SURVEY WITH DETAILED CASE STUDIES OF THE
        GEZIRA SCHEME, THE VOLTA RIVER PROJECT, TRANSPORT,
        ECONOMIC INTEGRATION IN EAST AFRICA, LIBERIA, MADA-
        GASCAR AND OTHERS. FINAL CHAPTER EXAMINES DEVELOPMENT
        POTENTIALS BY COUNTRY WITH A GOOD SUMMARY TABLE.

LEWIS W ARTHUR
DEVELOPMENT PLANNING.
NEW YORK, HARPER AND ROW, 1966
071,072,
        DISCUSSES PRINCIPLES AND PROCESSES OF ECONOMIC PLAN-
        NING FOR DEVELOPMENT. PRESENTED IN NON-TECHNICAL LAN-
        GUAGE, BY A PROMINENT ECONOMIST.

STOLPER W
PLANNING WITHOUT FACTS.
CAMBRIDGE, HARVARD UNIVERSITY PRESS, 1966
072,128-08,
        PRACTICAL AND HARD-HEADED DISCUSSION OF PLANNING PRO-
        CESSES IN NIGERIAN FIRST DEVELOPMENT PLANS. AUTHOR
        WAS HEAD OF NIGERIAN PLANNING BUREAU FOR FOUR YEARS.

DEALS WITH PROBLEMS AND PROCESS OF PLANNING AND IMPLE-
MENTATION IN NIGERIA.

072

AFRICAN MONOGRAPHS
THE CHALLENGE OF DEVELOPMENT.
KENYA, EAST AFRICAN PUBLISHING HOUSE, 1968
072,
     REFERENCE

ARKADIE BRIAN VAN   FRANK CHARLES R
ECONOMIC ACCOUNTING AND DEVELOPMENT PLANNING.
EASTERN AFRICA, OXFORD UNIVERSITY PRESS, 1966
072,
     REFERENCE

ECONOMIC COMMISSION FOR AFRICA
CO-ORDINATION OF DEVELOPMENT PLANS IN AFRICA.
ECONOMIC BULLETIN FOR AFRICA 1 1964
072,
     REFERENCE

HAMILTON F E IAN
REGIONAL ECONOMIC ANALYSIS IN BRITAIN AND THE COMMONWEALTH-
A BIBLIOGRAPHIC GUIDE
NEW YORK, SCHOCKEN BOOKS, 1970
048,069,072,
     REFERENCE

LOKEN ROBERT D
MANPOWER DEVELOPMENT IN AFRICA.
NEW YORK, PRAEGER PUBLISHERS, 1969
072,
     REFERENCE

MAGENAU MARY S
A BIBLIOGRAPHY OF DEVELOPMENT PLANS IN AFRICA SOUTH OF THE
SAHARA
NEW HAVEN, YALE UNIVERSITY ECONOMIC GROWTH CENTER LIBRARY,
1966 5P.
072,
     REFERENCE

MAZRUI ALI A
IS AFRICAN DEVELOPMENT PLANNABLE CHAPTER 9.
IN ON HEROES AND UHURU-WORSHIP, LONDON, LONGMANS,
1967, PP 137-145
072,
     REFERENCE

OSER JACOB
PROMOTING ECONOMIC DEVELOPMENT-WITH ILLUSTRATIONS FROM KENYA
EVANSTON, NORTHWESTERN UNIVERSITY PRESS, 1967
072,117-08,
     REFERENCE

BURKE FRED G
TANGANYIKA PREPLANNING.
SYRACUSE, SYRACUSE UNIVERSITY PRESS, 1965
072,136-08,

CASE STUDY

072
   CLARK PAUL
   DEVELOPMENT STRATEGY IN AN EARLY STAGE ECONOMY-UGANDA
   JOURNAL OF MODERN AFRICAN STUDIES 4 1966 PP 47-64
   072,073,139-08,
      CASE STUDY

   DUWAJI GHAZI
   ECONOMIC DEVELOPMENT IN TUNISIA--THE IMPACT AND COURSE OF
   GOVERNMENT PLANNING.
   NEW YORK, PRAEGER PUBLISHERS, 1967
   072,138-08,
      CASE STUDY

   EL-KAMMASH MAGDI M
   ECONOMIC DEVELOPMENT AND PLANNING IN EGYPT.
   NEW YORK, PRAEGER PUBLISHERS, 1967
   072,140-08,
      CASE STUDY

   GREEN REGINALD H
   FOUR AFRICAN DEVELOPMENT PLANS-- GHANA, KENYA, NIGERIA,
   AND TANZANIA CHAPTER 20.
   IN EDITH WHETHAM AND JEAN CURRIE (EDS.), READINGS IN THE
   APPLIED ECONOMICS OF AFRICA, LONDON, CAMBRIDGE UNIVERSITY
   PRESS, 2, 1967, PP 21-32
   072,114-08,117-08,128-08,136-08,
      CASE STUDY

   REPUBLIC OF KENYA
   AFRICAN SOCIALISM AND ITS APPLICATION TO PLANNING IN KENYA
   NAIROBI, GOVERNMENT PRINTER, 1965
   054,072,077,117-08,
      CASE STUDY

   SKOROV GEORGE
   INTEGRATION OF EDUCATIONAL AND ECONOMIC PLANNING IN
   TANZANIA.
   PARIS, UNESCO, 1967
   072,136-08,
      CASE STUDY

   CHIN ROBERT
   THE UTILITY OF SYSTEM MODELS AND DEVELOPMENTAL MODELS
   CHAPTER 1.
   IN JASON L FINKLE AND RICHARD W GABLE, POLITICAL
   DEVELOPMENT AND SOCIAL CHANGE, NEW YORK, JOHN WILEY, 1966
   072,098,
      GENERAL THEORY

   DELL SIDNEY
   TRADE BLOCS AND COMMON MARKETS
   NEW YORK KNOPF 1963
   071,072,073,078,
      GENERAL THEORY

   HEILBRONER ROBERT
   THE ENGINEERING OF DEVELOPMENT.

IN LEWIS P FICKETT (ED), PROBLEMS OF THE DEVELOPING NATIONS,
NEW YORK, CROWELL, 1966, PP 53-63
072,
 GENERAL THEORY

072
ROSTOW W W
THE TAKE-OFF INTO SELF-SUSTAINED GROWTH CHAPTER 7.
IN JASON L FINKLE AND RICHARD W GABLE, POLITICAL
DEVELOPMENT AND SOCIAL CHANGE, NEW YORK, JOHN WILEY, 1966
072,
 GENERAL THEORY

SHILS EDWARD
THE CONCENTRATION AND DISPERSION OF CHARISMA-- THEIR
BEARING ON ECONOMIC POLICY IN UNDERDEVELOPED COUNTRIES.
WORLD POLITICS 11 OCT 1958 PP 1-19; ALSO WILLIAM J HANNA, ED,
INDEPENDENT BLACK AFRICA, CHICAGO, RAND MCNALLY, 1964, PP
389-406
072,
 GENERAL THEORY

73. DEVELOPMENT OF ECONOMIC SYSTEMS

073
ADELMAN IRMA   MORRIS CYNTHIA TAFT
SOCIETY, POLITICS, AND ECONOMIC DEVELOPMENT, A QUANTITATIVE
APPROACH.
BALTIMORE, JOHNS HOPKINS UNIVERSITY PRESS, 1967
073, 074,
 A STATISTICAL ANALYSIS OF SEVENTY-FOUR UNDERDEVELOPED
 COUNTRIES, ONE-THIRD OF WHICH ARE AFRICAN. USEFUL IN
 CONTRASTING THE POLITICAL, ECONOMIC, AND SOCIAL CHAR-
 ACTERISTICS OF COUNTRIES AT DIFFERENT STAGES OF DEVEL-
 OPMENT.

CLOWER ROBERT W   ET AL
GROWTH WITHOUT DEVELOPMENT, AN ECONOMIC SURVEY OF LIBERIA.
EVANSTON, NORTHWESTERN UNIVERISTY PRESS, 1966
CHAPTER 10 AND APPENDIX PP 259-335
073, 119-08,
 CASE STUDY OF A WEST AFRICAN ECONOMY (LIBERIA) AT THE
 BEGINNING STAGES OF ECONOMIC DEVELOPMENT AND MODERNI-
 ZATION. SPECIAL EMPHASIS ON WAY LIBERIA EXHIBITED
 POLITICAL, SOCIAL AND ECONOMIC STRUCTURAL TRANSFORMA-
 TIONS.

HUNTER GUY
THE BEST OF BOTH WORLDS- A CHALLENGE ON DEVELOPMENT POLICIES
IN AFRICA
LONDON AND NEW YORK, OXFORD UNIVERSITY PRESS, 1967
073, 075, 076,
 A SERIES OF ESSAYS FOCUSING ON THE TRANSFER OF
 TECHNOLOGY, INSTITUTIONS AND THE IDEAS AND VALUES
 CORRESPONDING TO THEM, FROM DEVELOPED TO DEVELOPING

COUNTRIES.AND ON THE EFFECTS OF THIS TRANSFER. MAJOR
SECTIONS OF THE HISTORICAL POSITION OF AFRICA AND THE
NATURE OF GROWTH.ECONOMIC GROWTH AND EMPLOYMENT.THE
RURAL ECONOMY.INSTITUTIONS AND EDUCATION.

073
MIDDLETON JOHN
THE EFFECTS OF ECONOMIC DEVELOPMENT ON TRADITIONAL POLITICAL
SYSTEMS IN AFRICA SOUTH OF THE SAHARA.
THE HAGUE,MOUTON,1966
053,073,
EXCELLENT SURVEY. HAS CHAPTERS ON TRADITIONAL AND
CHANGING ECONOMIC AND POLITICAL SYSTEMS OF AFRICA--
STUDIES OF CHANGE IN RURAL AREAS-- AND STUDIES OF
URBANISM AND URBANIZATION. AUTHOR IS PROFESSOR OF
URBAN ANTHROPOLOGY AT NEW YORK UNIVERSITY. FORTY PAGE
BIBLIOGRAPHY ARRANGED BY TOPIC, E.G. PEASANT COMMUNI-
TIES, ELITES AND SOCIAL CLASSES, NATIONALISM, URBANI-
ZATION, CHIEFSHIP AND GOVERNMENT.

ROBINSON E A G   ED
ECONOMIC DEVELOPMENT FOR AFRICA SOUTH OF THE SAHARA.
NEW YORK,ST MARTIN'S PRESS, 1964
073,
SYMPOSIUM FOR INTERNATIONAL ECONOMICS ASSOCIATION ON
VARIETY OF ECONOMIC AND TECHNICAL PROBLEMS OF PROG-
RESS. CONTRIBUTORS INCLUDE AFRICAN, EUROPEAN, AND
AMERICAN ECONOMISTS AND CIVIL SERVANTS. FIRST CHAP-
TER IS EXCELLENT SURVEY OF INDUSTRIALIZATION IN NINE
AFRICAN STATES.

SINGER HANS
INTERNATIONAL ECONOMIC DEVELOPMENT, GROWTH AND CHANGE.
NEW YORK MCGRAW HILL 1964
073,
SERIES OF ESSAYS BY DISTINGUISHED U.N. ECONOMIST WHO
HAS MADE CONTRIBUTIONS TO THEORY AND TO PRACTICAL POL-
ICIES OF ECONOMIC DEVELOPMENT. SEVERAL PAPERS ON
AFRICA. EXCELLENT THEORETICAL AND CONCEPTUAL FRAME-
WORK.

TANZANIA AFRICAN NATIONAL UNION
THE ARUSHA DECLARATION AND TANU'S POLICY ON SOCIALISM AND
SELF-RELIANCE.
DAR ES-SALAAM,GOVERNMENT PRINTER, 1967
058,060,070,073,136-04,
MAJOR STATEMENT OF THE POLITICAL PHILOSOPHY OF PRESI-
DENT JULIUS NYERERE WITH RESPECT TO THE PROBLEMS OF
MODERNIZATION AND INTERNATIONAL FINANCING OF ECONOMIC
DEVELOPMENT. ASSERTS THAT NEW AFRICAN STATES MUST
GENERATE THEIR OWN FINANCING, CONTROL THEIR OWN ECONO-
MIES, AND BUILD UPON THEIR STRENGTHS IN AGRICULTURE.

WHETHAM EDITH H   CURRIE JEAN I   EDS
READINGS IN THE APPLIED ECONOMICS OF AFRICA.
LONDON, CAMBRIDGE UNIVERSITY PRESS, 1, 1967
073,
VOLUME ONE ON MICRO-ECONOMICS CONTAINS EIGHTEEN RE-
PRINTED ARTICLES DEALING WITH RESOURCE USE IN AGRICUL-
TURE AND INDUSTRY, AND THE ROLE OF PRICES AND MARKETS

AS THEY AFFECT INCOME AND THE EXCHANGE OF GOODS AND
SERVICES.

073

WHETHAM EDITH H   CURRIE JEAN I   EDS
READINGS IN THE APPLIED ECONOMICS OF AFRICA.
LONDON. CAMBRIDGE UNIVERSITY PRESS, 2, 1967,
073,128-08,
        VOLUME TWO ON MACRO-ECONOMICS CONTAINS FOURTEEN RE-
        PRINTS OF ARTICLES DEALING WITH THE FRAMING AND IMPLE-
        MENTATION OF ECONOMIC POLICY. SECTIONS COVER THE
        PROBLEMS OF COMPILING AND USING NATIONAL ACCOUNTS--
        PUBLIC FINANCING, BANKING, AND THE BALANCE OF PAY-
        MENTS-- AND ECONOMIC DEVELOPMENT (POPULATION, EXPORT
        TRADE AND IMPORT SUBSTITUTION, EMPLOYMENT AND INFLA-
        TION).

WHETHAM EDITH H   CURRIE JEAN I
THE ECONOMICS OF AFRICAN COUNTRIES.
LONDON AND NEW YORK, INTERNATIONAL UNIVERSITY BOOKSELLERS,
INC., 1969
073,
        COMPANION TO PREVIOUSLY PUBLISHED TWO VOLUMES OF READ-
        INGS ON GENERAL TOPICS. CONTAINS MANY EXCELLENT CASE
        STUDIES OF ECONOMIC DEVELOPMENT IN AFRICAN COUNTRIES.
        INTRODUCTION REVIEWS CONCEPTS AND METHODS OF ECONOMIC
        ANALYSIS, FOLLOWED BY COVERAGE OF MICRO AND MACRO
        THEORY. CONCLUDES ON SUBJECT OF ECONOMIC DEVELOPMENT.

ARRIGHI GIOVANNI   SAUL JOHN S
SOCIALISM AND ECONOMIC DEVELOPMENT IN TROPICAL AFRICA.
THE JOURNAL OF MODERN AFRICAN STUDIES, VOL. 6, NO. 2, 1968,
PP. 141-69
073,
        REFERENCE

BELL P W
ECONOMIC THEORY--AN INTEGRATED TEXT WITH SPECIAL REFERENCE
TO TROPICAL AFRICA AND OTHER DEVELOPING AREAS.
LONDON AND NEW YORK, INTERNATIONAL UNIVERSITY BOOKSELLERS,
INC., 1969
073,
        REFERENCE

BERG ELLIOT J   BUTLER JEFFREY
TRADE UNIONS.
IN J S COLEMAN AND C G ROSBERG (EDS.), POLITICAL PARTIES
AND NATIONAL INTEGRATION IN TROPICAL AFRICA, BERKELEY,
UNIVERSITY OF CALIFORNIA PRESS, 1964
073,
        REFERENCE

BERG ELLIOT J
SOCIALISM AND ECONOMIC DEVELOPMENT IN TROPICAL AFRICA
QUARTERLY JOURNAL OF ECONOMICS 78 1964 PP 549-573
073,
        REFERENCE

BLAU G
COMMODITY EXPORT EARNINGS AND ECONOMIC GROWTH CHAPTER 19.

IN EDITH WHETHAM AND JEAN CURRIE (EDS.), READINGS IN THE
APPLIED ECONOMICS OF AFRICA, LONDON, CAMBRIDGE UNIVERSITY
PRESS, 2, 1967, PP 163-181
073,
        REFERENCE

073
  BOWLES SAMUEL
  PLANNING EDUCATIONAL SYSTEMS FOR ECONOMIC GROWTH
  CAMBRIDGE, HARVARD UNIVERSITY PRESS, 1969
  073,
        REFERENCE

  DAVIES IOAN
  AFRICAN TRADE UNIONS.
  BALTIMORE, PENGUIN BOOKS, 1966
  044,073,
        REFERENCE

  EISENSTADT S N
  MODERNIZATION AND CONDITIONS OF SUSTAINED GROWTH
  WORLD POLITICS 16 JULY 1964 PP 576-594
  037,073,
        REFERENCE

  GONCHAROV L
  URGENT PROBLEMS OF AFRICAN ECONOMIC DEVELOPMENT.
  THE JOURNAL OF MODERN AFRICAN STUDIES, VOL. 6, NO.4, 1968,
  PP. 475-83
  073,
        REFERENCE

  HELLEINER G K
  NEW FORMS OF FOREIGN INVESTMENT IN AFRICA.
  THE JOURNAL OF MODERN AFRICAN STUDIES, VOL. 6, NO. 1, 1968,
  PP. 17-27
  073,
        REFERENCE

  HERSKOVITS MELVILLE J   HARWITZ MITCHELL EDS
  ECONOMIC TRANSITION IN AFRICA
  EVANSTON, NORTHWESTERN UNIVERSITY PRESS, 1964
  010,073,
        REFERENCE

  HUNTER GUY
  AFRICAN LABOUR AND THE AFRICAN MANAGER CHAPTER 9.
  IN THE NEW SOCIETIES OF TROPICAL AFRICA, LONDON, OXFORD
  UNIVERSITY PRESS 1962, PP 193-236
  073,
        REFERENCE

  INTERNATIONAL BANK FOR RECONSTRUCTION AND DEVELOPMENT
  WORLD BANK AND IDA ANNUAL REPORT 1966/1967.
  WASHINGTON D C, INTERNATIONAL BANK FOR RECONSTRUCTION AND
  DEVELOPMENT, 1967, P 26
  073,
        REFERENCE

  KALDOR N

INTERNATIONAL TRADE AND ECONOMIC DEVELOPMENT
JOURNAL OF MODERN AFRICAN STUDIES 2 1964 PP 491-511
073,080,
        REFERENCE

073

    KAMARCK ANDREW M
    THE ECONOMICS OF AFRICAN DEVELOPMENT.
    NEW YORK, PRAEGER, 1967
    069,070,071,073,
        REFERENCE

    KILLICK A J
    INFLATION AND GROWTH CHAPTER 32.
    IN EDITH WHETHAM AND JEAN CURRIE (EDS) READINGS IN THE
    APPLIED ECONOMICS OF AFRICA, LONDON, CAMBRIDGE UNIVERSITY
    PRESS, 2, 1967, PP 215-228
    073,
        REFERENCE

    KIMBLE HELEN
    ON THE TEACHING OF ECONOMICS IN AFRICA
    JOURNAL OF MODERN AFRICAN STUDIES 7 1969 PP 713-741
    073,
        REFERENCE

    MARE W S
    AFRICAN TRADE UNIONS.
    LONDON, LONGMANS, 1949
    073,
        REFERENCE

    MOORE WILBERT E
    THE ADAPTATION OF AFRICAN LABOR SYSTEMS TO SOCIAL CHANGE.
    IN M J HERSKOVITS AND M HARWITZ (EDS.), ECONOMIC TRANSITION
    IN AFRICA, EVANSTON, NORTHWESTERN UNIVERSITY PRESS, 1964,
    PP 277-297
    073,
        REFERENCE

    NEUMARK S DANIEL
    THE CHARACTER AND POTENTIAL OF AFRICAN ECONOMIES CHAPTER 4.
    IN THE UNITED STATES AND AFRICA, BACKGROUND PAPERS OF THE
    13TH ASSEMBLY, THE AMERICAN ASSEMBLY, COLUMBIA UNIVERSITY,
    1958, PP 91-115
    073,
        REFERENCE

    NEWLYN W T
    MONEY IN AN AFRICAN CONTEXT.
    EASTERN AFRICA, OXFORD UNIVERSITY PRESS, 1967
    073,
        REFERENCE

    OKIGBO PIUS N C
    THE FISCAL SYSTEM AND THE GROWTH IN NATIONAL INCOME
    CHAPTER 26.
    IN EDITH WHETHAM AND JEAN CURRIE (EDS.), READINGS IN THE
    APPLIED ECONOMICS OF AFRICA, LONDON, CAMBRIDGE UNIVERSITY
    PRESS, 2, 1967, PP 126-140

073,
     REFERENCE

073

OLAKANPO O
DISTRIBUTIVE TRADE-A CRITIQUE OF GOVERNMENT POLICY CHAPTER
17.
IN EDITH WHETHAM AND JEAN CURRIE (EDS.),READINGS IN THE
APPLIED ECONOMICS OF AFRICA, LONDON, CAMBRIDGE UNIVERSITY
PRESS, 1, 1967, PP 193-204
073,
     REFERENCE

ORR CHARLES A
TRADE UNIONISM IN COLONIAL AFRICA.
JOURNAL OF MODERN AFRICAN STUDIES 4 1966 PP 65-81
073,
     REFERENCE

RIVKIN ARNOLD
THE POLITICS OF NATION-BUILDING-- PROBLEMS AND
PRECONDITIONS.
JOURNAL OF INTERNATIONAL AFFIARS 16 PP 131-143
073,
     REFERENCE

ROBSON PETER   LURY D A   EDS
THE ECONOMIES OF AFRICA.
EVANSTON, NORTHWESTERN UNIVERSITY PRESS, 1969
073,
     REFERENCE

SCHATZ SAYER P
GOVERNMENT LENDING TO AFRICAN BUSINESSMEN--INEPT INCENTIVES.
THE JOURNAL OF MODERN AFRICAN STUDIES, VOL. 6, NO. 4, 1968,
PP. 519-29
073,
     REFERENCE

SEERS DUDLEY
INTERNATIONAL AID-THE NEXT STEPS
JOURNAL OF MODERN AFRICAN STUDIES 2 1964 PP 471-489
073,080,
     REFERENCE

SMITH HADLEY E   ED
READINGS ON ECONOMIC DEVELOPMENT AND ADMINISTRATION IN
TANZANIA.
EASTERN AFRICA, OXFORD UNIVERSITY PRESS, 1966
073,136-08,
     REFERENCE

STEWART I G   ORD H W   EDS
AFRICAN PRIMARY PRODUCTS AND INTERNATIONAL TRADE.
EDINBURGH,UNIVERSITY PRESS,1965
069,073,
     REFERENCE

TAYLOR MILTON   ED
TAXATION FOR AFRICAN ECONOMIC DEVELOPMENT.

NEW YORK, AFRICANA PUBLISHING CORPORATION, 1970
073,
    REFERENCE

073
UNITED NATIONS
REPORT OF THE UNITED NATIONS CONFERENCE ON TRADE
AND DEVELOPMENT.
IN LEWIS P FICKETT (ED), PROBLEMS OF THE DEVELOPING NATIONS,
NEW YORK, CROWELL, 1966 PP 64-83
073,
    REFERENCE

UNITED NATIONS
ENLARGEMENT OF THE EXCHANGE ECONOMY IN TROPICAL AFRICA.
NEW YORK, UN DEPARTMENT OF ECONOMIC AFFAIRS (E/2557 ST/ECA/23
1954. II.C.4)
073,
    REFERENCE

WEST ROBERT L
LOOKING AT AFRICAN DEVELOPMENT--AN ANNOTATED OVERVIEW.
AFRICAN REPORT, MAY, 1968, P. 58
073,
    REFERENCE

WORTHINGTON E B
SCIENCE IN THE DEVELOPMENT OF AFRICA.
LONDON, COMMISSION FOR TECHNICAL COOPERATION IN AFRICA SOUTH
OF THE SAHARA, 1958
073,075,
    REFERENCE

YESUFU T M
THE SHORTAGE OF SKILLED LABOUR CHAPTER 12.
IN EDITH WHETHAM AND JEAN CURRIE (EDS.), READINGS IN THE
APPLIED ECONOMICS OF AFRICA, LONDON, CAMBRIDGE UNIVERSITY
PRESS, 1, 1967, PP 126-132
073,
    REFERENCE

BANTON MICHAEL P
ECONOMIC DEVELOPMENT AND SOCIAL CHANGE IN SIERRA LEONE.
ECONOMIC DEVELOPMENT AND CULTURAL CHANGE 2 1953 PP 135-138
073,131-08,
    CASE STUDY

BARBER WILLIAM J
ECONOMIC RATIONALITY AND BEHAVIOR PATTERNS IN AN
UNDERDEVELOPED AREA--A CASE STUDY OF AFRICAN ECONOMICS IN
THE RHODESIAS.
ENONOMIC DEVELOPMENT AND CULTURAL CHANGE 8 1960 PP 237-251
073,122-08,142-08,145-08,
    CASE STUDY

BELING WILLARD A
MODERNIZATION AND AFRICAN LABOR-- A TUNISIAN CASE STUDY.
NEW YORK, PRAEGER, 1965
073,138-08,
    CASE STUDY

073

CLARK PAUL
DEVELOPMENT STRATEGY IN AN EARLY STAGE ECONOMY-UGANDA
JOURNAL OF MODERN AFRICAN STUDIES 4 1966 PP 47-64
072,073,139-08,
      CASE STUDY

COX-GEORGE N A
FINANCE AND DEVELOPMENT IN WEST AFRICA -- THE SIERRA LEONE
EXPERIENCE.
LONDON DOBSON 1961
073,131-08,
      CASE STUDY

ELKAN WALTER
THE ECONOMIC DEVELOPMENT OF UGANDA.
LONDON, OXFORD UNIVERSITY PRESS, 1961
073,139-08,
      CASE STUDY

ENGBERG H L
COMMERCIAL BANKING IN EAST AFRICA CHAPTER 22.
IN EDITH WHETHAM AND JEAN CURRIE (EDS.), READINGS IN THE
APPLIED ECONOMICS OF AFRICA, LONDON, CAMBRIDGE UNIVERSITY
PRESS, 2, 1967, PP 48-69
073,
      CASE STUDY

FAIR T J D
A REGIONAL APPROACH TO ECONOMIC DEVELOPMENT IN KENYA.
SOUTH AFRICAN GEOGRAPHICAL JOURNAL 45 DECEMBER1963 PP 55-77
048,073,117-08,
      CASE STUDY

GHAI DHARAM P
TAXATION FOR DEVELOPMENT--A CASE STUDY OF UGANDA.
KENYA, EAST AFRICAN PUBLISHING HOUSE, 1966
073,139-08,
      CASE STUDY

GREEN L P   FAIR T J D
DEVELOPMENT IN AFRICA- A STUDY IN REGIONAL ANALYSIS WITH
SPECIAL REFERENCE TO SOUTHERN AFRICA
JOHANNESBURG,WITWATERSRAND UNIVERSITY PRESS, 1962
048,073,132-08,145-08,
      CASE STUDY

HANSEN B   MARZOUK G A
DEVELOPMENT AND ECONOMIC POLICY IN THE UAR
AMSTERDAM,NORTH HOLLAND PUBLISHING COMPANY, 1965
073,140-08,
      CASE STUDY

HELLEINER G K
THE FISCAL ROLE OF THE MARKETING BOARDS IN NIGERIAN
ECONOMIC DEVELOPMENT 1947-61 CHAPTER 23.
IN EDITH WHETHAM AND JEAN CURRIE (EDS.), READINGS IN THE
APPLIED ECONOMICS OF AFRICA, LONDON, CAMBRIDGE UNIVERSITY
PRESS, 2, 1967, PP 70-93

073,128-08,
CASE STUDY

073
INTERNATIONAL BANK FOR RECONSTRUCTION AND DEVELOPMENT
THE ECONOMIC DEVELOPMENT OF TANGANYIKA
BALTIMORE, JOHNS HOPKINS UNIVERSITY PRESS, 1961
073,136-08,
CASE STUDY

INTERNATIONAL BANK FOR RECONSTRUCTION AND DEVELOPMENT
THE ECONOMIC DEVELOPMENT OF KENYA
BALTIMORE, JOHNS HOPKINS UNIVERSITY PRESS, 1963
073,117-08,
CASE STUDY

INTERNATIONAL BANK FOR RECONSTRUCTION AND DEVELOPMENT
THE ECONOMIC DEVELOPMENT OF LIBYA
BALTIMORE, JOHNS HOPKINS UNIVERSITY PRESS, 1960
073,120-08,
CASE STUDY

INTERNATIONAL BANK FOR RECONSTRUCTION AND DEVELOPMENT
THE ECONOMIC DEVELOPMENT OF MOROCCO
BALTIMORE, JOHNS HOPKINS UNIVERSITY PRESS, 1966
073,126-08,
CASE STUDY

INTERNATIONAL BANK FOR RECONSTRUCTION AND DEVELOPMENT
THE ECONOMIC DEVELOPMENT OF UGANDA
BALTIMORE, JOHNS HOPKINS UNIVERSITY PRESS, 1962
073,139-08,
CASE STUDY

LAWSON R M
THE MARKETS FOR FOODS IN GHANA CHAPTER 16.
IN EDITH WHETHAM AND JEAN CURRIE (EDS.), READINGS IN THE
APPLIED ECONOMICS OF AFRICA, LONDON, CAMBRIDGE UNIVERSITY
PRESS, 1, 1967, PP 173-192
070,073,114-08,
CASE STUDY

MAY R S
DIRECT OVERSEAS INVESTMENT IN NIGERIA 1953-63 CHAPTER 8.
IN EDITH WHETHAM AND JEAN CURRIE (EDS.), READINGS IN THE
APPLIED ECONOMICS OF AFRICA, LONDON, CAMBRIDGE UNIVERSITY
PRESS, 1, 1967, PP 72-92
073,128-08,
CASE STUDY

OKIGBO PIUS N C
NIGERIAN NATIONAL ACCOUNTS 1950-7 CHAPTER 19.
IN EDITH WHETHAM AND JEAN CURRIE (EDS.), READINGS IN THE
APPLIED ECONOMICS OF AFRICA, LONDON, CAMBRIDGE UNIVERSITY
PRESS, 2, 1967, PP 1-20
073,128-08,
CASE STUDY

PERHAM MARGERY   ED
MINING, COMMERCE AND FINANCE IN NIGERIA.

IN ECONOMICS OF A TROPICAL DEPENDENCY, VOL 2, LONDON, FABER
1948
073,128-08,
     CASE STUDY

073

ROE ALAN R
THE FUTURE OF THE COMPANY IN TANZANINA DEVELOPMENT.
THE JOURNAL OF MODERN AFRICAN STUDIES, VOL. 7, NO. 1, 1969,
PP. 47-67
073,136-08,
     CASE STUDY

SCHATZ SAYER P
THE CAPITAL SHORTAGE ILLUSION-- GOVERNMENT LENDING IN
NIGERIA CHAPTER 9.
IN EDITH WHETHAM AND JEAN CURRIE (EDS.), READINGS IN THE
APPLIED ECONOMICS OF AFRICA, LONDON, CAMBRIDGE UNIVERSITY
PRESS, 1, 1967, PP 93-101
073, 128-08,
     CASE STUDY

TRACHTMAN LESTER N
THE LABOR MOVEMENT OF GHANA-- A STUDY IN POLITICAL
UNIONISM.
ECONOMIC DEVELOPMENT AND CULTURAL CHANGE 10 1962 PP 183-200
073,114-08,
     CASE STUDY

WARMINGTON W A
A WEST AFRICAN TRADE UNION.
LONDON, OXFORD UNIVERSITY PRESS, 1960
A CASE STUDY OF THE CAMEROONS DEVELOPMENT CORPORATION
WORKERS' UNIONS AND ITS RELATIONS WITH THE EMPLOYERS
073,104-08,
     CASE STUDY

WILLIAMS J W
THE ECONOMY OF GHANA CHAPTER 6.
IN CALVIN B HOOVER, ECONOMIC SYSTEMS OF THE COMMONWEALTH,
DURHAM, DUKE UNIVERSITY PRESS, 1962, PP 238-261
073,114-08,
     CASE STUDY

AMIN SAMIR
LE DEVELOPPEMENT ECONOMIQUE ET SOCIALE DE LA COTE D'IVOIRE
DAKAR IDEP 1966
073,116-08,
     LESS ACCESSIBLE

AMIN SAMIR
TROIS EXPERIENCES AFRICAINES DE DEVELOPPEMENT-LE MALI,LA
GUINEE,ET LA GHANA
PARIS PRESSES UNIVERSITAIRES DE FRANCE 1965
073,123-08,115-08,114-08,
     LESS ACCESSIBLE

BADOUIN R
LES MODIFICATIONS DES STRUCTURES ECONOMIQUES INTERNES DANS
LES ETATS DE L'AFRIQUE OCCIDENTAL (MODIFICATIONS OF THE

INTERNAL ECONOMIC STRUCTURES OF THE WEST AFRICAN STATES).
ANNALES AFRICAINES 1960 PP 61-82
073,
       LESS ACCESSIBLE

073

AMIN SAMIR
L'ECONOMIE DU MAGHREB VOLUME 1- LA COLONISATION ET LA
DECOLONISATION VOLUME 2-LES PERSPECTIVE D AVENIR
PARIS,EDITIONS DE MINUIT, 1966
073,101-08,126-08,138-08,
       LESS ACCESSIBLE

ADELMAN IRMA
THEORIES OF ECONOMIC GROWTH AND DEVELOPMENT.
STANFORD,STANFORD UNIVERSITY PRESS, 1961
073,
       GENERAL THEORY

APTER DAVID E
SYSTEM, PROCESS, AND THE POLITICS OF ECONOMIC DEVELOPMENT.
IN JASON L FINKLE AND RICHARD W GABLE, POLITICAL
DEVELOPMENT AND SOCIAL CHANGE, NEW YORK, JOHN WILEY, 1966
073,074,
       GENERAL THEORY

AVRAMOVIC D
POSTWAR ECONOMIC GROWTH FOR LOW INCOME COUNTRIES.
WASHINGTON D C,INTERNATIONAL BANK FOR RECONSTRUCTION AND
DEVELOPMENT,1963, P 20
073,
       GENERAL THEORY

BLACK CYRIL E
THE DYNAMICS OF MODERNIZATION.
NEW YORK,HARPER AND ROW, 1966
037,073,
       GENERAL THEORY

DELL SIDNEY
TRADE BLOCS AND COMMON MARKETS
NEW YORK,KNOPF,1963
071,072,073,078,
       GENERAL THEORY

HAGEN EVERETT E
HOW ECONOMIC GROWTH BEGINS-- A THEORY OF SOCIAL CHANGE
CHAPTER 4.
IN JASON L FINKLE AND RICHARD W GABLE, POLITICAL
DEVELOPMENT AND SOCIAL CHANGE, NEW YORK, JOHN WILEY, 1966
037,073,
       GENERAL THEORY

HAGEN EVERETT E
THE ECONOMICS OF DEVELOPMENT.
HOMEWOOD, ILLINOIS, IRWIN PRESS,1968
071,073,
       GENERAL THEORY

HIRSCHMAN A O

THE STRATEGY OF ECONOMIC DEVELOPMENT
NEW HAVEN, YALE UNIVERSITY PRESS, 1968
071,073,
        GENERAL THEORY

073
    HOOVER CALVIN B   ED
    ECONOMIC SYSTEMS OF THE COMMONWEALTH.
    DURHAM, DUKE UNIVERSITY PRESS, 1962
    073,
        GENERAL THEORY

    HOSELITZ BERTHOLD
    ECONOMIC GROWTH AND DEVELOPMENT CHAPTER 8.
    IN JASON L FINKLE AND RICHARD W GABLE, POLITICAL
    DEVELOPMENT AND SOCIAL CHANGE, NEW YORK, JOHN WILEY, 1966
    037,073,
        GENERAL THEORY

    LEIBENSTEIN HARVEY
    ECONOMIC BACKWARDNESS AND ECONOMIC GROWTH.
    NEW YORK, JOHN WILEY, 1963
    073,
        GENERAL THEORY

    MOORE WILBERT E   FELDMAN ARNOLD S
    LABOR COMMITMENT AND SOCIAL CHANGE IN DEVELOPING AREAS.
    NEW YORK, SOCIAL SCIENCE RESEARCH COUNCIL, 1960
    073,
        GENERAL THEORY

    MYINT H
    THE ECONOMICS OF THE DEVELOPING COUNTRIES.
    NEW YORK, PRAEGER, 1964
    071,073,
        GENERAL THEORY

    MYRDAL GUNNAR
    RICH LANDS AND POOR.
    NEW YORK, HARPER, 1957 (ESP. CHAPTERS 1-3)
    037,071,073,
        GENERAL THEORY

    ROBERTS B C
    LABOUR IN THE TROPICAL TERRITORIES OF THE COMMONWEALTH.
    DURHAM, NORTH CAROLINA, DUKE UNIVERSITY PRESS, 1964
    073,
        GENERAL THEORY

74. POPULATION PRESSURE AND SOCIAL FACTORS IN DEVELOPMENT

074
    ADELMAN IRMA   MORRIS CYNTHIA TAFT
    SOCIETY, POLITICS, AND ECONOMIC DEVELOPMENT, A QUANTITATIVE
    APPROACH.

BALTIMORE, JOHNS HOPKINS UNIVERSITY PRESS, 1967
073,074,
        A STATISTICAL ANALYSIS OF SEVENTY-FOUR UNDERDEVELOPED
        COUNTRIES, ONE-THIRD OF WHICH ARE AFRICAN. USEFUL IN
        CONTRASTING THE POLITICAL, ECONOMIC, AND SOCIAL CHAR-
        ACTERISTICS OF COUNTRIES AT DIFFERENT STAGES OF DEVEL-
        OPMENT.

074
BRASS WILLIAM   COALE ANSLEY J   ET AL
THE DEMOGRAPHY OF TROPICAL AFRICA
PRINCETON, PRINCETON UNIVERSITY PRESS, 1968
074,
        CO-AUTHORED WITH PAUL DEMENY, DON F HEISEL, FRANK LORI,
           ANATOLE ROMANIUK, AND ETIENNE VAN DER WALLE. EXCELLENT
        SURVEY INCLUDES CURRENTLY AVAILABLE DATA ON AGE AND
        SEX COMPOSITION,FERTILITY AND MORTALITY. FIVE CASE
        STUDIES FOLLOWED BY FIVE GENERAL DEMOGRAPHIC CHAPTERS
        FOCUSING ON DATA COLLECTION AND USE

CALDWELL JOHN C   OKONJO C   EDS
THE POPULATION OF TROPICAL AFRICA.
LONDON, LONGMANS, 1968
053,074,076,
        RECORD OF FIRST AFRICAN POPULATION CONFERENCE AT THE
        UNIVERSITY OF IBADAN, 1966. FIRST SECTION EXAMINES
        BASIC DEMOGRAPHIC DATA, PROBLEMS OF COLLECTION, AND
        ROLE OF MIGRATION AND URBANIZATION. SECOND SECTION
        COVERS POPULATION GROWTH AND ECONOMIC DEVELOPMENT,
        PARTICULARLY WITH RESPECT TO PLANNING. TOTAL OF
        FORTY-SIX CONTRIBUTORY ARTICLES.

HANCE WILLIAM A
THE RACE BETWEEN POPULATION AND RESOURCES.
AFRICA REPORT 13 NO 1 JANUARY 1968
074,
        CHALLENGES PREVAILING VIEW THAT AFRICA IS NOT FACED
        WITH PROBLEMS OF OVERPOPULATION, ALTHOUGH AUTHOR IS
        OPTIMISTIC ABOUT FUTURE. DESCRIBES INDICATORS OF POP-
        ULATION PRESSURE AND GIVES EXAMPLES OF PARTICULAR DEN-
        SITY PROBLEMS (PARTS OF THE SAHARA, NORTHEASTERN
        GHANA, EASTERN REGION OF NIGERIA, SOKOTO PROVINCE OF
        NIGERIA, AFRICAN RESERVES IN RHODESIA). EXCELLENT
        MAP-- A TENTATIVE DEPICTION OF POPULATION PRESSURE IN
        1966.

HOLT ROBERT T   TURNER JOHN E
THE POLITICAL BASIS OF ECONOMIC DEVELOPMENT.
PRINCETON, VAN NOSTRAND, 1966
074,
        FORMULATES CONCEPTUAL FRAMEWORK FOR ANALYSIS OF POLI-
        TICAL FACTORS IN ECONOMIC GROWTH. FRAMEWORK APPLIED
        IN EMPIRICAL ANALYSES OF FRANCE, CHINA, JAPAN, AND
        ENGLAND. NOT SPECIFICALLY FOCUSED ON AFRICA.

UNESCO
SOCIAL IMPLICATIONS OF INDUSTRIALIZATION AND URBANIZATION
IN AFRICA SOUTH OF THE SAHARA.
PARIS, UNESCO, 1956
047,071,074,

FIRST MAJOR SYMPOSIUM ON PROBLEMS OF URBANIZATION AND
INDUSTRIALIZATION IN AFRICA. INCLUDES INTRODUCTORY
ESSAY BY DARYLL FORDE, AND SECTIONS ON SOCIAL EFFECTS
ON ECONOMIC DEVELOPMENT AND URBANIZATION, INCLUDING
NUMEROUS CASE STUDIES FROM ALL PARTS OF AFRICA SOUTH
OF THE SAHARA.

074

ADELMAN IRMA   DALTON GEORGE   MORRIS CYNTHIA TAFT
SOCIETY, POLITICS, AND ECONOMIC DEVELOPMENT IN AFRICA.
IN CARTER, GWENDOLEN M. AND ANN PADEN (EDS), EXPANDING
HORIZONS IN AFRICAN STUDIES, EVANSTON, NORTHWESTERN
UNIVERSITY PRESS, 1969, PP. 209-242
074,100.
        REFERENCE

APTER DAVID E
NATIONALISM GOVERNMENT AND ECONOMIC GROWTH.
ECONOMIC DEVELOPMENT AND CULTURAL CHANGE 7 1959 PP 117-136
074,
        REFERENCE

BALANDIER GEORGES
DESEQUILIBRES SOCIO-CULTURELS ET MODERNISATION DES PAYS
SOUS-DEVELOPEES (SOCIO-CULTURAL DISEQUILIBRIUMS AND
MODERNIZATION OF THE UNDERDEVELOPED COUNTRIES).
CAHIERS INTERNATIONAUX DE SOCIOLOGIE 20 JANUARY-JUNE 1956
PP 30-44
074,
        REFERENCE

BANTON MICHAEL P   DOSSER D G M
THE BALANCE BETWEEN SOCIAL AND ECONOMIC DEVELOPMENT
IN AFRICA SOUTH OF THE SAHARA.
INFORMATION 27 1961 PP 5-23
074,
        REFERENCE

CALDWELL JOHN C
POPULATION GROWTH AND FAMILY CHANGE IN AFRICA.
NEW YORK, HUMANITIES PRESS,INC., 1968
074,
        REFERENCE

ENDOZIEN J C
MALARIA, POPULATION GROWTH AND ECONOMIC DEVELOPMENT IN
AFRICA.
IN LALAGE BOWN AND MICHAEL CROWDER (EDS.), PROCEEDINGS OF
THE FIRST INTERNATIONAL CONGRESS OF AFRICANISTS, ACCRA,
1962, LONDON, LONGMANS, 1964, PP 329-333
074,
        REFERENCE

HARBISON F
THE AFRICAN UNIVERSITY AND HUMAN RESOURCES DEVELOPMENT
JOURNAL OF MODERN AFRICAN STUDIES 3 1965 PP 53-62
074,075,
        REFERENCE

INTER-AFRICAN LABOUR INSTITUTE

THE HUMAN FACTORS OF PRODUCTIVITY IN AFRICA.
LONDON, COMMISSION FOR TECHNICAL CO-OPERATION IN AFRICA
SOUTH OF THE SAHARA, 1952, 2ND EDITION, 1960
074,
        REFERENCE

074
LORIMER FRANK   BRASS WILLIAM   VAN DE WALLE E
DEMOGRAPHY.
IN ROBERT A LYSTAD (ED), THE AFRICAN WORLD, NEW YORK,
PRAEGER, 1966, PP 271-303
069,074,
        REFERENCE

LORIMER FRANK   KARP MARK   EDS
POPULATION IN AFRICA.
BOSTON, BOSTON UNIVERSITY PRESS, 1960
069,074,
        REFERENCE

MAIR LUCY P
THE GROWTH OF ECONOMIC INDIVIDUALISM IN AFRICAN SOCIETY.
JOURNAL OF THE ROYAL AFRICAN SOCIETY 33 1934 PP 261-273
074,
        REFERENCE

RADO E R
MANPOWER EDUCATION AND ECONOMIC GROWTH
JOURNAL OF MODERN AFRICAN STUDIES 4 1966 PP 83-93
074,075,
        REFERENCE

VILAKAZI ABSOLOM L
SOCIAL RESEARCH AND PROBLEMS OF AFRICAN ECONOMIC AND SOCIAL
DEVELOPMENT.
IN LALAGE BOWN AND MICHAEL CROWDER (EDS.), PROCEEDINGS OF
THE FIRST INTERNATIONAL CONGRESS OF AFRICANISTS, ACCRA,
1962, LONDON, LONGMANS, 1964, PP 184-189
074,
        REFERENCE

WILLIAMS P
THE COST AND FINANCE OF EDUCATION CHAPTER 27.
IN EDITH WHETHAM AND JEAN CURRIE (EDS.), READINGS IN THE
APPLIED ECONOMICS OF AFRICA, LONDON, CAMBRIDGE UNIVERSITY
PRESS, 2, 1967, PP 141-148
074,
        REFERENCE

ARDENER EDWIN   ED
SOCIAL AND DEMOGRAPHIC PROBLEMS OF THE SOUTHERN
CAMEROONS PLANTATION AREA.
IN AIDAN SOUTHALL (ED.), SOCIAL CHANGE IN MODERN AFRICA,
LONDON, OXFORD UNIVERSITY PRESS, 1961, PP 83-97
074,104-08,
        CASE STUDY

HUNTER GUY
EDUCATION FOR A DEVELOPING REGION, A STUDY IN EAST AFRICA
NEW YORK, OXFORD, FOR INSTITUTE OF RACE RELATIONS, LONDON, 1964

074,
       CASE STUDY

074

MCLOUGHLIN P F M
THE SUDAN'S THREE TOWNS--A DEMOGRAPHIC AND ECONOMIC PROFILE
OF AN AFRICAN URBAN COMPLEX
ECONOMIC DEVELOPMENT AND CULTURAL CHANGE 12 1963 AND 1964,
PP 70-83, 158-173, 286-304
046,074,134-05,
       CASE STUDY

OMINDE S H
LAND AND POPULATION MOVEMENTS IN KENYA
EVANSTON, NORTHWESTERN UNIVERSITY PRESS, 1968
074,117-08,
       CASE STUDY

RICHARDS AUDREY I   ED
ECONOMIC DEVELOPMENT AND TRIBAL CHANGE-- A STUDY OF
IMMIGRANT LABOUR IN BUGANDA.
CAMBRIDGE, HEFFER, 1956
074,139-08,
       CASE STUDY

SMOCK AUDREY   SMOCK DAVID
ETHNICITY AND ATTITUDES TOWARD DEVELOPMENT IN EASTERN
NIGERIA
JOURNAL OF THE DEVELOPING AREAS 3 1969 PP 499-512
074,
       CASE STUDY

TREWARTHA G T   ZELINSKY W
POPULATION PATTERNS IN TROPICAL AFRICA.
ANNALS OF THE ASSOCIATION OF AMERICAN GEOGRAPHERS WASHINGTON
VOL 44 JUNE 1954 PP 135-193
069,074,
       CASE STUDY

APTER DAVID E
SYSTEM, PROCESS, AND THE POLITICS OF ECONOMIC DEVELOPMENT.
IN JASON L FINKLE AND RICHARD W GABLE, POLITICAL
DEVELOPMENT AND SOCIAL CHANGE, NEW YORK, JOHN WILEY, 1966
073,074,
       GENERAL THEORY

HAUSER PHILIP M
CULTURAL AND PERSONAL OBSTACLES TO ECONOMIC DEVELOPMENT IN
THE LESS DEVELOPED AREAS.
HUMAN ORGANIZATION 18 SUMMER 1959 PP 78-84
074,
       GENERAL THEORY

HOSELITZ BERTHOLD
SOME REFLECTIONS ON THE SOCIAL AND CULTURAL CONDITIONS OF
ECONOMIC PRODUCTIVITY.
CIVILIZATIONS 12 1962 PP 489-498
074,
       GENERAL THEORY

NASH MANNING
SOME SOCIAL AND CULTURAL ASPECTS OF ECONOMIC DEVELOPMENT
CHAPTER 8.
IN JASON L FINKLE AND RICHARD W GABLE, POLITICAL
DEVELOPMENT AND SOCIAL CHANGE, NEW YORK, JOHN WILEY, 1966
074,
    GENERAL THEORY

074

PESHKIN ALAN   COHEN RONALD
THE VALUES OF MODERNIZATION
JOURNAL OF THE DEVELOPING AREAS 2 1967 PP 7-22
074,
    GENERAL THEORY

SADIE J L
THE SOCIAL ANTHROPOLOGY OF ECONOMIC DEVELOPMENT.
ECONOMIC JOURNAL 70 JUNE 1960 PP 294-303
074,
    GENERAL THEORY

SPENGLER J J
ECONOMIC DEVELOPMENT -- POLITICAL PRECONDITIONS AND
POLITICAL CONSEQUENCES CHAPTER 7.
IN JASON L FINKLE AND RICHARD W GABLE, POLITICAL
DEVELOPMENT AND SOCIAL CHANGE, NEW YORK, JOHN WILEY, 1966
074,
    GENERAL THEORY

TANGRI SHANTI
URBANIZATION, POLITICAL STABILITY AND ECONOMIC GROWTH
CHAPTER 9.
IN JASON L FINKLE AND RICHARD W GABLE, POLITICAL
DEVELOPMENT AND SOCIAL CHANGE, NEW YORK, JOHN WILEY, 1966
047,074,
    GENERAL THEORY

BARBOUR K M   PROTHERO R MANSELL   EDS
ESSAYS ON AFRICAN POPULATION.
LONDON, ROUTLEDGE AND KEGAN PAUL, 1961
069,074,
    REFERENCE

75. TECHNOLOGY AND NATION-BUILDING

075

COCKCROFT SIR JOHN
TECHNOLOGY FOR DEVELOPING COUNTRIES
LONDON, OVERSEAS DEVELOPMENT INSTITUTE
075,
    GOOD INTRODUCTION TO THE ROLE OF TECHNOLOGY. MAJOR
    FOCUS ON CURRENT RESEARCH IN AND POTENTIALS FOR THE
    ADAPTATION OF INDUSTRIAL TECHNOLOGIES TO DEVELOPING
    COUNTRIES. ALSO CONTAINS A REVIEW OF THE WORK OF THE
    TROPICAL PRODUCTS INSTITUTE

075

HUNTER GUY
THE BEST OF BOTH WORLDS- A CHALLENGE ON DEVELOPMENT POLICIES
IN AFRICA
LONDON AND NEW YORK, OXFORD UNIVERSITY PRESS, 1967
073,075,076,
        A SERIES OF ESSAYS FOCUSING ON THE TRANSFER OF
        TECHNOLOGY,INSTITUTIONS AND THE IDEAS AND VALUES
        CORRESPONDING TO THEM,FROM DEVELOPED TO DEVELOPING
        COUNTRIES,AND ON THE EFFECTS OF THIS TRANSFER. MAJOR
        SECTIONS OF THE HISTORICAL POSITION OF AFRICA AND THE
        NATURE OF GROWTH,ECONOMIC GROWTH AND EMPLOYMENT,THE
        RURAL ECONOMY,INSTITUTIONS AND EDUCATION.

WOLSTENHOLME G   O CONNOR M   EDS
MAN AND AFRICA
LONDON,J AND A CHURCHILL,1965
075,
        SYMPOSIUM SPONSORED BY CIBA FOUNDATION AND HAILE
        SELASSIE I PRIZE TRUST.ARTICLES ON CLIMATE AND WATER
        RESOURCES,EPEDEMIOLOGY AND HEALTH SERVICES,TRANSPORT
        AND COMMUNICATIONS,BIOLOGY,EDUCATION,AGRICULTURE,
        CONSERVATION AND COMPREHENSIVE ENVIRONMENTAL
        DEVELOPMENT.

BAFFOUR R P
SCIENCE AND TECHNOLOGY IN RELATION TO AFRICA≠S DEVELOPMENT.
IN LALAGE BOWN AND MICHAEL CROWDER (EDS.), PROCEEDINGS OF
THE FIRST INTERNATIONAL CONGRESS OF AFRICANISTS, ACCRA,
1962, LONDON, LONGMANS, 1964, PP 301-308
037,075,
        REFERENCE

BROWN R
HEALTH AND DISEASE IN AFRICA.
TRANSITION 6 26 1966 PP 28-33
069,075,
        REFERENCE

CLOUDSLEY THOMPSON
TSETSE-- THE SCOURGE OF AFRICA.
LONDON,SCIENCE NEWS,PENGUIN BOOKS,1959, PP 69-78
069,075,
        REFERENCE

COLBOURNE MICHAEL
MALARIA IN AFRICA.
LONDON, OXFORD UNIVERSITY PRESS, 1966
075,
        REFERENCE

DECRAEMER WILLY   FOX RENEE C
THE EMERGING PHYSICIAN.
PALO ALTO, HOOVER INSTITUTION PRESS, 1969
075,
        REFERENCE

GINZBERG E   ED
TECHNOLOGY AND SOCIAL CHANGE

NEW YORK, COLUMBIA UNIVERSITY PRESS, 1964
037,075,
     REFERENCE

075
  GOUROU PIERRE   BEAVER S H   LABORDE E D
  THE TROPICAL WORLD-- ITS SOCIAL AND ECONOMIC CONDITIONS AND
  ITS FUTURE STATUS.
  LONDON, LONGMANS, 4TH EDITION, 1966
  069,075,
     REFERENCE

  GRAY ROBERT F
  MEDICAL RESEARCH-- SOME ANTHROPOLOGICAL ASPECTS.
  IN ROBERT A LYSTAD (ED), THE AFRICAN WORLD, NEW YORK,
  PRAEGER, 1966,
  075,100,
     REFERENCE

  HARBISON F
  THE AFRICAN UNIVERSITY AND HUMAN RESOURCES DEVELOPMENT
  JOURNAL OF MODERN AFRICAN STUDIES 3 1965 PP 53-62
  074,075,
     REFERENCE

  KING MAURICE
  A MEDICAL LABORATORY FOR DEVELOPING COUNTRIES.
  KAMPALA, INTERNATIONAL UNIVERSITY BOOKSELLERS, INC., 1968
  075,
     REFERENCE

  KIRKWOOD KENNETH
  BRITAIN AND AFRICA.
  BALTIMORE, JOHNS HOPKINS PRESS, 1965
  082,
  075,
     REFERENCE

  LYSTAD ROBERT A
  R AND D AT THE GRASS ROOTS.
  AFRICA REPORT, MAY 1968, P. 12
  075,
     REFERENCE

  MCNOWN JOHN S
  ENGINEERING EDUCATION IN SUBSAHARAN AFRICA.
  NEW YORK, PRAEGER, 1968
  075,
     REFERENCE

  MOXON JAMES
  VOLTA--MAN'S GREATEST LAKE.
  NEW YORK, PRAEGER PUBLISHERS, 1969
  075,114-08,
     REFERENCE

  OTIENO N C
  CURRENT PROBLEMS IN THE EDUCATION OF AN AFRICAN SCIENTIST
  AND THE ROLE SUCH A SCIENTIST COULD PLAY IN THE ECONOMIC
  AND SOCIAL DEVELOPMENT OF AFRICA.

IN LALAGE BOWN AND MICHAEL CROWDER (EDS.), PROCEEDINGS OF
THE FIRST INTERNATIONAL CONGRESS OF AFRICANISTS, ACCRA,
1962, LONDON, LONGMANS, 1964, PP 309-317
075,
        REFERENCE

075

   PROTHERO R MANSELL
   MIGRANTS AND MALARIA.
   LONDON, LONGMANS, 1965
   069,075,
        REFERENCE

   PROTHERO R MANSELL
   POPULATION MOVEMENT AND PROBLEMS OF MALARIA ERADICATION IN
   AFRICA.
   WORLD HEALTH ORGANIZATION BULLETIN 24 1961 PP 405-425
   069,075,
        REFERENCE

   RADO E R
   MANPOWER EDUCATION AND ECONOMIC GROWTH
   JOURNAL OF MODERN AFRICAN STUDIES 4 1966 PP 83-93
   074,075,
        REFERENCE

   ROBINSON M E
   THE FOOD POTENTIAL OF AFRICA.
   CHICAGO, FOOD AND CONTAINER INSTITUTE OF THE ARMED FORCES,
   12 1960
   069,075,
        REFERENCE

   RODIER J
   HYDROLOGY IN AFRICA.
   NEW YORK, UNESCO, 1953
   069,075,
        REFERENCE

   RODIER J
   THE BIBLIOGRAPHY OF AFRICAN HYDROLOGY.
   PARIS, UNESCO, 1963
   069,075,
        REFERENCE

   WARREN M W   RUBIN N
   DAMS IN AFRICA-AN INTERDISCIPLINARY STUDY OF MAN-MADE LAKES
   IN AFRICA
   LONDON, FRANK CASS, 1968
   075,
        REFERENCE

   WEISS CHARLES JR
   A BIOPHYSICIST LOOKS AT SCIENCE IN AFRICA.
   AFRICA REPORT, JANUARY 1968, P. 13
   075,
        REFERENCE

   WORTHINGTON E B
   SCIENCE IN THE DEVELOPMENT OF AFRICA.

LONDON, COMMISSION FOR TECHNICAL COOPERATION IN AFRICA SOUTH
OF THE SAHARA, 1958
073,075,
          REFERENCE

075
    EAST AFRICAN ACADEMY
    PROCEEDINGS OF THE EAST AFRICAN ACADEMY. D.F. OWEN ED.
    NAIROBI, EAST AFRICAN PUBLISHING HOUSE, 1967
    075,099,
          CASE STUDY

    OWEN D F   ED
    RESEARCH AND DEVELOPMENT IN EAST AFRICA.
    NAIROBI, EAST AFRICAN ACADEMY, EAST AFRICAN INSTITUTE PRESS
    LTD., 1966
    075,100,
          CASE STUDY

    BRANSON JACK
    ECONOMIC AND SOCIAL CONSIDERATIONS IN ADAPTING TECHNOLOGIES
    FOR DEVELOPING COUNTRIES.
    TECHNOLOGY AND CULTURE 4 WINTER 1963 PP 22-29
    075,
          GENERAL THEORY

    LEWIS W ARTHUR
    EDUCATION FOR SCIENTIFIC PROFESSIONS IN THE POOR COUNTRIES.
    DAEDALUS 91 SPRING 1962 PP 310-318
    042,075,
          GENERAL THEORY

    NADER CLAIRE   ZAHLAN A B   EDS
    SCIENCE AND TECHNOLOGY IN DEVELOPING COUNTRIES
    NEW YORK, CAMBRIDGE UNIVERSITY PRESS, 1969
    075,
          GENERAL THEORY

    BARBICHON G
    THE DIFFUSION OF SCIENTIFIC AND TECHNICAL KNOWLEDGE--
    PROCEEDINGS OF THE IBADAN CONFERENCE ON THE PROBLEMS OF
    SOCIAL PSYCHOLOGY IN DEVELOPING NATIONS.
    JOURNAL OF SOCIAL ISSUES 12 1966, 1 1967
    075,
          REFERENCE

    HUNTER GUY
    THE NEW SOCIETIES OF TROPICAL AFRICA.
    LONDON, OXFORD UNIVERSITY PRESS, 1962
    053,075,
          REFERENCE

76. STUDY QUESTIONS: CONSOLIDATION OF NATION-STATES

CALDWELL JOHN C   OKONJO C   EDS
THE POPULATION OF TROPICAL AFRICA.
LONDON,LONGMANS,1968
053,074,076,

>   RECORD OF FIRST AFRICAN POPULATION CONFERENCE AT THE
>   UNIVERSITY OF IBADAN, 1966. FIRST SECTION EXAMINES
>   BASIC DEMOGRAPHIC DATA, PROBLEMS OF COLLECTION, AND
>   ROLE OF MIGRATION AND URBANIZATION. SECOND SECTION
>   COVERS POPULATION GROWTH AND ECONOMIC DEVELOPMENT,
>   PARTICULARLY WITH RESPECT TO PLANNING. TOTAL OF
>   FORTY-SIX CONTRIBUTORY ARTICLES.

076

CARTER GWENDOLEN M   ED
NATIONAL UNITY AND REGIONALISM IN EIGHT AFRICAN STATES--
NIGERIA, NIGER, CONGO, GABON, CENTRAL AFRICAN REPUBLIC,
CHAD, UGANDA, ETHIOPIA.
ITHACA,CORNELL UNIVERSITY PRESS,1966
057,076,

>   CASE STUDIES OF THE CONFLICTS BETWEEN REGIONALISM AND
>   THE DESIRE FOR NATIONAL UNITY. AUTHORS FOLLOW COMMON
>   OUTLINE WHICH INCLUDES HISTORICAL BACKGROUND, LAND AND
>   PEOPLE, THE POLITICAL PROCESS, CONTEMPORARY PROBLEMS,
>   EXTERNAL AFFAIRS, AND BIBLIOGRAPHY. CONCLUSION SYN-
>   THESIZES MAJOR POINTS OF INDIVIDUAL STUDIES.

COWAN L GRAY
THE DILEMMAS OF AFRICAN INDEPENDENCE.
NEW YORK,WALKER,1968
002,076,

>   COMPLETELY REVISED EDITION OF EARLIER WORK. AUTHOR
>   HAS FOUR SECTIONS-- NATIONALISM AND AFTER, PROSPECT
>   FOR POLITICAL DEVELOPMENT, AFRICA S ECONOMIC FUTURE,
>   AND FOREIGN POLICIES OF THE AFRICAN STATES. AUTHOR IS
>   PROFESSOR OF GOVERNMENT AT COLUMBIA UNIVERSITY.
>   SECOND HALF OF BOOK IS REFERENCE DATA ON AFRICA COM-
>   PILED BY A. E. STIEFBOLD AND S. MCNAMARA, WHICH
>   INCLUDES MAPS, VITAL STATISTICS, AND CAPSULE DESCRIP-
>   TIONS OF STATE/REGIONAL ORGANIZATIONS.

DEUTSCH KARL W   FOLTZ WILLIAM J   EDS
NATION-BUILDING.
ATHERTON PRESS,1966
057,076,

>   A MAJOR RECENT ANTHOLOGY DEALING WITH NATION-BUILDING
>   THROUGH-OUT THE WORLD, INCLUDING EUROPE. ESSAY BY
>   RUPERT EMERSON ON NATION-BUILDING IN AFRICA GIVES
>   CLEAR OVERVIEW OF ETHNICITY, PLURALISM, AND TRIBALISM
>   IN MODERN CONTEXT. ALSO ASSESSES RELIGION AND OTHER
>   CULTURAL PATTERNS AS THEY AFFECT NATIONAL INTEGRATION
>   INTRODUCTORY ESSAY BY DEUTSCH IS EXCELLENT SUMMARY OF
>   CONCEPTS AND DEFINITIONS. SELECT BIBLIOGRAPHY OF
>   RECENT WORKS ON NATION-BUILDING.

HANNA WILLIAM J   ED
INDEPENDENT BLACK AFRICA.
CHICAGO,RAND MCNALLY,1964
076,097,

>   REPRINTS OF MAJOR ARTICLES BY WELL-KNOWN SCHOLARS,
>   AND AFRICAN STATESMEN. SECTIONS INCLUDE-- CHANGE

(PERSONALITY, URBANIZATION), REACTION TO CHANGE (DE-
COLONIZATION, NATIONALISM), CONTINUITY (TRADITIONAL-
ISM, MODERNIZATION, ELITES, ELECTIONS), TERRITORIAL
UNITY (CHARISMA, SINGLE PARTY SYSTEMS, POLITICAL
OPPOSITION, INTELLECTUALS, CORRUPTION), LARGER UNITY
(PAN-AFRICANISM, NEGRITUDE, UNITED NATIONS, REGIONS).

076

HUNTER GUY
THE BEST OF BOTH WORLDS- A CHALLENGE ON DEVELOPMENT POLICIES
IN AFRICA
LONDON AND NEW YORK, OXFORD UNIVERSITY PRESS, 1967
073,075,076,
 A SERIES OF ESSAYS FOCUSING ON THE TRANSFER OF
 TECHNOLOGY,INSTITUTIONS AND THE IDEAS AND VALUES
 CORRESPONDING TO THEM,FROM DEVELOPED TO DEVELOPING
 COUNTRIES.AND ON THE EFFECTS OF THIS TRANSFER. MAJOR
 SECTIONS OF THE HISTORICAL POSITION OF AFRICA AND THE
 NATURE OF GROWTH.ECONOMIC GROWTH AND EMPLOYMENT,THE
 RURAL ECONOMY,INSTITUTIONS AND EDUCATION.

LEGUM COLIN   ED
AFRICA-- HANDBOOK TO A CONTINENT.
NEW YORK, PRAEGER, 1966
056,076,
 CAPSULE SUMMARY OF EACH AFRICAN STATE INCLUDES VITAL
 STATISTICS ON POLITICS, ECONOMICS, DEMOGRAPHY, AND
 COLONIAL HISTORY. SECOND PART IS SUMMARY OF MAJOR
 TOPICS-- INTERNATIONAL RELATIONS, ART, LITERATURE,
 RELIGION, ECONOMICS, EDUCATION, LAW, TRADE UNIONS,
 PRESS, UNITED NATION ACTIVITIES IN AFRICA. EDITOR
 IS BRITISH JOURNALIST WITH LONG AFRICAN EXPERIENCE.

MARKOVITZ IRVING L ED
AFRICAN POLITICS AND SOCIETY
NEW YORK,THE FREE PRESS, 1970
076,
 VOLUME CONSISTS OF 27 SELECTIONS FROM EXISTING JOURNAL
 LITERATURE ON ALL ASPECTS OF NATION-BUILDING,INCLUDING
 ARTICLES BY-CHEIKH ANTA DIOP,MICHAEL CROWDER,AIME
 CESAIRE,EDUARDO MONDLANE,PAULA BROWN,MAX GLUCKMAN,
 JEAN SURET-CANAL,GICHA MBEE,J.S.COLEMAN,GEORGE
 SHEPPERSON,JEAN PIERRE N'DIAYE,CARL ROSBERG AND JOHN
 NOTTIMGHAM,DAVID APTER,FRED GREENE,CRAWFORD YOUNG,
 COLIM LEGUM,I.L.MARKOVITZ,SAMIR AMIN,TOM MBOYA,S.J.
 PATEL,CRANFORD PRATT,STANLEY TRAPIDO,RUPERT EMERSON.

MCEWAN PETER J   ED
TWENTIETH CENTURY AFRICA.
LONDON, OXFORD UNIVERSITY PRESS, 1968
002,076,
 REPRINTS OF MAJOR ARTICLES BY WELL-KNOWN SCHOLARS.
 ARRANGED REGIONALLY-- WEST AFRICA, NORTH AFRICA,
 EGYPT, ETHIOPIA, EAST AFRICA, SOUTH AFRICA, SOUTHERN
 RHODESIA. ZAMBIA AND MALAWI. CONCLUDED WITH SECTION
 ON NATIONALISM AND PAN-AFRICANISM. CHRONOLOGICAL
 TABLE. BOOK IS INTENDED FOR TEXTBOOK USE AT
 UNIVERSITY LEVEL. EXTREMELY USEFUL FOR INTRODUCTION
 TO CASE STUDIES. LAST OF THREE-VOLUME SERIES ON
 AFRICAN HISTORY.

076

MCEWAN PETER J   SUTCLIFFE ROBERT B   EDS
MODERN AFRICA.
NEW YORK, THOMAS CROWELL, 1965
002,076,097,
        EXCELLENT SELECTION OF REPRINTS, ARRANGED THEMATICALLY
        AS AN INTRODUCTION TO AFRICAN STUDIES. TWO MAJOR SEC-
        TIONS TO THE BOOK-- THE TRADITIONAL BACKGROUND, AND
        THE CONTEMPORARY SCENE. FORMER DEALS WITH TRADITIONAL
        SOCIAL STRUCTURE, VALUE SYSTEMS, TRIBAL GOVERNMENT,
        AND TRADITIONAL ECONOMIC SYSTEMS. SECOND PART DEALS
        WITH RISE OF NATIONS, POLITICS, ECONOMIC AND SOCIAL
        CHANGE, AND ROLE OF AFRICA IN WORLD AFFAIRS.

POST KENNETH W J
THE NEW STATES OF WEST AFRICA
BALTIMORE, PENGUIN BOOKS, REVISED EDITION, 1968
076,
        EXCELLENT SUMMARY BY BRITISH POLITICAL SCIENTIST WITH
        TEACHING EXPERIENCE AT UNIVERSITY COLLEGE IBADAN.
        COVERS THE MAJOR THEMES OF NATION-BUILDING-THE PATH TO
        INDEPENDENCE.THE HEIRS TO THE THRONE,NATIONAL UNITY
        AND THE OPPOSITION,THE INSTITUTIONS OF GOVERNMENT,
        ECONOMIC DEVELOPMENT,EDUCATION AND MANPOWER,FOREIGN
        RELATIONS,CONCLUSION.

WALLERSTEIN I M
THE POLITICS OF INDEPENDENCE.
NEW YORK, VINTAGE, 1961
056,076,
        INTERPRETS TOTALITY OF AFRICAN HISTORICAL DEVELOPMENT
        IN CLEAR AND INSIGHTFUL PERSPECTIVE. FOCUSES ON THE
        PERIOD OF NATIONALISM AND INDEPENDENCE. AUTHOR IS
        PROFESSOR OF SOCIOLOGY AT COLUMBIA UNIVERSITY.

DODGE DOROTHY
AFRICAN POLITICS IN PERSPECTIVE.
NEW YORK, VAN NOSTRAND-REINHOLD, 1966
076,
        REFERENCE

HODDER B W   HARRIS D R   EDS
AFRICA IN TRANSITION-GEOGRAPHICAL ESSAYS
LONDON, METHUEN, 1967
069,076,
        REFERENCE

HOWE RUSSELL WARREN
BLACK AFRICA-- AFRICA SOUTH OF THE SAHARA FROM PRE-
HISTORY TO INDEPENDENCE.
CHICAGO, WALKER, 1967
036,076,
        REFERENCE

JORDAN ROBERT S
GOVERNMENT AND POWER IN WEST AFRICA
NEW YORK, AFRICANA PUBLISHING CORPORATION, 1969
076,
        REFERENCE

076
    MAZRUI ALI A
    HAS AFRICA'S INDEPENDENCE CHANGED THE WORLD CHAPTER 14.
    IN ON HEROES AND UHURU-WORSHIP LONDON LONGMANS
    1967 PP 231-244
    076,
        REFERENCE

    WELCH CLAUDE E   ED
    POLITICAL MODERNIZATION-- A READER IN COMPARATIVE POLITICAL
    CHANGE.
    BELMONT, CALIFORNIA, WADSWORTH PUBLISHING COMPANY, 1967
    076,
        REFERENCE

    AKE CLAUDE
    A THEORY OF POLITICAL INTEGRATION
    HOMEWOOD, ILLINOIS, THE DORSEY PRESS, 1967
    057,076,
        GENERAL THEORY

    LEYS COLIN   ED
    POLITICS AND CHANGE IN DEVELOPING COUNTRIES
    NEW YORK, CAMBRIDGE UNIVERSITY PRESS, 1970
    076,
        GENERAL THEORY

    MAIR LUCY P
    NEW NATIONS.
    LONDON, WEIDENFELD AND NICOLSON, 1963
    076,
        GENERAL THEORY

PART V
Africa and
the Modern World

77. CONCEPTS OF SUPRANATIONALISM

077
  FRIEDLAND WILLIAM H ROSBERG CARL G   EDS
  AFRICAN SOCIALISM.
  LONDON, OXFORD UNIVERSITY PRESS, 1965
  060,077,
       MAJOR SOURCE OF WRITINGS AND ESSAYS ON AFRICAN SOCIAL-
       ISM.

  HAZLEWOOD ARTHUR
  PROBLEMS OF INTEGRATION AMONG AFRICAN STATES CHAPTER 1.
  IN AFRICAN INTEGRATION AND DISINTEGRATION, LONDON, OXFORD
  UNIVERSITY PRESS, 1967, PP 3-25 (INTRODUCTION)
  077,
       ESTABLISHES FRAMEWORK AND PERSPECTIVE FOR LARGER VOL-
       UME EDITED BY AUTHOR. EXAMINES THEORY OF CUSTOMS
       UNIONS, ECONOMIC DEVELOPMENT POLICIES, EXTENSION OF
       MARKETS, INVESTMENT PRIORITIES, EXTERNAL TARIFFS, E-
       QUALIZATION, AND GENERAL PROBLEMS OF ECONOMIC INTEGRA-
       TION. LITTLE SPECIFICALLY ON POLITICAL INTEGRATION.

  HOSKYNS CATHERINE
  THE AFRICAN STATES AND THE UNITED NATIONS, 1958-1964.
  INTERNATIONAL AFFAIRS 40 3 JULY 1964 PP 466-480
  077,081,
       FOUR PARTS-- 1) AFRICA AT THE UNITED NATIONS-- 2) PAN-

AFRICAN, AFRO-ASIAN, AND EURAFRICAN MOVEMENTS--
3) AFRICA S RELATIONS WITH INDIA AND THE SOVIET
UNION-- 4) AMERICAN POLICY IN AFRICA. GOOD DATA ON
EVENTS AND TRENDS UP TO ABOUT 1962. AUTHOR IS PROFES-
SOR AT JOHNS HOPKINS SCHOOL OF ADVANCED INTERNATIONAL
STUDIES.

077

JAMES C L R
A HISTORY OF PAN-AFRICAN REVOLT
WASHINGTON, D. C., DRUM AND SPEAR PRESS, 1969
077,079,
> AUTHOR IS WEST INDIAN WHO HAS ACTIVELY PARTICIPATED
> IN MANY OF THE KEY EVENTS IN PAN-AFRICAN HISTORY.
> DEALS WITH BLACK RESISTANCE TO OPPRESSION IN
> AMERICA, THE WEST INDIES, AND AFRICA. AVAILABLE
> IN PAPERBACK.

LEGUM COLIN
PAN-AFRICANISM-A SHORT POLITICAL GUIDE.
NEW YORK, PRAEGER, 1962
077,079,
> EXCELLENT BACKGROUND TO THE DEVELOPMENT OF PAN-AFRI-
> CAN IDEAS AND MOVEMENT. DEALS WITH EARLY PAN-AFRICAN
> CONFERENCES IN EUROPE AND THE INFLUENCE OF THE DIAS-
> PORA ON PAN-AFRICANISM (INCLUDING THE BACK TO AFRICA
> MOVEMENTS). PROVIDES SUMMARY OF THE SUPRA-NATIONAL
> GROUPINGS IN AFRICA FROM 1960-63 (CASABLANCA AND MON-
> ROVIA GROUPS), AND THE INTERNATIONAL ROLE OF AFRICAN
> LABOR. ASSESSES LITERARY AND CULTURAL MANIFESTATIONS
> OF PAN-AFRICANISM.

MAZRUI ALI A
TOWARDS A PAX AFRICANA-- A STUDY OF IDEOLOGY AND AMBITION.
LONDON, WEIDENFELD AND NICOLSON, 1967
CHICAGO, UNIVERSITY OF CHICAGO PRESS, 1967
060,077,099,
> THREE MAJOR SECTIONS-- 1) IDEOLOGY AND IDENTITY (IDI-
> OM OF SELF-DETERMINATION, PRINCIPLE OF RACIAL SOVER-
> EIGNTY, CONCEPT WE ARE ALL AFRICANS , NEO-DEPENDENCY,
> PRINCIPLE OF CONTINENTAL JURISDICTION, AND PAN-AFRICAN
> IMPLICATIONS OF SOCIALISM AND ONE-PARTY STATE)-- 2)
> DILEMNAS OF STATEHOOD (PEACE VERSUS HUMAN RIGHTS, NON-
> ALIGNMENT, PAN-AFRICANISM AND COLD WAR, CONCEPT OF
> PAX AFRICANA)-- 3) APPENDICES (CHARTER OF ORGANIZA-
> TION OF AFRICAN UNITY).

NYE JOSEPH S
PAN AFRICANISM AND EAST AFRICAN INTEGRATION.
CAMBRIDGE, HARVARD UNIVERSITY PRESS, 1965
077,
> EXAMINES BACKGROUND AND FUTURE POTENTIAL OF EAST
> AFRICAN INTEGRATION, WITH SPECIAL REFERENCE TO ISSUES
> OF PAN-AFRICANISM. PROVIDES COLONIAL ERA BACKGROUND,
> AND EXAMINES EUROPEAN THEORIES OF INTEGRATION IN
> EAST AFRICAN CONTEXT. DISCUSSES ADAPTATION OF PRE-
> INDEPENDENCE REGIONAL STRUCTURES SUCH AS THE COMMON
> SERVICES ORGANIZATION.

D'ARBOUSSIER G

DEVELOPMENTS IN FRENCH-SPEAKING WEST AFRICA CHAPTER 5.
IN DAVID P CURRIE, FEDERALISM AND THE NEW NATIONS OF AFRICA,
CHICAGO,UNIVERSITY OF CHICAGO PRESS,1964,PP 117-136,
DISCUSSION PP 137-152
077,
        REFERENCE

077

    DIOP ALIOUNE
    REMARKS ON AFRICAN PERSONALITY AND NEGRITUDE
    IN AMERICAN SOCIETY OF AFRICAN CULTURE,PAN-AFRICANISM
    RECONSIDERED,BERKELEY,UNIVERSITY OF CALIFORNIA PRESS,1962
    PP 337-345
    039,054,077,079,
        REFERENCE

    DRAKE ST CLAIR
    PAN-AFRICANISM NEGRITUDE AND THE AFRICAN PERSONALITY.
    BOSTON UNIVERSITY GRADUATE JOURNAL 10 1961 PP 38-51, IN
    WILLIAM J HANNA,INDEPENDENT BLACK AFRICA,CHICAGO,RAND
    MCNALLY,1964,PP 530-541
    039,054,077,
        REFERENCE

    GREEN REGINALD H   KRISHNA K G V
    ECONOMIC CO-OPERATION IN AFRICA.
    LONDON,OXFORD UNIVERSITY PRESS,1967
    077,078,080,
        REFERENCE

    HOUPHOUET-BOIGNY F
    BLACK AFRICA AND THE FRENCH UNION.
    IN PHILIP W QUIGG (ED.), AFRICA. NEW YORK, PRAEGER, 1964,
    PP 263-271
    077,116-04,
        REFERENCE

    HUGHES A J
    EAST AFRICA-- THE SEARCH FOR UNITY-- KENYA, TANGANYIKA,
    UGANDA AND ZANZIBAR.
    MIDDLESEX,HARMONDSWORTH,1963
    077,117-09,136-09,139-09,
        REFERENCE

    JOHNSON CAROL A
    POLITICAL AND REGIONAL GROUPINGS IN AFRICA.
    IN WILLIAM J HANNA (ED), INDEPENDENT BLACK AFRICA, CHICAGO,
    RAND MCNALLY, 1964, PP 555-587
    077,
        REFERENCE

    NYERERE JULIUS K
    UJAMAA--ESSAYS ON SOCIALISM
    NEW YORK,OXFORD UNIVERSITY PRESS,1969
    060,077,
        REFERENCE

    POVOLNY M
    AFRICA IN SEARCH OF UNITY-- MODEL AND REALITY.
    BACKGROUND 9 FEBRUARY 1966 PP 297-318

077,
        REFERENCE

077
LEWIS I M
PAN AFRICANISM AND PAN SOMALISM
JOURNAL OF MODERN AFRICAN STUDIES 1 1963 PP 147-162
059,077,133-09,
        CASE STUDY

LINTON NEVILLE
NYERERE'S ROAD TO SOCIALISM
CANADIAN JOURNAL OF AFRICAN STUDIES 2 1968 PP 1-6
077,136-07,
        CASE STUDY

MAZRUI ALI A
TANZANIA VERSUS EAST AFRICA CHAPTER 6.
IN ON HEROES AND UHURU-WORSHIP, LONDON, LONGMANS,
1967, PP 73-95
077,136-09,
        CASE STUDY

NYERERE JULIUS K
ESSAYS ON SOCIALISM.
LONDON AND NEW YORK. INTERNATIONAL BOOKSELLERS, INC., 1969
060,077,136-04,
        CASE STUDY

REPUBLIC OF KENYA
AFRICAN SOCIALISM AND ITS APPLICATION TO PLANNING IN KENYA
NAIROBI GOVERNMENT PRINTER 1965
054,072,077,117-08,
        CASE STUDY

SOJA EDWARD
COMMUNICATIONS AND TERRITORIAL INTEGRATION IN EAST AFRICA-
AN INTRODUCTION TO TRANSACTION FLOW ANALYSIS
EAST LAKES GEOGRAPHER 4 1968 PP 39-57
048,059,077,
        CASE STUDY

GONIDEC P F
LA COMMUNAUTE (THE COMMUNITY).
PUBLIC LAW, SUMMER, 1960, PP. 177-189
077,
        LESS ACCESSIBLE

DEUTSCH KARL W
MAIN FINDINGS-- INTEGRATION AS A PROCESS.
IN KARL DEUTSCH ET AL, POLITICAL COMMUNITY AND THE NORTH
ATLANTIC AREA, PRINCETON, NEW JERSEY, PRINCETON UNIVERSITY
PRESS, 1968 (PAPERBACK), PP 70-116
077,
        GENERAL THEORY

HAAS ERNST B
FUNCTIONALISM AND THE THEORY OF INTEGRATION.
IN ERNST B HASS, BEYOND THE NATION-STATE-- FUNCTIONALISM AND
INTERNATIONAL ORGANIZATION, STANFORD CALIFORNIA, STANFORD

UNIVERSITY PRESS, 1964, PP 3-138
077,
        GENERAL THEORY

077
   FOLTZ WILLIAM J
   FROM FRENCH WEST AFRICA TO THE MALI FEDERATION.
   NEW HAVEN, YALE UNIVERSITY PRESS, 1965
   077,123-09,130-09,

   NYERERE JULIUS K
   FREEDOM AND UNITY--UHURU NA UMOJA.
   LONDON, OXFORD UNIVERSITY PRESS, 1967
   060,077,136-04,

78. EMERGENT PATTERNS OF REGIONALISM

078
   BELASSA BELA
   THE THEORY OF ECONOMIC INTEGRATION
   HOMEWOOD, ILLINOIS, IRWIN PRESS, 1961
   071,078,
        DISCUSSES THEORETICAL ASPECTS OF INTER-STATE ECONOMIC
        INTEGRATION WITH SPECIAL REFERENCE TO THE TYPES OF
        ORGANIZATIONAL ARRANGEMENTS ACCOMMODATING SUCH LINKAGE
        DISTINGUISHES BETWEEN CUSTOMS UNION (TARIFF VERSUS
        OUTSIDERS), COMMON MARKET (FREE COMMODITY MOVEMENTS),
        ECONOMIC UNION (FREE FACTOR FLOW), AND TOTAL UNIFICATION--
        MONETARY, FISCAL, AND SOCIAL

   CHITEPO HERBERT W
   DEVELOPMENTS IN CENTRAL AFRICA.
   IN DAVID P CURRIE (ED), FEDERALISM AND THE NEW NATIONS OF
   AFRICA, CHICAGO, UNIVERSITY OF CHICAGO PRESS, 1964, PP 3-28
   078,087,122-06,142-06,145-06,
        DISCUSSES THE FEDERATION OF RHODESIA AND NYASALAND
        WHICH WAS ESTABLISHED DESPITE AFRICAN PROTESTS IN
        1953. AUTHOR SKETCHES ETHNIC AND DEMOGRAPHIC ASPECTS
        OF FEDERATION. PROCEEDINGS OF DISCUSSION WITH CONFER-
        ENCE PARTICIPANTS IS INCLUDED. AUTHOR IS LONDON
        TRAINED LAWYER, AND CURRENT LEADER OF NATIONALIST
        MOVEMENT IN RHODESIA (ZIMBABWE).

   HAZLEWOOD ARTHUR   ED
   AFRICAN INTEGRATION AND DISINTEGRATION-- POLITICAL AND
   ECONOMIC CASE STUDIES.
   LONDON, OXFORD UNIVERSITY PRESS, 1967
   059,078,
        EXCELLENT COLLECTION OF ORIGINAL ARTICLES. ANALYSES
        OF ECONOMIC UNIONS, ACTUAL AND PROJECTED, IN EQUATOR-
        IAL AFRICA, EAST AFRICA, SENEGAL-GAMBIA, POLITICAL
        UNIONS EXTANT AND DEFUNCT NIGERIA, CENTRAL AFRICAN
        FEDERATION, SOMALI REPUBLIC, CAMEROONS, AND WIDER
        GROUPINGS FRENCH-SPEAKING AFRICA, PAN-AFRICANISM.
        INTRODUCTORY ESSAY BY EDITOR, ECONOMIST AND SENIOR RE-

SEARCH STATISTICIAN AT OXFORD UNIVERSITY.   MAPS,
BIBLIOGRAPHY.

078

MORGENTHAU RUTH SCHACHTER
FROM AOF FEDERATION TO SOVEREIGN NATIONS
IN RUTH SCHACHTER MORGENTHAU POLITICAL PARTIES IN FRENCH-
SPEAKING WEST AFRICA, OXFORD, CLARENDON PRESS, 1964, PP 301-329
078,

> AUTHOR DEALS WITH BACKGROUND TO INTERTERRITORIAL MOVE-
> MENTS, ASPECTS OF DECISION-MAKING AS TO FUTURE REGION-
> AL LINKAGES, THE EXPERIENCE OF THE MALI FEDERATION,
> AND THE END OF WEST AFRICAN FEDERATION WITH INDEPEN-
> DENCE. AUTHOR DID EXTENSIVE FIELD RESEARCH DURING
> 1950'S IN FRENCH WEST AFRICA, AND IS PROFESSOR AT
> BRANDEIS UNIVERSITY.

ROBSON PETER
ECONOMIC INTEGRATION IN AFRICA
LONDON, ALLEN & UNWIN; EVANSTON, NORTHWESTERN UNIVERSITY PRESS, 1968
071,078,

> AUTHOR DEALS WITH FIVE MAJOR TOPICS-(1) THE ECONOMICS
> OF INTEGRATION AMONG LESS DEVELOPED COUNTRIES (2) THE
> ECONOMIC SETTING IN AFRICA AND THE PROBLEMS OF
> INTEGRATION (3) ECONOMIC INTEGRATION IN EAST AFRICA
> (4) ECONOMIC INTEGRATION IN EQUATORIAL AFRICA (5)
> OTHER INITIATIVES FOR ECONOMIC INTEGRATION IN AFRICA.
> MOST COMPREHENSIVE VOLUME AVAILABLE ON ECONOMIC
> INTEGRATION BETWEEN AFRICAN STATES.

WIDSTRAND CARL   ED
AFRICAN BOUNDARY PROBLEMS
UPPSALA,THE SCANDANAVIAN INSTITUTE OF AFRICAN STUDIES;AND NEW
YORK,AFRICANA PUBLISHING CORPORATION,1969
059,078,080,

> A COMPREHENSIVE COLLECTION OF PAPERS ON BOUNDARIES AND
> THE LAW,THE ECONOMICS OF BOUNDARIES,THE OAU AND
> AFRICAN BOUNDARIES,FOREIGN AND MILITARY POLITICS,
> STATUS QUO VERSUS IRRIDENTISM,THE SOUTHERN BORDER,
> INTER-AFRICAN ECONOMIC COOPERATION,COLONIALISM AND
> TERRITORIAL CONFLICTS.EDITOR SURVEYS AFRICAN
> BOUNDARY PROBLEMS IN FINAL CHAPTER. APPENDIXES MAP AND
> LIST BOUNDARY DISPUTES AND CHART LENGTH AND STATUS OF
> ALL.

ZARTMAN I WILLIAM
INTERNATIONAL RELATIONS IN THE NEW AFRICA.
NEW JERSEY, PRENTICE-HALL, 1966
059,078,080,

> BEST INTRODUCTION TO AFRICAN INTERNATIONAL RELATIONS
> ON POLITICAL LEVEL. DISCUSSES AFRICAN STATE ALLIANCES
> IN THE PRE-INDEPENDENCE AND POST-COLONIAL PERIODS, AS
> WELL AS REGIONAL RELATIONS WITHIN THE ORGANIZATION OF
> AFRICAN UNITY (OAU). ANALYZES CRITERIA FOR AFRICAN
> STATE POLICY (NATIONAL SECURITY, SUBNATIONAL INTERESTS
> IDEOLOGY) AND THE PATTERNS OF INTRA-AFRICAN POLICY
> (ESPECIALLY BOUNDARY PROBLEMS).

ADERIBIGBE A B
WEST AFRICAN INTEGRATION-- AN HISTORICAL PERSPECTIVE.

NIGERIAN JOURNAL OF ECONOMIC AND SOCIAL STUDIES 5 MARCH 1963
PP 9-14
078,
        REFERENCE

078
    ADERIBIGBE A B
    SYMPOSIUM ON WEST AFRICAN INTEGRATION.
    NIGERIAN JOURNAL OF ECONOMIC AND SOCIAL STUDIES 5 MARCH
    1963
    078,
        REFERENCE

    BANEFIELD JANE
    THE STRUCTURE AND ADMINISTRATION OF THE EAST AFRICAN COMMON
    SERVICES ORGANIZATION.
    IN COLIN LEYS AND P ROBSON (EDS), FEDERATION IN EAST AFRICA--
    OPPORTUNITIES AND PROBLEMS, NAIROBI, OXFORD UNIVERSITY PRESS,
    1965, PP 30-40
    078,117-09,136-09,139-09,
        REFERENCE

    BAUER P T
    WEST AFRICAN TRADE-- A STUDY OF COMPETITION, OLIGOPOLY
    AND MONOPOLY IN A CHANGING ECONOMY.
    CAMBRIDGE, CAMBRIDGE UNIVERSITY PRESS, 1954
    078,
        REFERENCE

    BELSHAW D G R
    AGRICULTURAL PRODUCTION AND TRADE IN THE EAST AFRICAN COMMON
    MARKET.
    IN COLIN LEYS AND P ROBSON (EDS), FEDERATION IN EAST AFRICA--
    OPPORTUNITIES AND PROBLEMS, NAIROBI, OXFORD UNIVERSITY PRESS,
    1965, PP 83-101
    078,
        REFERENCE

    BERG ELLIOT J
    THE ECONOMIC BASIS OF POLITICAL CHOICE IN FRENCH WEST
    AFRICA.
    IN WILLIAM J HANNA (ED), INDEPENDENT BLACK AFRICA, CHICAGO,
    RAND MCNALLY, 1964, PP 607-634
    078,
        REFERENCE

    BIRCH A H
    OPPORTUNITIES AND PROBLEMS OF FEDERATION.
    IN COLIN LEYS AND P ROBSON (EDS), FEDERATION IN EAST AFRICA--
    OPPORTUNITIES AND PROBLEMS, NAIROBI, OXFORD UNIVERSITY PRESS,
    1965, PP 6-29
    078,
        REFERENCE

    CURRIE DAVID P
    FEDERALISM AND THE NEW NATIONS OF AFRICA.
    CHICAGO, UNIVERSITY OF CHICAGO PRESS, 1964
    061,078,
        REFERENCE

ECONOMIC COMMISSION FOR AFRICA
INTRA-AFRICAN TRADE.
E/CN IY/STC/20 1963
078,
     REFERENCE

078

ECONOMIC COMMISSION FOR AFRICA
STUDIES OF EXISTING AFRICAN CUSTOMS UNIONS.
ECONOMIC BULLETIN FOR AFRICA 2 1962
078,
     REFERENCE

EWING A F
PROSPECTS FOR ECONOMIC INTEGRATION IN AFRICA.
JOURNAL OF MODERN AFRICAN STUDIES 5 MAY 1967 PP 53-67
078,
     REFERENCE

GREEN REGINALD H   KRISHNA K G V
ECONOMIC CO-OPERATION IN AFRICA.
LONDON,OXFORD UNIVERSITY PRESS,1967
077,078,080,
     REFERENCE

HAZLEWOOD ARTHUR
THE ECONOMICS OF FEDERATION AND DISSOLUTION IN CENTRAL
AFRICA CHAPTER 6.
IN AFRICAN INTEGRATION AND DISINTEGRATION, LONDON, OXFORD
UNIVERSITY PRESS, 1967, PP 185-250
078,
     REFERENCE

HAZLEWOOD ARTHUR
THE COORDINATION OF TRANSPORT POLICY.
IN COLIN LEYS AND P ROBSON (EDS), FEDERATION IN EAST AFRICA--
OPPORTUNITIES AND PROBLEMS, NAIROBI, OXFORD UNIVERSITY PRESS,
1965, PP 111-123
078,
     REFERENCE

JULIENNE ROLAND
THE EXPERIENCE OF INTEGRATION IN FRENCH-SPEAKING AFRICA
CHAPTER 9.
IN ARTHUR HAZLEWOOD, AFRICAN INTEGRATION AND DISINTEGRATION,
LONDON, OXFORD UNIVERSITY PRESS, 1967, PP 339-353
078,
     REFERENCE

MAZRUI ALI A
POLITICAL COMMITMENT AND ECONOMIC INTEGRATION CHAPTER 5.
IN ON HEROES AND UHURU-WORSHIP, LONDON, LONGMANS,
1967. PP 63-72
078,
     REFERENCE

MBOYA TOM
EAST AFRICAN LABOUR POLICY AND FEDERATION.
IN COLIN LEYS AND P ROBSON (EDS), FEDERATION IN EAST AFRICA--
OPPORTUNITIES AND PROBLEMS, NAIROBI, OXFORD UNIVERSITY PRESS,

1965, PP 102-110
078,117-04,
        REFERENCE

078
  NDEGWA PHILIP
  THE COMMON MARKET AND DEVELOPMENT IN EAST AFRICA.
  NAIROBI, THE EAST AFRICAN PUBLISHING HOUSE, 1965
  078,080,082,
        REFERENCE

  NEWMAN PETER
  THE ECONOMICS OF INTEGRATION IN EAST AFRICA.
  IN COLIN LEYS AND P ROBSON (EDS), FEDERATION IN EAST AFRICA--
  OPPORTUNITIES AND PROBLEMS, NAIROBI, OXFORD UNIVERSITY PRESS,
  1965, PP 56-71
  078,
        REFERENCE

  NYE JOSEPH S
  ECONOMIC INTEGRATION CHAPTER 5.
  IN PAN-AFRICANISM AND EAST AFRICAN INTEGRATION, CAMBRIDGE
  MASS, HARVARD UNIVERSTIY PRESS, 1965
  078,
        REFERENCE

  NYE JOSEPH S
  THE EXTENT AND VIABILITY OF EAST AFRICAN COOPERATION.
  IN COLIN LEYS AND P ROBSON (EDS), FEDERATION IN EAST AFRICA--
  OPPORTUNITIES AND PROBLEMS, NAIROBI, OXFORD UNIVERSITY PRESS,
  1965, PP 41-55
  078,
        REFERENCE

  OKONDO PETER J
  PROSPECTS OF FEDERALISM IN EAST AFRICA CHAPTER 2.
  IN DAVID P CURRIE, FEDERALISM AND THE NEW NATIONS OF AFRICA,
  CHICAGO, UNIVERSITY OF CHICAGO PRESS, 1964, PP 29-38
  078,
        REFERENCE

  ONITIRI H M A
  TOWARDS A WEST AFRICAN ECONOMIC COMMUNITY.
  NIGERIAN JOURNAL OF ECONOMIC AND SOCIAL STUDIES 5 MARCH
  1963 PP 27-54
  078,
        REFERENCE

  OUDES BRUCE J
  OCAM COMES OF AGE.
  AFRICA REPORT, FEBRUARY, 1968
  078,
        REFERENCE

  ROBSON PETER
  ECONOMIC INTEGRATION IN EQUATORIAL AFRICA CHAPTER 2.
  IN ARTHUR HAZLEWOOD, AFRICAN INTEGRATION AND DISINTEGRATION,
  LONDON, OXFORD UNIVERSITY PRESS, 1967, PP 27-69
  078,105-09,106-09,107-09,112-09,
        REFERENCE

078

ROBSON PETER
ECONOMIC INTEGRATION IN SOUTHERN AFRICA.
THE JOURNAL OF MODERN AFRICAN STUDIES 5 4 DECEMBER 1967 PP
469-490
078,
        REFERENCE

BANDA HASTINGS K   NKUMBULA HARRY M
FEDERATION IN CENTRAL AFRICA.
LONDON 1951
078,122-04,
        CASE STUDY

BOUADIB ABDERRAHIM
PROSPECTS FOR A UNITED MAGHRIB.
IN WILLIAM H LEWIS,NEW FORCES IN AFRICA,GEORGETOWN
COLLOQUIUM ON AFRICA PAPERS,WASHINGTON,PUBLIC AFFAIRS
PRESS,1962,PP 101-113
078,
        CASE STUDY

DIENG DIAKHA
FROM UAM TO OCAM.
AFRICAN FORUM I 2 1965
078,
        CASE STUDY

ELKAN WALTER
EAST AFRICAN ECONOMIC COMMUNITY
IN LEGUM AND DRYSDALE, AFRICA CONTEMPORARY RECORD.
LONDON, AFRICA RESEARCH LIMITED, 1969, P. 13-17
078,
        CASE STUDY

FRANCK THOMAS M
EAST AFRICAN FEDERATION.
IN THOMAS FRANCK (ED), WHY FEDERATIONS FAIL, NEW YORK, NEW
YORK UNIVERSITY PRESS, 1968, PP. 3-36
078,
        CASE STUDY

HAZLEWOOD ARTHUR
ECONOMIC INTEGRATION IN EAST AFRICA CHAPTER 3.
IN AFRICAN INTEGRATION AND DISINTEGRATION, LONDON, OXFORD
UNIVERSITY PRESS, 1967, PP 69-114
078,
        CASE STUDY

HAZLEWOOD ARTHUR   HENDERSON P D   EDS
NYASALAND-- THE ECONOMICS OF FEDERATION.
OXFORD,BLACKWELL,1960
078,122-09,
        CASE STUDY

KIANO J GIKONYO
THE EMERGENT EAST AFRICAN FEDERATION CHAPTER 3.
IN DAVID P CURRIE, FEDERALISM AND THE NEW NATIONS OF AFRICA
CHICAGO, UNIVERSITY OF CHICAGO PRESS, 1964, PP 61-74

078,
     CASE STUDY

078
   LEBON J H G
   THE CONTROL AND UTILIZATION OF NILE WATERS--A PROBLEM OF
   POLITICAL GEOGRAPHY.
   REVIEW OF THE GEOGRAPHICAL INSTITUTE OF THE UNIVERSITY OF
   ISTANBUL 1960 PP 32-49
   078,134-09,140-09,
        CASE STUDY

   MEAD DONALD C
   ECONOMIC CO-OPERATION IN EAST AFRICA.
   JOURNAL OF MODERN AFRICAN STUDIES, VOL. 7, NO. 2, 1969, PP.
   277-287
   078,
        CASE STUDY

   NDEGWA PHILIP
   THE COMMON MARKET AND DEVELOPMENT IN EAST AFRICA.
   KENYA, EAST AFRICAN PUBLISHING HOUSE, 1968
   078,
        CASE STUDY

   O CONNOR A M
   A WIDER EASTERN AFRICAN UNION--SOME GEOGRAPHICAL ASPECTS.
   THE JOURNAL OF MODERN AFRICAN STUDIES, VOL. 6, NO. 4, 1968,
   PP. 485-493
   078,
        CASE STUDY

   PLESSZ NICHOLAS G
   PROBLEMS AND PROSPECTS OF ECONOMIC INTEGRATION IN WEST
   AFRICA
   MONTREAL, MCGILL-QUEEN'S, 1968
   078,
        CASE STUDY

   RICHARDS AUDREY I
   SOME EFFECTS OF THE INTRODUCTION OF INDIVIDUAL FREEHOLD
   INTO BUGANDA.
   IN D BIEBUYCK (ED), AFRICAN AGRARIAN SYSTEMS, LONDON,
   OXFORD UNIVERSITY PRESS, 1963, PP 267-280
   078,139-08,
        CASE STUDY

   ROBSON PETER
   PROBLEMS OF INTEGRATION BETWEEN SENEGAL AND
   GAMBIA CHAPTER 4.
   IN ARTHUR HAZLEWOOD, AFRICAN INTEGRATION AND DISINTEGRATION,
   LONDON, OXFORD UNIVERSITY PRESS, 1967, PP 115-128
   078,113-09,130-09,
        CASE STUDY

   ROBSON PETER
   THE PROBLEMS OF SENEGAMBIA.
   JOURNAL OF MODERN AFRICAN STUDIES 3 1965
   078,113-09,130-09,
        CASE STUDY

078
   ROSBERG CARL G
   THE FEDERATION OF RHODESIA AND NYASALAND-- PROBLEMS OF
   DEMOCRATIC GOVERNMENT.
   ANNALS OF THE AMERICAN ACADEMY OF POLITICAL AND SOCIAL
   SCIENCES 306 1956 PP 98-105
   078,
         CASE STUDY

   ROTHCHILD DONALD S   ED
   POLITICS OF INTEGRATION-AN EAST AFRICAN DOCUMENTARY
   NAIROBI, EAST AFRICAN PUBLISHING HOUSE, 1968
   078,
         CASE STUDY

   SEGAL AARON
   THE INTEGRATION OF DEVELOPING COUNTRIES--SOME THOUGHTS ON
   EAST AFRICA AND CENTRAL AMERICA.
   JOURNAL OF COMMON MARKET STUDIES, VOL. V, NO. 3, MARCH 1967,
   PP. 252-282
   078,
         CASE STUDY

   SPIRO HERBERT J
   THE FEDERATION OF RHODESIA AND NYASALAND.
   IN THOMAS FRANCK (ED), WHY FEDERATIONS FAIL, NEW YORK, NEW
   YORK UNIVERSITY PRESS, 1968, PP. 37-90
   078,122-06,145-06,
         CASE STUDY

   SANDS WILLIAM
   PROSPECTS FOR A UNITED MAGHRIB
   IN TIBOR KEREKES (ED), THE ARAB MIDDLE EAST AND MUSLIM
   AFRICA, NEW YORK, PRAEGER, 1961
   078,101-09,120-09,126-09,138-09,
         CASE STUDY

   BUSTIN EDOUARD
   LA DECENTRALISATION ADMINISTRATIVE ET L'EVOLUTION DES
   STRUCTURES POLITIQUES EN AFRIQUE ORIENTALE BRITANNIQUE
   (ADMINISTRATIVE DECENTRALIZATION AND THE EVOLUTION OF
   OF POLITICAL STRUCTURES IN BRITISH EAST AFRICA).
   LIEGE, UNIVERSITE DE LIEGE, 1958
   078,
         LESS ACCESSIBLE

   BARBERA MARIO   HAAS ERNST B
   THE OPERATIONALIZATION OF SOME VARIABLES RELATED TO REGIONAL
   INTEGRATION--A RESEARCH NOTE.
   INTERNATIONAL ORGANIZATION, VOL. XXIII, NO. 1, 1969, PP. 150
   160
   078,
         GENERAL THEORY

   DELL SIDNEY
   TRADE BLOCS AND COMMON MARKETS
   NEW YORK, KNOPF, 1963
   071,072,073,078,
         GENERAL THEORY

078

FISHER WILLIAM E
AN ANALYSIS OF THE DEUTSCH SOCIOCAUSAL PARADIGM OF POLITICAL
INTEGRATION.
INTERNATIONAL ORGANIZATION, SPRING, 1969, VOL. XXIII, NO. 2,
PP. 254-290
078,
      GENERAL THEORY

NYE JOSEPH S
COMPARATIVE REGIONAL INTEGRATION--CONCEPT AND MEASUREMENT.
INTERNATIONAL ORGANIZATION, VOL. XXII, NO. 4, 1968, PP. 855-
880
078,
      GENERAL THEORY

RUSSETT BRUCE M
INTERNATIONAL REGIONS AND THE INTERNATIONAL SYSTEM
CHICAGO, RAND MCNALLY, 1967
078,
      GENERAL THEORY

SCHMITTER PHILIPPE C
FURTHER NOTES ON OPERATIONALIZING SOME VARIABLES RELATED TO
REGIONAL INTEGRATION.
INTERNATIONAL ORGANIZATION, SPRING, 1969, VOL. XXIII, NO. 2,
PP. 327-336
078,
      GENERAL THEORY

SCHMITTER PHILIPPE C
THREE NEO-FUNCTIONAL HYPOTHESES ABOUT INTERNATIONAL
INTEGRATION.
INTERNATIONAL ORGANIZATION, VOL. XXIII, NO. 1, 1969, PP. 161
-166
078,
      GENERAL THEORY

GHAI DHARAM P
TERRITORIAL DISTRIBUTION OF THE BENEFITS AND COSTS OF THE
EAST AFRICAN COMMON MARKET.
IN COLIN LEYS AND P ROBSON (EDS), FEDERATION IN EAST AFRICA--
OPPORTUNITIES AND PROBLEMS, NAIROBI, OXFORD UNIVERSITY PRESS,
1965, PP 72-82
078,

LEYS COLIN   ROBSON PETER   EDS
FEDERATION IN EAST AFRICA-- OPPORTUNITIES AND PROBLEMS.
NAIROBI, OXFORD UNIVERSITY PRESS, 1965
078,
      REFERENCE

392

79. PAN-AFRICANISM AND CONTINENTAL UNITY

GREEN REGINALD H   SEIDMAN ANN
UNITY OR POVERTY THE ECONOMICS OF PAN-AFRICANISM.
BALTIMORE, PENGUIN, 1968
071,079,
     ARGUES FOR THE NECESSITY OF ECONOMIC CO-OPERATION TO
     COUNTER SUCH PROBLEMS OF BALKANIZATION AS OVERDEPEN-
     DENCE ON EXPORTS, LIMITED MARKETS, ECONOMIC ISOLATION
     AND NEO-COLONIALISM . GREEN IS CURRENTLY ECONOMIC
     ADVISER TO THE TREASURY OF TANZANIA.

JAMES C L R
A HISTORY OF PAN-AFRICAN REVOLT
WASHINGTON, D. C., DRUM AND SPEAR PRESS, 1969
077,079,
     AUTHOR IS WEST INDIAN WHO HAS ACTIVELY PARTICIPATED
     IN MANY OF THE KEY EVENTS IN PAN-AFRICAN HISTORY.
     DEALS WITH BLACK RESISTANCE TO OPPRESSION IN
     AMERICA, THE WEST INDIES, AND AFRICA. AVAILABLE
     IN PAPERBACK.

LEGUM COLIN
PAN-AFRICANISM A SHORT POLITICAL GUIDE.
NEW YORK, PRAEGER, 1962
077,079,
     EXCELLENT BACKGROUND TO THE DEVELOPMENT OF PAN-AFRI-
     CAN IDEAS AND MOVEMENT. DEALS WITH EARLY PAN-AFRICAN
     CONFERENCES IN EUROPE AND THE INFLUENCE OF THE DIAS-
     PORA ON PAN-AFRICANISM (INCLUDING THE BACK TO AFRICA
     MOVEMENTS). PROVIDES SUMMARY OF THE SUPRA-NATIONAL
     GROUPINGS IN AFRICA FROM 1960-63 (CASABLANCA AND MON-
     ROVIA GROUPS), AND THE INTERNATIONAL ROLE OF AFRICAN
     LABOR. ASSESSES LITERARY AND CULTURAL MANIFESTATIONS
     OF PAN-AFRICANISM.

WALLERSTEIN I M
AFRICA-- THE POLITICS OF UNITY.
NEW YORK, RANDOM HOUSE, 1967
002,079,080,097,
     SEQUEL TO AUTHOR S PREVIOUS BOOK ON POLITICS OF
     INDEPENDENCE. IS INTERPRETATION OF MAJOR POLITICAL
     DEVELOPMENTS IN AFRICA FROM 1957 TO 1965, SEEN IN PER-
     SPECTIVE OF SOCIAL CHANGE. DISTINGUISHES BETWEEN
     MOVEMENTS AND ALLIANCES IN THE EFFORTS OF AFRICAN
     STATES TO ACHIEVE WIDER UNITY. INTERPRETS FIRST AND
     SECOND CONGO CRISES, ORGANIZATION OF AFRICAN UNITY,
     RHODESIA AND SOUTH AFRICAN PROBLEMS, AND REGIONAL
     UNITY PATTERNS.

ABRAHAM W E
THE PROSPECTS FOR PAN-AFRICANISM.
IN PETER J MCEWAN AND ROBERT B SUTCLIFFE (EDS), MODERN AFRICA,
NEW YORK, THOMAS CROWELL, 1965, PP 406-412
079,
     REFERENCE

AMERICAN SOCIETY OF AFRICAN CULTURE
PAN-AFRICANISM RECONSIDERED.
BERKELEY, UNIVERSITY OF CALIFORNIA PRESS, 1962

079,
        REFERENCE

079
ANDRIAN CHARLES F
THE PAN-AFRICAN MOVEMENT--THE SEARCH FOR ORGANIZATION AND
COMMUNITY.
PHYLON 23 SPRING 1962 PP 5-27
079,
        REFERENCE

APTER DAVID E   COLEMAN JAMES S
PAN-AFRICANISM OR NATIONALISM IN AFRICA.
IN AMERICAN SOCIETY OF AFRICAN CULTURE, PAN-AFRICANISM
RECONSIDERED, BERKELEY, UNIVERSITY OF CALIFORNIA PRESS, 1962
PP 81-115
079,
        REFERENCE

APTER DAVID E   COLEMAN JAMES S
PAN-AFRICANISM OR NATIONALISM.
IN PETER J MCEWAN AND ROBERT B SUTCLIFFE (EDS), MODERN AFRICA,
NEW YORK, THOMAS CROWELL, 1965, PP 413-423
079,
        REFERENCE

AZIKIWE NNAMDI
THE FUTURE OF PAN-AFRICANISM.
PRESENCE AFRICAINE FIRST TRIMESTER 1962 PP 5-31
079,128-04,
        REFERENCE

AZIKIWE NNAMDI
REALITIES OF AFRICAN UNITY.
AFRICAN FORUM I 1 1965 PP 7-22
079,128-04,
        REFERENCE

BALANDIER GEORGES
OBSERVATIONS ON THE POLITICAL REGROUPING OF AFRICA.
IN WILLIAM J HANNA (ED), INDEPENDENT BLACK AFRICA, CHICAGO,
RAND MCNALLY, 1964, PP 588-594
079,
        REFERENCE

CERVENKA ZDENEK
THE ORGANIZATION OF AFRICAN UNITY AND ITS CHARTER.
NEW YORK, PRAEGER PUBLISHERS, 1969
079,080,
        REFERENCE

DIOP ALIOUNE
REMARKS ON AFRICAN PERSONALITY AND NEGRITUDE
IN AMERICAN SOCIETY OF AFRICAN CULTURE,PAN-AFRICANISM
RECONSIDERED,BERKELEY,UNIVERSITY OF CALIFORNIA PRESS,1962,
PP 337-345
039,054,077,079,
        REFERENCE

DUIGNAN PETER

PAN-AFRICANISM-- A BIBLIOGRAPHIC ESSAY.
AFRICAN FORUM I 1 1965 PP 105-107
079,
        REFERENCE

079
   EMERSON RUPERT   KILSON MARTIN L
   INTER-AFRICAN PROBLEMS AND PAN-AFRICANISM CHP 4.
   IN THE POLITICAL AWAKENING OF AFRICA, ENGLEWOOD CLIFFS,
   NEW JERSEY, PRENTICE-HALL, 1965
   079,
        REFERENCE

   EMERSON RUPERT
   PAN-AFRICANISM.
   IN NORMAN J PADELFORD AND RUPERT EMERSON (EDS), AFRICA AND
   WORLD ORDER, NEW YORK, PRAEGER, 1963, PP 7-22, INTERNATIONAL
   ORGANIZATION 16 SPRING 1962 PP 275-290
   079,
        REFERENCE

   HAILE SELASSIE 1
   TOWARDS AFRICAN UNITY.
   JOURNAL OF MODERN AFRICAN STUDIES 1 SEPTEMBER 1963
   PP 281-292
   079,
        REFERENCE

   HENRY PAUL-MARC
   PAN-AFRICANISM-- A DREAM COME TRUE.
   IN PHILIP W QUIGG (ED.), AFRICA, NEW YORK, PRAEGER, 1964,
   079,
        REFERENCE

   HOSKYNS CATHERINE
   PAN-AFRICANISM AND INTEGRATION CHAPTER 10.
   IN ARTHUR HAZLEWOOD, AFRICAN INTEGRATION AND DISINTEGRATION,
   LONDON, OXFORD UNIVERSITY PRESS, 1967, PP 354-393
   079,
        REFERENCE

   KENYATTA JOMO
   AFRICAN SOCIALISM AND AFRICAN UNITY.
   AFRICAN FORUM I 1 1965 PP 23-37
   079,117-04,
        REFERENCE

   KLOMAN ERASMUS H
   AFRICAN UNIFICATION MOVEMENTS.
   IN NORMAN J PADELFORD AND RUPERT EMERSON (EDS), AFRICA AND
   WORLD ORDER, NEW YORK, PRAEGER, 1963, PP 119-135
   079,
        REFERENCE

   LEFEVER ERNEST W
   UNCERTAIN MANDATE-- POLITICS OF THE UN CONGO OPERATION.
   BALTIMORE, JOHNS HOPKINS UNIVERSITY PRESS, 1967
   079,081,108-09,
        REFERENCE

LEGUM COLIN
PAN-AFRICANISM AND NATIONALISM CHP 30.
IN JC ANENE AND GODFREY BROWN, AFRICA IN THE 19TH AND 20TH
CENTURIES, LONDON, NELSON IUP, 1966
079,
        REFERENCE

079
LEGUM COLIN
THE CHANGING IDEAS OF PAN-AFRICANISM.
AFRICAN FORUM I 2 1965 PP 50-61
079,
        REFERENCE

LOGAN RAYFORD W
THE HISTORICAL ASPECTS OF PAN-AFRICANISM 1900-1945.
IN AMERICAN SOCIETY FOR AFRICAN CULTURE, PAN-AFRICANISM
RECONSIDERED, BERKELEY, UNIVERSITY OF CALIFORNIA PRESS, 1962,
PP 37-52
079,
        REFERENCE

LOGAN RAYFORD W
THE HISTORICAL ASPECTS OF PAN-AFRICANISM-- A PERSONAL CHRON-
ICLE.
AFRICAN FORUM I 1 1965 PP 90-104
030,079,
        REFERENCE

LUTHULI ALBERT
AFRICA AND FREEDOM CHAPTER 1.
IN AFRICA'S FREEDOM, NEW YORK, BARNES AND NOBLE,
1964, PP 9-23
079,089,132-04,
        REFERENCE

MARCUM JOHN A
PAN-AFRICANISM OR FRAGMENTATION.
IN WILLIAM H LEWIS, NEW FORCES IN AFRICA, GEORGETOWN
COLLOQUIUM ON AFRICA PAPERS, WASHINGTON, PUBLIC AFFAIRS
PRESS ,1962, PP 25-41
079,
        REFERENCE

MAZRUI ALI A
ON THE CONCEPT OF   'WE ARE ALL AFRICANS'.
AMERICAN POLITICAL SCIENCE REVIEW 57 MARCH 1963 PP 88-97
079,
        REFERENCE

MEZU S O   ED
MTHE PHILOSOPHY OF PAN-AFRICANISM.
WASHINGTON, GEORGETOWN UNIVERSITY PRESS, 1965
079,
        REFERENCE

MOHAN JITENDRA
GHANA, THE CONGO AND THE UNITED NATIONS
JOURNAL OF MODERN AFRICAN STUDIES 7 1969 PP 369-406
079,081,

REFERENCE

079
  NELKIN DOROTHY
  SOCIALIST SOURCES OF PAN-AFRICAN IDEOLOGY CHAPTER 4.
  IN WILLIAM FRIEDLAND AND CARL ROSBERG (EDS), AFRICAN
  SOCIALISM, STANFORD CALIFORNIA, STANFORD UNIVERSITY PRESS,
  1964, PP 63-79
  079,084,
        REFERENCE

  NYERERE JULIUS K
  THE NATURE AND REQUIREMENTS OF AFRICAN UNITY.
  AFRICAN FORUM I 1 1965 PP 38-52
  079, 136-04,
        REFERENCE

  PADELFORD NORMAN J
  THE ORGANIZATION OF AFRICAN UNITY.
  INTERNATIONAL ORGANIZATION 18 SUMMER 1964 PP 521-542
  079,
        REFERENCE

  PADMORE GEORGE
  PAN-AFRICANISM OR COMMUNISM.
  PARIS DENNIS DOBSON 1960
  079,084,
        REFERENCE

  PADMORE GEORGE   ED
  HISTORY OF THE PAN-AFRICAN CONGRESS.
  LONDON HAMMERSMITH 1963
  079,
        REFERENCE

  PANOFSKY HANS E
  PAN-AFRICANISM-- A BIBLIOGRAPHIC NOTE ON ORGANIZATIONS.
  AFRICAN FORUM I 2 1965 PP 62-64
  079,
        REFERENCE

  QUAISON-SACKEY ALEX
  AFRICAN UNITY CHAPTER 3.
  IN AFRICA UNBOUND, NEW YORK, PRAEGER, 1963, PP 59-99
  079,
        REFERENCE

  SHEPPERSON GEORGE
  PAN-AFRICANISM-- SOME HISTORICAL NOTES.
  PHYLON 23 WINTER 1962 PP 346-358
  079,
        REFERENCE

  TELLI DIALLO
  THE ORGANIZATION OF AFRICAN UNITY IN HISTORICAL PERSPEC-
  TIVES.
  AFRICAN FORUM I 2 1965 PP 7-27
  079,080,
        REFERENCE

THOMPSON V BAKPETU
AFRICA AND UNITY--THE EVOLUTION OF PAN-AFRICANISM.
LONDON, INTERNATIONAL UNIVERSITY BOOKSELLERS, INC., 1969
079,
        REFERENCE

079
WALLERSTEIN I M
PAN-AFRICANISM AS PROTEST.
IN MORTON A KAPLAN, THE REVOLUTION IN WORLD POLITICS,
NEW YORK, JOHN WILEY, 1962, PP 137-151
079,
        REFERENCE

WALLERSTEIN I M
LARGER UNITIES-- PAN-AFRICANISM AND REGIONAL FEDERATIONS.
IN PETER J MCEWAN AND ROBERT B SUTCLIFFE (EDS), MODERN AFRICA,
NEW YORK, THOMAS CROWELL, 1965, PP 217-228
079,
        REFERENCE

WELCH CLAUDE E
DREAM OF UNITY-PAN-AFRICANISM AND POLITICAL UNIFICATION IN
WEST AFRICA
ITHACA, CORNELL UNIVERSITY PRESS, 1966
054,059,079,
        REFERENCE

COX RICHARD
PAN-AFRICANISM IN PRACTICE-- AN EAST AFRICAN STUDY--
PAFMESCA 1958-1964.
LONDON, OXFORD UNIVERSITY PRESS, 1964
079,
        CASE STUDY

KIANO J GIKONYO
FROM PAFMECA TO PAFMECSA--AND BEYOND.
AFRICAN FORUM I 2 1965 PP 36-49
079,
        CASE STUDY

VAN BILSEN A A A J
SOME ASPECTS OF THE CONGO PROBLEM.
INTERNATIONAL AFFAIRS 38 1962 PP 41-51
079,
        CASE STUDY

HAMA BOUBOU
ENQUETE SUR LES FONDEMENTS ET LA GENESE DE L'UNITE AFRICAINE
(INQUIRY ON THE FOUNDATIONS AND EARLY DEVELOPMENT OF AFRICAN
UNITY).
PARIS, PRESENCE AFRICAINE, 1966
079,127-04,
        LESS ACCESSIBLE

80. INTERNATIONAL ORGANIZATIONS
IN AFRICA

LEGUM COLIN   DRYSDALE JOHN
AFRICA CONTEMPORARY RECORD.
LONDON, AFRICA RESEARCH LIMITED, 1969
002,062,080,081,087,
> BEST EXISTING GENERAL REFERENCE FOR DETAILS OF EACH
> AFRICAN COUNTRY IN THE FIELDS OF FOREIGN RELATIONS,
> GOVERNMENT AND ECONOMICS. IT IS WRITTEN FOR THE SPE-
> CIALIST, BUT CAN BE USED BY THE TEACHER AS WELL.

OKIGBO PIUS N C
AFRICA AND THE COMMON MARKET.
EVANSTON, NORTHWESTERN UNIVERSITY PRESS, 1967
080,082,
> AUTHOR IS HIGH-LEVEL NIGERIAN DIPLOMAT/SCHOLAR. PRI-
> MARY FOCUS ON RELATIONSHIPS BETWEEN NIGERIA AND UNITED
> KINGDOM IN POST-COLONIAL PERIOD. ALSO DISCUSSES MAJOR
> ISSUES OF EUROPEAN COMMON MARKET AS THEY AFFECT AFRI-
> CAN STATES. SURVEYS EXISTING AFRICAN CUSTOMS UNIONS,
> AND POSSIBILITIES FOR A CONTINENTAL AFRICAN COMMON
> MARKET.

WALLERSTEIN I M
AFRICA-- THE POLITICS OF UNITY.
NEW YORK, RANDOM HOUSE, 1967
002,079,080,097,
> SEQUEL TO AUTHOR'S PREVIOUS BOOK ON POLITICS OF
> INDEPENDENCE. IS INTERPRETATION OF MAJOR POLITICAL
> DEVELOPMENTS IN AFRICA FROM 1957 TO 1965, SEEN IN PER-
> SPECTIVE OF SOCIAL CHANGE. DISTINGUISHES BETWEEN
> MOVEMENTS AND ALLIANCES IN THE EFFORTS OF AFRICAN
> STATES TO ACHIEVE WIDER UNITY. INTERPRETS FIRST AND
> SECOND CONGO CRISES, ORGANIZATION OF AFRICAN UNITY,
> RHODESIA AND SOUTH AFRICAN PROBLEMS, AND REGIONAL
> UNITY PATTERNS.

WIDSTRAND CARL   ED
AFRICAN BOUNDARY PROBLEMS
UPPSALA,THE SCANDANAVIAN INSTITUTE OF AFRICAN STUDIES,AND NEW
YORK,AFRICANA PUBLISHING CORPORATION,1969
059,078,080,
> A COMPREHENSIVE COLLECTION OF PAPERS ON BOUNDARIES AND
> THE LAW,THE ECONOMICS OF BOUNDARIES,THE OAU AND
> AFRICAN BOUNDARIES,FOREIGN AND MILITARY POLITICS,
> STATUS QUO VERSUS IRRIDENTISM,THE SOUTHERN BORDER,
> INTER-AFRICAN ECONOMIC COOPERATION,COLONIALISM AND
> TERRITORIAL CONFLICTS.EDITOR SURVEYS AFRICAN
> BOUNDARY PROBLEMS IN FINAL CHAPTER. APPENDIXES MAP AND
> LIST BOUNDARY DISPUTES AND CHART LENGTH AND STATUS OF
> ALL.

ZARTMAN I WILLIAM
INTERNATIONAL RELATIONS IN THE NEW AFRICA.
NEW JERSEY, PRENTICE-HALL, 1966

059,078,080,
BEST INTRODUCTION TO AFRICAN INTERNATIONAL RELATIONS
ON POLITICAL LEVEL. DISCUSSES AFRICAN STATE ALLIANCES
IN THE PRE-INDEPENDENCE AND POST-COLONIAL PERIODS, AS
WELL AS REGIONAL RELATIONS WITHIN THE ORGANIZATION OF
AFRICAN UNITY (OAU). ANALYZES CRITERIA FOR AFRICAN
STATE POLICY (NATIONAL SECURITY, SUBNATIONAL INTERESTS
IDEOLOGY) AND THE PATTERNS OF INTRA-AFRICAN POLICY
(ESPECIALLY BOUNDARY PROBLEMS).

080

CERVENKA ZDENEK
THE ORGANIZATION OF AFRICAN UNITY AND ITS CHARTER.
NEW YORK, PRAEGER PUBLISHERS, 1969
079,080,
REFERENCE

GREEN REGINALD H   KRISHNA K G V
ECONOMIC CO-OPERATION IN AFRICA.
LONDON, OXFORD UNIVERSITY PRESS, 1967
077,078,080,
REFERENCE

GREGG ROBERT W
THE UN REGIONAL ECONOMIC COMMISSIONS AND INTEGRATION IN THE
UNDERDEVELOPED AREAS
IN J S NYE (ED), INTERNATIONAL REGIONALISM, BOSTON, LITTLE,
BROWN, 1968, PP 304-332
080,081,
REFERENCE

KALDOR N
INTERNATIONAL TRADE AND ECONOMIC DEVELOPMENT
JOURNAL OF MODERN AFRICAN STUDIES 2 1964 PP 491-511
073,080,
REFERENCE

MAZRUI ALI A
AFRICAN ATTITUDES TO THE EUROPEAN ECONOMIC COMMUNITY.
LONDON, INTERNATIONAL AFFAIRS, VOL. 38, NO. 1, JANUARY,
1963, PP. 24-35
080,082,
REFERENCE

MONDLANE EDUARDO
THE STRUGGLE FOR MOZAMBIQUE.
BALTIMORE, PENGUIN BOOKS, 1969
080,087,144-06,
REFERENCE

NDEGWA PHILIP
THE COMMON MARKET AND DEVELOPMENT IN EAST AFRICA.
NAIROBI, THE EAST AFRICAN PUBLISHING HOUSE, 1965
078,080,082,
REFERENCE

PADELFORD NORMAN J EMERSON RUPERT   EDS
AFRICA AND WORLD ORDER.
NEW YORK, PRAEGER, 1963
080,

REFERENCE

080

RIVKIN ARNOLD
AFRICA AND THE EUROPEAN COMMON MARKET.
DENVER, UNIVERSITY OF DENVER PRESS, 1966, PP 67
080,082,
        REFERENCE

SEERS DUDLEY
INTERNATIONAL AID-THE NEXT STEPS
JOURNAL OF MODERN AFRICAN STUDIES 2 1964 PP 471-489
073,080,
        REFERENCE

TELLI DIALLO
THE ORGANIZATION OF AFRICAN UNITY IN HISTORICAL PERSPEC-
TIVES.
AFRICAN FORUM I 2 1965 PP 7-27
079,080,
        REFERENCE

81. AFRICA AT THE UNITED NATIONS

081

HOSKYNS CATHERINE
THE AFRICAN STATES AND THE UNITED NATIONS, 1958-1964.
INTERNATIONAL AFFAIRS 40 3 JULY 1964 PP 466-480
077,081,
        FOUR PARTS-- 1) AFRICA AT THE UNITED NATIONS-- 2) PAN-
        AFRICAN, AFRO-ASIAN, AND EURAFRICAN MOVEMENTS--
        3) AFRICA S RELATIONS WITH INDIA AND THE SOVIET
        UNION-- 4) AMERICAN POLICY IN AFRICA. GOOD DATA ON
        EVENTS AND TRENDS UP TO ABOUT 1962. AUTHOR IS PROFES-
        SOR AT JOHNS HOPKINS SCHOOL OF ADVANCED INTERNATIONAL
        STUDIES.

HOVET THOMAS JR
AFRICA IN THE UNITED NATIONS
EVANSTON, NORTHWESTERN UNIVERSITY PRESS, 1963
081,
        ANALYSIS OF U.N. VOTING RECORDS UP TO 1963. MANY
        TABLES, INCLUDING APPENDIX SHOWING VOTES ON HUNDREDS
        OF ISSUES FOR ALL U.N. MEMBERS. GOOD STUDY OF BOTH
        AFRICAN STATES AND THE U.N. ITSELF.

LEGUM COLIN   DRYSDALE JOHN
AFRICA CONTEMPORARY RECORD.
LONDON, AFRICA RESEARCH LIMITED, 1969
002,062,080,081,087,
        BEST EXISTING GENERAL REFERENCE FOR DETAILS OF EACH
        AFRICAN COUNTRY IN THE FIELDS OF FOREIGN RELATIONS,
        GOVERNMENT AND ECONOMICS. IT IS WRITTEN FOR THE SPE-
        CIALIST, BUT CAN BE USED BY THE TEACHER AS WELL.

MAZRUI ALI A
THE UNITED NATIONS AND SOME AFRICAN POLITICAL ATTITUDES
CHAPTER 12.
IN ON HEROES AND UHURU-WORSHIP, LONDON, LONGMANS,
1967 PP 183-208; ALSO INTERNATIONAL ORGANIZATION 18 1964
PP 514-515
     081,
          AUTHOR ASSESSES IMPACT OF AFRICAN SOVEREIGNTY ON UNI-
          TED NATIONS AND VICE VERSA. PROVIDES BACKGROUND ON
          LEAGUE OF NATIONS AND COLONIAL TERRITORIES, ESPECIALLY
          WITH REGARD TO PRINCIPLES OF SELF-DETERMINATION
          AND HUMAN RIGHTS. ASSESSES AFRICAN REACTION TO ISSUE
          OF MEMBERSHIP OF CHINA AND SOUTH AFRICA. DISCUSSES
          U.N. VOTING SYSTEM, AND AFRICAN NON-ALIGNMENT ON COLD
          WAR ISSUES. SUGGESTS U.N. MIGHT BE EFFECTIVE AID
          CHANNEL TO AFRICA.

081
   ELLIS WILLIAM W   SALZBERG JOHN
   AFRICA AND THE U N-- A STATISTICAL NOTE.
   AMERICAN BEHAVIORAL SCIENTIST 8 APRIL 1965 PP 30-32
   081,
         REFERENCE

   FOELL EARL W
   AFRICA'S VANISHING ACT AT THE UN-WHERE DOES THE UNITED
   STATES STAND ON AFRICAN QUESTIONS
   AFRICA REPORT NOVEMBER 1969 PP 31-33
   081,
         REFERENCE

   GORDENKER LEON
   THE UN SECRETARY GENERAL AND THE MAINTENANCE OF THE PEACE
   NEW YORK, COLUMBIA UNIVERSITY PRESS, 1967
   081,
         REFERENCE

   GREGG ROBERT W
   THE UN REGIONAL ECONOMIC COMMISSIONS AND INTEGRATION IN THE
   UNDERDEVELOPED AREAS
   IN J S NYE (ED), INTERNATIONAL REGIONALISM, BOSTON, LITTLE,
   BROWN, 1968, PP 304-332
   080,081,
         REFERENCE

   GROSS ERNEST A
   ADLAI STEVENSON, THE UNITED NATIONS, AND AFRICA.
   AFRICAN FORUM I 2 FALL 1965 PP 3-6
   081,
         REFERENCE

   HOVET THOMAS JR
   AFRICAN POLITICS IN THE UNITED NATIONS.
   IN HERBERT J SPIRO, ED., AFRICA-THE PRIMACY OF POLITICS,
   NEW YORK, RANDOM HOUSE, 1966, PP 116-149
   081,
         REFERENCE

   KAREFA-SMART JOHN
   AFRICA AND THE UNITED NATIONS.

INTERNATIONAL ORGANIZATION 19 3 SUMMER 1965 PP 764-773
081,131-04,
        REFERENCE

081

KAY DAVID A
THE IMPACT OF AFRICAN STATES IN THE UNITED NATIONS.
INTERNATIONAL ORGANIZATION, VOL. XXIII, NO. 1, WINTER, 1969,
PP. 20-47
081,
        REFERENCE

LEFEVER ERNEST W
UNCERTAIN MANDATE-- POLITICS OF THE UN CONGO OPERATION.
BALTIMORE, JOHNS HOPKINS UNIVERSITY PRESS, 1967
079,081,108-09,
        REFERENCE

LOGAN RAYFORD W
THE AFRICAN MANDATES IN WORLD POLITICS.
WASHINGTON, PUBLIC AFFAIRS PRESS, 1948
081,
        REFERENCE

MAZRUI ALI A
AFRICAN DOCTRINES OF NON-INTERVENTION CHAPTER 3.
IN ON HEROES AND UHURU-WORSHIP, LONDON, LONGMANS,
1967, PP 35-49
081,
        REFERENCE

MCKAY VERNON
AFRICAN DIPLOMACY-- STUDIES IN THE DETERMINANTS OF FOREIGN
POLICY.
NEW YORK, PRAEGER, 1966
081,
        REFERENCE

MOHAN JITENDRA
GHANA, THE CONGO AND THE UNITED NATIONS
JOURNAL OF MODERN AFRICAN STUDIES 7 1969 PP 369-406
079,081,
        REFERENCE

OLYMPIO SYLVANUS
AFRICAN PROBLEMS AND THE COLD WAR.
IN PHILIP W QUIGG (ED.), AFRICA, NEW YORK, PRAEGER, 1964,
PP 292-301
081,137-04,
        REFERENCE

QUIGG PHILIP W   ED
AFRICA-- A FOREIGN AFFAIRS READER.
NEW YORK, PRAEGER, 1964
081,
        REFERENCE

RIVKIN ARNOLD
THE AFRICAN PRESENCE IN WORLD AFFAIRS.
NEW YORK, FREE PRESS, 1963, PP 67-94, PP 118-129

081,
        REFERENCE

081

SPENCER JOHN
AFRICA AT THE U N-- SOME OBSERVATIONS.
IN WILLIAM J HANNA (ED), INDEPENDENT BLACK AFRICA, CHICAGO,
RAND MCNALLY, 1964, PP 542-544
081,
        REFERENCE

THIAM DOUDOU
THE FOREIGN POLICY OF AFRICAN STATES.
NEW YORK, PRAEGER, 1965
081,130-09,
        REFERENCE

WEIGERT KATHLEEN M   RIGGS ROBERT E
AFRICA AND UNITED NATIONS ELECTIONS--AN AGGREGATE DATA
ANALYSIS.
INTERNATIONAL ORGANIZATION, VOL. XXIII, NO. 1, WINTER, 1969,
PP. 1-17
081,
        REFERENCE

YOUNG CRAWFORD
POLITICS IN THE CONGO--DECOLONIZATION AND INDEPENDENCE.
PRINCETON, NEW JERSEY, PRINCETON UNIVERSITY PRESS. 1965
054,061,081,108-07,
        REFERENCE

CARROLL F
SOUTH WEST AFRICA AND THE UNITED NATIONS
LEXINGTON, UNIVERSITY OF KENTUCKY PRESS, 1967
081,146-09,
        CASE STUDY

FIRST RUTH
SOUTH WEST AFRICA
BALTIMORE, PENGUIN, 1963
081,146-11,
        CASE STUDY

GARDINIER DAVID E
CAMEROON.   UNITED NATIONS CHALLENGE TO FRENCH POLICY.
LONDON, OXFORD UNIVERSITY PRESS, 1963
081,104-02,
        CASE STUDY

HIDAYATULLAH M
SOUTH WEST AFRICA CASE
NEW YORK, ASIA PUBLISHING HOUSE, 1968
081,146-09,
        CASE STUDY

081

    QUAISON-SACKEY ALEX
    AFRICA AND THE UNITED NATIONS-- OBSERVATIONS OF A GHANAIAN
    DIPLOMAT.
    ARICAN FORUM I 1 1965 PP 53-68
    081,114-09,
         CASE STUDY

    SEGAL RONALD   FIRST RUTH   EDS
    SOUTH-WEST AFRICA- TRAVESTY OF TRUST
    LONDON,OXFORD UNIVERSITY PRESS,1967,INTERNATIONAL CONFERENCE
    ON SOUTH-WEST AFRICA,OXFORD 1966
    081,146-07,146-11,
         CASE STUDY

    WELLINGTON J H
    SOUTH WEST AFRICA AND ITS HUMAN ISSUES.
    LONDON AND NEW YORK, OXFORD UNIVERSITY PRESS, 1967
    081,
         CASE STUDY

    YOUNG CRAWFORD
    THE CONGO REBELLION.
    AFRICA REPORT 10 APRIL 1965 PP 6-11
    064,081,108-06,
         CASE STUDY

    WAINHOUSE DAVID W
    REMNANTS OF EMPIRE-- THE UNITED NATIONS AND THE END OF
    COLONIALISM.
    NEW YORK,HARPER AND ROW, 1964
    081,087,
         GENERAL THEORY

    MCKAY VERNON
    AFRICA IN WORLD POLITICS.
    NEW YORK, HARPER AND ROW, 1963
    081,083,084,085,

82. AFRICA AND THE FORMER METROPOLES

082

    NKRUMAH KWAME
    NEO-COLONIALISM, THE LAST STAGE OF IMPERIALISM.
    NEW YORK, INTERNATIONAL PUBLISHERS,1965
    060,082,114-04,
         BOOK WRITTEN WHILE AUTHOR WAS PRESIDENT OF GHANA.
         DEVELOPS CONCEPT OF NEOCOLONIALISM AS CONTINUED
         CONTROL OVER AFRICAN STATES BY EUROPEAN POWERS,
         DESPITE FORMAL INDEPENDENCE. DETAILS THE PATTERN OF
         INTERNATIONAL CAPITALISM IN AFRICA, ESPECIALLY IN THE
         CONGO AND SOUTHERN AFRICA. THE BOOK IS AN IDEOLOGICAL
         DOCUMENT, ALTHOUGH THE ECONOMIC AND FINANCIAL DATA IS
         REASONABLY ACCURATE.

082

OKIGBO PIUS N C
AFRICA AND THE COMMON MARKET.
EVANSTON, NORTHWESTERN UNIVERSITY PRESS, 1967
080,082,
      AUTHOR IS HIGH-LEVEL NIGERIAN DIPLOMAT/SCHOLAR. PRI-
      MARY FOCUS ON RELATIONSHIPS BETWEEN NIGERIA AND UNITED
      KINGDOM IN POST-COLONIAL PERIOD. ALSO DISCUSSES MAJOR
      ISSUES OF EUROPEAN COMMON MARKET AS THEY AFFECT AFRI-
      CAN STATES. SURVEYS EXISTING AFRICAN CUSTOMS UNIONS,
      AND POSSIBILITIES FOR A CONTINENTAL AFRICAN COMMON
      MARKET.

ANONYMOUS
FRANCE'S NEW ROLE IN AFRICA.
THE WORLD TODAY 20 9 SEPTEMBER 1965 PP 382-387
082,
      REFERENCE

ANONYMOUS
FRANCO-AFRICAN MILITARY COOPERATION.
AFRICA REPORT, JUNE, 1968, P. 22
082,
      REFERENCE

BERG ELLIOT J
THE ECONOMICS OF INDEPENDENCE IN FRENCH-SPEAKING WEST
AFRICA.
IN PETER J MCEWAN AND ROBERT B SUTCLIFFE (EDS), MODERN AFRICA,
NEW YORK, THOMAS CROWELL, 1965
082,
      REFERENCE

CROCKER CHESTER A
FRANCE'S CHANGING MILITARY INTERESTS.
AFRICA REPORT, JUNE, 1968, P.16
082,
      REFERENCE

FOLTZ WILLIAM J
MILITARY INFLUENCES ON AFRICAN FOREIGN POLICIES.
NEW YORK, PRAEGER, 1966
082,
      REFERENCE

HATCH JOHN
THE HISTORY OF BRITISH-AFRICAN RELATIONS.
NEW YORK, INTERNATIONAL UNIVERSITY BOOKSELLERS, INC., 1969
082,
      REFERENCE

HOLMES J
THE IMPACT ON THE COMMONWEALTH OF THE EMERGENCE OF AFRICA.
INTERNATIONAL ORGANIZATION 16 2 SPRING 1962 PP 291-302
082,
      REFERENCE

KAMARCK ANDREW M
THE AFRICAN ECONOMY AND INTERNATIONAL TRADE CHAPTER 5.

IN THE UNITED STATES AND AFRICA, BACKGROUND PAPERS OF THE
13TH ASSEMBLY, THE AMERICAN ASSEMBLY, COLUMBIA UNIVERSITY,
1958, PP 117-138
082,083,
            REFERENCE

082

    KIRKWOOD KENNETH
    BRITAIN AND AFRICA.
    BALTIMORE, JOHNS HOPKINS PRESS, 1965
    082,
    075,
            REFERENCE

    LANDIER SIMONE
    THE CHANGING FRENCH MILITARY ROLE IN AFRICA.
    AFRICA REPORT 9 NOVEMBER 1964 P 21
    082,
            REFERENCE

    MAZRUI ALI A
    THE ANGLO-AFRICAN COMMONWEALTH.
    NEW YORK, PERGAMON, 1967
    082,
            REFERENCE

    MAZRUI ALI A
    AFRICAN ATTITUDES TO THE EUROPEAN ECONOMIC COMMUNITY.
    LONDON, INTERNATIONAL AFFAIRS, VOL. 38, NO. 1, JANUARY,
    1963, PP. 24-35
    080,082,
            REFERENCE

    MORTIMER EDWARD
    FRANCE AND THE AFRICANS 1944-1960--A POLITICAL HISTORY.
    LONDON, INTERNATIONAL UNIVERSITY BOOKSELLERS, INC., 1969
    082,
            REFERENCE

    NDEGWA PHILIP
    THE COMMON MARKET AND DEVELOPMENT IN EAST AFRICA.
    NAIROBI, THE EAST AFRICAN PUBLISHING HOUSE, 1965
    078,080,082,
            REFERENCE

    RIVKIN ARNOLD
    AFRICA AND THE WEST-- ELEMENTS OF FREE-WORLD POLICY.
    NEW YORK, FREDERICK A PRAEGER, 1962
    082,083,
            REFERENCE

    RIVKIN ARNOLD
    AFRICA AND THE EUROPEAN COMMON MARKET.
    DENVER, UNIVERSITY OF DENVER PRESS, 1966 PP 67
    080,082,
            REFERENCE

    RIVKIN ARNOLD
    AFRICAN PROBLEMS OF TRADE AND AID.
    CURRENT HISTORY 43 251 JULY 1962 PP 29-34

082,083,
       REFERENCE

082
   ROBINSON KENNETH
   FRENCH AFRICA AND THE FRENCH UNION.
   IN C G HAINES (ED), AFRICA TODAY, BALTIMORE,JOHNS HOPKINS
   PRESS, 1955
   082,
       REFERENCE

   WEINSTEIN BRIAN
   THE FRENCH COMMUNITY-- DOES IT EXIST?
   CURRENT HISTORY 50 296 APRIL 1966 PP 214-220
   082,
       REFERENCE

   ZARTMAN I WILLIAM
   THE EEC'S NEW DEAL WITH AFRICA
   AFRICA REPORT 15 FEBRUARY 1970 PP 28-31
   082,
       REFERENCE

   HOWELL JOHN
   AN ANALYSIS OF KENYAN FOREIGN POLICY.
   THE JOURNAL OF MODERN AFRICAN STUDIES, VOL. 6, NO. 1, 1968,
   PP. 29-48
   082,117-09,
       CASE STUDY

   LEGUM COLIN
   BRITAIN'S YEAR IN AFRICA.
   IN LEGUM AND DRYSDALE, AFRICA CONTEMPORARY RECORD,
   LONDON, AFRICA RESEARCH LIMITED, 1969, P. 22-26
   082,
       CASE STUDY

   PHILLIPS CLAUDE JR
   THE DEVELOPMENT OF NIGERIAN FOREIGN POLICY.
   EVANSTON ILLINOIS, NORTHWESTERN UNIVERSITY PRESS 1964
   082,128-09,
       CASE STUDY

   THOMPSON W SCOTT
   GHANA'S FOREIGN POLICY,1957-1966- DIPLOMACY,IDEOLOGY AND THE
   NEW STATE
   PRINCETON,PRINCETON UNIVERSITY PRESS,1969
   060,082,083,084,085,114-09,
       CASE STUDY

   WHITEMAN K
   FRANCE'S YEAR IN AFRICA.
   IN LEGUM AND DRYSDALE, 1969, P. 27-31
   082,
       CASE STUDY

   ATEMENGUE JOSEPH   ED
   A QUOI SERT LA COOPERATION FRANCO-AFRICAINE--LE PROBLEME
   VOL I (WHAT SHALL BE THE NATURE OF FRANCO-AFRICAN COOPERA-
   TION VOL I)

DES AVANTAGES CONCRETS TIRES DE LA COOPERATION FRANCO-
AFRICAINE VOL II (CONCRETE ADVANTAGES TO BE HAD FROM FRANCO-
AFRICAN COOPERATION VOL II).
PARIS, INTERNATIONAL UNIVERSITY BOOKSELLERS, INC., 1969
082,
    LESS ACCESSIBLE

082
    GUIFFRAY R
    LE FRANCAIS EN AFRIQUE (THE FRENCH IN AFRICA).
    PARIS, LAROUSSE; NEW YORK, INTERNATIONAL UNIVERSITY BOOKSEL-
    LERS,INC., 1969
    082,
        LESS ACCESSIBLE

    BARKER D
    BRITISH AID TO DEVELOPING NATIONS.
    LONDON, H.M.S.O., 1964
    082,
        GENERAL THEORY

    HAYTER THERESA
    FRENCH AID.
    LONDON OVERSEAS DEVELOPMENT INSTITUTE 1966
    082,
        GENERAL THEORY

83. AFRICA AND THE UNITED STATES

083
    HANCE WILLIAM A   ED
    SOUTHERN AFRICA AND THE UNITED STATES.
    NEW YORK, COLUMBIA UNIVERSITY PRESS, 1968
    083,089,132-09,
        INCLUDES CONTRIBUTIONS BY WILLIAM HANCE, MCKAY, LEO
        KUPER, AND EDWIN MUNGER. EDITOR'S SUMMARY EXAMINES
        SEVERAL PROPOSALS AS TO HOW AMERICAN POLICY MIGHT IN-
        FLUENCE SOUTH AFRICA. DISMISSES MULTILATERAL SANC-
        TIONS, MILITARY ACTION, AND ECONOMIC DISENGAGEMENT,
        BUT ARGUES FOR CONSTRUCTIVE POSSIBILITIES (E.G. CON-
        TINUED POLICY OPPOSITION TO APARTHEID).

    NIELSEN WALDEMAR
    THE GREAT POWERS AND AFRICA
    NEW YORK, PRAEGER, 1969
    083, 097,
        A GENERAL AND FAIRLY BALANCED BUT CONSERVATIVE
        ASSESSMENT OF AFRICAS ROLE IN THE MODERN WORLD
        PARTICULARLY FROM THE PERSPECTIVE OF THE GREAT POWERS.
        COVERS WIDE RANGE OF TOPICS AND PROVIDES GOOD INTRO-
        DUCTION TO AFRICAN RELATIONS WITH THE UNITED STATES,
        SOVIET UNION, COMMUNIST CHINA, THE FORMER METROPOLES,
        AND THE UNITED NATIONS.

    AFRICA REPORT

U.S. ECONOMIC AID TO AFRICA 1950-1964.
AFRICA REPORT 9 DECEMBER 1964 PP 8-12
083,
        REFERENCE

083
DUNCAN PATRICK
TOWARD A WORLD POLICY FOR SOUTH AFRICA.
IN PHILIP W QUIGG (ED.), AFRICA, NEW YORK, PRAEGER, 1964,
PP 248-260
083,089,132-09,
        REFERENCE

EMERSON RUPERT
THE CHARACTER OF AMERICAN INTERESTS IN AFRICA CHAPTER 1.
IN THE UNITED STATES AND AFRICA, BACKGROUND PAPERS OF THE
13TH ASSEMBLY, THE AMERICAN ASSEMBLY, COLUMBIA UNIVERSITY,
1958, PP 1-24
083,
        REFERENCE

GALLAGHER CHARLES F
THE UNITED STATES AND NORTH AFRICA
CAMBRIDGE MASS HARVARD UNIVERSITY PRESS 1963
083,101-09,126-09,138-09,
        REFERENCE

HOWARD LAWRENCE C
THE UNITED STATES AND AFRICA-- TRADE AND INVESTMENT.
IN AMSAC, AFRICA SEEN BY AMERICAN NEGROES, PARIS,
PRESENCE AFRICAINE, 1958 , PP 279-302
083,
        REFERENCE

KAMARCK ANDREW M
THE AFRICAN ECONOMY AND INTERNATIONAL TRADE CHAPTER 5.
IN THE UNITED STATES AND AFRICA, BACKGROUND PAPERS OF THE
13TH ASSEMBLY, THE AMERICAN ASSEMBLY, COLUMBIA UNIVERSITY,
1958, PP 117-138
082,083,
        REFERENCE

MCKAY VERNON
THE AFRICAN OPERATIONS OF UNITED STATES GOVERNMENT AGENCIES.
IN THE UNITED STATES AND AFRICA, BACKGROUND PAPERS OF THE
13TH ASSEMBLY, THE AMERICAN ASSEMBLY, COLUMBIA UNIVERSITY,
1958, PP 193-203 (APPENDIX)
083,
        REFERENCE

MCKAY VERNON
EXTERNAL POLITICAL PRESSURES ON AFRICA TODAY CHAPTER 3.
IN THE UNITED STATES AND AFRICA, BACKGROUND PAPERS OF THE
13TH ASSEMBLY, THE AMERICAN ASSEMBLY, COLUMBIA UNIVERSITY,
1958, PP 63-88
083,
        REFERENCE

WILLIAMS G MENNEN
AFRICA FOR THE AFRICANS
GRAND RAPIDS, MICH., INTERNATIONAL UNIVERSITY BOOKSELLERS, 1969
083,
        REFERENCE

083

PAYNE WILLIAM
AMERICAN PRESS COVERAGE OF AFRICA.
AFRICA REPORT JANUARY 1966 PP 44-48
083,
        REFERENCE

RIVKIN ARNOLD
AFRICA AND THE WEST-- ELEMENTS OF FREE-WORLD POLICY.
NEW YORK, FREDERICK A PRAEGER, 1962
082,083,
        REFERENCE

RIVKIN ARNOLD
AFRICAN PROBLEMS OF TRADE AND AID.
CURRENT HISTORY 43 251 JULY 1962 PP 29-34
082,083,
        REFERENCE

SHEPHERD GEORGE W
UNITED STATES AND NON-ALIGNED AFRICA.
DENVER, INTERNATIONAL UNIVERSITY BOOKSELLERS, INC., 1969
083,
        REFERENCE

WALLERSTEIN I M
FROM NIXON TO NIXON- IS AMERICA'S OUTMODED POLICY TOWARDS A
CHANGING AFRICA ABOUT TO CROSS A NEW FRONTIER
AFRICA REPORT NOVEMBER 1969 PP 28-30
083,
        REFERENCE

WILLIAMS G MENNEN
DIPLOMATIC RAPPORT BETWEEN AFRICA AND THE UNITED STATES.
ANNALS OF THE AMERICAN ACADEMY OF POLITICAL AND SOCIAL SCI-
ENCE 354 JULY 1964 PP 54-64
083,
        REFERENCE

BIXLER RAYMOND W
THE FOREIGN POLICY OF THE UNITED STATES IN LIBERIA.
NEW YORK PAGEANT PRESS 1957
083,119-09,
        CASE STUDY

MORROW JOHN H
FIRST AMERICAN AMBASSADOR TO GUINEA.
NEW BRUNSWICK, NEW JERSEY, RUTGERS UNIVERSITY PRESS, 1968
083,115-09,
        CASE STUDY

MUNGER EDWIN S
JOHN VORSTER AND THE UNITED STATES
AMERICAN UNIVERSITIES FIELD STAFF REPORTS 12 1968
083,132-09,

CASE STUDY

083

THOMPSON W SCOTT
GHANA'S FOREIGN POLICY,1957-1966- DIPLOMACY,IDEOLOGY AND THE
NEW STATE
PRINCETON, PRINCETON UNIVERSITY PRESS, 1969
060,082,083,084,085,114-09,
        CASE STUDY

EMERSON RUPERT
AFRICA AND UNITED STATES POLICY.
ENGLEWOOD CLIFFS,N.J., PRENTICE-HALL, 1967
083,
        GENERAL THEORY

LEIGHTON RICHARD M   SANDERS RALPH
AID'S PUBLIC SAFETY CIVIC ACTION AND COMMUNITY DEVELOPMENT
PROGRAM.
IN LEWIS P FICKETT   (ED), PROBLEMS OF THE DEVELOPING NATIONS,
NEW YORK, CROWELL, 1966, PP 116-122
083,
        GENERAL THEORY

RIVKIN ARNOLD
PRINCIPAL ELEMENTS OF U.S. POLICY TOWARDS UNDERDEVELOPED
COUNTRIES.
INTERNATIONAL AFFAIRS 37 4 OCTOBER 1961 PP 452-464
083,
        GENERAL THEORY

MCKAY VERNON
AFRICA IN WORLD POLITICS.
NEW YORK,HARPER AND ROW, 1963
081,083,084,085,

84. AFRICA AND THE COMMUNIST BLOC

084

BRZEZINSKI Z   ED
AFRICA AND THE COMMUNIST WORLD.
STANFORD,CALIFORNIA, STANFORD UNIVERSITY PRESS, 1963
084,
        CONTRIBUTORS TO THIS VOLUME EXPERTS IN VARIOUS SOVIET
        BLOC COUNTRIES. SUMMARIZE THE POLICIES AND ACTIVITES
        IN AFRICA OF SOVIET UNION, EASTERN EUROPE IN GENERAL,
        YUGOSLAVIA, AND CHINA. ALL ASSESS COLD WAR IMPLICA-
        TIONS FOR AFRICA.

MORISON DAVID
THE U S S R AND AFRICA
LONDON,OXFORD UNIVERSITY PRESS,1964
084,
        EXPLORES EXTENT OF UNDERSTANDING AND INTERPRETATION OF
        AFRICA IN THE SOVIET UNION, AND THE IMPACT OF AFRICA

ON SOVIET THINKING. DESCRIBES SOVIET EFFORT TO ADJUST
IDEOLOGY TO MEET NEEDS OF NEW AFRICAN STATES. APPEN-
DIX GIVES SUMMARY OF SOVIET POLICY AND ACTIVITY IN
EACH OF THE NEW AFRICAN STATES. AUTHOR IS EDITOR OF
MIZAN NEWSLETTER, OXFORD.

084

ALEXANDRE PIERRE
MARXISM AND AFRICAN CULTURAL TRADITION.
IN LEOPOLD LABEDZ   (ED.), POLYCENTRISM-- THE NEW FACTOR IN
INTERNATIONAL COMMUNISM, NEW YORK. PRAEGER, 1962, PP 173-
186
084,
        REFERENCE

BASS ROBERT   BASS ELIZABETH
EASTERN EUROPE
IN BRZEZINSKI (ED), AFRICA AND THE COMMUNIST WORLD,
STANFORD UNIVERSITY PRESS, 1963, PP 84-115
084,
        REFERENCE

BRZEZINSKI Z
YUGOSLAVIA.
IN Z BRZEZINSKI (ED), AFRICA AND THE COMMUNIST WORLD,
STANFORD, CALIFORNIA, STANFORD UNIVERSITY PRESS, 1963,
PP 116-141
084,
        REFERENCE

BRZEZINSKI Z
CONCLUSION-- THE AFRICAN CHALLENGE.
IN Z BRZEZINSKI (ED), AFRICA AND THE COMMUNIST WORLD,
STANFORD, CALIFORNIA, STANFORD UNIVERSITY PRESS, 1963,
PP 204-230
084,
        REFERENCE

COOLEY JOHN K
EAST WIND OVER AFRICA-- RED CHINA'S AFRICAN OFFENSIVE.
NEW YORK, WALKER, 1965
084,
        REFERENCE

DALLIN ALEXANDER
THE SOVIET UNION-- POLITICAL ACTIVITY.
IN Z BRZEZINSKI (ED), AFRICA AND THE COMMUNIST WORLD,
STANFORD, CALIFORNIA, STANFORD UNIVERSITY PRESS, 1963
PP 7-48
084,
        REFERENCE

HEVI EMMANUEL J
THE DRAGON'S EMBRACE-- THE CHINESE COMMUNISTS AND AFRICA.
NEW YORK, PRAEGER, 1967
084,098,
        REFERENCE

KLINGHOFFER ARTHUR J
THE SOVIET VIEW OF AFRICAN SOCIALISM

AFRICAN AFFAIRS 67 1968 PP 197-208
084,
        REFERENCE

084
LAQUEUR WALTER Z
COMMUNISM AND NATIONALISM IN TROPICAL AFRICA.
IN PHILIP W QUIGG (ED.), AFRICA, NEW YORK, PRAEGER, 1964,
PP 182-195
084,
        REFERENCE

LEGVOLD ROBERT
MOSCOW'S CHANGING VIEW OF AFRICA'S REVOLUTIONARY REGIMES.
AFRICA REPORT, MARCH/APRIL, 1969, PP. 54-58
084,
        REFERENCE

LOWENTHAL RICHARD
CHINA.
IN Z BRZEZINSKI (ED), AFRICA AND THE COMMUNIST WORLD,
STANFORD, CALIFORNIA, STANFORD UNIVERSITY PRESS, 1963,
PP 142-203
084,
        REFERENCE

NELKIN DOROTHY
SOCIALIST SOURCES OF PAN-AFRICAN IDEOLOGY CHAPTER 4.
IN WILLIAM FRIEDLAND AND CARL ROSBERG (EDS), AFRICAN
SOCIALISM, STANFORD, CALIFORNIA, STANFORD UNIVERSITY PRESS,
1964, PP 63-79
079,084,
        REFERENCE

PADMORE GEORGE
PAN-AFRICANISM OR COMMUNISM.
PARIS, DENNIS DOBSON, 1960
079,084,
        REFERENCE

POTEKHIN I I
FRONTIERS NATIONS AND GROUPINGS CHP 3.
IN AFRICA'S FUTURE-- THE SOVIET VIEW, SUPPLEMENT TO MIZAN
NEWSLETTER, 4 APRIL 1961
084,
        REFERENCE

POTEKHIN I I
THE FORMATION OF NATIONS IN AFRICA.
MARXISM TODAY 2 1958 PP 308-314
084,
        REFERENCE

POTEKHIN I I
AFRICAN PROBLEMS.
TORONTO, PROGRESS BOOKS, 1969
084,
        REFERENCE

SCALAPINO ROBERT A

SINO-SOVIET COMPETITION IN AFRICA.
FOREIGN AFFAIRS 42 4 JULY 1964 PP 640-654
084,
        REFERENCE

084

SCHATTEN F
COMMUNISM IN AFRICA.
LONDON, ALLEN AND UNWIN, 1966.
084,
        REFERENCE

STOKKE BAARD RICHARD
SOVIET AND EASTERN EUROPEAN TRADE AND AID IN AFRICA.
NEW YORK, PRAEGER, 1967
084,
        REFERENCE

ADIE W A C
CHINA'S REVIVED INTEREST IN AFRICA.
IN LEGUM AND DRYSDALE (AFRICA CONTEMPORARY RECORD),
1969, P.45-48
084,
        CASE STUDY

HYDAN GORAN
MAO AND MWALIMU--THE SOLDIER AND THE TEACHER AS
REVOLUTIONARY
TRANSITION 7 1968 PP 24-30
084,136-04,
        CASE STUDY

KLINGHOFFER ARTHUR J
WHY THE SOVIETS CHOSE SIDES IN THE NIGERIAN WAR.
AFRICA REPORT, FEBRUARY, 1968, P. 48
065,084,128-06,
        CASE STUDY

MARSH WILLIAM W
EAST GERMANY AND AFRICA.
AFRICA REPORT, MARCH/APRIL, 1969, PP. 59-64
084,
        CASE STUDY

MORISON DAVID
 SOVIET UNION AND AFRICA, 1968
IN LEGUM AND DRYSDALE, AFRICA CONTEMPORARY RECORD,
LONDON. AFRICA RESEARCH LIMITED, 1969, P. 38-42
084,
        CASE STUDY

THOMPSON W SCOTT
GHANA'S FOREIGN POLICY,1957-1966- DIPLOMACY,IDEOLOGY AND THE
NEW STATE
PRINCETON PRINCETON UNIVERSITY PRESS 1969
060,082,083,084,085,114-09,
        CASE STUDY

ERLICH ALEXANDER   SONNE CHRISTIAN R
THE SOVIET UNION-- ECONOMIC ACTIVITY.

IN Z BRZEZINSKI (ED), AFRICA AND THE COMMUNIST WORLD,
STANFORD, CALIFORNIA, STANFORD UNIVERSITY PRESS, 1963,
PP 49-83
084,
        LESS ACCESSIBLE

084
  ECKSTEIN A
  COMMUNIST CHINA S ECONOMIC GROWTH AND FOREIGN TRADE.
  NEW YORK MCGRAW HILL 1966
  084,
        GENERAL THEORY

  GOLDMAN MARSHALL
  COMMUNIST FOREIGN AID-- SUCCESSES AND SHORTCOMINGS.
  CURRENT HISTORY 51 300 AUGUST 1966 PP 78-87
  084,
        GENERAL THEORY

  MCKAY VERNON
  AFRICA IN WORLD POLITICS.
  NEW YORK HARPER AND ROW 1963
  081,083,084,085,

85. AFRICA AND THE THIRD WORLD

085
  EAST AFRICAN INSTITUTE OF SOCIAL AND CULTURAL AFFAIRS
  RACIAL AND COMMUNAL TENSIONS IN EAST AFRICA.
  KENYA, EAST AFRICAN PUBLISHING HOUSE, 1966
  057,085,
        CONFERENCE ESSAYS IN PAPERBACK, GIVE WIDE RANGE OF CO-
        VERAGE ON RACIAL AND ETHNIC PROBLEMS IN EAST AFRICA--
        PRIMARILY BY AFRICAN SCHOLARS. TOPICS INCLUDE--ROLE
        OF ASIANS IN EAST AFRICA, RACIAL CONSCIOUSNESS AMONG
        AFRICANS, TRIBALISM AS A FACTOR IN INTERNATIONAL TEN-
        SIONS, ECONOMIC ASPECTS OF RACE RELATIONS, AND CULTURAL
        TENSIONS IN A MIXED SOCIETY.

  FANON FRANTZ
  BLACK SKIN, WHITE MASKS-- THE EXPERIENCES OF A BLACK
  MAN IN A WHITE WORLD.
  NEW YORK, GROVE PRESS, 1967
  041,085,088,101-03,
        AUTHOR IS BLACK PSYCHIATRIST WHO WORKED IN ALGERIA
        DURING FRENCH-ALGERIAN WAR. BOOK BEGINS WITH FACT OF
        HIS OWN BLACKNESS, AND HOSTILITY OF WHITE WORLD.
        GIVES PSYCHOPATHOLOGICAL AND PHILOSOPHICAL ANALYSIS OF
        STATE OF BEING BLACK IN SUCH A WORLD. CRITICIZES
        MANNONI. EXPLORES LITERATURE, DREAMS, CASE HISTORIES,
        AND SPECIAL ISSUE OF BLACK MEN AND WHITE WOMEN.

  MAZRUI ALI A
  AFRICA AND THE THIRD WORLD CHAPTER 13
  IN ON HEROES AND UHURU-WORSHIP, LONDON, LONGMANS, 1967, 209-230

085,

ANALYZES CONCEPT AND ORIGINS OF THIRD WORLDISM IN
AFRICA.BRIEFLY DISCUSSES THE EROSION OF PAN-NEGROISM,
INDIA'S POVERTY AND AFRICAN RESISTANCE,CHINAS EXAMPLE
AND AFRICAN REVOLUTIONARIES,AFRICAS LINKS WITH LATIN
AMERICA. CONCLUDES CONCEPT COULD REMAIN FORM OF
FELLOWSHIP BUT TOO COMPETITIVE AS BASIS FOR
INTEGRATION.

085

AMIJI HATIM
THE ASIAN MINORITIES
IN KRITZECK AND LEWIS, PP 139-181
085,
REFERENCE

GHAI DHARAM P
PORTRAIT OF A MINORITY.
NAIROBI,   OXFORD UNIVERSITY PRESS, 1965
085,
REFERENCE

LEGUM COLIN
BANDUNG.
IN PAN-AFRICANISM, LONDON, PALL MALL PRESS, 1962
085,
REFERENCE

MANGAT J S
A HISTORY OF THE ASIANS IN EAST AFRICA.
LONDON, OXFORD UNIVERSITY PRESS, 1969
085,
REFERENCE

MAZRUI ALI A
SOCIALISM AND SILENCE IN THE THIRD WORLD CHAPTER 10.
IN ON HEROES AND UHURU-WORSHIP, LONDON, LONGMANS,
1967, PP 146-156
085,
REFERENCE

MORRIS H S
THE INDIANS IN UGANDA
CHICAGO,UNIVERSITY OF CHICAGO PRESS,1968
085,139-06,
REFERENCE

POWER PAUL
GANDHI IN SOUTH AFRICA
JOURNAL OF MODERN AFRICAN STUDIES 7 1969 PP 441-456
085,
REFERENCE

THEROUX PAUL
HATING THE ASIANS
TRANSITION 7 1967 PP 46-51
085,
REFERENCE

DATTA A K

INDIA AND AFRICA-- A LETTER.
GOVERNMENT AND OPPOSITION CLEVELAND 2 NO 4 1968 PP 612-620
085,
        CASE STUDY

085
    DOTSON FLOYD   LILLIAN O
    THE INDIAN MINORITY OF ZAMBIA, RHODESIA, AND MALAWI.
    NEW HAVEN, CONN. (YALE), MCGILL-QUEEN'S PRESS, 1969
    085,142-06,145-06,122-06,
        CASE STUDY

    LEGUM COLIN
    JAPAN AND AFRICA, 1968.
    IN LEGUM AND DRYSDALE, AFRICA CONTEMPORARY RECORD,
    LONDON, AFRICA RESEARCH LIMITED, 1969, P. 43-45
    085,
        CASE STUDY

    THOMPSON W SCOTT
    GHANA'S FOREIGN POLICY,1957-1966- DIPLOMACY,IDEOLOGY AND THE
    NEW STATE
    PRINCETON,PRINCETON UNIVERSITY PRESS, 1969
    060,082,083,084,085,114-09,
        CASE STUDY

    MCKAY VERNON
    AFRICA IN WORLD POLITICS.
    NEW YORK, HARPER AND ROW, 1963
    081,083,084,085,

86. AFRICA AND THE MIDDLE EAST

086
    KEREKES TIBOR
    THE ARAB MIDDLE EAST AND MUSLIM AFRICA.
    NEW YORK, PRAEGER, 1961
    086,
        EXCELLENT INTRODUCTION TO THE ROLE OF MODERN ISLAMIC
        FACTOR IN ARAB-AFRICAN RELATIONS, ESSAYS BY LEADING
        ISLAMICISTS (GIBB AND HOURANI) PROVIDE INSIGHT INTO
        SOCIAL CHANGE WITHIN THE ARAB MUSLIM WORLD. CHAPTER
        BY WILLIAM LEWIS ON ISLAM AND NATIONALISM IN AFRICA
        RELATES DEMOGRAPHIC AND POLITICAL PATTERNS IN AFRICA
        TO THE ISLAMIC FACTOR. NOW SLIGHTLY DATED IN TERMS OF
        DETAILS.

    ABU-LUGHOD IBRAHIM
    THE ISLAMIC FACTOR IN AFRICAN POLITICS.
    ORBIS 8 2 SUMMER 1964 PP 425-44
    086,140-09,
        REFERENCE

    BAULIN JACQUES
    THE ARAB ROLE IN AFRICA.

BALTIMORE,1962
086,
        REFERENCE

086

    DECALO SAMUEL.
    ISRAEL AND AFRICA-- A SELECTED BIBLIOGRAPHY.
    THE JOURNAL OF MODERN AFRICAN STUDIES 5 3 NOVEMBER 1967 PP
    385-400
    086,
        REFERENCE

    KREININ MORDECHAI E
    ISRAEL AND AFRICA-- A STUDY IN TECHNICAL COOPERATION.
    NEW YORK,PRAEGER,1964
    086,
        REFERENCE

    LAUFER
    ISRAEL IN AFRICA.
    20TH CENTURY FUND
    086,
        REFERENCE

    MAZRUI ALI A
    AFRICA AND EGYPT'S FOUR CIRCLES CHAPTER 7.
    IN ON HEROES AND UHURU-WORSHIP, LONDON, LONGMANS,
    1967, PP 96-112
    086,140-09,
        REFERENCE

    MCKAY VERNON
    THE IMPACT OF ISLAM ON RELATIONS AMONG THE NEW AFRICAN
    STATES.
    IN J H PROCTOR (ED), ISLAM AND INTERNATIONAL RELATIONS, NEW
    YORK,PRAEGER,1965,PP 158-191
    086,
        REFERENCE

    SEGAL AARON
    ISRAEL IN AFRICA.
    AFRICA REPORT 8 4 APRIL 1963 PP 19-21
    086,
        REFERENCE

    FALLERS LLOYD A
    COMMENTS ON THE LEBANESE IN WEST AFRICA .
    SOC. HIST., VOL. IV, NO. 3, APRIL, 1962, PP. 334-336
    086,
        CASE STUDY

    ISMAEL TAREQ Y
    RELIGION AND U A R AFRICAN POLICY.
    THE JOURNAL OF MODERN AFRICAN STUIDES, VOL. 6, NO. 1, 1968,
    PP. 49-57
    086,140-09,
        CASE STUDY

    NASSER GAMAL ABDEL
    THE PHILOSOPHY OF THE REVOLUTION.

BUFFALO, NEW YORK, SMITH, KEYNES AND MARSHALL PUBLISHERS,
ENGLISH VERSION, 1959
086,140-04,
     CASE STUDY

086
   WINDER R BAYLEY
   THE LEBANESE IN WEST AFRICA.
   IMMIGRANTS AND ASSOCIATIONS, FALLERS, L.A. (ED.), 1967,
   PP. 103-154
   086,
      CASE STUDY

87. THE REMNANTS OF COLONIALISM

087
   CHITEPO HERBERT W
   DEVELOPMENTS IN CENTRAL AFRICA.
   IN DAVID P CURRIE (ED), FEDERALISM AND THE NEW NATIONS OF
   AFRICA, CHICAGO, UNIVERSITY OF CHICAGO PRESS, 1964, PP 3-28
   078,087,122-06,142-06,145-06,
      DISCUSSES THE FEDERATION OF RHODESIA AND NYASALAND
      WHICH WAS ESTABLISHED DESPITE AFRICAN PROTESTS IN
      1953. AUTHOR SKETCHES ETHNIC AND DEMOGRAPHIC ASPECTS
      OF FEDERATION. PROCEEDINGS OF DISCUSSION WITH CONFER-
      ENCE PARTICIPANTS IS INCLUDED. AUTHOR IS LONDON
      TRAINED LAWYER, AND CURRENT LEADER OF NATIONALIST
      MOVEMENT IN RHODESIA (ZIMBABWE).

   DAVIDSON BASIL
   THE LIBERATION OF GUINE-- ASPECTS OF AN AFRICAN RE-
   VOLUTION.
   BALTIMORE, PENGUIN, 1969
   087,144-11,
      EXCELLENT ASSESSMENT OF LIBERATION MOVEMENT IN PORTU-
      GUESE GUINEA. AUTHOR SPENT EXTENSIVE PERIODS AMONG
      THE REBEL GROUPS AND OFFERS NOT ONLY A DESCRIPTION OF
      THEIR ACTIVITIES BUT A BASIC POLITICAL AND PHILOSO-
      PHICAL STATEMENT ON THE NATURE OF COLONIALISM WHICH
      SOME HAVE COMPARED WITH THE WRITINGS OF FRANTZ FANON.

   DUFFY JAMES
   PORTUGUESE AFRICA.
   CAMBRIDGE, HARVARD UNIVERSITY PRESS, 1959
   027,087,088,144-06,
      DEALS PRIMARILY WITH ANGOLA AND MOZAMBIQUE. FIRST
      SCHOLARLY HISTORY OF PORTUGUESE CONTACT WITH AFRICA
      FROM EARLIEST TIME (FIFTEENTH CENTURY) TO MID-TWENTI-
      ETH CENTURY. DEALS WITH THE REALITY, OFTEN HARSH, OF
      PORTUGUESE CONTACT RATHER THAN WITH THE OFFICIAL POLI-
      CY AND COLONIAL IDEALS ESPOUSED BY LISBON.

   LEGUM COLIN   DRYSDALE JOHN
   AFRICA CONTEMPORARY RECORD.
   LONDON, AFRICA RESEARCH LIMITED, 1969

002,062,080,081,087,
    BEST EXISTING GENERAL REFERENCE FOR DETAILS OF EACH
    AFRICAN COUNTRY IN THE FIELDS OF FOREIGN RELATIONS,
    GOVERNMENT AND ECONOMICS. IT IS WRITTEN FOR THE SPE-
    CIALIST, BUT CAN BE USED BY THE TEACHER AS WELL.

087
    ABSHIRE DAVID M   SAMUELS MICHAEL A   EDS
    PORTUGUESE AFRICA--A HANDBOOK.
    NEW YORK, PRAEGER PUBLISHERS, 1969
    087,144-11,
        REFERENCE

    DEBOSSCHERE G
    NEO-COLONIALISM
    PRESENCE AFRICAINE 10 38 1962 (ENGLISH EDITION) PP 26-35
    087,
        REFERENCE

    DUFFY JAMES
    PORTUGAL IN AFRICA.
    IN PHILIP W QUIGG (ED.), AFRICA, NEW YORK, PRAEGER, 1964,
    PP 86-102
    035,087,144-06,
        REFERENCE

    DUFFY JAMES
    PORTUGAL'S AFRICAN TERRITORIES--PRESENT REALITIES.
    NEW YORK, CARNEGIE ENDOWMENT FOR INTERNATIONAL PEACE, 1962,
    39 PAGES
    087,
        REFERENCE

    FRANCK THOMAS M
    RACE AND NATIONALISM--THE STRUGGLE FOR POWER IN RHODESIA-
    NYASALAND
    NEW YORK FORDHAM UNIVERSITY PRESS 1960
    087,122-07,142-07,145-07,
        REFERENCE

    FRANCK THOMAS M
    MUST WE LOSE ZIMBABWE?
    AFRICAN FORUM 2 3 1967 PP 17-33
    087,145-06,
        REFERENCE

    GONCHAROV L
    NEW FORMS OF COLONISATION IN AFRICA.
    JOURNAL OF MODERN AFRICAN STUDIES 1 4 1963 PP 467-74
    087,
        REFERENCE

    HOWE MARVINE
    PORTUGAL AT WAR
    AFRICA REPORT NOVEMBER 1969 PP 16-21
    087,
        REFERENCE

    KAUNDA KENNETH
    CRISIS IN SOUTHERN AFRICA.

AFRICAN FORUM 2 3 1967 PP 11-16
087,142-04,
        REFERENCE

087
    MARCUM JOHN A
    THE ANGOLAN REVOLUTION VOLUME 1- THE ANATOMY OF AN EXPLOSION
    CAMBRIDGE, MASS, MIT PRESS, 1969
    087,144-11,
        REFERENCE

    MONDLANE EDUARDO
    THE STRUGGLE FOR MOZAMBIQUE.
    BALTIMORE, PENGUIN BOOKS, 1969
    080,087,144-06,
        REFERENCE

    PARKER   JOHN
    EXPANDING GUERILLA WARFARE.
    IN LEGUM AND DRYSDALE, AFRICA CONTEMPORARY RECORD,
    087,
        REFERENCE

    PELISSIER RENE
    SPANISH GUINEA-- AN INTRODUCTION.
    RACE 6 2 OCTOBER 1964 PP 117-128
    087, 111-01,
        REFERENCE

    POTEKHIN I I
    PROBLEMS OF ECONOMIC INDEPENDENCE OF AFRICAN COUNTRIES.
    IN LALAGE BOWN AND MICHAEL CROWDER (EDS.), PROCEEDINGS OF
    THE FIRST INTERNATIONAL CONGRESS OF AFRICANISTS, ACCRA,
    1962, LONDON, LONGMANS, 1964, PP 171-183
    087,
        REFERENCE

    SHAMUYARIRA NATHAN M
    THE NATIONALIST MOVEMENT IN ZIMBABWE.
    AFRICAN FORUM 2 3 1967 PP 34-42
    087,145-06,
        REFERENCE

    BARNETT DONALD
    ANGOLA--REPORT FROM HANOI II.
    RAMPARTS, APRIL 1969, PP. 49-54
    087,
        CASE STUDY

    BOWMAN LARRY W
    STRAINS IN THE RHODESIAN FRONT.
    AFRICAN REPORT, DECEMBER, 1968, P. 16
    087,145-06,
        CASE STUDY

    CHILCOTE RONALD H
    EMERGING NATIONALISM IN PORTUGUESE AFRICA.
    PALO ALTO, CALIFORNIA, HOOVER INSTITUTION PRESS, 1969
    087,144-12,
        CASE STUDY

087

CHILCOTE RONALD H
THE POLITICAL THOUGHT OF AMILCAR CABRAL.
THE JOURNAL OF MODERN AFRICAN STUDIES, VOL. 6, NO. 3, 1968,
PP. 373-388
087,144-04,
    CASE STUDY

CHILCOTE RONALD H
PORTUGUESE AFRICA
ENGLEWOOD CLIFFS, PRENTICE-HALL, 1967
087,144-11,
    CASE STUDY

CLEMENTS FRANK
RHODESIA--A STUDY OF THE DETERIORATION OF A WHITE SOCIETY.
NEW YORK, PRAEGER, 1969
087,145-06,
    CASE STUDY

DUFFY JAMES
PORTUGAL IN AFRICA
BALTIMORE, PENGUIN, 1962
027,087,088,144-06,
    CASE STUDY

FLOYD BARRY
LAND APPORTIONMENT IN SOUTHERN RHODESIA.
GEOGRAPHIC REVIEW LII OCTOBER 1962 PP 566-582
087,145-08,
    CASE STUDY

GANN LEWIS H
A HISTORY OF SOUTHERN RHODESIA.
LONDON, 1965
087,145-02,
    CASE STUDY

GRAY RICHARD
THE TWO NATIONS-- ASPECTS OF THE DEVELOPMENT OF RACE
RELATIONS IN THE RHODESIAS AND NYASALAND.
LONDON,OXFORD UNIVERSITY PRESS,1960
087,088,122-06,142-06,145-06,
    CASE STUDY

INSTITUTE OF   RACE RELATIONS
ANGOLA--A SYMPOSIUM--VIEWS OF A REVOLT.
LONDON, OXFORD UNIVERSITY PRESS, 1962
087,144-06,
    CASE STUDY

LEYS COLIN
EUROPEAN POLITICS IN SOUTHERN RHODESIA.
OXFORD,CLARENDON PRESS,1959
087,145-06,
    CASE STUDY

MARCUM JOHN A
A MARTYR FOR MOZAMBIQUE.

AFRICA REPORT, MARCH/APRIL, 1969, PP. 6-9
087,144-06,
       CASE STUDY

087

MASON PHILIP
THE BIRTH OF A DILEMMA-- THE CONQUEST AND SETTLEMENT OF
RHODESIA.
LONDON, OXFORD UNIVERSITY PRESS, 1958
087,145-06,
       CASE STUDY

MORRIS   ELIZABETH
PORTUGAL'S YEAR IN AFRICA.
IN LEGUM AND DRYSDALE, AFRICA CONTEMPORARY RECORD.
LONDON, AFRICA RESEARCH LIMITED, 1969, P. 49-52
087,
       CASE STUDY

NYERERE JULIUS K
INDEPENDENCE MEANS POWER.
AFRICA REPORT, DECEMBER, 1968, P. 22
087,136-04,
       CASE STUDY

RAKE ALAN
BLACK GUERRILLAS IN RHODESIA.
AFRICAN REPORT, DECEMBER, 1968, P. 23
087,145-06,
       CASE STUDY

RODER W
THE DIVISION OF LAND RESOURCES IN SOUTHERN RHODESIA.
ANNALS OF THE ASSOCIATION OF AMERICAN GEOGRAPHERS 54 MARCH
1964 PP 42-52
087,145-06,
       CASE STUDY

SHAMUYARIRA NATHAN M
CRISIS IN RHODESIA.
LONDON, 1965
087,145-06,
       CASE STUDY

THOMPSON VIRGINIA   ADLOFF RICHARD
DJIBOUTI AND THE HORN OF AFRICA.
STANFORD, STANFORD UNIVERSITY PRESS, 1968
087,133-09,143-11,
       CASE STUDY

WHEELER DOUGLAS L   PELISSIER RENE
ANGOLA.
LONDON, PALL MALL PRESS, 1970
087,144-11,
       CASE STUDY

ZARTMAN I WILLIAM
GUINEA-- THE QUIET WAR GOES ON.
AFRICA REPORT, 12 NOVEMBER 1967, PP 67-72
087,115-09,

CASE STUDY

087

ANDRADE MARIO
LE NATIONALISME ANGOLAIS (ANGOLESE NATIONALISM).
PRESENCE AFRICAINE, 14 JULY 1964, PP 7-23
087,
        LESS ACCESSIBLE

TWITCHETT K J
COLONIALISM-- AN ATTEMPT AT UNDERSTANDING IMPERIAL,
COLONIAL AND NEO-COLONIAL RELATIONSHIPS.
POPULATION STUDIES 13 OCTOBER 1965 PP 300-323
087,
        GENERAL THEORY

WAINHOUSE DAVID W
REMNANTS OF EMPIRE-- THE UNITED NATIONS AND THE END OF
COLONIALISM.
NEW YORK, HARPER AND ROW, 1964
081,087,
        GENERAL THEORY

CHALIAND GERARD
ARMED STRUGGLE IN AFRICA-- WITH THE GUERILLAS IN 'PORTU-
GUESE' GUINEA.
NEW YORK MONTHLY REVIEW PRESS 1969
087,144-07,144-09,

88. RACE RELATIONS IN SOUTHERN AFRICA

088

DUFFY JAMES
PORTUGUESE AFRICA.
CAMBRIDGE, HARVARD UNIVERSITY PRESS, 1959
027,087,088,144-06,
        DEALS PRIMARILY WITH ANGOLA AND MOZAMBIQUE. FIRST
        SCHOLARLY HISTORY OF PORTUGUESE CONTACT WITH AFRICA
        FROM EARLIEST TIME (FIFTEENTH CENTURY) TO MID-TWENTI-
        ETH CENTURY. DEALS WITH THE REALITY, OFTEN HARSH, OF
        PORTUGUESE CONTACT RATHER THAN WITH THE OFFICIAL POLI-
        CY AND COLONIAL IDEALS ESPOUSED BY LISBON.

FANON FRANTZ
BLACK SKIN, WHITE MASKS-- THE EXPERIENCES OF A BLACK
MAN IN A WHITE WORLD.
NEW YORK GROVE PRESS 1967
041,085,088,101-03,
        AUTHOR IS BLACK PSYCHIATRIST WHO WORKED IN ALGERIA
        DURING FRENCH-ALGERIAN WAR. BOOK BEGINS WITH FACT OF
        HIS OWN BLACKNESS, AND HOSTILITY OF WHITE WORLD.
        GIVES PSYCHOPATHOLOGICAL AND PHILOSOPHICAL ANALYSIS OF
        STATE OF BEING BLACK IN SUCH A WORLD. CRITICIZES
        MANNONI. EXPLORES LITERATURE, DREAMS, CASE HISTORIES,
        AND SPECIAL ISSUE OF BLACK MEN AND WHITE WOMEN.

088

MANNONI DOMINIQUE O
PROSPERO AND CALIBAN-- THE PSYCHOLOGY OF COLONIZATION.
LONDON, METHUEN AND COMPANY, 1956 (NEW YORK, PRAEGER, 1964)
035,041,088,121-03,
>AUTHOR ASSESSES PSYCHOLOGICAL IMPACT OF COLONIAL RE-
>LATIONSHIP ON BOTH THE EUROPEAN IN AFRICA AND ON THE
>INDIGENOUS POPULATIONS. FOCUSED ON MADAGASCAR, BUT
>HAS BROAD INSIGHTS INTO THE NATURE OF COLONIAL SYSTEMS
>IN OTHER AREAS. SUGGESTS THAT SUPERIOR-SUBORDINATE
>RELATIONSHIP IS DAMAGING TO BOTH AFRICANS AND EUROPE-
>ANS. BOOK IS IMPRESSIONISTIC RATHER THAN BASED ON
>SPECIFIC RESEARCH.

VAN DEN BERGHE P
RACE AND RACISM-- A COMPARATIVE PERSPECTIVE.
NEW YORK, JOHN WILEY, 1967
030,088,132-06,
>AUTHOR PROVIDES THEORETICAL INTRODUCTION TO ISSUE OF
>RACE, INCLUDING CRITIQUE OF DOMINANT TRENDS IN RACE
>RELATIONS, DEFINITIONS, ORIGINS AND DISTRIBUTION OF
>RACISM, RACE AND PERSONALITY, RACE AS DIFFERENTIATION
>AND STRATIFICATION, A TYPOLOGY OF RACE RELATIONS, AND
>RACE AND THE THEORY OF PLURALISM AND CONFLICT. CASE
>STUDIES INCLUDE MEXICO, BRAZIL, THE UNITED STATES, AND
>SOUTH AFRICA. ATTEMPTS ANALYTICAL COMPARISON.

BIESHEUVEL SIMON
THE MEASUREMENT OF AFRICAN ATTITUDES TOWARDS EUROPEAN
ETHICAL CONCEPTS, CUSTOMS, LAWS AND ADMINISTRATION OF
JUSTICE.
JOURNAL OF THE NATIONAL INSTITUTE OF PERSONNEL RESEARCH 6
1955 PP 5-17
088,
>REFERENCE

BROWN WILLIAM O   LEWIS HYLAN
RACIAL SITUATIONS AND ISSUES IN AFRICA CHAPTER 6.
IN THE UNITED STATES AND AFRICA, BACKGROUND PAPERS OF THE
13TH ASSEMBLY, THE AMERICAN ASSEMBLY, COLUMBIA UNIVERSITY,
1958, PP 141-163
088,
>REFERENCE

DE BLIJ HARM J
AFRICA SOUTH
EVANSTON, NORTHWESTERN UNIVERSITY PRESS, 1962
088,
>REFERENCE

FANON FRANTZ
STUDIES IN A DYING COLONIALISM.
NEW YORK, MONTHLY REVIEW PRESS, 1959
088,
>REFERENCE

KEATLEY PATRICK
THE POLITICS OF PARTNERSHIP.
BALTIMORE, PENGUIN, 1963

088,145-11,
        REFERENCE

088
    LEVINE ROBERT A
    ANTI-EUROPEAN VIOLENCE IN AFRICA-- A COMPARATIVE ANALYSIS.
    JOURNAL OF CONFLICT RESOLUTION, 3 DECEMBER 1959,
    PP 420-429
    088,117-06,
        REFERENCE

    MALINOWSKI B
    THE DYNAMICS OF CULTURE CHANGE-- AN INQUIRY INTO
    RACE RELATIONS IN AFRICA.
    NEW HAVEN, YALE UNIVERSITY PRESS, 1945
    088,
        REFERENCE

    MAZRUI ALI A
    EXTERNAL EVENTS AND INTERNAL RACIAL TENSION CHAPTER 4.
    IN ON HEROES AND UHURU-WORSHIP, LONDON, LONGMANS,
    1967, PP 50-60
    088,
        REFERENCE

    RICHARDSON HENRY J
    MALAWI- BETWEEN BLACK AND WHITE AFRICA
    AFRICA REPORT, 15 FEBRUARY 1970, PP 18-21
    088,122-09,
        REFERENCE

    ARDENER EDWIN
    SOME IBO ATTITUDES TO SKIN PIGMENTATION.
    MAN, 54, 1954, PP 70-73
    088,128-03,
        CASE STUDY

    CHIDZERO BERNARD T
    REACTIONS TO MULTI-RACIALISM CHP 8.
    IN TANGANYIKA AND INTERNATIONAL TRUSTEESHIP, NEW YORK,
    OXFORD UNIVERSITY PRESS, 1961
    088,136-06,
        CASE STUDY

    CHIDZERO BERNARD T
    CENTRAL AFRICA-- THE RACE QUESTION AND THE FRANCHISE.
    RACE 1 1955 PP 53-60
    088,122-06,142-06,
        CASE STUDY

    DUFFY JAMES
    PORTUGAL IN AFRICA
    BALTIMORE, PENGUIN, 1962
    027,087,088,144-06,
        CASE STUDY

    GRAY RICHARD
    THE TWO NATIONS-- ASPECTS OF THE DEVELOPMENT OF RACE
    RELATIONS IN THE RHODESIAS AND NYASALAND.
    LONDON, OXFORD UNIVERSITY PRESS, 1960

087,088,122-06,142-06,145-06,
     CASE STUDY

088

HALPERN JACK
SOUTH AFRICA'S HOSTAGES-- BASUTOLAND, BECHUANALAND,
AND SWAZILAND.
BALTIMORE, PENGUIN, 1965
032,088,102-07,118-07,135-07,
     CASE STUDY

HOLLINGSWORTH L W
THE ASIANS OF EAST AFRICA.
NEW YORK, ST MARTIN'S, 1960
088,
     CASE STUDY

JAHODA GUSTAV
NATIONALITY PREFERENCES AND NATIONAL STEREOTYPES IN GHANA
INDEPENDENCE.
JOURNAL OF SOCIAL PSYCHOLOGY 50 1959 PP 165-174
088,114-06,
     CASE STUDY

JAHODA GUSTAV
WHITE MAN-- A STUDY OF THE ATTITUDE OF AFRICANS TO EUROPEANS
IN GHANA DURING INDEPENDENCE.
LONDON, OXFORD UNIVERSITY PRESS, 1961
041,088,114-06,
     CASE STUDY

MAZRUI ALI A
EXTERNAL EVENTS AND INTERNAL COMMUNAL TENSIONS.
IN LAWRENCE SAGINI (ED) RACIAL AND COMMUNAL TENSIONS IN EAST
AFRICA, NAIROBI EAST AFRICAN PUBLISHING HOUSE, 1966, PP 70-76
088,
     CASE STUDY

MITCHELL J CLYDE
WHITE-COLLAR WORKERS AND SUPERVISORS IN A PLURAL SOCIETY.
CIVILIZATIONS 10 1960 PP 293-306
088,
     CASE STUDY

PRATT R CRANFORD
MULTI-RACIALISM AND LOCAL GOVERNMENT IN TANGANYIKA.
RACE 2 1960 PP 33-49
088,136-06,
     CASE STUDY

ROGERS CYRIL A
A STUDY OF RACE ATTITUDES IN NIGERIA.
RHODES-LIVINGSTONE JOURNAL 26 1959 PP 51-64
088,128-06,
     CASE STUDY

ROGERS CYRIL A   FRANTZ CHARLES
RACIAL THEMES IN SOUTHERN RHODESIA-THE ATTITUDES OF THE
WHITE POPULATION
NEW HAVEN, YALE UNIVERSITY PRESS, 1962

```
088,145-07,
      CASE STUDY
```

088

```
   BETTELHEIM BRUNO     JANOWITZ MORRIS
   ETHNIC TOLERANCE-- A FUNCTION OF SOCIAL AND PERSONAL
   CONTROL.
   THE AMERICAN JOURNAL OF SOCIOLOGY 55 SEPTEMBER 1949
   PP 137-145 (BOBBS-MERRILL REPRINT 24)
   088,
         GENERAL THEORY
```

```
   DAEDALUS               ED
   COLOR AND RACE.
   SPECIAL ISSUE OF THE JOURNAL OF THE AMERICAN ACADEMY OF ARTS
   AND SCIENCES, SPRING 1967
   088,
         GENERAL THEORY
```

```
   ERIKSON ERIK H
   THE CONCEPT OF IDENTITY IN RACE RELATIONS.
   IN THE NEGRO AMERICAN,TALCOTT PARSONS AND KENNETH CLARK EDS,
   BOSTON,HOUGHTON MIFFLIN, 1966, PP 227-253
   088,
         GENERAL THEORY
```

```
   FRAZIER E FRANKLIN
   RACE AND CULTURE CONTACTS IN THE MODERN WORLD.
   BOSTON,BEACON PRESS,1965
   088,
         GENERAL THEORY
```

```
   KOHN HANS
   RACIALISM CHAPTER 9.
   IN POLITICAL IDEOLOGIES OF THE TWENTIETH CENTURY, NEW YORK,
   HARPER, 1966,  3RD EDITION REV
   088,
         GENERAL THEORY
```

```
   LITTLE KENNETH
   RACE AND SOCIETY.
   PARIS,UNESCO,1958
   088,
         GENERAL THEORY
```

89. POLITICS AND RACE IN SOUTH AFRICA

089

```
   BROOKES EDGAR H
   APARTHEID-A DOCUMENTARY STUDY OF MODERN SOUTH AFRICA
   NEW YORK,BARNES AND NOBLE,1968
   089,
         INCLUDES SELECTIONS FROM MAJOR DOCUMENTARY SOURCES AND
         SPEECHES ON THE MEANING OF APARTHEID, THE POPULATION
         REGISTRATION ACT, BANTU EDUCATION, UNIVERSITY EDUCA-
```

TION, THE CHURCHES, WORK AND VOTING, THE GROUP AREAS
ACT, AND SOCIAL CONSEQUENCES.

089

CARTER GWENDOLEN M
AFRICAN CONCEPTS OF NATIONALISM IN SOUTH AFRICA.
MELVILLE HERSKOVITS MEMORIAL LECTURE, EDINBURGH, EDINBURGH
UNIVERSITY PRESS, MARCH 1965
054,089,132-06,
        SHORT ESSAY ON THE DISTINCTIVENESS OF SOUTH AFRICAN
        NATIONALISM IN SETTING OBJECTIVES AND TACTICS.
        DISTINGUISHING FEATURES INCLUDE CONFRONTATION WITH
        LOCAL WHITE POWER STRUCTURE-- WITH A COMPETING WHITE
        (AFRIKANER) NATIONALISM-- WITH A DYNAMIC AND FAR
        REACHING INDUSTRIAL AND COMMERCIAL STRUCTURE-- AND WITH
        A CONTEXT IN WHICH THE POLITICAL RIGHTS OF AFRICANS
        HAVE BECOME INCREASINGLY RESTRICTED.

CARTER GWENDOLEN M   KARIS THOMAS   STULTZ NEWELL M
SOUTH AFRICA'S TRANSKEI-- THE POLITICS OF DOMESTIC COLONIAL-
IALISM.
EVANSTON, NORTHWESTERN UNIVERSITY PRESS, 1967 (LONDON,
HEINEMANN EDUCATIONAL BOOKS)
089,132-06,
        AUTHORS DISCUSS THE SETTING OF DOMESTIC COLONIALISM,
        THE THEORY AND PROGRAMS OF SEPARATE DEVELOPMENT, LEG-
        ISLATIVE PROVISIONS, AND BACKGROUND TO THE ESTABLISH-
        MENT OF THE TRANSKEI BANTUSTAN.   ALSO DISCUSSED ARE
        SUBSEQUENT DEVELOPMENTS--CONSTITUTION MAKING, THE 1963
        ELECTIONS, RISE OF POLITICAL PARTIES. ALL SET WITHIN
        CONTEXT OF SOUTH AFRICAN DOMESTIC AND FOREIGN POLICY.

HANCE WILLIAM A   ED
SOUTHERN AFRICA AND THE UNITED STATES.
NEW YORK, COLUMBIA UNIVERSITY PRESS, 1968
083,089,132-09,
        INCLUDES CONTRIBUTIONS BY WILLIAM HANCE, MCKAY, LEO
        KUPER, AND EDWIN MUNGER. EDITOR'S SUMMARY EXAMINES
        SEVERAL PROPOSALS AS TO HOW AMERICAN POLICY MIGHT IN-
        FLUENCE SOUTH AFRICA. DISMISSES MULTILATERAL SANC-
        TIONS, MILITARY ACTION, AND ECONOMIC DISENGAGEMENT,
        BUT ARGUES FOR CONSTRUCTIVE POSSIBILITIES (E.G. CON-
        TINUED POLICY OPPOSITION TO APARTHEID).

LEGUM COLIN   LEGUM MARGARET
THE BITTER CHOICE--EIGHT SOUTH AFRICANS RESISTANCE TO
TYRANNY
CLEVELAND AND NEW YORK WORLD 1968
032, 089,
        AUTHORS--SOUTH AFRICAN EXILES BANNED FROM RETURNING
        SINCE 1964--ASSESS THE PATTERNS OF REACTION AND
        RESISTANCE TO APARTHEID OF AUTHOR ALAN PATON, NOBEL
        PRIZE WINNER ALBERT LUTÚLI, NELSON MANDELA, ROBERT
        SOBUKWE, C F B NAUDE, NANA SITA, DENNIS BRUTUS, AND
        MICHAEL SCOTT

SIMONS H J   SIMONS R E
CLASS AND COLOR IN SOUTH AFRICA 1850-1950
BALTIMORE, PENGUIN, 1969
032,089,

A RECENT SOCIAL AND HISTORICAL ANALYSIS OF THE LABOR
AND NATIONAL MOVEMENTS IN SOUTH AFRICA.FOCUSES ON
REACTION AND RESISTENCE OF VARIOUS AFRICAN,INDIAN,
AND COLOURED GROUPS AND THE CLASS STRUGGLES INVOLVED
IN SOCIALIST AND COMMUNIST PARTICIPATION IN AND
INTERPRETATION OF SOUTH AFRICAN PROBLEMS.

089
STULTZ NEWELL M
THE POLITICS OF SECURITY-SOUTH AFRICA UNDER VERWOERD 1961-6
JOURNAL OF MODERN AFRICAN STUDIES 7 1969 PP 3-20
089,132-07,
    A GOOD REVIEW OF THIS RECENT PERIOD WHICH EXAMINES THE
    MANY POLITICAL CHANGES WHICH TOOK PLACE AFTER THE
    ESTABLISHMENT OF THE REPUBLIC. COVERS INCREASING
    COERCION,CHANGING IDEOLOGY AND THE CENTRALIZATION OF
    DECISION-MAKING.

BALLINGER MARGARET
FROM UNION TO APARTHEID--A TREK TO ISOLATION.
NEW YORK, PRAEGER PUBLISHERS, 1969
089,132-02,
    REFERENCE

BOWMAN LARRY W
THE SUBORDINATE STATE SYSTEM OF SOUTHERN AFRICA
INTERNATIONAL STUDIES QUARTERLY 12 1968 PP 231-261
089,
    REFERENCE

BROWN DOUGLAS
AGAINST THE WORLD-- ATTITUDES OF WHITE SOUTH AFRICA.
GARDEN CITY, DOUBLEDAY,1969
089,
    REFERENCE

CARTER GWENDOLEN M
SOUTH AFRICA--SEGMENTED BUT INTERDEPENDENT.
AFRICA REPORT, MAY, 1968, P. 15-18
089,132-06,
    REFERENCE

CARTER GWENDOLEN M
THE POLITICS OF INEQUALITY.
NEW YORK,PRAEGER,1952;REVISED ED,1962
089,132-07,
    REFERENCE

DRURY ALLEN
A VERY STRANGE SOCIETY
NEW YORK,POCKET BOOKS,1968
089,
    REFERENCE

DUNCAN PATRICK
TOWARD A WORLD POLICY FOR SOUTH AFRICA.
IN PHILIP W QUIGG (ED.), AFRICA, NEW YORK, PRAEGER, 1964,
PP 248-260
083,089,132-09,
    REFERENCE

089

DUNCAN PATRICK
RACE QUESTIONS IN SOUTH AFRICA.
IN PHILIP W QUIGG (ED.), AFRICA, NEW YORK, PRAEGER, 1964,
PP 199-214
089,132-06,
        REFERENCE

FAIR T J D   SHAFFER N M
POPULATION PATTERNS AND POLICIES IN SOUTH AFRICA, 1951-1960
ECONOMIC GEOGRAPHY, 40 JULY 1964 PP 261-274
089,132-06,
        REFERENCE

FEIT EDWARD
AFRICAN OPPOSITION IN SOUTH AFRICA.
PALO ALTO, CALIFORNIA, HOOVER INSTITUTION PRESS, 1967
032,089,132-07,
        REFERENCE

FRYE WILLIAM
IN WHITEST AFRICA--THE DYNAMICS OF APARTHEID
ENGLEWOOD CLIFFS, PRENTICE-HALL, 1968
032,089,
        REFERENCE

HEPPLE ALEXANDER
VERWOERD.
HARMONDSWORTH, ENGLAND, PENGUIN BOOKS, 1967
089,132-04,
        REFERENCE

HORWITZ RALPH
THE POLITICAL ECONOMY OF SOUTH AFRICA.
NEW YORK, PRAEGER, 1967
089,132-08,
        REFERENCE

HORWOOD O P F   BURROWS JOHN R
THE SOUTH AFRICAN ECONOMY CHAPTER 11.
IN CALVIN B HOOVER, ECONOMIC SYSTEMS OF THE COMMONWEALTH,
DURHAM, DUKE UNIVERSITY PRESS, 1962, PP 462-500
089,132-08,
        REFERENCE

HOUGHTON D HOBART
THE SOUTH AFRICAN ECONOMY.
CAPE TOWN, OXFORD UNIVERSITY PRESS, 1967
089,132-08,
        REFERENCE

KARIS THOMAS
THE TREASON TRIAL IN SOUTH AFRICA- A GUIDE TO THE MICROFILM
RECORD OF THE TRIAL
STANFORD, HOOVER INSTITUTION PRESS, 1968
089,
        REFERENCE

KUPER LEO

AN AFRICAN BOURGEOSIE--RACE, CLASS AND POLITICS IN SOUTH
AFRICA.
NEW HAVEN, CONN., YALE UNIVERSITY PRESS, 1969
089,132-03,
       REFERENCE

089

   KUPER LEO
   DURBAN--A STUDY IN RACIAL ECOLOGY.
   NEW YORK (COLUMBIA), MCGILL-QUEEN'S PRESS, 1969
   089,132-05,
       REFERENCE

   LUTHULI ALBERT
   AFRICA AND FREEDOM CHAPTER 1.
   IN AFRICA,S FREEDOM, NEW YORK, BARNES AND NOBLE,
   1964, PP 9-23
   079,089,132-04,
       REFERENCE

   PATON ALAN
   CRY,THE BELOVED COUNTRY
   NEW YORK,SCRIBNER,1948
   032,089,
       REFERENCE

   PATTEN J W
   ALTERNATIVE TO APARTHEID IN SOUTH AFRICA.
   IN PHILIP W QUIGG (ED.), AFRICA, NEW YORK, PRAEGER, 1964,
   PP 231-247
   089,132-06,
       REFERENCE

   SCHREINER O D
   POLITICAL POWER IN SOUTH AFRICA.
   IN PETER J MCEWAN AND ROBERT B SUTCLIFFE (EDS), MODERN AFRICA,
   NEW YORK,THOMAS CROWELL, 1965, PP 229-238
   089,132-06,
       REFERENCE

   SOLOMON LAURENCE
   THE ECONOMIC BACKGROUND TO THE REVIVAL OF AFRIKANER NATION-
   ALISM.
   IN JEFFREY BUTLER (ED),BOSTON UNIVERSITY PAPERS IN AFRICAN
   HISTORY VOL I, BOSTON,BOSTON UNIVERSITY PRESS,1964,PP 217-
   242
   089,132-06,
       REFERENCE

   UNITED NATIONS
   MILITARY AND POLICE FORCES IN THE REPUBLIC OF SOUTH AFRICA.
   ST/PSCA/SER. A/3A/AC. 115/S. 203-204, 1967, 15 PAGES
   089,132-06,
       REFERENCE

   VAN DEN BERGHE P
   SOUTH AFRICA- A STUDY OF CONFLICT
   MIDDLETOWN, CONNECTICUT,WESLEYAN UNIVERSITY PRESS,1965
   032,089,
       REFERENCE

089

WALSHE A P
THE ORIGIN OF AFRICAN POLITICAL CONSCIOUSNESS IN SOUTH
AFRICA
JOURNAL OF MODERN AFRICAN STUDIES 7 1969 PP 583-610
032,089,
        REFERENCE

BROOKFIELD H C   TATHAM M A
THE DISTRIBUTION OF RACIAL GROUPS IN DURBAN--THE BACKGROUND
OF APARTHEID IN A SOUTH AFRICAN CITY.
GEOGRAPHICAL REVIEW 47 JANUARY 1957 PP 44-65
089,132-05,
        CASE STUDY

BRUTUS DENNIS
LETTERS TO MARTHA AND OTHER POEMS FROM A SOUTH AFRICAN
PRISON.
NEW YORK, HUMANITIES PRESS, INC., 1968
089,132-04,
        CASE STUDY

DERIDDER J C
THE PERSONALITY OF THE URBAN AFRICAN IN SOUTH AFRICA.
NEW YORK,HUMANITIES PRESS,1961
041, 089; 132-05,
        CASE STUDY

MAYER PHILIP
TOWNSMEN OR TRIBESMEN-- CONSERVATISM AND THE PROCESS OF
URBANIZATION IN A SOUTH AFRICAN CITY.
CAPETOWN,OXFORD UNIVERSITY PRESS,1961
047,089,132-05,
        CASE STUDY

PATON ALAN
THE LONG VIEW.
NEW YORK, PRAEGER, 1968
089,132-07,
        CASE STUDY

SCHWAB WILLIAM B
THE GROWTH AND CONFLICTS OF RELIGION IN A MODERN YORUBA
COMMUNITY.
ZAIRE 6 8 OCTOBER 1952 PP 829-35
089,128-03,
        CASE STUDY

BANTON MICHAEL P
RACE RELATIONS.
LONDON, TAVISTOCK, 1968
006,030,089,
        GENERAL THEORY

HANCOCK SIR WILLIAM
SMUTS-THE SANGUINE YEARS,1870-1919 VOLUME 1
NEW YORK,OXFORD,1962
032,089,132-02,

90. CONTEMPORARY AFRICAN LITERATURE

090

ACHEBE CHINUA
THINGS FALL APART.
NEW YORK, MCDOWELL OBELENSKY, 1959 (LONDON, HEINEMANN
EDUCATIONAL BOOKS)
090,128-10,
> THE ACHEBE CYCLE IS EXCELLENT BASIS FOR INTRODUCTORY
> STUDY OF AFRICAN LITERATURE. TO BE READ IN ORDER
> OF EVENTS, NOT OF PUBLICATION. STYLE OF ACHEBE IS
> EASY TO GRASP AT FIRST READING AND THEREFORE
> THOROUGHLY AVAILABLE TO WESTERN READERSHIP. REALISTIC
> HUMOROUS, ACHEBE IS IBO, IBADAN UNIVERSITY EDUCATED
> AND CYCLE SEEMS TO BE A CELEBRATION OF HIS OWN BACK-
> GROUND EXPERIENCE. GREAT UNDERSTANDING OF TRIBAL
> ORGANIZATION, CUSTOM, ART,MUSIC, ETC.

ARMAH AYI KWEI
THE BEAUTIFUL ONES ARE NOT YET BORN.
NEW YORK, COLLIER BOOKS (MACMILLAN), 1969 (LONDON,
HEINEMANN EDUCATIONAL BOOKS)
090,114-10,
> CANDID ACCOUNT OF THE YEARS IN GHANA UNDER THE SINGLE
> PARTY SYSTEM, INCLUDING THE DISCREPANCY BETWEEN RICH
> (POLITICIANS) AND POOR. PROTAGONIST IS A BUS DRIVER.
> BOOK IS LESS A POLITICAL STATEMENT THAN A STATEMENT OF
> BITTER CYNICISM ABOUT THE NOUVEAU RICHE IN URBAN AFRICA
> AUTHOR IS A YOUNG HARVARD GRADUATE.

BEIER ULLI   ED
INTRODUCTION TO AFRICAN LITERATURE-- AN ANTHOLOGY OF
CRITICAL WRITING FROM BLACK ORPHEUS.
EVANSTON, NORTHWESTERN UNIVERSITY PRESS, 1967
090,
> FREE-WHEELING SELECTION OF ESSAYS ON THE BOOKS AND
> RELATED TOPICS, E.G. INDIGENOUS YORUBA POETRY.
> ORAL TRADITIONS, LOCAL DRAMA, ETC.

BETI MONGO
MISSION TO KALA.
TRANSLATED BY PETER GREEN. IBADAN, HEINEMANN EDUCATIONAL
BOOKS LTD, 1964
090,104-10,
> WRY, IMAGINATIVE, INTELLECTUAL. MONGO BETI SEEMS TO
> REPRESENT THE AFRICAN WRITER AS ALIENATED FROM BOTH
> EUROPEAN AND AFRICAN CULTURE. HE IS PART OF THE
> NEGRITUDE MOVEMENT, BUT HAS GONE BEYOND OTHERS IN
> IN HIS REJECTION OF THE MYTHOLOGICAL ASPECTS OF
> TRADITIONAL AFRICAN CULTURE. HE EMERGES AS A
> REALIST, A HUMORIST, AND INDEPENDENT THINKER. HE IS
> CAMEROONIAN, OF BETE ETHNIC BACKGROUND. ALTHOUGH
> THIS IS NOT SPECIFICALLY EVIDENT IN HIS WRITINGS.

CARTEY WILFRED
WHISPERS FROM A CONTINENT--THE LITERATURE OF CONTEMPORARY

BLACK AFRICA.
NEW YORK, RANDOM HOUSE. 1969
090,

BEAUTIFULLY WRITTEN, PERSONALISTIC ACCOUNT WHICH WEAVES
THE AUTHOR'S RESPONSE TOGETHER WITH THE WHISPERS WHICH
HE HEARS FROM THE WRITERS OF CONTEMPORARY BLACK AFRICA.
THEMATIC ORGANIZATION INCLUDES AUTOBIOGRAPHY, DISILLUS-
IONMENT AND BREAKUP OF THE COLONIAL WORLD, ALIENATION,
THE LOST GENERATION, THE URBAN REALITY, THE SEARCH, THE
HOMECOMING, NEGRITUDE, BELIEF AND MAN'S FAITH.

090

EKWENSI CYPRIAN
PEOPLE OF THE CITY.
LONDON, HEINEMANN EDUCATIONAL BOOKS LTD, 1964
090,128-10,

FROM THE WESTERN POINT OF VIEW, SLIGHTLY ECCENTRIC,
WITH REGARD TO STYLE, CONSTRUCTION, ETC. YET,
PERHAPS MORE TRULY REPRESENTATIVE OF GRASS-ROOTS
LITERATURE IN NIGERIA IN ENGLISH, THAN ACHEBE. HE
MIGHT BE CALLED THE CITY NOVELIST, BECAUSE HIS BEST
WORKS SEEM TO DEAL WITH THE PROBLEMS OF TRANSITION
IN THE NEW URBAN CENTERS. IBO, TRAINED AS A
PHARMACIST. SEEMS TO BE THE LONE WOLF IN TERMS OF
LITERARY RELATIONS WITH OTHER WRITERS.

GLEASON JUDITH
THIS AFRICA.
EVANSTON, NORTHWESTERN UNIVERSITY PRESS, 1965
090,

EXCELLENT HISTORICAL CONTEXT, WITH REGARD TO
COLONIAL EVENTS ETC. BASIC COMMENTARY OF MOST
IMPORTANT BOOKS.

LAYE CAMARA   TRANSLATED BY   JAMES KIRKUP
THE AFRICAN CHILD.
LONDON, COLLINS LTD, 1965
090,115-10,

AN EXCELLENT INTRODUCTION TO THE WARMTH, COMMUNAL-
ITY OF THE AFRICAN TRADITIONAL BACKGROUND. AUTOBIO-
GRAPHICAL, NOSTALGIC, POIGNANT. ORIGINALLY FROM
GUINEA, HE STUDIED IN FRANCE. WHILE WORKING IN AN
AUTOMOBILE FACTORY NEAR PARIS, WROTE THIS BOOK IN
PASSIONATE MEMORY OF HIS BOYHOOD. AWARE OF THE
SEPARATION FROM HIS BOYHOOD, HE IS CREATING A WHOLLY
PERSONAL LITERARY IMAGE OF AFRICA.

NGUGI JAMES
THE RIVER BETWEEN.
IBADAN, HEINEMANN EDUCATIONAL BOOKS LTD, 1965
090,117-10,

FROM KENYA, HE CONSTRUCTS AN IMAGINATIVE PARABLE
OF THE CONFRONTATION OF EUROPEAN AND AFRICAN
CULTURES. HE WRITES AS A KIKUYU AWARE OF THE
PROBLEMS OF ACCEPTING OR NOT ACCEPTING EUROPEAN
WAYS.

OYONO FERDINAND   TRANSLATED BY   REED JOHN
HOUSEBOY.
LONDON, HEINEMANN EDUCATIONAL BOOKS LTD, 1966

(NEW YORK, MACMILLAN, 1970)
090,

  MOST NEARLY DESERVES THE TITLE OF PROTEST LITERATURE,
  EMERGING FROM WEST AFRICA. WRITTEN IN THE FORM OF
  A DIARY, DRAMATIZES THE AFRICAN VIEW OF THE COLONIAL
  SITUATION. IT IS SAVAGE IN ITS INSIGHTS. OYONO IS
  FROM THE CAMEROONS, AND STUDIED IN PARIS. HE IS NOW
  IN THE CAMEROONIAN DIPLOMATIC SERVICE.

090

PIETERSE COSMO   MUNRO DONALD   EDS
PROTEST AND CONFLICT IN AFRICAN LITERATURE
NEW YORK, AFRICANA PUBLISHING CORPORATION, 1969
090,091,

  CENTRAL THEME EXAMINED IN FOUR LITERARY TIME PHASES-
     1890-1925,1925-1940,1940-1960,POST-INDEPENDENCE.
  COVERS,WITH EXAMPLES,THE POLITICS OF NEGRITUDE,THE
  POLITICAL AND CULTURAL REVOLUTION,SATIRE IN NIGERIA,
  A MIRROR OF INTEGRATION,THE IDEA OF ASSIMILATION,
  PROTEST AGAINST APARTHEID,GENERATIONS IN CONFLICT,THE
  PROTEST TRADITION. BACKGROUND AND LIST OF PUBLISHED
  WORKS FOR MOST AFRICAN WRITERS.

SENGHOR LEOPOLD S
SELECTED POEMS.
NEW YORK, ATHENEUM, 1966
090,130-10,

  WITH AIME CESAIRE, ESSENTIAL TO AN UNDERSTANDING OF
  NEGRITUDE AND THE CREATIVE RESULTS OF THAT LITERARY
  PHILOSOPHIC MOVEMENT. MAIN LITERARY WORKS ARE IN FORM
  OF POETRY. FIRST DIRECT ARTICULATION OF BLACK CON-
  SCIOUSNESS IN AFRICAN CREATIVE WRITING. FORTHRIGHT,
  POWERFUL, AND AFFIRMATIVE IN HIS STATEMENT THAT BLACK
  IS BEAUTIFUL. AUTHOR IS PRESIDENT OF SENEGAL.

SOYINKA WOLE
THE SWAMP DWELLERS.
IN FIVE PLAYS, LONDON, OXFORD UNIVERSITY PRESS, 1964
090,128-10,

  INTERNATIONALLY IMPORTANT, AS DRAMATIST, POET, AND
  NOVELIST. USING LOCAL MATERIAL, HE IS PERHAPS THE
  MOST SOPHISTICATED IN HIS DETACHMENT AND LITERARY
  METHODS. HE IS MODERN, EXPERIMENTAL, AND AT THE
  AT THE SAME TIME THOROUGHLY AFRICAN. HE IS YORUBA,
  IBADAN EDUCATED, WIDELY TRAVELED, POLITICALLY ACTIVE.

TUTUOLA AMOS
THE PALM-WINE DRINKARD.
NEW YORK, GROVE PRESS INC, 1953
090,128-10,

  FIRST NIGERIAN WRITER OF IMPORTANCE. THE PALM
  WINE DRINKARD AND MY LIFE IN THE BUSH OF GHOSTS
  EMBODY COLLECTION OF ORAL TRADITIONAL LITERATURE
  WITH LOOSE FRAMEWORK OF PICARESQUE ADVENTURE.
  JOURNEYS IMAGINATIVELY INTO RACIAL SUBCONSCIOUS.
  ARTICULATING WITH IMMEDIACY AND FASCINATION THE RICH
  ORAL MYTHS AND LEGENDS OF HIS PEOPLE, THE YORUBA.

VANSINA JAN
ORAL TRADITION, A STUDY OF HISTORICAL METHODOLOGY.

CHICAGO, ALDINE, 1961
012,090,
>   PIONEER EXPLORATION OF METHODS NECESSARY TO PROCESS
>   ORAL TESTIMONY. MUCH OF TECHNIQUE BASED ON AUTHOR≠S
>   FIELD RESEARCH IN CONGO AREA. DEALS WITH TRADITION AS
>   A CHAIN OF TESTIMONIES, PROBLEMS OF UNDERSTANDING TES-
>   TIMONY, EVALUATION OF TESTIMONY, AND THE DIFFERENT
>   TYPES OF TESTIMONY RELATED TO HISTORICAL KNOWLEDGE
>   (POETRY, FORMULAE, LISTS, TALES, COMMENTARIES). AU-
>   THOR IS PROFESSOR OF AFRICAN HISTORY AT WISCONSIN.

090

WAUTHIER CLAUDE
THE LITERATURE AND THOUGHT OF MODERN AFRICA.
LONDON, PALL MALL, 1966 (NEW YORK, PRAEGER, 1967)
090,091,
>   AUTHOR IS CORRESPONDENT IN AFRICA FOR AGENCE FRANCE-
>   PRESSE, CHAPTERS COVER PROBLEM OF LINGUA FRANCA, AND
>   'RETURN TO ORIGINS'--THE REVOLT AGAINST COLONIALISM AND
>   THE SEARCH FOR THE POLITICAL KINGDOM--THE EMERGENCE OF
>   A NEW AFRICA(NEGRITUDE, THE AFRICAN PROLETARIAT, THE
>   LIMITATIONS OF REVOLUTIONS). VERY READABLE TEXT WITH
>   GOOD BIBLIOGRAPHY.

ABRAHAMS PETER
A WREATH FOR UDOMO.
LONDON, FABER AND FABER, 1956
090,132-10,
>   REFERENCE

ABRAHAMS PETER
TELL FREEDOM.
NEW YORK, ALFRED A KNOPF, 1954
090,132-10,
>   REFERENCE

ABRAHAMS PETER
A NIGHT OF THEIR OWN.
NEW YORK, ALFRED A KNOPF, 1965
090,132-10,
>   REFERENCE

ABRASH BARBARA
BLACK AFRICAN LITERATURE IN ENGLISH SINCE 1952-- WORKS AND
CRITICISM.
NEW YORK, JOHNSON REPRINT CORP, 1967
090,
>   REFERENCE

ACHEBE CHINUA
ARROW OF GOD.
LONDON, HEINEMANN EDUCATIONAL BOOKS LTD, 1964
090,128-10,
>   REFERENCE

ACHEBE CHINUA
NO LONGER AT EASE.
LONDON, HEINEMANN EDUCATIONAL BOOKS LTD, 1962
090,128-10,
>   REFERENCE

090

ACHEBE CHINUA
MAN OF THE PEOPLE.
LONDON, HEINEMANN EDUCATIONAL BOOKS LTD, 1966
090,128-10,
        REFERENCE

ACHEBE CHINUA
THE NOVELIST AS TEACHER.
FIRST CONFERENCE ON COMMONWEALTH LITERATURE, JOHN PRESS ED
LONDON, HEINEMANN EDUCATIONAL BOOKS LTD, 1965, PP 201-205
090,128-10,
        REFERENCE

ALLEN SAMUEL W
TENDENCIES IN AFRICAN POETRY.
IN AMSAC, AFRICA SEEN BY AMERICAN NEGROES, PARIS,
PRESENCE AFRICAINES, 1958, PP. 175-198
090,094,
        REFERENCE

ARMAH AYI KWEI
FRAGMENTS
BOSTON, HOUGHTON-MIFFLIN, 1969
090,
        REFERENCE

ARMSTRONG ROBERT P
THE ARTS IN HUMAN CULTURE--THEIR SIGNIFICANCE AND THEIR
STUDY.
IN CARTER, GWENDOLEN M. AND ANN PADEN (EDS), EXPANDING
HORIZONS IN AFRICAN STUDIES, EVANSTON, NORTHWESTERN
UNIVERSITY PRESS, 1969, PP. 119-127
090,093,100,
        REFERENCE

BEIER ULLI   ED
POLITICAL SPIDER--AN ANTHOLOGY OF STORIES FROM 'BLACK
ORPHEUS'.
NEW YORK, AFRICANA PUBLISHING CORPORATION, 1969
090,
        REFERENCE

COLE ROBERT W
KOSSOH TOWN BOY.
CAMBRIDGE, CAMBRIDGE UNIVERSITY PRESS, 1960
090,
        REFERENCE

COOK MERCER   HENDERSON STEPHEN E
THE MILITANT BLACK WRITER IN AFRICA AND THE UNITED STATES.
MADISON, UNIVERSITY OF WISCONSIN PRESS, 1969
090,094,
        REFERENCE

EKWENSI CYPRIAN
JAGUA NANA.
LONDON, HUTCHINSON AND CO, 1964
090,128-10,

REFERENCE

090
FONLON BERNARD
THE KAMPALA CONFERENCE.
IN ALBERT H BERRIAN AND RICHARD A LOND (EDS), NEGRITUDE--
ESSAYS AND STUDIES, HAMPTON, VIRGINIA, HAMPTON INSTITUTE
PRESS, 1967, PP 102-115
090,
        REFERENCE

HUGHES LANGSTON   ED
POEMS FROM BLACK AFRICA.
BLOOMINGTON, INDIANA UNIVERSITY PRESS, 1963
090,
        REFERENCE

IRELE ABIOLA   ED
LECTURES AFRICAINES--A PROSE ANTHOLOGY OF AFRICAN WRITING
IN FRENCH.
LONDON, INTERNATIONAL UNIVERSITY BOOKSELLERS, INC., 1969
090,
        REFERENCE

JACKSON IRENE D
NEGRITUDE-- A STUDY IN OUTLINE.
IN ALBERT BERRIAN AND RICHARD LONG (EDS), NEGRITUDE--
ESSAYS AND STUDIES, HAMPTON, VIEGINIA, HAMPTON INSTITUTE
PRESS, 1967, PP 1-7
090,
        REFERENCE

KILLAM G D
THE NOVELS OF CHINUA ACHEBE.
NEW YORK, AFRICANA PUBLISHING CORPORATION, 1970
090,128-10,
        REFERENCE

LAGUMA ALEX
AND A THREEFOLD CORD.
EVANSTON, NORTHWESTERN UNIVERSITY PRESS, 1967 (LONDON,
HEINEMANN EDUCATIONAL BOOKS)
090,132-10,
        REFERENCE

LAGUMA ALEX
A WALK IN THE NIGHT.
IBADAN, MBARI PUBLICATIONS; EVANSTON, NORTHWESTERN UNIVERSITY PRESS, 1962
090,132-10,
        REFERENCE

MODISANE BLOKE
BLAME ME ON HISTORY.
LONDON, THAMES AND HUDSON, 1963
090,132-10,
        REFERENCE

MOORE GERALD   ED
AFRICAN LITERATURE AND THE UNIVERSITIES.
IBADAN, IBADAN UNIVERSITY PRESS, 1965

090,
    REFERENCE

090
  MOORE GERALD   BEIER ULLI   EDS
  MODERN POETRY FROM AFRICA.
  BALTIMORE, PENGUIN, 1963
  090,
      REFERENCE

  MPHAHLELE EZEKIEL
  AFRICAN LITERATURE.
  IN LALAGE BOWN AND MICHAEL CROWDER (EDS.), PROCEEDINGS OF
  THE FIRST INTERNATIONAL CONGRESS OF AFRICANISTS, ACCRA,
  1962, LONDON, LONGMANS, 1964, PP 220-232
  090,132-10,
      REFERENCE

  MPHAHLELE EZEKIEL
  DOWN SECOND AVENUE.
  LONDON, FABER AND FABER, 1959
  090,132-10,
      REFERENCE

  POVEY JOHN F
  CANONS OF CRITICISM FOR NEO-AFRICAN LITERATURE.
  IN PROCEEDINGS OF THE CONFERENCE ON AFRICAN LANGUAGES AND
  LITERATURES, NORTHWESTERN UNIVERSITY, 1966, UNITED STATES
  OFFICE OF EDUCATION, NO. OE-6-14-018, PP 73-90
  090,
      REFERENCE

  RAMSARAN JOHN A
  MODERN AFRICAN WRITING IN ENGLISH.
  IN PROCEEDINGS OF THE CONFERENCE ON AFRICAN LANGUAGES AND
  LITERATURES, NORTHWESTERN UNIVERSITY, 1966, UNITED STATES
  OFFICE OF EDUCATION, NO. OE-6-14-018, PP 105-114
  090,
      REFERENCE

  RAMSARAN JOHN A
  BIBLIOGRAPHY OF AFRICAN LITERATURE.
  IBADAN, UNIVERSITY OF IBADAN PRESS, 1965
  090,093,
      REFERENCE

  RIVE RICHARD
  THE QUARTET.
  NEW YORK, CROWN PUBLISHERS, 1963
  090,
      REFERENCE

  SHELTON AUSTIN J   ED
  THE AFRICAN ASSERTION-- A CRITICAL ANTHOLOGY OF
  AFRICAN LITERATURE.
  NEW YORK, ODYSSEY PRESS, 1968
  090,
      REFERENCE

  SNYDER EMILE

THE TEACHING OF MODERN AFRICAN LITERATURE WRITTEN IN A
WESTERN LANGUAGE.
IN PROCEEDINGS OF THE CONFERENCE ON AFRICAN LANGUAGES AND
LITERATURES, NORTHWESTERN UNIVERSITY, 1966, UNITED STATES
OFFICE OF EDUCATION NO. OE-6-14-018, PP 92-102
090,
        REFERENCE

090
    SOYINKA WOLE
    DANCE OF THE FORESTS.
    LONDON, OXFORD UNIVERSITY PRESS, 1963
    013,090,
        REFERENCE

    SOYINKA WOLE
    KONGI'S HARVEST.
    LONDON, OXFORD UNIVERSITY PRESS,1967
    090,128-10,
        REFERENCE

    TAIWO ODELELE
    INTRODUCTION TO WEST AFRICAN LITERATURE.
    LONDON, NELSON, 1967
    090,
        REFERENCE

    THOMAS L V
    THE PRINCIPAL THEMES OF NEGRITUDE.
    IN ALBERT BERRIAN AND RICHARD LONG (EDS), NEGRITUDE--
    ESSAYS AND STUDIES, HAMPTON, VIRGINIA, HAMPTON INSTITUTE
    PRESS, 1967, PP 39-47
    090,
        REFERENCE

    TUCKER MARTIN
    AFRICA IN MODERN LITERATURE-- A SURVEY OF CONTEMPORARY
    WRITING IN ENGLISH.
    NEW YORK, F UNGAR PUBLISHING COMPANY, 1967
    090,
        REFERENCE

    TUTUOLA AMOS
    SIMBI AND THE SATYR OF THE DARK JUNGLE
    LONDON, FABER AND FABER, 1955
    090,
        REFERENCE

    TUTUOLA AMOS
    MY LIFE IN BUSH OF GHOSTS
    LONDON, FABER AND FABER, 1954
    090,
        REFERENCE

    TUTUOLA AMOS
    FEATHER WOMEN OF JUNGLE
    LONDON, FABER AND FABER, 1962
    090,
        REFERENCE

TUTUOLA AMOS
THE BRAVE AFRICAN HUNTRESS
LONDON, FABER AND FABER, 1958
090,
        REFERENCE

090
TUTUOLA AMOS
AJAIYI THIS INHERITED POVERTY
LONDON, FABER AND FABER, 1967
090,
        REFERENCE

WASTBERG PER   ED
THE WRITER IN MODERN AFRICA-AFRICAN-SCANDANAVIAN WRITER≠S
CONFERENCE.STOCKHOLM 1967
NEW YORK, AFRICANA PUBLISHING CORPORATION, AND SCANDANAVIAN
INSTITUTE OF AFRICAN STUDIES, 1969
090,
        REFERENCE

ZELL HANS M   ED
THE LITERATURE OF AFRICA.
NEW YORK, AFRICANA PUBLISHING CORPORATION, 1970
090,
        REFERENCE

ABRAHAMS PETER
MINE BOY.
NEW YORK, MACMILLAN CO., 1970   (LONDON, HEINEMANN
EDUCATIONAL BOOKS)
090,132-10,
        CASE STUDY

ABRAHAMS PETER
TELL FREEDOM.
NEW YORK, MACMILLAN CO., 1970
090,132-10,
        CASE STUDY

BETI MONGO
KING LAZAROUS.
NEW YORK, MACMILLAN CO., 1970   (LONDON, HEINEMANN
EDUCATIONAL BOOKS)
090,104-10,
        CASE STUDY

COLLINS HAROLD R
AMOS TUTUOLA.
NEW YORK, TWAYNE, 1969
090,
        CASE STUDY

KANE CHEIKH HAMIDOU
AMBIGOUS ADVENTURE.
NEW YORK, MACMILLAN CO., 1969
090,130-10,
        CASE STUDY

LARSON CHARLES R

NIGERIAN DRAMA COMES OF AGE.
AFRICA REPORT, MAY, 1968, P. 55
090,128-10,
        CASE STUDY

090

LAURENCE MARGARET
LONG DRUMS AND CANNONS-NIGERIAN DRAMATISTS AND NOVELISTS
LONDON, MACMILLAN, 1968; AND NEW YORK, PRAEGER, 1969
090,128-10,
        CASE STUDY

LAYE CAMARA
RADIANCE OF THE KING.
NEW YORK, MACMILLAN CO., 1970
090,115-10,
        CASE STUDY

NGUGI JAMES
WEEP NOT, CHILD.
NEW YORK, MACMILLAN CO., 1969   (LONDON, HEINEMANN
EDUCATIONAL BOOKS)
090,117-10,
        CASE STUDY

NGUGI JAMES
THE BLACK HERMIT.
NEW YORK, HUMANITIES PRESS INC., 1968   (LONDON, HEINEMANN
EDUCATIONAL BOOKS)
090,117-10,
        CASE STUDY

OKARA GABRIEL
THE VOICE.
NEW YORK, AFRICANA PUBLISHING CORPORATION, 1969 (LONDON,
HEINEMAN EDUCATIONAL BOOKS)
090,128-10,
        CASE STUDY

OKIGBO CHRISTOPHER
LABYRINTHS WITH 'PATHS OF THUNDER'.
NEW YORK, AFRICANA PUBLISHING CORPORATION, 1970 (LONDON,
HEINEMANN EDUCATIONAL BOOKS)
090,128-10,
        CASE STUDY

RIVE RICHARD
EMERGENCY.
NEW YORK, MACMILLAN CO., 1970
090,
        CASE STUDY

SHEPPERSON GEORGE
THE LITERATURE OF BRITISH CENTRAL AFRICA.
RHODES LIVINGSTONE JOURNAL 23 1958 PP 12-46
090,122-10,142-10,145-10,
        CASE STUDY

SOYINKA WOLE
THREE PLAYS.

IBADAN, MBARI PUBLISHERS, 1963
090,128-10,
      CASE STUDY

090
   SOYINKA WOLE
   THE INTERPRETERS.
   LONDON, HEINEMANN EDUCATIONAL BOOKS 1965
   090,128-10,
         CASE STUDY

   SOYINKA WOLE   FAGUNWA D O
   THE FOREST OF A THOUSAND DAEMONS.
   NEW YORK, HUMANITIES PRESS, INC., 1968
   090,128-10,
         CASE STUDY

   ARMSTRONG ROBERT P
   THE CHARACTERISTICS AND COMPREHENSION OF A NATIONAL
   LITERATURE.
   IN PROCEEDINGS OF THE CONFERENCE ON AFRICAN LANGUAGES AND
   LITERATURES, NORTHWESTERN UNIVERSITY, 1966, UNITED STATES
   OFFICE OF EDUCATION, NO. OE-6-14-018, PP 117-132
   090,
         LESS ACCESSIBLE

   BARATTE THERESE
   BIBLIOGRAPHIE, AUTEURS AFRICAINS ET MALGACHES DE LANGUE
   FRANCAISE (BIBLIOGRAPHY, FRENCH-SPEAKING AFRICAN AND MALA-
   GASY AUTHORS).
   PARIS, OFFICE DE COOPERATION RADIOPHONIQUE, 1968
   090,
         LESS ACCESSIBLE

   BETI MONGO
   LE PAUVRE CHRIST DE BOMBA.
   PARIS, R LAFFONT, 1956
   090,104-10,
         LESS ACCESSIBLE

   OYONO FERDINAND
   LA VIEUX NEGRE ET LA MEDAILLE.
   PARIS, JULLIARD, 1956
   090,104-10,
         LESS ACCESSIBLE

   GARRETT NAOMI M
   POETS OF NEGRITUDE.
   IN ALBERT BERRIAN AND RICHARD LONG (EDS), NEGRITUDE--
   ESSAYS AND STUDIES, HAMPTON, VIRGINIA, HAMPTON INSTITUTE
   PRESS, 1967, PP 89-101
   090,
         REFERENCE

   KEITA BODEBA
   POEMES AFRICAINS.
   PARIS, SEGHERS, 1958
   090,115-10,

91. CONTEMPORARY SOCIAL THOUGHT

091

ABRAHAM W E
THE MIND OF AFRICA.
CHICAGO, UNIVERSITY OF CHICAGO PRESS, 1962 (LONDON,
WEIDENFELD AND NICOLSON)
040,060,091,099,114-01,
     AUTHOR IS GHANAIAN SCHOLAR AND PHILOSOPHER, FORMER
     VICE-CHANCELLOR OF THE UNIVERSITY OF GHANA. BOOK AS-
     SESSES THE IDEA OF LATENT IDEOLOGY, OR CULTURAL BE-
     LIEFS. DRAWS ON PARADIGM OF ASHANTI SOCIETY TO GEN-
     ERALIZE ABOUT AFRICAN PERSONALITY-CULTURE PATTERNS.
     BRILLIANT THEORETICAL ANALYSIS, AND GOOD HISTORICAL
     SURVEY OF AFRICA BEFORE, DURING AND AFTER COLONIALISM.
     WEAKEST ON EXTRAPOLATION FROM ASHANTI CASE STUDY.

NKRUMAH KWAME
HANDBOOK OF REVOLUTIONARY WARFARE.
NEW YORK, INTERNATIONAL PUBLISHERS, INC., 1969
060,091,114-04,
     DEALS WITH PRINCIPLES OF GUERRILLA WARFARE--ORGANIZA-
     TION OF PEOPLE, TECHNICAL ASPECTS OF ARMS AND HEALTH.
     WRITTEN BY FORMER PRESIDENT OF GHANA WHO IS IN EXILE IN
     GUINEA. SPECIAL FOCUS ON LIBERATION IN SOUTHERN AFRICA.

PIETERSE COSMO   MUNRO DONALD   EDS
PROTEST AND CONFLICT IN AFRICAN LITERATURE
NEW YORK, AFRICANA PUBLISHING CORPORATION, 1969
090,091,
     CENTRAL THEME EXAMINED IN FOUR LITERARY TIME PHASES-
        1890-1925,1925-1940,1940-1960,POST-INDEPENDENCE.
     COVERS,WITH EXAMPLES,THE POLITICS OF NEGRITUDE,THE
     POLITICAL AND CULTURAL REVOLUTION,SATIRE IN NIGERIA,
     A MIRROR OF INTEGRATION,THE IDEA OF ASSIMILATION,
     PROTEST AGAINST APARTHEID,GENERATIONS IN CONFLICT,THE
     PROTEST TRADITION. BACKGROUND AND LIST OF PUBLISHED
     WORKS FOR MOST AFRICAN WRITERS.

WAUTHIER CLAUDE
THE LITERATURE AND THOUGHT OF MODERN AFRICA.
LONDON, PALL MALL, 1966 (NEW YORK, PRAEGER, 1967)
090,091,
     AUTHOR IS CORRESPONDENT IN AFRICA FOR AGENCE FRANCE-
     PRESSE, CHAPTERS COVER PROBLEM OF LINGUA FRANCA, AND
     'RETURN TO ORIGINS'--THE REVOLT AGAINST COLONIALISM AND
     THE SEARCH FOR THE POLITICAL KINGDOM--THE EMERGENCE OF
     A NEW AFRICA(NEGRITUDE, THE AFRICAN PROLETARIAT, THE
     LIMITATIONS OF REVOLUTIONS). VERY READABLE TEXT WITH
     GOOD BIBLIOGRAPHY.

CESAIRE AIME
RETURN TO MY NATIVE LAND.
PARIS, PRESENCE AFRICAINE, 1968
054,091,
     REFERENCE

091

FANON FRANTZ
THE WRETHCHED OF THE EARTH
NEW YORK, GROVE PRESS, 1963
060,091,101-03,
        REFERENCE

JULY ROBERT W
THE ORIGINS OF MODERN AFRICAN THOUGHT--ITS DEVELOPMENT IN
WEST AFRICA DURING THE NINETEENTH AND TWENTIETH CENTURIES.
NEW YORK, PRAEGER, 1967
091,
        REFERENCE

LEVINE VICTOR T
GENERATIONAL CONFLICT AND POLITICS IN AFRICA--A PARADIGM.
CIVILISATIONS, VOL. XVIII, 1968, NO. 3, PP. 399-420
091,
        REFERENCE

SITHOLE NDABANINGI
AFRICAN NATIONALISM.
LONDON, OXFORD UNIVERSITY PRESS, 1968
054,091,145-04,
        REFERENCE

AZIKIWE NNAMDI
ZIK-- A SELECTION FROM THE SPEECHES OF DOCTOR NNAMDI AZIKIWE
CAMBRIDGE,ENGLAND, CAMBRIDGE UNIVERSITY PRESS, 1961
044,060,091,096,128-04,
        CASE STUDY

CESAIRE AIME
DISCOURS SUR LE COLONIALISME.
PARIS, PRESENCE AFRICAINE. 1955
091,
        CASE STUDY

CESAIRE AIME
TOUSSAINT LOUVERTURE.
PARIS, PRESENCE AFRICAINE, 1961
091,
        CASE STUDY

CESAIRE AIME
LA TRAGEDIE DU ROI CHRISTOPHE (THE TRAGEDY OF KING
CHRISTOPHER).
PARIS, PRESENCE AFRICAINE, 1963
091,
        CASE STUDY

EDWARDS PAUL   INTRODUCTION
LETTERS OF THE LATE IGNATIUS SANCHO, AN AFRICAN.
NEW YORK, HUMANITIES PRESS, INC., 1968, 5TH EDITION-1803
091,
        CASE STUDY

FANON FRANTZ
TOWARD THE AFRICAN REVOLUTION

NEW YORK, GROVE PRESS, 1967
091,
     CASE STUDY

091
   GROHS G K   REVIEW
   FRANTZ FANON AND THE AFRICAN REVOLUTION.
   THE JOURNAL OF MODERN AFRICAN STUDIES, VOL. 6, NO. 4, PP.
   543-556, 1968
   091,
     CASE STUDY

   HAMA BOUBOU
   KOTIA-NIMA RENCONTRE AVEC L'EUROPE.
   PARIS, PRESENCE AFRICAINE, 1968
   091,127-04,
     CASE STUDY

   HAMA BOUBOU
   ESSAI D'ANALYSE DE L'EDUCATION AFRICAINE.
   PARIS, PRESENCE AFRICAINE, 1968
   091,127-04,
     CASE STUDY

   AWOLOWO OBAFEMI
   THE PATH TO ECONOMIC FREEDOM IN DEVELOPING COUNTRIES.
   LECTURE DELIVERED AT THE UNIVERSITY OF LAGOS ON MARCH 15TH,
   1968, 23 PAGES, PAMPHLET
   091,128-04,
     LESS ACCESSIBLE

   AZIKIWE NNAMDI
   TRIBALISM--A PRAGMATIC INSTRUMENT FOR NATIONAL UNITY.
   LECTURE DELIVERED UNIVERSITY OF NIGERIA, FRIDAY, MAY 15TH,
   1964, 30 PAGES, PAMPHLET
   091,128-04,
     LESS ACCESSIBLE

   DIOP CHEIKH ANTA
   ANTERIORITE DES CIVILISATIONS NEGRES--MYTHE OU VERITE
   HISTORIQUE.
   PARIS, PRESENCE AFRICAINE, 1967
   091,099,
     LESS ACCESSIBLE

   SENGHOR LEOPOLD S
   LES FONDEMENTS DE L'AFRICANITE OU NEGRITUDE ET ARABITE.
   PARIS, PRESENCE AFRICAINE, 1967
   091,130-04,
     LESS ACCESSIBLE

   RIEFF PHILIP   ED
   ON INTELLECTUALS.
   NEW YORK, DOUBLEDAY AND CO., 1969
   091,
     GENERAL THEORY

   SHILS EDWARD
   INTELLECTUALS, PUBLIC OPINION AND ECONOMIC DEVELOPMENT.
   WORLD POLITICS, 10 JAN 1958, PP 232-255; ALSO WILLIAM J HANNA,

ED, INDEPENDENT BLACK AFRICA, CHICAGO, RAND MCNALLY, 1964, PP
472-494
091,
        GENERAL THEORY

92. URBAN DESIGN AND ARCHITECTURE

092
    KULTERMANN U
    NEW ARCHITECTURE IN AFRICA.
    NEW YORK, UNIVERSE BOOKS, 1963, PP 26-180
    092,
        EXCELLENT INTRODUCTORY TEXT WITH COUNTRY-BY-COUNTRY
        COMMENTARY. SECOND PART OF VOLUME CONSISTS OF 180
        PAGES OF STUNNING FULL-PAGE BLACK-AND-WHITE PHOTO-
        GRAPHIC PLATES ILLUSTRATING ALL ASPECTS OF THE NEW,
         MODERNISTIC ARCHITECTURE WHICH IS EMERGING THROUGH-
        OUT AFRICA. AUTHOR IS DIRECTOR OF THE MUSEUM FOR
        MODERN ART IN LEVELKUSEN.

    OJO G J AFOLABI
    YORUBA PALACES
    LONDON, UNIVERSITY OF LONDON PRESS, 1966
    092,
        INTRIGUING STUDY OF YORUBA PALACE ARCHITECTURE AND
        DESIGN AS WELL AS HISTORICAL BACKGROUND. AUTHOR IS
        CHAIRMAN,DEPARTMENT OF GEOGRAPHY,UNIVERSITY OF IFE,
        NIGERIA.

    PRUSSIN LABELLE
    THE ARCHITECTURE OF ISLAM IN WEST AFRICA.
    AFRICAN ARTS 1 2 WINTER 1968 PP 32-35, 70-74
    092,
        THE AUTHOR IS AN ARCHITECT WHO HAS LIVED IN AFRICA FOR
        SEVERAL YEARS. DISCUSSES THE PLACE OF ARCHITECTURE
        WITHIN CONTEXT OF AFRICAN ARTS, THE BUILDING TECHNOLO-
        GY OF SUB-SAHARAN AFRICA, THE SAVANNA ENVIRONMENT
        WHICH HAS PRODUCED THE GREAT ISLAMIC MOVEMENTS OF THE
        PAST, AND THE STYLES OF MOSQUE CONSTRUCTION IN THE
        WEST/CENTRAL SUDANIC ZONE. EXCELLENT PHOTOGRAPHS AND
        MAP OF MOSQUE DISTRIBUTION.

    GARLAKE PETER
    EARLY ISLAMIC ARCHITECTURE OF THE EAST AFRICAN COAST.
    NAIROBI, OXFORD PRESS, 1966
    092,
        REFERENCE

    KIRKMAN JAMES S
    THE ARAB CITY OF GEDI-- EXCAVATIONS AT THE GREAT MOSQUE
    ARCHITECTURE AND FINDS.
    LONDON, OXFORD UNIVERSITY PRESS, 1954
    092,117-02,
        REFERENCE

KULTURMANN U
NEW DIRECTIONS IN AFRICAN ARCHITECTURE.
NEW YORK, GEORGE BRAZILLER, 1969
092,
      REFERENCE

092
   AMARTEIFIO G W   BUTCHER D A P   WHITHAM DAVID
   TEMA MANHEAN--A STUDY OF RESETTLEMENT.
   GHANA, GHANA UNIVERSITIES PRESS, 1966
   092,114-05,
        CASE STUDY

   ANONYMOUS
   GREATER KANO PLANNING AUTHORITY PLANS.
   THE WEST AFRICAN BUILDER AND ARCHITECT 4 5 SEPTEMBER-OCTOBER
   1964 PP 85-95
   092,128-05,
        CASE STUDY

   BETTS RAYMOND F
   THE PROBLEM OF THE MEDINA IN THE URBAN PLANNING OF DAKAR
   SENEGAL
   AFRICAN URBAN NOTES, VOL IV, NO. 3, SEPT. 1969, PP. 5-15
   045,092,
        CASE STUDY

   BIDDER IRMGAARD
   LALIBELA-- THE MONOLITHIC CHURCHES OF ETHIOPIA.
   NEW YORK, PRAEGER, 1960
   092,110-01,
        CASE STUDY

   CHECCHI AND COMPANY
   A DEVELOPMENT STUDY AND PRELIMINARY DESIGNS FOR AN INDUS-
   TRIAL PARK IN MONROVIA.
   WASHINGTON, D.C., CHECCHI AND COMPANY, 1964
   092,119-05,
        CASE STUDY

   CONNAH G
   ARCHAEOLOGICAL RESEARCH IN BENIN CITY, 1961-1964.
   JOURNAL OF THE HISTORICAL SOCIETY OF NIGERIA 2 1964
   PP 465-477
   092,128-02,
        CASE STUDY

   ENGESTROM TOR
   ORIGIN OF PRE-ISLAMIC ARCHITECTURE IN WEST AFRICA.
   ETHNOS 24 1959 PP 64-69
   092,
        CASE STUDY

   KIRKMAN JAMES S
   GEDI, THE PALACE.
   THE HAGUE, MOUTON, 1963
   092,117-05,
        CASE STUDY

   LOCK MAX

A SURVEY AND PLAN OF THE CAPITAL TERRITORY FOR THE GOVERN-
MENT OF NORTHERN NIGERIA.
NEW YORK, PRAEGER, 1967
092,128-05,
        CASE STUDY

092
    MUENCH C Z   MUENCH L H
    PLANNING AND COUNTER-PLANNING IN NIGERIA--LAGOS AND IBADAN
    JOURNAL OF THE AMERICAN INSTITUTE OF PLANNERS 34 1968
    PP 374-381
    092,
        CASE STUDY

    TREVALLION B A W
    METROPOLITAN KANO-- REPORT ON THE TWENTY YEAR DEVELOPMENT
    PLAN 1963-1983.
    OXFORD, PERGAMON PRESS, 1966
    092,128-05,
        CASE STUDY

    TERRASSE H
    LA MASQUEE AL-QUARADUIYIR A FES (THE QUADIRIYYA MOSQUE AT
    FEZ).
    PARIS, KLINCKSIECK, 1969
    092,126-01,
        LESS ACCESSIBLE

    EDILIZIA MODERNA
    ARCHITECTURE.
    MILAN, ISSUE 89-90, 1967
    092,
        GENERAL THEORY

    RUDOFSY BERNARD
    ARCHITECTURE WITHOUT ARCHITECTS.
    MUSEUM OF MODERN ART, NEW YORK, DOUBLEDAY, 1965
    092,
        GENERAL THEORY

93. VISUAL ARTS AND MUSIC

093
    BEIER ULLI
    CONTEMPORARY ART IN AFRICA.
    NEW YORK, PRAEGER PUBLISHERS, 1968
    093,
        EASILY THE BEST SURVEY OF CONTEMPORARY AFRICAN ART
        CURRENTLY AVAILABLE. INTRODUCTION SURVEYS THE SOCIAL
        AND HISTORICAL BACKGROUND. PART ONE COVERS THE AFRI-
        CAN RENAISSANCE (MAINLY SUDAN, ETHIOPIA, NIGERIA,
        GHANA, CONGO, MOZAMBIWUE, KENYA AND RHODESIA). TWO--
        THE DEVELOPMENTS AT OSHOGBO. 11 COLOR PLATES, 99
        MONOCHROMES.

MERRIAM ALAN P
AFRICAN MUSIC ON LP-AN ANNOTATED DISCOGRAPHY
EVANSTON, NORTHWESTERN UNIVERSITY PRESS, 1970
015,093,
     A LISTING OF COMMERCIALLY AVAILABLE RECORDINGS OF
     AFRICAN MUSIC UP THROUGH 1965. INFORMATION IS GIVEN
     ON THE ARTISTS FOR EACH RECORDING AND THERE ARE 18
     INDEXES LISTING THE RECORDINGS BY COUNTRY,ETHNIC GROUP
     LANGUAGE,PERFORMERS,MUSICAL INSTRUMENTS,TYPES OF
     MUSIC AND SONGS,ETC.

093
   AFRICAN STUDIES ASSOCIATION
   AFRICAN FILM BIBLIOGRAPHY 1965.
   AFRICAN STUDIES ASSOCIATION, OCCASIONAL PAPERS NO. 1, 1966
   049,093,
      REFERENCE

   ARMSTRONG ROBERT P
   THE ARTS IN HUMAN CULTURE--THEIR SIGNIFICANCE AND THEIR
   STUDY.
   IN CARTER, GWENDOLEN M. AND ANN PADEN (EDS), EXPANDING
   HORIZONS IN AFRICAN STUDIES, EVANSTON, NORTHWESTERN
   UNIVERSITY PRESS, 1969, PP. 119-127
   090,093,100,
      REFERENCE

   BROWN EVELYN S
   AFRICA'S CONTEMPORARY ART AND ARTISTS.
   NEW YORK, HARMON FOUNDATION, 1966
   093,
      REFERENCE

   CROWLEY DANIEL J
   TRADITIONAL AND CONTEMPORARY ART IN AFRICA.
   IN CARTER, GWENDOLEN M. AND ANN PADEN (EDS), EXPANDING
   HORIZONS IN AFRICAN STUDIES, EVANSTON, NORTHWESTERN
   UNIVERSITY PRESS, 1969
   014,093,100,
      REFERENCE

   EAST N B
   AFRICAN THEATRE--A CHECKLIST OF CRITICAL MATERIALS.
   NEW YORK, AFRICANA PUBLISHING CORPORATION, 1970
   093,
      REFERENCE

   ELKAN WALTER
   THE EAST AFRICAN TRADE IN WOODCARVING.
   AFRICA 28 1958 PP 314-323
   093,
      REFERENCE

   ENWONWU BEN
   PROBLEMS OF THE AFRICAN ARTIST TODAY.
   PRESENCE AFRICAINE NS 8-10 1956 PP 147-178
   093,
      REFERENCE

   MORGENTHAU HENRY

GUIDES TO AFRICAN FILMS.
AFRICA REPORT, MAY 1968, PP 52-54
093,
     REFERENCE

093
MORGENTHAU HENRY
ON FILMS AND FILMMAKERS
AFRICA REPORT, 14 MAY-JUNE, 1969, PP 71-75
049,093,
     REFERENCE

NJAU ELIMO P
AFRICAN ART.
IN LALAGE BOWN AND MICHAEL CROWDER (EDS.), PROCEEDINGS OF
THE FIRST INTERNATIONAL CONGRESS OF AFRICANISTS, ACCRA,
1962, LONDON, LONGMANS, 1964, PP 235-242
093,
     REFERENCE

NKETIA J H KWABENA
ARTISTIC VALUES IN AFRICAN MUSIC
COMPOSER, JOURNAL OF THE COMPOSERS GUILD OF GREAT BRITAIN
19 1966 PP16-19
015,093,
     REFERENCE

RAMSARAN JOHN A
BIBLIOGRAPHY OF AFRICAN LITERATURE.
IBADAN, UNIVERSITY OF IBADAN PRESS 1965
090,093,
     REFERENCE

ROUCH JEAN
THE AWAKENING AFRICAN CINEMA.
THE UNESCO COURIER, MARCH 1962
093,
     REFERENCE

SIEBER ROY
THE VISUAL ARTS.
IN ROBERT A LYSTAD (ED), THE AFRICAN WORLD, NEW YORK,
PRAEGER, 1966, PP 442-451
014,093,
     REFERENCE

SINGH J   ED
AFRICAN FILM
NAIROBI, DRUM PUBLICATIONS, 1968
049,093,
     REFERENCE

SOCIETY OF AFRICAN CULTURE-PARIS
COLLOQUIUM ON NEGRO ART.
PARIS, PRESENCE AFRICAINE, 1968
093,
     REFERENCE

BEIER ULLI
ART IN NIGERIA 1960.

CAMBRIDGE, CAMBRIDGE UNIVERSITY PRESS, 1960
014,093,128-01,
        CASE STUDY

093
    SOWANDE FELA
    OYIGIYIGI-INTRODUCTION,THEME AND VARIATIONS ON A YORUBA FOLK
    THEME FOR ORGAN
    NEW YORK, RICORDI, 1958
    015,093,
            CASE STUDY

    TRAORE B
    LE THEATRE NEGRO-AFRICAINE ET SES FONCTIONS SOCIALES (BLACK
    AFRICAN THEATER AND ITS SOCIAL FUNCTIONS).
    PARIS, PRESENCE AFRICAINE, 1958
    093,
            LESS ACCESSIBLE

94. AFRICA AND AFRO-AMERICAN IDENTITY

094
    AMERICAN SOCIETY OF AFRICAN CULTURE
    AFRICA SEEN BY AMERICAN NEGROES.
    PARIS, PRESENCE AFRICAINE, 1958
    094,
            ESSAYS BY 23 WELL-KNOWN BLACK AMERICAN SCHOLARS AND
            WRITERS ON ALL ASPECTS OF AFRO-AMERICAN CULTURE CON-
            TACT. FIRST SECTION ON ANALYSIS OF AFRICAN SOCIETIES
            (DRAKE, KILSON, SMYTHE, HANSBERRY, TURNER). SECOND
            SECTION ON AFRICAN ART, DANCE, LITERATURE-- THIRD ON
            AFRO-AMERICAN RELATIONS WITH AFRICA (LOGAN, IVY, BOND,
            FRAZIER, DUBOIS, HILL). ALTHOUGH WRITTEN IN LATE
            1950 S, VOLUME REMAINS FUNDAMENTAL INTRODUCTION TO
            SUBJECT.

    AMERICAN SOCIETY OF AFRICAN CULTURE
    THE AMERICAN NEGRO WRITER AND HIS ROOTS.
    NEW YORK, AMSAC, 1960
    094,
            VOLUME INCLUDES SELECTED PAPERS FROM THE FIRST CONFER-
            ENCE OF NEGRO WRITERS, 1959. CONTRIBUTORS INCLUDE
            SAUNDERS REDDING, SAMUEL ALLEN, JOHN HENRIK CLARKE,
            JULIAN MAYFIELD, ARTHUR DAVIS, LANGSTON HUGHES, WILLIAM
            BRANCH, ARNA BONTEMPS, LOFTEN MITCHELL, SARAH WRIGHT,
            AND JOHN KILLENS.

    HILL ADELAIDE C   KILSON MARTIN L   EDS
    APROPOS OF AFRICA--SENTIMENTS OF NEGRO AMERICAN LEADERS ON
    AFRICA FROM THE 1800'S TO THE 1950'S.
    NEW YORK, HUMANITIES PRESS INC., 1969
    094,
            EXCELLENT AND STIRRING ANTHOLOGY OF NOTES AND WRITINGS
            OF BLACK LEADERS OVER PAST 150 YEARS, CHARTING THE
            HISTORY OF RELATIONS BETWEEN BLACK AMERICA AND BLACK

AFRICA. A TIMELY, COMPREHENSIVE AND EXCITING SURVEY
BY TWO OUTSTANDING BLACK AMERICAN SOCIAL SCIENTISTS.

094

KILSON MARTIN L
THE INTELLECTUAL VALIDITY OF STUDYING THE BLACK EXPERIENCE.
IN BLACK STUDIES IN THE UNIVERSITY, ARMSTEAD ROBINSON ET AL
(EDS), NEW HAVEN, YALE UNIVERSITY PRESS, 1969, PP. 13-36
094,

AUTHOR TEACHES AT HARVARD, AND ARGUES THAT SCHOLARS
SHOULD BE CONCERNED WITH STUDYING HUMAN EXPERIENCE
AMONG BLACK PEOPLES, RATHER THAN SPECIFICALLY BLACK
EXPERIENCE .

REDDING SAUNDERS
THEY CAME IN CHAINS
PHILADELPHIA J.B.LIPPINCOTT 1950
030,094,

AUTHOR IS WELL-KNOWN AFRO-AMERICAN WRITER,WHOSE
PORTRAIT OF BLACK MEN IN THE AMERICAS IS INFORMED BY
HIS EXTENSIVE KNOWLEDGE OF AFRICAN HISTORY,HIS
LITERARY INSIGHTS,AND HIS KNOWLEDGE OF AMERICAN
HISTORY.VOLUME,WHICH IS NOW SLIGHTLY DATED,COVERS
PERIOD 1619-1950.

ROBINSON ARMSTEAD   FOSTER CRAIG   OGILVIE DONALD
BLACK STUDIES IN THE UNIVERSITY--A SYMPOSIUM.
NEW HAVEN, YALE UNIVERSITY PRESS, 1969
002,094,095,

VOLUME PRESENTS A VARIETY OF VIEWPOINTS, YET ALL BY
PERSONS WITH EXPERIENCE IN BLACK STUDIES. RECORD OF
SYMPOSIUM BY BLACK STUDENT ALLIANCE AT YALE IN MAY
1968 CONCERNED WITH THE INADEQUACIES WHICH HAVE TYPI-
FIED THE INTELLECTUAL TREATMENT OF THE AFRO-AMERICAN
EXPERIENCE.

ALBERT ALAN
A STUDY IN BROWN.
IN ALBERT BERRIAN AND RICHARD LONG (EDS), NEGRITUDE--
ESSAYS AND STUDIES, HAMPTON, VIRGINIA, HAMPTON INSTITUTE
PRESS, 1967, PP 79-88
094,

REFERENCE

ALLEN SAMUEL W
TENDENCIES IN AFRICAN POETRY.
IN AMSAC, AFRICA SEEN BY AMERICAN NEGROES, PARIS,
PRESENCE AFRICAINES, 1958, PP 175-198
090,094,

REFERENCE

BALDWIN JAMES
THE FIRE NEXT TIME.
NEW YORK, DIAL PRESS, 1963
094,

REFERENCE

BENNETT LERONE
CONFRONTATION-BLACK AND WHITE
BALTIMORE, PENGUIN,1966,REVISED EDITION,1968

030,094,
        REFERENCE

094

BLAIR THOMAS L
DU BOIS AND THE CENTURY OF AFRICAN LIBERATION.
IN ALBERT BERRIAN AND RICHARD LONG (EDS), NEGRITUDE--
ESSAYS AND STUDIES, HAMPTON, VIRGINIA, HAMPTON INSTITUTE
PRESS, 1967, PP 8-14
094,
        REFERENCE

CARMICHAEL STOKELY   HAMILTON CHARLES
BLACK POWER-- THE POLITICS OF LIBERATION IN AMERICA.
NEW YORK, RANDOM HOUSE, 1967
094,095,
        REFERENCE

CLEAVER ELDRIDGE
POST-PRISON WRITINGS AND SPEECHES-EDITED AND WITH AN
APPRAISAL BY ROBERT SCHAER
NEW YORK, RANDOM HOUSE, 1969
094,095,
        REFERENCE

COOK MERCER   HENDERSON STEPHEN E
THE MILITANT BLACK WRITER IN AFRICA AND THE UNITED STATES.
MADISON, UNIVERSITY OF WISCONSIN PRESS, 1969
090,094,
        REFERENCE

DRAKE ST CLAIR
THE AMERICAN NEGRO≠S RELATION TO AFRICA.
AFRICA TODAY, 14 DECEMBER 1967, PP 12-15
094,
        REFERENCE

DRAKE ST CLAIR
AN APPROACH TO THE EVALUATION OF AFRICAN SOCIETIES.
IN AMSAC, AFRICA SEEN BY AMERICAN NEGROES, PARIS ,
PRESENCE AFRICAINE, 1958, PP 11-34
094,
        REFERENCE

DU BOIS W E B
WORLDS OF COLOR.
IN PHILIP W QUIGG (ED.), AFRICA, NEW YORK, PRAEGER, 1964,
PP 30-52
094,
        REFERENCE

EASUM DONALD B
THE CALL FOR BLACK STUDIES.
AFRICA REPORT, MAY-JUNE, 1969, PP. 16-28
094,
        REFERENCE

EMERSON RUPERT   KILSON MARTIN L
THE AMERICAN DILEMMA IN A CHANGING WORLD-- THE RISE OF
AFRICA AND THE NEGRO AMERICAN.

IN THE NEGRO AMERICAN, TALCOTT PARSONS AND KENNETH CLARK, EDS,
BOSTON, HOUGHTON MIFFLIN, 1966, PP 626-655
094,
        REFERENCE

094

ESSIEN-UDOM E U
BLACK NATIONALISM--A SEARCH FOR IDENTITY IN AMERICA.
NEW YORK, DELL PUBLISHERS, 1965 (ORIGINALLY UNIVERSITY OF
CHICAGO PRESS, 1962)
094,096,
        REFERENCE

FARMER JAMES
AN AMERICAN NEGRO LEADER'S VIEW OF AFRICAN UNITY.
AFRICAN FORUM I 1 1965 PP 69-89
094,
        REFERENCE

FRAZIER E FRANKLIN
POTENTIAL AMERICAN NEGRO CONTRIBUTIONS TO AFRICAN
SOCIAL DEVELOPMENT.
IN AMSAC, AFRICA SEEN BY AMERICAN NEGROES, PARIS,
PRESENCE AFRICAINE, 1958, PP 263-278
094,
        REFERENCE

HAMMOND PETER B
AFRO-AMERICAN INDIANS AND AFRO-ASIANS--CULTURAL CONTACTS
BETWEEN AFRICA AND THE PEOPLES OF ASIA AND ABORIGINAL
AMERICA.
IN CARTER, GWENDOLEN M. AND ANN PADEN (EDS), EXPANDING
HORIZONS IN AFRICAN STUDIES, EVANSTON, NORTHWESTERN
UNIVERSITY PRESS, 1969, PP. 275-290
030,094,100,
        REFERENCE

IVY JAMES W
TRADITIONAL NAACP INTEREST IN AFRICA.
IN AMSAC, AFRICA SEEN BY AMERICAN NEGROES, PARIS,
PRESENCE AFRICAINE, 1958, PP 229-246
094,
        REFERENCE

JEANPIERRE W A
AFRICAN NEGRITUDE-- BLACK AMERICAN SOUL.
AFRICA TODAY 14 DECEMBER 1967 PP 10-11
094,
        REFERENCE

KARENGA MAULANA RON
THE BLACK COMMUNITY AND THE UNIVERSITY--A COMMUNITY
ORGANIZER'S PERSPECTIVE.
IN BLACK STUDIES IN THE UNIVERSITY, ARMSTEAD ROBINSON ET AL
(EDS), NEW HAVEN, YALE UNIVERSITY PRESS, 1969, PP. 37-54
094,
        REFERENCE

LEMELLE TILDEN
THE IDEOLOGY OF BLACKNESS AFRICAN-AMERICAN STYLE.

AFRICA TODAY, 14 DECEMBER 1967, PP 2-4
094,
        REFERENCE

094
    LINCOLN ERIC C
    THE BLACK MUSLIMS IN AMERICA.
    BOSTON, BEACON PRESS, 1961
    094,095,
        REFERENCE

    LOGAN RAYFORD W
    THE AMERICAN NEGRO'S VIEW OF AFRICA.
    IN AMSAC, AFRICA SEEN BY AMERICAN NEGROES, PARIS,
    PRESENCE AFRICAINE, 1958, PP 217-228
    094,
        REFERENCE

    MILLER ELIZABETH
    THE NEGRO IN AMERICA, A BIBLIOGRAPHY.
    CAMBRIDGE, HARVARD UNIVERSITY PRESS, 1968
    030,094,
        REFERENCE

    PORTER DOROTHY B
    A BIBIOGRAPHICAL CHECKLIST OF AMERICAN NEGRO WRITERS
    ABOUT AFRICA.
    IN AMSAC, AFRICA SEEN BY AMERICAN NEGROES, PARIS,
    PRESENCE AFRICAINE, 1958, PP 379-399
    094,
        REFERENCE

    SHEPPERSON GEORGE
    NOTES ON NEGRO AMERICAN INFLUENCES ON THE EMERGENCE OF
    AFRICAN NATIONALISM.
    IN WILLIAM J HANNA (ED), INDEPENDENT BLACK AFRICA, CHICAGO,
    RAND MCNALLY, 1964, PP 192-207
    094,
        REFERENCE

    STUCKEY STERLING
    AFRICAN AND AFRO-AMERICAN RELATIONSHIPS--RESEARCH POSSIBIL-
    ITIES.
    IN CARTER, GWENDOLEN M. AND ANN PADEN (EDS), EXPANDING
    HORIZONS IN AFRICAN STUDIES, EVANSTON, NORTHWESTERN
    UNIVERSITY PRESS, 1969, PP. 291-302
    030,094,100,
        REFERENCE

    WARREN ROBERT PENN
    WHO SPEAKS FOR THE NEGRO.
    NEW YORK, HARCOURT, BRACE AND WORLD, 1965
    094,
        REFERENCE

    BALDWIN JAMES
    TELL ME HOW LONG THE TRAIN'S BEEN GONE.
    NEW YORK, THE DIAL PRESS, 1968
    094,
        CASE STUDY

094

    BALDWIN JAMES
    NOBODY KNOWS MY NAME.
    NEW YORK, THE DIAL PRESS, 1961
    094,
            CASE STUDY

    BROOKS GWENDOLYN
    IN THE MECCA.
    NEW YORK, HARPER AND ROW PUBLISHERS, 1968
    094,
            CASE STUDY

    CLARKE JOHN HENRIK
    MALCOLM X, THE MAN AND HIS TIMES
    NEW YORK, MACMILLAN, 1969
    094,
            CASE STUDY

    CLEAVER ELDRIDGE
    SOUL ON ICE.
    NEW YORK, MCGRAW-HILL BOOK COMPANY, 1968
    094,
            CASE STUDY

    DU BOIS W E B
    THE SOULS OF BLACK FOLK.
    LONDON, LONGMANS, 1965
    094,
            CASE STUDY

    DU BOIS W E B
    THE WORLD AND AFRICA.
    NEW YORK, THE VIKING PRESS, 1947
    094,
            CASE STUDY

    DU BOIS W E B
    THE AUTOBIOGRAPHY OF W E B DUBOIS.
    NEW YORK, INTERNATIONAL PUBLISHERS, 1968
    094,
            CASE STUDY

    DU BOIS W E B
    THE SUPPRESSION OF THE SLAVE-TRADE TO THE UNITED STATES
    OF AMERICA, 1638-1870
    NEW YORK, SCHOCKEN BOOKS, 1969
    094,
            CASE STUDY

    DU BOIS W E B
    DUSK OF DAWN-AN ESSAY TOWARD AN AUTOBIOGRAPHY OF A RACE
    CONCEPT
    NEW YORK, HARCOURT, BRACE, 1940
    094,
            CASE STUDY

    DU BOIS W E B
    DARKWATER-VOICES FROM WITHIN THE VEIL

NEW YORK HARCOURT BRACE 1921
094,
        CASE STUDY

094

    HOOKER JAMES R
    BLACK REVOLUTIONARY-- GEORGE PADMORE≠S PATH FROM COMMUNISM
    TO PAN-AFRICANISM.
    NEW YORK, PRAEGER, 1967
    094,095,
            CASE STUDY

    JONES LEROI
    BLACK MAGIC POETRY, 1961-1967
    NEW YORK, BOBBS-MERRILL, 1969
    094,
        CASE STUDY

    JONES LEROI
    FOUR BLACK REVOLUTIONARY PLAYS
    NEW YORK, BOBBS-MERRILL, 1969
    094,
        CASE STUDY

    MALCOLM X   EPPS ARCHIE EDITOR
    THE SPEECHES OF MALCOLM X AT HARVARD.
    NEW YORK, WILLIAM MORROW AND COMPANY, INC., 1968
    094,
        CASE STUDY

    WRIGHT RICHARD
    BLACK POWER.
    NEW YORK, HARPER, 1954
    094,
        CASE STUDY

    FACULTY OF ARTS AND SCIENCES HARVARD   UNIVERSITY
    REPORT OF THE FACULTY COMMITTEE ON AFRICAN AND AFRO-AMERICAN
    STUDIES--JANUARY 20, 1969.
    CAMBRIDGE, HARVARD UNIVERSITY PRESS, 1969
    094,
        LESS ACCESSIBLE

    X MALCOLM
    THE AUTOBIOGRAPHY OF MALCOLM X.
    NEW YORK GROVE PRESS 1965
    094,095,
        CASE STUDY

95. AFRICA AND AFRO-AMERICAN SOCIAL CHANGE

095

CRONON EDMOND DAVID
BLACK MOSES--THE STORY OF MARCUS GARVEY AND THE UNIVERSAL
NEGRO IMPROVEMENT ASSOCIATION.
MADISON, UNIVERSITY OF WISCONSIN PRESS, 1955
095,
    SYMPATHETIC STUDY OF THE WEST INDIAN LEADER WHO INSPI-
    RED MANY BLACK AMERICANS IN THE 1920 S TO ORGANIZE
    THEMSELVES FOR RETURN TO AFRICA. AVAILABLE IN
    PAPERBACK.

ROBINSON ARMSTEAD   FOSTER CRAIG   OGILVIE DONALD
BLACK STUDIES IN THE UNIVERSITY--A SYMPOSIUM.
NEW HAVEN, YALE UNIVERSITY PRESS, 1969
002,094,095,
    VOLUME PRESENTS A VARIETY OF VIEWPOINTS, YET ALL BY
    PERSONS WITH EXPERIENCE IN BLACK STUDIES. RECORD OF
    SYMPOSIUM BY BLACK STUDENT ALLIANCE AT YALE IN MAY
    1968 CONCERNED WITH THE INADEQUACIES WHICH HAVE TYPI-
    FIED THE INTELLECTUAL TREATMENT OF THE AFRO-AMERICAN
    EXPERIENCE.

BARBOUR FLOYD B
BLACK POWER REVOLT, ESSAYS.
BOSTON, PORTER SARGENT, 1968
095,
    REFERENCE

BARBOUR FLOYD B   ED
THE BLACK POWER REVOLT
NEW YORK, MACMILLAN, 1969
095,
    REFERENCE

BENNETT LERONE
PIONEERS IN PROTEST
BALTIMORE, PENGUIN, 1969
030,095,
    REFERENCE

BENNETT LERONE
THE NEGRO MOOD.
CHICAGO, JOHNSON PUBLISHING CO, 1964
030, 095,
      REFERENCE

095

CARMICHAEL STOKELY HAMILTON CHARLES
BLACK POWER-- THE POLITICS OF LIBERATION IN AMERICA.
NEW YORK, RANDOM HOUSE, 1967
094, 095,
      REFERENCE

CLEAVER ELDRIDGE
POST-PRISON WRITINGS AND SPEECHES-EDITED AND WITH AN
APPRAISAL BY ROBERT SCHAER
NEW YORK, RANDOM HOUSE, 1969
094, 095,
      REFERENCE

DELANY M R   CAMPBELL ROBERT
SEARCH FOR A PLACE--BLACK SEPARATISM AND AFRICA, 1860.
ANN ARBOR, UNIVERSITY OF MICHIGAN PRESS, 1969
095,
      REFERENCE

DRAKE ST CLAIR
SOCIAL AND ECONOMIC STATUS.
IN THE NEGRO AMERICAN, TALCOTT PARSONS AND KENNETH CLARK, EDS,
BOSTON, HOUGHTON MIFFLIN, 1966, PP 3-46
095,
      REFERENCE

KING MARTIN LUTHER
WHERE DO WE GO FROM HERE-CHAOS OR COMMUNITY
BOSTON, BEACON PRESS, 1968
095,
      REFERENCE

LINCOLN ERIC C
THE BLACK MUSLIMS IN AMERICA.
BOSTON, BEACON PRESS, 1961
094, 095,
      REFERENCE

MARINE GENE
THE BLACK PANTHERS
NEW YORK, NEW AMERICAN LIBRARY-SIGNET BOOKS, 1969
095,
      REFERENCE

SILBERMANN CHARLES
CRISIS IN BLACK AND WHITE.
NEW YORK, RANDOM HOUSE, 1964
095,
      REFERENCE

BROWN H RAP
DIE NIGGER DIE
NEW YORK, THE DIAL PRESS, 1969

095,
        CASE STUDY

095

GARVEY AMY JACQUES
THE PHILOSOPHY AND OPINIONS OF MARCUS GARVEY.
NEW YORK, THE UNIVERSAL PUBLISHING HOUSE, 1926;REPRINTED
LONDON, FRANK CASS, 1967
095,
        CASE STUDY

HOOKER JAMES R
BLACK REVOLUTIONARY-- GEORGE PADMORE S PATH FROM COMMUNISM
TO PAN-AFRICANISM.
NEW YORK PRAEGER 1967
094,095,
        CASE STUDY

JULY ROBERT W
NINETEENTH-CENTURY NEGRITUDE-- EDWARD W BLYDEN.
JOURNAL OF AFRICAN HISTORY 5 1964 PP 87-98
095,
        CASE STUDY

MCKISSICK FLOYD
THREE-FIFTHS A MAN
NEW YORK MACMILLAN 1969
095,
        CASE STUDY

SHERRILL ROBERT
BIRTH OF A BLACK NATION.
ESQUIRE, JANUARY, 1969, VOL. LXXI, NO. 1, PP. 70-77
095,
        CASE STUDY

STEEL   RONALD
LETTER FROM OAKLAND. THE PANTHERS.
THE NEW YORK REVIEW OF BOOKS,VOL XIII, NO. 4, SEPTEMBER 11,
1969, PP. 14-25
095,
        CASE STUDY

X MALCOLM
THE AUTOBIOGRAPHY OF MALCOLM X.
NEW YORK GROVE PRESS 1965
094,095,
        CASE STUDY

96. AFRICAN INTERPRETATIONS OF MULTIRACIAL AMERICA

096

CLARK J P
AMERICA, THEIR AMERICA.
LONDON, HEINEMANN EDUCATIONAL BOOKS, 1969; AND NEW YORK,
AFRICANA PUBLISHING CORP, 1969
096,128-10,
    CRITICAL APPRAISAL BY OUTSTANDING NIGERIAN POET OF HIS
    EXPERIENCE AS GRADUATE STUDENT AT PRINCETON UNIVERSI-
    TY. WELL-WRITTEN FIRST PERSON DISCUSSION OF ALL AS-
    PECTS OF AMERICAN SOCIETY, INCLUDING CHAPTER ON THE
    BLACKS IN WHICH HE REACTS TO JAMES MEREDITH, AMSAC,
    BLACK MUSLIM ELIJAH MUHAMMAD, JAMES BALDWIN, NAACP,
    AND HARLEM.

ESSIEN-UDOM E U
THE RELATIONSHIP OF AFRO-AMERICANS TO AFRICAN NATIONALISM--
AN HISTORICAL INTERPRETATION.
FREEDOMWAYS 2 4 FALL 1962 PP 391-408
096,
    AUTHOR IS NIGERIAN (PROFESSOR OF POLITICAL SCIENCE,
    UNIVERSITY COLLEGE IBADAN, NIGERIA) WHO DID DOCTORAL
    DISSERTATION AT UNIVERSITY OF CHICAGO. THIS ARTICLE
    REFUTES IDEA OF SUPPOSED ESTRANGEMENT BETWEEN AFRICANS
    AND AFRO-AMERICANS. ARTICLE TRACES HISTORY OF RELA-
    TIONSHIP BETWEEN AFRO-AMERICANS AND AFRICA IN 19TH AND
    20TH CENTURIES.

KLINEBERG OTTO   ZAVALLONI MARISA
NATIONALISM AND TRIBALISM AMONG AFRICAN STUDENTS.
NEW YORK, HUMANITIES PRESS INC., 1969
096,
    ATTITUDINAL STUDY OF LARGE SAMPLE OF AFRICAN STUDENTS
    IN THE UNITED STATES AS TO THEIR VIEWS OF ETHNICITY AND
    NATIONALISM. ALSO GIVES SOME INDICATION OF REACTION OF
    STUDENTS TO THE UNITED STATES.

OBICHERE BONIFACE
AFRICAN HISTORY AND WESTERN CIVILIZATION.
IN BLACK STUDIES IN THE UNIVERSITY, ARMSTEAD ROBINSON ET AL
(EDS), NEW HAVEN, YALE UNIVERSITY PRESS, 1969, PP. 83-103

096,099,
    BIAFRAN SCHOLAR WITH EXPERIENCE IN BRITAIN AND THE
    UNITEDSTATES, DISCUSSES THE WAY IN WHICH AFRICAN HIS-
    TORY HAS BEEN PERCEIVED BY WESTERN SCHOLARS. SOME HE
    CITES AS EXAMPLES OF GROSS ETHNOCENTRISM, AND OTHERS HE
    COMMENDS FOR THEIR CONTRIBUTION TO THE RECONSTRUCTION
    OF THE AFRICAN PAST.

096
  CLENDENEN CLARENCE COLLINS ROBERT O   DUIGNAN PETER
  AMERICANS IN AFRICA, 1865-1900.
  PALO ALTO, CALIFORNIA, HOOVER INSTITUTION PRESS, 1966
  096,
      REFERENCE

  ESSIEN-UDOM E U
  BLACK NATIONALISM--A SEARCH FOR IDENTITY IN AMERICA.
  NEW YORK, DELL PUBLISHERS, 1965 (ORIGINALLY UNIVERSITY OF
  CHICAGO PRESS, 1962)
  094,096,
      REFERENCE

  NAKASA N
  SOUTH AFRICAN IMPRESSION OF HARLEM.
  NEW YORK TIMES MAGAZINE, FEBRUARY 7, 1965, P 40
  096,
      REFERENCE

  NKRUMAH KWAME
  NEO-COLONIALISM--THE LAST STAGE OF IMPERIALISM.
  LONDON, HEINEMAN EDUCATIONAL BOOKS, 1965
  096,114-04,
      REFERENCE

  AZIKIWE NNAMDI
  ZIK-- A SELECTION FROM THE SPEECHES OF DOCTOR NNAMDI AZIKIWE
  CAMBRIDGE, ENGLAND, CAMBRIDGE UNIVERSITY PRESS, 1961
  044,060,091,096,128-04,
      CASE STUDY

  MBOYA TOM
  THE AMERICAN NEGRO CANNOT LOOK TO AFRICA FOR AN ESCAPE.
  THE NEW YORK TIMES MAGAZINE, JULY 13, 1969, SECTION 6, PP.
  30-44
  096,117-04,
      CASE STUDY

  NKRUMAH KWAME
  GHANA--THE AUTOBIOGRAPHY OF KWAME NKRUMAH.
  NEW YORK, NELSON, 1957
  096,114-04,
      CASE STUDY

  OKEDIJI FRANCIS O
  SOME CORRELATES OF ETHNIC COHESIVENESS-- AFRICAN STUDENTS≠
  ADJUSTMENT IN TWO U S COMMUNITIES.
  NIGERIAN JOURNAL OF ECONIMIC AND SOCIAL STUDIES 7 NOVEMBER
  1965 PP 347-362
  096,
      CASE STUDY

096

NDIAYE JEAN-PIERRE
ENQUETE SUR LES ETUDIANTS NOIRS EN FRANCE (STUDY OF BLACK
STUDENTS IN FRANCE)
PARIS, EDITIONS REALITES AFRICAINES, 1962
043,096,
        LESS ACCESSIBLE

BRUYN SEVERYN T
THE HUMAN PERSPECTIVE IN SOCIOLOGY-- THE METHOD OF
PARTICIPANT OBSERVATION.
ENGLEWOOD CLIFFS, N J, PRENTICE-HALL, 1966
096,
        GENERAL THEORY

FANI-KAYODE REMI
BLACKISM.
LAGOS (NIGERIA) 1965
096,

97. STUDY QUESTIONS: AFRICA AND THE MODERN WORLD

097

HANNA WILLIAM J   ED
INDEPENDENT BLACK AFRICA.
CHICAGO, RAND MCNALLY, 1964
076,097,
        REPRINTS OF MAJOR ARTICLES BY WELL-KNOWN SCHOLARS,
        AND AFRICAN STATESMEN. SECTIONS INCLUDE-- CHANGE
        (PERSONALITY, URBANIZATION), REACTION TO CHANGE (DE-
        COLONIZATION, NATIONALISM), CONTINUITY (TRADITIONAL-
        ISM, MODERNIZATION, ELITES, ELECTIONS), TERRITORIAL
        UNITY (CHARISMA, SINGLE PARTY SYSTEMS, POLITICAL
        OPPOSITION, INTELLECTUALS, CORRUPTION), LARGER UNITY
        (PAN-AFRICANISM, NEGRITUDE, UNITED NATIONS, REGIONS).

MAZRUI ALI A
ON HEROES AND UHURU-WORSHIP
LONDON, LONGMANS, 1967
002,097,
        ESSAYS ON INDEPENDENT AFRICA BY PROFESSOR AND HEAD OF
        DEPARTMENT OF POLITICAL SCIENCE,MAKERERE UNIVERSITY
        COLLEGE,UGANDA.SEPARATELY NOTED CHAPTERS GROUPED INTO
        4 SECTIONS-THE TRIALS OF SELF DETERMINATION.PROBLEMS
        OF UNITY,IDEOLOGY AND DEVELOPMENT,AFRICA AND WORLD
        POLITICS.READABLE,WELL-WRITTEN AND VERY THOUGHT
        PROVOKING.

MCEWAN PETER J   SUTCLIFFE ROBERT B   EDS
MODERN AFRICA.
NEW YORK, THOMAS CROWELL, 1965
002,076,097,
        EXCELLENT SELECTION OF REPRINTS, ARRANGED THEMATICALLY
        AS AN INTRODUCTION TO AFRICAN STUDIES. TWO MAJOR SEC-

TIONS TO THE BOOK-- THE TRADITIONAL BACKGROUND, AND
THE CONTEMPORARY SCENE. FORMER DEALS WITH TRADITIONAL
SOCIAL STRUCTURE, VALUE SYSTEMS, TRIBAL GOVERNMENT,
AND TRADITIONAL ECONOMIC SYSTEMS. SECOND PART DEALS
WITH RISE OF NATIONS, POLITICS, ECONOMIC AND SOCIAL
CHANGE, AND ROLE OF AFRICA IN WORLD AFFAIRS.

097

NIELSEN WALDEMAR
THE GREAT POWERS AND AFRICA
NEW YORK, PRAEGER, 1969
083, 097,
    A GENERAL AND FAIRLY BALANCED BUT CONSERVATIVE
    ASSESSMENT OF AFRICAS ROLE IN THE MODERN WORLD
    PARTICULARLY FROM THE PERSPECTIVE OF THE GREAT POWERS.
    COVERS WIDE RANGE OF TOPICS AND PROVIDES GOOD INTRO-
    DUCTION TO AFRICAN RELATIONS WITH THE UNITED STATES,
    SOVIET UNION, COMMUNIST CHINA, THE FORMER METROPOLES,
    AND THE UNITED NATIONS.

WALLERSTEIN I M
AFRICA-- THE POLITICS OF UNITY.
NEW YORK, RANDOM HOUSE, 1967
002, 079, 080, 097,
    SEQUEL TO AUTHOR S PREVIOUS BOOK ON POLITICS OF
    INDEPENDENCE. IS INTERPRETATION OF MAJOR POLITICAL
    DEVELOPMENTS IN AFRICA FROM 1957 TO 1965, SEEN IN PER-
    SPECTIVE OF SOCIAL CHANGE. DISTINGUISHES BETWEEN
    MOVEMENTS AND ALLIANCES IN THE EFFORTS OF AFRICAN
    STATES TO ACHIEVE WIDER UNITY. INTERPRETS FIRST AND
    SECOND CONGO CRISES, ORGANIZATION OF AFRICAN UNITY,
    RHODESIA AND SOUTH AFRICAN PROBLEMS, AND REGIONAL
    UNITY PATTERNS.

GOOD ROBERT C
CHANGING PATTERNS OF AFRICAN INTERNATIONAL RELATIONS.
AMERICAN POLITICAL SCIENCE REVIEW, VOL. LVIII, SEPT., 1969,
NO. 3, PP. 632-641
097,
    REFERENCE

LEGUM COLIN   ED
CONFRONTATION BETWEEN THE DEVELOPED AND DEVELOPING
COUNTRIES.
NEW YORK, INTERNATIONAL UNIVERSITY BOOKSELLERS, INC., 1969
097,
    REFERENCE

SAID ABDUL A
THE AFRICAN PHENOMENON.
BOSTON, ALLYN AND BACON INC, 1968
097,
    REFERENCE

EPILOGUE
Social Science
and Africa

98. AFRICA AND THE CONCEPT OF SOCIAL SCIENCE

098

    BALANDIER GEORGES
    AMBIGUOUS AFRICA-CULTURES IN COLLISION
    NEW YORK, MERIDIAN BOOKS, 1966
    098,
        AUTHOR IS HEAD OF AFRICAN STUDIES CENTER AT SORBONNE
        AND OUTSTANDING FRENCH SOCIOLOGIST.HE RECOUNTS IN
        PERSONALISTIC MANNER THE FACTORS WHICH LED HIM TO
        APPROACH AFRICA AND HIS EXPERIENCE IN DIFFERENT PARTS
        OF FRENCH-SPEAKING WEST AND EQUATORIAL AFRICA.BOOK WAS
        ORIGINALLY PUBLISHED IN FRENCH IN 1957 BUT STANDS AS
        EXCELLENT ACCOUNT OF PARTICIPANT OBSERVATION METHODS
        TRANSLATED BY HELEN WEAVER

    BOWEN ELENORE SMITH
    RETURN TO LAUGHTER
    GARDEN CITY, NEW YORK, DOUBLEDAY AND COMPANY, 1964
    098,
        AUTHOR'S NAME A PSEUDONYM FOR LAURA BOHANNAN WHO GIVES
        PERSONALISTIC ACCOUNT OF HER FIELD WORK AMONG THE TIV
        OF NIGERIA.THIS PAPERBACK VOLUME IS A CLASSIC IN
        PARTICIPANT OBSERVATION APPROACHES,ALTHOUGH IT IS
        WRITTEN AS A NOVEL

    DEXTER LEWIS

ELITE AND SPECIALIZED INTERVIEWING.
EVANSTON, NORTHWESTERN UNIVERSITY PRESS, 1970
098,
     METHODOLOGY BOOK--DISCUSSES METHODS OF ELITE, IN-DEPTH
     INTERVIEWING VIS-A-VIS SURVEY-TYPE INTERVIEWING. SET
     PARTICULARLY IN U.S. AND CANADA, BUT BROAD PRINCIPLES
     AND TECHNIQUES ARE WIDELY APPLICABLE, GIVEN ALLOWANCE
     FOR CULTURAL DIFFERENCES. CONTAINS GOOD BIBLIOGRAPHY
     OF INTERVIEWING BOOKS AND CASE STUDIES WHERE INTERVIEW
     WAS THE SIGNIFICANT MEANS OF DATA COLLECTION.

098

ELLIS WILLIAM W
WHITE ETHICS AND BLACK POWER.
CHICAGO, ALDINE PUBLISHING COMPANY, 1969
098,
     AUTHOR IS COMPETENT IN WIDE RANGE OF SOCIAL SCIENCE
     TECHNIQUES, BUT STRESSES PARTICIPANT OBSERVATION.
     HENCE, QUERIES WHETHER WHITE SOCIAL SCIENTISTS CAN WORK
     IN BLACK COMMUNITIES, BECAUSE OF ETHNOCENTRISM AND
     VESTED INTERESTS OF THE WHITE-RICH ESTABLISHMENT IN THE
     RESULTS OF SOCIAL SCIENCE. AUTHOR ELABORATES THESE
     VIEWS IN INTRODUCTION TO CASE STUDY OF WEST SIDE ORGAN-
     IZATION IN CHICAGO.

GIBSON GORDON D
A BIBLIOGRAPHY OF ANTHROPOLOGICAL BIBLIOGRAPHIES-AFRICA
CURRENT ANTHROPOLOGY 10 1969 PP 527-566
001,098,
     RECENT SPECIALIZED LIST OF OVER 870 BIBLIOGRAPHIC
     REFERENCES ON AFRICA DEALING PRIMARILY WITH ANTHROPO-
     LOGY AND HISTORY. AN EXCELLENT SOURCE FOR COUNTRY
     CASE STUDIES. SPECIAL SECTIONS ON GENERAL SOURCES,
     LIBRARY COLLECTIONS, PERIODICALS, ARCHEOLOGY, PREHIS-
     TORY, THE ARTS, HISTORY, LINGUISTICS, RELIGION, SOCIAL
     SCIENCES. SHOULD BE REFERRED TO FOR CASE STUDY REFER-
     ENCE.

HORTON ROBIN
AFRICAN TRADITIONAL THOUGHT AND WESTERN SCIENCE PART 1-FROM
TRADITION TO SCIENCE, PART 2- THE CLOSED AND OPEN
PREDICAMENT
AFRICA 37 1967 PP 50-71 AND 155-187
013,040,098,
     EXCELLENT ARTICLES. FIRST DEVELOPS AN APPROACH TO
     TRADITIONAL AFRICAN THOUGHT WHICH STRESSES ITS CROSS-
     CULTURAL SIMILARITIES,PARTICULARLY WITH WESTERN
     THOUGHT AND ESPECIALLY IN RELIGION. SECOND EXAMINES
     DIFFERENCES BETWEEN TRADITIONAL AND SCIENTIFIC
     THOUGHT,FOCUSING ON AWARENESS OF ALTERNATIVES TO THE
     ESTABLISHED BODY OF THEORETICAL TENETS.

KENYATTA JOMO
FACING MT KENYA--THE RURAL LIFE OF THE KIKUYU.
NEW YORK, VINTAGE BOOKS, 1964
010,060,098,117-01,
     A MAJOR ANTHROPOLOGICAL CASE STUDY OF KIKUYU LIFE BY
     THE PRESIDENT OF THE REPUBLIC OF KENYA. STILL A STAN-
     DARD REFERENCE WORK, IT DERIVES FROM RESEARCH IN THE
     1930'S AT THE LONDON SCHOOL OF ECONOMICS UNDER THE

FAMOUS ANTHROPOLOGIST, BRONISLAW MALINOWSKI (WHO WROTE
THE INTRODUCTION). FASCINATING READING FOR ITS INSIGHTS
NOT ONLY INTO THE KIKUYU BUT ALSO INTO THE THOUGHTS
AND EXPERIENCES OF THE AUTHOR.

098

LEVINE ROBERT A
DREAMS AND DEEDS.
CHICAGO, UNIVERSITY OF CHICAGO PRESS, 1966
038,041,098,128-03,
A SYSTEMATIC ANALYSIS OF PERSONALITY FACTORS RELATED
TO DIFFERENCES IN MODERNIZING ATTITUDES AMONG THE
THREE MAJOR ETHNIC GROUPS IN NIGERIA-- IBO, YORUBA,
AND HAUSA. BASED ON ANALYSIS OF DREAM REPORTS AND
WRITTEN ESSAYS BY NIGERIAN STUDENTS. FINDINGS INDI-
CATE DISTINCT ETHNIC DIFFERENCES IN MOTIVATION. HIGH-
LY CONTROVERSIAL, PARTICULARLY IN NIGERIA.

MORRISON DONALD G   ET AL
BLACK AFRICA- A HANDBOOK FOR COMPARATIVE ANALYSIS
NEW YORK, FREE PRESS, 1970
002,058,064,098,
CO-EDITED BY R.C.MITCHELL,H.M.STEVENSON AND J.N.PADEN.
COMPREHENSIVE DATA SOURCE BOOK FOR 32 SUB-SAHARAN
STATES PART 1-DETAILED DATA FOR OVER 200 VARIABLES
INCLUDING ANALYSIS OF BASIC PATTERNS PART 2- COUNTRY
PROFILES OF BASIC INFORMATION ON URBAN,ECONOMIC AND
POLITICAL PATTERNS PART 3-ESSAYS ON DATA RELIABILITY,
BASES OF ETHNIC CLASSIFICATION,PATTERNS AND PROCESSES
OF NATURAL INTEGRATION.

CURTIN PHILIP D
THE ARCHIVES OF TROPICAL AFRICA-- A RECONNAISSANCE.
JOURNAL OF AFRICAN HISTORY 1 1960 PP 129-147
098,099,
REFERENCE

DADZIE E W   STRICKLAND J T
DIRECTORY OF ARCHIVES, LIBRARIES AND SCHOOLS OF
LIBRARIANSHIP IN AFRICA.
UNESCO,1965
098,099,
REFERENCE

DUIGNAN PETER
HANDBOOK OF AMERICAN RESOURCES FOR AFRICAN STUDIES.
STANFORD, HOOVER INSTITUTE,1967
098,099,
REFERENCE

FLEMING WILLIAM G
AMERICAN POLITICAL SCIENCE AND AFRICAN POLITICS
JOURNAL OF MODERN AFRICAN STUDIES 7 1969 PP 495-512
098,
REFERENCE

HARE NATHAN
A RADICAL PERSPECTIVE ON SOCIAL SCIENCE CURRICULA.
IN BLACK STUDIES IN THE UNIVERSITY, ARMSTEAD ROBINSON ET AL
(EDS), NEW HAVEN, YALE UNIVERSITY PRESS, 1969, PP. 104-121

098,
REFERENCE

098

HEVI EMMANUEL J
THE DRAGON'S EMBRACE-- THE CHINESE COMMUNISTS AND AFRICA.
NEW YORK, PRAEGER, 1967
084,098,
REFERENCE

SEGALL MARSHALL H
THE GROWTH OF PSYCHOLOGY IN AFRICAN STUDIES.
IN CARTER, GWENDOLEN M. AND ANN PADEN (EDS), EXPANDING
HORIZONS IN AFRICAN STUDIES, EVANSTON, NORTHWESTERN
UNIVERSITY PRESS, 1969, PP. 47-65
039,098,100,
REFERENCE

WICKERT FREDERIC R   ED
READINGS IN AFRICAN PSYCHOLOGY FROM FRENCH LANGUAGE SOURCES.
EAST LANSING, MICHIGAN STATE UNIVERSITY PRESS, 1967
039,040,098,
REFERENCE

NADEL S F
A FIELD EXPERIMENT IN RACIAL PSYCHOLOGY.
BRITISH JOURNAL OF PSYCHOLOGY 28 1937 PP 195-211
098,
CASE STUDY

O≠BRIEN CONNOR C
TO KATANGA AND BACK--A U.N. CASE HISTORY.
NEW YORK, SIMON AND SCHUSTER, 1962
098,108-06,
CASE STUDY

VANSINA JAN
THE FUNCTIONS OF ORAL TRADITIONS AND THEIR INFLUENCE ON THE
HISTORICAL CONTENT OF THESE SOURCES.
SALISBURY, SOUTHERN RHODESIA, HISTORIANS IN TROPICAL AFRICA,
UNIVERSITY COLLEGE OF RHODESIA AND NYASALAND, 1962
PP 119-126
098,
LESS ACCESSIBLE

ALMOND GABRIEL A
A DEVELOPMENTAL APPROACH TO POLITICAL SYSTEMS.
WORLD POLITICS 17 JANUARY 1965 PP 183-214
098,
GENERAL THEORY

ALMOND GABRIEL A
POLITICAL SYSTEMS AND POLITICAL CHANGE.
AMERICAN BEHAVIORAL SCIENTIST 16 JUNE 1963 PP 3-10
098,
GENERAL THEORY

ALMOND GABRIEL A   POWELL G B
COMPARATIVE POLITICS-- A DEVELOPMENTAL APPROACH.
BOSTON, LITTLE, BROWN AND COMPANY, 1966

098,
        GENERAL THEORY

098
    ALMOND GABRIEL A
    A DEVELOPMENTAL APPROACH TO POLITICAL SYSTEMS CHAPTER 3.
    IN JASON L FINKLE AND RICHARD W GABLE, POLITICAL
    DEVELOPMENT AND SOCIAL CHANGE, NEW YORK, JOHN WILEY, 1966
    098,
        GENERAL THEORY

    ALMOND GABRIEL A
    COMPARATIVE POLITICAL SYSTEMS.
    THE JOURNAL OF POLITICS 18 AUGUST 1956 PP 391-409
    (BOBBS-MERRILL REPRINT PS-6)
    098,
        GENERAL THEORY

    APTER DAVID E
    A COMPARATIVE METHOD FOR THE STUDY OF POLITICS.
    THE AMERICAN JOURNAL OF SOCIOLOGY 64 NOVEMBER 1958 (BOBBS-
    MERRILL REPRINT PS-8) ABSTRACT
    098,
        GENERAL THEORY

    BANTON MICHAEL P
    ROLES-- AN INTRODUCTION TO THE STUDY OF SOCIAL RELATIONS.
    NEW YORK, BASIC BOOKS, 1965
    098,
        GENERAL THEORY

    BUCKLEY WALTER   ED
    MODERN SYSTEMS RESEARCH FOR THE BEHAVIORAL SCIENTIST.
    CHICAGO, ALDINE, 1968
    098,
        GENERAL THEORY

    CAMPBELL DONALD T   LEVINE ROBERT A
    A PROPOSAL FOR COOPERATIVE CROSS-CULTURAL RESEARCH ON
    ETHNOCENTRISM.
    JOURNAL OF CONFLICT RESOLUTION 5 MARCH 1961 PP 82-108
    098,
        GENERAL THEORY

    CHILD IRVIN L
    SOCIALIZATION CHP 18.
    IN GARDNER LINDZEY (ED), HANDBOOK OF SOCIAL PSYCHOLOGY 2
    CAMBRIDGE MASS, ADDISON-WESLEY, 1954
    098,
        GENERAL THEORY

    CHIN ROBERT
    THE UTILITY OF SYSTEM MODELS AND DEVELOPMENTAL MODELS
    CHAPTER 1.
    IN JASON L FINKLE AND RICHARD W GABLE, POLITICAL
    DEVELOPMENT AND SOCIAL CHANGE, NEW YORK, JOHN WILEY, 1966
    072,098,
        GENERAL THEORY

    CHU GODWIN C

PROBLEMS OF CROSS-CULTURAL COMMUNICATIONS RESEARCH.
JOURNALISM QUARTERLY 41 AUTUMN 1964 PP 557-562
098,
        GENERAL THEORY

098

COHEN RONALD
BRITTLE MARRIAGE IS A STABLE SYSTEM
IN PAUL BOHANNAN, DIVORCE AND AFTER, NEW YORK, NATURAL HISTORY
PRESS, 1970
098,
        GENERAL THEORY

CUTRIGHT PHILLIPS
NATIONAL POLITICAL DEVELOPMENT-- MEASUREMENT AND ANALYSIS.
AMERICAN SOCIOLOGICAL REVIEW   APRIL 1963 PP 253-264
098,
        GENERAL THEORY

DUDLEY B J O
POLITICAL THEORY AND POLITICAL SCIENCE.
NIGERIAN JOURNAL OF ECONOMIC AND SOCIAL STUDIES 7 NOVEMBER
1965 PP 257-272
098,
        GENERAL THEORY

GALTUNG JOHAN
THEORY AND METHODS OF SOCIAL RESEARCH.
NEW YORK, COLUMBIA UNIVERSITY PRESS, 1967
098,
        GENERAL THEORY

HOPKINS RAYMOND F
AGGREGATE DATA AND THE STUDY OF POLITICAL DEVELOPMENT.
THE JOURNAL OF POLITICS, FEB., 1969, VOL. 31, NO. 1, PP. 71-
95
098,
        GENERAL THEORY

LAZARSFELD PAUL F   ROSENBERG MORRIS   EDS
THE LANGUAGE OF SOCIAL RESEARCH.
NEW YORK, FREE PRESS, 1955
098,
        GENERAL THEORY

MACKENZIE NORMAN
A GUIDE TO THE SOCIAL SCIENCES.
LONDON, WEIDENFELD AND NICOLSON, 1966
098,
        GENERAL THEORY

MERRITT RICHARD L
SYSTEMS AND THE DISINTEGRATION OF EMPIRES.
YEARBOOK OF THE SOCIETY FOR GENERAL SYSTEMS RESEARCH 8 1963
PP 91-103
098,
        GENERAL THEORY

MITCHELL ROBERT E
SURVEY MATERIALS COLLECTED IN THE DEVELOPING COUNTRIES--

SAMPLING, MEASUREMENT, AND INTERVIEWING OBSTACLES TO INTRA-
AND INTER-NATIONAL COMPARISONS.
INTERNATIONAL SOCIAL SCIENCE JOURNAL 17 1965
PP 665-685
098,
        GENERAL THEORY

098
   NAROLL RAOUL R
   DATA QUALITY CONTROL-A NEW RESEARCH TECHNIQUE
   NEW YORK,THE FREE PRESS,1962
   098,
        GENERAL THEORY

   PYE LUCIAN W
   ASPECTS OF POLITICAL DEVELOPMENT.
   BOSTON,LITTLE,BROWN,1966
   098,
        GENERAL THEORY

   PYE LUCIAN W
   THE NATURE OF TRANSITIONAL POLITICS CHAPTER 15.
   IN JASON L FINKLE AND RICHARD W GABLE, POLITICAL
   DEVELOPMENT AND SOCIAL CHANGE, NEW YORK, JOHN WILEY, 1966
   098,
        GENERAL THEORY

   PYE LUCIAN W
   THE CONCEPT OF POLITICAL DEVELOPMENT CHAPTER 3.
   IN JASON L FINKLE AND RICHARD W GABLE, POLITICAL
   DEVELOPMENT AND SOCIAL CHANGE, NEW YORK, JOHN WILEY, 1966
   098,
        GENERAL THEORY

   PYE LUCIAN W
   THE NON-WESTERN POLITICAL PROCESS.
   IN WILLIAM J HANNA (ED), INDEPENDENT BLACK AFRICA, CHICAGO,
   RAND MCNALLY, 1964, PP 372-388
   098,
        GENERAL THEORY

   RADCLIFFE-BROWN A R
   ON THE CONCEPT OF FUNCTION IN SOCIAL SCIENCE.
   AMERICAN ANTHROPOLOGIST 37 JULY-SEPTEMBER 1935
   (BOBBS-MERRILL REPRINT S-227)
   098,
        GENERAL THEORY

   RIGGS FRED W
   THE THEORY OF DEVELOPING POLITIES.
   WORLD POLITICS 16 OCTOBER 1963 PP 147-171
   037,098,
        GENERAL THEORY

   RIGGS FRED W
   ADMINISTRATION IN DEVELOPING COUNTRIES-THE THEORY OF
   PRISMATIC SOCIETY
   BOSTON,HOUGHTON MIFFLIN,1964
   062,063,098,
        GENERAL THEORY

098

ROKKAN   STEIN   ED
COMPARATIVE RESEARCH ACROSS CULTURES AND NATIONS
PARIS/THE HAGUE, MOUTON, 1968
098,
      GENERAL THEORY

SMITH M G
PRE-INDUSTRIAL STRATIFICATION SYSTEMS.
IN NEIL J. SMELSER AND SEYMOUR LIPSET EDS. SOCIAL
STRUCTURE AND MOBILITY IN ECONOMIC DEVELOPMENT. CHICAGO,
ALDINE PUBLISHING CO, 1966, PP 141-176
098,
      GENERAL THEORY

SNOW PETER G
A SCALOGRAM ANALYSIS OF POLITICAL DEVELOPMENT.
AMERICAN BEHAVIORAL SCIENTIST 9 MARCH 1966 PP 33-36
098,
      GENERAL THEORY

SUTTON FRANCIS X
ANALIZING SOCIAL SYSTEMS CHAPTER 1.
IN JASON L FINKLE AND RICHARD W GABLE, POLITICAL
DEVELOPMENT AND SOCIAL CHANGE, NEW YORK, JOHN WILEY, 1966
098,
      GENERAL THEORY

COHEN RONALD
POLITICAL ANTHROPOLOGY--- THE FUTURE OF A PIONEER.
ANTHROPOLOGICAL QUARTERLY 38 1965 PP 117-131, NORTHWESTERN
UNIVERSITY PROGRAM OF AFRICAN STUDIES, REPRINT SERIES 4
009,098,100,
      REFERENCE
      CASE STUDY

99. CONDUCTING SOCIAL RESEARCH IN AFRICA

099

ABRAHAM W E
THE MIND OF AFRICA.
CHICAGO, UNIVERSITY OF CHICAGO PRESS, 1962 (LONDON,
WEIDENFELD AND NICOLSON)
040,060,091,099,114-01,
      AUTHOR IS GHANAIAN SCHOLAR AND PHILOSOPHER, FORMER
      VICE-CHANCELLOR OF THE UNIVERSITY OF GHANA. BOOK AS-
      SESSES THE IDEA OF LATENT IDEOLOGY, OR CULTURAL BE-
      LIEFS. DRAWS ON PARADIGM OF ASHANTI SOCIETY TO GEN-
      ERALIZE ABOUT AFRICAN PERSONALITY-CULTURE PATTERNS.
      BRILLIANT THEORETICAL ANALYSIS, AND GOOD HISTORICAL
      SURVEY OF AFRICA BEFORE, DURING AND AFTER COLONIALISM.
      WEAKEST ON EXTRAPOLATION FROM ASHANTI CASE STUDY.

DIOP CHEIKH ANTA

THE CULTURAL UNITY OF NEGRO-AFRICA.
PARIS, PRESENCE AFRICAINE, 1962
016,039,054,099,
        AUTHOR IS SENEGALESE SCHOLAR WHO HAS UNDERTAKEN
        RESEARCH ON THE HISTORY OF THE AFRICAN CONTINENT WITH
        A VIEW TO STRESSING SIMILARITIES RATHER THAN
        DIFFERENCES AMONG THE VARIOUS ETHNIC SOCIETIES. FROM
        THESE SMILARITIES HE PROPOSES CERTAIN CULTURE-PERSON-
        ALITY PATTERNS WHICH HE FEELS DISTINGUISH AFRICANS
        FROM EUROPEANS.

099
    FORTES MEYER   EVANS-PRITCHARD E E EDS
    AFRICAN POLITICAL SYSTEMS.
    LONDON, OXFORD UNIVERSITY PRESS, 1940 (1962)
    009,099,
        FIRST COMPREHENSIVE CLASSIFICATION OF TRADITIONAL
        AFRICAN POLITICAL SYSTEMS. CATEGORIES INCLUDE HUNTING
        BANDS, SEGMENTARY LINEAGE SOCIETIES, AND CENTRALIZED
        STATES. COUNTERACTS STEREOTYPE OF SMALL-SCALE SOCIE-
        TIES NOT HAVING GOVERNMENT BY DESCRIBING HOW POLITICAL
        FUNCTIONS ARE PERFORMED WITHOUT NECESSITY OF CENTRAL-
        IZED AUTHORITY. SUPPORTED BY CASE STUDIES FROM LEAD-
        ING ANTHROPOLOGISTS.

    LEVINE ROBERT A
    AFRICA.
    IN FRANCES K HSU, ED., PSYCHOLOGICAL ANTHROPOLOGY, HOMEWOOD
    ILLINOIS, DORSEY PRESS, 1961 PP 48-92
    039,099,100,
        A MAJOR SURVEY OF PYCHOLOGICAL RESEARCH WHICH ATTEMPTS
        TO DERIVE BROAD GENERALIZATIONS ABOUT AFRICAN PERSON-
        ALITY DEVELOPMENT IN CHILDHOOD AND ADOLESCENCE, APPLI-
        CATION OF TAT IN SOUTH AFRICA AND CONGO, PERSONALITY
        AND ACCULTRUATION. PSYCHOCULTURAL INTERPRETATIONS OF
        RITUAL, WITCHCRAFT AND DREAMS, MENTAL ILLNESS.

    MAZRUI ALI A
    TOWARDS A PAX AFRICANA-- A STUDY OF IDEOLOGY AND AMBITION.
    LONDON, WEIDENFELD AND NICOLSON, 1967
    CHICAGO, UNIVERSITY OF CHICAGO PRESS, 1967
    060,077,099,
        THREE MAJOR SECTIONS-- 1) IDEOLOGY AND IDENTITY (IDI-
        OM OF SELF-DETERMINATION, PRINCIPLE OF RACIAL SOVER-
        EIGNTY, CONCEPT WE ARE ALL AFRICANS , NEO-DEPENDENCY,
        PRINCIPLE OF CONTINENTAL JURISDICTION, AND PAN-AFRICAN
        IMPLICATIONS OF SOCIALISM AND ONE-PARTY STATE)-- 2)
        DILEMNAS OF STATEHOOD (PEACE VERSUS HUMAN RIGHTS, NON-
        ALIGNMENT, PAN-AFRICANISM AND COLD WAR, CONCEPT OF
         PAX AFRICANA)-- 3) APPENDICES (CHARTER OF ORGANIZA-
        TION OF AFRICAN UNITY).

    OBICHERE BONIFACE
    AFRICAN HISTORY AND WESTERN CIVILIZATION.
    IN BLACK STUDIES IN THE UNIVERSITY, ARMSTEAD ROBINSON ET AL
    (EDS), NEW HAVEN, YALE UNIVERSITY PRESS, 1969, PP. 83-103
    096,099,
        BIAFRAN SCHOLAR WITH EXPERIENCE IN BRITAIN AND THE
        UNITEDSTATES, DISCUSSES THE WAY IN WHICH AFRICAN HIS-
        TORY HAS BEEN PERCEIVED BY WESTERN SCHOLARS. SOME HE

CITES AS EXAMPLES OF GROSS ETHNOCENTRISM, AND OTHERS HE
COMMENDS FOR THEIR CONTRIBUTION TO THE RECONSTRUCTION
OF THE AFRICAN PAST.

099

BATTUTA IBN
THE TRAVELS OF IBN BATTUTA. (TRANS BY HAR GIBB)
CAMBRIDGE, CAMBRIDGE UNIVERSITY PRESS, 1958
099,
        REFERENCE

CARTER GWENDOLEN M
AFRICAN STUDIES IN THE UNITED STATES.
IN PROCEEDINGS OF THE CONFERENCE ON AFRICAN LANGUAGES AND
LITERATURES, NORTHWESTERN UNIVERSITY, 1966, UNITED STATES
OFFICE OF EDUCATION NO. OE-6-14-018, PP 2-7
099,100,
        REFERENCE

COHEN RONALD   VANSINA JAN   ZOLBERG ARISTIDE R
ORAL HISTORY IN AFRICA.
EVANSTON ILLINOIS, NORTHWESTERN UNIVERSITY, PROGRAM OF
AFRICAN STUDIES, REPRINT SERIES, 2, NO.1 SEPTEMBER 1965
012,099,
        REFERENCE

CURTIN PHILIP D
THE ARCHIVES OF TROPICAL AFRICA-- A RECONNAISSANCE.
JOURNAL OF AFRICAN HISTORY 1 1960 PP 129-147
098,099,
        REFERENCE

DADZIE E W   STRICKLAND J T
DIRECTORY OF ARCHIVES, LIBRARIES AND SCHOOLS OF
LIBRARIANSHIP IN AFRICA.
UNESCO,1965
098,099,
        REFERENCE

DELAMATER J   ET AL
SOCIAL PSYCHOLOGICAL RESEARCH IN DEVELOPING COUNTRIES
JOURNAL OF SOCIAL ISSUES 24 1968 PP 1-298
041,099,
        REFERENCE

DUIGNAN PETER
HANDBOOK OF AMERICAN RESOURCES FOR AFRICAN STUDIES.
STANFORD,HOOVER INSTITUTE,1967
098,099,
        REFERENCE

FAGE JOHN D
THE USE OF ORAL EVIDENCE IN WEST AFRICAN HISTORY.
BULLETIN OF THE INSTITUTE OF HISTORICAL RESEARCH 31 1958
PP 33-35
099,
        REFERENCE

FIRTH RAYMOND W
SOCIAL PROBLEMS AND RESEARCH IN WEST AFRICA.

AFRICA LONDON 17 1947 PP 77-91, 17, 1947, PP 170-180
099,
        REFERENCE

099
    GALTUNG JOHAN
    SCIENTIFIC COLONIALISM
    TRANSACTION 30 1967 PP 11-19
    099,
        REFERENCE

    HANNA WILLIAM J
    THE CROSS-CULTURAL STUDY OF LOCAL POLITICS.
    CIVILIZATIONS 16 1966 PP 12-20
    099,
        REFERENCE

    HANNA WILLIAM J
    IMAGE-MAKING IN FIELD RESEARCH-- SOME TACTICAL AND ETHNIC
    PROBLEMS OF RESEARCH IN TROPICAL AFRICA.
    AMERICAN BEHAVIORAL SCIENTIST 8 JANUARY 1965 PP 15-20
    099,
        REFERENCE

    HANNA WILLIAM J   HANNA JUDITH L
    THE PROBLEM OF ETHNICITY AND FACTIONALISM IN AFRICAN
    SURVEY RESEARCH.
    PUBLIC OPINION QUARTERLY 30 SUMMER 1966 PP 290-294
    099,
        REFERENCE

    HERSKOVITS MELVILLE J
    THE DEVELOPMENT OF AFRICANIST STUDIES IN EUROPE AND
    AMERICA.
    IN LALAGE BOWN AND MICHAEL CROWDER (EDS.), PROCEEDINGS OF
    THE FIRST INTERNATIONAL CONGRESS OF AFRICANISTS, ACCRA,
    1962, LONDON, LONGMANS, 1964
    099,
        REFERENCE

    HILL ADELAIDE C
    AFRICAN STUDIES PROGRAMS IN THE UNITED STATES.
    IN AMSAC, AFRICA SEEN BY AMERICAN NEGROES, PARIS,
    PRESENCE AFRICAINE, 1958, PP 361-378
    099,
        REFERENCE

    KAMARCK ANDREW M
    ECONOMICS AND ECONOMIC DEVELOPMENT.
    IN ROBERT A LYSTAD (ED), THE AFRICAN WORLD, NEW YORK,
    PRAEGER, 1966, PP 221-244
    099,100,
        REFERENCE

    MAQUET JACQUES J
    PROBLEMES DES SCIENCES HUMAINES EN AFRIQUE CENTRALE,
    (PROBLEMS OF THE HUMAN SCIENCES IN CENTRAL AFRICA).
    INSTITUT DE RECHERCHE SCIENTIFIQUE D'AFRIQUE CENTRALE
    8TH RAPPORT 1955 PP 83-95
    099,

REFERENCE

099

MCKELVEY JOHN J
AGRICULTURAL RESEARCH.
IN ROBERT A LYSTAD (ED), THE AFRICAN WORLD, NEW YORK,
PRAEGER, 1966, PP 317-351
099,100,
        REFERENCE

OLIVER ROLAND
REFLECTIONS ON THE SOURCES OF EVIDENCE FOR THE PRECOLONIAL
HISTORY OF EAST AFRICA.
HISTORIANS IN TROPICAL AFRICA SALISBURY S R UNIVERSITY
COLLEGE OF RHODESIA AND NYASALAND 1962 PP 322-336
099,
        REFERENCE

PEARSON J D   JONES RUTH   EDS
THE BIBLIOGRAPHY OF AFRICA-PROCEEDINGS AND PAPERS OF THE
INTERNATIONAL CONFERENCE OF AFRICAN BIBLIOGRAPHY NAIROBI
DECEMBER 1967
NEW YORK, AFRICANA PUBLISHING CORPORATION, 1969
099,
        REFERENCE

VANSINA JAN   ET AL   EDS
THE HISTORIAN IN TROPICAL AFRICA.
LONDON, OXFORD UNIVERSITY PRESS, 1964
036,099,
        REFERENCE

AFRICANUS LEO
THE HISTORY AND DESCRIPTION OF AFRICA. (TRANS BY JOHN PORY
IN 1600)
LONDON, HAKLUYT SOCIETY, 1896
099,
        CASE STUDY

ARNETT E J
THE RISE OF THE SOKOTO FULANI (TRANSLATION OF MUHAMMAD
BELLO, INFAQ AL-MAISUR)
KANO, 1929
099,128-01,
        CASE STUDY

BALANDIER GEORGES
SOCIOLOGIE ACTUELLE DE L'AFRIQUE NOIRE(SOCIOLOGY OF BLACK
AFRICA).
PARIS, PRESSES UNIVERSITAIRES DE FRANCE, 1955 (NEW YORK,
1969)
099,
        CASE STUDY

BARTH HEINRICH
TRAVELS AND DISCOVERIES IN NORTH AND CENTRAL AFRICA 1849-
1855
LONDON, CASS, 1968, 3 VOLUMES
027,099,
        CASE STUDY

099

BRADBURY R E
THE HISTORICAL USES OF COMPARATIVE ETHNOGRAPHY WITH SPECIAL
REFERENCE TO BENIN AND THE YORUBA.
IN VANSINA   (ED.), THE HISTORIAN IN TROPICAL AFRICA, LONDON,
OXFORD UNIVERSITY PRESS, 1964, PP 145-164
099,128-02,
        CASE STUDY

BUSIA KOFI A
THE POSITION OF THE CHIEF IN THE MODERN POLITICAL SYSTEM OF
ASHANTI.
LONDON, OXFORD UNIVERSITY PRESS, 1951
061,099,114-01,
        CASE STUDY

DANQUAH JOSEPH B
THE AKAN DOCTRINE OF GOD.
NEW YORK, HUMANITIES PRESS INC., 1968
099,114-01,
        CASE STUDY

DENHAM DIXON   CLAPPERTON HUGH   OUDNEY WALTER
NARRATIVE OF TRAVELS AND DISCOVERIES IN NORTHERN AND CENTRAL
AFRICA IN THE YEARS 1822, 1823 AND 1824.
LONDON, CAMBRIDGE UNIVERSITY PRESS, 1966, 3 VOLUMES
E W BOVILL, (ED.)
027,099,
        CASE STUDY

DIAMOND STANLEY
NIGERIAN DISCOVERY-- THE POLITICS OF FIELD WORK.
IN A VIDICH, ET AL (EDS.), REFLECTIONS ON COMMUNITY STUDIES,
NEW YORK, JOHN WILEY, 1964, PP 119-154
099,128-01,
        CASE STUDY

EAST AFRICAN ACADEMY
PROCEEDINGS OF THE EAST AFRICAN ACADEMY. D.F. OWEN ED.
NAIROBI, EAST AFRICAN PUBLISHING HOUSE, 1967
075,099,
        CASE STUDY

LANDER RICHARD   LANDER J
JOURNAL OF AN EXPEDITION TO EXPLORE THE COURSE AND
TERMINATION OF THE NIGER.
NEW YORK, HARPER AND BROTHERS, 1837
027,099,
        CASE STUDY

PALMER SIR HERBERT R
SUDANESE MEMOIRS.
LONDON, F. CASS, 1967
099,128-02,
        CASE STUDY

POWDERMAKER H
NORTHERN RHODESIA, NOW ZAMBIA, PART 5.
IN STRANGER AND FRIEND, NEW YORK, W W NORTON,

1966, PP 235-306
099,142-03,
     CASE STUDY

099
RATTRAY ROBERT S
ASHANTI LAW AND CONSTITUTION.
OXFORD, CLARENDON PRESS, 1929
026,066,099,114-01,
     CASE STUDY

SCHAPERA ISAAC
SOME PROBLEMS OF ANTHROPOLIGICAL RESEARCH IN KENYA COLONY.
LONDON,INTERNATIONAL AFRICAN INSTITUTE,1949
099,117-01,
     CASE STUDY

AFIGBO A E
ORAL TRADITION AND HISTORY IN EASTERN NIGERIA.
AFRICAN NOTES 3 APRIL 1966 PP 12-20
099,
     LESS ACCESSIBLE

BA AMADOU HAMPATE
L'EMPIRE PEUL DE MACINA 1818-1853.
BAMAKO, INSTITUT FRANCAIS D'AFRIQUE NOIRE, CENTRE DU SOUDAN
1955
099,123-02,
     LESS ACCESSIBLE

DELAFOSSE MAURICE
LES NOIRS DE L'AFRIQUE.
PARIS, PAYOT, 1941
099,
     LESS ACCESSIBLE

DESCHAMPS HUBERT J
TRADITIONS ORALES ET ARCHIVES AU GABON-- CONTRIBUTION A
L'ETHNO-HISTOIRE (ORAL TRADITIONS AND ARCHIVES IN GABON--
CONTRIBUTION TO ETHNO-HISTORY).
PARIS, L'HOMME D'OUTRE-MER, 6 BERGER-LEVROULT, 1962
099,112-02,
     LESS ACCESSIBLE

DIOP CHEIKH ANTA
L'AFRIQUE NOIRE PRE-COLONIALE (PRE-COLONIAL BLACK AFRICA).
PARIS, PRESENCE AFRICAINE, 1960
054,099,
     LESS ACCESSIBLE

DIOP CHEIKH ANTA
ANTERIORITE DES CIVILISATIONS NEGRES--MYTHE OU VERITE
HISTORIQUE.
PARIS, PRESENCE AFRICAINE, 1967
091,099,
     LESS ACCESSIBLE

HAMA BOUBOU
HISTOIRE TRADITIONNELLE D'UN PEUPLE--LES ZARMA-SONGHAY.
PARIS, PRESENCE AFRICAINE, 1967

099,127-04,
    LESS ACCESSIBLE

099
HAMA BOUBOU
RECHERCHES SUR L'HISTOIRE DES TOUAREG SAHARIENS ET
SOUDANAIS.
PARIS, PRESENCE AFRICAINE, 1967
099,127-04,
    LESS ACCESSIBLE

HAMA BOUBOU
HISTOIRE DU GOBIR ET DE SOKOTO.
PARIS, PRESENCE AFRICAINE, 1967
099,127-04,
    LESS ACCESSIBLE

HAMA BOUBOU
HISTOIRE DES SONGHAY.
PARIS, PRESENCE AFRICAINE, 1968
099,
    LESS ACCESSIBLE

HAMA BOUBOU
CONTRIBUTION A L'HISTOIRE DES PEUL.
PARIS, PRESENCE AFRICAINE
099,127-04,
    LESS ACCESSIBLE

ROUCH JEAN
PROBLEMES RELATIFS A L'ETUDE DES MIGRATIONS
TRADITIONNELLES ET DES MIGRATIONS ACTUELLES EN AFRIQUE
OCCIDENTALE (PROBLEMS RELATIVE TO THE STUDY OF
TRADITIONAL AND PRESENT DAY MIGRATIONS IN WEST AFRICA).
BULLETIN DE L'INSTITUT FRANCAIS D'AFRIQUE NOIRE 22
1960 PP 369-378
099,
    LESS ACCESSIBLE

LEVINE ROBERT A
ANTHROPOLOGY AND THE STUDY OF CONFLICT-- AN INTRODUCTION.
JOURNAL OF CONFLICT RESOLUTION 5 1961 PP 3-15
099,
    GENERAL THEORY

MIDDLETON JOHN   ED
MYTH AND COSMOS.
GARDEN CITY, NEW YORK, THE NATURAL HISTORY PRESS, 1967
012,013,099,
    GENERAL THEORY

KI-ZERBO JOSEPH
LE MONDE AFRICAIN NOIR--HISTOIRE ET CIVILISATION.
ABIDJAN/PARIS, CEDA/HATIER, 1963
099,141-02,

100. RESEARCH FRONTIERS IN AFRICA

100

BOWN LALAGE   CROWDER MICHAEL   EDS
THE PROCEEDINGS OF THE FIRST INTERNATIONAL CONGRESS OF
AFRICANISTS.
LONDON,LONGMANS,1964;ALSO EVANSTON,NORTHWESTERN UNIVERSITY
PRESS,1964
100,
        PROCEEDINGS OF THE INTERNATIONAL CONFERENCE HELD IN
        GHANA IN DECEMBER 1962. AFRICANIST SCHOLARS FROM
        THROUGHOUT THE WORLD PRESENTED PAPERS ON VARIOUS IS-
        SUES OF RESEARCH IN AFRICA (HISTORY, LANGUAGES, RELIG-
        ION, SOCIAL AND ECONOMIC PROBLEMS, LITERATURE, ART AND
        MUSIC, POLITICAL INSTITUTIONS, SCIENCE AND TECHNOLOGY,
        EDUCATION AND PSYCHOLOGY).

CARTER GWENDOLEN M PADEN ANN   EDS
EXPANDING HORIZONS IN AFRICAN STUDIES.
EVANSTON, NORTHWESTERN UNIVERSITY PRESS, 1969
002,100,
        TWENTIETH ANNIVERSARY CONFERENCE AT PROGRAM OF AFRICAN
        STUDIES, NORTHWESTERN UNIVERSITY. SCHOLARS FROM ALL
        FIELDS PARTICIPATED AND GAVE THEIR VIEWS AS TO RESEARCH
        PRIORITIES IN AFRICA IN THE NEXT TWENTY YEARS.

FAGE JOHN D   ED
AFRICA DISCOVERS HER PAST
NEW YORK,OXFORD UNIVERSITY PRESS,1969
036, 100,
        VOLUME OF ESSAYS ASSESSES CURRENT METHODS AND
        FINDINGS OF RESEARCH IN AFRICAN HISTORY. ESPECIALLY
        GOOD ON COMPARATIVE ANALYSIS OF ORAL, DOCUMENTARY, AND
        ARCHEOLOGICAL SOURCES. ALSO EXAMINES THE DEVELOPMENT
        OF HISTORICAL WRITING AND RESEARCH IN THE VARIOUS
        REGIONS OF AFRICA.

LEVINE ROBERT A
AFRICA.
IN FRANCES K HSU,ED., PSYCHOLOGICAL ANTHROPOLOGY, HOMEWOOD,
ILLINOIS, DORSEY PRESS, 1961 PP 48-92
039,099,100,
        A MAJOR SURVEY OF PYCHOLOGICAL RESEARCH WHICH ATTEMPTS
        TO DERIVE BROAD GENERALIZATIONS ABOUT AFRICAN PERSON-
        ALITY DEVELOPMENT IN CHILDHOOD AND ADOLESCENCE, APPLI-
        CATION OF TAT IN SOUTH AFRICA AND CONGO, PERSONALITY
        AND ACCULTRUATION. PSYCHOCULTURAL INTERPRETATIONS OF
        RITUAL, WITCHCRAFT AND DREAMS, MENTAL ILLNESS.

LYSTAD ROBERT A   ED
THE AFRICAN WORLD.
NEW YORK,PRAEGER,1965
100,
        PURPOSE OF BOOK IS TO SUMMARIZE CURRENT STAGE OF
        ACADEMIC RESEARCH ON AFRICA IN MOST OF THE MAJOR
        DISCIPLINES. THREE PARTS-- 1) HISTORICAL AND SOCIO-

STRUCTURAL (PRE-HISTORY, HISTORY, ANTHROPOLOGY,
SOCIOLOGY, POLITICAL SCIENCE, LAW, EDUCATION, ECONO-
MICS)-- 2) PHYSICO-BIOLOGICAL (GEOGRAPHY, DEMOGRAPHY,
BIOLOGY, AGRICULTURE, MEDICINE)-- AND 3) PSYCHO-
CULTURAL (PSYCHOLOGY, LINGUISTICS, VISUAL ARTS, MUSIC,
DANCE, FOLKLORE, AND LITERATURE).

100

ADELMAN IRMA   DALTON GEORGE   MORRIS CYNTHIA TAFT
SOCIETY, POLITICS, AND ECONOMIC DEVELOPMENT IN AFRICA.
IN CARTER, GWENDOLEN M. AND ANN PADEN (EDS), EXPANDING
HORIZONS IN AFRICAN STUDIES, EVANSTON, NORTHWESTERN
UNIVERSITY PRESS, 1969, PP. 209-242
074,100,
        REFERENCE

ARMSTRONG ROBERT P
THE ARTS IN HUMAN CULTURE--THEIR SIGNIFICANCE AND THEIR
STUDY.
IN CARTER, GWENDOLEN M. AND ANN PADEN (EDS) EXPANDING
HORIZONS IN AFRICAN STUDIES, EVANSTON, NORTHWESTERN
UNIVERSITY PRESS, 1969, PP. 119-127
090,093,100,
        REFERENCE

BALANDIER GEORGES
AFRICANISM CONFRONTED WITH PROBLEMS OF POLITICAL
ANTHROPOLOGY AND POLITICAL SOCIOLOGY.
IN LALAGE BOWN AND MICHAEL CROWDER (EDS.), PROCEEDINGS OF
THE FIRST INTERNATIONAL CONGRESS OF AFRICANISTS, ACCRA,
1962, LONDON, LONGMANS, 1964, PP 267-271
100,
        REFERENCE

BEATTIE J H M
ETHNOGRAPHIC AND SOCIOLOGICAL RESEARCH IN EAST AFRICA.
AFRICA(LONDON)26 1956 PP 265-276
100,
        REFERENCE

BENTSI-ENCHILL K
PROBLEMS IN THE CONSTRUCTION OF VIABLE CONSTITUTIONAL
STRUCTURES IN AFRICA.
IN CARTER, GWENDOLEN M. AND ANN PADEN (EDS), EXPANDING
HORIZONS IN AFRICAN STUDIES, EVANSTON, NORTHWESTERN
UNIVERSITY PRESS, 1969, PP. 173-180
068,100,
        REFERENCE

BERRY JACK   GREENBERG JOSEPH H
SOCIOLINGUISTIC RESEARCH IN AFRICA.
AFRICAN STUDIES BULLETIN SEPTEMBER 1966 PP 1-9
100,
        REFERENCE

BERRY JACK
THE MADINA PROJECT--SOCIOLINGUISTIC RESEARCH IN GHANA.
IN GWENDOLEN CARTER AND ANN PADEN (EDS), EXPANDING HORIZONS
IN AFRICAN STUDIES,EVANSTON, NORTHWESTERN UNIVERSITY PRESS,
1969

100,114-03,
     REFERENCE

100

CARTER GWENDOLEN M
AFRICAN STUDIES IN THE UNITED STATES.
IN PROCEEDINGS OF THE CONFERENCE ON AFRICAN LANGUAGES AND
LITERATURES, NORTHWESTERN UNIVERSITY, 1966, UNITED STATES
OFFICE OF EDUCATION NO. OE-6-14-018, PP 2-7
099,100,
     REFERENCE

CARTER GWENDOLEN M
THE CHANGING ROLE OF THE AFRICANIST.
AFRICA REPORT, JANUARY 1968, P. 60
100,
     REFERENCE

CLIGNET REMI
SOCIAL AREA ANALYSIS OF DOUALA AND YAOUNDE.
IN CARTER, GWENDOLEN M. AND ANN PADEN (EDS), EXPANDING
HORIZONS IN AFRICAN STUDIES, EVANSTON, NORTHWESTERN
UNIVERSITY PRESS, 1969, PP. 315-320
100,104-05,
     REFERENCE

CROWLEY DANIEL J
TRADITIONAL AND CONTEMPORARY ART IN AFRICA.
IN CARTER, GWENDOLEN M. AND ANN PADEN (EDS), EXPANDING
HORIZONS IN AFRICAN STUDIES, EVANSTON, NORTHWESTERN
UNIVERSITY PRESS, 1969
014,093,100,
     REFERENCE

DIKE K O
THE IMPORTANCE OF AFRICAN STUDIES.
IN LALAGE BOWN AND MICHAEL CROWDER (EDS.), PROCEEDINGS OF
THE FIRST INTERNATIONAL CONGRESS OF AFRICANISTS, ACCRA,
1962, LONDON, LONGMANS, 1964, PP 19-28
100,
     REFERENCE

EAST AFRICAN INSTITUTE OF SOCIAL AND CULTURAL AFFAIRS
RESEARCH PRIORITIES FOR EAST AFRICA.
KENYA, EAST AFRICAN PUBLISHING HOUSE, 1966
100,
     REFERENCE

FAGE JOHN D
HISTORY.
IN ROBERT A LYSTAD (ED), THE AFRICAN WORLD, NEW YORK,
PRAEGER, 1966, PP 40-56
100,
     REFERENCE

FALLERS LLOYD A
POLITICAL SOCIOLOGY AND THE ANTHROPOLOGICAL STUDY OF
AFRICAN POLITIES.
ARCHIVES EUROPEENNES DE SOCIOLOGIE 4 1963 PP 311-329
100,

REFERENCE

100

FERNANDEZ JAMES W
CONTEMPORARY AFRICAN RELIGION--CONFLUENTS OF INQUIRY.
IN CARTER, GWENDOLEN M. AND ANN PADEN (EDS), EXPANDING
HORIZONS IN AFRICAN STUDIES, EVANSTON, NORTHWESTERN
UNIVERSITY PRESS, 1969, PP. 27-46
013,050,100,
        REFERENCE

FORD RICHARD B
AFRICA AND THE SCHOOLS
AFRICA REPORT MAY/JUNE 1969 PP 76-77
100,
        REFERENCE

FRANCK THOMAS M
SOME THOUGHTS ON LEGAL STUDIES IN AFRICA.
AMERICAN BEHAVIORAL SCIENTIST 5 APRIL 1962 PP 18-19
066,100,
        REFERENCE

FRASER C GERALD
BLACK CAUCUS DELIBERATIONS AT MONTREAL-WHO SHOULD CONTROL
AFRICAN STUDIES AND FOR WHAT ENDS
AFRICA REPORT DECEMBER 1969 PP20-21
100,
        REFERENCE

GLICKMAN HARVEY
POLITICAL SCIENCE.
IN ROBERT A LYSTAD (ED), THE AFRICAN WORLD, NEW YORK,
PRAEGER, 1966, PP 131-165
100,
        REFERENCE

GOULD PETER
GEOGRAPHY, SPATIAL PLANNING, AND AFRICA--THE RESPONSIBILIT-
IES OF THE NEXT TWENTY YEARS.
IN CARTER, GWENDOLEN M. AND ANN PADEN (EDS), EXPANDING
HORIZONS IN AFRICAN STUDIES, EVANSTON, NORTHWESTERN
UNIVERSITY PRESS, 1969, PP. 181-203
048,100,
        REFERENCE

GRAY ROBERT F
MEDICAL RESEARCH-- SOME ANTHROPOLOGICAL ASPECTS.
IN ROBERT A LYSTAD (ED), THE AFRICAN WORLD, NEW YORK,
PRAEGER, 1966,
075,100,
        REFERENCE

GULLIVER P H
ANTHROPOLOGY.
IN ROBERT A LYSTAD (ED), THE AFRICAN WORLD, NEW YORK,
PRAEGER, 1966, PP 57-106
100,
        REFERENCE

HAMMOND PETER B
AFRO-AMERICAN INDIANS AND AFRO-ASIANS--CULTURAL CONTACTS
BETWEEN AFRICA AND THE PEOPLES OF ASIA AND ABORIGINAL
AMERICA.
IN CARTER, GWENDOLEN M. AND ANN PADEN (EDS), EXPANDING
HORIZONS IN AFRICAN STUDIES, EVANSTON, NORTHWESTERN
UNIVERSITY PRESS, 1969, PP. 275-290
030,094,100,
        REFERENCE

100
    HAYNES JANE B
    ASA MEETING DISRUPTED BY RACIAL CRISIS
    AFRICA REPORT DECEMBER 1969 PP 16-17
    100,
        REFERENCE

    KAMARCK ANDREW M
    ECONOMICS AND ECONOMIC DEVELOPMENT.
    IN ROBERT A LYSTAD (ED), THE AFRICAN WORLD, NEW YORK,
    PRAEGER, 1966, PP 221-244
    099,100,
        REFERENCE

    KIMAMBO ISARIA N
    HISTORICAL RESEARCH IN MAINLAND TANZANIA.
    IN CARTER, GWENDOLEN M. AND ANN PADEN (EDS) EXPANDING
    HORIZONS IN AFRICAN STUDIES, EVANSTON, NORTHWESTERN
    UNIVERSITY PRESS, 1969, PP. 75-90
    100,136-02,
        REFERENCE

    MAZRUI ALI A
    POLITICAL SCIENCE AND THE DECLINE OF AFRICAN NATIONALISM.
    IN CARTER, GWENDOLEN M. AND ANN PADEN (EDS) EXPANDING
    HORIZONS IN AFRICAN STUDIES, EVANSTON, NORTHWESTERN
    UNIVERSITY PRESS, 1969, PP. 147-156
    004,100,
        REFERENCE

    MAZRUI ALI A
    EUROPEAN EXPLORATION AND AFRICAS SELF DISCOVERY
    JOURNAL OF MODERN AFRICAN STUDIES 7 1969 PP 661-676
    027,038,100,
        REFERENCE

    MCKELVEY JOHN J
    AGRICULTURAL RESEARCH.
    IN ROBERT A LYSTAD (ED), THE AFRICAN WORLD, NEW YORK,
    PRAEGER, 1966, PP 317-351
    099,100,
        REFERENCE

    MITCHELL ROBERT C   MORRISON DONALD G   PADEN JOHN N
    NATIONAL INTEGRATION AND STABILITY IN AFRICA.
    IN CARTER, GWENDOLEN M. AND ANN PADEN (EDS) EXPANDING
    HORIZONS IN AFRICAN STUDIES, EVANSTON, NORTHWESTERN
    UNIVERSITY PRESS, 1969, PP. 329-336
    100,
        REFERENCE

100

MOWLANA HAMID
COMMUNICATIONS MEDIA IN AFRICA--A CRITIQUE IN RETROSPECT AND
PROSPECT.
IN CARTER, GWENDOLEN M. AND ANN PADEN (EDS), EXPANDING
HORIZONS IN AFRICAN STUDIES, EVANSTON, NORTHWESTERN
UNIVERSITY PRESS, 1969, PP. 259-274
049,100,
        REFERENCE

RESNICK IDRIAN N   CLARKE JOHN HENRIK   ET AL
DIALOG-THE FUTURE OF AFRICAN STUDIES AFTER MONTREAL
AFRICA REPORT DECEMBER 1969 PP 22-27
100,
        REFERENCE

SCANLON DAVID G
EDUCATION.
IN ROBERT A LYSTAD (ED), THE AFRICAN WORLD, NEW YORK,
PRAEGER, 1966, PP 199-220
100,
        REFERENCE

SCHNEIDER HAROLD K
A FORMALIST VIEW OF AFRICAN ECONOMIC ANTHROPOLOGY.
IN CARTER, GWENDOLEN M. AND ANN PADEN (EDS), EXPANDING
HORIZONS IN AFRICAN STUDIES, EVANSTON, NORTHWESTERN
UNIVERSITY PRESS, 1969, PP. 243-255
010,100,
        REFERENCE

SEGALL MARSHALL H
THE GROWTH OF PSYCHOLOGY IN AFRICAN STUDIES.
IN CARTER, GWENDOLEN M. AND ANN PADEN (EDS), EXPANDING
HORIZONS IN AFRICAN STUDIES, EVANSTON, NORTHWESTERN
UNIVERSITY PRESS, 1969, PP. 47-65
039,098,100,
        REFERENCE

SOJA EDWARD W
TRANSACTION FLOWS AND NATIONAL UNITY--THE NIGERIAN CASE.
IN CARTER, GWENDOLEN M. AND ANN PADEN (EDS), EXPANDING
HORIZONS IN AFRICAN STUDIES, EVANSTON, NORTHWESTERN
UNIVERSITY PRESS, 1969, PP. 321-328
100,128-06,
        REFERENCE

STUCKEY STERLING
AFRICAN AND AFRO-AMERICAN RELATIONSHIPS--RESEARCH POSSIBIL-
ITIES.
IN CARTER, GWENDOLEN M. AND ANN PADEN (EDS), EXPANDING
HORIZONS IN AFRICAN STUDIES, EVANSTON, NORTHWESTERN
UNIVERSITY PRESS, 1969, PP. 291-302
030,094,100,
        REFERENCE

UCHENDU VICTOR C
PRIORITY ISSUES FOR SOCIAL ANTHROPOLOGICAL RESEARCH IN
AFRICA IN THE NEXT TWO DECADES.

IN CARTER, GWENDOLEN M. AND ANN PADEN (EDS), EXPANDING
HORIZONS IN AFRICAN STUDIES, EVANSTON, NORTHWESTERN
UNIVERSITY PRESS, 1969, PP. 3-23
016,100,
    REFERENCE

100

WACHSMANN KLAUS
ETHNOMUSICOLOGY IN AFRICAN STUDIES--THE NEXT TWENTY YEARS.
IN CARTER, GWENDOLEN M. AND ANN PADEN (EDS), EXPANDING
HORIZONS IN AFRICAN STUDIES, EVANSTON, NORTHWESTERN
UNIVERSITY PRESS, 1969, PP. 131-142
015,100,
    REFERENCE

WILLETT FRANK
ARCHAEOLOGY IN AFRICA.
IN CARTER, GWENDOLEN M. AND ANN PADEN (EDS), EXPANDING
HORIZONS IN AFRICAN STUDIES, EVANSTON, NORTHWESTERN
UNIVERSITY PRESS, 1969, PP. 91-110
036,100,
    REFERENCE

YOUNG ROLAND A
POLITICAL RESEARCH IN THE NEW AFRICAN NATIONS.
THE AMERICAN BEHAVIORAL SCIENTIST APRIL 1962 PP 3-5
100,
    REFERENCE

ZAKE S JOSHUA L
REVISION AND UNIFICATION OF AFRICAN LEGAL SYSTEMS--THE
UGANDA EXPERIENCE.
IN CARTER, GWENDOLEN M. AND ANN PADEN (EDS), EXPANDING
HORIZONS IN AFRICAN STUDIES, EVANSTON, NORTHWESTERN
UNIVERSITY PRESS, 1969, PP. 157-168
066, 100, 139-06,
    REFERENCE

BIOBAKU SABURI O
THE PROBLEM OF TRADITIONAL HISTORY WITH SPECIAL REFERENCES
TO YORUBA TRADITIONS.
JOURNAL OF THE HISTORICAL SOCIETY OF NIGERIA 1 1956
PP 43-47
100,128-02,
    CASE STUDY

EAST AFRICAN INSTITUTE OF SOCIAL AND CULTURAL AFFAIRS
RESEARCH PRIORITIES FOR EAST AFRICA.
NAIROBI EAST AFRICAN PUBLISHING HOUSE CONTEMPORARY
AFRICAN MONOGRAPH SERIES NO 5 1966
100,
    CASE STUDY

OWEN D F   ED
RESEARCH AND DEVELOPMENT IN EAST AFRICA.
NAIROBI, EAST AFRICAN ACADEMY, EAST AFRICAN INSTITUTE PRESS,
LTD. 1966
075,100,
    CASE STUDY

COHEN RONALD
ANTHROPOLOGY AND POLITICAL SCIENCE-- COURTSHIP OR MARRIAGE.
AMERICAN BEHAVIORAL SCIENTIST NOVEMBER 1967
100,
    GENERAL THEORY

100
D'ANDRADE ROY G
ANTHROPOLOGICAL STUDIES OF DREAMS.
IN FRANCIS L K HSU, (ED), PSYCHOLOGICAL ANTHROPOLOGY,
HOMEWOOD, ILLINOIS, DORSEY PRESS, 1961, PP 296-332
100,
    GENERAL THEORY

THOMAS B E
GEOGRAPHY.
IN ROBERT A LYSTAD (ED), THE AFRICAN WORLD, NEW YORK,
PRAEGER, 1966, PP 245-270
100,
    GENERAL THEORY

COHEN RONALD
POLITICAL ANTHROPOLOGY--- THE FUTURE OF A PIONEER.
ANTHROPOLOGICAL QUARTERLY 38 1965 PP 117-131, NORTHWESTERN
UNIVERSITY PROGRAM OF AFRICAN STUDIES REPRINT SERIES 4
009,098,100,
    REFERENCE
    CASE STUDY

II

Country-by-Country
Case-Study References

Independent States

101. ALGERIA

101-01
   LAJOUX JEAN D
   THE ROCK PAINTINGS OF TASSILI. (TRANS BY G D LIVERSAGE)
   CLEVELAND, WORLD PUBLISHING COMPANY, 1963
   014,101-01,

101-02
   GORDON DAVID C
   THE PASSING OF FRENCH ALGERIA.
   NEW YORK, OXFORD UNIVERSITY PRESS. 1966
   033,055,056,101-02,

101-03
   FANON FRANTZ
   BLACK SKIN, WHITE MASKS-- THE EXPERIENCES OF A BLACK
   MAN IN A WHITE WORLD.
   NEW YORK, GROVE PRESS, 1967
   041,085,088,101-03,

   FANON FRANTZ
   THE WRETCHED OF THE EARTH
   NEW YORK, GROVE PRESS, 1963
   060,091,101-03,

   GORDON DAVID C
   WOMEN OF ALGERIA-- AN ESSAY ON CHANGE.
   CAMBRIDGE, MASS, HARVARD, 1968
   101-03,

101-04
   SAADALLAH BELKACEM
   THE RISE OF THE ALGERIAN ELITE, 1900-24.
   THE JOURNAL OF MODERN AFRICAN STUDIES 5 MAY 1967 PP 69-77
   044,101-04,

101-06
   CLARCK MICHAEL K
   ALGERIA IN TURMOIL--A HISTORY OF THE REBELLION.
   NEW YORK, PRAEGER, 1959
   055,101-06,

   HUMBARACI ARSLAN
   ALGERIA A REVOLUTION THAT FAILED.
   LONDON, PALL MALL PRESS, 1966
   101-06,

101-08
   THOMAS B E

TRADE ROUTES OF ALGERIA AND THE SAHARA.
BERKELEY, UNIVERSITY OF CALIFORNIA PRESS, 1957
048,101-08,

101-08
    AMIN SAMIR
    L'ECONOMIE DU MAGHREB VOLUME 1- LA COLONISATION ET LA
    DECOLONISATION VOLUME 2-LES PERSPECTIVE D'AVENIR
    PARIS, EDITIONS DE MINUIT, 1966
    073,101-08,126-08,138-08,

101-09
    GALLAGHER CHARLES F
    THE UNITED STATES AND NORTH AFRICA
    CAMBRIDGE, MASS, HARVARD UNIVERSITY PRESS, 1963
    083,101-09,126-09,138-09,

    SANDS WILLIAM
    PROSPECTS FOR A UNITED MAGHRIB
    IN TIBOR KEREKES (ED), THE ARAB MIDDLE EAST AND MUSLIM
    AFRICA, NEW YORK, PRAEGER, 1961
    078,101-09,120-09,126-09,138-09,

101-11
    BRACE RICHARD M
    MOROCCO ALGERIA TUNISIA
    ENGLEWOOD CLIFFS, PRENTICE-HALL, 1964
    101-11,126-11,138-11,

101-12
    AFRICAN BIBLIOGRAPHIC CENTER
    ALGERIAN PANORAMA-A SELECTED BIBLIOGRAPHIC SURVEY 1965-1966
    WASHINGTON VOLUME 5 NUMBER 2 1967
    101-12,

102. BOTSWANA

102-01
    SCHAPERA ISAAC   ED
    PRAISE PEOMS OF TSWANA CHIEFS.
    OXFORD, CLARENDON PRESS, 1965
    012,102-01,

    SCHAPERA ISAAC
    A HANDBOOK OF TSWANA LAW AND CUSTOM
    NEW YORK, OXFORD UNIVERSITY PRESS, 1955
    102-01,

    SCHAPERA ISAAC
    MARRIED LIFE IN AN AFRICAN TRIBE
    EVANSTON, NORTHWESTERN UNIVERSITY PRESS, 1966
    102-01,

    SCHAPERA ISAAC
    THE TSWANA

LONDON, INTERNATIONAL AFRICAN INSTITUTE, 1953
102-01,

102-01
VAN DER POST L
THE HEART OF THE HUNTER
NEW YORK, MORROW, 1961
102-01,

102-02
SMITH EDWIN W
GREAT LION OF BECHUANALAND
LONDON, INDEPENDENT PRESS, 1957
031,102-02,

102-03
SCHAPERA ISAAC
MIGRANT LABOUR AND TRIBAL LIFE-- A STUDY OF CONDITIONS
IN THE BECHUANALAND PROTECTORATE.
LONDON, OXFORD UNIVERSITY PRESS, 1947
038,102-03,

102-04
GABATSHWANE S M
TSHEKEDI KHAMA OF BECHUANALAND-- GREAT STATESMAN AND
POLITICIAN.
CAPETOWN, OXFORD UNIVERSITY PRESS, 1961
102-04,

102-07
BREUTZ P L
TSWANA LOCAL GOVERNMENT TODAY.
SOCIOLOGUS 8 1958 PP 140-154
062,102-07,

HALPERN JACK
SOUTH AFRICA'S HOSTAGES-- BASUTOLAND, BECHUANALAND,
AND SWAZILAND.
BALTIMORE, PENGUIN, 1965
032,088,102-07,118-07,135-07,

MACARTNEY W A J
BOTSWANA GOES TO THE POLLS
AFRICAN REPORT, DECEMBER 1969, PP 28-30
063,102-07,

PROCTOR J H
THE HOUSE OF CHIEFS AND THE POLITICAL DEVELOPMENT OF
BOTSWANA
JOURNAL OF MODERN AFRICAN STUDIES 6 1968 PP 59-79
062, 102-07,

AFRICAN INSTITUTE
POLITICAL DEVELOPMENTS IN BECHUANALAND PROTECTORATE.
INTERNATIONAL BULLETIN II FEBRUARY 1964
102-07,

102-09
MUNGER EDWIN S
BECHUANALAND PAN-AFRICANIST OUTPOST OR BANTU HOMELAND.

LONDON, OXFORD UNIVERSITY PRESS, 1965
102-09,

102-11
   GREAT BRITAIN   COLONIAL OFFICE
   BECHUANALAND PROTECTORATE, REPORT FOR THE YEARS 1961-62.
   LONDON, HER MAJESTY'S STATIONERY OFFICE, 1964
   102-11,

   GREAT BRITAIN   COLONIAL OFFICE
   BECHUANALAND PROTECTORATE REPORT FOR THE YEAR 1963.
   LONDON, HER MAJESTY'S STATIONERY OFFICE, 1965
   102-11,

   STEVENS RICHARD P
   LESOTHO BOTSWANA AND SWAZILAND.
   LONDON, PALL MALL PRESS, 1967
   102-11, 118-11, 135-11,

102-12
   MIDDLETON CORAL
   BECHUANALAND--A BIBLIOGRAPHY.
   CAPETOWN, UNIVERSITY OF CAPETOWN SCHOOL OF LIBRARIANSHIP, 1965
   102-12,

   WEBSTER JOHN B   ET AL
   A SUPPLEM NT TO A BIBLIOGRAPHY ON BECHUANALAND.
   SYRACUSE, NEW YORK, MAXWELL SCHOOL OF PUBLIC AFFAIRS, PRO-
   GRAM OF EASTERN AFRICAN STUDIES, AUGUST 12, 1968
   102-12,

103. BURUNDI

103-01
   ALBERT ETHEL M
   UNE ETUDE DE VALEURS EN URUNDI-A STUDY OF VALUES IN URUNDI
   CAHIERS D'ETUDES AFRICAINES 2 1960. PP 148-160
   013, 103-01,

103-02
   LOUIS WILLIAM ROGER
   RUANDA-URUNDI-- 1884-1919.
   OXFORD, CLARENDON PRESS, 1963
   033, 103-02, 129-02,

103-03
   ALBERT ETHEL M
   SOCIO-ECONOMIC ORGANIZATION AND RECEPTIVITY TO CHANGE-SOME
   DIFFERENCES BETWEEN RUANDA AND URUNDI
   SOUTHWESTERN JOURNAL OF ANTHROPOLOGY 16 1960 PP 46-74
   013, 038, 103-03, 129-03,

103-05
   BAECK LOUIS
   ETUDE SOCIO-ECONOMIQUE DU CENTRE EXTRA COUTUMIER D'USUMBURA.

BRUXELLES, ACADEMY OF RORAL SCIENCES COLONIALES, 1957
103-05,

103-05
    VAN DE WALLE E
    FACTEURS ET INDICES DE STABILISATION ET D URBANIZATION A
    A USUMBURA RUANDA-URUNDI.
    RECHERCHES ECONOMIQUE DE LOUVAIN 27 2   1961
    103-05,

103-07
    CART H P
    CONCEPTION DES RAPPORTS POLITIQUES AU BURUNDI.
    ETUDES CONGOLAISES 9 2   MARCH-APRIL 1966
    103-07,

    LEMARCHAND RENE
    SOCIAL AND POLITICAL CHANGES IN BURUNDI.
    IN G.M. CARTER, ED, FIVE AFRICAN STATES--RESPONSES TO
    DIVERSITY, ITHACA, CORNELL UNIVERSITY PRESS, 1963
    103-07,

    WEBSTER JOHN B
    THE CONSTITUTIONS OF BURUNDI MALAGASY AND RWANDA.
    SYRACUSE NEW YORK MAXWELL GRADUATE SCHOOL OF PUBLIC AFFAIRS
    THE PROGRAM OF EASTERN STUDIES, NO. 3, FEB., 1964
    066,103-07,121-07,129-07,

    WEBSTER JOHN B
    THE POLITICAL DEVELOPMENT OF RWANDA AND BURUNDI.
    SYRACUSE, NEW YORK, MAXWELL GRADUATE SCHOOL OF PUBLIC AFFAIRS
    PROGRAM OF EASTERN AFRICAN STUDIES, NO. 16, JUNE, 1966
    103-07,129-07,

103-11
    ANONYMOUS
    BURUNDI AT CLOSE RANGE.
    AFRICA REPORT MARCH 1965
    103-11,

    LEMARCHAND RENE
    RWANDA BURUNDI.
    LONDON, PALL MALL PRESS, 1970
    103-11, 129-11,

103-12
    CLEMENT JOSEPH R
    ESSAI DE BIBLIOGRAPHIE DU RUANDA-URUNDI.
    USUMBURA, N.P., 1959
    103-12,

104. CAMEROON

104-01
    ARDENER EDWIN   ARDENER S   WARMINGTON W A

PLANTATION AND VILLAGE IN THE CAMEROONS.
LONDON, OXFORD UNIVERSITY PRESS, 1960
047,104-01,

104-01
ALEXANDRE PIERRE
APERCU SOMMAIRE SUR LE PIDGIN A 70 DU CAMEROUN.
COLLOQUE SUR LE MULTILINGUISME, BRAZZAVILLE, CCTA, 1962
104-01,

BAHOKEN JEAN CALVIN
CLAIRIERES METAPHYSIQUES AFRICAINES: ESSAI SUR LA
PHILOSOPHIE ET LA RELIGION CHEZ LES BANTU DU SUB-CAMEROUN-
LA CONNAISSANCE DE NYAMBEO L'OETRE SUPREME ET LES INFLUENCES
DES IDEES PHILOSOPHIQUES AT RELIGIEUSES SUR LA SOCIETE ET
LES INSTITUTIONS.
PARIS, PRESENCE AFRICAINE, 1967
104-01,

LECOQ RAYMOND
LES BAMILIKE (THE BAMILIKE).
PARIS, PRESENCE AFRICAINE, 1953
104-01,

MOHAMADOU ELDRIDGE
CONTES ET POEMES FOULBE DE LA BENOUE NORD-CAMEROUN.
YAOUNDE, EDITIONS ABBIA-CLE, 1965
104-01,

MOUME ETIA ISSAC
LES FABLES DE DOUALA CAMEROUN. EN LANGUE FRANCAISE ET DOUALA
BERGERAC, IMP CASTANET, 1930
104-01,

MVENG ENGELBERT
L'ART D'AFRIQUE NOIRE. LITURGIE COSMIQUE ET LANGAGE
RELIGEUX.
PARIS, MAME, 1964
104-01,

PERRAULT GILLES
LES FANG DU PAYS YAOUNDE.
LES CAHIERS D'OUTRE-MER, OCTOBER-DECEMBER 1949
104-01,

104-02
GARDINIER DAVID E
CAMEROON. UNITED NATIONS CHALLENGE TO FRENCH POLICY.
LONDON, OXFORD UNIVERSITY PRESS, 1963
081,104-02,

FROELICH JEAN C
CAMEROUN TOGO TERRITOIRES SOUS TUTELLE.
PARIS, BERGER-LEVRAULT, 1956
104-02,137-02,

MOHAMADOU ELDRIDGE
L'HISTOIRE DE TIBATI.
YAOUNDE, EDITIONS ABBIA, 1965
104-02,

104-02
MVENG ENGELBERT
HISTOIRE DU CAMEROUN.
PARIS, PRESENCE AFRICAINE, 1963
104-02,

NJOYA SULTAN
HISTOIRE ET COUTUMES DES BAMUM.
YAOUNDE, INSTITUT FRANCAIS DE AFRIQUE NOIRE CENTRE, CAMEROON
1952
104-02,

104-03
ALEXANDRE PIERRE
CAMEROUN
IN KRITZECK AND LEWIS, PP 270-277
104-03,

BALA MBARGA HENRI
PROBLEMES AFRICAINS DE L'EDUCATION PRECEDE DE L'ETUDE DU
CAS DU CAMEROUN.
PARIS, HACHETTE, 1962
104-03,

JOHNSON WILLARD R
AFRICAN-SPEAKING AFRICA--LESSONS FROM THE CAMEROON.
AFRICAN FORUM V. I NO 2 FALL 1965
104-03,

LACROIX PIERRE
L'ISLAM PEUL DE L'ADAMAWA.
IN LEWIS, ISLAM IN TROPICAL AFRICA, LONDON, OXFORD UNIVERSITY
PRESS, 1966, P. 401-407
104-03,

104-04
AHIDJO AHMADOU
CONTRIBUTION TO NATIONAL CONSTRUCTION.
PARIS, PRESENCE AFRICAINE, 1964
054,060,104-04,

104-05
CLIGNET REMI
SOCIAL AREA ANALYSIS OF DOUALA AND YAOUNDE.
IN CARTER, GWENDOLEN M. AND ANN PADEN (EDS), EXPANDING
HORIZONS IN AFRICAN STUDIES, EVANSTON, NORTHWESTERN
UNIVERSITY PRESS, 1969, PP. 315-320
100,104-05,

GARDINIER DAVID E
URBAN POLITICS IN DOUALA, CAMEROON, 1944-1955
AFRICAN URBAN NOTES, VOL IV, NO. 3, SEPT. 1969, PP. 20-29
047,104-05,

104-06
ARDENER EDWIN
THE NATURE OF THE REUNIFICATION OF CAMEROON CHAPTER 8.
IN ARTHUR HAZLEWOOD, AFRICAN INTEGRATION AND DISINTEGRATION,
LONDON, OXFORD UNIVERSITY PRESS, 1967, PP 285-337

054,104-06,

104-06
JOHNSON WILLARD R
CAMEROON FEDERATION--POLITICAL INTEGRATION IN A FRAGMENTARY
SOCIETY.
PRINCETON, NEW JERSEY, PRINCETON UNIVERSITY PRESS, 1970
057,059,104-06,

LEVINE VICTOR T
THE CAMEROONS FROM MANDATE TO INDEPENDENCE.
BERKELEY UNIVERSITY OF CALIFORNIA PRESS 1964
055,104-06,

104-07
GONIDEC P F
LES INSTITUTIONS POLITIQUE DE LA REPUBLIQUE FEDERAL DU
CAMAROUN (THE POLITICAL INSTITUTIONS OF THE FEDERAL
REPUBLIC OF THE CAMEROONS).
CIVILIZATIONS 11 1961 PP 370-395 AND 12 1962 PP 13-26
062,104-07,

JOHNSON WILLARD R
THE CAMEROON FEDERATION--POLITICAL UNION BETWEEN ENGLISH
AND FRENCH SPEAKING AFRICA.
IN WILLIAM LEWIS ED FRENCH SPEAKING AFRICA,NEW YORK,WALKER
1965
104-07,

LEVINE VICTOR T
CAMEROON.
IN G.M. CARTER,ED,FIVE AFRICAN STATES-- RESPONSES TO
DIVERSITY, ITHACA, CORNELL UNIVERSITY PRESS, 1963,
104-07,

LEVINE VICTOR T
CAMEROON.
IN J.S. COLEMAN AND C.G. ROSBERG EDS POLITICAL PARTIES AND
NATIONAL INTEGRATION IN TROPICAL AFRICA. LOS ANGELES,
UNIVERSITY OF CALIFORNIA PRESS, 1964
104-07,

104-08
UNITED NATIONS
INDUSTRIAL DEVELOPMENT IN AFRICA
NEW YORK UNITED NATIONS 1967
071,104-08,110-08,117-08,127-08,134-08,140-08,142-08,

ARDENER EDWIN   ED
SOCIAL AND DEMOGRAPHIC PROBLEMS OF THE SOUTHERN
CAMEROONS PLANTATION AREA.
IN AIDAN SOUTHALL (ED.), SOCIAL CHANGE IN MODERN AFRICA,
LONDON,OXFORD UNIVERSITY PRESS,1961, PP 83-97
074,104-08,

KABERRY PHYLLIS M
SOME PROBLEMS OF LAND TENURE IN NSAW, SOUTHERN CAMEROONS.
JOURNAL OF AFRICAN ADMINISTRATION 12 JANUARY 1960 PP 21-28
070,104-08,

MEEK CHARLES K
LAND TENURE AND LAND ADMINISTRATION IN NIGERIA AND THE
CAMEROONS.
LONDON, HER MAJESTY'S STATIONERY OFFICE, 1957
010,070,104-08,128-08,

104-08
  WARMINGTON W A
  A WEST AFRICAN TRADE UNION.
  LONDON OXFORD UNIVERSITY PRESS 1960
  A CASE STUDY OF THE CAMEROONS DEVELOPMENT CORPORATION
  WORKERS? UNIONS AND ITS RELATIONS WITH THE EMPLOYERS
  073,104-08,

  WELLS F A   WARMINGTON W A
  STUDIES IN INDUSTRIALIZATION--NIGERIA AND THE CAMEROONS.
  LONDON, OXFORD UNIVERSITY PRESS, 1962
  071,104-08,128-08,

104-10
  BETI MONGO
  MISSION TO KALA.
  TRANSLATED BY PETER GREEN, IBADAN, HEINEMANN EDUCATIONAL
  BOOKS LTD, 1964
  090,104-10,

  BETI MONGO
  KING LAZAROUS.
  NEW YORK, MACMILLAN CO., 1970   (LONDON, HEINEMANN
  EDUCATIONAL BOOKS)
  090,104-10,

  BETI MONGO
  LE PAUVRE CHRIST DE BOMBA.
  PARIS, R LAFFONT, 1956
  090,104-10,

  OYONO FERDINAND
  LA VIEUX NEGRE ET LA MEDAILLE.
  PARIS, JULLIARD, 1956
  090,104-10,

  BETI MONGO
  ECRIVAIN CAMEROUNAIS. TEXTES COMMENTES PAR ROGER MERCIER ET
  M ET S BATTESTINI.
  PARIS, F NATHAN, 1964, COLLECTION LITTERATURE AFRICAINE-- 5
  104-10,

  BETI MONGO
  LE ROI MIRACULE.
  PARIS, CORREA BUCHER CHASTEL, 1958
  104-10,

  BETI MONGO
  MISSION TERMINEE.
  PARIS, CORREA BUCHER CHASTEL, 1957
  104-10,

  BETI MONGO
  VILLE CRUELLE.

PARIS,EDITIONS AFRICAINES, 1954
104-10,

104-10
EPANYA YONDO ELOLONGUE
KAMERUN KAMERUN.
PARIS,PRESENCE AFRICAINE, 1960
104-10,

OYONO FERDINAND
CHEMIN D? EUROPE.
PARIS, JULLIARD, 1960
104-10,

OYONO FERDINAND
ECRIVAIN CAMEROUNAIS. TEXTES COMMENTES PAR ROGER MERCIER ET
M AND S BATTESTINI.
PARIS, F NATHAN, 1964
104-10,

104-11
LUSIGNAN GUY DE
FRENCH-SPEAKING AFRICA SINCE INDEPENDENCE.
NEW YORK, PRAEGER PUBLISHERS, 1969
056,061,104-11,105-11,106-11,107-11,109-11,112-11,
115-11,116-11,123-11,137-11,141-11,

104-12
WITHERELL JULIAN 1
OFFICIAL PUBLICATIONS OF THE FRENCH EQUATORIAL AFRICA,
FRENCH CAMEROUNS AND TOGO, 1949-1958.
WASHINGTON,LIBRARY OF CONGRESS,AFRICAN SECTION,1964
104-12,105-12,106-12,107-12,112-12,137-12,

105. CENTRAL AFRICAN REPUBLIC

105-01
SAMARIN WILLIAM J
UNE LINGUA CENTRAFRICAINE.
COLLOQUE SUR LE MULTILINGUISME, BRAZZAVILLE, 1962
105-01,

105-03
BALLARD JOHN A
EQUATORIAL AFRICA
IN KRITZECK AND LEWIS PP 278-286
105-03,106-03,107-03,112-03,

105-06
BALLARD JOHN A
FOUR EQUATORIAL STATES--THE CONGO, GABON, CENTRAL AFRICAN
REPUBLIC, CHAD.
IN GWENDOLEN M CARTER (ED.), NATIONAL UNITY AND REGIONALISM
IN EIGHT AFRICAN STATES, ITHACA, CORNELL UNIVERSITY PRESS,
1966, PP 231-329

105-06,106-06,107-06,112-06,

105-09
   ROBSON PETER
   ECONOMIC INTEGRATION IN EQUATORIAL AFRICA CHAPTER 2.
   IN ARTHUR HAZLEWOOD, AFRICAN INTEGRATION AND DISINTEGRATION,
   LONDON, OXFORD UNIVERSITY PRESS, 1967, PP 27-69
   078,105-09,106-09,107-09,112-09,

105-10
   BAMBOTE PIERRE
   LE DUR AVENIR.
   BANGUI, IMP. CENTRALE D'AFRIQUE, 1965
   105-10,

   BAMBOTE PIERRE
   LA POESIE EST DANS L'HISTOIRE.
   PARIS, OSWALD, 1960
   105-10,

105-11
   LUSIGNAN GUY DE
   FRENCH-SPEAKING AFRICA SINCE INDEPENDENCE.
   NEW YORK, PRAEGER PUBLISHERS, 1969
   056,061,104-11,105-11,106-11,107-11,109-11,112-11,
   115-11,116-11,123-11,137-11,141-11,

   THOMPSON VIRGINIA   ADLOFF RICHARD
   THE EMERGING STATES OF FRENCH EQUATORIAL AFRICA.
   STANFORD, STANFORD UNIVERSITY PRESS, 1960
   105-11,107-11,112-11,106-11,

105-12
   WITHERELL JULIAN T
   OFFICIAL PUBLICATIONS OF THE FRENCH EQUATORIAL AFRICA,
   FRENCH CAMEROUNS AND TOGO, 1949-1958.
   WASHINGTON LIBRARY OF CONGRESS AFRICAN SECTION 1964
   104-12,105-12,106-12,107-12,112-12,137-12,

106. CHAD

106-01
   ADLER ALFRED
   LES DAY DE BOUNA (THE DAY OF BOUNA).
   ETUDES ET DOCUMENTS TCHADIENS SERIES A 1,INSTITUT NATIONAL
   TCHADIEN POUR LES SCIENCES HUMAINES,FORT LAMY,1966
   106-01,

   CHAPELLE JEAN
   LA RELIGION DES TOUBOUS (TUBU RELIGION) CHAPTER 9.
   IN NOMADES NOIRS DU SAHARA, PARIS, LIBRARIE PLON, 1957
   013,106-01,

   LE ROUVREUR ALBERT
   SAHELIENS ET SAHARIENS DU TCHAD

PARIS, BERGER-LEVRAULT, 1962
106-01,

106-01
LEBEUF ANNIE
LES POPULATIONS DU CHAD.
PARIS, PRESSES UNIVERSITAIRES DE FRANCE, 1959
106-01,

TUBIANA MARIE-JOSE
CONTES ZAGHAWA--TRENTE-SEPT CONTES ET DEUX LEGENDES
RECUEILLIS AU TCHAD--PREFACE DE MICHEL LEIRS--OUVRAGE PUBLIE
AVEC LE CONCOURS DU CENTRE NATIONAL DE LA RECHERCHE
SCIENTIFIQUE.
PARIS, LES QUATRE-JEUDIS, 1962
106-01,

106-02
ARKELL A J
THE HISTORY OF DARFUR 1200-1700 A D.
SUDAN NOTES AND RECORDS 32 1951 PP 37-70, PP 207-238
ALSO 33 1952 PP 129-155, PP 244-275
024,106-02,

ARKELL A J
THE MEDIEVAL HISTORY OF DARFUR IN ITS RELATION TO OTHER
CULTURES AND TO THE NILOTIC SUDAN.
SUDAN NOTES AND RECORDS 40 1959 PP 44-47
024,106-02,

MARTIN B G
KANEM, BORNU, AND THE FAZZAN--NOTES ON THE POLITICAL HISTORY
OF A TRADE SOURCE.
JOURNAL OF AFRICAN HISTORY, X, 1, 1969, PP. 15-27
024,106-02,

ROBINSON ARTHUR E
THE ARAB DYNASTY OF DAR FOR (DARFUR),AD 1448-1874 OR
AH 852-1201.
JOURNAL OF THE AFRICAN SOCIETY 27 1927 PP 353-363
28 1928 PP 55-67, 274-280, 379-384 AND
29 1929 PP 53-70, 164-180
024,106-02,

LEBEUF JEAN PAUL   MASSON-DEFOURRET A M
LA CIVILIZATION DU CHAD.
PARIS, PAYOT, 1950
106-02,

106-03
BALLARD JOHN A
EQUATORIAL AFRICA
IN KRITZECK AND LEWIS, PP 278-286
105-03,106-03,107-03,112-03,

106-06
BALLARD JOHN A
FOUR EQUATORIAL STATES--THE CONGO, GABON, CENTRAL AFRICAN
REPUBLIC, CHAD.
IN GWENDOLEN M CARTER (ED.), NATIONAL UNITY AND REGIONALISM

IN EIGHT AFRICAN STATES, ITHACA, CORNELL UNIVERSITY PRESS,
1966, PP 231-329
105-06,106-06,107-06,112-06,

106-09
   ROBSON PETER
   ECONOMIC INTEGRATION IN EQUATORIAL AFRICA CHAPTER 2.
   IN ARTHUR HAZLEWOOD, AFRICAN INTEGRATION AND DISINTEGRATION,
   LONDON, OXFORD UNIVERSITY PRESS, 1967, PP 27-69
   078,105-09,106-09,107-09,112-09,

106-10
   BEBNONE PALOU
   KALTOUMA--PIECE EN UN ACTE.
   PARIS, L'AVANT-SCENE-THEATRE, 1965
   106-10,

   SEID JOSEPH BRAHIM
   UN ENFANT DU TCAD--RECIT.
   PARIS, ED. SAGEREP, 1967
   106-10,

106-11
   LUSIGNAN GUY DE
   FRENCH-SPEAKING AFRICA SINCE INDEPENDENCE.
   NEW YORK, PRAEGER PUBLISHERS, 1969
   056,061,104-11,105-11,106-11,107-11,109-11,112-11,
   115-11,116-11,123-11,137-11,141-11,

   HUGOT PIERRE
   LE TCHAD.
   PARIS, NOUVELLES EDITIONS LATINES, 1965
   106-11,

   THOMPSON VIRGINIA   ADLOFF RICHARD
   THE EMERGING STATES OF FRENCH EQUATORIAL AFRICA.
   STANFORD, STANFORD UNIVERSITY PRESS, 1960
   105-11,107-11,112-11,106-11,

   THOMPSON VIRGINIA   ADLOFF RICHARD
   CHAD.
   IN V. THOMPSON AND R. ADLOFF, THE EMERGING STATES OF FRENCH
   EQUATORIAL AFRICA, STANFORD, STANFORD UNIVERSITY PRESS, 1960
   106-11,

106-12
   WITHERELL JULIAN T
   OFFICIAL PUBLICATIONS OF THE FRENCH EQUATORIAL AFRICA,
   FRENCH CAMEROUNS AND TOGO, 1949-1958.
   WASHINGTON,LIBRARY OF CONGRESS,AFRICAN SECTION,1964
   104-12,105-12,106-12,107-12,112-12,137-12,

107. CONGO-BRAZZAVILLE

BALLARD JOHN A
EQUATORIAL AFRICA
IN KRITZECK AND LEWIS, PP 278-286
105-03,106-03,107-03,112-03,

107-05
VENNETIER PIERRE
L'URBANISATION ET SES CONSEQUENCES AU CONGO (BRAZZAVILLE).
IN LES CAHIERS D'OUTRE MER, 16, 63, JULY-SEPT., 1963
107-05,

107-06
BALLARD JOHN A
FOUR EQUATORIAL STATES--THE CONGO, GABON, CENTRAL AFRICAN
REPUBLIC, CHAD.
IN GWENDOLEN M CARTER (ED.), NATIONAL UNITY AND REGIONALISM
IN EIGHT AFRICAN STATES, ITHACA, CORNELL UNIVERSITY PRESS,
1966, PP 231-329
105-06,106-06,107-06,112-06,

107-09
ROBSON PETER
ECONOMIC INTEGRATION IN EQUATORIAL AFRICA CHAPTER 2.
IN ARTHUR HAZLEWOOD, AFRICAN INTEGRATION AND DISINTEGRATION,
LONDON, OXFORD UNIVERSITY PRESS, 1967, PP 27-69
078,105-09,106-09,107-09,112-09,

107-10
MALONGA JEAN
COEUR D'ARYENNE.
PARIS, PRESENCE AFRICAINE, 1955
107-10,

MALONGA JEAN
LA LEGENDE DE M°PFOUMOU MA MAZONO.
PARIS, PRESENCE AFRICAINE. 1954
107-10,

TCHICAYA U TAM'SI G
EPITOME--PREFACE DE L S SENGHOR.
HONFLEU, PIERRE JEAN OSWALD, NOUVELLE EDITION, 1968
107-10,

TCHICAYA U TAM'SI G
FEU DE BROUSSE.
PARIS, CARACTERES, 1956;NEW EDITION BY PIERRE JEAN OSWALD
107-10,

TCHICAYA U TAM'SI G
LE MAUVIS SANG.
PARIS, CARACTERES, 1956;NEW EDITION BY PIERRE JEAN OSWALD

107-10,

TCHICAYA U TAM'SI G
LE VENTRE.
PARIS, PRESENCE AFRICAINE, 1964
107-10,

TCHICAYA U TAM'SI G

EPITOME.
TUNIS, SOCIETE NATIONALE D'EDITION ET DE DIFFUSION, 1962
HONFLEU, PIERRE JEAN OSWALD, NEW EDITION, 1968
107-10.

107-10
TCHICAYA U TAM'SI G
A TRICHE COEUR.
PARIS, ED. HAUTE-FEUILLE, 1958; NEW EDITION IN 1968 BY
PIERRE JEAN OSWALD
107-10.

TCHICAYA U TAM'SI G
L'ARC MUSICAL.
HONFLEUR, PIERRE JEAN OSWALD, FORTHCOMING
107-10.

TCHICAYA U TAM'SI G
TRESOR AFRICAIN (ANTHOLOGIE DE LEGENDES AFRICAINES).
PARIS, SEGHERS, FORTHCOMING
107-10,

107-11
LUSIGNAN GUY DE
FRENCH-SPEAKING AFRICA SINCE INDEPENDENCE.
NEW YORK, PRAEGER PUBLISHERS, 1969
056,061,104-11,105-11,106-11,107-11,109-11,112-11,
115-11,116-11,123-11,137-11,141-11,

THOMPSON VIRGINIA   ADLOFF RICHARD
THE EMERGING STATES OF FRENCH EQUATORIAL AFRICA.
STANFORD, STANFORD UNIVERSITY PRESS, 1960
105-11,107-11,112-11,106-11,

THOMPSON VIRGINIA   ADLOFF RICHARD
CONGO-BRAZZAVILLE.
IN V. THOMPSON AND R. ADLOFF, THE EMERGING STATES OF FRENCH
EQUATORIAL AFRICA, STANFORD, STANFORD UNIVERSITY PRESS, 1960
107-11,

107-12
PERROT C   SAUVALLE H
REPUBLIQUE DU CONGO--BRAZZAVILLE--REPERTOIRE
BIBLIOGRAPHIQUE.
PARIS, BUREAU POUR LE DEVELOPMENT DE LA PRODUCTION AGRICOLE,
1965
107-12,

WITHERELL JULIAN T
OFFICIAL PUBLICATIONS OF THE FRENCH EQUATORIAL AFRICA,
FRENCH CAMEROUNS AND TOGO, 1949-1958.
WASHINGTON, LIBRARY OF CONGRESS, AFRICAN SECTION, 1964
104-12,105-12,106-12,107-12,112-12,137-12,

108. CONGO-KINSHASA

108-01
  VANSINA JAN
  INTRODUCTION A L'ETHNOGRAPHE DU CONGO.
  BRUXELLES, EDITIONS UNIVERSITAIRES DU CONGO, NO. 1, 1966
  003,108-01,

  DOUGLAS MARY
  THE LELE OF THE KASAI.
  LONDON, OXFORD UNIVERSITY PRESS, 1963
  108-01,

  MERRIAM ALAN P
  THE CONCEPT OF CULTURE CLUSTERS APPLIED TO THE BELGIAN
  CONGO.
  SOUTHWESTERN JOURNAL OF ANTHROPOLOGY VOL 15 1959 PP 373-395
  004,108-01,

  HOTTOT R
  TEKE FETISHES.
  JOURNAL OF THE ROYAL ANTHROPOLOGICAL INSTITUTE 86
  1956 PP 25-36
  014,108-01,

  KOPYTOFF IGOR
  EXTENSION OF CONFLICT AS A METHOD OF CONFLICT RESOLUTION
  AMONG THE SUKU OF THE CONGO.
  JOURNAL OF CONFLICT RESOLUTION 5 MARCH 1961, PP 61-69
  057,108-01,

  POLOME EDGAR
  CULTURAL LANGUAGES AND CONTACT VERNACULARS IN THE REPUBLIC
  OF THE CONGO.
  TEXAS STUDIES IN LITERATURE AND LANGUAGE, 1963
  108-01,

  MAESEN ALBERT
  UMBANGU, ART DU CONGO AU MUSEE ROYAL DU CONGO BELGE
  (UMBANGU, CONGO ART IN THE ROYAL MUSEUM OF THE BELGIAN
  CONGO).
  BRUXELLES, MUSEE ROYAL DE L'AFRIQUE CENTRALE, 1960
  014,108-01,

  TURNBULL COLIN M
  THE FOREST PEOPLE
  NEW YORK, SIMON AND SCHUSTER, 1961
  108-01,

  TURNBULL COLIN M
  WAYWARD SERVANTS, THE TWO WORLDS OF THE AFRICAN PYGMIES
  NEW YORK, NATIONAL HISTORY PRESS, DIST. BY DOUBLEDAY, 1965
  108-01,

108-02
  MOREL E D

RED RUBBER-THE STORY OF THE RUBBER SLAVE TRADE FLOURISHING
ON THE CONGO IN THE YEAR OF GRACE 1906
LONDON, FISHER UNWIN, 1906
035,108-02,

108-02
VANSINA JAN
KINGDOMS OF THE SAVANNA.
MADISON, UNIVERSITY OF WISCONSIN, 1968
025,108-02,

ACHERSON NEAL
THE KING INCORPORATED, LEOPOLD II IN THE AGE OF TRUSTS
NEW YORK, DOUBLEDAY, 1964
033,108-02,

ANSTEY ROGER T
BRITAIN IN THE CONGO IN THE 19TH CENTURY.
OXFORD, CLARENDON PRESS, 1962
033,108-02,

ANSTEY ROGER T
KING LEOPOLD'S LEGACY-- THE CONGO UNDER BELGIAN RULE.
LONDON, OXFORD UNIVERSITY PRESS, 1966
033,108-02,

RYCKMANS PIERRE
BELGIAN COLONIALISM .
IN PHILIP Q QUIGG (ED), AFRICA, NEW YORK, PRAEGER, 1964,
PP 71-83; ALSO FOREIGN AFFAIRS 34 1955 PP 89-101
035,108-02,

SLADE RUTH
KING LEOPOLD'S CONGO.
LONDON, OXFORD UNIVERSITY PRESS, 1962
035,108-02,

GIDE ANDRE
VOYAGE AU CONGO (VOYAGE TO THE CONGO).
PARIS, GALLIMARD, 1929
035,108-02,

VANSINA JAN
NOTES SUR L'ORIGINE DU ROYAUME DE KONGO (NOTES ON THE
ORIGIN OF THE KINGDOM OF KONGO).
JOURNAL OF AFRICAN HISTORY 4 1963 PP 33-38
025,108-02,

108-03
ANDERSSON EFRIAM
MESSIANIC POPULAR MOVEMENTS IN THE LOWER CONGO.
UPSALA, ALMQUIST AND WIKSELL, 1958
(STUDIA ETHNOGRAPHICA UPSALIENSIA, 14)
051,108-03,

DOUGLAS MARY
THE LELE--RESISTANCE TO CHANGE.
IN BOHANNAN AND DALTON (EDS), MARKETS IN AFRICA, DOUBLEDAY,
1965
010,108-03,

108-03
   FABIAN JOHANNES
   CHARISMA AND CULTURAL CHANGE-THE CASE OF THE JAMAA MOVEMENT
   IN KATANGA(CONGO REPUBLIC)
   COMPARATIVE STUDIES IN SOCIETY AND HISTORY 11 1969 PP155-173
   051,108-03,

   FEHDERAU HAROLD W
   KIMBANGUISM-- PROPHETIC CHRISTIANITY IN THE CONGO.
   PRACTICAL ANTHROPOLOGY 9 1962 PP 157-178
   051,108-03,

   KNAPEN M TH
   SOME RESULTS OF AN ENQUIRY INTO THE INFLUENCE OF CHILD-
   TRAINING ON THE DEVELOPMENT OF PERSONALITY IN A BACINGO
   SOCIETY (BELGIAN CONGO).
   JOURNAL OF SOCIAL PSYCHOLOGY 47 1958 PP 223-229
   040,108-03,

   LEBLANC MARIA
   ACCULTURATION OF ATTITUDE AND PERSONALITY AMONG KATANGESE
   WOMEN.
   JOURNAL OF SOCIAL PSYCHOLOGY 47 1958 PP 257-264
   041,108-03,

   ROTBERG ROBERT I
   PLYMOUTH BRETHREN AND THE OCCUPATION OF KATANGA 1886-1907.
   JOURNAL OF AFRICAN HISTORY 5 1964 PP 285-297
   050,108-03,

   SLADE RUTH
   ENGLISH SPEAKING MISSIONS IN THE CONGO INDEPENDENT STATE--
   1878-1908.
   BRUXELLES, ACADEMIE ROYALE DES SCIENCES COLONIALES,1959
   050,108-03,

   CHOME JULES
   LA PASSION DE SIMON KIMBANGU 1921-1951 (THE PASSION OF
   SIMON KIMBANGU 1921-1951).
   BRUXELLES, AMIS DE PRESENCE AFRICAINE, 1959
   051,108-03,

   CEULEMANS P
   INTRODUCTION DE L INFLUENCE DE L ISLAM AU CONGO.
   IN LEWIS, ISLAM IN TROPICAL AFRICA, LONDON, OXFORD UNIVERSIT
   PRESS, 1966, P. 174-192
   108-03,

   MULAGO VINCENT   THEUWS T
   AUTOUR DU MOUVEMENT DE LA JAMAA.
   LEOPOLDVILLE, CENTRE D'ETUDES PASTORALES, 1960
   108-03,

108-04
   LUMUMBA PATRICE
   CONGO, MY COUNTRY.
   NEW YORK, PRAEGER PUBLISHERS, 1962
   060,108-04,

LUMUMBA PATRICE
RESUME DE LA CONFERENCE DONEE LE 13 AVRIL 1958 AUX MEMBRES
DE LA FEDERATION DES BATETELA.
LEOPOLDVILLE, RONEOTYPE, 1958
108-04,

108-04
SKURNIK W A E
AFRICAN POLITICAL THOUGHT--LUMUMBA, NKRUMAH, AND TOURE.
DENVER, COLORADO, INTERNATIONAL UNIVERSITY BOOKSELLERS, INC.
   1968
060,108-04,114-04,115-04,

VAN LIERDE JEAN
LA PENSEE POLITIQUE DE PATRICE LUMUMBA.   (THE POLITICAL
THOUGHT OF PATRICE LUMUMBA).
PARIS, PRESENCE AFRICAINE, 1963
060,108-04,

KALONJI ALBERT D
MA LUTTE AU KASAI, POUR LA VERITE AU SERVICE DE LA JUSTICE.
BARCELONA, C.A.G.S.A., 1964
108-04,

KANZA THOMAS
LE CONGO A LA VEILLE DE SON INDEPENDANCE OU PROPOS D UN
CONGOLAIS DESILLUSIONNE.
BRUXELLES, LES AMIS DE PRESENCE AFRICAINE, 1959
108-04,

KANZA THOMAS
PROPOS D UN CONGOLAIS NAIF--DISCOURS SUR LA VOCATION
COLONIALE DANS L'AFRIQUE DE DEMAIN.
BRUXELLES, LES AMIS DE PRESENCE AFRICAINE, 1959, P. 43
108-04,

KASAVUBU JOSEPH
MESSAGE ADRESSE A LA NATION PAR LE PRESIDENT DE LA
REPUBLIQUE.
LEOPOLDVILLE, IMP. DE LA REPUBLIQUE DU CONGO, 1962
108-04,

LUMUMBA PATRICE
LE CONGO, TERRE D'AVENIR EST-IL MENACE.
BRUXELLES, OFFICE DE PUBLICITE, 1961
108-04,

LUMUMBA PATRICE
LA PENSEE POLITIQUE DE PATRICE LUMUMBA--PREFACE DE JEAN-PAUL
SARTRE--TEXTES RECUEILLIS ET PRESENTES PAR JEAN VAN LIERDE.
PARIS, PRESENCE AFRICAINE, XLV, 1963
108-04,

LUMUMBA PATRICE
LA VERITE SUR LE CRIME ODIEUX DES COLONIALISTES.
MOSCOW, LES EDITIONS EN LANGUES ETRANGERES, 1961
108-04,

LUMUMBA PATRICE
PROPOS DE M PATRICE LUMUMBA, PREMIER MINISTRE DE LA

REPUBLIQUE DU CONGO.
BRUXELLES, COMMISSION DE COORDINATION, 1965
108-04,

108-04
TSHOMBE MOISE
BILAN DE DEUX ANS D'INDEPENDANCE--RAPPORT SUR LES
REALISATIONS DE GOUVERNEMENT KATANGAIS DE 1960-1962--
DISCOURS PRONONCE A L'ASSEMBLEE NATIONALE, LE 7 SEPTEMBRE
1962.
ELISABETHVILLE, SECRETARIAT D'ETAT A L'INFORMATION, SERVICE
DE EDUCATION DE LA MASSE, 1962
108-04,

TSHOMBE MOISE
QUINZE MOIS DE GOVERNEMENT DE CONGO.
PARIS, ED. DE LA TABLE RONDE, 1966
108-04,

108-05
PONS VALDO
STANLEYVILLE-AN AFRICAN URBAN COMMUNITY UNDER BELGIAN
ADMINISTRATION
NEW YORK, OXFORD UNIVERSITY PRESS, 1969
046,108-05,

FORTHOME G
MARRIAGE ET INDUSTRIALISATION-- EVOLUTION DE LA MENTALITE
DANS UNE CITE DE TRAVAILLEURS D ELISABETHVILLE (MARRIAGE
AND INDUSTRIALIZATION-- EMERGENCE OF THE MENTALITY IN A
WORKER'S DOMAIN OF ELISABETHVILLE).
LIEGE, H VALLIANT-CARMANNE, 1957
047,108-05,

ANONYMOUS
ZAIRE.
SPECIAL EDITION ON LEOPOLDVILLE, JUNE, 1956
108-05,

BAECK LOUIS
LEOPOLDVILLE--PHENOMENE URBAIN AFRICAIN.
ZAIRE, X, 1956.
108-05,

ECONOMIC COMMISSION FOR AFRICA
LEOPOLDVILLE AND LAGOS--COMPARATIVE STUDY OF CONDITIONS IN
1960.
IN GERALD BREESE (ED), THE CITY IN NEWLY DEVELOPING
COUNTRIES, PRENTICE-HALL, NEW JERSEY, 1969
108-05,128-05,

PONS VALDO
CHANGING SIGNIFICANCE OF ETHNIC AFFILIATIONS AND OF
WESTERNIZATION IN THE AFRICA SETTLEMENT PATTERNS IN
STANLEYVILLE.
IN SOCIAL IMPLICATIONS OF INDUSTRIALIZATION AND URBANIZATION
IN SOUTH OF THE SAHARA, PARIS, UNESCO, 1956
108-05,

PONS VALDO

THE GROWTH OF STANLEYVILLE AND THE COMPOSITION OF ITS
AFRICAN POPULATION.
IN SOCIAL IMPLICATIONS OF INDUSTRIALIZATION AND URBANIZATION
IN AFRICA SOUTH OF THE SAHARA, PARIS,UNESCO, 1956
108-05,

108-06
MAZRUI ALI A
EDMUND BURKE AND REFLECTIONS ON THE REVOLUTION IN THE CONGO.
IN ON HEROES AND UHURU-WORSHIP, LONDON, LONGMANS, 1967
064,108-06,

BRAUSCH GEORGES
BELGIAN ADMINISTRATION IN THE CONGO.
LONDON, OXFORD UNIVERSITY PRESS, 1961
035,108-06,

BUSTIN EDOUARD
THE QUEST FOR POLITICAL STABILITY IN THE CONGO--
SOLDIERS, BUREAUCRATS AND POLITICIANS.
IN HERBERT J SPIRO, ED., AFRICA THE PRIMACY OF POLITICS,
NEW YORK, RANDOM HOUSE, 1966, PP 16-48
064,108-06,

CROWLEY DANIEL J
POLITICS AND TRIBALISM IN THE KATANGA.
WESTERN POLITICAL QUARTERLY 16 MAY 1963 PP 68-78
007,108-06,

LEGUM COLIN
CONGO DISASTER.
HARMONDSWORTH, PENGUIN, 1961
064,108-06,

LEMARCHAND RENE
THE BASES OF NATIONALISM AMONG THE BAKONGO.
AFRICA 31 OCTOBER 1961 PP 344-354
055,108-06,

LEMARCHAND RENE
THE LIMITS OF SELF-DETERMINATION-- THE CASE OF THE KATANGA
SECESSION.
AMERICAN POLITICAL SCIENCE REVIEW 56 JUNE 1962 PP 404-416
059,108-06,

LIBOIS JULES G
KATANGA SECESSION.
MADISON, UNIVERSITY OF WISCONSIN PRESS, 1966
057,059,108-06,

O'BRIEN CONNOR C
TO KATANGA AND BACK--A U.N. CASE HISTORY.
NEW YORK, SIMON AND SCHUSTER, 1962
098,108-06,

REYNER ANTHONY S
THE REPUBLIC OF THE CONGO-- DEVELOPMENT OF ITS INTERNATIONAL
BOUNDARIES.
PITTSBURGH, DUQUESNE UNIVERSITY PRESS, 1961, AFRICAN REPRINT
SERIES, 9

059,108-06,

108-06
VERHAEGEN BENOIT
REBELLIONS AU CONGO. REBELLIONS OF THE CONGO.
BRUSSELS,CENTRE DE RECHERCHE ET D'INFORMATION SOCIO-
POLITIQUES,1 1966
064,108-06,

WILLAME JEAN-CLAUDE
MILITARY INTERVENTION IN THE CONGO.
AFRICA REPORT 11 NOVEMBER 1966 PP 41-45
064,108-06,

YOUNG CRAWFORD
THE CONGO REBELLION.
AFRICA REPORT 10 APRIL 1965 PP 6-11
064,081,108-06,

BIEBUYCK DANIEL   DOUGLAS MARY
CONGO-TRIBES AND PARTIES.
LONDON, ROYAL ANTHROPOLOGICAL INSTITUTE, 1961
108-06,

LEMARCHAND RENE
CONGO.
IN COLEMAN, J.S. AND ROSBERG, C.G. (EDS), POLITICAL PARTIES
AND NATIONAL INTEGRATION IN TROPICAL AFRICA, LOS ANGELES,
UNIVERSITY OF CALIFORNIA PRESS, 1964
108-06,

POLOME EDGAR
THE CHOICE OF OFFICIAL LANGUAGES IN THE DEMOCRATIC REPUBLIC
OF THE CONGO.
IN JOSHUA A. FISHMAN, CHARLES A. FERGUSON AND JYOTIRINDRA
DAS GUPTA (EDS), LANGUAGE PROBLEMS OF DEVELOPING NATIONS,
NEW YORK, JOHN WILEY AND SONS, INC., 1968
108-06,

108-07
YOUNG CRAWFORD
POLITICS IN THE CONGO--DECOLONIZATION AND INDEPENDENCE.
PRINCETON, NEW JERSEY, PRINCETON UNIVERSITY PRESS, 1965
054,061,081,108-07,

LEMARCHAND RENE
POLITICAL AWAKENING IN THE BELGIAN CONGO.
BERKELEY UNIVERSITY OF CALIFORNIA PRESS 1964
055,108-07,

WEISS HERBERT
POLITICAL PROTEST IN THE CONGO--THE PARTI SOLIDAIRE AFRICAIN
DURING THE INDEPENDENCE STRUGGLE.
PRINCETON, PRINCETON UNIVERSITY PRESS, 1967
061,108-07,

ASSOCIATION DES ANCIENS ETUDIANTS DE L'INUTOM
L'EVOLUTION POLITIQUE DU CONGO BELGE ET LES AUTORITES
INDIGENES (POLITICAL EVOLUTION OF THE BELGIAN CONGO AND THE
NATIVE AUTHORITIES).

PROBLEMS DE L'AFRIQUE CENTRALE 13 1959 PP 3-77
035,108-07,

108-07
  BUSTIN EDOUARD
  CONGO.
  IN G.M. CARTER (ED), FIVE AFRICAN STATES--RESPONSES TO
  DIVERSITY, ITHACA, CORNELL UNIVERSITY PRESS, 1963
  108-07,

  C R I S P
  CONGO--POLITICAL DOCUMENTS OF A DEVELOPING NATION.
  PRINCETON, PRINCETON UNIVERSITY PRESS, 1966
  108-07,

  C R I S P
  CONGO 1965--POLITICAL DOCUMENTS OF A DEVELOPING NATION.
  PRINCETON, PRINCETON UNIVERSITY PRESS, 1967
  108-07,

  HOSKYNS CATHERINE
  THE CONGO SINCE INDEPENDENCE.
  LONDON, OXFORD UNIVERSITY PRESS, 1965
  108-07,

108-08
  MIRACLE MARVIN P
  AGRICULTURE IN THE CONGO BASIN--TRADITION AND CHANGE IN
  AFRICAN RURAL ECONOMIES.
  MADISON, UNIVERSITY OF WISCONSIN PRESS, 1967
  070,108-08,

  LACROIX J L
  INDUSTRIALISATION AU CONGO-LA TRANFORMATION DES STRUCTURES
  ECONOMIQUE
  PARIS, EDITIONS MOUTON, 1967
  071,108-08,

108-09
  LEFEVER ERNEST W
  UNCERTAIN MANDATE-- POLITICS OF THE UN CONGO OPERATION.
  BALTIMORE, JOHNS HOPKINS UNIVERSITY PRESS, 1967
  079,081,108-09,

108-10
  BOLAMBA A R
  ETUDES SOCIALES--LES PROBLEMES DE L EVOLUTION DE LA FEMME
  NOIRE.
  ELIZABETHVILLE, ED. DE L'ESSOR DU CONGO, 1949, P. 171
  108-10,

  BOLAMBA A R
  PREMIERS ESSAIS--POEMES--PREFACE D'OLIVIER DE BOUVEIGNES
  (FIRST ESSAYS--POEMS--PREFACE D'OLIVER DE BOVEIGNES).
  ELIZABETHVILLE, ED. DE L ESSOR DU CONGO, 1947
  108-10,

108-12
  HOSKYNS CATHERINE
  SOURCES FOR A STUDY OF THE CONGO SINCE INDEPENDENCE.

JOURNAL OF MODERN AFRICAN STUDIES, VOL. 1, NO. 3, 1963
108-12,

109. DAHOMEY

109-01
   CARROLL KEVIN
   YORUBA RELIGIOUS SCULPTURE-- PAGAN AND CHRISTIAN SCULPTURE
   IN NIGERIA AND DAHOMEY.
   NEW YORK, PRAEGER, 1967
   014,109-01,128-01,

   ARGYLE W J
   THE FON OF DAHOMEY-- A HISTORY AND ETHNOGRAPHY OF
   OF THE OLD KINGDOM.
   OXFORD, CLARENDON PRESS, 1966
   026,109-01,

   HERSKOVITS MELVILLE J   HERSKOVITS FRANCES S
   DAHOMEAN NARRATIVE-A CROSS CULTURAL ANALYSIS
   EVANSTON, NORTHWESTERN UNIVERSITY PRESS, 1958
   012,109-01,

   HIMMELHEBER HANS
   SCULPTORS AND SCULPTURES OF THE DAN.
   IN LALAGE BOWN AND MICHAEL CROWDER (EDS.), PROCEEDINGS OF
   THE FIRST INTERNATIONAL CONGRESS OF AFRICANISTS, ACCRA,
   1962, LONDON . LONGMANS, 1964, PP 243-255
   014,109-01,

   GOVERNMENT OF FRANCE
   COUTUMIERS JURIDIQUES DE L'AFRIQUE OCCIDENTALE FRANCAISE--
   MAURITANIE, NIGER, COTE D'IVOIRE, DAHOMEY, GUINEE FRANCAISE
   (FRENCH WEST AFRICAN JURIDIC CUSTOMS-- MAURITANIA, NIGER
   IVORY COAST, DAHOMEY, FRENCH GUINEA) .
   PARIS, LIBRAIRIE LAROSE, 1939 VOL3
   066,109-01,115-01,116-01,124-01,127-01,

   HIMMELHEBER HANS
   LE SYSTEME DE LA RELIGION DES DAN (THE RELIGIOUS SYSTEM OF
   THE DAN).
   IN RENCONTRES INTERNATIONALES DE ROUAKE, LES RELIGIONS
   AFRICAINES TRADITIONNELLES, PARIS, EDITIONS DU SEUIL, 1965,
   PP 75-96
   013,109-01,

   TIDJANI A S
   NOTES SUR LE MARIAGE AU DAHOMEY.
   PORTO-NOVO, IFAN-DAHOMEY, 1951
   109-01,

109-02
   AKINJOGBIN I A
   DAHOMEY AND ITS NEIGHBORS, 1708-1818.
   NEW YORK AND LONDON, CAMBRIDGE UNIVERSITY PRESS, 1967

026,109-02,

109-02
   HERSKOVITS MELVILLE J
   DAHOMEY-- AN ANCIENT WEST AFRICAN KINGDOM.
   EVANSTON,NORTHWESTERN UNIVERSITY PRESS, 1967
   013,026,109-02,

   NEWBURY COLIN W
   AN EARLY ENQUIRY INTO SLAVERY AND CAPTIVITY IN DAHOMEY.
   ZAIRE 14 1960 PP 53-67
   028,109-02,

   GEAY J
   ORIGINE, FORMATION ET HISTOIRE DU ROYAUME DE PORTO-NOVO
   (THE ORIGIN, FORMATION AND HISTORY OF THE KINGDOM OF
   PORTO-NOVO).
   BULLETIN DU COMITE D'ETUDES HISTORIQUES ET SCIENTIFIQUES DE
   L'AFRIQUE OCCIDENTALE FRANCAISE 7 1924 PP 619-634
   026,109-02,

   RAMIN JEAN CHARLES KOUBETTI V   GUILHEM MARCEL
   HISTOIRE DU DAHOMEY.
   PARIS, L'AFRIQUE-LE MONDE, COURS MOYEN, LIGEL, 1964
   109-02,

109-04
   TARDITS M CLAUDE
   PARENTE ET CLASSE SOCIALE A PORTO-NOVO, DAHOMEY.
   IN LLOYD, THE NEW ELITES OF TROPICAL AFRICA, LONDON, OXFORD
   UNIVERSITY PRESS, 1966, P. 184-198
   109-04,

   TEVOEDJRE ALBERT
   CONTRIBUTION A UNE SYNTHESE SUR LE PROBLEME DE LA FORMATION
   DES CADRES AFRICAINS EN VUE DE LA CROISSANCE ECONOMIQUE.
   PARIS, DILOUTREMER, 1965
   109-04,

   TEVOEDJRE ALBERT
   L'AFRIQUE REVOLTEE.
   PARIS, PRESENCE AFRICAINE, 1958.
   109-04,

109-05
   LOMBARD J
   COTONOU, VILLE AFRICAINE.
   ETUDES DAHOMEENES, 10, 1953
   109-05,

109-06
   LEMARCHAND RENE
   DAHOMEY--COUP WITHIN A COUP.
   AFRICA REPORT, JUNE, 1968, P. 46
   064,109-06,

109-07
   MORGENTHAU RUTH SCHACHTER
   POLITICAL PARTIES IN FRENCH-SPEAKING WEST AFRICA.
   OXFORD, OXFORD UNIVERSITY PRESS, 1964

055,058,061,109-07,123-07,130-07,

109-07
    THOMPSON VIRGINIA
    DAHOMEY.
    IN G.M. CARTER (ED) FIVE AFRICAN STATES--RESPONSES TO
    DIVERSITY, ITHACA, CORNELL UNIVERSITY PRESS, 1963
    109-07,

109-11
    LUSIGNAN GUY DE
    FRENCH-SPEAKING AFRICA SINCE INDEPENDENCE.
    NEW YORK, PRAEGER PUBLISHERS, 1969
    056,061,104-11,105-11,106-11,107-11,109-11,112-11,
    115-11,116-11,123-11,137-11,141-11,

110. ETHIOPIA

110-01
    BIDDER IRMGAARD
    LALIBELA-- THE MONOLITHIC CHURCHES OF ETHIOPIA.
    NEW YORK, PRAEGER, 1960
    092,110-01,

    PAULOS TSADUA ABBA
    FETHA NEGAST--THE LAW OF THE KINGS.
    ADDIS ABABA, INTERNATIONAL UNIVERSITY BOOKSELLERS,INC., 1968
    066,110-01,

    POWNE MICHAEL
    ETHIOPIAN MUSIC--AN INTRODUCTION.
    LONDON, OXFORD UNIVERSITY PRESS, 1968
    015,110-01,

    CERULLI ERNESTA
    PEOPLES OF SOUTH-WEST ETHIOPIA AND ITS BORDERLAND
    LONDON, INTERNATIONAL AFRICAN INSTITUTE, 1956
    110-01,

    HUNTINGFORD G W B
    THE GALLA OF ETHIOPIA-THE KINGDOMS OF KAFA AND JANJERS
    LONDON, INTERNATIONAL AFRICAN INSTITUTE, 1956
    110-01,

    LIPSKY GEORGE ARTHUR
    ETHIOPIA--ITS PEOPLE, ITS SOCIETY, ITS CULTURE.
    NEW HAVEN, HRAF PRESS, 1962
    110-01,

    SIMOONS FREDERICK J
    NORTHWEST ETHIOPIA,PEOPLES AND ECONOMY
    MADISON,UNIVERSITY OF WISCONSIN PRESS, 1960
    110-01,

110-02

PANKHURST RICHARD
ITALIAN SETTLEMENT POLICY IN ERITREA AND ITS REPERCUSSIONS,
1889-1894.
IN JEFFREY BUTLER (ED), BOSTON UNIVERSITY PAPERS IN AFRICAN
HISTORY VOL I, BOSTON, BOSTON UNIVERSITY PRESS, 1964, PP 119-
154
033,110-02,

110-02
LEROY JULES
ETHIOPIAN PAINTING--IN THE LATE MIDDLE AGES AND DURING THE
GONDAR DYNASTY.
NEW YORK, PRAEGER, 1967
014,110-02,

LEWIS HERBERT S
A GALLA MONARCHY-- JIMMA ABBA JIFAR, ETHIOPIA, 1830-1932.
MADISON UNIVERSITY OF WISCONSIN PRESS 1965
009,110-02,

PAEZ PERO
THE GLORIOS VICTORIES OF AMDA SEYON, KING OF ETHIOPIA,
TOGETHER WITH THE HISTORY OF THE EMPEROR ADN CEON OTHERWISE
CALLED GABRA MAZCAL.
LONDON, OXFORD UNIVERSITY PRESS, 1965
012,110-02,

PANKHURST RICHARD   ED
THE ETHIOPIAN ROYAL CHRONICLES.
LONDON, OXFORD UNIVERSITY PRESS, 1967
012,110-02,

SANDERSON G N
THE FOREIGN POLICY OF THE NEGUS MENELIK, 1896-1898.
JOURNAL OF AFRICAN HISTORY 5 1964 PP 87-98
034,110-02,

ULLENDORFF EDWARD
ETHIOPIA AND THE BIBLE.
LONDON, OXFORD UNIVERSITY PRESS, 1968
050,110-02,

JONES ARNOLD   MARTIN HUGH   MONROE ELIZABETH
A HISTORY OF ETHIOPIA
OXFORD, CLARENDON PRESS, 1955, SECOND EDITION
110-02;

110-03
ALAPINI M
LE CULTE DE VODOUN ET DE ORICHA CHEZ LES FON ET LES NAGO
DU DAHOMEY (THE CULT OF VODOUN AND ORICHA AMONG THE FON AND
THE NAGO OF DAHOMEY).
IN COLLOQUE SUR LES RELIGIONS, ABIDJAN, APRIL, 1961, PARIS,
PRESENCE AFRICAINE, 1962, PP 91-96
051,110-03,

110-04
LEVINE DONALD N
CLASS CONSCIOUSNESS AND CLASS SOLIDARITY IN THE NEW ETHIOPIA
ELITES.

IN LLOYD, THE NEW ELITES OF TROPICAL AFRICA, LONDON, OXFORD
UNIVERSITY PRESS, 1966, P. 212-327
110-04,

110-04
   MOSLEY LEONARD
   HAILE SELASSIE-THE CONQUERING LION
   ENGLEWOOD CLIFFS,N.J,PRENTICE-HALL,1965
   110-04,

110-05
   HORVATH RONALD J
   THE WANDERING CAPITALS OF ETHIOPIA.
   JOURNAL OF AFRICAN HISTORY, X, 2, 1969, PP. 205-219
   045,110-05,

   PANKHURST RICHARD
   MENELIK AND THE FOUNDATION OF ADDIS ABABA.
   JOURNAL OF AFRICAN HISTORY 2 1961 PP 103-117
   045,110-05,

   DERUS JACQUES
   ADDIS ABABA, GENESE D UN CAPITALE IMPERIALE.
   IN REVUE BELGE DE GEOGRAPHIE, 88, 3, APRIL 1965
   110-05,

110-06
   CLAPHAM CHRISTOPHER
   THE ETHIOPIAN COUP D'ETAT OF DECEMBER 1960.
   THE JOURNAL OF MODERN AFRICAN STUDIES, VOL. 6, NO. 4, 1968,
   PP. 495-507
   064,110-06,

   DEMOZ ABRAHAM
   AMHARIC FOR MODERN USE.
   JOURNAL OF THE FACULTY OF EDUCATION, HAILE SELASSIE UNIVER-
   SITY, 196
   110-06,

   LOWENSTEIN STEVEN
   MATERIALS FOR THE STUDY OF THE PENAL LAW OF ETHIOPIA.
   EASTERN AFRICA, OXFORD UNIVERSITY PRESS, 1965
   067,110-06,

   PANKHURST ESTELLE
   ETHIOPIA AND ERITREA-- LAST PHASE OF THE REUNION STRUGGLE
   1941-1952.
   WOODFORD GREEN, LALIBELA HOUSE 1953
   059,110-06,

   REDDEN KENNETH R
   THE LEGAL SYSTEM OF ETHIOPIA.
   CHARLOTTESVILLE, VIRGINIA, THE MICHIE COMPANY, 1968
   066,110-06,

110-07
   HESS ROBERT L   LOEWENBERG GERHARD
   THE ETHIOPIAN NO-PARTY STATE--A NOTE ON THE FUNCTIONS OF
   POLITICAL PARTIES IN DEVELOPING STATES.
   JASON L. FINKLE AND RICHARD W. GABLE (EDS), POLITICAL

DEVELOPMENT AND SOCIAL CHANGE, JOHN WILEY AND SONS, INC.,
NEW YORK, 1966, PP. 530-535
061,110-07,

110-07
   LEVINE DONALD N
   ETHIOPIA--IDENTITY, AUTHORITY, AND REALISM.
   LUCIAN W. PYE AND SIDNEY VERBA (EDS), POLITICAL CULTURE AND
   POLITICAL DEVELOPMENT, PRINCETON, NEW JERSEY, PRINCETON
   UNIVERSITY PRESS, 1965
   061,110-07,

   GREENFIELD RICHARD
   ETHIOPIA--A NEW POLITICAL HISTORY.
   LONDON, PALL MALL, 1967
   034,110-07,

   PERHAM MARGERY
   THE GOVERNMENT OF ETHIOPIA.
   LONDON, FABER, 1948; 2D EDITION, EVANSTON, NORTHWESTERN
   UNIVERSITY PRESS, 1969
   110-07,

   TREVASKIS G K N
   ERITREA-A COLONY IN TRANSITION 1941-1952
   LONDON, OXFORD, FOR ROYAL INSTITUTE OF INTERNATIONAL
   AFFAIRS, 1960
   110-07,

110-08
   UNITED NATIONS
   INDUSTRIAL DEVELOPMENT IN AFRICA
   NEW YORK, UNITED NATIONS, 1967
   071,104-08,110-08,117-08,127-08,134-08,140-08,142-08,

   MANN H S
   LAND TENURE IN CHORE.
   ADDIS ABABA, INSTITUTE OF ETHIOPIAN STUDIES, HAILE
   SELASSIE UNIVERSITY, WITH OXFORD UNIVERSITY PRESS, 1965
   070,110-08,

   PANKHURST RICHARD
   TRANSPORTATION AND COMMUNICATIONS IN ETHIOPIA 1835-1935.
   JOURNAL OF TRANSPORT HISTORY 5 1961 PP 69-88, 6 1962 PP166-
   181, 233-254
   048,110-08,

110-11
   LEVINE DONALD N
   WAX AND GOLD--TRADITION AND INNOVATION IN ETHIOPIAN CULTURE.
   CHICAGO, UNIVERSITY OF CHICAGO PRESS, 1966
   110-11,

   PANKHURST ESTELLE
   ETHIOPIA--A CULTURAL HISTORY.
   ESSEX, LALEBELA HOUSE, 1955
   110-11,

110-12
   AFRICAN BIBLIO   CENTER

ETHIOPIA, 1950-1962--A SELECT BIBLIOGRAPHY.
WASHINGTON, AFRICAN BIBLIOGRAPHIC CENTER, 1963
110-12,

110-12
   DELANEY ANNETTE
   ETHIOPIA SURVEY--A SELECTED BIBLIOGRAPHY.
   WASHINGTON, AFRICAN BIBLIOGRAPHIC CENTER, 1964
   110-12,

   MATTHEW DANIEL G   COMP
   A CURRENT BIBLIOGRAPHY ON ETHIOPIAN AFFIARS--A SELECT
   BIBLIOGRAPHY FROM 1950-1964.
   WASHINGTON, AFRICAN BIBLIOGRAPHIC CENTER, 1965
   110-12,

   WRIGHT STEPHEN G
   A BIBLIOGRAPHY OF PRE-1963 PRINTED MATERIAL PRODUCED IN
   ETHIOPIA.
   ADDIS ABABA, INSTITUTE OF ETHIOPIAN STUDIES, HAILE SELASSIE
   I UNIVERSITY, 1964
   110-12,

111. EQUATORIAL GUINEA

111-01
   PELISSIER RENE
   SPANISH GUINEA-- AN INTRODUCTION.
   RACE 6 2 OCTOBER 1964 PP 117-128
   087, 111-01,

111-07
   PELISSIER RENE
   UNCERTAINTIES IN SPANISH GUINEA
   AFRICA REPORT MARCH 1968 PP 16-18
   111-07,

   ANONYMOUS
   AFRICAN POLITICAL PARTIES IN EQUATORIAL GUINEA 1968.
   AFRICA REPORT, MARCH 18, 1968
   061,111-07,

112. GABON

112-01
   RAPONDA-WALKER ANDRE   SILLANS ROGER
   RITES ET CROYANCES DES PEUPLES DU GABON, ESSAI SUR LES
   PRATIQUES RELIGIEUSES DE AUTREFOIS ET D'AUJORD'HUI.
   PARIS, PRESENCE AFRICAINE, 1962
   112-01,

112-02

DESCHAMPS HUBERT J
TRADITIONS ORALES ET ARCHIVES AU GABON-- CONTRIBUTION A
L'ETHNO-HISTOIRE (ORAL TRADITIONS AND ARCHIVES IN GABON--
CONTRIBUTION TO ETHNO-HISTORY).
PARIS L'HOMME D'OUTRE-MER 6 BERGER-LEVROULT 1962
099,112-02,

RAPONDA-WALKER ANDRE
NOTES D'HISTOIRE DU GABON.
MONTPELLIER, IMPRIMERIE CHARITE, 1960
112-02,

112-03

BALANDIER GEORGES
ASPECTS DE L'EVOLUTION SOCIALE CHEZ LES FANG
(ASPECTS OF SOCIAL EVOLUTION AMONG THE FANG).
CAHIERS INTERNATIONAUX DE SOCIOLOGIE 9 1950 PP 76-106
038,112-03,

BALANDIER GEORGES   PAUVERT J C
LES VILLAGES GABONAIS-- ASPECTS DEMOGRAPHIQUES, ECONOMIQUES
SOCIOLOGIQUES, PROJETS DE MODERNISATION (GABON VILLAGES--
DEMOGRAPHIC, ECONOMIC AND SOCIOLOGICAL ASPECTS, PROJECTS
OF MODERNIZATION).
BRAZZAVILLE, INSTITUT DES ETUDES CONTRFICAINES, 1952
070,112-03,

BALLARD JOHN A
EQUATORIAL AFRICA
IN KRITZECK AND LEWIS, PP 278-286
105-03,106-03,107-03,112-03,

112-04

AUBAME HILAIRE
RENAISSANCE GABONAISE, PROGRAMME ET REGROUPEMENT DES
VILLAGES.
BRAZZAVILLE, IMPRIMERIE OFFICIELLE, 1947
112-04,

112-06

ANONYMOUS
GABON-- PUTSCH OR COUP D'ETAT.
AFRICA REPORT 9 MARCH 1964 PP 12-15
064,112-06,

ANONYMOUS
COUP FOILED IN GABON.
WEST AFRICA FEBRUARY 22 1964 P 207
064,112-06,

WEINSTEIN BRIAN
GABON--NATION-BUILDING ON THE OGOOUE.
CAMBRIDGE, MASSACHUSETTS INSTITUTE OF TECHNOLOGY PRESS, 1966
048,057,112-06,

BALLARD JOHN A
FOUR EQUATORIAL STATES--THE CONGO, GABON, CENTRAL AFRICAN
REPUBLIC, CHAD.

IN GWENDOLEN M CARTER (ED.), NATIONAL UNITY AND REGIONALISM
IN EIGHT AFRICAN STATES, ITHACA, CORNELL UNIVERSITY PRESS,
1966, PP 231-329
105-06,106-06,107-06,112-06,

112-08
  HANCE WILLIAM A
  GABON AND ITS MAIN GATEWAYS-- LIBREVILLE AND PORT GENTIL.
  TIJDSCHRIFT VOOR ECONOMISHE EN SOCIALE GEOGRAFIE (AMSTERDAM)
  52STE JAARGANG NOVEMBER 1961 PP 286-295
  048,112-08,

  HILLING D
  THE CHANGING ECONOMY OF GABON--DEVELOPMENTS IN A NEW
  AFRICAN REPUBLIC.
  GEOGRAPHY, 48, 219, APRIL, 1963
  112-08,

112-09
  ROBSON PETER
  ECONOMIC INTEGRATION IN EQUATORIAL AFRICA CHAPTER 2.
  IN ARTHUR HAZLEWOOD, AFRICAN INTEGRATION AND DISINTEGRATION,
  LONDON, OXFORD UNIVERSITY PRESS, 1967, PP 27-69
  078,105-09,106-09,107-09,112-09,

112-10
  RAPONDA-WALKER ANDRE
  CONTES GABONAIS--NOUVELLE EDITION REVUE ET AUGMENTEE--
  ACCOMPAGNEE DE 47 COMPOSITIONS ORIGINALES DE ROGER L
  SILLANS.
  PARIS, PRESENCE AFRICAINE, 1967
  112-10,

112-11
  LUSIGNAN GUY DE
  FRENCH-SPEAKING AFRICA SINCE INDEPENDENCE.
  NEW YORK, PRAEGER PUBLISHERS, 1969
  056,061,104-11,105-11,106-11,107-11,109-11,112-11,
  115-11,116-11,123-11,137-11,141-11,

  CHARBONNIER FRANCOIS
  GABON, TERRE D AVENIR.
  PARIS, ENCYCLOPEDIE D'OUTRE-MER, 1957
  112-11,

  THOMPSON VIRGINIA   ADLOFF RICHARD
  THE EMERGING STATES OF FRENCH EQUATORIAL AFRICA.
  STANFORD, STANFORD UNIVERSITY PRESS, 1960
  105-11,107-11,112-11,106-11,

112-12
  WEINSTEIN BRIAN
  GABON--A BIBLIOGRAPHIC ESSAY.
  AFRICANA NEWSLETTER, VOL. 1, NOV. 4, 1963
  112-12,

  WITHERELL JULIAN T
  OFFICIAL PUBLICATIONS OF THE FRENCH EQUATORIAL AFRICA,
  FRENCH CAMEROUNS AND TOGO, 1949-1958.
  WASHINGTON, LIBRARY OF CONGRESS, AFRICAN SECTION, 1964

104-12,105-12,106-12,107-12,112-12,137-12,

113. GAMBIA

113-02
 GAILEY HARRY A
 A HISTORY OF THE GAMBIA.
 LONDON, ROUTLEDGE AND KEGAN PAUL, 1964
 113-02,

113-05
 VAN DER PLAS C O
 REPORT OF A SOCIO-ECONOMIC SURVEY OF BATHURST AND KOMBO ST
 MARY IN THE GAMBIA.
 NEW YORK, UNITED NATIONS, 1956
 113-05,

113-06
 RICE BERKELEY
 ENTER GAMBIA-- THE BIRTH OF AN IMPROBABLE NATION.
 BOSTON,HOUGHTON MIFFLIN,1967
 056,113-06,

113-08
 LITTLE KENNETH
 THE ORGANIZATION OF COMMUNAL FARMS IN THE GAMBIA.
 JOURNAL OF AFRICAN ADMINISTRATION 1 1949 PP 76-82
 070,113-08,

113-09
 ROBSON PETER
 PROBLEMS OF INTEGRATION BETWEEN SENEGAL AND
 GAMBIA CHAPTER 4.
 IN ARTHUR HAZLEWOOD, AFRICAN INTEGRATION AND DISINTEGRATION,
 LONDON, OXFORD UNIVERSITY PRESS, 1967, P   115-128
 078,113-09,130-09,

 ROBSON PETER
 THE PROBLEMS OF SENEGAMBIA.
 JOURNAL OF MODERN AFRICAN STUDIES 3 1965
 078,113-09,130-09,

113-12
 GAMBLE DAVID P
 BIBLIOGRAPHY OF THE GAMBIA.
 LONDON, N.P., 1958
 113-12,

 GAILEY HARRY A
 BIBLIOGRAPHIC ESSAYS--THE GAMBIA.
 AFRICAN NEWSLETTER, VOL. 2, NO. 1, 1964
 113-12,

114. GHANA

114-01

ABRAHAM W E
THE MIND OF AFRICA.
CHICAGO, UNIVERSITY OF CHICAGO PRESS, 1962 (LONDON,
WEIDENFELD AND NICOLSON)
040,060,091,099,114-01.

WILKS IVOR
ASHANTI GOVERNMENT, IN DARYLL FORDE AND P M KABERRY (EDS),
WEST AFRICAN KINGDOMS IN THE NINETEENTH CENTURY.
LONDON, OXFORD UNIVERSITY PRESS, 1967
026,038,114-01,

BARRINGTON KAYE
BRINGING UP CHILDREN IN GHANA.
LONDON, GEORGE ALLEN AND UNWIN, 1962
008,114-01,

BUSIA KOFI A
THE POSITION OF THE CHIEF IN THE MODERN POLITICAL SYSTEM OF
ASHANTI.
LONDON, OXFORD UNIVERSITY PRESS, 1951
061,099,114-01,

DANQUAH JOSEPH B
GOLD COAST-- AKAN LAWS AND CUSTOMS AND THE AKIM ABUAKWA
CONSTITUTION.
LONDON, ROUTLEDGE, 1928
066,114-01,

DANQUAH JOSEPH B
THE AKAN DOCTRINE OF GOD.
NEW YORK, HUMANITIES PRESS INC., 1968
099,114-01,

FIELD M J
SEARCH FOR SECURITY-- AN ETHNO-PSYCHIATRIC STUDY OF
RURAL GHANA.
EVANSTON, NORTHWESTERN UNIVERSITY PRESS, 1960; ALSO LONDON,
FABER AND FABER, 1960
040,114-01,

FORTES MEYER
THE WEB OF KINSHIP AMONG THE TALLENSI.
LONDON, OXFORD UNIVERSITY PRESS, 1949
008,114-01,

GOLDWATER ROBERT
SENUFO SCULPTURE FROM WEST AFRICA.
GREENWICH, CONNECTICUT, THE MUSEUM OF PRIMITIVE ART, 1964
014,114-01,

HAYFORD CASELY
GOLD COAST NATIVE INSTITUTIONS.

LONDON LONGMANS 1967
056,114-01,

114-01
LYSTAD MARY H
TRADITIONAL VALUES OF GHANAIAN CHILDREN.
AMERICAN ANTHROPOLOGIST 42 1960 PP 454-464
040,114-01,

LYSTAD ROBERT A
MARRIAGE AND KINSHIP AMONG THE ASHANTI AND THE AGNI--
A STUDY OF DIFFERENTIAL ACCULTURATION CHAPTER 10.
IN WILLIAM BASCOM AND MELVILLE HERSKOVITS, CONTINUTY AND
CHANGE IN AFRICAN CULTURES, CHICAGO, UNIVERSITY OF CHICAGO
PRESS, 1962, PP 187-204
008,114-01,

MCCALL DANIEL F
SLAVERY IN ASHANTI.
TRANS-ACTION, 1967
028,114-01,

MEYEROWITZ EVA L
THE AKAN OF GHANA-- THEIR ANCIENT BELIEFS.
LONDON, FABER, 1958
013,114-01,

OLLENNU NII AMAA
PRINCIPLES OF CUSTOMARY LAND LAW IN GHANA.
LONDON, SWEET AND MAXWELL, 1962
066,114-01,

RATTRAY ROBERT S
RELIGION AND ART IN ASHANTI.
LONDON, OXFORD UNIVERSITY PRESS, 1959
013,114-01,

RATTRAY ROBERT S
ASHANTI LAW AND CONSTITUTION.
OXFORD, CLARENDON PRESS, 1929
026,066,099,114-01,

SARBAH JOHN MENSAH
FANTI NATIONAL CONSTITUTION.
NEW YORK, HUMANITIES PRESS INC., 1968
066,114-01,

SARBAH JOHN MENSAH
FANTI CUSTOMARY LAWS.
NEW YORK, HUMANITIES PRESS INC., 1968
066,114-01,

WILKS IVOR
AKAMU AND OTUBLOHUM-- AN EIGHTEENTH CENTURY AKAN
MARRIAGE ARRANGEMENT.
AFRICA 29 1959 PP 391-404
026,114-01,

FORTES MEYER
THE DYNAMICS OF CLANSHIP AMONG THE TALLENSI.

LONDON, OXFORD UNIVERSITY PRESS, 1945
008, 114-01,

114-01
  ANONYMOUS
  1960 POPULATION CENSUS OF GHANA.
  SPECIAL REPORT E, TRIBES IN GHANA, CENSUS OFFICE ACCRA, 1964
  114-01,

  DANQUAH JOSEPH B
  THE CULTURE OF AKAN.
  AFRICA, 22, 1952, PP. 360-366
  114-01,

114-02
  FAGE JOHN D
  GHANA--A HISTORICAL INTERPRETATION.
  MADISON, UNIVERSITY OF WISCONSIN PRESS, 1959
  114-02,

  GOODY JACK
  ETHNOHISTORY AND THE AKAN OF GHANA.
  AFRICA 29 1959 PP 67-81
  026,114-02,

  AGYEMAN-DUAH J
  MAMPONG ASHANTI-- A TRADITIONAL HISTORY TO THE REIGN OF NANA
  SAFO KANTANKA.
  TRANSACTIONS OF THE HISTORICAL SOCIETY OF GHANA 4 1960
  PP 21-25
  026,114-02,

  BOWDICH THOMAS E
  MISSION FROM CAPE COAST CASTLE TO ASHANTEE WITH A
  STATISTICAL ACCOUNT OF THE KINGDOM AND GEOGRAPHICAL NOTICES
  OF OTHER PARTS OF THE INTERIOR OF AFRICA.
  LONDON, CASS, 1967
  026,114-02,

  BRAIMAH J A   GOODY J R
  SALAGA--THE STRUGGLE FOR POWER.
  LONDON, LONGMANS, GREEN AND COMPANY LIMITED, 1967
  026,114-02,

  CLARIDGE W WALTON
  A HISTORY OF THE GOLD COAST AND ASHANTI.
  LONDON, CASS, 1964
  026,114-02,

  DUPUIS JOSEPH
  JOURNAL OF A RESIDENCE IN ASHANTEE.
  LONDON, CASS, 1967
  026,114-02,

  LLOYD ALAN
  THE DRUMS OF KUMASI-- THE STORY OF THE ASHANTI WARS.
  LONDON, LONGMANS, 1964
  026,114-02,

  NATHAN MATHEW

THE GOLD COAST AT THE END OF THE SEVENTEENTH CENTURY UNDER
THE DANES AND THE DUTCH.
JOURNAL OF THE AFRICAN SOCIETY IV 1904 PP 1-32
027,114-02,

114-02
  PRESTAGE EDGAR
  THE ASHANTI QUESTION AND THE BRITISH-- EIGHTEENTH-CENTURY
  ORIGINS.
  THE JOURNAL OF AFRICAN HISTORY II 1961 PP 35-60
  033,114-32,
  033, 114-02,

  PRIESTLEY MARGARET WILKS IVOR
  THE ASHANTI KINGS IN THE EIGHTEENTH CENTURY-- A REVISED
  CHRONOLOGY.
  THE JOURNAL OF AFRICAN HISTORY 1 1960 PP 83-92
  026,114-02,

  TORDOFF WILLIAM
  THE ASHANTI CONFEDERACY.
  JOURNAL OF AFRICAN HISTORY 3 1962 PP 399-417
  026,114-02,

  TORDOFF WILLIAM
  THE EXILE AND THE REPATRIATION OF NANA PREMPEH 1 OF ASHANTI
  1896-1924.,
  TRANSACTIONS OF THE HISTORICAL SOCIETY OF GHANA 4 1960
  PP 33-58
  026,114-02,

  TORDOFF WILLIAM
  ASHANTI UNDER THE PREMPEHS, 1888-1935.
  LONDON, OXFORD UNIVERSITY PRESS, 1965
  026,114-02,

  WILKS IVOR
  THE RISE OF THE AKWAMU EMPIRE 1650-1710.
  TRANSACTIONS OF THE HISTORICAL SOCIETY OF GHANA 3 1957
  PP 99-136
  026,114-02,

  WILKS IVOR
  A NOTE ON THE TRADITIONAL HISTORY OF MAMPONG.
  TRANSACTIONS OF THE HISTORICAL SOCIETY OF GHANA 4 1960
  PP 26-29
  026,114-02,

  WILKS IVOR
  THE NORTHERN FACTOR IN ASHANTI HISTORY.
  LEGON, INSTITUTE OF AFRICAN STUDIES, UNIVERSITY COLLEGE OF
  GHANA, 1961
  026,114-02,

  COOMBS DOUGLAS
  THE GOLD COAST BRITAIN AND THE NETHERLANDS 1850-1874.
  LONDON, OXFORD UNIVERSITY PRESS, 1963
  027,114-02,

  DICKSON K B

A HISTORICAL GEOGRAPHY OF GHANA
CAMBRIDGE, UNIVERSITY PRESS, 1969
114-02,

114-02
    WARD W E F
    A HISTORY OF GHANA.
    LONDON, ALLEN AND UNWIN, 1966
    114-02,

114-03
    BERRY JACK
    THE MADINA PROJECT--SOCIOLINGUISTIC RESEARCH IN GHANA.
    IN GWENDOLEN CARTER AND ANN PADEN (EDS), EXPANDING HORIZONS
    IN AFRICAN STUDIES, EVANSTON, NORTHWESTERN UNIVERSITY PRESS,
    1969
    100,114-03,

    HARVEY WILLIAM B
    LAW AND SOCIAL CHANGE IN GHANA.
    PRINCETON, PRINCETON UNIVERSITY PRESS, 1966
    067,114-03,

    APTER DAVID E
    THE ROLE OF TRADITIONALISM IN THE POLITICAL
    MODERNIZATION OF GHANA AND UGANDA.
    WORLD POLITICS 13 OCT 1960 PP 45-68 ALSO WILLIAM J HANNA, ED,
    INDEPENDENT BLACK AFRICA, CHICAGO, RAND MCNALLY, 1964, PP
    254-277
    055,114-03,139-03,

    BROKENSHA DAVID
    SOCIAL CHANGE AT LARTEH, GHANA.
    LONDON, OXFORD UNIVERSITY PRESS, 1966
    038,114-03,

    CHRISTENSEN JAMES
    THE ADAPTIVE FUNCTIONS OF FANTI PRIESTHOOD CHAPTER 13.
    IN WILLIAM BASCOM AND MELVILLE HERSKOVITS, CONTINUTY AND
    CHANGE IN AFRICAN CULTURES, CHICAGO, UNIVERSITY OF CHICAGO
    PRESS, 1962, PP 238-256
    051,114-03,

    CURLE ADAM
    NATIONALISM AND HIGHER EDUCATION IN GHANA.
    UNIVERSITIES QUARTERLY 16 JUNE 1962 PP 229-242
    042,114-03,

    CURLE ADAM
    EDUCATIONAL PROBLEMS OF DEVELOPING SOCIETIES--WITH CASE
    STUDIES OF GHANA AND PAKISTAN.
    NEW YORK, PRAEGER PUBLISHERS, 1969
    043,114-03,

    DZOBO N K
    THE BRAIN CRISIS IN THE TEACHING PROFESSION IN GHANA.
    IN COLIN LEGUM AND JOHN DRYSDALE, AFRICA CONTEMPORARY
    RECORD, AFRICA RESEARCH LIMITED, LONDON, 1969, PP.875-77
    043,114-03,

FOSTER PHILIP
EDUCATION   AND SOCIAL CHANGE IN GHANA.
CHICAGO, UNIVERSITY OF CHICAGO PRESS, 1965
044,114-03,

114-03
  GOODY JACK
  ANOMIE IN ASHANTI.
  AFRICA 26 1957 PP 356-363
  044,114-03,

  JAHODA GUSTAV
   BOYS' IMAGES OF MARRIAGE PARTNERS AND GIRLS' SELF IMAGES
  IN GHANA.
  SOCIOLOGUS 8 1958 PP 155-169
  040,114-03,

  LYSTAD MARY H
  PAINTINGS OF GHANAIAN CHILDREN.
  AFRICA 30 1960 PP 238-242
  040,114-03,

  ROUCH JEAN
  SECOND GENERATION MIGRANTS IN GHANA AND THE IVORY COAST.
  IN AIDAN SOUTHALL (ED.), SOCIAL CHANGE IN MODERN AFRICA.
  LONDON, OXFORD UNIVERSITY PRESS, 1961
  046,114-03,116-03,

  SMITH NOEL
  THE PRESBYTERIAN CHURCH OF GHANA 1835-1960--A YOUNGER CHURCH
  IN A CHANGING SOCIETY.
  GHANA, GHANA UNIVERSITIES PRESS, 1966
  050,114-03,

  TIMOTHY BANKHOLE
  KWAME NKRUMAH-- HIS RISE TO POWER.
  LONDON, ALLEN AND UNWIN, 1963
  060,114-03,

  WILLIAMSON SIDNEY G
  AKAN RELIGION AND THE CHRISTIAN FAITH.
  GHANA, GHANA UNIVERSITIES PRESS, 1965
  050,114-03,

  HODGKIN THOMAS
  THE ISLAMIC LITERARY TRADITION IN GHANA.
  IN LEWIS, ISLAM IN TROPICAL AFRICA, LONDON, OXFORD UNIVERSIT
  PRESS, 1966, P. 442-462
  052,114-03,

  WILKS IVOR
  THE POSITION OF MUSLIMS IN METROPOLITAN ASHANTI IN THE EARLY
  NINETEENTH CENTURY.
  IN LEWIS, ISLAM IN TROPICAL AFRICA, LONDON, OXFORD UNIVERSIT
  PRESS, 1966, P. 318-341
  114-03,

114-04
  AFRIFA A A COLONEL
  THE GHANA COUP, 24TH FEBRUARY, 1966.

LONDON, FRANK CASS AND COMPANY, 1966, PREFACE BY KOFI A BUSIA,
INTRODUCTION BY TIBOR SZAMUELY
064,114-04,

114-04
   BUSIA KOFI A
   AFRICA IN SEARCH OF DEMOCRACY.
   NEW YORK PRAEGER 1967
   LONDON, ROUTLEDGE AND KEGAN PAUL, 1967
   060,114-04,

   NKRUMAH KWAME
   NEO-COLONIALISM. THE LAST STAGE OF IMPERIALISM.
   NEW YORK, INTERNATIONAL PUBLISHERS, 1965
   060,082,114-04,

   NKRUMAH KWAME
   DARK DAYS IN GHANA.
   NEW YORK, INTERNATIONAL PUBLISHERS, 1968
   064,114-04,

   NKRUMAH KWAME
   GHANA--THE AUTOBIOGRAPHY OF KWAME NKRUMAH.
   NEW YORK, NELSON, 1957
   044,114-04,

   NKRUMAH KWAME
   HANDBOOK OF REVOLUTIONARY WARFARE.
   NEW YORK, INTERNATIONAL PUBLISHERS, INC., 1969
   060,091,114-04,

   BUSIA KOFI A
   PURPOSEFUL EDUCATION FOR AFRICA.
   THE HAGUE, MOUTON, 1964
   042, 114-04,

   NKRUMAH KWAME
   NEO-COLONIALISM--THE LAST STAGE OF IMPERIALISM.
   LONDON, HEINEMAN EDUCATIONAL BOOKS, 1965
   096,114-04,

   BRETTON HENRY L
   CURRENT POLITICAL THOUGHT AND PRACTICE IN GHANA.
   AMERICAN POLITICAL SCIENCE REVIEW 52 MARCH 1958 PP 46-63
   060,114-04,

   BRETTON HENRY L
   THE RISE AND FALL OF KWAME NKRUMAH.
   NEW YORK, PRAEGER, 1966
   061,114-04,

   BUSIA KOFI A
   THE CHALLENGE OF AFRICA.
   NEW YORK, PRAEGER, 1962
   060, 114-04,

   JAHODA GUSTAV
   SOCIAL ASPIRATIONS, MAGIC AND WITCHCRAFT IN GHANA - A SOCIAL
   PSYCHOLOGICAL INTERPRETATION.
   IN LLOYD, THE NEW ELITES OF TROPICAL AFRICA, LONDON, OXFORD

UNIVERSITY PRESS, 1966, P. 199-215
041,114-04,

114-04
MAZRUI ALI A
NKRUMAH-- THE LENINIST CZAR CHAPTER 8.
IN ON HEROES AND UHURU-WORSHIP, LONDON, LONGMANS,
1967, PP 113-134
061,114-04,

NKRUMAH KWAME
CONSCIENCISM-- PHILOSOPHY AND IDEOLOGY FOR DECOLONIZATION
AND DEVELOPMENT WITH PARTICULAR REFERENCE TO THE AFRICAN
REVOLUTION.
LONDON, HEINEMANN, 1964
013,060,114-04,

NKRUMAH KWAME
MOVEMENT FOR COLONIAL FREEDOM.
PHYLON 16 1955 PP 397-409
060,114-04,

NKRUMAH KWAME
CHALLENGE OF THE CONGO-- A CASE STUDY OF FOREIGN PRESSURES
IN AN INDEPENDENT STATE.
NEW YORK, INTERNATIONAL PUBLISHERS, 1967
060,114-04,

NKRUMAH KWAME
I SPEAK OF FREEDOM.
NEW YORK, PRAEGER, 1961 (LONDON, HEINEMANN EDUCATIONAL BOOKS)
060,114-04,

NKRUMAH KWAME
AFRICAN PROSPECT.
IN PHILIP W QUIGG (ED.), AFRICA, NEW YORK, PRAEGER, 1964,
PP 272-282
060,114-04,

NKRUMAH KWAME
GHANA--THE AUTOBIOGRAPHY OF KWAME NKRUMAH.
NEW YORK, NELSON, 1957
096,114-04,

O'CONNELL JAMES
SENGHOR, NKRUMAH AND AZIKIWE-- UNITY AND DIVERSITY IN THE
WEST AFRICAN STATES.
NIGERIAN JOURNAL OF ECONOMIC AND SOCIAL STUDIES 5 MARCH
1963 PP 77-93
044,114-04,128-04,130-04,

PADMORE GEORGE
THE GOLD COAST REVOLUTION-- THE STRUGGLE OF AN AFRICAN
PEOPLE FROM SLAVERY TO FREEDOM.
LONDON, D DOBSON, 1953
060,114-04,

SKURNIK W A E
AFRICAN POLITICAL THOUGHT--LUMUMBA, NKRUMAH, AND TOURE.
DENVER, COLORADO, INTERNATIONAL UNIVERSITY BOOKSELLERS, INC.

    1968
    060,108-04,114-04,115-04,

114-04
    SPARK
    SOME ESSENTIAL FEATURES OF NKRUMAISM.
    NEW YORK, INTERNATIONAL PUBLISHERS, 1965
    THE SPARK-JOURNAL OF THE CONVENTION PEOPLE'S PARTY, GHANA
    BY THE EDITORS
    060,114-04,

    DZIRASA STEPHEN
    THE POLITICAL THOUGHT OF DR KWAME NKRUMAH.
    ACCRA,GUINEA PRESS
    060,114-04,

    DE GRAFT-JOHNSON K
    THE EVOLUTION OF ELITES IN GHANA.
    IN LLOYD, THE NEW ELITES OF TROPICAL AFRICA, LONDON, OXFORD
    UNIVERSITY PRESS, 1966, P. 104-117
    114-04,

    PRIESTLEY MARGARET
    THE EMERGENCE OF AN ELITE - A CASE STUDY OF A WEST COAST FAMILY
    IN LLOYD, THE NEW ELITES OF TROPICAL AFRICA, LONDON, OXFORD
    UNIVERSITY PRESS, 1966, P. 87-103
    114-04,

114-05
    AMARTEIFIO G W   BUTCHER D A P   WHITHAM DAVID
    TEMA MANHEAN--A STUDY OF RESETTLEMENT.
    GHANA, GHANA UNIVERSITIES PRESS, 1966
    092,114-05,

    BOATENG E A
    THE GROWTH AND FUNCTIONS OF ACCRA.
    BULLETIN OF THE GHANA GEOGRAPHICAL ASSOCIATION 4 JULY 1959
    PP 4-15
    045,114-05,

    CALDWELL JOHN C
    AFRICAN RURAL-URBAN MIGRATION--THE MOVEMENT TO GHANA'S
    TOWNS.
    NEW YORK (COLUMBIA), MCGILL-QUEENS UNIVERSITY PRESS, 1969
    045,114-05,

    GOULD PETER
    THE DEVELOPMENT OF THE TRANSPORTATION PATTERN IN GHANA
    EVANSTON,DEPARTMENT OF GEOGRAPHY,NORTHWESTERN UNIVERSITY
    PRESS,1960
    048,114-05,

    MCNULTY MICHAEL
    URBAN STRUCTURE AND DEVELOPMENT-THE URBAN SYSTEM OF GHANA
    JOURNAL OF THE DEVELOPING AREAS,3 1969 PP 159-176
    047,048,114-05,

    ROUCH JEAN
    MIGRATION AU GOLD COAST (MIGRATION TO THE GOLD COAST).
    JOURNAL DE LA SOCIETE DES AFRICANISTES 26 1956 PP 33-196

045,114-05,

114-05
   ACQUAH IONE
   ACCRA SURVEY.
   LONDON, UNIVERSITY OF LONDON PRESS, 1958
   114-05,

   GHANA MIN OF HOUSING
   ACCRA--A PLAN FOR THE TOWN.
   ACCRA, GOVERNMENT PRINTER, 1958
   114-05,

   GOLD COAST GOV STAT
   KUMASI SURVEY OF POPULATION AND HOUSEHOLD BUDGETS, 1955.
   ACCRA, GOVERNMENT PRINTER, 1956
   114-05,

   GOLD COAST GOV STAT
   SECONDI-TAKORADI SURVEY OF POPULATION AND HOUSEHOLD BUDGETS.
   ACCRA, GOVERNMENT PRINTER, 1956
   114-05,

   MCELRATH DENNIS
   SOCIETAL SCALE AND SOCIAL DIFFERENTIATION--ACCRA, GHANA.
   THE NEW URBANIZATION, EDS. SCOTT GREER, ET AL., NEW YORK,
   ST. MARTINS PRESS, 1968
   037,114-05,

   NYARKO K A J
   THE DEVELOPMENT OF KUMASI.
   BULL. GHANA GEOG. ASSOC., 4, 1, 1959
   114-05,

114-06
   ANKRAH J A
   100 DAYS IN GHANA.
   AFRICA REPORT, JUNE, 1966, PP. 21-23
   064,114-06,

   APTER DAVID E
   THE DEVELOPMENT OF GHANA NATIONALISM.
   UNITED ASIA 9 1957 PP 23-30
   055,114-06,

   ARDEN-CLARKE C
   GOLD COAST INTO GHANA, SOME PROBLEMS OF TRANSITION.
   INTERNATIONAL AFFAIRS 34 1958 PP 49-56
   056,114-06,

   BOAHEN A ADU
   THE ROOTS OF GHANAIAN NATIONALISM.
   JOURNAL OF AFRICAN HISTORY 5 1964 PP 127-132
   055,114-06,

   HARVEY WILLIAM B
   THE EVOLUTION OF GHANA LAW SINCE INDEPENDENCE.
   LAW AND CONTEMPORARY PROBLEMS 27 1962 PP 581-604
   066,114-06,

JAHODA GUSTAV
NATIONALITY PREFERENCES AND NATIONAL STEREOTYPES IN GHANA
INDEPENDENCE.
JOURNAL OF SOCIAL PSYCHOLOGY 50 1959 PP 165-174
088,114-06,

114-06
JAHODA GUSTAV
WHITE MAN-- A STUDY OF THE ATTITUDE OF AFRICANS TO EUROPEANS
IN GHANA DURING INDEPENDENCE.
LONDON, OXFORD UNIVERSITY PRESS, 1961
041,088,114-06,

JONES-QUARTEY K A
PRESS AND NATIONALISM IN GHANA.
UNITED ASIA 9 FEBRUARY 1957 PP 55-60
055,114-06,

KIMBLE DAVID A
A POLITICAL HISTORY OF GHANA-- THE RISE OF GOLD COAST
NATIONALISM 1850-1958.
OXFORD, CLARENDON PRESS, 1963
055,114-06,

OWIREDU P A
PROPOSALS FOR A NATIONAL LANGUAGE FOR GHANA.
AFRICAN AFFAIRS 63 APRIL 1964 PP 142-145
056,114-06,

AMONOO R F
PROBLEMS OF GHANAIAN LINGUE FRANCHE.
IN SPENCER, JOHN (ED), LANGUAGE IN AFRICA, PAPERS OF THE
LEVERHULME CONFERENCE ON UNIVERSITIES AND THE LANGUAGE
PROBLEMS OF TROPICAL AFRICA, CAMBRIDGE, CAMBRIDGE UNIVERSITY
PRESS, 1963
114-06,

ANSRE GILBERT
A STUDY ON THE OFFICIAL LANGUAGE IN GHANA.
COLLOQUE SUR LE MULTILINGUISME, BRAZZAVILLE, 1962
114-06,

114-07
APTER DAVID E   LYSTAD ROBERT A
BUREAUCRACY, PARTY, AND CONSTITUTIONAL DEMOCRACY-- AN EXAM-
INATION OF POLITICAL ROLE SYSTEMS IN GHANA.
IN GWENDOLEN M CARTER AND WILLIAM O BROWN (EDS) TRANSITION
IN AFRICA-- STUDIES IN POLITICAL ADAPTATION BOSTON BOSTON
UNIVERSITY PRESS 1958 PP 16-43
062,114-07,

APTER DAVID E
GHANA IN TRANSITION.
NEW YORK, ATHENEUM, 1963
056,058,114-07,

APTER DAVID E
GHANA.
JAMES S. COLEMAN AND CARL G. ROSBERG JR. (EDS), POLITICAL
PARTIES AND NATIONAL INTEGRATION IN TROPICAL AFRICA,

BERKELEY, UNIVERSITY OF CALIFORNIA PRESS, 1966
058,062,114-07,

114-07
AUSTIN DENNIS
ELECTIONS IN AN AFRICAN RURAL AREA.
IN WILLIAM J HANNA (ED), INDEPENDENT BLACK AFRICA, CHICAGO,
RAND MCNALLY, 1964, PP 341-362
063,114-07,

AUSTIN DENNIS
POLITICS IN GHANA 1946-1960.
LONDON, OXFORD UNIVERSITY PRESS, 1964
055,114-07,

BENNETT GEORGE
THE GOLD COAST GENERAL ELECTION OF 1954.
PARLIAMENTARY AFFAIRS 7 1954 PP 430-439
063,114-07,

BOURRET F M
GHANA-- THE ROAD TO INDEPENDENCE 1919-1957.
STANFORD, STANFORD UNIVERSITY PRESS 1960
055,056,114-07,

CARD EMILY
GHANA PREPARES FOR CIVILIAN RULE.
AFRICA REPORT, APRIL 9, 1968
064,114-07,

LEE J M
PARLIAMENT IN REPUBLICAN GHANA.
PARLIAMENTARY AFFAIRS 16 AUTUMN 1963 PP 376-395
062,114-07,

OMARI T PETER
KWAME NKRUMAH--THE ANATOMY OF AN AFRICAN DICTATORSHIP.
NEW YORK, AFRICANA PUBLISHING CORPORATION, 1970
061,114-07,

RUBIN LESLIE   MURRAY PAULA
THE CONSTITUTION AND GOVERNMENT OF GHANA.
LONDON, SWEET AND MAXWELL, 1961
068,114-07,

114-08
MOXON JAMES
VOLTA--MAN'S GREATEST LAKE.
NEW YORK, PRAEGER PUBLISHERS, 1969
075,114-08,

BENTSI-ENCHILL K
GHANA LAND LAW.
LONDON SWEET AND MAXWELL 1964
010, 066, 114-08,

GREEN REGINALD H
FOUR AFRICAN DEVELOPMENT PLANS-- GHANA, KENYA, NIGERIA,
AND TANZANIA CHAPTER 20.
IN EDITH WHETHAM AND JEAN CURRIE   (EDS.) READINGS IN THE

APPLIED ECONOMICS OF AFRICA, LONDON, CAMBRIDGE UNIVERSITY
PRESS, 2, 1967, PP 21-32
072,114-08,117-08,128-08,136-08,

114-08
HILL P
THREE TYPES OF SOUTHERN GHANAIAN COCOA FARMER.
IN D BIEBUYCK, ED., AFRICAN AGRARIAN SYSTEMS, LONDON,
LONDON, OXFORD UNIVERSITY PRESS, 1963, PP 203-233
070,114-08,

HILL P
MIGRANT COCOA FARMERS OF SOUTHERN GHANA.
CAMBRIDGE, CAMBRIDGE UNIVERSITY PRESS, 1963
070,114-08,

HILL P
THE MIGRATION OF SOUTHERN GHANAIAN COCOA FARMERS.
BULLETIN OF THE GHANA GEOGRAPHICAL ASSOCIATION 5 JULY 1960
PP 9-19
070,114-08,

LAWSON R M
THE MARKETS FOR FOODS IN GHANA CHAPTER 16.
IN EDITH WHETHAM AND JEAN CURRIE, (EDS.), READINGS IN THE
APPLIED ECONOMICS OF AFRICA, LONDON, CAMBRIDGE UNIVERSITY
PRESS, 1, 1967, PP 173-192
070,073,114-08,

TRACHTMAN LESTER N
THE LABOR MOVEMENT OF GHANA-- A STUDY IN POLITICAL
UNIONISM.
ECONOMIC DEVELOPMENT AND CULTURAL CHANGE 10 1962 PP 183-200
073,114-08,

WILLIAMS J W
THE ECONOMY OF GHANA CHAPTER 6.
IN CALVIN B HOOVER, ECONOMIC SYSTEMS OF THE COMMONWEALTH,
DURHAM, DUKE UNIVERSITY PRESS, 1962, PP 238-261
073,114-08,

AMIN SAMIR
TROIS EXPERIENCES AFRICAINES DE DEVELOPPEMENT-LE MALI,LA
GUINEE.ET LA GHANA
PARIS,PRESSES UNIVERSITAIRES DE FRANCE,1965
073,123-08,115-08,114-08,

BIRMINGHAM WALTER   ET AL   EDS
A STUDY OF CONTEMPORARY GHANA--VOL 1 THE ECONOMY OF
GHANA ; VOL 2 SOME ASPECTS OF SOCIAL STRUCTURE.
LONDON,ALLEN AND UNWIN;AND EVANSTON,NORTHWESTERN UNIVERSITY
PRESS,1966
114-08,

114-09
QUAISON-SACKEY ALEX
AFRICA AND THE UNITED NATIONS-- OBSERVATIONS OF A GHANAIAN
DIPLOMAT.
AFRICAN FORUM I 1 1965 PP 53-68
081,114-09,

114-09
THOMPSON W SCOTT
GHANA?S FOREIGN POLICY,1957-1966- DIPLOMACY,IDEOLOGY AND THE
NEW STATE
PRINCETON,PRINCETON UNIVERSITY PRESS, 1969
060,082,083,084,085,114-09,

114-10
ARMAH AYI KWEI
THE BEAUTIFUL ONES ARE NOT YET BORN.
NEW YORK, COLLIER BOOKS (MACMILLAN), 1969   (LONDON,
HEINEMANN EDUCATIONAL BOOKS)
090,114-10,

114-12
JOHNSON ALBERT F
A BIBLIOGRAPHY OF GHANA, 1930-1961.
LONDON, LONGMANS, 1964
114-12,

LANCEY M W DE
THE GHANA-GUINEA-MALI UNION--A BIBLIOGRAPHIC ESSAY.
AFRICAN STUDIES BULLETIN, 9, 2, SEPTEMBER, 1966
114-12,115-12,123-12,

PITCHER G M
BIBLIOGRAPHY OF GHANA 1957-1959.
KUMASI, KWAME NKRUMAH UNIVERSITY OF SCIENCE AND TECHNOLOGY,
1960
114-12,

114-32
PRESTAGE EDGAR
THE ASHANTI QUESTION AND THE BRITISH-- EIGHTEENTH-CENTURY
ORIGINS.
THE JOURNAL OF AFRICAN HISTORY II 1961 PP 35-60
033,114-32,
033, 114-02,

115. GUINEA

115-01
SOW ALFA IBRAHIM
CHRONIQUES ET RECITS DU FOUTA DJALON (CHRONICLES AND
RECITATIONS OF FUTA JALLON).
PARIS, KLINCKSIECK, NEW YORK, INTERNATIONAL UNIVERSITY BOOK-
SELLERS, 1968
012,115-01,

GOVERNMENT OF FRANCE
COUTUMIERS JURIDIQUES DE L'AFRIQUE OCCIDENTALE FRANCAISE--
MAURITANIE, NIGER, COTE D'IVOIRE, DAHOMEY, GUINEE FRANCAISE
(FRENCH WEST AFRICAN JURIDIC CUSTOMS-- MAURITANIA, NIGER
IVORY COAST, DAHOMEY, FRENCH GUINEA) .

PARIS, LIBRAIRIE LAROSE, 1939, VOL3
066,109-01,115-01,116-01,124-01,127-01,

115-01
   SOW ALFA IBRAHIM
   LA FEMME, LA VACHE, LA FOI--ECRIVAINS ET POETES DU FOUTA-
   DJALON.
   PARIS, JULLIARD, 1966
   115-01,

115-02
   NIANE DJIBRIL T   SURET-CANALE J
   HISTOIRE DE L'AFRIQUE OCCIDENTALE.
   PARIS, PRESENCE AFRICAINE, 1962
   115-02,

115-03
   MARTY PAUL
   L'ISLAM EN GUINNEE-- FOUTA DJALLON (ISLAM IN GUINEA-- FOUTA
   DJALON).
   PARIS, EDITIONS ERNEST LEROUX, 1921
   021,115-03,

115-04
   SKURNIK W A E
   AFRICAN POLITICAL THOUGHT--LUMUMBA, NKRUMAH, AND TOURE.
   DENVER, COLORADO, INTERNATIONAL UNIVERSITY BOOKSELLERS, INC.
    1968
   060,108-04,114-04,115-04,

   TOURE SEKOU
   AFRICA'S FUTURE AND THE WORLD.
   IN PHILIP W QUIGG (ED.), AFRICA, NEW YORK, PRAEGER, 1964
   PP 314-326
   060,115-04,

   WALLERSTEIN I M
   THE POLITICAL IDEOLOGY OF THE PDG.
   PRESENCE AFRICAINE 12 JANUARY 1962 PP 30-41
   060,115-04,

   CESAIRE AIME
   LA PENSEE POLITIQUE DE SEKOU TOURE (THE POLITICAL THOUGHT
   OF SEKOU TOURE).
   PRESENCE AFRICAINE 29 JANUARY 1960
   060,115-04,

   FISCHER GEORGES
   QUELQUES ASPECTS DE LA DOCTRINE POLITIQUE GUINEENE (SOME
   ASPECTS OF GUINEA POLITICAL DOCTRINE).
   CIVILIZATIONS 9 1959 PP 457-478
   060,115-04,

   TOURE SEKOU
   GUINEE, PRELUDE A L'INDEPENDANCE.
   PARIS, PRESENCE AFRICAINE, 1959
   115-04,

   TOURE SEKOU
   L'AFRIQUE ET LA REVOLUTION.

PARIS, PRESENCE AFRICAINE, 1966
115-04,

115-04
   TOURE SEKOU
   LA GUINEE ET L'EMANCIPATION AFRICAINE--L'ACTION POLITIQUE DU
   PARTI DEMOCRATIQUE DE GUINEE.
   PARIS, PRESENCE AFRICAINE, 1959
   115-04,

   TOURE SEKOU
   LA REVOLUTION GUINEENNE ET LE PROGRES SOCIAL.
   CONAKRY, IMP. PATRICE LUMUMBA, 1963
   115-04,

   TOURE SEKOU
   POEMES MILITANTS, PARTI DEMOCRATIQUE DE GUINEE.
   CONAKRY, IMP. PATRICE LUMUMBA, 1964
   115-04,

   TOURE SEKOU
   REPUBLIQUE DE GUINEE--LA LUTTE DU PARTI DEMOCRATIQUE DE
   GUINEE POUR L'EMANCIPATION AFRICAINE.
   CONAKRY, IMP. PATRICE LUMUMBA, 1959
   115-04,

115-05
   COLLFUS O
   CONAKRY EN 1951-52--ETUDE HUMAINE ET ECONOMIQUE.
   ETUDES GUINEENNES, 10, 11, 1952
   115-05,

115-06
   DU BOIS VICTOR D
   THE ROLE OF THE ARMY IN GUINEA.
   AFRICA REPORT 8 JANUARY 1963 PP 3-5
   064,115-06,

   DU BOIS VICTOR D
   GUINEA.
   IN COLEMAN, J.S. AND ROSBERG, C.G. (EDS), POLITICAL PARTIES
   AND NATIONAL INTEGRATION IN TROPICAL AFRICA, LOS ANGELES,
   UNIVERSITY OF CALIFORNIA PRESS, 1964
   115-06,

115-07
   ANONYMOUS
   CHANGING RELATIONS AMONG GUINEA, THE IVORY COAST AND MALI.
   AMERICAN UNIVERSITIES FIELD STAFF, VOL. V, NO. 8, 1962
   115-07,

115-08
   AMIN SAMIR
   TROIS EXPERIENCES AFRICAINES DE DEVELOPPEMENT-LE MALI,LA
   GUINEE,ET LA GHANA
   PARIS, PRESSES UNIVERSITAIRES DE FRANCE, 1965
   073,123-08,115-08,114-08,

   DUMONT RENE
   RECONVERSION DE L'ECONOMIE AGRIOLE EN GUINEE EN COTE

D'IVOIRE ET AU MALI.
PARIS, PRESSES UNIVERSITAIRES DE FRANCE, 1961
115-08, 123-08,

115-09
MORROW JOHN H
FIRST AMERICAN AMBASSADOR TO GUINEA.
NEW BRUNSWICK, NEW JERSEY, RUTGERS UNIVERSITY PRESS, 1968
083,115-09,

ZARTMAN I WILLIAM
GUINEA-- THE QUIET WAR GOES ON.
AFRICA REPORT 12 NOVEMBER 1967 PP 67-72
087,115-09,

TOURE SEKOU
EXPERIENCE GUINEENNE ET UNITE AFRICAINE (GUINEAN EXPERIENCE
AND AFRICAN UNITY).
PARIS, PRESENCE AFRICAINE, 1959
057,115-09,

115-10
LAYE CAMARA   TRANSLATED BY   JAMES KIRKUP
THE AFRICAN CHILD.
LONDON COLLINS LTD 1965
090,115-10,

LAYE CAMARA
RADIANCE OF THE KING.
NEW YORK, MACMILLAN CO., 1970
090,115-10,

FODEBA KEITA
AUBE AFRICAINE.
PARIS, SEGHERS, 1965
115-10,

FODEBA KEITA
LE MAITRE D'ECOLE, SUIVI DE MINUIT.
PARIS, SEGHER, 1952
115-10,

KEITA BODEBA
POEMES AFRICAINS.
PARIS, SEGHERS, 1958
090,115-10,

KEITA FODEBA   HUET MICHEL
LES HOMMES DE LA DANSE.
LAUSANNE, LA GUILDE DE LIVRE, 1954
115-10,

LAYE CAMARA
DRAMOUSS.
PARIS, PLON, 1966
115-10,

LAYE CAMARA
ECRIVAIN GUINEEN--TEXTES COMMENTES PAR ROGER MERCIER ET M ET
S BATTESTINI.

PARIS, F. NATHAN, 1964
115-10,

115-11
   LUSIGNAN GUY DE
   FRENCH-SPEAKING AFRICA SINCE INDEPENDENCE.
   NEW YORK, PRAEGER PUBLISHERS, 1969
   056,061,104-11,105-11,106-11,107-11,109-11,112-11,
   115-11,116-11,123-11,137-11,141-11,

115-12
   LANCEY M W DE
   THE GHANA-GUINEA-MALI UNION--A BIBLIOGRAPHIC ESSAY.
   AFRICAN STUDIES BULLETIN, 9, 2, SEPTEMBER, 1966
   114-12,115-12,123-12,

   ORG FOR ECON COOP   ECON COOP AND DEVEL
   BIBLIOGRAPHY ON GUINEA.
   PARIS, O.E.C.D. DEVELOPMENT CENTRE, 1965
   115-12,

116. IVORY COAST

116-01
   HOLAS B
   L'IMAGE DU MONDE BETE (THE BETE IMAGE OF THE WORLD).
   PARIS, PRESSES UNIVERSITAIRE DE FRANCE, NEW YORK,
   INTERNATIONAL UNIVERSITY BOOKSELLERS, 1968
   013,116-01,

   KOBBEN A J F
   LAND AS AN OBJECT OF GAIN IN A NON-LITERATE SOCIETY--
   LAND TENURE AMONG THE BETE AND DIDA (IVORY COAST).
   IN D BIEBUYCK (ED.), AFRICAN AGRARIAN SYSTEMS, LONDON,
   OXFORD UNIVERSITY PRESS, 1963, PP 245-266
   010,070,116-01,

   GOVERNMENT OF FRANCE
   COUTUMIERS JURIDIQUES DE L'AFRIQUE OCCIDENTALE FRANCAISE--
   MAURITANIE, NIGER, COTE D'IVOIRE, DAHOMEY, GUINEE FRANCAISE
   (FRENCH WEST AFRICAN JURIDIC CUSTOMS-- MAURITANIA, NIGER
   IVORY COAST, DAHOMEY, FRENCH GUINEA) .
   PARIS, LIBRAIRIE LAROSE, 1939, VOL3
   066,109-01,115-01,116-01,124-01,127-01,

   HOLAS B
   CULTURES MATERIELLES DE LA COTE D'IVOIRE (MATERIAL CULTURE
   OF THE IVORY COAST).
   PARIS, PRESSES UNIVERSITAIRE DE FRANCE, 1960
   014,116-01,

   AMON D'ABY J F
   CROYANCES RELIGIEUSES ET COUTUMES JURIDIQUES DES AGNI DE LA
   COTE-D'IVOIRE.
   PARIS, G. P. MAISONNEUVE ET LAROSE, 1960

116-01,

116-03
  CLIGNET REMI   FOSTER PHILIP
  THE FORTUNATE FEW.
  EVANSTON, NORTHWESTERN UNIVERSITY PRESS, 1966
  039,043,116-03,

  CLIGNET REMI
  MANY WIVES, MANY POWERS--AUTHORITY AND POWER IN POLYGYNOUS
  FAMILIES.
  EVANSTON, NORTHWESTERN UNIVERSITY PRESS, 1970
  046,116-03,

  CLIGNET REMI   FOSTER PHILIP
  THE SOCIAL, ECONOMIC AND EDUCATIONAL SCENE IN THE IVORY
  COAST CHAPTER 2.
  IN THE FORTUNATE FEW,EVANSTON, NORTHWESTERN UNIVERSITY
  PRESS 1966
  042,116-03,

  ROUCH JEAN
  SECOND GENERATION MIGRANTS IN GHANA AND THE IVORY COAST.
  IN AIDAN SOUTHALL (ED.), SOCIAL CHANGE IN MODERN AFRICA.
  LONDON, OXFORD UNIVERSITY PRESS, 1961
  046,114-03,116-03,

  HOLAS B
  LE SEPARATISME RELIGIEUX EN AFRIQUE NOIRE-- L'EXAMPLE
  DE LA COTE D'IVOIRE (RELIGIOUS SEPARATISM IN BLACK AFRICA--
  THE EXAMPLE OF THE IVORY COAST).
  PARIS,PRESSES UNIVERSITAIRES DE FRANCE, 1965
  051,116-03,

  MARTY PAUL
  ETUDES SUR L'ISLAM EN COTE D'IVOIRE (STUDIES ON ISLAM IN
  THE IVORY COAST).
  PARIS,EDITIONS ERNEST LEROUX,1922
  021, 116-03,

116-04
  HOUPHOUET-BOIGNY F
  BLACK AFRICA AND THE FRENCH UNION.
  IN PHILIP W QUIGG (ED.), AFRICA, NEW YORK, PRAEGER, 1964,
  PP 263-271
  077,116-04,

116-05
  ANONYMOUS
  SOCIETE POUR L'ETUDE TECHNIQUE D'AMENAGEMENTS PLANIFIES
  RAPPORT SUR LE PLAN D'ABIDJAN.
  ABIDJAN, MINISTERE DES TRAVAUX PUBLICS, 1959
  116-05,

  BERNUS EDMOND
  ABIDJAN--NOTE SUR L'AGGOMERATION D'ABIDJAN ET SA POPULATION.
  BULL. IFAN, SERIES B, 24, 1-2, 1962
  116-05,

  BERNUS EDMOND

NOTE ON ABIDJAN.
IN CSA MEETING OF SPECIALISTS ON URBANIZATION AND ITS SOCIAL
ASPECTS, ABIDJAN, 1961, LONDON, CCTA, 1961
116-05,

116-05
GENNET C
PLAN DIRECTEUR D'URBANISME D'ABIDJAN.
INDUSTRIES ET TRAVAUS D'OUTRE-MER, 10, 100, MARCH, 1962
116-05,

116-06
ZOLBERG ARISTIDE R
PATTERNS OF NATIONAL INTEGRATION.
THE JOURNAL OF MODERN AFRICAN STUDIES, 5, 4, 1967, PP 449-67
055,058,116-06,123-06,

ALEXANDER A S JR
THE IVORY COAST CONSTITUTION--AN ACCELERATOR, NOT A BRAKE.
THE JOURNAL OF MODERN AFRICAN STUDIES, VOL. I, NO. 3, SEPT.
1963, PP. 293-312
068,116-06,

ZOLBERG ARISTIDE R
MASS PARTIES AND NATIONAL INTEGRATION--THE CASE OF IVORY
COAST.
JOURNAL OF POLITICS 25 FEBRUARY 1963 PP 36-48
057,116-06,

ZOLBERG ARISTIDE R
ONE PARTY GOVERNMENT IN THE IVORY COAST.
PRINCETON, PRINCETON UNIVERSITY PRESS 1964 (AND 1969)
058,061,116-06,

116-07
THOMPSON VIRGINIA
IVORY COAST.
IN G. M. CARTER (ED), AFRICAN ONE-PARTY STATES, ITHACA,
CORNELL UNIVERSITY PRESS, 1962
116-07,

116-08
AMIN SAMIR
LE DEVELOPPEMENT ECONOMIQUE ET SOCIALE DE LA COTE D'IVOIRE
DAKAR, IDEP, 1966
073,116-08,

116-10
AMON D'ABY J F
LA COURONNE AUX ENCHERES, DRAME SOCIAL EN TROIS ACTES ET SIX
TABLEAUX.
PARIS, ED. LES PARAGRAPHES LITTERAIRES, 1957
116-10,

AMON D'ABY J F   DADIE BERNARD   GADEAU G COFFI
LE THEATRE POPULAIRE EN REPUBLIQUE DE COTE-D'IVOIRE--OEUVRES
CHOISIES.
ABIDJAN, CERCLE CULTUREL ET FOLKLORIQUE DE LA COTE-D'IVOIRE
1965
116-10,

116-10
    DADIE BERNARD
    ASSEMIEN DEHYLE--CHRONIQUE AGNI.
    PARIS, L'AVANT-SCENE-THEATRE, NO. 343, OCT. 15, 1965, PP. 37
    -43
    116-10,

    DADIE BERNARD
    ECRIVAIN IVOIREN--TEXTES COMMENTES PAR ROGER MERCIER ET M ET
    S BATTESTINI.
    PARIS, F. NATHAN, 1964
    116-10,

    DADIE BERNARD
    HOMMES DE TOUS LES CONTINENTS, POEMS.
    PARIS, PRESENCE AFRICAINE, 1967
    116-10,

    DADIE BERNARD
    LEGENDES AFRICAINES.
    PARIS, SEGHERS, 1954
    116-10,

    DADIE BERNARD
    LEGENDES ET POEMES--AFRIQUE DEBOUT, LEGENDES AFRICAINES,
    CLIMBIE, LA RONDE DES JOURS.
    PARIS, SEGHERS, 1966
    116-10,

    DADIE BERNARD
    LE PAGNE NOIR, CONTES AFRICAINES.
    PARIS, PRESENCE AFRICAINE, 1955
    116-10,

    DADIE BERNARD
    LA RONDE DES JOURS.
    PARIS, SEGHERS, 1956
    116-10,

    DADIE BERNARD
    PATRON DE NEW YORK.
    PARIS, PRESENCE AFRICAINE, 1964
    116-10,

    DADIE BERNARD
    UN NEGRE A PARIS.
    PARIS, PRESENCE AFRICAINE, 1959
    116-10,

116-11
    LUSIGNAN GUY DE
    FRENCH-SPEAKING AFRICA SINCE INDEPENDENCE.
    NEW YORK, PRAEGER PUBLISHERS, 1969
    056,061,104-11,105-11,106-11,107-11,109-11,112-11,
    115-11,116-11,123-11,137-11,141-11,

116-12
    NOVACCO N   COMP
    ESSAI D'UNE BIBLIOGRAPHIE SUR LA COTE D'IVOIRE.

PARIS, CENTRE DE DEVELOPPMENT DE L'ORGANISATION DE
COOPERATION ET DE DEVELOPPMENT ECONOMIQUES, IV, 1964
116-12,

117. KENYA

117-01
   KENYATTA JOMO
   FACING MT KENYA--THE RURAL LIFE OF THE KIKUYU.
   NEW YORK, VINTAGE BOOKS, 1964
   010,060,098,117-01,

   HARRIES LYNDON
   POEMS FROM KENYA--GNOMIC VERSES IN SWAHILI BY AHMAD NASSIR
   BIN JUMA BHALO.
   MADISON, UNIVERSITY OF WISCONSIN PRESS, 1966
   012,117-01,

   LEVINE ROBERT A
   GUSII SEX OFFENCES-- A STUDY IN SOCIAL CONTROL.
   AMERICAN ANTHROPOLOGIST 61 1959 PP 965-990
   008,117-01,

   LEVINE ROBERT A
   WEALTH AND POWER IN GUSIILAND.
   IN PAUL BOHANNAN AND GEORGE DALTON (EDS.), MARKETS IN
   AFRICA, EVANSTON, NORTHWESTERN UNIVERSITY PRESS, 1962, PP
   520-536
   010,117-01,

   SCHAPERA ISAAC
   SOME PROBLEMS OF ANTHROPOLIGICAL RESEARCH IN KENYA COLONY.
   LONDON INTERNATIONAL AFRICAN INSTITUTE 1949
   099,117-01,

   WHITELEY W H   MULI M G
   PRACTICAL INTRODUCTION TO KAMBA.
   LONDON, OXFORD UNIVERSITY PRESS, 1962
   011,117-01,

   HUNTINGFORD G W B
   THE NANDI OF KENYA-TRIBAL CONTROL IN A PASTORAL SOCIETY
   LONDON,ROUTLEDGE AND KEGAN PAUL,1953
   117-01,

   LAMBERT HAROLD E
   KIKUYU SOCIAL AND POLITICAL INSTITUTIONS.
   LONDON, OXFORD UNIVERSITY PRESS, 1956
   117-01,

   MIDDLETON JOHN   KERSHAW GREET
   THE KIKUYU AND KAMBA OF KENYA
   LONDON, INTERNATIONAL AFRICAN INSTITUTE, 1956
   117-01,

OSOGO JOHN
A HISTORY OF THE BALUYIA.
LONDON, OXFORD UNIVERSITY PRESS, 1966
117-01,

117-01
   WERE GIDEON S
   A HISTORY OF THE ABALUYIA OF WESTERN KENYA.
   KENYA, EAST AFRICAN PUBLISHING HOUSE, 1967
   117-01,

117-02
   BENNETT GEORGE
   SETTLERS AND POLITICS IN KENYA UP TO 1945.
   IN VINCENT HARLOW AND E M CHILVER (EDS), HISTORY OF EAST
   AFRICA VOL II, OXFORD, CLARENDON PRESS, 1965, PP 265-332
   035,117-02,

   KIRKMAN JAMES S
   THE ARAB CITY OF GEDI-- EXCAVATIONS AT THE GREAT MOSQUE
   ARCHITECTURE AND FINDS.
   LONDON, OXFORD UNIVERSITY PRESS, 1954
   092,117-02,

   MIDDLETON JOHN
   KENYA-- CHANGES IN AFRICAN LIFE, 1912-1945.
   IN VINCENT HARLOW AND E M CHILVER (EDS), HISTORY OF EAST
   AFRICA VOL II, OXFORD, CLARENDON PRESS, 1965, PP 333-394
   035,117-02,

   DILLEY MARJORIE R
   BRITISH POLICY IN KENYA COLONY
   LONDON, FRANK CASS, 1966, SECOND EDITION
   035,117-02,

   HUXLEY ELSPETH
   WHITE MAN S COUNTRY-- LORD DELAMERE AND THE MAKING OF KENYA.
   LONDON, CHATTO AND WINDUS, 1953
   035,117-02,

   MORGAN W T W
   THE 'WHITE HIGHLANDS' OF KENYA.
   GEOGRAPHICAL JOURNAL 129 JUNE 1963 PP 140-155
   035,117-02,

   MUNGEAM G H
   BRITISH RULE IN KENYA 1895-1912
   OXFORD, CLARENDON PRESS, 1967
   035,117-02,

117-03
   GULLIVER P H   ED
   TRADITION AND TRANSITION IN EAST AFRICA--STUDIES OF THE
   TRIBAL FACTOR IN THE MODERN ERA.
   BERKELEY, UNIVERSITY OF CALIFORNIA PRESS, 1969
   007,117-03,136-03,139-03,

   KOPF DAVID   VON DER MUHLL G
   POLITICAL SOCIALIZATION IN KENYA AND TANZANIA.
   JOURNAL OF MODERN AFRICAN STUDIES 5 MAY 1967 PP 13-51

043,117-03,136-03,

117-03
   SOJA EDWARD W
   THE GEOGRAPHY OF MODERNIZATION IN KENYA.
   SYRACUSE, SYRACUSE UNIVERSITY PRESS, 1968
   038,047,048,117-03,

   CHAGULA W K
   THE ROLE OF THE ELITE, THE INTELLIGENTSIA AND EDUCATED EAST
   AFRICANS, IN THE DEVELOPMENT OF UGANDA, KENYA AND TANZANIA.
   KAMPALA, EAST AFRICAN ACADEMY, SECOND FOUNDATION LECTURE, 1966
   044,117-03,136-03,139-03,

   HACHTEN WILLIAM A
   THE PRESS IN A ONE-PARTY STATE--KENYA SINCE
   INDEPENDENCE.
   JOURNALISM QUARTERLY 42 SPRING 1965 PP 262-266
   049,117-03,

   MIDDLETON JOHN
   KENYA-- ADMINISTRATION AND CHANGES IN AFRICAN LIFE
   1912-45 CHAPTER 7.
   IN ROLAND OLIVER AND GERVASE MATHEW, HISTORY OF EAST
   AFRICA, 2, LONDON, OXFORD UNIVERSITY PRESS, 1965,
   PP 333-392
   035,117-03,

   OGOT BETHWELL A   WELBOURN F B
   A PLACE TO FEEL AT HOME--A STUDY OF TWO INDEPENDENT CHURCHES
   IN WESTERN KENYA.
   LONDON, OXFORD UNIVERSITY PRESS, 1966
   051,117-03,

   ROTHCHILD DONALD S
   ETHNIC INEQUALITIES IN KENYA
   JOURNAL OF MODERN AFRICAN STUDIES 7 1969 PP 689-711
   057,117-03,

   BAXTER P T W
   ACCEPTANCE AND REJECTION OF ISLAM AMONG THE BORAN OF THE
   NORTHERN FRONTIER DISTRICT OF KENYA.
   IN LEWIS, ISLAM IN TROPICAL AFRICA, LONDON, OXFORD UNIVERSIT
   PRESS, 1966, P. 233-252
   117-03,

117-04
   KENYATTA JOMO
   SUFFERING WITHOUT BITTERNESS--THE FOUNDING OF THE KENYA
   NATION.
   KENYA, EAST AFRICAN PUBLISHING HOUSE, 1968
   044,117-04,

   MBOYA TOM
   FREEDOM AND AFTER.
   BOSTON, LITTLE, BROWN, AND COMPANY, 1963
   044,060,117-04,

   KENYATTA JOMO
   AFRICAN SOCIALISM AND AFRICAN UNITY.

AFRICAN FORUM I 1 1965 PP 23-37
079,117-04,

117-04
MBOYA TOM
EAST AFRICAN LABOUR POLICY AND FEDERATION.
IN COLIN LEYS AND P ROBSON (EDS), FEDERATION IN EAST AFRICA--
OPPORTUNITIES AND PROBLEMS NAIROBI OXFORD UNIVERSITY PRESS
1965 PP 102-110
078,117-04,

STABLER ERNEST
EDUCATION SINCE UHURU-- THE SCHOOLS OF KENYA.
MIDDLETOWN, CONN, WESLEYAN UNIVERSITY PRESS, 1969
042,117-04,

KENYATTA JOMO
HARAMBEE--THE PRIME MINISTER OF KENYA≠S SPEECHES 1963-1964.
LONDON, OXFORD UNIVERSITY PRESS, 1964
060,117-04,

MBOYA TOM
THE PARTY SYSTEM AND DEMOCRACY IN AFRICA.
IN PHILIP W QUIGG (ED.), AFRICA, NEW YORK, PRAEGER, 1964
PP 327-338
060,117-04,

MBOYA TOM
AFRICAN SOCIALISM CHAPTER 6.
IN AFRICA'S FREEDOM, NEW YORK, BARNES AND NOBLE, 1964,
PP 78-87
060,117-04,

MBOYA TOM
TENSIONS IN AFRICAN DEVELOPMENT CHAPTER 4.
IN AFRICA'S FREEDOM, NEW YORK, BARNES AND NOBLE, 1964,
PP 55-66
060,117-04,

MBOYA TOM
VISION IN AFRICA.
IN WILLIAM J HANNA (ED), INDEPENDENT BLACK AFRICA, CHICAGO,
RAND MCNALLY, 1964, PP 515-520
060,117-04,

MBOYA TOM
THE AMERICAN NEGRO CANNOT LOOK TO AFRICA FOR AN ESCAPE.
THE NEW YORK TIMES MAGAZINE, JULY 13, 1969, SECTION 6, PP.
30-44
096,117-04,

117-05
DE BLIJ HARM J
MOMBASA-- AN AFRICAN CITY.
EVANSTON, NORTHWESTERN UNIVERSITY PRESS, 1968
045,117-05,

GUTKIND PETER C W
THE ENERGY OF DESPAIR--SOCIAL ORGANIZATION OF THE UNEMPLOYED
IN TWO AFRICAN CITIES-- LAGOS AND NAIROBI.

CIVILISATIONS, VOL. XVII, 1967, PP. 186-380
043,128-05,117-05,

117-05
    KIRKMAN JAMES S
    GEDI, THE PALACE.
    THE HAGUE, MOUTON,1963
    092,117-05,

    MORGAN W T W   ED
    NAIROBI--CITY AND REGION
    NEW YORK, OXFORD UNIVERSITY PRESS. 1967
    117-05,

    WILSON GORDON
    MOMBASA--A MODERN COLONIAL MUNICIPALITY.
    IN A.W. SOUTHALL (ED) SOCIAL CHANGE IN MODERN AFRICA,
    LONDON, OXFORD UNIVERSITY PRESS, 1961
    117-05,

117-06
    ITOTE WARUHIU
    'MAU MAU' GENERAL.
    KENYA, EAST AFRICAN PUBLISHING HOUSE, 1967
    055,117-06,

    ROSBERG CARL G   NOTTINGHAM JOHN
    THE MYTH OF MAU-MAU-- NATIONALISM IN KENYA.
    NEW YORK, PRAEGER,1966
    055,117-06,

    LEVINE ROBERT A
    ANTI-EUROPEAN VIOLENCE IN AFRICA-- A COMPARATIVE ANALYSIS.
    JOURNAL OF CONFLICT RESOLUTION 3 DECEMBER 1959
    PP 420-429
    088,117-06,

    CORFIELD F D
    HISTORICAL SURVEY OF THE ORIGINS AND GROWTH OF MAU MAU.
    NAIROBI,GOVERNMENT PRINTER,1960
    055,117-06,

    KILSON MARTIN L
    LAND AND POLITICS IN KENYA-- AN ANALYSIS OF AFRICAN
    POLITICS IN A PLURAL SOCIETY.
    WESTERN POLITICAL QUARTERLY 10 SEPTEMBER 1957 PP 559-581
    055,117-06,

    KILSON MARTIN L
    BEHIND THE MAU MAU REBELLION.
    DISSENT 3 SUMMER 1956 PP 264-275
    055,117-06,

    KOINAGE MBIYU
    THE PEOPLE OF KENYA SPEAK FOR THEMSELVES.
    DETROIT, KENYA PUBLICATION FUND,1955
    055,117-06,

    LEAKEY L S B
    MAU MAU AND THE KIKUYU.

LONDON, METHUEN, 1954
055,117-06,

117-06
LEGUM COLIN
KENYA'S LITTLE GUERRILLA WAR HEATS UP.
AFRICA REPORT 12 APRIL 1967 P 39
059,117-06,

PERHAM MARGERY   HUXLEY ELSPETH
RACE AND POLITICS IN KENYA.
LONDON, FABER, 1944
035,117-06,

HARRIES LYNDON
SWAHILI IN MODERN EAST AFRICA.
IN J. A. FISHMAN, CHAS. A. FERGUSON AND JYOTIRINDRA DAS
GUPTA (EDS), LANGUAGE PROBLEMS OF DEVELOPING NATIONS
117-06,

KARIUKI JOSIAH M
MAU MAU DETAINEE--THE ACCOUNT BY A KENYA AFRICAN OF HIS
EXPERIENCES IN DETENTION CAMPS 1953-1960.
LONDON. OXFORD UNIVERSITY PRESS, 1963
055,117-06,

117-07
BENNETT GEORGE   ROSBERG CARL G
THE KENYATTA ELECTION-- KENYA 1960-1961.
LONDON, OXFORD UNIVERSITY PRESS, 1961
063,117-07,

BENNETT GEORGE
KENYA'S FRUSTRATED ELECTION.
WORLD TODAY 17 1961 PP 254-261
063,117-07,

BURKE FRED G
POLITICAL EVOLUTION IN KENYA CHAPTER 5.
IN STANLEY DIAMOND AND FRED G BURKE (EDS.), THE
TRANSFORMATION OF EAST AFRICA, NEW YORK, BASIC BOOKS, 1966
055,117-07,

ENGHOLM G F
AFRICAN ELECTIONS IN KENYA, MARCH 1957, CHAPTER 7.
IN W J MACKENZIE AND KENNETH ROBINSON, FIVE ELECTIONS IN
AFRICA, LONDON. OXFORD UNIVERSITY PRESS, 1960
063,117-07,

SANGER CLYDE   NOTTINGHAM JOHN
THE KENYA GENERAL ELECTION OF 1963.
JOURNAL OF MODERN AFRICAN STUDIES 2 1964 PP 1-40
063,117-07,

BENNETT GEORGE
KENYA--A POLITICAL HISTORY.
LONDON, OXFORD UNIVERSITY PRESS, 1963
117-07,

117-08

UNITED NATIONS
INDUSTRIAL DEVELOPMENT IN AFRICA
NEW YORK, UNITED NATIONS, 1967
071,104-08,110-08,117-08,127-08,134-08,140-08,142-08,

117-08
    OSER JACOB
    PROMOTING ECONOMIC DEVELOPMENT-WITH ILLUSTRATIONS FROM KENYA
    EVANSTON, NORTHWESTERN UNIVERSITY PRESS, 1967
    072,117-08,

    CLAYTON E S
    AGRARIAN DEVELOPMENT IN PEASANT ECONOMIES-- SOME LESSONS
    FROM KENYA.
    LONDON OXFORD UNIVERSITY PRESS 1964
    070,117-08,

    FAIR T J D
    A REGIONAL APPROACH TO ECONOMIC DEVELOPMENT IN KENYA.
    SOUTH AFRICAN GEOGRAPHICAL JOURNAL 45 DECEMBER1963 PP 55-77
    048,073,117-08,

    GREEN REGINALD H
    FOUR AFRICAN DEVELOPMENT PLANS-- GHANA, KENYA, NIGERIA,
    AND TANZANIA CHAPTER 20.
    IN EDITH WHETHAM AND JEAN CURRIE, (EDS.), READINGS IN THE
    APPLIED ECONOMICS OF AFRICA, LONDON, CAMBRIDGE UNIVERSITY
    PRESS, 2, 1967, PP 21-32
    072,114-08,117-08,128-08,136-08,

    HENNINGS R O
    SOME TRENDS AND PROBLEMS OF AFRICAN LAND TENURE IN KENYA.
    JOURNAL OF AFRICAN ADMINISTRATION 4 OCTOBER 1952 PP 122-134
    070,117-08,

    INTERNATIONAL BANK FOR RECONSTRUCTION AND DEVELOPMENT
    THE ECONOMIC DEVELOPMENT OF KENYA
    BALTIMORE, JOHNS HOPKINS UNIVERSITY PRESS,1963
    073,117-08,

    NORTH A C   ET-AL
    AFRICAN LAND TENURE DEVELOPMENTS IN KENYA AND UGANDA AND
    THEIR APPLICATION TO NORTHERN RHODESIA.
    JOURNAL OF AFRICAN ADMINISTRATION 13 OCTOBER 1961
    PP 211-219
    070,117-08,139-08,142-08,

    OMINDE S H
    LAND AND POPULATION MOVEMENTS IN KENYA
    EVANSTON,NORTHWESTERN UNIVERSITY PRESS,1968
    074,117-08,

    PEDRAZA G J W
    LAND CONSOLIDATION IN THE KIKUYU AREA OF KENYA CHAPTER 6.
    IN EDITH WHETHAM AND JEAN CURRIE, (EDS.), READINGS IN THE
    APPLIED ECONOMICS OF AFRICA, LONDON, CAMBRIDGE UNIVERSITY
    PRESS, 1, 1967, PP 58-71
    070,117-08,

    REPORT WORKING PARTY

WHO CONTROLS INDUSTRY IN KENYA.
KENYA, EAST AFRICAN PUBLISHING HOUSE, 1968
071,117-08,

117-08
REPUBLIC OF KENYA
AFRICAN SOCIALISM AND ITS APPLICATION TO PLANNING IN KENYA
NAIROBI,GOVERNMENT PRINTER,1965
054,072,077,117-08,

117-09
BANEFIELD JANE
THE STRUCTURE AND ADMINISTRATION OF THE EAST AFRICAN COMMON
SERVICES ORGANIZATION.
IN COLIN LEYS AND P ROBSON (EDS), FEDERATION IN EAST AFRICA--
OPPORTUNITIES AND PROBLEMS,NAIROBI, OXFORD UNIVERSITY PRESS,
1965,PP 30-40
078,117-09,136-09,139-09,

CASTAGNO A A JR
THE SOMALI-KENYA CONTROVERSY
JOURNAL OF MODERN AFRICAN STUDIES 2 1964 PP 165-188
059, 117-09, 133-09,

HUGHES A J
EAST AFRICA-- THE SEARCH FOR UNITY-- KENYA, TANGANYIKA,
UGANDA AND ZANZIBAR.
MIDDLESEX, HARMONDSWORTH, 1963
077,117-09,136-09,139-09,

HOWELL JOHN
AN ANALYSIS OF KENYAN FOREIGN POLICY.
THE JOURNAL OF MODERN AFRICAN STUDIES, VOL. 6, NO. 1, 1968,
PP. 29-48
082,117-09,

117-10
NGUGI JAMES
THE RIVER BETWEEN.
IBADAN,HEINEMANN EDUCATIONAL BOOKS LTD,1965
090,117-10,

NGUGI JAMES
WEEP NOT, CHILD.
NEW YORK, MACMILLAN CO., 1969   (LONDON, HEINEMANN
EDUCATIONAL BOOKS)
090,117-10,

NGUGI JAMES
THE BLACK HERMIT.
NEW YORK, HUMANITIES PRESS INC., 1968   (LONDON, HEINEMANN
EDUCATIONAL BOOKS)
090,117-10,

117-12
BROWN EDWARD E   WEBSTER JOHN B
A BIBLIOGRAPHY ON POLITICS AND GOVERNMENT IN KENYA.
NEW YORK, SYRACUSE UNIVERSITY PROGRAM OF EASTERN AFRICAN
STUDIES, 1965
117-12,

117-12
   LIBRARY OF CONGRESS
   OFFICIAL PUBLICATIONS OF BRITISH EAST AFRICA, PART 3, KENYA
   AND ZANZIBAR.
   WASHINGTON, LIBRARY OF CONGRESS, 1962
   117-12,

   MOSES LARRY
   KENYA, UGANDA, TANGANYIKA 1960-1964--A BIBLIOGRAPHY.
   WASHINGTON, DEPT. OF STATE, EXTERNAL RESEARCH STAFF, 1964
   117-12,139-12,

   WEBSTER JOHN B
   A BIBLIOGRAPHY ON KENYA.
   NEW YORK, SYRACUSE UNIVERSITY PROGRAM OF EASTERN AFRICAN
   STUDIES, 1967
   117-12,

118. LESOTHO

118-01
   DUNCAN PATRICK
   SOTHO LAWS AND CUSTOMS.
   CAPE TOWN, OXFORD UNIVERSITY PRESS, 1960
   066,118-01,

   ASHTON HUGH
   THE BASUTO.
   LONDON, OXFORD UNIVERSITY PRESS, 1967
   118-01,

118-02
   LYE WILLIAM F
   THE DIFAQANE-THE MFECANE IN THE SOUTHERN SOTHO AREA 1822-24
   JOURNAL OF AFRICAN HISTORY 8 1967 PP 107-131
   031,118-02,132-02,

118-07
   HALPERN JACK
   SOUTH AFRICA'S HOSTAGES-- BASUTOLAND, BECHUANALAND,
   AND SWAZILAND.
   BALTIMORE, PENGUIN,1965
   032,088,102-07,118-07,135-07,

   HUGHES P
   THE INTRODUCTION OF LOCAL GOVERNMENT TO BASUTOLAND.
   JOURNAL OF LOCAL ADMIN. OVERSEAS, 2, 3, JULY, 1963
   118-07,

118-09
   SPENCE JOHN EDWARD
   LESOTHO--THE POLITICS OF DEPENDENCE.
   LONDON, OXFORD UNIVERSITY PRESS, 1968
   118-09,

118-11
  STEVENS RICHARD P
  LESOTHO BOTSWANA AND SWAZILAND.
  LONDON, PALL MALL PRESS, 1967
  102-11, 118-11, 135-11,

119. LIBERIA

119-01
  HAIR P E H
  NOTES ON THE DISCOVERY OF THE VAI SCRIPT WITH A
  BIBLIOGRAPHY.
  SIERRA LEONE LANGUAGE REVIEW 2 1963 PP 36-49
  012,119-01,

119-02
  HARGREAVES JOHN D
  AFRICAN COLONIZATION IN THE NINETEENTH CENTURY-- LIBERIA AND
  SIERRA LEONE.
  IN JEFFREY BUTLER (ED), BOSTON UNIVERSITY PAPERS IN AFRICAN
  HISTORY VOLUME I, BOSTON, BOSTON UNIVERSITY PRESS, 1964, PP 55-
  76
  029,119-02,131-02,

  AZIKIWE NNAMDI
  IN DEFENCE OF LIBERIA.
  JOURNAL OF NEGRO HISTORY 17 JANUARY 1932 PP 30-49
  029,119-02,128-04,

  LYNCH HOLLIS R
  EDWARD WILMOT BLYDEN--PAN-NEGRO PATRIOT 1832-1912.
  LONDON, OXFORD UNIVERSITY PRESS, 1967
  029,030,119-02,

  MOWER J H
  THE REPUBLIC OF LIBERIA.
  THE JOURNAL OF NEGRO HISTORY XXXII 1947 PP 265-306
  029,119-02,

  STAUDENRAUS P J
  THE AFRICAN COLONIZATION MOVEMENT.1816-1865
  NEW YORK, COLUMBIA UNIVERSITY PRESS, 1961
  029,119-02,

  WESLEY CHARLES H
  THE STRUGGLE FOR THE RECOGNITION OF HAITI AND LIBERIA AS
  INDEPENDENT REPUBLICS.
  THE JOURNAL OF NEGRO HISTORY II 1917 PP 369-383
  029,119-02,

  AZIKIWE NNAMDI
  LIBERIA IN WORLD POLITICS.
  LONDON, A H STOCKWELL, 1934
  029,119-02,128-04,

119-03
   GAY J   COLE M
   THE NEW MATHEMATICS AND THE OLD CULTURE
   NEW YORK,HOLT,RINEHART AND WINSTON,1967
   041,119-03,

119-04
   TOWNSEND E REGINALD ED
   THE OFFICIAL PAPERS OF WILLIAM V S TUBMAN, PRESIDENT OF THE
   REPUBLIC OF LIBERIA.
   NEW YORK, HUMANITIES PRESS INC., 1968
   060,119-04,

119-05
   CHECCHI AND COMPANY
   A DEVELOPMENT STUDY AND PRELIMINARY DESIGNS FOR AN INDUS-
   TRIAL PARK IN MONROVIA.
   WASHINGTON, D.C., CHECCHI AND COMPANY, 1964
   092,119-05,

   FRAENKEL MERRAN
   TRIBE AND CLASS IN MONROVIA.
   LONDON, OXFORD UNIVERSITY PRESS, 1964
   119-05,

   WOOD DONALD S
   THE PATTERN OF SETTLEMENT AND DEVELOPMENT IN LIBERIA.
   JOURNAL OF GEOGRAPHY, VOL. 62, 9, DECEMBER, 1963
   119-05,

119-06
   LIEBENOW J GUS
   LIBERIA.
   IN COLEMAN, J.S. AND ROSBERG, C. G. (EDS), POLITICAL PARTIES
   AND NATIONAL INTEGRATION IN TROPICAL AFRICA, LOS ANGELES,
   UNIVERSITY OF CALIFORNIA PRESS, 1964
   119-06,

119-07
   LIEBENOW J GUS
   LIBERIA--THE EVOLUTION OF PRIVILEGE.
   ITHACA, CORNELL UNIVERSITY PRESS, 1969
   029,058,119-07,

   HUBERICH CHARLES H
   THE POLITICAL AND LEGISLATIVE HISTORY OF LIBERIA.
   NEW YORK, NEW YORK CENTRAL BOOK CO., 1947
   119-07,

   LIEBENOW J GUS
   LIBERIA.
   IN G.M. CARTER (ED) AFRICAN ONE-PARTY STATES, ITHACA,
   CORNELL UNIVERSITY PRESS, 1962
   119-07,

119-08
   CLOWER ROBERT W   ET AL
   GROWTH WITHOUT DEVELOPMENT, AN ECONOMIC SURVEY OF LIBERIA.
   EVANSTON,NORTHWESTERN UNIVERISTY PRESS,1966

CHAPTER 10 AND APPENDIX PP 259-335
073,119-08,

119-09
BIXLER RAYMOND W
THE FOREIGN POLICY OF THE UNITED STATES IN LIBERIA.
NEW YORK, PAGEANT PRESS, 1957
083,119-09,

119-12
LIBRARY OF CONGRESS
LIBERIA--A SELECTED LIST OF REFERENCES.
WASHINGTON, LIBRARY OF CONGRESS, 1942
119-12,

SOLOMON MARVIN D   D AZEVEDO   COMPS
A GENERAL BIBLIOGRAPHY OF THE REPUBLIC OF LIBERIA.
EVANSTON, NORTHWESTERN UNIVERSITY PRESS, 1962
119-12,

120. LIBYA

120-01
PETERS E L
SOME STRUCTURAL ASPECTS OF THE FEUDS AMONG THE CAMEL-HERDING
BEDOUIN OF CYRENAICA.
AFRICA 37 1967 PP 260-282
009,120-01,

EVANS-PRITCHARD E E
THE SANUSI OF CYRENAICA.
OXFORD, CLARENDON PRESS, 1949
120-01,

120-07
KHADDURI MAJID
MODERN LIBYA-- A STUDY IN POLITICAL DEVELOPMENT.
BALTIMORE, JOHNS HOPKINS UNIVERSITY PRESS, 1963
120-07,

120-08
INTERNATIONAL BANK FOR RECONSTRUCTION AND DEVELOPMENT
THE ECONOMIC DEVELOPMENT OF LIBYA
BALTIMORE, JOHNS HOPKINS UNIVERSITY PRESS, 1960
073,120-08,

120-09
SANDS WILLIAM
PROSPECTS FOR A UNITED MAGHRIB
IN TIBOR KEREKES (ED), THE ARAB MIDDLE EAST AND MUSLIM
AFRICA, NEW YORK, PRAEGER, 1961
078,101-09,120-09,126-09,138-09,

120-11
WRIGHT JOHN

```
LIBYA.
NEW YORK, PRAEGER, 1969
120-11,
```

121. MALAGASY REPUBLIC (MADAGASCAR)

121-01
```
RAHAJASON RAYMOND C
ESSAI SUR LA LANGUE MALGACHE.
TANANANRIVE, IMP. IARIVO, 1962
121-01.
```

```
RAMANDRAIVONONA DESI
LE MALGACHE, SA LANGUE ET SA RELIGION.
PARIS, PRESENCE AFRICAINE, 1959
121-01,
```

121-02
```
KENT R K
MADAGASCAR AND AFRICA 1-THE PROBLEM OF THE BARA 2-THE
SAKALAVA, MAROSERANA, DADY AND TROMBA BEFORE 1700, 3-THE
ANTEIMORO
JOURNAL OF AFRICAN HISTORY 9 1968 PP 387-408, 527-546 AND
10 1969 PP 45-65
121-02,
```

```
RANAIVO GUY DE P
BIOGRAPHIE ET HISTOIRE SOCIALE DE MADAGASCAR.
NIMES, IMP. MAUGER, 1954
121-02,
```

121-03
```
MANNONI DOMINIQUE O
PROSPERO AND CALIBAN-- THE PSYCHOLOGY OF COLONIZATION.
LONDON, METHUEN AND COMPANY, 1956 (NEW YORK, PRAEGER, 1964)
035,041,088,121-03,
```

121-06
```
JUMEAUX R
ESSAI D ANALYSE DU NATIONALISME MALGACHE ESSAY ANALYZING
MALAGASY NATIONALISM.
L'AFRIQUE ET L'ASIE 40 1957 PP 31-42
055,121-06,
```

121-07
```
WEBSTER JOHN B
THE CONSTITUTIONS OF BURUNDI MALAGASY AND RWANDA.
SYRACUSE, NEW YORK, MAXWELL GRADUATE SCHOOL OF PUBLIC AFFAIRS,
THE PROGRAM OF EASTERN STUDIES, NO. 3, FEB., 1964
066,103-07,121-07,129-07,
```

121-10
```
RABEMANANJARA JACQUE
AGAPES DES DIEUX--TRITRIVA, TRAGEIDE MALGACHE.
PARIS, PRESENCE AFRICAINE, 1962
```

121-10,

121-10
    RABEMANANJARA JACQUE
    ANTIDOTE. POEMES.
    PARIS, PRESENCE AFRICAINE. 1961
    121-10,

    RABEMANANJARA JACQUE
    ANTSA.
    PARIS, PRESENCE AFRICAINE, 1962
    121-10,

    RABEMANANJARA JACQUE
    LAMBA--POEME.
    PARIS, PRESENCE AFRICAINE, 1966 (2ND EDITION)
    121-10,

    RABEMANANJARA JACQUE
    LES BOUTRIERS DE L AURORE--TRAGEDIE EN 3 ACTES, 6 TABLEAUX.
    PARIS, PRESENCE AFRICAINE, 1957
    121-10,

    RABEMANANJARA JACQUE
    LES DIEUX MALGACHES, VERSION DESTINEE A LA SCENE.
    PARIS, HACHETTE, 1964 (2ND EDITION)
    121-10,

    RABEMANANJARA JACQUE
    NATIONALISME ET PROBLEMES MALGACHES.
    PARIS, PRESENCE AFRICAINE, 1958
    121-10,

    RABEMANANJARA JACQUE
    RITES MILLENAIRES.
    PARIS, SEGHERS, 1955
    121-10,

    RABEMANANJARA JACQUE
    TEMOIGNAGE MALGACHE ET COLONIALISME.
    PARIS, PRESENCE AFRICAINE, 1956
    121-10,

    RAKOTO-RATSIMAMANGA LORIN CLAUDE-MARIE
    POETES MALGACHES DE LANGUE FRANCAISE.
    PARIS, PRESENCE AFRICAINE, 1956
    121-10,

121-11
    THOMPSON VIRGINIA   ADLOFF RICHARD
    THE MALAGASY REPUBLIC--MADAGASCAR TODAY.
    STANFORD, STANFORD UNIVERSITY PRESS, 1965
    121-11,

122. MALAWI

122-01
    MITCHELL J CLYDE
    AFRICAN TRIBES AND LANGUAGES OF THE FEDERATION OF RHODESIA
    AND NYASALAND.
    SALISBURY, FEDERAL GOVERNMENT PRINTERS, RHODESIA AND
    122-01,142-01,

122-02
    STOKES E   BROWN RICHARD   EDS
    THE ZAMBESIAN PAST-STUDIES IN CENTRAL AFRICAN HISTORY
    MANCHESTER MANCHESTER UNIVERSITY PRESS 1966
    025,122-02,142-02,145-02,

    MAIR LUCY P
    NATIVE ADMINISTRATION IN CENTRAL NYASALAND.
    LONDON,HIS MAJESTY'S STATIONERY OFFICE, 1952
    035,122-02,

    MWASE GEORGE SIMEON ROTBERG ROBERT   ED
    STRIKE A BLOW AND DIE.
    CAMBRIDGE, HARVARD UNIVERSITY PRESS, 1967
    034, 122-02,

    SHEPPERSON GEORGE   PRICE THOMAS
    INDEPENDENT AFRICAN-- JOHN CHILEMBWE AND THE ORIGINS SETTING
    AND SIGNIFICANCE OF THE NYASALAND RISING OF 1915.
    EDINBURGH,EDINBURGH UNIVERSITY PRESS, 1958
    034,122-02,

122-03
    SHEPPERSON GEORGE
    NYASALAND AND THE MILLENIUM.
    IN SYLVIA L THRUPP (ED), MILLENNIAL DREAMS IN ACTION,
    THE HAGUE, MOUTON, 1962, PP 144-159
    051,122-03,

    WISHLADE R L
    SECTARIANISM IN SOUTHERN NYASALAND.
    LONDON,OXFORD UNIVERSITY PRESS,1965
    051,122-03,

    SHEPPERSON GEORGE
    THE JUMBE OF KOTA KOTA AND SOME ASPECTS OF THE HISTORY OF
    ISLAM IN BRITISH CENTRAL AFRICA.
    IN LEWIS, ISLAM IN TROPICAL AFRICA, LONDON, OXFORD UNIVERSITY
    PRESS, 1966, P. 193-207
    122-03,

122-04
    BANDA HASTINGS K   NKUMBULA HARRY M
    FEDERATION IN CENTRAL AFRICA.
    LONDON,1951
    078,122-04,

CHISIZA D K
THE OUTLOOK FOR CONTEMPORARY AFRICA CHAPTER 3.
IN AFRICA'S FREEDOM, NEW YORK, BARNES AND NOBLE, 1964,
PP 38-54
060,122-04,

122-04
    CHISIZA D K
    AFRICA-- WHAT LIES AHEAD.
    NEW YORK AFRICAN AMERICAN INSTITUTE 1962
    LONDON, COMMAND 1030, HER MAJESTY'S STATIONERY OFFICE, 1960
    060,122-04,

122-05
    BETTISON DAVID G   RIGBY P J A
    PATTERNS OF INCOME AND EXPENDITURE IN BLANTYRE-LIMBE,
    NYASALAND.
    LUSAKA, RHODES-LIVINGSTONE INSTITUTE, 1961
    122-05,

122-06
    CHITEPO HERBERT W
    DEVELOPMENTS IN CENTRAL AFRICA.
    IN DAVID P CURRIE (ED), FEDERALISM AND THE NEW NATIONS OF
    AFRICA. CHICAGO, UNIVERSITY OF CHICAGO PRESS, 1964, PP 3-28
    078,087,122-06,142-06,145-06,

    CHIDZERO BERNARD T
    CENTRAL AFRICA-- THE RACE QUESTION AND THE FRANCHISE.
    RACE 1 1955 PP 53-60
    088,122-06,142-06,

    DOTSON FLOYD   LILLIAN O
    THE INDIAN MINORITY OF ZAMBIA, RHODESIA, AND MALAWI.
    NEW HAVEN, CONN. (YALE), MCGILL-QUEEN'S PRESS, 1969
    085,142-06,145-06,122-06,

    GRAY RICHARD
    THE TWO NATIONS-- ASPECTS OF THE DEVELOPMENT OF RACE
    RELATIONS IN THE RHODESIAS AND NYASALAND.
    LONDON OXFORD UNIVERSITY PRESS 1960
    087,088,122-06,142-06,145-06,

    ROTBERG ROBERT I
    THE RISE OF NATIONALISM IN CENTRAL AFRICA-- THE MAKING
    OF MALAWI AND ZAMBIA, 1873-1964.
    CAMBRIDGE HARVARD UNIVERSITY PRESS 1966
    055,122-06,142-06,

    SPIRO HERBERT J
    THE FEDERATION OF RHODESIA AND NYASALAND.
    IN THOMAS FRANCK (ED), WHY FEDERATIONS FAIL, NEW YORK, NEW
    YORK UNIVERSITY PRESS, 1968, PP. 37-90
    078,122-06,145-06,

122-07
    FRANCK THOMAS M
    RACE AND NATIONALISM--THE STRUGGLE FOR POWER IN RHODESIA-
    NYASALAND
    NEW YORK, FORDHAM UNIVERSITY PRESS, 1960

087,122-07,142-07,145-07,

122-07
   MAIR LUCY P
   THE NYASALAND ELECTIONS OF 1961.
   LONDON, ATHLONE PRESS, 1962
   063,122-07,

   LIEBENOW J GUS
   FEDERALISM IN RHODESIA AND NYASALAND.
   IN WILLIAM LIVINGSTON (ED), FEDERALISM IN THE COMMONWEALTH,
   LONDON, 1963
   122-07,

   SPIRO HERBERT J
   RHODESIA AND NYASALAND.
   IN G.M. CARTER (ED), FIVE AFRICAN STATES--RESPONSES TO
   DIVERSITY, ITHACA, CORNELL UNIVERSITY PRESS, 1963
   122-07,

122-08
   BARBER WILLIAM J
   ECONOMIC RATIONALITY AND BEHAVIOR PATTERNS IN AN
   UNDERDEVELOPED AREA--A CASE STUDY OF AFRICAN ECONOMICS IN
   THE RHODESIAS.
   ENONOMIC DEVELOPMENT AND CULTURAL CHANGE 8 1960 PP 237-251
   073,122-08,142-08,145-08,

   DEAN EDWIN
   THE SUPPLY RESPONSES OF AFRICAN FARMERS-- THEORY
   AND MEASUREMENT IN MALAWI.
   AMSTERDAM NORTH-HOLLAND PUBLISHING CO. 1966
   070,122-08,

122-09
   RICHARDSON HENRY J
   MALAWI- BETWEEN BLACK AND WHITE AFRICA
   AFRICA REPORT 15 FEBRUARY 1970 PP 18-21
   088,122-09,

   HAZLEWOOD ARTHUR   HENDERSON P D   EDS
   NYASALAND-- THE ECONOMICS OF FEDERATION.
   OXFORD, BLACKWELL, 1960
   078,122-09,

122-10
   SHEPPERSON GEORGE
   THE LITERATURE OF BRITISH CENTRAL AFRICA.
   RHODES-LIVINGSTONE JOURNAL 23 1958 PP 12-46
   090,122-10,142-10,145-10,

122-11
   PIKE JOHN
   MALAWI.
   LONDON, PALL MALL PRESS, 1968
   122-11,

122-12
   BROWN EDWARD E   ET AL
   A BIBLIOGRAPHY OF MALAWI.

NEW YORK, SYRACUSE UNIVERSITY, 1965
122-12,

122-12
WALKER AUDREY A   ED
THE RHODESIAS AND NYASALAND--A GUIDE TO OFFICIAL PUBLICA-
TIONS.
WASHINGTON, U.S. GOVERNMENT PRINTING OFFICE, 1965
122-12,142-12,

123. MALI

123-01
GOVERNMENT OF FRANCE
COUTUMIERS JURIDIQUE DE L'AFRIQUE OCCIDENTALE FRANCAISE--
SOUDAN (FRENCH WEST AFRICAN JURIDIC CUSTOMS-- SUDAN).
PARIS, LAROSE EDITEURS, 1939, VOL 2
066,123-01,

BA AMADOU HAMPATE   DIETERLEN GERMAINE
KOUMEN--TEXTE INITIATIQUE DES PASTEURS PEULS.
PARIS, MOUTON ET CIE, 1961
123-01,

TRAVELE MOUSSA
PETIT MANUEL FRANCAIS-BAMBARA.
PARIS, LIBRAIRIE ORIENTALISTE PAUL GEUTHNER, 1955
123-01,

123-02
OLORUNTIMEHIN B O
RESISTANCE MOVEMENTS IN THE TUKULOR EMPIRE.
CAHIERS D'ETUDES AFRICAINES, VOL. VIII, 1968, NO. 29,
PP. 123-143
034,123-02,

ROUCH JEAN
SONGHAY.
IN P J M MCEWAN (ED) AFRICA FROM EARLY TIMES TO 1800, LONDON,
OXFORD UNIVERSITY PRESS, 1968, PP 59-89
022,123-02,

DECRAENE PHILIPPE
LE MALI MEDIEVAL (MEDIEVAL MALI).
CIVILISATIONS 12 1962 PP 250-258
022,123-02,

BROWN WILLIAM A
TOWARD A CHRONOLOGY FOR THE CALIPHATE OF HAMDULLAHI (MASINA)
CAHIERS D'ETUDES AFRICAINE, VOL. VIII, NO. 31, 1968, PP. 428
434
024,123-02,

HAMA BOUBOU
HISTOIRE DES SONGHAY (HISTORY OF THE SONGHAY).

PARIS, PRESENCE AFRICAINE, 1968
022,123-02,

123-02
   NIANE DJUBRIL T
   SUNDIATA--AN EPIC OF OLD MALI (TRANSLATED BY G D PICKETT)
   LONDON, LONGMANS, 1965
   022,123-02,

   BA AMADOU HAMPATE   DAGET JACQUES
   L'EMPIRE PEUL DE MACINA 1818-1853.   THE FULANI EMPIRE OF
   MACINA 1818-1853).
   BAMAKO, INSTITUT FRANCAIS D'AFRIQUE NOIRE, CENTRE DU SOUDAN,
   ETUDES SOUDANAISES 3 1962
   024,123-02,

   BA AMADOU HAMPATE
   L'EMPIRE PEUL DE MACINA 1818-1853.
   BAMAKO, INSTITUT FRANCAIS D'AFRIQUE NOIRE, CENTRE DU SOUDAN,
   1955
   099,123-02,

   MONTEIL CHARLES
   LES EMPIRES DU MALI (THE EMPIRES OF MALI).
   BULLETIN DU COMITE D'ETUDES HISTORIQUES ET SCIENTIFIQUES DE
   L'AFRIQUE OCCIDENTALE FRANCAISE 12 1929 PP 191-447
   022,123-02,

   MONTEIL CHARLES
   UNE CITE SOUDANAISE-- DJENNE METROPOLE DU DELTA CENTRAL
   DU NIGER (A SUDANESE CITY-- JENNE, METROPOLIS OF THE
   CENTRAL NIGER DELTA).
   SOCIETE D'EDITIONS DE GEOGRAPHIE MARITIME ET COLONIALE, PARIS,
   1932
   022,123-02,

   NIANE DJUBRIL T
   RECHERCHES SUR L'EMPIRE DU MALI AU MOYEN AGE (RESEARCH
   ON THE MALI EMPIRE IN THE MIDDLE AGES).
   RECHERCHES AFRICAINES 2 1961 PP 31-51
   022,123-02,

   ROUCH JEAN
   CONTRIBUTION A L'HISTOIRE DES SONGHAY (A CONTRIBUTION TO
   THE HISTORY OF SONGHAI).
   DAKAR, INSTITUT FRANCAIS D'AFRIQUE NOIRE, MEMOIRE 29, 1953
   022,123-02,

   BA AMADOU HAMPATE   CARDAIRE MARCEL
   TIERNO BOKAR, LE SAGE DE BANDIAGARA.
   PARIS, PRESENCE AFRICAINE, 1957
   123-02,

   TRAORE ANDRE   GUILHEM MARCEL
   MALI--RECITS HISTORIQUES--3EME ET 4EME ANNEES DU CYCLE
   FONDAMENTAL.
   PARIS, LIGEL, 1964
   123-02,

123-03

MARTY PAUL
ETUDES SUR L'ISLAM ET LES TRIBUS DU SOUDAN (STUDIES ON
ISLAM AND THE SUDANIC TRIBES).
PARIS, EDITIONS ERNEST LEROUX, 1920
021,123-03,

123-03
MARTY PAUL
LA REGION DE KAYES, LE PAYS BAMBARA, LE SAHEL DE NIORO VOL4
(THE KAYES REGION, BAMBARA COUNTRY, THE NIORO SAVANNAH).
IN ETUDES SUR L'ISLAM ET LES TRIBUS DU SOUDAN, PARIS,
EDITIONS ERNEST LEROUX, 1920
021,123-03,

MOREAU R L
LES MARABOUTS DE DORI (THE MARABOUS OF DORI).
ARCHIVES DE SOCIOLOGIE DES RELIGIONS 17 JANUARY 1964
PP 113-134
052,123-03,

123-04
MADIERA KIETA
THE SINGLE PARTY IN AFRICA.
PRESENCE AFRICAINE 30 FEBRUARY 1960 PP 3-24
060,061,065,123-04,

SNYDER FRANCIS G
THE POLITICAL THOUGHT OF MODIBO KEITA.
JOURNAL OF MODERN AFRICAN STUDIES 5 MAY 1967 PP 79-106
054,123-04,

123-05
MEILLASSOUX CLAUDE
URBANIZATION OF AN AFRICAN COMMUNITY--VOLUNTARY ASSOCIATIONS
IN BAMAKO.
SEATTLE, UNIVERSITY OF WASHINGTON PRESS, 1968
046,123-05,

MINER HORACE M
THE PRIMITIVE CITY OF TIMBUCTOO
GARDEN CITY,   DOUBLEDAY, 1965
045,123-05,

VILLIEN-ROSSI MARIE
BAMAKO, CAPITALE DU MALI.
BULLETIN IFAN, 28, B, 1-2, JAN.-APR., 1966)
123-05,

123-06
ZOLBERG ARISTIDE R
PATTERNS OF NATIONAL INTEGRATION.
THE JOURNAL OF MODERN AFRICAN STUDIES, 5, 4, 1967, PP 449-67
055,058,116-06,123-06,

HAZARD JOHN N
MALI'S SOCIALISM AND THE SOVIET LEGAL MODEL.
YALE LAW JOURNAL, LXXVII, 1967, PP. 28-69
068,123-06,

SNYDER FRANCIS G

AN ERA ENDS IN MALI.
AFRICA REPORT, MARCH/APRIL, 1969, PP. 16-53
064,123-06,

123-06
   DEPUIS J
   UN PROBLEME DE MINORITE-- LES NOMADES DANS L'ETAT SOUDANAISE
   (A MINORITY PROBLEM-- NOMADES IN THE STATE OF SUDAN).
   L'AFRIQUE ET L'ASIE 50 1960 PP 19-44
   057,123-06,

   HODGKIN THOMAS   MORGENTHAU RUTH SCHACHTER
   MALI.
   IN COLEMAN, J.S. AND ROSBERG, C.G. (ED), POLITICAL PARTIES
   AND NATIONAL INTEGRATION IN TROPICAL AFRICA, LOS ANGELES,
   UNIVERSITY OF CALIFORNIA PRESS, 1964
   123-06,

123-07
   SNYDER FRANCIS G
   ONE-PARTY GOVERNMENT IN MALI-- TRANSITION TOWARD CONTROL.
   NEW HAVEN, YALE UNIVERSITY PRESS, 1965
   061,123-07,

   MORGENTHAU RUTH SCHACHTER
   POLITICAL PARTIES IN FRENCH-SPEAKING WEST AFRICA.
   OXFORD, OXFORD UNIVERSITY PRESS, 1964
   055,058,061,109-07,123-07,130-07,

123-08
   REPUBLIQUE DU MALI
   COMPTES ECONOMIQUES DE LA REPUBLIQUE DU MALI 1959.
   MINISTERE DU PLAN ET DE LA COORDINATION, BAMAKO,
   GOVERNMENT PRINTER, 1962
   123-08,

   AMIN SAMIR
   TROIS EXPERIENCES AFRICAINES DE DEVELOPPEMENT-LE MALI,LA
   GUINEE,ET LA GHANA
   PARIS PRESSES UNIVERSITAIRES DE FRANCE 1965
   073,123-08,115-08,114-08,

   DUMONT RENE
   RECONVERSION DE L'ECONOMIE AGRIOLE EN GUINEE EN COTE
   D'IVOIRE ET AU MALI.
   PARIS, PRESSES UNIVERSITAIRES DE FRANCE, 1961
   115-08, 123-08,

123-09
   FOLTZ WILLIAM J
   FROM FRENCH WEST AFRICA TO THE MALI FEDERATION.
   NEW HAVEN. YALE UNIVERSITY PRESS, 1965
   077,123-09,130-09,

123-10
   SISSOKO FILY-DABO
   COUPS DE SAGAIE, CONTROVERSES SUR L'UNION FRANCAISE.
   PARIS, ED. DE LA TOUR DU GUET, 1957
   123-10,

SISSOKO FILY-DABO
CRAYONS ET PORTRAITS.
MULHOUSE, IMP. UNION, 1953
123-10,

123-10
  SISSOKO FILY-DABO
  HARMAKHIS--POEMES DU TERROIR AFRICAIN.
  PARIS, ED. DE LA TOUR DU GUET, 1955
  123-10,

  SISSOKO FILY-DABO
  LA PASSION DE DJIME.
  PARIS, ED. DE LA TOUR DU GUET, 1956
  123-10,

  SISSOKO FILY-DABO
  LA SAVANE ROUGE.
  AVIGNON, LES PRESSES UNIVERSELLES, 1962
  123-10,

  SISSOKO FILY-DABO
  POEMES DE L AFRIQUE NOIRE FEUX DE BROUSSE HARMAKHIS--FLEURS
  ET CHARDONS.
  PARIS, DEBRESSE, 1963
  123-10,

  SISSOKO FILY-DABO
  SAGESSE NOIRE, SENTENCES ET PROVERBES MALINKES.
  PARIS, ED. DE LA TOUR DU GUET, 1955, SVIII
  123-10,

123-11
  LUSIGNAN GUY DE
  FRENCH-SPEAKING AFRICA SINCE INDEPENDENCE.
  NEW YORK, PRAEGER PUBLISHERS, 1969
  056,061,104-11,105-11,106-11,107-11,109-11,112-11,
  115-11,116-11,123-11,137-11,141-11,

123-12
  BRASSEUR PAULE
  BIBLIOGRAPHIE GENRALE DU MALI
  DAKAR, IFAN, 1964
  123-12,

  CUTTER C H
  MALI--A BIBLIOGRAPHIC INTRODUCTION.
  AFRICAN STUDIES BULLETIN, 9, 3, DEC., 1966
  123-12,

  LANCEY M W DE
  THE GHANA-GUINEA-MALI UNION--A BIBLIOGRAPHIC ESSAY.
  AFRICAN STUDIES BULLETIN, 9, 2, SEPTEMBER, 1966
  114-12,115-12,123-12,

124. MAURITANIA

124-01
   GOVERNMENT OF FRANCE
   COUTUMIERS JURIDIQUES DE L'AFRIQUE OCCIDENTALE FRANCAISE--
   MAURITANIE, NIGER, COTE D'IVOIRE, DAHOMEY, GUINEE FRANCAISE
   (FRENCH WEST AFRICAN JURIDIC CUSTOMS-- MAURITANIA, NIGER
   IVORY COAST, DAHOMEY, FRENCH GUINEA) .
   PARIS, LIBRAIRIE LAROSE, 1939, VOL3
   066,109-01,115-01,116-01,124-01,127-01,

124-03
   MARTY PAUL
   ETUDES SUR L'ISLAM ET LES TRIBUS MAURES-- LES BRAKNA
   (STUDIES ON ISLAM AND THE MAURITANIAN TRIBES-- THE BRAKNA.
   PARIS, EDITIONS ERNEST LEROUX, 1921
   021,124-03,

   GERTEINY ALFRED G
   MAURITANIA
   IN KRITZECK AND LEWIS, PP 319-332
   124-03,

124-07
   MOORE CLEMENT H
   ONE-PARTYISM IN MAURITANIA.
   JOURNAL OF MODERN AFRICAN STUDIES 3 OCTOBER 1965 PP 409-420
   061,124-07,

124-10
   BA OUMAR
   DIALOGUE OU D'UNE RIVE A L'AUTRE (POEMES).
   SAINT-LOUIS, IFAN   (ETUDES MAURITANIENNES), N.D.
   124-10,

   BA OUMAR
   FAUT-IL GARDER LA LANGUE FRANCAISE.
   SAINT-LOUIS, IFAN, 1966
   124-10,

   BA OUMAR
   MON MEILLEUR CHEF DE CANTON--TEMOIGNAGE.
   LYON, IMP. NICOLON, 1966
   124-10,

   BA OUMAR
   NOTES SUR LA DEMOCRATIE EN PAYS TOUCOULEUR.
   SAINT-LOUIS, IFAN, 1966
   124-10,

   BA OUMAR
   POEMES PEUL MODERNES.
   NOUAKCHOTT, IMP. MAURITANIENNE, 1965
   124-10,

   BA OUMAR

PRESQUE GRIFFONAGES OU LA FRANCOPHONIE.
SAINT-LOUIS, IFAN, 1966
124-10.

124-11
  GERTEINY ALFRED G
  MAURITANIA.
  LONDON, PALL MALL PRESS, 1967
  124-11.

  HAMIDOUN MOKTAR OULD
  PRECIS SUR LA MAURITANIE.
  SAINT-LOUIS, IFAN, 1952
  124-11.

124-12
  TOUPET CHARLES
  ORIENTATION BIBLIOGRAPHIQUE SUR LA MAURITANIE.
  DAKAR, INSTITUT FRANCAISE D'AFRIQUE NOIRE, 1958
  124-12.

125. MAURITIUS

125-02
  BARNWELL PATRICK J   TOUSSAINT AUGUSTE
  A SHORT HISTORY OF MAURITIUS
  NEW YORK AND LONDON,LONGMANS,GREEN FOR THE GOVERNMENT OF
  MAURITIUS, 1949
  125-02.

125-03
  TITMUSS RICHARD M   ABEL-SMITH B
  SOCIAL AND POPULATION GROWTH IN MAURITIUS
  LONDON,METHUEN,1961, REPORT TO THE GOVERNMENT OF MAURITIUS ;
  REPRINTED 1968
  125-03.

126. MOROCCO

126-01
  MIKESELL M W
  THE ROLE OF TRIBAL MARKETS IN MOROCCO--EXAMPLES FROM THE
  (NORTHERN ZONE).
  GEOGRAPHICAL REVIEW 48 OCTOBER 1958 PP 494-511
  010,126-01.

  TERRASSE H
  LA MASQUEE AL-QUARADUIYIR A FES (THE QUADIRIYYA MOSQUE AT
  FEZ).
  PARIS, KLINCKSIECK, 1969

092,126-01,

126-03
   GELLNER ERNEST
   TRIBALISM AND SOCIAL CHANGE IN NORTH AFRICA.
   IN WILLIAM H LEWIS (ED), FRENCH-SPEAKING AFRICA, THE SEARCH
   FOR IDENTITY, NEW YORK WALKER AND CO 1965 PP 107-118
   006,126-03,

   ABUN-NASR JAMIL
   THE SALAFIYYA MOVEMENT IN MOROCCO-- THE RELIGIOUS BASES
   OF THE MOROCCAN NATIONALIST MOVEMENT.
   IN IMMANUEL WALLERSTEIN, SOCIAL CHANGE THE COLONIAL
   SITUATION, NEW YORK, JOHN WILEY AND SONS, 1966
   052,126-03,

   LEWIS WILLIAM H
   FEUDING AND SOCIAL CHANGE IN MOROCCO.
   JOURNAL OF CONFLICT RESOLUTION 5 1961 PP 43-54
   008,126-03,

126-06
   HALSTEAD JOHN P
   REBIRTH OF A NATION-THE ORIGINS AND RISE OF MOROCCAN
   NATIONALISM,1912-1944
   CAMBRIDGE,MASS,HARVARD UNIVERSITY PRESS,1967
   055,126-06,

   ASHFORD DOUGLAS E
   NATIONAL DEVELOPMENT AND LOCAL REFORM-POLITICAL PARTITION
   IN MOROCCO,TUNISIA,AND PAKISTAN
   PRINCETON,PRINCETON UNIVERSITY PRESS
   126-06,138-06,

126-07
   ASHFORD DOUGLAS E
   POLITICAL CHANGE IN MOROCCO.
   PRINCETON, NEW JERSEY, PRINCETON UNIVERSITY PRESS, 1961
   126-07,

126-08
   INTERNATIONAL BANK FOR RECONSTRUCTION AND DEVELOPMENT
   THE ECONOMIC DEVELOPMENT OF MOROCCO
   BALTIMORE, JOHNS HOPKINS UNIVERSITY PRESS,1966
   073,126-08,

   AMIN SAMIR
   L'ECONOMIE DU MAGHREB VOLUME 1- LA COLONISATION ET LA
   DECOLONISATION VOLUME 2-LES PERSPECTIVE D'AVENIR
   PARIS,EDITIONS DE MINUIT, 1966
   073,101-08,126-08,138-08,

126-09
   GALLAGHER CHARLES F
   THE UNITED STATES AND NORTH AFRICA
   CAMBRIDGE, MASS,HARVARD UNIVERSITY PRESS, 1963
   083,101-09,126-09,138-09,

   SANDS WILLIAM
   PROSPECTS FOR A UNITED MAGHRIB

IN TIBOR KEREKES (ED), THE ARAB MIDDLE EAST AND MUSLIM
AFRICA, NEW YORK, PRAEGER, 1961
078,101-09,120-09,126-09,138-09,

126-11
   BRACE RICHARD M
   MOROCCO ALGERIA TUNISIA
   ENGLEWOOD CLIFFS, PRENTICE-HALL, 1964
   101-11,126-11,138-11,

127. NIGER

127-01
   RODD FRANCIS
   PEOPLE OF THE VEIL.
   LONDON, MACMILLAN, 1926
   127-01,

   NICOLAISEN JOHANNES
   ECOLOGY AND CULTURE OF THE PASTORAL TUAREG-- WITH SPECIAL
   REFERENCE TO THE TUAREG OF AHAGGAR AND AIR.
   COPENHAGEN, THE NATIONAL MUSEUM OF COPENHAGEN,
   ETHNOGRAPHICAL SERIES 9, 1963
   010,127-01,

   GOVERNMENT OF FRANCE
   COUTUMIERS JURIDIQUES DE L AFRIQUE OCCIDENTALE FRANCAISE--
   MAURITANIE, NIGER, COTE D IVOIRE, DAHOMEY, GUINEE FRANCAISE
   (FRENCH WEST AFRICAN JURIDIC CUSTOMS-- MAURITANIA, NIGER
   IVORY COAST, DAHOMEY, FRENCH GUINEA) .
   PARIS LIBRAIRIE LAROSE 1939 VOL3
   066,109-01,115-01,116-01,124-01,127-01,

   NICOLAISEN JOHANNES
   STRUCTURES POLITIQUES ET SOCIALES DES TOUAREG DE L AIR ET
   DE L AHAGGAR. (POLITICAL AND SOCIAL STRUCTURES OF THE TUAREG)
   ETUDES NIGERIENNES, 7, NIAMEY, INSTITUT FRANCAIS D'AFRIQUE
   NOIRE, 1963
   009,127-01,

   ROUCH JEAN
   LA RELIGION ET LA MAGIE SONGHAY (RELIGION AND MAGIC OF
   SONGHAY).
   PARIS, PRESSES UNIVERSITAIRES DE FRANCE, 1960
   013,127-01,

   BERNUS EDMOND
   QUELQUES ASPECTS DE L'EVOLUTION DES TOUAREG DE L'QUEST DE LA
   REPUBLIQUE DU NIGER.
   NIAMEY, IFAN, ETUDES NIGERIENNES, 9, 1963
   127-01,

   HAMA BOUBOU
   CONTRIBUTION A LA CONNAISSANCE DE L'HISTOIRE DES PEUL.
   PARIS, PRESENCE AFRICAINE, 1968

127-01,128-01,

127-01
     HAMA BOUBOU
     RECHERCHE SUR L'HISTOIRE DES TOUAREG SAHARIENS ET
     SOUDANAIS.
     PARIS, PRESENCE AFRICAINE, 1967
     127-01,

127-02
     HAMA BOUBOU   GUILHEM MARCEL
     HISTOIRE DU NIGER.
     PARIS, L'AFRIQUE-LE MONDE, COURS MOYEN, 1965
     127-02,

     HAMA BOUBOU   GUILHEM MARCEL
     NIGER--RECITS HISTORIQUES--COURS ELEMENTAIRE.
     PARIS, LIGEL, 1964
     127-02,

     URVOY YVES
     HISTOIRE DES POPULATIONS DU SOUDAN CENTRAL--COLONIE DU
     NIGER.
     PARIS, LAROSE, 1936
     127-02,

127-03
     MARTY PAUL
     L'ISLAM ET LES TRIBUS DANS LA COLONIE DU NIGER-- EXTRAIT
     DE LA REVUE DES ETUDES ISLAMIQUES (ISLAM AND THE TRIBES
     OF NIGER COLONY-- EXTRACT FROM THE REVIEW OF ISLAMIC
     STUDIES).
     PARIS, LIBRERIE ORIENTALISTE PAUL GEUTHNER, 1931
     021,127-03,

127-04
     HAMA BOUBOU
     KOTIA-NIMA RENCONTRE AVEC L'EUROPE.
     PARIS, PRESENCE AFRICAINE, 1968
     091,127-04,

     HAMA BOUBOU
     ESSAI D'ANALYSE DE L'EDUCATION AFRICAINE.
     PARIS, PRESENCE AFRICAINE, 1968
     091,127-04,

     HAMA BOUBOU
     ENQUETE SUR LES FONDEMENTS ET LA GENESE DE L'UNITE AFRICAINE
     (INQUIRY ON THE FOUNDATIONS AND EARLY DEVELOPMENT OF AFRICAN
     UNITY).
     PARIS, PRESENCE AFRICAINE, 1966
     079,127-04,

     HAMA BOUBOU
     HISTOIRE TRADITIONNELLE D'UN PEUPLE--LES ZARMA-SONGHAY.
     PARIS, PRESENCE AFRICAINE, 1967
     099,127-04,

     HAMA BOUBOU
     RECHERCHES SUR L'HISTOIRE DES TOUAREG SAHARIENS ET

    SOUDANAIS.
    PARIS, PRESENCE AFRICAINE, 1967
    099,127-04,

127-04
    HAMA BOUBOU
    HISTOIRE DU GOBIR ET DE SOKOTO.
    PARIS, PRESENCE AFRICAINE, 1967
    099,127-04,

    HAMA BOUBOU
    CONTRIBUTION A L'HISTOIRE DES PEUL.
    PARIS, PRESENCE AFRICAINE
    099,127-04,

127-05
    BERNUS SUZANNE
    NIAMEY--POPULATION ET HABITAT.
    PARIS, IFAN-CNRS, N.D.
    127-05,

    VAN HOEY LEO F
    THE COERCIVE PROCESS OF URBANIZATION--THE CASE OF NIGER.
    IN THE NEW URBANIZATION, ED. SCOTT GREER, ET AL., NEW YORK,
    SAINT MARTINS PRESS, 1968
    127-05,

127-06
    THOMPSON VIRGINIA
    NIGER.
    IN G.M. CARTER (ED), NATIONAL UNITY AND REGIONALISM IN EIGHT
    AFRICAN STATES, ITHACA, CORNELL UNIVERSITY PRESS, 1966
    127-06,

127-08
    UNITED NATIONS
    INDUSTRIAL DEVELOPMENT IN AFRICA
    NEW YORK, UNITED NATIONS, 1967
    071,104-08,110-08,117-08,127-08,134-08,140-08,142-08,

127-11
    BONARDI PIERRE
    LA REPUBLIQUE DU NIGER--NAISSANCE D'UN ETAT.
    PARIS, AGENCE PARISIENNE DE DISTRIBUTION, 1960
    127-11,

128. NIGERIA

128-01
    BOHANNAN LAURA   BOHANNAN PAUL
    THE TIV OF CENTRAL NIGERIA.
    LONDON, INTERNATIONAL AFRICAN INSTITUTE, 1953
    014,128-01,

    CARROLL KEVIN

YORUBA RELIGIOUS SCULPTURE-- PAGAN AND CHRISTIAN SCULPTURE
IN NIGERIA AND DAHOMEY.
NEW YORK,PRAEGER,1967
014,109-01,128-01,

128-01
 SMITH M G
 GOVERNMENT IN ZAZZAU, 1800-1950.
 LONDON,OXFORD UNIVERSITY PRESS, 1960
 024,128-01,

 SMITH MARY
 BABA OF KARO--A WOMAN OF THE MOSLEM HAUSA.
 NEW YORK, PRAEGER, 1964
 008,128-01,

 WILLETT FRANK
 IFE IN THE HISTORY OF WEST AFRICAN SCULPTURE.
 NEW YORK,MCGRAW HILL, 1967
 014,128-01,

 AMES DAVID W
 PROFESSIONALS AND AMATEURS-- THE MUSICIANS OF ZARIA AND
 OBIMO.
 AFRICAN ARTS 1 2 WINTER 1968 PP 41-45, 80-84
 015,128-01,

 ARNETT E J
 THE RISE OF THE SOKOTO FULANI (TRANSLATION OF MUHAMMAD
 BELLO, INFAQ AL-MAISUR)
 KANO, 1929
 099,128-01,

 BABALOLA S A
 THE CONTENT AND FORM OF YORUBA IJALA.
 LONDON, OXFORD UNIVERSITY PRESS, 1966
 012,128-01,

 BEIER ULLI
 THE STORY OF SACRED WOOD CARVINGS FROM ONE SMALL
 YORUBA TOWN.
 LAGOS, NIGERIA, MARINA, NIGERIA MAGAZINE, 1957
 E W MACROW, (ED.)
 128-01,

 BEIER ULLI
 NIGERIAN MUD SCULPTURE.
 CAMBRIDGE,CAMBRIDGE UNIVERSITY PRESS,1963
 014,128-01,

 BEIER ULLI
 ART IN NIGERIA 1960.
 CAMBRIDGE, CAMBRIDGE UNIVERSITY PRESS, 1960
 014,093,128-01,

 BEN AMOS PAULA
 BIBLIOGRAPHY OF BENIN ART.
 NEW YORK, INTERNATIONAL UNIVERSITY BOOKSELLERS, INC., 1968
 014,128-01,

BOHANNAN PAUL
JUSTICE AND JUDGMENT AMONG THE TIV.
LONDON, OXFORD UNIVERSITY PRESS, 1957
066,128-01,

128-01
BOHANNAN PAUL   BOHANNAN LAURA
TIV ECONOMY.
EVANSTON, NORTHWESTERN UNIVERSITY PRESS, 1968
010,128-01,

BRADBURY R E
THE BENIN KINGDOM AND THE EDO-SPEAKING PEOPLES OF SOUTH-
WESTERN NIGERIA.
LONDON, OXFORD UNIVERSITY PRESS, 1957
026,128-01,

BRADBURY R E
CHRONOLOGICAL PROBLEMS IN THE STUDY OF BENIN HISTORY.
JOURNAL OF THE HISTORICAL SOCIETY OF NIGERIA 1 1959
PP 263-287
026,128-01,

COCKER G B A
FAMILY PROPERTY AMONG THE YORUBAS.
LAGOS, AFRICAN UNIVERSITIES PRESS, 1966
008,128-01,

COHEN RONALD
FAMILY LIFE IN BORNU.
ANTHROPOLOGICA 9 NO. 1 1967 PP 21-42
008,128-01,

COHEN RONALD
MARRIAGE INSTABILITY AMONG THE KANURI OF NORTHERN NIGERIA.
AMERICAN ANTHROPOLOGIST 63 1961 PP 1231-1249
008,128-01,

COHEN RONALD
SOME ASPECTS OF INSTITUTIONALIZED EXCHANGE-- A KANURI
EXAMPLE.
CAHIERS D'ETUDES AFRICAINES 5 1965 PP 353-369
010,128-01,

COHEN RONALD
THE DYNAMICS OF FEUDALISM IN BORNU.
IN J BUTLER (ED), BOSTON UNIVERSITY PUBLICATIONS IN AFRICAN
HISTORY VOL 2, BOSTON, BOSTON UNIVERSITY PRESS, 1966
PP 87-105
024,128-01,

COHEN RONALD
POWER, AUTHORITY, AND PERSONAL SUCCESS IN ISLAM AND BORNU.
IN M SWARTZ,   V TURNER, AND A TUDEN (EDS), POLITICAL
ANTHROPOLOGY, CHICAGO, ALDINE, 1966, PP 129-139
009,128-01,

COHEN RONALD
SOCIAL STRATIFICATION IN BORNU.
IN A TUDEN AND L PLOTNICOV (EDS), CLASS AND STATUS IN SUB-

SAHARAN AFRICA, NEW YORK, FREE PRESS, 1968
008,128-01,

128-01
  COHEN RONALD
  THE KANURI OF BORNU.
  NEW YORK, HOLT, RINEHART AND WINSTON, 1967
  008,024,128-01,

  COHEN RONALD
  SLAVERY AMONG THE KANURI.
  TRANS ACTION, 1967
  028,128-01,

  CORDWELL JUSTINE M
  NATURALISM AND STYLIZATION IN YORUBA ART.
  MAGAZINE OF ART 46 1953 PP 220-226
  014,128-01,

  DERRETT DUNCAN J
  STUDIES IN THE LAWS OF SUCCESSION IN NIGERIA.
  LONDON, OXFORD UNIVERSITY PRESS, 1965
  066,128-01,

  DIAMOND STANLEY
  NIGERIAN DISCOVERY-- THE POLITICS OF FIELD WORK.
  IN A VIDICH, ET AL (EDS.), REFLECTIONS ON COMMUNITY STUDIES,
  NEW YORK, JOHN WILEY, 1964, PP 119-154
  099,128-01,

  FAGG WILLIAM
  NIGERIAN IMAGES.
  NEW YORK, PRAEGER, 1963
  014,020,128-01,

  FORDE C DARYLL   SCOTT R
  THE NATIVE ECONOMIES OF NIGERIA.
  LONDON, FABER, 1946
  010,128-01,

  GREEN MARGARET
  A DESCRIPTIVE GRAMMAR OF IGBO.
  BERLIN, AKADEMIE-VERLAG, 1963
  011,128-01,

  GREENBERG JOSEPH H
  THE INFLUENCE OF ISLAM ON A SUDANESE RELIGION.
  SEATTLE, UNIVERSITY OF WASHINGTON PRESS, 1969
  013,128-01,

  HODDER B W
  RURAL PERIODIC DAY MARKETS IN PART OF YORUBALAND, WESTERN
  NIGERIA.
  INSTITUTE OF BRITISH GEOGRAPHERS, PAPERS AND TRANSACTIONS
  29 1961 PP 149-159
  010,128-01,

  HORTON ROBIN
  KALABARI SCULPTURE.
  LAGOS, NIGERIA, DEPARTMENT OF ANTIQUITIES, 1965

014,128-01,

128-01
    ISICHEI ELIZABETH
    HISTORICAL CHANGE IN AN IBO POLITY ASABA TO 1885.
    IN JOURNAL OF AFRICAN HISTORY VOL 10 1969 P 421
    009,128-01,

    JOHNSTON H A S   ED
    A SELECTION OF HAUSA STORIES.
    LONDON, OXFORD UNIVERSITY PRESS, 1966
    012,128-01,

    KIRK-GREENE A H M
    HAUSA BA DABO BANE--A COLLECTION OF 500 PROVERBS.
    IBADAN, OXFORD UNIVERSITY PRESS, 1966
    012,128-01,

    LASEBIKAN E L
    LEARNING YORUBA.
    LONDON, OXFORD UNIVERSITY PRESS, 1958
    011,128-01,

    LEITH-ROSS SYLVIA
    AFRICAN WOMEN-- A STUDY OF THE IBO OF NIGERIA.
    LONDON, ROUTLEDGE AND KEGAN PAUL, 1963
    008,128-01,

    LLOYD PETER C
    YORUBA MYTHS-- A SOCIOLOGIST'S INTERPRETATION.
    ODU 2 1956 PP 20-28
    013,128-01,

    LLOYD PETER C
    SACRED KINGSHIP AND GOVERNMENT AMONG THE YORUBA.
    AFRICA 30 1960 PP 221-237
    009,128-01,

    LLOYD PETER C
    CRAFT ORGANIZATIONS IN YORUBA TOWNS.
    AFRICA, VOL. XXIII, 1953
    010,128-01,

    LLOYD PETER C
    YORUBA LAND LAW.
    LONDON, OXFORD UNIVERSITY PRESS, 1962
    066,128-01,

    NADEL S F
    NUPE RELIGION.
    LONDON, ROUTLEDGE AND KEGAN PAUL LTD, 1954
    013,128-01,

    NADEL S F
    A BLACK BYZANTIUM, THE KINGDOM OF NUPE IN NIGERIA.
    OXFORD, OXFORD UNIVERSITY PRESS, 1942
    009,010,128-01,

    OTTENBERG SIMON
    DOUBLE DESCENT IN AN AFRICAN SOCIETY--THE AFIKPO VILLAGE-

GROUP.
SEATTLE, UNIVERSITY OF WASHINGTON PRESS, 1968
008,128-01,

128-01
ROSMAN ABRAHAM
SOCIAL STRUCTURE AND ACCULTURATION AMONG THE KANURI
OF BORNU PROVINCE, NORTHERN NIGERIA.
TRANSACTIONS OF THE NEW YORK ACADEMY OF SCIENCE 21 MAY
1958 PP 620-630
038,128-01,

SIEBER ROY
SCULPTURE OF NORTHERN NIGERIA.
NEW YORK, MUSEUM OF PRIMITIVE ART, 1961
014,128-01,

SKINNER NEIL
HAUSA READINGS--SELECTIONS FROM EDGAR≠S TATSUNIYOYI.
MADISON, UNIVERSITY OF WISCONSIN PRESS, 1968
012,128-01,

SKINNER NEIL   TRANS AND ED
HAUSA TALES AND TRADITIONS.
NEW YORK, AFRICANA PUBLISHING CORPORATION, 1969
012,128-01,

SMITH M G
THE HAUSA--MARKETS IN A PEASANT ECONOMY.
IN BOHANNAN AND DALTON (EDS) MARKETS IN AFRICA, DOUBLEDAY,
1965.
010,128-01,

SMITH ROBERT
KINGDOMS OF THE YORUBA
LONDON, METHUEN, 1969
026,128-01,

TAYLOR F W
A PRACTICAL HAUSA GRAMMAR.
LONDON, OXFORD UNIVERSITY PRESS, 1959
011,128-01,

UCHENDU VICTOR C
SLAVERY IN SOUTHEAST NIGERIA.
TRANS-ACTION, 1967
028,128-01,

UMEASIEGBU REMS NNA
THE WAY WE LIVED--IBO CUSTOMS AND STORIES.
NEW YORK, HUMANITIES PRESS INC., 1969 (LONDON, HEINEMANN
EDUCATIONAL BOOKS)
012,128-01,

WILLETT FRANK
IFE AND ITS ARCHAEOLOGY.
THE JOURNAL OF AFRICAN HISTORY 1 1960 PP 231-248
014,020,026,128-01,

WILLETT FRANK   PICTON J

ON THE IDENTIFICATION OF INDIVIDUAL CARVERS, A STUDY OF
ANCESTOR SHRINE CARVINGS FROM OWO, NIGERIA.
MAN 2 1967
014,128-01,

128-01
    BEIER ULLI
    THE HISTORICAL AND PSYCHOLOGICAL SIGNIFICANCE OF YORUBA
    MYTHS.
    ODU, A JOURNAL OF YORUBA AND RELATED STUDIES 1 N C PP 17-25
    012,128-01,

    FAGG WILLIAM
    DE L'ART DES YORUBA (ON THE ART OF YORUBA).
    L'ART NEGRE, PRESENCE AFRICAINE 10-11 PARIS 1951 PP 103-135
    014,128-01,

    PADEN JOHN N
    KANO HAUSA POETRY.
    KANO STUDIES 1 SEPTEMBER 1965 PP 33-39
    012,128-01,

    PALAU MARTI M
    LE ROI-DIEU AU BENIN (THE GOD-KING OF BENIN).
    PARIS BERGER-LEVRAULT 1964
    026,128-01,

    SMITH M G
    CO-OPERATION IN HAUSA SOCIETY.
    INFORMATION VOL 11 1957 PP 2-20
    009,128-01,

    BOHANNAN PAUL
    THE TIV OF NIGERIA.
    IN JAMES L GIBBS JR. (ED) PEOPLES OF AFRICA, NEW YORK, HOLT
    RINEHART AND WINSTON, 1965, PP. 513-546
    128-01,

    GREEN MARGARET
    IBO VILLIAGE AFFAIRS.
    NEW YORK, PRAEGER, 1964
    128-01,

    HAMA BOUBOU
    CONTRIBUTION A LA CONNAISSANCE DE L HISTOIRE DES +EUL.
    PARIS, PRESENCE AFRICAINE, 1968
    127-01,128-01,

    HOPEN E EDWARD
    THE PASTORAL FULBE FAMILY IN GWANDU.
    LONDON, OXFORD UNIVERSITY PRESS, 1958
    128-01,

    LLOYD PETER C
    THE YORUBA OF NIGERIA.
    IN JAMES L GIBBS JR. (ED), PEOPLES OF AFRICA, NEW YORK, HOLT
    RINEHART AND WINSTON, 1965, PP. 547-582
    128-01,

    OTTENBERG PHOEBE

THE AFIKPO IBO OF EASTERN NIGERIA.
IN JAMES L GIBBS JR. (ED), PEOPLES OF AFRICA, NEW YORK, HOLT
RINEHART AND WINSTON, 1965, PP. 1-40
128-01,

128-01
   SMITH M G
   THE HAUSA OF NORTHERN NIGERIA.
   IN JAMES L GIBBS JR. (ED), PEOPLES OF AFRICA, NEW YORK, HOLT,
   RINEHART AND WINSTON, 1965, PP. 119-156
   128-01,

   STENNING DERRICK J
   THE PASTORAL FULANI OF NORTHERN NIGERIA.
   IN JAMES L. GIBBS (ED), PEOPLES OF AFRICA, NEW YORK, HOLT
   RINEHART AND WINSTON, 1965 PP. 361-402
   128-01,

   STENNING DERRICK J
   SAVANNAH NOMADS--A STUDY OF THE WODAABE PASTORAL FULANI OF
   WESTERN BORNU PROVINCE NORTHERN REGION NIGERIA.
   LONDON, OXFORD UNIVERSITY PRESS, 1959
   128-01,

   TALBOT PERCY A
   THE PEOPLES OF SOUTHERN NIGERIA.
   LONDON, CASS, 1966
   128-01,

128-02
   JOHNSTON H A S
   THE FULANI EMPIRE OF SOKOTO.
   LONDON, OXFORD UNIVERSITY PRESS, 1967
   024,052,128-02,

   LAST MURRAY
   THE SOKOTO CALIPHATE.
   LONDON, LONGMANS, GREEN AND COMPANY LTD., 1967
   024,128-02,

   HISKETT MERVIN
   KITAB AL-FARQ-- A WORK ON THE HABE KINGDOMS ATTRIBUTED TO
   UTHMAN DAN FODIO.
   BULLETIN OF THE SCHOOL OF ORIENTAL AND AFRICAN STUDIES 23
   1960 PP 558-579
   024,128-02,

   HOGBEN S J   KIRK-GREENE A H M
   THE EMIRATES OF NORTHERN NIGERIA-- A PRELIMINARY SURVEY OF
   HISTORICAL TRADITIONS.
   LONDON, OXFORD UNIVERSITY PRESS, 1966
   024,128-02,

   KIRK-GREENE A H M   ED
   LUGARD AND THE AMALGAMATION OF NIGERIA--A DOCUMENTARY
   RECORD.
   LONDON, FRANK CASS AND COMPANY LIMITED, 1968
   035,128-02,

   MUFFETT DAVID M J

CONCERNING BRAVE CAPTAINS-- BEING A HISTORY OF THE BRITISH
OCCUPATION OF KANO AND SOKOTO AND OF THE LAST STAND OF THE
FULANI FORCES.
LONDON, A DEUTSCH, 1964
034,128-02,

128-02
ABDULLAHI IBN M
TAZYIN AL WARAQAT.
IBADAN, UNIVERSITY OF IBADAN PRESS, 1964 (TRANSLATED AND
EDITED. MERVYN HISKETT)
024,128-02,

AJAYI J F ADE   SMITH ROBERT
YORUBA WARFARE IN THE 19TH CENTURY.
CAMBRIDGE, ENGLAND, CAMBRIDGE UNIVERSITY PRESS, 1964
026,128-02,

AJAYI J F ADE
THE BRITISH OCCUPATION OF LAGOS 1851-1861.
NIGERIA MAGAZINE 69 1961 PP 96-105
033,128-02,

ALAGOA EBIEGBERI J
THE SMALL BRAVE CITY STATE-- A HISTORY OF NEMBRE-BRASS IN
THE NIGER DELTA.
MADISON, UNIVERSITY OF WISCONSIN PRESS, 1964
026,128-02,

BIOBAKU SABURI O
THE PROBLEM OF TRADITIONAL HISTORY WITH SPECIAL REFERENCES
TO YORUBA TRADITIONS.
JOURNAL OF THE HISTORICAL SOCIETY OF NIGERIA 1 1956
PP 43-47
100,128-02,

BIVAR A D H
THE WATHIQAT AHL AL-SUDAN-- A MANIFESTO OF THE FULANI JIHAD.
JOURNAL OF AFRICAN HISTORY 2 1961 PP 235-243
024,128-02,

BIVAR A D H   HISKETT MERVIN
THE ARABIC LITERATURE OF NIGERIA TO 1804-- A PROVISIONAL
ACCOUNT.
BULLETIN OF THE SCHOOL OF ORIENTAL AND AFRICAN STUDIES 25
1962 PP 104-148
021,060,128-02,

BIVAR A D H   SHINNIE P L
OLD KANURI CAPITALS.
JOURNAL OF AFRICAN HISTORY 3 1962 PP 1-10
024,128-02,

BRADBURY R E
THE HISTORICAL USES OF COMPARATIVE ETHNOGRAPHY WITH SPECIAL
REFERENCE TO BENIN AND THE YORUBA.
IN VANSINA (ED.), THE HISTORIAN IN TROPICAL AFRICA, LONDON,
OXFORD UNIVERSITY PRESS, 1964, PP 145-164
099,128-02,

CAMERON SIR D
MY TANGANYIKA SERVICE AND SOME NIGERIA.
LONDON, ALLEN AND UNWIN, 1939
035,128-02,136-02,

128-02
COHEN RONALD
THE BORNU KING LISTS.
IN J BUTLER (ED), BOSTON UNIVERSITY PUBLICATIONS IN AFRICAN
HISTORY VOL 2, BOSTON, BOSTON UNIVERSITY PRESS, 1966,
PP 41-83
024,128-02,

COHEN RONALD   BRENNER LOUIS
BORNU IN THE 19TH CENTURY.
IN A AJAYI AND MICHAEL CROWDER (EDS), THE HISTORY OF WEST
AFRICA, OXFORD, CLARENDON PRESS, 1968
024,128-02,

CONNAH G
ARCHAEOLOGICAL RESEARCH IN BENIN CITY, 1961-1964.
JOURNAL OF THE HISTORICAL SOCIETY OF NIGERIA 2 1964
PP 465-477
092,128-02,

DIKE K O
BENIN-- A GREAT FOREST KINGDOM OF MEDIEVAL NIGERIA.
PRACTICAL ANTHROPOLOGY 8 1961 PP 31-35
026,128-02,

DIKE K O
TRADE AND POLITICS IN THE NIGER DELTA 1830-1885.
OXFORD, CLARENDON PRESS, 1956
027,128-02,

EGHAREVBA JACOB
A SHORT HISTORY OF BENIN.
IBADAN UNIVERSITY PRESS, 1960
026,128-02,

FAGG BERNARD
THE NOK CULTURE IN PREHISTORY.
JOURNAL OF THE HISTORICAL SOCIETY OF NIGERIA 1 1959
PP 288-293
020,128-02,

HEUSSLER ROBERT
THE BRITISH IN NORTHERN NIGERIA.
LONDON, OXFORD UNIVERSITY PRESS, 1968
035,128-02,

JOHNSON SAMUEL
THE HISTORY OF THE YORUBAS FROM THE EARLIEST TIMES TO THE
BEGINNING OF THE BRITISH PROTECTORATE.
LONDON, ROUTLEDGE AND KEGAN PAUL, 1966   (O JOHNSON, ED.)
026,128-02,

JONES GWILYN I
THE TRADING STATES OF THE OIL RIVERS-- A STUDY OF
POLITICAL DEVELOPMENT IN EASTERN NIGERIA.

LONDON, OXFORD UNIVERSITY PRESS, 1963
027,035,128-02,

128-02
KIRK-GREENE A H M
THE PRINCIPLES OF NATIVE ADMINISTRATION IN NIGERIA--
SELECTED DOCUMENTS 1900-1947.
LONDON, OXFORD UNIVERSITY PRESS, 1965
035,128-02,

PALMER SIR HERBERT R
SUDANESE MEMOIRS.
LONDON, F. CASS. 1967
099,128-02,

PERHAM MARGERY
NATIVE ADMINISTRATION IN NIGERIA.
LONDON, OXFORD UNIVERSITY PRESS, 1961
035,128-02,

PHILLIPS EARL
THE EGBA AT ABEOKUTA--ACCULTURATION AND POLITICAL CHANGE,
1830-1870.
JOURNAL OF AFRICAN HISTORY, X, 1, 1969, PP. 117-131
026,128-02,

RYDER A F C
MISSIONARY ACTIVITY IN THE KINGDOM OF WARRI TO THE EARLY
NINETEENTH CENTURY.
JOURNAL OF THE HISTORICAL SOCIETY OF NIGERIA 22 1960 PP 2-
27
027,128-02,

SHAW C T
NIGERIA'S PAST UNEARTHED.
WEST AFRICAN REVIEW DECEMBER 1960 PP 30-37
026,128-02,

SHAW C T
IGBO-UKWU-AN ACCOUNT OF ARCHEOLOGICAL DISCOVERIES IN
EASTERN NIGERIA
LONDON, FABER AND FABER; AND EVANSTON, NORTHWESTERN UNIVERSITY
PRESS, 1970
020,026,128-02,

WILLETT FRANK
INVESTIGATIONS AT OLD OYO, 1956-1957-- AN INTERIM REPORT.
JOURNAL OF THE HISTORICAL SOCIETY OF NIGERIA 2 1960 PP 57-77
026,128-02,

EL MASRI F H
THE LIFE OF SHEHU USUMAN DAN FODIO BEFORE THE JIHAD.
JOURNAL OF THE HISTORICAL SOCIETY OF NIGERIA 2 DECEMBER
1963 PP 435-448
024,128-02,

URVOY YVES
HISTOIRE DE L'EMPIRE DU BORNU (HISTORY OF THE EMPIRE OF
BORNU).
PARIS LAROSE 1949 (IFAN MEMOIRES 7)

024,128-02,

128-02
   CROWDER MICHAEL
   THE STORY OF NIGERIA.
   LONDON, FABER AND FABER, 1962
   128-02,

128-03
   ABERNETHY DAVID B
   THE POLITICAL DILEMMA OF POPULAR EDUCATION--AN AFRICAN CASE.
   PALO ALTO, STANFORD UNIVERSITY PRESS, 1969
   042,128-03,

   LEVINE ROBERT A
   DREAMS AND DEEDS.
   CHICAGO, UNIVERSITY OF CHICAGO PRESS, 1966
   038,041,098,128-03,

   MELSON ROBERT   WOLPE HOWARD   EDS
   NIGERIA-MODERNIZATION AND THE POLITICS OF COMMUNALISM.
   EAST LANSING, MICHIGAN STATE UNIVERSITY PRESS, 1970
   006,065,128-03,

   WOLFF HANS
   LANGUAGE, ETHNIC IDENTITY, AND SOCIAL CHANGE IN SOUTHERN
   NIGERIA.
   ANTHROPOLOGICAL LINGUISTICS JANUARY 1967
   006,128-03,

   AFRICAN NEWSLETTER
   THE PRESS OF NIGERIA.
   AFRICAN NEWSLETTER 1 NUMBER 3 SUMMER 1963 PP 40-45
   049,128-03,

   ARDENER EDWIN
   SOME IBO ATTITUDES TO SKIN PIGMENTATION.
   MAN 54 1954 PP 70-73
   088,128-03,

   COHEN ABNER
   THE POLITICS OF MYSTICISM IN SOME LOCAL COMMUNITIES.
   LOCAL-LEVEL POLITICS, MARC J. SWARTZ (ED.), CHICAGO, ALDINE
   PUBLISHING CO., 1968, PP. 361-376
   052,128-03,

   COHEN RONALD
   CONFLICT AND CHANGE IN A NORTHERN NIGERIAN EMIRATE.
   IN G ZOLLSCHAN AND D HIRSCH (EDS). EXPLORATIONS IN SOCIAL
   CHANGE,BOSTON, HOUGHTON MIFFLIN, 1964
   024,128-03,

   ELIAS T O
   THE IMPACT OF ENGLISH LAW ON NIGERIAN CUSTOMARY LAW.
   LUGARD LECTURES, CMS NIGERIA, 1958
   066,128-03,

   IKEJIANI OKECHUKWU   ED
   EDUCATION IN NIGERIA.
   NEW YORK, PRAEGER, 1965

042,128-03,

128-03
KEAY ELLIOT A   RICHARDSON SAMUEL
THE NATIVE AND CUSTOMARY COURTS OF NIGERIA.
LONDON, SWEET AND MAXWELL, 1966
066,128-03,

LAMBO T ADEOYE
THE ROLE OF CULTURAL FACTORS IN PARANOID PSYCHOSES AMONG
THE YORUBA TRIBE.
JOURNAL OF MENTAL SCIENCE 101 1955 PP 239-265
040,128-03,

LEIGHTON A H   ET-AL
PSYCHIATRIC DISORDER AMONG THE YORUBA-- A REPORT FROM THE
CORNELL ARO-MENTAL HEALTH RESEARCH PROJECT IN THE WESTERN
REGION NIGERIA.
ITHACA, CORNELL UNIVERSITY PRESS, 1963
041,128-03,

LEVINE ROBERT A   KLEIN N   OWEN C
FATHER-CHILD RELATIONSHIPS AND CHANGING LIFE-STYLES IN
IBADAN, NIGERIA.
IN HORACE MINER (ED), THE CITY IN MODERN AFRICA, NEW YORK,
PRAEGER, 1967
040,128-03,

LLOYD PETER C
SOME MODERN DEVELOPMENTS IN YORUBA CUSTOMARY LAW.
JOURNAL OF AFRICAN ADMINISTRATION 12 JANUARY 1960 PP 11-20
066,128-03,

MACKAY IAN K
BROADCASTING IN NIGERIA.
IBADAN. IBADAN UNIVERSITY PRESS, 1964
049,128-03,

MARIOGHAE MICHAEL   FERGUSON JOHN
NIGERIA UNDER THE CROSS.
LONDON, THE HIGHWAY PRESS, 1965
050,128-03,

MESSENGER JOHN C
REINTERPRETATIONS OF CHRISTIAN AND INDIGENOUS BELIEF IN A
NIGERIAN NATIVIST CHURCH.
AMERICAN ANTHROPOLOGIST 62 APRIL 1960 PP 268-278
051,128-03,

MESSENGER JOHN C
RELIGIOUS ACCULTURATION AMONG THE ANANG IBIBIO CHAPTER 15.
IN WILLIAM BASCOM AND MELVILLE HERSKOVITS, CONTINUITY AND
CHANGE IN AFRICAN CULTURES, CHICAGO, UNIVERSITY OF CHICAGO
PRESS, 1962, PP 279-299
051,128-03,

MINER HORACE M
CULTURE CHANGE UNDER PRESSURE-- A HAUSA CASE.
HUMAN ORGANIZATION 19 FALL 1960 PP 164-167
041,128-03,

128-03

OTTENBERG PHOEBE
THE CHANGING ECONOMIC POSITION OF WOMEN AMONG THE AFIKPO
IBO CHAPTER 11.
IN WILLIAM BASCOM AND MELVILLE HERSKOVITS, CONTINUTY AND
CHANGE IN AFRICAN CULTURES, CHICAGO, UNIVERSITY OF CHICAGO
PRESS, 1962, PP 205-223
038,128-03,

OTTENBERG SIMON
IBO RECEPTIVITY TO CHANGE CHAPTER 7.
IN WILLIAM BASCOM AND MELVILLE HERSKOVITS, CONTINUTY AND
CHANGE IN AFRICAN CULTURES, CHICAGO, UNIVERSITY OF CHICAGO
PRESS, 1962, PP 130-143
038,128-03,

PARRINDER GEOFFREY
INDIGENOUS CHURCHES IN NIGERIA.
WEST AFRICAN REVIEW 31 SEPTEMBER 1960 PP 87-93
LONDON, AFRICA RESEARCH LIMITED, 1969, P. 53-54
051,128-03,

PEEL J D Y
ALADURA--A RELIGIOUS MOVEMENT AMONG THE YORUBA.
LONDON, OXFORD UNIVERSITY PRESS, 1968
051,128-03,

SCARRITT JAMES R
THE IMPACT OF NATIONALISM.
IN POLITICAL CHANGE IN A TRADITIONAL AFRICAN CLAN-- A
STRUCTURAL-FUNCTIONAL ANALYSIS OF THE NSITS OF NIGERIA
DENVER MONOGRAPH SERIES IN WORLD AFFAIRS 3 1964-5UNIVERSITY
OF DENVER
038,128-03,

SCHACHT JOSEPH
ISLAM IN NORTHERN NIGERIA.
STUDIA ISLAMICA 8 SUMMER 1957 PP 123-146
052,128-03,

SCHWAB WILLIAM B
THE GROWTH AND CONFLICTS OF RELIGION IN A MODERN YORUBA
COMMUNITY.
ZAIRE 6 8 OCTOBER 1952 PP 829-35
089,128-03,

TURNER HAROLD
AFRICAN INDEPENDENT CHURCH-- THE LIFE AND FAITH OF THE
CHURCH OF THE LORD (ALADURA).
LONDON, OXFORD UNIVERSITY PRESS, 1967
051,128-03,

WEBSTER J B
THE AFRICAN CHURCHES AMONG THE YORUBA 1888-1922.
OXFORD, CLARENDON PRESS, 1964
051,128-03,

WEILER HANS N
ERZIEHUNGSWESEN AND POLITIK IN NIGERIA, EDUCATION AND

POLITICS IN NIGERIA (BILINGUAL EDITION)
FREIBURG IM BREISGAU,   VERLAG ROMBACH, 1964
042,043,128-03,

128-03

AJAYI J F ADE
CHRISTIAN MISSIONS IN NIGERIA.
EVANSTON, NORTHWESTERN UNIVERSITY PRESS. 1965
050,128-03,

HISKETT MERVYN
NORTHERN NIGERIA
IN KRITZECK AND LEWIS, PP 287-300
128-03,

128-04

AWOLOWO OBAFEMI
AWO--THE AUTOBIOGRAPHY OF CHIEF OBAFEMI AWOLOWO.
CAMBRIDGE. CAMBRIDGE UNIVERSITY PRESS, 1960
044,128-04,

AZIKIWE NNAMDI
THE FUTURE OF PAN-AFRICANISM.
PRESENCE AFRICAINE FIRST TRIMESTER 1962 PP 5-31
079,128-04,

AZIKIWE NNAMDI
ETHICS OF COLONIAL IMPERIALISM.
JOURNAL OF NEGRO HISTORY 16 JULY 1931 PP 287-308
035,128-04,

AZIKIWE NNAMDI
IN DEFENCE OF LIBERIA.
JOURNAL OF NEGRO HISTORY 17 JANUARY 1932 PP 30-49
029,119-02,128-04,

AZIKIWE NNAMDI
REALITIES OF AFRICAN UNITY.
AFRICAN FORUM I 1 1965 PP 7-22
079,128-04,

AWOLOWO OBAFEMI
PATH TO NIGERIAN FREEDOM.
LONDON, FABER, 1966
055,128-04,

AWOLOWO OBAFEMI
THE PEOPLES REPUBLIC.
NIGERIA, OXFORD UNIVERSITY PRESS. 1969
068,128-04,

AWOLOWO OBAFEMI
THOUGHTS ON NIGERIAN CONSTITUTION.
NIGERIA, OXFORD UNIVERSITY PRESS,1966
054,068,128-04,

AZIKIWE NNAMDI
NIGERIAN POLITICAL INSTITUTIONS.
JOURNAL OF NEGRO HISTORY 14 1929 PP 328-340
060,128-04,

128-04

AZIKIWE NNAMDI
THE DEVELOPMENT OF POLITICAL PARTIES IN NIGERIA.
LONDON 1957 (1792 OFFICE OF THE COMMISSIONER IN THE U K
FOR THE EASTERN REGION OF NIGERIA)
061,128-04,

AZIKIWE NNAMDI
ZIK-- A SELECTION FROM THE SPEECHES OF DOCTOR NNAMDI AZIKIWE
CAMBRIDGE, ENGLAND, CAMBRIDGE UNIVERSITY PRESS, 1961
044,060,091,096,128-04,

BALEWA ABUBAKAR T
NIGERIA LOOKS AHEAD.
IN PHILIP W QUIGG (ED.), AFRICA, NEW YORK, PRAEGER, 1964
PP 302-313
060,128-04,

BELLO AHMADU
MY LIFE.
CAMBRIDGE, ENGLAND, CAMBRIDGE UNIVERSITY PRESS, 1962
044,128-04,

IKEOTUONYE VINCENT
ZIK OF NEW AFRICA.
LONDON, P R MACMILLAN, 1961
044,128-04,

LLOYD BARBARA B
EDUCATION AND FAMILY LIFE IN THE DEVELOPMENT OF CLASS
IDENTIFICATION AMONG THE YORUBA.
IN LLOYD, THE NEW ELITES OF TROPICAL AFRICA, LONDON, OXFORD
UNIVERSITY PRESS, 1966, P. 163-183
043,128-04,

O≠CONNELL JAMES
SENGHOR, NKRUMAH AND AZIKIWE⊗- UNITY AND DIVERSITY IN THE
WEST AFRICAN STATES.
NIGERIAN JOURNAL OF ECONOMIC AND SOCIAL STUDIES 5 MARCH
1963 PP 77-93
044,114-04,128-04,130-04,

OMER-COOPER J D   ET-AL
NIGERIAN MARXISM AND SOCIAL PROGRESS.
NIGERIAN JOURNAL OF ECONOMIC AND SOCIAL STUDIES 6 JULY
1964 PP 133-198 SYMPOSIUM ON NIGERIA
060,128-04,

SMYTHE HUGH H
AFRICAN ELITE IN NIGERIA.
IN AMSAC, AFRICA SEEN BY AMERICAN NEGROES, PARIS,
PRESENCE AFRICAINE, 1958, PP 71-82
044,128-04,

AWOLOWO OBAFEMI
THE PATH TO ECONOMIC FREEDOM IN DEVELOPING COUNTRIES.
LECTURE DELIVERED AT THE UNIVERSITY OF LAGOS ON MARCH 15TH,
1968, 23 PAGES, PAMPHLET
091,128-04,

128-04
    AZIKIWE NNAMDI
    TRIBALISM--A PRAGMATIC INSTRUMENT FOR NATIONAL UNITY.
    LECTURE DELIVERED UNIVERSITY OF NIGERIA, FRIDAY, MAY 15TH,
    1964, 30 PAGES, PAMPHLET
    091,128-04.

    AZIKIWE NNAMDI
    LIBERIA IN WORLD POLITICS.
    LONDON, A H STOCKWELL,1934
    029,119-02,128-04,

    LLOYD PETER C
    CLASS CONSCIOUSNESS AMONG THE YORUBA.
    IN LLOYD, THE NEW ELITES OF TROPICAL AFRICA, LONDON, OXFORD
    UNIVERSITY PRESS, 1966, P. 328-341
    044,128-04.

128-05
    COHEN ABNER
    CUSTOM AND POLITICS IN URBAN AFRICA--A STUDY OF HAUSA
    MIGRANTS IN YORUBA TOWNS.
    BERKELEY, UNIVERSITY OF CALIFORNIA PRESS, 1969
    007,128-05,

    LLOYD PETER C   MABOGUNJE AKIN L   AWE B
    THE CITY OF IBADAN-- A SYMPOSIUM ON ITS STRUCTURE AND
    DEVELOPMENT.
    CAMBRIDGE,CAMBRIDGE UNIVERSITY PRESS,1967
    026,045,128-05.

    MABOGUNJE AKIN L
    URBANIZATION IN NIGERIA.
    NEW YORK, AFRICANA PUBLISHING CORPORATION, 1969
    045,047,128-05,

    PLOTNICOV LEONARD
    STRANGERS TO THE CITY-- URBAN MAN IN JOS, NIGERIA.
    PITTSBURGH,UNIVERSITY OF PITTSBURGH PRESS,1967
    046,128-05,

    PADEN JOHN N
    URBAN PLURALISM, INTEGRATION, AND ADAPTATION OF COMMUNAL I-
    DENTITY IN KANO, NIGERIA.
    IN RONALD COHEN AND JOHN MIDDLETON (EDS),FROM TRIBE TO NA-
    TION IN AFRICA. SAN FRANCISCO, CHANDLER, 1970
    006,128-05,

    ABIODUN JOSEPHINE O
    CENTRAL PLACE STUDY IN ABEOKUTA PROVINCE,SOUTHWEST NIGERIA
    JOURNAL OF REGIONAL SCIENCE 8 1968
    047,048,128-05,

    AKINOLA R A
    THE INDUSTRIAL STRUCTURE OF IBADAN.
    NIGERIAN GEOGRAPHICAL JOURNAL IBADAN 7 DECEMBER 1964
    PP 115-130
    046,128-05,

ANONYMOUS
GREATER KANO PLANNING AUTHORITY PLANS.
THE WEST AFRICAN BUILDER AND ARCHITECT 4 5 SEPTEMBER-OCTOBER
1964 PP 85-95
092,128-05,

128-05
GUTKIND PETER C W
THE ENERGY OF DESPAIR--SOCIAL ORGANIZATION OF THE UNEMPLOYED
IN TWO AFRICAN CITIES-- LAGOS AND NAIROBI.
CIVILISATIONS. VOL. XVII, 1967, PP. 186-380
043,128-05,117-05,

LOCK MAX
A SURVEY AND PLAN OF THE CAPITAL TERRITORY FOR THE GOVERN-
MENT OF NORTHERN NIGERIA.
NEW YORK, PRAEGER, 1967
092,128-05,

MABOGUNJE AKIN L
THE EVOLUTION OF RURAL SETTLEMENT IN EGBA DIVISION, NIGERIA.
JOURNAL OF TROPICAL GEOGRAPHY, SINGAPORE AND KUALA LUMPUR
13 DECEMBER 1959 PP 65-77
045,128-05,

MABOGUNJE AKIN L
THE GROWTH OF RESIDENTIAL DISTRICTS IN IBADAN.
GEOGRAPHICAL REVIEW JANUARY 1962 PP 56-77
046,128-05,

MABOGUNJE AKIN L
URBANIZATION IN NIGERIA-A CONSTRAINT ON ECONOMIC DEVELOPMENT
ECONOMIC DEVELOPMENT AND CULTURAL CHANGE 13 1965 PP 413-438
047,128-05,

MCDONELL G
THE DYNAMICS OF GEOGRAPHIC CHANGE--THE CASE OF KANO.
ANNALS OF THE ASSOCIATION OF AMERICAN GEOGRAPHERS
5J SEPTEMBER 1964 PP 355-371
046,128-05,

TREVALLION B A W
METROPOLITAN KANO-- REPORT ON THE TWENTY YEAR DEVELOPMENT
PLAN 1963-1983.
OXFORD, PERGAMON PRESS, 1966
092,128-05,

BARBER C R
IGBO-ORA--A TOWN IN TRANSITION.
NIGERIA, OXFORD UNIVERSITY PRESS, 1966
128-05,

ECONOMIC COMMISSION FOR AFRICA
LEOPOLDVILLE AND LAGOS--COMPARATIVE STUDY OF CONDITIONS IN
1960.
IN GERALD BREESE (ED), THE CITY IN NEWLY DEVELOPING
COUNTRIES, PRENTICE-HALL, NEW JERSEY, 1969
108-05,128-05,

MABOGUNJE AKIN L

YORUBA TOWNS.
IBADAN, IBADAN UNIVERSITY PRESS, 1962
128-05,

128-05
    MARRIS PETER
    FAMILY AND SOCIAL CHANGE IN AN AFRICAN CITY (LAGOS).
    EVANSTON, NORTHWESTERN UNIVERSITY PRESS, 1962
    128-05,

    SCHWAB WILLIAM B
    SOCIAL SURVEY OF LAGOS.
    AMERICAN ANTHROPOLOGIST, VOL.66, 2, APRIL, 1964
    128-05,

    WILLIAMS BABATUNDE   WALSH ANNMARIE H
    URBAN GOVERNMENT FOR METROPOLITAN LAGOS.
    NEW YORK, PRAEGER, 1967
    128-05,

128-06
    LEGUM COLIN   DRYSDALE JOHN
    NIGERIAN CIVIL WAR.
    COLIN LEGUM AND JOHN DRYSDALE, AFRICA CONTEMPORARY RECORD,
    LONDON, AFRICA RESEARCH LIMITED, 1969, PP. 645-688
    065,128-06,

    OJUKWU C ODUMEGWU
    BIAFRA--SELECTED SPEECHES WITH JOURNAL OF EVENTS.
    NEW YORK, HARPER AND ROW, 1969
    065,128-06,

    ADEBANJO TIMOTHY
    BEYOND THE CONFLICT.
    AFRICA REPORT, FEB., 1968, P. 12
    065,128-06,

    DIAMOND STANLEY
    THE BIAFRAN POSSIBILITY.
    AFRICA REPORT, FEB., 1968, P. 16
    065,128-06,

    FERGUSON JOHN
    THE LESSONS OF BIAFRA.
    THE CHRISTIAN CENTURY, AUGUST 14, 1968, PP. 1013-1017
    065,128-06,

    LINDSAY KENNEDY
    HOW BIAFRA PAYS FOR THE WAR.
    VENTURE, MARCH 1969
    065,128-06,

    O'CONNELL JAMES
    THE SCOPE OF THE TRAGEDY.
    AFRICA REPORT, FEB., 1968, P. 8
    065,128-06,

    OJUKWU C ODUMEGWU
    RANDOM THOUGHTS OF C ODUMEGWU OJUKWU, GENERAL OF THE
    PEOPLES ARMY, BIAFRA.

NEW YORK, HARPER AND ROW, 1969
065,128-06,

128-06
SKLAR RICHARD L
CONTRADICTIONS IN THE NIGERIAN POLOTICAL SYSTEM.
THE JOURNAL OF MODERN AFRICAN STUDIES, VOL. 3, NO. 2, 1965,
PP. 201-13
065,128-06,

SOJA EDWARD W
TRANSACTION FLOWS AND NATIONAL UNITY--THE NIGERIAN CASE.
IN CARTER, GWENDOLEN M. AND ANN PADEN (EDS), EXPANDING
HORIZONS IN AFRICAN STUDIES, EVANSTON, NORTHWESTERN
UNIVERSITY PRESS, 1969, PP. 321-328
100,128-06,

AKIWOWO AKINSOLA
THE SOCIOLOGY OF NIGERIAN TRIBALISM.
PHYLON 25 SUMMER 1964 PP 155-163
057,128-06,

ANDERSON J N D
RETURN TO NIGERIA-- JUDICIAL AND LEGAL DEVELOPMENTS IN THE
NORTHERN REGION.
INTERNATIONAL AND COMPARATIVE LAW QUARTERLY JANUARY 1963
PP 282-294
067,128-06,

COLEMAN JAMES S
NIGERIA BACKGROUND TO NATIONALISM.
BERKELEY, UNIVERSITY OF CALIFORNIA PRESS, 1958
055,128-06,

DILLON WILTON S
NIGERIA'S TWO REVOLUTIONS.
AFRICA REPORT 11 MARCH 1966 PP 9-14
065,128-06,

ELIAS T O
THE NIGERIAN LEGAL SYSTEM.
LONDON, ROUTLEDGE AND KEGAN PAUL, 1963, 2ND REV. ED.
066,128-06,

GREAT BRITAIN   COLONIAL OFFICE
REPORT OF THE COMMISSION TO ENQUIRE INTO THE FEARS OF
MINORITIES AND THE MEANS OF ALLAYING THEM.
HER MAJESTY'S STATIONERY OFFICE, COMMAND 505, JULY 1958
057,128-06,

JARVIS STEVEN
NIGERIA AND BIAFRA.
AFRICA TODAY 14 DECEMBER 1967 PP 16-18
065,128-06,

KLINGHOFFER ARTHUR J
WHY THE SOVIETS CHOSE SIDES IN THE NIGERIAN WAR.
AFRICA REPORT, FEBRUARY, 1968, P. 48
065,084,128-06,

LLOYD PETER C
TRIBALSIM IN NIGERIA.
IN A A DUBB (ED), THE MULTI-TRIBAL SOCIETY, 16TH RHODES-
LIVINGSTON INSTITUTE CONFERENCE PROCEEDINGS 1962 LUSAKA
PP 133-147
057,128-06,

128-06
MUFFETT DAVID J M
THE FAILURE OF ELITE-MASS COMMUNICATION--SOME PROBLEMS
CONFRONTING THE MILITARY REGIMES AND CIVIL SERVICES OF
NIGERIA.
THE SOUTH ATLANTIC QUARTERLY, VOL. LXVII, NO. 1, WINTER 1968
  PP. 125-140
058,128-06,

NAFZIGER E WAYNE
INTER-REGIONAL ECONOMIC RELATIONS IN THE NIGERIAN FOOTWEAR
INDUSTRY.
THE JOURNAL OF MODERN AFRICAN STUDIES, VOL 6, NO. 4, 1968,
PP. 531-542
057,128-06,

O'CONNELL JAMES
POLITICAL INTEGRATION-- THE NIGERIAN CASE CHAPTER 5.
IN ARTHUR HAZLEWOOD, AFRICAN INTEGRATION AND DISINTEGRATION,
LONDON, OXFORD UNIVERSITY PRESS, 1967, P   129-184
057,128-06,

PADEN JOHN N
LANGUAGE PROBLEMS OF NATIONAL INTEGRATION IN NIGERIA-- THE
SPECIAL POSITION OF HAUSA.
IN JOSHUA A FISHMAN, CHARLES FERGUSON, AND JYOTIRINDRA DAS
GUPTA (EDS), LANGUAGE PROBLEMS IN DEVELOPING NATIONS, NEW
YORK, JOHN WILEY, 1968, P. 199-214
057,128-06,

PARK ANDREW E W
THE SOURCES OF NIGERIAN LAW.
LAGOS, AFRICAN UNIVERSITIES PRESS, 1963
066,128-06,

POST KENNETH W J
NATIONALISM AND POLITICS IN NIGERIA-- A MARXIST APPROACH.
NIGERIAN JOURNAL OF ECONOMIC AND SOCIAL STUDIES 6 JULY
1964 PP 169-176
054,128-06,

ROGERS CYRIL A
A STUDY OF RACE ATTITUDES IN NIGERIA.
RHODES-LIVINGSTONE JOURNAL 26 1959 PP 51-64
088,128-06,

ROTHCHILD DONALD S
SAFE GUARDING NIGERIAN MINORITIES.
INSTITUTE OF AFRICAN AFFAIRS PUBLICATION, PHILADELPHIA,
UNIVERSITY OF PENSYLVANIA, 1964
057,128-06,

SKLAR RICHARD L

THE CONTRIBUTION OF TRIBALISM TO NATIONALISM IN WESTERN
NIGERIA.
IN IMMANUEL WALLERSTEIN, SOCIAL CHANGE, THE COLONIAL
SITUATION, NEW YORK, JOHN WILEY AND SONS, 1966, PP 290-300
057,128-06,

128-06
  AKIWOWO AKINSOLA
  THE SOCIOLOGICAL RELEVANCE OF TRIBALISM TO THE BUILDING OF
  THE NIGERIAN NATION.
  SIXTH WORLD CONGRESS OF SOCIOLOGY, EVIAN, FRANCE, SEPT. 4-11
    1966, 32 PAGES
  065,128-06,

  DEBONNEVILLE FLORIS
  LA MORT DU BIAFRA (THE DEATH OF BIAFRA).
  PARIS, R. SOLAR, 1968
  065,128-06,

  SCHWARTZ FREDERICK A
  NIGERIA--THE TRIBES, THE NATION OT THE RACE,THE POLITICS OF
  INDEPENDENCE.
  CAMBRIDGE, MASSACHUSETTS INSTITUTE OF TECHNOLOGY PRESS,
  1965
  065,128-06,

  WHITAKER C S   SKLAR RICHARD L
  NIGERIA.
  IN G.M. CARTER (ED) NATIONAL UNITY AND REGIONALISM IN EIGHT
  AFRICAN STATES. ITHACA, CORNELL UNIVERSITY PRESS, 1966
  065,128-06,

128-07
  SKLAR RICHARD L
  NIGERIAN POLITICS--THE ORDEAL OF CHIEF AWOLOWO, 1960-65.
  GWENDOLEN M. CARTER (ED), POLOTICS IN AFRICA--7 CASES, NEW
  YORK, HARCOURT, BRACE AND WORLD INC., 1966, PP. 119-166
  065,128-07,

  ALUKO S A
  FEDERAL ELECTION CRISIS 1964-- AN ANALYSIS.
  ONITSHA,ETUDO LTD,1965
  061,064,128-07,

  AWA EME O
  FEDERAL GOVERNMENT IN NIGERIA.
  BERKELEY,UNIVERSITY OF CALIFORNIA PRESS,1964
  061,128-07,

  BRAND J A
  THE MID-WEST STATE MOVEMENT IN NIGERIAN POLITICS-- A STUDY
  IN PARTY FORMATION.
  POLITICAL STUDIES 13 OCTOBER 1965 PP 346-365
  061,128-07,

  BRETTON HENRY L
  POLITICAL INFLUENCE IN SOUTHERN NIGERIA.
  IN HERBERT J SPIRO, ED., AFRICA—THE PRIMACY OF POLITICS,
  NEW YORK, RANDOM HOUSE, 1966, PP 49-84
  063,128-07,

128-07

DENT M J
ELECTIONS IN NORTHERN NIGERIA.
JOURNAL OF LOCAL ADMINISTRATION OVERSEAS OCTOBER 1962
PP 213-224
063,128-07,

DUDLEY B J O
THE NOMINATION OF PARLIAMENTARY CANDIDATES IN
NORTHERN NIGERIA.
JOURNAL OF COMMONWEALTH POLITICAL STUDIES, 2 NOVEMBER, 1963
LONDON, LEICESTER UNIVERSITY PRESS, PP 45-58
063,128-07,

DUDLEY B J O
PARTIES AND POLITICS IN NORTHERN NIGERIA.
LONDON, FRANK CASS AND CO. LTD.; NEW YORK, HUMANITIES PRESS,
1968
061,128-07,

ELECTORAL COMMISSION
REPORT ON THE NIGERIA FEDERAL ELECTIONS, DECEMBER 1959.
LAGOS, FEDERAL GOVERNMENT PRINTER 1960
063,128-07,

EZERA KALU
CONSTITUTIONAL DEVELOPMENTS IN NIGERIA.
CAMBRIDGE, CAMBRIDGE UNIVERSITY PRESS, 1964
068,128-07,

LLOYD PETER C
THE DEVELOPMENT OF POLITICAL PARTIES IN WESTERN NIGERIA.
AMERICAN POLITICAL SCIENCE REVIEW 49 SEPTEMBER 1955
PP 693-707
062,128-07,

LLOYD PETER C
SOME COMMENTS ON THE ELECTIONS IN NIGERIA.
JOURNAL OF AFRICAN ADMINISTRATION 4 1952 PP 82-92
063,128-07,

MACKINTOSH JOHN P
FEDERALISM IN NIGERIA.
POLITICAL STUDIES 10 OCTOBER 1962 PP 223-247
061,128-07,

MACKINTOSH JOHN P
ELECTORAL TRENDS AND THE TENDENCY TO A ONE PARTY
SYSTEM IN NIGERIA.
JOURNAL OF COMMONWEALTH POLITICAL STUDIES 1 NOVEMBER 1962
PP 194-210
063,128-07,

MACKINTOSH JOHN P   ED
NIGERIAN GOVERNMENT AND POLITICS.
EVANSTON, NORTHWESTERN UNIVERSITY PRESS, 1966
061,128-07,

O'CONNELL JAMES

THE NORTHERN REGIONAL ELECTIONS, 1961, AN ANALYSIS.
NIGERIAN JOURNAL OF ECONOMIC AND SOCIAL STUDIES 4 JULY
JULY 1962
063,128-07,

128-07
  OLUSANYA G O
  THE ROLE OF EX-SERVICEMEN IN NIGERIAN POLITICS.
  THE JOURNAL OF MODERN AFRICAN STUDIES, VOL. 6, NO. 2, 1968
  PP. 221-32
  063,128-07,

  POST KENNETH W J
  THE NIGERIAN FEDERAL ELECTION OF 1959--POLITICS AND
  ADMINISTRATION IN A DEVELOPING POLITICAL SYSTEM.
  LONDON, OXFORD UNIVERSITY PRESS (FOR NISER), 1963
  063,128-07,

  PRICE J H
  THE EASTERN REGION OF NIGERIA CHAPTER 4.
  IN W J MACKENZIE AND KENNETH ROBINSON, FIVE ELECTIONS IN
  AFRICA, LONDON, OXFORD UNIVERSITY PRESS, 1960
  063,128-07,

  SKLAR RICHARD L
  NIGERIAN POLITICAL PARTIES-- POWER IN AN EMERGENT AFRICAN
  NATION.
  PRINCETON, NEW JERSEY, PRINCETON UNIVERSITY PRESS, 1963
  061, 128-07,

  SMOCK AUDREY CHAPMAN
  THE N.C.N.C. AND ETHNIC UNIONS IN BIAFRA.
  THE JOURNAL OF MODERN AFRICAN STUDIES, 7, 1, 1969
  007,128-07,

  TAMUNO TEKENA N
  NIGERIA AND ELECTIVE REPRESENTATION 1923-1947.
  LONDON, HEINEMANN, 1966
  056,063,128-07,

  WHEARE JOAN
  THE NIGERIAN LEGISLATIVE COUNCIL.
  LONDON, FABER, 1950
  061,128-07,

  WHITAKER C S
  THE POLITICS OF TRADITION-CONTINUITY AND CHANGE IN NORTHERN
  NIGERIA
  PRINCETON, NEW JERSEY, PRINCETON UNIVERSITY PRESS, 1970
  061,128-07,

  ROYAL INSTITUTE OF INTERNATIONAL AFFAIRS
  NIGERIA--THE POLITICAL AND ECONOMIC BACKROUND.
  LONDON. OXFORD UNIVERSITY PRESS, 1960
  128-07,

128-08
  STOLPER W
  PLANNING WITHOUT FACTS.
  CAMBRIDGE, HARVARD UNIVERSITY PRESS, 1966

072,128-08,

128-08
WHETHAM EDITH H   CURRIE JEAN I   EDS
READINGS IN THE APPLIED ECONOMICS OF AFRICA.
LONDON, CAMBRIDGE UNIVERSITY PRESS, 2, 1967,
073,128-08,

FLOYD BARRY
EASTERN NIGERIA--A GEOGRAPHICAL REVIEW.
NEW YORK, PRAEGER PUBLISHERS, 1969
065,128-08,

BALDWIN K D S
THE MARKETING OF COCOA IN WESTERN NIGERIA, WITH SPECIAL
REFERENCE TO THE POSITION OF MIDDLEMEN.
LONDON,OXFORD UNIVERSITY PRESS,1954
070,128-08,

COOK ARTHUR NORTON
BRITISH ENTERPRISE IN NIGERIA.
PHILADELPHIA,UNIVERSITY OF PENNSYLVANIA PRESS,1943
035,128-08,

FOGG C DAVIS
ECONOMIC AND SOCIAL FACTORS AFFECTING THE DEVELOPMENT OF
SMALL HOLDER AGRICULTURE IN EASTERN NIGERIA CHAPTER 3.
IN EDITH WHETHAM AND JEAN CURRIE (EDS.) READINGS IN THE
APPLIED ECONOMICS OF AFRICA, LONDON, CAMBRIDGE UNIVERSITY
PRESS, 1, 1967, PP 25-31
070,128-08,

GALLETTI R   BALDWIN K D S   DINA I O
NIGERIAN COCOA FARMERS-- AN ECONOMIC SURVEY OF YORUBA
COCOA FARMING FAMILIES.
LONDON,OXFORD UNIVERSITY PRESS,1956
070,128-08,

GREEN REGINALD H
FOUR AFRICAN DEVELOPMENT PLANS-- GHANA, KENYA, NIGERIA,
AND TANZANIA CHAPTER 20.
IN EDITH WHETHAM AND JEAN CURRIE (EDS.), READINGS IN THE
APPLIED ECONOMICS OF AFRICA, LONDON, CAMBRIDGE UNIVERSITY
PRESS, 2, 1967, PP 21-32
072,114-08,117-08,128-08,136-08,

HELLEINER G K
E FISCAL ROLE OF THE MARKETING BOARDS IN NIGERIAN
ECONOMIC DEVELOPMENT 1947-61 CHAPTER 23.
IN EDITH WHETHAM AND JEAN CURRIE (EDS.), READINGS IN THE
APPLIED ECONOMICS OF AFRICA, LONDON, CAMBRIDGE UNIVERSITY
PRESS, 2, 1967, PP 70-93
073,128-08,

KILBY PETER
COMPETITION IN THE NIGERIAN BREAD INDUSTRY CHAPTER 15.
IN EDITH WHETHAM AND JEAN CURRIE (EDS.), READINGS IN THE
APPLIED ECONOMICS OF AFRICA, LONDON, CAMBRIDGE UNIVERSITY
PRESS, 1, 1967, PP 164-172
071,128-08,

128-08
  KILBY PETER
  INDUSTRIALIZATION IN AN OPEN ECONOMY--NIGERIA 1945-1966.
  CAMBRIDGE, UNIVERSITY PRESS, 1969
  044,071,128-08,

  MAY R S
  DIRECT OVERSEAS INVESTMENT IN NIGERIA 1953-63 CHAPTER 8.
  IN EDITH WHETHAM AND JEAN CURRIE (EDS.), READINGS IN THE
  APPLIED ECONOMICS OF AFRICA, LONDON, CAMBRIDGE UNIVERSITY
  PRESS, 1, 1967, PP 72-92
  073,128-08,

  MEEK CHARLES K
  LAND TENURE AND LAND ADMINISTRATION IN NIGERIA AND THE
  CAMEROONS.
  LONDON HER MAJESTY'S STATIONERY OFFICE 1957
  010,070,104-08,128-08,

  NETTING ROBERT
  HILL FARMERS OF NIGERIA--CULTURAL ECOLOGY OF THE KOFYAR OF
  THE JOS PLATEAU.
  SEATTLE, UNIVERSITY OF WASHINGTON, 1968
  070,128-08,

  OKIGBO PIUS N C
  NIGERIAN NATIONAL ACCOUNTS 1950-7 CHAPTER 19.
  IN EDITH WHETHAM AND JEAN CURRIE (EDS.), READINGS IN THE
  APPLIED ECONOMICS OF AFRICA, LONDON, CAMBRIDGE UNIVERSITY
  PRESS, 2, 1967, PP 1-20
  073,128-08,

  OLUWASANMI H A
  AGRICULTURE AND NIGERIAN ECONOMIC DEVELOPMENT.
  NIGERIA, OXFORD UNIVERSITY PRESS, 1966
  070,128-08,

  ONYEMELUKWE CLEMENT
  PROBLEMS OF INDUSTRIAL PLANNING AND MANAGEMENT IN NIGERIA.
  NEW YORK (COLUMBIA), MCGILL-QUEENS, 1969
  071,128-08,

  PERHAM MARGERY   ED
  MINING, COMMERCE AND FINANCE IN NIGERIA.
  IN ECONOMICS OF A TROPICAL DEPENDENCY, VOL 2, LONDON, FABER
  1948
  073,128-08,

  SCHATZ SAYER P
  THE CAPITAL SHORTAGE ILLUSION-- GOVERNMENT LENDING IN
  NIGERIA CHAPTER 9.
  IN EDITH WHETHAM AND JEAN CURRIE (EDS.), READINGS IN THE
  APPLIED ECONOMICS OF AFRICA, LONDON, CAMBRIDGE UNIVERSITY
  PRESS, 1, 1967, PP 93-101
  073, 128-08,

  UGOH S U
  THE NIGERIAN CEMENT INDUSTRY CHAPTER 10.
  IN EDITH WHETHAM AND JEAN CURRIE (EDS.), READINGS IN THE

APPLIED ECONOMICS OF AFRICA, LONDON, CAMBRIDGE UNIVERSITY
PRESS, 1, 1967, PP 102-113
071,128-08.

128-08
WELLS F A   WARMINGTON W A
STUDIES IN INDUSTRIALIZATION--NIGERIA AND THE CAMEROONS.
LONDON, OXFORD UNIVERSITY PRESS, 1962
071,104-08,128-08,

YESUFU T M
AN INTRODUCTION TO INDUSTRIAL RELATIONS IN NIGERIA.
LONDON, OXFORD UNIVERSITY PRESS, 1962
071,128-08,

128-09
PHILLIPS CLAUDE JR
THE DEVELOPMENT OF NIGERIAN FOREIGN POLICY.
EVANSTON, ILLINOIS, NORTHWESTERN UNIVERSITY PRESS 1964
082,128-09,

128-10
ACHEBE CHINUA
THINGS FALL APART.
NEW YORK, MCDOWELL OBELENSKY, 1959   (LONDON, HEINEMANN
EDUCATIONAL BOOKS)
090,128-10,

CLARK J P
AMERICA, THEIR AMERICA.
LONDON, HEINEMANN EDUCATIONAL BOOKS, 1969; AND NEW YORK,
AFRICANA PUBLISHING CORP, 1969
096,128-10,

EKWENSI CYPRIAN
PEOPLE OF THE CITY.
LONDON, HEINEMANN EDUCATIONAL BOOKS LTD, 1964
090,128-10,

SOYINKA WOLE
THE SWAMP DWELLERS.
IN FIVE PLAYS, LONDON, OXFORD UNIVERSITY PRESS, 1964
090,128-10,

TUTUOLA AMOS
THE PALM-WINE DRINKARD.
NEW YORK, GROVE PRESS INC, 1953
090,128-10,

ACHEBE CHINUA
ARROW OF GOD.
LONDON, HEINEMANN EDUCATIONAL BOOKS LTD., 1964
090,128-10,

ACHEBE CHINUA
NO LONGER AT EASE.
LONDON, HEINEMANN EDUCATIONAL BOOKS LTD, 1962
090,128-10,

ACHEBE CHINUA

MAN OF THE PEOPLE.
LONDON, HEINEMANN EDUCATIONAL BOOKS LTD, 1966
090,128-10,

128-10
ACHEBE CHINUA
THE NOVELIST AS TEACHER.
FIRST CONFERENCE ON COMMONWEALTH LITERATURE, JOHN PRESS, ED,
LONDON, HEINEMANN EDUCATIONAL BOOKS LTD, 1965, PP 201-205
090,128-10,

EKWENSI CYPRIAN
JAGUA NANA.
LONDON, HUTCHINSON AND CO, 1964
090,128-10,

KILLAM G D
THE NOVELS OF CHINUA ACHEBE.
NEW YORK, AFRICANA PUBLISHING CORPORATION, 1970
090,128-10,

SOYINKA WOLE
KONGI'S HARVEST.
LONDON, OXFORD UNIVERSITY PRESS, 1967
090,128-10,

LARSON CHARLES R
NIGERIAN DRAMA COMES OF AGE.
AFRICA REPORT, MAY, 1968, P. 55
090,128-10,

LAURENCE MARGARET
LONG DRUMS AND CANNONS-NIGERIAN DRAMATISTS AND NOVELISTS
LONDON, MACMILLAN, 1968; AND NEW YORK, PRAEGER, 1969
090,128-10,

OKARA GABRIEL
THE VOICE.
NEW YORK, AFRICANA PUBLISHING CORPORATION, 1969 (LONDON,
HEINEMAN EDUCATIONAL BOOKS)
090,128-10,

OKIGBO CHRISTOPHER
LABYRINTHS WITH 'PATHS OF THUNDER'.
NEW YORK, AFRICANA PUBLISHING CORPORATION, 1970 (LONDON,
HEINEMANN EDUCATIONAL BOOKS)
090,128-10,

SOYINKA WOLE
THREE PLAYS.
IBADAN, MBARI PUBLISHERS, 1963
090,128-10,

SOYINKA WOLE
THE INTERPRETERS.
LONDON, HEINEMANN EDUCATIONAL BOOKS 1965
090,128-10,

SOYINKA WOLE   FAGUNWA D O
THE FOREST OF A THOUSAND DAEMONS.

NEW YORK, HUMANITIES PRESS, INC., 1968
090,128-10,

128-11
SCHWARZ WALTER
NIGERIA.
LONDON, PALL MALL PRESS, 1968
128-11,

128-12
ANONYMOUS
NIGERIAN THESES.
IBADAN, IBADAN UNIVERSITY PRESS, 1965
128-12,

CONOVER HELEN F
NIGERIAN OFFICIAL PUBLICATIONS, 1869-1959-- A GUIDE.
WASHINGTON, LIBRARY OF CONGRESS, 1959
128-12,

DIPEOLU J O
BIBLIOGRAPHICAL SOURCES FOR NIGERIAN STUDIES.
EVANSTON, NORTHWESTERN UNIVERSITY PRESS, 1966
128-12,

KEMP JULIET D
A LIST OF BOOKS, ARTICLES AND GOVERNMENT PUBLICATIONS ON THE
ECONOMY OF NIGERIA 1960-62.
IBADAN, NIGERIAN INSTITUTE OF SOCIAL AND ECONOMIC RESEARCH,
128-12,

LOCKWOOD SHARON B
A GUIDE TO OFFICIAL PUBLICATIONS--NIGERIA.
WASHINGTON, LIBRARY OF CONGRESS, 1966
128-12,

129. RWANDA

129-01
COUPEZ A   KAMANZI THOMAS   EDS
LITTERATURE COURTOISE DU RWANDA (COURT LITERATURE OF
RWANDA).
LONDON AND NEW YORK, INTERNATIONAL UNIVERSITY BOOKSELLERS,
INC., 1969
012,129-01,

SMET G
COMMERCE, MARCHE ET SPECULATION CHEZ LES BARUNDI, COMMERCE
MARKETING AND SPECULATION AMONG THE BARUNDI,.
REVUE DE L'INSTITUT DE SOCIOLOGIE SOLVAY 18 1938 PP 53-57
010,129-01,

DE HEUSCH LUC
LE RWANDA ET LA CIVILISATION INTERLACUSTRE.
BRUXELLES, EDITIONS OF L'INSTITUTE DE SOCIOLOGIE DE

L'UNIVERSITE LIBRE OF BRUXELLES, 1966
129-01,

129-01
KAGAME ALEXIS
LE CODE DES INSTITUTIONS POLITIQUES DU RWANDA PRECOLONIAL.
BRUXELLES, INSTITUT ROYAL COLONIAL BELGE, 1952
129-01,

KAGAME ALEXIS
LA LANGUE DU RWANDA ET BURUNDI EXPLIQUEE AUX AUTOCHTONES.
KABGAYI (RWANDA), ED. MORALES, 1960
129-01,

KAGAME ALEXIS
LES ORGANISATIONS SOCIO-FAMILIALES DE L'ANCIEN RWANDA.
BRUXELLES, ACADEMIE ROYALE DES SCIENCES COLONIALES, 1954
129-01,

KAGAME ALEXIS
LA PHILOSOPHIE BANTU-RWANDAISE DE L'ETRE.
BRUXELLES, ACADEMIE ROYALE DES SCIENCES COLONIALES, 1956
129-01,

KAMANZI THOMAS   NKONGORI LAURENT
PROVERBES DU RWANDA.
TERVUREN, MUSEE ROYAL DU CONGO BELGE, 1957
129-01,

MAQUET JACQUES J
THE PREMISE OF INEQUALITY IN RUANDA.
LONDON, OXFORD UNIVERSITY PRESS, 1961
057,129-01,

129-02
LOUIS WILLIAM ROGER
RUANDA-URUNDI-- 1884-1919.
OXFORD, CLARENDON PRESS, 1963
033,103-02,129-02,

VANSINA JAN
L'EVOLUTION DU ROYAUME RWANDA DES ORIGINES A 1900   (EV-
OLUTION OF THE KINGDOM OF RWANDA FROM ITS ORIGINS TO 1900).
BRUXELLES, ACADEMIE ROYALE DE SCIENCES D'OUTRE MER, 1962
025,129-02,

KAGAME ALEXIS
HISTOIRE DU RWANDA.
LEVERVILLE (CONGO), BIBLIOTHEQUE DE L'ETIOLE, 1958
129-02,

KAGAME ALEXIS
L'HISTOIRE DES ARMEES BOVINES DANS L'ANCIEN RWANDA.
BRUXELLES, ACADEMIE ROYALE DES SCIENCES D'OUTRE-MER, 1961
129-02,

KAGAME ALEXIS
LES MILICES DU RWANDA PRECOLONIAL.
BRUXELLES, ACADEMIE ROYALE DES SCIENCES D'OUTRE-MER, 1963
129-02,

129-02
   KAGAME ALEXIS
   LA NOTION DE GENERATION APPLIQUEE A LA GENEALOGIE DYNASTIQUE
   ET A L'HISTOIRE DU RWANDA DES XEME ET XLEME SIECLES A NOS
   JOURS.
   BRUXELLES, ACADEMIE ROYALE DES SCIENCES COLONIALES, 1959
   129-02,

129-03
   ALBERT ETHEL M
   SOCIO-ECONOMIC ORGANIZATION AND RECEPTIVITY TO CHANGE-SOME
   DIFFERENCES BETWEEN RUANDA AND URUNDI
   SOUTHWESTERN JOURNAL OF ANTHROPOLOGY 16 1960 PP 46-74
   013, 038, 103-03, 129-03,

129-04
   KAYIBANDA GREGOIRE
   LE PRESIDENT KAYIBANDA VOUS PARLE.
   KIGALI, SERVICE DE L'INFORMATION, 1964
   129-04,

129-06
   LEMARCHAND RENE
   REVOLUTIONARY PHENOMENA IN STRATIFIED SOCIETIES--RWANDA AND
   ZANZIBAR.
   CIVILISATIONS, VOL XVIII, NO. 1, 1968, PP. 16-51
   057,129-06,136-06,

129-07
   WEBSTER JOHN B
   THE CONSTITUTIONS OF BURUNDI, MALAGASY, AND RWANDA.
   SYRACUSE, NEW YORK, MAXWELL GRADUATE SCHOOL OF PUBLIC AFFAIRS,
   THE PROGRAM OF EASTERN STUDIES, NO. 3, FEB., 1964
   066,103-07,121-07,129-07,

   WEBSTER JOHN B
   THE POLITICAL DEVELOPMENT OF RWANDA AND BURUNDI.
   SYRACUSE,NEW YORK,MAXWELL GRADUATE SCHOOL OF PUBLIC AFFAIRS,
   PROGRAM OF EASTERN AFRICAN STUDIES, NO. 16, JUNE, 1966
   103-07,129-07,

129-10
   KAGAME ALEXIS
   AVEC UN TROUBADOUR DU RWANDA.
   BRUXELLES. ED. UNIVERSITAIRES, 1949
   129-10.

   KAGAME ALEXIS
   BREF APERCU SUR LA POESIE DYNASTIQUE DU RWANDA.
   BRUXELLES. ED. UNIVERSITARIES, 1950
   129-10.

   KAGAME ALEXIS
   LA DIVINE PASTORALE--TRADUCTION FRANCAISE PAR L'AUTEUR DE LA
   PREMIER VEILLE D'UNE EPOPEE ECRITE EN LANGUE RWANDAISE.
   BRUXELLES, ED. DU MARAIS, 1952
   129-10.

   KAGAME ALEXIS

LA NAISSANCE DE L'UNIVERS (DUEXIEME VEILLE DE LA DIVINE
PASTORALE).
BRUXELLES, ED. DU MARAIS, 1955
129-10,

129-10
  KAGAME ALEXIS
  LA POESIE DYNASTIQUE AU RWANDA.
  BRUXELLES, INSTITUT ROYAL COLONIAL BEIGE, 1951
  129-10,

  KAMANZI THOMAS   COUPEZ A
  POEMES DYNASTIQUES RWANDA.
  BUJUMBURA, UNIVERSITE OFFICILLE, 1965
  129-10,

129-11
  LEMARCHAND RENE
  RWANDA BURUNDI.
  LONDON, PALL MALL PRESS, 1970
  103-11, 129-11,

130. SENEGAL

130-01
  AMES DAVID W
  WOLOF CO-OPERATIVE WORK GROUPS CHAPTER 12.
  IN WILLIAM BASCOM AND MELVILLE HERSKOVITS, CONTINUTY AND
  CHANGE IN AFRICAN CULTURES, CHICAGO, UNIVERSITY OF CHICAGO
  PRESS, 1962, PP 224-237
  010,130-01,

  DIOP BIRAGO
  TALES OF AMADOU KOUMBA.
  LONDON, OXFORD UNIVERSITY PRESS, 1966
  012,130-01,

  GOVERNMENT OF FRANCE
  COUTUMIERS JURIDIQUES DE L'AFRIQUE OCCIDENTALE FRANCAISE--
  SENEGAL (FRENCH WEST AFRICAN JURIDIC CUSTOMS-- SENEGAL).
  PARIS, LIBRAIRIE LAROSE, 1939, VOL1
  066,130-01,

  GRAVAND R P
  LA DIGNITE SERERE (SERERE DIGNITY).
  IN COLLOQUE SUR LES RELIGIONS, ABIDJAN, APRIL, 1961, PARIS,
  PRESENCE AFRICAINE, 1962, PP 87-90
  013,130-01,

130-02
  KLEIN MARTIN A
  ISLAM AND IMPERIALISM IN SENEGAL-- SINE-SALOUM, 1847-1941.
  STANFORD, CALIFORNIA, STANFORD UNIVERSITY PRESS, 1967
  034,130-02,

CROWDER MICHAEL
SENEGAL-- A STUDY IN FRENCH ASSIMILATION POLICY.
LONDON, OXFORD UNIVERSITY, 1962 (REVISED, METHUEN, 1967)
035,130-02,

130-02
FAIDHERBE LOUIS L
LE SENEGAL-- LA FRANCE DANS L'AFRIQUE OCCIDENTAL
(SENEGAL-- FRANCE IN WEST AFRICA).
PARIS, HACHETTE, 1889
027,130-02,

CISSE DIA AMADOU
LES DERNIERS JOURS DE LAT DIOR--LA MORT DU DAMEL.
PARIS, PRESENCE AFRICAINE, 1965
130-02,

130-03
BEHRMAN LUCY
MUSLIM BROTHERHOODS AND POLITICS IN SENEGAL
CAMBRIDGE, HARVARD UNIVERSITY PRESS, 1970
052,130-03,

O'BRIEN DONAL CRUISE
LE TALIBE MOURIDE--ETUDE D'UN CAS DE DEPENDANCE SOCIALE
(THE MOURIDE DISCIPLE-STUDY OF A CASE OF SOCIAL DEPENDENCE).
CAHIERS D'ETUDES AFRICANES, VOL. IX, NO. 35, 1969, PP. 502-
507
052,130-03,

GAUCHER JOSEPH
LES DEBUTS DE L'ENSEIGNMENT EN AFRIQUE FRANCOPHONE--JEAN
DARD ET L'ECOLE MUTELLE DE SAINT-LOUIS DU SENEGAL (THE
BEGINNINGS OF EDUCATION IN FRENCH-SPEAKING AFRICA--JEAN
DARD AND THE MUTUAL SCHOOL AT SAINT-LOUIS IN SENEGAL).
PARIS, INTERNATIONAL UNIVERSITY BOOKSELLERS, INC., 1968
042,130-03,

GRAVAND R P
CONTRIBUTION DU CHRISTIANISME A L'AFFIRMATION DE LA
PERSONNALITE AFRICAINE EN PAYS SERERE (CONTRIBUTION OF
CHRISTIANITY TO THE AFFIRMATION OF THE AFRICAN PERSONALITY
IN SERERE COUNTRY).
IN COLLOQUE SUR LES RELIGIONS, ABIDJAN, APRIL, 1961, PARIS
PRESENCE AFRICAINE, 1962, PP 209-214
039,050,130-03,

MARTY PAUL
ETUDES SUR L'ISLAM AU SENEGAL-- LES DOCTRINES ET LES
INSTITUTIONS (STUDIES ON ISLAM IN SENEGAL-- THE DOCTRINES
AND THE INSTITUTIONS).
COLLECTIONS DE LA REVUE DU MONDE, PARIS, MAISON ERNEST
LEROUX, 1917
021,130-03,

MONTEIL VINCENT
UNE CONFRERIE MUSULMANE-- LES MOURIDES DU SENEGAL (A MUSLIM
BROTHERHOOD-- THE MOURIDES OF SENEGAL).
ARCHIVES DE SOCIOLOGIE DES RELIGIONS 14 JULY 1962 PP 77-102
052,130-03,

130-03
  MONTEIL VINCENT
  LAT DIOR-- DAMAL DU KAYOR (1842-1886) ET L'ISLAMISATION DES
  WOLOFS (LAT DIOR-- DAMAL OF KAYOR (1842-1886) THE
  ISLAMIZATION OF THE WOLOF).
  ARCHIVES DE SOCIOLOGIE DES RELIGIONS 16 JULY 1963 PP 77-104
  052,130-03,

  SY CHEIKH TIDIANE
  LA CONFRERIE SENEGALAISE DES MOURIDES (THE SENEGAL
  BROTHERHOOD OF MOURIDES).
  PARIS, PRESENCE AFRICAINE, 1969
  052,130-03,

  LY ABDOULAYE
  UN NAVIRE DE COMMERCE SUR LA COTE SENEGAMBIENNE EN 1685.
  DAKAR, IFAN, 1964
  130-03,

130-04
  DIA MAMADOU   TRANSLATED BY   COOK MERCER
  THE AFRICAN NATIONS AND WORLD SOLIDARITY.
  LONDON,THAMES AND HUDSON,1962
  054,060,130-04,

  GUEYE LAMINE
  ITINERAIRE AFRICAIN (AFRICAN ITINERARY).
  PARIS, PRESENCE AFRICAINE, 1966
  044,060,130-04,

  MARKOVITZ IRVING L
  LEOPOLD SENGHOR AND THE POLITICS OF NEGRITUDE.
  NEW YORK, ATHENEUM, 1969   (LONDON, HEINEMANN
  EDUCATIONAL BOOKS)
  044,054,130-04,

  O CONNELL JAMES
  SENGHOR, NKRUMAH AND AZIKIWE-- UNITY AND DIVERSITY IN THE
  WEST AFRICAN STATES.
  NIGERIAN JOURNAL OF ECONOMIC AND SOCIAL STUDIES 5 MARCH
  1963 PP 77-93
  044,114-04,128-04,130-04,

  SENGHOR LEOPOLD S
  ON AFRICAN SOCIALISM.
  NEW YORK,PRAEGER,1964
  013,054,060,130-04,

  SENGHOR LEOPOLD S
  WEST AFRICA IN EVOLUTION.
  FOREIGN AFFAIRS 39 1960-61 PP 240-246,ALSO PHILIP W QUIGG,
  ED,AFRICA,NEW YORK,PRAEGER,1964,PP 283-291
  060,130-04,

  MILICENT ERNEST   SORDE MONIQUE
  LEOPOLD SEDAR SENGHOR ET LA NAISSANCE DE L'AFRIQUE MODERNE
  (LEOPOLD SEDAR SENGHOR AND THE BIRTH OF MODERN AFRICA).
  PARIS, INTERNATIONAL UNIVERSITY BOOKSELLERS, INC., 1969
  044,130-04,

130-04

SENGHOR LEOPOLD S
LES FONDEMENTS DE L'AFRICANITE OU NEGRITUDE ET ARABITE.
PARIS, PRESENCE AFRICAINE, 1967
091,130-04,

D ARBOUSSIER GABRIEL
L AFRIQUE VERS L UNITE.
PARIS. ED. SAINT-PAUL, 1961
130-04.

DIA MAMADOU
CONTRIBUTION A L'ETUDE DU MOUVEMENT COOPERATIF EN AFRIQUE
NOIRE.
PARIS, PRESENCE AFRICAINE, 1962 (3RD EDITION.
130-04,

DIA MAMADOU
L'ECONOMIE AFRICAINE, ETUDES ET PROBLEMES NOUVEAUX.
PARIS, P. U. F., 1957
130-04,

DIA MAMADOU
NATIONS AFRICAINES ET SOLIDARITE MONDIALE.
PARIS, P.U.F., 1963 (2ND EDITION)
130-04,

DIA MAMADOU
REFLEXIONS SUR L'ECONOMIE DE L' AFRIQUE NOIRE--NOUVELLE ED-
ITION REVUE ET AUGMENTEE.
PARIS, PRESENCE AFRICAINE, 1961
130-04.

SENGHOR LEOPOLD S
CHANTS D'OMBRE, SUIVIS DE HOSTIES NOIRES.
PARIS, SEUIL, 1956 (2ND EDITION)
130-04.

SENGHOR LEOPOLD S
CONGRES CONSTITUTIF DU P. F, A. (PARTI DE LA FEDERATION
AFRICAINE), DAKAR, 1-3, JUILLET 1959--RAPPORT SUR LA
DOCTRINE ET LE PROGRAMME DU PARTI.
PARIS, PRESENCE AFRICAINE, 1959
130-04,

SENGHOR LEOPOLD S
ETHIOPIQUES.
PARIS, SEUIL, 1956
130-04,

SENGHOR LEOPOLD S
A AFRIQUE A L' O.N.U.--ALLOCUTION DU PRESIDENT DE LA
REPUBLIQUE DU SENEGAL A LA XVIEME SESSION DE L'ASSEMBLEE
GENERALE DES NATIONS UNIES TENUE LE 31 OCTOBRE 1961.
PARIS, PRESENCE AFRICAINE, 1961
130-04.

SENGHOR LEOPOLD S
LIBERTE--NEGRITUDE ET HUMANISME.

PARIS, SEUIL, 1964
130-04,

130-04
SENGHOR LEOPOLD S
NATION ET VOIE AFRICAINE DU SOCIALISME.
PARIS, PRESENCE AFRICAINE, 1961
130-04,

SENGHOR LEOPOLD S
NOCTURNES. TRANS BY CLIVE WAKE AND JOHN REED
LONDON, HEINEMANN EDUCATIONAL BOOKS, 1970 (ORIGINALLY
NOCTURNES, PARIS, SEUIL, 1961)
130-04,

SENGHOR LEOPOLD S
PIERRE TEILHARD DE CHARDIN ET LA POLITIQUE AFRICAINE.
PARIS, SEUIL, 1962
130-04,

SENGHOR LEOPOLD S
POETE SENEGALAIS--TEXTES COMMENTES PAR ROGER MERCIER ET M ET
S BATTESTINI.
PARIS, F. NATHAN, 1964
130-04,

SENGHOR LEOPOLD S
CHANTS POUR NAET.
PARIS, SEGHERS, 1949
130-04,

THIAM DOUDOU
LA PORTEE DE LA CITOYENNETE FRANCAISE DANS LES TERRITOIRES D'
OUTRE-MER.
PARIS, ED. AFRICAINES, 1953
130-04,

130-05
MERCIER PAUL
EVOLUTION OF SENEGALESE ELITES
INTERNATIONAL SOCIAL SCIENCE BULLETIN 8 1956 PP 441-451
043,130-05,

MOURER HENRY
ADMINISTRATIVE PROBLEMS OF URBANIZATION IN AFRICA--ADDITION-
AL NOTE ON SENEGAL (DAKAR).
ADDIS ABABA, WORKSHOP ON URBANIZATION IN AFRICA, 1962
130-05,

BOUTILLIER J L
LES RAPPORTS DU SYSTEME FONCIER TOUCOULEUR ET
L'ORGANISATION SOCIALE ET ECONOMIQUE TRADITIONNELLE-- LEUR
EVOLUTION ACTUELLE (THE PRODUCTIVITY OF TOUCOULEUR FARMERS--
ITS CONTEMPORARY EVOLUTION FROM THE TRADITIONAL SOCIAL AND
ECONOMIC SYSTEM).
IN D BIEBUYCK, ED., AFRICAN AGRARIAN SYSTEMS, LONDON,
OXFORD UNIVERSITY PRESS 1963, PP 116-136
070,130-05,

CHARPY JACQUES

LA FONDATION DE DAKAR (THE FOUNDATION OF DAKAR) 1845-1857-
1869.
PARIS, LAROSE, 1958
045,130-05,

130-05
DIOP ABDOULAYE B
SOCIETE TOUCOULEUR ET MIGRATION (TUCOLOR SOCIETY AND
MIGRATION).
DAKAR, INSTITUT FRANCAIS D'AFRIQUE NOIRE, 1965
070,130-05,

VAN DER VAEREN-AGUESSY D
LES FEMMES COMMERCANTES AU DETAIL SUR LES MARCHES DAKAROIS.
IN LLOYD, THE NEW ELITES OF TROPICAL AFRICA, LONDON, OXFORD
UNIVERSITY PRESS, 1966, P. 244-255
046,130-05,

MERCIER PAUL
LE GROUPMENT EUROPEAN DE DAKAR--ORIENTATION D UNE ENQUETE.
CAHIERS INTERNATIONAUX DE SOCIOLOGIE, 2, 19, 1955
130-05,

PETEREC RICHARD J
DAKAR AND WEST AFRICAN ECONOMIC DEVELOPMENT.
NEW YORK AND LONDON, COLUMBIA UNIVERSITY PRESS, 1967
130-05,

130-06
FOLTZ WILLIAM J
SENEGAL.
IN COLEMAN, J.S. AND ROSBERG, C.G. (EDS), POLITICAL PARTIES
AND NATIONAL INTEGRATION IN TROPICAL AFRICA, LOS ANGELES,
130-06,

130-07
MILICENT ERNEST
SENEGAL.
IN G.M. CARTER (ED) AFRICAN ONE-PARTY STATES, ITHACA,
CORNELL UNIVERSITY PRESS, 1962
130-07,

ROBINSON KENNETH
SENEGAL--THE ELECTION TO THE TERRITORIAL ASSEMBLY MARCH
1957, CHAPTER 6.
IN W J MACKENZIE AND KENNETH ROBINSON, FIVE ELECTIONS IN
AFRICA, OXFORD, CLARENDON PRESS, 1960
063,130-07,

MORGENTHAU RUTH SCHACHTER
POLITICAL PARTIES IN FRENCH-SPEAKING WEST AFRICA.
OXFORD, OXFORD UNIVERSITY PRESS, 1964
055,058,061,109-07,123-07,130-07,

NDIAYE MASSATA
LE SENEGAL A L'HEURE DE L'INDEPENDANCE.
DOULLENS, IMP. DESSAINT, 1962
130-07,

130-08

FOUQUET J
LA TRAITE DES ARACHIDES DANS LE PAYS DE KAOLACK, ET DES
CONSEQUENCES ECONOMIQUES, SOCIALES ET JURIDIQUES,
(THE CULTIVATION OF GROUND NUTS IN KAOLACK COUNTRY, AND THE
CONSEQUENCES, ECONOMIC, SOCIAL AND JURIDIC).
SAINT LOUIS DU SENEGAL, INSTITUT FRANCAIS D' AFRIQUE NOIRE,
1958
070,130-08,

130-08
FOUQUET JOSEPH
LA TRAITE DES ARACHIDES DANS LE PAYS DE KAOLACK, ET SES
CONSEQUENCES ECONOMIQUES, SOCIALES ET JURIDIQUE.
SAINT-LOUIS, CENTRE IFAN-SENEGAL, 1958
130-08,

LY ABDOULAYE
LA COMPAGNIE DU SENEGAL.
PARIS, PRESENCE AFRICAINE, 1958
130-08,

130-09
THIAM DOUDOU
THE FOREIGN POLICY OF AFRICAN STATES.
NEW YORK, PRAEGER, 1965
081,130-09,

ROBSON PETER
PROBLEMS OF INTEGRATION BETWEEN SENEGAL AND
GAMBIA CHAPTER 4.
IN ARTHUR HAZLEWOOD, AFRICAN INTEGRATION AND DISINTEGRATION,
LONDON, OXFORD UNIVERSITY PRESS, 1967, P   115-128
078,113-09,130-09,

ROBSON PETER
THE PROBLEMS OF SENEGAMBIA.
JOURNAL OF MODERN AFRICAN STUDIES 3 1965
078,113-09,130-09,

FOLTZ WILLIAM J
FROM FRENCH WEST AFRICA TO THE MALI FEDERATION.
NEW HAVEN, YALE UNIVERSITY PRESS, 1965
077,123-09,130-09,

130-10
SENGHOR LEOPOLD S
SELECTED POEMS.
NEW YORK, ATHENEUM, 1966
090,130-10,

KANE CHEIKH HAMIDOU
AMBIGOUS ADVENTURE.
NEW YORK, MACMILLAN CO., 1969
090,130-10,

DIOP ALIOUNE   DIOP CHEIKH ANTA
CULTURE ET COLONIALISME.
PARIS, LA NEF DE PARIS, 1957
130-10,

DIOP BIRAGO
ECRIVAIN SENEGALAIS--TEXTES COMMENTES PAR ROGER MERCIER ET
M ET S BATTESTINI.
PARIS, F. NATHAN, 1964
130-10.

130-10
DIOP BIRAGO
LEURRES ET LEURS--POEMES.
PARIS, PRESENCE AFRICAINE, 1967 (2ND EDITION)
130-10.

DIOP DAVID
COUPS DE PILON.
PARIS, PRESENCE AFRICAINE, 1961
130-10,

DIOP OUSMANE SOCE
CONTES ET LEDENDES D'AFRIQUE NOIRE.
PARIS. NOUVELLES EDITIONS LATINES, 1962
130-10.

DIOP OUSMANE SOCE
KARIM. ROMAN SENEGALAIS, SUIVI DE CONTES ET LEGENDES
D AFRIQUE NOIRE.
PARIS, NOUVELLES EDITIONS LATINES, 1966
130-10.

DIOP OUSMANE SOCE
MIRAGES DE PARIS.
PARIS, NOUVELLES EDITIONS LATINES, 1965
130-10,

DIOP OUSMANE SOCE
RYTHMES DU KHALAM.
PARIS. NOUVELLES EDITIONS LATINES, 1962
130-10.

KANE CHEIKH HAMIDOU
ECRIVAIN SENEGALAIS--TEXTES COMMENTES PAR ROGER MERCIER ET
M ET S BATTESTINI.
PARIS, F. NATHAN, 1964
130-10.

SEMBENE OUSMANE
GOD'S BITS OF WOOD TRANS BY FRANCIS PRICE
LONDON, HEINEMANN EDUCATIONAL BOOKS, 1970 (ORIGINALLY
LES BOUTS DE DIEU. PARIS, LE LIVRE CONTEMPORAIN, 1960)
130-10,

SEMBENE OUSMANE
LE DOCKER NOIR.
PARIS. NOUVELLES EDITIONS DEBRESSE, 1956
130-10,

SEMBENE OUSMANE
L'HARMATTAN.
PARIS, PRESENCE AFRICAINE, 1964
130-10.

SEMBENE OUSMANE
O PAYS, MON BEAU PEUPLE.
PARIS, AMIOT-DUMONT, 1957
130-10,

130-10
   SEMBENE OUSMANE
   VOLTAIQUES, NOUVELLES.
   PARIS, PRESENCE AFRICAINE, 1962
   130-10,

130-11
   DESCHAMPS HUBERT J
   LE SENEGAL ET LA GAMBIE.
   PARIS, PRESSES UNIVERSITAIRES DE FRANCE, 1964
   130-11,

   O'BRIEN DONAL CRUISE
   SENEGAL.
   LONDON, PALL MALL PRESS, 1970
   130-11,

130-12
   ABI-SAAB ROSEMARY
   ELEMENTS DE BIBLIOGRAPHIE--LE SENEGAL, DES ORIGINES A
   L'INDEPENDENCE.
   GENEVA-AFRIQUE, VOL. 3, NO. 2, 1964
   130-12,

   JOHNSON G WESLEY
   BIBLIOGRAPHIC ESSAYS--SENEGAL.
   AFRICANA NEWSLETTER, VOL. 2, NO. 1, 1964
   130-12,

   PORGES LAURENCE
   ELEMENTS DE BIBLIOGRAPHIE SENEGALAISE, 1959-1963.
   DAKAR, ARCHIVES NATIONALES, CENTRE DE DOCUMENTATION, 1964
   130-12,

131. SIERRA LEONE

131-01
   DAWSON J L M
   TRADITIONAL CONCEPTS OF MENTAL HEALTH IN SIERRA LEONE.
   THE JOURNAL OF THE SIERRA LEONE SOCIETY NO. 18 JANUARY 1966
   PP 18-28
   040,131-01,

   FINNEGAN RUTH   ED
   LIMBA STORIES AND STORY-TELLING.
   LONDON, OXFORD UNIVERSITY PRESS, 1967
   012,131-01,

   HARRIS W T   SAWYER HARRY
   THE SPRINGS OF MENDE BELIEF AND CONDUCT.

FREETOWN, SIERRA LEONE UNIVERSITY PRESS, 1968
013,131-01,

131-01
FINNEGAN RUTH
SURVEY OF THE LIMBA PEOPLE OF NORTHERN SIERRA LEONE.
LONDON, HER MAJESTYS STATIONERY OFFICE, 1965
131-01,

LITTLE KENNETH
THE MENDE OF SIERRA LEONE-A WEST AFRICAN PEOPLE IN
TRANSITION
LONDON, ROUTLEDGE AND KEGAN PAUL, 1951
131-01,

131-02
HARGREAVES JOHN D
AFRICAN COLONIZATION IN THE NINETEENTH CENTURY-- LIBERIA AND
SIERRA LEONE.
IN JEFFREY BUTLER (ED), BOSTON UNIVERSITY PAPERS IN AFRICAN
HISTORY VOLUME I, BOSTON, BOSTON UNIVERSITY PRESS, 1964, PP 55-
76
029,119-02,131-02.

PETERSON JOHN
PROVINCE OF FREEDOM--A HISTORY OF SIERRA LEONE 1787-1870.
EVANSTON, NORTHWESTERN UNIVERSITY PRESS, 1969
029,131-02,

FYFE CHRISTOPHER
A HISTORY OF SIERRA LEONE.
LONDON, OXFORD UNIVERSITY PRESS, 1962
029,131-02,

KUP A P
EARLY PORTUGESE TRADE IN THE SIERRA LEONE AND GREAT
SCARCIES RIVERS.
BOLETIM CULTURAL DA GUINE PORTUGUESA XVIII 1963 PP 107-124
027,131-02,

131-03
DORJAHN VERNON R
THE CHANGING POLITICAL SYSTEM OF TEMNE.
IN IMMANUEL WALLERSTEIN (ED.) SOCIAL CHANGE-- THE
COLONIAL SITUATION, NEW YORK, ROBERT WILEY, 1966
PP 171-209
038,131-03,

VOORHOEVE J
CREOLE LANGUAGES AND COMMUNICATION.
COLLOQUE SUR LE MULTILINGUISME, BRAZZAVILLE, 1962
131-03,

131-04
KAREFA-SMART JOHN
AFRICA AND THE UNITED NATIONS.
INTERNATIONAL ORGANIZATION 19 3 SUMMER 1965 PP 764-773
081,131-04,

LITTLE KENNETH

ATTITUDES TOWARDS MARRIAGE AND THE FAMILY AMONG EDUCATED YOU
SIERRA LEONEANS.
IN LLOYD, THE NEW ELITES OF TROPICAL AFRICA, LONDON, OXFORD
UNIVERSITY PRESS, 1966, P. 139-162
131-04,

131-05
BANTON MICHAEL P
THE ORIGINS OF TRIBAL ADMINISTRATION IN FREETOWN.
SIERRA LEONE STUDIES 2 1954 PP 109-119
046,131-05,

BANTON MICHAEL P
WEST AFRICAN CITY--A STUDY OF TRIBAL LIFE IN FREETOWN.
LONDON. OXFORD UNIVERSITY PRESS, 1957
045,131-05,

FYFE CHRISTOPHER   JONES ELDRED   EDS
FREETOWN--A SYMPOSIUM.
FREETOWN, SIERRA LEONE UNIVERSITY PRESS, 1968
045,131-05,

HARVEY MILTON
IMPLICATIONS OF MIGRATION TO FREETOWN-- A STUDY OF THE
RELATIONSHIP BETWEEN MIGRANTS, HOUSING AND OCCUPATION.
CIVILISATIONS, VOL. XVIII, NO. 2, 1968, PP. 247-69
047,131-05,

HARVEY MILTON
SIERRA LEONES LARGEST PROVINCIAL TOWN.
SIERRA LEONE STUDIES, NO. 18, JAN. 1966
131-05,

JARRETT H R
THE PORT AND TOWN OF FREETOWN.
GEOGRAPHY, 40, 2, 1955
131-05,

PORTER ARTHUR T
CREOLEDOM--A STUDY OF THE DEVELOPMENT OF FREETOWN SOCIETY.
LONDON, OXFORD UNIVERSITY PRESS, 1963
131-05,

131-06
RIDDELL J BARRY
THE SPATIAL DYNAMICS OF MODERNIZATION IN SIERRA LEONE
EVANSTON, NORTHWESTERN UNIVERSITY PRESS, 1970
038,048,131-06,

KILSON MARTIN L
SIERRA LEONE.
IN COLEMAN, J.S. AND ROSBERG, C.G. (EDS), POLITICAL PARTIES
AND NATIONAL INTEGRATION IN TROPICAL AFRICA, LOS ANGELES,
UNIVERSITY OF CALIFORNIA PRESS, 1964
131-06,

131-07
SCOTT D J
THE SIERRE LEONE ELECTION MAY, 1957 CHAPTER 5.
IN W J MACKENZIE AND KENNETH ROBINSON, FIVE ELECTIONS IN

AFRICA, LONDON, OXFORD UNIVERSITY PRESS, 1960
063,131-07,

131-08
  BANTON MICHAEL P
  ECONOMIC DEVELOPMENT AND SOCIAL CHANGE IN SIERRA LEONE.
  ECONOMIC DEVELOPMENT AND CULTURAL CHANGE 2 1953 PP 135-138
  073,131-08,

  COX-GEORGE N A
  FINANCE AND DEVELOPMENT IN WEST AFRICA -- THE SIERRA LEONE
  EXPERIENCE.
  LONDON, DOBSON, 1961
  073,131-08,

  VAN DER LAAN H L
  THE SIERRA LEONE DIAMONDS.
  FREETOWN, UNIVERSITY OF SIERRA LEONE, 1965
  069,131-08,

  SAYLOR RALPH GERALD
  THE ECONOMIC SYSTEM OF SIERRA LEONE.
  DURHAM, DUKE UNIVERSITY PRESS, 1967
  131-08,

131-12
  WILLIAMS GEOFFREY J
  A BIBLIOGRAPHY OF SIERRA LEONE
  NEW YORK, AFRICANA PUBLISHING CORPORATION, 1969
  131-12,

132. SOUTH AFRICA

132-01
  THOMPSON LEONARD   ED
  AFRICAN SOCIETIES IN SOUTHERN AFRICA.
  NEW YORK, OXFORD UNIVERSITY PRESS, 1970
  031,132-01,

  STUART JAMES   ED
  IZIBONGO, ZULU PRAISE-POEMS.
  OXFORD, CLARENDON PRESS, 1968
  012,132-01,

  SCHAPERA ISAAC   ED
  THE BANTU-SPEAKING TRIBES OF SOUTH AFRICA.
  LONDON, ROUTLEDGE AND KEGAN PAUL, 1937
  132-01,

132-02
  OMER-COOPER J D
  THE ZULU AFTERMATH-- A NINETEENTH-CENTURY REVOLUTION
  IN BANTU AFRICA.
  LONDON, LONGMANS, 1966
  032,034,132-02,

132-02
   WILSON MONICA   THOMPSON LEONARD   EDS
   THE OXFORD HISTORY OF SOUTH AFRICA. VOL I   SOUTH AFRICA
   TO 1870
   LONDON, OXFORD UNIVERSITY PRESS, 1970
   031,032,132-02,

   BALLINGER MARGARET
   FROM UNION TO APARTHEID--A TREK TO ISOLATION.
   NEW YORK, PRAEGER PUBLISHERS, 1969
   089,132-02,

   LYE WILLIAM F
   THE DIFAQANE-THE MFECANE IN THE SOUTHERN SOTHO AREA 1822-24
   JOURNAL OF AFRICAN HISTORY 8 1967 PP 107-131
   031,118-02,132-02,

   BECKER PETER
   RULE OF FEAR,THE LIFE AND TIMES OF DINGANE KING OF THE ZULU
   LONDON, LONGMANS, GREEN, 1964
   031,132-02,

   BINNS C T
   THE LAST ZULU KING
   LONDON, LONGMANS, GREEN, 1963
   031,132-02,

   SMITH K W
   THE FALL OF THE BAPEDI OF THE NORTH-EASTERN TRANSVAAL.
   JOURNAL OF AFRICAN HISTORY, X, 1, 1969, PP. 237-252.
   031,132-02,

   WALKER ERIC
   A HISTORY OF SOUTHERN AFRICA.
   LONDON, LONGMANS, 1957
   031,132-02,

   GALBRAITH JOHN S
   RELUCTANT EMPIRE,BRITISH POLICY ON THE SOUTH AFRICAN
   FRONTIER,1834-1854
   BERKELEY, UNIVERSITY OF CALIFORNIA PRESS, 1963
   032,132-02,

   HANCOCK SIR WILLIAM
   SMUTS-THE SANGUINE YEARS,1870-1919 VOLUME 1
   NEW YORK, OXFORD, 1962
   032,089,132-02,

132-03
   KUPER LEO
   AN AFRICAN BOURGEOSIE--RACE, CLASS AND POLITICS IN SOUTH
   AFRICA.
   NEW HAVEN, CONN., YALE UNIVERSITY PRESS, 1969
   089,132-03,

   GLUCKMAN MAX
   ANALYSIS OF A SOCIAL SITUATION IN MODERN ZULULAND.
   MANCHESTER, MANCHESTER UNIVERSITY PRESS, 1958
   038,132-03,

132-03

   LOUDON J B
   PSYCHOGENIC DISORDER AND SOCIAL CONFLICT AMONG THE ZULU.
   IN MARVIN K OPLER (ED.), CULTURE AND MENTAL HEALTH, NEW YORK
   MACMILLAN. PP 351-369
   041,132-03,

   SCHAPERA ISAAC
   ECONOMIC CHANGES IN SOUTH AFRICAN NATIVE LIFE.
   AFRICA,1928;ALSO G DALTON (ED.), TRIBAL AND PEASANT SOCIETIES,
   DOUBLEDAY, 1967
   010,132-03,

   SCOTCH NORMAN A
   A PRELIMINARY REPORT ON THE RELATION OF SOCIOCULTURAL
   FACTORS TO HYPERTENSION AMONG THE ZULU.
   ANNALS OF THE NEW YORK ACADEMY OF SCIENCES 134 1960
   PP 1000-1009
   041,132-03,

   SUNDKLER BENGT
   BANTU PROPHETS IN SOUTH AFRICA.
   LONDON, OXFORD UNIVERSITY PRESS (2ND ED), 1961
   051,132-03,

   DE BLIJ HARM J
   SOUTH AFRICA
   IN KRITZECK AND LEWIS, PP 243-249
   132-03,

132-04

   HEPPLE ALEXANDER
   VERWOERD.
   HARMONDSWORTH, ENGLAND, PENGUIN BOOKS 1967
   089,132-04,

   LUTHULI ALBERT
   AFRICA AND FREEDOM CHAPTER 1.
   IN AFRICA'S FREEDOM, NEW YORK, BARNES AND NOBLE,
   1964. PP 9-23
   079,089,132-04,

   BRUTUS DENNIS
   LETTERS TO MARTHA AND OTHER POEMS FROM A SOUTH AFRICAN
   PRISON.
   NEW YORK, HUMANITIES PRESS, INC., 1968
   089,132-04,

   BENSON MARY
   CHIEF LUTULI OF SOUTH AFRICA.
   LONDON, OXFORD UNIVERSITY PRESS, 1963
   132-04,

132-05

   KUPER LEO
   DURBAN--A STUDY IN RACIAL ECOLOGY.
   NEW YORK (COLUMBIA), MCGILL-QUEEN'S PRESS, 1969
   089,132-05,

BROOKFIELD H C   TATHAM M A
THE DISTRIBUTION OF RACIAL GROUPS IN DURBAN--THE BACKGROUND
OF APARTHEID IN A SOUTH AFRICAN CITY.
GEOGRAPHICAL REVIEW 47 JANUARY 1957 PP 44-65
089,132-05,

132-05
DAVIES R J
THE SOUTH AFRICAN URBAN HIERARCHY
SOUTH AFRICAN GEOGRAPHICAL JOURNAL 49 1967 PP 9-19
047,048,132-05,

DERIDDER J C
THE PERSONALITY OF THE URBAN AFRICAN IN SOUTH AFRICA.
NEW YORK, HUMANITIES PRESS, 1961
041, 089, 132-05,

MAYER PHILIP
TOWNSMEN OR TRIBESMEN-- CONSERVATISM AND THE PROCESS OF
URBANIZATION IN A SOUTH AFRICAN CITY.
CAPETOWN, OXFORD UNIVERSITY PRESS, 1961
047,089,132-05,

132-06
CARTER GWENDOLEN M
AFRICAN CONCEPTS OF NATIONALISM IN SOUTH AFRICA.
MELVILLE HERSKOVITS MEMORIAL LECTURE, EDINBURGH, EDINBURGH
UNIVERSITY PRESS, MARCH 1965
054,089,132-06,

CARTER GWENDOLEN M KARIS THOMAS   STULTZ NEWELL M
SOUTH AFRICA S TRANSKEI-- THE POLITICS OF DOMESTIC COLONIAL-
IALISM.
EVANSTON, NORTHWESTERN UNIVERSITY PRESS, 1967 (LONDON,
HEINEMANN EDUCATIONAL BOOKS)
089,132-06,

VAN DEN BERGHE P
RACE AND RACISM-- A COMPARATIVE PERSPECTIVE.
NEW YORK JOHN WILEY 1967
030,088,132-06,

CARTER GWENDOLEN M
SOUTH AFRICA--SEGMENTED BUT INTERDEPENDENT.
AFRICA REPORT, MAY, 1968, P. 15-18
089,132-06,

DUNCAN PATRICK
RACE QUESTIONS IN SOUTH AFRICA.
IN PHILIP W QUIGG (ED.), AFRICA, NEW YORK, PRAEGER, 1964,
PP 199-214
089,132-06,

FAIR T J D   SHAFFER N M
POPULATION PATTERNS AND POLICIES IN SOUTH AFRICA, 1951-1960
ECONOMIC GEOGRAPHY, 40 JULY 1964 PP 261-274
089,132-06,

PATTEN J W
ALTERNATIVE TO APARTHEID IN SOUTH AFRICA.

IN PHILIP W QUIGG (ED.), AFRICA, NEW YORK, PRAEGER, 1964,
PP 231-247
089,132-06,

132-06
   SCHREINER O D
   POLITICAL POWER IN SOUTH AFRICA.
   IN PETER J MCEWAN AND ROBERT B SUTCLIFFE (EDS), MODERN AFRICA,
   NEW YORK, THOMAS CROWELL, 1965 PP 229-238
   089,132-06,

   SOLOMON LAURENCE
   THE ECONOMIC BACKGROUND TO THE REVIVAL OF AFRIKANER NATION-
   ALISM.
   IN JEFFREY BUTLER (ED), BOSTON UNIVERSITY PAPERS IN AFRICAN
   HISTORY VOL I. BOSTON, BOSTON UNIVERSITY PRESS, 1964, PP 217-
   242
   089,132-06,

   UNITED NATIONS
   MILITARY AND POLICE FORCES IN THE REPUBLIC OF SOUTH AFRICA.
   ST/PSCA/SER. A/3A/AC. 115/S. 203-204, 1967, 15 PAGES
   089,132-06,

132-07
   STULTZ NEWELL M
   THE POLITICS OF SECURITY-SOUTH AFRICA UNDER VERWOERD 1961-6
   JOURNAL OF MODERN AFRICAN STUDIES 7 1969 PP 3-20
   089,132-07,

   CARTER GWENDOLEN M
   THE POLITICS OF INEQUALITY.
   NEW YORK, PRAEGER, 1952; REVISED ED, 1962
   089,132-07,

   FEIT EDWARD
   AFRICAN OPPOSITION IN SOUTH AFRICA.
   PALO ALTO. CALIFORNIA, HOOVER INSTITUTION PRESS, 1967
   032,089,132-07,

   ROUX EDWARD
   TIME LONGER THAN ROPE--A HISTORY OF THE BLACK MAN≠S STRUGGLE
   FOR FREEDOM IN SOUTH AFRICA.
   MADISON, WISCONSIN, UNIVERSITY OF WISCONSIN PRESS, 1966
   032,132-07,

   PATON ALAN
   THE LONG VIEW.
   NEW YORK, PRAEGER, 1968
   089,132-07,

   HEPPLE ALEXANDER
   SOUTH AFRICA--A POLITICAL AND ECONOMIC HISTORY.
   LONDON, PALL MALL PRESS, 1966
   132-07,

   MAYER PHILIP
   THE TRIBAL ELITE AND THE TRANSKEIAN ELECTIONS OF 1963.
   IN LLOYD, THE NEW ELITES OF TROPICAL AFRICA, LONDON, OXFORD
   UNIVERSITY PRESS, 1966. P. 286-311

132-07,

132-08
    COLE MONICA
    SOUTH AFRICA.
    LONDON,METHUEN,1966 (REVISED EDITION)
    069,132-08,

    HORWITZ RALPH
    THE POLITICAL ECONOMY OF SOUTH AFRICA.
    NEW YORK,PRAEGER,1967
    089,132-08,

    HORWOOD O P F   BURROWS JOHN R
    THE SOUTH AFRICAN ECONOMY CHAPTER 11.
    IN CALVIN B HOOVER, ECONOMIC SYSTEMS OF THE COMMONWEALTH,
    DURHAM, DUKE UNIVERSITY PRESS, 1962, PP 462-500
    089,132-08,

    HOUGHTON D HOBART
    THE SOUTH AFRICAN ECONOMY.
    CAPE TOWN, OXFORD UNIVERSITY PRESS, 1967
    089,132-08,

    GREEN L P   FAIR T J D
    DEVELOPMENT IN AFRICA- A STUDY IN REGIONAL ANALYSIS WITH
    SPECIAL REFERENCE TO SOUTHERN AFRICA
    JOHANNESBURG, WITWATERSRAND UNIVERSITY PRESS,1962
    048,073,132-08,145-08,

132-09
    HANCE WILLIAM A   ED
    SOUTHERN AFRICA AND THE UNITED STATES.
    NEW YORK,COLUMBIA UNIVERSITY PRESS,1968
    083,089,132-09,

    AUSTIN DENNIS
    BRITAIN AND SOUTH AFRICA.
    LONDON, OXFORD UNIVERSITY PRESS, 1966
    032, 033, 132-09,

    DUNCAN PATRICK
    TOWARD A WORLD POLICY FOR SOUTH AFRICA.
    IN PHILIP W QUIGG (ED.), AFRICA, NEW YORK, PRAEGER, 1964,
    PP 248-260
    083,089,132-09,

    MUNGER EDWIN S
    JOHN VORSTER AND THE UNITED STATES
    AMERICAN UNIVERSITIES FIELD STAFF REPORTS 12 1968
    083,132-09,

132-10
    ABRAHAMS PETER
    A WREATH FOR UDOMO.
    LONDON,FABER AND FABER,1956
    090,132-10,

    ABRAHAMS PETER
    TELL FREEDOM.

NEW YORK, ALFRED A KNOPF, 1954
090,132-10,

132-10
ABRAHAMS PETER
A NIGHT OF THEIR OWN.
NEW YORK, ALFRED A KNOPF, 1965
090,132-10,

LAGUMA ALEX
AND A THREEFOLD CORD.
EVANSTON, NORTHWESTERN UNIVERSITY PRESS. 1967 (LONDON,
HEINEMANN EDUCATIONAL BOOKS)
090,132-10,

LAGUMA ALEX
A WALK IN THE NIGHT.
IBADAN, MBARI; EVANSTON, NORTHWESTERN UNIV. PRESS, 1962
090,132-10,

MODISANE BLOKE
BLAME ME ON HISTORY.
LONDON, THAMES AND HUDSON, 1963
090,132-10,

MPHAHLELE EZEKIEL
AFRICAN LITERATURE.
IN LALAGE BOWN AND MICHAEL CROWDER (EDS.), PROCEEDINGS OF
THE FIRST INTERNATIONAL CONGRESS OF AFRICANISTS, ACCRA,
1962, LONDON, LONGMANS, 1964, PP 220-232
090,132-10,

MPHAHLELE EZEKIEL
DOWN SECOND AVENUE.
LONDON FABER AND FABER 1959
090,132-10,

ABRAHAMS PETER
MINE BOY.
NEW YORK, MACMILLAN CO., 1970   (LONDON, HEINEMANN
EDUCATIONAL BOOKS)
090,132-10,

ABRAHAMS PETER
TELL FREEDOM.
NEW YORK, MACMILLAN CO., 1970
090,132-10,

133. SOMALI REPUBLIC

133-01
ANDRZEJEWSKI B W   LEWIS I M
SOMALI POETRY.
LONDON, OXFORD UNIVERSITY PRESS. 1964
012,133-01,

133-01
  LEWIS I M
  A PASTORAL DEMOCRACY.
  LONDON, OXFORD UNIVERSITY PRESS, 1961
  009,133-01,

  LEWIS I M
  THE NORTHERN PASTORAL SOMALI OF THE HORN.
  IN JAMES L GIBBS JR (ED), PEOPLES OF AFRICA, NEW YORK, HOLT,
  RINEHART AND WINSTON, 1965 PP. 319-360
  133-01,

  LEWIS I M
  PEOPLES OF THE HORN OF AFRICA-SOMALI,AFAR,SANO
  LONDON, INTERNATIONAL AFRICAN INSTITUTE, 1955
  133-01,

133-02
  HESS ROBERT L
  THE   MAD MULLAH   AND NORTHERN SOMALIA.
  JOURNAL OF AFRICAN HISTORY 5 1964 PP 415-433
  034,133-02,

133-03
  LEWIS I M
  LINEAGE CONTINUITY AND MODERN COMMERCE IN NORTHERN
  SOMALILAND.
  IN PAUL BOHANNAN AND GEORGE DALTON (EDS.), MARKETS IN
  AFRICA, EVANSTON, NORTHWESTERN UNIVERSITY PRESS, 1962, PP
  365-385
  038,133-03,

  LEWIS I M
  CONFORMITY AND CONTRAST IN SOMALI ISLAM.
  IN LEWIS, ISLAM IN TROPICAL AFRICA, LONDON, OXFORD UNIVERSIT
  PRESS, 1966, P. 253-267
  133-03,

133-06
  LEWIS I M
  THE CLASSIFICATION OF AFRICAN POLITICAL SYSTEMS.
  RHODES-LIVINGSTONE JOURNAL 25 MARCH 1959 PP 59-69
  009,133-06,

  LEWIS I M
  INTEGRATION IN THE SOMALI REPUBLIC CHAPTER 7.
  IN ARTHUR HAZLEWOOD, AFRICAN INTEGRATION AND DISINTEGRATION,
  LONDON, OXFORD UNIVERSITY PRESS, 1967, PP 251-284
  055,133-06,

  LEWIS I M
  THE MODERN HISTORY OF SOMALILAND-- FROM NATION TO STATE.
  LONDON, WEIDENFELD AND NICOLSON, 1965
  055,133-06,

  ANDRZEJEWSKI B W
  SPEECH AND WRITING DICHOTOMY AS THE PATTERN OF MULTILINGUAL-
  ISM IN THE SOMALI REPUBLIC.
  COLLOQUE SUR LE MULTILINGUISME, BRAZZAVILLE, 1962

133-06,

133-06
    CASTAGNO A A JR
    SOMALI.
    IN COLEMAN. J.S. AND ROSBERG, C.G. (EDS), POLITICAL PARTIES
    AND NATIONAL INTEGRATION IN TROPICAL AFRICA, LOS ANGELES,
    UNIVERSITY OF CALIFORNIA PRESS, 1964
    133-06,

133-07
    CASTAGNO A A JR
    SOMALIA GOES MILITARY
    AFRICA REPORT 15 FEBRUARY 1970 PP 25-27
    064,133-07,

    LEGUM COLIN
    SOMALI LIBERATION SONGS.
    JOURNAL OF MODERN AFRICAN STUDIES, 1, 4, DEC. 1963
    133-07,

133-08
    KARP MARK
    THE ECONOMICS OF TRUSTEESHIP IN SOMALIA.
    BOSTON, BOSTON UNIVERSITY PRESS, 1960
    133-08,

133-09
    CASTAGNO A A JR
    THE SOMALI-KENYA CONTROVERSY
    JOURNAL OF MODERN AFRICAN STUDIES 2 1964 PP 165-188
    059, 117-09, 133-09,

    LEWIS I M
    PAN AFRICANISM AND PAN SOMALISM
    JOURNAL OF MODERN AFRICAN STUDIES 1 1963 PP 147-162
    059,077,133-09,

    THOMPSON VIRGINIA   ADLOFF RICHARD
    DJIBOUTI AND THE HORN OF AFRICA.
    STANFORD, STANFORD UNIVERSITY PRESS, 1968
    087,133-09,143-11,

    TOUVAL SAADIA
    SOMALI NATIONALISM-- INTERNATIONAL POLITICS AND THE DRIVE
    FOR UNITY IN THE HORN OF AFRICA.
    CAMBRIDGE,MASS,HARVARD UNIVERSITY PRESS,1963
    054,055,133-09,

    DRYSDALE JOHN
    THE SOMALI DISPUTE
    NEW YORK,PRAEGER,1964
    133-09,

133-10
    LAURENCE MARGARET   ED
    A TREE FOR POVERTY,SOMALI POETRY AND PROSE
    NAIROBI,EAGLE PRESS,1954
    133-10,

SYAD WILLIAM
5HAMSINE, POEMES--PREFACE BY LEOPOLD SEDAR SENGHOR.
PARIS. PRESENCE AFRICAINE, 1959
133-10,

133-11
CASTAGNO A A JR
SOMALIA
NEW YORK, CARNEGIE ENDOWMENT BY COLUMBIA UNIVERSITY PRESS
1959
133-11,

133-12
CONOVER HELEN F
OFFICIAL PUBLICATIONS OF SOMALILAND, 1941-1959--A GUIDE.
WASHINGTON, LIBRARY OF CONGRESS, 1960
133-12,

134. SUDAN

134-01
EVANS-PRITCHARD E E
THE ZANDE STATE.
JOURNAL OF THE ROYAL ANTHROPOLOGICAL INSTITUTE 93 1963
PP 134-154
009,134-01,

EVANS-PRITCHARD E E
KINSHIP AND MARRIAGE AMONG THE NUER.
LONDON, OXFORD UNIVERSITY PRESS, 1953
008,134-01,

EVANS-PRITCHARD E E
THE ZANDE TRICKSTER.
LONDON, OXFORD UNIVERSITY PRESS, 1967
012,134-01,

EVANS-PRITCHARD E E
WITCHCRAFT, ORACLES, AND MAGIC AMONG THE AZANDE.
LONDON, OXFORD UNIVERSITY PRESS, 1951
013,134-01,

EVANS-PRITCHARD E E
NUER RELIGION
LONDON, OXFORD UNIVERSITY PRESS, 1956
013,134-01,

FARRAN CHARLES
MATRIMONIAL LAWS OF THE SUDAN.
LONDON BUTTERWORTHS 1963
066,134-01,

HOWELL P P
A MANUEL OF NUER LAW.
LONDON OXFORD UNIVERSITY PRESS 1954

066,134-01,

134-01
LIENHARDT GODFREY
DIVINITY AND EXPERIENCE--THE RELIGION OF THE DINKA.
LONDON, OXFORD UNIVERSITY PRESS, 1961
013,134-01,

BUTT AUDREY J
THE NILOTES OF THE SUDAN AND UGANDA.
LONDON, INTERNATIONAL AFRICAN INSTITUTE, 1952
134-01,

EVANS-PRITCHARD E E
THE NUER--A DESCRIPTION OF THE MODES OF LIVLIHOOD AND
POLITICAL INSTITUTIONS OF A NILOTIC PEOPLE.
LONDON, OXFORD UNIVERSITY PRESS, 1940
134-01,

EVANS-PRITCHARD E E
THE POLITICAL SYSTEM OF THE ANUAX OF THE ANGLO-EGYPTIAN
SUDAN
LONDON, LUND, 1940
134-01,

134-02
ABD AL-MAGID A
SOME GENERAL ASPECTS OF THE ARABIZATION OF THE SUDAN.
SUDAN NOTES AND RECORDS 40 1959 PP 48-74
021,134-02,

COLLINS ROBERT O
KING LEOPOLD, ENGLAND AND THE UPPER NILE, 1899-1909.
NEW HAVEN, CONN. (YALE), MCGILL-QUEEN'S PRESS, 1969
033,134-02,

HASAN YUSUF F
THE ARABS AND THE SUDAN FROM THE SEVENTH TO THE EARLY
SIXTEENTH CENTURY.
EDINBURGH, THE UNIVERSITY PRESS, 1967
021,134-02,

SHINNIE P L
MEROE, A CIVILIZATION OF THE SUDAN.
LONDON, THAMES AND HUDSON, 1967
020,134-02,

ALLEN BERNARD M
GORDON AND THE SUDAN.
LONDON, MACMILLAN, 1931
033,134-02,

COLLINS ROBERT O
THE SOUTHERN SUDAN, 1883-1898-- A STRUGGLE FOR CONTROL.
NEW HAVEN, YALE UNIVERSITY PRESS, 1962
033,134-02,

HOLT PETER M
THE MAHDIST STATE IN THE SUDAN -- 1881-1898.
OXFORD, CLARENDON PRESS, 1958

034,134-02,

134-02
   THEOBALD A B
   THE MAHDIYA-- A HISTORY OF THE ANGLO-EGYPTIAN SUDAN 1881-
   1899.
   LONDON, LONGMANS, 1951
   034,052,134-02,

   EL-MAHDI MANDOUR
   SHORT HISTORY OF THE SUDAN.
   LONDON, OXFORD UNIVERSITY PRESS, 1965
   134-02,

   HOLT PETER M
   A MODERN HISTORY OF THE SUDAN.
   NEW YORK, GROVE PRESS, 1961
   134-02,

134-03
   TRIMINGHAM J S
   ISLAM IN THE SUDAN.
   LONDON, FRANK CASS LTD, 1965
   021,134-03,

   BIOBAKU SABURI O   AL-HAJJ MUHAMMAD
   THE SUDANESE MAHDIYYA AND THE NIGER-CHAD REGION.
   IN LEWIS, ISLAM IN TROPICAL AFRICA, LONDON, OXFORD UNIVERSIT
   PRESS, 1966, P. 425-441
   052,134-03,

   NORMAN DANIEL
   THE SUDAN
   IN KRITZECK AND LEWIS, PP 202-213
   134-03,

   STEVENSON R C
   SOME ASPECTS OF THE SPREAD OF ISLAM IN THE NUBA MOUNTAINS.
   IN LEWIS, ISLAM IN TROPICAL AFRICA, LONDON, OXFORD UNIVERSIT
   PRESS, 1966, P. 208-232
   134-03,

134-04
   BESHIR MOHAMED O
   EDUCATIONAL DEVELOPMENT IN THE SUDAN
   NEW YORK, OXFORD UNIVERSITY PRESS, 1969
   042,134-04,

134-05
   MCLOUGHLIN P F M
   THE SUDAN'S THREE TOWNS--A DEMOGRAPHIC AND ECONOMIC PROFILE
   OF AN AFRICAN URBAN COMPLEX
   ECONOMIC DEVELOPMENT AND CULTURAL CHANGE 12 1963 AND 1964,
   PP 70-83, 158-173, 286-304
   046,074,134-05,

   HENIN R A
   THE FUTURE POPULATION SIZE OF KHARTOUM, KHARTOUM NORTH,
   OMDURMAN, AND PORT SUDAN.
   SUDAN NOTES AND RECORDS, 42, 1961

134-05,

134-05
   REHFISCH F
   A STUDY OF SOME SOUTHERN MIGRANTS IN OMDURMAN.
   SUDAN NOTES AND RECORDS, 43, 1962
   134-05,

   REHFISCH F
   A UNRECORDED POPULATION COUNT OF OMDURMAN.
   SUDAN NOTES, 46, 1965
   134-05,

134-06
   BESHIR MOHAMED O
   THE SUDAN-- A MILITARY SURRENDER.
   AFRICA REPORT 9 DECEMBER 1964 PP 3-10
   064,134-06,

   HOLT PETER M
   SUDANESE NATIONALISM AND SELF DETERMINATION.
   IN WALTER LAQUEUR, THE MIDDLE EAST IN TRANSITION, NEW YORK,
   PRAEGER, 1958, PP 166-182
   055,134-06,

   KILNER PETER
   MILITARY GOVERNMENT IN SUDAN--THE PAST THREE YEARS.
   WORLD TODAY 18 JUNE 1962 PP 259-268
   064,134-06,

   KILNER PETER
   A YEAR OF ARMY RULE IN THE SUDAN.
   THE WORLD TODAY 15 1959 PP 430-441
   064,134-06,

   SHARMA B S
   THE SUDAN.
   THE POLITICS OF DEMILITARISATION, UNIVERSITY OF LONDON
   APRIL-MAY 1966 PP 32-40
   INSTITUTE OF COMMONWEALTH STUDIES
   064,134-06,

   JERNUDD BJORN
   LINGUISTIC INTEGRATION AND NATIONAL DEVELOPMENT--A CASE
   STUDY OF THE JEBEL MARRA AREA, SUDAN.
   IN JOSHUA A. FISHMAN, CHARLES A. FERGUSON AND JYOTIRINDRA
   DAS GUPTA (EDS) LANGUAGE PROBLEMS OF DEVELOPING NATIONS, NEW
   YORK, JOHN WILEY AND SONS,INC., 1968
   134-06,

   MURRAY W A
   ENGLISH IN THE SUDAN--TRENDS AND POLOTICS--RELATIONS WITH
   ARABIC.
   IN JOHN SPENCER (ED) LANGUAGE IN AFRICA, CAMBRIDGE,
   CAMBRIDGE UNIVERSITY PRESS, 1963
   134-06,

   ODUHO JOSEPH   DENG WILLIAM
   THE PROBLEM OF THE SOUTHERN SUDAN.
   LONDON, OXFORD UNIVERSITY PRESS, 1963

134-06,

134-08
    UNITED NATIONS
    INDUSTRIAL DEVELOPMENT IN AFRICA
    NEW YORK, UNITED NATIONS, 1967
    071,104-08,110-08,117-08,127-08,134-08,140-08,142-08,

    SCHLIPPE P
    SHIFTING CULTIVATION IN AFRICA.
    LONDON, ROUTLEDGE AND KEGAN PAUL, 1956
    069,134-08,

    KHIDER MAHASSIN   SIMPSON MORAG C
    CO-OPERATIVES AND AGRICULTURAL DEVELOPMENT IN THE SUDAN.
    THE JOURNAL OF MODERN AFRICAN STUDIES, VOL. 6, NO. 4, 1968,
    PP. 509-18
    070,134-08,

    LEBON J H G
    LAND USE IN SUDAN.
    MONOGRAPH 4, SIR DUDLEY STAMP (ED.) GEOGRAPHICAL
    PUBLICATIONS, BUDE, 1965
    070,134-08,

    MCLOUGHLIN P F M
    THE SUDAN S GEZIRA SCHEME-- AN ECONOMIC PROFILE.
    SOCIAL AND ECONOMIC STUDIES 12 1963 PP 179-199
    070,134-08,

    REINING CONRAD C
    THE ZANDE SCHEME--AN ANTHROPOLOGICAL CASE STUDY OF ECONOMIC
    DEVELOPMENT IN AFRICA.
    EVANSTON, NORTHWESTERN UNIVERSITY PRESS, 1966
    070,134-08,

    VAN DER KOLFT G H
    THE SOCIAL ASPECTS OF THE GEZIRA SCHEME IN THE SUDAN.
    AMSTERDAM, TROPENINSTITUUT, 1953
    070,134-08,

    GAITSKELL ARTHUR
    GEZIRA, A STORY OF DEVELOPMENT IN THE SUDAN
    NEW YORK, HUMANITIES PRESS, 1959
    134-08,

134-09
    LEBON J H G
    THE CONTROL AND UTILIZATION OF NILE WATERS--A PROBLEM OF
    POLITICAL GEOGRAPHY.
    REVIEW OF THE GEOGRAPHICAL INSTITUTE OF THE UNIVERSITY OF
    ISTANBUL 1960 PP 32-49
    078,134-09,140-09,

    FABUMI L A
    THE SUDAN IN ANGLO-EGYPTIAN RELATIONS-A CASE STUDY IN POWER
    POLITICS 1800-1956
    LONDON, LONGMANS, GREEN, 1960
    134-09,

134-11
    BARBOUR K M
    THE REPUBLIC OF THE SUDAN.
    LONDON, UNIVERSITY OF LONDON PRESS, 1961
    134-11.

134-11
    HENDERSON K D D
    SUDAN REPUBLIC
    NEW YORK, PRAEGER, 1966
    134-11.

    SAID BEWSHIR M
    THE SUDAN--CROSSROADS OF AFRICA.
    LONDON, BODLEY HEAD, 1967
    134-11.

134-12
    EL NASRI ABDEL R
    A BIBLIOGRAPHY OF THE SUDAN 1938-1958.
    LONDON, OXFORD UNIVERSITY PRESS, 1962
    134-12.

    HILL RICHARD L
    A BIBLIOGRAPHY OF THE ANGLO-EGYPTIAN SUDAN FROM THE
    EARLIEST TIMES TO 1937
    LONDON, OXFORD UNIVERSITY PRESS, 1939
    134-12.

    IBRAHIM ASMA   EL NASRI ABDEL R
    SUDAN BIBLIOGRAPHY, 1959-1963.
    SUDAN NOTES AND RECORDS, NO. 46, 1965
    134-12.

    MATTHEWS D G
    A CURRENT BIBLIOGRAPHY ON SUDANESE AFFAIRS, 1960-64.
    WASHINGTON, AFRICAN BIBLIOGRAPHIC CENTER, 1965
    134-12.

135. SWAZILAND

135-01
    KUPER HILDA
    AN AFRICAN ARISTOCRACY.
    LONDON, OXFORD UNIVERSITY PRESS, 1961
    009,135-01.

    KUPER HILDA
    THE SWAZI
    LONDON, INTERNATIONAL AFRICAN INSTITUTE, 1952
    135-01.

135-07
    HALPERN JACK
    SOUTH AFRICA'S HOSTAGES-- BASUTOLAND, BECHUANALAND,

AND SWAZILAND.
BALTIMORE, PENGUIN, 1965
032,088,102-07,118-07,135-07,

135-08
FAIR T J D   MURDOCK G   JONES H M
DEVELOPMENT IN SWAZILAND-A REGIONAL ANALYSIS
JOHANNESBURG,WITWATERSRAND UNIVERSITY PRESS,1969
135-08,

HOLLEMAN J F   ED
EXPERIMENT IN SWAZILAND
DURBAN,INSTITUTE OF SOCIAL RESEARCH,UNIVERSITY OF NATAL,1962
135-08,

135-11
BARKER
SWAZILAND
NEW YORK,BRITISH INFORMATION SERVICE,CORONA LIBRARY,1965
135-11,

STEVENS RICHARD P
LESOTHO, BOTSWANA, AND SWAZILAND.
LONDON,PALL MALL PRESS,1967
102-11, 118-11, 135-11,

136. TANZANIA

136-01
WILSON GODFREY
THE NYAKYUSA OF SOUTH-WESTERN TANGANYIKA.
IN E. COLSON AND M. GLICKMAN (EDS), SEVEN TRIBES OF BRITISH
CENTRAL AFRICA, MANCHESTER, UNIVERSITY OF MANCHESTER PRESS,
1951, PP. 253-291
136-01,

ABRAHAMS R G
THE POLITICAL ORGANIZATION OF UNYAMWEZI.
LONDON AND NEW YORK, CAMBRIDGE MONOGRAPHS IN SOCIAL ANTHRO-
POLOGY, 1967
009,136-01,

CORY HANS
SUKUMA LAW AND CUSTOM.
LONDON,OXFORD UNIVERSITY PRESS,1953
066,136-01,

RIGBY P J A
CATTLE AND KINSHIP AMONG THE GOGO--A SEMIPASTORAL SOCIETY OF
CENTRAL TANZANIA.
ITHACA, CORNELL UNIVERSITY PRESS, 1969
008,136-01,

WILSON MONICA
GOOD COMPANY-A STUDY OF NYAKYUSU AGE VILLAGES

LONDON,OXFORD UNIVERSITY PRESS,1951
009,136-01,

136-01
ABRAHAMS R G
THE PEOPLES OF GREATER UNYAMWEZI,TANZANIA-NYAMWEZI,SUKUMA,
SUMBROOA,KIMBU,KONONGO
LONDON,INTERNATIONAL AFRICAN INSTITUTE,1967
136-01.

BEIDELMAN T O
THE MATRILINEAL PEOPLES OF EASTERN TANZANIA-ZARAMO,LIGURU,
KAGURU,NGULU,ETC.
LONDON INTERNATIONAL AFRICAN INSTITUTE 1967
136-01,

WILLIS R G
THE FIPA AND RELATED PEOPLES OF SOUTH-WEST TANZANIA AND
NORTH-EAST ZAMBIA
LONDON,INTERNATIONAL AFRICAN INSTITUTE,1966
136-01,

WINANS EDGAR V
SHAMBALA-THE CONSTITUTION OF A TRADITIONAL STATE
BERKELEY,UNIVERSITY OF CALIFORNIA PRESS,1962
136-01.

136-02
KIMAMBO ISARIA N
A POLITICAL HISTORY OF THE PARE KINGDOM
NAIROBI,EAST AFRICAN PUBLISHING HOUSE,1969
023,136-02,

AUSTEN RALPH A
NORTHWEST TANZANIA UNDER GERMAN AND BRITISH RULE.
NEW HAVEN, CONN. (YALE), MCGILL-QUEEN'S PRESS, 1969
035,136-02,

DORMAN M H
THE KILWA CIVILIZATION AND THE KILWA RUINS.
TANGANYIKA NOTES AND RECORDS 6 1938 PP 61-71
023,136-02,

GRAY JOHN M
EARLY PORTUGUESE VISITORS OF KILWA.
TANGANYIKA NOTES AND RECORDS 52 1959 PP 117-128
023,136-02,

ILIFFE JOHN
TANGANYIKA UNDER GERMAN RULE 1905-1912.
LONDON, CAMBRIDGE UNIVERSITY PRESS. 1969
035,136-02,

KIMAMBO ISARIA N
HISTORICAL RESEARCH IN MAINLAND TANZANIA.
IN CARTER, GWENDOLEN M. AND ANN PADEN (EDS), EXPANDING
HORIZONS IN AFRICAN STUDIES, EVANSTON, NORTHWESTERN
UNIVERSITY PRESS, 1969, PP. 75-90
100,136-02,

BELL R M
THE MAJI-MAJI REBELLION IN THE LIWALE DISTRICT.
TANGANYIKA NOTES AND RECORDS 28 1950 PP 38-57
034,136-02,

136-02
CAMERON SIR D
MY TANGANYIKA SERVICE AND SOME NIGERIA.
LONDON, ALLEN AND UNWIN, 1939
035,128-02,136-02,

CHIDZERO BERNARD T
TANGANYIKA AND INTERNATIONAL TRUSTEESHIP.
LONDON, OXFORD UNIVERSITY PRESS, 1961
035,136-02,

CHITTICK H NEVILLE
KILWA AND THE ARAB SETTLEMENT OF THE EAST AFRICAN COAST.
THE JOURNAL OF AFRICAN HISTORY 4 1963 PP 179-190
023,136-02,

FLINT J E
ZANZIBAR, 1890-1950.
IN VINCENT HARLOW AND E M CHILVER (EDS), HISTORY OF EAST
AFRICA VOL II, OXFORD, CLARENDON PRESS, 1965, PP 641-671
035,136-02,

ILIFFE JOHN
THE ORGANIZATION OF THE MAJI MAJI REBELLION.
THE JOURNAL OF AFRICAN HISTORY 8 1967 PP 495-512
034,136-02,

INGHAM KENNETH
TANGANYIKA-- SLUMP AND SHORT-TERM GOVERNORS, 1932-1945.
IN VINCENT HARLOW AND E M CHILVER (EDS), HISTORY OF EAST
AFRICA VOL II, OXFORD, CLARENDON PRESS, 1965, PP 594-624
035,136-02,

INGHAM KENNETH
TANGANYIKA-- THE MANDATE AND CAMEROUN, 1919-1931.
IN VINCENT HARLOW AND E M CHILVER (EDS), HISTORY OF EAST
AFRICA VOL II, OXFORD, CLARENDON PRESS, 1965, PP. 543-593
035,136-02,

MIDDLETON JOHN
SLAVERY IN ZANZIBAR.
TRANS-ACTION, 1967
028,136-02,

PERHAM MARGERY
THE SYSTEM OF NATIVE ADMINISTRATION IN TANGANYIKA.
AFRICA 2 1931 PP 302-312
035,136-02,

ROBERTS A   ED
TANZANIA BEFORE 1900
NAIROBI, EAST AFRICAN PUBLISHING HOUSE, 1968
025,136-02,

SULLIVAN CAPT G L

DHOW CHASING IN ZANZIBAR WATERS (1873).
NEW YORK, HUMANITIES PRESS, INC., 1967 (NEW INTRODUCTION)
028,136-02,

136-02
CHITTICK H NEVILLE
NOTES ON KILWA.
TANGANYIKA NOTES AND RECORDS 53 1959 PP 179-203
023,136-02,

KIMAMBO ISARIA N   TEMU A J   EDS
A HISTORY OF TANZANIA
NAIROBI,EAST AFRICAN PUBLISHING HOUSE,1969
136-02,

136-03
GOULD PETER
TANZANIA 1920-1963-THE SPATIAL IMPRESS OF THE MODERNIZATION
PROCESS
WORLD POLITICS 22 1970 PP 149-170
048,136-03,

GULLIVER P H   ED
TRADITION AND TRANSITION IN EAST AFRICA--STUDIES OF THE
TRIBAL FACTOR IN THE MODERN ERA.
BERKELEY, UNIVERSITY OF CALIFORNIA PRESS, 1969
007,117-03,136-03,139-03,

KOPF DAVID   VON DER MUHLL G
POLITICAL SOCIALIZATION IN KENYA AND TANZANIA.
JOURNAL OF MODERN AFRICAN STUDIES 5 MAY 1967 PP 13-51
043,117-03,136-03,

CHAGULA W K
THE ROLE OF THE ELITE, THE INTELLIGENTSIA AND EDUCATED EAST
AFRICANS, IN THE DEVELOPMENT OF UGANDA, KENYA AND TANZANIA.
KAMPALA,EAST AFRICAN ACADEMY, SECOND FOUNDATION LECTURE,1966
044,117-03,136-03,139-03,

RESNICK IDRIAN N   ED
TANZANIA--REVOLUTION BY EDUCATION.
NEW YORK, HUMANITIES PRESS INC., 1968
043,136-03,

YOUNG ROLAND A   FOSBROOKE H
SMOKE IN THE HILLS-- POLITICAL TENSION IN THE MOROGORO
DISTRICT OF TANGANYIKA.
EVANSTON,ILLINOIS,NORTHWESTERN UNIVERSITY PRESS,1960
(LAND AND POLITICS AMONG THE LUGURU OF TANGANYIKA,LONDON,
ROUTLEDGE AND KEGAN PAUL,1960)
067,136-03,

LIENHARDT PETER
A CONTROVERSY OVER ISLAMIC CUSTOM IN KILWA KIVINJE, TANZANIA
IN LEWIS, ISLAM IN TROPICAL AFRICA, LONDON, OXFORD UNIVERSIT
PRESS, 1966, P. 374-386
136-03,

RIGBY P J A
SOCIOLOGICAL FACTORS IN THE CONTACT OF THE GOGO OF CENTRAL

TANZANIA WITH ISLAM.
IN LEWIS, ISLAM IN TROPICAL AFRICA, LONDON, OXFORD UNIVERSITY
PRESS, 1966, P. 268-295
136-03,

136-03
SCHILDKNECHT FRANK
TANZANIA
IN KRITZECK AND LEWIS, PP 227-242
136-03,

136-04
TANZANIA AFRICAN NATIONAL UNION,
THE ARUSHA DECLARATION AND TANU'S POLICY ON SOCIALISM AND
SELF-RELIANCE.
DAR ES-SALAAM, GOVERNMENT PRINTER, 1967
058,060,070,073,136-04,

NYERERE JULIUS K
THE RELATIONSHIP BETWEEN THE CIVIL SERVICE, POLITICAL
PARTIES AND MEMBERS OF LEGISLATIVE COUNCIL.
INTERNATIONAL AFFAIRS 36 JANUARY 1960 PP 43-47
062,136-04,

NYERERE JULIUS K
THE NATURE AND REQUIREMENTS OF AFRICAN UNITY.
AFRICAN FORUM I 1 1965 PP 38-52
079, 136-04,

GOVERNMENT OF TANZANIA
REPORT OF THE PRESIDENTIAL COMMISSION ON THE ESTABLISHMENT
OF A DEMOCRATIC ONE-PARTY STATE.
DAR ES SALAAM,1965
061,136-04,

HYDAN GORAN
MAO AND MWALIMU--THE SOLDIER AND THE TEACHER AS
REVOLUTIONARY
TRANSITION 7 1968 PP 24-30
084,136-04,

NYERERE JULIUS K
UJAMAA-- THE BASIS OF AFRICAN SOCIALISM CHAPTER 5.
IN AFRICA'S FREEDOM, NEW YORK, BARNES AND NOBLE, 1964,
PP 67-77
060, 136-04,

NYERERE JULIUS K
THE AFRICAN AND DEMOCRACY.
IN WILLIAM J HANNA (ED), INDEPENDENT BLACK AFRICA, CHICAGO,
RAND MCNALLY, 1964, PP 521-527
060, 136-04,

NYERERE JULIUS K
TANGANYIKA TODAY-- THE NATIONALIST VIEW.
INTERNATIONAL AFFAIRS 36 1960 PP43-47
060,136-04,

NYERERE JULIUS K
INDEPENDENCE MEANS POWER.

AFRICA REPORT, DECEMBER, 1968, P. 22
087,136-04,

136-04
   NYERERE JULIUS K
   ESSAYS ON SOCIALISM.
   LONDON AND NEW YORK, INTERNATIONAL BOOKSELLERS, INC., 1969
   060,077,136-04,

   NYERERE JULIUS K
   FREEDOM AND UNITY--UHURU NA UMOJA.
   LONDON, OXFORD UNIVERSITY PRESS, 1967
   060,077,136-04,

136-05
   DE BLIJ HARM J
   DAR ES SALAAM.
   EVANSTON, NORTHWESTERN UNIVERSITY PRESS, 1963
   045,136-05,

   ANONYMOUS
   A SURVEY OF DAR ES SALAAM--A REVIEW.
   AFRICA, VOL. 34, NO. 4
   136-05,

   LESLIE J A K
   A SURVEY OF DAR ES SALAAM.
   LONDON, OXFORD UNIVERSITY PRESS, 1963
   136-05,

136-06
   CHIDZERO BERNARD T
   THE PLURAL SOCIETY OF TANGANYIKA CHP 7.
   IN TANGANYIKA AND INTERNATIONAL TRUSTEESHIP, NEW YORK,
   OXFORD UNIVERSITY PRESS, 1961
   057,136-06,

   CHIDZERO BERNARD T
   REACTIONS TO MULTI-RACIALISM CHP 8.
   IN TANGANYIKA AND INTERNATIONAL TRUSTEESHIP, NEW YORK,
   OXFORD UNIVERSITY PRESS, 1961
   088,136-06,

   COTRAN EUGENE
   SOME RECENT DEVELOPMENTS IN THE TANGANYIKA JUDICIAL
   SYSTEM.
   JOURNAL OF AFRICAN LAW 6 SPRING PP 19-28
   066,136-06,

   GULLIVER P H
   THE ARUSHA--ECONOMIC AND SOCIAL CHANGE.
   IN BOHANNAN AND DALTON (EDS), MARKETS IN AFRICA, DOUBLEDAY,
   1965
   010,136-06,

   KYLE KEITH
   COUP IN ZANZIBAR.
   AFRICA REPORT 9 FEBRUARY 1964 PP 18-20
   064,136-06,

LEMARCHAND RENE
REVOLUTIONARY PHENOMENA IN STRATIFIED SOCIETIES--RWANDA AND
ZANZIBAR.
CIVILISATIONS, VOL XVIII, NO. 1, 1968, PP. 16-51
057,129-06,136-06,

136-06
LOFCHIE MICHAEL
ZANZIBAR-- BACKGROUND TO REVOLUTION.
PRINCETON NEW JERSEY PRINCETON UNIVERSITY PRESS 1965
055,136-06,

OKELLO JOHN
REVOLUTION IN ZANZIBAR.
KENYA, EAST AFRICAN PUBLISHING HOUSE, 1967
057,059,136-06,

PRATT R CRANFORD
MULTI-RACIALISM AND LOCAL GOVERNMENT IN TANGANYIKA.
RACE 2 1960 PP 33-49
088,136-06,

136-07
CLIFFE LIONEL   ED
ONE-PARTY DEMOCRACY-- THE 1965 TANZANIA GENERAL ELECTIONS.
NAIROBI, EAST AFRICAN PUBLISHING HOUSE, 1967
063,136-07,

BATES M L
TANGANYIKA.
IN G.M. CARTER (ED) AFRICAN ONE-PARTY STATES, ITHACA,
CORNELL UNIVERSITY PRESS, 1962
136-07,

BIENEN HENRY
TANZANIA-- PARTY TRANSFORMATION AND ECONOMIC DEVELOPMENT.
PRINCETON, PRINCETON UNIVERSITY PRESS, 1967
061,136-07,

DRYDEN STANLEY
LOCAL ADMINISTRATION IN TANZANIA.
KENYA, EAST AFRICAN PUBLISHING HOUSE, 1968
062,136-07,

LIEBENOW J GUS
COLONIAL RULE AND POLITICAL DEVELOPMENT IN TANZANIA-THE
CASE OF THE MAKONDE
EVANSTON NORTHWESTERN UNIVERSITY PRESS 1970
035,055,063,136-07,

LINTON NEVILLE
NYERERE'S ROAD TO SOCIALISM
CANADIAN JOURNAL OF AFRICAN STUDIES 2 1968 PP 1-6
077,136-07,

LOFCHIE MICHAEL
PARTY CONFLICT IN ZANZIBAR.
JOURNAL OF MODERN AFRICAN STUDIES 1 1963 PP 185-207
061,136-07,

MAZRUI ALI A
ANTI-MILITARISM AND POLITICAL MILITANCY IN TANZANIA
JOURNAL OF CONFLICT RESOLUTION 12 1968 PP269-284
061,136-07,

136-07
BENNETT GEORGE
AN OUTLINE OF HISTORY OF TANU.
MAKERERE JOURNAL 7 1962 PP 15-32
055,136-07,

LEYS COLIN
TANGANYIKA--THE REALITIES OF INDEPENDENCE.
INTERNATIONAL JOURNAL 17, 1962
136-07,

TAYLOR JAMES C   1
THE POLITICAL DEVELOPMENT OF TANGANYIKA.
LONDON, OXFORD UNIVERSITY PRESS;   STANFORD, STANFORD
UNIVERSITY PRESS, 1963
136-07,

136-08
SMITH HADLEY E   ED
READINGS ON ECONOMIC DEVELOPMENT AND ADMINISTRATION IN
TANZANIA.
EASTERN AFRICA, OXFORD UNIVERSITY PRESS, 1966
073,136-08,

BURKE FRED G
TANGANYIKA PREPLANNING.
SYRACUSE, SYRACUSE UNIVERSITY PRESS, 1965
072,136-08,

FRIEDLAND WILLIAM H
VUTA KAMBA--THE DEVELOPMENT OF TRADE UNIONS IN TANGANYIKA.
PALO ALTO, CALIFORNIA, HOOVER INSTITUTION PRESS, 1969
063,136-08,

FUGGLES-COUCHMAN N
AGRICULTURAL CHANGE IN TANGANYIKA.
STANFORD, STANFORD UNIVERSITY FOOD RESEARCH INSTITUTE, 1964
070,136-08,

GREEN REGINALD H
FOUR AFRICAN DEVELOPMENT PLANS-- GHANA, KENYA, NIGERIA,
AND TANZANIA CHAPTER 20.
IN EDITH WHETHAM AND JEAN CURRIE, (EDS.) READINGS IN THE
APPLIED ECONOMICS OF AFRICA, LONDON, CAMBRIDGE UNIVERSITY
PRESS, 2, 1967, PP 21-32
072,114-08,117-08,128-08,136-08,

GULLIVER P H
LAND TENURE AND SOCIAL CHANGE AMONG THE NYAKYUSA--
AN ESSAY IN APPLIED ANTHROPOLOGY IN SOUTH-WEST TANGANYIKA.
KAMPALA, EAST AFRICAN INSTITUTE OF SOCIAL RESEARCH, 1958
070,136-08,

HANCE WILLIAM A   VAN DONGEN I S
DAR ES SALAAM, THE PORT AND ITS TRIBUTARY.

ANNALS OF THE ASSOCIATION OF AMERICAN GEOGRAPHERS
48 DECEMBER 1958 PP 419-435
048,136-08,

136-08
INTERNATIONAL BANK FOR RECONSTRUCTION AND DEVELOPMENT
THE ECONOMIC DEVELOPMENT OF TANGANYIKA
BALTIMORE,JOHNS HOPKINS UNIVERSITY PRESS, 1961
073,136-08,

MIDDLETON JOHN
LAND TENURE IN ZANZIBAR.
LONDON,HER MAJESTY'S STATIONERY OFFICE, 1961
070,136-08,

ROE ALAN R
THE FUTURE OF THE COMPANY IN TANZANIAN DEVELOPMENT.
THE JOURNAL OF MODERN AFRICAN STUDIES, VOL. 7, NO. 1, 1969,
PP. 47-67
073,136-08,

RUTHENBERG HANS
AGRICULTURAL DEVELOPMENT IN TANGANYIKA.
BERLIN,SPRINGER-VERLAG, 1964
070,136-08,

SKOROV GEORGE
INTEGRATION OF EDUCATIONAL AND ECONOMIC PLANNING IN
TANZANIA.
PARIS,UNESCO,1967
072,136-08,

SMITH HADLEY E   ED
AGRICULTURAL DEVELOPMENT IN TANZANIA.
LONDON,OXFORD UNIVERSITY PRESS,1965
INSTITUTE OF PUBLIC ADMINISTRATION,DAR-ES-SALAAM,STUDY 2
070,136-08,

136-09
BANEFIELD JANE
THE STRUCTURE AND ADMINISTRATION OF THE EAST AFRICAN COMMON
SERVICES ORGANIZATION.
IN COLIN LEYS AND P ROBSON (EDS),FEDERATION IN EAST AFRICA--
OPPORTUNITIES AND PROBLEMS,NAIROBI,OXFORD UNIVERSITY PRESS,
1965 PP 30-40
078,117-09,136-09,139-09,

HUGHES A J
EAST AFRICA-- THE SEARCH FOR UNITY-- KENYA, TANGANYIKA,
UGANDA AND ZANZIBAR.
MIDDLESEX,HARMONDSWORTH,1963
077,117-09,136-09,139-09,

NYERERE JULIUS K
WHY TANZANIA RECOGNIZED BIAFRA.
AFRICA REPORT, JUNE 27, 1968
065,136-09,

DUDBRIDGE B J   GRIFFITHS J E S
THE DEVELOPMENT OF LOCAL GOVERNMENT IN SUKUMALAND.

JOURNAL OF AFRICAN ADMINISTRATION 3 JULY 1951 PP 141-146
062,136-09,

136-09
    MAZRUI ALI A
    TANZANIA VERSUS EAST AFRICA CHAPTER 6.
    IN ON HEROES AND UHURU-WORSHIP, LONDON, LONGMANS,
    1967, PP 73-95
    077,136-09,

136-11
    LONSDALE JOHN
    THE TANZANIAN EXPERIMENT
    AFRICAN AFFAIRS 67 1968 PP 330-344
    063,070,136-11,

    CLIFFE LIONEL
    TANZANIA.
    LONDON, PALL MALL PRESS, 1970
    136-11,

    MIDDLETON JOHN
    ZANZIBAR
    NEW YORK, OXFORD, 1965
    136-11,

    MOFFETT JOHN PERRY   ED
    HANDBOOK OF TANGANYIKA.
    DAR-ES-SALAAM, GOVERNMENT PRINTER (2ND EDITION), 1958
    136-11,

136-12
    KURIA LUCAS   WEBSTER JOHN R
    A BIBLIOGRAPHY ON ANTHROPOLOGY AND SOCIOLOGY IN TANZANIA AND
    EAST AFRICA.
    NEW YORK. SYRACUSE UNIVERSITY PROGRAM OF EASTERN AFRICAN
    STUDIES, 1966
    136-12,

137. TOGO

137-01
    CARDINALL ALLAN W   ED
    TALES TOLD IN TOGOLAND-- TO WHICH IS ADDED THE MYTHICAL AND
    TRADITIONAL HISTORY OF DAGOMBA BY E F TAMAKLOE.
    LONDON, OXFORD UNIVERSITY PRESS, 1931
    012,137-01,

    FROELICH JEAN C
    LES POPULATIONS DE NORD-TOGO.
    PRESSES UNIVERSITAIRES DE FRANCE, 1963
    137-01,

137-02
    FROELICH JEAN C

CAMEROUN TOGO TERRITOIRES SOUS TUTELLE.
PARIS, BERGER-LEVRAULT, 1956
104-02,137-02,

137-02
FROELICH JEAN C
CAMEROUN, TOGO, TERRITORIES SOUS TUTELLE.
PARIS, BERGER-LEVRAULT, 1956
137-02,

KWAKUME HENRY
PRECIS D'HISTOIRE DU PEUPLE EWE.
LOME, IMP. DE L'ECOLE PROFESSIONELLE, N.D.
137-02,

137-03
DEBRUNNER HANS
A CHURCH BETWEEN COLONIAL POWERS--A STUDY OF THE CHURCH IN
TOGO.
LONDON, LUTTERWORTH PRESS, 1965
050,137-03,

137-04
OLYMPIO SYLVANUS
AFRICAN PROBLEMS AND THE COLD WAR.
IN PHILIP W QUIGG (ED.), AFRICA, NEW YORK, PRAEGER, 1964,
PP 292-301
081,137-04,

NSOUGAN AGBLEMAGNON
MASSES ET ELITES EN AFRIQUE NOIRE - LE CAS DU TOGO.
IN LLOYD, THE NEW ELITES OF TROPICAL AFRICA, LONDON, OXFORD
UNIVERSITY PRESS, 1966, P. 118-125
137-04,

137-06
ANONYMOUS
CONVULSIONS WITHIN TOGO.
PAN AFRICA NO. 93 JANUARY 6, 1967 P 9
064,137-06,

137-08
ENJALBERT H
PAYSANS NOIRS-- LES KABRE DU NORD-TOGO
(BLACK PEASANTS-- THE KABRE OF NORTHERN TOGO).
CAHIERS D'OUTRE-MER 9 APRIL JUNE 1956 PP 137-180
070,137-08,

137-10
AKAKPO TYPAMM PAUL
POEMES ET CONTES D'AFRIQUE.
PARIS, CERCLE DE LA POESIE ET DE LA PEINTURE, 1958
137-10,

ANANOU DAVID
LE FILS DU FETICHE--ROMAN.
PARIS, NOUVELLES EDITIONS LATINES, 1955
137-10,

137-11

LUSIGNAN GUY DE
FRENCH-SPEAKING AFRICA SINCE INDEPENDENCE.
NEW YORK, PRAEGER PUBLISHERS, 1969
056,061,104-11,105-11,106-11,107-11,109-11,112-11,
115-11,116-11,123-11,137-11,141-11,

137-11
  CORNEVIN ROBERT
  LE TOGO, NATION-PILOTE.
  PARIS, NOUVELLES EDITIONS LATINES. 1963
  137-11,

  LA DOCUMENTATION FRANCAISE
  LA REPUBLIQUE DU TOGO.
  NOTES ET ETUDES DOCUMENTAIRES, NO. 2736, OCT. 5, 1960
  137-11,

137-12
  WITHERELL JULIAN T
  OFFICIAL PUBLICATIONS OF THE FRENCH EQUATORIAL AFRICA,
  FRENCH CAMEROUNS AND TOGO, 1949-1958.
  WASHINGTON, LIBRARY OF CONGRESS, AFRICAN SECTION, 1964
  104-12,105-12,106-12,107-12,112-12,137-12,

138. TUNISIA

138-06
  ASHFORD DOUGLAS E
  NATIONAL DEVELOPMENT AND LOCAL REFORM-POLITICAL PARTITION
  IN MOROCCO,TUNISIA,AND PAKISTAN
  PRINCETON, PRINCETON UNIVERSITY PRESS
  126-06,138-06,

138-07
  MOORE CLEMENT H
  THE NEO-DESTOUR PARTY OF TUNISIA-- A STRUCTURE FOR
  DEMOCRACY CHAPTER 15.
  IN JASON L FINKLE AND RICHARD W GABLE, POLITICAL
  DEVELOPMENT AND SOCIAL CHANGE, NEW YORK, JOHN WILEY, 1966
  061,138-07,

  MOORE CLEMENT H   HOCHSCHILD ARLIE R
  STUDENT UNIONS IN NORTH AFRICAN POLITICS.
  DAEDALUS, WINTER 1968, PP. 21-50
  063,138-07,

  GALLAGHER CHARLES F
  TUNISIA.
  IN G.M. CARTER (ED) AFRICAN ONE-PARTY STATES, ITHACA, NEW
  YORK, CORNELL UNIVERSITY PRESS. 1962
  138-07,

  MICAUD CHARLES A
  TUNISIA--THE POLITICS OF MODERNIZATION.
  NEW YORK, PRAEGER, 1964

138-07,

138-07
    MOORE CLEMENT H
    THE NEO-DESTOUR PARTY OF TUNISIA--A STRUCTURE FOR DEMOCRACY
    CHAPTER 15.
    IN JASON L. FINKLE AND RICHARD W GABLE, POLITICAL
    DEVELOPMENT AND SOCIAL CHANGE, NEW YORK, JOHN WILEY, 1966
    138-07,

138-08
    BELING WILLARD A
    MODERNIZATION AND AFRICAN LABOR-- A TUNISIAN CASE STUDY.
    NEW YORK, PRAEGER, 1965
    073,138-08,

    DUWAJI GHAZI
    ECONOMIC DEVELOPMENT IN TUNISIA--THE IMPACT AND COURSE OF
    GOVERNMENT PLANNING.
    NEW YORK, PRAEGER PUBLISHERS, 1967
    072,138-08,

    AMIN SAMIR
    L)ECONOMIE DU MAGHREB VOLUME 1- LA COLONISATION ET LA
    DECOLONISATION VOLUME 2-LES PERSPECTIVE D'AVENIR
    PARIS, EDITIONS DE MINUIT, 1966
    073,101-08,126-08,138-08,

138-09
    GALLAGHER CHARLES F
    THE UNITED STATES AND NORTH AFRICA
    CAMBRIDGE, MASS, HARVARD UNIVERSITY PRESS, 1963
    083,101-09,126-09,138-09,

    SANDS WILLIAM
    PROSPECTS FOR A UNITED MAGHRIB
    IN TIBOR KEREKES (ED), THE ARAB MIDDLE EAST AND MUSLIM
    AFRICA, NEW YORK PRAEGER 1961
    078,101-09,120-09,126-09,138-09,

138-11
    MOORE CLEMENT H
    TUNISIA SINCE INDEPENDENCE.
    BERKELEY, UNIVERSITY OF CALIFORNIA PRESS, 1965
    138-11,

    BRACE RICHARD M
    MOROCCO ALGERIA TUNISIA
    ENGLEWOOD CLIFFS, PRENTICE-HALL, 1964
    101-11,126-11,138-11,

139. UGANDA

139-01
    AINSWORTH MARY D

INFANCY IN UGANDA.
BALTIMORE, JOHNS HOPKINS PRESS, 1967
040,139-01,

139-01
CHESSWAS J D
THE ESSENTIALS OF LUGANDA.
EAST AFRICA, OXFORD UNIVERSITY PRESS, 1968
011,139-01,

MIDDLETON JOHN
LUGBARA RELIGION-RITUAL AND AUTHORITY AMONG AN EAST AFRICAN
PEOPLE
LONDON,OXFORD FOR INTERNATIONAL AFRICAN INSTITUTE, 1960
013,139-01,

MORRIS HENRY F
THE HEROIC RECITATIONS OF THE BAHIMA OF ANKOLE.
LONDON, OXFORD UNIVERSITY PRESS, 1964
012,015,139-01,

ROSCOE J
THE BAGANDA
LONDON,FRANK CASS,SECOND EDITION, 1965
025,139-01,

TROWELL MARGARET   WACHSMANN KLAUS
TRIBAL CRAFTS OF UGANDA
LONDON, OXFORD UNIVERSITY PRESS, 1953
014,139-01,

BEATTIE J H M
THE NYORO.
IN AUDREY I. RICHARDS (ED). EAST AFRICAN CHIEFS, LONDON,
FABER AND FABER, 1960, PP. 98-123
139-01,

FALLERS LLOYD A
THE SOGA.
IN A.I. RICHARDS (ED), EAST AFRICAN CHIEFS, LONDON, FABER
AND FABER, 1960, PP. 78-97
139-01,

FALLERS M C
THE EASTERN LACUSTRINE BANTU-GANDA,SOGA
LONDON, INTERNATIONAL AFRICAN INSTITUTE, 1960
139-01,

GIRLING F K
THE ACHOLI OF UGANDA.
LONDON, HER MAJESTY'S STATIONERY OFFICE, 1960
139-01.

SOUTHWALD MARTIN
THE GANDA OF UGANDA.
IN JAMES L. GIBBS JR. (ED), PEOPLES OF AFRICA, NEW YORK,
HOLT, RINEHART AND WINSTON, 1965, PP. 81-118
139-01.

139-02

LOW DAVID A   PRATT R CRANFORD
BUGANDA AND BRITISH OVERRULE 1900-1955.
LONDON, OXFORD UNIVERSITY PRESS, 1960
035, 139-02,

139-02
    LOW DAVID A
    UGANDA-- THE ESTABLISHMENT OF THE PROTECTORATE, 1894-1919.
    IN VINCENT HARLOW AND E M CHILVER (EDS), HISTORY OF EAST
    AFRICA VOL II, OXFORD, CLARENDON PRESS, 1965, PP 57-122
    033, 139-02,

    LUGARD FREDERICK D
    THE STORY OF THE UGANDA PROTECTORATE.
    LONDON, H MARSHALL, 1901
    033, 139-02,

    OLIVER ROLAND
    ANCIENT CAPITAL SITES OF ANKOLE.
    THE UGANDA JOURNAL 23 1959 PP 51-63
    025, 139-02,

    PRATT R CRANFORD
    ADMINISTRATION AND POLITICS IN UGANDA, 1919-1945.
    IN VINCENT HARLOW AND E M CHILVER (EDS), HISTORY OF EAST
    AFRICA VOL II, OXFORD, CLARENDON PRESS, 1965, PP 476-542
    035, 139-02,

    ADIMOLA A B
    THE LAMOGI REBELLION 1911-1912.
    THE UGANDA JOURNAL 18 1954 PP 166-177
    034, 139-02,

    INGHAM KENNETH
    THE MAKING OF MODERN UGANDA.
    LONDON, ALLEN AND UNWIN, 1958
    139-02,

139-03
    GULLIVER P H   ED
    TRADITION AND TRANSITION IN EAST AFRICA--STUDIES OF THE
    TRIBAL FACTOR IN THE MODERN ERA.
    BERKELEY, UNIVERSITY OF CALIFORNIA PRESS, 1969
    007, 117-03, 136-03, 139-03,

    APTER DAVID E
    THE ROLE OF TRADITIONALISM IN THE POLITICAL
    MODERNIZATION OF GHANA AND UGANDA.
    WORLD POLITICS 13 OCT 1960 PP 45-68; ALSO WILLIAM J HANNA, ED,
    INDEPENDENT BLACK AFRICA, CHICAGO, RAND MCNALLY, 1964, PP
    254-277
    055, 114-03, 139-03,

    CHAGULA W K
    THE ROLE OF THE ELITE, THE INTELLIGENTSIA AND EDUCATED EAST
    AFRICANS, IN THE DEVELOPMENT OF UGANDA, KENYA AND TANZANIA.
    KAMPALA, EAST AFRICAN ACADEMY, SECOND FOUNDATION LECTURE, 1966
    044, 117-03, 136-03, 139-03,

    FALLERS LLOYD A

THE KING'S MEN-- LEADERSHIP AND STATUS IN BUGANDA ON THE
EVE OF INDEPENDENCE.
LONDON, OXFORD UNIVERSITY PRESS, 1964
034,038,139-03,

139-03
FALLERS LLOYD A
CHANGING CUSTOMARY LAW IN BUSOGA DISTRICT OF UGANDA.
JOUNRAL OF AFRICAN ADMINISTRATION 8 JULY 1956 PP 139-144
066,139-03,

FALLERS LLOYD A
THE PREDICAMENT OF THE MODERN AFRICAN CHIEF-- AN
INSTANCE FROM UGANDA.
AMERICAN ANTHROPOLOGIST 57 1955 PP 290-305; ALSO WILLIAM J
HANNA, ED, INDEPENDENT BLACK AFRICA, CHICAGO, RAND MCNALLY,
1964, PP 278-296
038,139-03,

MIDDLETON JOHN
SOCIAL CHANGE AMONG THE LUGBARA OF UGANDA.
CIVILIZATIONS 10 1960 PP 446-456
038, 139-03,

LEWENKOPF MARTIN
UGANDA
IN KRITZECK AND LEWIS, PP 214-226
139-03,

WINGARD PETER
PROBLEMS OF THE MEDIA OF INSTRUCTION IN SOME UGANDA SCHOOL
CLASSES--A PRELIMINARY SURVEY.
IN JOHN SPENCER (ED), LANGUAGE IN AFRICA, PAPERS OF THE
LEVERHULME CONFERENCE ON UNIVERSITIES AND THE LANGUAGE
PROBLEMS OF TROPICAL AFRICA, CAMBRIDGE, CAMBRIDGE UNIVERSITY
PRESS, 1963
139-03,

139-04
KUMALO C
AFRICAN ELITES IN INDUSTRIAL BUREAUCRACY.
IN LLOYD, THE NEW ELITES OF TROPICAL AFRICA, LONDON, OXFORD
UNIVERSITY PRESS, 1966. P. 216-229
071,139-04,

MUTESA II
THE DESECRETION OF MY KINGDOM.
LONDON, CONSTABLE, 1967
054,064,139-04,

SOUTHALL AIDAN
THE CONCEPT OF ELITES AND THEIR FORMATION IN UGANDA.
IN LLOYD, THE NEW ELITES OF TROPICAL AFRICA, LONDON, OXFORD
UNIVERSITY PRESS, 1966. P. 342-366
044,139-04,

139-05
LARIMORE A E
THE ALIEN TOWN--PATTERNS OF SETTLEMENT IN BUSOGA, UGANDA.
UNIVERSITY OF CHICAGO, DEPT OF GEOGRAPHY RESEARCH PAPERS,

AUGUST 1958 PP 1-210
046,139-05,

139-05
    MUNGER EDWIN S
    RELATIONAL PATTERNS OF KAMPALA, UGANDA.
    UNIVERSITY OF CHICAGO,DEPT OF GEOGRAPHY RESEARCH PAPERS,
    SEPTEMBER 1951 PP 1-178
    048,139-05,

    PARKIN DAVID J
    TYPES OF URBAN AFRICAN MARRIAGE IN KAMPALA.
    AFRICA 36 JULY 1966 PP 269-285
    047,139-05,

    PARKIN DAVID J
    NEIGHBORS AND NATIONALS IN AN AFRICAN CITY WARD.
    BERKELEY, UNIVERSITY OF CALIFORNIA, 1969
    046,139-05,

    SOFER CYRIL   SOFER RHONA
    JINJA TRANSFORMED--A SOCIAL SURVEY OF A MULTI-RACIAL
    TOWNSHIP.
    EAST AFRICAN STUDIES NO. 4, KAMPALA, EAST AFRICAN INSTITUTE
    OF SOCIAL RESEARCH, 1955
    139-05,

    SOFER CYRIL   SOFER RHONA
    RECENT POPULATION GROWTH IN JINJA.
    UGANDA JOURNAL, 17, 1, 1953
    139-05,

    SOUTHALL AIDAN
    DETERMINANTS OF THE SOCIAL STRUCTURE OF AFRICAN URBAN
    POPULATIONS, WITH SPECIAL REFERENCE TO KAMPALA, (UGANDA)
    (1956).
    IN IMMANUEL WALLERSTEIN, SOCIAL CHANGE-- THE COLONIAL
    SITUATION, NEW YORK, WILEY, 1966, PP 321-339
    046,139-05,

    SOUTHALL AIDAN
    KAMPALA-MENGO.
    IN THE CITY IN MODERN AFRICA, HORACE MINER (ED), PRAEGER,
    1967
    139-05,

    SOUTHALL AIDAN
    SOME PROBLEMS OF STATISTICAL ANALYSIS IN COMMUNITY STUDIES,
    ILLUSTRATED FROM KAMPALA, UGANDA.
    IN SOCIAL IMPLICATIONS OF INDUSTRIALIZATION AND URBANIZATION
    IN AFRICA SOUTH OF THE SAHARA, PARIS, UNESCO, 1956
    139-05,

    SOUTHALL AIDAN
    TOWNSMEN IN THE MAKING--KAMPALA AND ITS SUBURBS.
    EAST AFRICAN STUDIES NO. 9, KAMPALA, EAST AFRICAN INSTITUTE
    OF SOCIAL RESEARCH, 1957
    139-05,

    TEMPLE P H

KAMPALA--INFLUENCES UPON ITS GROWTH AND DEVELOPMENT.
EAST AFRICAN INSTITUTE OF SOCIAL RESEARCH CONFERENCE PAPER,
JUNE, 1963
139-05.

139-06
EPSTEIN ARNOLD L
JUDICIAL TECHNIQUES AND THE JUDICIAL PROCESS-- A STUDY IN
AFRICAN CUSTOMARY LAW.
MANCHESTER MANCHESTER UNIVERSITY PRESS 1954
066,139-06,

MORRIS H S
THE INDIANS IN UGANDA
CHICAGO UNIVERSITY OF CHICAGO PRESS 1968
085,139-06,

ZAKE S JOSHUA L
REVISION AND UNIFICATION OF AFRICAN LEGAL SYSTEMS--THE
UGANDA EXPERIENCE.
IN CARTER, GWENDOLEN M. AND ANN PADEN (EDS) EXPANDING
HORIZONS IN AFRICAN STUDIES, EVANSTON, NORTHWESTERN
UNIVERSITY PRESS, 1969, PP. 157-168
066, 100, 139-06,

APTER DAVID E
THE POLITICAL KINGDOM IN UGANDA A STUDY IN BUREAUCRATIC
NATIONALISM.
PRINCETON PRINCETON UNIVERSITY PRESS 1961 REVISED 1967
055,139-06,

FALLERS LLOYD A
POPULISM AND NATIONALISM-- A COMMENT ON D A LOWS THE ADVENT
OF POPULISM IN BUGANDA.
COMPARATIVE STUDIES IN SOCIETY AND HISTORY 6 JULY 1964
055,139-06,
PP 445-448

FALLERS LLOYD A
IDEOLOGY AND CULTURE IN UGANDA NATIONALISM.
AMERICAN ANTHROPOLOGIST 63 1961 PP 677-686
060,139-06,

HAYDON E S
LAW AND JUSTICE IN BUGANDA.
LONDON BUTTERWORTHS 1960
AFRICAN LAW SERIES NO. 2
066,139-06,

LOW DAVID A
THE ADVENT OF POPULISM IN BUGANDA.
COMPARATIVE STUDIES IN SOCIETY AND HISTORY 6 JULY 1964
PP 424-444
055,139-06,

PRATT R CRANFORD
NATIONALISM IN UGANDA.
POLITICAL STUDIES   JUNE 1961 PP 157-178
055,139-06,

YOUNG CRAWFORD
THE OBOTE REVOLUTION.
AFRICA REPORT 11 JUNE 1966 PP 8-14
064,139-06,

139-06
   FALLERS LLOYD A
   LAW WITHOUT PRECEDENT--LEGAL IDEAS IN ACTION IN THE COURTS
   OF COLONIAL BUSOGA.
   CHICAGO AND LONDON, THE UNIVERSITY OF CHICAGO PRESS, 1969
   066,139-06,

139-07
   ENGHOLM G F
   THE WESTMINSTER MODEL IN UGANDA.
   INTERNATIONAL JOURNAL 18 AUTUMN 1963 PP 468-487
   062,139-07,

   LEYS COLIN
   POLITICIANS AND POLICIES-- AN ESSAY IN AXCHOLI
   UGANDA 1962-65.
   NAIROBI KENYA THE EAST AFRICAN PUBLISHING HOUSE 1967
   061,139-07,

   LOW DAVID A
   POLITICAL PARTIES IN UGANDA 1949-1962.
   LONDON 1962
   055,139-07,

   BURKE FRED G
   LOCAL GOVERNMENT AND POLITICS IN UGANDA.
   SYRACUSE, SYRACUSE UNIVERSITY PRESS, 1964
   139-07,

139-08
   CLARK PAUL
   DEVELOPMENT STRATEGY IN AN EARLY STAGE ECONOMY-UGANDA
   JOURNAL OF MODERN AFRICAN STUDIES 4 1966 PP 47-64
   072,073,139-08,

   ELKAN WALTER
   THE ECONOMIC DEVELOPMENT OF UGANDA.
   LONDON, OXFORD UNIVERSITY PRESS, 1961
   073,139-08,

   FALLERS LLOYD A
   THE POLITICS OF LANDHOLDING IN BUSOGA.
   ECONOMIC DEVELOPMENT AND CULTURAL CHANGE 3 1955 PP 260-270
   070,139-08,

   GHAI DHARAM P
   TAXATION FOR DEVELOPMENT--A CASE STUDY OF UGANDA.
   KENYA, EAST AFRICAN PUBLISHING HOUSE, 1966
   073,139-08,

   HOYLE B S
   THE ECONOMIC EXPANSION OF JINJA, UGANDA.
   GEOGRAPHICAL REVIEW L111 JULY 1963 PP 377-388
   071,139-08,

INTERNATIONAL BANK FOR RECONSTRUCTION AND DEVELOPMENT
THE ECONOMIC DEVELOPMENT OF UGANDA
BALTIMORE JOHNS HOPKINS UNIVERSITY PRESS 1962
073,139-08,

139-08
    LAWRANCE J C D
    A PILOT SCHEME FOR LAND TITLES IN UGANDA.
    JOURNAL OF AFRICAN ADMINISTRATION 12 JULY 1960 PP 135-143
    070,139-08,

    MASEFIELD G B
    AGRICULTURAL CHANGE IN UGANDA, 1945-1960, CHAPTER 5.
    IN EDITH WHETHAM AND JEAN CURRIE, (EDS.) READINGS IN THE
    APPLIED ECONOMICS OF AFRICA, LONDON, CAMBRIDGE UNIVERSITY
    PRESS, 1, 1967, PP 38-57
    070,139-08,

    NORTH A C   ET-AL
    AFRICAN LAND TENURE DEVELOPMENTS IN KENYA AND UGANDA AND
    THEIR APPLICATION TO NORTHERN RHODESIA.
    JOURNAL OF AFRICAN ADMINISTRATION 13 OCTOBER 1961
    PP 211-219
    070,117-08,139-08,142-08,

    RICHARDS AUDREY I   ED
    ECONOMIC DEVELOPMENT AND TRIBAL CHANGE-- A STUDY OF
    IMMIGRANT LABOUR IN BUGANDA.
    CAMBRIDGE HEFFER 1956
    074,139-08,

    RICHARDS AUDREY I
    SOME EFFECTS OF THE INTRODUCTION OF INDIVIDUAL FREEHOLD
    INTO BUGANDA.
    IN D BIEBUYCK (ED), AFRICAN AGRARIAN SYSTEMS, LONDON,
    OXFORD UNIVERSITY PRESS, 1963, PP 267-280
    078,139-08,

139-09
    BANEFIELD JANE
    THE STRUCTURE AND ADMINISTRATION OF THE EAST AFRICAN COMMON
    SERVICES ORGANIZATION.
    IN COLIN LEYS AND P ROBSON (EDS) FEDERATION IN EAST AFRICA--
    OPPORTUNITIES AND PROBLEMS NAIROBI OXFORD UNIVERSITY PRESS
    1965 PP 30-40
    078,117-09,136-09,139-09,

    HUGHES A J
    EAST AFRICA-- THE SEARCH FOR UNITY-- KENYA, TANGANYIKA,
    UGANDA AND ZANZIBAR.
    MIDDLESEX HARMONDSWORTH 1963
    077,117-09,136-09,139-09,

    ROTHCHILD DONALD S   ROGIN MICHAEL
    UGANDA.
    IN CARTER, G.M. NATIONAL UNITY AND REGIONALISM IN EIGHT
    AFRICAN STATES, ITHACA, CORNELL UNIVERSITY PRESS, 1966
    139-09,

139-11

GERTZEL CHERRY
UGANDA.
LONDON, PALL MALL PRESS, 1970
139-11,

139-12
ANONYMOUS
CATALOGUES OF GOVERNMENT PUBLICATIONS PUBLISHED PRIOR TO
1ST JANUARY, 1965 .
ENTEBBE, GOVERNMENT PRINTER, 1965
139-12,

KURIA LUCAS   RAGHEB ISIS   WEBSTER JOHN B
A BIBLIOGRAPHY ON POLITICS AND GOVERNMENT IN UGANDA.
COMPILED BY LUCAS KURIA, ISIS RAGHEB AND JOHN WEBSTER, NEW
YORK, SYRACUSE UNIVERSITY PROGRAM OF EASTERN AFRICAN STUDIES
, 1965
139-12,

LANGLANDS BRYAN W
UGANDA BIBLIOGRAPHY, 1961-1962.
UGANDA JOURNAL, 27, 2, SEPT. 1963
139-12,

MOSES LARRY
KENYA, UGANDA, TANGANYIKA 1960-1964--A BIBLIOGRAPHY.
WASHINGTON, DEPT. OF STATE, EXTERNAL RESEARCH STAFF, 1964
117-12,139-12,

PECKHAM ROBERT   RAGHEB ISIS   SOUTHALL AIDAN
A BIBLIOGRAPHY ON ANTHROPOLOGY AND SOCIOLOGY IN UGANDA.
NEW YORK, SYRACUSE UNIVERSITY PROGRAM OF EASTERN AFRICAN
STUDIES, 1965
139-12,

140. UNITED ARAB REPUBLIC (EGYPT)

140-02
ALDRED CYRIL
THE EGYPTIANS-- ANCIENT PEOPLE AND PLACES.
NEW YORK PRAEGER 1961
020,140-02,

MONTET PIERRE
ETERNAL EGYPT.
NEW YORK, PRAEGER PUBLISHERS, 1969
020,140-02,

140-04
ABU-LUGHOD IBRAHIM
THE TRANSFORMATION OF THE EGYPTIAN ELITE.
THE MIDDLE EAST JOURNAL, SUMMER, 1967, PP. 325-343
044,140-04,

NASSER GAMAL ABDEL

THE PHILOSOPHY OF THE REVOLUTION.
BUFFALO, NEW YORK, SMITH, KEYNES AND MARSHALL PUBLISHERS,
ENGLISH VERSION, 1959
086,140-04,

140-06
AHMED JAMAL M
THE INTELLECTUAL ORIGINS OF EGYPTIAN NATIONALISM.
NEW YORK OXFORD UNIVERSITY PRESS 1960
054,140-06,

BINDER LEONARD
EGYPT--THE INTEGRATIVE REVOLUTION.
IN LUCIEN W PYE AND S VERBA (EDS), POLITICAL CULTURE AND
POLITICAL DEVELOPMENT, PRINCETON, PRINCETON UNIVERSITY PRESS,
1965, PP 396-449
057,140-06.

SAFRAN N
EGYPT IN SEARCH OF POLITICAL COMMUNITY.
CAMBRIDGE, HARVARD UNIVERSITY PRESS, 1961
140-06,

140-07
BINDER LEONARD
POLITICAL RECRUITMENT AND PARTICIPATION IN EGYPT.
JOSEPH LA POLOMBARA AND MYRON WEINER (EDS), POLITICAL
PARTIES AND POLITICAL DEVELOPMENT. PRINCETON, NEW JERSEY,
PRINCETON UNIVERSITY PRESS, 1966
063,140-07,

140-08
UNITED NATIONS
INDUSTRIAL DEVELOPMENT IN AFRICA
NEW YORK, UNITED NATIONS, 1967
071,104-08,110-08,117-08,127-08,134-08,140-08,142-08,

EL-KAMMASH MAGDI M
ECONOMIC DEVELOPMENT AND PLANNING IN EGYPT.
NEW YORK, PRAEGER PUBLISHERS, 1967
072,140-08,

HANSEN B   MARZOUK G A
DEVELOPMENT AND ECONOMIC POLICY IN THE UAR
AMSTERDAM, NORTH HOLLAND PUBLISHING COMPANY, 1965
073,140-08,

140-09
ABU-LUGHOD IBRAHIM
THE ISLAMIC FACTOR IN AFRICAN POLITICS.
ORBIS 8 2 SUMMER 1964 PP 425-44
086,140-09,

MAZRUI ALI A
AFRICA AND EGYPT'S FOUR CIRCLES CHAPTER 7.
IN ON HEROES AND UHURU-WORSHIP, LONDON, LONGMANS.
1967, PP 96-112
086,140-09,

ISMAEL TAREQ Y

RELIGION AND U A R AFRICAN POLICY.
THE JOURNAL OF MODERN AFRICAN STUIDES, VOL. 6, NO. 1, 1968,
PP. 49-57
086,140-09,

140-09
   LEBON J H G
   THE CONTROL AND UTILIZATION OF NILE WATERS--A PROBLEM OF
   POLITICAL GEOGRAPHY.
   REVIEW OF THE GEOGRAPHICAL INSTITUTE OF THE UNIVERSITY OF
   ISTANBUL 1960 PP 32-49
   078,134-09,140-09,

140-11
   MANSFIELD PETER
   NASSER'S EGYPT.
   BALTIMORE, PENGUIN, 1966
   140-11,

   VATIKIOTIS P J
   THE MODERN HISTORY OF EGYPT
   LONDON, WEIDENFELD AND NICOLSON, 1969
   140-11,

141. UPPER VOLTA

141-01
   SKINNER ELLIOTT P
   TRADITIONAL AND MODERN PATTERNS OF SUCCESSION TO POLITICAL
   OFFICE AMONG THE MOSSI OF THE VOLTAIC REPUBLIC.
   JOURNAL OF HUMAN RELATIONS 8 1960 PP 394-406
   009,141-01,

   DIM DELOBSOM AA
   L'EMPIRE DU MOGHO-NABA--COUTIMES DES MOSSI DE LA
   HAUTE-VOLTA.
   PARIS, DOMAT-MONCHRESTIEN, 1932
   141-01,

   KABORE GOMKOUDOUGOU
   ORGANISATION POLITIQUE TRADITIONNELLE ET EVOLUTION POLITIQUE
   DES MOSSI DE OUGADOUGOU.
   PARIS, CENTRE VOLTAIQUE DE LA RECHERCHE SCIENTIFIQUE, 1966
   141-01,

141-02
   KI-ZERBO JOSEPH
   LE MONDE AFRICAIN NOIR--HISTOIRE ET CIVILISATION.
   ABIDJAN/PARIS, CEDA/HATIER, 1963
   099,141-02,

   TOE SYLVAIN   GUILHEM MARCEL
   HAUTE-VOLTA--RECITS HISTORIQUES--COURS ELEMENTAIRE.
   PARIS, LIGEL, 1964
   141-02,

141-02
TOE SYLVAIN   GUILHEM MARCEL   HEBERT JEAN
HISTOIRE DE LA HAUTE-VOLTA.
PARIS. L'AFRIQUE-LE MONDE. COURS MOYEN. LIGEL, 1964
141-02.

141-03
LEVTZION NEHEMIA
MUSLIMS AND CHIEFS IN WEST AFRICA.
OXFORD, CLARENDON PRESS, 1968
024,141-03.

SKINNER ELLIOTT P
CHRISTIANITY AND ISLAM AMONG THE MOSSI.
AMERICAN ANTHROPOLOGIST 60 DECEMBER 1958 PP 1102-1119
050,052,141-03,

SKINNER ELLIOTT P
INTERGENERATIONAL CONFLICT AMONG THE MOSSI-- FATHER
AND SON.
JOURNAL OF CONFLICT RESOLUTION 5 1961 PP 55-60
043,141-03,

SKINNER ELLIOTT P
LABOUR MIGRATION AND ITS RELATIONSHIP TO SOCIOCULTURAL
CHANGE IN MOSSI SOCIETY.
AFRICA (LONDON) 30 1960 PP 375-401
038,141-03,

SKINNER ELLIOTT P
ISLAM IN MOSSI SOCIETY.
IN LEWIS, ISLAM IN TROPICAL AFRICA, LONDON, OXFORD,UNIVERSIT
PRESS, 1966, P. 350-373
141-03,

141-07
SKINNER ELLIOTT P
THE MOSSI OF THE UPPER VOLTA-- THE POLITICAL DEVELOPMENT OF
A SUDANESE PEOPLE.
STANFORD,STANFORD UNIVERSITY PRESS,1964
061,141-07,

141-08
GERADIN B
LE DEVELOPMENT DE LA HAUTE-VOLTA.
PARIS, ISEA, 1964
141-08,

HAMMOND PETER B
YATENGA,TECHNOLOGY IN THE CULTURE OF A WEST AFRICAN KINGDOM
GLENCOE,ILL.FREE PRESS 1966
010,141-08,

141-11
LUSIGNAN GUY DE
FRENCH-SPEAKING AFRICA SINCE INDEPENDENCE.
NEW YORK, PRAEGER PUBLISHERS, 1969
056,061,104-11,105-11,106-11,107-11,109-11,112-11,
115-11,116-11,123-11,137-11,141-11,

141-11
    LA DOCUMENTATION FRANCAISE
    LA REPUBLIQUE DE HAUTE-VOLTA.
    NOTES ET ETUDES DOCUMENTAIRES, 2693, AUGUST, 1960
    141-11.

142. ZAMBIA

142-01
    COLSON ELIZABETH
    THE PLATEAU TONGA OF NORTHERN RHODESIA.
    IN SEVEN TRIBES OF BRITISH CENTRAL AFRICA, LONDON, OXFORD
    UNIVERSITY PRESS, 1951, PP. 94-162
    142-01.

    COLSON ELIZABETH
    INCORPORATION IN TONGA.
    IN R COHEN AND J MIDDLETON,EDS, FROM TRIBE TO NATION IN
    AFRICA, SAN FRANCISCO, CHANDLER, 1968
    038,142-01.

    COLSON ELIZABETH
    TRADE AND WEALTH AMONG THE TONGA.
    IN P J BOHANNAN AND GEORGE DALTON, EDS., MARKETS IN
    AFRICA, EVANSTON, NORTHWESTERN UNIVERSITY PRESS, 1962,
    PP 606-616
    010,142-01.

    GLUCKMAN MAX
    THE IDEAS OF BAROTSE JURISPRUDENCE.
    NEW HAVEN, YALE UNIVERSITY PRESS, 1965
    066,142-01.

    GLUCKMAN MAX
    THE JUDICIAL PROCESS AMONG THE BAROTSE OF NORTHERN RHODESIA.
    NEW YORK, FREE PRESS, 1955
    066,142-01.

    RICHARDS AUDREY I
    LAND, LABOUR AND DIET IN NORTHERN RHODESIA-- AN ECONOMIC
    STUDY OF THE BEMBA TRIBE.
    LONDON, ROUTLEDGE AND KEGAN PAUL, 1939
    010,142-01.

    SCUDDER T
    THE ECOLOGY OF THE GWEMBE TONGA.
    MANCHESTER, MANCHESTER UNIVERSITY PRESS, 1962
    010,142-01.

    TUDEN ARTHUR
    ILA SLAVERY (ZAMBIA).
    TRANS-ACTION, 1967
    028,142-01.

BARNES JAMES A
THE FORT JAMESON NGONI.
IN ELIZABETH COLSON AND MAX GLUCKMAN (EDS), SEVEN TRIBES OF
BRITISH CENTRAL AFRICA, LONDON, OXFORD UNIVERSITY PRESS,
1951
142-01.

142-01
MITCHELL J CLYDE
AFRICAN TRIBES AND LANGUAGES OF THE FEDERATION OF RHODESIA
AND NYASALAND.
SALISBURY, FEDERAL GOVERNMENT PRINTERS, RHODESIA AND
122-01,142-01,

142-02
CAPLAN GERALD L
BAROTSELAND'S SCRAMBLE FOR PROTECTION.
JOURNAL OF AFRICAN HISTORY, X, 2, 1969, PP. 277-294
032,142-02,

STOKES E   BROWN RICHARD   EDS
THE ZAMBESIAN PAST-STUDIES IN CENTRAL AFRICAN HISTORY
MANCHESTER MANCHESTER UNIVERSITY PRESS 1966
025,122-02,142-02,145-02,

FAGAN BRIAN M
IRON AGE CULTURES IN ZAMBIA--TWO VOLUMES
LONDON, 1967-69
019,142-02,

VAN VELSEN J
THE ESTABLISHMENT OF THE ADMINISTRATION IN TONGALAND.
SALISBURY, HISTORIANS IN TROPICAL AFRICA, UNIVERSITY
COLLEGE OF RHODESIA AND NYASALAND, 1962, PP 177-196
035,142-02,

FAGAN BRIAN M   ED
A SHORT HISTORY OF ZAMBIA.
LONDON, OXFORD UNIVERSITY PRESS, 1966
142-02,

GANN LEWIS H
HISTORY OF NORTHERN RHODESIA-EARLY DAYS TO 1953
LONDON, CHATTO AND WINDUS, 1964
142-02,

142-03
BARNES JAMES A
POLITICS IN A CHANGING SOCIETY-- A POLITICAL HISTORY OF THE
FORT JAMESON NGONI.
NEW YORK, OXFORD UNIVERSITY PRESS, 1954
038,142-03,

DAVIDSON S
PSYCHIATRIC WORK AMONG THE BEMBA.
RHODES-LIVINGSTONE JOURNAL 7 1949 PP 75-86
043,142-03,

LONG NORMAN
SOCIAL CHANGE AND THE INDIVIDUAL--A STUDY OF THE SOCIAL AND

RELIGIOUS RESPONSES TO INNOVATION IN A ZAMBIAN RURAL
COMMUNITY.
NEW YORK, HUMANITIES PRESS, INC., 1968
051,142-03,

142-03
MOFFAT R L
AFRICAN COURTS AND NATIVE CUSTOMARY LAW IN THE URBAN AREAS
OF NORTHERN RHODESIA.
JOURNAL OF AFRICAN ADMINISTRATION 9 APRIL 1957 PP 71-78
066,142-03,

POWDERMAKER H
NORTHERN RHODESIA, NOW ZAMBIA, PART 5.
IN STRANGER AND FRIEND, NEW YORK, W W NORTON,
1966, PP 235-306
099,142-03,

ROTBERG ROBERT I
CHRISTIAN MISSIONARIES AND THE CREATION OF NORTHERN
RHODESIA, 1800-1924.
PRINCETON, PRINCETON UNIVERSITY PRESS, 1965
050,142-03,

ROTBERG ROBERT I
MISSIONARIES AS CHIEFS AND ENTREPRENEURS-- NORTHER RHODESIA,
1887-1924.
IN JEFFREY BUTLER (ED), BOSTON UNIVERSITY PAPERS IN AFRICAN
HISTORY VOL I, BOSTON, BOSTON UNIVERSITY PRESS, 1964, PP 195-
216
041,142-03,

TAYLOR JOHN   LEHMANN D A
CHRISTIANS OF THE COPPERBELT-- THE GROWTH OF CHURCH IN
NORTHERN RHODESIA.
LONDON, SUDAN CHRISTIAN MISSION PRESS, 1961
050,142-03,

VAN VELSEN J
LABOUR MIGRATION AS A POSITIVE FACTOR IN THE CONTINUITY
OF TONGA TRIBAL SOCIETY.
ECONOMIC DEVELOPMENT AND CULTURAL CHANGE 8 1960 PP 265-278
038,142-03.

JONES A D
SOCIAL NETWORKS OF FARMERS AMONG THE PLATEAU TONGA OF ZAMBIA
IN LLOYD, THE NEW ELITES OF TROPICAL AFRICA, LONDON, OXFORD
UNIVERSITY PRESS, 1966, P. 272-285
142-03,

KAY GEORGE
A SOCIAL GEOGRAPHY OF ZAMBIA.
LONDON, UNIVERSITY OF LONDON PRESS, 1967
142-03,

RICHARDSON I
LINGUISTIC CHANGE IN AFRICA WITH SPECIAL REFERENCE TO THE
BEMBA-SPEAKING AREA OF NORTHERN RHODESIA.
COLLOQUE SUR LE MULTILINGUISME, BRAZZAVILLE, 1962
142-03,

142-04

KAUNDA KENNETH
CRISIS IN SOUTHERN AFRICA.
AFRICAN FORUM 2 3 1967 PP 11-16
087,142-04.

KAUNDA KENNETH
SOME PERSONAL REFLECTIONS CHAPTER 2.
IN AFRICA'S FREEDOM, NEW YORK, BARNES AND NOBLE, 1964,
PP 24-37
044,142-04.

KAUNDA KENNETH
ZAMBIA SHALL BE FREE.
NEW YORK PRAEGER 1963 (LONDON, HEINEMANN EDUCATIONAL BOOKS)
060,142-04.

KAUNDA KENNETH
ZAMBIA--INDEPENDENCE AND BEYOND.
LONDON, NELSON, 1966
054,060,142-04.

142-05

EPSTEIN ARNOLD L
POLITICS IN AN URBAN AFRICAN COMMUNITY.
MANCHESTER, MANCHESTER UNIVERSITY PRESS, 1958
007,046,142-05.

BARBER WILLIAM J
URBANISATION AND ECONOMIC GROWTH--THE CASES OF TWO WHITE
SETTLER TERRITORIES.
IN THE CITY IN MODERN AFRICA, HORACE MINER (ED), NEW YORK,
FREDERICK A. PRAEGER, 1967
142-05.

BETTISON DAVID G
NUMERICAL DATA ON AFRICAN DWELLERS IN LUSAKA, NORTHERN
RHODESIA.
LUSAKA, RHODES-LIVINGSTONE INSTITUTE, 1959
142-05.

MITCHELL J CLYDE
AFRICAN URBANIZATION IN NDOLA AND LUANSHYA.
LUSAKA, RHODES-LIVINGSTONE INSTITUTE, 1954
142-05.

142-06

CHITEPO HERBERT W
DEVELOPMENTS IN CENTRAL AFRICA.
IN DAVID P CURRIE (ED), FEDERALISM AND THE NEW NATIONS OF
AFRICA, CHICAGO, UNIVERSITY OF CHICAGO PRESS, 1964, PP 3-28
078,087,122-06,142-06,145-06.

CAPLAN GERALD L
BAROTSELAND--THE SECESSIONIST CHALLENGE TO ZAMBIA.
THE JOURNAL OF MODERN AFRICAN STUDIES, VOL. 6, NO. 3, 1968,
PP. 343-360
057,142-06.

CHIDZERO BERNARD T
CENTRAL AFRICA-- THE RACE QUESTION AND THE FRANCHISE.
RACE 1 1955 PP 53-60
088,122-06,142-06,

142-06
DOTSON FLOYD   LILLIAN O
THE INDIAN MINORITY OF ZAMBIA, RHODESIA, AND MALAWI.
NEW HAVEN, CONN. (YALE), MCGILL-QUEEN'S PRESS, 1969
085,142-06,145-06,122-06,

GRAY RICHARD
THE TWO NATIONS-- ASPECTS OF THE DEVELOPMENT OF RACE
RELATIONS IN THE RHODESIAS AND NYASALAND.
LONDON, OXFORD UNIVERSITY PRESS, 1960
087,088,122-06,142-06,145-06,

ROTBERG ROBERT I
THE RISE OF NATIONALISM IN CENTRAL AFRICA-- THE MAKING
OF MALAWI AND ZAMBIA, 1873-1964.
CAMBRIDGE, HARVARD UNIVERSITY PRESS, 1966
055,122-06,142-06,

142-07
FRANCK THOMAS M
RACE AND NATIONALISM--THE STRUGGLE FOR POWER IN RHODESIA-
NYASALAND
NEW YORK, FORDHAM UNIVERSITY PRESS, 1960
087,122-07,142-07,145-07,

BARNES JAMES A
SOME ASPECTS OF POLITICAL DEVELOPMENT AMONG THE FORT
JAMESON NGONI.
AFRICAN STUDIES 7 1948 PP 99-109
061,142-07,

COLSON ELIZABETH
MODERN POLITICAL ORGANIZATION OF THE PLATEAU TONGA.
AFRICAN STUDIES 7 1948 PP 85-98
061,142-07,

MULFORD DAVID C
THE NORTHERN RHODESIA GENERAL ELECTION 1962.
EASTERN AFRICA, OXFORD UNIVERSITY PRESS, 1964
063,142-07,

MULFORD DAVID C
ZAMBIA--THE POLITICS OF INDEPENDENCE 1957-1964.
OXFORD, OXFORD UNIVERSITY PRESS, 1967
142-07,

142-08
UNITED NATIONS
INDUSTRIAL DEVELOPMENT IN AFRICA
NEW YORK, UNITED NATIONS, 1967
071,104-08,110-08,117-08,127-08,134-08,140-08,142-08,

BARBER WILLIAM J
ECONOMIC RATIONALITY AND BEHAVIOR PATTERNS IN AN
UNDERDEVELOPED AREA--A CASE STUDY OF AFRICAN ECONOMICS IN

THE RHODESIAS.
ECONOMIC DEVELOPMENT AND CULTURAL CHANGE 8 1960 PP 237-251
073,122-08,142-08,145-08,

142-08
FORTMAN BASTIAAN DE ED
AFTER MULUNGUSHI--THE ECONOMICS OF ZAMBIAN HUMANISM.
KENYA, EAST AFRICAN PUBLISHING HOUSE. 1969
060,142-08,

HAEFELE E T   STEINBERG E B
GOVERNMENT CONTROLS ON TRANSPORT-AN AFRICAN CASE (ZAMBIA)
WASHINGTON, BROOKINGS INSTITUTE, 1965
048,142-08,

NORTH A C   ET-AL
AFRICAN LAND TENURE DEVELOPMENTS IN KENYA AND UGANDA AND
THEIR APPLICATION TO NORTHERN RHODESIA.
JOURNAL OF AFRICAN ADMINISTRATION 13 OCTOBER 1961
PP 211-219
070,117-08,139-08,142-08,

142-10
SHEPPERSON GEORGE
THE LITERATURE OF BRITISH CENTRAL AFRICA.
RHODES-LIVINGSTONE JOURNAL 23 1958 PP 12-46
090,122-10,142-10,145-10,

142-11
HALL RICHARD
ZAMBIA.
LONDON, PALL MALL PRESS, 1967
142-11,

142-12
WALKER AUDREY A   ED
THE RHODESIAS AND NYASALAND--A GUIDE TO OFFICIAL PUBLICA-
TIONS.
WASHINGTON, U.S. GOVERNMENT PRINTING OFFICE, 1965
122-12,142-12,

Nonindependent States
or Territories

143. FRENCH AND SPANISH REMNANTS

143-11
   THOMPSON VIRGINIA   ADLOFF RICHARD
   DJIBOUTI AND THE HORN OF AFRICA.
   STANFORD, STANFORD UNIVERSITY PRESS, 1968
   087,133-09,143-11,

144. PORTUGUESE TERRITORIES

144-02
   BIRMINGHAM DAVID
   THE PORTUGUESE CONQUEST OF ANGOLA.
   LONDON, OXFORD UNIVERSITY PRESS, 1965
   027, 144-02,

   HAMMOND R J
   PORTUGAL AND AFRICA, 1815-1910.
   STANFORD, STANFORD UNIVERSITY, OXFORD UNIVERSITY PRESS, 1966
   033, 144-02

   BIRMINGHAM DAVID
   TRADE AND CONFLICT IN ANGOLA-- THE MBUNDU AND THEIR
   NEIGHBOURS UNDER THE INFLUENCE OF THE PORTUGUESE 1483-1790.
   LONDON, OXFORD UNIVERSITY PRESS, 1966
   027, 144-02,

   NEWITT M D D
   THE PORTUGUESE ON THE ZAMBEZI--AN HISTORICAL INTERPRETATION
   OF THE PRAZO SYSTEM.
   JOURNAL OF AFRICAN HISTORY, X, 1, 1969, PP. 67-85
   027, 144-02,

144-04

CHILCOTE RONALD H
THE POLITICAL THOUGHT OF AMILCAR CABRAL.
THE JOURNAL OF MODERN AFRICAN STUDIES, VOL. 6, NO. 3, 1968,
PP. 373-388
087,144-04,

LUKHERO M B
THE SOCIAL CHARACTERISTICS OF AN EMERGENT ELITE IN HARARE.
IN LLOYD, THE NEW ELITES OF TROPICAL AFRICA, LONDON, OXFORD
UNIVERSITY PRESS, 1966, P. 126-138
144-04,

144-05

DE BLIJ HARM J
THE FUNCTIONAL STRUCTURE AND CENTRAL BUSINESS DISTRICT OF
LOURENCO MARQUES, MOZAMBIQUE.
ECONOMIC GEOGRAPHY, 38 JANUARY 1962 PP 56-77
046,144-05,

HANCE WILLIAM A   VAN DONGEN I S
LOURENCO MARQUES IN DELAGOA BAY.
ECONOMIC GEOGRAPHY 33 JULY 1957 PP 238-256
048,144-05,

144-06

DUFFY JAMES
PORTUGUESE AFRICA.
CAMBRIDGE, HARVARD UNIVERSITY PRESS, 1959
027,087,088,144-06,

DUFFY JAMES
PORTUGAL IN AFRICA.
IN PHILIP W QUIGG (ED.), AFRICA, NEW YORK, PRAEGER, 1964,
PP 86-102
035,087,144-06,

144-06

MONDLANE EDUARDO
THE STRUGGLE FOR MOZAMBIQUE.
BALTIMORE, PENGUIN BOOKS, 1969
080,087,144-06,

DUFFY JAMES
PORTUGAL IN AFRICA
BALTIMORE, PENGUIN, 1962
027,087,088,144-06,

INSTITUTE OF   RACE RELATIONS
ANGOLA--A SYMPOSIUM--VIEWS OF A REVOLT.
LONDON, OXFORD UNIVERSITY PRESS, 1962
087,144-06,

MARCUM JOHN A
A MARTYR FOR MOZAMBIQUE.
AFRICA REPORT, MARCH/APRIL, 1969, PP. 6-9
087,144-06,

144-07
   BOXER CHARLES RALPH
   PORTUGUESE SOCIETY IN THE TROPICS--THE MUNICIPAL COUNCILS
   OF GOA, MACAO. BAHIA AND LUANDA 1510-1800.
   MADISON, UNIVERSITY OF WISCONSIN PRESS, 1965
   027, 144-07,

   CHALIAND GERARD
   ARMED STRUGGLE IN AFRICA-- WITH THE GUERILLAS IN 'PORTU-
   GUESE' GUINEA.
   NEW YORK, MONTHLY REVIEW PRESS, 1969
   087,144-07,144-09,

144-09
   CHALIAND GERARD
   ARMED STRUGGLE IN AFRICA-- WITH THE GUERILLAS IN 'PORTU-
   GUESE' GUINEA.
   NEW YORK, MONTHLY REVIEW PRESS, 1969
   087,144-07,144-09,

144-11
   DAVIDSON BASIL
   THE LIBERATION OF GUINE-- ASPECTS OF AN AFRICAN RE-
   VOLUTION.
   BALTIMORE, PENGUIN, 1969
   087,144-11,

   ABSHIRE DAVID M   SAMUELS MICHAEL A   EDS
   PORTUGUESE AFRICA--A HANDBOOK.
   NEW YORK, PRAEGER PUBLISHERS, 1969
   087,144-11,

   MARCUM JOHN A

   THE ANGOLAN REVOLUTION VOLUME 1- THE ANATOMY OF AN EXPLOSION
   CAMBRIDGE, MASS, MIT PRESS, 1969
   087,144-11,

144-11
   CHILCOTE RONALD H
   PORTUGUESE AFRICA
   ENGLEWOOD CLIFFS, PRENTICE-HALL, 1967
   087,144-11,

   WHEELER DOUGLAS L   PELISSIER RENE
   ANGOLA.
   LONDON, PALL MALL PRESS, 1970
   087,144-11,

144-12
   CHILCOTE RONALD H
   EMERGING NATIONALISM IN PORTUGUESE AFRICA.
   PALO ALTO, CALIFORNIA, HOOVER INSTITUTION PRESS, 1969
   087,144-12,

145. RHODESIA (ZIMBABWE)

145-01
HOLLEMAN J F
SHONA CUSTOMARY LAW.
NEW YORK, HUMANITIES PRESS INC., 1969
066, 145-01,

KUPER HILDA   HUGHES A J B   VAN VELSEN J
THE SHONA AND NDEBELE OF SOUTHERN RHODESIA
LONDON, INTERNATIONAL AFRICAN INSTITUTE, 1954
145-01,

145-02
SUMMERS ROGER
ZIMBABWE-- A RHODESIAN MYSTERY.
CAPE TOWN, THOMAS NELSON AND SONS, 1963
025, 145-02,

RANGER TERENCE O
REVOLT IN SOUTHERN RHODESIA, 1896-97--A STUDY IN AFRICAN
RESISTANCE.
EVANSTON, NORTHWESTERN UNIVERSITY PRESS, 1967 (LONDON,
HEINEMANN EDUCATIONAL BOOKS)
034, 145-02,

STOKES E   BROWN RICHARD   EDS
THE ZAMBESIAN PAST-STUDIES IN CENTRAL AFRICAN HISTORY
MANCHESTER, MANCHESTER UNIVERSITY PRESS, 1966
025, 122-02, 142-02, 145-02,

ABRAHAM D P
THE EARLY POLITICAL HISTORY OF THE KINGDOMS OF MWENE MUTAPA
850-1589.

HISTORIANS IN TROPICAL AFRICA-- PROCEEDINGS, SALISBURY,
SOUTHERN RHODESIA. UNIVERSITY COLLEGE OF RHODESIA AND
NAYASALAND, 1962, PP 61-92
025, 145-02,

145-02
FAGAN BRIAN M
ZIMBABWE--A CENTURY OF DISCOVERY.
AFRICAN ARTS, SPRING 1969, VOL II, NO. 3, PP. 20-24, CONT.
85-86
025, 145-02,

GANN LEWIS H
A HISTORY OF SOUTHERN RHODESIA.
LONDON, 1965
087, 145-02,

RANGER TERENCE O
TRADITIONAL AUTHORITIES AND THE RISE OF MODERN POLITICS IN
SOUTHERN RHODESIA 1898-1930.
CONFERENCE OF THE HISTORY OF CENTRAL AFRICAN PEOPLES, LUSAKA
1963, RHODES-LIVINGSTONE INSTITUTE. 1963
033, 145-02,

145-04
   SITHOLE NDABANINGI
   AFRICAN NATIONALISM.
   LONDON, OXFORD UNIVERSITY PRESS, 1968
   054,091,145-04,

145-06
   CHITEPO HERBERT W
   DEVELOPMENTS IN CENTRAL AFRICA.
   IN DAVID P CURRIE (ED), FEDERALISM AND THE NEW NATIONS OF
   AFRICA, CHICAGO,UNIVERSITY OF CHICAGO,PRESS, 1964, PP 3-28
   078,087,122-06,142-06,145-06,

   FRANCK THOMAS M
   MUST WE LOSE ZIMBABWE?
   AFRICAN FORUM 2 3 1967 PP 17-33
   087,145-06,

   SHAMUYARIRA NATHAN M
   THE NATIONALIST MOVEMENT IN ZIMBABWE.
   AFRICAN FORUM 2 3 1967 PP 34-42
   087,145-06,

   BOWMAN LARRY W
   STRAINS IN THE RHODESIAN FRONT.
   AFRICA REPORT, DECEMBER, 1968, P. 16
   087,145-06,

   CLEMENTS FRANK
   RHODESIA--A STUDY OF THE DETERIORATION OF A WHITE SOCIETY.
   NEW YORK, PRAEGER, 1969
   087,145-06,

   DOTSON FLOYD   LILLIAN O
   THE INDIAN MINORITY OF ZAMBIA, RHODESIA, AND MALAWI.
   NEW HAVEN, CONN. (YALE), MCGILL-QUEEN'S PRESS, 1969

   085,142-06,145-06,122-06,

145-06
   GRAY RICHARD
   THE TWO NATIONS-- ASPECTS OF THE DEVELOPMENT OF RACE
   RELATIONS IN THE RHODESIAS AND NYASALAND.
   LONDON,OXFORD UNIVERSITY PRESS,1960
   087,088,122-06,142-06,145-06,

   LEYS COLIN
   EUROPEAN POLITICS IN SOUTHERN RHODESIA.
   OXFORD,CLARENDON PRESS, 1959
   087,145-06,

   MASON PHILIP
   THE BIRTH OF A DILEMMA-- THE CONQUEST AND SETTLEMENT OF
   RHODESIA.
   LONDON,OXFORD UNIVERSITY PRESS, 1958
   087,145-06,

   RAKE ALAN
   BLACK GUERRILLAS IN RHODESIA.
   AFRICA REPORT, DECEMBER, 1968, P. 23
   087,145-06,

RODER W
THE DIVISION OF LAND RESOURCES IN SOUTHERN RHODESIA.
ANNALS OF THE ASSOCIATION OF AMERICAN GEOGRAPHERS 54 MARCH
1964 PP 42-52
087,145-06,

SHAMUYARIRA NATHAN M
CRISIS IN RHODESIA.
LONDON,1965
087,145-06,

SPIRO HERBERT J
THE FEDERATION OF RHODESIA AND NYASALAND.
IN THOMAS FRANCK (ED), WHY FEDERATIONS FAIL, NEW YORK, NEW
YORK UNIVERSITY PRESS, 1968, PP. 37-90
078,122-06,145-06,

MARSHALL CHARLES B
CRISIS OVER RHODESIA--A SKEPTICAL VIEW.
BALTIMORE SCHOOL OF ADVANCED INTERNATIONAL STUDIES, JOHNS
BALTIMORE, JOHNS HOPKINS PRESS, 1967
145-06,

145-07
FRANCK THOMAS M
RACE AND NATIONALISM--THE STRUGGLE FOR POWER IN RHODESIA-
NYASALAND
NEW YORK,FORDHAM UNIVERSITY PRESS, 1960
087,122-07,142-07,145-07,

ROGERS CYRIL A   FRANTZ CHARLES
RACIAL THEMES IN SOUTHERN RHODESIA-THE ATTITUDES OF THE
WHITE POPULATION
NEW HAVEN,YALE UNIVERSITY PRESS,1962
088,145-07,

145-08
BARBER WILLIAM J
ECONOMIC RATIONALITY AND BEHAVIOR PATTERNS IN AN
UNDERDEVELOPED AREA--A CASE STUDY OF AFRICAN ECONOMICS IN
THE RHODESIAS.
ENONOMIC DEVELOPMENT AND CULTURAL CHANGE 8 1960 PP 237-251
073,122-08,142-08,145-08,

FLOYD BARRY
LAND APPORTIONMENT IN SOUTHERN RHODESIA.
GEOGRAPHIC REVIEW LII OCTOBER 1962 PP 566-582
087,145-08,

GREEN L P   FAIR T J D
DEVELOPMENT IN AFRICA- A STUDY IN REGIONAL ANALYSIS WITH
SPECIAL REFERENCE TO SOUTHERN AFRICA
JOHANNESBURG,WITWATERSRAND UNIVERSITY PRESS, 1962
048,073,132-08,145-08,

145-10
SHEPPERSON GEORGE
THE LITERATURE OF BRITISH CENTRAL AFRICA.
RHODES-LIVINGSTONE JOURNAL 23 1958 PP 12-46
090,122-10,142-10,145-10,

145-11
    KEATLEY PATRICK
    THE POLITICS OF PARTNERSHIP.
    BALTIMORE, PENGUIN, 1963
    088,145-11,

146. SOUTH-WEST AFRICA (NAMIBIA)

146-07
    SEGAL RONALD   FIRST RUTH   EDS
    SOUTH-WEST AFRICA- TRAVESTY OF TRUST
    LONDON, OXFORD UNIVERSITY PRESS, 1967, INTERNATIONAL CONFERENCE
    ON SOUTH-WEST AFRICA, OXFORD, 1966
    081,146-07,146-11,

146-09
    CARROLL F
    SOUTH WEST AFRICA AND THE UNITED NATIONS
    LEXINGTON, UNIVERSITY OF KENTUCKY PRESS, 1967
    081,146-09,

    HIDAYATULLAH M
    SOUTH WEST AFRICA CASE
    NEW YORK, ASIA PUBLISHING HOUSE, 1968
    081,146-09,

    MAZERICK CARROLL F
    SOUTH WEST AFRICA AND THE UNITED NATIONS
    NEW YORK, UNIVERSITY PRESS OF KENTUCKY, 1968

    081,146-09,

146-11
    FIRST RUTH
    SOUTH WEST AFRICA
    BALTIMORE, PENGUIN, 1963
    081,146-11,

    SEGAL RONALD   FIRST RUTH   EDS
    SOUTH-WEST AFRICA- TRAVESTY OF TRUST
    LONDON, OXFORD UNIVERSITY PRESS, 1967, INTERNATIONAL CONFERENCE
    ON SOUTH-WEST AFRICA, OXFORD, 1966
    081,146-07,146-11,

III

Author Index

A

ABD AL-MAGID A
    ABD AL-MAGID A
    SOME GENERAL ASPECTS OF THE ARABIZATION OF THE SUDAN.
    SUDAN NOTES AND RECORDS 40 1959 PP 48-74
    021,134-02,

ABDULLAHI IBN M
    ABDULLAHI IBN M
    TAZYIN AL WARAQAT.
    IBADAN UNIVERSITY OF IBADAN PRESS 1964 (TRANSLATED AND
    EDITED, MERVYN HISKETT)
    024,128-02,

ABEL-SMITH B
    TITMUSS RICHARD M   ABEL-SMITH B
    SOCIAL AND POPULATION GROWTH IN MAURITIUS
    LONDON METHUEN 1961 REPORT TO THE GOVERNMENT OF MAURITIUS

REPRINTED 1968
125-03,

ABERCROMBIE K C
    ABERCROMBIE K C
    THE TRANSITION FROM SUBSISTENCE TO MARKET AGRICULTURE IN
    AFRICA SOUTH OF THE SAHARA CHAPTER 1.
    IN EDITH WHETHAM AND JEAN CURRIE (EDS.), READINGS IN THE
    APPLIED ECONOMICS OF AFRICA, LONDON, CAMBRIDGE UNIVERSITY
    PRESS, 1, 1967, PP 1-11
    070,

ABERNETHY DAVID B
    ABERNETHY DAVID B
    THE POLITICAL DILEMMA OF POPULAR EDUCATION--AN AFRICAN CASE.
    PALO ALTO, STANFORD UNIVERSITY PRESS, 1969
    042,128-03,

ABI-SAAB ROSEMARY
    ABI-SAAB ROSEMARY
    ELEMENTS DE BIBLIOGRAPHIE--LE SENEGAL, DES ORIGINES A
    L'INDEPENDENCE.
    GENEVA-AFRIQUE, VOL. 3, NO. 2, 1964
    130-12,

ABIODUN
    ABIODUN JOSEPHINE O
    CENTRAL PLACE STUDY IN ABEOKUTA PROVINCE,SOUTHWEST NIGERIA
    JOURNAL OF REGIONAL SCIENCE 8 1968
    047,048,128-05,

ABRAHAM D P
    ABRAHAM D P
    THE EARLY POLITICAL HISTORY OF THE KINGDOMS OF MWENE MUTAPA
    850-1589.
    HISTORIANS IN TROPICAL AFRICA-- PROCEEDINGS,SALISBURY,
    SOUTHERN RHODESIA, UNIVERSITY COLLEGE OF RHODESIA AND
    NAYASALAND, 1962, PP 61-92
    025,145-02,

ABRAHAM W E
    ABRAHAM W E
    THE MIND OF AFRICA.
    CHICAGO,UNIVERSITY OF CHICAGO PRESS,1962 (LONDON,
    WEIDENFELD AND NICOLSON)
    040,060,091,099,114-01,

    ABRAHAM W E
    THE PROSPECTS FOR PAN-AFRICANISM.
    IN PETER J MCEWAN AND ROBERT B SUTCLIFFE (EDS),MODERN AFRICA,
    NEW YORK, THOMAS CROWELL,1965,PP 406-412
    079,

    ABRAHAM W E
    IDEOLOGY AND SOCIETY CHAPTER 1.
    IN THE MIND OF AFRICA,LONDON,WEIDENFELD AND NICOLSON,
    1962,PP 11-43
    060,

ABRAHAMS PETER

ABRAHAMS PETER
A WREATH FOR UDOMO.
LONDON, FABER AND FABER, 1956
090,132-10,

ABRAHAMS PETER
   ABRAHAMS PETER
   TELL FREEDOM.
   NEW YORK, ALFRED A KNOPF, 1954
   090,132-10,

   ABRAHAMS PETER
   A NIGHT OF THEIR OWN.
   NEW YORK, ALFRED A KNOPF, 1965
   090,132-10,

   ABRAHAMS PETER
   MINE BOY.
   NEW YORK, MACMILLAN CO., 1970   (LONDON, HEINEMANN
   EDUCATIONAL BOOKS)
   090,132-10,

   ABRAHAMS PETER
   TELL FREEDOM.
   NEW YORK, MACMILLAN CO., 1970
   090,132-10,

ABRAHAMS R G
   ABRAHAMS R G
   THE POLITICAL ORGANIZATION OF UNYAMWEZI.
   LONDON AND NEW YORK, CAMBRIDGE MONOGRAPHS IN SOCIAL ANTHRO-
   POLOGY, 1967
   009,136-01,

   ABRAHAMS R G
   THE PEOPLES OF GREATER UNYAMWEZI,TANZANIA-NYAMWEZI,SUKUMA,
   SUMBROOA,KIMBU,KONONGO
   LONDON, INTERNATIONAL AFRICAN INSTITUTE, 1967
   136-01,

ABRAHAMSSON H
   ABRAHAMSSON H
   THE ORIGIN OF DEATH-STUDIES IN AFRICAN MYTHOLOGY
   UPPSALA, ALQUIST AND WIKSELL, 1951
   012,

ABRASH BARBARA
   ABRASH BARBARA
   BLACK AFRICAN LITERATURE IN ENGLISH SINCE 1952-- WORKS AND
   CRITICISM.
   NEW YORK, JOHNSON REPRINT CORP, 1967
   090,

ABSHIRE DAVID M
   ABSHIRE DAVID M   SAMUELS MICHAEL A   EDS
   PORTUGUESE AFRICA--A HANDBOOK.
   NEW YORK, PRAEGER PUBLISHERS, 1969
   087,144-11,

ABU-LUGHOD IBRAHIM

ABU-LUGHOD IBRAHIM
NATIONALISM IN A NEW PERSPECTIVE-- THE AFRICAN CASE.
IN HERBERT J SPIRO, ED, PATTERNS OF AFRICAN DEVELOPMENT
ENGLEWOOD CLIFFS, PRENTICE-HALL, 1967, PP 35-62
054,

ABU-LUGHOD IBRAHIM
    ABU-LUGHOD IBRAHIM
    THE ISLAMIC FACTOR IN AFRICAN POLITICS.
    ORBIS 8 2 SUMMER 1964 PP 425-44
    086,140-09,

    ABU-LUGHOD IBRAHIM
    THE TRANSFORMATION OF THE EGYPTIAN ELITE.
    THE MIDDLE EAST JOURNAL, SUMMER, 1967, PP. 325-343
    044,140-04,

ABUN-NASR JAMIL
    ABUN-NASR JAMIL
    THE TIJANIYYA--A SUFI ORDER IN THE MODERN WORLD.
    LONDON, OXFORD UNIVERSITY PRESS, 1965
    052,

    ABUN-NASR JAMIL
    THE SALAFIYYA MOVEMENT IN MOROCCO-- THE RELIGIOUS BASES
    OF THE MOROCCAN NATIONALIST MOVEMENT.
    IN IMMANUEL WALLERSTEIN, SOCIAL CHANGE THE COLONIAL
    SITUATION, NEW YORK, JOHN WILEY AND SONS, 1966
    052,126-03,

ACADEMY
    EAST AFRICAN ACADEMY
    PROCEEDINGS OF THE EAST AFRICAN ACADEMY. D.F. OWEN ED.
    NAIROBI, EAST AFRICAN PUBLISHING HOUSE, 1967
    075,099,

ACHEBE CHINUA
    ACHEBE CHINUA
    THINGS FALL APART.
    NEW YORK, MCDOWELL OBELENSKY, 1959   (LONDON, HEINEMANN
    EDUCATIONAL BOOKS)
    090,128-10,

    ACHEBE CHINUA
    ARROW OF GOD.
    LONDON, HEINEMANN EDUCATIONAL BOOKS LTD., 1964
    090,128-10,

    ACHEBE CHINUA
    NO LONGER AT EASE.
    LONDON, HEINEMANN EDUCATIONAL BOOKS LTD, 1962
    090,128-10,

    ACHEBE CHINUA
    MAN OF THE PEOPLE.
    LONDON, HEINEMANN EDUCATIONAL BOOKS LTD, 1966
    090,128-10,

    ACHEBE CHINUA
    THE NOVELIST AS TEACHER.

FIRST CONFERENCE ON COMMONWEALTH LITERATURE JOHN PRESS ED
LONDON, HEINEMANN EDUCATIONAL BOOKS LTD, 1965, PP 201-205
090,128-10,

ACHERSON NEAL
    ACHERSON NEAL
    THE KING INCORPORATED,LEOPOLD II IN THE AGE OF TRUSTS
    NEW YORK,DOUBLEDAY, 1964
    033,108-02,

ACQUAH IONE
    ACQUAH IONE
    ACCRA SURVEY.
    LONDON, UNIVERSITY OF LONDON PRESS, 1958
    114-05,

ADAM THOMAS R
    ADAM THOMAS R
    GOVERNMENT AND POLITICS IN AFRICA SOUTH OF THE SAHARA.
    NEW YORK, RANDOM, HOUSE 1965
    061,

ADAMS MARGARET
    ADAMS MARGARET
    THE BRITISH ATTITUDE TO GERMAN COLONIZATION 1880-1885.
    BULLETIN OF THE INSTITUTE OF HISTORICAL RESEARCH 15 1937
    PP 190-193
    033,

ADEBANJO TIMOTHY
    ADEBANJO TIMOTHY
    BEYOND THE CONFLICT.
    AFRICA REPORT, FEB., 1968, P. 12
    065,128-06,

ADEDEJI ADEBAYO
    ADEDEJI ADEBAYO   ED
    PROBLEMS AND TECHNIQUES OF ADMINISTRATIVE TRAINING IN
    AFRICA.
    IFE, NIGERIA, AND NEW YORK, INTERNATIONAL UNIVERSITY BOOK-
    SELLERS, INC., 1969
    062,

ADELAJA KOLA
    ADELAJA KOLA
    SOURCES IN AFRICAN POLITICAL THOUGHT.
    PRESENCE AFRICAINE, NO. 70, 2ND QUARTER, 1969, PP. 7-26
    060,

ADELMAN IRMA
    ADELMAN IRMA   MORRIS CYNTHIA TAFT
    SOCIETY, POLITICS, AND ECONOMIC DEVELOPMENT, A QUANTITATIVE
    APPROACH.
    BALTIMORE, JOHNS HOPKINS UNIVERSITY PRESS,1967
    073,074,

    ADELMAN IRMA   DALTON GEORGE   MORRIS CYNTHIA TAFT
    SOCIETY, POLITICS, AND ECONOMIC DEVELOPMENT IN AFRICA.
    IN CARTER, GWENDOLEN M. AND ANN PADEN (EDS), EXPANDING
    HORIZONS IN AFRICAN STUDIES, EVANSTON, NORTHWESTERN

UNIVERSITY PRESS, 1969, PP. 209-242
074,100,

ADELMAN IRMA
ADELMAN IRMA
THEORIES OF ECONOMIC GROWTH AND DEVELOPMENT.
STANFORD,STANFORD UNIVERSITY PRESS,1961
073,

ADERIBIGBE A B
ADERIBIGBE A B
WEST AFRICAN INTEGRATION-- AN HISTORICAL PERSPECTIVE.
NIGERIAN JOURNAL OF ECONOMIC AND SOCIAL STUDIES 5 MARCH 1963
PP 9-14
078,

ADERIBIGBE A B
SYMPOSIUM ON WEST AFRICAN INTEGRATION.
NIGERIAN JOURNAL OF ECONOMIC AND SOCIAL STUDIES 5 MARCH
1963
078,

ADIE W A C
ADIE W A C
CHINA'S REVIVED INTEREST IN AFRICA.
IN LEGUM AND DRYSDALE (AFRICA CONTEMPORARY RECORD),
1969, P.45-48
084,

ADIMOLA A B
ADIMOLA A B
THE LAMOGI REBELLION 1911-1912.
THE UGANDA JOURNAL 18 1954 PP 166-177
034,139-02,

ADLER ALFRED
ADLER ALFRED
LES DAY DE BOUNA (THE DAY OF BOUNA).
ETUDES ET DOCUMENTS TCHADIENS SERIES A 1,INSTITUT NATIONAL
TCHADIEN POUR LES SCIENCES HUMAINES,FORT LAMY,1966
106-01,

ADLER RENATA
ADLER RENATA
LETTER FROM BIAFRA.
THE NEW YORKER, OCT. 4, 1969, PP. 47-113
065,

ADLOFF RICHARD
THOMPSON VIRGINIA   ADLOFF RICHARD
DJIBOUTI AND THE HORN OF AFRICA.
STANFORD, STANFORD UNIVERSITY PRESS, 1968
087,133-09,143-11,

THOMPSON VIRGINIA   ADLOFF RICHARD
THE EMERGING STATES OF FRENCH EQUATORIAL AFRICA.
STANFORD, STANFORD UNIVERSITY PRESS, 1960
105-11,107-11,112-11,106-11,

THOMPSON VIRGINIA   ADLOFF RICHARD

CHAD.
IN V. THOMPSON AND R. ADLOFF, THE EMERGING STATES OF FRENCH
EQUATORIAL AFRICA, STANFORD, STANFORD UNIVERSITY PRESS, 1960
106-11,

ADLOFF RICHARD
THOMPSON VIRGINIA   ADLOFF RICHARD
CONGO-BRAZZAVILLE.
IN V. THOMPSON AND R. ADLOFF, THE EMERGING STATES OF FRENCH
EQUATORIAL AFRICA, STANFORD, STANFORD UNIVERSITY PRESS, 1960
107-11,

THOMPSON VIRGINIA   ADLOFF RICHARD
THE MALAGASY REPUBLIC--MADAGASCAR TODAY.
STANFORD, STANFORD UNIVERSITY PRESS, 1965
121-11,

ADU A L
ADU A L
THE CIVIL SERVICE IN NEW AFRICAN STATES.
NEW YORK, PRAEGER, 1965
062,

ADY P H
ADY P H
REGIONAL ECONOMIC ATLAS OF AFRICA.
OXFORD, CLARENDON PRESS, 1965
069,

AFIGBO A E
AFIGBO A E
ORAL TRADITION AND HISTORY IN EASTERN NIGERIA.
AFRICAN NOTES 3 APRIL 1966 PP 12-20
099,

AFRICA
ECONOMIC COMMISSION FOR AFRICA
INTRA-AFRICAN TRADE.
E/CN   IY/STC/20 1963
078,

ECONOMIC COMMISSION FOR AFRICA
STUDIES OF EXISTING AFRICAN CUSTOMS UNIONS.
ECONOMIC BULLETIN FOR AFRICA 2 1962
078,

ECONOMIC COMMISSION FOR AFRICA
CO-ORDINATION OF DEVELOPMENT PLANS IN AFRICA.
ECONOMIC BULLETIN FOR AFRICA 1 1964
072,

ECONOMIC COMMISSION FOR AFRICA
TRANSPORT PROBLEMS IN RELATION TO ECONOMIC DEVELOPMENT IN
WEST AFRICA.
NEW YORK, U N DOCUMENT NO 62.11.K.2,1963
048,

EAST AFRICA ROYAL COMMISSION
EAST AFRICA ROYAL COMMISSION 1953-1955 REPORT.
LONDON, HER MAJESTY'S STATIONERY OFFICE, COMMAND PAPER NO 9475

REPRINT 482 1961
035,045,

AFRICA
ECONOMIC COMMISSION FOR AFRICA
LEOPOLDVILLE AND LAGOS--COMPARATIVE STUDY OF CONDITIONS IN
1960.
IN GERALD BREESE (ED),THE CITY IN NEWLY DEVELOPING
COUNTRIES, PRENTICE HALL, NEW JERSEY, 1969
108-05,128-05,

AFRICA REPORT
AFRICA REPORT
U.S. ECONOMIC AID TO AFRICA 1950-1964.
AFRICA REPORT 9 DECEMBER 1964 PP 8-12
083,

AFRICAN
AMERICAN SOCIETY OF AFRICAN CULTURE
AFRICA SEEN BY AMERICAN NEGROES.
PARIS,PRESENCE AFRICAINE,1958
094,

AMERICAN SOCIETY OF AFRICAN CULTURE
THE AMERICAN NEGRO WRITER AND HIS ROOTS.
NEW YORK, AMSAC, 1960
094,

EAST AFRICAN INSTITUTE OF SOCIAL AND CULTURAL AFFAIRS
RACIAL AND COMMUNAL TENSIONS IN EAST AFRICA.
KENYA, EAST AFRICAN PUBLISHING HOUSE, 1966
057,085,

TANZANIA AFRICAN NATIONAL UNION
THE ARUSHA DECLARATION AND TANU S POLICY ON SOCIALISM AND
SELF-RELIANCE.
DAR ES-SALAAM,GOVERNMENT PRINTER,1967
058,060,070,073,136-04,

AFRICAN STUDIES ASSOCIATION
AFRICAN FILM BIBLIOGRAPHY 1965.
AFRICAN STUDIES ASSOCIATION,OCCASIONAL PAPERS NO. 1,1966
049,093,

AMERICAN SOCIETY OF AFRICAN CULTURE
THE AMERICAN NEGRO BIBLIOGRAPHY.
NEW YORK, AMERICAN SOCIETY OF AFRICAN CULTURE, 1967
030,

AMERICAN SOCIETY OF AFRICAN CULTURE
COLLOQUIUM ON NEGRO ART--THE FUNCTION AND SIGNIFICANCE OF
NEGRO AFRICAN ART IN THE LIFE OF THE PEOPLE AND FOR THE
PEOPLE.
PARIS, INTERNATIONAL UNIVERSITY BOOKSELLERS, INC., 1969
014,

AMERICAN SOCIETY OF AFRICAN CULTURE
PAN-AFRICANISM RECONSIDERED.
BERKELEY,UNIVERSITY OF CALIFORNIA PRESS,1962
079,

AFRICAN
    EAST AFRICAN INSTITUTE OF SOCIAL AND CULTURAL AFFAIRS
    RESEARCH PRIORITIES FOR EAST AFRICA.
    KENYA, EAST AFRICAN PUBLISHING HOUSE, 1966
    100,

    EAST AFRICAN ACADEMY
    PROCEEDINGS OF THE EAST AFRICAN ACADEMY. D.F. OWEN ED.
    NAIROBI, EAST AFRICAN PUBLISHING HOUSE, 1967
    075,099,

    EAST AFRICAN INSTITUTE OF SOCIAL AND CULTURAL AFFAIRS
    RESEARCH PRIORITIES FOR EAST AFRICA.
    NAIROBI EAST AFRICAN PUBLISHING HOUSE CONTEMPORARY
    AFRICAN MONOGRAPH SERIES NO 5 1966
    100,

    AFRICAN BIBLIOGRAPHIC CENTER
    ALGERIAN PANORAMA-A SELECTED BIBLIOGRAPHIC SURVEY 1965-1966
    WASHINGTON, VOLUME 5 NUMBER 2, 1967
    101-12,

AFRICAN BIBLIO
    AFRICAN BIBLIO   CENTER
    ETHIOPIA, 1950-1962--A SELECT BIBLIOGRAPHY.
    WASHINGTON, AFRICAN BIBLIOGRAPHIC CENTER, 1963
    110-12,

AFRICAN INSTITUTE
    AFRICAN INSTITUTE
    POLITICAL DEVELOPMENTS IN BECHUANALAND PROTECTORATE.
    INTERNATIONAL BULLETIN II   FEBRUARY 1964
    102-07,

AFRICAN MONOGRAPHS
    AFRICAN MONOGRAPHS
    THE CHALLENGE OF DEVELOPMENT.
    KENYA, EAST AFRICAN PUBLISHING HOUSE, 1968
    072,

AFRICAN NEWSLETTER
    AFRICAN NEWSLETTER
    THE PRESS OF NIGERIA.
    AFRICAN NEWSLETTER 1 NUMBER 3 SUMMER 1963 PP 40-45
    049,128-03,

AFRICANUS LEO
    AFRICANUS LEO
    THE HISTORY AND DESCRIPTION OF AFRICA. (TRANS BY JOHN PORY
    IN 1600)
    LONDON, HAKLUYT SOCIETY, 1896
    099,

AFRIFA A A COLONEL
    AFRIFA A A COLONEL
    THE GHANA COUP, 24TH FEBRUARY, 1966.
    LONDON, FRANK CASS AND COMPANY, 1966, PREFACE BY KOFI A BUSIA
    INTRODUCTION BY TIBOR SZAMUELY
    064,114-04,

AFRIKA-INSTITUUT
    AFRIKA-INSTITUUT
    THE FUTURE OF CUSTOMARY LAW IN AFRICA.
    LEIDEN,UNIVERSITAIRE PERS LEIDEN,1956
    066,

AGYEMAN-DUAH J
    AGYEMAN-DUAH J
    MAMPONG ASHANTI-- A TRADITIONAL HISTORY TO THE REIGN OF NANA
    SAFO KANTANKA.
    TRANSACTIONS OF THE HISTORICAL SOCIETY OF GHANA 4 1960
    PP 21-25
    026,114-02,

AHIDJO AHMADOU
    AHIDJO AHMADOU
    CONTRIBUTION TO NATIONAL CONSTRUCTION.
    PARIS, PRESENCE AFRICAINE, 1964
    054,060,104-04,

AHMED JAMAL M
    AHMED JAMAL M
    THE INTELLECTUAL ORIGINS OF EGYPTIAN NATIONALISM.
    NEW YORK,OXFORD UNIVERSITY PRESS,1960
    054,140-06,

AHN PETER M
    AHN PETER M
    WEST AFRICAN AGRICULTURE.
    LONDON, OXFORD UNIVERSITY PRESS, 1969
    070,

AINSLIE ROSALYNDE
    AINSLIE ROSALYNDE
    THE PRESS IN AFRICA-- COMMUNICATIONS PAST AND PRESENT.
    LONDON,GOLLANCZ,1966
    049,

AINSWORTH LEONARD
    AINSWORTH LEONARD   AINSWORTH MARY D
    ACULTURATION IN EAST AFRICA.
    JOURNAL OF SOCIAL PSYCHOLOGY 57 1962 PP 391-432
    041,

    AINSWORTH LEONARD
    RIGIDITY, STRESS, AND ACCULTURATION.
    JOURNAL OF SOCIAL PSYCHOLOGY 49 1959 PP 131-136
    041,

AINSWORTH MARY D
    AINSWORTH LEONARD   AINSWORTH MARY D
    ACULTURATION IN EAST AFRICA.
    JOURNAL OF SOCIAL PSYCHOLOGY 57 1962 PP 391-432
    041,

    AINSWORTH MARY D
    INFANCY IN UGANDA.
    BALTIMORE,JOHNS HOPKINS PRESS,1967
    040,139-01,

AJAYI J F ADE
    AJAYI J F ADE   ESPIE IAN   EDS
    A THOUSAND YEARS OF WEST AFRICAN HISTORY-- A HANDBOOK FOR
    TEACHERS AND STUDENTS.
    IBADAN,IBADAN UNIVERSITY PRESS; ALSO LONDON, THOMAS NELSON
    AND SONS, 1965
    001,036,

    AJAYI J F ADE   WEBSTER J B
    THE EMERGENCE OF A NEW ELITE IN AFRICA
    IN CHAPTER 9 IN J C ANENE AND GODFREY BROWN,AFRICA IN THE
    NINETEENTH AND TWENTIETH CENTURIES,LONDON,NELSON AND IBADAN
    UNIVERSITY PRESS,1966
    044,

    AJAYI J F ADE   SMITH ROBERT
    YORUBA WARFARE IN THE 19TH CENTURY.
    CAMBRIDGE,ENGLAND,CAMBRIDGE UNIVERSITY PRESS,1964
    026,128-02,

    AJAYI J F ADE
    THE BRITISH OCCUPATION OF LAGOS 1851-1861.
    NIGERIA MAGAZINE 69 1961 PP 96-105
    033,128-02,

    AJAYI J F ADE
    CHRISTIAN MISSIONS IN NIGERIA.
    EVANSTON, NORTHWESTERN UNIVERSITY PRESS, 1965
    050,128-03,

AKAKPO TYPAMM PAUL
    AKAKPO TYPAMM PAUL
    POEMES ET CONTES D≠AFRIQUE.
    PARIS, CERCLE DE LA POESIE ET DE LA PEINTURE, 1958
    137-10,

AKE CLAUDE
    AKE CLAUDE
    POLITICAL INTEGRATION AND THE MASS-ELITE GAP
    IN CLAUDE AKE, A THEORY OF POLITICAL INTEGRATION
    HOMEWOOD, ILLINOIS, THE DORSEY PRESS, 1967, PP 68-81
    058,

    AKE CLAUDE
    A THEORY OF POLITICAL INTEGRATION
    HOMEWOOD ILLINOIS THE DORSEY PRESS 1967
    057,076,

AKINJOGBIN I A
    AKINJOGBIN I A
    DAHOMEY AND ITS NEIGHBORS, 1708-1818.
    NEW YORK AND LONDON, CAMBRIDGE UNIVERSITY PRESS, 1967
    026,109-02,

AKINOLA R A
    AKINOLA R A
    THE INDUSTRIAL STRUCTURE OF IBADAN.
    NIGERIAN GEOGRAPHICAL JOURNAL IBADAN 7 DECEMBER 1964
    PP 115-130

046,128-05,

AKIWOWO AKINSOLA
    AKIWOWO AKINSOLA
    THE SOCIOLOGY OF NIGERIAN TRIBALISM.
    PHYLON 25 SUMMER 1964 PP 155-163
    057,128-06,

    AKIWOWO AKINSOLA
    THE SOCIOLOGICAL RELEVANCE OF TRIBALISM TO THE BUILDING OF
    THE NIGERIAN NATION.
    SIXTH WORLD CONGRESS OF SOCIOLOGY, EVIAN, FRANCE, SEPT. 4-11
      1966, 32 PAGES
    065,128-06,

AL-HAJJ MUHAMMAD
    BIOBAKU SABURI O   AL-HAJJ MUHAMMAD
    THE SUDANESE MAHDIYYA AND THE NIGER-CHAD REGION.
    IN LEWIS, ISLAM IN TROPICAL AFRICA, LONDON, OXFORD UNIVERSITY
    PRESS, 1966, P. 425-441
    052,134-03,

AL-RAZZAZ MUNIF
    AL-RAZZAZ MUNIF
    THE EVOLUTION OF THE MEANING OF NATIONALISM.
    GARDEN CITY, NEW YORK, DOUBLEDAY, 1963
    054,

ALAGOA EBIEGBERI J
    ALAGOA EBIEGBERI J
    THE SMALL BRAVE CITY STATE-- A HISTORY OF NEMBRE-BRASS IN
    THE NIGER DELTA.
    MADISON, UNIVERSITY OF WISCONSIN PRESS, 1964
    026,128-02,

ALAPINI M
    ALAPINI M
    LE CULTE DE VODOUN ET DE ORICHA CHEZ LES FON ET LES NAGO
    DU DAHOMEY (THE CULT OF VODOUN AND ORICHA AMONG THE FON AND
    THE NAGO OF DAHOMEY).
    IN COLLOQUE SUR LES RELIGIONS, ABIDJAN, APRIL, 1961, PARIS,
    PRESENCE AFRICAINE, 1962, PP 91-96
    051,110-03,

ALBERT ALAN
    ALBERT ALAN
    A STUDY IN BROWN.
    IN ALBERT BERRIAN AND RICHARD LONG (EDS), NEGRITUDE--
    ESSAYS AND STUDIES, HAMPTON, VIRGINIA, HAMPTON INSTITUTE
    PRESS, 1967, PP 79-88
    094,

ALBERT ETHEL M
    ALBERT ETHEL M
    UNE ETUDE DE VALEURS EN URUNDI-A STUDY OF VALUES IN URUNDI
    CAHIERS D'ETUDES AFRICAINES 2 1960 PP 148-160
    013,103-01,

    ALBERT ETHEL M
    SOCIO-ECONOMIC ORGANIZATION AND RECEPTIVITY TO CHANGE-SOME

DIFFERENCES BETWEEN RUANDA AND URUNDI
SOUTHWESTERN JOURNAL OF ANTHROPOLOGY 16 1960 PP 46-74
013, 038, 103-03, 129-03,

ALBINO RONALD C
    ALBINO RONALD C   THOMPSON VIRGINIA
    THE EFFECTS OF SUDDEN WEANING ON ZULU CHILDREN.
    BRITISH JOURNAL OF MEDICAL PSYCHOLOGY 29 1956 PP 177-210
    040,

ALDRED CYRIL
    ALDRED CYRIL
    THE EGYPTIANS-- ANCIENT PEOPLE AND PLACES.
    NEW YORK, PRAEGER, 1961
    020,140-02,

ALEXANDER A S JR
    ALEXANDER A S JR
    THE IVORY COAST CONSTITUTION--AN ACCELERATOR, NOT A BRAKE.
    THE JOURNAL OF MODERN AFRICAN STUDIES, VOL. I, NO. 3, SEPT.
    1963, PP. 293-312
    068,116-06,

ALEXANDRE PIERRE
    ALEXANDRE PIERRE
    MARXISM AND AFRICAN CULTURAL TRADITION.
    IN LEOPOLD LABEDZ (ED.), POLYCENTRISM-- THE NEW FACTOR IN
    INTERNATIONAL COMMUNISM, NEW YORK, PRAEGER, 1962, PP 173-
    186
    084,

    ALEXANDRE PIERRE
    PROBLEMES LINGUISTIQUES DES ETATS NEGRO-AFRICAINES A L≠HEURE
    DE L'INDEPENDANCE(LINGUISTIC PROBLEMS OF NEGRO AFRICAN
    STATES AT THE TIME OF INDEPENDENCE).
    CAHIERS D'ETUDES AFRICAINES 2 1961 PP 177-195
    056,

    ALEXANDRE PIERRE
    APERCU SOMMAIRE SUR LE PIDGIN A 70 DU CAMEROUN.
    COLLOQUE SUR LE MULTILINGUISME, BRAZZAVILLE, CCTA, 1962
    104-01,

    ALEXANDRE PIERRE
    CAMEROUN
    IN KRITZECK AND LEWIS, PP 270-277
    104-03,

ALIMEN HENRIETTA
    ALIMEN HENRIETTA
    THE PREHISTORY OF AFRICA.
    LONDON, HUTCHINSON PRESS, 1957
    018,

ALLAN WILLIAM H
    ALLAN WILLIAM H
    THE AFRICAN HUSBANDMAN.
    EDINBURGH, OLIVER AND BOYD, 1965
    010,070,

ALLARD G O
    ALLARD G O   HURST VERNON J
    BRAZIL-GABON GEOLOGIC LINK SUPPORTS CONTINENTAL DRIFT-NEWLY
    DISCOVERED TECTONIC PROVINCE IN BRAZIL MATCHES PROVINCE IN
    GABON
    SCIENCE 163 1969 PP 528-532
    017,

ALLEN BERNARD M
    ALLEN BERNARD M
    GORDON AND THE SUDAN.
    LONDON, MACMILLAN, 1931
    033,134-02,

ALLEN SAMUEL W
    ALLEN SAMUEL W
    TENDENCIES IN AFRICAN POETRY.
    IN AMSAC, AFRICA SEEN BY AMERICAN NEGROES, PARIS,
    PRESENCE AFRICAINES, 1958, PP 175-198
    090,094,

ALLISON PHILIP
    ALLISON PHILIP
    AFRICAN STONE SCULPTURE.
    NEW YORK, PRAEGER, 1968
    014,

ALLOTT ANTHONY
    ALLOTT ANTHONY
    ENGLISH LAW IN AFRICA PT 1.
    IN ESSAYS IN AFRICAN LAW, LONDON, BUTTERWORTHS, 1960
    066,

    ALLOTT ANTHONY
    CUSTOMARY LAW AND ITS ADMINISTRATION PT 2.
    IN ESSAYS IN AFRICAN LAW, LONDON, BUTTERWORTHS, 1960
    066,

    ALLOTT ANTHONY
    THE CHANGING LAW IN A CHANGING AFRICA.
    SOCIOLOGUS 11 1961 PP 115-131
    067,

    ALLOTT ANTHONY
    THE UNITY OF AFRICAN LAW.
    JOURNAL OF AFRICAN ADMINISTRATION 11 APRIL 1959 PP 72-83
    067,

    ALLOTT ANTHONY
    THE CODIFICATION OF THE LAW OF CIVIL WRONGS IN COMMON-
    LAW AFRICAN COUNTRIES.
    SOCIOLOGUS NEW SERIES 16 1966 PP 101-121
    066,

    ALLOTT ANTHONY   READ J S
    THE LEGAL STATUS OF WOMEN IN AFRICA-- IN PRACTICE,
    PROCEDURE AND EVIDENCE IN THE NATIVE, AFRICAN, LOCAL
    OR CUSTOMARY COURTS.
    JOURNAL OF AFRICAN LAW 5 AUTUMN 1961 PP 125-138
    066,

ALLOTT ANTHONY
   ALLOTT ANTHONY
   THE PLACE OF AFRICAN CUSTOMARY LAW IN MODERN AFRICAN LEGAL
   SYSTEMS.
   IN LALAGE BOWN AND MICHAEL CROWDER (EDS.), PROCEEDINGS OF
   THE FIRST INTERNATIONAL CONGRESS OF AFRICANISTS, ACCRA,
   1962, LONDON, LONGMANS, 1964, PP 190-196
   067,

   ALLOTT ANTHONY   ED
   THE FUTURE OF LAW IN AFRICA.
   LONDON, BUTTERWORTH, 1960
   067,

ALMOND GABRIEL A
   ALMOND GABRIEL A
   A DEVELOPMENTAL APPROACH TO POLITICAL SYSTEMS.
   WORLD POLITICS 17 JANUARY 1965 PP 183-214
   098,

   ALMOND GABRIEL A
   POLITICAL SYSTEMS AND POLITICAL CHANGE.
   AMERICAN BEHAVIORAL SCIENTIST 16 JUNE 1963 PP 3-10
   098,

   ALMOND GABRIEL A   POWELL G B
   COMPARATIVE POLITICS-- A DEVELOPMENTAL APPROACH.
   BOSTON, LITTLE, BROWN AND COMPANY, 1966
   098,

   ALMOND GABRIEL A
   A DEVELOPMENTAL APPROACH TO POLITICAL SYSTEMS CHAPTER 3.
   IN JASON L FINKLE AND RICHARD W GABLE, POLITICAL
   DEVELOPMENT AND SOCIAL CHANGE, NEW YORK, JOHN WILEY, 1966
   098,

   ALMOND GABRIEL A
   COMPARATIVE POLITICAL SYSTEMS.
   THE JOURNAL OF POLITICS 18 AUGUST 1956 PP 391-409
   (BOBBS-MERRILL REPRINT PS-6)
   098,

ALPERS EDWARD A
   ALPERS EDWARD A
   MUTAPA AND MALAWI POLITICAL SYSTEMS.
   IN TERENCE RANGER (ED), ASPECTS OF CENTRAL AFRICAN HISTORY,
   EVANSTON, NORTHWESTERN UNIVERSITY PRESS, 1968, PP 1-28
   025,

   ALPERS EDWARD A
   THE EAST AFRICAN SLAVE TRADE.
   NAIROBI, EAST AFRICAN PUBLISHING HOUSE, 1967
   023,028,

ALTMAN RALPH C
   ALTMAN RALPH C   ED
   MASTERPIECES FROM THE SIR HENRY WELLCOME COLLECTION AT UCLA.
   LOS ANGELES, MUSEUM AND LABORATORIES OF ETHNIC ARTS AND TECH-
   NOLOGY, UCLA, 1966

014,

ALUKO S A
  ALUKO S A
  FEDERAL ELECTION CRISIS 1964-- AN ANALYSIS.
  ONITSHA, ETUDO LTD 1965
  061,064,128-07,

AMANN HANS
  AMANN HANS
  ENERGY SUPPLY AND ECONOMIC DEVELOPMENT IN EAST AFRICA.
  NEW YORK, HUMANITIES PRESS INC., 1969
  069,

AMARTEIFIO G W
  AMARTEIFIO G W   BUTCHER D A P   WHITHAM DAVID
  TEMA MANHEAN--A STUDY OF RESETTLEMENT.
  GHANA, GHANA UNIVERSITIES PRESS, 1966
  092,114-05,

AMENUMEY D E K
  AMENUMEY D E K
  GERMAN ADMINISTRATION IN SOUTHERN TOGO.
  IN JOURNAL OF AFRICAN HISTORY VOL 10 1969 P 623
  035,

AMERICAN
  AMERICAN SOCIETY OF AFRICAN CULTURE
  AFRICA SEEN BY AMERICAN NEGROES.
  PARIS, PRESENCE AFRICAINE, 1958
  094,

  AMERICAN SOCIETY OF AFRICAN CULTURE
  THE AMERICAN NEGRO WRITER AND HIS ROOTS.
  NEW YORK, AMSAC, 1960
  094,

  AMERICAN SOCIETY OF AFRICAN CULTURE
  THE AMERICAN NEGRO BIBLIOGRAPHY.
  NEW YORK, AMERICAN SOCIETY OF AFRICAN CULTURE, 1967
  030,

  AMERICAN SOCIETY OF AFRICAN CULTURE
  COLLOQUIUM ON NEGRO ART--THE FUNCTION AND SIGNIFICANCE OF
  NEGRO AFRICAN ART IN THE LIFE OF THE PEOPLE AND FOR THE
  PEOPLE.
  PARIS, INTERNATIONAL UNIVERSITY BOOKSELLERS, INC., 1969
  014,

  AMERICAN SOCIETY OF AFRICAN CULTURE
  PAN-AFRICANISM RECONSIDERED.
  BERKELEY, UNIVERSITY OF CALIFORNIA PRESS, 1962
  079,

AMES DAVID W
  AMES DAVID W
  WOLOF CO-OPERATIVE WORK GROUPS CHAPTER 12.
  IN WILLIAM BASCOM AND MELVILLE HERSKOVITS, CONTINUTY AND
  CHANGE IN AFRICAN CULTURES, CHICAGO, UNIVERSITY OF CHICAGO
  PRESS, 1962, PP 224-237

010,130-01,

AMES DAVID W
  AMES DAVID W
  PROFESSIONALS AND AMATEURS-- THE MUSICIANS OF ZARIA AND
  OBIMO.
  AFRICAN ARTS 1 2 WINTER 1968 PP 41-45, 80-84
  015,128-01,

AMIJI HATIM
  AMIJI HATIM
  THE ASIAN MINORITIES
  IN KRITZECK AND LEWIS, PP 139-181
  085,

AMIN SAMIR
  AMIN SAMIR
  LE DEVELOPPEMENT ECONOMIQUE ET SOCIALE DE LA COTE D'IVOIRE
  DAKAR, IDEP, 1966
  073,116-08,

  AMIN SAMIR
  TROIS EXPERIENCES AFRICAINES DE DEVELOPPEMENT-LE MALI,LA
  GUINEE,ET LA GHANA
  PARIS, PRESSES UNIVERSITAIRES DE FRANCE, 1965
  073,123-08,115-08,114-08,

  AMIN SAMIR
  L ECONOMIE DU MAGHREB VOLUME 1- LA COLONISATION ET LA
  DECOLONISATION VOLUME 2-LES PERSPECTIVE D≠AVENIR
  PARIS, EDITIONS DE MINUIT, 1966
  073,101-08,126-08,138-08,

AMON D'ABY J F
  AMON D'ABY J F
  CROYANCES RELIGIEUSES ET COUTUMES JURIDIQUES DES AGNI DE LA
  COTE-D'IVOIRE.
  PARIS, G. P. MAISONNEUVE ET LAROSE, 1960
  116-01,

  AMON D'ABY J F
  LA COURONNE AUX ENCHERES, DRAME SOCIAL EN TROIS ACTES ET SIX
  TABLEAUX.
  PARIS, ED. LES PARAGRAPHES LITTERAIRES, 1957
  116-10,

  AMON D ABY J F   DADIE BERNARD   GADEAU G COFFI
  LE THEATRE POPULAIRE EN REPUBLIQUE DE COTE-D'IVOIRE--OEUVRES
  CHOISIES.
  ABIDJAN, CERCLE CULTUREL ET FOLKLORIQUE DE LA COTE-D'IVOIRE
  1965
  116-10,

AMONOO R F
  AMONOO R F
  PROBLEMS OF GHANAIAN LINGUE FRANCHE.
  IN SPENCER, JOHN (ED), LANGUAGE IN AFRICA, PAPERS OF THE
  LEVERHULME CONFERENCE ON UNIVERSITIES AND THE LANGUAGE
  PROBLEMS OF TROPICAL AFRICA, CAMBRIDGE, CAMBRIDGE UNIVERSITY
  PRESS, 1963

114-06,

ANANOU DAVID
   ANANOU DAVID
   LE FILS DU FETICHE--ROMAN.
   PARIS, NOUVELLES EDITIONS LATINES, 1955
   137-10,

ANDERSON CHARLES
   ANDERSON CHARLES   VON DER MEHDEN FRED YOUNG CRAWFORD
   ISSUES OF POLITICAL DEVELOPMENT.
   ENGLEWOOD CLIFFS, N.J., PRENTICE-HALL, 1967
   002,

ANDERSON J N D
   ANDERSON J N D
   ISLAMIC LAW IN AFRICA.
   LONDON, HER MAJESTY'S STATIONARY OFFICE 1 1954
   066,

   ANDERSON J N D
   RELATIONSHIP BETWEEN ISLAMIC AND CUSTOMARY LAW IN AFRICA.
   JOURNAL OF AFRICAN ADMINISTRATION 12 OCTOBER 1960
   PP 228-234
   066,

   ANDERSON J N D
   MUSLIM PROCEDURE AND EVIDENCE.
   JOURNAL OF AFRICAN ADMINISTRATION 1 JULY 1949 PP 123-129
   066,

   ANDERSON J N D
   HOMICIDE IN ISLAMIC LAW.
   LONDON UNIVERSITY, BULLITIN OF THE SCHOOL OF ORIENTAL AND
   AFRICAN STUDIES 13 1951 PP 811-828
   066,

   ANDERSON J N D
   COLONIAL LAW IN TROPICAL AFRICA-- THE CONFLICT BETWEEN
   ENGLISH, ISLAMIC AND CUSTOMARY LAW.
   INDIANA LAW JOURNAL 35 1960 PP 433-442
   067,

   ANDERSON J N D
   THE LEGAL TRADITION
   IN KRITZECK AND LEWIS, PP 35-53
   021,

   ANDERSON J N D
   RETURN TO NIGERIA-- JUDICIAL AND LEGAL DEVELOPMENTS IN THE
   NORTHERN REGION.
   INTERNATIONAL AND COMPARATIVE LAW QUARTERLY JANUARY 1963
   PP 282-294
   067,128-06,

   ANDERSON J N D
   ISLAMIC LAW IN THE MODERN WORLD.
   NEW YORK, NEW YORK UNIVERSITY PRESS, 1959
   066,

ANDERSSON EFRIAM
    ANDERSSON EFRIAM
    MESSIANIC POPULAR MOVEMENTS IN THE LOWER CONGO.
    UPSALA,ALMQUIST AND WIKSELL, 1958
    (STUDIA ETHNOGRAPHICA UPSALIENSIA, 14)
    051,108-03,

ANDRADE MARIO
    ANDRADE MARIO
    LE NATIONALISME ANGOLAIS (ANGOLESE NATIONALISM).
    PRESENCE AFRICAINE 14 JULY 1964 PP 7-23
    087,

ANDRIAN CHARLES F
    ANDRIAN CHARLES F
    THE PAN-AFRICAN MOVEMENT--THE SEARCH FOR ORGANIZATION AND
    COMMUNITY.
    PHYLON 23 SPRING 1962 PP 5-27
    079,

ANDRZEJEWSKI B W
    ANDRZEJEWSKI B W   LEWIS I M
    SOMALI POETRY.
    LONDON, OXFORD UNIVERSITY PRESS, 1964
    012,133-01,

    ANDRZEJEWSKI B W
    SPEECH AND WRITING DICHOTOMY AS THE PATTERN OF MULTILINGUAL-
    ISM IN THE SOMALI REPUBLIC.
    COLLOQUE SUR LE MULTILINGUISME, BRAZZAVILLE, 1962
    133-06,

ANENE JOSEPH C
    ANENE JOSEPH C   BROWN GODFREY N   EDS
    AFRICA IN THE NINETEENTH AND TWENTIETH CENTURIES-- A HAND-
    BOOK FOR TEACHERS AND STUDENTS.
    IBADAN,IBADAN UNIVERSITY PRESS;ALSO LONDON,THOMAS NELSON AND
    SONS,1966
    001,

ANKRAH J A
    ANKRAH J A
    100 DAYS IN GHANA.
    AFRICA REPORT, JUNE, 1966, PP. 21-23
    064,114-06,

ANONYMOUS
    ANONYMOUS
    FRANCE'S NEW ROLE IN AFRICA.
    THE WORLD TODAY 20 9 SEPTEMBER 1965 PP 382-387
    082,

    ANONYMOUS
    FRANCO-AFRICAN MILITARY COOPERATION.
    AFRICA REPORT, JUNE, 1968, P. 22
    082,

    ANONYMOUS
    GABON-- PUTSCH OR COUP D'ETAT.
    AFRICA REPORT 9 MARCH 1964 PP 12-15

064,112-06,

ANONYMOUS
   ANONYMOUS
   CONVULSIONS WITHIN TOGO.
   PAN AFRICA NO. 93 JANUARY 6, 1967 P 9
   064,137-06,

   ANONYMOUS
   COUP FOILED IN GABON.
   WEST AFRICA FEBRUARY 22 1964 P 207
   064,112-06,

   ANONYMOUS
   GREATER KANO PLANNING AUTHORITY PLANS.
   THE WEST AFRICAN BUILDER AND ARCHITECT 4 5 SEPTEMBER-OCTOBER
   1964 PP 85-95
   092,128-05,

   ANONYMOUS
   AFRICAN POLITICAL PARTIES IN EQUATORIAL GUINEA 1968.
   AFRICA REPORT, MARCH 18, 1968
   061,111-07,

   ANONYMOUS
   TABLE RONDE SUR LES LANGUES AFRICAINES (ROUND TABLE ON
   AFRICAN LANGUAGES).
   PRESENCE AFRICAINE, NO. 67, 3RD QUARTER, 1968, PP. 53-156
   011,

   ANONYMOUS
   BURUNDI AT CLOSE RANGE.
   AFRICA REPORT MARCH 1965
   103-11,

   ANONYMOUS
   ZAIRE.
   SPECIAL EDITION ON LEOPOLDVILLE, JUNE, 1956
   108-05,

   ANONYMOUS
   1960 POPULATION CENSUS OF GHANA.
   SPECIAL REPORT E TRIBES IN GHANA, CENSUS OFFICE, ACCRA, 1964
   114-01,

   ANONYMOUS
   CHANGING RELATIONS AMONG GUINEA, THE IVORY COAST AND MALI.
   AMERICAN UNIVERSITIES FIELD STAFF, VOL. V, NO. 8, 1962
   115-07,

   ANONYMOUS
   SOCIETE POUR L'ETUDE TECHNIQUE D'AMENAGEMENTS PLANIFIES
   RAPPORT SUR LE PLAN D ABIDJAN.
   ABIDJAN, MINISTERE DES TRAVAUX PUBLICS, 1959
   116-05,

   ANONYMOUS
   NIGERIAN THESES.
   IBADAN, IBADAN UNIVERSITY PRESS, 1965
   128-12,

ANONYMOUS
   ANONYMOUS
   A SURVEY OF DAR ES SALAAM--A REVIEW.
   AFRICA, VOL. 34, NO. 4
   136-05,

   ANONYMOUS
   CATALOGUES OF GOVERNMENT PUBLICATIONS PUBLISHED PRIOR TO
   1ST JANUARY, 1965 .
   ENTEBBE, GOVERNMENT PRINTER, 1965
   139-12,

ANSCHEL KURT R
   ANSCHEL KURT R   BRANNON RUSSELL H   SMITH ELSON D
   AGRICULTURAL COOPERATIVES AND MARKETS IN DEVELOPING
   COUNTRIES.
   NEW YORK, PRAEGER PUBLISHERS, 1969
   070,

ANSRE GILBERT
   BIRNIE J R   ANSRE GILBERT   EDS
   PROCEEDINGS OF THE CONFERENCE ON THE STUDY OF GHANAIAN
   LANGUAGES.
   ACCRA, INTERNATIONAL UNIVERSITY BOOKSELLERS,INC., 1968
   011,

   ANSRE GILBERT
   A STUDY ON THE OFFICIAL LANGUAGE IN GHANA.
   COLLOQUE SUR LE MULTILINGUISME, BRAZZAVILLE, 1962
   114-06,

ANSTEY ROGER T
   ANSTEY ROGER T
   BRITAIN IN THE CONGO IN THE 19TH CENTURY.
   OXFORD, CLARENDON PRESS, 1962
   033,108-02,

   ANSTEY ROGER T
   KING LEOPOLD)S LEGACY-- THE CONGO UNDER BELGIAN RULE.
   LONDON,OXFORD UNIVERSITY PRESS, 1966
   033,108-02,

APOKO ANNA
   LIJEMBE JOSEPH A   APOKO ANNA   MUTUKU NZIOKI J
   AN EAST AFRICAN CHILDHOOD--THREE VERSIONS.
   LONDON, OXFORD UNIVERSITY PRESS, 1967
   008,

APTER DAVID E
   APTER DAVID E
   THE POLITICS OF MODERNIZATION.
   CHICAGO, UNIVERSITY OF CHICAGO PRESS, 1965
   037,061,

   APTER DAVID E   ED
   IDEOLOGY AND DISCONTENT.
   NEW YORK, FREE PRESS OF GLENCOE, 1964
   060

APTER DAVID E
NATIONALISM GOVERNMENT AND ECONOMIC GROWTH.
ECONOMIC DEVELOPMENT AND CULTURAL CHANGE 7 1959 PP 117-136
074,

APTER DAVID E
    APTER DAVID E   COLEMAN JAMES S
    PAN-AFRICANISM OR NATIONALISM IN AFRICA.
    IN AMERICAN SOCIETY OF AFRICAN CULTURE, PAN-AFRICANISM
    RECONSIDERED, BERKELEY, UNIVERSITY OF CALIFORNIA PRESS, 1962
    PP 81-115
    079,

    APTER DAVID E   COLEMAN JAMES S
    PAN-AFRICANISM OR NATIONALISM.
    IN PETER J MCEWAN AND ROBERT B SUTCLIFFE (EDS) MODERN AFRICA,
    NEW YORK, THOMAS CROWELL, 1965, PP 413-423
    079,

    APTER DAVID E
    THE POLITICAL KINGDOM IN UGANDA A STUDY IN BUREAUCRATIC
    NATIONALISM.
    PRINCETON, PRINCETON UNIVERSITY PRESS, 1961; REVISED 1967
    055,139-06,

    APTER DAVID E
    THE ROLE OF TRADITIONALISM IN THE POLITICAL
    MODERNIZATION OF GHANA AND UGANDA.
    WORLD POLITICS 13 OCT 1960 PP 45-68 ALSO WILLIAM J HANNA, ED,
    INDEPENDENT BLACK AFRICA, CHICAGO, RAND MCNALLY, 1964, PP
    254-277
    055,114-03,139-03,

    APTER DAVID E
    THE DEVELOPMENT OF GHANA NATIONALISM.
    UNITED ASIA 9 1957 PP 23-30
    055,114-06,

    APTER DAVID E   LYSTAD ROBERT A
    BUREAUCRACY, PARTY, AND CONSTITUTIONAL DEMOCRACY-- AN EXAM-
    INATION OF POLITICAL ROLE SYSTEMS IN GHANA.
    IN GWENDOLEN M CARTER AND WILLIAM O BROWN (EDS) TRANSITION
    IN AFRICA-- STUDIES IN POLITICAL ADAPTATION, BOSTON, BOSTON
    UNIVERSITY PRESS, 1958, PP 16-43
    062,114-07,

    APTER DAVID E
    GHANA IN TRANSITION.
    NEW YORK, ATHENEUM, 1963
    056,058,114-07,

    APTER DAVID E
    GHANA.
    JAMES S. COLEMAN AND CARL G. ROSBERG JR. (EDS), POLITICAL
    PARTIES AND NATIONAL INTEGRATION IN TROPICAL AFRICA,
    BERKELEY, UNIVERSITY OF CALIFORNIA PRESS, 1966
    058,062,114-07,

    APTER DAVID E
    THE POLITICAL PARTY AS A MODERNIZING INSTRUMENT CHP 6.

IN THE POLITICS OF MODERNIZATION, CHICAGO, CHICAGO
UNIVERSITY PRESS,1965
061,

APTER DAVID E
    APTER DAVID E
    SOME REFLECTIONS ON THE ROLE OF A POLITICAL OPPOSITION IN
    NEW NATIONS.
    COMPARATIVE STUDIES IN SOCIETY AND HISTORY 4 JANUARY 1962
    PP 154-168;ALSO WILLIAM J HANNA, ED, INDEPENDENT BLACK AFRICA,
    CHICAGO, RAND MCNALLY,1964, PP 456-471
    061,

    APTER DAVID E
    SYSTEM, PROCESS, AND THE POLITICS OF ECONOMIC DEVELOPMENT.
    IN JASON L FINKLE AND RICHARD W GABLE, POLITICAL
    DEVELOPMENT AND SOCIAL CHANGE, NEW YORK, JOHN WILEY, 1966
    073,074,

    APTER DAVID E
    A COMPARATIVE METHOD FOR THE STUDY OF POLITICS.
    THE AMERICAN JOURNAL OF SOCIOLOGY 64 NOVEMBER 1958 (BOBBS-
    MERRILL REPRINT PS-8) ABSTRACT
    098,

APTHEKER HERBERT
    APTHEKER HERBERT
    A DOCUMENTARY HISTORY OF THE NEGRO PEOPLE IN THE UNITED
    STATES.
    NEW YORK, CITADEL PRESS, 1951
    030,

    APTHEKER HERBERT
    NEGRO SLAVE REVOLTS IN THE U.S.
    NEW YORK,INTERNATIONAL PUBLISHERS,1939
    030,

APTHORPE RAYMOND J
    APTHORPE RAYMOND J
    POLITICAL CHANGE, CENTRALIZATION AND ROLE DIFFERENTIATION.
    CIVILISATIONS 10 1960 PP 217-224
    038,

    APTHORPE RAYMOND J
    THE INTRODUCTION OF BUREAUCRACY INTO AFRICAN POLITIES.
    JOURNAL OF AFRICAN ADMINISTRATION 12 JULY 1960 PP 125-134
    062,

    APTHORPE RAYMOND J   ED
    FROM TRIBAL RULE TO MODERN GOVERNMENT-- THE 13TH
    CONFERENCE OF THE RHODES-LIVINGSTONE INSTITUTE FOR SOCIAL
    RESEARCH.
    LUSAKA, RHODES-LIVINGSTONE INSTITUTE, 1959
    038,

ARBERRY A J
    ARBERRY A J
    SUFISM, AN ACCOUNT OF THE MYSTICS OF ISLAM.
    LONDON, GEORGE ALLEN AND UNWIN, 1950
    021,

ARBOUSSIER
  D'ARBOUSSIER GABRIEL
  L AFRIQUE VERS L UNITE.
  PARIS, ED. SAINT-PAUL, 1961
  130-04,

ARDEN-CLARKE C
  ARDEN-CLARKE C
  GOLD COAST INTO GHANA, SOME PROBLEMS OF TRANSITION.
  INTERNATIONAL AFFAIRS 34 1958 PP 49-56
  056,114-06,

ARDENER EDWIN
  ARDENER EDWIN
  SOME IBO ATTITUDES TO SKIN PIGMENTATION.
  MAN 54 1954 PP 70-73
  088,128-03,

  ARDENER EDWIN
  THE NATURE OF THE REUNIFICATION OF CAMEROON CHAPTER 8.
  IN ARTHUR HAZLEWOOD, AFRICAN INTEGRATION AND DISINTEGRATION,
  LONDON, OXFORD UNIVERSITY PRESS, 1967, PP 285-337
  054,104-06,

  ARDENER EDWIN   ARDENER S   WARMINGTON W A
  PLANTATION AND VILLAGE IN THE CAMEROONS.
  LONDON, OXFORD UNIVERSITY PRESS, 1960
  047,104-01,

  ARDENER EDWIN   ED
  SOCIAL AND DEMOGRAPHIC PROBLEMS OF THE SOUTHERN
  CAMEROONS PLANTATION AREA.
  IN AIDAN SOUTHALL (ED.), SOCIAL CHANGE IN MODERN AFRICA,
  LONDON, OXFORD UNIVERSITY PRESS, 1961, PP 83-97
  074,104-08,

ARDENER S
  ARDENER EDWIN   ARDENER S   WARMINGTON W A
  PLANTATION AND VILLAGE IN THE CAMEROONS.
  LONDON, OXFORD UNIVERSITY PRESS, 1960
  047,104-01,

ARELSON E
  ARELSON E
  THE PORTUGESE IN SOUTHEAST AFRICA 1600-1700
  JOHANNESBURG, WITWATERSRAND UNIVERSITY PRESS, 1960
  027,

ARGYLE W J
  ARGYLE W J
  THE FON OF DAHOMEY-- A HISTORY AND ETHNOGRAPHY OF
  OF THE OLD KINGDOM.
  OXFORD, CLARENDON PRESS, 1966
  026,109-01,

ARKADIE BRIAN VAN
  ARKADIE BRIAN VAN   FRANK CHARLES R
  ECONOMIC ACCOUNTING AND DEVELOPMENT PLANNING.
  EASTERN AFRICA, OXFORD UNIVERSITY PRESS, 1966

072,

ARKELL A J
   ARKELL A J
   A HISTORY OF THE SUDAN FROM THE EARLIEST TIMES TO 1821
   LONDON,ATHLONE PRESS, 1955
   020,

   ARKELL A J
   THE HISTORY OF DARFUR 1200-1700 A D.
   SUDAN NOTES AND RECORDS 32 1951 PP 37-70, PP 207-238
   ALSO 33 1952 PP 129-155, PP 244-275
   024,106-02,

   ARKELL A J
   THE MEDIEVAL HISTORY OF DARFUR IN ITS RELATION TO OTHER
   CULTURES AND TO THE NILOTIC SUDAN.
   SUDAN NOTES AND RECORDS 40 1959 PP 44-47
   024,106-02,

ARMAH AYI KWEI
   ARMAH AYI KWEI
   THE BEAUTIFUL ONES ARE NOT YET BORN.
   NEW YORK, COLLIER BOOKS (MACMILLAN), 1969   (LONDON,
   HEINEMANN EDUCATIONAL BOOKS)
   090,114-10,

   ARMAH AYI KWEI
   FRAGMENTS
   BOSTON, HOUGHTON-MIFFLIN, 1969
   090,

ARMSTRONG ROBERT P
   ARMSTRONG ROBERT P
   GUINEAISM.
   TRI-QUARTERLY 5 1966 PP 137-146
   014,015,

   ARMSTRONG ROBERT P
   THE ARTS IN HUMAN CULTURE--THEIR SIGNIFICANCE AND THEIR
   STUDY.
   IN CARTER, GWENDOLEN M. AND ANN PADEN (EDS), EXPANDING
   HORIZONS IN AFRICAN STUDIES, EVANSTON, NORTHWESTERN
   UNIVERSITY PRESS, 1969, PP. 119-127
   090,093,100,

   ARMSTRONG ROBERT P
   THE CHARACTERISTICS AND COMPREHENSION OF A NATIONAL
   LITERATURE.
   IN PROCEEDINGS OF THE CONFERENCE ON AFRICAN LANGUAGES AND
   LITERATURES, NORTHWESTERN UNIVERSITY, 1966, UNITED STATES
   OFFICE OF EDUCATION, NO. OE-6-14-018, PP 117-132
   090,

ARNETT E J
   ARNETT E J
   THE RISE OF THE SOKOTO FULANI (TRANSLATION OF MUHAMMAD
   BELLO, INFAQ AL-MAISUR)
   KANO, 1929
   099,128-01,

ARNOLD ROSEMARY
    ARNOLD ROSEMARY
    A PORT OF TRADE-- WHYDAH ON THE GUINEA COAST.
    IN K POLANYI, C M ARENSBERG AND H W PEARSON (EDS.), TRADE AND
    MARKET IN THE EARLY EMPIRES, GLENCOE, ILLINOIS, THE FREE
    PRESS, 1957
    010,

ARRIGHI GIOVANNI
    ARRIGHI GIOVANNI   SAUL JOHN S
    SOCIALISM AND ECONOMIC DEVELOPMENT IN TROPICAL AFRICA.
    THE JOURNAL OF MODERN AFRICAN STUDIES, VOL. 6, NO. 2, 1968,
    PP. 141-69
    073,

ASHBY ERIC
    ASHBY ERIC
    AFRICAN UNIVERSITIES AND THE WESTERN TRADITION.
    CAMBRIDGE, MASSACHUSETTS, HARVARD UNIVERSITY PRESS, 1964
    042,

    ASHBY ERIC
    UNIVERSITIES-- BRITISH, INDIAN, AFRICAN, A STUDY IN THE ECO-
    LOGY OF HIGHER EDUCATION.
    CAMBRIDGE, MASSACHUSETTS, HARVARD UNIVERSITY PRESS, 1966
    042,

ASHFORD DOUGLAS E
    ASHFORD DOUGLAS E
    POLITICAL CHANGE IN MOROCCO.
    PRINCETON, NEW JERSEY, PRINCETON UNIVERSITY PRESS, 1961
    126-07,

    ASHFORD DOUGLAS E
    NATIONAL DEVELOPMENT AND LOCAL REFORM-POLITICAL PARTITION
    IN MOROCCO, TUNISIA, AND PAKISTAN
    PRINCETON, PRINCETON UNIVERSITY PRESS
    126-06, 138-06,

ASHTON HUGH
    ASHTON HUGH
    THE BASUTO.
    LONDON, OXFORD UNIVERSITY PRESS, 1967
    118-01,

ASIEGBU
    ASIEGBU JOHNSON U J
    SLAVERY AND THE POLITICS OF LIBERATION 1787-1861.
    NEW YORK, AFRICANA PUBLISHING CORPORATION, 1970
    030,

ASIKA U
    ASIKA U
    ENOUGH IS ENOUGH.
    FEDERAL MINISTRY OF INFORMATION, DEC., 1967, 16 PAGES
    065,

ASSOCIATION
    AFRICAN STUDIES ASSOCIATION

AFRICAN FILM BIBLIOGRAPHY 1965.
AFRICAN STUDIES ASSOCIATION OCCASIONAL PAPERS NO. 1 1966
049,093,

ASSOCIATION
ASSOCIATION DES ANCIENS ETUDIANTS DE L'INUTOM
L'EVOLUTION POLITIQUE DU CONGO BELGE ET LES AUTORITES
INDIGENES (POLITICAL EVOLUTION OF THE BELGIAN CONGO AND THE
NATIVE AUTHORITIES).
PROBLEMS DE L'AFRIQUE CENTRALE 13 1959 PP 3-77
035,108-07,

ATEMENGUE JOSEPH
ATEMENGUE JOSEPH   ED
A QUOI SERT LA COOPERATION FRANCO-AFRICAINE--LE PROBLEME
VOL I (WHAT SHALL BE THE NATURE OF FRANCO-AFRICAN COOPERA-
TION VOL I)
DES AVANTAGES CONCRETS TIRES DE LA COOPERATION FRANCO-
AFRICAINE VOL II (CONCRETE ADVANTAGES TO BE HAD FROM FRANCO-
AFRICAN COOPERATION VOL II).
PARIS, INTERNATIONAL UNIVERSITY BOOKSELLERS, INC., 1969
082,

ATMORE ANTHONY
OLIVER ROLAND   ATMORE ANTHONY
THE LAST YEARS OF COLONIAL RULE, 1940-1960.
IN AFRICA SINCE 1800, CAMBRIDGE, CAMBRIDGE UNIVERSITY PRESS,
1967, PP 213-222
056,

OLIVER ROLAND   ATMORE ANTHONY
THE INTER-WAR PERIOD, 1918-1938
IN AFRICA SINCE 1800, CAMBRIDGE, CAMBRIDGE UNIVERSITY PRESS,
1967, PP 160-171
035,

OLIVER ROLAND   ATMORE ANTHONY
COLONIAL RULE IN TROPICAL AFRICA-- SOCIAL AND RELIGIOUS
DEVELOPMENTS.
IN AFRICA SINCE 1800, CAMBRIDGE, CAMBRIDGE UNIVERSITY PRESS,
1967, PP 141-159
035,050,

OLIVER ROLAND   ATMORE ANTHONY
COLONIAL RULE IN TROPICAL AFRICA-- POLITICAL AND ECONOMIC
DEVELOPMENTS, 1885-1914.
IN AFRICA SINCE 1800, CAMBRIDGE, CAMBRIDGE UNIVERSITY PRESS,
1967, PP 128-140
033,

OLIVER ROLAND   ATMORE ANTHONY
THE PARTITION OF AFRICA ON THE GROUND, 1891-1901.
IN AFRICA SINCE 1800, CAMBRIDGE, CAMBRIDGE UNIVERSITY PRESS,
1967, PP 114-127
033,

OLIVER ROLAND   ATMORE ANTHONY
THE PARTITION OF AFRICA ON PAPER, 1879-1891.
IN AFRICA SINCE 1800, CAMBRIDGE, CAMBRIDGE UNIVERSITY PRESS,
1967, PP 103-114

033,

ATMORE ANTHONY
    OLIVER ROLAND   ATMORE ANTHONY
    WEST AFRICA BEFORE THE COLONIAL PERIOD, 1800-1875.
    IN AFRICA SINCE 1800, CAMBRIDGE, CAMBRIDGE UNIVERSITY PRESS,
    1967, PP 29-42
    026,

AUBAME HILAIRE
    AUBAME HILAIRE
    RENAISSANCE GABONAISE, PROGRAMME ET REGROUPEMENT DES
    VILLAGES.
    BRAZZAVILLE, IMPRIMERIE OFFICIELLE, 1947
    112-04,

AUSTEN RALPH A
    AUSTEN RALPH A
    NORTHWEST TANZANIA UNDER GERMAN AND BRITISH RULE.
    NEW HAVEN, CONN. (YALE), MCGILL-QUEEN'S PRESS, 1969
    035,136-02,

    AUSTEN RALPH A
    NOTES ON THE PRE-HISTORY OF TANU.
    MAKERERE JOURNAL 9 1963 PP 1-6
    055,

AUSTIN DENNIS
    AUSTIN DENNIS
    POLITICAL CONFLICT IN AFRICA.
    GOVERNMENT AND OPPOSITION CLEVELAND 2 NO 4 1968 PP 487-490
    064,

    AUSTIN DENNIS
    BRITAIN AND SOUTH AFRICA.
    LONDON, OXFORD UNIVERSITY PRESS, 1966
    032, 033, 132-09,

    AUSTIN DENNIS
    ELECTIONS IN AN AFRICAN RURAL AREA.
    IN WILLIAM J HANNA (ED), INDEPENDENT BLACK AFRICA, CHICAGO,
    RAND MCNALLY, 1964, PP 341-362
    063,114-07,

    AUSTIN DENNIS
    POLITICS IN GHANA 1946-1960.
    LONDON, OXFORD UNIVERSITY PRESS, 1964
    055,114-07,

    AUSTIN DENNIS
    THE UNCERTAIN FRONTIER-GHANA-TOGO
    JOURNAL OF MODERN AFRICAN STUDIES 1 1963 PP 139-145
    059,

AVRAMOVIC D
    AVRAMOVIC D
    POSTWAR ECONOMIC GROWTH FOR LOW INCOME COUNTRIES.
    WASHINGTON,D C,INTERNATIONAL BANK FOR RECONSTRUCTION AND
    DEVELOPMENT, 1963 P 20
    073,

AWA EME O
    AWA EME O
    FEDERAL GOVERNMENT IN NIGERIA.
    BERKELEY,UNIVERSITY OF CALIFORNIA PRESS,1964
    061,128-07,

AWE B
    LLOYD PETER C   MABOGUNJE AKIN L   AWE B
    THE CITY OF IBADAN-- A SYMPOSIUM ON ITS STRUCTURE AND
    DEVELOPMENT.
    CAMBRIDGE,CAMBRIDGE UNIVERSITY PRESS,1967
    026,045,128-05,

AWOLOWO OBAFEMI
    AWOLOWO OBAFEMI
    AWO--THE AUTOBIOGRAPHY OF CHIEF OBAFEMI AWOLOWO.
    CAMBRIDGE, CAMBRIDGE UNIVERSITY PRESS, 1960
    044,128-04,

    AWOLOWO OBAFEMI
    PATH TO NIGERIAN FREEDOM.
    LONDON, FABER, 1966
    055,128-04,

    AWOLOWO OBAFEMI
    THE PEOPLES REPUBLIC.
    NIGERIA, OXFORD UNIVERSITY PRESS, 1969
    068,128-04,

    AWOLOWO OBAFEMI
    THOUGHTS ON NIGERIAN CONSTITUTION.
    NIGERIA, OXFORD UNIVERSITY PRESS,1966
    054,068,128-04,

    AWOLOWO OBAFEMI
    THE PATH TO ECONOMIC FREEDOM IN DEVELOPING COUNTRIES.
    LECTURE DELIVERED AT THE UNIVERSITY OF LAGOS ON MARCH 15TH,
    1968, 23 PAGES, PAMPHLET
    091,128-04,

AXELSON E
    AXELSON E   ED
    SOUTH AFRICAN EXPLORERS
    LONDON, OXFORD UNIVERSITY PRESS, 1954
    027,

AYANDELE E A
    AYANDELE E A
    NATIONALIST MOVEMENTS IN NORTH AFRICA CHP 12.
    IN JC ANENE AND GODFREY BROWN,AFRICA IN THE 19TH AND 20TH
    CENTURIES,LONDON, NELSON IUP, 1966
    054,

    AYANDELE E A
    THE MISSIONARY IMPACT ON MODERN NIGERIA.
    LONDON, LONGMANS, 1964
    050,

AYDELOTTE W O

AYDELOTTE W O
BISMARCK AND THE BRITISH COLONIAL POLICY-- THE PROBLEM OF
SOUTHWEST AFRICA 1883-1885.
PHILADELPHIA,UNIVERSITY OF PENNSYLVANIA PRESS,1937
033,

AZEVEDO
BOXER CHARLES RALPH DE AZEVEDO CARLOS
FORT JESUS AND THE PORTUGESE IN MOMBASA 1593-1729
LONDON,HOLLIS AND CARTER,1960
023,027,

AZIKIWE NNAMDI
AZIKIWE NNAMDI
THE FUTURE OF PAN-AFRICANISM.
PRESENCE AFRICAINE FIRST TRIMESTER 1962 PP 5-31
079,128-04,

AZIKIWE NNAMDI
ETHICS OF COLONIAL IMPERIALISM.
JOURNAL OF NEGRO HISTORY 16 JULY 1931 PP 287-308
035,128-04,

AZIKIWE NNAMDI
IN DEFENCE OF LIBERIA.
JOURNAL OF NEGRO HISTORY 17 JANUARY 1932 PP 30-49
029,119-02,128-04,

AZIKIWE NNAMDI
REALITIES OF AFRICAN UNITY.
AFRICAN FORUM I 1 1965 PP 7-22
079,128-04,

AZIKIWE NNAMDI
NIGERIAN POLITICAL INSTITUTIONS.
JOURNAL OF NEGRO HISTORY 14 1929 PP 328-340
060,128-04,

AZIKIWE NNAMDI
THE DEVELOPMENT OF POLITICAL PARTIES IN NIGERIA.
LONDON 1957 (1792 OFFICE OF THE COMMISSIONER IN THE U K
FOR THE EASTERN REGION OF NIGERIA)
061,128-04,

AZIKIWE NNAMDI
ZIK-- A SELECTION FROM THE SPEECHES OF DOCTOR NNAMDI AZIKIWE
CAMBRIDGE,ENGLAND,CAMBRIDGE UNIVERSITY PRESS,1961
044,060,091,096,128-04,

AZIKIWE NNAMDI
TRIBALISM--A PRAGMATIC INSTRUMENT FOR NATIONAL UNITY.
LECTURE DELIVERED UNIVERSITY OF NIGERIA, FRIDAY, MAY 15TH,
1964, 30 PAGES, PAMPHLET
091,128-04,

AZIKIWE NNAMDI
LIBERIA IN WORLD POLITICS.
LONDON,A H STOCKWELL,1934
029,119-02,128-04,

B

BA AMADOU HAMPATE
  BA AMADOU HAMPATE
  THE FULBE OR FULANI OF MALI AND THEIR CULTURE
  ABBIA, JULY-DECEMBER 1966, NO. 14-15, PP. 55-87
  013,

  BA AMADOU HAMPATE
  L'ISLAM ET L'AFRIQUE NOIRE (ISLAM AND BLACK AFRICA).
  IN COLLOQUE SUR LES RELIGIONS, ABIDJAN, APRIL, 1961, PARIS,
  PRESENCE AFRICAINE, 1962, PP 101-118
  052,

  BA AMADOU HAMPATE
  ANIMISME EN SAVANE AFRICAINE (ANIMISM IN THE AFRICAN
  SAVANAH).
  IN RENCONTRES INTERNATIONALES DE BOUAKE, LES RELIGIONS
  AFRICAINES TRADITIONNELLES, PARIS, EDITIONS DU SEUIL, 1965,
  PP 33-55
  013,

  BA AMADOU HAMPATE   DAGET JACQUES
  L'EMPIRE PEUL DE MACINA 1818-1853. (THE FULANI EMPIRE OF
  MACINA 1818-1853).
  BAMAKO,INSTITUT FRANCAIS D'AFRIQUE NOIRE, CENTRE DU SOUDAN,
  ETUDES SOUDANAISES 3 1962
  024,123-02,

  BA AMADOU HAMPATE
  L'EMPIRE PEUL DE MACINA 1818-1853.
  BAMAKO, INSTITUT FRANCAIS D'AFRIQUE NOIRE, CENTRE DU SOUDAN
  1955
  099,123-02,

  BA AMADOU HAMPATE   DIETERLEN GERMAINE
  KOUMEN--TEXTE INITIATIQUE DES PASTEURS PEULS.
  PARIS, MOUTON ET CIE, 1961
  123-01,

  BA AMADOU HAMPATE   CARDAIRE MARCEL
  TIERNO BOKAR, LE SAGE DE BANDIAGARA.
  PARIS, PRESENCE AFRICAINE, 1957
  123-02,

BA OUMAR
  BA OUMAR
  DIALOGUE OU D'UNE RIVE A L'AUTRE (POEMES).
  SAINT-LOUIS, IFAN, (ETUDES MAURITANIENNES), N.D.
  124-10,

  BA OUMAR
  FAUT-IL GARDER LA LANGUE FRANCAISE.
  SAINT-LOUIS, IFAN, 1966
  124-10,

  BA OUMAR

MON MEILLEUR CHEF DE CANTON--TEMOIGNAGE.
LYÓN, IMP. NICOLON, 1966
124-10,

BA OUMAR
  BA OUMAR
  NOTES SUR LA DEMOCRATIE EN PAYS TOUCOULEUR.
  SAINT-LOUIS, IFAN, 1966
  124-10,

  BA OUMAR
  POEMES PEUL MODERNES.
  NOUAKCHOTT, IMP. MAURITANIENNE, 1965
  124-10,

  BA OUMAR
  PRESQUE GRIFFONAGES OU LA FRANCOPHONIE.
  SAINT-LOUIS, IFAN, 1966
  124-10,

BAADE HANS W
  BAADE HANS W   ED
  AFRICAN LAW-- NEW LAW FOR NEW NATIONS.
  DOBBS FERRY, NEW YORK, OCEANA PUBLICATIONS, 1963
  067,

BABALOLA S A
  BABALOLA S A
  THE CONTENT AND FORM OF YORUBA IJALA.
  LONDON, OXFORD UNIVERSITY PRESS, 1966
  012,128-01,

BACHRACH PETER
  BACHRACH PETER
  THE THEORY OF DEMOCRATIC ELITISM.
  BOSTON, LITTLE, BROWN AND COMPANY, 1966
  044,

BADOUIN R
  BADOUIN R
  LES MODIFICATIONS DES STRUCTURES ECONOMIQUES INTERNES DANS
  LES ETATS DE L'AFRIQUE OCCIDENTAL (MODIFICATIONS OF THE
  INTERNAL ECONOMIC STRUCTURES OF THE WEST AFRICAN STATES).
  ANNALES AFRICAINES 1960 PP 61-82
  073,

BAECK LOUIS
  BAECK LOUIS
  ETUDE SOCIO-ECONOMIQUE DU CENTRE EXTRA COUTUMIER D≠USUMBURA.
  BRUXELLES, ACADEMY OF RORAL SCIENCES COLONIALES 1957
  103-05,

  BAECK LOUIS
  LEOPOLDVILLE--PHENOMENE URBAIN AFRICAIN.
  ZAIRE, X, 1956.
  108-05,

BAETA C G
  BAETA C G   ED
  CHRISTIANITY IN TROPICAL AFRICA.

LONDON,OXFORD UNIVERSITY PRESS, 1968
050,

BAFFOUR R P
   BAFFOUR R P
   SCIENCE AND TECHNOLOGY IN RELATION TO AFRICA'S DEVELOPMENT.
   IN LALAGE BOWN AND MICHAEL CROWDER (EDS.). PROCEEDINGS OF
   THE FIRST INTERNATIONAL CONGRESS OF AFRICANISTS, ACCRA,
   1962, LONDON, LONGMANS, 1964, PP 301-308
   037,075,

BAHOKEN
   BAHOKEN JEAN CALVIN
   LA CONTRIBUTION DES RELIGIONS A L'EXPRESSION CULTURELLE DE
   LA PERSONNALITE AFRICAINE (THE CONTRIBUTION OF RELIGION TO
   THE CULTURAL EXPRESSION OF THE AFRICAN PERSONALITY).
   IN COLLOQUE SUR LES RELIGIONS, ABIDJAN, APRIL, 1961, PARIS,
   PRESENCE AFRICAINE, 1962, PP 155-168
   013,039,

   BAHOKEN JEAN CALVIN
   CLAIRIERES METAPHYSIQUES AFRICAINES. ESSAI SUR LA
   PHILOSOPHIE ET LA RELIGION CHEZ LES BANTU DU SUB-CAMEROUN-
   LA CONNAISSANCE DE NYAMBEO L'OETRE SUPREME ET LES INFLUENCES
   DES IDEES PHILOSOPHIQUES AT RELIGIEUSES SUR LA SOCIETE ET
   LES INSTITUTIONS.
   PARIS, PRESENCE AFRICAINE, 1967
   104-01,

BAKER S J K
   BAKER S J K
   THE EAST AFRICAN ENVIRONMENT.
   HISTORY OF EAST AFRICA 1 CHAPTER 1 1963 PP 1-22
   069,

   BAKER S J K
   THE POPULATION GEOGRAPHY OF EAST AFRICA.
   EAST AFRICAN GEOGRAPHICAL REVIEW KAMPALA APRIL 1963 PP 1-6
   069,

BALA MBARGA HENRI
   BALA MBARGA HENRI
   PROBLEMES AFRICAINS DE L EDUCATION PRECEDE DE L#ETUDE DU
   CAS DU CAMEROUN.
   PARIS, HACHETTE, 1962
   104-03,

BALANDIER GEORGES
   BALANDIER GEORGES
   AMBIGUOUS AFRICA-CULTURES IN COLLISION
   NEW YORK, MERIDIAN BOOKS, 1966
   098,

   BALANDIER GEORGES
   MESSIANISMES ET NATIONALISMES EN AFRIQUE NOIRE (MESSIANIC
   CULTS AND NATIONALISM IN BLACK AFRICA).
   CAHIERS INTERNATIONAUX DE SOCIOLOGIE 14 1953 PP41-65(ENGLISH
   TRANSLATION-- VANDENBERGHE)
   050,051,

BALANDIER GEORGES
LA SITUATION COLONIALE-- APPROCHE THEORETIQUE
(THE COLONIAL SITUATION-- THEORETICAL APPROACH).
CAHIERS INTERNATIONAUX DE SOCIOLOGIE 11 1951 PP 44-79.
IN PIERRE VAN DEN BERGHE, AFRICA-- SOCIAL PROBLEMS OF
035,

BALANDIER GEORGES
BALANDIER GEORGES
DESEQUILIBRES SOCIO-CULTURELS ET MODERNISATION DES PAYS
SOUS-DEVELOPEES (SOCIO-CULTURAL DISEQUILIBRIUMS AND
MODERNIZATION OF THE UNDERDEVELOPED COUNTRIES).
CAHIERS INTERNATIONAUX DE SOCIOLOGIE 20 JANUARY-JUNE 1956
PP 30-44
074,

BALANDIER GEORGES
AFRICANISM CONFRONTED WITH PROBLEMS OF POLITICAL
ANTHROPOLOGY AND POLITICAL SOCIOLOGY.
IN LALAGE BOWN AND MICHAEL CROWDER (EDS.), PROCEEDINGS OF
THE FIRST INTERNATIONAL CONGRESS OF AFRICANISTS, ACCRA,
1962, LONDON, LONGMANS, 1964, PP 267-271
100,

BALANDIER GEORGES
OBSERVATIONS ON THE POLITICAL REGROUPING OF AFRICA.
IN WILLIAM J HANNA (ED), INDEPENDENT BLACK AFRICA, CHICAGO,
RAND MCNALLY, 1964, PP 588-594
079,

BALANDIER GEORGES
SOCIOLOGIE ACTUELLE DE L'AFRIQUE NOIRE(SOCIOLOGY OF BLACK
AFRICA).
PARIS, PRESSES UNIVERSITAIRES DE FRANCE, 1955 (NEW YORK,
1969)
099,

BALANDIER GEORGES
DAILY LIFE IN THE KINGDOM OF THE CONGO- TRANS FROM THE
FRENCH BY H WEAVER
NEW YORK, PANTHEON BOOKS, 1968
028,

BALANDIER GEORGES
CONTRIBUTION A L'ETUDE DES NATIONALISMES EN AFRIQUE NOIRE
(CONTRIBUTIONS TO THE STUDY OF NATIONALISM IN BLACK AFRICA).
ZAIRE 8 1954 PP 379-389
055,

BALANDIER GEORGES
ASPECTS DE L'EVOLUTION SOCIALE CHEZ LES FANG
(ASPECTS OF SOCIAL EVOLUTION AMONG THE FANG).
CAHIERS INTERNATIONAUX DE SOCIOLOGIE 9 1950 PP 76-106
038,112-03,

BALANDIER GEORGES   PAUVERT J C
LES VILLAGES GABONAIS-- ASPECTS DEMOGRAPHIQUES, ECONOMIQUES
SOCIOLOGIQUES, PROJETS DE MODERNISATION (GABON VILLAGES--
DEMOGRAPHIC, ECONOMIC AND SOCIOLOGICAL ASPECTS, PROJECTS
OF MODERNIZATION).

BRAZZAVILLE, INSTITUT DES ETUDES CONTRFICAINES, 1952
070,112-03,

BALDWIN JAMES
    BALDWIN JAMES
    THE FIRE NEXT TIME.
    NEW YORK, DIAL PRESS, 1963
    094,

    BALDWIN JAMES
    TELL ME HOW LONG THE TRAIN'S BEEN GONE.
    NEW YORK, THE DIAL PRESS, 1968
    094,

    BALDWIN JAMES
    NOBODY KNOWS MY NAME.
    NEW YORK, THE DIAL PRESS, 1961
    094,

BALDWIN K D S
    BALDWIN K D S
    THE MARKETING OF COCOA IN WESTERN NIGERIA, WITH SPECIAL
    REFERENCE TO THE POSITION OF MIDDLEMEN.
    LONDON, OXFORD UNIVERSITY PRESS, 1954
    070,128-08,

    GALLETTI R   BALDWIN K D S   DINA I O
    NIGERIAN COCOA FARMERS-- AN ECONOMIC SURVEY OF YORUBA
    COCOA FARMING FAMILIES.
    LONDON, OXFORD UNIVERSITY PRESS, 1956
    070,128-08,

BALEWA ABUBAKAR T
    BALEWA ABUBAKAR T
    NIGERIA LOOKS AHEAD.
    IN PHILIP W QUIGG (ED.), AFRICA, NEW YORK, PRAEGER, 1964
    PP 302-313
    060,128-04,

BALLARD JOHN A
    BALLARD JOHN A
    FOUR EQUATORIAL STATES--THE CONGO, GABON, CENTRAL AFRICAN
    REPUBLIC, CHAD.
    IN GWENDOLEN M CARTER (ED.), NATIONAL UNITY AND REGIONALISM
    IN EIGHT AFRICAN STATES, ITHACA, CORNELL UNIVERSITY PRESS,
    1966, PP 231-329
    105-06,106-06,107-06,112-06,

    BALLARD JOHN A
    EQUATORIAL AFRICA
    IN KRITZECK AND LEWIS, PP 278-286
    105-03,106-03,107-03,112-03,

BALLINGER MARGARET
    BALLINGER MARGARET
    FROM UNION TO APARTHEID--A TREK TO ISOLATION.
    NEW YORK, PRAEGER PUBLISHERS, 1969
    089,132-02,

BAMBOTE PIERRE

BAMBOTE PIERRE
LE DUR AVENIR.
BANGUI, IMP. CENTRALE D'AFRIQUE, 1965
105-10,

BAMBOTE PIERRE
BAMBOTE PIERRE
LA POESIE EST DANS L'HISTOIRE.
PARIS, OSWALD, 1960
105-10,

BANDA HASTINGS K
BANDA HASTINGS K   NKUMBULA HARRY M
FEDERATION IN CENTRAL AFRICA.
LONDON, 1951
078,122-04,

BANDI HANS G
BANDI HANS G   ET-AL
THE ART OF THE STONE AGE.   (TRANS BY ANN E KEEP)
LONDON, METHUEN; NEW YORK, ART OF THE WORLD SERIES, 1961
014,

BANDINEL JAMES
BANDINEL JAMES
SOME ACCOUNT OF THE TRADE IN SLAVES FROM AFRICA AS
CONNECTED WITH EUROPE AND AMERICA.
LONDON, LONGMAN, BROWN, 1842
028,

BANEFIELD JANE
BANEFIELD JANE
THE STRUCTURE AND ADMINISTRATION OF THE EAST AFRICAN COMMON
SERVICES ORGANIZATION.
IN COLIN LEYS AND P ROBSON (EDS), FEDERATION IN EAST AFRICA--
OPPORTUNITIES AND PROBLEMS, NAIROBI, OXFORD UNIVERSITY PRESS,
1965, PP 30-40
078,117-09,136-09,139-09,

BANFIELD EDWARD C
BANFIELD EDWARD C
THE POLITICAL IMPLICATIONS OF METROPOLITAN GROWTH.
DAEDALUS, THE JOURNAL OF THE AMERICAN ACADEMY OF ARTS AND
SCIENCES 90 WINTER 1960 PP 61-78 (BOBBS-MERRILL REPRINT S-7)
047,

BANTON MICHAEL P
BANTON MICHAEL P
AFRICAN PROPHETS.
RACE 5 OCTOBER 1963 PP 42-55
051,

BANTON MICHAEL P   DOSSER D G M
THE BALANCE BETWEEN SOCIAL AND ECONOMIC DEVELOPMENT
IN AFRICA SOUTH OF THE SAHARA.
INFORMATION 27 1961 PP 5-23
074,

BANTON MICHAEL P
ECONOMIC DEVELOPMENT AND SOCIAL CHANGE IN SIERRA LEONE.

ECONOMIC DEVELOPMENT AND CULTURAL CHANGE 2 1953 PP 135-138
073,131-08,

BANTON MICHAEL P
    BANTON MICHAEL P
    THE ORIGINS OF TRIBAL ADMINISTRATION IN FREETOWN.
    SIERRA LEONE STUDIES 2 1954 PP 109-119
    046,131-05,

    BANTON MICHAEL P
    WEST AFRICAN CITY--A STUDY OF TRIBAL LIFE IN FREETOWN.
    LONDON, OXFORD UNIVERSITY PRESS, 1957
    045,131-05,

    BANTON MICHAEL P   ED
    ANTHROPOLOGICAL APPROACHES TO THE STUDY OF RELIGION.
    ASSOCIATION OF SOCIAL ANTHROPOLOGISTS MONOGRAPHS 3
    LONDON, TAVISTOCK PUBLICATION
    NEW YORK, PRAEGER, 1966
    013,

    BANTON MICHAEL P
    ROLES-- AN INTRODUCTION TO THE STUDY OF SOCIAL RELATIONS.
    NEW YORK, BASIC BOOKS, 1965
    098,

    BANTON MICHAEL P
    RACE RELATIONS.
    LONDON, TAVISTOCK, 1968
    006,030,089,

BARATTE THERESE
    BARATTE THERESE
    BIBLIOGRAPHIE, AUTEURS AFRICAINS ET MALGACHES DE LANGUE
    FRANCAISE (BIBLIOGRAPHY, FRENCH-SPEAKING AFRICAN AND MALA-
    GASY AUTHORS).
    PARIS, OFFICE DE COOPERATION RADIOPHONIQUE, 1968
    090,

BARBER C R
    BARBER C R
    IGBO-ORA--A TOWN IN TRANSITION.
    NIGERIA, OXFORD UNIVERSITY PRESS, 1966
    128-05,

BARBER WILLIAM J
    BARBER WILLIAM J
    THE AGRICULTURAL ECONOMY OF EAST AFRICA.
    CAMBRIDGE, HARVARD UNIVERSITY PRESS, 1964
    070,

    BARBER WILLIAM J
    ECONOMIC RATIONALITY AND BEHAVIOR PATTERNS IN AN
    UNDERDEVELOPED AREA--A CASE STUDY OF AFRICAN ECONOMICS IN
    THE RHODESIAS.
    ENONOMIC DEVELOPMENT AND CULTURAL CHANGE 8 1960 PP 237-251
    073,122-08,142-08,145-08,

    BARBER WILLIAM J
    URBANISATION AND ECONOMIC GROWTH--THE CASES OF TWO WHITE

SETTLER TERRITORIES.
IN THE CITY IN MODERN AFRICA, HORACE MINER (ED), NEW YORK,
FREDERICK A. PRAEGER, 1967
142-05,

BARBERA MARIO
    BARBERA MARIO   HAAS ERNST B
    THE OPERATIONALIZATION OF SOME VARIABLES RELATED TO REGIONAL
    INTEGRATION--A RESEARCH NOTE.
    INTERNATIONAL ORGANIZATION, VOL. XXIII, NO. 1, 1969, PP. 150
    160
    078,

BARBICHON G
    BARBICHON G
    THE DIFFUSION OF SCIENTIFIC AND TECHNICAL KNOWLEDGE--
    PROCEEDINGS OF THE IBADAN CONFERENCE ON THE PROBLEMS OF
    SOCIAL PSYCHOLOGY IN DEVELOPING NATIONS.
    JOURNAL OF SOCIAL ISSUES 12 1966, 1 1967
    075,

BARBOUR FLOYD B
    BARBOUR FLOYD B
    BLACK POWER REVOLT, ESSAYS.
    BOSTON, PORTER SARGENT, 1968
    095,

    BARBOUR FLOYD B   ED
    THE BLACK POWER REVOLT
    NEW YORK, MACMILLAN, 1969
    095,

BARBOUR K M
    BARBOUR K M   PROTHERO R MANSELL   EDS
    ESSAYS ON AFRICAN POPULATION.
    LONDON, ROUTLEDGE AND KEGAN PAUL, 1961
    069,074,

    BARBOUR K M
    THE REPUBLIC OF THE SUDAN.
    LONDON, UNIVERSITY OF LONDON PRESS, 1961
    134-11,

BARKER
    BARKER
    SWAZILAND
    NEW YORK, BRITISH INFORMATION SERVICE, CORONA LIBRARY, 1965
    135-11,

BARKER D
    BARKER D
    BRITISH AID TO DEVELOPING NATIONS.
    LONDON, H.M.S.O., 1964
    082,

BARNES JAMES A
    BARNES JAMES A
    POLITICS IN A CHANGING SOCIETY-- A POLITICAL HISTORY OF THE
    FORT JAMESON NGONI.
    NEW YORK, OXFORD UNIVERSITY PRESS, 1954

038,142-03,

BARNES JAMES A
    BARNES JAMES A
    SOME ASPECTS OF POLITICAL DEVELOPMENT AMONG THE FORT
    JAMESON NGONI.
    AFRICAN STUDIES 7 1948 PP 99-109
    061,142-07,

    BARNES JAMES A
    THE FORT JAMESON NGONI.
    IN ELIZABETH COLSON AND MAX GLUCKMAN (EDS), SEVEN TRIBES OF
    BRITISH CENTRAL AFRICA, LONDON, OXFORD UNIVERSITY PRESS,
    1951
    142-01,

BARNETT DONALD
    BARNETT DONALD
    ANGOLA--REPORT FROM HANOI II.
    RAMPARTS, APRIL 1969, PP. 49-54
    087,

BARNWELL PATRICK J
    BARNWELL PATRICK J TOUSSAINT AUGUSTE
    A SHORT HISTORY OF MAURITIUS
    NEW YORK AND LONDON, LONGMANS, GREEN, FOR THE GOVERNMENT OF
    MAURITIUS, 1949
    125-02,

BARRETT DAVID B
    BARRETT DAVID B
    SCHISM AND RENEWAL IN AFRICA--AN ANALYSIS OF SIX THOUSAND
    CONTEMPORARY RELIGIOUS MOVEMENTS.
    NAIROBI, OXFORD UNIVERSITY PRESS, 1968
    051,

    BARRETT DAVID B
    CHURCH GROWTH AND INDEPENDENCY AS ORGANIC PHENOMENA-- AN
    ANALYSIS OF TWO HUNDRED AFRICAN TRIBES.
    IN C G BAETA (ED), CHRISTIANITY IN TROPICAL AFRICA, LONDON,
    OXFORD UNIVERSITY PRESS, 1968, PP 269-288
    051,

BARRINGTON KAYE
    BARRINGTON KAYE
    BRINGING UP CHILDREN IN GHANA.
    LONDON, GEORGE ALLEN AND UNWIN, 1962
    008,114-01,

BARRY H
    BARRY H
    REGIONAL AND WORLDWIDE VARIATIONS IN CULTURE.
    ETHNOLOGY 7 1968 PP 207-217
    040,

BARTH HEINRICH
    BARTH HEINRICH
    TRAVELS AND DISCOVERIES IN NORTH AND CENTRAL AFRICA 1849-
    1855
    LONDON, CASS, 1968, 3 VOLUMES

027,099,

BARTON FRANK
    BARTON FRANK
    THE PRESS IN AFRICA
    NAIROBI, EAST AFRICA PUBLISHING HOUSE, 1966
    049,

BASCOM WILLIAM R
    BASCOM WILLIAM R   HERSKOVITS MELVILLE J
    CONTINUITY AND CHANGE IN AFRICAN CULTURES.
    CHICAGO, UNIVERSITY OF CHICAGO PRESS, 1962
    038,

    BASCOM WILLIAM R
    FOLKLORE AND LITERATURE.
    IN ROBERT A LYSTAD (ED), THE AFRICAN WORLD, NEW YORK,
    PREAGER, 1965, PP 469-492
    012,

    BASCOM WILLIAM R   HERSKOVITS MELVILLE J
    THE PROBLEM OF STABILITY AND CHANGE IN AFRICAN CULTURE
    CHAPTER 1.
    IN CONTINUITY AND CHANGE IN AFRICAN CULTURES, CHICAGO,
    UNIVERSITY OF CHICAGO PRESS, 1962, PP 1-14
    038,

    BASCOM WILLIAM R
    AFRICAN ARTS EXHIBITION CATALOGUE
    BERKELEY, UNIVERSITY OF CALIFORNIA PRESS, 1967
    014,

    BASCOM WILLIAM R
    THE URBAN AFRICAN AND HIS WORLD.
    CAHIERS D'ETUDES AFRICAINES 4 APRIL 1963 PP 163-185
    046,

    BASCOM WILLIAM R
    TRIBALISM NATIONALISM AND PAN-AFRICANISM.
    ANNALS OF THE AMERICAN ACADEMY OF POLITICAL AND SOCIAL
    SCIENCE PHILADELPHIA JULY 1962 PP 21-29
    055,

BASS ELIZABETH
    BASS ROBERT   BASS ELIZABETH
    EASTERN EUROPE
    IN BRZEZINSKI (ED), AFRICA AND THE COMMUNIST WORLD,
    STANFORD, UNIVERSITY PRESS, 1963 PP 84-115
    084,

BASS ROBERT
    BASS ROBERT   BASS ELIZABETH
    EASTERN EUROPE
    IN BRZEZINSKI (ED) AFRICA AND THE COMMUNIST WORLD
    STANFORD UNIVERSITY PRESS 1963 PP 84-115
    084,

BASSIR OLUMBE
    BASSIR OLUMBE
    LE QUAKERISME ET LA PERSONNALITE AFRICAINE (THE QUAKER FAITH

AND THE AFRICAN PERSONALITY).
COLLOQUE SUR LES RELIGIONS, ABIDJAN, APRIL, 1961, PARIS,
PRESENCE AFRICAINE, 1962, PP 173-178
050,

BASTIAAN
    FORTMAN BASTIAAN DE ED
    AFTER MULUNGUSHI--THE ECONOMICS OF ZAMBIAN HUMANISM.
    KENYA, EAST AFRICAN PUBLISHING HOUSE, 1969
    060,142-03,

BASTIDE ROGER
    BASTIDE ROGER
    VARIATIONS ON NEGRITUDE.
    PRESENCE AFRICAINE 36 1ST TRIMESTRE 1961 PP 7-17
    ALSO ALBERT BERRIAN RICHARD LONG, EDS, NEGRITUDE-- ESSAYS AND
    STUDIES, HAMPTON, VIRGINIA, HAMPTON INSTITUTE PRESS, 1967, PP
    69-78
    054,

    BASTIDE ROGER
    LES AMERICQUES NOIRES-- LES CIVILIXATIONS (THE BLACK AMERI-
    CAS-- THE CIVILIZATIONS).
    AFRICAINES DANS LE NOUVEAU MONDE PARIS PAYOT 1967
    030,

    BASTIDE ROGER
    RELIGIONS AFRICAINES ET STRUCTURES DE CIVILISATION (AFRICAN
    RELIGIONS AND STRUCTURES OF CIVILISATION).
    PRESENCE AFRICAINE, NO. 66, 2ND QUARTER, 1968, PP. 98-111
    013,

BASTIN
    BASTIN MARIE-LOUISE
    ART DECORATIF TSHOKWE. (CHOKWE DECORATIVE ART).
    LISBON, COMPANHIA DE DIAMANTES DE ANGOLA 1961 2 VOLUMES
    014,

BATES M L
    BATES M L
    TANGANYIKA.
    IN G.M. CARTER (ED) AFRICAN ONE-PARTY STATES, ITHACA,
    CORNELL UNIVERSITY PRESS, 1962
    136-07,

BATTUTA IBN
    BATTUTA IBN
    THE TRAVELS OF IBN BATTUTA. (TRANS BY HAR GIBB)
    CAMBRIDGE, CAMBRIDGE UNIVERSITY PRESS, 1958
    099,

BAUER P T
    BAUER P T
    WEST AFRICAN TRADE-- A STUDY OF COMPETITION, OLIGOPOLY
    AND MONOPOLY IN A CHANGING ECONOMY.
    CAMBRIDGE, CAMBRIDGE UNIVERSITY PRESS, 1954
    078,

BAULIN JACQUES
    BAULIN JACQUES

THE ARAB ROLE IN AFRICA.
BALTIMORE 1962
086,

BAUMANN H
   BAUMANN H   WESTERMANN D
   LES PEUPLES LES CIVILISATIONS DE L AFRIQUE NOIRE (THE
   PEOPLES AND THE CIVILIZATIONS OF BLACK AFRICA).
   PARIS, PAYOT, 1962
   003,

BAXTER P T W
   BAXTER P T W
   ACCEPTANCE AND REJECTION OF ISLAM AMONG THE BORAN OF THE
   NORTHERN FRONTIER DISTRICT OF KENYA.
   IN LEWIS, ISLAM IN TROPICAL AFRICA, LONDON, OXFORD UNIVERSIT
   PRESS, 1966, P. 233-252
   117-03,

BAYLEY DAVID H
   BAYLEY DAVID H
   PUBLIC LIBERTIES IN THE NEW STATES.
   CHICAGO, RAND MCNALLY AND COMPANY, 1964
   068,

BEACHEY R W
   BEACHEY R W
   THE ARMS TRADE IN EAST AFRICA IN THE LATE
   NINETEENTH CENTURY.
   JOURNAL OF AFRICAN HISTORY 3 1962 PP 451-467
   034,

BEATTIE J H M
   BEATTIE J H M
   ETHNOGRAPHIC AND SOCIOLOGICAL RESEARCH IN EAST AFRICA.
   AFRICA LONDON 26 1956 PP 265-276
   100,

   BEATTIE J H M
   CHECKS ON THE ABUSE OF POLITICAL POWER IN SOME AFRICAN
   STATES-- A PRELIMINARY FRAMEWORK FOR ANALYSIS.
   SOCIOLOGUS 9 1959 PP 97-115
   009,

   BEATTIE J H M   MIDDLETON JOHN   EDS
   SPIRIT MEDIUMSHIP AND SOCIETY IN AFRICA
   NEW YORK, AFRICANA PUBLISHING CORPORATION, 1969
   013,

   BEATTIE J H M
   THE NYORO.
   IN AUDREY I. RICHARDS (ED), EAST AFRICAN CHIEFS, LONDON,
   FABER AND FABER, 1960, PP. 98-123
   139-01,

BEAVER S H
   GOUROU PIERRE   BEAVER S H   LABORDE E D
   THE TROPICAL WORLD-- ITS SOCIAL AND ECONOMIC CONDITIONS AND
   ITS FUTURE STATUS.
   LONDON, LONGMANS, 4TH EDITION, 1966

069,075,

BEBEY F
   BEBEY F
   MUSIQUE DE L'AFRIQUE--UN DISQUE D'ACCOMPAGNEMENT (MUSIC OF
   AFRICA--WITH AN ACCOMPANYING RECORD).
   PARIS, HORIZONS DE FRANCE, NEW YORK, INTERNATIONAL
   UNIVERSITY BOOKSELLERS, 1969
   015,

BEBNONE PALOU
   BEBNONE PALOU
   KALTOUMA--PIECE EN UN ACTE.
   PARIS, L'AVANT-SCENE-THEATRE, 1965
   106-10,

BECKER PETER
   BECKER PETER
   RULE OF FEAR,THE LIFE AND TIMES OF DINGANE KING OF THE ZULU
   LONDON, LONGMANS, GREEN, 1964
   031,132-02,

BECKINGHAM C F
   BECKINGHAM C F   HUNTINGFORD G W B
   PRESTER JOHN OF THE INDIES.
   LONDON, 1961
   027,

BECKMANN MARTIN J
   BECKMANN MARTIN J
   CITY HIERARCHIES AND DISTRIBUTION OF CITY SIZE.
   ECONOMIC DEVELOPMENT AND CULTURAL CHANGE 6 APRIL 1958
   B-M REPRINT S-338
   047,

BEETHAM T A
   BEETHAM T A
   CHRISTIANITY AND THE NEW AFRICA.
   LONDON, PALL MALL PRESS, 1967
   050,

BEHRMAN LUCY
   BEHRMAN LUCY
   MUSLIM BROTHERHOODS AND POLITICS IN SENEGAL
   CAMBRIDGE, HARVARD UNIVERSITY PRESS, 1970
   052,130-03,

BEIDELMAN T O
   BEIDELMAN T O
   THE MATRILINEAL PEOPLES OF EASTERN TANZANIA-ZARAMO,LIGURU,
   KAGURU,NGULU,ETC.
   LONDON, INTERNATIONAL AFRICAN INSTITUTE, 1967
   136-01,

BEIER ULLI
   BEIER ULLI   ED
   INTRODUCTION TO AFRICAN LITERATURE-- AN ANTHOLOGY OF
   CRITICAL WRITING FROM BLACK ORPHEUS.
   EVANSTON, NORTHWESTERN UNIVERSITY PRESS, 1967
   090,

BEIER ULLI
   BEIER ULLI
   CONTEMPORARY ART IN AFRICA.
   NEW YORK, PRAEGER PUBLISHERS, 1968
   093,

   BEIER ULLI   ED
   POLITICAL SPIDER--AN ANTHOLOGY OF STORIES FROM   BLACK
   ORPHEUS .
   NEW YORK, AFRICANA PUBLISHING CORPORATION, 1969
   090,

   MOORE GERALD   BEIER ULLI   EDS
   MODERN POETRY FROM AFRICA.
   BALTIMORE, PENGUIN, 1963
   090,

   BEIER ULLI
   THE STORY OF SACRED WOOD CARVINGS FROM ONE SMALL
   YORUBA TOWN.
   LAGOS, NIGERIA, MARINA "NIGERIA MAGAZINE," 1957
   E W MACROW, (ED.)
   128-01,

   BEIER ULLI
   NIGERIAN MUD SCULPTURE.
   CAMBRIDGE, CAMBRIDGE UNIVERSITY PRESS, 1963
   014,128-01,

   BEIER ULLI
   ART IN NIGERIA 1960.
   CAMBRIDGE, CAMBRIDGE UNIVERSITY PRESS, 1960
   014,093,128-01,

   BEIER ULLI
   THE HISTORICAL AND PSYCHOLOGICAL SIGNIFICANCE OF YORUBA
   MYTHS.
   ODU, A JOURNAL OF YORUBA AND RELATED STUDIES 1 N C PP 17-25
   012,128-01,

BELASSA BELA
   BELASSA BELA
   THE THEORY OF ECONOMIC INTEGRATION
   HOMEWOOD, ILLINOIS, IRWIN PRESS, 1961
   071,078,

BELING WILLARD A
   BELING WILLARD A
   MODERNIZATION AND AFRICAN LABOR-- A TUNISIAN CASE STUDY.
   NEW YORK, PRAEGER, 1965
   073,138-08,

BELL DANIEL
   BELL DANIEL
   THE END OF IDEOLOGY IN THE WEST--AN EPILOGUE.
   IN THE END OF IDEOLOGY, GLENCOE ILLINOIS, FREE
   PRESS, 1962, PP 393-404
   060,

BELL P W
    BELL P W
    ECONOMIC THEORY--AN INTEGRATED TEXT WITH SPECIAL REFERENCE
    TO TROPICAL AFRICA AND OTHER DEVELOPING AREAS.
    LONDON AND NEW YORK, INTERNATIONAL UNIVERSITY BOOKSELLERS,
    INC., 1969
    073,

BELL R M
    BELL R M
    THE MAJI-MAJI REBELLION IN THE LIWALE DISTRICT.
    TANGANYIKA NOTES AND RECORDS 28 1950 PP 38-57
    034,136-02,

BELL WENDELL
    BELL WENDELL
    SOCIAL CHANGE AND ELITES IN AN EMERGENT NATION.
    IN BARRINGER GEORGE BLANKSTEN RAYMOND MACK, SOCIAL CHANGE
    IN DEVELOPING AREAS, CAMBRIDGE, MASS, SCHENKMAN PUBLISHING
    COMPANY, 1965, PP 155-204
    043,

BELLAH ROBERT
    BELLAH ROBERT
    RELIGIOUS SYSTEMS.
    IN EVON Z. VOGT AND ETHEL M. ALBERT (EDS), PEOPLE OF RIMROCK
    --A STUDY OF VALUES IN FIVE CULTURES, CAMBRIDGE, HARVARD
    UNIVERSITY PRESS, 1966, P. 227
    013,

BELLO AHMADU
    BELLO AHMADU
    MY LIFE.
    CAMBRIDGE, ENGLAND, CAMBRIDGE UNIVERSITY PRESS, 1962
    044,128-04,

BELSHAW D G R
    BELSHAW D G R
    AGRICULTURAL PRODUCTION AND TRADE IN THE EAST AFRICAN COMMON
    MARKET.
    IN COLIN LEYS AND P ROBSON (EDS), FEDERATION IN EAST AFRICA--
    OPPORTUNITIES AND PROBLEMS, NAIROBI, OXFORD UNIVERSITY PRESS,
    1965 PP 83-101
    078,

BEN AMOS PAULA
    BEN AMOS PAULA
    BIBLIOGRAPHY OF BENIN ART.
    NEW YORK, INTERNATIONAL UNIVERSITY BOOKSELLERS, INC., 1968
    014,128-01,

BENEZET ANTHONY
    BENEZET ANTHONY
    SOME HISTORICAL ACCOUNT OF GUINEA. ITS SITUATION, PRODUCE
    AND THE GENERAL DISPOSITION OF ITS INHABITANTS, WITH AN
    INQUIRY INTO THE RISE AND PROGRESS OF THE SLAVE TRADE.
    PHILADELPHIA, J CRUKSHANK, 1771
    028,

BENNETT GEORGE

BENNETT GEORGE   ROSBERG CARL G
THE KENYATTA ELECTION-- KENYA 1960-1961.
LONDON, OXFORD UNIVERSITY PRESS, 1961
063,117-07,

BENNETT GEORGE
    BENNETT GEORGE
    SETTLERS AND POLITICS IN KENYA UP TO 1945.
    IN VINCENT HARLOW AND E M CHILVER (EDS), HISTORY OF EAST
    AFRICA VOL II, OXFORD, CLARENDON PRESS, 1965, PP 265-332
    035,117-02,

    BENNETT GEORGE
    THE GOLD COAST GENERAL ELECTION OF 1954.
    PARLIAMENTARY AFFAIRS 7 1954 PP 430-439
    063,114-07,

    BENNETT GEORGE
    KENYA'S FRUSTRATED ELECTION.
    WORLD TODAY 17 1961 PP 254-261
    063,117-07,

    BENNETT GEORGE
    AN OUTLINE OF HISTORY OF TANU.
    MAKERERE JOURNAL 7 1962 PP 15-32
    055,136-07,

    BENNETT GEORGE
    KENYA--A POLITICAL HISTORY.
    LONDON, OXFORD UNIVERSITY PRESS, 1963
    117-07,

BENNETT LERONE
    BENNETT LERONE
    BEFORE THE MAYFLOWER-A HISTORY OF THE NEGRO IN AMERICA,
    1619-1964
    BALTIMORE, PENGUIN, REVISED EDITION, 1966
    030,

    BENNETT LERONE
    PIONEERS IN PROTEST
    BALTIMORE, PENGUIN, 1969
    030,095,

    BENNETT LERONE
    CONFRONTATION-BLACK AND WHITE
    BALTIMORE, PENGUIN, 1966; REVISED EDITION, 1968
    030,094,

    BENNETT LERONE
    THE NEGRO MOOD.
    CHICAGO, JOHNSON PUBLISHING CO, 1964
    030,095,

BENNETT NORMAN
    BENNETT NORMAN   ED
    LEADERSHIP IN EASTERN AFRICA-- SIX POLITICAL BIOGRAPHIES.
    BROOKLINE, MASS, BOSTON UNIVERSITY PRESS, 1968
    034,

MCCALL DANIEL F   BENNETT NORMAN   BUTLER JEFFREY
EASTERN AFRICAN HISTORY
NEW YORK, PRAEGER, 1969
036,

BENNETT NORMAN
    MCCALL DANIEL F   BENNETT NORMAN   BUTLER JEFFREY
    WESTERN AFRICAN HISTORY
    NEW YORK, PRAEGER, 1969
    036,

BENSON MARY
    BENSON MARY
    CHIEF LUTULI OF SOUTH AFRICA.
    LONDON, OXFORD UNIVERSITY PRESS, 1963
    132-04,

BENTSI-ENCHILL K
    BENTSI-ENCHILL K
    PROBLEMS IN THE CONSTRUCTION OF VIABLE CONSTITUTIONAL
    STRUCTURES IN AFRICA.
    IN CARTER, GWENDOLEN M. AND ANN PADEN (EDS) EXPANDING
    HORIZONS IN AFRICAN STUDIES, EVANSTON, NORTHWESTERN
    UNIVERSITY PRESS, 1969, PP. 173-180
    068,100,

    BENTSI-ENCHILL K
    GHANA LAND LAW.
    LONDON, SWEET AND MAXWELL, 1964
    010, 066, 114-08,

BERCHER L
    BERCHER L
    LA RISALA PAR IBIN ABI ZAYD AL QAYRAWANI-- TEXTE ET
    TRADUCTION (THE RISALA BY IBIN ABI ZAYD AL QAYRAWANI--
    TEXT AND TRANSLATION).
    ALGIERS 1945
    066,

BERG ELLIOT J
    BERG ELLIOT J
    THE ECONOMICS OF THE MIGRANT LABOR SYSTEM.
    IN HILDA KUPER, (ED.), URBANIZATION AND MIGRATION IN
    WEST AFRICA, BERKELEY, UNIVERSITY OF CALIFORNIA PRESS, 1965,
    PP 160-181
    071,

    BERG ELLIOT J
    THE ECONOMIC BASIS OF POLITICAL CHOICE IN FRENCH WEST
    AFRICA.
    IN WILLIAM J HANNA (ED), INDEPENDENT BLACK AFRICA, CHICAGO,
    RAND MCNALLY, 1964, PP 607-634
    078,

    BERG ELLIOT J   BUTLER JEFFREY
    TRADE UNIONS.
    IN J S COLEMAN AND C G ROSBERG, (EDS.), POLITICAL PARTIES
    AND NATIONAL INTEGRATION IN TROPICAL AFRICA, BERKELEY,
    UNIVERSITY OF CALIFORNIA PRESS, 1964
    073,

BERG ELLIOT J
    BERG ELLIOT J
    THE ECONOMICS OF INDEPENDENCE IN FRENCH-SPEAKING WEST
    AFRICA.
    IN PETER J MCEWAN AND ROBERT B SUTCLIFFE (EDS), MODERN AFRICA,
    NEW YORK, THOMAS CROWELL, 1965
    082,

    BERG ELLIOT J
    THE DEVELOPMENT OF A LABOR FORCE IN SUB-SAHARAN AFRICA.
    ECONOMIC DEVELOPMENT AND CULTURAL CHANGE, PART I, JULY, 1965
    PP. 394-412
    071,

    BERG ELLIOT J
    SOCIALISM AND ECONOMIC DEVELOPMENT IN TROPICAL AFRICA
    QUARTERLY JOURNAL OF ECONOMICS 78 1964 PP 549-573
    073,

BERG F J
    BERG F J
    THE SWAHILI COMMUNITY OF MOMBASA, 1500-1900
    JOURNAL OF AFRICAN HISTORY 9 1968 PP 35-56
    023,

BERGER MORROE
    BERGER MORROE
    IDEOLOGIES NATIONAL AND INTERNATIONAL CHAPTER 9.
    IN THE ARAB WORLD TODAY, GARDEN CITY, NEW YORK, DOUBLEDAY,
    1964, PP 322-384
    060,

BERNUS EDMOND
    BERNUS EDMOND
    ABIDJAN--NOTE SUR L'AGGOMERATION D'ABIDJAN ET SA POPULATION.
    BULL. IFAN, SERIES B, 24, 1-2, 1962
    116-05,

    BERNUS EDMOND
    NOTE ON ABIDJAN.
    IN CSA MEETING OF SPECIALISTS ON URBANIZATION AND ITS SOCIAL
    ASPECTS, ABIDJAN,1961, LONDON, CCTA, 1961
    116-05,

    BERNUS EDMOND
    QUELQUES ASPECTS DE L EVOLUTION DES TOUAREG DE L QUEST DE LA
    REPUBLIQUE DU NIGER.
    NIAMEY, IFAN, ETUDES NIGERIENNES, 9, 1963
    127-01,

BERNUS SUZANNE
    BERNUS SUZANNE
    NIAMEY--POPULATION ET HABITAT.
    PARIS, IFAN-CNRS, N.D.
    127-05,

BERRIAN ALBERT H
    BERRIAN ALBERT H   LONG RICHARD A   EDS
    NEGRITUDE--ESSAYS AND STUDIES.

HAMPTON, VIRGINIA, HAMPTON INSTITUTE PRESS, 1967
060,

BERRY BRIAN J L
 BERRY BRIAN J L GARRISON WILLIAM
 ALTERNATE EXPLANATIONS OF URBAN RANK-SIZE RELATIONSHIPS.
 ANNALS OF THE ASSOCIATION OF AMERICAN GEOGRAPHERS 48 MARCH
 1958 B-M REPRINT S-341
 047,

 BERRY BRIAN J L
 CITY SIZE DISTRIBUTIONS AND ECONOMIC DEVELOPMENT.
 IN K M BARBOUR AND R M PROTHERO (EDS.), ESSAYS ON
 ECONOMIC DEVELOPMENT AND CULTURAL CHANGE 9 JULY 1961
 B-M REPRINT S-340
 047,

BERRY JACK
 BERRY JACK GREENBERG JOSEPH H
 SOCIOLINGUISTIC RESEARCH IN AFRICA.
 AFRICAN STUDIES BULLETIN SEPTEMBER 1966 PP 1-9
 100,

 BERRY JACK
 THE MADINA PROJECT--SOCIOLINGUISTIC RESEARCH IN GHANA.
 IN GWENDOLEN CARTER AND ANN PADEN (EDS), EXPANDING HORIZONS
 IN AFRICAN STUDIES,EVANSTON, NORTHWESTERN UNIVERSITY PRESS,
 1969
 100,114-03,

BESHIR MOHAMED O
 BESHIR MOHAMED O
 THE SUDAN-- A MILITARY SURRENDER.
 AFRICA REPORT 9 DECEMBER 1964 PP 3-10
 064,134-06,

 BESHIR MOHAMED O
 EDUCATIONAL DEVELOPMENT IN THE SUDAN
 NEW YORK,OXFORD UNIVERSITY PRESS, 1969
 042,134-04,

BETHELL LESLIE
 BETHELL LESLIE
 THE MIXED COMMISSIONS FOR THE SUPPRESSION OF THE TRANS-
 ATLANTIC SLAVE TRADE IN THE NINETEENTH CENTURY
 JOURNAL OF AFRICAN HISTORY 7 1966 PP 79-93
 029,

BETI MONGO
 BETI MONGO
 MISSION TO KALA.
 TRANSLATED BY PETER GREEN, IBADAN, HEINEMANN EDUCATIONAL
 BOOKS LTD, 1964
 090,104-10,

 BETI MONGO
 KING LAZAROUS.
 NEW YORK, MACMILLAN CO., 1970 (LONDON, HEINEMANN
 EDUCATIONAL BOOKS)
 090,104-10,

BETI MONGO
    BETI MONGO
    LE PAUVRE CHRIST DE BOMBA.
    PARIS, R LAFFONT, 1956
    090,104-10,

    BETI MONGO
    ECRIVAIN CAMEROUNAIS. TEXTES COMMENTES PAR ROGER MERCIER ET
    M ET S BATTESTINI.
    PARIS, F NATHAN, 1964, COLLECTION LITTERATURE AFRICAINE-- 5
    104-10,

    BETI MONGO
    LE ROI MIRACULE.
    PARIS, CORREA BUCHER CHASTEL, 1958
    104-10,

    BETI MONGO
    MISSION TERMINEE.
    PARIS, CORREA BUCHER CHASTEL, 1957
    104-10,

    BETI MONGO
    VILLE CRUELLE.
    PARIS, EDITIONS AFRICAINES, 1954
    104-10,

BETTELHEIM BRUNO
    BETTELHEIM BRUNO   JANOWITZ MORRIS
    ETHNIC TOLERANCE-- A FUNCTION OF SOCIAL AND PERSONAL
    CONTROL.
    THE AMERICAN JOURNAL OF SOCIOLOGY 55 SEPTEMBER 1949
    PP 137-145 (BOBBS-MERRILL REPRINT 24)
    088,

BETTISON DAVID G
    BETTISON DAVID G   RIGBY P J A
    PATTERNS OF INCOME AND EXPENDITURE IN BLANTYRE-LIMBE,
    NYASALAND.
    LUSAKA, RHODES-LIVINGSTONE INSTITUTE, 1961
    122-05,

    BETTISON DAVID G
    NUMERICAL DATA ON AFRICAN DWELLERS IN LUSAKA, NORTHERN
    RHODESIA.
    LUSAKA, RHODES-LIVINGSTONE INSTITUTE, 1959
    142-05,

BETTS RAYMOND F
    BETTS RAYMOND F
    THE PROBLEM OF THE MEDINA IN THE URBAN PLANNING OF DAKAR
    SENEGAL
    AFRICAN URBAN NOTES, VOL IV, NO. 3, SEPT. 1969, PP. 5-15
    045,092,

BIBERSON P
    BIBERSON P
    HUMAN EVOLUTION IN MOROCCO, IN THE FRAMEWORK OF THE
    PALEOCLIMATIC VARIATIONS OF THE ATLANTIC PLEISTOCENE.

IN F CLARK HOWELL AND FRANCOIS BOURLIERE (EDS.), AFRICAN
ECOLOGY AND HUMAN EVOLUTION, CHICAGO, ALDINE, 1966,
PP 417-447
018,

BIDDER IRMGAARD
   BIDDER IRMGAARD
   LALIBELA-- THE MONOLITHIC CHURCHES OF ETHIOPIA.
   NEW YORK PRAEGER 1960
   092,110-01,

BIEBUYCK DANIEL
   BIEBUYCK DANIEL   ED
   TRADITION AND CREATIVITY IN TRIBAL ART.
   BERKELEY, UNIVERSITY OF CALIFORNIS PRESS, 1969
   014,

   BIEBUYCK DANIEL
   AFRICAN AGRARIAN SYSTEMS.
   LONDON, OXFORD UNIVERSITY PRESS, 1963
   010,070,

   BIEBUYCK DANIEL   DOUGLAS MARY
   CONGO-TRIBES AND PARTIES.
   LONDON, ROYAL ANTHROPOLOGICAL INSTITUTE, 1961
   108-06,

BIENEN HENRY
   BIENEN HENRY
   TANZANIA-- PARTY TRANSFORMATION AND ECONOMIC DEVELOPMENT.
   PRINCETON, PRINCETON UNIVERSITY PRESS, 1967
   061,136-07,

BIESHEUVEL SIMON
   BIESHEUVEL SIMON
   THE MEASUREMENT OF AFRICAN ATTITUDES TOWARDS EUROPEAN
   ETHICAL CONCEPTS, CUSTOMS, LAWS AND ADMINISTRATION OF
   JUSTICE.
   JOURNAL OF THE NATIONAL INSTITUTE OF PERSONNEL RESEARCH 6
   1955 PP 5-17
   088,

BINDER LEONARD
   BINDER LEONARD
   POLITICAL RECRUITMENT AND PARTICIPATION IN EGYPT.
   JOSEPH LA POLOMBARA AND MYRON WEINER (EDS), POLITICAL
   PARTIES AND POLITICAL DEVELOPMENT, PRINCETON, NEW JERSEY,
   PRINCETON UNIVERSITY PRESS, 1966
   063,140-07,

   BINDER LEONARD
   EGYPT--THE INTEGRATIVE REVOLUTION.
   IN LUCIEN W PYE AND S VERBA (EDS), POLITICAL CULTURE AND
   POLITICAL DEVELOPMENT, PRINCETON, PRINCETON UNIVERSITY PRESS,
   1965, PP 396-449
   057,140-06,

   BINDER LEONARD
   THE IDEOLOGICAL REVOLUTION IN THE MIDDLE EAST.
   NEW YORK, WILEY, 1964

060,

BINNS C T
   BINNS C T
   DINIZULU-THE DEATH OF THE HOUSE OF SHAKA
   LONDON, LONGMANS, 1968
   031,

   BINNS C T
   THE LAST ZULU KING
   LONDON, LONGMANS, GREEN, 1963
   031,132-02,

BIOBAKU SABURI O
   BIOBAKU SABURI O
   THE PROBLEM OF TRADITIONAL HISTORY WITH SPECIAL REFERENCES
   TO YORUBA TRADITIONS.
   JOURNAL OF THE HISTORICAL SOCIETY OF NIGERIA 1 1956
   PP 43-47
   100,128-02,

   BIOBAKU SABURI O   AL-HAJJ MUHAMMAD
   THE SUDANESE MAHDIYYA AND THE NIGER-CHAD REGION.
   IN LEWIS, ISLAM IN TROPICAL AFRICA, LONDON, OXFORD UNIVERSIT
   PRESS, 1966, P. 425-441
   052,134-03,

BIRCH A H
   BIRCH A H
   OPPORTUNITIES AND PROBLEMS OF FEDERATION.
   IN COLIN LEYS AND P ROBSON (EDS), FEDERATION IN EAST AFRICA--
   OPPORTUNITIES AND PROBLEMS, NAIROBI, OXFORD UNIVERSITY PRESS,
   1965 PP 6-29
   078,

BIRMINGHAM DAVID
   BIRMINGHAM DAVID
   THE PORTUGUESE CONQUEST OF ANGOLA.
   LONDON, OXFORD UNIVERSITY PRESS, 1965
   027, 144-02,

   BIRMINGHAM DAVID
   TRADE AND CONFLICT IN ANGOLA-- THE MBUNDU AND THEIR
   NEIGHBOURS UNDER THE INFLUENCE OF THE PORTUGUESE 1483-1790.
   LONDON, OXFORD UNIVERSITY PRESS, 1966
   027, 144-02,

BIRMINGHAM WALTER
   BIRMINGHAM WALTER   ET AL   EDS
   A STUDY OF CONTEMPORARY GHANA--VOL 1 THE ECONOMY OF
   GHANA ; VOL 2 SOME ASPECTS OF SOCIAL STRUCTURE
   LONDON, ALLEN AND UNWIN; AND EVANSTON, NORTHWESTERN UNIVERSITY
   PRESS, 1966
   114-08,

BIRNBAUM NORMAN
   BIRNBAUM NORMAN
   THE SOCIOLOGICAL STUDY OF IDEOLOGY-- 1940-1960.
   CURRENT SOCIOLOGY 9 1960 PP 91-126
   060,

BIRNIE J R
    BIRNIE J R   ANSRE GILBERT   EDS
    PROCEEDINGS OF THE CONFERENCE ON THE STUDY OF GHANAIAN
    LANGUAGES.
    ACCRA, INTERNATIONAL UNIVERSITY BOOKSELLERS,INC., 1968
    011,

BISHOP WALTER W
    BISHOP WALTER W
    THE LATER TERTIARY AND PLEISTOCENE IN EASTERN EQUATORIAL
    AFRICA.
    IN F CLARK HOWELL AND FRANCOIS BOURLIERE (EDS.), AFRICAN
    ECOLOGY AND HUMAN EVOLUTION, CHICAGO, ALDINE, 1966,
    PP 246-275
    018,

    BISHOP WALTER W   CLARK J DESMOND
    BACKGROUND TO EVOLUTION IN AFRICA
    CHICAGO, UNIVERSITY OF CHICAGO PRESS, 1966
    018,

BIVAR A D H
    BIVAR A D H
    THE WATHIQAT AHL AL-SUDAN-- A MANIFESTO OF THE FULANI JIHAD.
    JOURNAL OF AFRICAN HISTORY 2 1961 PP 235-243
    024,128-02,

    BIVAR A D H   HISKETT MERVIN
    THE ARABIC LITERATURE OF NIGERIA TO 1804-- A PROVISIONAL
    ACCOUNT.
    BULLETIN OF THE SCHOOL OF ORIENTAL AND AFRICAN STUDIES 25
    1962 PP 104-148
    021,060,128-02,

    BIVAR A D H   SHINNIE P L
    OLD KANURI CAPITALS.
    JOURNAL OF AFRICAN HISTORY 3 1962 PP 1-10
    024,128-02,

BIXLER RAYMOND W
    BIXLER RAYMOND W
    THE FOREIGN POLICY OF THE UNITED STATES IN LIBERIA.
    NEW YORK, PAGEANT PRESS, 1957
    083,119-09,

BLACK CYRIL E
    BLACK CYRIL E
    THE DYNAMICS OF MODERNIZATION.
    NEW YORK, HARPER AND ROW, 1966
    037,073,

BLACKMER DONALD
    MILLIKAN MAX F   BLACKMER DONALD   EDS
    RESISTANCE AND CONFLICT IN THE MODERNIZATION PROCESS CHP 3.
    IN EMERGING NATIONS, CENTER FOR INTERNATIONAL STUDIES, MIT,
    BOSTON, LITTLE, BROWN, 1961; ALSO LEWIS P FICKETT, ED, PROBLEMS
    OF THE DEVELOPING NATIONS, NEW YORK, CROWELL, 1966, PP 12-20
    037,

BLAIR THOMAS L
  BLAIR THOMAS L
  DU BOIS AND THE CENTURY OF AFRICAN LIBERATION.
  IN ALBERT BERRIAN AND RICHARD LONG (EDS), NEGRITUDE--
  ESSAYS AND STUDIES, HAMPTON, VIRGINIA, HAMPTON INSTITUTE
  PRESS, 1967, PP 8-14
  094,

BLAKE JOHN W
  BLAKE JOHN W
  EUROPEAN BEGINNINGS IN WEST AFRICA 1454-1578.
  LONDON, LONGMANS, GREEN, 1937
  027,

  BLAKE JOHN W
  EUROPEANS IN WEST AFRICA 1450-1560.
  LONDON, HAKLUYT SOCIETY, 1942, 2 VOLUMES
  (TRANSLATED AND EDITED, JOHN W BLAKE)
  027,

BLANCHET ANDRE
  BLANCHET ANDRE
  L'ITINERAIRE DES PARTIS AFRICAINES DEPUIS BAMAKO
  GUIDEBOOK OF AFRICAN PARTIES SINCE BAMAKO.
  PARIS, PLON, 1958
  061,

BLAU G
  BLAU G
  COMMODITY EXPORT EARNINGS AND ECONOMIC GROWTH CHAPTER 19.
  IN EDITH WHETHAM AND JEAN CURRIE (EDS.), READINGS IN THE
  APPLIED ECONOMICS OF AFRICA, LONDON, CAMBRIDGE UNIVERSITY
  PRESS, 2, 1967, PP 163-181
  073,

BLONDEL J
  BLONDEL J
  CONSTITUTIONAL CHANGES IN FORMER FRENCH BLACK AFRICA.
  PARLIAMENTARY AFFAIRS 14 1961 PP 507-517
  068,

BLYDEN EDWARD W
  BLYDEN EDWARD W
  AFRICAN LIFE AND CUSTOMS.
  LONDON, INTERNATIONAL UNIVERSITY BOOKSELLERS, INC., 1969
  030,

  BLYDEN EDWARD W
  CHRISTIANITY, ISLAM AND THE NEGRO RACE.
  EDINBURGH, UNIVERSITY PRESS, 1967
  030,

BOAHEN A ADU
  BOAHEN A ADU
  BRITAIN, THE SAHARA, AND THE WESTERN SUDAN, 1788-1861.
  OXFORD, CLARENDON PRESS, 1964
  024,

  BOAHEN A ADU
  THE ROOTS OF GHANAIAN NATIONALISM.

JOURNAL OF AFRICAN HISTORY 5 1964 PP 127-132
055,114-06,

BOAS FRANZ
    BOAS FRANZ
    PRIMITIVE ART.
    NEW YORK, DOVER, 1955
    014,

BOATENG E A
    BOATENG E A
    THE GROWTH AND FUNCTIONS OF ACCRA.
    BULLETIN OF THE GHANA GEOGRAPHICAL ASSOCIATION 4 JULY 1959
    PP 4-15
    045,114-05,

BOHANNAN LAURA
    BOHANNAN LAURA   BOHANNAN PAUL
    THE TIV OF CENTRAL NIGERIA.
    LONDON, INTERNATIONAL AFRICAN INSTITUTE, 1953
    014,128-01,

    BOHANNAN PAUL   BOHANNAN LAURA
    TIV ECONOMY.
    EVANSTON, NORTHWESTERN UNIVERSITY PRESS, 1968
    010,128-01,

BOHANNAN PAUL
    BOHANNAN LAURA   BOHANNAN PAUL
    THE TIV OF CENTRAL NIGERIA.
    LONDON, INTERNATIONAL AFRICAN INSTITUTE, 1953
    014,128-01,

    BOHANNAN PAUL
    AFRICA AND AFRICANS
    NEW YORK, NATURAL HISTORY PRESS, 1964
    001,003,010,016,

    BOHANNAN PAUL   DALTON GEORGE   ED
    MARKETS IN AFRICA.
    EVANSTON, NORTHWESTERN UNIVERSITY PRESS, 1965
    010,

    BOHANNAN PAUL
    THE PEOPLES OF AFRICA CHP 5.
    IN AFRICA AND AFRICANS, NEW YORK, THE NATURAL HISTORY PRESS,
    1964
    003,

    BOHANNAN PAUL
    THE IMPACT OF MONEY ON AN AFRICAN SUBSISTENCE ECONOMY.
    JOURNAL OF ECONOMIC HISTORY 19 DECEMBER 1959 PP 481-503
    010,

    BOHANNAN PAUL   ED
    AFRICAN HOMICIDE AND SUICIDE.
    PRINCETON, NEW JERSEY, PRINCETON UNIVERSITY PRESS, 1960
    041,

    BOHANNAN PAUL

LAND USE,LAND TENURE AND LAND REFORM
IN HERSKOVITS AND HARWITZ (EDS), ECONOMIC TRANSITION IN
AFRICA,EVANSTON,NORTHWESTERN UNIVERSITY PRESS,1964
PP 133-150
010,

BOHANNAN PAUL
   BOHANNAN PAUL
   JUSTICE AND JUDGMENT AMONG THE TIV.
   LONDON, OXFORD UNIVERSITY PRESS, 1957
   066,128-01,

   BOHANNAN PAUL
   AFRICA'S LAND.
   IN G DALTON (ED.) TRIBAL AND PEASANT SOCIETIES, DOUBLEDAY,
   1967
   010,

   BOHANNAN PAUL   BOHANNAN LAURA
   TIV ECONOMY.
   EVANSTON,NORTHWESTERN UNIVERSITY PRESS, 1968
   010,128-01,

   BOHANNAN PAUL   ED
   LAW AND WARFARE-- STUDIES IN THE ANTHROPOLOGY OF CONFLICT.
   GARDEN CITY,NEW YORK,NATURAL HISTORY PRESS,1967
   009,

   BOHANNAN PAUL   MIDDLETON JOHN   EDS
   MARRIAGE, FAMILY AND RESIDENCE.
   GARDEN CITY, NEW YORK, INTERNATIONAL UNIVERSITY BOOKSELLERS,
   INC., 1968
   008,

   BOHANNAN PAUL
   THE TIV OF NIGERIA.
   IN JAMES L GIBBS JR. (ED), PEOPLES OF AFRICA, NEW YORK, HOLT
   RINEHART AND WINSTON, 1965, PP. 513-546
   128-01,

BOLAMBA A R
   BOLAMBA A R
   ETUDES SOCIALES--LES PROBLEMES DE L'EVOLUTION DE LA FEMME
   NOIRE.
   ELIZABETHVILLE, ED. DE L'ESSOR DU CONGO, 1949, P. 171
   108-10,

   BOLAMBA A R
   PREMIERS ESSAIS--POEMES--PREFACE D'OLIVIER DE BOUVEIGNES
   (FIRST ESSAYS--POEMS--PREFACE D'OLIVER DE BOVEIGNES).
   ELIZABETHVILLE, ED. DE L'ESSOR DU CONGO, 1947
   108-10,

BONARDI PIERRE
   BONARDI PIERRE
   LA REPUBLIQUE DU NIGER--NAISSANCE D'UN ETAT.
   PARIS, AGENCE PARISIENNE DE DISTRIBUTION, 1960
   127-11,

BOOTH ALAN R

BOOTH ALAN R
THE UNITED STATES AFRICAN SQUADRON 1843-1861.
IN JEFFREY BUTLER (ED), BOSTON UNIVERSITY PAPERS IN AFRICAN
HISTORY VOL I, BOSTON, BOSTON UNIVERSITY PRESS, 1964, PP 77-118
029,

BOUADIB ABDERRAHIM
BOUADIB ABDERRAHIM
PROSPECTS FOR A UNITED MAGHRIB.
IN WILLIAM H LEWIS, NEW FORCES IN AFRICA, GEORGETOWN
COLLOQUIUM ON AFRICA, PAPERS, WASHINGTON, PUBLIC AFFAIRS
PRESS, 1962, PP 101-113
078,

BOUCHE DENISE
BOUCHE DENISE
LES VILLAGES DE LIBERTE EN AFRIQUE NOIRE, 1887-1910. (THE
LIBERTY SETTLEMENTS IN BLACK AFRICA, 1887-1910).
PARIS, MOUTON, 1968
030,

BOURLIERE FRANCOIS
HOWELL F CLARK   BOURLIERE FRANCOIS   EDS
AFRICAN ECOLOGY AND HUMAN EVOLUTION.
CHICAGO, ALDINE, 1966
018,019,

BOURRET F M
BOURRET F M
GHANA-- THE ROAD TO INDEPENDENCE 1919-1957.
STANFORD, STANFORD UNIVERSITY PRESS 1960
055,056,114-07,

BOUTILLIER J L
BOUTILLIER J L
LES RAPPORTS DU SYSTEME FONCIER TOUCOULEUR ET
L'ORGANISATION SOCIALE ET ECONOMIQUE TRADITIONNELLE-- LEUR
EVOLUTION ACTUELLE (THE PRODUCTIVITY OF TOUCOULEUR FARMERS--
ITS CONTEMPORARY EVOLUTION FROM THE TRADITIONAL SOCIAL AND
ECONOMIC SYSTEM).
IN D BIEBUYCK, ED., AFRICAN AGRARIAN SYSTEMS, LONDON,
OXFORD UNIVERSITY PRESS 1963, PP 116-136
070,130-05,

BOVILL EDWARD W
BOVILL EDWARD W
THE GOLDEN TRADE OF THE MOORS.
LONDON, OXFORD UNIVERSITY PRESS, 1958; SECOND EDITION, 1968
022,

BOVILL EDWARD W
THE MOORISH INVASION OF THE SUDAN.
JOURNAL OF THE AFRICAN SOCIETY 26 1926 PP 245-262 AND
27 1927 PP 47-56
021,

BOVILL EDWARD W   ED
MISSIONS TO THE NIGER-- THE JOURNAL OF FRIEDRICH
HORNEMANN'S TRAVELS-- (AND) THE LETTERS OF MAJOR ALEXANDER
GORDON LAING.

CAMBRIDGE,ENGLAND, UNIVERSITY PRESS,1964
027,

BOWDICH THOMAS E
    BOWDICH THOMAS E
    MISSION FROM CAPE COAST CASTLE TO ASHANTEE WITH A
    STATISTICAL ACCOUNT OF THE KINGDOM AND GEOGRAPHICAL NOTICES
    OF OTHER PARTS OF THE INTERIOR OF AFRICA.
    LONDON,CASS,1967
    026,114-02,

BOWEN
    BOWEN ELENORE SMITH
    RETURN TO LAUGHTER
    GARDEN CITY,NEW YORK,DOUBLEDAY AND COMPANY,1964
    098,

BOWLES   SAMUEL
    BOWLES   SAMUEL
    PLANNING EDUCATIONAL SYSTEMS FOR ECONOMIC GROWTH
    CAMBRIDGE, HARVARD UNIVERSITY PRESS, 1969
    073,

BOWMAN LARRY W
    BOWMAN LARRY W
    THE SUBORDINATE STATE SYSTEM OF SOUTHERN AFRICA
    INTERNATIONAL STUDIES QUARTERLY 12 1968 PP 231-261
    089,

    BOWMAN LARRY W
    STRAINS IN THE RHODESIAN FRONT.
    AFRICAN REPORT, DECEMBER, 1968, P. 16
    087,145-06,

BOWN LALAGE
    BOWN LALAGE   CROWDER MICHAEL   EDS
    THE PROCEEDINGS OF THE FIRST INTERNATIONAL CONGRESS OF
    AFRICANISTS.
    LONDON,LONGMANS,1964;ALSO EVANSTON,NORTHWESTERN UNIVERSITY
    PRESS,1964
    100,

BOXER
    BOXER CHARLES RALPH
    PORTUGUESE SOCIETY IN THE TROPICS--THE MUNICIPAL COUNCILS
    OF GOA, MACAO, BAHIA AND LUANDA 1510-1800.
    MADISON, UNIVERSITY OF WISCONSIN PRESS, 1965
    027, 144-07,

    BOXER CHARLES RALPH DE AZEVEDO CARLOS
    FORT JESUS AND THE PORTUGESE IN MOMBASA 1593-1729
    LONDON,HOLLIS AND CARTER,1960
    023,027,

BRACE RICHARD M
    BRACE RICHARD M
    MOROCCO ALGERIA TUNISIA
    ENGLEWOOD CLIFFS,PRENTICE-HALL,1964
    101-11,126-11,138-11,

BRADBURY R E
    BRADBURY R E
    THE BENIN KINGDOM AND THE EDO-SPEAKING PEOPLES OF SOUTH-
    WESTERN NIGERIA.
    LONDON OXFORD UNIVERSITY PRESS 1957
    026,128-01,

BRADBURY R E
    BRADBURY R E
    CHRONOLOGICAL PROBLEMS IN THE STUDY OF BENIN HISTORY.
    JOURNAL OF THE HISTORICAL SOCIETY OF NIGERIA 1 1959
    PP 263-287
    026,128-01,

    BRADBURY R E
    THE HISTORICAL USES OF COMPARATIVE ETHNOGRAPHY WITH SPECIAL
    REFERENCE TO BENIN AND THE YORUBA.
    IN VANSINA, (ED.) THE HISTORIAN IN TROPICAL AFRICA, LONDON,
    OXFORD UNIVERSITY PRESS, 1964, PP 145-164
    099,128-02,

BRAIMAH J A
    BRAIMAH J A   GOODY J R
    SALAGA--THE STRUGGLE FOR POWER.
    LONDON, LONGMANS, GREEN AND COMPANY LIMITED, 1967
    026,114-02,

BRAND J A
    BRAND J A
    THE MID-WEST STATE MOVEMENT IN NIGERIAN POLITICS-- A STUDY
    IN PARTY FORMATION.
    POLITICAL STUDIES 13 OCTOBER 1965 PP 346-365
    061,128-07,

BRANNEY L
    BRANNEY L
    TOWARD THE SYSTEMATIC INDIVIDUALISATION OF AFRICAN LAND
    TENURE.
    JOURNAL OF AFRICAN ADMINISTRATION 11 OCTOBER 1959 PP 208-14
    070,

BRANNON RUSSELL H
    ANSCHEL KURT R   BRANNON RUSSELL H   SMITH ELSON D
    AGRICULTURAL COOPERATIVES AND MARKETS IN DEVELOPING
    COUNTRIES.
    NEW YORK, PRAEGER PUBLISHERS, 1969
    070,

BRANSON JACK
    BRANSON JACK
    ECONOMIC AND SOCIAL CONSIDERATIONS IN ADAPTING TECHNOLOGIES
    FOR DEVELOPING COUNTRIES.
    TECHNOLOGY AND CULTURE 4 WINTER 1963 PP 22-29
    075,

BRASS WILLIAM
    BRASS WILLIAM   COALE ANSLEY J   ET AL
    THE DEMOGRAPHY OF TROPICAL AFRICA
    PRINCETON, PRINCETON UNIVERSITY PRESS, 1968
    074,

BRASS WILLIAM
    LORIMER FRANK   BRASS WILLIAM   VAN DE WALLE E
    DEMOGRAPHY.
    IN ROBERT A LYSTAD (ED), THE AFRICAN WORLD, NEW YORK,
    PRAEGER, 1966, PP 271-303
    069,074,

BRASSEUR PAULE
    BRASSEUR PAULE
    BIBLIOGRAPHIE GENRALE DU MALI
    DAKAR, IFAN,1964
    123-12,

BRAUSCH GEORGES
    BRAUSCH GEORGES
    AFRICAN ETHNOCRACIES-- SOME SOCIOLOGICAL IMPLICATIONS OF
    CONSTITUTIONAL CHANGE IN EMERGENT TERRITORIES OF AFRICA.
    CIVILISATIONS VOL XIII NO 1-2 1963 PP 82-95
    007,

    BRAUSCH GEORGES
    BELGIAN ADMINISTRATION IN THE CONGO.
    LONDON, OXFORD UNIVERSITY PRESS, 1961
    035,108-06,

BREESE GERALD
    BREESE GERALD
    URBANIZATION IN NEWLY DEVELOPING COUNTRIES.
    ENGLEWOOD CLIFFS,NJ,PRENTICE-HALL, 1966
    045,

    BREESE GERALD   ED
    THE CITY IN NEWLY DEVELOPING COUNTRIES.
    ENGLEWOOD CLIFFS,NJ,PRENTICE-HALL,1969
    045,

BRENNER LOUIS
    COHEN RONALD   BRENNER LOUIS
    BORNU IN THE 19TH CENTURY.
    IN A AJAYI AND MICHAEL CROWDER (EDS), THE HISTORY OF WEST
    AFRICA, OXFORD, CLARENDON PRESS, 1968
    024,128-02,

BRENTJES BURCHARD
    BRENTJES BURCHARD
    AFRICAN ROCK ART.
    LONDON, INTERNATIONAL UNIVERSITY BOOKSELLERS, INC., 1969
    014,

BRETTON HENRY L
    BRETTON HENRY L
    CURRENT POLITICAL THOUGHT AND PRACTICE IN GHANA.
    AMERICAN POLITICAL SCIENCE REVIEW 52 MARCH 1958 PP 46-63
    060,114-04,

    BRETTON HENRY L
    POLITICAL INFLUENCE IN SOUTHERN NIGERIA.
    IN HERBERT J SPIRO, ED., AFRICA THE PRIMACY OF POLITICS,
    NEW YORK, RANDOM HOUSE, 1966, PP 49-84

063,128-07,

BRETTON HENRY L
    BRETTON HENRY L
    THE RISE AND FALL OF KWAME NKRUMAH.
    NEW YORK, PRAEGER, 1966
    061,114-04,

BREUTZ P L
    BREUTZ P L
    TSWANA LOCAL GOVERNMENT TODAY.
    SOCIOLOGUS 8 1958 PP 140-154
    062,102-07,

BRIEN
    O'BRIEN DONAL CRUISE
    LE TALIBE MOURIDE--ETUDE D≠UN CAS DE DEPENDANCE SOCIALE
    (THE MOURIDE DISCIPLE-STUDY OF A CASE OF SOCIAL DEPENDENCE).
    CAHIERS D'ETUDES AFRICANES, VOL. IX, NO. 35, 1969, PP. 502-
    507
    052,130-03,

    O'BRIEN DONAL CRUISE
    SENEGAL.
    LONDON, PALL MALL PRESS, 1970
    130-11,

BRODE JOHN
    BRODE JOHN
    THE PROCESS OF MODERNIZATION--AN ANNOTATED BIBLIOGRAPHY ON
    THE SOCIOCULTURAL ASPECTS OF DEVELOPMENT.
    CAMBRIDGE, HARVARD UNIVERSITY PRESS, 1969
    037,

BROKENSHA DAVID
    BROKENSHA DAVID   ED
    ECOLOGY AND ECONOMIC DEVELOPMENT IN TROPICAL AFRICA.
    BERKELEY UNIVERSITY OF CALIFORNIA PRESS 1965
    RESEARCH SERIES NO. 9 INSTITUTE OF INTERNATIONAL STUDIES
    069,070,

    BROKENSHA DAVID
    SOCIAL CHANGE AT LARTEH, GHANA.
    LONDON, OXFORD UNIVERSITY PRESS, 1966
    038,114-03,

BROOKES EDGAR H
    BROOKES EDGAR H
    APARTHEID-A DOCUMENTARY STUDY OF MODERN SOUTH AFRICA
    NEW YORK, BARNES AND NOBLE, 1968
    089,

BROOKFIELD H C
    BROOKFIELD H C   TATHAM M A
    THE DISTRIBUTION OF RACIAL GROUPS IN DURBAN--THE BACKGROUND
    OF APARTHEID IN A SOUTH AFRICAN CITY.
    GEOGRAPHICAL REVIEW 47 JANUARY 1957 PP 44-65
    089,132-05,

BROOKS ANGIE E

BROOKS ANGIE E
POLITICAL PARTICIPATION OF WOMEN IN AFRICA SOUTH OF THE
SAHARA.
THE ANNALS OF THE AMERICAN ACADEMY OF POLITICAL AND SOCIAL
SCIENCE, JAN. 1968, PP. 82-85
063,

BROOKS GWENDOLYN
BROOKS GWENDOLYN
IN THE MECCA.
NEW YORK. HARPER AND ROW PUBLISHERS, 1968
094,

BROWN CHARLES E
BROWN CHARLES E
THE LIBYAN REVOLUTION SORTS ITSELF OUT
AFRICA REPORT DECEMBER 1969 PP 12-15
064,

BROWN DOUGLAS
BROWN DOUGLAS
AGAINST THE WORLD-- ATTITUDES OF WHITE SOUTH AFRICA.
GARDEN CITY, DOUBLEDAY, 1969
089,

BROWN EDWARD E
BROWN EDWARD E   WEBSTER JOHN B
A BIBLIOGRAPHY ON POLITICS AND GOVERNMENT IN KENYA.
NEW YORK, SYRACUSE UNIVERSITY PROGRAM OF EASTERN AFRICAN
STUDIES, 1965
117-12,

BROWN EDWARD E   ET AL
A BIBLIOGRAPHY OF MALAWI.
NEW YORK, SYRACUSE UNIVERSITY, 1965
122-12.

BROWN EVELYN S
BROWN EVELYN S
AFRICA'S CONTEMPORARY ART AND ARTISTS.
NEW YORK, HARMON FOUNDATION, 1966
093,

BROWN GODFREY N
ANENE JOSEPH C   BROWN GODFREY N   EDS
AFRICA IN THE NINETEENTH AND TWENTIETH CENTURIES-- A HAND-
BOOK FOR TEACHERS AND STUDENTS.
IBADAN, IBADAN UNIVERSITY PRESS; ALSO LONDON, THOMAS NELSON AND
SONS, 1966
001,

BROWN GODFREY N
BRITISH EDUCATIONAL POLICY IN WEST AND CENTRAL AFRICA.
JOURNAL OF MODERN AFRICAN STUDIES 2 1964 PP 365-377
042,

BROWN H RAP
BROWN H RAP
DIE NIGGER DIE
NEW YORK, THE DIAL PRESS, 1969

095,

BROWN R
   BROWN R
   HEALTH AND DISEASE IN AFRICA.
   TRANSITION 6 26 1966 PP 28-33
   069,075,

BROWN RICHARD
   STOKES E   BROWN RICHARD   EDS
   THE ZAMBESIAN PAST-STUDIES IN CENTRAL AFRICAN HISTORY
   MANCHESTER,MANCHESTER UNIVERSITY PRESS, 1966
   025,122-02,142-02,145-02,

BROWN WILLIAM A
   BROWN WILLIAM A
   TOWARD A CHRONOLOGY FOR THE CALIPHATE OF HAMDULLAHI (MASINA)
   CAHIERS D'ETUDES AFRICAINE, VOL. VIII, NO. 31, 1968, PP. 428
   434
   024,123-02,

BROWN WILLIAM O
   BROWN WILLIAM O   LEWIS HYLAN
   RACIAL SITUATIONS AND ISSUES IN AFRICA CHAPTER 6.
   IN THE UNITED STATES AND AFRICA, BACKGROUND PAPERS OF THE
   13TH ASSEMBLY, THE AMERICAN ASSEMBLY, COLUMBIA UNIVERSITY,
   1958, PP 141-163
   088,

BRUNSCHWIG HENRI
   BRUNSCHWIG HENRI
   L'EXPANSION ALLEMANDE OUTRE-MER DU XV SIECLE A NOS JOURS
   (GERMAN EXPANSION IN AFRICA FROM THE FIFTEENTH CENTURY TO
   MODERN TIMES).
   PARIS,PRESSES UNIVERSITAIRES DE FRANCE,1957
   027,033,

   BRUNSCHWIG HENRI
   MYTHES ET REALITES DE L IMPERIALISME COLONIAL FRANCAISE
   (FACTS AND FANCIES ABOUT FRENCH COLONIAL IMPERIALISM) 1871
   -1914.
   PARIS,A COLIN,1960
   033,

BRUTUS DENNIS
   BRUTUS DENNIS
   LETTERS TO MARTHA AND OTHER POEMS FROM A SOUTH AFRICAN
   PRISON.
   NEW YORK, HUMANITIES PRESS, INC., 1968
   089,132-04,

BRUYN SEVERYN T
   BRUYN SEVERYN T
   THE HUMAN PERSPECTIVE IN SOCIOLOGY-- THE METHOD OF
   PARTICIPANT OBSERVATION.
   ENGLEWOOD CLIFFS,N J,PRENTICE-HALL,1966
   096,

BRYAN M A
   WESTERMANN D   BRYAN M A

LANGUAGES OF WEST AFRICA.
LONDON, OXFORD UNIVERSITY PRESS, 1952
011,

BRZEZINSKI Z
    BRZEZINSKI Z   ED
    AFRICA AND THE COMMUNIST WORLD.
    STANFORD, CALIFORNIA, STANFORD UNIVERSITY PRESS, 1963
    084,

    BRZEZINSKI Z
    YUGOSLAVIA.
    IN Z BRZEZINSKI (ED), AFRICA AND THE COMMUNIST WORLD,
    STANFORD, CALIFORNIA, STANFORD UNIVERSITY PRESS, 1963,
    PP 116-141
    084,

    BRZEZINSKI Z
    CONCLUSION-- THE AFRICAN CHALLENGE.
    IN Z BRZEZINSKI (ED), AFRICA AND THE COMMUNIST WORLD,
    STANFORD, CALIFORNIA, STANFORD UNIVERSITY PRESS, 1963,
    PP 204-230
    084,

BUCKLEY WALTER
    BUCKLEY WALTER   ED
    MODERN SYSTEMS RESEARCH FOR THE BEHAVIORAL SCIENTIST.
    CHICAGO, ALDINE, 1968
    098,

BUELL RAYMOND L
    BUELL RAYMOND L
    THE NATIVE PROBLEM IN AFRICA.
    HAMDEN, CONNECTICUT, ARCHON PRESS, 1965
    035,

    BUELL RAYMOND L
    LIBERIA-- A CENTURY OF SURVIVAL 1847-1947.
    PHILADELPHIA, UNIVERSITY OF PENNSYLVANIA PRESS, 1947
    029,

BULMER-THOMAS IVOR
    BULMER-THOMAS IVOR
    DEVELOPMENT OF A MIDDLE CLASS IN TROPICAL AND SUB-TROPICAL
    COUNTRIES.
    BRUSSELS, INTERNATIONAL INSTITUTE OF DIFFERING CIVILIZATIONS,
    GENERAL REPORT, 1955, PP 356-364
    044,

BUNTING BRIAN
    BUNTING BRIAN
    THE RISE OF THE SOUTH AFRICAN REICH
    LONDON, PENGUIN, 1964
    031,032,

BURKE FRED G
    BURKE FRED G
    AFRICA'S QUEST FOR ORDER.
    ENGLEWOOD CLIFFS, PRENTICE-HALL, 1964
    061,

BURKE FRED G
    BURKE FRED G
    POLITICAL EVOLUTION IN KENYA CHAPTER 5.
    IN STANLEY DIAMOND AND FRED G BURKE (EDS.), THE
    TRANSFORMATION OF EAST AFRICA, NEW YORK, BASIC BOOKS, 1966
    055,117-07,

    BURKE FRED G
    TANGANYIKA PREPLANNING.
    SYRACUSE, SYRACUSE UNIVERSITY PRESS, 1965
    072,136-08,

    BURKE FRED G
    LOCAL GOVERNMENT AND POLITICS IN UGANDA.
    SYRACUSE, SYRACUSE UNIVERSITY PRESS, 1964
    139-07,

BURNS ALAN C
    BURNS ALAN C
    PARLIAMENT AS AN EXPORT.
    LONDON, ALLEN AND UNWIN, 1966
    068,

    BURNS ALAN C
    COLONIAL CIVIL SERVANT.
    LONDON, ALLEN AND UNWIN, 1949
    035,

BURNS D G
    BURNS D G
    AFRICAN EDUCATION.
    LONDON, OXFORD UNIVERSITY PRESS, 1965
    042,

BURROWS JOHN R
    HORWOOD O P F   BURROWS JOHN R
    THE SOUTH AFRICAN ECONOMY CHAPTER 11.
    IN CALVIN B HOOVER, ECONOMIC SYSTEMS OF THE COMMONWEALTH,
    DURHAM, DUKE UNIVERSITY PRESS, 1962, PP 462-500
    089,132-08,

BURTON RICHARD
    BURTON RICHARD
    THE LAKE REGIONS OF CENTRAL AFRICA.
    TWO VOLUMES, NEW YORK, HORIZON PRESS, 1961 (REPRINT)
    027,

BUSIA KOFI A
    BUSIA KOFI A
    AFRICA IN SEARCH OF DEMOCRACY.
    NEW YORK, PRAEGER, 1967
    LONDON, ROUTLEDGE AND KEGAN PAUL, 1967
    060,114-04,

    BUSIA KOFI A
    THE CHALLENGE OF NATIONALISM CHP 11.
    IN THE CHALLENGE OF AFRICA, NEW YORK, PRAEGER, 1962
    054,

BUSIA KOFI A
PURPOSEFUL EDUCATION FOR AFRICA.
THE HAGUE, MOUTON, 1964
042, 114-04,

BUSIA KOFI A
   BUSIA KOFI A
   THE CHALLENGE OF AFRICA.
   NEW YORK, PRAEGER, 1962
   060, 114-04,

   BUSIA KOFI A
   THE POSITION OF THE CHIEF IN THE MODERN POLITICAL SYSTEM OF
   ASHANTI.
   LONDON. OXFORD UNIVERSITY PRESS, 1951
   061,099,114-01,

BUSTIN EDOUARD
   BUSTIN EDOUARD
   THE QUEST FOR POLITICAL STABILITY IN THE CONGO--
   SOLDIERS, BUREAUCRATS AND POLITICIANS.
   IN HERBERT J SPIRO, ED., AFRICA THE PRIMACY OF POLITICS,
   NEW YORK, RANDOM HOUSE, 1966, PP 16-48
   064,108-06,

   BUSTIN EDOUARD
   LA DECENTRALISATION ADMINISTRATIVE ET L'EVOLUTION DES
   STRUCTURES POLITIQUES EN AFRIQUE ORIENTALE BRITANNIQUE
   (ADMINISTRATIVE DECENTRALIZATION AND THE EVOLUTION OF
   OF POLITICAL STRUCTURES IN BRITISH EAST AFRICA).
   LIEGE, UNIVERSITE DE LIEGE, 1958
   078,

   BUSTIN EDOUARD
   CONGO.
   IN G.M. CARTER (ED), FIVE AFRICAN STATES--RESPONSES TO
   DIVERSITY, ITHACA, CORNELL UNIVERSITY PRESS, 1963
   108-07,

BUTCHER D A P
   AMARTEIFIO G W   BUTCHER D A P   WHITHAM DAVID
   TEMA MANHEAN--A STUDY OF RESETTLEMENT.
   GHANA, GHANA UNIVERSITIES PRESS, 1966
   092,114-05,

BUTLER JEFFREY
   BERG ELLIOT J   BUTLER JEFFREY
   TRADE UNIONS.
   IN J S COLEMAN AND C G ROSBERG (EDS.), POLITICAL PARTIES
   AND NATIONAL INTEGRATION IN TROPICAL AFRICA, BERKELEY,
   UNIVERSITY OF CALIFORNIA PRESS, 1964
   073,

   MCCALL DANIEL F   BENNETT NORMAN   BUTLER JEFFREY
   EASTERN AFRICAN HISTORY
   NEW YORK, PRAEGER, 1969
   036,

   MCCALL DANIEL F   BENNETT NORMAN   BUTLER JEFFREY
   WESTERN AFRICAN HISTORY

NEW YORK, PRAEGER, 1969
036,

BUTT AUDREY J
    BUTT AUDREY J
    THE NILOTES OF THE SUDAN AND UGANDA.
    LONDON, INTERNATIONAL AFRICAN INSTITUTE, 1952
    134-01,

BUTZER KARL W
    BUTZER KARL W   HANSEN CARL L
    DESERT AND RIVER IN NUBIA-GEOMORPHOLOGY AND PREHISTORIC
    ENVIRONMENTS AT THE ASWAN RESERVOIR
    MADISON, UNIVERSITY OF WISCONSIN PRESS, 1968
    017,018,020,

BUXTON THOMAS F
    BUXTON THOMAS F
    THE AFRICAN SLAVE TRADE.
    LONDON, J MURRAY, 1839
    028,

C

CRISP
    CRISP
    CONGO--POLITICAL DOCUMENTS OF A DEVELOPING NATION.
    PRINCETON, PRINCETON UNIVERSITY PRESS, 1966
    108-07,

    CRISP
    CONGO 1965--POLITICAL DOCUMENTS OF A DEVELOPING NATION.
    PRINCETON, PRINCETON UNIVERSITY PRESS, 1967
    108-07,

CAILLIE RENE
    CAILLIE RENE
    TRAVELS THROUGH CENTRAL AFRICA TO TIMBUCTOO AND ACROSS THE
    GREAT DESERT TO MOROCCO PERFORMED IN THE YEARS 1824-1828.
    LONDON, 1830, 2V.
    027,

CAIRNS H A C
    CAIRNS H A C
    PRELUDE TO IMPERIALISM-BRITISH REACTIONS TO CENTRAL AFRICAN
    SOCIETY 1840-1890
    LONDON, ROUTLEDGE AND KEGAN PAUL, 1965
    033,

CALDWELL JOHN C
    CALDWELL JOHN C   OKONJO C   EDS
    THE POPULATION OF TROPICAL AFRICA.
    LONDON, LONGMANS, 1968
    053,074,076,

    CALDWELL JOHN C

POPULATION GROWTH AND FAMILY CHANGE IN AFRICA.
NEW YORK, HUMANITIES PRESS,INC., 1968
074,

CALDWELL JOHN C
    CALDWELL JOHN C
    AFRICAN RURAL-URBAN MIGRATION--THE MOVEMENT TO GHANA≠S
    TOWNS.
    NEW YORK (COLUMBIA), MCGILL-QUEENS UNIVERSITY PRESS, 1969
    045,114-05,

    CALDWELL JOHN C
    AFRICAN RURAL-URBAN MIGRATION THE MOVEMENT TO GHANA≠S TOWNS
    NEW YORK, COLUMBIA UNIVERSITY PRESS,1969
    047,

CALLAWAY ARCHIBALD
    CALLAWAY ARCHIBALD
    UNEMPLOYMENT AMONG AFRICAN SCHOOL LEAVERS
    JOURNAL OF MODERN AFRICAN STUDIES 1 1963 PP 351-371
    044,

CAMERON SIR D
    CAMERON SIR D
    MY TANGANYIKA SERVICE AND SOME NIGERIA.
    LONDON, ALLEN AND UNWIN,1939
    035,128-02,136-02,

CAMPBELL DONALD T
    SEGALL MARSHALL H   CAMPBELL DONALD T   HERSKOVITS MELVILLE
    THE INFLUENCE OF CULTURE ON VISUAL PERCEPTION
    INDIANAPOLIS, BOBBS-MERRILL,1966
    040,

    CAMPBELL DONALD T   LEVINE ROBERT A
    A PROPOSAL FOR COOPERATIVE CROSS-CULTURAL RESEARCH ON
    ETHNOCENTRISM.
    JOURNAL OF CONFLICT RESOLUTION 5 MARCH 1961 PP 82-108
    098,

CAMPBELL ROBERT
    DELANY M R   CAMPBELL ROBERT
    SEARCH FOR A PLACE--BLACK SEPARATISM AND AFRICA, 1860.
    ANN ARBOR, UNIVERSITY OF MICHIGAN PRESS, 1969
    095,

CAPLAN GERALD L
    CAPLAN GERALD L
    BAROTSELAND'S SCRAMBLE FOR PROTECTION.
    JOURNAL OF AFRICAN HISTORY, X, 2, 1969, PP. 277-294
    032,142-02,

    CAPLAN GERALD L
    BAROTSELAND--THE SECESSIONIST CHALLENGE TO ZAMBIA.
    THE JOURNAL OF MODERN AFRICAN STUDIES, VOL. 6, NO. 3, 1968,
    PP. 343-360
    057,142-06,

CARD EMILY
    CARD EMILY

GHANA PREPARES FOR CIVILIAN RULE.
AFRICA REPORT, APRIL 9, 1968
064,114-07,

CARDAIRE MARCEL
    BA AMADOU HAMPATE   CARDAIRE MARCEL
    TIERNO BOKAR, LE SAGE DE BANDIAGARA.
    PARIS, PRESENCE AFRICAINE, 1957
    123-02,

CARDINALL ALLAN W
    CARDINALL ALLAN W   ED
    TALES TOLD IN TOGOLAND-- TO WHICH IS ADDED THE MYTHICAL AND
    TRADITIONAL HISTORY OF DAGOMBA BY E F TAMAKLOE.
    LONDON, OXFORD UNIVERSITY PRESS, 1931
    012,137-01,

CARLSTON KENNETH S
    CARLSTON KENNETH S
    SOCIAL THEORY AND AFRICAN TRIBAL ORGANIZATION.
    URBANA, UNIVERSITY OF ILLINOIS PRESS, 1968
    009,

CARMICHAEL STOKELY
    CARMICHAEL STOKELY HAMILTON CHARLES
    BLACK POWER-- THE POLITICS OF LIBERATION IN AMERICA.
    NEW YORK, RANDOM HOUSE, 1967
    094,095,

CARNELL FG
    CARNELL FG
    POLITICAL IMPLICATIONS OF FEDERALISM IN NEW STATES.
    IN FEDERALISM AND ECONOMIC GROWTH IN UNDERDEVELOPED
    COUNTRIES, SYMPOSIUM BY UK HICKS AND OTHERS, LONDON, OXFORD
    UNIVERSITY PRESS, 1961, PP 16-69
    061,

CAROTHERS J C
    CAROTHERS J C
    THE AFRICAN MIND IN HEALTH AND DISEASE.
    GENEVA, WORLD HEALTH ORGANIZATION, MONOGRAPH SERIES, NO 17,
    1953
    039,

CARPENTER GEORGE
    CARPENTER GEORGE
    THE ROLE OF CHRISTIANITY AND ISLAM IN CONTEMPORARY AFRICA.
    IN CHARLES G HAINES (ED), AFRICA TODAY, BALTIMORE, THE JOHNS
    HOPKINS PRESS, 1955, PP 90-112
    050,

CARPENTER RHYS
    CARPENTER RHYS
    A TRANS-SAHARAN CARAVAN ROUTE IN HERODOTUS.
    AMERICAN JOURNAL OF ARCHAEOLOGY 60 1956 PP 231-242
    020,

CARRINGTON JOHN F
    CARRINGTON JOHN F
    TALKING DRUMS OF AFRICA

LONDON, CAREY KINGSGATE PRESS, 1949
015,

CARROLL F
    CARROLL F
    SOUTH WEST AFRICA AND THE UNITED NATIONS
    LEXINGTON, UNIVERSITY OF KENTUCKY PRESS, 1967
    081,146-09,

CARROLL KEVIN
    CARROLL KEVIN
    YORUBA RELIGIOUS SCULPTURE-- PAGAN AND CHRISTIAN SCULPTURE
    IN NIGERIA AND DAHOMEY.
    NEW YORK, PRAEGER, 1967
    014,109-01,128-01,

CART H P
    CART H P
    CONCEPTION DES RAPPORTS POLITIQUES AU BURUNDI.
    ETUDES CONGOLAISES 9 2 MARCH-APRIL 1966
    103-07,

CARTER GWENDOLEN M
    CARTER GWENDOLEN M
    AFRICAN CONCEPTS OF NATIONALISM IN SOUTH AFRICA.
    MELVILLE HERSKOVITS MEMORIAL LECTURE, EDINBURGH, EDINBURGH
    UNIVERSITY PRESS, MARCH 1965
    054,089,132-06,

    CARTER GWENDOLEN M   ED
    NATIONAL UNITY AND REGIONALISM IN EIGHT AFRICAN STATES--
    NIGERIA, NIGER, CONGO, GABON, CENTRAL AFRICAN REPUBLIC,
    CHAD, UGANDA, ETHIOPIA.
    ITHACA, CORNELL UNIVERSITY PRESS, 1966
    057,076,

    CARTER GWENDOLEN M
    INDEPENDENCE FOR AFRICA.
    NEW YORK, PRAEGER, 1960
    056,

    CARTER GWENDOLEN M   KARIS THOMAS   STULTZ NEWELL M
    SOUTH AFRICA'S TRANSKEI-- THE POLITICS OF DOMESTIC COLONIAL-
    IALISM.
    EVANSTON, NORTHWESTERN UNIVERSITY PRESS, 1967 (LONDON,
    HEINEMANN EDUCATIONAL BOOKS)
    089,132-06,

    CARTER GWENDOLEN M   PADEN ANN   EDS
    EXPANDING HORIZONS IN AFRICAN STUDIES.
    EVANSTON, NORTHWESTERN UNIVERSITY PRESS, 1969
    002,100,

    CARTER GWENDOLEN M
    AFRICAN STUDIES IN THE UNITED STATES.
    IN PROCEEDINGS OF THE CONFERENCE ON AFRICAN LANGUAGES AND
    LITERATURES, NORTHWESTERN UNIVERSITY, 1966, UNITED STATES
    OFFICE OF EDUCATION NO. OE-6-14-018, PP 2-7
    099,100,

CARTER GWENDOLEN M
AFRICAN ONE-PARTY STATES.
IN PETER J MCEWAN AND ROBERT B SUTCLIFFE (EDS), MODERN AFRICA,
NEW YORK, THOMAS CROWELL, 1965, PP 201-209
061,

CARTER GWENDOLEN M
    CARTER GWENDOLEN M
    SOUTH AFRICA--SEGMENTED BUT INTERDEPENDENT.
    AFRICA REPORT, MAY, 1968, P. 15-18
    089,132-06,

    CARTER GWENDOLEN M
    THE CHANGING ROLE OF THE AFRICANIST.
    AFRICA REPORT, JANUARY 1968, P. 60
    100,

    CARTER GWENDOLEN M
    THE POLITICS OF INEQUALITY.
    NEW YORK, PRAEGER, 1952; REVISED ED, 1962
    089,132-07,

    CARTER GWENDOLEN M ED
    AFRICAN ONE-PARTY STATES.
    ITHACA, CORNELL UNIVERSITY PRESS, 1962
    061,

    CARTER GWENDOLEN M ED
    POLITICS IN AFRICA--SEVEN CASES.
    NEW YORK, HARCOURT, BRACE AND WORLD, 1966
    061,

CARTEY WILFRED
    CARTEY WILFRED
    WHISPERS FROM A CONTINENT--THE LITERATURE OF CONTEMPORARY
    BLACK AFRICA.
    NEW YORK, RANDOM HOUSE, 1969
    090,

CASTAGNO A A JR
    CASTAGNO A A JR
    THE SOMALI-KENYA CONTROVERSY
    JOURNAL OF MODERN AFRICAN STUDIES 2 1964 PP 165-188
    059, 117-09, 133-09,

    CASTAGNO A A JR
    SOMALIA GOES MILITARY
    AFRICA REPORT 15 FEBRUARY 1970 PP 25-27
    064,133-07,

    CASTAGNO A A JR
    SOMALI.
    IN COLEMAN, J.S. AND ROSBERG, C.G. (EDS), POLITICAL PARTIES
    AND NATIONAL INTEGRATION IN TROPICAL AFRICA, LOS ANGELES,
    UNIVERSITY OF CALIFORNIA PRESS, 1964
    133-06,

    CASTAGNO A A JR
    SOMALIA
    NEW YORK CARNEGIE ENDOWMENT BY COLUMBIA UNIVERSITY PRESS

1959
133-11,

CAYTON HORACE
    DRAKE ST CLAIR   CAYTON HORACE
    BLACK METROPOLIS.
    NEW YORK, HARCOURT BRACE, 1945
    030,

CERULLI ERNESTA
    CERULLI ERNESTA
    PEOPLES OF SOUTH-WEST ETHIOPIA AND ITS BORDERLAND
    LONDON, INTERNATIONAL AFRICAN INSTITUTE, 1956
    110-01.

CERVENKA ZDENEK
    CERVENKA ZDENEK
    THE ORGANIZATION OF AFRICAN UNITY AND ITS CHARTER.
    NEW YORK, PRAEGER PUBLISHERS, 1969
    079,080,

CESAIRE AIME
    CESAIRE AIME
    RETURN TO MY NATIVE LAND.
    PARIS, PRESENCE AFRICAINE. 1968
    054,091,

    CESAIRE AIME
    LETTER TO MAURICE THOREZ.
    PARIS, PRESENCE AFRICAINE. 1956
    054,

    CESAIRE AIME
    DISCOURS SUR LE COLONIALISME.
    PARIS, PRESENCE AFRICAINE, 1955
    091,

    CESAIRE AIME
    TOUSSAINT LOUVERTURE.
    PARIS, PRESENCE AFRICAINE, 1961
    091,

    CESAIRE AIME
    LA TRAGEDIE DU ROI CHRISTOPHE (THE TRAGEDY OF KING
    CHRISTOPHER).
    PARIS, PRESENCE AFRICAINE, 1963
    091,

    CESAIRE AIME
    LA PENSEE POLITIQUE DE SEKOU TOURE (THE POLITICAL THOUGHT
    OF SEKOU TOURE).
    PRESENCE AFRICAINE 29 JANUARY 1960
    060,115-04,

    CESAIRE AIME
    DISCOURS SUR LE COLONIALISME (DISCOURSE ON COLONIALISM).
    PRESENCE AFRICAINE,
    054,

CEULEMANS P

CEULEMANS P
INTRODUCTION DE L'INFLUENCE DE L'ISLAM AU CONGO.
IN LEWIS, ISLAM IN TROPICAL AFRICA, LONDON, OXFORD UNIVERSITY
PRESS, 1966, P. 174-192
108-03,

CHAGULA W K
CHAGULA W K
THE ROLE OF THE ELITE, THE INTELLIGENTSIA AND EDUCATED EAST
AFRICANS, IN THE DEVELOPMENT OF UGANDA, KENYA AND TANZANIA.
KAMPALA, EAST AFRICAN ACADEMY, SECOND FOUNDATION LECTURE, 1966
044,117-03,136-03,139-03,

CHALIAND GERARD
CHALIAND GERARD
ARMED STRUGGLE IN AFRICA-- WITH THE GUERILLAS IN 'PORTU-
GUESE' GUINEA.
NEW YORK, MONTHLY REVIEW PRESS, 1969
087,144-07,144-09,

CHAMBERS ROBERT
CHAMBERS ROBERT
SETTLEMENT SCHEMES IN TROPICAL AFRICA--A STUDY OF
ORGANIZATIONS AND DEVELOPMENTS.
NEW YORK, PRAEGER PUBLISHERS, 1969
070,

CHAPELLE JEAN
CHAPELLE JEAN
LA RELIGION DES TOUBOUS (TUBU RELIGION) CHAPTER 9.
IN NOMADES NOIRS DU SAHARA, PARIS, LIBRARIE PLON, 1957
013,106-01,

CHAPELLE JEAN
REGARDS SUR LE PASSE (A LOOK AT THE PAST) CHAPTER 1.
NOMADES NOIRS DU SAHARA, PARIS, LIBRARIE PLON, 1957
005,

CHAPELLE JEAN
L≠ORGANISATION CLANIQUE (CLAN ORGANIZATION) CHAPTER 8.
IN NOMADES NOIRS DU SAHARA, PARIS, LIBRARIE PLON, 1957
008,009,

CHAPELLE JEAN
LA VIE EN SOCIETE (SOCIAL LIFE) CHAPTER 7.
IN NOMADES NOIRS DU SAHARA, PARIS, LIBRARIE PLON, 1957
008,

CHAPELLE JEAN
DE LA NAISSANCE A LA MORT (LIFE-CYCLE) CHAPTER 6.
IN NOMADES NOIRS DU SAHARA, PARIS, LIBRARIE PLON, 1957
008,

CHAPLIN J H
CHAPLIN J H
A NOTE ON CENTRAL AFRICAN DREAM CONCEPTS.
MAN 58 1958 PP 90-92
040,

CHAPMAN

SMOCK AUDREY CHAPMAN
THE N.C.N.C. AND ETHNIC UNIONS IN BIAFRA.
THE JOURNAL OF MODERN AFRICAN STUDIES, 7, 1, 1969
007,128-07,

CHARBONNIER
CHARBONNIER FRANCOIS
GABON, TERRE D AVENIR.
PARIS, ENCYCLOPEDIE D'OUTRE-MER, 1957
112-11,

CHARPY JACQUES
CHARPY JACQUES
LA FONDATION DE DAKAR (THE FOUNDATION OF DAKAR) 1845-1857-
1869.
PARIS, LAROSE,1958
045,130-05,

CHECCHI
CHECCHI AND COMPANY
A DEVELOPMENT STUDY AND PRELIMINARY DESIGNS FOR AN INDUS-
TRIAL PARK IN MONROVIA.
WASHINGTON, D.C., CHECCHI AND COMPANY, 1964
092,119-05,

CHESSWAS J D
CHESSWAS J D
THE ESSENTIALS OF LUGANDA.
EAST AFRICA, OXFORD UNIVERSITY PRESS, 1968
011,139-01,

CHIDZERO BERNARD T
CHIDZERO BERNARD T
AFRICAN NATIONALISM IN EAST AND CENTRAL AFRICA.
INTERNATIONAL AFFAIRS 36 OCTOBER PP 464-475
055,

CHIDZERO BERNARD T
THE PLURAL SOCIETY OF TANGANYIKA CHP 7.
IN TANGANYIKA AND INTERNATIONAL TRUSTEESHIP, NEW YORK,
OXFORD UNIVERSITY PRESS, 1961
057,136-06,

CHIDZERO BERNARD T
REACTIONS TO MULTI-RACIALISM CHP 8.
IN TANGANYIKA AND INTERNATIONAL TRUSTEESHIP, NEW YORK,
OXFORD UNIVERSITY PRESS, 1961
088,136-06,

CHIDZERO BERNARD T
CENTRAL AFRICA-- THE RACE QUESTION AND THE FRANCHISE.
RACE 1 1955 PP 53-60
088,122-06,142-06,

CHIDZERO BERNARD T
TANGANYIKA AND INTERNATIONAL TRUSTEESHIP.
LONDON, OXFORD UNIVERSITY PRESS, 1961
035,136-02,

CHILCOTE RONALD H

CHILCOTE RONALD H
EMERGING NATIONALISM IN PORTUGUESE AFRICA.
PALO ALTO, CALIFORNIA, HOOVER INSTITUTION PRESS, 1969
087,144-12,

CHILCOTE RONALD H
CHILCOTE RONALD H
THE POLITICAL THOUGHT OF AMILCAR CABRAL.
THE JOURNAL OF MODERN AFRICAN STUDIES, VOL. 6, NO. 3, 1968,
PP. 373-388
087,144-04,

CHILCOTE RONALD H
PORTUGUESE AFRICA
ENGLEWOOD CLIFFS, PRENTICE-HALL, 1967
087,144-11,

CHILD IRVIN L
CHILD IRVIN L
SOCIALIZATION CHP 18.
IN GARDNER LINDZEY (ED), HANDBOOK OF SOCIAL PSYCHOLOGY 2
CAMBRIDGE MASS, ADDISON-WESLEY, 1954
098,

CHILDE V GORDON
CHILDE V GORDON
A SHORT INTRODUCTION TO ARCHAEOLOGY.
NEW YORK, MACMILLAN, 1958
018,

CHILVER E M
CHILVER E M   KABERRY PHYLLIS M
FROM TRIBUTE TO TAX IN A TIKAR CHIEFDOM.
AFRICA (LONDON) 30 1960 PP 1-19
038,

CHIN ROBERT
CHIN ROBERT
THE UTILITY OF SYSTEM MODELS AND DEVELOPMENTAL MODELS
CHAPTER 1.
IN JASON L FINKLE AND RICHARD W GABLE, POLITICAL
DEVELOPMENT AND SOCIAL CHANGE, NEW YORK, JOHN WILEY, 1966
072,098,

CHING JAMES C
CHING JAMES C
MASS COMMUNICATION IN THE REPUBLIC OF CONGO.
JOURNALISM QUARTERLY 41 SPRING 1964 PP 237-244
049,

CHISIZA D K
CHISIZA D K
THE OUTLOOK FOR CONTEMPORARY AFRICA CHAPTER 3.
IN AFRICA'S FREEDOM, NEW YORK, BARNES AND NOBLE, 1964,
PP 38-54
060,122-04,

CHISIZA D K
AFRICA-- WHAT LIES AHEAD.
NEW YORK, AFRICAN AMERICAN INSTITUTE, 1962

LONDON, COMMAND 1030, HER MAJESTY'S STATIONERY OFFICE, 1960
060,122-04,

CHITEPO HERBERT W
   CHITEPO HERBERT W
   DEVELOPMENTS IN CENTRAL AFRICA.
   IN DAVID P CURRIE (ED), FEDERALISM AND THE NEW NATIONS OF
   AFRICA, CHICAGO, UNIVERSITY OF CHICAGO PRESS, 1964, PP 3-28
   078,087,122-06,142-06,145-06,

CHITTICK H NEVILLE
   CHITTICK H NEVILLE
   THE SHIRAZI COLONIZATION OF EAST AFRICA
   JOURNAL OF AFRICAN HISTORY 6 1965 PP 275-294
   023,

   CHITTICK H NEVILLE
   KILWA AND THE ARAB SETTLEMENT OF THE EAST AFRICAN COAST.
   THE JOURNAL OF AFRICAN HISTORY 4 1963 PP 179-190
   023,136-02,

   CHITTICK H NEVILLE
   NOTES ON KILWA.
   TANGANYIKA NOTES AND RECORDS 53 1959 PP 179-203
   023,136-02,

CHOME JULES
   CHOME JULES
   LA PASSION DE SIMON KIMBANGU 1921-1951 (THE PASSION OF
   SIMON KIMBANGU 1921-1951).
   BRUXELLES, AMIS DE PRESENCE AFRICAINE, 1959
   051,108-03,

CHRISTENSEN JAMES
   CHRISTENSEN JAMES
   THE ADAPTIVE FUNCTIONS OF FANTI PRIESTHOOD CHAPTER 13.
   IN WILLIAM BASCOM AND MELVILLE HERSKOVITS, CONTINUTY AND
   CHANGE IN AFRICAN CULTURES, CHICAGO, UNIVERSITY OF CHICAGO
   PRESS, 1962, PP 238-256
   051,114-03,

CHU GODWIN C
   CHU GODWIN C
   PROBLEMS OF CROSS-CULTURAL COMMUNICATIONS RESEARCH.
   JOURNALISM QUARTERLY 41 AUTUMN 1964 PP 557-562
   098,

CHURCH
   CHURCH R J HARRISON
   WEST AFRICA-A STUDY OF THE ENVIRONMENT AND OF MAN'S USE
   OF IT.
   LONDON, LONGMANS, GREEN, 1960 AND 1966
   069,

   CHURCH R J HARRISON
   GEOGRAPHICAL FACTORS IN THE DEVELOPMENT OF TRANSPORT IN
   AFRICA.
   NEW YORK, UNITED NATIONS TRANSPORT AND COMMUNICATIONS REVIEW
   2 NO 3 1949 PP 3-11
   048,

CHURCH
    CHURCH R J HARRISON ET AL
    AFRICA AND THE ISLANDS.
    NEW YORK, WILEY, 1964
    069,

    CHURCH R J HARRISON
    AFRICAN BOUNDARIES
    CHAPTER 21 IN W G EAST AND A E MOODIE(EDS), THE CHANGING
    WORLD,LONDON 1956
    059,

    CHURCH R J HARRISON
    ENVIRONMENT AND POLICIES IN WEST AFRICA
    PRINCETON, VAN NOSTRAND, 1963
    069,

CISSE DIA AMADOU
    CISSE DIA AMADOU
    LES DERNIERS JOURS DE LAT DIOR--LA MORT DU DAMEL.
    PARIS, PRESENCE AFRICAINE, 1965
    130-02,

CLAPHAM
    CLAPHAM CHRISTOPHER
    THE ETHIOPIAN COUP D'ETAT OF DECEMBER 1960.
    THE JOURNAL OF MODERN AFRICAN STUDIES, VOL. 6, NO. 4, 1968,
    PP. 495-507
    064,110-06,

CLAPPERTON HUGH
    CLAPPERTON HUGH
    JOURNAL OF A SECOND EXPEDITION INTO THE INTERIOR OF AFRICA
    FROM THE BIGHT OF BENIN TO SOCCATOO.
    LONDON, CASS, 1966
    027,

    DENHAM DIXON   CLAPPERTON HUGH   OUDNEY WALTER
    NARRATIVE OF TRAVELS AND DISCOVERIES IN NORTHERN AND CENTRAL
    AFRICA IN THE YEARS 1822, 1823 AND 1824.
    LONDON, CAMBRIDGE UNIVERSITY PRESS,1966,3 VOLUMES
    E W BOVILL, (ED.)
    027,099,

CLARCK MICHAEL K
    CLARCK MICHAEL K
    ALGERIA IN TURMOIL--A HISTORY OF THE REBELLION.
    NEW YORK, PRAEGER, 1959
    055,101-06,

CLARIDGE W WALTON
    CLARIDGE W WALTON
    A HISTORY OF THE GOLD COAST AND ASHANTI.
    LONDON, CASS, 1964
    026,114-02,

CLARK GRAHAM D
    CLARK GRAHAM D
    ARCHAEOLOGY AND SOCIETY

NEW YORK, BARNES AND NOBLE, 1965
018.

CLARK J DESMOND
    CLARK J DESMOND
    THE SPREAD OF FOOD PRODUCTION IN SUB-SAHARAN AFRICA.
    JOURNAL OF AFRICAN HISTORY 3 1962 PP 211-228
    019.

    BISHOP WALTER W   CLARK J DESMOND
    BACKGROUND TO EVOLUTION IN AFRICA
    CHICAGO, UNIVERSITY OF CHICAGO PRESS, 1966
    018.

    CLARK J DESMOND
    CULTURE AND ECOLOGY IN PREHISTORIC AFRICA.
    IN DAVID BROKENSHA (ED.), ECOLOGY AND ECONOMIC DEVELOPMENT
    IN TROPICAL AFRICA, BERKELEY, UNIVERSITY OF CALIFORNIA,
    1965, PP 13-28
    019.

    CLARK J DESMOND
    PREHISTORY.
    IN ROBERT A LYSTAD (ED), THE AFRICAN WORLD, NEW YORK,
    PREAGER, 1966, PP 11-39
    018.

    CLARK J DESMOND
    THE PREHISTORIC ORIGINS OF AFRICAN CULTURE,
    JOURNAL OF AFRICAN HISTORY VOL 5 NO 2 1964 PP 161-183
    018.

    CLARK J DESMOND
    ATLAS OF AFRICAN PREHISTORY.
    CHICAGO, UNIVERSITY OF CHICAGO, 1967
    018.

    CLARK J DESMOND
    AFRICA SOUTH OF THE SAHARA
    IN BRAIDWOOD AND WILLEY, COURSES TOWARD URBAN LIFE, VIKING
    FUND PUBLICATIONS IN ANTHROPOLOGY, CHICAGO, ALDINE, 1962
    018.

    CLARK J DESMOND
    THE PREHISTORY OF SOUTHERN AFRICA
    HARMONDSWORTH, PENGUIN, 1959; REVISED, 1970
    018.

    HOWELL F CLARK   CLARK J DESMOND
    ACHEULIAN HUNTER-GATHERERS OF SUB-SAHARAN AFRICA.
    IN F CLARK HOWELL AND FRANCOIS BOURLIERE (EDS.), AFRICAN
    ECOLOGY AND HUMAN EVOLUTION, CHICAGO, ALDINE, 1966,
    PP 458-533
    018.

CLARK J P
    CLARK J P
    AMERICA, THEIR AMERICA.
    LONDON, HEINEMANN EDUCATIONAL BOOKS, 1969; AND NEW YORK,
    AFRICANA PUBLISHING CORP, 1969

096,128-10,

CLARK KENNETH
    CLARK KENNETH
    DARK GHETTO, DILEMMAS OF SOCIAL POWER.
    NEW YORK, HARPER AND ROW, 1965
    030,

    PARSONS TALCOTT   CLARK KENNETH   EDS
    THE NEGRO AMERICAN.
    BOSTON, HOUGHTON MIFFLIN, DAEDALUS LIBRARY, 7 1966
    030,

CLARK PAUL
    CLARK PAUL
    DEVELOPMENT STRATEGY IN AN EARLY STAGE ECONOMY-UGANDA
    JOURNAL OF MODERN AFRICAN STUDIES 4 1966 PP 47-64
    072,073,139-08,

CLARK W E LE-GROS
    CLARK W E LE-GROS
    MAN-APES OR APE MEN THE STORY OF DISCOVERIES IN AFRICA
    NEW YORK, HOLT, RINEHART AND WINSTON, 1967
    018,

CLARKE F A S
    HAYWOOD AUSTIN   CLARKE F A S
    THE HISTORY OF THE ROYAL WEST AFRICAN FRONTIER FORCE.
    ALDERSHOT, GALE AND POLDEN LIMITED, 1964
    033,

CLARKE J I
    CLARKE J I
    OIL IN LIBYA--SOME IMPLICATIONS.
    ECONOMIC GEOGRAPHY 39 JANUARY 1963 PP 40-59
    069,

CLARKE JOHN HENRIK
    RESNICK IDRIAN N   CLARKE JOHN HENRIK   ET AL
    DIALOG-THE FUTURE OF AFRICAN STUDIES AFTER MONTREAL
    AFRICA REPORT DECEMBER 1969 PP 22-27
    100,

    CLARKE JOHN HENRIK
    MALCOLM X. THE MAN AND HIS TIMES
    NEW YORK, MACMILLAN, 1969
    094,

    CLARKE JOHN HENRIK
    HARLEM, A COMMUNITY IN TRANSITION.
    NEW YORK, CITADEL PRESS, 1964
    030,

CLARKSON THOMAS
    CLARKSON THOMAS
    AN ESSAY ON THE COMPARATIVE EFFICIENCY OF REGULATION OR
    ABOLITION AS APPLIED TO THE SLAVE TRADE.
    LONDON, J PHILLIPS, 1789
    029,

CLARKSON THOMAS
THE SUBSTANCE OF THE EVIDENCE OF SUNDRY PERSONS ON THE SLAVE
TRADE COLLECTED IN THE COURSE OF A TOUR MADE IN THE AUTUMN
OF THE YEAR 1788.
LONDON,1789
028,

CLAYTON E S
   CLAYTON E S
   ECONOMIC AND TECHNICAL OPTIMA IN PEASANT AGRICULTURE CHAPTER
   2.
   IN EDITH WHETHAM AND JEAN CURRIE (EDS.), READINGS IN THE
   APPLIED ECONOMICS OF AFRICA, LONDON, CAMBRIDGE UNIVERSITY
   PRESS, 1, 1967, PP 12-24
   070,

   CLAYTON E S
   AGRARIAN DEVELOPMENT IN PEASANT ECONOMIES-- SOME LESSONS
   FROM KENYA.
   LONDON,OXFORD UNIVERSITY PRESS,1964
   070,117-08,

CLEAVER ELDRIDGE
   CLEAVER ELDRIDGE
   POST-PRISON WRITINGS AND SPEECHES-EDITED AND WITH AN
   APPRAISAL BY ROBERT SCHAER
   NEW YORK,RANDOM HOUSE,1969
   094,095,

   CLEAVER ELDRIDGE
   SOUL ON ICE.
   NEW YORK, MCGRAW-HILL BOOK COMPANY, 1968
   094,

CLEMENT
   ONYEMELUKWE CLEMENT
   PROBLEMS OF INDUSTRIAL PLANNING AND MANAGEMENT IN NIGERIA.
   NEW YORK (COLUMBIA), MCGILL-QUEENS, 1969
   071,128-08,

CLEMENT JOSEPH R
   CLEMENT JOSEPH R
   ESSAI DE BIBLIOGRAPHIE DU RUANDA-URUNDI.
   USUMBURA,N.P., 1959
   103-12,

CLEMENTS FRANK
   CLEMENTS FRANK
   RHODESIA--A STUDY OF THE DETERIORATION OF A WHITE SOCIETY.
   NEW YORK, PRAEGER, 1969
   087,145-06,

CLENDENEN CLARENCE
   CLENDENEN CLARENCE   COLLINS ROBERT O   DUIGNAN PETER
   AMERICANS IN AFRICA, 1865-1900.
   PALO ALTO, CALIFORNIA, HOOVER INSTITUTION PRESS, 1966
   096,

   DUIGNAN PETER   CLENDENEN CLARENCE
   THE UNITED STATES AND THE AFRICAN SLAVE TRADE 1619-1862.

STANFORD HOOVER INSTITUTE 1963
029,

CLIFFE LIONEL
   CLIFFE LIONEL   ED
   ONE-PARTY DEMOCRACY-- THE 1965 TANZANIA GENERAL ELECTIONS.
   NAIROBI,EAST AFRICAN PUBLISHING HOUSE,1967
   063,136-07,

   CLIFFE LIONEL
   TANZANIA.
   LONDON, PALL MALL PRESS, 1970
   136-11,

CLIGNET REMI
   CLIGNET REMI   FOSTER PHILIP
   THE FORTUNATE FEW.
   EVANSTON,NORTHWESTERN UNIVERSITY PRESS,1966
   039,043,116-03,

   CLIGNET REMI   FOSTER PHILIP
   FRENCH AND BRITISH COLONIAL EDUCATION IN AFRICA.
   COMPARATIVE EDUCATIONAL REVIEW 8 1964 PP 191-198
   042,

   CLIGNET REMI
   ETHNICITY SOCIAL DIFFERENTIATION AND SECONDARY SCHOOLING
   IN WEST AFRICA.
   CAHIERS D'ETUDES AFRICAINES 7 1967 PP 361-378
   043,

   CLIGNET REMI   FOSTER PHILIP
   INTRODUCTION.
   IN REMI CLIGNET AND PHILIP FOSTER, THE FORTUNATE FEW,
   EVANSTON, NORTHWESTERN UNIVERSITY PRESS, 1966, PP 3-22
   043,

   CLIGNET REMI
   SOCIAL AREA ANALYSIS OF DOUALA AND YAOUNDE.
   IN CARTER, GWENDOLEN M. AND ANN PADEN (EDS), EXPANDING
   HORIZONS IN AFRICAN STUDIES, EVANSTON, NORTHWESTERN
   UNIVERSITY PRESS, 1969. PP. 315-320
   100,104-05,

   CLIGNET REMI
   MANY WIVES, MANY POWERS--AUTHORITY AND POWER IN POLYGYNOUS
   FAMILIES.
   EVANSTON, NORTHWESTERN UNIVERSITY PRESS, 1970
   046,116-03,

   CLIGNET REMI   SWEEN JOYCE
   SOCIAL CHANGE AND TYPE OF MARRIAGE.
   AMERICAN JOURNAL OF SOCIOLOGY, VOL. 74, NO. 1, JULY 1969,
   PP. 123-145
   046,

   CLIGNET REMI   FOSTER PHILIP
   THE HIERARCHY OF POSTPRIMARY SCHOOLS-- ITS IMPACT ON ETHNIC
   AND SOCIAL RECRUITMENT OF STUDENTS CHAPTER 4.
   IN REMI CLIGNET AND PHILIP FOSTER, THE FORTUNATE FEW,

EVANSTON NORTHWESTERN UNIVERSITY PRESS 1965
043,

CLIGNET REMI
    CLIGNET REMI   FOSTER PHILIP
    THE ETHNIC, SOCIAL AND CULTURAL ORIGIN OF STUDENTS IN THE
    POSTPRIMARY SCHOOL CHAPTER 3.
    IN REMI CLIGNET AND PHILIP FOSTER. THE FORTUNATE FEW
    EVANSTON, NORTHWESTERN UNIVERSITY PRESS , 1966
    043,

    CLIGNET REMI   FOSTER PHILIP
    THE SOCIAL, ECONOMIC AND EDUCATIONAL SCENE IN THE IVORY
    COAST CHAPTER 2.
    IN THE FORTUNATE FEW,EVANSTON, NORTHWESTERN UNIVERSITY
    PRESS 1966
    042,116-03,

    CLIGNET REMI   FOSTER PHILIP
    LA PREEMINENCE DE L'ENSEIGNEMENT CLASSIQUE EN COTE D'IVOIRE
    UN EXAMPLE D'ASSIMILATION (THE PREEMINENCE OF THE CLASSICAL
    EDUCATION IN THE IVORY COAST-- AN EXAMPLE OF ASSIMILATION).
    REVUE FRANCAISE DE SOCIOLOGIE 7 1966 PP 32-47
    043,

    CLIGNET REMI
    REFLEXIONS SUR LES PROBLEMS DE PSYCHOLOGIE EN AFRIQUE
    (REFLECTIONS ON THE PROBLEMS OF PSYCHOLOGY IN AFRICA).
    BULLETIN DE L'INSTITUT NATIONAL D'ORIENTATION
    PROFESSIONNELLE 18 1962 PP 86-94
    041,

CLOUDSLEY THOMPSON
    CLOUDSLEY THOMPSON
    TSETSE-- THE SCOURGE OF AFRICA.
    LONDON,SCIENCE NEWS,PENGUIN BOOKS,1959, PP 69-78
    069,075,

CLOWER ROBERT W
    CLOWER ROBERT W   ET AL
    GROWTH WITHOUT DEVELOPMENT, AN ECONOMIC SURVEY OF LIBERIA.
    EVANSTON,NORTHWESTERN UNIVERISTY PRESS,1966
    CHAPTER 10 AND APPENDIX PP 259-335
    073,119-08,

COALE ANSLEY J
    BRASS WILLIAM   COALE ANSLEY J   ET AL
    THE DEMOGRAPHY OF TROPICAL AFRICA
    PRINCETON,PRINCETON UNIVERSITY PRESS,1968
    074,

COCKCROFT SIR JOHN
    COCKCROFT SIR JOHN
    TECHNOLOGY FOR DEVELOPING COUNTRIES
    LONDON,OVERSEAS DEVELOPMENT INSTITUTE
    075,

COCKER G B A
    COCKER G B A
    FAMILY PROPERTY AMONG THE YORUBAS.

LAGOS, AFRICAN UNIVERSITIES PRESS, 1966
008,128-01,

COHEN ABNER
  COHEN ABNER
  CUSTOM AND POLITICS IN URBAN AFRICA--A STUDY OF HAUSA
  MIGRANTS IN YORUBA TOWNS.
  BERKELEY, UNIVERSITY OF CALIFORNIA PRESS, 1969
  007,128-05,

  COHEN ABNER
  POLITICS OF THE KOLA TRADE CHAPTER 14.
  IN EDITH WHETHAM AND JEAN CURRIE (EDS.), READINGS IN THE
  APPLIED ECONOMICS OF AFRICA, LONDON, CAMBRIDGE UNIVERSITY
  PRESS, 1, 1967, PP 153-163
  038,

  COHEN ABNER
  THE POLITICS OF MYSTICISM IN SOME LOCAL COMMUNITIES.
  LOCAL-LEVEL POLITICS, MARC J. SWARTZ (ED.), CHICAGO, ALDINE
  PUBLISHING CO., 1968, PP. 361-376
  052,128-03,

  COHEN ABNER
  POLITICAL ANTHROPOLOGY--THE ANALYSIS OF THE SYMBOLISM OF
  POWER RELATIONS.
  MAN, VOL. 4, NO. 2, JUNE, 1969, PP. 215-235
  009,

COHEN ANDREW
  COHEN ANDREW
  BRITISH POLICY IN CHANGING AFRICA.
  LONDON, ROUTLEDGE AND KEGAN PAUL, 1959
  035,

COHEN RONALD
  COHEN RONALD   MIDDLETON JOHN   EDS
  COMPARATIVE POLITICAL SYSTEMS-- A READER IN POLITICAL
  ANTHROPOLOGY.
  NEW YORK, NATURAL HISTORY PRESS, 1967
  009,

  COHEN RONALD   MIDDLETON JOHN   EDS
  FROM TRIBE TO NATION IN AFRICA.
  SAN FRANCISCO, CHANDLER, 1970
  004,006,057,

  COHEN RONALD
  THE JUST-SO SO-- A SPURIOUS TRIBAL GROUP IN WESTERN SUDANIC
  HISTORY.
  MAN 62 1962 PP 153-154
  005,

  COHEN RONALD   VANSINA JAN   ZOLBERG ARISTIDE R
  ORAL HISTORY IN AFRICA.
  EVANSTON ILLINOIS, NORTHWESTERN UNIVERSITY, PROGRAM OF
  AFRICAN STUDIES, REPRINT SERIES, 2, NO.1 SEPTEMBER 1965
  012,099,

  COHEN RONALD

SLAVERY IN AFRICA.
TRANS-ACTION (SPECIAL SUPPLEMENT) 4 1967 PP 44-56
010,028,

COHEN RONALD
    COHEN RONALD
    FAMILY LIFE IN BORNU.
    ANTHROPOLOGICA 9 NO. 1 1967 PP 21-42
    008,128-01,

    COHEN RONALD
    MARRIAGE INSTABILITY AMONG THE KANURI OF NORTHERN NIGERIA.
    AMERICAN ANTHROPOLOGIST 63 1961 PP 1231-1249
    008,128-01,

    COHEN RONALD
    THE SUCCESS THAT FAILED-- AN EXPERIMENT IN CULTURE CHANGE
    IN AFRICA.
    ANTHROPOLOGICA 4 1962 PP 1-15
    070,

    COHEN RONALD
    CONFLICT AND CHANGE IN A NORTHERN NIGERIAN EMIRATE.
    IN G ZOLLSCHAN AND D HIRSCH (EDS), EXPLORATIONS IN SOCIAL
    CHANGE,BOSTON, HOUGHTON MIFFLIN, 1964
    024,128-03,

    COHEN RONALD
    SOME ASPECTS OF INSTITUTIONALIZED EXCHANGE-- A KANURI
    EXAMPLE.
    CAHIERS D'ETUDES AFRICAINES 5 1965 PP 353-369
    010,128-01,

    COHEN RONALD
    THE BORNU KING LISTS.
    IN J BUTLER (ED), BOSTON UNIVERSITY PUBLICATIONS IN AFRICAN
    HISTORY VOL 2, BOSTON, BOSTON UNIVERSITY PRESS, 1966,
    PP 41-83
    024,128-02,

    COHEN RONALD
    THE DYNAMICS OF FEUDALISM IN BORNU.
    IN J BUTLER (ED), BOSTON UNIVERSITY PUBLICATIONS IN AFRICAN
    HISTORY VOL 2, BOSTON, BOSTON UNIVERSITY PRESS, 1966
    PP 87-105
    024,128-01,

    COHEN RONALD
    POWER, AUTHORITY, AND PERSONAL SUCCESS IN ISLAM AND BORNU.
    IN M SWARTZ,   V TURNER, AND A TUDEN (EDS), POLITICAL
    ANTHROPOLOGY, CHICAGO, ALDINE, 1966, PP 129-139
    009,128-01,

    COHEN RONALD
    SOCIAL STRATIFICATION IN BORNU.
    IN A TUDEN AND L PLOTNICOV (EDS), CLASS AND STATUS IN SUB-
    SAHARAN AFRICA, NEW YORK, FREE PRESS, 1968
    008,128-01,

    COHEN RONALD   BRENNER LOUIS

BORNU IN THE 19TH CENTURY.
IN A AJAYI AND MICHAEL CROWDER (EDS), THE HISTORY OF WEST
AFRICA, OXFORD, CLARENDON PRESS, 1968
024,128-02,

COHEN RONALD
    COHEN RONALD
    THE KANURI OF BORNU.
    NEW YORK, HOLT, RINEHART AND WINSTON, 1967
    008,024,128-01,

    COHEN RONALD
    SLAVERY AMONG THE KANURI.
    TRANS-ACTION, 1967
    028,128-01,

    COHEN RONALD
    ANTHROPOLOGY AND POLITICAL SCIENCE-- COURTSHIP OR MARRIAGE.
    AMERICAN BEHAVIORAL SCIENTIST NOVEMBER 1967
    100,

    COHEN RONALD   SCHLEGEL A
    THE TRIBE AS A SOCIO-POLITICAL UNIT-- A CROSS CULTURAL
    EXAMINATION.
    IN HELM (ED), ESSAYS ON THE PROBLEM OF TRIBE, AMERICAN
    ETHNOLOGICAL SOCIETY, 1968, PP 120-149
    005,

    COHEN RONALD
    BRITTLE MARRIAGE IS A STABLE SYSTEM
    IN PAUL BOHANNAN, DIVORCE AND AFTER, NEW YORK, NATURAL HISTORY
    PRESS, 1970
    098,

    PESHKIN ALAN   COHEN RONALD
    THE VALUES OF MODERNIZATION
    JOURNAL OF THE DEVELOPING AREAS 2 1967 PP 7-22
    074,

    COHEN RONALD
    POLITICAL ANTHROPOLOGY--- THE FUTURE OF A PIONEER.
    ANTHROPOLOGICAL QUARTERLY 38 1965 PP 117-131, NORTHWESTERN
    UNIVERSITY PROGRAM OF AFRICAN STUDIES, REPRINT SERIES, 4
    009,098,100,

COLBOURNE MICHAEL
    COLBOURNE MICHAEL
    MALARIA IN AFRICA.
    LONDON, OXFORD UNIVERSITY PRESS, 1966
    075,

COLE M
    GAY J   COLE M
    THE NEW MATHEMATICS AND THE OLD CULTURE
    NEW YORK, HOLT, RINEHART AND WINSTON, 1967
    041,119-03,

COLE MONICA
    COLE MONICA
    SOUTH AFRICA.

LONDON, METHUEN, 1966 (REVISED EDITION)
069,132-08,

COLE ROBERT W
    COLE ROBERT W
    KOSSOH TOWN BOY.
    CAMBRIDGE, CAMBRIDGE UNIVERSITY PRESS, 1960
    090,

COLE SONIA
    COLE SONIA
    THE PREHISTORY OF EAST AFRICA.
    NEW YORK, MACMILLAN, 1963
    018,

COLE TAYLOR
    PIPER DONALD C   COLE TAYLOR   EDS
    POST PRIMARY EDUCATION AND POLITICAL AND ECONOMIC
    DEVELOPMENT.
    DURHAM, NORTH CAROLINA, DUKE UNIVERSITY PRESS, 1964
    042,

COLEMAN JAMES S
    COLEMAN JAMES S
    THE POLITICS OF SUB-SAHARAN AFRICA CHP 3.
    IN ALMOND AND COLEMAN (EDS), THE POLITICS OF DEVELOPING
    AREAS, PRINCETON, PRINCETON UNIVERSITY PRESS, 1960
    061,

    COLEMAN JAMES S   ROSBERG CARL G   EDS
    POLITICAL PARTIES AND NATIONAL INTEGRATION IN TROPICAL
    AFRICA.
    BERKELEY, CALIFORNIA, UNIVERSITY OF CALIFORNIA PRESS, 1964
    002,061,

    COLEMAN JAMES S
    NATIONALISM IN TROPICAL AFRICA.
    IN WILLIAM J HANNA (ED), INDEPENDENT BLACK AFRICA. CHICAGO,
    RAND MCNALLY, 1964, PP 208-234
    055,

    APTER DAVID E   COLEMAN JAMES S
    PAN-AFRICANISM OR NATIONALISM IN AFRICA.
    IN AMERICAN SOCIETY OF AFRICAN CULTURE, PAN-AFRICANISM
    RECONSIDERED, BERKELEY, UNIVERSITY OF CALIFORNIA PRESS, 1962
    PP 81-115
    079,

    APTER DAVID E   COLEMAN JAMES S
    PAN-AFRICANISM OR NATIONALISM.
    IN PETER J MCEWAN AND ROBERT B SUTCLIFFE (EDS), MODERN AFRICA,
    NEW YORK, THOMAS CROWELL, 1965, PP 413-423
    079,

    COLEMAN JAMES S
    THE EMERGENCE OF AFRICAN POLITICAL PARTIES.
    IN CHARLES G HAINES (ED), AFRICA TODAY, BALTIMORE, JOHNS
    HOPKINS PRESS, 1955, PP 225-255
    057,

COLEMAN JAMES S
THE CHARACTER AND VIABILITY OF AFRICAN POLITICAL SYSTEMS
CHAPTER 2.
IN THE UNITED STATES AND AFRICA, BACKGROUND PAPERS OF THE
13TH ASSEMBLY, THE AMERICAN ASSEMBLY, COLUMBIA UNIVERSITY,
1958, PP 27-62
061,

COLEMAN JAMES S
 COLEMAN JAMES S
 THE PROBLEM OF POLITICAL INTEGRATION IN EMERGENT AFRICA.
 WESTERN POLITICAL QUARTERLY 8 MARCH 1955 PP 44-58
 057,

 COLEMAN JAMES S
 NIGERIA BACKGROUND TO NATIONALISM.
 BERKELEY, UNIVERSITY OF CALIFORNIA PRESS, 1958
 055,128-06,

 COLEMAN JAMES S
 SOCIAL CLEAVAGE AND RELIGIOUS CONFLICT.
 JOURNAL OF SOCIAL ISSUES 12 1956 B-M REPRINT 47
 050,

 COLEMAN JAMES S
 CONCLUSION
 IN ALMOND AND COLEMAN THE POLITICS OF THE DEVELOPING AREAS
 PRINCETON, PRINCETON UNIVERSITY PRESS, 1960, PP 532-576
 046,

 COLEMAN JAMES S
 THE EDUCATION OF MODERN ELITES IN DEVELOPING COUNTRIES PT 3.
 IN JAMES S COLEMAN (ED), EDUCATION AND POLITICAL
 DEVELOPMENT, PRINCETON, NEW JERSEY, PRINCETON UNIVERSITY
 PRESS, 1965
 043,

COLLFUS O
 COLLFUS O
 CONAKRY EN 1951-52--ETUDE HUMAINE ET ECONOMIQUE.
 ETUDES GUINEENNES, 10, 11, 1952
 115-05,

COLLINS HAROLD R
 COLLINS HAROLD R
 AMOS TUTUOLA.
 NEW YORK, TWAYNE, 1969
 090,

COLLINS ROBERT O
 COLLINS ROBERT O   ED
 PROBLEMS IN AFRICAN HISTORY.
 ENGLEWOOD CLIFFS, NEW JERSEY, PRENTICE-HALL, INC., 1968
 009,019,020,036,

 CLENDENEN CLARENCE   COLLINS ROBERT O   DUIGNAN PETER
 AMERICANS IN AFRICA, 1865-1900.
 PALO ALTO, CALIFORNIA, HOOVER INSTITUTION PRESS, 1966
 096,

COLLINS ROBERT O
KING LEOPOLD, ENGLAND AND THE UPPER NILE, 1899-1909.
NEW HAVEN, CONN. (YALE), MCGILL-QUEEN·S PRESS, 1969
033,134-02,

COLLINS ROBERT O
COLLINS ROBERT O
THE SOUTHERN SUDAN, 1883-1898-- A STRUGGLE FOR CONTROL.
NEW HAVEN YALE UNIVERSITY PRESS 1962
033,134-02,

COLONIAL OFFICE
GREAT BRITAIN   COLONIAL OFFICE
REPORT OF THE COMMISSION TO ENQUIRE INTO THE FEARS OF
MINORITIES AND THE MEANS OF ALLAYING THEM.
HER MAJESTY'S STATIONERY OFFICE COMMAND 505 JULY 1958
057,128-06,

GREAT BRITAIN   COLONIAL OFFICE
BECHUANALAND PROTECTORATE, REPORT FOR THE YEARS 1961-62.
LONDON, HER MAJESTY'S STATIONERY OFFICE, 1964
102-11,

GREAT BRITAIN   COLONIAL OFFICE
BECHUANALAND PROTECTORATE REPORT FOR THE YEAR 1963.
LONDON, HER MAJESTY'S STATIONERY OFFICE, 1965
102-11,

COLSON ELIZABETH
COLSON ELIZABETH
THE PLATEAU TONGA OF NORTHERN RHODESIA.
IN SEVEN TRIBES OF BRITISH CENTRAL AFRICA, LONDON, OXFORD
UNIVERSITY PRESS, 1951, PP. 94-162
142-01,

COLSON ELIZABETH
INCORPORATION IN TONGA.
IN R COHEN AND J MIDDLETON, EDS, FROM TRIBE TO NATION IN
AFRICA, SAN FRANCISCO, CHANDLER, 1968
038,142-01,

COLSON ELIZABETH
MODERN POLITICAL ORGANIZATION OF THE PLATEAU TONGA.
AFRICAN STUDIES 7 1948 PP 85-98
061,142-07,

COLSON ELIZABETH
TRADE AND WEALTH AMONG THE TONGA.
IN P J BOHANNAN AND GEORGE DALTON, EDS., MARKETS IN
AFRICA, EVANSTON, NORTHWESTERN UNIVERSITY PRESS, 1962,
PP 606-616
010,142-01,

COMMISSION
ECONOMIC COMMISSION FOR AFRICA
INTRA-AFRICAN TRADE.
E/CN IY/STC/20 1963
078,

ECONOMIC COMMISSION FOR AFRICA

STUDIES OF EXISTING AFRICAN CUSTOMS UNIONS.
ECONOMIC BULLETIN FOR AFRICA 2 1962
078,

COMMISSION
ECONOMIC COMMISSION FOR AFRICA
CO-ORDINATION OF DEVELOPMENT PLANS IN AFRICA.
ECONOMIC BULLETIN FOR AFRICA 1 1964
072,

ECONOMIC COMMISSION FOR AFRICA
TRANSPORT PROBLEMS IN RELATION TO ECONOMIC DEVELOPMENT IN
WEST AFRICA.
NEW YORK, U N DOCUMENT NO 62.11.K.2 1963
048,

INTERNATIONAL COMMISSION OF JURISTS
AFRICAN CONFERENCE ON THE RULE OF LAW.
LAGOS, NIGERIA, 1961, INTERNATIONAL COMMISSION OF JURISTS.
068,

EAST AFRICA ROYAL COMMISSION
EAST AFRICA ROYAL COMMISSION 1953-1955 REPORT.
LONDON HER MAJESTY'S STATIONERY OFFICE COMMAND PAPER NO 9475
REPRINT 482 1961
035,045,

ELECTORAL COMMISSION
REPORT ON THE NIGERIA FEDERAL ELECTIONS, DECEMBER 1959.
LAGOS, FEDERAL GOVERNMENT PRINTER, 1960
063,128-07,

COMMISSION DE COOPERATION TECHNIQUE EN AFRIQUE
REPORT OF THE SYMPOSIUM ON MULTILINGUALISM (BRAZZAVILLE).
LONDON, COMMISSION DE COOPERATION TECHNIQUE EN AFRIQUE, 87
1962
011,

ECONOMIC COMMISSION FOR AFRICA
LEOPOLDVILLE AND LAGOS--COMPARATIVE STUDY OF CONDITIONS IN
1960.
IN GERALD BREESE (ED), THE CITY IN NEWLY DEVELOPING
COUNTRIES, PRENTICE-HALL, NEW JERSEY, 1969
108-05,128-05,

CONDON JOHN C
CONDON JOHN C
NATION BUILDING AND IMAGE BUILDING IN THE TANZANIAN PRESS
JOURNAL OF MODERN AFRICAN STUDIES 5 1967 PP 335-354
049,

CONNAH G
CONNAH G
ARCHAEOLOGICAL RESEARCH IN BENIN CITY, 1961-1964.
JOURNAL OF THE HISTORICAL SOCIETY OF NIGERIA 2 1964
PP 465-477
092,128-02,

CONOVER HELEN F
CONOVER HELEN F

NIGERIAN OFFICIAL PUBLICATIONS, 1869-1959-- A GUIDE.
WASHINGTON, LIBRARY OF CONGRESS, 1959
128-12,

CONOVER HELEN F
CONOVER HELEN F
OFFICIAL PUBLICATIONS OF SOMALILAND, 1941-1959--A GUIDE.
WASHINGTON, LIBRARY OF CONGRESS, 1960
133-12,

COOK ARTHUR NORTON
COOK ARTHUR NORTON
BRITISH ENTERPRISE IN NIGERIA.
PHILADELPHIA, UNIVERSITY OF PENNSYLVANIA PRESS, 1943
035,128-08,

COOK MERCER
DIA MAMADOU   TRANSLATED BY   COOK MERCER
THE AFRICAN NATIONS AND WORLD SOLIDARITY.
LONDON, THAMES AND HUDSON, 1962
054,060,130-04,

COOK MERCER   HENDERSON STEPHEN E
THE MILITANT BLACK WRITER IN AFRICA AND THE UNITED STATES.
MADISON, UNIVERSITY OF WISCONSIN PRESS, 1969
090,094,

COOKE C K
COOKE C K
THE ROCK PAINTINGS AND ENGRAVINGS OF AFRICA.
TARIKH 1 1966 PP 45-66
014,018,

COOLEY JOHN K
COOLEY JOHN K
EAST WIND OVER AFRICA-- RED CHINA'S AFRICAN OFFENSIVE.
NEW YORK, WALKER, 1965
084,

COOLEY WILLIAM D
COOLEY WILLIAM D
THE NEGRO LAND OF THE ARABS EXAMINED AND EXPLAINED OR
AN INQUIRY INTO THE EARLY HISTORY AND GEOGRAPHY OF CENTRAL
AFRICA.
NEW YORK, BARNES AND NOBLE, 1966
024,

COOMBS DOUGLAS
COOMBS DOUGLAS
THE GOLD COAST BRITAIN AND THE NETHERLANDS 1850-1874.
LONDON, OXFORD UNIVERSITY PRESS, 1963
027,114-02,

COPE J
COPE J
KING OF THE HOTTENTOTS-BIOGRAPHY OF A SOUTH AFRICAN
HOTTENTOT AT THE CAPE IN 1613
CAPE TOWN, TIMMINS, 1967
032,

CORDWELL JUSTINE M
    CORDWELL JUSTINE M
    THE PROBLEM OF PROCESS AND FORM IN WEST AFRICAN ART.
    PROCEEDINGS OF THE THIRD INTERNATIONAL WEST AFRICAN
    CONFERENCE, 1949, LAGOS, 1956, PP 53-60
    014,

CORDWELL JUSTINE M
    CORDWELL JUSTINE M
    NATURALISM AND STYLIZATION IN YORUBA ART.
    MAGAZINE OF ART 46 1953 PP 220-226
    014,128-01,

CORFIELD F D
    CORFIELD F D
    HISTORICAL SURVEY OF THE ORIGINS AND GROWTH OF MAU MAU.
    NAIROBI, GOVERNMENT PRINTER, 1960
    055,117-06,

CORNEVIN ROBERT
    CORNEVIN ROBERT
    LE TOGO, NATION-PILOTE.
    PARIS, NOUVELLES EDITIONS LATINES, 1963
    137-11,

CORY HANS
    CORY HANS
    REFORM OF TRIBAL POLITICAL INSTITUTIONS IN TANGANYIKA.
    JOURNAL OF AFRICAN ADMINISTRATION 12 APRIL 1960 PP 77-84
    038,

    CORY HANS
    SUKUMA LAW AND CUSTOM.
    LONDON, OXFORD UNIVERSITY PRESS, 1953
    066,136-01,

COTRAN EUGENE
    RUBIN NEVILLE   COTRAN EUGENE   EDS
    READINGS IN AFRICAN LAW--VOLS 1 AND 2.
    NEW YORK, INTERNATIONAL UNIVERSITY BOOKSELLERS,INC., 1970
    067,

    RUBIN NEVILLE   COTRAN EUGENE   EDS
    AN ANNUAL SURVEY OF AFRICAN LAW, VOL 1.
    NEW YORK, INTERNATIONAL UNIVERSITY BOOKSELLERS,INC., 1970
    067,

    COTRAN EUGENE
    SOME RECENT DEVELOPMENTS IN THE TANGANYIKA JUDICIAL
    SYSTEM.
    JOURNAL OF AFRICAN LAW 6 SPRING PP 19-28
    066,136-06,

    COTRAN EUGENE
    THE UNIFICATION OF LAWS IN EAST AFRICA.
    JOURNAL OF MODERN AFRICAN STUDIES 1 JUNE 1963 PP 209-220
    067,

COULSON NOEL J
    COULSON NOEL J

THE CONCEPT OF PROGRESS AND ISLAMIC LAW.
IN ROBERT BALLAH, RELIGION AND PROGRESS IN MODERN ASIA,
NEW YORK, FREE PRESS, 1965, PP 74-92
066,

COULT ALLAN D
    COULT ALLAN D
    LINEAGE SOLIDARITY, TRANSFORMATIONAL ANALYSIS AND THE MEAN-
    ING OF KINSHIP TERMINOLOGIES.
    MAN VOL 2 NO 1 MARCH 1967 PP 26-47
    004,

COUPEZ A
    COUPEZ A   KAMANZI THOMAS   EDS
    LITTERATURE COURTOISE DU RWANDA (COURT LITERATURE OF
    RWANDA).
    LONDON AND NEW YORK, INTERNATIONAL UNIVERSITY BOOKSELLERS,
    INC., 1969
    012,129-01,

    KAMANZI THOMAS   COUPEZ A
    POEMES DYNASTIQUES RWANDA.
    BUJUMBURA, UNIVERSITE OFFICILLE, 1965
    129-10,

COUPLAND REGINALD
    COUPLAND REGINALD
    EAST AFRICA AND ITS INVADERS FROM THE EARLIEST TIMES TO THE
    DEATH OF SEYYID SAID IN 1856.
    OXFORD, 1938
    023,

    COUPLAND REGINALD
    THE BRITISH ANTI-SLAVERY MOVEMENT.
    LONDON, CASS, 1964
    029,

    COUPLAND REGINALD
    THE EXPLOITATION OF EAST AFRICA 1856-1890.
    LONDON, 1939; REPRINTED, 1968, BY NORTHWESTERN UNIVERSITY PRESS
    027,

    COUPLAND REGINALD
    THE EXPLOITATION OF EAST AFRICA, 1856-1890.
    EVANSTON, NORTHWESTERN UNIVERSITY PRESS, 1939, 1967
    028,

COWAN L GRAY
    COWAN L GRAY
    THE DILEMMAS OF AFRICAN INDEPENDENCE.
    NEW YORK, WALKER, 1968
    002,076,

    COWAN L GRAY
    BRITISH AND FRENCH EDUCATION IN AFRICA-- A CRITICAL
    APPRAISAL CHP 8.
    IN DONALD PIPER AND TAYLOR COLE ,EDS., POST PRIMERY
    EDUCATION AND POLITICAL AND ECONOMIC DEVELOPMENT, DURHAM
    NORTH CAROLINA, DUKE UNIVERSITY PRESS, 1964
    042,

COWAN L GRAY
  COWAN L GRAY
  LOCAL GOVERNMENT IN WEST AFRICA.
  NEW YORK, COLUMBIA UNIVERSITY PRESS, 1958
  063,

  COWAN L GRAY   O CONNELL JAMES   SCANLON DAVID G
  EDUCATION AND NATION-BUILDING IN AFRICA.
  NEW YORK, PRAEGER, 1965
  042,043,

COWLEY MALCOLM
  MANNIX DANIEL   COWLEY MALCOLM
  BLACK CARGOES-- A HISTORY OF THE ATLANTIC SLAVE TRADE 1518-
  1865.
  NEW YORK, VIKING PRESS, 1962
  028,

COX RICHARD
  COX RICHARD
  PAN-AFRICANISM IN PRACTICE-- AN EAST AFRICAN STUDY--
  PAFMESCA 1958-1964.
  LONDON, OXFORD UNIVERSITY PRESS, 1964
  079,

COX-GEORGE N A
  COX-GEORGE N A
  FINANCE AND DEVELOPMENT IN WEST AFRICA -- THE SIERRA LEONE
  EXPERIENCE.
  LONDON, DOBSON, 1961
  073,131-08,

CROCKER CHESTER A
  CROCKER CHESTER A
  FRANCES CHANGING MILITARY INTERESTS.
  AFRICA REPORT, JUNE, 1968, P.16
  082,

CRONON
  CRONON EDMOND DAVID
  BLACK MOSES--THE STORY OF MARCUS GARVEY AND THE UNIVERSAL
  NEGRO IMPROVEMENT ASSOCIATION.
  MADISON, UNIVERSITY OF WISCONSIN PRESS, 1955
  095,

CROWDER MICHAEL
  BOWN LALAGE   CROWDER MICHAEL   EDS
  THE PROCEEDINGS OF THE FIRST INTERNATIONAL CONGRESS OF
  AFRICANISTS.
  LONDON, LONGMANS, 1964; ALSO EVANSTON, NORTHWESTERN UNIVERSITY
  PRESS, 1964
  100,

  CROWDER MICHAEL   IKIME OBARO   EDS
  WEST AFRICAN CHIEFS--THEIR CHANGING STATUS UNDER COLONIAL
  RULE AND INDEPENDENCE.
  NEW YORK, AFRICANA PUBLISHING CORPORATION, FORTHCOMING
  009,013,035,

CROWDER MICHAEL
WEST AFRICA UNDER COLONIAL RULE.
LONDON, HUTCHINSON; EVANSTON, NORTHWESTERN UNIVERSITY PRESS,
1968
034,035,

CROWDER MICHAEL
   CROWDER MICHAEL
   INDIRECT RULE FRENCH AND BRITISH STYLE.
   AFRICA 34 1964 PP 197-205
   035,

   CROWDER MICHAEL
   INDEPENDENCE AS A GOAL IN FRENCH WEST AFRICAN POLITICS, 1944
   -1960.
   FRENCH-SPEAKING AFRICA (LEWIS), NEW YORK, WALKER AND CO.,
   1965
   056,

   CROWDER MICHAEL
   SENEGAL-- A STUDY IN FRENCH ASSIMILATION POLICY.
   LONDON, OXFORD UNIVERSITY, 1962 (REVISED METHUEN 1967)
   035,130-02,

   CROWDER MICHAEL
   THE STORY OF NIGERIA.
   LONDON, FABER AND FABER, 1962
   128-02,

CROWE SYBIL E
   CROWE SYBIL E
   THE BERLIN WEST AFRICAN CONFERENCE, 1884-1885.
   LONDON, LONGMANS, 1942
   033,

CROWLEY DANIEL J
   CROWLEY DANIEL J
   TRADITIONAL AND CONTEMPORARY ART IN AFRICA.
   IN CARTER, GWENDOLEN M. AND ANN PADEN (EDS), EXPANDING
   HORIZONS IN AFRICAN STUDIES, EVANSTON, NORTHWESTERN
   UNIVERSITY PRESS, 1969
   014,093,100,

   CROWLEY DANIEL J
   POLITICS AND TRIBALISM IN THE KATANGA.
   WESTERN POLITICAL QUARTERLY 16 MAY 1963 PP 68-78
   007,108-06,

CRUM MASON
   CRUM MASON
   GULLAH-- NEGRO LIFE IN THE CAROLINA SEA ISLANDS.
   DURHAM, DUKE UNIVERSITY PRESS, 1940
   030,

CURLE ADAM
   CURLE ADAM
   NATIONALISM AND HIGHER EDUCATION IN GHANA.
   UNIVERSITIES QUARTERLY 16 JUNE 1962 PP 229-242
   042,114-03,

CURLE ADAM
EDUCATIONAL PROBLEMS OF DEVELOPING SOCIETIES--WITH CASE
STUDIES OF GHANA AND PAKISTAN.
NEW YORK, PRAEGER PUBLISHERS, 1969
043,114-03,

CURRIE DAVID P
  CURRIE DAVID P
  FEDERALISM AND THE NEW NATIONS OF AFRICA.
  CHICAGO, UNIVERSITY OF CHICAGO PRESS, 1964
  061,078,

CURRIE JEAN I
  WHETHAM EDITH H   CURRIE JEAN I   EDS
  READINGS IN THE APPLIED ECONOMICS OF AFRICA.
  LONDON, CAMBRIDGE UNIVERSITY PRESS, 1, 1967
  073,

  WHETHAM EDITH H   CURRIE JEAN I   EDS
  READINGS IN THE APPLIED ECONOMICS OF AFRICA.
  LONDON, CAMBRIDGE UNIVERSITY PRESS, 2, 1967,
  073,128-08,

  WHETHAM EDITH H   CURRIE JEAN I
  THE ECONOMICS OF AFRICAN COUNTRIES.
  LONDON AND NEW YORK, INTERNATIONAL UNIVERSITY BOOKSELLERS,
  INC., 1969
  073,

CURTIN PHILIP D
  CURTIN PHILIP D
  THE IMAGE OF AFRICA-- BRITISH IDEAS AND ACTION, 1780-1850.
  MADISON, UNIVERSITY OF WISCONSIN PRESS, 1964
  027,029,

  CURTIN PHILIP D
  AFRICAN HISTORY.
  NEW YORK, MACMILLAN CO, 1964
  036,

  CURTIN PHILIP D
  THE ATLANTIC SLAVE TRADE--A CENSUS.
  MADISON, UNIVERSITY OF WISCONSIN, 1969
  028,

  CURTIN PHILIP D
  THE ARCHIVES OF TROPICAL AFRICA-- A RECONNAISSANCE.
  JOURNAL OF AFRICAN HISTORY 1 1960 PP 129-147
  098,099,

  CURTIN PHILIP D   VANSINA JAN
  SOURCES OF THE 19TH CENTURY ATLANTIC SLAVE TRADE.
  JOURNAL OF AFRICAN HISTORY 5 1964 PP 185-208
  028,

  CURTIN PHILIP D
  AFRICA REMEMBERED-- NARRATIVES BY WEST AFRICANS FROM THE
  ERA OF THE SLAVE TRADE.
  MADISON, UNIVERSITY OF WISCONSIN PRESS, 1967
  028,030,

CUTRIGHT PHILLIPS
    CUTRIGHT PHILLIPS
    NATIONAL POLITICAL DEVELOPMENT-- MEASUREMENT AND ANALYSIS.
    AMERICAN SOCIOLOGICAL REVIEW   APRIL 1963 PP 253-264
    098,

CUTTER C H
    CUTTER C H
    MALI--A BIBLIOGRAPHIC INTRODUCTION.
    AFRICAN STUDIES BULLETIN, 9, 3, DEC., 1966
    123-12,

D

D'AZEVEDO
    SOLOMON MARVIN D   D AZEVEDO   COMPS
    A GENERAL BIBLIOGRAPHY OF THE REPUBLIC OF LIBERIA.
    EVANSTON, NORTHWESTERN UNIVERSITY PRESS, 1962
    119-12,

D'ANDRADE ROY G
    D'ANDRADE ROY G
    ANTHROPOLOGICAL STUDIES OF DREAMS.
    IN FRANCIS L K HSU (ED), PSYCHOLOGICAL ANTHROPOLOGY,
    HOMEWOOD, ILLINOIS, DORSEY PRESS, 1961, PP 296-332
    100,

D'ARBOUSSIER G
    D'ARBOUSSIER G
    DEVELOPMENTS IN FRENCH SPEAKING WEST AFRICA CHAPTER 5.
    IN DAVID P CURRIE, FEDERALISM AND THE NEW NATIONS OF AFRICA,
    CHICAGO, UNIVERSITY OF CHICAGO PRESS, 1964, PP 117-136
    DISCUSSION PP 137-152
    077,

D'HERTEFELT MARCEL
    D'HERTEFELT MARCEL
    THE RWANDA OF RWANDA.
    IN JAMES L. GIBBS JR. (ED), PEOPLES OF AFRICA, NEW YORK, HOLT
    RINEHART AND WINSTON, 1965, PP. 403-440

DAAKU K YEBOA
    DAAKU K YEBOA
    PRE-EUROPEAN CURRENCIES OF WEST AFRICA AND WESTERN SUDAN.
    GHANA NOTES AND QUERIES 2 1961 PP 12-14
    010,

DADIE BERNARD
    DADIE BERNARD
    FOLKLORE AND LITERATURE.
    IN LALAGE BOWN AND MICHAEL CROWDER (EDS.), PROCEEDINGS OF
    THE FIRST INTERNATIONAL CONGRESS OF AFRICANISTS, ACCRA,
    1962, LONDON, LONGMANS, 1964, PP 199-219
    012,

AMON D'ABY J F   DADIE BERNARD   GADEAU G COFFI
LE THEATRE POPULAIRE EN REPUBLIQUE DE COTE-D'IVOIRE--OEUVRES
CHOISIES.
ABIDJAN, CERCLE CULTUREL ET FOLKLORIQUE DE LA COTE-D'IVOIRE
1965
116-10,

DADIE BERNARD
    DADIE BERNARD
    ASSEMIEN DEHYLE--CHRONIQUE AGNI.
    PARIS, L'AVANT-SCENE-THEATRE, NO. 343, OCT. 15, 1965, PP. 37
    -43
    116-10,

    DADIE BERNARD
    ECRIVAIN IVOIREN--TEXTES COMMENTES PAR ROGER MERCIER ET M ET
    S BATTESTINI.
    PARIS, F. NATHAN, 1964
    116-10,

    DADIE BERNARD
    HOMMES DE TOUS LES CONTINENTS, POEMS.
    PARIS, PRESENCE AFRICAINE, 1967
    116-10,

    DADIE BERNARD
    LEGENDES AFRICAINES.
    PARIS, SEGHERS, 1954
    116-10,

    DADIE BERNARD
    LEGENDES ET POEMES--AFRIQUE DEBOUT, LEGENDES AFRICAINES,
    CLIMBIE, LA RONDE DES JOURS.
    PARIS, SEGHERS, 1966
    116-10,

    DADIE BERNARD
    LE PAGNE NOIR, CONTES AFRICAINES.
    PARIS, PRESENCE AFRICAINE, 1955
    116-10,

    DADIE BERNARD
    LA RONDE DES JOURS.
    PARIS, SEGHERS, 1956
    116-10,

    DADIE BERNARD
    PATRON DE NEW YORK.
    PARIS, PRESENCE AFRICAINE, 1964
    116-10,

    DADIE BERNARD
    UN NEGRE A PARIS.
    PARIS, PRESENCE AFRICAINE, 1959
    116-10,

DADZIE E W
    DADZIE E W   STRICKLAND J T
    DIRECTORY OF ARCHIVES, LIBRARIES AND SCHOOLS OF
    LIBRARIANSHIP IN AFRICA.

UNESCO 1965
098,099,

DAEDALUS
DAEDALUS   ED
COLOR AND RACE.
SPECIAL ISSUE OF THE JOURNAL OF THE AMERICAN ACADEMY OF ARTS
AND SCIENCES) SPRING 1967
088,

DAGET JACQUES
BA AMADOU HAMPATE   DAGET JACQUES
L'EMPIRE PEUL DE MACINA 1818-1853.   THE FULANI EMPIRE OF
MACINA 1818-1853).
BAMAKO,INSTITUT FRANCAIS D'AFRIQUE NOIRE,CENTRE DU SOUDAN,
ETUDES SOUDANAISES 3 1962
024,123-02,

DALLIN ALEXANDER
DALLIN ALEXANDER
THE SOVIET UNION-- POLITICAL ACTIVITY.
IN Z BRZEZINSKI (ED), AFRICA AND THE COMMUNIST WORLD,
STANFORD, CALIFORNIA, STANFORD UNIVERSITY PRESS, 1963
PP 7-48
084,

DALTON GEORGE
BOHANNAN PAUL   DALTON GEORGE   ED
MARKETS IN AFRICA.
EVANSTON, NORTHWESTERN UNIVERSITY PRESS, 1965
010,

DALTON GEORGE
THEORETICAL ISSUES IN ECONOMIC ANTHROPOLOGY.
CURRENT ANTHROPOLOGY VOL 10 NO 1 JANUARY 1969
010,

ADELMAN IRMA   DALTON GEORGE   MORRIS CYNTHIA TAFT
SOCIETY, POLITICS, AND ECONOMIC DEVELOPMENT IN AFRICA.
IN CARTER, GWENDOLEN M. AND ANN PADEN (EDS) EXPANDING
HORIZONS IN AFRICAN STUDIES, EVANSTON, NORTHWESTERN
UNIVERSITY PRESS, 1969, PP. 209-242
074,100,

DALTON GEORGE   ED
TRIBAL AND PEASANT ECONOMIES-- READINGS IN ECONOMIC
ANTHROPOLOGY.
GARDEN CITY, NEW YORK, NATURAL HISTORY PRESS,1967
010,

DALTON GEORGE   ED
PRIMITIVE, ARCHAIC, AND MODERN ECONOMIES-- ESSAYS OF KARL
POLANYI.
NEW YORK, DOUBLEDAY, 1968
010,

DALTON GEORGE
TRADITIONAL PRODUCTION IN PRIMITIVE AFRICAN ECONOMIES.
QUARTERLY JOURNAL OF ECONOMICS AUGUST 1962 ALSO G DALTON
TRIBAL AND PEASANT ECONOMIES, DOUBLEDAY, 1967

010,

DAMMANN E
DAMMANN E
THE INFLUENCE OF RELIGION ON AFRICAN LANGUAGES.
IN LALAGE BOWN AND MICHAEL CROWDER (EDS.), PROCEEDINGS OF
THE FIRST INTERNATIONAL CONGRESS OF AFRICANISTS, ACCRA,
1962, LONDON, LONGMANS, 1964, PP 115-123
011,

DANIELOU R P
DANIELOU R P
CATHOLICISME ET PERSONNALITE CULTURELLE DES PEUPLES
(CATHOLICISM AND CULTURAL PERSONALITY OF PEOPLES).
IN COLLOQUE SUR LES RELIGIONS, ABIDJAN, APRIL, 1961, PARIS,
PRESENCE AFRICAINE, 1962, PP 215-218
039,

DANIELS S G H
DANIELS S G H
THE LATER STONE AGE.
TARIKH 1 1966 PP 20-32
018,

DANIELS W C EKOW
DANIELS W C EKOW
THE INFLUENCE OF EQUITY IN WEST AFRICAN LAW.
INTERNATIONAL AND COMPARATIVE LAW QUARTERLY 2 1962 PP 31-58
066,

DANIELS W C EKOW
THE COMMON LAW IN WEST AFRICA.
LONDON, BUTTERWORTHS, 1964
066,

DANQUAH JOSEPH B
DANQUAH JOSEPH B
GOLD COAST-- AKAN LAWS AND CUSTOMS AND THE AKIM ABUAKWA
CONSTITUTION.
LONDON,ROUTLEDGE, 1928
066,114-01,

DANQUAH JOSEPH B
THE AKAN DOCTRINE OF GOD.
NEW YORK, HUMANITIES PRESS INC., 1968
099,114-01,

DANQUAH JOSEPH B
THE CULTURE OF AKAN.
AFRICA, 22, 1952, PP. 360-366
114-01,

DARK PHILIP J C
FORMAN W   FORMAN B   DARK PHILIP J C
BENIN ART
LONDON, PAUL HAMLYN, 1960
014,

DATTA A K
DATTA A K

INDIA AND AFRICA-- A LETTER.
GOVERNMENT AND OPPOSITION CLEVELAND 2 NO 4 1968 PP 612-620
085,

DAVIDSON BASIL
    DAVIDSON BASIL   EDITORS OF TIME-LIFE
    AFRICAN KINGDOMS.
    NEW YORK, TIME INCORPORATED, 1966
    036,

    DAVIDSON BASIL
    THE AFRICAN SLAVE TRADE.
    BOSTON, ATLANTIC-LITTLE, BROWN, 1961
    028,

    DAVIDSON BASIL
    THA AFRICAN PAST-- CHRONICLES FROM ANTIQUITY TO
    MODERN TIMES.
    BOSTON, LITTLE, BROWN, 1964; PENGUIN, 1966
    036,

    DAVIDSON BASIL
    WHICH WAY AFRICA-- THE SEARCH FOR A NEW SOCIETY.
    HARMONSWORTH, MIDDLESEX, PENGUIN BOOKS, 1964
    002,

    DAVIDSON BASIL
    AFRICA-- HISTORY OF A CONTINENT.
    LONDON, WEIDENFELD AND NICOLSON, 1966; ALSO NEW YORK, MCMILLAN,
    1966
    001,

    DAVIDSON BASIL
    THE LOST CITIES OF AFRICA.
    BOSTON, LITTLE, BROWN AND CO., 1959
    036,

    DAVIDSON BASIL
    AFRICA IN HISTORY.
    NEW YORK, MACMILLAN, 1968
    001,028,036,

    DAVIDSON BASIL
    THE GROWTH OF AFRICAN CIVILIZATION-A HISTORY OF WEST AFRICA
    1000-1800
    GARDEN CITY, NEW YORK, DOUBLEDAY ANCHOR BOOKS, 1969
    022,026,

    DAVIDSON BASIL
    A HISTORY OF EAST AND CENTRAL AFRICA-TO THE LATE
    NINETEENTH CENTURY
    GARDEN CITY, NEW YORK, DOUBLEDAY ANCHOR, 1969
    023,025,

    DAVIDSON BASIL
    THE LIBERATION OF GUINE-- ASPECTS OF AN AFRICAN RE-
    VOLUTION.
    BALTIMORE, PENGUIN, 1969
    087,144-11,

DAVIDSON BASIL
THE AFRICAN GENIUS--AN INTRODUCTION TO AFRICAN AND CULTURAL
HISTORY.
BOSTON,LITTLE,BROWN,1969
016,

DAVIDSON S
DAVIDSON S
PSYCHIATRIC WORK AMONG THE BEMBA.
RHODES-LIVINGSTONE JOURNAL 7 1949 PP 75-86
043,142-03,

DAVIES IOAN
DAVIES IOAN
AFRICAN TRADE UNIONS.
BALTIMORE,PENGUIN BOOKS,1966
044,073,

DAVIES KENNETH G
DAVIES KENNETH G
THE ROYAL AFRICAN COMPANY.
LONDON,LONGMANS,1957
033,

DAVIES OLIVER
DAVIES OLIVER
LIFE AND DEVELOPMENT AMONG THE EARLIEST HUMANS IN AFRICA.
TARIKH 1 1966 PP 12-19
018,

DAVIES OLIVER
THE NEOLITHIC REVOLUTION IN TROPICAL AFRICA.
TRANSACTIONS OF THE HISTORICAL SOCIETY OF GHANA 4 1960
PP 14-20
019,

DAVIES OLIVER
WEST AFRICA BEFORE THE EUROPEANS
LONDON,METHUEN,1967
019,022,026,

DAVIES R J
DAVIES R J
THE SOUTH AFRICAN URBAN HIERARCHY
SOUTH AFRICAN GEOGRAPHICAL JOURNAL 49 1967 PP 9-19
047,048,132-05,

DAVIS ALLISON
DAVIS ALLISON   GARDINER B   GARDINER M R
DEEP SOUTH.
CHICAGO,UNIVERSITY OF CHICAGO PRESS,1941
030,

DAVIS JOHN P
DAVIS JOHN P   ED
THE AMERICAN NEGRO REFERENCE BOOK.
THE PHELPS-STOKES FUND, ENGLEWOOD CLIFFS,NEW JERSEY, 1966
030,

DAWSON J L M

DAWSON J L M
TRADITIONAL CONCEPTS OF MENTAL HEALTH IN SIERRA LEONE.
THE JOURNAL OF THE SIERRA LEONE SOCIETY NO. 18 JANUARY 1966
PP 18-28
040,131-01,

DE ANDRADE MARIO
DE ANDRADE MARIO
LE NATIONALISME ANGOLAIS (ANGOLAN NATIONALISM).
PRESENCE AFRICAINE 42 1962 PP 5-24
055,

DE BLIJ HARM J
DE BLIJ HARM J
A GEOGRAPHY OF SUB-SAHARAN AFRICA.
CHICAGO, RAND MCNALLY, 1964, CH. 1
017, 069

DE BLIJ HARM J
AFRICA SOUTH
EVANSTON, NORTHWESTERN UNIVERSITY PRESS, 1962
088,

DE BLIJ HARM J
THE FUNCTIONAL STRUCTURE AND CENTRAL BUSINESS DISTRICT OF
LOURENCO MARQUES, MOZAMBIQUE.
ECONOMIC GEOGRAPHY, 38 JANUARY 1962 PP 56-77
046,144-05,

DE BLIJ HARM J
MOMBASA-- AN AFRICAN CITY.
EVANSTON, NORTHWESTERN UNIVERSITY PRESS, 1968
045,117-05,

DE BLIJ HARM J
DAR ES SALAAM.
EVANSTON, NORTHWESTERN UNIVERSITY PRESS, 1963
045,136-05,

DE BLIJ HARM J
SOUTH AFRICA
IN KRITZECK AND LEWIS, PP 243-249
132-03,

DE GRAFT-JOHNSON J
DE GRAFT-JOHNSON J
AFRICAN GLORY-- THE STORY OF VANISHED NEGRO CIVILIZATIONS.
NEW YORK, WALKER, 1966
036,

DE GRAFT-JOHNSON K
DE GRAFT-JOHNSON K
THE EVOLUTION OF ELITES IN GHANA.
IN LLOYD, THE NEW ELITES OF TROPICAL AFRICA, LONDON, OXFORD
UNIVERSITY PRESS, 1966, P. 104-117

114-04,

DE HEINZELIN J
    DE HEINZELIN J
    OBSERVATIONS ON THE ABSOLUTE CHRONOLOGY OF THE UPPER
    PLEISTOCENE.
    IN F CLARK HOWELL AND FRANCOIS BOURLIERE (EDS.), AFRICAN
    ECOLOGY AND HUMAN EVOLUTION, CHICAGO, ALDINE, 1966,
    PP 285-303
    018,

DE HEUSCH LUC
    DE HEUSCH LUC
    LE RWANDA ET LA CIVILISATION INTERLACUSTRE.
    BRUXELLES, EDITIONS OF L'INSTITUTE DE SOCIOLOGIE DE
    L'UNIVERSITE LIBRE OF BRUXELLES, 1966
    129-01,

DE KIEWIET C W
    DE KIEWIET C W
    A HISTORY OF SOUTH AFRICA--SOCIAL AND ECONOMIC
    NEW YORK, OXFORD UNIVERSITY PRESS, 1967
    031,032,

    DE KIEWIET C W
    THE IMPERIAL FACTOR IN SOUTH AFRICA-A STUDY IN POLITICS AND
    ECONOMICS
    CAMBRIDGE, UNIVERSITY PRESS, 1937
    031,032,

DE KUN NICHOLAS A
    DE KUN NICHOLAS A
    THE MINERAL RESOURCES OF AFRICA.
    NEW YORK, AMERICAN ELSEVIER PUBLISHING CO, 1965
    069,

DE SMITH S A
    DE SMITH S A
    INTEGRATION OF LEGAL SYSTEMS.
    IN COLIN LEYS AND P ROBSON (EDS), FEDERATION IN EAST AFRICA--
    OPPORTUNITIES AND PROBLEMS NAIROBI OXFORD UNIVERSITY PRESS
    1965 PP 158-171
    067,

    DE SMITH S A
    FEDERALISM, HUMAN RIGHTS AND THE PROTECTION OF MINORITIES
    CHAPTER 11.
    IN DAVID P CURRIE, FEDERALISM AND THE NEW NATIONS OF AFRICA,
    CHICAGO, UNIVERSITY OF CHICAGO PRESS, 1964, PP 279-314
    057,

DE WILDE JOHN C
    DE WILDE JOHN C   ET AL
    EXPERIENCES WITH AGRICULTURAL DEVELOPMENT IN TROPICAL
    AFRICA, 2 VOLUMES
    BALTIMORE, JOHNS HOPKINS PRESS, 1967
    070,

DEAN EDWIN
    DEAN EDWIN

THE SUPPLY RESPONSES OF AFRICAN FARMERS-- THEORY
AND MEASUREMENT IN MALAWI.
AMSTERDAM, NORTH-HOLLAND PUBLISHING CO, 1966
070,122-08,

DEBONNEVILLE
DEBONNEVILLE FLORIS
LA MORT DU BIAFRA (THE DEATH OF BIAFRA).
PARIS, R. SOLAR, 1968
065,128-06,

DEBOSSCHERE G
DEBOSSCHERE G
NEO-COLONIALISM
PRESENCE AFRICAINE 10 38 1962 (ENGLISH EDITION) PP 26-35
087,

DEBRAH E M
DEBRAH E M
THE PSYCHOLOGY OF AFRICAN NATIONALISM.
IN WILLIAM H LEWIS, NEW FORCES IN AFRICA, GEORGETOWN
COLLOQUIUM ON AFRICA, PAPERS, WASHINGTON, PUBLIC AFFAIRS
PRESS, 1961, PP 51-66
054,

DEBRUNNER HANS
DEBRUNNER HANS
A CHURCH BETWEEN COLONIAL POWERS--A STUDY OF THE CHURCH IN
TOGO.
LONDON, BUTTERWORTH PRESS, 1965
050,137-03,

DECALO SAMUEL.
DECALO SAMUEL.
ISRAEL AND AFRICA-- A SELECTED BIBLIOGRAPHY.
THE JOURNAL OF MODERN AFRICAN STUDIES 5 3 NOVEMBER 1967 PP
385-400
086,

DECRAEMER WILLY
DECRAEMER WILLY   FOX RENEE C
THE EMERGING PHYSICIAN.
PALO ALTO, HOOVER INSTITUTION PRESS, 1969
075,

DECRAENE PHILIPPE
DECRAENE PHILIPPE
LE MALI MEDIEVAL (MEDIEVAL MALI).
CIVILISATIONS 12 1962 PP 250-258
022,123-02,

DELAFOSSE MAURICE
DELAFOSSE MAURICE
LES NOIRS DE L'AFRIQUE.
PARIS, PAYOT, 1941
099,

DELAMATER J
DELAMATER J   ET AL
SOCIAL PSYCHOLOGICAL RESEARCH IN DEVELOPING COUNTRIES

JOURNAL OF SOCIAL ISSUES 24 1968 PP 1-298
041,099,

DELANEY ANNETTE
    DELANEY ANNETTE
    ETHIOPIA SURVEY--A SELECTED BIBLIOGRAPHY.
    WASHINGTON, AFRICAN BIBLIOGRAPHIC CENTER, 1964
    110-12,

DELANGE JACQUELINE
    LEIRIS MICHEL   DELANGE JACQUELINE
    AFRICAN ART
    LONDON, THAMES AND HUDSON, 1968
    014,

DELANY M R
    DELANY M R   CAMPBELL ROBERT
    SEARCH FOR A PLACE--BLACK SEPARATISM AND AFRICA, 1860.
    ANN ARBOR, UNIVERSITY OF MICHIGAN PRESS, 1969
    095,

DELAVIGNETTE R L
    DELAVIGNETTE R L
    FREEDOM AND AUTHORITY IN FRENCH WEST AFRICA.
    LONDON, OXFORD UNIVERSITY PRESS, 1950
    035,

DELCOURT ANDRE
    DELCOURT ANDRE
    LA FRANCE ET LES ETABLISSEMENTS FRANCAIS AU SENEGAL ENTRE
    1713 ET 1763 (FRANCE AND FRENCH SETTLEMENTS IN SENEGAL
    BETWEEN 1713 AND 1763).
    DAKAR, INSTITUT FRANCAIS D AFRIQUE NOIRE, 1952
    027,

DELL SIDNEY
    DELL SIDNEY
    TRADE BLOCS AND COMMON MARKETS
    NEW YORK KNOPF 1963
    071,072,073,078,

DEMOZ ABRAHAM
    DEMOZ ABRAHAM
    AMHARIC FOR MODERN USE.
    JOURNAL OF THE FACULTY OF EDUCATION, HAILE SELASSIE UNIVER-
    SITY, 196
    110-06,

DENG WILLIAM
    ODUHO JOSEPH   DENG WILLIAM
    THE PROBLEM OF THE SOUTHERN SUDAN.
    LONDON, OXFORD UNIVERSITY PRESS, 1963
    134-06,

DENHAM DIXON
    DENHAM DIXON   CLAPPERTON HUGH   OUDNEY WALTER
    NARRATIVE OF TRAVELS AND DISCOVERIES IN NORTHERN AND CENTRAL
    AFRICA IN THE YEARS 1822, 1823 AND 1824.
    LONDON, CAMBRIDGE UNIVERSITY PRESS, 1966, 3 VOLUMES
    E W BOVILL, (ED.)

027,099,

DENT M J
   DENT M J
   ELECTIONS IN NORTHERN NIGERIA.
   JOURNAL OF LOCAL ADMINISTRATION OVERSEAS OCTOBER 1962
   PP 213-224
   063,128-07,

DEPUIS J
   DEPUIS J
   UN PROBLEME DE MINORITE-- LES NOMADES DANS L'ETAT SOUDANAISE
   (A MINORITY PROBLEM-- NOMADES IN THE STATE OF SUDAN).
   L'AFRIQUE ET L'ASIE 50 1960 PP 19-44
   057,123-06,

DERIDDER J C
   DERIDDER J C
   THE PERSONALITY OF THE URBAN AFRICAN IN SOUTH AFRICA.
   NEW YORK, HUMANITIES PRESS,1961
   041, 089, 132-05,

DERRETT DUNCAN J
   DERRETT DUNCAN J
   STUDIES IN THE LAWS OF SUCCESSION IN NIGERIA.
   LONDON, OXFORD UNIVERSITY PRESS, 1965
   066,128-01,

DERUS JACQUES
   DERUS JACQUES
   ADDIS ABABA, GENESE D UN CAPITALE IMPERIALE.
   IN REVUE BELGE DE GEOGRAPHIE, 88, 3, APRIL 1965
   110-05,

DERWENT DAVID F
   DERWENT DAVID F
   GROWTH POLE AND GROWTH CENTER CONCEPTS-A REVIEW,EVALUATION,
   AND BIBLIOGRAPHY
   BERKELEY,CENTER FOR PLANNING AND DEVELOPMENT RESEARCH,
   WORKING PAPER NUMBER 89,1968
   071,

DESAI RAM
   DESAI RAM   ED
   CHRISTIANITY IN AFRICA AS SEEN BY THE AFRICANS
   DENVER,SWALLOW,   1962
   050,

DESCHAMPS HUBERT J
   DESCHAMPS HUBERT J
   METHODES ET DOCTRINES COLONIALES DE LA FRANCE (FRENCH
   COLONIAL DOCTRINES AND METHODS).
   PARIS LIBRERIE ARMAND COLIN 1953
   035,

   DESCHAMPS HUBERT J
   TRADITIONS ORALES ET ARCHIVES AU GABON-- CONTRIBUTION A
   L'ETHNO-HISTOIRE (ORAL TRADITIONS AND ARCHIVES IN GABON--
   CONTRIBUTION TO ETHNO-HISTORY).
   PARIS L'HOMME D'OUTRE-MER 6 BERGER-LEVROULT 1962

099,112-02,

DESCHAMPS HUBERT J
    DESCHAMPS HUBERT J
    LE SENEGAL ET LA GAMBIE.
    PARIS, PRESSES UNIVERSITAIRES DE FRANCE, 1964
    130-11,

DESHLER W
    DESHLER W
    CATTLE IN AFRICA DISTRIBUTION TYPES AND PROBLEMS.
    THE GEOGRAPHICAL REVIEW AMERICAN GEOGRAPHICAL SOCIETY 53
    JANUARY 1963 PP 52-58
    010,069,070,

    DESHLER W
    LIVESTOCK TRYPANOSOMIASIS AND HUMAN SETTLEMENT IN
    NORTHEASTERN UGANDA.
    GEOGRAPHICAL REVIEW 50 OCTOBER 1960 PP 541-554
    069,

DEUTSCH KARL W
    DEUTSCH KARL W   FOLTZ WILLIAM J   EDS
    NATION-BUILDING.
    ATHERTON PRESS, 1966
    057,076,

    DEUTSCH KARL W
    NATIONALISM AND SOCIAL COMMUNICATIONS-- AN INQUIRY INTO
    THE FOUNDATIONS OF NATIONALITY.
    NEW YORK, JOHN WILEY, 1953; CAMBRIDGE, MASSACHUSETTS INSTITUTE
    OF TECHNOLOGY PRESS, 1966
    048,

    DEUTSCH KARL W
    SHIFTS IN THE BALANCE OF COMMUNICATION FLOWS.
    IN NELSON POLSBY, ROBERT DENTLER, AND PAUL SMITH, POLITICS
    AND SOCIAL LIFE. BOSTON, HOUGHTON MIFFLIN, 1963
    048,

    DEUTSCH KARL W
    SOCIAL MOBILIZATION AND POLITICAL DEVELOPMENT CHAPTER 6.
    IN JASON L FINKLE AND RICHARD W GABLE, POLITICAL
    DEVELOPMENT AND SOCIAL CHANGE, NEW YORK, JOHN WILEY, 1966
    037,

    DEUTSCH KARL W
    MAIN FINDINGS-- INTEGRATION AS A PROCESS.
    IN KARL DEUTSCH ET AL, POLITICAL COMMUNITY AND THE NORTH
    ATLANTIC AREA, PRINCETON, NEW JERSEY, PRINCETON UNIVERSITY
    PRESS, 1968 (PAPERBACK), PP 70-116
    077,

    DEUTSCH KARL W
    NATIONALISM AND ITS ALTERNATIVES
    NEW YORK, ALFRED KNOPF, 1969
    054,

DEVORE IRVEN
    DEVORE IRVEN   WASHBURN S L

BABOON ECOLOGY AND HUMAN EVOLUTION.
IN F CLARK HOWELL AND FRANCOIS BOURLIERE (EDS.), AFRICAN
ECOLOGY AND HUMAN EVOLUTION, CHICAGO, ALDINE, 1966,
PP 335-367
018,

DEVORE IRVEN
    LEE RICHARD B   DEVORE IRVEN   EDS
    MAN THE HUNTER
    CHICAGO,ALDINE,1968
    005, 009,

DEXTER LEWIS
    DEXTER LEWIS
    ELITE AND SPECIALIZED INTERVIEWING.
    EVANSTON, NORTHWESTERN UNIVERSITY PRESS, 1970
    098,

DIA MAMADOU
    DIA MAMADOU   TRANSLATED BY   COOK MERCER
    THE AFRICAN NATIONS AND WORLD SOLIDARITY.
    LONDON, THAMES AND HUDSON, 1962
    054,060,130-04,

    DIA MAMADOU
    TOWARDS A NEW DEFINITION OF NATION CHP 1.
    IN THE AFRICAN NATIONS AND WORLD SOLIDARITY, NEW YORK,
    PRAEGER, 1961
    054,

    DIA MAMADOU
    CONTRIBUTION A L' ETUDE DU MOUVEMENT COOPERATIF EN AFRIQUE
    NOIRE.
    PARIS, PRESENCE AFRICAINE. 1962 (3RD EDITION.
    130-04,

    DIA MAMADOU
    L'ECONOMIE AFRICAINE, ETUDES ET PROBLEMES NOUVEAUX.
    PARIS, P. U. F., 1957
    130-04,

    DIA MAMADOU
    NATIONS AFRICAINES ET SOLIDARITE MONDIALE.
    PARIS, P.U.F., 1963 (2ND EDITION)
    130-04,

    DIA MAMADOU
    REFLEXIONS SUR L' ECONOMIE DE L' AFRIQUE NOIRE--NOUVELLE ED-
    ITION REVUE ET AUGMENTEE.
    PARIS, PRESENCE AFRICAINE, 1961
    130-04,

DIAMOND STANLEY
    DIAMOND STANLEY
    THE BIAFRAN POSSIBILITY.
    AFRICA REPORT, FEB., 1968, P. 16
    065,128-06,

    DIAMOND STANLEY
    NIGERIAN DISCOVERY-- THE POLITICS OF FIELD WORK.

IN A VIDICH, ET AL (EDS.) REFLECTIONS ON COMMUNITY STUDIES,
NEW YORK, JOHN WILEY, 1964, PP 119-154
099,128-01,

DICKINSON ROBERT E
   DICKINSON ROBERT E
   CITY AND REGION-A GEOGRAPHIC INTERPRETATION
   LONDON, ROUTLEDGE AND KEGAN PAUL, 1964
   047,

DICKSON K B
   DICKSON K B
   A HISTORICAL GEOGRAPHY OF GHANA
   CAMBRIDGE, UNIVERSITY PRESS, 1969
   114-02,

DICKSON KWESI
   DICKSON KWESI
   BASES ETHIQUES ET SPIRITUELLES DE L'HUMANISME ANIMISTE
   (ETHICAL AND SPIRITUAL BASES OF ANIMISTIC HUMANISM).
   IN COLLOQUE SUR LES RELIGIONS, ABIDJAN, APRIL, 1961, PARIS,
   PRESENCE AFRICAINE, 1962, PP 81-86
   013,

DIENG DIAKHA
   DIENG DIAKHA
   FROM UAM TO OCAM.
   AFRICAN FORUM I 2 1965
   078,

DIETERLEN GERMAINE
   FORTES MEYER   DIETERLEN GERMAINE   EDS
   AFRICAN SYSTEMS OF THOUGHT
   LONDON, OXFORD UNIVERSITY PRESS ,1965, INTERNATIONAL AFRICAN
   INSTITUTE
   013,

   BA AMADOU HAMPATE   DIETERLEN GERMAINE
   KOUMEN--TEXTE INITIATIQUE DES PASTEURS PEULS.
   PARIS, MOUTON ET CIE, 1961
   123-01,

DIETZ BETTY W
   DIETZ BETTY W   OLATUNJI
   MUSICAL INSTRUMENTS OF AFRICA, THEIR NATURE, USE, AND
   PLACE IN THE LIFE OF A DEEPLY MUSICAL PEOPLE.
   NEW YORK, JOHN DAY, 1965
   015,

DIFFIE BAILEY W
   DIFFIE BAILEY W
   PRELUDE TO EMPIRE-- PORTUGAL OVERSEAS BEFORE HENRY THE
   NAVIGATOR.
   LINCOLN, UNIVERSITY OF NEBRASKA PRESS, 1960
   027,

DIKE K O
   DIKE K O
   THE STUDY OF AFRICAN HISTORY.
   IN LALAGE BOWN AND MICHAEL CROWDER (EDS.), PROCEEDINGS OF

THE FIRST INTERNATIONAL CONGRESS OF AFRICANISTS, ACCRA,
1962, LONDON,LONGMANS, 1964, PP 55-67
036,

DIKE K O
    DIKE K O
    THE IMPORTANCE OF AFRICAN STUDIES.
    IN LALAGE BOWN AND MICHAEL CROWDER (EDS.), PROCEEDINGS OF
    THE FIRST INTERNATIONAL CONGRESS OF AFRICANISTS, ACCRA,
    1962, LONDON, LONGMANS, 1964, PP 19-28
    100,

    DIKE K O
    BENIN-- A GREAT FOREST KINGDOM OF MEDIEVAL NIGERIA.
    PRACTICAL ANTHROPOLOGY 8 1961 PP 31-35
    026,128-02,

    DIKE K O
    TRADE AND POLITICS IN THE NIGER DELTA 1830-1885.
    OXFORD, CLARENDON PRESS,1956
    027,128-02,

DILLEY MARJORIE R
    DILLEY MARJORIE R
    BRITISH POLICY IN KENYA COLONY
    LONDON,FRANK CASS,1966 ,SECOND EDITION
    035,117-02,

DILLON WILTON S
    DILLON WILTON S
    UNIVERSITIES AND NATION-BUILDING IN AFRICA.
    JOURNAL OF MODERN AFRICAN STUDIES 1 MARCH 1963 PP 75-89
    042,058,

    DILLON WILTON S
    NIGERIA'S TWO REVOLUTIONS.
    AFRICA REPORT 11 MARCH 1966 PP 9-14
    065,128-06,

DIM DELOBSOM AA
    DIM DELOBSOM AA
    L'EMPIRE DU MOGHO-NABA--COUTIMES DES MOSSI DE LA
    HAUTE-VOLTA.
    PARIS, DOMAT-MONCHRESTIEN, 1932
    141-01,

DINA I O
    GALLETTI R   BALDWIN K D S   DINA I O
    NIGERIAN COCOA FARMERS-- AN ECONOMIC SURVEY OF YORUBA
    COCOA FARMING FAMILIES.
    LONDON,OXFORD UNIVERSITY PRESS,1956
    070,128-08,

DIOP ABDOULAYE B
    DIOP ABDOULAYE B
    SOCIETE TOUCOULEUR ET MIGRATION (TUCOLOR SOCIETY AND
    MIGRATION).
    DAKAR,INSTITUT FRANCAIS D'AFRIQUE NOIRE,1965
    070,130-05,

DIOP ALIOUNE
   DIOP ALIOUNE
   REMARKS ON AFRICAN PERSONALITY AND NEGRITUDE
   IN AMERICAN SOCIETY OF AFRICAN CULTURE,PAN-AFRICANISM
   RECONSIDERED,BERKELEY,UNIVERSITY OF CALIFORNIA PRESS, 1962
   PP 337-345
   039,054,077,079,

DIOP ALIOUNE
   DIOP ALIOUNE   DIOP CHEIKH ANTA
   CULTURE ET COLONIALISME.
   PARIS, LA NEF DE PARIS, 1957
   130-10,

DIOP BIRAGO
   DIOP BIRAGO
   TALES OF AMADOU KOUMBA.
   LONDON, OXFORD UNIVERSITY PRESS, 1966
   012,130-01,

   DIOP BIRAGO
   ECRIVAIN SENEGALAIS--TEXTES COMMENTES PAR ROGER MERCIER ET
   M ET S BATTESTINI.
   PARIS, F. NATHAN, 1964
   130-10,

   DIOP BIRAGO
   LEURRES ET LEURS--POEMES.
   PARIS, PRESENCE AFRICAINE, 1967 (2ND EDITION)
   130-10,

DIOP CHEIKH ANTA
   DIOP CHEIKH ANTA
   THE CULTURAL UNITY OF NEGRO-AFRICA.
   PARIS, PRESENCE AFRICAINE, 1962
   016,039,054,099,

   DIOP CHEIKH ANTA
   LES FONDEMENTS CULTURELS, TECHNIQUES ET INDUSTRIELS D·UN
   FUTUR, ETAT FEDERAL D'AFRIQUE NOIRE.
   PARIS, PRESENCE AFRICAINE, 1960
   054,

   DIOP CHEIKH ANTA
   L'AFRIQUE NOIRE PRE-COLONIALE (PRE-COLONIAL BLACK AFRICA).
   PARIS, PRESENCE AFRICAINE, 1960
   054,099,

   DIOP CHEIKH ANTA
   NATIONS NEGRES ET CULTURE (BLACK NATIONS AND CULTURE).
   PARIS, EDITIONS AFRICAINES, 1955
   054,

   DIOP CHEIKH ANTA
   ANTERIORITE DES CIVILISATIONS NEGRES--MYTHE OU VERITE
   HISTORIQUE.
   PARIS, PRESENCE AFRICAINE, 1967
   091,099,

   DIOP ALIOUNE   DIOP CHEIKH ANTA

CULTURE ET COLONIALISME.
PARIS, LA NEF DE PARIS, 1957
130-10,

DIOP DAVID
DIOP DAVID
COUPS DE PILON.
PARIS, PRESENCE AFRICAINE, 1961
130-10,

DIOP OUSMANE SOCE
DIOP OUSMANE SOCE
CONTES ET LEDENDES D'AFRIQUE NOIRE.
PARIS, NOUVELLES EDITIONS LATINES, 1962
130-10,

DIOP OUSMANE SOCE
KARIM, ROMAN SENEGALAIS, SUIVI DE CONTES ET LEGENDES
D'AFRIQUE NOIRE.
PARIS, NOUVELLES EDITIONS LATINES, 1966
130-10,

DIOP OUSMANE SOCE
MIRAGES DE PARIS.
PARIS, NOUVELLES EDITIONS LATINES, 1965
130-10,

DIOP OUSMANE SOCE
RYTHMES DU KHALAM.
PARIS, NOUVELLES EDITIONS LATINES. 1962
130-10,

DIPEOLU J O
DIPEOLU J O
BIBLIOGRAPHICAL SOURCES FOR NIGERIAN STUDIES.
EVANSTON, NORTHWESTERN UNIVERSITY PRESS, 1966
128-12,

DIXEY FRANK
DIXEY FRANK
THE EAST AFRICAN RIFT SYSTEM.
LONDON, HER MAJESTY'S STATIONERY OFFICE, 1956
017,

DOCUMENTATION
LA DOCUMENTATION FRANCAISE
LA REPUBLIQUE DU TOGO.
NOTES ET ETUDES DOCUMENTAIRES, NO. 2736, OCT. 5, 1960
137-11,

LA DOCUMENTATION FRANCAISE
LA REPUBLIQUE DE HAUTE-VOLTA.
NOTES ET ETUDES DOCUMENTAIRES, 2693, AUGUST, 1960
141-11,

DODGE DOROTHY
DODGE DOROTHY
AFRICAN POLITICS IN PERSPECTIVE.
NEW YORK, VAN NOSTRAND REINHOLD, 1966
076,

DOLE GERTRUDE E
   DOLE GERTRUDE E
   TRIBE AS THE AUTONOMOUS UNIT
   IN HELM(EDS), ESSAYS ON THE PROBLEM OF TRIBE, AMERICAN
   ETHNOLOGICAL SOCIETY, 1968, PP 83-100
   005,

DONNAN ELIZABETH
   DONNAN ELIZABETH   ED
   DOCUMENTS ILLUSTRATIVE OF THE HISTORY OF THE SLAVE TRADE
   TO AMERICA.
   NEW YORK, OCTAGON, 1965
   028,

DOOB LEONARD W
   DOOB LEONARD W
   PSYCHOLOGY.
   IN ROBERT A LYSTAD (ED), THE AFRICAN WORLD, NEW YORK,
   PRAEGER, 1966, PP 373-415
   039,

   DOOB LEONARD W
   FROM TRIBALISM TO NATIONALISM IN AFRICA.
   JOURNAL OF INTERNATIONAL AFFAIRS 16 1962 PP 144-155
   007,

   DOOB LEONARD W
   COMMUNICATION IN AFRICA--A SEARCH FOR BOUNDARIES.
   NEW HAVEN, YALE UNIVERSITY PRESS, 1961
   049,

   DOOB LEONARD W
   THE PSYCHOLOGICAL PRESSURE ON MODERN AFRICANS.
   IN PETER J MCEWAN AND ROBERT B SUTCLIFFE (EDS), MODERN AFRICA,
   NEW YORK, THOMAS CROWELL, 1965, PP 376-392
   041,

   DOOB LEONARD W
   ANTS WILL NOT EAT YOUR FINGERS- A SELECTION OF TRADITIONAL
   AFRICAN POEMS
   NEW YORK, WALKER, 1966
   012,

   DOOB LEONARD W   ED
   A CROCODILE HAS ME BY THE LEG-- AFRICAN POEMS.
   NEW YORK, WALKER, 1967
   012,

DORJAHN VERNON R
   DORJAHN VERNON R
   THE CHANGING POLITICAL SYSTEM OF TEMNE.
   IN IMMANUEL WALLERSTEIN (ED.), SOCIAL CHANGE-- THE
   COLONIAL SITUATION, NEW YORK, ROBERT WILEY, 1966
   PP 171-209
   038,131-03,

DORMAN M H
   DORMAN M H
   THE KILWA CIVILIZATION AND THE KILWA RUINS.

TANGANYIKA NOTES AND RECORDS 6 1938 PP 61-71
023,136-02,

DOSSER D G M
BANTON MICHAEL P   DOSSER D G M
THE BALANCE BETWEEN SOCIAL AND ECONOMIC DEVELOPMENT
IN AFRICA SOUTH OF THE SAHARA.
INFORMATION 27 1961 PP 5-23
074,

DOTSON FLOYD
DOTSON FLOYD   LILLIAN O
THE INDIAN MINORITY OF ZAMBIA, RHODESIA, AND MALAWI.
NEW HAVEN, CONN. (YALE), MCGILL-QUEENS PRESS, 1969
085,142-06,145-06,122-06,

DOUGLAS FREDERICK
DOUGLAS FREDERICK
NARRATIVE OF THE LIFE OF FREDERICK DOUGLAS, AN AMERICAN
SLAVE, WRITTEN BY HIMSELF.
CAMBRIDGE, HARVARD UNIVERSITY PRESS, 1960
030,

DOUGLAS M
FORDE C DARYLL   DOUGLAS M
PRIMITIVE ECONOMICS.
IN H L SHAPIRO (ED.) MAN, CULTURE. AND SOCIETY, OXFORD
UNIVERSITY PRESS, 1956 ALSO G DALTON (ED.) TRIBAL AND
PEASANT ECONOMIES, DOUBLEDAY, 1967
010,

DOUGLAS MARY
DOUGLAS MARY
THE LELE OF THE KASAI.
LONDON, OXFORD UNIVERSITY PRESS, 1963
108-01,

DOUGLAS MARY
THE LELE--RESISTANCE TO CHANGE.
IN BOHANNAN AND DALTON (EDS), MARKETS IN AFRICA, DOUBLEDAY,
1965
010,108-03,

BIEBUYCK DANIEL   DOUGLAS MARY
CONGO-TRIBES AND PARTIES.
LONDON, ROYAL ANTHROPOLOGICAL INSTITUTE, 1961
108-06,

DOW GEORGE F
DOW GEORGE F   ED
SLAVE SHIPS AND SLAVING.
SALEM, MARINE RESEARCH SOCIETY, 1927
028,

DOWD JEROME
DOWD JEROME
THE AFRICAN SLAVE TRADE.
JOURNAL OF NEGRO HISTORY 2 1917 PP 1-20
028,

DRAKE RICHARD
    DRAKE RICHARD
    OF RICHARD DRAKE.
    NEW YORK, DEWITT, 1960
    028,

DRAKE ST CLAIR
    DRAKE ST CLAIR
    PAN-AFRICANISM NEGRITUDE AND THE AFRICAN PERSONALITY.
    BOSTON UNIVERSITY GRADUATE JOURNAL 10 1961 PP 38-51, IN
    WILLIAM J HANNA, INDEPENDENT BLACK AFRICA, CHICAGO, RAND
    MCNALLY, 1964, PP 530-541
    039,054,077,

    DRAKE ST CLAIR
    THE AMERICAN NEGRO'S RELATION TO AFRICA.
    AFRICA TODAY 14 DECEMBER 1967 PP 12-15
    094,

    DRAKE ST CLAIR
    THE RESPONSIBILITY OF MEN OF CULTURE FOR DESTROYING THE
    HAMITIC MYTH.
    PRESENCE AFRICAINE 1 1959 PP 228-243
    003,

    DRAKE ST CLAIR
    AN APPROACH TO THE EVALUATION OF AFRICAN SOCIETIES.
    IN AMSAC, AFRICA SEEN BY AMERICAN NEGROES, PARIS ,
    PRESENCE AFRICAINE, 1958, PP 11-34
    094,

    DRAKE ST CLAIR
    SOCIAL AND ECONOMIC STATUS.
    IN THE NEGRO AMERICAN, TALCOTT PARSONS AND KENNETH CLARK, EDS,
    BOSTON, HOUGHTON MIFFLIN 1966 PP 3-46
    095,

    DRAKE ST CLAIR   CAYTON HORACE
    BLACK METROPOLIS.
    NEW YORK, HARCOURT BRACE, 1945
    030,

DRURY ALLEN
    DRURY ALLEN
    A VERY STRANGE SOCIETY
    NEW YORK, POCKET BOOKS, 1968
    089,

DRYDEN STANLEY
    DRYDEN STANLEY
    LOCAL ADMINISTRATION IN TANZANIA.
    KENYA, EAST AFRICAN PUBLISHING HOUSE, 1968
    062,136-07,

DRYSDALE JOHN
    LEGUM COLIN   DRYSDALE JOHN
    AFRICA CONTEMPORARY RECORD.
    LONDON, AFRICA RESEARCH LIMITED, 1969
    002,062,080,081,087,

LEGUM COLIN   DRYSDALE JOHN
NIGERIAN CIVIL WAR.
COLIN LEGUM AND JOHN DRYSDALE, AFRICA CONTEMPORARY RECORD,
LONDON, AFRICA RESEARCH LIMITED, 1969, PP. 645-688
065,128-06,

DRYSDALE JOHN
    DRYSDALE JOHN
    THE SOMALI DISPUTE
    NEW YORK, PRAEGER, 1964
    133-09,

DU BOIS VICTOR D
    DU BOIS VICTOR D
    NEW STATES AND AN OLD CHURCH.
    IN KALMAN SILVERT, ED, CHURCHES AND STATES-- THE RELIGIOUS IN-
    STITUTION AND MODERNIZATION, NEW YORK, AMERICAN
    UNIVERSITIES FIELD STAFF INC, 1967, PP 51-80
    050,

    DU BOIS VICTOR D
    THE ROLE OF THE ARMY IN GUINEA.
    AFRICA REPORT 8 JANUARY 1963 PP 3-5
    064,115-06,

    DU BOIS VICTOR D
    GUINEA.
    IN COLEMAN, J.S. AND ROSBERG, C.G. (EDS), POLITICAL PARTIES
    AND NATIONAL INTEGRATION IN TROPICAL AFRICA, LOS ANGELES,
    UNIVERSITY OF CALIFORNIA PRESS, 1964
    115-06,

DU BOIS W E B
    DU BOIS W E B
    WORLDS OF COLOR.
    IN PHILIP W QUIGG (ED.), AFRICA, NEW YORK, PRAEGER, 1964,
    PP 30-52
    094,

    DU BOIS W E B
    BLACK RECONSTITUTION IN AMERICA.
    LONDON, FRANK CASS AND CO. LTD., 1966
    030,

    DU BOIS W E B
    LIBERIA THE LEAGUE AND THE UNITED STATES.
    IN AFRICA SEEN BY AMERICAN NEGROES, NEW YORK, AMERICAN
    SOCIETY OF AFRICAN CULTURE, 1963 PP 329-344
    029,

    DU BOIS W E B
    THE SOULS OF BLACK FOLK.
    LONDON, LONGMANS, 1965
    094,

    DU BOIS W E B
    THE WORLD AND AFRICA.
    NEW YORK, THE VIKING PRESS, 1947
    094,

DU BOIS W E B
THE AUTOBIOGRAPHY OF W E B DUBOIS.
NEW YORK, INTERNATIONAL PUBLISHERS, 1968
094,

DU BOIS W E B
DU BOIS W E B
THE SUPPRESSION OF THE SLAVE-TRADE TO THE UNITED STATES
OF AMERICA, 1638-1870
NEW YORK, SCHOCKEN BOOKS, 1969
094,

DU BOIS W E B
DUSK OF DAWN-AN ESSAY TOWARD AN AUTOBIOGRAPHY OF A RACE
CONCEPT
NEW YORK, HARCOURT BRACE, 1940
094,

DU BOIS W E B
DARKWATER-VOICES FROM WITHIN THE VEIL
NEW YORK, HARCOURT BRACE, 1921
094,

DU SAUTOY PETER
DU SAUTOY PETER
THE PLANNING AND ORGANIZATION OF ADULT LITERACY PROGRAMMES
IN AFRICA.
PARIS, UNESCO, 1966
042,

DU TOIT A L
DU TOIT A L
OUR WANDERING CONTINENTS
LONDON, OLIVER AND BOYD, 1937
017,

DUBE S C
DUBE S C
BUREAUCRACY AND NATION BUILDING IN TRADITIONAL SOCIETIES
CHAPTER 12.
IN JASON L FINKLE AND RICHARD W GABLE, POLITICAL
DEVELOPMENT AND SOCIAL CHANGE, NEW YORK, JOHN WILEY, 1966
062,

DUDBRIDGE B J
DUDBRIDGE B J   GRIFFITHS J E S
THE DEVELOPMENT OF LOCAL GOVERNMENT IN SUKUMALAND.
JOURNAL OF AFRICAN ADMINISTRATION 3 JULY 1951 PP 141-146
062,136-09,

DUDLEY B J O
DUDLEY B J O
THE NOMINATION OF PARLIAMENTARY CANDIDATES IN
NORTHERN NIGERIA.
JOURNAL OF COMMONWEALTH POLITICAL STUDIES, 2 NOVEMBER, 1963
LONDON, LEICESTER UNIVERSITY PRESS, PP 45-58
063,128-07,

DUDLEY B J O
PARTIES AND POLITICS IN NORTHERN NIGERIA.

LONDON, FRANK CASS AND CO. LTD., NEW YORK, HUMANITIES PRESS,
1968
061,128-07,

DUDLEY B J O
   DUDLEY B J O
   POLITICAL THEORY AND POLITICAL SCIENCE.
   NIGERIAN JOURNAL OF ECONOMIC AND SOCIAL STUDIES 7 NOVEMBER
   1965 PP 257-272
   098,

   DUDLEY B J O
   THE CONCEPT OF FEDERALISM.
   NIGERIAN JOURNAL OF ECONOMIC AND SOCIAL STUDIES 5 MARCH
   1963 PP 95-103
   061,

DUFFY JAMES
   DUFFY JAMES
   PORTUGUESE AFRICA.
   CAMBRIDGE, HARVARD UNIVERSITY PRESS, 1959
   027,087,088,144-06,

   DUFFY JAMES   MANNERS ROBERT   EDS
   AFRICA SPEAKS.
   PRINCETON, VAN NOSTRAND, 1961
   060,

   DUFFY JAMES
   PORTUGAL IN AFRICA.
   IN PHILIP W QUIGG (ED.), AFRICA, NEW YORK, PRAEGER, 1964,
   PP 86-102
   035,087,144-06,

   DUFFY JAMES
   PORTUGAL'S AFRICAN TERRITORIES--PRESENT REALITIES.
   NEW YORK, CARNEGIE ENDOWMENT FOR INTERNATIONAL PEACE, 1962,
   39 PAGES
   087,

   DUFFY JAMES
   A QUESTION OF SLAVERY-LABOUR POLICIES IN PORTUGESE AFRICA
   AND THE BRITISH PROTEST,1850-1920
   CAMBRIDGE, HARVARD UNIVERSITY PRESS, 1967
   029,

   DUFFY JAMES
   PORTUGAL IN AFRICA
   BALTIMORE, PENGUIN, 1962
   027,087,088,144-06,

DUIGNAN PETER
   GANN LEWIS H   DUIGNAN PETER
   THE HISTORY AND POLITICS OF COLONIALISM, 1870-1914
   VOL 1--COLONIALISM IN AFRICA, 1870-1960
   CAMBRIDGE, UNIVERSITY PRESS 1969
   033,

   CLENDENEN CLARENCE COLLINS ROBERT O   DUIGNAN PETER
   AMERICANS IN AFRICA, 1865-1900.

PALO ALTO, CALIFORNIA, HOOVER INSTITUTION PRESS, 1966
096,

DUIGNAN PETER
   DUIGNAN PETER
   HANDBOOK OF AMERICAN RESOURCES FOR AFRICAN STUDIES.
   STANFORD, HOOVER INSTITUTE, 1967
   098,099,

   DUIGNAN PETER   CLENDENEN CLARENCE
   THE UNITED STATES AND THE AFRICAN SLAVE TRADE 1619-1862.
   STANFORD, HOOVER INSTITUTE, 1963
   029,

   DUIGNAN PETER
   PAN-AFRICANISM-- A BIBLIOGRAPHIC ESSAY.
   AFRICAN FORUM I 1 1965 PP 105-107
   079,

   GANN LEWIS H   DUIGNAN PETER
   BURDEN OF EMPIRE--AN APPRAISAL OF WESTERN COLONIALISM IN
   AFRICA SOUTH OF THE SAHARA.
   NEW YORK, PRAEGER, 1967
   035,

DUMONT RENE
   DUMONT RENE
   FALSE START IN AFRICA.
   NEW YORK, PRAEGER PUBLISHERS, 1969
   037,053,070,

   DUMONT RENE
   RECONVERSION DE L ECONOMIE AGRIOLE EN GUINEE EN COTE
   D'IVOIRE ET AU MALI.
   PARIS, PRESSES UNIVERSITAIRES DE FRANCE, 1961
   115-08, 123-08,

DUNCAN PATRICK
   DUNCAN PATRICK
   TOWARD A WORLD POLICY FOR SOUTH AFRICA.
   IN PHILIP W QUIGG (ED.), AFRICA, NEW YORK, PRAEGER, 1964,
   PP 248-260
   083,089,132-09,

   DUNCAN PATRICK
   RACE QUESTIONS IN SOUTH AFRICA.
   IN PHILIP W QUIGG (ED.), AFRICA, NEW YORK, PRAEGER, 1964,
   PP 199-214
   089,132-06,

   DUNCAN PATRICK
   SOTHO LAWS AND CUSTOMS.
   CAPE TOWN, OXFORD UNIVERSITY PRESS, 1960
   066,118-01,

DUNHAM DOWS
   DUNHAM DOWS
   NOTES ON THE HISTORY OF KUSH 850 BC - AD 350.
   AMERICAN JOURNAL OF ARCHAEOLOGY 50 1946 PP 378-388
   020,

DUPUIS JOSEPH
    DUPUIS JOSEPH
    JOURNAL OF A RESIDENCE IN ASHANTEE.
    LONDON, CASS, 1967
    026,114-02,

DURKHEIM EMILE
    DURKHEIM EMILE
    THE ELEMENTARY FORMS OF RELIGIOUS LIFE.
    NEW YORK, MACMILLAN, 1965, PP 1-33
    013,

    DURKHEIM EMILE
    THE DIVISION OF LABOR IN SOCIETY.
    GLENCOE, ILLINOIS, FREE PRESS, 1964, PP 70-110, 111-132, 200-232
    010,

DUSTAN ELIZABETH
    DUSTAN ELIZABETH   ED
    TWELVE NIGERIAN LANGUAGES.
    NEW YORK, INTERNATIONAL BOOKSELLERS, INC., 1969
    011,

DUVERGER MAURICE
    DUVERGER MAURICE
    POLITICAL PARTIES-- THEIR ORGANIZATION AND ACTIVITY IN THE
    MODERN STATE.
    NEW YORK, JOHN WILEY AND SONS, 1962
    061,

DUWAJI GHAZI
    DUWAJI GHAZI
    ECONOMIC DEVELOPMENT IN TUNISIA--THE IMPACT AND COURSE OF
    GOVERNMENT PLANNING.
    NEW YORK, PRAEGER PUBLISHERS, 1967
    072,138-08,

DZIRASA STEPHEN
    DZIRASA STEPHEN
    THE POLITICAL THOUGHT OF DR KWAME NKRUMAH.
    ACCRA, GUINEA PRESS
    060,114-04,

DZOBO N K
    DZOBO N K
    THE BRAIN CRISIS IN THE TEACHING PROFESSION IN GHANA.
    IN COLIN LEGUM AND JOHN DRYSDALE, AFRICA CONTEMPORARY
    RECORD, AFRICA RESEARCH LIMITED, LONDON, 1969, PP.875-77
    043,114-03,

E

EAST
    EAST AFRICAN INSTITUTE OF SOCIAL AND CULTURAL AFFAIRS
    RACIAL AND COMMUNAL TENSIONS IN EAST AFRICA.

KENYA, EAST AFRICAN PUBLISHING HOUSE, 1966
057,085,

EAST
    EAST AFRICAN INSTITUTE OF SOCIAL AND CULTURAL AFFAIRS
    RESEARCH PRIORITIES FOR EAST AFRICA.
    KENYA, EAST AFRICAN PUBLISHING HOUSE, 1966
    100,

    EAST AFRICA ROYAL COMMISSION
    EAST AFRICA ROYAL COMMISSION 1953-1955 REPORT.
    LONDON, HER MAJESTY'S STATIONERY OFFICE, COMMAND PAPER NO 9475,
    REPRINT 482, 1961
    035,045,

    EAST AFRICAN ACADEMY
    PROCEEDINGS OF THE EAST AFRICAN ACADEMY. D.F. OWEN ED.
    NAIROBI, EAST AFRICAN PUBLISHING HOUSE, 1967
    075,099,

    EAST AFRICAN INSTITUTE OF SOCIAL AND CULTURAL AFFAIRS
    RESEARCH PRIORITIES FOR EAST AFRICA.
    NAIROBI, EAST AFRICAN PUBLISHING HOUSE, CONTEMPORARY
    AFRICAN MONOGRAPH SERIES, NO 5, 1966
    100,

EAST N B
    EAST N B
    AFRICAN THEATRE--A CHECKLIST OF CRITICAL MATERIALS.
    NEW YORK, AFRICANA PUBLISHING CORPORATION, 1970
    093,

EASUM DONALD B
    EASUM DONALD B
    THE CALL FOR BLACK STUDIES.
    AFRICA REPORT, MAY/JUNE, 1969, PP. 16-28
    094,

ECKSTEIN A
    ECKSTEIN A
    COMMUNIST CHINA S ECONOMIC GROWTH AND FOREIGN TRADE.
    NEW YORK, MCGRAW-HILL, 1966
    084,

ECON COOP AND DEVEL
    ORG FOR ECON COOP   ECON COOP AND DEVEL
    BIBLIOGRAPHY ON GUINEA.
    PARIS, O.E.C.D. DEVELOPMENT CENTRE, 1965
    115-12,

ECONOMIC
    ECONOMIC COMMISSION FOR AFRICA
    INTRA-AFRICAN TRADE.
    E/CN   IY/STC/20 1963
    078,

    ECONOMIC COMMISSION FOR AFRICA
    STUDIES OF EXISTING AFRICAN CUSTOMS UNIONS.
    ECONOMIC BULLETIN FOR AFRICA 2 1962
    078,

ECONOMIC
   ECONOMIC COMMISSION FOR AFRICA
   CO-ORDINATION OF DEVELOPMENT PLANS IN AFRICA.
   ECONOMIC BULLETIN FOR AFRICA 1 1964
   072,

   ECONOMIC COMMISSION FOR AFRICA
   TRANSPORT PROBLEMS IN RELATION TO ECONOMIC DEVELOPMENT IN
   WEST AFRICA.
   NEW YORK, U N DOCUMENT NO 62.11.K.2, 1963
   048,

   ECONOMIC COMMISSION FOR AFRICA
   LEOPOLDVILLE AND LAGOS--COMPARATIVE STUDY OF CONDITIONS IN
   1960.
   IN GERALD BREESE (ED), THE CITY IN NEWLY DEVELOPING
   COUNTRIES, PRENTICE HALL, NEW JERSEY, 1969
   108-05,128-05,

EDGERTON R B
   EDGERTON R B
   AN ECOLOGICAL VIEW OF WITCHCRAFT IN FOUR AFRICAN SOCIETIES.
   AFRICAN STUDIES ASSOCIATION MEETINGS, PHILADELPHIA, OCTOBER
   1965
   040,

   EDGERTON R B
   CULTURAL VERSUS ECOLOGICAL FACTORS IN THE EXPRESSION OF
   VALUES, ATTITUDES AND PERSONALITY CHARACTERISTICS.
   AMERICAN ANTHROPOLOGIST 67 1965A PP 442-447
   040,

EDILIZIA MODERNA
   EDILIZIA MODERNA
   ARCHITECTURE.
   MILAN ISSUE 89-90 1967
   092,

EDINBURGH
   EDINBURGH UNIVERSITY
   THE TRANSATLANTIC SLAVE TRADE FROM WEST AFRICA
   CENTRE OF AFRICAN STUDIES,PAPERS AND DISCUSSION REPORTS
   CONTRIBUTED TO A SEMINAR HELD JUNE 4-5,1965
   028,

EDITORS OF TIME-LIFE
   DAVIDSON BASIL   EDITORS OF TIME-LIFE
   AFRICAN KINGDOMS.
   NEW YORK, TIME INCORPORATED, 1966
   036,

EDMOND
   CRONON EDMOND DAVID
   BLACK MOSES--THE STORY OF MARCUS GARVEY AND THE UNIVERSAL
   NEGRO IMPROVEMENT ASSOCIATION.
   MADISON, UNIVERSITY OF WISCONSIN PRESS, 1955
   095,

EDWARDS PAUL

EDWARDS PAUL   INTRODUCTION
LETTERS OF THE LATE IGNATIUS SANCHO, AN AFRICAN.
NEW YORK, HUMANITIES PRESS, INC., 1968, 5TH EDITION-1803
091,

EGHAREVBA JACOB
    EGHAREVBA JACOB
    A SHORT HISTORY OF BENIN.
    IBADAN UNIVERSITY PRESS, 1960
    026,128-02,

EISENSTADT S N
    EISENSTADT S N
    FROM GENERATION TO GENERATION-AGE GROUPS AND SOCIAL
    STRUCTURE
    NEW YORK, FREE PRESS, 1964; ORIGINALLY PUBLISHED 1956
    009,

    EISENSTADT S N
    MODERNIZATION-PROTEST AND CHANGE
    ENGLEWOOD CLIFFS, NEW JERSEY, PRENTICE-HALL, 1966
    037,

    EISENSTADT S N
    MODERNIZATION AND CONDITIONS OF SUSTAINED GROWTH
    WORLD POLITICS 16 JULY 1964 PP 576-594
    037,073,

    EISENSTADT S N
    COMMUNICATION SYSTEMS AND SOCIAL STRUCTURE-- AN
    EXPLORATORY COMPARATIVE STUDY.
    PUBLIC OPINION QUARTERLY 19 SUMMER 1955 PP 153-167
    048,

    EISENSTADT S N
    INITIAL INSTITUTIONAL PATTERNS OF POLITICAL MODERNIZATION--
    A COMPARATIVE STUDY.
    CIVILIZATIONS 12 1962 PP 461-473 AND 13 1963 PP 15-29
    062,

    EISENSTADT S N
    BREAKDOWNS OF MODERNIZATION CHAPTER 16.
    IN JASON L FINKLE AND RICHARD W GABLE, POLITICAL
    DEVELOPMENT AND SOCIAL CHANGE, NEW YORK, JOHN WILEY, 1966
    037,

    EISENSTADT S N
    PRIMITIVE POLITICAL SYSTEMS-- A PRELIMINARY COMPARATIVE
    ANALYSIS.
    AMERICAN ANTHROPOLOGIST 61 1959 PP 200-220. REPRINTED
    IN WILLIAM J HANNA (ED), INDEPENDENT BLACK AFRICA, CHICAGO,
    RAND MCNALLY, 1964, PP 60-85
    009,

EKOLLO PASTEUR
    EKOLLO PASTEUR
    ILLUSTRATION DU GENIE AFRICAINE AU SIEN DE LA COMMUNAUTE
    PROTESTANTE EN AFRIQUE (ILLUSTRATION OF THE AFRICAN SPIRIT
    IN THE BOSOM OF THE PROTESTANT COMMUNITY IN AFRICA).
    IN COLLOQUE SUR LES RELIGIONS, ABIDJAN, APRIL, 1961, PARIS

PRESENCE AFRICAINE, 1962, PP 147-154
050,

EKWENSI CYPRIAN
EKWENSI CYPRIAN
PEOPLE OF THE CITY.
LONDON, HEINEMANN EDUCATIONAL BOOKS LTD, 1964
090,128-10,

EKWENSI CYPRIAN
JAGUA NANA.
LONDON, HUTCHINSON AND CO, 1964
090,128-10,

EL MASRI F H
EL MASRI F H
THE LIFE OF SHEHU USUMAN DAN FODIO BEFORE THE JIHAD.
JOURNAL OF THE HISTORICAL SOCIETY OF NIGERIA 2 DECEMBER
1963 PP 435-448
024,128-02,

EL NASRI ABDEL R
EL NASRI ABDEL R
A BIBLIOGRAPHY OF THE SUDAN 1938-1958.
LONDON, OXFORD UNIVERSITY PRESS, 1962
134-12,

IBRAHIM ASMA   EL NASRI ABDEL R
SUDAN BIBLIOGRAPHY, 1959-1963.
SUDAN NOTES AND RECORDS, NO. 46, 1965
134-12,

EL-KAMMASH MAGDI M
EL-KAMMASH MAGDI M
ECONOMIC DEVELOPMENT AND PLANNING IN EGYPT.
NEW YORK, PRAEGER PUBLISHERS, 1967
072,140-08,

EL-MAHDI MANDOUR
EL-MAHDI MANDOUR
SHORT HISTORY OF THE SUDAN.
LONDON, OXFORD UNIVERSITY PRESS, 1965
134-02,

ELECTORAL
ELECTORAL COMMISSION
REPORT ON THE NIGERIA FEDERAL ELECTIONS, DECEMBER 1959.
LAGOS, FEDERAL GOVERNMENT PRINTER 1960
063,128-07,

ELIAS T O
ELIAS T O
THE FORM AND CONTENT OF COLONIAL LAW.
INTERNATIONAL AND COMPARATIVE LAW QUARTERLY 3 1954
PP 645-651
066,

ELIAS T O
THE NATURE OF AFRICAN CUSTOMARY LAW.
MANCHESTER, MANCHESTER UNIVERSITY PRESS, 1956

066,

ELIAS T O
    ELIAS T O
    THE IMPACT OF ENGLISH LAW ON NIGERIAN CUSTOMARY LAW.
    LUGARD LECTURES, CMS NIGERIA, 1958
    066,128-03,

    ELIAS T O
    THE NIGERIAN LEGAL SYSTEM.
    LONDON, ROUTLEDGE AND KEGAN PAUL, 1963, 2ND REV. ED.
    066,128-06,

ELISOFON ELIOT
    ELISOFON ELIOT   FAGG WILLIAM
    THE SCULPTURE OF AFRICA.
    NEW YORK, PRAEGER, 1958
    014,

ELKAN WALTER
    ELKAN WALTER
    AN AFRICAN LABOUR FORCE CHAPTER 7.
    IN EDITH WHETHAM AND JEAN CURRIE (EDS.), READINGS IN THE
    APPLIED ECONOMICS OF AFRICA, LONDON, CAMBRIDGE UNIVERSITY
    PRESS, 1, 1967, PP 67-71
    069,

    ELKAN WALTER
    THE EAST AFRICAN TRADE IN WOODCARVING.
    AFRICA 28 1958 PP 314-323
    093,

    ELKAN WALTER
    THE ECONOMIC DEVELOPMENT OF UGANDA.
    LONDON, OXFORD UNIVERSITY PRESS, 1961
    073,139-08,

    ELKAN WALTER
    EAST AFRICAN ECONOMIC COMMUNITY
    IN LEGUM AND DRYSDALE, AFRICA CONTEMPORARY RECORD,
    LONDON, AFRICA RESEARCH LIMITED, 1969, P. 13-17
    078,

    ELKAN WALTER
    MIGRANTS AND PROLETARIANS, URBAN LABOUR IN THE
    ECONOMIC DEVELOPMENT OF UGANDA.
    LONDON, OXFORD UNIVERSITY PRESS, 1960
    046,

ELKINS STANLEY
    ELKINS STANLEY
    SLAVERY A PROBLEM IN AMERICAN INSTITUTIONAL AND
    INTELLECTUAL LIFE.
    CHICAGO, UNIVERSITY OF CHICAGO PRESS, 1959
    029,030,

ELLIS WILLIAM W
    ELLIS WILLIAM W
    WHITE ETHICS AND BLACK POWER.
    CHICAGO, ALDINE PUBLISHING COMPANY, 1969

098,

ELLIS WILLIAM W
   ELLIS WILLIAM W   SALZBERG JOHN
   AFRICA AND THE U N-- A STATISTICAL NOTE.
   AMERICAN BEHAVIORAL SCIENTIST 8 APRIL 1965 PP 30-32
   081,

ELLISON R E
   ELLISON R E
   THREE FORGOTTEN EXPLORERS OF THE LATTER HALF OF THE
   NINETEENTH CENTURY, WITH SPECIAL REFERENCE TO THEIR
   JOURNEYS TO BORNU.
   JOURNAL OF THE HISTORICAL SOCIETY OF NIGERIA I 1959 PP
   322-330
   024,

EMERSON
   EMERSON RUPERT   KILSON MARTIN L   EDS
   THE POLITICAL AWAKENING OF AFRICA.
   ENGLEWOOD CLIFFS, NJ, PRENTICE-HALL, 1965
   060,

EMERSON RUPERT
   EMERSON RUPERT
   NATIONALISM AND POLITICAL DEVELOPMENT.
   JOURNAL OF POLITICS 22 FEBRUARY 1960 PP 3-28
   ALSO IN FINKLE J L AND GABLE R W, POLITICAL DEVELOPMENT AND
   SOCIAL CHANGE, NEW YORK, JOHN WILEY, 1966, CH 5
   054,

   EMERSON RUPERT
   CRUCIAL PROBLEMS INVOLVED IN NATION-BUILDING IN AFRICA.
   JOURNAL OF NEGRO EDUCATION 30 1961 PP 193-205
   055,

   EMERSON RUPERT   KILSON MARTIN L
   IDEAS AND CONTEXT OF AFRICAN NATIONALISM CHP 2.
   IN THE POLITICAL AWAKENING OF AFRICA, ENGELWOOD CLIFFS,
   NEW JERSEY, PRENTICE-HALL, 1965
   054,

   EMERSON RUPERT   KILSON MARTIN L
   INTER-AFRICAN PROBLEMS AND PAN-AFRICANISM CHP 4.
   IN THE POLITICAL AWAKENING OF AFRICA, ENGLEWOOD CLIFFS,
   NEW JERSEY, PRENTICE-HALL, 1965
   079,

   EMERSON RUPERT
   POLITICAL MODERNIZATION-- THE SINGLE-PARTY SYSTEM.
   MONOGRAPH NO 1, DENVER, DENVER UNIVERSITY PRESS, 1964
   061,

   EMERSON RUPERT
   THE CHARACTER OF AMERICAN INTERESTS IN AFRICA CHAPTER 1.
   IN THE UNITED STATES AND AFRICA, BACKGROUND PAPERS OF THE
   13TH ASSEMBLY, THE AMERICAN ASSEMBLY, COLUMBIA UNIVERSITY,
   1958, PP 1-24
   083,

EMERSON RUPERT   KILSON MARTIN L
THE AMERICAN DILEMMA IN A CHANGING WORLD-- THE RISE OF
AFRICA AND THE NEGRO AMERICAN.
IN THE NEGRO AMERICAN, TALCOTT PARSONS AND KENNETH CLARK, EDS,
BOSTON, HOUGHTON MIFFLIN, 1966, PP 626-655
094,

EMERSON RUPERT
    EMERSON RUPERT
    PARTIES AND NATIONAL INTEGRATION IN AFRICA.
    IN J LAPALOMBARA AND M WEINER (EDS), POLITICAL PARTIES IN
    POLITICAL DEVELOPMENT PRINCETON, NEWJERSEY, PRINCETON
    UNIVERSITY PRESS, 1966, PP 267-302
    057,

    EMERSON RUPERT
    PAN-AFRICANISM.
    IN NORMAN J PADELFORD AND RUPERT EMERSON (EDS), AFRICA AND
    WORLD ORDER, NEW YORK, PRAEGER, 1963, PP 7-22; INTERNATIONAL
    ORGANIZATION 16 SPRING 1962 PP 275-290
    079,

    PADELFORD NORMAN J EMERSON RUPERT   EDS
    AFRICA AND WORLD ORDER.
    NEW YORK, PRAEGER, 1963
    080,

    EMERSON RUPERT
    AFRICA AND UNITED STATES POLICY.
    ENGLEWOOD CLIFFS, N.J., PRENTICE-HALL, 1967
    083,

    EMERSON RUPERT
    FROM EMPIRE TO NATION.
    CAMBRIDGE, MASS, HARVARD UNIVERSITY PRESS, 1960
    054,

EMERY W B
    EMERY W B
    ARCHAIC EGYPT
    BALTIMORE, PENGUIN, 1963
    020,

ENDOZIEN J C
   ENDOZIEN J C
   MALARIA, POPULATION GROWTH AND ECONOMIC DEVELOPMENT IN
   AFRICA.
   IN LALAGE BOWN AND MICHAEL CROWDER (EDS.), PROCEEDINGS OF
   THE FIRST INTERNATIONAL CONGRESS OF AFRICANISTS, ACCRA,
   1962, LONDON, LONGMANS, 1964, PP 329-333
   074,

ENGBERG H L
   ENGBERG H L
   COMMERCIAL BANKING IN EAST AFRICA CHAPTER 22.
   IN EDITH WHETHAM AND JEAN CURRIE (EDS.),READINGS IN THE
   APPLIED ECONOMICS OF AFRICA, LONDON, CAMBRIDGE UNIVERSITY
   PRESS, 2, 1967, PP 48-69
   073,

ENGESTROM TOR
   ENGESTROM TOR
   ORIGIN OF PRE-ISLAMIC ARCHITECTURE IN WEST AFRICA.
   ETHNOS 24 1959 PP 64-69
   092,

ENGHOLM G F
   ENGHOLM G F
   AFRICAN ELECTIONS IN KENYA, MARCH 1957, CHAPTER 7.
   IN W J MACKENZIE AND KENNETH ROBINSON, FIVE ELECTIONS IN
   AFRICA, LONDON, OXFORD UNIVERSITY PRESS, 1960
   063,117-07,

   ENGHOLM G F
   THE WESTMINSTER MODEL IN UGANDA.
   INTERNATIONAL JOURNAL 18 AUTUMN 1963 PP 468-487
   062,139-07,

ENJALBERT H
   ENJALBERT H
   PAYSANS NOIRS-- LES KABRE DU NORD-TOGO
   (BLACK PEASANTS-- THE KABRE OF NORTHERN TOGO).
   CAHIERS D'OUTRE-MER 9 APRIL JUNE 1956 PP 137-180
   070,137-08,

ENKE STEPHEN
   ENKE STEPHEN
   AGRICULTURAL INNOVATIONS AND COMMUNITY DEVELOPMENT.
   IN LEWIS P FICKETT (ED), PROBLEMS OF THE DEVELOPING NATIONS,
   NEW YORK, CROWELL, 1966, PP 21-51

070,

ENWONWU BEN
   ENWONWU BEN
   PROBLEMS OF THE AFRICAN ARTIST TODAY.
   PRESENCE AFRICAINE, NS 8-10,1956 PP 147-178
   093,

EPANYA
   EPANYA YONDO ELOLONGUE
   KAMERUN KAMERUN.
   PARIS,PRESENCE AFRICAINE,1960
   104-10,

EPPS ARCHIE EDITOR
   MALCOLM X   EPPS ARCHIE EDITOR
   THE SPEECHES OF MALCOLM X AT HARVARD.
   NEW YORK, WILLIAM MORROW AND COMPANY, INC., 1968
   094,

EPSTEIN ARNOLD L
   EPSTEIN ARNOLD L
   URBANIZATION AND SOCIAL CHANGE IN AFRICA.
   CURRENT ANTHROPOLOGY 8 NO 4 OCTOBER 1967 PP 275-283
   007,046,

   EPSTEIN ARNOLD L
   JUDICIAL TECHNIQUES AND THE JUDICIAL PROCESS-- A STUDY IN
   AFRICAN CUSTOMARY LAW.
   MANCHESTER,MANCHESTER UNIVERSITY PRESS, 1954
   066,139-06,

   EPSTEIN ARNOLD L
   POLITICS IN AN URBAN AFRICAN COMMUNITY.
   MANCHESTER,MANCHESTER UNIVERSITY PRESS, 1958
   007,046,142-05,

ERIKSON ERIK H
   ERIKSON ERIK H
   CHILDHOOD AND SOCIETY.
   NEW YORK, NORTON, 1964 (REVISED EDITION) CHAPTERS 8-10
   008,

   ERIKSON ERIK H
   THE CONCEPT OF IDENTITY IN RACE RELATIONS.
   IN THE NEGRO AMERICAN,TALCOTT PARSONS AND KENNETH CLARK, EDS,
   BOSTON, HOUGHTON MIFFLIN,1966, PP 227-253
   088,

ERLICH ALEXANDER
   ERLICH ALEXANDER   SONNE CHRISTIAN R
   THE SOVIET UNION-- ECONOMIC ACTIVITY.
   IN Z BRZEZINSKI (ED), AFRICA AND THE COMMUNIST WORLD,
   STANFORD, CALIFORNIA, STANFORD UNIVERSITY PRESS, 1963,
   PP 49-83
   084,

ESPIE IAN
   AJAYI J F ADE   ESPIE IAN   EDS
   A THOUSAND YEARS OF WEST AFRICAN HISTORY-- A HANDBOOK FOR

TEACHERS AND STUDENTS.
IBADAN, IBADAN UNIVERSITY PRESS; ALSO LONDON, THOMAS NELSON
AND SONS, 1965
001,036,

ESSIEN-UDOM E U
    ESSIEN-UDOM E U
    THE RELATIONSHIP OF AFRO-AMERICANS TO AFRICAN NATIONALISM--
    AN HISTORICAL INTERPRETATION.
    FREEDOMWAYS 2 4 FALL 1962 PP 391-408
    096,

    ESSIEN-UDOM E U
    BLACK NATIONALISM--A SEARCH FOR IDENTITY IN AMERICA.
    NEW YORK, DELL PUBLISHERS, 1965 (ORIGINALLY UNIVERSITY OF
    CHICAGO PRESS, 1962)
    094,096,

ET COMP
    WALKER AUDREY A   ET COMP
    THE RHODESIAS AND NYASALAND--A GUIDE TO OFFICIAL PUBLICA-
    TIONS.
    WASHINGTON, U.S. GOVERNMENT PRINTING OFFICE, 1965
    142-12,

EVANS J L
    EVANS J L
    CHILDREN IN AFRICA-A REVIEW OF PSYCHOLOGICAL RESEARCH
    NEW YORK, TEACHER'S COLLEGE PRESS, FORTHCOMING
    040,

    SEGALL MARSHALL H   EVANS J L
    LEARNING TO CLASSIFY BY COLOR AND FUNCTION-A STUDY IN
    CONCEPT FORMATION BY GANDA CHILDREN
    JOURNAL OF SOCIAL PSYCHOLOGY 77 1969 PP 35-53
    040,

EVANS-PRITCHARD
    FORTES MEYER   EVANS-PRITCHARD E
    VALUES IN AFRICAN TRIBAL LIFE.
    IN PETER J MCEWAN AND ROBERT B SUTCLIFFE (EDS), MODERN AFRICA,
    NEW YORK, THOMAS CROWELL, 1965, PP 55-57
    013,

    EVANS-PRITCHARD E E
    THE ZANDE STATE.
    JOURNAL OF THE ROYAL ANTHROPOLOGICAL INSTITUTE 93 1963
    PP 134-154
    009,134-01,

    EVANS-PRITCHARD E E
    KINSHIP AND MARRIAGE AMONG THE NUER.
    LONDON, OXFORD UNIVERSITY PRESS, 1953
    008,134-01,

    EVANS-PRITCHARD E E
    THE ZANDE TRICKSTER.
    LONDON, OXFORD UNIVERSITY PRESS, 1967
    012,134-01,

EVANS-PRITCHARD E E
WITCHCRAFT, ORACLES, AND MAGIC AMONG THE AZANDE.
LONDON, OXFORD UNIVERSITY PRESS, 1951
013,134-01,

EVANS-PRITCHARD
  EVANS-PRITCHARD E E
  NUER RELIGION
  LONDON, OXFORD UNIVERSITY PRESS, 1956
  013,134-01,

  EVANS-PRITCHARD E E
  THE POSITION OF WOMEN IN PRIMITIVE SOCIETIES AND OTHER
  ESSAYS IN SOCIAL ANTHROPOLOGY.
  NEW YORK, FREE PRESS, 1965
  008,

  EVANS-PRITCHARD E E
  THE SANUSI OF CYRENAICA.
  OXFORD, CLARENDON PRESS, 1949
  120-01,

  EVANS-PRITCHARD E E
  THE NUER--A DESCRIPTION OF THE MODES OF LIVLIHOOD AND
  POLITICAL INSTITUTIONS OF A NILOTIC PEOPLE.
  LONDON, OXFORD UNIVERSITY PRESS, 1940
  134-01,

  EVANS-PRITCHARD E E
  THE POLITICAL SYSTEM OF THE ANUAX OF THE ANGLO-EGYPTIAN
  SUDAN
  LONDON, LUND, 1940
  134-01,

EVANS-PRITCHARD E E
  FORTES MEYER   EVANS-PRITCHARD E E EDS
  AFRICAN POLITICAL SYSTEMS.
  LONDON, OXFORD UNIVERSITY PRESS, 1940 (1962)
  009,099,

EWING A F
  EWING A F
  INDUSTRY IN AFRICA
  LONDON, OXFORD UNNIVERSITY PRESS, 1968
  071,

  EWING A F
  PROSPECTS FOR ECONOMIC INTEGRATION IN AFRICA.
  JOURNAL OF MODERN AFRICAN STUDIES 5 MAY 1967 PP 53-67
  078,

EZERA KALU
  EZERA KALU
  CONSTITUTIONAL DEVELOPMENTS IN NIGERIA.
  CAMBRIDGE, CAMBRIDGE UNIVERSITY PRESS, 1964
  068,128-07,

F

FABIAN JOHANNES
   FABIAN JOHANNES
   CHARISMA AND CULTURAL CHANGE-THE CASE OF THE JAMAA MOVEMENT
   IN KATANGA(CONGO REPUBLIC)
   COMPARATIVE STUDIES IN SOCIETY AND HISTORY 11 1969 PP155-173
   051,108-03,

FABUMI L A
   FABUMI L A
   THE SUDAN IN ANGLO-EGYPTIAN RELATIONS-A CASE STUDY IN POWER
   POLITICS 1800-1956
   LONDON,LONGMANS, GREEN,1960
   134-09,

FACULTY
   FACULTY OF ARTS AND SCIENCES HARVARD   UNIVERSITY
   REPORT OF THE FACULTY COMMITTEE ON AFRICAN AND AFRO-AMERICAN
   STUDIES--JANUARY 20, 1969.
   CAMBRIDGE, HARVARD UNIVERSITY PRESS, 1969
   094,

FAGAN BRIAN M
   FAGAN BRIAN M
   RADIOCARBON DATES FOR SUB-SAHARAN AFRICA VI.
   JOURNAL OF AFRICAN HISTORY, X, 1, 1969, PP. 149-169
   019,

   FAGAN BRIAN M
   PRE-EUROPEAN IRON WORKING IN CENTRAL AFRICA WITH SPECIAL
   REFERENCE TO NORTHERN RHODESIA.
   JOURNAL OF AFRICAN HISTORY 2 1961 PP 199-210
   019,

   FAGAN BRIAN M
   THE IRON AGE SEQUENCE IN THE SOUTHERN PROVINCE OF NORTHERN
   RHODESIA.
   JOURNAL OF AFRICAN HISTORY 4 1963 PP 157-177
   019,

   FAGAN BRIAN M
   SOUTHERN AFRICA IN THE IRON AGE.
   LONDON,THAMES AND HUDSON,1965
   019,025,

   FAGAN BRIAN M
   EARLY TRADE AND RAW MATERIALS IN SOUTH CENTRAL AFRICA
   JOURNAL OF AFRICAN HISTORY, X, 1, 1969, PP. 1-13
   019,

   FAGAN BRIAN M
   ZIMBABWE--A CENTURY OF DISCOVERY.
   AFRICAN ARTS, SPRING 1969, VOL II, NO. 3, PP. 20-24, CONT.
   85-86
   025,145-02,

FAGAN BRIAN M
    IRON AGE CULTURES IN ZAMBIA--TWO VOLUMES
    LONDON, 1967-69
    019,142-02,

FAGAN BRIAN M
    FAGAN BRIAN M   ED
    A SHORT HISTORY OF ZAMBIA.
    LONDON, OXFORD UNIVERSITY PRESS, 1966
    142-02,

FAGE JOHN D
    FAGE JOHN D
    AN ATLAS OF AFRICAN HISTORY
    LONDON, EDWARD ARNOLD, 1958
    036,

    FAGE JOHN D   ED
    AFRICA DISCOVERS HER PAST
    NEW YORK, OXFORD UNIVERSITY PRESS, 1969
    036, 100,

    FAGE JOHN D
    A HISTORY OF WEST AFRICA
    NEW YORK, CAMBRIDGE UNIVERSITY PRESS, 1969
    022, 026, 036,

    OLIVER ROLAND   FAGE JOHN D
    A SHORT HISTORY OF AFRICA.
    BALTIMORE, PENGUIN BOOKS, 1962
    001,036,

    OLIVER ROLAND   FAGE JOHN D
    THIRD CONFERENCE ON AFRICAN HISTORY AND ARCHAEOLOGY-- 1961.
    THE JOURNAL OF AFRICAN HISTORY VOL III NO 2 1962 (ENTIRE
    VOLUME)
    018,019,

    FAGE JOHN D
    HISTORY.
    IN ROBERT A LYSTAD (ED), THE AFRICAN WORLD, NEW YORK,
    PRAEGER, 1966, PP 40-56
    100,

    FAGE JOHN D
    ANCIENT GHANA-- A REVIEW OF THE EVIDENCE.
    TRANSACTIONS OF THE HISTORICAL SOCIETY OF GHANA 3 1957
    PP 77-98
    022,

    FAGE JOHN D
    THE USE OF ORAL EVIDENCE IN WEST AFRICAN HISTORY.
    BULLETIN OF THE INSTITUTE OF HISTORICAL RESEARCH 31 1958
    PP 33-35
    099,

    FAGE JOHN D
    REVIEW OF MURDOCK-- AFRICA, ITS PEOPLE AND THEIR CULTURE
    HISTORY.
    THE JOURNAL OF AFRICAN HISTORY VOL 2 NO 2 1961 PP 299-309

003,

FAGE JOHN D
    FAGE JOHN D
    SOME THOUGHTS ON STATE FORMATION IN THE WESTERN SUDAN BEFORE
    THE SEVENTEENTH CENTURY.
    IN JEFFREY BUTLER (ED) BOSTON UNIVERSITY PAPERS IN AFRICAN
    HISTORY VOL I, BOSTON, BOSTON UNIVERSITY PRESS, 1964, PP 17-34
    022,

    FAGE JOHN D
    GHANA--A HISTORICAL INTERPRETATION.
    MADISON, UNIVERSITY OF WISCONSIN PRESS, 1959
    114-02,

    FAGE JOHN D
    SLAVERY AND THE SLAVE TRADE IN THE CONTEXT OF WEST AFRICAN
    HISTORY.
    IN JOURNAL OF AFRICAN HISTORY VOL 10 1969 P 393
    028,

    FAGE JOHN D
    SOME THOUGHTS ON MIGRATION AND URBAN SETTLEMENT CHAPTER 3.
    IN HILDA KUPER (ED), URBANIZATION AND MIGRATION IN WEST
    AFRICA, BERKELEY, UNIVERSITY OF CALIFORNIA PRESS,1965
    046,

FAGEN RICHARD R
    FAGEN RICHARD R
    POLITICS AND COMMUNICATION.
    BOSTON, LITTLE, BROWN AND COMPANY, 1966
    048,

    FAGEN RICHARD R
    RELATIONS OF COMMUNICATION GROWTH TO NATIONAL POLITICAL
    SYSTEMS IN THE LESS DEVELOPED COUNTRIES.
    JOURNALISM QUARTERLY 41 WINTER 1964 PP 87-94
    048,

FAGG BERNARD
    FAGG BERNARD
    THE NOK CULTURE IN PREHISTORY.
    JOURNAL OF THE HISTORICAL SOCIETY OF NIGERIA 1 1959
    PP 288-293
    020,128-02,

FAGG WILLIAM
    ELISOFON ELIOT   FAGG WILLIAM
    THE SCULPTURE OF AFRICA.
    NEW YORK, PRAEGER, 1958
    014,

    FAGG WILLIAM
    THE ART OF WESTERN AFRICA-- SCULPTURE AND TRIBAL MASKS.
    NEW YORK AND TORONTO, MENTOR UNESCO ART BOOK MQ 772, 1967
    014,

    FAGG WILLIAM
    TRIBES AND FORMS IN AFRICAN ART.
    LONDON, METHUEN,1965

014,

FAGG WILLIAM
    FAGG WILLIAM
    THE ART OF CENTRAL AFRICA-- SCULPTURE AND TRIBAL MASKS.
    NEW YORK AND TORONTO, MENTOR UNESCO ART BOOK, MQ773, 1967
    014,

    FAGG WILLIAM
    ON THE NATURE OF AFRICAN ART.
    MEMOIRS AND PROCEEDING OF THE MANCHESTER LITERATURE AND
    PHILOSOPHICAL SOCIETY, 94, PP 93-104, 1953
    REPRINTED IN COLIN LEGUM, AFRICA, A HANDBOOK TO THE
    CONTINENT, LONDON, A BLOND, 1961, PP 414-424
    014,

    FAGG WILLIAM
    THE STUDY OF AFRICAN ART.
    BULLETIN OF THE ALLEN MEMORIAL ART MUSEUM 12 1955-56
    PP 44-61 OBERLIN COLLEGE
    014,

    FAGG WILLIAM
    AFRICAN TRIBAL IMAGES
    CLEVELAND, CASE WESTERN RESERVE, 1968
    014,

    FAGG WILLIAM
    NIGERIAN IMAGES.
    NEW YORK, PRAEGER, 1963
    014,020,128-01,

    FAGG WILLIAM
    DE L'ART DES YORUBA (ON THE ART OF YORUBA).
    L'ART NEGRE, PRESENCE AFRICAINE 10-11 PARIS 1951 PP 103-135
    014,128-01,

FAGUNWA D O
    SOYINKA WOLE   FAGUNWA D O
    THE FOREST OF A THOUSAND DAEMONS.
    NEW YORK, HUMANITIES PRESS, INC., 1968
    090,128-10,

FAIDHERBE LOUIS L
    FAIDHERBE LOUIS L
    LE SENEGAL-- LA FRANCE DANS L'AFRIQUE OCCIDENTAL
    (SENEGAL-- FRANCE IN WEST AFRICA).
    PARIS, HACHETTE, 1889
    027,130-02,

FAIR T J D
    FAIR T J D   SHAFFER N M
    POPULATION PATTERNS AND POLICIES IN SOUTH AFRICA, 1951-1960
    ECONOMIC GEOGRAPHY, 40 JULY 1964 PP 261-274
    089,132-06,

    FAIR T J D
    A REGIONAL APPROACH TO ECONOMIC DEVELOPMENT IN KENYA.
    SOUTH AFRICAN GEOGRAPHICAL JOURNAL 45 DECEMBER1963 PP 55-77
    048,073,117-08,

FAIR T J D
   GREEN L P   FAIR T J D
   DEVELOPMENT IN AFRICA- A STUDY IN REGIONAL ANALYSIS WITH
   SPECIAL REFERENCE TO SOUTHERN AFRICA
   JOHANNESBURG,WITWATERSRAND UNIVERSITY PRESS,1962
   048,073,132-08,145-08,

   FAIR T J D   MURDOCK G   JONES H M
   DEVELOPMENT IN SWAZILAND-A REGIONAL ANALYSIS
   JOHANNESBURG,WITWATERSRAND UNIVERSITY PRESS,1969
   135-08,

FAIRSERVIS WALTER
   FAIRSERVIS WALTER
   THE ANCIENT KINGDOMS OF THE NILE AND THE DOOMED MONUMENTS
   OF NUBIA.
   NEW YORK,THOMAS CROWELL,1962
   020,

FALCONBRIDGE A
   FALCONBRIDGE A
   AN ACCOUNT OF THE SLAVE TRADE ON THE COAST OF AFRICA.
   LONDON, J PHILLIPS,1788
   028,

FALLERS LLOYD A
   FALLERS LLOYD A
   CUSTOMARY LAW IN THE NEW AFRICAN STATES.
   LAW AND CONTEMPORARY PROBLEMS 27 1962 PP 605-616
   066,

   FALLERS LLOYD A
   ARE AFRICAN CULTIVATORS TO BE CALLED PEASANTS.
   CURRENT ANTHROPOLOGY 2 1961 PP 108-110
   070,

   FALLERS LLOYD A
   POLITICAL SOCIOLOGY AND THE ANTHROPOLOGICAL STUDY OF
   AFRICAN POLITIES.
   ARCHIVES EUROPEENNES DE SOCIOLOGIE 4 1963 PP 311-329
   100,

   FALLERS LLOYD A
   POPULISM AND NATIONALISM-- A COMMENT ON D A LOWS THE ADVENT
   OF POPULISM IN BUGANDA.
   COMPARATIVE STUDIES IN SOCIETY AND HISTORY 6 JULY 1964
   055,139-06,
   PP 445-448

   FALLERS LLOYD A
   BANTU BUREAUCRACY.
   CHICAGO,UNIVERSITY OF CHICAGO PRESS,1965
   009,

   FALLERS LLOYD A   FALLERS M C
   HOMICIDE AND SUICIDE IN BUSOGA.
   IN PAUL BOHANNAN (ED), AFRICAN HOMICIDE AND SUICIDE,
   PRINCETON, PRINCETON UNIVERSITY PRESS, 1960, PP 65-93
   041,

FALLERS LLOYD A
   FALLERS LLOYD A
   THE KING'S MEN-- LEADERSHIP AND STATUS IN BUGANDA ON THE
   EVE OF INDEPENDENCE.
   LONDON, OXFORD UNIVERSITY PRESS, 1964
   034,038,139-03,

   FALLERS LLOYD A
   CHANGING CUSTOMARY LAW IN BUSOGA DISTRICT OF UGANDA.
   JOUNRAL OF AFRICAN ADMINISTRATION 8 JULY 1956 PP 139-144
   066,139-03,

   FALLERS LLOYD A
   THE PREDICAMENT OF THE MODERN AFRICAN CHIEF-- AN
   INSTANCE FROM UGANDA.
   AMERICAN ANTHROPOLOGIST 57 1955 PP 290-305; ALSO WILLIAM J
   HANNA, ED, INDEPENDENT BLACK AFRICA, CHICAGO, RAND MCNALLY,
   1964, PP 278-296
   038,139-03,

   FALLERS LLOYD A
   THE POLITICS OF LANDHOLDING IN BUSOGA.
   ECONOMIC DEVELOPMENT AND CULTURAL CHANGE 3 1955 PP 260-270
   070,139-08,

   FALLERS LLOYD A
   IDEOLOGY AND CULTURE IN UGANDA NATIONALISM.
   AMERICAN ANTHROPOLOGIST 63 1961 PP 677-686
   060,139-06,

   FALLERS LLOYD A
   COMMENTS ON 'THE LEBANESE IN WEST AFRICA'.
   SOC. HIST., VOL. IV, NO. 3, APRIL, 1962, PP. 334-336
   086,

   FALLERS LLOYD A   LEVY MARION J
   THE FAMILY-- SOME COMPARATIVE CONSIDERATIONS.
   IN PETER HAMMOND, ED., CULTURAL AND SOCIAL ANTHROPOLOGY,
   NEW YORK, MACMILLAN CO., 1964, PP 163-166
   008,

   FALLERS LLOYD A   ED
   IMMIGRANTS AND ASSOCIATIONS.
   THE HAGUE, MOUTON, 1967
   046,047,

   FALLERS LLOYD A
   THE SOGA.
   IN A.I. RICHARDS (ED), EAST AFRICAN CHIEFS, LONDON, FABER
   AND FABER, 1960, PP. 78-97
   139-01,

   FALLERS LLOYD A
   LAW WITHOUT PRECEDENT--LEGAL IDEAS IN ACTION IN THE COURTS
   OF COLONIAL BUSOGA.
   CHICAGO AND LONDON, THE UNIVERSITY OF CHICAGO PRESS, 1969
   066,139-06,

FALLERS M C

FALLERS LLOYD A   FALLERS M C
HOMICIDE AND SUICIDE IN BUSOGA.
IN PAUL BOHANNAN (ED), AFRICAN HOMICIDE AND SUICIDE,
PRINCETON, PRINCETON UNIVERSITY PRESS, 1960, PP 65-93
041,

FALLERS M C
    FALLERS M C
    THE EASTERN LACUSTRINE BANTU-GANDA,SOGA
    LONDON,INTERNATIONAL AFRICAN INSTITUTE,1960
    139-01,

FANI-KAYODE REMI
    FANI-KAYODE REMI
    BLACKISM.
    LAGOS (NIGERIA), 1965
    096,

FANON FRANTZ
    FANON FRANTZ
    BLACK SKIN, WHITE MASKS-- THE EXPERIENCES OF A BLACK
    MAN IN A WHITE WORLD.
    NEW YORK,GROVE PRESS,1967
    041,085,088,101-03,

    FANON FRANTZ
    STUDIES IN A DYING COLONIALISM.
    NEW YORK,MONTHLY REVIEW PRESS,1959
    088,

    FANON FRANTZ
    THE WRETHCHED OF THE EARTH
    NEW YORK,GROVE PRESS,1963
    060,091,101-03,

    FANON FRANTZ
    TOWARD THE AFRICAN REVOLUTION
    NEW YORK,GROVE PRESS,1967
    091,

FAO
    UNITED NATIONS   FAO
    REPORT ON THE POSSIBILITIES OF AFRICAN RURAL DEVELOPMENT
    IN RELATION TO ECONOMIC AND SOCIAL GROWTH.
    ROME,FAO,1961
    070,

FARMER JAMES
    FARMER JAMES
    AN AMERICAN NEGRO LEADER S VIEW OF AFRICAN UNITY.
    AFRICAN FORUM I 1 1965 PP 69-89
    094,

FARNSWORTH E A
    FARNSWORTH E A
    LAW REFORM IN A DEVELOPING COUNTRY-- A NEW CODE OF
    OBLIGATIONS FOR SENEGAL.
    JOURNAL OF AFRICAN LAW 8 SPRING 1964 PP 6-19
    067,

FARRAN CHARLES
    FARRAN CHARLES
    MATRIMONIAL LAWS OF THE SUDAN.
    LONDON, BUTTERWORTHS, 1963
    066,134-01,

FARUKI KEMAL A
    FARUKI KEMAL A
    ISLAMIC JURISPRUDENCE.
    KARACHI, 1962
    066,

FEHDERAU HAROLD W
    FEHDERAU HAROLD W
    KIMBANGUISM-- PROPHETIC CHRISTIANITY IN THE CONGO.
    PRACTICAL ANTHROPOLOGY 9 1962 PP 157-178
    051,108-03,

FEIERMAN S
    FEIERMAN S
    THE SHAMBAA
    IN A ROBERTS, ED, TANZANIA BEFORE 1900, NAIROBI, 1968, PP 1-15
    023,

FEIT EDWARD
    FEIT EDWARD
    AFRICAN OPPOSITION IN SOUTH AFRICA.
    PALO ALTO, CALIFORNIA, HOOVER INSTITUTION PRESS, 1967
    032,089,132-07,

FELDMAN ARNOLD S
    MOORE WILBERT E   FELDMAN ARNOLD S
    LABOR COMMITMENT AND SOCIAL CHANGE IN DEVELOPING AREAS.
    NEW YORK, SOCIAL SCIENCE RESEARCH COUNCIL, 1960
    073,

FELDMAN SUSAN
    FELDMAN SUSAN   ED
    AFRICAN MYTHS AND TALES
    NEW YORK, DELL PUBLISHING COMPANY, 1963
    012,

FERGUSON J H
    FERGUSON J H
    LATIN AMERICA-- THE BALANCE OF RACE REDRESSED.
    NEW YORK, OXFORD UNIVERSITY PRESS, 1961
    030,

FERGUSON JOHN
    FERGUSON JOHN
    THE LESSONS OF BIAFRA.
    THE CHRISTIAN CENTURY, AUGUST 14, 1968, PP. 1013-1017
    065,128-06,

    MARIOGHAE MICHAEL   FERGUSON JOHN
    NIGERIA UNDER THE CROSS.
    LONDON, THE HIGHWAY PRESS, 1965
    050,128-03,

FERNANDEZ JAMES W

FERNANDEZ JAMES W
CONTEMPORARY AFRICAN RELIGION--CONFLUENTS OF INQUIRY.
IN CARTER, GWENDOLEN M. AND ANN PADEN (EDS), EXPANDING
HORIZONS IN AFRICAN STUDIES, EVANSTON, NORTHWESTERN
UNIVERSITY PRESS, 1969, PP. 27-46
013,050,100,

FERNANDEZ JAMES W
  FERNANDEZ JAMES W
  THE SHAKA COMPLEX
  TRANSITION 29 1967 PP 11-14
  041,

FICKETT LEWIS P
  FICKETT LEWIS P   ED
  PROBLEMS OF THE DEVELOPING NATIONS.
  NEW YORK, CROWELL, 1966
  055,

  FICKETT LEWIS P
  COMPARATIVE CASE STUDIES--ALGERIA TUNISIA.
  IN PROBLEMS OF THE DEVELOPING NATIONS, NEW YORK, CROWELL,
  1966, PP. 141-167 AND 163-171

FIELD M J
  FIELD M J
  SEARCH FOR SECURITY-- AN ETHNO-PSYCHIATRIC STUDY OF
  RURAL GHANA.
  EVANSTON, NORTHWESTERN UNIVERSITY PRESS, 1960; ALSO LONDON,
  FABER AND FABER, 1960
  040,114-01,

FINER S E
  FINER S E
  MILITARY DISENGAGEMENT FROM POLITICS.
  THE POLITICS OF DEMILITARISATION, UNIVERSITY OF LONDON
  APRIL-MAY 1966
  INSTITUTE OF COMMONWEALTH STUDIES
  064,

FINKLE JASON L
  FINKLE JASON L   GABLE RICHARD W   EDS
  POLITICAL DEVELOPMENT AND SOCIAL CHANGE.
  NEW YORK, JOHN WILEY, 1966
  037,

FINNEGAN RUTH
  FINNEGAN RUTH   ED
  LIMBA STORIES AND STORY-TELLING.
  LONDON, OXFORD UNIVERSITY PRESS, 1967
  012,131-01,

  FINNEGAN RUTH
  SURVEY OF THE LIMBA PEOPLE OF NORTHERN SIERRA LEONE.
  LONDON, HER MAJESTYS STATIONERY OFFICE, 1965
  131-01,

FIRST RUTH
  FIRST RUTH
  SOUTH WEST AFRICA

BALTIMORE PENGUIN 1963
081,146-11,

FIRST RUTH
  SEGAL RONALD   FIRST RUTH   EDS
  SOUTH-WEST AFRICA- TRAVESTY OF TRUST
  LONDON OXFORD UNIVERSITY PRESS 1967 INTERNATIONAL CONFERENCE
  ON SOUTH-WEST AFRICA,OXFORD 1966
  081,146-07,146-11,

FIRTH RAYMOND W
  FIRTH RAYMOND W
  SOCIAL PROBLEMS AND RESEARCH IN WEST AFRICA.
  AFRICA LONDON 17 1947 PP 77-91, 17, 1947, PP 170-180
  099,

FISCHER GEORGES
  FISCHER GEORGES
  QUELQUES ASPECTS DE LA DOCTRINE POLITIQUE GUINEENE (SOME
  ASPECTS OF GUINEA POLITICAL DOCTRINE).
  CIVILIZATIONS 9 1959 PP 457-478
  060,115-04,

FISHER HUMPHREY J
  FISHER HUMPHREY J
  SEPARATISM IN WEST AFRICA
  IN KRITZECK AND LEWIS, PP 127-138
  052,

  FISHER HUMPHREY J
  AHMADIYYAH, A STUDY IN CONTEMPORARY ISLAM ON THE WEST
  AFRICAN COAST.
  LONDON, OXFORD UNIVERSITY PRESS, 1963
  052,

FISHER WILLIAM E
  FISHER WILLIAM E
  AN ANALYSIS OF THE DEUTSCH SOCIOCAUSAL PARADIGM OF POLITICAL
  INTEGRATION.
  INTERNATIONAL ORGANIZATION, SPRING, 1969, VOL. XXIII, NO. 2,
  PP. 254-290
  078,

FISHMAN JOSHUA
  FISHMAN JOSHUA   ET AL   EDS
  LANGUAGE PROBLEMS OF DEVELOPING NATIONS.
  NEW YORK, JOHN WILEY AND SONS, 1968
  011,049,

  FISHMAN JOSHUA
  NATIONAL LANGUAGES AND LANGUAGES OF WIDER COMMUNICATION IN
  THE DEVELOPING NATIONS.
  ANTHROPOLOGICAL LINGUSITICS, VOL II, NO. 4, APRIL 1969, PP.
  111-135
  049,

FLEMING WILLIAM G
  FLEMING WILLIAM G
  AMERICAN POLITICAL SCIENCE AND AFRICAN POLITICS
  JOURNAL OF MODERN AFRICAN STUDIES 7 1969 PP 495-512

098,

FLINT J E
    FLINT J E
    ZANZIBAR, 1890-1950.
    IN VINCENT HARLOW AND E M CHILVER (EDS) HISTORY OF EAST
    AFRICA VOL II,OXFORD,CLARENDON PRESS, 1965, PP 641-671
    035,136-02,

FLOYD BARRY
    FLOYD BARRY
    EASTERN NIGERIA--A GEOGRAPHICAL REVIEW.
    NEW YORK, PRAEGER PUBLISHERS, 1969
    065,128-08,

    FLOYD BARRY
    LAND APPORTIONMENT IN SOUTHERN RHODESIA.
    GEOGRAPHIC REVIEW LII OCTOBER 1962 PP 566-582
    087,145-08,

FODEBA KEITA
    FODEBA KEITA
    AUBE AFRICAINE.
    PARIS, SEGHERS, 1965
    115-10,

    FODEBA KEITA
    LE MAITRE D ECOLE, SUIVI DE MINUIT.
    PARIS, SEGHER, 1952
    115-10,

FODOR ISTVAN
    FODOR ISTVAN
    LINGUISTIC PROBLEMS AND ≠LANGUAGE PLANNING≠ IN AFRICA.
    LINGUISTICS, 25, SEPT. 1966, PP. 18-33
    049,

    FODOR ISTVAN
    LA CLASSIFICATION DES LANGUES NEGRO-AFRICAINES ET LA THEORIE
    DE J H GREENBERG (THE CLASSIFICATION OF THE BLACK AFRICAN
    LANGUAGES AND THE THEORY OF J H GREENBERG).
    CAHIER D'ETUDES AFRICAINES, VOL. VIII, NO. 32, 1968, PP.
    617-31
    011,

    FODOR ISTVAN
    THE PROBLEMS IN THE CLASSIFICATION OF THE AFRICAN LANGUAGES.
    BUDAPEST CENTER FOR AFRO-ASIAN RESEARCH OF THE HUNGARIAN
    ACADEMY OF SCIENCES NO 5 1966
    011,

FOELL EARL W
    FOELL EARL W
    AFRICA'S VANISHING ACT AT THE UN-WHERE DOES THE UNITED
    STATES STAND ON AFRICAN QUESTIONS
    AFRICA REPORT NOVEMBER 1969 PP 31-33
    081,

FOGG C DAVIS
    FOGG C DAVIS

ECONOMIC AND SOCIAL FACTORS AFFECTING THE DEVELOPMENT OF
SMALL HOLDER AGRICULTURE IN EASTERN NIGERIA CHAPTER 3.
IN EDITH WHETHAM AND JEAN CURRIE (EDS.), READINGS IN THE
APPLIED ECONOMICS OF AFRICA, LONDON, CAMBRIDGE UNIVERSITY
PRESS, 1, 1967, PP 25-31
070,128-08,

FOLTZ WILLIAM J
   DEUTSCH KARL W   FOLTZ WILLIAM J   EDS
   NATION-BUILDING.
   ATHERTON PRESS,1966
   057,076,

   FOLTZ WILLIAM J
   THE RADICAL LEFT IN FRENCH SPEAKING WEST AFRICA.
   IN WILLIAM H LEWIS, EMERGING AFRICA, WASHINGTON, PUBLIC
   AFFAIRS PRESS, 1963, PP 29-42
   060,

   FOLTZ WILLIAM J
   BUILDING THE NEWEST NATIONS.
   IN LEWIS P FICKETT (ED),PROBLEMS OF THE DEVELOPING NATIONS,
   NEW YORK, CROWELL, 1966 PP 124-137
   057,

   FOLTZ WILLIAM J
   MILITARY INFLUENCES ON AFRICAN FOREIGN POLICIES.
   NEW YORK, PRAEGER, 1966
   082,

   FOLTZ WILLIAM J
   FROM FRENCH WEST AFRICA TO THE MALI FEDERATION.
   NEW HAVEN, YALE UNIVERSITY PRESS, 1965
   077,123-09,130-09,

   FOLTZ WILLIAM J
   SENEGAL.
   IN COLEMAN, J.S. AND ROSBERG, C.G. (EDS), POLITICAL PARTIES
   AND NATIONAL INTEGRATION IN TROPICAL AFRICA, LOS ANGELES,
   130-06,

FONLON BERNARD
   FONLON BERNARD
   THE KAMPALA CONFERENCE.
   IN ALBERT H BERRIAN AND RICHARD A LOND (EDS), NEGRITUDE--
   ESSAYS AND STUDIES, HAMPTON, VIRGINIA, HAMPTON INSTITUTE
   PRESS, 1967, PP 102-115
   090,

FORD RICHARD B
   FORD RICHARD B
   AFRICA AND THE SCHOOLS
   AFRICA REPORT MAY/JUNE 1969 PP 76-77
   100,

FORDE
   RADCLIFFE-BROWN A R FORDE C DARYLL   EDS
   AFRICAN SYSTEMS OF KINSHIP AND MARRIAGE.
   LONDON, OXFORD UNIVERSITY PRESS, 1950
   008,

FORDE
    FORDE C DARYLL   SCOTT R
    THE NATIVE ECONOMIES OF NIGERIA.
    LONDON, FABER, 1946
    010,128-01,

FORDE C DARYLL
    FORDE C DARYLL
    AFRICAN WORLDS--STUDIES IN THE COSMOLOGICAL IDEAS AND
    SOCIAL VALUES OF AFRICAN PEOPLES.
    LONDON, OXFORD UNIVERSITY PRESS, 1965
    013,

    FORDE C DARYLL   KABERRY PHYLLIS M   EDS
    WEST AFRICAN KINGDOMS IN THE NINETEENTH CENTURY.
    LONDON, OXFORD UNIVERSITY PRESS, 1967
    026,036,

    FORDE C DARYLL
    THE SOCIAL IMPACT OF INDUSTRIALIZATION AND URBAN CONDITIONS
    IN AFRICA SOUTH OF THE SAHARA.
    INTERNATIONAL SOCIAL SCIENCE BULLETIN 7 WINTER 1955
    PP 114-127
    047,071,

    FORDE C DARYLL
    THE CONDITIONS OF SOCIAL DEVELOPMENT IN WEST AFRICA.
    CIVILISATIONS 3 1953 PP 471-489
    038,

    FORDE C DARYLL   DOUGLAS M
    PRIMITIVE ECONOMICS.
    IN H L SHAPIRO (ED.), MAN, CULTURE, AND SOCIETY, OXFORD
    UNIVERSITY PRESS, 1956; ALSO G DALTON (ED.), TRIBAL AND
    PEASANT ECONOMIES, DOUBLEDAY, 1967
    010,

    FORDE C DARYLL
    AFRICAN MODES OF THINKING.
    IN PETER J MCEWAN AND ROBERT B SUTCLIFFE (EDS), MODERN AFRICA,
    NEW YORK, THOMAS CROWELL, 1965, PP 58-62
    013,

    FORDE C DARYLL
    YAKU STUDIES.
    LONDON, OXFORD UNIVERSITY PRESS, 1964
    008,

FORDE ENID
    FORDE ENID
    THE POPULATION OF GHANA-A STUDY OF THE SPATIAL RELATIONSHIPS
    OF SOCIOCULTURAL AND ECONOMIC CHARACTERISTICS
    EVANSTON, DEPARTMENT OF GEOGRAPHY, NORTHWESTERN UNIVERSITY
    PRESS, 1968
    048,

FORDHAM PAUL
    FORDHAM PAUL
    THE GEOGRAPHY OF AFRICAN AFFAIRS

BALTIMORE, PENGUIN, 1965
069,

FORMAN B
  FORMAN W   FORMAN B   DARK PHILIP J C
  BENIN ART
  LONDON, PAUL HAMLYN, 1960
  014,

FORMAN W
  FORMAN W   FORMAN B   DARK PHILIP J C
  BENIN ART
  LONDON, PAUL HAMLYN, 1960
  014,

FORSYTH FREDERICK
  FORSYTH FREDERICK
  THE BIAFRA STORY.
  BALTIMORE, PENGUIN, 1969
  065,

FORTES
  FORTES MEYER   EVANS-PRITCHARD E
  VALUES IN AFRICAN TRIBAL LIFE.
  IN PETER J MCEWAN AND ROBERT B SUTCLIFFE (EDS), MODERN AFRICA,
  NEW YORK, THOMAS CROWELL, 1965, PP 55-57
  013,

FORTES MEYER
  FORTES MEYER   EVANS-PRITCHARD E E EDS
  AFRICAN POLITICAL SYSTEMS.
  LONDON, OXFORD UNIVERSITY PRESS, 1940 (1962)
  009,099,

  FORTES MEYER   DIETERLEN GERMAINE   EDS
  AFRICAN SYSTEMS OF THOUGHT
  LONDON, OXFORD UNIVERSITY PRESS, 1965, INTERNATIONAL AFRICAN
  INSTITUTE
  013,

  FORTES MEYER
  THE STRUCTURE OF UNILINEAL DECENT GROUPS.
  IN SIMON AND PHOEBE OTTENBERG EDS, CULTURES AND SOCIETIES
  OF AFRICA. NEW YORK, RANDOM HOUSE, 1960, PP 163-190
  008,

  FORTES MEYER
  THE NOTION OF FATE IN WEST AFRICA.
  IN PETER J MCEWAN AND ROBERT B SUTCLIFFE (EDS), MODERN AFRICA,
  NEW YORK, THOMAS CROWELL, 1965, PP 75-78
  013,

  FORTES MEYER
  OEDIPUS AND JOB IN WEST AFRICA.
  CAMBRIDGE, CAMBRIDGE UNIVERSITY PRESS, 1959
  013,

  FORTES MEYER
  THE WEB OF KINSHIP AMONG THE TALLENSI.
  LONDON, OXFORD UNIVERSITY PRESS, 1949

008,114-01,

FORTES MEYER
   FORTES MEYER
   THE DYNAMICS OF CLANSHIP AMONG THE TALLENSI.
   LONDON, OXFORD UNIVERSITY PRESS, 1945
   008, 114-01,

   FORTES MEYER
   THE ASHANTI SOCIAL SURVEY-- A PRELIMINARY REPORT.
   RHODES-LIVINGSTONE JOURNAL 6 1948 PP 1-36
   038,

   FORTES MEYER
   INTRODUCTION.
   IN J GOODY ED, THE DEVELOPMENT CYCLE IN DOMESTIC GROUPS,
   CAMBRIDGE PAPERS IN SOCIAL ANTHROPOLOGY, NO. 1, CAMBRIDGE,
   CAMBRIDGE UNIVERSITY PRESS, 1961
   008,

FORTHOME G
   FORTHOME G
   MARRIAGE ET INDUSTRIALISATION-- EVOLUTION DE LA MENTALITE
   DANS UNE CITE DE TRAVAILLEURS D'ELISABETHVILLE (MARRIAGE
   AND INDUSTRIALIZATION-- EMERGENCE OF THE MENTALITY IN A
   WORKER*S DOMAIN OF ELISABETHVILLE).
   LIEGE, H VALLIANT-CARMANNE, 1957
   047,108-05,

FORTMAN
   FORTMAN BASTIAAN DE ED
   AFTER MULUNGUSHI--THE ECONOMICS OF ZAMBIAN HUMANISM.
   KENYA, EAST AFRICAN PUBLISHING HOUSE, 1969
   060,142-08,

FORTUNE GEORGE
   FORTUNE GEORGE
   THE CONTRIBUTIONS OF LINGUISTICS TO ETHNOHISTORY.
   HISTORIANS IN TROPICAL AFRICA, PROCEEDINGS, SALISBURY,
   SOUTHERN RHODESIA, UNIVERSITY COLLEGE OF RHODESIA AND
   NYASALAND , 1962, PP 17-30
   011,

FOSBROOKE H
   YOUNG ROLAND A   FOSBROOKE H
   SMOKE IN THE HILLS-- POLITICAL TENSION IN THE MOROGORO
   DISTRICT OF TANGANYIKA.
   EVANSTON, ILLINOIS, NORTHWESTERN UNIVERSITY PRESS, 1960
   (LAND AND POLITICS AMONG THE LUGURU OF TANGANYIKA, LONDON,
   ROUTLEDGE AND KEGAN PAUL, 1960)
   067,136-03,

FOSTER CRAIG
   ROBINSON ARMSTEAD   FOSTER CRAIG   OGILVIE DONALD
   BLACK STUDIES IN THE UNIVERSITY--A SYMPOSIUM.
   NEW HAVEN, YALE UNIVERSITY PRESS, 1969
   002,094,095,

FOSTER PHILIP
   CLIGNET REMI   FOSTER PHILIP

THE FORTUNATE FEW.
EVANSTON, NORTHWESTERN UNIVERSITY PRESS, 1966
039,043,116-03,

FOSTER PHILIP
    CLIGNET REMI   FOSTER PHILIP
    FRENCH AND BRITISH COLONIAL EDUCATION IN AFRICA.
    COMPARATIVE EDUCATIONAL REVIEW 8 1964 PP 191-198
    042,

    CLIGNET REMI   FOSTER PHILIP
    INTRODUCTION.
    IN REMI CLIGNET AND PHILIP FOSTER, THE FORTUNATE FEW,
    EVANSTON, NORTHWESTERN UNIVERSITY PRESS, 1966, PP 3-22
    043,

    CLIGNET REMI   FOSTER PHILIP
    THE HIERARCHY OF POSTPRIMARY SCHOOLS-- ITS IMPACT ON ETHNIC
    AND SOCIAL RECRUITMENT OF STUDENTS CHAPTER 4.
    IN REMI CLIGNET AND PHILIP FOSTER, THE FORTUNATE FEW,
    EVANSTON, NORTHWESTERN UNIVERSITY PRESS, 1965
    043,

    CLIGNET REMI   FOSTER PHILIP
    THE ETHNIC, SOCIAL AND CULTURAL ORIGIN OF STUDENTS IN THE
    POSTPRIMARY SCHOOL CHAPTER 3.
    IN REMI CLIGNET AND PHILIP FOSTER, THE FORTUNATE FEW,
    EVANSTON, NORTHWESTERN UNIVERSITY PRESS , 1966
    043,

    CLIGNET REMI   FOSTER PHILIP
    THE SOCIAL, ECONOMIC AND EDUCATIONAL SCENE IN THE IVORY
    COAST CHAPTER 2.
    IN THE FORTUNATE FEW,EVANSTON, NORTHWESTERN UNIVERSITY
    PRESS 1966
    042,116-03,

    FOSTER PHILIP
    EDUCATION   AND SOCIAL CHANGE IN GHANA.
    CHICAGO, UNIVERSITY OF CHICAGO PRESS, 1965
    044,114-03,

    FOSTER PHILIP
    STATUS POWER AND EDUCATION IN A TRADITIONAL COMMUNITY.
    SCHOOL REVIEW 72 1964 PP 158-172
    041,

    CLIGNET REMI   FOSTER PHILIP
    LA PREEMINENCE DE L'ENSEIGNEMENT CLASSIQUE EN COTE D'IVOIRE
    UN EXAMPLE D'ASSIMILATION (THE PREEMINENCE OF THE CLASSICAL
    EDUCATION IN THE IVORY COAST-- AN EXAMPLE OF ASSIMILATION).
    REVUE FRANCAISE DE SOCIOLOGIE 7 1966 PP 32-47
    043,

FOTE H MEMEL
    FOTE H MEMEL
    RAPPORT SUR LA CIVILISATION ANIMISTE (A REPORT ON THE
    ANIMIST CIVILISATION).
    IN COLLOQUE SUR LES RELIGIONS, ABIDJAN, 5-12 APRIL, 1961,
    PARIS, PRESENCE AFRICAINE, 1962

013,

FOUQUET J
 FOUQUET J
 LA TRAITE DES ARACHIDES DANS LE PAYS DE KAOLACK, ET SES
 CONSEQUENCES ECONOMIQUES, SOCIALES ET JURIDIQUES,
 (THE CULTIVATION OF GROUND NUTS IN KAOLACK COUNTRY, AND THE
 CONSEQUENCES, ECONOMIC, SOCIAL AND JURIDIC).
 SAINT LOUIS DU SENEGAL, INSTITUT FRANCAIS D'AFRIQUE NOIRE,
 1958
 070,130-08,

FOURNIER F
 FOURNIER F
 THE SOILS OF AFRICA.
 PARIS, UNESCO, 1963, PP 221-248
 069,

FOX IRENE K
 FOX IRENE K   ET-AL
 EAST AFRICAN CHILDHOOD-- THREE EXPERIENCES.
 NEW YORK, OXFORD UNIVERSITY PRESS, 1967
 040,

FOX RENEE C
 DECRAEMER WILLY   FOX RENEE C
 THE EMERGING PHYSICIAN.
 PALO ALTO, HOOVER INSTITUTION PRESS, 1969
 075,

FRAENKEL MERRAN
 FRAENKEL MERRAN
 TRIBE AND CLASS IN MONROVIA.
 LONDON, OXFORD UNIVERSITY PRESS, 1964
 119-05,

FRANCAISE
 LA DOCUMENTATION FRANCAISE
 LA REPUBLIQUE DU TOGO.
 NOTES ET ETUDES DOCUMENTAIRES, NO. 2736, OCT. 5, 1960
 137-11,

 LA DOCUMENTATION FRANCAISE
 LA REPUBLIQUE DE HAUTE-VOLTA.
 NOTES ET ETUDES DOCUMENTAIRES, 2693, AUGUST, 1960
 141-11,

FRANCE
 GOVERNMENT OF FRANCE
 COUTUMIERS JURIDIQUES DE L'AFRIQUE OCCIDENTALE FRANCAISE--
 MAURITANIE, NIGER, COTE D'IVOIRE, DAHOMEY, GUINEE FRANCAISE
 (FRENCH WEST AFRICAN JURIDIC CUSTOMS-- MAURITANIA, NIGER
 IVORY COAST, DAHOMEY, FRENCH GUINEA) .

PARIS LIBRAIRIE LAROSE 1939 VOL3
066,109-01,115-01,116-01,124-01,127-01,

FRANCE
GOVERNMENT OF FRANCE
COUTUMIERS JURIDIQUE DE L'AFRIQUE OCCIDENTALE FRANCAISE--
SOUDAN (FRENCH WEST AFRICAN JURIDIC CUSTOMS-- SUDAN).
PARIS LAROSE EDITEURS 1939 VOL 2
066,123-01,

GOVERNMENT OF FRANCE
COUTUMIERS JURIDIQUES DE L'AFRIQUE OCCIDENTALE FRANCAISE--
SENEGAL (FRENCH WEST AFRICAN JURIDIC CUSTOMS-- SENEGAL).
PARIS LIBRAIRIE LAROSE 1939 VOL1
066,130-01,

FRANCIS E K
FRANCIS E K
THE ETHNIC FACTOR IN NATION-BUILDING.
SOCIAL FORCES, VOL. 46, NO. 3, MARCH, 1968, PP. 338-346
057,

FRANCK
SNOWDEN FRANCK M JR
BLACKS IN ANTIQUITY--ETHIOPIANS IN THE GRECO-ROMAN
EXPERIENCE.
CAMBRIDGE, HARVARD UNIVERSITY PRESS, 1969
020,027,

FRANCK THOMAS M
FRANCK THOMAS M
SOME THOUGHTS ON LEGAL STUDIES IN AFRICA.
AMERICAN BEHAVIORAL SCIENTIST 5 APRIL 1962 PP 18-19
066,100,

FRANCK THOMAS M
RACE AND NATIONALISM--THE STRUGGLE FOR POWER IN RHODESIA-
NYASALAND
NEW YORK FORDHAM UNIVERSITY PRESS 1960
087,122-07,142-07,145-07,

FRANCK THOMAS M
MUST WE LOSE ZIMBABWE .
AFRICAN FORUM 2 3 1967 PP 17-33
087,145-06,

FRANCK THOMAS M
EAST AFRICAN FEDERATION.
IN THOMAS FRANCK (ED), WHY FEDERATIONS FAIL, NEW YORK, NEW
YORK UNIVERSITY PRESS, 1968, PP. 3-36
078,

FRANCK THOMAS M
COMPARATIVE CONSTITUTIONAL PROCESS--CASES AND MATERIALS--
FUNDAMENTAL RIGHTS IN THE COMMON LAW NATIONS.
NEW YORK, PRAEGER PUBLISHING COMPANY, 1968
068,

FRANK CHARLES R
    ARKADIE BRIAN VAN   FRANK CHARLES R
    ECONOMIC ACCOUNTING AND DEVELOPMENT PLANNING.
    EASTERN AFRICA, OXFORD UNIVERSITY PRESS, 1966
    072,

FRANKLIN JOHN H
    FRANKLIN JOHN H
    FROM SLAVERY TO FREEDOM A HISTORY OF NEGRO AMERICANS.
    NEW YORK, ALFRED A. KNOPF, 1968
    030,

    FRANKLIN JOHN H   STARR ISADORE
    THE NEGRO IN TWENTIETH CENTURY AMERICA.
    NEW YORK, VINTAGE BOOKS, 1967
    030,

FRANTZ CHARLES
    FRANTZ CHARLES
    THE AFRICAN PERSONALITY-- MYTH AND REALITY.
    JOURNAL OF HUMAN RELATIONS 8 1960 PP 455-464
    039,

    ROGERS CYRIL A   FRANTZ CHARLES
    RACIAL THEMES IN SOUTHERN RHODESIA-THE   ATTITUDES OF THE
    WHITE POPULATION
    NEW HAVEN, YALE UNIVERSITY PRESS, 1962
    088,145-07,

FRASER C GERALD
    FRASER C GERALD
    BLACK CAUCUS DELIBERATIONS AT MONTREAL-WHO SHOULD CONTROL
    AFRICAN STUDIES AND FOR WHAT ENDS
    AFRICA REPORT DECEMBER 1969 PP20-21
    100,

FRAZIER E FRANKLIN
    FRAZIER E FRANKLIN
    URBANIZATION AND ITS EFFECTS UPON THE TASK OF NATION -
    BUILDING IN AFRICA SOUTH OF THE SAHARA.
    JOURNAL OF NEGRO EDUCATION 30 SUMMER 1961 PP 214-222
    047,

    FRAZIER E FRANKLIN
    POTENTIAL AMERICAN NEGRO CONTRIBUTIONS TO AFRICAN
    SOCIAL DEVELOPMENT.
    IN AMSAC, AFRICA SEEN BY AMERICAN NEGROES, PARIS,
    PRESENCE AFRICAINE, 1958, PP 263-278
    094,

    FRAZIER E FRANKLIN
    THE NEGRO FAMILY IN THE UNITED STATES.
    NEW YORK, DRYDEN PRESS, 1948
    030,

    FRAZIER E FRANKLIN

RACE AND CULTURE CONTACTS IN THE MODERN WORLD.
BOSTON, BEACON PRESS, 1965
088,

FREEMAN-GRENVILLE
   FREEMAN-GRENVILLE G S P
   THE COAST-- 1498-1840.
   IN ROLAND OLIVER AND GERVASE MATHEW (EDS), HISTORY OF EAST
   AFRICA VOLUME ONE, OXFORD, CLARENDON PRESS, 1963, PP 129-168
   023,

   FREEMAN-GRENVILLE G S P
   EAST AFRICAN COIN FINDS AND THEIR HISTORICAL SIGNIFICANCE.
   JOURNAL OF AFRICAN HISTORY 1 1960 PP 31-43
   023,

   FREEMAN-GRENVILLE G S
   THE EAST AFRICAN COAST-SELECT DOCUMENTS FROM THE FIRST TO
   THE EARLIER NINETEENTH CENTURY
   LONDON, OXFORD UNIVERSITY PRESS, 1962
   023,

   FREEMAN-GRENVILLE G S
   THE MEDIEVAL HISTORY OF THE COAST OF TANGANYIKA
   LONDON, OXFORD UNIVERSITY PRESS, 1962
   023,

   FREEMAN-GRENVILLE G S P
   SWAHILI LITERATURE AND THE HISTORY AND ARCHAEOLOGY OF THE
   EAST AFRICAN COAST.
   JOURNAL OF THE EAST AFRICAN SWAHILI COMMITTEE 28/2 1958
   PP 7-25
   023,

FREITAG RUTH S
   FREITAG RUTH S
   AGRICULTURAL DEVELOPMENT SCHEMES IN SUB-SAHARAN AFRICA- A
   BIBLIOGRAPHY
   WASHINGTON, LIBRARY OF CONGRESS, 1963
   070,

FRIED MORTON H
   FRIED MORTON H
   ON THE CONCEPTS OF TRIBE AND TRIBAL SOCIETY.
   IN HELM (ED), ESSAYS ON THE PROBLEM OF TRIBE, AMERICAN
   ETHNOLOGICAL SOCIETY, 1968
   005,

   FRIED MORTON H
   THE EVOLUTION OF POLITICAL SOCIETY
   NEW YORK, RANDOM HOUSE, 1967
   004, 009,

FRIEDLAND
   FRIEDLAND WILLIAM H ROSBERG CARL G   EDS
   AFRICAN SOCIALISM.
   LONDON, OXFORD UNIVERSITY PRESS, 1965
   060, 077,

   FRIEDLAND WILLIAM H

UNIONS, LABOR AND INDUSTRIAL RELATIONS IN AFRICA.
ITHACA,CORNELL UNIVERSITY PRESS,1965,ANNOTATED BIBLIOGRAPHY
071,

FRIEDLAND
    FRIEDLAND WILLIAM H
    SOME SOURCES OF TRADITIONALISM AMONG MODERN AFRICAN ELITES.
    IN WILLIAM J HANNA (ED), INDEPENDENT BLACK AFRICA, CHICAGO,
    RAND MCNALLY, 1964, PP 363-369
    044,

    FRIEDLAND WILLIAM H
    VUTA KAMBA--THE DEVELOPMENT OF TRADE UNIONS IN TANGANYIKA.
    PALO ALTO, CALIFORNIA, HOOVER INSTITUTION PRESS, 1969
    063,136-08,

FRIEDMANN G
    FRIEDMANN G
    THE SOCIAL CONSEQUENCES OF TECHNICAL PROGRESS.
    INTERNATIONAL SOCIAL SCIENCE BULLETIN 4 1952 PP 243-260
    037,

FRIEDRICH CARL J
    FRIEDRICH CARL J
    SOME REFLECTIONS ON CONSTITUTIONALISM FOR EMERGENT POLITICAL
    ORDERS.
    IN HERBERT J SPIRO (ED), PATTERNS OF AFRICAN DEVELOPMENT,
    ENGLEWOOD CLIFFS, NJ, PRENTICE-HALL, 1967, PP 9-34
    068,

FROELICH JEAN C
    FROELICH JEAN C
    LES MUSULMANS D'AFRIQUE NOIRE (THE MUSLIMS OF BLACK
    AFRICA).
    PARIS EDITIONS DE L'ORANTE 1962
    021,052,

    FROELICH JEAN C
    L'IMPORTANCE ET L'INFLUENCE DE L'ISLAM DU CHRISTIANISME ET
    DES SECTES EN AFRIQUE NOIRE (THE IMPORTANCE AND THE
    INFLUENCE OF ISLAM, OF CHRISTIANITY AND SECTS IN BLACK
    AFRICA).
    EUROPE-FRANCE OUTREMER 396 1963 PP 36-40
    052,

    FROELICH JEAN C
    ESSAI SUR LES CAUSES ET METHODES DE L'ISLAMISATION DE
    L'AFRIQUE DE L'OUEST DU XI SIECLE AU XX SIECLE.
    IN LEWIS, ISLAM IN TROPICAL AFRICA, LONDON, OXFORD UNIVERSITY
    PRESS, 1966, P. 160-173
    052,

    FROELICH JEAN C
    CAMEROUN TOGO TERRITOIRES SOUS TUTELLE.
    PARIS, BERGER-LEVRAULT, 1956
    104-02,137-02,

    FROELICH JEAN C
    CAMEROUN, TOGO, TERRITORIES SOUS TUTELLE.
    PARIS,BERGER-LEBRAULT, 1956

137-02,

FROELICH JEAN C
    FROELICH JEAN C
    LES POPULATIONS DE NORD-TOGO.
    PRESSES UNIVERSITAIRES DE FRANCE, 1963
    137-01,

FRYE WILLIAM
    FRYE WILLIAM
    IN WHITEST AFRICA--THE DYNAMICS OF APARTHEID
    ENGLEWOOD CLIFFS, PRENTICE-HALL, 1968
    032,089,

FUGGLES-COUCHMAN N
    FUGGLES-COUCHMAN N
    AGRICULTURAL CHANGE IN TANGANYIKA.
    STANFORD, STANFORD UNIVERSITY, FOOD RESEARCH INSTITUTE, 1964
    070,136-08,

FULLARD HAROLD
    FULLARD HAROLD   ED
    MODERN COLLEGE ATLAS FOR AFRICA
    LONDON, PHILIP AND SON, 1961
    069,

FULLER CHARLES E
    FULLER CHARLES E
    ETHNOHISTORY IN THE STUDY OF CULTURE CHANGE IN SOUTHEAST
    AFRICA CHAPTER 6.
    IN WILLIAM BASCOM AND MELVILLE HERSKOVITS, CONTINUTY AND
    CHANGE IN AFRICAN CULTURES, CHICAGO, UNIVERSITY OF CHICAGO
    PRESS, 1962, PP 113-129
    038,

FURNIVALL JOHN S
    FURNIVALL JOHN S
    COLONIAL POLICY AND PRACTICE.
    CAMBRIDGE, ENGLAND, CAMBRIDGE UNIVERSITY PRESS, 1948
    035,057,

FURON R
    FURON R
    GEOLOGY OF AFRICA TRANSLATED BY A HALLAN AND L A STEVENS
    NEW YORK, HAFNER, 1963
    017,069,

FYFE CHRISTOPHER
    FYFE CHRISTOPHER
    A HISTORY OF SIERRA LEONE.
    LONDON, OXFORD UNIVERSITY PRESS, 1962
    029,131-02,

    FYFE CHRISTOPHER   JONES ELDRED   EDS
    FREETOWN--A SYMPOSIUM.
    FREETOWN, SIERRA LEONE UNIVERSITY PRESS, 1968
    045,131-05,

FYZEE A A A
    FYZEE A A A

OUTLINES OF MUHAMMADAN LAW.
LONDON, OXFORD UNIVERSITY PRESS, 1955
066,

G

GABATSHWANE S M
   GABATSHWANE S M
   TSHEKEDI KHAMA OF BECHUANALAND-- GREAT STATESMAN AND
   POLITICIAN.
   CAPETOWN, OXFORD UNIVERSITY PRESS, 1961
   102-04,

GABEL CREIGHTON
   GABEL CREIGHTON   NORMAN BENNETT   EDS
   RECONSTRUCTING AFRICAN CULTURE HISTORY.
   BROOKLINE, BOSTON UNIVERSITY PRESS, 1967
   036,

GABLE RICHARD W
   FINKLE JASON L   GABLE RICHARD W   EDS
   POLITICAL DEVELOPMENT AND SOCIAL CHANGE.
   NEW YORK, JOHN WILEY, 1966
   037,

GADEAU G COFFI
   AMON D'ABY J F   DADIE BERNARD   GADEAU G COFFI
   LE THEATRE POPULAIRE EN REPUBLIQUE DE COTE-D'IVOIRE--OEUVRES
   CHOISIES.
   ABIDJAN, CERCLE CULTUREL ET FOLKLORIQUE DE LA COTE-D'IVOIRE
   1965
   116-10,

GAILEY HARRY A
   GAILEY HARRY A
   BIBLIOGRAPHIC ESSAYS--THE GAMBIA.
   AFRICAN NEWSLETTER, VOL. 2, NO. 1, 1964
   113-12,

   GAILEY HARRY A
   A HISTORY OF THE GAMBIA.
   LONDON, ROUTLEDGE AND KEGAN PAUL, 1964
   113-02,

GAITSKELL ARTHUR
   GAITSKELL ARTHUR
   GEZIRA, A STORY OF DEVELOPMENT IN THE SUDAN
   NEW YORK, HUMANITIES PRESS, 1959
   134-08,

GALBRAITH JOHN S
   GALBRAITH JOHN S
   RELUCTANT EMPIRE, BRITISH POLICY ON THE SOUTH AFRICAN
   FRONTIER, 1834-1854
   BERKELEY, UNIVERSITY OF CALIFORNIA PRESS, 1963
   032, 132-02,

GALLAGHER
    GALLAGHER CHARLES F
    THE UNITED STATES AND NORTH AFRICA
    CAMBRIDGE, MASS, HARVARD UNIVERSITY PRESS, 1963
    083,101-09,126-09,138-09,

    GALLAGHER CHARLES F
    TUNISIA.
    IN G.M. CARTER (ED) AFRICAN ONE-PARTY STATES, ITHACA, NEW
    YORK, CORNELL UNIVERSITY PRESS, 1962
    138-07,

GALLAGHER JOHN
    ROBINSON RONALD   GALLAGHER JOHN
    AFRICA AND THE VICTORIANS-- THE CLIMAX OF IMPERIALISM IN THE
    DARK CONTINENT.
    NEW YORK, ST MARTIN'S, 1961
    033,

GALLETTI R
    GALLETTI R   BALDWIN K D S   DINA I O
    NIGERIAN COCOA FARMERS-- AN ECONOMIC SURVEY OF YORUBA
    COCOA FARMING FAMILIES.
    LONDON, OXFORD UNIVERSITY PRESS, 1956
    070,128-08,

GALTUNG JOHAN
    GALTUNG JOHAN
    SCIENTIFIC COLONIALISM
    TRANSACTION 30 1967 PP 11-19
    099,

    GALTUNG JOHAN
    THEORY AND METHODS OF SOCIAL RESEARCH.
    NEW YORK, COLUMBIA UNIVERSITY PRESS, 1967
    098,

GAMBLE DAVID P
    GAMBLE DAVID P
    BIBLIOGRAPHY OF THE GAMBIA.
    LONDON, N.P., 1958
    113-12,

GANN LEWIS H
    GANN LEWIS H   DUIGNAN PETER
    THE HISTORY AND POLITICS OF COLONIALISM, 1870-1914
    VOL 1--COLONIALISM IN AFRICA, 1870-1960
    CAMBRIDGE, UNIVERSITY PRESS 1969
    033,

    GANN LEWIS H   DUIGNAN PETER
    BURDEN OF EMPIRE--AN APPRAISAL OF WESTERN COLONIALISM IN
    AFRICA SOUTH OF THE SAHARA.
    NEW YORK, PRAEGER, 1967
    035,

    GANN LEWIS H
    A HISTORY OF SOUTHERN RHODESIA.
    LONDON, 1965

087,145-02,

GANN LEWIS H
    GANN LEWIS H
    HISTORY OF NORTHERN RHODESIA-EARLY DAYS TO 1953
    LONDON, CHATTO AND WINDUS, 1964
    142-02,

GARDINER A
    GARDINER A
    EGYPT OF THE PHAROAHS
    OXFORD, CLARENDON PRESS, 1961
    020,

GARDINER B
    DAVIS ALLISON   GARDINER B   GARDINER M R
    DEEP SOUTH.
    CHICAGO, UNIVERSITY OF CHICAGO PRESS, 1941
    030,

GARDINER M R
    DAVIS ALLISON   GARDINER B   GARDINER M R
    DEEP SOUTH.
    CHICAGO, UNIVERSITY OF CHICAGO PRESS, 1941
    030,

GARDINIER DAVID E
    GARDINIER DAVID E
    CAMEROON.   UNITED NATIONS CHALLENGE TO FRENCH POLICY.
    LONDON, OXFORD UNIVERSITY PRESS, 1963
    081,104-02,

    GARDINIER DAVID E
    URBAN POLITICS IN DOUALA, CAMEROON, 1944-1955
    AFRICAN URBAN NOTES, VOL IV, NO. 3, SEPT. 1969, PP. 20-29
    047,104-05,

GARIGUE PHILIP
    GARIGUE PHILIP
    THE WEST AFRICAN STUDENTS UNION.
    AFRICA 23 1953 PP 55-69
    044,

GARLAKE PETER
    GARLAKE PETER
    EARLY ISLAMIC ARCHITECTURE OF THE EAST AFRICAN COAST.
    NAIROBI, OXFORD PRESS, 1966
    092,

GARN STANLEY M
    GARN STANLEY M
    HUMAN RACES
    SPRINGFIELD, ILLINOIS, CHARLES C THOMAS, 1965
    018,

GARRETT NAOMI M
    GARRETT NAOMI M
    POETS OF NEGRITUDE.
    IN ALBERT BERRIAN AND RICHARD LONG (EDS), NEGRITUDE--
    ESSAYS AND STUDIES, HAMPTON, VIRGINIA, HAMPTON INSTITUTE

PRESS, 1967, PP 89-101
090,

GARRISON WILLIAM
   BERRY BRIAN J L   GARRISON WILLIAM
   ALTERNATE EXPLANATIONS OF URBAN RANK-SIZE RELATIONSHIPS.
   ANNALS OF THE ASSOCIATION OF AMERICAN GEOGRAPHERS 48 MARCH
   1958 B-M REPRINT .S-341
   047,

GARVEY AMY JACQUES
   GARVEY AMY JACQUES
   THE PHILOSOPHY AND OPINIONS OF MARCUS GARVEY.
   NEW YORK, THE UNIVERSAL PUBLISHING HOUSE, 1926 REPRINTED
   LONDON, FRANK CASS, 1967
   095,

GASKIN L J P
   GASKIN L J P   ED
   A SELECT BIBLIOGRAPHY OF MUSIC IN AFRICA.
   LONDON INTERNATIONAL AFRICAN INSTITUTE 1965 AFRICAN
   BIBLIOGRAPHY SERIES B
   015,

   GASKIN L J P
   A BIBLIOGRAPHY OF AFRICAN ART.
   LONDON, INTERNATIONAL AFRICAN INSTITUTE, 1965
   014,

GAUCHER JOSEPH
   GAUCHER JOSEPH
   LES DEBUTS DE L'ENSEIGNMENT EN AFRIQUE FRANCOPHONE--JEAN
   DARD ET L'ECOLE MUTELLE DE SAINT-LOUIS DU SENEGAL (THE
   BEGINNINGS OF EDUCATION IN FRENCH-SPEAKING AFRICA--JEAN
   DARD AND THE MUTUAL SCHOOL AT SAINT-LOUIS IN SENEGAL).
   PARIS, INTERNATIONAL UNIVERSITY BOOKSELLERS, INC., 1968
   042,130-03,

GAVIN R J
   GAVIN R J
   THE MAKING OF MODERN AFRICA
   VOL I--THE NINETEENTH CENTURY TO THE PARTITION.
   NEW YORK, HUMANITIES PRESS, 1969
   036,

GAY J
   GAY J   COLE M
   THE NEW MATHEMATICS AND THE OLD CULTURE
   NEW YORK, HOLT, RINEHART AND WINSTON, 1967
   041,119-03,

GEAY J
   GEAY J
   ORIGINE, FORMATION ET HISTOIRE DU ROYAUME DE PORTO-NOVO
   (THE ORIGIN, FORMATION AND HISTORY OF THE KINGDOM OF
   PORTO-NOVO).
   BULLETIN DU COMITE D'ETUDES HISTORIQUES ET SCIENTIFIQUES DE
   L'AFRIQUE OCCIDENTALE FRANCAISE 7 1924 PP 619-634
   026,109-02,

GEERTZ CLIFFORD
    GEERTZ CLIFFORD   ED
    OLD SOCIETIES AND NEW STATES--THE QUEST FOR MODERNITY
    IN ASIA AND AFRICA.
    NEW YORK FREE PRESS, 1963
    037,

GEERTZ CLIFFORD
    GEERTZ CLIFFORD
    THE INTEGRATION REVOLUTION--PRIMORDIAL SENTIMENTS AND CIVIL
    POLITICS IN THE NEW STATES.
    IN OLD SOCIETIES AND NEW STATES, NEW YORK, FREE PRESS OF
    GLENCOE, 1963, PP 105-158
    057,

GELLNER ERNEST
    GELLNER ERNEST
    TRIBALISM AND SOCIAL CHANGE IN NORTH AFRICA.
    IN WILLIAM H LEWIS (ED), FRENCH-SPEAKING AFRICA, THE SEARCH
    FOR IDENTITY, NEW YORK, WALKER AND CO, 1965, PP 107-118
    006,126-03,

    GELLNER ERNEST
    NATIONALISM CHP 7.
    IN THOUGHT AND CHANGE, CHICAGO, UNIVERSITY OF CHICAGO
    PRESS, 1965
    054,

GENNET C
    GENNET C
    PLAN DIRECTEUR D'URBANISME D'ABIDJAN.
    INDUSTRIES ET TRAVAUS D'OUTRE-MER, 10, 100, MARCH, 1962
    116-05,

GENOVESE EUGENE D
    GENOVESE EUGENE D
    THE LEGACY OF SLAVERY AND THE ROOTS OF BLACK NATIONALISM.
    STUDIES ON THE LEFT 6 1966 PP 3-65
    030,

    GENOVESE EUGENE D
    THE POLITICAL ECONOMY OF SLAVERY.
    NEW YORK, PANTHEON BOOKS, 1956
    028,

GERADIN B
    GERADIN B
    LE DEVELOPMENT DE LA HAUTE-VOLTA.
    PARIS, ISEA, 1964
    141-08,

GERBRANDS A
    GERBRANDS A
    ART AS AN ELEMENT OF CULTURE, ESPECIALLY IN NEGRO AFRICA.
    LEIDEN, E J BRILL, 1957
    014,

GERTEINY ALFRED G
    GERTEINY ALFRED G
    MAURITANIA.

LONDON, PALL MALL PRESS, 1967
124-11,

GERTEINY ALFRED G
   GERTEINY ALFRED G
   MAURITANIA
   IN KRITZECK AND LEWIS, PP 319-332
   124-03,

GERTZEL CHERRY
   GERTZEL CHERRY
   UGANDA.
   LONDON, PALL MALL PRESS, 1970
   139-11,

GHAI DHARAM P
   GHAI DHARAM P
   PORTRAIT OF A MINORITY.
   EASTERN AFRICA, OXFORD UNIVERSITY PRESS, 1965
   085,

   GHAI DHARAM P
   TAXATION FOR DEVELOPMENT--A CASE STUDY OF UGANDA.
   KENYA, EAST AFRICAN PUBLISHING HOUSE, 1966
   073,139-08,

   GHAI DHARAM P
   TERRITORIAL DISTRIBUTION OF THE BENEFITS AND COSTS OF THE
   EAST AFRICAN COMMON MARKET.
   IN COLIN LEYS AND P ROBSON (EDS), FEDERATION IN EAST AFRICA--
   OPPORTUNITIES AND PROBLEMS, NAIROBI, OXFORD UNIVERSITY PRESS,
   1965, PP 72-82
   078,

GHAI YASH
   GHAI YASH
   SOME LEGAL ASPECTS OF AN EAST AFRICAN FEDERATION.
   IN COLIN LEYS AND P ROBSON (EDS), FEDERATION IN EAST AFRICA--
   OPPORTUNITIES AND PROBLEMS, NAIROBI, OXFORD UNIVERSITY PRESS,
   1965, PP 172-182
   067,

   GHAI YASH
   PROSPECTS FOR ASIANS IN EAST AFRICA.
   IN LAWRENCE SAGINI (ED) RACIAL AND COMMUNAL TENSIONS IN EAST
   AFRICA, NAIROBI, EAST AFRICAN PUBLISHING HOUSE, 1966, PP 9-26
   057,

GHANA
   GHANA MIN OF HOUSING
   ACCRA--A PLAN FOR THE TOWN.
   ACCRA, GOVERNMENT PRINTER, 1958
   114-05,

GIBB H A R
   GIBB H A R
   STUDIES ON THE CIVILIZATION OF ISLAM-EDITED BY S.J.SHAW AND
   W.R.POLK
   BOSTON, BEACON PRESS, 1962
   021,

GIBBS JAMES JR
   GIBBS JAMES JR   ED
   PEOPLES OF AFRICA.
   NEW YORK, HOLT, RINEHART AND WINSTON, 1965
   004,016,

GIBSON GORDON D
   GIBSON GORDON D
   A BIBLIOGRAPHY OF ANTHROPOLOGICAL BIBLIOGRAPHIES-AFRICA
   CURRENT ANTHROPOLOGY 10 1969 PP 527-566
   001,098,

GIDE ANDRE
   GIDE ANDRE
   VOYAGE AU CONGO (VOYAGE TO THE CONGO).
   PARIS, GALLIMARD, 1929
   035,108-02,

GIFFORD PROSSER
   GIFFORD PROSSER   LOUIS WILLIAM ROGER
   BRITAIN AND GERMANY IN AFRICA--IMPERIAL RIVALRY AND COLONIAL
   RULE.
   NEW HAVEN, CONN. (YALE), MCGILL-QUEEN'S PRESS, 1969
   033,

GILLARD D R
   GILLARD D R
   SALISBURY S AFRICAN POLICY AND THE HELIGOLAND OFFER OF 1890.
   THE ENGLISH HISTORICAL REVIEW 75 1960 PP 631-653
   033,

GINZBERG E
   GINZBERG E   ED
   TECHNOLOGY AND SOCIAL CHANGE
   NEW YORK, COLUMBIA UNIVERSITY PRESS, 1964
   037,075,

GIRLING F K
   GIRLING F K
   THE ACHOLI OF UGANDA.
   LONDON, HER MAJESTY'S STATIONERY OFFICE, 1960
   139-01,

GLEASON JUDITH
   GLEASON JUDITH
   THIS AFRICA.
   EVANSTON, NORTHWESTERN UNIVERSITY PRESS, 1965
   090,

GLICKMAN HARVEY
   GLICKMAN HARVEY
   POLITICAL SCIENCE.
   IN ROBERT A LYSTAD (ED), THE AFRICAN WORLD, NEW YORK,
   PRAEGER, 1966, PP 131-165
   100,

GLOCK CHARLES Y
   GLOCK CHARLES Y   STARK RODNEY
   RELIGION AND SOCIETY IN TENSION.

CHICAGO, RAND MCNALLY, 1965
013,

GLUCKMAN MAX
    GLUCKMAN MAX
    POLITICS LAW AND RITUAL IN TRIBAL SOCIETY.
    CHICAGO, ALDINE PUBLISHING COMPANY, 1965
    009,

    GLUCKMAN MAX
    TRIBALISM IN MODERN BRITISH CENTRAL AFRICA.
    IN IMMANUEL WALLERSTEIN, SOCIAL CHANGE, THE COLONIAL
    SITUATION, NEW YORK, JOHN WILEY AND SONS, 1966, PP 251-264
    007,

    GLUCKMAN MAX
    CUSTOM AND CONFLICT IN AFRICA.
    OXFORD, BLACKWELL, 1955
    009,

    GLUCKMAN MAX
    THE LOGIC OF WITCHCRAFT.
    IN PETER J MCEWAN AND ROBERT B SUTCLIFFE (EDS), MODERN AFRICA,
    NEW YORK, THOMAS CROWELL, 1965, PP 79-92
    013,

    GLUCKMAN MAX   ED
    IDEAS AND PROCEDURES IN AFRICAN CUSTOMARY LAW.
    LONDON, OXFORD UNIVERSITY PRESS, 1969
    066,

    GLUCKMAN MAX
    THE IDEAS OF BAROTSE JURISPRUDENCE.
    NEW HAVEN, YALE UNIVERSITY PRESS, 1965
    066,142-01,

    GLUCKMAN MAX
    THE JUDICIAL PROCESS AMONG THE BAROTSE OF NORTHERN RHODESIA.
    NEW YORK, FREE PRESS, 1955
    066,142-01,

    GLUCKMAN MAX
    ANALYSIS OF A SOCIAL SITUATION IN MODERN ZULULAND.
    MANCHESTER, MANCHESTER UNIVERSITY PRESS, 1958
    038,132-03,

    GLUCKMAN MAX   ED
    IDEAS AND PROCEEDURES IN AFRICAN CUSTOMARY LAW--STUDIES PRE-
    SENTED AND DISCUSSED AT THE EIGTH INTERNATIONAL AFRICAN SEM-
    INAR AT THE HAILE SELLASSIE I UNIVERSITY, ADDIS ABABA,
    JANUARY 1966.
    LONDON, OXFORD UNIVERSITY PRESS, 1969
    066,

GLUCKMAN MAY
    GLUCKMAN MAY
    THE RISE OF A ZULU EMPIRE
    SCIENTIFIC AMERICAN 202 1960 PP 157-168
    031,

GOLD
   GOLD COAST GOV STAT
   KUMASI SURVEY OF POPULATION AND HOUSEHOLD BUDGETS, 1955.
   ACCRA, GOVERNMENT PRINTER, 1956
   114-05,

GOLD
   GOLD COAST GOV STAT
   SECONDI-TAKORADI SURVEY OF POPULATION AND HOUSEHOLD BUDGETS.
   ACCRA, GOVERNMENT PRINTER, 1956
   114-05,

GOLDMAN MARSHALL
   GOLDMAN MARSHALL
   COMMUNIST FOREIGN AID-- SUCCESSES AND SHORTCOMINGS.
   CURRENT HISTORY 51 300 AUGUST 1966 PP 78-87
   084,

GOLDWATER ROBERT
   GOLDWATER ROBERT
   SENUFO SCULPTURE FROM WEST AFRICA.
   GREENWICH, CONNECTICUT, THE MUSEUM OF PRIMITIVE ART, 1964
   014,114-01,

GOMKOUDOUGOU
   KABORE GOMKOUDOUGOU
   ORGANISATION POLITIQUE TRADITIONNELLE ET EVOLUTION POLITIQUE
   DES MOSSI DE OUGADOUGOU.
   PARIS, CENTRE VOLTAIQUE DE LA RECHERCHE SCIENTIFIQUE, 1966
   141-01,

GONCHAROV L
   GONCHAROV L
   NEW FORMS OF COLONISATION IN AFRICA.
   JOURNAL OF MODERN AFRICAN STUDIES 1 4 1963 PP 467-74
   087,

   GONCHAROV L
   URGENT PROBLEMS OF AFRICAN ECONOMIC DEVELOPMENT.
   THE JOURNAL OF MODERN AFRICAN STUDIES, VOL. 6, NO.4, 1968,
   PP. 475-83
   073,

GONIDEC P F
   GONIDEC P F
   LES INSTITUTIONS POLITIQUE DE LA REPUBLIQUE FEDERAL DU
   CAMAROUN (THE POLITICAL INSTITUTIONS OF THE FEDERAL
   REPUBLIC OF THE CAMAROONS).
   CIVILIZATIONS 11 1961 PP 370-395 AND 12 1962 PP 13-26
   062,104-07,

   GONIDEC P F
   LA COMMUNAUTE (THE COMMUNITY).
   PUBLIC LAW, SUMMER, 1960, PP. 177-189
   077,

GOOD ROBERT C
   GOOD ROBERT C
   CHANGING PATTERNS OF AFRICAN INTERNATIONAL RELATIONS.
   AMERICAN POLITICAL SCIENCE REVIEW, VOL. LVIII, SEPT., 1969,

NO. 3, PP. 632-641
097,

GOODWIN A J H
   SCHAPERA ISAAC   GOODWIN A J H
   WORK AND WEALTH.
   IN I SCHAPERA (ED.) THE BANTU-SPEAKING TRIBES OF SOUTH
   AFRICA, LONDON, ROUTLEDGE, 1937
   010,

GOODY J R
   BRAIMAH J A   GOODY J R
   SALAGA--THE STRUGGLE FOR POWER.
   LONDON, LONGMANS, GREEN AND COMPANY LIMITED, 1967
   026,114-02,

GOODY JACK
   GOODY JACK
   COMPARATIVE STUDIES IN KINSHIP.
   PALO ALTO, STANFORD UNIVERSITY PRESS, 1969
   008,

   GOODY JACK
   ETHNOHISTORY AND THE AKAN OF GHANA.
   AFRICA 29 1959 PP 67-81
   026,114-02,

   GOODY JACK
   ANOMIE IN ASHANTI.
   AFRICA 26 1957 PP 356-363
   044,114-03,

   GOODY JACK
   DEATH, PROPERTY AND THE ANCESTORS--A STUDY OF THE MORTUARY
   CUSTOMS OF THE LODAGAA OF WEST AFRICA.
   STANFORD, STANFORD UNIVERSITY PRESS, 1962
   013,

GORDENKER LEON
   GORDENKER LEON
   THE UN SECRETARY GENERAL AND THE MAINTENANCE OF THE PEACE
   NEW YORK, COLUMBIA UNIVERSITY PRESS, 1967
   081,

GORDON DAVID C
   GORDON DAVID C
   NORTH AFRICA?S FRENCH LEGACY 1954-1962.
   CAMBRIDGE, MASS, HARVARD UNIVERSITY PRESS, 1962
   035,

   GORDON DAVID C
   THE PASSING OF FRENCH ALGERIA.
   NEW YORK, OXFORD UNIVERSITY PRESS. 1966
   033,055,056,101-02,

   GORDON DAVID C
   WOMEN OF ALGERIA-- AN ESSAY ON CHANGE.
   CAMBRIDGE, MASS, HARVARD, 1968
   101-03,

GORDON MILTON M
   GORDON MILTON M
   ASSIMILATION IN AMERICA-- THEORY AND REALITY.
   DAEDALUS 90 SPRING 1961 (BOBBS-MERRILL REPRINT S-407)
   057,

GORDON MILTON M
   GORDON MILTON M
   ASSIMILATION IN AMERICAN LIFE-- THE ROLE OF RACE, RELIGION
   AND NATIONAL ORIGINS.
   NEW YORK, OXFORD UNIVERSITY PRESS. 1964
   057,

GOUILLY ALPHONSE
   GOUILLY ALPHONSE
   L'ISLAM DANS L'AFRIQUE OCCIDENTALE FRANCAISE (ISLAM IN
   FRENCH WEST AFRICA).
   PARIS, EDITIONS LAROSE, 1952
   021,052,

GOULD PETER
   GOULD PETER
   TANZANIA 1920-1963-THE SPATIAL IMPRESS OF THE MODERNIZATION
   PROCESS
   WORLD POLITICS 22 1970 PP 149-170
   048,136-03,

   TAAFFE E J   MORRILL R L   GOULD PETER
   TRANSPORT EXPANSION IN UNDERDEVELOPED COUNTRIES--A
   COMPARATIVE ANALYSIS.
   GEOGRAPHICAL REVIEW 53 OCTOBER 1963 PP 503-529
   048,

   GOULD PETER
   GEOGRAPHY, SPATIAL PLANNING, AND AFRICA--THE RESPONSIBILIT-
   IES OF THE NEXT TWENTY YEARS.
   IN CARTER, GWENDOLEN M. AND ANN PADEN (EDS), EXPANDING
   HORIZONS IN AFRICAN STUDIES, EVANSTON, NORTHWESTERN
   UNIVERSITY PRESS, 1969, PP. 181-203
   048,100,

   GOULD PETER   ED
   AFRICA CONTINENT OF CHANGE
   BELMONT, CALIFORNIA, WADSWORTH PUBLISHING COMPANY, 1961
   038,

   GOULD PETER
   A NOTE ON RESEARCH INTO THE DIFFUSION OF DEVELOPMENT
   JOURNAL OF MODERN AFRICAN STUDIES 2 1964 PP 123-125
   048,

   GOULD PETER
   THE DEVELOPMENT OF THE TRANSPORTATION PATTERN IN GHANA
   EVANSTON, DEPARTMENT OF GEOGRAPHY, NORTHWESTERN UNIVERSITY
   PRESS, 1960
   048,114-05,

GOUROU PIERRE
   GOUROU PIERRE   BEAVER S H   LABORDE E D
   THE TROPICAL WORLD-- ITS SOCIAL AND ECONOMIC CONDITIONS AND

ITS FUTURE STATUS.
LONDON, LONGMANS, 4TH EDITION, 1966
069,075,

GOVERNMENT
GOVERNMENT OF TANZANIA
REPORT OF THE PRESIDENTIAL COMMISSION ON THE ESTABLISHMENT
OF A DEMOCRATIC ONE-PARTY STATE.
DAR ES SALAAM, 1965
061,136-04,

GOVERNMENT OF FRANCE
COUTUMIERS JURIDIQUES DE L'AFRIQUE OCCIDENTALE FRANCAISE--
MAURITANIE, NIGER, COTE D'IVOIRE, DAHOMEY, GUINEE FRANCAISE
(FRENCH WEST AFRICAN JURIDIC CUSTOMS-- MAURITANIA, NIGER
IVORY COAST, DAHOMEY, FRENCH GUINEA) .
PARIS,LIBRAIRIE LAROSE, 1939 VOL3
066,109-01,115-01,116-01,124-01,127-01,

GOVERNMENT OF FRANCE
COUTUMIERS JURIDIQUE DE L'AFRIQUE OCCIDENTALE FRANCAISE--
SOUDAN (FRENCH WEST AFRICAN JURIDIC CUSTOMS-- SUDAN).
PARIS, LAROSE EDITEURS, 1939, VOL 2
066,123-01,

GOVERNMENT OF FRANCE
COUTUMIERS JURIDIQUES DE L'AFRIQUE OCCIDENTALE FRANCAISE--
SENEGAL (FRENCH WEST AFRICAN JURIDIC CUSTOMS-- SENEGAL).
PARIS LIBRAIRIE LAROSE,1939 VOL1
066,130-01,

GOWER L C B
GOWER L C B
INDEPENDENT AFRICA--THE CHALLENGE TO THE LEGAL PROFESSION.
CAMBRIDGE, HARVARD UNIVERSITY PRESS, 1968
067,

GRAHAM J
GRAHAM J
THE SLAVE TRADE,DEPOPULATION AND HUMAN SACRIFICE IN BENIN
HISTORY
CAHIERS D'ETUDES AFRICAINES 5 1965 PP 317-324
028,

GRAVAND R P
GRAVAND R P
CONTRIBUTION DU CHRISTIANISME A L'AFFIRMATION DE LA
PERSONNALITE AFRICAINE EN PAYS SERERE (CONTRIBUTION OF
CHRISTIANITY TO THE AFFIRMATION OF THE AFRICAN PERSONALITY
IN SERERE COUNTRY).
IN COLLOQUE SUR LES RELIGIONS, ABIDJAN, APRIL, 1961, PARIS,
PRESENCE AFRICAINE, 1962, PP 209-214
039,050,130-03,

GRAVAND R P
LA DIGNITE SERERE (SERERE DIGNITY).
IN COLLOQUE SUR LES RELIGIONS, ABIDJAN, APRIL, 1961, PARIS,
PRESENCE AFRICAINE, 1962, PP 87-90
013,130-01,

GRAY JOHN M
  GRAY JOHN M
  EARLY PORTUGUESE VISITORS OF KILWA.
  TANGANYIKA NOTES AND RECORDS 52 1959 PP 117-128
  023,136-02,

GRAY JOHN M
  GRAY JOHN M
  HISTORY OF ZANZIBAR FROM THE MIDDLE AGES TO 1856
  LONDON, OXFORD UNIVERSITY PRESS, 1962
  023,

GRAY RICHARD
  GRAY RICHARD
  THE TWO NATIONS-- ASPECTS OF THE DEVELOPMENT OF RACE
  RELATIONS IN THE RHODESIAS AND NYASALAND.
  LONDON, OXFORD UNIVERSITY PRESS, 1960
  087,088,122-06,142-06,145-06,

GRAY ROBERT F
  GRAY ROBERT F
  MEDICAL RESEARCH-- SOME ANTHROPOLOGICAL ASPECTS.
  IN ROBERT A LYSTAD (ED), THE AFRICAN WORLD, NEW YORK,
  PRAEGER, 1966,
  075,100,

  GRAY ROBERT F
  POLITICAL PARTIES IN NEW AFRICAN NATIONS-- AN
  ANTHROPOLOGICAL VIEW.
  COMPARATIVE STUDIES IN SOCIETY AND HISTORY 4 JULY 1963
  PP 449-465
  061,

  GRAY ROBERT F
  POLITICAL PARTIES IN NEW AFRICAN STATES-- A REPLY TO
  LUCY MAIR.
  COMPARATIVE STUDIES IN SOCIETY AND HISTORY 6 JANUARY 1964
  PP 230-232
  061,

GREAT BRITAIN
  GREAT BRITAIN
  BIBLIOGRAPHY OF PUBLISHED SOURCES RELATING TO
  AFRICAN LAND TENURE.
  LONDON, HER MAJESTY'S STATIONERY OFFICE, 1950
  070,

  GREAT BRITAIN   COLONIAL OFFICE
  REPORT OF THE COMMISSION TO ENQUIRE INTO THE FEARS OF
  MINORITIES AND THE MEANS OF ALLAYING THEM.
  HER MAJESTY'S STATIONERY OFFICE, COMMAND 505, JULY 1958
  057,128-06,

  GREAT BRITAIN   COLONIAL OFFICE
  BECHUANALAND PROTECTORATE, REPORT FOR THE YEARS 1961-62.
  LONDON, HER MAJESTY'S STATIONERY OFFICE, 1964
  102-11,

  GREAT BRITAIN   COLONIAL OFFICE
  BECHUANALAND PROTECTORATE REPORT FOR THE YEAR 1963.

LONDON, HER MAJESTY'S STATIONERY OFFICE, 1965
102-11,

GREEN L P
  GREEN L P   FAIR T J D
  DEVELOPMENT IN AFRICA- A STUDY IN REGIONAL ANALYSIS WITH
  SPECIAL REFERENCE TO SOUTHERN AFRICA
  JOHANNESBURG WITWATERSRAND UNIVERSITY PRESS 1962
  048,073,132-08,145-08,

GREEN MARGARET
  GREEN MARGARET
  A DESCRIPTIVE GRAMMAR OF IGBO.
  BERLIN, AKADEMIE-VERLAG, 1963
  011,128-01,

  GREEN MARGARET
  IBO VILLIAGE AFFAIRS.
  NEW YORK, PRAEGER, 1964
  128-01,

GREEN REGINALD H
  GREEN REGINALD H   SEIDMAN ANN
  UNITY OR POVERTY THE ECONOMICS OF PAN-AFRICANISM.
  BALTIMORE, PENGUIN, 1968
  071,079,

  GREEN REGINALD H   KRISHNA K G V
  ECONOMIC CO-OPERATION IN AFRICA.
  LONDON, OXFORD UNIVERSITY PRESS, 1967
  077,078,080,

  GREEN REGINALD H
  FOUR AFRICAN DEVELOPMENT PLANS-- GHANA, KENYA, NIGERIA,
  AND TANZANIA CHAPTER 20.
  IN EDITH WHETHAM AND JEAN CURRIE. (EDS.), READINGS IN THE
  APPLIED ECONOMICS OF AFRICA, LONDON, CAMBRIDGE UNIVERSITY
  PRESS, 2, 1967, PP 21-32
  072,114-08,117-08,128-08,136-08,

GREENBERG JOSEPH H
  GREENBERG JOSEPH H
  STUDIES IN AFRICAN LINGUISTIC CLASSIFICATION.
  NEW YORK, VIKING PRESS, COMPASS BOOKS,1955
  003,011,

  GREENBERG JOSEPH H
  THE LANGUAGES OF AFRICA.
  BLOOMINGTON, INDIANA UNIVERSITY PRESS,1963
  003,011,

  GREENBERG JOSEPH H
  URBANISM,MIGRATION AND LANGUAGE
  CHAPTER 4 IN HILDA KUPER (ED),URBANIZATION AND MIGRATION IN
  WEST AFRICA,BERKELEY,UNIVERSITY OF CALIFORNIA PRESS,1965
  007,046,

  BERRY JACK   GREENBERG JOSEPH H
  SOCIOLINGUISTIC RESEARCH IN AFRICA.
  AFRICAN STUDIES BULLETIN SEPTEMBER 1966 PP 1-9

100,

GREENBERG JOSEPH H
GREENBERG JOSEPH H
LANGUAGES AND HISTORY IN AFRICA.
PRESENCE AFRICAINE 17 JANUARY 1963 PP 114-122
003,

GREENBERG JOSEPH H
LINGUISTICS CHAPTER 15.
IN ROBERT A LYSTAD (ED), THE AFRICAN WORLD, NEW YORK,
PRAEGER 1965 PP 416-441
011,

GREENBERG JOSEPH H
AFRICA AS A LINGUISTIC AREA CHAPTER 2.
IN WILLIAM BASCOM AND MELVILLE HERSKOVITS, CONTINUTY AND
CHANGE IN AFRICAN CULTURES, CHICAGO, UNIVERSITY OF CHICAGO
PRESS, 1962, PP 15-27
003,011,

GREENBERG JOSEPH H
THE HISTORY AND PRESENT STATUS OF AFRICAN LINGUISTIC
STUDIES.
IN LALAGE BOWN AND MICHAEL CROWDER (EDS.), PROCEEDINGS OF
THE FIRST INTERNATIONAL CONGRESS OF AFRICANISTS, ACCRA,
1962, LONDON, LONGMANS, 1964, PP 83-96
011,

GREENBERG JOSEPH H
THE NEGRO KINGDOMS OF THE SUDAN.
TRANSACTIONS OF THE NEW YORK ACADEMY OF SCIENCES 11 1949
PP 126-135
024,

GREENBERG JOSEPH H
HISTORICAL INFERENCES FROM LINGUISTIC RESEARCH IN SUB-SAHA-
RAN AFRICA.
IN JEFFREY BUTLER (ED), BOSTON UNIVERSITY PAPERS IN AFRICAN
HISTORY VOL I, BOSTON, BOSTON UNIVERSITY PRESS, 1964, PP 1-16
011,

GREENBERG JOSEPH H
THE INFLUENCE OF ISLAM ON A SUDANESE RELIGION.
SEATTLE, UNIVERSITY OF WASHINGTON PRESS, 1969
013,128-01,

GREENFIELD RICHARD
GREENFIELD RICHARD
ETHIOPIA--A NEW POLITICAL HISTORY.
LONDON, PALL MALL, 1967
034,110-07,

GREER SCOTT
GREER SCOTT   MCELRATH DENNIS   MINAR DAVID
THE NEW URBANIZATION.
NEW YORK, ST MARTIN'S PRESS, 1968
046,

GREGG ROBERT W

GREGG ROBERT W
THE UN REGIONAL ECONOMIC COMMISSIONS AND INTEGRATION IN THE
UNDERDEVELOPED AREAS
IN J S NYE (ED), INTERNATIONAL REGIONALISM, BOSTON, LITTLE,
BROWN, 1968, PP 304-332
080,081,

GREGORY J W
GREGORY J W
THE GREAT RIFT VALLEY
LONDON, JOHN MURRAY, 1896
017,

GRENVILLE J A S
GRENVILLE J A S
LORD SALISBURY AND FOREIGN POLICY-- THE CLOSE OF THE
NINETEENTH CENTURY.
LONDON, ATHLONE PRESS, 1964
033,

GRIAULE MARCEL
GRIAULE MARCEL
FOLK ARTS OF BLACK AFRICA
NEW YORK, TUDOR, 1950
014,

GRIAULE MARCEL
CONVERSATION WITH OGOTEMMELI
NEW YORK, OXFORD, 1965
013,

GRIFFITHS J E S
DUDBRIDGE B J   GRIFFITHS J E S
THE DEVELOPMENT OF LOCAL GOVERNMENT IN SUKUMALAND.
JOURNAL OF AFRICAN ADMINISTRATION 3 JULY 1951 PP 141-146
062,136-09,

GRIMSHAW ALLEN D
GRIMSHAW ALLEN D
URBAN RACIAL VIOLENCE IN THE UNITED STATES CHANGING
ECOLOGICAL CONSIDERATIONS.
THE AMERICAN JOURNAL OF SOCIOLOGY 66 SEPTEMBER 1960
PP 109-119
030,

GROHS G K
GROHS G K   REVIEW
FRANTZ FANON AND THE AFRICAN REVOLUTION.
THE JOURNAL OF MODERN AFRICAN STUDIES, VOL. 6, NO. 4, PP.
543-556, 1968
091,

GROSS ERNEST A
GROSS ERNEST A
ADLAI STEVENSON, THE UNITED NATIONS, AND AFRICA.
AFRICAN FORUM I 2 FALL 1965 PP 3-6
081,

GROVE A T
GROVE A T

AFRICA SOUTH OF THE SAHARA
LONDON, OXFORD UNIVERSITY PRESS, 1967
017,069,

GROVE A T
  GROVE A T   PULLAN R A
  SOME ASPECTS OF THE PLEISTOCENE PALEOGEOGRAPHY OF THE
  CHAD BASIN.
  IN F CLARK HOWELL AND FRANCOIS BOURLIERE (EDS.), AFRICAN
  ECOLOGY AND HUMAN EVOLUTION, CHICAGO, ALDINE, 1966,
  PP 230-245
  018,

  GROVE A T   WARREN A
  QUATERNARY LANDFORMS AND THE CLIMATE ON THE SOUTH SIDE OF
  THE SAHARA
  GEOGRAPHICAL JOURNAL 134 1968 PP 194-208
  017,

  GROVE A T
  POPULATION DENSITIES AND AGRICULTURE IN NORTHERN NIGERIA.
  AFRICAN POPULATION, NEW YORK, PRAEGER, 1962, PP 115-136
  069,

GROVE DAVID
  GROVE DAVID   HUSZAR LASZLO
  THE TOWNS OF GHANA--THE ROLE OF SERVICE CENTRES IN REGIONAL
  PLANNING.
  ACCRA, GHANA UNIVERSITIES PRESS, 1964

GROVES C P
  GROVES C P
  THE PLANING OF CHRISTIANITY IN AFRICA.
  LONDON, 4 VOLUMES, 1948-58.
  050,

GRUNDY KENNETH W
  GRUNDY KENNETH W
  POLITICAL POWER AND ECONOMIC THEORY IN RADICAL WEST
  AFRICA.
  ORBIS 8 SUMMER 1964 PP 405-424
  060,

  GRUNDY KENNETH W
  CONFLICTING IMAGES OF THE MILITARY IN AFRICA
  NAIROBI, EAST AFRICAN PUBLISHING HOUSE, 1968
  064,

  GRUNDY KENNETH W
  THE CLASS STRUGGLE IN AFRICA-- AN EXAMINATION OF
  CONFLICTING THEORIES.
  JOURNAL OF MODERN AFRICAN STUDIES 2 NOVEMBER 1964 PP 379-394
  058,

GUEYE LAMINE
  GUEYE LAMINE
  ITINERAIRE AFRICAIN (AFRICAN ITINERARY).
  PARIS, PRESENCE AFRICAINE, 1966
  044,060,130-04,

GUIFFRAY R
    GUIFFRAY R
    LE FRANCAIS EN AFRIQUE (THE FRENCH IN AFRICA).
    PARIS, LAROUSSE, NEW YORK, INTERNATIONAL UNIVERSITY BOOKSEL-
    LERS,INC., 1969
    082,

GUILHEM MARCEL
    HAMA BOUBOU   GUILHEM MARCEL
    HISTOIRE DU NIGER.
    PARIS, L'AFRIQUE-LE MONDE, COURS MOYEN, 1965
    127-02,

    HAMA BOUBOU   GUILHEM MARCEL
    NIGER--RECITS HISTORIQUES--COURS ELEMENTAIRE.
    PARIS, LIGEL, 1964
    127-02,

    RAMIN JEAN CHARLES KOUBETTI V   GUILHEM MARCEL
    HISTOIRE DU DAHOMEY.
    PARIS, L'AFRIQUE-LE MONDE, COURS MOYEN, LIGEL, 1964
    109-02,

    TOE SYLVAIN   GUILHEM MARCEL
    HAUTE-VOLTA--RECITS HISTORIQUES--COURS ELEMENTAIRE.
    PARIS, LIGEL, 1964
    141-02,

    TOE SYLVAIN   GUILHEM MARCEL   HEBERT JEAN
    HISTOIRE DE LA HAUTE-VOLTA.
    PARIS, L'AFRIQUE-LE MONDE, COURS MOYEN, LIGEL, 1964
    141-02,

    TRAORE ANDRE   GUILHEM MARCEL
    MALI--RECITS HISTORIQUES--3EME ET 4EME ANNEES DU CYCLE
    FONDAMENTAL.
    PARIS, LIGEL, 1964
    123-02,

GULLIVER P H
    GULLIVER P H
    ANTHROPOLOGY.
    IN ROBERT A LYSTAD (ED), THE AFRICAN WORLD, NEW YORK,
    PRAEGER, 1966, PP 57-106
    100,

    GULLIVER P H
    REVIEW OF MURDOCK-- AFRICA, ITS PEOPLES AND THEIR CULTURE
    HISTORY.
    AMERICAN ANTHROPOLOGIST VOL 62 1960 PP 900-903
    003,

    GULLIVER P H   ED
    TRADITION AND TRANSITION IN EAST AFRICA--STUDIES OF THE
    TRIBAL FACTOR IN THE MODERN ERA.
    BERKELEY, UNIVERSITY OF CALIFORNIA PRESS, 1969
    007,117-03,136-03,139-03,

    GULLIVER P H
    LAND SHORTAGE, SOCIAL CHANGE AND SOCIAL CONFLICT IN EAST

AFRICA.
JOURNAL OF CONFLICT RESOLUTION 5 WINTER 1961 PP 16-26
070,

GULLIVER P H
  GULLIVER P H
  LABOUR MIGRATION IN A RURAL ECONOMMY CHAPTER 4.
  IN EDITH WHETHAM AND JEAN CURRIE (EDS.), READINGS IN THE
  APPLIED ECONOMICS OF AFRICA, LONDON, CAMBRIDGE UNIVERSITY
  PRESS, 1, 1967, PP 32-37
  070,

  GULLIVER P H
  LAND TENURE AND SOCIAL CHANGE AMONG THE NYAKYUSA--
  AN ESSAY IN APPLIED ANTHROPOLOGY IN SOUTH-WEST TANGANYIKA.
  KAMPALA, EAST AFRICAN INSTITUTE OF SOCIAL RESEARCH, 1958
  070,136-08,

  GULLIVER P H
  THE ARUSHA--ECONOMIC AND SOCIAL CHANGE.
  IN BOHANNAN AND DALTON (EDS), MARKETS IN AFRICA, DOUBLEDAY,
  1965
  010,136-06,

  GULLIVER P H
  THE FAMILY HERDS-- A STUDY OF TWO PASTORAL TRIBES.
  LONDON, RUTLEDGE, 1955
  010,

GUTHRIE MALCOLM
  GUTHRIE MALCOLM
  COMPARATIVE BANTU--AN INTRODUCTION TO THE COMPARATIVE
  LINGUISTICS AND PREHISTORY OF THE BANTU LANGUAGE.
  HANTS, ENGLAND, GREGG PRESS LTD., 1969
  011,019,

  GUTHRIE MALCOLM
  BANTU ORIGINS-- A TENTATIVE NEW HYPOTHESIS.
  THE JOURNAL OF AFRICAN LANGUAGES 1 1962 PP 9-21
  019,

  GUTHRIE MALCOLM
  A TWO-STAGE METHOD OF COMPARATIVE BANTU STUDY.
  AFRICAN LANGUAGE STUDIES 3 1962 PP 1-24
  019,

  GUTHRIE MALCOLM
  REVIEW OF GREENBERG S LANGUAGES OF AFRICA.
  JOURNAL OF AFRICAN HISTORY 5 1 1964
  003,

GUTKIND PETER C W
  GUTKIND PETER C W
  AFRICAN URBANISM, MOBILITY AND THE SOCIAL NETWORK.
  INTERNATIONAL JOURNAL OF COMPARATIVE SOCIOLOGY 6 1965 PP
  48-60 SPECIAL ISSUE ON KINSHIP AND GEOGRAPHICAL
  MOBILITY, R PIDDINGTON, GUEST ED
  046,

  GUTKIND PETER C W

THE AFRICAN URBAN MILIEU-- A FORCE IN RAPID CHANGE.
CIVILISATIONS 12 1962 PP 167-195
046,

GUTKIND PETER C W
    GUTKIND PETER C W
    AFRICAN URBAN CHIEFS-- AGENTS OF STABILITY OR CHANGE IN
    AFRICAN URBAN LIFE.
    ANTHROPOLOGICA 8 1966 PP 249-268
    046,

    GUTKIND PETER C W
    AFRICAN URBAN LIFE.
    ANTHROPOLOGICA 8 1966 PP 249-268
    046,

    GUTKIND PETER C W
    ACCOMODATION AND CONFLICT IN AN AFRICAN PERI-URBAN AREA.
    ANTHROPOLOGICA 4 1962 PP 163-174
    047,

    GUTKIND PETER C W
    THE ENERGY OF DESPAIR--SOCIAL ORGANIZATION OF THE UNEMPLOYED
    IN TWO AFRICAN CITIES-- LAGOS AND NAIROBI.
    CIVILISATIONS, VOL. XVII, 1967, PP. 186-380
    043,128-05,117-05,

GUTTERIDGE WILLIAM
    GUTTERIDGE WILLIAM
    THE PLACE OF THE ARMED FORCES IN SOCIETY IN AFRICAN STATES.
    RACE 4 NOVEMBER 1962 PP 22-33
    064,

    GUTTERIDGE WILLIAM
    THE NATURE OF NATIONALISM IN BRITISH WEST AFRICA.
    WESTERN POLITICAL QUARTERLY 11 1958 PP 574-582
    055,

    GUTTERIDGE WILLIAM
    THE POLITICAL ROLE OF AFRICAN ARMED FORCES-- THE IMPACT
    OF FOREIGN MILITARY ASSISTANCE.
    AFRICAN AFFAIRS 66 APRIL 1967 PP 93-103
    064,

    GUTTERIDGE WILLIAM
    ARMED FORCES IN NEW STATES.
    LONDON, OXFORD UNIVERSITY PRESS, 1962
    064,

GWASSA G C K
    GWASSA G C K   ILIFFE JOHN   EDS
    RECORDS OF THE MAJI MAJI RISING.
    NAIROBI, EAST AFRICAN PUBLISHING HOUSE, AND EVANSTON,
    NORTHWESTERN UNIVERSITY PRESS, 1967
    034,

H

HAAS ERNST B
    BARBERA MARIO   HAAS ERNST B
    THE OPERATIONALIZATION OF SOME VARIABLES RELATED TO REGIONAL
    INTEGRATION--A RESEARCH NOTE.
    INTERNATIONAL ORGANIZATION, VOL. XXIII, NO. 1, 1969, PP. 150
    160
    078,

    HAAS ERNST B
    FUNCTIONALISM AND THE THEORY OF INTEGRATION.
    IN ERNST B HASS, BEYOND THE NATION-STATE-- FUNCTIONALISM AND
    INTERNATIONAL ORGANIZATION, STANFORD, CALIFORNIA, STANFORD
    UNIVERSITY PRESS, 1964, PP 3-138
    077,

HACHTEN WILLIAM A
    HACHTEN WILLIAM A
    THE PRESS IN A ONE-PARTY STATE--KENYA SINCE
    INDEPENDENCE.
    JOURNALISM QUARTERLY 42 SPRING 1965 PP 262-266
    049,117-03,

HAEFELE E T
    HAEFELE E T   STEINBERG E B
    GOVERNMENT CONTROLS ON TRANSPORT-AN AFRICAN CASE (ZAMBIA)
    WASHINGTON, BROOKINGS INSTITUTE, 1965
    048,142-08,

HAGEN EVERETT E
    HAGEN EVERETT E
    PLANNING FOR ECONOMIC DEVELOPMENT.
    HOMEWOOD, ILLINOIS, IRWIN PRESS, 1963
    072,

    HAGEN EVERETT E
    HOW ECONOMIC GROWTH BEGINS-- A THEORY OF SOCIAL CHANGE
    CHAPTER 4.
    IN JASON L FINKLE AND RICHARD W GABLE, POLITICAL
    DEVELOPMENT AND SOCIAL CHANGE, NEW YORK, JOHN WILEY, 1966
    037,073,

    HAGEN EVERETT E
    THE ECONOMICS OF DEVELOPMENT.
    HOMEWOOD, ILLINOIS, IRWIN PRESS, 1968
    071,073,

    HAGEN EVERETT E
    ON THE THEORY OF SOCIAL CHANGE
    HOMEWOOD, ILLINOIS, DORSEY PRESS, 1962
    037,

HAGGETT PETER
    HAGGETT PETER
    LOCATIONAL ANALYSIS IN HUMAN GEOGRAPHY
    NEW YORK, ST. MARTINS PRESS, 1965

048,

HAILE SELASSIE 1
   HAILE SELASSIE 1
   TOWARDS AFRICAN UNITY.
   JOURNAL OF MODERN AFRICAN STUDIES 1 SEPTEMBER 1963
   PP 281-292
   079,

HAILEY LORD
   HAILEY LORD
   AN AFRICAN SURVEY-- A STUDY OF PROBLEMS ARISING IN AFRICA
   SOUTH OF THE SAHARA.
   LONDON, OXFORD UNIVERSITY PRESS, 1957
   035,

   HAILEY LORD
   NATIVE ADMINISTRATION IN BRITISH AFRICAN TERRITORIES.
   LONDON, HER MAJESTYS STATIONERY OFFICE, 1950-1953 5VOLS
   035,

HAIR P E H
   HAIR P E H
   NOTES ON THE DISCOVERY OF THE VAI SCRIPT WITH A
   BIBLIOGRAPHY.
   SIERRA LEONE LANGUAGE REVIEW 2 1963 PP 36-49
   012,119-01,

HALL RICHARD
   HALL RICHARD
   ZAMBIA.
   LONDON, PALL MALL PRESS, 1967
   142-11,

HALLETT ROBIN
   HALLETT ROBIN   ED
   THE NIGER JOURNAL OF RICHARD AND JOHN LANDER.
   LONDON, ROUTLEDGE AND KEGAN PAUL, 1965
   027,

   HALLETT ROBIN
   AFRICA TO 1875
   ANN ARBOR, UNIVERSITY OF MICHIGAN PRESS, 1969
   036,

   HALLETT ROBIN
   THE EUROPEAN APPROACH TO THE INTERIOR OF AFRICA IN THE
   EIGHTEENTH CENTURY.
   THE JOURNAL OF AFRICAN HISTORY IV 1963 PP 191-206
   027,

HALPERN JACK
   HALPERN JACK
   SOUTH AFRICA'S HOSTAGES-- BASUTOLAND, BECHUANALAND,
   AND SWAZILAND.
   BALTIMORE, PENGUIN, 1965
   032,088,102-07,118-07,135-07,

HALPERN MANFRED
   HALPERN MANFRED

THE POLITICS OF SOCIAL CHANGE IN THE MIDDLE EAST AND NORTH
AFRICA.
PRINCETON, NEW JERSEY, PRINCETON UNIVERSITY PRESS, 1965
038,

HALSTEAD JOHN P
    HALSTEAD JOHN P
    REBIRTH OF A NATION-THE ORIGINS AND RISE OF MOROCCAN
    NATIONALISM,1912-1944
    CAMBRIDGE,MASS.HARVARD UNIVERSITY PRESS 1967
    055,126-06,

HAMA BOUBOU
    HAMA BOUBOU
    KOTIA-NIMA RENCONTRE AVEC L'EUROPE.
    PARIS, PRESENCE AFRICAINE, 1968
    091,127-04,

    HAMA BOUBOU
    ESSAI D'ANALYSE DE L'EDUCATION AFRICAINE.
    PARIS, PRESENCE AFRICAINE, 1968
    091,127-04,

    HAMA BOUBOU
    HISTOIRE DES SONGHAY (HISTORY OF THE SONGHAY).
    PARIS, PRESENCE AFRICAINE, 1968
    022,123-02,

    HAMA BOUBOU
    ENQUETE SUR LES FONDEMENTS ET LA GENESE DE L'UNITE AFRICAINE
    (INQUIRY ON THE FOUNDATIONS AND EARLY DEVELOPMENT OF AFRICAN
    UNITY).
    PARIS PRESENCE AFRICAINE 1966
    079,127-04,

    HAMA BOUBOU
    HISTOIRE TRADITIONNELLE D'UN PEUPLE--LES ZARMA-SONGHAY.
    PARIS, PRESENCE AFRICAINE, 1967
    099,127-04,

    HAMA BOUBOU
    RECHERCHES SUR L'HISTOIRE DES TOUAREG SAHARIENS ET
    SOUDANAIS.
    PARIS, PRESENCE AFRICAINE, 1967
    099,127-04,

    HAMA BOUBOU
    HISTOIRE DU GOBIR ET DE SOKOTO.
    PARIS, PRESENCE AFRICAINE, 1967
    099,127-04,

    HAMA BOUBOU
    HISTOIRE DES SONGHAY.
    PARIS, PRESENCE AFRICAINE, 1968
    099,

    HAMA BOUBOU
    CONTRIBUTION A L'HISTOIRE DES PEUL.
    PARIS, PRESENCE AFRICAINE
    099,127-04,

HAMA BOUBOU
    HAMA BOUBOU
    CONTRIBUTION A LA CONNAISSANCE DE L'HISTOIRE DES PEUL.
    PARIS, PRESENCE AFRICAINE, 1968
    127-01,128-01,

    HAMA BOUBOU   GUILHEM MARCEL
    HISTOIRE DU NIGER.
    PARIS, L'AFRIQUE-LE MONDE, COURS MOYEN, 1965
    127-02,

    HAMA BOUBOU   GUILHEM MARCEL
    NIGER--RECITS HISTORIQUES--COURS ELEMENTAIRE.
    PARIS, LIGEL, 1964
    127-02,

    HAMA BOUBOU
    RECHERCHE SUR L'HISTOIRE DES TOUAREG SAHARIENS ET
    SOUDANAIS.
    PARIS, PRESENCE AFRICAINE, 1967
    127-01,

HAMDAN G
    HAMDAN G
    CAPITALS OF THE NEW AFRICA.
    ECONOMIC GEOGRAPHY 40 JULY 1964 PP 239-253
    045,

HAMIDOUN
    HAMIDOUN MOKTAR OULD
    PRECIS SUR LA MAURITANIE.
    SAINT-LOUIS, IFAN, 1952
    124-11,

HAMILTON CHARLES
    CARMICHAEL STOKELY HAMILTON CHARLES
    BLACK POWER-- THE POLITICS OF LIBERATION IN AMERICA.
    NEW YORK, RANDOM HOUSE 1967
    094,095,

HAMILTON F E IAN
    HAMILTON F E IAN
    REGIONAL ECONOMIC ANALYSIS IN BRITAIN AND THE COMMONWEALTH-
    A BIBLIOGRAPHIC GUIDE
    NEW YORK, SCHOCKEN BOOKS, 1970
    048,069,072,

HAMMOND PETER B
    HAMMOND PETER B
    AFRO-AMERICAN INDIANS AND AFRO-ASIANS--CULTURAL CONTACTS
    BETWEEN AFRICA AND THE PEOPLES OF ASIA AND ABORIGINAL
    AMERICA.
    IN CARTER. GWENDOLEN M. AND ANN PADEN (EDS), EXPANDING
    HORIZONS IN AFRICAN STUDIES, EVANSTON, NORTHWESTERN
    UNIVERSITY PRESS, 1969, PP. 275-290
    030,094,100,

    HAMMOND PETER B
    ECONOMIC CHANGE AND MOSSI ACCULTURATION CHAPTER 13.

IN WILLIAM BASCOM AND MELVILLE HERSKOVITS, CONTINUTY AND
CHANGE IN AFRICAN CULTURES, CHICAGO, UNIVERSITY OF CHICAGO
PRESS, 1958, PP 238-256
038,

HAMMOND PETER B
    HAMMOND PETER B
    YATENGA,TECHNOLOGY IN THE CULTURE OF A WEST AFRICAN KINGDOM
    GLENCOE,ILL,FREE PRESS,1966
    010,141-08,

HAMMOND R J
    HAMMOND R J
    PORTUGAL AND AFRICA, 1815-1910.
    STANFORD, STANFORD UNIVERSITY, OXFORD UNIVERSITY PRESS, 1966
    033, 144-02

HAMMOND-TOOKE W D
    HAMMOND-TOOKE W D
    THE TRANSKEIAN COUNCIL SYSTEM 1895-1955-AN APPRAISAL
    JOURNAL OF AFRICAN HISTORY 9 1968 PP 455-477
    032,

HANCE WILLIAM A
    HANCE WILLIAM A
    AFRICAN ECONOMIC DEVELOPMENT.
    NEW YORK,PRAEGER,1967 (REVISED EDITION)
    048,069,072,

    HANCE WILLIAM A
    THE GEOGRAPHY OF MODERN AFRICA.
    NEW YORK,COLUMBIA UNIVERSITY PRESS,1964
    069,

    HANCE WILLIAM A
    THE RACE BETWEEN POPULATION AND RESOURCES.
    AFRICA REPORT 13 NO 1 JANUARY 1968
    074,

    HANCE WILLIAM A   ED
    SOUTHERN AFRICA AND THE UNITED STATES.
    NEW YORK,COLUMBIA UNIVERSITY PRESS,1968
    083,089,132-09,

    HANCE WILLIAM A   KOTSCHAP V   PETEREC RICHARD J
    SOURCE AREAS OF EXPORT PRODUCTION IN TROPICAL AFRICA.
    GEOGRAPHIC REVIEW 51 OCTOBER 1961 PP 487-499
    069,

    HANCE WILLIAM A
    GABON AND ITS MAIN GATEWAYS-- LIBREVILLE AND PORT GENTIL.
    TIJDSCHRIFT VOOR ECONOMISHE EN SOCIALE GEOGRAFIE AMSTERDAM
    52STE JAARGANG NOVEMBER 1961 PP 286-295
    048,112-08,

    HANCE WILLIAM A   VAN DONGEN I S
    DAR ES SALAAM, THE PORT AND ITS TRIBUTARY.
    ANNALS OF THE ASSOCIATION OF AMERICAN GEOGRAPHERS
    48 DECEMBER 1958 PP 419-435
    048,136-08,

HANCE WILLIAM A
    HANCE WILLIAM A   VAN DONGEN I S
    LOURENCO MARQUES IN DELAGOA BAY.
    ECONOMIC GEOGRAPHY 33 JULY 1957 PP 238-256
    048,144-05,

    HANCE WILLIAM A   VAN DONGEN I S
    THE PORT OF LOBITO AND THE BENGUELA RAILWAY.
    GEOGRAPHICAL REVIEW 46 OCTOBER 1956 PP 460-487
    048,

    HANCE WILLIAM A   VAN DONGEN I S
    MATADI, FOCUS OF BELGIAN AFRICAN TRANSPORT.
    ANNALS OF THE ASSOCIATION OF AMERICAN GEOGRAPHERS 48
    MARCH 1958 PP 41-72
    48 MARCH 1958 PP 41-72
    048,

HANCOCK
    HANCOCK SIR WILLIAM
    SMUTS-THE SANGUINE YEARS,1870-1919 VOLUME 1
    NEW YORK, OXFORD, 1962
    032,089,132-02,

HANNA JUDITH L
    HANNA WILLIAM J   HANNA JUDITH L
    THE PROBLEM OF ETHNICITY AND FACTIONALISM IN AFRICAN
    SURVEY RESEARCH.
    PUBLIC OPINION QUARTERLY 30 SUMMER 1966 PP 290-294
    099,

    HANNA WILLIAM J   HANNA JUDITH L
    THE INTEGRATIVE ROLE OF URBAN AFRICA≠S MIDDLEPLACES AND
    MIDDLEMEN.
    CIVILISATIONS, VOL. XVII, 1967, PP. 12-30
    046,

HANNA WILLIAM J
    HANNA WILLIAM J   ED
    INDEPENDENT BLACK AFRICA.
    CHICAGO, RAND MCNALLY, 1964
    076,097,

    HANNA WILLIAM J
    THE CROSS-CULTURAL STUDY OF LOCAL POLITICS.
    CIVILIZATIONS 16 1966 PP 12-20
    099,

    HANNA WILLIAM J
    IMAGE-MAKING IN FIELD RESEARCH-- SOME TACTICAL AND ETHNIC
    PROBLEMS OF RESEARCH IN TROPICAL AFRICA.
    AMERICAN BEHAVIORAL SCIENTIST 8 JANUARY 1965 PP 15-20
    099,

    HANNA WILLIAM J   HANNA JUDITH L
    THE PROBLEM OF ETHNICITY AND FACTIONALISM IN AFRICAN
    SURVEY RESEARCH.
    PUBLIC OPINION QUARTERLY 30 SUMMER 1966 PP 290-294
    099,

HANNA WILLIAM J
  HANNA WILLIAM J
  STUDENTS.
  IN JAMES S. COLEMAN AND CARL G. ROSBERG (EDS), POLITICAL PAR-
  TIES AND NATIONAL INTEGRATION IN TROPICAL AFRICA, BERKELY,
  UNIVERSITY OF CALIFORNIA PRESS, 1964, PP 413-511
  042,

  HANNA WILLIAM J
  THE STUDY OF URBAN AFRICA-- A REVIEW ESSAY.
  JOURNAL OF LOCAL ADMINISTRATION OVERSEAS 5 APRIL 1966 PP
  124-7
  047,

  HANNA WILLIAM J   HANNA JUDITH L
  THE INTEGRATIVE ROLE OF URBAN AFRICA≠S MIDDLEPLACES AND
  MIDDLEMEN.
  CIVILISATIONS, VOL. XVII, 1967, PP. 12-30
  046,

HANNIGAN A ST A
  HANNIGAN A ST A
  THE IMPOSITION OF WESTERN LAW FORMS UPON PRIMITIVE
  SOCIETIES.
  COMPARATIVE STUDIES IN SOCIETY AND HISTORY 4 NOVEMBER 1961
  PP 1-9
  066,

HANNING HUGH
  HANNING HUGH
  LESSONS FROM THE ARMS RACE.
  AFRICA REPORT, FEB., 1968, P. 42
  065,

HANSBERRY W L
  HANSBERRY W L
  ANCIENT KUSH, OLD AETHEOPIA AND THE BILAD ES SUDAN.
  JOURNAL OF HUMAN RELATIONS 8 1960 PP 357-387
  020,

  HANSBERRY W L
  INDIGENOUS AFRICAN RELIGIONS.
  IN AMSAC, AFRICA SEEN BY AMERICAN NEGROES, PARIS,
  PRESENCE AFRICAINE, 1958, PP 83-100
  013,

HANSEN B
  HANSEN B   MARZOUK G A
  DEVELOPMENT AND ECONOMIC POLICY IN THE UAR
  AMSTERDAM, NORTH HOLLAND PUBLISHING COMPANY, 1965
  073,140-08,

HANSEN CARL L
  BUTZER KARL W   HANSEN CARL L
  DESERT AND RIVER IN NUBIA-GEOMORPHOLOGY AND PREHISTORIC
  ENVIRONMENTS AT THE ASWAN RESERVOIR
  MADISON, UNIVERSITY OF WISCONSIN PRESS, 1968
  017,018,020,

HAPGOOD DAVID
    MILLIKAN MAX F   HAPGOOD DAVID
    NO EAST HARVEST-- THE DILEMMA OF AGRICULTURE IN UNDERDEVEL-
    OPED COUNTRIES.
    BOSTON, LITTLE, BROWN, 1967
    070,

HARBISON F
    HARBISON F
    THE AFRICAN UNIVERSITY AND HUMAN RESOURCES DEVELOPMENT
    JOURNAL OF MODERN AFRICAN STUDIES 3 1965 PP 53-62
    074,075,

HARE NATHAN
    HARE NATHAN,
    A RADICAL PERSPECTIVE ON SOCIAL SCIENCE CURRICULA.
    IN BLACK STUDIES IN THE UNIVERSITY, ARMSTEAD ROBINSON ET AL
    (EDS), NEW HAVEN, YALE UNIVERSITY PRESS, 1969, PP. 104-121
    098,

HARGREAVES JOHN D
    HARGREAVES JOHN D
    AFRICAN COLONIZATION IN THE NINETEENTH CENTURY-- LIBERIA AND
    SIERRA LEONE.
    IN JEFFREY BUTLER (ED), BOSTON UNIVERSITY PAPERS IN AFRICAN
    HISTORY VOLUME I, BOSTON, BOSTON UNIVERSITY PRESS, 1964, PP 55-
    76
    029,119-02,131-02,

    HARGREAVES JOHN D
    PRELUDE TO THE PARTITION OF WEST AFRICA.
    NEW YORK, ST MARTIN'S, 1963
    029,033,

    HARGREAVES JOHN D
    THE ESTABLISHMENT OF THE SIERRA LEONE PROTECTORATE AND THE
    INSURRECTION OF 1898.
    THE CAMBRIDGE HISTORICAL JOURNAL 12 1956 PP 56-80
    029,

HARRIES LYNDON
    HARRIES LYNDON
    SWAHILI POETRY.
    OXFORD, CLARENDON PRESS, 1962
    012,023,

    HARRIES LYNDON
    POEMS FROM KENYA--GNOMIC VERSES IN SWAHILI BY AHMAD NASSIR
    BIN JUMA BHALO.
    MADISON, UNIVERSITY OF WISCONSIN PRESS, 1966
    012,117-01,

    HARRIES LYNDON
    THE FOUNDING OF RABAI-- A SWAHILI CHRONICLE BY MIDANI BIN
    MWIDAD.
    SWAHILI 31 1960 PP 140-149
    023,

    HARRIES LYNDON
    SWAHILI IN MODERN EAST AFRICA.

IN J. A. FISHMAN, CHAS. A. FERGUSON AND JYOTIRINDRA DAS
GUPTA (EDS), LANGUAGE PROBLEMS OF DEVELOPING NATIONS, NEW
117-06,

HARRIS D R
    HODDER B W   HARRIS D R   EDS
    AFRICA IN TRANSITION-GEOGRAPHICAL ESSAYS
    LONDON, METHUEN, 1967
    069,076,

HARRIS MARVIN
    HARRIS MARVIN
    PATTERNS OF RACE IN THE AMERICAS.
    NEW YORK, WALKER, 1964
    030,

HARRIS W T
    HARRIS W T   SAWYER HARRY
    THE SPRINGS OF MENDE BELIEF AND CONDUCT.
    FREETOWN, SIERRA LEONE UNIVERSITY PRESS, 1968
    013,131-01,

HARTWIG GERALD W
    HARTWIG GERALD W
    EAST AFRICAN PLASTIC ART TRADITION-A DISCUSSION OF THE
    LITERATURE
    GENEVE-AFRIQUE 7 1968 PP 31-52
    014,

HARVARD
    FACULTY OF ARTS AND SCIENCES HARVARD   UNIVERSITY
    REPORT OF THE FACULTY COMMITTEE ON AFRICAN AND AFRO-AMERICAN
    STUDIES--JANUARY 20, 1969.
    CAMBRIDGE, HARVARD UNIVERSITY PRESS, 1969
    094,

HARVEY MILTON
    HARVEY MILTON
    IMPLICATIONS OF MIGRATION TO FREETOWN-- A STUDY OF THE
    RELATIONSHIP BETWEEN MIGRANTS, HOUSING AND OCCUPATION.
    CIVILISATIONS, VOL. XVIII, NO. 2, 1968, PP. 247-69
    047,131-05,

    HARVEY MILTON
    SIERRA LEONES LARGEST PROVINCIAL TOWN.
    SIERRA LEONE STUDIES, NO. 18, JAN. 1966
    131-05,

HARVEY WILLIAM B
    HARVEY WILLIAM B
    LAW AND SOCIAL CHANGE IN GHANA.
    PRINCETON, PRINCETON UNIVERSITY PRESS, 1966
    067,114-03,

    HARVEY WILLIAM B
    THE EVOLUTION OF GHANA LAW SINCE INDEPENDENCE.
    LAW AND CONTEMPORARY PROBLEMS 27 1962 PP 581-604
    066,114-06,

HARWITZ

HERSKOVITS MELVILLE J   HARWITZ MITCHELL EDS
ECONOMIC TRANSITION IN AFRICA
EVANSTON, NORTHWESTERN UNIVERSITY PRESS, 1964
010,073,

HASAN YUSUF F
   HASAN YUSUF F
   THE PENETRATION OF ISLAM IN THE EASTERN SUDAN.
   IN LEWIS, ISLAM IN TROPICAL AFRICA, LONDON, OXFORD
   UNIVERSITY PRESS, 1966, PP 144-159
   021,

   HASAN YUSUF F
   THE ARABS AND THE SUDAN FROM THE SEVENTH TO THE EARLY
   SIXTEENTH CENTURY.
   EDINBURGH, THE UNIVERSITY PRESS, 1967
   021,134-02,

HATCH JOHN
   HATCH JOHN
   AFRICA THE REBIRTH OF SELF-RULE.
   LONDON, OXFORD UNIVERSITY PRESS, 1967
   056,

   HATCH JOHN
   THE HISTORY OF BRITISH-AFRICAN RELATIONS.
   NEW YORK, INTERNATIONAL UNIVERSITY BOOKSELLERS, INC., 1969
   082,

HAUSER M A
   HAUSER M A
   L'EMERGENCE DE CADRES DE BASE AFRICAINS DANS L'INDUSTRIE.
   IN LLOYD, THE NEW ELITES OF TROPICAL AFRICA, LONDON, OXFORD
   UNIVERSITY PRESS, 1966, P. 230-243
   071,

HAUSER PHILIP M
   HAUSER PHILIP M
   CULTURAL AND PERSONAL OBSTACLES TO ECONOMIC DEVELOPMENT IN
   THE LESS DEVELOPED AREAS.
   HUMAN ORGANIZATION 18 SUMMER 1959 PP 78-84
   074,

HAYCOCK B G
   HAYCOCK B G
   THE KINGSHIP OF CUSH IN THE SUDAN
   COMPARATIVE STUDIES IN SOCIETY AND HISTORY 7 1965 PP 461-80
   020,

HAYDON E S
   HAYDON E S
   LAW AND JUSTICE IN BUGANDA.
   LONDON, BUTTERWORTHS, 1960
   AFRICAN LAW SERIES NO. 2
   066,139-06,

HAYES CARLTON J
   HAYES CARLTON J
   NATIONALISM-- A RELIGION.
   NEW YORK, MACMILLAN, 1960

054,

HAYFORD CASELY
    HAYFORD CASELY
    GOLD COAST NATIVE INSTITUTIONS.
    LONDON, LONGMANS, 1967
    056,114-01,

HAYNES JANE B
    HAYNES JANE B
    ASA MEETING DISRUPTED BY RACIAL CRISIS
    AFRICA REPORT DECEMBER 1969 PP 16-17
    100,

HAYTER THERESA
    HAYTER THERESA
    FRENCH AID.
    LONDON, OVERSEAS DEVELOPMENT INSTITUTE, 1966
    082,

HAYWOOD AUSTIN
    HAYWOOD AUSTIN   CLARKE F A S
    THE HISTORY OF THE ROYAL WEST AFRICAN FRONTIER FORCE.
    ALDERSHOT, GALE AND POLDEN LIMITED, 1964
    033,

HAZARD JOHN N
    HAZARD JOHN N
    MALI≠S SOCIALISM AND THE SOVIET LEGAL MODEL.
    YALE LAW JOURNAL, LXXVII, 1967, PP. 28-69
    068,123-06,

HAZLEWOOD ARTHUR
    HAZLEWOOD ARTHUR
    PROBLEMS OF INTEGRATION AMONG AFRICAN STATES CHAPTER 1.
    IN AFRICAN INTEGRATION AND DISINTEGRATION, LONDON, OXFORD
    UNIVERSITY PRESS, 1967, PP 3-25 (INTRODUCTION)
    077,

    HAZLEWOOD ARTHUR   ED
    AFRICAN INTEGRATION AND DISINTEGRATION-- POLITICAL AND
    ECONOMIC CASE STUDIES.
    LONDON, OXFORD UNIVERSITY PRESS, 1967
    059,078,

    HAZLEWOOD ARTHUR
    THE ECONOMICS OF FEDERATION AND DISSOLUTION IN CENTRAL
    AFRICA CHAPTER 6.
    IN AFRICAN INTEGRATION AND DISINTEGRATION, LONDON, OXFORD
    UNIVERSITY PRESS, 1967, PP 185-250
    078,

    HAZLEWOOD ARTHUR
    THE COORDINATION OF TRANSPORT POLICY.
    IN COLIN LEYS AND P ROBSON (EDS), FEDERATION IN EAST AFRICA--
    OPPORTUNITIES AND PROBLEMS, NAIROBI, OXFORD UNIVERSITY PRESS,
    1965, PP 111-123
    078,

    HAZLEWOOD ARTHUR

ECONOMIC INTEGRATION IN EAST AFRICA CHAPTER 3.
IN AFRICAN INTEGRATION AND DISINTEGRATION, LONDON, OXFORD
UNIVERSITY PRESS, 1967, PP 69-114
078,

HAZLEWOOD ARTHUR
HAZLEWOOD ARTHUR   HENDERSON P D   EDS
NYASALAND-- THE ECONOMICS OF FEDERATION.
OXFORD, BLACKWELL, 1960
078,122-09,

HEBERT JEAN
TOE SYLVAIN   GUILHEM MARCEL   HEBERT JEAN
HISTOIRE DE LA HAUTE-VOLTA.
PARIS, L'AFRIQUE-LE MONDE, COURS MOYEN, LIGEL, 1964
141-02,

HEILBRONER ROBERT
HEILBRONER ROBERT
THE ENGINEERING OF DEVELOPMENT.
IN LEWIS P FICKETT (ED) PROBLEMS OF THE DEVELOPING NATIONS,
NEW YORK, CROWELL, 1966, PP 53-63
072,

HEINTZEN HARRY
HEINTZEN HARRY
THE ROLE OF ISLAM IN THE ERA OF NATIONALISM.
IN WILLIAM H LEWIS, NEW FORCES IN AFRICA, GEORGETOWN
COLLOQUIUM ON AFRICA PAPERS, WASHINGTON, PUBLIC AFFAIRS
PRESS, 1962, PP 42-50
055,

HELLEINER G K
HELLEINER G K
AGRICULTURAL PLANNING IN EAST AFRICA.
NAIROBI, EAST AFRICAN PUBLISHING HOUSE, 1968
070,

HELLEINER G K
NEW FORMS OF FOREIGN INVESTMENT IN AFRICA.
THE JOURNAL OF MODERN AFRICAN STUDIES, VOL. 6, NO. 1, 1968,
PP. 17-27
073,

HELLEINER G K
E FISCAL ROLE OF THE MARKETING BOARDS IN NIGERIAN
ECONOMIC DEVELOPMENT 1947-61 CHAPTER 23.
IN EDITH WHETHAM AND JEAN CURRIE (EDS.) READINGS IN THE
APPLIED ECONOMICS OF AFRICA, LONDON, CAMBRIDGE UNIVERSITY
PRESS, 2, 1967, PP 70-93
073,128-08,

HELM JUNE ED.
HELM JUNE ED.
ESSAYS ON THE PROBLEM OF TRIBE-- PROCEEDINGS OF THE
ANNUAL SPRING MEETINGS OF THE AMERICAN ETHNOLOGICAL
SOCIETY, SAN FRANCISCO, 1967.
SEATTLE, UNIVERSITY OF WASHINGTON PRESS, 1968
005,

HENDERSON
    HENDERSON WILLIAM O
    STUDIES IN GERMAN COLONIAL HISTORY.
    LONDON, CASS, 1962
    035,

HENDERSON
    HENDERSON WILLIAM O
    GERMAN EAST AFRICA, 1884-1918.
    IN VINCENT HARLOW AND E M CHILVER (EDS) HISTORY OF EAST
    AFRICA VOL II, OXFORD, CLARENDON PRESS, 1965, PP 123-162
    033,

HENDERSON K D D
    HENDERSON K D D
    SUDAN REPUBLIC
    NEW YORK, PRAEGER, 1966
    134-11,

HENDERSON P D
    HAZLEWOOD ARTHUR   HENDERSON P D   EDS
    NYASALAND-- THE ECONOMICS OF FEDERATION.
    OXFORD, BLACKWELL, 1960
    078,122-09,

HENDERSON STEPHEN E
    COOK MERCER   HENDERSON STEPHEN E
    THE MILITANT BLACK WRITER IN AFRICA AND THE UNITED STATES.
    MADISON, UNIVERSITY OF WISCONSIN PRESS, 1969
    090,094,

HENIN R A
    HENIN R A
    THE FUTURE POPULATION SIZE OF KHARTOUM, KHARTOUM NORTH,
    OMDURMAN, AND PORT SUDAN.
    SUDAN NOTES AND RECORDS, 42, 1961
    134-05,

HENNINGS R O
    HENNINGS R O
    SOME TRENDS AND PROBLEMS OF AFRICAN LAND TENURE IN KENYA.
    JOURNAL OF AFRICAN ADMINISTRATION 4 OCTOBER 1952 PP 122-134
    070,117-08,

HENRY PAUL-MARC
    HENRY PAUL-MARC
    PAN-AFRICANISM-- A DREAM COME TRUE.
    IN PHILIP W QUIGG (ED.), AFRICA, NEW YORK, PRAEGER, 1964,
    079,

HEPPLE ALEXANDER
    HEPPLE ALEXANDER
    VERWOERD.
    HARMONDSWORTH, ENGLAND, PENGUIN BOOKS, 1967
    089,132-04,

    HEPPLE ALEXANDER
    SOUTH AFRICA--A POLITICAL AND ECONOMIC HISTORY.
    LONDON, PALL MALL PRESS, 1966
    132-07,

HERD NORMAN
    HERD NORMAN
    1922-THE REVOLT ON THE RAND
    NEW YORK, HUMANITIES PRESS, 1966
    032,

HERSKOVITS
    HERSKOVITS MELVILLE J
    THE HUMAN FACTOR IN CHANGING AFRICA.
    NEW YORK, ALFRED A KNOPF, 1962
    001,038,045,047,

    HERSKOVITS MELVILLE J
    THE BASELINE OF CHANGE.
    IN M J HERSKOVITS, THE HUMAN FACTOR IN CHANGING AFRICA, KNOPF
    NEW YORK, 1962, CHAP 3, 4
    003,

    HERSKOVITS MELVILLE J
    REVIEW OF J C CAROTHERS, THE AFRICAN MIND IN HEALTH AND
    DISEASE.
    MAN 26 1954 PP 388-389
    039,

    HERSKOVITS MELVILLE J
    NATIVE SELF-GOVERNMENT.
    IN PHILIP W QUIGG (ED.), AFRICA, NEW YORK, PRAEGER, 1964,
    PP 103-113
    035,

    HERSKOVITS MELVILLE J
    THE DEVELOPMENT OF AFRICANIST STUDIES IN EUROPE AND
    AMERICA.
    IN LALAGE BOWN AND MICHAEL CROWDER (EDS.), PROCEEDINGS OF
    THE FIRST INTERNATIONAL CONGRESS OF AFRICANISTS, ACCRA,
    1962, LONDON, LONGMANS, 1964
    099,

    HERSKOVITS MELVILLE J
    ON THE PROVENIENCE OF NEW WORLD NEGROES.
    SOCIAL FORCES 12 1933
    030,

    HERSKOVITS MELVILLE J
    THE CONTRIBUTION OF AFROAMERICAN STUDIES TO AFRICANIST
    RESEARCH.
    AMERICAN ANTHROPOLOGIST 50 1948 PP1-10
    030,

    HERSKOVITS MELVILLE J
    BACKGROUND OF AFRICAN ART.
    DENVER, DENVER ART MUSEUM, 1945
    014,

HERSKOVITS
    HERSKOVITS MELVILLE J
    THE MYTH OF THE NEGRO PAST.
    BOSTON, BEACON PRESS, 1962
    030,

    HERSKOVITS MELVILLE J
    THE AHISTORICAL APPROACH TO AFRO-AMERICAN STUDIES-- A
    CRITIQUE.
    AMERICAN ANTHROPOLOGIST 62 1960 PP 559-568
    030,

    HERSKOVITS MELVILLE J
    THE PRESENT STATUS AND NEEDS OF AFROAMERICAN RESEARCH.
    JOURNAL OF NEGRO HISTORY 36 1951 PP 123-147
    030,

    HERSKOVITS MELVILLE J
    PROBLEM METHOD AND THEORY IN AFRO-AMERICAN STUDIES.
    PHYLON 7 1946 PP 337-354
    030,

    HERSKOVITS MELVILLE J
    PEOPLES AND CULTURES OF SUB-SAHARAN AFRICA.
    IN PETER J MCEWAN AND ROBERT B SUTCLIFFE (EDS), MODERN AFRICA,
    NEW YORK, THOMAS CROWELL, 1965, PP 15-25
    003,

    HERSKOVITS MELVILLE J
    THE AMERICAN NEGRO.
    BLOOMINGTON, INDIANA UNIVERSITY PRESS, 1964
    030,

    HERSKOVITS MELVILLE J
    THE NEW WORLD NEGRO--SELECTED PAPERS
    BLOOMINGTON, INDIANA UNIVERSITY PRESS, 1966
    030,

    HERSKOVITS MELVILLE J   HARWITZ MITCHELL EDS
    ECONOMIC TRANSITION IN AFRICA
    EVANSTON, NORTHWESTERN UNIVERSITY PRESS, 1964
    010,073,

    HERSKOVITS MELVILLE J
    REDISCOVERY AND INTEGRATION-- RELIGION AND THE
    ARTS CHAPTER 13.
    IN THE HUMAN FACTOR IN CHANGING AFRICA, NEW YORK, ALFRED
    A KNOPF, 1962, PP 417-450
    051,

    HERSKOVITS MELVILLE J
    DAHOMEY-- AN ANCIENT WEST AFRICAN KINGDOM.
    EVANSTON, NORTHWESTERN UNIVERSITY PRESS, 1967
    013,026,109-02,

    HERSKOVITS MELVILLE J   HERSKOVITS FRANCES S
    DAHOMEAN NARRATIVE-A CROSS CULTURAL ANALYSIS
    EVANSTON, NORTHWESTERN UNIVERSITY PRESS, 1958
    012,109-01,

HERSKOVITS
    HERSKOVITS MELVILLE J
    LA STRUCTURE DES RELIGIONS AFRICAINES (THE STRUCTURE OF
    AFRICAN RELIGIONS).
    IN COLLOQUE SUR LES RELIGIONS, ABIDJAN, APRIL, 1961, PARIS,
    PRESENCE AFRICAINE, 1962, PP 71-80
    013,

    HERSKOVITS MELVILLE J
    THE CULTURE AREAS OF AFRICA.
    AFRICA 3 JAN 1930 PP 59-77
    003,

HERSKOVITS MELVILLE
    BASCOM WILLIAM R   HERSKOVITS MELVILLE J
    CONTINUITY AND CHANGE IN AFRICAN CULTURES.
    CHICAGO, UNIVERSITY OF CHICAGO PRESS, 1962
    038,

    BASCOM WILLIAM R   HERSKOVITS MELVILLE J
    THE PROBLEM OF STABILITY AND CHANGE IN AFRICAN CULTURE
    CHAPTER 1.
    IN CONTINUITY AND CHANGE IN AFRICAN CULTURES, CHICAGO,
    UNIVERSITY OF CHICAGO PRESS, 1962, PP 1-14
    038,

    SEGALL MARSHALL H   CAMPBELL DONALD T   HERSKOVITS MELVILLE
    THE INFLUENCE OF CULTURE ON VISUAL PERCEPTION
    INDIANAPOLIS, BOBBS-MERRILL, 1966
    040,

HESS ROBERT L
    HESS ROBERT L
    THE MAD MULLAH AND NORTHERN SOMALIA.
    JOURNAL OF AFRICAN HISTORY 5 1964 PP 415-433
    034,133-02,

    HESS ROBERT L   LOEWENBERG GERHARD
    THE ETHIOPIAN NO-PARTY STATE--A NOTE ON THE FUNCTIONS OF
    POLITICAL PARTIES IN DEVELOPING STATES.
    JASON L. FINKLE AND RICHARD W. GABLE (EDS), POLITICAL
    DEVELOPMENT AND SOCIAL CHANGE, JOHN WILEY AND SONS, INC.,
    NEW YORK, 1966, PP. 530-535
    061,110-07,

    HESS ROBERT L
    ITALIAN COLONIALISM IN SOMALIA
    CHICAGO, UNIVERSITY OF CHICAGO PRESS, 1966
    035,

HEUSSLER ROBERT
    HEUSSLER ROBERT
    THE BRITISH IN NORTHERN NIGERIA.
    LONDON, OXFORD UNIVERSITY PRESS, 1968
    035,128-02,

HEVI EMMANUEL J
    HEVI EMMANUEL J
    THE DRAGON'S EMBRACE-- THE CHINESE COMMUNISTS AND AFRICA.

NEW YORK PRAEGER 1967
084,098,

HIDAYATULLAH M
    HIDAYATULLAH M
    SOUTH WEST AFRICA CASE
    NEW YORK, ASIA PUBLISHING HOUSE, 1968
    081,146-09,

HIERNAUX J
    HIERNAUX J
    SOME ECOLOGICAL FACTORS EFFECTING HUMAN POPULATIONS
    IN SUB-SAHARAN AFRICA.
    IN F CLARK HOWELL AND FRANCOIS BOURLIERE (EDS.), AFRICAN
    ECOLOGY AND HUMAN EVOLUTION, CHICAGO, ALDINE, 1966,
    PP 534-546
    018,

    HIERNAUX J
    BANTU EXPANSION-THE EVIDENCE FROM PHYSICAL ANTHROPOLOGY
    CONFRONTED WITH LINGUISTIC AND ARCHAEOLOGICAL EVIDENCE
    JOURNAL OF AFRICAN HISTORY 4 1968 PP 505-515
    019,

    HIERNAUX J
    LA DIVERSITE HUMAINE EN AFRIQUE SUBSAHARIENNE
    UNIVERSITE LIBRE DE BRUXELLES,EDITIONS DE L'INSTITUT DE
    SOCIOLOGIE, 1968
    018,

HIERTZLER J R
    HIERTZLER J R
    SEA FLOOR SPREADING
    SCIENTIFIC AMERICAN 219 1968 PP 60-70
    017,

HILL ADELAIDE C
    HILL ADELAIDE C   KILSON MARTIN L   EDS
    APROPOS OF AFRICA--SENTIMENTS OF NEGRO AMERICAN LEADERS ON
    AFRICA FROM THE 1800'S TO THE 1950'S.
    NEW YORK, HUMANITIES PRESS INC., 1969
    094,

    HILL ADELAIDE C
    AFRICAN STUDIES PROGRAMS IN THE UNITED STATES.
    IN AMSAC, AFRICA SEEN BY AMERICAN NEGROES, PARIS,
    PRESENCE AFRICAINE, 1958, PP 361-378
    099,

HILL P
    HILL P
    THREE TYPES OF SOUTHERN GHANAIAN COCOA FARMER.
    IN D BIEBUYCK, ED., AFRICAN AGRARIAN SYSTEMS, LONDON,
    LONDON, OXFORD UNIVERSITY PRESS, 1963, PP 203-233
    070,114-08,

    HILL P
    MIGRANT COCOA FARMERS OF SOUTHERN GHANA.
    CAMBRIDGE,CAMBRIDGE UNIVERSITY PRESS,1963
    070,114-08,

HILL P
   HILL P
   THE MIGRATION OF SOUTHERN GHANAIAN COCOA FARMERS.
   BULLETIN OF THE GHANA GEOGRAPHICAL ASSOCIATION 5 JULY 1960
   PP 9-19
   070,114-08,

HILL RICHARD L
   HILL RICHARD L
   A BIBLIOGRAPHY OF THE ANGLO-EGYPTIAN SUDAN FROM THE
   EARLIEST TIMES TO 1937
   LONDON, OXFORD UNIVERSITY PRESS,1939
   134-12,

HILLIARD F H
   HILLIARD F H
   A SHORT HISTORY OF EDUCATION IN BRITISH WEST AFRICA.
   LONDON, THOMAS NELSON, 1957
   042,

HILLING D
   HILLING D
   THE CHANGING ECONOMY OF GABON--DEVELOPMENTS IN A NEW
   AFRICAN REPUBLIC.
   GEOGRAPHY, 48, 219, APRIL, 1963
   112-08,

HIMMELHEBER HANS
   HIMMELHEBER HANS
   SCULPTORS AND SCULPTURES OF THE DAN.
   IN LALAGE BOWN AND MICHAEL CROWDER (EDS.), PROCEEDINGS OF
   THE FIRST INTERNATIONAL CONGRESS OF AFRICANISTS, ACCRA,
   1962, LONDON , LONGMANS, 1964, PP 243-255
   014,109-01,

   HIMMELHEBER HANS
   LE SYSTEME DE LA RELIGION DES DAN (THE RELIGIOUS SYSTEM OF
   THE DAN).
   IN RENCONTRES INTERNATIONALES DE BOUAKE, LES RELIGIONS
   AFRICAINES TRADITIONNELLES, PARIS, EDITIONS DU SEUIL, 1965,
   PP 75-96
   013,109-01,

   HIMMELHEBER HANS
   NEGERKUNST AND NEGERKUNSTLER (NEGRO ART AND NEGRO ARTISTS).
   BRUNSWICK, KLINCKHARDT AND BIERMANN,1960
   014,

HIRSCHMAN A O
   HIRSCHMAN A O
   THE STRATEGY OF ECONOMIC DEVELOPMENT
   NEW HAVEN, YALE UNIVERSITY PRESS, 1968
   071,073,

HISKETT MERVIN
   HISKETT MERVIN
   KITAB AL-FARQ-- A WORK ON THE HABE KINGDOMS ATTRIBUTED TO
   UTHMAN DAN FODIO.
   BULLETIN OF THE SCHOOL OF ORIENTAL AND AFRICAN STUDIES 23

1960 PP 558-579
024,128-02,

HISKETT MERVIN
HISKETT MERVIN
AN ISLAMIC TRADITION OF REFORM IN THE WESTERN SUDAN
FROM THE SIXTEENTH TO THE EIGHTEENTH CENTURY.
BULLETIN OF THE SCHOOL OF ORIENTAL AND AFRICAN STUDIES 25
1962 PP 577-596
052,

BIVAR A D H   HISKETT MERVIN
THE ARABIC LITERATURE OF NIGERIA TO 1804-- A PROVISIONAL
ACCOUNT.
BULLETIN OF THE SCHOOL OF ORIENTAL AND AFRICAN STUDIES 25
1962 PP 104-148
021,060,128-02,

HISKETT MERVYN
HISKETT MERVYN
NORTHERN NIGERIA
IN KRITZECK AND LEWIS PP 287-300
128-03,

HOARE MIKE
HOARE MIKE
NO PLACE FOR MERCENARIES.
AFRICA REPORT, FEB. 1968, P. 44
065,

HOCHSCHILD ARLIE R
MOORE CLEMENT H   HOCHSCHILD ARLIE R
STUDENT UNIONS IN NORTH AFRICAN POLITICS.
DAEDALUS, WINTER 1968, PP. 21-50
063,138-07,

HODDER B W
HODDER B W   HARRIS D R   EDS
AFRICA IN TRANSITION-GEOGRAPHICAL ESSAYS
LONDON,METHUEN,1967
069,076,

HODDER B W   UKWU U I
MARKETS IN WEST AFRICA
IBADAN UNIVERSITY PRESS,1969
010,

HODDER B W
RURAL PERIODIC DAY MARKETS IN PART OF YORUBALAND, WESTERN
NIGERIA.
INSTITUTE OF BRITISH GEOGRAPHERS, PAPERS AND TRANSACTIONS
29 1961 PP 149-159
010,128-01,

HODGKIN THOMAS
HODGKIN THOMAS
NATIONALISM IN COLONIAL AFRICA.
NEW YORK UNIVERSITY PRESS,1965
055,

HODGKIN THOMAS
AFRICAN POLITICAL PARTIES.
BALTIMORE, PENGUIN, 1961
058,061,

HODGKIN THOMAS
HODGKIN THOMAS
ISLAM AND NATIONAL MOVEMENTS IN WEST AFRICA.
JOURNAL OF AFRICAN HISTORY 3 1962 PP323-327
055,

HODGKIN THOMAS
PROPHETS AND PRIESTS CHAPTER 3.
IN NATIONALISM AND COLONIAL AFRICA, NEW YORK, NEW
YORK UNIVERSITY PRESS, 1965
050,

HODGKIN THOMAS
THE NEW WEST AFRICA STATE SYSTEM.
UNIVERSITY OF TORONTO QUARTERLY 31 OCTOBER 1961 PP 74-82
061,

HODGKIN THOMAS
A NOTE ON WEST AFRICAN POLITICAL PARTIES.
IN WHAT ARE THE PROBLEMS OF PARLIAMENTARY GOVERNMENT IN
WEST AFRICA, THE HANSARD SOCIETY, LONDON, CHISWICK PRESS
1958 PP 51-62
061,

HODGKIN THOMAS
A NOTE ON THE LANGUAGE OF AFRICAN NATIONALISM.
IN WILLIAM J HANNA (ED), INDEPENDENT BLACK AFRICA, CHICAGO,
RAND MCNALLY, 1964, PP 235-252
IN K KIRKWOOD (ED), ST ANTHONY'S PAPERS, 10, SOUTHERN
ILLINOIS UNIVERSITY PRESS, 1961, PP 22-40
055,

HODGKIN THOMAS
WELFARE ACTIVITIES OF AFRICAN POLITICAL PARTIES.
IN PETER J MCEWAN AND ROBERT B SUTCLIFFE (EDS), MODERN AFRICA,
NEW YORK, THOMAS CROWELL, 1965, PP 194-200
061,

HODGKIN THOMAS
THE AFRICAN MIDDLE CLASS
IN WALLERSTEIN, SOCIAL CHANGE-THE COLONIAL SITUATION, NEW YORK,
JOHN WILEY AND SONS, 1966, PP 359-362; AND IN CORONA 8 1956
PP 85-88
044,

HODGKIN THOMAS
THE RELEVANCE OF 'WESTERN' IDEAS FOR NEW AFRICAN STATES--
THE ELITE MASSES MYTH.
IN JR PENNOCK, SELF GOVERNMENT IN MODERNIZING NATIONS,
NEW YORK, PRENTICE-HALL, 1964
058,

HODGKIN THOMAS   MORGENTHAU RUTH SCHACHTER
MALI.
IN COLEMAN, J.S. AND ROSBERG, C.G. (ED), POLITICAL PARTIES

AND NATIONAL INTEGRATION IN TROPICAL AFRICA, LOS ANGELES,
UNIVERSITY OF CALIFORNIA PRESS, 1964
123-06,

HODGKIN THOMAS
    HODGKIN THOMAS
    THE ISLAMIC LITERARY TRADITION IN GHANA.
    IN LEWIS, ISLAM IN TROPICAL AFRICA, LONDON, OXFORD UNIVERSITY
    PRESS, 1966, P. 442-462
    052,114-03,

HOEBEL E ADAMSON
    HOEBEL E ADAMSON
    THREE STUDIES OF AFRICAN LAW.
    STANFORD LAW REVIEW 8 1961 PP 418-442
    066,

HOGBEN S J
    HOGBEN S J   KIRK-GREENE A H M
    THE EMIRATES OF NORTHERN NIGERIA-- A PRELIMINARY SURVEY OF
    HISTORICAL TRADITIONS.
    LONDON, OXFORD UNIVERSITY PRESS, 1966
    024,128-02,

HOLAS B
    HOLAS B
    L'IMAGE DU MONDE BETE (THE BETE IMAGE OF THE WORLD).
    PARIS, PRESSES UNIVERSITAIRE DE FRANCE, NEW YORK,
    INTERNATIONAL UNIVERSITY BOOKSELLERS, 1968
    013,116-01,

    HOLAS B
    LE SEPARATISME RELIGIEUX EN AFRIQUE NOIRE-- L'EXAMPLE
    DE LA COTE D'IVOIRE (RELIGIOUS SEPARATISM IN BLACK AFRICA--
    THE EXAMPLE OF THE IVORY COAST).
    PARIS, PRESSES UNIVERSITAIRES DE FRANCE, 1965
    051,116-03,

    HOLAS B
    CULTURES MATERIELLES DE LA COTE D'IVOIRE (MATERIAL CULTURE
    OF THE IVORY COAST).
    PARIS, PRESSES UNIVERSITAIRE DE FRANCE, 1960
    014,116-01,

HOLDEN E
    HOLDEN E
    BLYDEN OF LIBERIA-AN ACCOUNT OF THE LIFE AND LABOUR OF
    EDWARD WILMOT BLYDEN
    NEW YORK, VANTAGE PRESS, 1966
    029,030,

HOLLEMAN J F
    HOLLEMAN J F
    SHONA CUSTOMARY LAW.
    NEW YORK, HUMANITIES PRESS INC., 1969
    066, 145-01,

    HOLLEMAN J F   ED
    EXPERIMENT IN SWAZILAND
    DURBAN INSTITUTE OF SOCIAL RESEARCH UNIVERSITY OF NATAL 1962

135-08,

HOLLINGSWORTH L W
    HOLLINGSWORTH L W
    THE ASIANS OF EAST AFRICA.
    NEW YORK, ST MARTIN'S, 1960
    088,

HOLMES J
    HOLMES J
    THE IMPACT ON THE COMMONWEALTH OF THE EMERGENCE OF AFRICA.
    INTERNATIONAL ORGANIZATION 16 2 SPRING 1962 PP 291-302
    082,

HOLT PETER M
    HOLT PETER M
    SUDANESE NATIONALISM AND SELF DETERMINATION.
    IN WALTER LAQUEUR, THE MIDDLE EAST IN TRANSITION, NEW YORK,
    PRAEGER, 1958, PP 166-182
    055,134-06,

    HOLT PETER M
    THE MAHDIST STATE IN THE SUDAN -- 1881-1898.
    OXFORD, CLARENDON PRESS, 1958
    034,134-02,

    HOLT PETER M
    A MODERN HISTORY OF THE SUDAN.
    NEW YORK, GROVE PRESS, 1961
    134-02,

HOLT ROBERT T
    HOLT ROBERT T   TURNER JOHN E
    THE POLITICAL BASIS OF ECONOMIC DEVELOPMENT.
    PRINCETON, VAN NOSTRAND, 1966
    074,

HOLY L
    HOLY L
    MASKS AND FIGURES FROM EASTERN AND SOUTHERN AFRICA
    LONDON, HAMLYN, 1967
    014,

HOOKER JAMES R
    HOOKER JAMES R
    BLACK REVOLUTIONARY-- GEORGE PADMORE'S PATH FROM COMMUNISM
    TO PAN-AFRICANISM.
    NEW YORK, PRAEGER, 1967
    094,095,

HOOVER CALVIN B
    HOOVER CALVIN B   ED
    ECONOMIC SYSTEMS OF THE COMMONWEALTH.
    DURHAM, DUKE UNIVERSITY PRESS, 1962
    073,

HOPEN E EDWARD
    HOPEN E EDWARD
    THE PASTORAL FULBE FAMILY IN GWANDU.
    LONDON, OXFORD UNIVERSITY PRESS, 1958

128-01,

HOPKINS KEITH
   HOPKINS KEITH
   CIVIL-MILITARY RELATIONS IN DEVELOPING COUNTRIES.
   BRITISH JOURNAL OF SOCIOLOGY 17 JUNE 1966 PP 165-182
   064,

HOPKINS RAYMOND F
   HOPKINS RAYMOND F
   AGGREGATE DATA AND THE STUDY OF POLITICAL DEVELOPMENT.
   THE JOURNAL OF POLITICS, FEB., 1969, VOL. 31, NO. 1, PP. 71-
   95
   098,

HOPKINSON TOM
   HOPKINSON TOM
   THE PRESS IN AFRICA.
   IN AFRICA-A HANDBOOK TO THE CONTINENT, COLIN LEGUM, NEW YORK
   PRAEGER,1966
   049,

HORNBOSTEL
   VON HORNBOSTEL ERICH
   AFRICAN NEGRO MUSIC
   AFRICA 1 1928 PP 30-62
   015,

HORTON ROBIN
   HORTON ROBIN
   AFRICAN TRADITIONAL THOUGHT AND WESTERN SCIENCE PART 1-FROM
   TRADITION TO SCIENCE, PART 2- THE CLOSED AND OPEN
   PREDICAMENT
   AFRICA 37 1967 PP 50-71 AND 155-187
   013,040,098,

   HORTON ROBIN
   RITUAL MAN IN AFRICA
   AFRICA 34 1964 PP 85-104
   013,

   HORTON ROBIN
   KALABARI SCULPTURE.
   LAGOS,NIGERIA,DEPARTMENT OF ANTIQUITIES,1965
   014,128-01,

   HORTON ROBIN
   GOD,MAN AND THE LAND IN A NORTHERN IBO VILLAGE GROUP
   AFRICA 26 1956 PP 17-28
   013,

   HORTON ROBIN
   THE KALABARI WORLD-VIEW- AN OUTLINE AND INTERPRETATION
   AFRICA 32 1962 PP 197-220
   013,

   HORTON ROBIN
   DESTINY AND THE UNCONSCIOUS IN WEST AFRICA.
   AFRICA 31 1961 PP 110-116
   013,

HORVATH RONALD J
   HORVATH RONALD J
   THE WANDERING CAPITALS OF ETHIOPIA.
   JOURNAL OF AFRICAN HISTORY, X, 2, 1969, PP. 205-219
   045,110-05,

HORWITZ RALPH
   HORWITZ RALPH
   THE POLITICAL ECONOMY OF SOUTH AFRICA.
   NEW YORK, PRAEGER, 1967
   089,132-08,

HORWOOD O P F
   HORWOOD O P F   BURROWS JOHN R
   THE SOUTH AFRICAN ECONOMY CHAPTER 11.
   IN CALVIN B HOOVER, ECONOMIC SYSTEMS OF THE COMMONWEALTH,
   DURHAM, DUKE UNIVERSITY PRESS, 1962, PP 462-500
   089,132-08,

HOSELITZ BERTHOLD
   HOSELITZ BERTHOLD
   SOME REFLECTIONS ON THE SOCIAL AND CULTURAL CONDITIONS OF
   ECONOMIC PRODUCTIVITY.
   CIVILIZATIONS 12 1962 PP 489-498
   074,

   HOSELITZ BERTHOLD
   ECONOMIC GROWTH AND DEVELOPMENT CHAPTER 8.
   IN JASON L FINKLE AND RICHARD W GABLE, POLITICAL
   DEVELOPMENT AND SOCIAL CHANGE, NEW YORK, JOHN WILEY, 1966
   037,073,

HOSKYNS CATHERINE
   HOSKYNS CATHERINE
   THE AFRICAN STATES AND THE UNITED NATIONS, 1958-1964.
   INTERNATIONAL AFFAIRS 40 3 JULY 1964 PP 466-480
   077,081,

   HOSKYNS CATHERINE
   PAN-AFRICANISM AND INTEGRATION CHAPTER 10.
   IN ARTHUR HAZLEWOOD, AFRICAN INTEGRATION AND DISINTEGRATION,
   LONDON, OXFORD UNIVERSITY PRESS, 1967, PP 354-393
   079,

   HOSKYNS CATHERINE
   THE CONGO SINCE INDEPENDENCE.
   LONDON, OXFORD UNIVERSITY PRESS, 1965
   108-07,

   HOSKYNS CATHERINE
   SOURCES FOR A STUDY OF THE CONGO SINCE INDEPENDENCE.
   JOURNAL OF MODERN AFRICAN STUDIES, VOL. 1, NO. 3, 1963
   108-12,

HOTTOT R
   HOTTOT R
   TEKE FETISHES.
   JOURNAL OF THE ROYAL ANTHROPOLOGICAL INSTITUTE 86
   1956 PP 25-36

014,108-01,

HOUGHTON D HOBART
    HOUGHTON D HOBART
    THE SOUTH AFRICAN ECONOMY.
    CAPE TOWN, OXFORD UNIVERSITY PRESS, 1967
    089,132-08,

HOUPHOUET-BOIGNY F
    HOUPHOUET-BOIGNY F
    BLACK AFRICA AND THE FRENCH UNION.
    IN PHILIP W QUIGG (ED.), AFRICA, NEW YORK, PRAEGER, 1964,
    PP 263-271
    077,116-04,

HOUSING
    GHANA MIN OF HOUSING
    ACCRA--A PLAN FOR THE TOWN.
    ACCRA, GOVERNMENT PRINTER, 1958
    114-05,

HOVET THOMAS JR
    HOVET THOMAS JR
    AFRICA IN THE UNITED NATIONS
    EVANSTON, NORTHWESTERN UNIVERSITY PRESS, 1963
    081,

    HOVET THOMAS JR
    AFRICAN POLITICS IN THE UNITED NATIONS.
    IN HERBERT J SPIRO, ED., AFRICA THE PRIMACY OF POLITICS,
    NEW YORK, RANDOM HOUSE, 1966, PP 116-149
    081,

HOWARD C
    HOWARD C
    WEST AFRICAN EXPLORERS
    LONDON, OXFORD UNIVERSITY PRESS, 1951
    027,

HOWARD LAWRENCE C
    HOWARD LAWRENCE C
    THE UNITED STATES AND AFRICA-- TRADE AND INVESTMENT.
    IN AMSAC, AFRICA SEEN BY AMERICAN NEGROES, PARIS,
    PRESENCE AFRICAINE, 1958 , PP 279-302
    083,

HOWE
    HOWE RUSSELL WARREN
    BLACK AFRICA-- AFRICA SOUTH OF THE SAHARA FROM PRE-
    HISTORY TO INDEPENDENCE.
    CHICAGO, WALKER, 1967
    036,076,

HOWE C WALTER
    HOWE C WALTER
    AFRICAN APPROACHES TO THE DEVELOPMENT OF HIGHER EDUCATION
    CHP 7.
    IN DONALD PIPER AND TAYLOR COLE ,EDS. , POST PRIMARY
    EDUCATION AND POLITICAL AND ECONOMIC DEVELOPMENT, DURHAM
    NORTH CAROLINA, DUKE UNIVERSITY PRESS, 1964

042,

HOWE MARVINE
    HOWE MARVINE
    PORTUGAL AT WAR
    AFRICA REPORT NOVEMBER 1969 PP 16-21
    087,

HOWELL F CLARK
    HOWELL F CLARK   BOURLIERE FRANCOIS   EDS
    AFRICAN ECOLOGY AND HUMAN EVOLUTION.
    CHICAGO,ALDINE,1966
    018,019,

    HOWELL F CLARK   CLARK J DESMOND
    ACHEULIAN HUNTER-GATHERERS OF SUB-SAHARAN AFRICA.
    IN F CLARK HOWELL AND FRANCOIS BOURLIERE (EDS.), AFRICAN
    ECOLOGY AND HUMAN EVOLUTION, CHICAGO, ALDINE, 1966,
    PP 458-533
    018,

    HOWELL F CLARK
    EARLY MAN
    NEW YORK, TIME INC, LIFE NATURE LIBRARY, 1965
    018,

HOWELL JOHN
    HOWELL JOHN
    AN ANALYSIS OF KENYAN FOREIGN POLICY.
    THE JOURNAL OF MODERN AFRICAN STUDIES, VOL. 6, NO. 1, 1968,
    PP. 29-48
    082,117-09,

HOWELL P P
    HOWELL P P
    A MANUEL OF NUER LAW.
    LONDON,OXFORD UNIVERSITY PRESS,1954
    066,134-01,

HOYLE B S
    HOYLE B S
    NEW OIL REFINERY CONSTRUCTION IN AFRICA.
    GEOGRAPHY, JOURNAL OF THE GEOGRAPHICAL ASSOCIATION 48
    APRIL 1963 PP 190-194
    069,

    HOYLE B S
    THE ECONOMIC EXPANSION OF JINJA, UGANDA.
    GEOGRAPHICAL REVIEW L111 JULY 1963 PP 377-388
    071,139-08,

HUBERICH CHARLES H
    HUBERICH CHARLES H
    THE POLITICAL AND LEGISLATIVE HISTORY OF LIBERIA.
    NEW YORK, NEW YORK CENTRAL BOOK CO., 1947
    119-07,

HUET MICHEL
    KEITA FODEBA   HUET MICHEL
    LES HOMMES DE LA DANSE.

LAUSANNE, LA GUILDE DE LIVRE, 1954
115-10,

HUGHES A J
   HUGHES A J
   EAST AFRICA-- THE SEARCH FOR UNITY-- KENYA, TANGANYIKA,
   UGANDA AND ZANZIBAR.
   MIDDLESEX HARMONDSWORTH 1963
   077,117-09,136-09,139-09,

HUGHES A J B
   KUPER HILDA   HUGHES A J B   VAN VELSEN J
   THE SHONA AND NDEBELE OF SOUTHERN RHODESIA
   LONDON INTERNATIONAL AFRICAN INSTITUTE 1954
   145-01,

HUGHES LANGSTON
   HUGHES LANGSTON   MELTZER MILTON
   A PICTORIAL HISTORY OF THE NEGRO IN AMERICA.
   NEW YORK, CROWN, 1963
   030,

   HUGHES LANGSTON   ED
   POEMS FROM BLACK AFRICA.
   BLOOMINGTON, INDIANA UNIVERSITY PRESS, 1963
   090,

HUGHES P
   HUGHES P
   THE INTRODUCTION OF LOCAL GOVERNMENT TO BASUTOLAND.
   JOURNAL OF LOCAL ADMIN. OVERSEAS, 2, 3, JULY, 1963
   118-07,

HUGOT PIERRE
   HUGOT PIERRE
   LE TCHAD.
   PARIS, NOUVELLES ÉDITIONS LATINES, 1965
   106-11,

HUMBARACI ARSLAN
   HUMBARACI ARSLAN
   ALGERIA-A REVOLUTION THAT FAILED.
   LONDON, PALL MALL PRESS, 1966
   101-06,

HUNTER GUY
   HUNTER GUY
   THE BEST OF BOTH WORLDS- A CHALLENGE ON DEVELOPMENT POLICIE
   IN AFRICA
   LONDON AND NEW YORK, OXFORD UNIVERSITY PRESS, 1967
   073,075,076,

   HUNTER GUY
   AFRICAN LABOUR AND THE AFRICAN MANAGER CHAPTER 9.
   IN THE NEW SOCIETIES OF TROPICAL AFRICA, LONDON, OXFORD
   UNIVERSITY PRESS, 1962, PP 193-236
   073,

   HUNTER GUY
   FROM THE OLD CULTURE TO THE NEW.

IN PETER J MCEWAN AND ROBERT B SUTCLIFFE (EDS), MODERN AFRICA,
NEW YORK, THOMAS CROWELL, 1965, PP 315-325
038,

HUNTER GUY
HUNTER GUY
EDUCATION FOR A DEVELOPING REGION.A STUDY IN EAST AFRICA
NEW YORK, OXFORD, FOR INSTITUTE OF RACE RELATIONS, LONDON, 1964
074,

HUNTER GUY
THE NEW SOCIETIES OF TROPICAL AFRICA.
LONDON, OXFORD UNIVERSITY PRESS, 1962
053,075,

HUNTER MONICA
HUNTER MONICA
REACTION TO CONQUEST.
LONDON. OXFORD UNIVERSITY PRESS, 1961
032,

HUNTINGFORD G W B
HUNTINGFORD G W B
THE PEOPLING OF THE INTERIOR BY ITS MODERN INHABITANTS
IN ROLAND OLIVER AND GERVASE MATHEW (EDS), HISTORY OF EAST
AFRICA VOLUME ONE.OXFORD, CLARENDON PRESS, 1963, PP 58-93
025,

BECKINGHAM C F   HUNTINGFORD G W B
PRESTER JOHN OF THE INDIES.
LONDON, 1961
027,

HUNTINGFORD G W B
THE NANDI OF KENYA-TRIBAL CONTROL IN A PASTORAL SOCIETY
LONDON, ROUTLEDGE AND KEGAN PAUL, 1953
117-01,

HUNTINGFORD G W B
THE GALLA OF ETHIOPIA-THE KINGDOMS OF KAFA AND JANJERO
LONDON, INTERNATIONAL AFRICAN INSTITUTE, 1956
110-01,

HUNTINGTON SAMUEL
HUNTINGTON SAMUEL
POLITICAL DEVELOPMENT AND POLITICAL DECAY.
WORLD POLITICS 17 APRIL 1965 PP 386-430
062,

HUNTINGTON SAMUEL
THE POLITICAL MODERNIZATION OF TRADITIONAL MONARCHIES.
DAEDALUS 95 SUMMER 1966 PP 763-788
037,

HUNTINGTON SAMUEL
POLITICAL ORDER IN CHANGING SOCIETIES.
NEW HAVEN. CONN, YALE. UNIVERSITY PRESS, 1969
064,

HUNWICK JOHN

HUNWICK JOHN
RELIGION AND STATE IN THE SONGHAY EMPIRE, 1464-1591.
IN LEWIS, ISLAM IN TROPICAL AFRICA, LONDON, OXFORD UNIVERSITY
PRESS, 1966, P. 296-317
022,038,

HUNWICK JOHN
HUNWICK JOHN
RELIGION AND STATE.
IN I.M. LEWIS ISLAM IN TROPICAL AFRICA,LONDON, OXFORD
UNIVERSITY PRESS, 1966
038,

HURLEY PATRICK M
HURLEY PATRICK M
THE CONFIRMATION OF CONTINENTAL DRIFT.
SCIENTIFIC AMERICAN 218 NO. 4 1968 PP 52-68
017,

HURLEY PATRICK M   ET AL
TEST OF CONTINENTAL DRIFT BY COMPARISON OF RADIOMETRIC AGES.
SCIENCE, VOL. 157, NO. 3788, AUGUST 4, 1967
017,

HURST VERNON J
ALLARD G O   HURST VERNON J
BRAZIL-GABON GEOLOGIC LINK SUPPORTS CONTINENTAL DRIFT-NEWLY
DISCOVERED TECTONIC PROVINCE IN BRAZIL MATCHES PROVINCE IN
GABON
SCIENCE 163 1969 PP 528-532
017,

HUSZAR LASZLO
GROVE DAVID   HUSZAR LASZLO
THE TOWNS OF GHANA--THE ROLE OF SERVICE CENTRES IN REGIONAL
PLANNING.
ACCRA, GHANA UNIVERSITIES PRESS, 1964

HUTCHINSON T W
HUTCHINSON T W   ET AL   EDS
AFRICA AND LAW-- DEVELOPING LEGAL SYSTEMS IN AFRICAN
COMMONWEALTH NATIONS.
MADISON,UNIVERSITY OF WISCONSIN,PRESS 1968
067,

HUXLEY ELSPETH
HUXLEY ELSPETH
WHITE MAN'S COUNTRY-- LORD DELAMERE AND THE MAKING OF KENYA.
LONDON,CHATTO AND WINDUS,1953
035,117-02,

PERHAM MARGERY   HUXLEY ELSPETH
RACE AND POLITICS IN KENYA.
LONDON,FABER,1944
035,117-06,

HYDAN GORAN
HYDAN GORAN
MAO AND MWALIMU--THE SOLDIER AND THE TEACHER AS
REVOLUTIONARY

TRANSITION 7 1968 PP 24-30
084,136-04,

HYMES DELL
    HYMES DELL
    LINGUISTIC PROBLEMS IN DEFINING THE CONCEPT OF TRIBE
    IN HELMS (ED), ESSAYS ON THE PROBLEM OF TRIBE,AMERICAN
    ETHNOLOGICAL SOCIETY,1968, PP 23-48
    007,

I

IBN BATTUTA
    IBN BATTUTA
    THE TRAVELS OF IBN BATTUTA.
    TRANS. H A R GIBB. CAMBRIDGE, CAMBRIDGE UNIVERSITY PRESS,
    1962
    022,

IBRAHIM ASMA
    IBRAHIM ASMA   EL NASRI ABDEL R
    SUDAN BIBLIOGRAPHY, 1959-1963.
    SUDAN NOTES AND RECORDS, NO. 46, 1965
    134-12,

IDOWU BOLAJI
    IDOWU BOLAJI
    TOWARDS AN INDIGENOUS CHURCH.
    LONDON, OXFORD UNIVERSITY PRESS, 1965
    050,

IKEJIANI OKECHUKWU
    IKEJIANI OKECHUKWU   ED
    EDUCATION IN NIGERIA.
    NEW YORK, PRAEGER, 1965
    042,128-03,

IKEOTUONYE VINCENT
    IKEOTUONYE VINCENT
    ZIK OF NEW AFRICA.
    LONDON, P R MACMILLAN, 1961
    044,128-04,

IKIME OBARO
    CROWDER MICHAEL   IKIME OBARO   EDS
    WEST AFRICAN CHIEFS--THEIR CHANGING STATUS UNDER COLONIAL
    RULE AND INDEPENDENCE.
    NEW YORK, AFRICANA PUBLISHING CORPORATION, FORTHCOMING
    009,013,035,

    IKIME OBARO
    MERCHANT PRINCE OF THE NIGER DELTA-THE RISE AND FALL OF NANA
    OLOMU,LAST GOVERNOR OF THE BENIN RIVER
    NEW YORK, AFRICAN PUBLISHING CORPORATION, 1969
    034,

ILIFFE JOHN
    ILIFFE JOHN
    TANGANYIKA UNDER GERMAN RULE 1905-1912.
    LONDON, CAMBRIDGE UNIVERSITY PRESS, 1969
    035,136-02,

ILIFFE JOHN
    GWASSA G C K   ILIFFE JOHN   EDS
    RECORDS OF THE MAJI MAJI RISING.
    NAIROBI, EAST AFRICAN PUBLISHING HOUSE; AND EVANSTON,
    NORTHWESTERN UNIVERSITY PRESS, 1967
    034,

    ILIFFE JOHN
    THE ORGANIZATION OF THE MAJI MAJI REBELLION.
    THE JOURNAL OF AFRICAN HISTORY 8 1967 PP 495-512
    034,136-02,

INGHAM KENNETH
    INGHAM KENNETH
    A HISTORY OF EAST AFRICA
    NEW YORK, PRAEGER, 1967
    036,

    INGHAM KENNETH
    TANGANYIKA-- SLUMP AND SHORT-TERM GOVERNORS, 1932-1945.
    IN VINCENT HARLOW AND E M CHILVER (EDS), HISTORY OF EAST
    AFRICA VOL II, OXFORD, CLARENDON PRESS, 1965, PP 594-624
    035,136-02,

    INGHAM KENNETH
    TANGANYIKA-- THE MANDATE AND CAMEROUN, 1919-1931.
    IN VINCENT HARLOW AND E M CHILVER (EDS), HISTORY OF EAST
    AFRICA VOL II, OXFORD, CLARENDON PRESS, 1965, PP 543-593
    035,136-02,

    INGHAM KENNETH
    THE MAKING OF MODERN UGANDA.
    LONDON, ALLEN AND UNWIN, 1958
    139-02,

INSTITUTE OF
    INSTITUTE OF   RACE RELATIONS
    ANGOLA--A SYMPOSIUM--VIEWS OF A REVOLT.
    LONDON, OXFORD UNIVERSITY PRESS, 1962
    087,144-06,

INSTITUTE OF AFRICA
    USSR ACAD SCIENCES   INSTITUTE OF AFRICA
    A HISTORY OF AFRICA 1914-1967
    MOSCOW, NAUKA PUBLISHING HOUSE, CENTRAL DEPARTMENT OF ORIENTAL
    LITERATURE, 1968
    036,

INTER-AFRICAN
    INTER-AFRICAN LABOUR INSTITUTE
    THE HUMAN FACTORS OF PRODUCTIVITY IN AFRICA.
    LONDON, COMMISSION FOR TECHNICAL CO-OPERATION IN AFRICA
    SOUTH OF THE SAHARA, 1952; 2ND EDITION, 1960
    074,

INTER-AFRICAN
    INTER-AFRICAN LABOUR INSTITUTE
    MIGRANT LABOUR IN AFRICA SOUTH OF THE SAHARA
    NEW YORK, INTERNATIONAL PUBLICATIONS SERVICE, 1963
    6TH INTER-AFRICAN LABOUR CONFERENCE ABIDJAN 1961
    SCIENTIFIC COUNCIL FOR AFRICA SOUTH OF THE SAHARA NO. 79
    069,

INTERNATIONAL
    INTERNATIONAL BANK FOR RECONSTRUCTION AND DEVELOPMENT
    WORLD BANK AND IDA ANNUAL REPORT 1966/1967.
    WASHINGTON D C, INTERNATIONAL BANK FOR RECONSTRUCTION AND
    DEVELOPMENT, 1967, P 26
    073,

    INTERNATIONAL COMMISSION OF JURISTS
    AFRICAN CONFERENCE ON THE RULE OF LAW.
    LAGOS, NIGERIA, 1961, INTERNATIONAL COMMISSION OF JURISTS.
    068,

    INTERNATIONAL LABOUR OFFICE
    TRANSITION FROM TRIBAL TO MODERN FORMS OF SOCIAL AND
    ECONOMIC ORGANIZATION.
    GENEVE, INTERNATIONAL LABOR ORGANIZATION, 1952
    038,

    INTERNATIONAL BANK FOR RECONSTRUCTION AND DEVELOPMENT
    THE ECONOMIC DEVELOPMENT OF TANGANYIKA
    BALTIMORE, JOHNS HOPKINS UNIVERSITY PRESS, 1961
    073,136-08,

    INTERNATIONAL BANK FOR RECONSTRUCTION AND DEVELOPMENT
    THE ECONOMIC DEVELOPMENT OF KENYA
    BALTIMORE, JOHNS HOPKINS UNIVERSITY PRESS, 1963
    073,117-08,

    INTERNATIONAL BANK FOR RECONSTRUCTION AND DEVELOPMENT
    THE ECONOMIC DEVELOPMENT OF LIBYA
    BALTIMORE, JOHNS HOPKINS UNIVERSITY PRESS, 1960
    073,120-08,

    INTERNATIONAL BANK FOR RECONSTRUCTION AND DEVELOPMENT
    THE ECONOMIC DEVELOPMENT OF MOROCCO
    BALTIMORE, JOHNS HOPKINS UNIVERSITY PRESS, 1966
    073,126-08,

    INTERNATIONAL BANK FOR RECONSTRUCTION AND DEVELOPMENT
    THE ECONOMIC DEVELOPMENT OF UGANDA
    BALTIMORE, JOHNS HOPKINS UNIVERSITY PRESS, 1962
    073,139-08,

    ROYAL INSTITUTE OF INTERNATIONAL AFFAIRS
    NIGERIA--THE POLITICAL AND ECONOMIC BACKROUND.
    LONDON, OXFORD UNIVERSITY PRESS, 1960
    128-07,

INUTOM
    ASSOCIATION DES ANCIENS ETUDIANTS DE L'INUTOM
    L'EVOLUTION POLITIQUE DU CONGO BELGE ET LES AUTORITES

INDIGENES (POLITICAL EVOLUTION OF THE BELGIAN CONGO AND THE
NATIVE AUTHORITIES).
PROBLEMS DE L'AFRIQUE CENTRALE 13 1959 PP 3-77
035,108-07,

IRELE ABIOLA
    IRELE ABIOLA
    NEGRITUDE OR BLACK CULTURAL NATIONALISM.
    JOURNAL OF MODERN AFRICAN STUDIES 3 OCTOBER 1965 PP 321-348
    054,

    IRELE ABIOLA   ED
    LECTURES AFRICAINES--A PROSE ANTHOLOGY OF AFRICAN WRITING
    IN FRENCH.
    LONDON, INTERNATIONAL UNIVERSITY BOOKSELLERS, INC., 1969
    090,

IRVINE FREDERICK R
    IRVINE FREDERICK R
    WEST AFRICAN AGRICULTURE.
    LONDON AND NEW YORK, INTERNATIONAL UNIVERSITY BOOKSELLERS,
    INC., 1969
    070,

ISICHEI ELIZABETH
    ISICHEI ELIZABETH
    HISTORICAL CHANGE IN AN IBO POLITY ASABA TO 1885.
    IN JOURNAL OF AFRICAN HISTORY VOL 10 1969 P 421
    009,128-01,

ISMAEL TAREQ Y
    ISMAEL TAREQ Y
    RELIGION AND U A R AFRICAN POLICY.
    THE JOURNAL OF MODERN AFRICAN STUIDES, VOL. 6, NO. 1, 1968,
    PP. 49-57
    086,140-09,

ITOTE WARUHIU
    ITOTE WARUHIU
    'MAU MAU' GENERAL.
    KENYA, EAST AFRICAN PUBLISHING HOUSE, 1967
    055,117-06,

IVY JAMES W
    IVY JAMES W
    TRADITIONAL NAACP INTEREST IN AFRICA.
    IN AMSAC, AFRICA SEEN BY AMERICAN NEGROES, PARIS,
    PRESENCE AFRICAINE, 1958, PP 229-246
    094,

J

JACKSON IRENE D
    JACKSON IRENE D
    NEGRITUDE-- A STUDY IN OUTLINE.
    IN ALBERT BERRIAN AND RICHARD LONG (EDS), NEGRITUDE--

ESSAYS AND STUDIES, HAMPTON, VIRGINIA, HAMPTON INSTITUTE
PRESS, 1967, PP 1-7
090,

JACOB PHILIP E
    JACOB PHILIP E   TOSCANO JAMES V
    THE INTEGRATION OF POLITICAL COMMUNITIES.
    PHILADELPHIA LIPPINCOTT 1964
    048,057,

JAHN JANHEINZ
    JAHN JANHEINZ
    MUNTU
    NEW YORK, GROVE PRESS, 1961
    030,

JAHODA GUSTAV
    JAHODA GUSTAV
    IMMINENT JUSTICE AMONG WEST AFRICAN CHILDREN.
    JOURNAL OF SOCIAL PSYCHOLOGY 47 1958 PP 241-248
    040,

    JAHODA GUSTAV
    LOVE MARRIAGE AND SOCIAL CHANGE.
    AFRICA 24 1959 PP 177-190
    041,

    JAHODA GUSTAV
    NATIONALITY PREFERENCES AND NATIONAL STEREOTYPES IN GHANA
    INDEPENDENCE.
    JOURNAL OF SOCIAL PSYCHOLOGY 50 1959 PP 165-174
    088,114-06,

    JAHODA GUSTAV
    'BOYS' IMAGES OF MARRIAGE PARTNERS AND GIRLS' SELF IMAGES
    IN GHANA.
    SOCIOLOGUS 8 1958 PP 155-169
    040,114-03,

    JAHODA GUSTAV
    WHITE MAN-- A STUDY OF THE ATTITUDE OF AFRICANS TO EUROPEANS
    IN GHANA DURING INDEPENDENCE.
    LONDON, OXFORD UNIVERSITY PRESS, 1961
    041,088,114-06,

    JAHODA GUSTAV
    SOCIAL ASPIRATIONS, MAGIC AND WITCHCRAFT IN GHANA - A SOCIAL
    PSYCHOLOGICAL INTERPRETATION.
    IN LLOYD, THE NEW ELITES OF TROPICAL AFRICA, LONDON, OXFORD
    UNIVERSITY PRESS, 1966, P. 199-215
    041,114-04,

    JAHODA GUSTAV
    ASSESSMENT OF ABSTRACT BEHAVIOR IN A NON-WESTERN CULTURE.
    JOURNAL OF ABNORMAL AND SOCIAL PSYCHOLOGY 53 1956 PP 237-243
    040,

JAIN SHARAD C
    JAIN SHARAD C
    AGRICULTURAL DEVELOPMENT OF AFRICAN NATIONS.

BOMBAY, INTERNATIONAL UNIVERSITY BOOKSELLERS,INC., 1968
070,

JAMES
TAYLOR JAMES C   1
THE POLITICAL DEVELOPMENT OF TANGANYIKA.
LONDON, OXFORD UNIVERSITY PRESS AND STANFORD, STANFORD
UNIVERSITY PRESS, 1963
136-07,

JAMES C L R
JAMES C L R
A HISTORY OF PAN-AFRICAN REVOLT
WASHINGTON, D. C., DRUM AND SPEAR PRESS, 1969
077,079,

JAMES KIRKUP
LAYE CAMARA   TRANSLATED BY   JAMES KIRKUP
THE AFRICAN CHILD.
LONDON, COLLINS LTD, 1965
090,115-10,

JANOWITZ MORRIS
BETTELHEIM BRUNO   JANOWITZ MORRIS
ETHNIC TOLERANCE-- A FUNCTION OF SOCIAL AND PERSONAL
CONTROL.
THE AMERICAN JOURNAL OF SOCIOLOGY 55 SEPTEMBER 1949
PP 137-145 (BOBBS-MERRILL REPRINT 24)
088,

JANOWITZ MORRIS
CHANGING PATTERNS OF ORGANIZATIONAL AUTHORITY--
THE MILITARY ESTABLISHMENT.
ADMINISTRATIVE SCIENCE QUARTERLY 3 MARCH 1959
064,

JANOWITZ MORRIS
THE MILITARY IN THE POLITICAL DEVELOPMENT OF NEW NATIONS.
CHICAGO,UNIVERSITY OF CHICAGO PRESS,1964,TABLES 1 AND 2
P 52
064,

JANOWITZ MORRIS
MILITARY ELITES AND THE STUDY OF WAR.
JOURNAL OF CONFLICT RESOLUTION 1 MARCH 1957 PP 9-18
(BOBBS-MERRILL REPRINT 134)
064,

JARRETT H R
JARRETT H R
THE PORT AND TOWN OF FREETOWN.
GEOGRAPHY, 40, 2, 1955
131-05,

JARVIS STEVEN
JARVIS STEVEN
NIGERIA AND BIAFRA.
AFRICA TODAY 14 DECEMBER 1967 PP 16-18
065,128-06,

JEANPIERRE W A
 JEANPIERRE W A
 AFRICAN NEGRITUDE-- BLACK AMERICAN SOUL.
 AFRICA TODAY 14 DECEMBER 1967 PP 10-11
 094,

JERNUDD BJORN
 JERNUDD BJORN
 LINGUISTIC INTEGRATION AND NATIONAL DEVELOPMENT--A CASE
 STUDY OF THE JEBEL MARRA AREA, SUDAN.
 IN JOSHUA A. FISHMAN, CHARLES A. FERGUSON AND JYOTIRINDRA
 DAS GUPTA (EDS), LANGUAGE PROBLEMS OF DEVELOPING NATIONS, NEW
 YORK, JOHN WILEY AND SONS,INC., 1968
 134-06,

JEUNE AFRIQUE
 JEUNE AFRIQUE   EDS
 AFRICA 1969-70 A REFERENCE VOLUME ON THE AFRICAN CONTINENT
 NEW YORK, AFRICANA PUBLISHING CORPORATION, 1969
 002,

JOHNSON
 ASIEGBU JOHNSON U J
 SLAVERY AND THE POLITICS OF LIBERATION 1787-1861.
 NEW YORK, AFRICANA PUBLISHING CORPORATION, 1970
 030,

JOHNSON ALBERT F
 JOHNSON ALBERT F
 A BIBLIOGRAPHY OF GHANA, 1930-1961.
 LONDON, LONGMANS, 1964
 114-12,

JOHNSON CAROL A
 JOHNSON CAROL A
 POLITICAL AND REGIONAL GROUPINGS IN AFRICA.
 IN WILLIAM J HANNA (ED), INDEPENDENT BLACK AFRICA, CHICAGO,
 RAND MCNALLY, 1964, PP 555-587
 077,

JOHNSON G WESLEY
 JOHNSON G WESLEY
 BIBLIOGRAPHIC ESSAYS--SENEGAL.
 AFRICANA NEWSLETTER, VOL. 2, NO. 1, 1964
 130-12,

JOHNSON SAMUEL
 JOHNSON SAMUEL
 THE HISTORY OF THE YORUBAS FROM THE EARLIEST TIMES TO THE
 BEGINNING OF THE BRITISH PROTECTORATE.
 LONDON, ROUTLEDGE AND KEGAN PAUL, 1966 (O JOHNSON, ED.)
 026,128-02,

JOHNSON WILLARD R
 JOHNSON WILLARD R
 CAMEROON FEDERATION--POLITICAL INTEGRATION IN A FRAGMENTARY
 SOCIETY.
 PRINCETON, NEW JERSEY, PRINCETON UNIVERSITY PRESS, 1970
 057,059,104-06,

JOHNSON WILLARD R
AFRICAN-SPEAKING AFRICA--LESSONS FROM THE CAMEROON.
AFRICAN FORUM V. I NO 2 FALL 1965
104-03,

JOHNSON WILLARD R
   JOHNSON WILLARD R
   THE CAMEROON FEDERATION--POLITICAL UNION BETWEEN ENGLISH
   AND FRENCH SPEAKING AFRICA.
   IN WILLIAM LEWIS,ED,FRENCH SPEAKING AFRICA,NEW YORK,WALKER,
   1965
   104-07,

JOHNSTON H A S
   JOHNSTON H A S
   THE FULANI EMPIRE OF SOKOTO.
   LONDON, OXFORD UNIVERSITY PRESS, 1967
   024,052,128-02,

   JOHNSTON H A S   ED
   A SELECTION OF HAUSA STORIES.
   LONDON, OXFORD UNIVERSITY PRESS, 1966
   012,128-01,

JOLLY RICHARD
   JOLLY RICHARD   ED
   EDUCATION IN AFRICA--RESEARCH AND ACTION.
   KENYA, EAST AFRICAN PUBLISHING HOUSE, 1969
   042,

JONES LEROI
   JONES LEROI
   BLACK MAGIC POETRY, 1961-1967
   NEW YORK, BOBBS-MERRILL, 1969
   094,

   JONES LEROI
   FOUR BLACK REVOLUTIONARY PLAYS
   NEW YORK, BOBBS-MERRILL, 1969
   094,

JONES A D
   JONES A D
   SOCIAL NETWORKS OF FARMERS AMONG THE PLATEAU TONGA OF ZAMBIA
   IN LLOYD, THE NEW ELITES OF TROPICAL AFRICA, LONDON, OXFORD
   UNIVERSITY PRESS, 1966, P. 272-285
   142-03,

JONES A M
   JONES A M
   STUDIES IN AFRICAN MUSIC-2 VOLS
   LONDON AND NEW YORK, OXFORD UNIVERSITY PRESS, 1959
   015,

   JONES A M
   AFRICAN RHYTHM
   AFRICA 24 1954 PP 26-47
   015,

   JONES A M

AFRICA AND INDONESIA
LEIDEN BRILL 1964
019,

JONES A M
   JONES A M
   INDONESIA AND AFRICA-- THE XYLOPHONE AS CULTURE-INDICATOR.·
   JOURNAL OF THE ROYAL ANTHROPOLOGICAL INSTITUTE 89 1959
   PP 155-168
   019,

JONES ARNOLD
   JONES ARNOLD   MARTIN HUGH   MONROE ELIZABETH
   A HISTORY OF ETHIOPIA
   OXFORD,CLARENDON PRESS,1955,SECOND EDITION
   110-02,

JONES ELDRED
   FYFE CHRISTOPHER   JONES ELDRED   EDS
   FREETOWN--A SYMPOSIUM.
   FREETOWN, SIERRA LEONE UNIVERSITY PRESS, 1968
   045,131-05,

JONES GWILYN I
   JONES GWILYN I
   THE TRADING STATES OF THE OIL RIVERS-- A STUDY OF
   POLITICAL DEVELOPMENT IN EASTERN NIGERIA.
   LONDON,OXFORD UNIVERSITY PRESS,1963
   027,035,128-02,

   JONES GWILYN I
   THE TRADING STATES OF THE OIL RIVERS-- A STUDY OF POLITICAL
   DEVELOPMENT IN EASTERN NIGERIA.
   LONDON, OXFORD UNIVERSITY PRESS, 1963
   035,

JONES H M
   FAIR T J D   MURDOCK G   JONES H M
   DEVELOPMENT IN SWAZILAND-A REGIONAL ANALYSIS
   JOHANNESBURG,WITWATERSRAND UNIVERSITY PRESS,1969
   135-08,

JONES RUTH
   PEARSON J D   JONES RUTH   EDS
   THE BIBLIOGRAPHY OF AFRICA-PROCEEDINGS AND PAPERS OF THE
   INTERNATIONAL CONFERENCE OF AFRICAN BIBLIOGRAPHY NAIROBI
   DECEMBER 1967
   NEW YORK,AFRICANA PUBLISHING CORPORATION,1969
   099,

JONES W O
   JONES W O
   FOOD AND AFRICULTURAL ECONOMICS OF TROPICAL AFRICA-- A
   SUMMARY VIEW.
   FOOD RESEARCH INSTITUTE BULLETIN(STANFORD UNIVERSITY) VOL.II
   NO. 1 1961
   010,

JONES WILLIAM O
   JONES WILLIAM O

INCREASING AGRICULTURAL PRODUCTIVITY IN TROPICAL AFRICA.
IN E F JOULSON (ED), ECONOMIC DEVELOPMENT IN AFRICA, OXFORD,
BLACKWELL, 1965
070,

JONES WILLIAM O
  JONES WILLIAM O
  MANIOC IN AFRICA.
  STANFORD UNIVERSITY, FOOD RESEARCH INSTITUTE, NO 2, 1951
  069,

JONES-QUARTEY K A
  JONES-QUARTEY K A
  PRESS AND NATIONALISM IN GHANA.
  UNITED ASIA 9 FEBRUARY 1957 PP 55-60
  055,114-06,

JORDAN A C
  JORDAN A C
  TALE, TELLER, AND AUDIENCE IN AFRICAN SPOKEN NARRATIVE.
  IN PROCEEDINGS OF THE CONFERENCE ON AFRICAN LANGUAGES AND
  LITERATURES, NORTHWESTERN UNIVERSITY, 1966, UNITED STATES
  OFFICE OF EDUCATION, NO. OE-6-14-018, PP 33-43
  012,

JORDAN ROBERT S
  JORDAN ROBERT S
  GOVERNMENT AND POWER IN WEST AFRICA
  NEW YORK, AFRICANA PUBLISHING CORPORATION, 1969
  076,

JORDAN WINTHROP
  JORDAN WINTHROP
  WHITE OVER BLACK AMERICAN ATTITUDES TOWARD THE NEGRO
  1550-1812.
  CHAPEL HILL, UNIVERSITY OF NORTH CAROLINA PRESS, 1967
  030,

JOSEPHINE
  ABIODUN JOSEPHINE O
  CENTRAL PLACE STUDY IN ABEOKUTA PROVINCE, SOUTHWEST NIGERIA
  JOURNAL OF REGIONAL SCIENCE 8 1968
  047,048,128-05,

JULIENNE ROLAND
  JULIENNE ROLAND
  THE EXPERIENCE OF INTEGRATION IN FRENCH-SPEAKING AFRICA
  CHAPTER 9.
  IN ARTHUR HAZLEWOOD, AFRICAN INTEGRATION AND DISINTEGRATION,
  LONDON, OXFORD UNIVERSITY PRESS, 1967, PP 339-353
  078,

JULY ROBERT W
  JULY ROBERT W
  THE ORIGINS OF MODERN AFRICAN THOUGHT--ITS DEVELOPMENT IN
  WEST AFRICA DURING THE NINETEENTH AND TWENTIETH CENTURIES.
  NEW YORK, PRAEGER, 1967
  091,

  JULY ROBERT W

NINETEENTH-CENTURY NEGRITUDE-- EDWARD W BLYDEN.
JOURNAL OF AFRICAN HISTORY 5 1964 PP 87-98
095,

JUMEAUX R
JUMEAUX R
ESSAI D'ANALYSE DU NATIONALISME MALGACHE ESSAY ANALYZING
MALAGASY NATIONALISM.
L'AFRIQUE ET L'ASIE 40 1957 PP 31-42
055,121-06,

JUNKER HERMANN
JUNKER HERMANN
THE FIRST APPEARANCE OF THE NEGROES IN HISTORY.
THE JOURNAL OF EGYPTIAN ARCHAEOLOGY 7 1921 PP 121-132
018,

JURISTS
INTERNATIONAL COMMISSION OF JURISTS
AFRICAN CONFERENCE ON THE RULE OF LAW.
LAGOS NIGERIA 1961,INTERNATIONAL COMMISSION OF JURISTS.
068,

K

KABERRY PHYLLIS M
FORDE C DARYLL   KABERRY PHYLLIS M   EDS
WEST AFRICAN KINGDOMS IN THE NINETEENTH CENTURY.
LONDON,OXFORD UNIVERSITY PRESS,1967
026,036,

KABERRY PHYLLIS M
PRIMITIVE STATES.
BRITISH JOURNAL OF SOCIOLOGY 8 SEPTEMBER 1957 PP 224-234
009,

CHILVER E M   KABERRY PHYLLIS M
FROM TRIBUTE TO TAX IN A TIKAR CHIEFDOM.
AFRICA (LONDON) 30 1960 PP 1-19
038,

KABERRY PHYLLIS M
SOME PROBLEMS OF LAND TENURE IN NSAW, SOUTHERN CAMEROONS.
JOURNAL OF AFRICAN ADMINISTRATION 12 JANUARY 1960 PP 21-28
070,104-08,

KABORE
KABORE GOMKOUDOUGOU
ORGANISATION POLITIQUE TRADITIONNELLE ET EVOLUTION POLITIQUE
DES MOSSI DE OUGADOUGOU.
PARIS, CENTRE VOLTAIQUE DE LA RECHERCHE SCIENTIFIQUE, 1966
141-01,

KAGAME ALEXIS
KAGAME ALEXIS
AVEC UN TROUBADOUR DU RWANDA.

BRUXELLES, ED. UNIVERSITAIRES, 1949
129-10,

KAGAME ALEXIS
KAGAME ALEXIS
BREF APERCU SUR LA POESIE DYNASTIQUE DU RWANDA.
BRUXELLES, ED. UNIVERSITARIES, 1950
129-10,

KAGAME ALEXIS
HISTOIRE DU RWANDA.
LEVERVILLE (CONGO), BIBLIOTHEQUE DE L'ETIOLE, 1958
129-02,

KAGAME ALEXIS
LE CODE DES INSTITUTIONS POLITIQUES DU RWANDA PRECOLONIAL.
BRUXELLES, INSTITUT ROYAL COLONIAL BELGE, 1952
129-01,

KAGAME ALEXIS
LA DIVINE PASTORALE--TRADUCTION FRANCAISE PAR L AUTEUR DE LA
PREMIER VEILLE D'UNE EPOPEE ECRITE EN LANGUE RWANDAISE.
BRUXELLES, ED. DU MARAIS, 1952
129-10,

KAGAME ALEXIS
L'HISTOIRE DES ARMEES BOVINES DANS L'ANCIEN RWANDA.
BRUXELLES, ACADEMIE ROYALE DES SCIENCES D OUTRE-MER, 1961
129-02,

KAGAME ALEXIS
LA LANGUE DU RWANDA ET BURUNDI EXPLIQUEE AUX AUTOCHTONES.
KABGAYI (RWANDA), ED. MORALES, 1960
129-01,

KAGAME ALEXIS
LES MILICES DU RWANDA PRECOLONIAL.
BRUXELLES, ACADEMIE ROYALE DES SCIENCES D OUTRE-MER, 1963
129-02,

KAGAME ALEXIS
LA NAISSANCE DE L'UNIVERS (DUEXIEME VEILLE DE LA DIVINE
PASTORALE).
BRUXELLES, ED. DU MARAIS, 1955
129-10,

KAGAME ALEXIS
LA NOTION DE GENERATION APPLIQUEE A LA GENEALOGIE DYNASTIQUE
ET A L'HISTOIRE DU RWANDA DES XEME ET XLEME SIECLES A NOS
JOURS.
BRUXELLES, ACADEMIE ROYALE DES SCIENCES COLONIALES, 1959
129-02,

KAGAME ALEXIS
LES ORGANISATIONS SOCIO-FAMILIALES DE L'ANCIEN RWANDA.
BRUXELLES, ACADEMIE ROYALE DES SCIENCES COLONIALES, 1954
129-01,

KAGAME ALEXIS
LA PHILOSOPHIE BANTU-RWANDAISE DE L'ETRE.

BRUXELLES, ACADEMIE ROYALE DES SCIENCES COLONIALES, 1956
129-01,

KAGAME ALEXIS
KAGAME ALEXIS
LA POESIE DYNASTIQUE AU RWANDA.
BRUXELLES, INSTITUT ROYAL COLONIAL BEIGE, 1951
129-10,

KALDOR N
KALDOR N
INTERNATIONAL TRADE AND ECONOMIC DEVELOPMENT
JOURNAL OF MODERN AFRICAN STUDIES 2 1964 PP 491-511
073,080,

KALONJI ALBERT D
KALONJI ALBERT D
MA LUTTE AU KASAI, POUR LA VERITE AU SERVICE DE LA JUSTICE.
BARCELONE, C.A.G.S.A., 1964
108-04,

KAMANZI THOMAS
COUPEZ A   KAMANZI THOMAS   EDS
LITTERATURE COURTOISE DU RWANDA (COURT LITERATURE OF
RWANDA).
LONDON AND NEW YORK, INTERNATIONAL UNIVERSITY BOOKSELLERS,
INC., 1969
012,129-01,

KAMANZI THOMAS   COUPEZ A
POEMES DYNASTIQUES RWANDA.
BUJUMBURA, UNIVERSITE OFFICILLE, 1965
129-10,

KAMANZI THOMAS   NKONGORI LAURENT
PROVERBES DU RWANDA.
TERVUREN, MUSEE ROYAL DU CONGO BELGE, 1957
129-01,

KAMARCK ANDREW M
KAMARCK ANDREW M
ECONOMICS AND ECONOMIC DEVELOPMENT.
IN ROBERT A LYSTAD (ED), THE AFRICAN WORLD, NEW YORK,
PRAEGER, 1966, PP 221-244
099,100,

KAMARCK ANDREW M
THE ECONOMICS OF AFRICAN DEVELOPMENT.
NEW YORK, PRAEGER, 1967
069,070,071,073,

KAMARCK ANDREW M
THE AFRICAN ECONOMY AND INTERNATIONAL TRADE CHAPTER 5.
IN THE UNITED STATES AND AFRICA, BACKGROUND PAPERS OF THE
13TH ASSEMBLY, THE AMERICAN ASSEMBLY, COLUMBIA UNIVERSITY,
1958, PP 117-138
082,083,

KANE
KANE CHEIKH HAMIDOU

AMBIGOUS ADVENTURE.
NEW YORK, MACMILLAN CO., 1969
090,130-10,

KANE
KANE CHEIKH HAMIDOU
ECRIVAIN SENEGALAIS--TEXTES COMMENTES PAR ROGER MERCIER ET
M ET S BATTESTINI.
PARIS, F. NATHAN, 1964
130-10,

KANYA-FORSTNER A S
KANYA-FORSTNER A S
THE CONQUEST OF WESTERN SUDAN--A STUDY IN FRENCH MILITARY
IMPERIALISM.
CAMBRIDGE, UNIVERSITY PRESS, 1969
033,

NEWBURY COLIN W   KANYA-FORSTNER A S
FRENCH POLICY AND THE ORIGINS OF THE SCRAMBLE FOR WEST
AFRICA.
JOURNAL OF AFRICAN HISTORY, X,2, 1969, PP. 253-276
033,

KANZA THOMAS
KANZA THOMAS
LE CONGO A LA VEILLE DE SON INDEPENDANCE OU PROPOS D' UN
CONGOLAIS DESILLUSIONNE.
BRUXELLES, LES AMIS DE PRESENCE AFRICAINE, 1959
108-04,

KANZA THOMAS
PROPOS D UN CONGOLAIS NAIF--DISCOURS SUR LA VOCATION
COLONIALE DANS L'AFRIQUE DE DEMAIN.
BRUXELLES, LES AMIS DE PRESENCE AFRICAINE, 1959, P. 43
108-04,

KAPIL RAVI L
KAPIL RAVI L
ON THE CONFLICT POTENTIAL OF INHERITED BOUNDARIES IN AFRICA.
WORLD POLITICS 18 JULY 1966 PP 656-673
059,

KAREFA-SMART JOHN
KAREFA-SMART JOHN
AFRICA AND THE UNITED NATIONS.
INTERNATIONAL ORGANIZATION 19 3 SUMMER 1965 PP 764-773
081,131-04,

KARENGA
KARENGA MAULANA RON
THE BLACK COMMUNITY AND THE UNIVERSITY--A COMMUNITY
ORGANIZER'S PERSPECTIVE.
IN BLACK STUDIES IN THE UNIVERSITY, ARMSTEAD ROBINSON ET AL
(EDS), NEW HAVEN, YALE UNIVERSITY PRESS, 1969, PP. 37-54
094,

KARIS THOMAS
CARTER GWENDOLEN M   KARIS THOMAS   STULTZ NEWELL M
SOUTH AFRICA S TRANSKEI-- THE POLITICS OF DOMESTIC COLONIAL-

IALISM.
EVANSTON, NORTHWESTERN UNIVERSITY PRESS, 1967 (LONDON,
HEINEMANN EDUCATIONAL BOOKS)
089,132-06,

KARIS THOMAS
    KARIS THOMAS
    THE TREASON TRIAL IN SOUTH AFRICA- A GUIDE TO THE MICROFILM
    RECORD OF THE TRIAL
    STANFORD, HOOVER INSTITUTION PRESS, 1968
    089,

KARIUKI JOSIAH M
    KARIUKI JOSIAH M
    MAU MAU DETAINEE--THE ACCOUNT BY A KENYA AFRICAN OF HIS
    EXPERIENCES IN DETENTION CAMPS 1953-1960.
    LONDON, OXFORD UNIVERSITY PRESS, 1963
    055,117-06,

KARP MARK
    LORIMER FRANK   KARP MARK   EDS
    POPULATION IN AFRICA.
    BOSTON, BOSTON UNIVERSITY PRESS, 1960
    069,074,

    KARP MARK
    THE ECONOMICS OF TRUSTEESHIP IN SOMALIA.
    BOSTON, BOSTON UNIVERSITY PRESS, 1960
    133-08,

KASAVUBU JOSEPH
    KASAVUBU JOSEPH
    MESSAGE ADRESSE A LA NATION PAR LE PRESIDENT DE LA
    REPUBLIQUE.
    LEOPOLDVILLE, IMP. DE LA REPUBLIQUE DU CONGO, 1962
    108-04,

KATZ ELIHU
    KATZ ELIHU
    THE TWO-STEP FLOW OF COMMUNICATION.
    PUBLIC OPINION QUARTERLY 21 SPRING 1957 PP 61-78
    048,

KAUNDA KENNETH
    KAUNDA KENNETH
    CRISIS IN SOUTHERN AFRICA.
    AFRICAN FORUM 2 3 1967 PP 11-16
    087,142-04,

    KAUNDA KENNETH
    SOME PERSONAL REFLECTIONS CHAPTER 2.
    IN AFRICA'S FREEDOM, NEW YORK, BARNES AND NOBLE, 1964,
    PP 24-37
    044,142-04,

    KAUNDA KENNETH
    ZAMBIA SHALL BE FREE.
    NEW YORK, PRAEGER, 1963 (LONDON, HEINEMANN EDUCATIONAL BOOKS)
    060,142-04,

KAUNDA KENNETH
ZAMBIA--INDEPENDENCE AND BEYOND.
LONDON, NELSON, 1966
054,060,142-04,

KAY DAVID A
KAY DAVID A
THE IMPACT OF AFRICAN STATES IN THE UNITED NATIONS.
INTERNATIONAL ORGANIZATION, VOL. XXIII, NO. 1, WINTER, 1969,
PP. 20-47
081,

KAY GEORGE
KAY GEORGE
A SOCIAL GEOGRAPHY OF ZAMBIA.
LONDON, UNIVERSITY OF LONDON PRESS, 1967
142-03,

KAYIBANDA GREGOIRE
KAYIBANDA GREGOIRE
DISCOURS PRONONCES PAR SON EXCELLENCE MR GR KAYIBANDA,
PRESIDENT DE LA REPUBLIQUE RWANDAISE EN DIVERSES
CIRCONSTANCES.
KIGALI, SERVICE DE L'INFORMATION, 1963

KAYIBANDA GREGOIRE
LE PRESIDENT KAYIBANDA VOUS PARLE.
KIGALI, SERVICE DE L'INFORMATION, 1964
129-04,

KEATLEY PATRICK
KEATLEY PATRICK
THE POLITICS OF PARTNERSHIP.
BALTIMORE,PENGUIN,1963
088,145-11,

KEAY ELLIOT A
KEAY ELLIOT A   RICHARDSON SAMUEL
THE NATIVE AND CUSTOMARY COURTS OF NIGERIA.
LONDON,SWEET AND MAXWELL,1966
066,128-03,

KEDOURIE ELIE
KEDOURIE ELIE
NATIONALISM.
LONDON,HUTCHISON,1960
054,

KEIL CHARLES
KEIL CHARLES
URBAN BLUES.
CHICAGO,UNIVERSITY OF CHICAGO PRESS,1966
030,

KEITA FODEBA
KEITA FODEBA
POEMES AFRICAINS.
PARIS, SEGHERS, 1958
090,115-10,

KEITA FODEBA
   KEITA FODEBA   HUET MICHEL
   LES HOMMES DE LA DANSE.
   LAUSANNE, LA GUILDE DE LIVRE, 1954
   115-10,

KEMP JULIET D
   KEMP JULIET D
   A LIST OF BOOKS, ARTICLES AND GOVERNMENT PUBLICATIONS ON THE
   ECONOMY OF NIGERIA 1960-62.
   IBADAN, NIGERIAN INSTITUTE OF SOCIAL AND ECONOMIC RESEARCH,
   128-12,

KENT R K
   KENT R K
   MADAGASCAR AND AFRICA 1-THE PROBLEM OF THE BARA 2-THE
   SAKALAVA,MAROSERANA,DADY AND TROMBA BEFORE 1700, 3-THE
   ANTEIMORO
   JOURNAL OF AFRICAN HISTORY 9 1968 PP 387-408,527-546 AND
   10 1969 PP 45-65
   121-02,

KENWORTHY JOAN M
   KENWORTHY JOAN M
   RAINFALL AND WATER RESOURCES OF EAST AFRICA.
   LONDON GEOGRAPHERS AND THE TROPICS 1964 PP 111-136
   069,

KENYATTA JOMO
   KENYATTA JOMO
   SUFFERING WITHOUT BITTERNESS--THE FOUNDING OF THE KENYA
   NATION.
   KENYA, EAST AFRICAN PUBLISHING HOUSE, 1968
   044,117-04,

   KENYATTA JOMO
   FACING MT KENYA--THE RURAL LIFE OF THE KIKUYU.
   NEW YORK, VINTAGE BOOKS, 1964
   010,060,098,117-01,

   KENYATTA JOMO
   AFRICAN SOCIALISM AND AFRICAN UNITY.
   AFRICAN FORUM I 1 1965 PP 23-37
   079,117-04,

   KENYATTA JOMO
   HARAMBEE--THE PRIME MINISTER OF KENYA'S SPEECHES 1963-1964.
   LONDON,OXFORD UNIVERSITY PRESS,1964
   060,117-04,

KEREKES TIBOR
   KEREKES TIBOR
   THE ARAB MIDDLE EAST AND MUSLIM AFRICA.
   NEW YORK,PRAEGER,1961
   086,

KERSHAW GREET
   MIDDLETON JOHN   KERSHAW GREET
   THE KIKUYU AND KAMBA OF KENYA
   LONDON,INTERNATIONAL AFRICAN INSTITUTE,1956

117-01,

KHADDURI MAJID
  KHADDURI MAJID
  NATURE AND SOURCES OF LAW PP 9-18.
  IN THE LAW OF WAR AND PEACE IN ISLAM, BALTIMORE, JOHNS
  HOPKINS PRESS, 1955
  066,

  KHADDURI MAJID
  MODERN LIBYA-- A STUDY IN POLITICAL DEVELOPMENT.
  BALTIMORE, JOHNS HOPKINS UNIVERSITY PRESS, 1963
  120-07,

KHALIL SIDI
  KHALIL SIDI   TRANS BY   RUXTON
  MALIKI LAW
  LONDON, LUZAC AND CO., 1916
  021,066,

KHIDER MAHASSIN
  KHIDER MAHASSIN   SIMPSON MORAG C
  CO-OPERATIVES AND AGRICULTURAL DEVELOPMENT IN THE SUDAN.
  THE JOURNAL OF MODERN AFRICAN STUDIES, VOL. 6, NO. 4, 1968,
  PP. 509-18
  070,134-08,

KI-ZERBO JOSEPH
  KI-ZERBO JOSEPH
  THE NEGRO-AFRICAN PERSONALITY.
  IN ALBERT BERRIAN AND RICHARD LONG (EDS), NEGRITUDE--
  ESSAYS AND STUDIES, HAMPTON, VIRGINIA, HAMPTON INSTITUTE
  PRESS, 1967, PP 56-62
  039,

  KI-ZERBO JOSEPH
  AFRICAN PERSONALITY AND THE NEW AFRICAN SOCIETY.
  IN WILLIAM J HANNA (ED), INDEPENDENT BLACK AFRICA, CHICAGO,
  RAND MCNALLY, 1964, PP 46-59
  039,

  KI-ZERBO JOSEPH
  LE MONDE AFRICAIN NOIR--HISTOIRE ET CIVILISATION.
  ABIDJAN/PARIS, CEDA/HATIER, 1963
  099,141-02,

KIANO J GIKONYO
  KIANO J GIKONYO
  THE EMERGENT EAST AFRICAN FEDERATION CHAPTER 3.
  IN DAVID P CURRIE, FEDERALISM AND THE NEW NATIONS OF AFRICA
  CHICAGO, UNIVERSITY OF CHICAGO PRESS, 1964, PP 61-74
  078,

  KIANO J GIKONYO
  FROM PAFMECA TO PAFMECSA--AND BEYOND.
  AFRICAN FORUM I 2 1965 PP 36-49
  079,

KILBY PETER
  KILBY PETER

AFRICAN LABOUR PRODUCTIVITY RECONSIDERED.
ECONOMIC JOURNAL 17 JUNE 1961 1961 PP 273-291
071,

KILBY PETER
  KILBY PETER
  COMPETITION IN THE NIGERIAN BREAD INDUSTRY CHAPTER 15.
  IN EDITH WHETHAM AND JEAN CURRIE (EDS.), READINGS IN THE
  APPLIED ECONOMICS OF AFRICA, LONDON, CAMBRIDGE UNIVERSITY
  PRESS, 1, 1967, PP 164-172
  071,128-08,

  KILBY PETER
  INDUSTRIALIZATION IN AN OPEN ECONOMY--NIGERIA 1945-1966.
  CAMBRIDGE, UNIVERSITY PRESS, 1969
  044,071,128-08,

KILLAM G D
  KILLAM G D
  THE NOVELS OF CHINUA ACHEBE.
  NEW YORK, AFRICANA PUBLISHING CORPORATION, 1970
  090,128-10,

KILLICK A J
  KILLICK A J
  INFLATION AND GROWTH CHAPTER 32.
  IN EDITH WHETHAM AND JEAN CURRIE (EDS), READINGS IN THE
  APPLIED ECONOMICS OF AFRICA, LONDON, CAMBRIDGE UNIVERSITY
  PRESS, 2, 1967, PP 215-228
  073,

KILNER PETER
  KILNER PETER
  MILITARY GOVERNMENT IN SUDAN--THE PAST THREE YEARS.
  WORLD TODAY 18 JUNE 1962 PP 259-268
  064,134-06,

  KILNER PETER
  A YEAR OF ARMY RULE IN THE SUDAN.
  THE WORLD TODAY 15 1959 PP 430-441
  064,134-06,

KILSON
  EMERSON RUPERT   KILSON MARTIN L   EDS
  THE POLITICAL AWAKENING OF AFRICA.
  ENGLEWOOD CLIFFS, NJ, PRENTICE-HALL, 1965
  060,

KILSON MARTIN L
  KILSON MARTIN L
  THE INTELLECTUAL VALIDITY OF STUDYING THE BLACK EXPERIENCE.
  IN BLACK STUDIES IN THE UNIVERSITY, ARMSTEAD ROBINSON ET AL
  (EDS), NEW HAVEN, YALE UNIVERSITY PRESS, 1969, PP. 13-36
  094,

  EMERSON RUPERT   KILSON MARTIN L
  IDEAS AND CONTEXT OF AFRICAN NATIONALISM CHP 2.
  IN THE POLITICAL AWAKENING OF AFRICA, ENGELWOOD CLIFFS,
  NEW JERSEY, PRENTICE-HALL, 1965
  054,

KILSON MARTIN L
  EMERSON RUPERT   KILSON MARTIN L
  INTER-AFRICAN PROBLEMS AND PAN-AFRICANISM CHP 4.
  IN THE POLITICAL AWAKENING OF AFRICA, ENGLEWOOD CLIFFS,
  NEW JERSEY, PRENTICE HALL, 1965
  079,

  EMERSON RUPERT   KILSON MARTIN L
  THE AMERICAN DILEMMA IN A CHANGING WORLD-- THE RISE OF
  AFRICA AND THE NEGRO AMERICAN.
  IN THE NEGRO AMERICAN,TALCOTT PARSONS AND KENNETH CLARK,EDS,
  BOSTON,HOUGHTON MIFFLIN,1966,PP 626-655
  094,

  KILSON MARTIN L
  NATIONALISM AND SOCIAL CLASSES IN BRITISH WEST AFRICA.
  JOURNAL OF POLITICS 20 MAY 1958 PP 368-387
  055,

  KILSON MARTIN L
  AFRICAN POLITICAL CHANGE AND THE MODERNIZATION PROCESS.
  JOURNAL OF MODERN AFRICAN STUDIES 1 DECEMBER 1963
  PP 425-440
  037,

  KILSON MARTIN L
  SOCIAL FORCES IN WEST AFRICAN POLITICAL DEVELOPMENT.
  JOURNAL OF HUMAN RELATIONS 8 1960 PP 576-598
  063,

  KILSON MARTIN L
  THE MASSES, THE ELITE, AND POST-COLONIAL POLITICS IN
  AFRICA CHAPTER 14.
  IN JASON L FINKLE AND RICHARD W GABLE, POLITICAL
  DEVELOPMENT AND SOCIAL CHANGE, NEW YORK, JOHN WILEY, 1966
  058,

  KILSON MARTIN L
  THE RISE OF NATIONALIST ORGANIZATIONS AND PARTIES IN
  BRITISH WEST AFRICA.
  IN AFRICA SEEN BY AMERICAN NEGROES, NEW YORK, AMERICAN
  SOCIETY OF AFRICAN CULTURE, 1963, PP 35-69
  055,

  KILSON MARTIN L
  AUTHORITARIANISM AND SINGLE PARTY TENDENCIES IN TROPICAL
  AFRICA.
  WORLD POLITICS JANUARY 1963 PP 262-294
  061,

  KILSON MARTIN L
  LAND AND POLITICS IN KENYA-- AN ANALYSIS OF AFRICAN
  POLITICS IN A PLURAL SOCIETY.
  WESTERN POLITICAL QUARTERLY 10 SEPTEMBER 1957 PP 559-581
  055,117-06,

  KILSON MARTIN L
  BEHIND THE MAU MAU REBELLION.
  DISSENT 3 SUMMER 1956 PP 264-275

055,117-06,

KILSON MARTIN L
    KILSON MARTIN L
    THE ANALYSIS OF AFRICAN NATIONALISM.
    WORLD POLITICS APRIL 1958 PP 484-497
    054,

    KILSON MARTIN L
    POLITICAL CHANGE IN A WEST AFRICAN STATE--A STUDY OF THE
    MODERNIZATION PROCESS IN SIERRA LEONE.
    CAMBRIDGE, HARVARD UNIVERSITY PRESS, 1966

    KILSON MARTIN L
    SIERRA LEONE.
    IN COLEMAN, J.S. AND ROSBERG, C.G. (EDS), POLITICAL PARTIES
    AND NATIONAL INTEGRATION IN TROPICAL AFRICA, LOS ANGELES,
    UNIVERSITY OF CALIFORNIA PRESS, 1964
    131-06,

KILSON MARTIN L   ED
    HILL ADELAIDE C   KILSON MARTIN L   EDS
    APROPOS OF AFRICA--SENTIMENTS OF NEGRO AMERICAN LEADERS ON
    AFRICA FROM THE 1800'S TO THE 1950'S.
    NEW YORK, HUMANITIES PRESS INC., 1969
    094,

KIMAMBO ISARIA N
    KIMAMBO ISARIA N
    A POLITICAL HISTORY OF THE PARE KINGDOM
    NAIROBI, EAST AFRICAN PUBLISHING HOUSE, 1969
    023,136-02,

    KIMAMBO ISARIA N
    HISTORICAL RESEARCH IN MAINLAND TANZANIA.
    IN CARTER, GWENDOLEN M. AND ANN PADEN (EDS), EXPANDING
    HORIZONS IN AFRICAN STUDIES, EVANSTON, NORTHWESTERN
    UNIVERSITY PRESS, 1969, PP. 75-90
    100,136-02,

    KIMAMBO ISARIA N   TEMU A J   EDS
    A HISTORY OF TANZANIA
    NAIROBI, EAST AFRICAN PUBLISHING HOUSE, 1969
    136-02,

KIMBLE DAVID A
    KIMBLE DAVID A
    A POLITICAL HISTORY OF GHANA-- THE RISE OF GOLD COAST
    NATIONALISM 1850-1958.
    OXFORD, CLARENDON PRESS, 1963
    055,114-06,

KIMBLE GEORGE
    KIMBLE GEORGE
    TROPICAL AFRICA.
    NEW YORK, TWENTIETH CENTURY FUND, 1960, TWO VOLUMES (CONDENSED
    VERSION, NEW YORK, DOUBLEDAY ANCHOR, 1962)
    069,

    KIMBLE GEORGE

EDUCATIONAL PROBLEMS IN SUB-SAHARAN AFRICA.
IN PETER J MCEWAN AND ROBERT B SUTCLIFFE (EDS), MODERN AFRICA,
NEW YORK, THOMAS CROWELL, 1965, PP 354-365
042,

KIMBLE GEORGE
  KIMBLE GEORGE
  SOME PROBLEMS OF SOCIAL CHANGE.
  IN PETER J MCEWAN AND ROBERT B SUTCLIFFE (EDS), MODERN AFRICA,
  NEW YORK, THOMAS CROWELL, 1965, PP 305-314
  038,

KIMBLE HELEN
  KIMBLE HELEN
  ON THE TEACHING OF ECONOMICS IN AFRICA
  JOURNAL OF MODERN AFRICAN STUDIES 7 1969 PP 713-741
  073,

KING COLIN
  TEMPELS RES PLACID   TRANSLATED BY   KING COLIN
  LA PHILOSOPHIE BANTOUE (BANTU PHILOSOPHY).
  PARIS, PRESENCE AFRICAINE, 2ND ED., 1961
  013,

KING KENNETH J
  KING KENNETH J
  AFRICA AND THE SOUTHERN STATES OF THE USA NOTES ON J H
  OLDHAM AND AMERICAN NEGRO EDUCATION FOR AFRICANS.
  IN JOURNAL OF AFRICAN HISTORY VOL 10 1969 P 659-677
  030,

KING LESTER C
  KING LESTER C
  MORPHOLOGY OF THE EARTH.
  NEW YORK, HAFNER, 1967, 2ND. ED.
  017,

KING MARTIN LUTHER
  KING MARTIN LUTHER
  WHERE DO WE GO FROM HERE-CHAOS OR COMMUNITY
  BOSTON, BEACON PRESS, 1968
  095,

KING MAURICE
  KING MAURICE
  A MEDICAL LABORATORY FOR DEVELOPING COUNTRIES.
  KAMPALA, INTERNATIONAL UNIVERSITY BOOKSELLERS, INC., 1968
  075,

KIRK-GREENE A H M
  HOGBEN S J   KIRK-GREENE A H M
  THE EMIRATES OF NORTHERN NIGERIA-- A PRELIMINARY SURVEY OF
  HISTORICAL TRADITIONS.
  LONDON, OXFORD UNIVERSITY PRESS, 1966
  024,128-02,

  KIRK-GREENE A H M   ED
  LUGARD AND THE AMALGAMATION OF NIGERIA--A DOCUMENTARY
  RECORD.
  LONDON, FRANK CASS AND COMPANY LIMITED, 1968

035,128-02,

KIRK-GREENE A H M
    KIRK-GREENE A H M
    BUREAUCRATIC CADRES IN A TRADITIONAL MILIEU.
    IN JAMES S COLEMAN (ED), EDUCATION AND POLITICAL DEVELOPMENT,
    PRINCETON, NEW JERSEY, PRINCETON UNIVERSITY PRESS, 1965
    PP 372-407
    062,

    KIRK-GREENE A H M
    THE PRINCIPLES OF NATIVE ADMINISTRATION IN NIGERIA--
    SELECTED DOCUMENTS 1900-1947.
    LONDON, OXFORD UNIVERSITY PRESS, 1965
    035,128-02,

    KIRK-GREENE A H M.
    HAUSA BA DABO BANE--A COLLECTION OF 500 PROVERBS.
    IBADAN, OXFORD UNIVERSITY PRESS, 1966
    012,128-01,

KIRKMAN JAMES S
    KIRKMAN JAMES S
    THE ARAB CITY OF GEDI-- EXCAVATIONS AT THE GREAT MOSQUE
    ARCHITECTURE AND FINDS.
    LONDON, OXFORD UNIVERSITY PRESS, 1954
    092,117-02,

    KIRKMAN JAMES S
    MEN AND MONUMENTS ON THE EAST AFRICAN COAST.
    LONDON, BUTTERWORTH PRESS, 1964
    023,

    KIRKMAN JAMES S
    GEDI, THE PALACE.
    THE HAGUE, MOUTON, 1963
    092,117-05,

KIRKWOOD KENNETH
    KIRKWOOD KENNETH
    BRITAIN AND AFRICA.
    BALTIMORE, JOHNS HOPKINS PRESS, 1965
    082,
    075,

KISHNER I
    MUNSTERBERGER W   KISHNER I
    HASARDS OF CULTURE CLASH-- A REPORT ON THE HISTORY AND
    DYNAMICS OF A PSYCHOTIC EPISODE IN A WEST AFRICAN EXCHANGE
    STUDENT.
    IN W MUNSTERBERGER AND S AXERAD,   EDS, THE PSYCHO-
    ANALYTIC STUDY OF SOCIETY 4 NEW YORK INTERNATIONAL
    UNIVERSITIES PRESS, PP 99-123
    041,

KITCHEN HELEN
    KITCHEN HELEN
    THE ARMIES OF AFRICA, PART 2.
    IN A HANDBOOK OF AFRICAN AFFAIRS, NEW, PRAEGER, 1964,
    PP 188-239

064,

KITCHEN HELEN
    KITCHEN HELEN
    THE PRESS IN AFRICA.
    WASHINGTON, RUTH SLOAN ASS., 1956
    049,

    KITCHEN HELEN   ED
    THE EDUCATED AFRICAN-- A COUNTRY BY COUNTRY SURVEY OF EDU-
    CATIONAL DEVELOPMENT IN AFRICA.
    NEW YORK, PRAEGER, 1962
    042,

KIWANUKA M S
    KIWANUKA M S
    THE EMPIRE OF BUNYORO KITARA
    CANADIAN JOURNAL OF AFRICAN STUDIES 2 1968 PP 27-48
    025,

KJERSMEIER CARL
    KJERSMEIER CARL
    CENTRES DE STYLE DE LA SCULPTURE NEGRE AFRICAINE
    (STYLE CENTERS OF NEGRO AFRICAN SCULPTURE)
    PARIS, A MORANCE, 1935-8; AND NEW YORK, HACKER, 1967
    014,

KLEIN HERBERT S
    KLEIN HERBERT S
    THE TRADE IN AFRICAN SLAVES TO RIO DE JANEIRO 1795-1811
    ESTIMATES OF MORTALITY AND PATTERNS OF VOYAGES.
    IN JOURNAL OF AFRICAN HISTORY VOL 10 1969 P 533
    028,

KLEIN MARTIN A
    KLEIN MARTIN A
    ISLAM AND IMPERIALISM IN SENEGAL-- SINE-SALOUM, 1847-1941.
    STANFORD, CALIFORNIA, STANFORD UNIVERSITY PRESS, 1967
    034,130-02,

KLEIN N
    LEVINE ROBERT A   KLEIN N   OWEN C
    FATHER-CHILD RELATIONSHIPS AND CHANGING LIFE-STYLES IN
    IBADAN, NIGERIA.
    IN HORACE MINER (ED), THE CITY IN MODERN AFRICA, NEW YORK,
    PRAEGER, 1967
    040,128-03,

KLINEBERG OTTO
    KLINEBERG OTTO   ZAVALLONI MARISA
    NATIONALISM AND TRIBALISM AMONG AFRICAN STUDENTS.
    NEW YORK, HUMANITIES PRESS INC., 1969
    096,

KLINGELHOFER E L
    KLINGELHOFER E L
    A BIBLIOGRAPHY OF PSYCHOLOGICAL RESEARCH AND WRITINGS ON
    AFRICA
    UPPSALA, SCANDANAVIAN INSTITUTE OF AFRICAN STUDIES, 1967
    040,

KLINGHOFFER
  KLINGHOFFER ARTHUR J
  THE SOVIET VIEW OF AFRICAN SOCIALISM
  AFRICAN AFFAIRS 67 1968 PP 197-208
  084,

  KLINGHOFFER ARTHUR J
  WHY THE SOVIETS CHOSE SIDES IN THE NIGERIAN WAR.
  AFRICA REPORT, FEBRUARY, 1968, P. 48
  065,084,128-06,

KLOMAN ERASMUS H
  KLOMAN ERASMUS H
  AFRICAN UNIFICATION MOVEMENTS.
  IN NORMAN J PADELFORD AND RUPERT EMERSON (EDS), AFRICA AND
  WORLD ORDER, NEW YORK, PRAEGER, 1963, PP 119-135
  079,

KNAPEN M TH
  KNAPEN M TH
  SOME RESULTS OF AN ENQUIRY INTO THE INFLUENCE OF CHILD-
  TRAINING ON THE DEVELOPMENT OF PERSONALITY IN A BACINGO
  SOCIETY (BELGIAN CONGO).
  JOURNAL OF SOCIAL PSYCHOLOGY 47 1958 PP 223-229
  040,108-03,

KNAPPERT JAN
  KNAPPERT JAN
  LANGUAGE PROBLEMS OF THE NEW NATIONS OF AFRICA.
  AFRICA QUARTERLY, JULY-SEPT., 1965, VOL. V, NO. 2
  011,

KNIGHT M M
  KNIGHT M M
  FRENCH COLONIAL POLICY-- THE DECLINE OF ASSOCIATION.
  JOURNAL OF MODERN HISTORY 5 1933 PP 208-224
  035,

KOBBEN A J F
  KOBBEN A J F
  LAND AS AN OBJECT OF GAIN IN A NON-LITERATE SOCIETY--
  LAND TENURE AMONG THE BETE AND DIDA (IVORY COAST).
  IN D BIEBUYCK (ED.), AFRICAN AGRARIAN SYSTEMS, LONDON,
  OXFORD UNIVERSITY PRESS, 1963, PP 245-266
  010,070,116-01,

KOHN HANS
  KOHN HANS
  THE IDEA OF NATIONALISM.
  NEW YORK, MACMILLAN, 1961
  054,

  KOHN HANS
  RACIALISM CHAPTER 9.
  IN POLITICAL IDEOLOGIES OF THE TWENTIETH CENTURY, NEW YORK,
  HARPER, 1966, 3RD EDITION REV
  088,

KOINAGE MBIYU

KOINAGE MBIYU
THE PEOPLE OF KENYA SPEAK FOR THEMSELVES.
DETROIT, KENYA PUBLICATION FUND, 1955
055,117-06,

KOMAROVSKY MIRRA
KOMAROVSKY MIRRA
THE VOLUNTARY ASSOCIATIONS OF URBAN DWELLERS.
AMERICAN SOCIOLOGICAL REVIEW 11 DECEMBER 1946 PP 686-698
(BOBBS-MERRILL REPRINT 151)
046,

KOPF DAVID
KOPF DAVID   VON DER MUHLL G
POLITICAL SOCIALIZATION IN KENYA AND TANZANIA.
JOURNAL OF MODERN AFRICAN STUDIES 5 MAY 1967 PP 13-51
043,117-03,136-03,

KOPYTOFF IGOR
KOPYTOFF IGOR
CLASSIFICATION OF RELIGIOUS MOVEMENTS-ANALYTICAL AND
SYNTHETIC
IN SYMPOSIUM ON NEW APPROACHES TO THE STUDY OF RELIGION,
PROCEEDINGS OF THE 1964 ANNUAL SPRING MEETING OF THE
AMERICAN ETHNOLOGICAL SOCIETY,SEATTLE 1964 PP 77-90
051,

KOPYTOFF IGOR
EXTENSION OF CONFLICT AS A METHOD OF CONFLICT RESOLUTION
AMONG THE SUKU OF THE CONGO.
JOURNAL OF CONFLICT RESOLUTION 5 MARCH 1961, PP 61-69
057,108-01,

KOTSCHAP V
HANCE WILLIAM A   KOTSCHAP V   PETEREC RICHARD J
SOURCE AREAS OF EXPORT PRODUCTION IN TROPICAL AFRICA.
GEOGRAPHIC REVIEW 51 OCTOBER 1961 PP 487-499
069,

KOUBETTI V
RAMIN JEAN CHARLES   KOUBETTI .V   GUILHEM MARCEL
HISTOIRE DU DAHOMEY.
PARIS, L'AFRIQUE-LE MONDE, COURS MOYEN, LIGEL, 1964
109-02,

KRADER LAWRENCE
KRADER LAWRENCE
THE FORMATION OF THE STATE.
ENGLEWOOD CLIFFS, NEW JERSEY, PRENTICE-HALL, 1968
006,009,

KRAUS JON
KRAUS JON
ARMS AND POLITICS IN GHANA
IN CLAUDE WELCH (ED), SOLDIER AND STATE IN AFRICA, EVANSTON
NORTHWESTERN UNIVERSITY PRESS, 1970
064,

KREININ
KREININ MORDECHAI E

ISRAEL AND AFRICA-- A STUDY IN TECHNICAL COOPERATION.
NEW YORK,PRAEGER,1964
086,

KRISHNA K G V
   GREEN REGINALD H   KRISHNA K G V
   ECONOMIC CO-OPERATION IN AFRICA.
   LONDON,OXFORD UNIVERSITY PRESS,1967
   077,078,080,

KRITZECK JAMES
   KRITZECK JAMES   LEWIS WILLIAM H   EDS
   ISLAM IN AFRICA
   NEW YORK,VAN NOSTRAND-REINHOLD COMPANY,1969
   021,052,

KULTERMANN U
   KULTERMANN U
   NEW ARCHITECTURE IN AFRICA.
   NEW YORK,UNIVERSE BOOKS,1963,PP 26-180
   092,

KULTURMANN U
   KULTURMANN U
   NEW DIRECTIONS IN AFRICAN ARCHITECTURE.
   NEW YORK, GEORGE BRAZILLER, 1969
   092,

KUMALO C
   KUMALO C
   AFRICAN ELITES IN INDUSTRIAL BUREAUCRACY.
   IN LLOYD, THE NEW ELITES OF TROPICAL AFRICA, LONDON, OXFORD
   UNIVERSITY PRESS, 1966, P. 216-229
   071,139-04,

KUP A P
   KUP A P
   A HISTORY OF SIERRA LEONE 1400-1787
   NEW YORK,CAMBRIDGE UNIVERSITY PRESS,1961
   028,

   KUP A P
   EARLY PORTUGESE TRADE IN THE SIERRA LEONE AND GREAT
   SCARCIES RIVERS.
   BOLETIM CULTURAL DA GUINE PORTUGUESA XVIII 1963 PP 107-124
   027,131-02,

KUPER HILDA
   KUPER HILDA   KUPER LEO   EDS
   AFRICAN LAW-- ADAPTATION AND DEVELOPMENT.
   BERKELEY,UNIVERSITY OF CALIFORNIA PRESS,1965
   066,067,

   KUPER HILDA   ED
   URBANIZATION AND MIGRATION IN WEST AFRICA.
   BERKELEY,UNIVERSITY OF CALIFORNIA PRESS,1965
   046,

   KUPER HILDA
   AN AFRICAN ARISTOCRACY.

    LONDON, OXFORD UNIVERSITY PRESS, 1961
    009,135-01,

KUPER HILDA
    KUPER HILDA   HUGHES A J B   VAN VELSEN J
    THE SHONA AND NDEBELE OF SOUTHERN RHODESIA
    LONDON,INTERNATIONAL AFRICAN INSTITUTE, 1954
    145-01;

    KUPER HILDA
    THE SWAZI
    LONDON,INTERNATIONAL AFRICAN INSTITUTE,1952
    135-01,

KUPER LEO
    KUPER HILDA   KUPER LEO   EDS
    AFRICAN LAW-- ADAPTATION AND DEVELOPMENT.
    BERKELEY,UNIVERSITY OF CALIFORNIA PRESS,1965
    066,067,

    KUPER LEO   SMITH M G   EDS
    PLURALISM IN AFRICA.
    BERKELEY AND LOS ANGELES, UNIVERSITY OF CALIFORNIA PRESS,
    1969
    006,007,016,057,

    KUPER LEO
    SOCIOLOGY-- SOME ASPECTS OF URBAN PLURAL SOCIETIES.
    IN ROBERT A LYSTAD (ED), THE AFRICAN WORLD, NEW YORK,
    PRAEGER, 1966, PP 107-130
    046,

    KUPER LEO
    AN AFRICAN BOURGEOSIE--RACE, CLASS AND POLITICS IN SOUTH
    AFRICA.
    NEW HAVEN, CONN.., YALE UNIVERSITY PRESS, 1969
    089,132-03,

    KUPER LEO
    DURBAN--A STUDY IN RACIAL ECOLOGY.
    NEW YORK (COLUMBIA), MCGILL-QUEEN'S PRESS, 1969
    089,132-05,

    KUPER LEO
    PASSIVE RESISTANCE IN SOUTH AFRICA
    NEW HAVEN,YALE UNIVERSITY PRESS,1967
    032,

    KUPER LEO
    PASSIVE RESISTANCE IN SOUTH AFRICA
    LONDON,JONATHAN CAPE,1956
    032,

KURIA LUCAS
    KURIA LUCAS   WEBSTER JOHN B
    A BIBLIOGRAPHY ON ANTHROPOLOGY AND SOCIOLOGY IN TANZANIA AND
    EAST AFRICA.
    NEW YORK, SYRACUSE UNIVERSITY PROGRAM OF EASTERN AFRICAN
    STUDIES, 1966
    136-12,

KURIA LUCAS
  KURIA LUCAS   RAGHEB ISIS   WEBSTER JOHN B
  A BIBLIOGRAPHY ON POLITICS AND GOVERNMENT IN UGANDA.
  COMPILED BY LUCAS KURIA, ISIS RAGHEB AND JOHN WEBSTER, NEW
  YORK, SYRACUSE UNIVERSITY PROGRAM OF EASTERN AFRICAN STUDIES
     1965
  139-12,

KURTEN BJORN
  KURTEN BJORN
  CONTINENTAL DRIFT AND EVOLUTION
  SCIENTIFIC AMERICAN 220 1969 PP 54-64
  017,

KWAKUME HENRY
  KWAKUME HENRY
  PRECIS D'HISTOIRE DU PEUPLE EWE.
  LOME, IMP. DE L'ECOLE PROFESSIONELLE, N.D.
  137-02,

KWAN KIAN
  SHIBUTANI TAMOTSU   KWAN KIAN
  ETHNIC STRATIFICATION-- A COMPARATIVE APPROACH.
  NEW YORK, MACMILLAN COMPANY, 1965
  004,057,

KYLE KEITH
  KYLE KEITH
  COUP IN ZANZIBAR.
  AFRICA REPORT 9 FEBRUARY 1964 PP 18-20
  064,136-06,

L

LA
  LA DOCUMENTATION FRANCAISE
  LA REPUBLIQUE DU TOGO.
  NOTES ET ETUDES DOCUMENTAIRES, NO. 2736, OCT. 5, 1960
  137-11,

  LA DOCUMENTATION FRANCAISE
  LA REPUBLIQUE DE HAUTE-VOLTA.
  NOTES ET ETUDES DOCUMENTAIRES, 2693, AUGUST, 1960
  141-11,

LABORDE E D
  GOUROU PIERRE   BEAVER S H   LABORDE E D
  THE TROPICAL WORLD-- ITS SOCIAL AND ECONOMIC CONDITIONS AND
  ITS FUTURE STATUS.
  LONDON, LONGMANS, 4TH EDITION, 1966
  069,075,

LABOUR
  INTER-AFRICAN LABOUR INSTITUTE
  THE HUMAN FACTORS OF PRODUCTIVITY IN AFRICA.

LONDON,COMMISSION FOR TECHNICAL CO-OPERATION IN AFRICA
SOUTH OF THE SAHARA ,1952; 2ND EDITION,1960
074,

LABOUR
    INTERNATIONAL LABOUR OFFICE
    TRANSITION FROM TRIBAL TO MODERN FORMS OF SOCIAL AND
    ECONOMIC ORGANIZATION.
    GENEVE,INTERNATIONAL LABOR ORGANIZATION,1952
    038,

    INTER-AFRICAN LABOUR INSTITUTE
    MIGRANT LABOUR IN AFRICA SOUTH OF THE SAHARA
    NEW YORK,INTERNATIONAL PUBLICATIONS SERVICE,1963
    6TH INTER-AFRICAN LABOUR CONFERENCE,ABIDJAN,1961
    SCIENTIFIC COUNCIL FOR AFRICA SOUTH OF THE SAHARA NO. 79
    069,

LACROIX J L
    LACROIX J L
    INDUSTRIALISATION AU CONGO-LA TRANFORMATION DES STRUCTURES
    ECONOMIQUE
    PARIS,EDITIONS MOUTON,1967
    071,108-08,

LACROIX PIERRE
    LACROIX PIERRE
    L ISLAM PEUL DE L ADAMAWA.
    IN LEWIS, ISLAM IN TROPICAL AFRICA, LONDON, OXFORD UNIVERSIT
    PRESS, 1966, P. 401-407
    104-03,

LAGUMA ALEX
    LAGUMA ALEX
    AND A THREEFOLD CORD.
    EVANSTON, NORTHWESTERN UNIVERSITY PRESS, 1967 (LONDON,
    HEINEMANN EDUCATIONAL BOOKS)
    090,132-10,

    LAGUMA ALEX
    A WALK IN THE NIGHT.
    IBADAN,MBARI PUBLICATIONS, 1962; EVANSTON, NORTHWESTERN
    090,132-10,

LAIRD MACGREGOR
    LAIRD MACGREGOR   OLDFIELD RICHARD
    NARRATIVE OF AN EXPEDITION INTO THE INTERIOR OF AFRICA BY
    THE RIVER NIGER IN THE STEAM VESSELS QUORRA AND ALBURKAH IN
    1832, 1833, AND 1834.
    LONDON,CASS,1966
    027,

LAJOUX JEAN D
    LAJOUX JEAN D
    THE ROCK PAINTINGS OF TASSILI. (TRANS BY G D LIVERSAGE)
    CLEVELAND,WORLD PUBLISHING COMPANY,1963
    014,101-01,

LAMBERT HAROLD E
    LAMBERT HAROLD E

KIKUYU SOCIAL AND POLITICAL INSTITUTIONS.
LONDON, OXFORD UNIVERSITY PRESS, 1956
117-01,

LAMBO T ADEOYE
LAMBO T ADEOYE
IMPORTANT AREAS OF IGNORANCE AND DOUBT IN THE PSYCHOLOGY OF
THE AFRICAN.
IN LALAGE BOWN AND MICHAEL CROWDER (EDS.), PROCEEDINGS OF
THE FIRST INTERNATIONAL CONGRESS OF AFRICANISTS, ACCRA,
1962, LONDON, LONGMANS, 1964, PP 337-344
040,

LAMBO T ADEOYE
THE ROLE OF CULTURAL FACTORS IN PARANOID PSYCHOSES AMONG
THE YORUBA TRIBE.
JOURNAL OF MENTAL SCIENCE 101 1955 PP 239-265
040,128-03,

LANCEY M w DE
LANCEY M w DE
THE GHANA-GUINEA-MALI UNION--A BIBLIOGRAPHIC ESSAY.
AFRICAN STUDIES BULLETIN, 9, 2, SEPTEMBER, 1966
114-12,115-12,123-12,

LANDER J
LANDER RICHARD   LANDER J
JOURNAL OF AN EXPEDITION TO EXPLORE THE COURSE AND
TERMINATION OF THE NIGER.
NEW YORK,HARPER AND BROTHERS,1837
027,099,

LANDER RICHARD
LANDER RICHARD   ED
RECORDS OF CAPTAIN CLAPPERTON'S LAST EXPEDITION TO AFRICA.
LONDON,CASS,1967, 2 VOLUMES
027,

LANDER RICHARD   LANDER J
JOURNAL OF AN EXPEDITION TO EXPLORE THE COURSE AND
TERMINATION OF THE NIGER.
NEW YORK,HARPER AND BROTHERS,1837
027,099,

LANDIER SIMONE
LANDIER SIMONE
THE CHANGING FRENCH MILITARY ROLE IN AFRICA.
AFRICA REPORT 9 NOVEMBER 1964 P 21
082,

LANGLANDS BRYAN W
LANGLANDS BRYAN W
UGANDA BIBLIOGRAPHY, 1961-1962.
UGANDA JOURNAL, 27, 2, SEPT. 1963
139-12,

LANTERNARI V
LANTERNARI V
SYNCRETISMES, MESSIANISMES, NEOTRADITIONALISMES-- POSTFACE
A UNE ETUDE DES MOUVEMENTS RELIGIEUX DE L'AFRIQUE NOIRE

(SYNCRETISM, MESSIANISM, NEO-TRADITIONALISM-- A REVIEW OF
A STUDY OF RELIGIOUS MOVEMENTS OF BLACK AFRICA).
ARCHIVES DE SOCIOLOGIE DES RELIGIONS 19 1965 PP 99-116
051,

LAPALOMBARA JOSEPH
    LAPALOMBARA JOSEPH   ED
    BUREAUCRACY AND POLITICAL DEVELOPMENT.
    PRINCETON,NEW JERSEY, PRINCETON UNIVERSITY PRESS,1963
    062,

    WEINER MYRON   LAPALOMBARA JOSEPH   EDS
    POLITICAL PARTIES AND POLITICAL DEVELOPMENT.
    PRINCETON, PRINCETON UNIVERSITY PRESS 1966
    061,

LAQUEUR WALTER Z
    LAQUEUR WALTER Z
    COMMUNISM AND NATIONALISM IN TROPICAL AFRICA.
    IN PHILIP W QUIGG (ED.), AFRICA, NEW YORK, PRAEGER, 1964,
    PP 182-195
    084,

    LAQUEUR WALTER Z
    REPORTING WEST AFRICA.
    NEW REPUBLIC 148 JANUARY 19 1963 PP 13-14
    049,

LARIMORE A E
    LARIMORE A E
    THE ALIEN TOWN--PATTERNS OF SETTLEMENT IN BUSOGA, UGANDA.
    UNIVERSITY OF CHICAGO,DEPT OF GEOGRAPHY RESEARCH PAPERS
    AUGUST 1958 PP 1-210
    046,139-05,

LARSON CHARLES R
    LARSON CHARLES R
    NIGERIAN DRAMA COMES OF AGE.
    AFRICA REPORT, MAY, 1968, P. 55
    090,128-10,

LASEBIKAN E L
    LASEBIKAN E L
    LEARNING YORUBA.
    LONDON, OXFORD UNIVERSITY PRESS, 1958
    011,128-01,

LASSWELL HAROLD
    LASSWELL HAROLD
    THE COMPARATIVE STUDY OF ELITES.
    STANFORD,CALIFORNIA,HOOVER INSTITUTE STUDIES,1952
    044,

    LASSWELL HAROLD   LERNER DANIEL
    WORLD REVOLUTIONARY ELITES
    CAMBRIDGE,MASS,MIT PRESS,1965
    044,

LAST MURRAY
    LAST MURRAY

THE SOKOTO CALIPHATE.
LONDON, LONGMANS, GREEN AND COMPANY LTD., 1967
024,128-02,

LAUFER
  LAUFER
  ISREAL IN AFRICA.
  20TH CENTURY FUND
  086,

LAURENCE MARGARET
  LAURENCE MARGARET
  LONG DRUMS AND CANNONS-NIGERIAN DRAMATISTS AND NOVELISTS
  LONDON,MACMILLAN, 1968; AND NEW YORK, PRAEGER, 1969
  090,128-10,

  LAURENCE MARGARET   ED
  A TREE FOR POVERTY.SOMALI POETRY AND PROSE
  NAIROBI,EAGLE PRESS,1954
  133-10,

LAVROFF D G
  LAVROFF D G   PEISER G
  LES CONSTITUTIONS AFRICAINES (AFRICAN CONSTITUTIONS), VOL-
  UME ONE.
  PARIS,A PEDONE,1961
  068,

LAWRANCE J C D
  LAWRANCE J C D
  A PILOT SCHEME FOR LAND TITLES IN UGANDA.
  JOURNAL OF AFRICAN ADMINISTRATION 12 JULY 1960 PP 135-143
  070,139-08,

LAWRENCE ARNOLD W
  LAWRENCE ARNOLD W
  TRADE CASTLES AND FORTS OF WEST AFRICA.
  LONDON, JONATHAN CAPE, 1963
  027,

LAWSON R M
  LAWSON R M
  THE MARKETS FOR FOODS IN GHANA CHAPTER 16.
  IN EDITH WHETHAM AND JEAN CURRIE (EDS.), READINGS IN THE
  APPLIED ECONOMICS OF AFRICA, LONDON, CAMBRIDGE UNIVERSITY
  PRESS, 1, 1967. PP 173-192
  070,073,114-08,

LAYE CAMARA
  LAYE CAMARA   TRANSLATED BY   JAMES KIRKUP
  THE AFRICAN CHILD.
  LONDON,COLLINS LTD, 1965
  090,115-10,

  LAYE CAMARA
  RADIANCE OF THE KING.
  NEW YORK, MACMILLAN CO., 1970
  090,115-10,

  LAYE CAMARA

DRAMOUSS.
PARIS, PLON, 1966
115-10,

LAYE CAMARA
LAYE CAMARA
ECRIVAIN GUINEEN--TEXTES COMMENTES PAR ROGER MERCIER ET M ET
S BATTESTINI.
PARIS, F. NATHAN, 1964
115-10,

LAZARSFELD PAUL F
LAZARSFELD PAUL F   ROSENBERG MORRIS   EDS
THE LANGUAGE OF SOCIAL RESEARCH.
NEW YORK, FREE PRESS, 1955
098,

LE MAY G M C
LE MAY G M C
BRITISH SUPREMACY IN SOUTH AFRICA-1899-1907
LONDON, OXFORD UNIVERSITY PRESS, 196J
032,

LE ROUVREUR ALBERT
LE ROUVREUR ALBERT
SAHELIENS ET SAHARIENS DU TCHAD
PARIS, BERGER-LEVRAULT, 1962
106-01,

LE TOURNEAU
LE TOURNEAU
ALMOHAD MOVEMENT IN NORTH AFRICA IN THE 12TH AND 13TH
CENTURIES.
PRINCETON, NEW JERSEY, PRINCETON UNIVERSITY PRESS, 1969
021,

LEAKEY L S B
LEAKEY L S B
THE PROGRESS AND EVOLUTION OF MAN IN AFRICA.
LONDON, OXFORD UNIVERSITY PRESS, 1961
018,

LEAKEY L S B   VANNE MORRIS-GOODALL
UNVEILING MAN'S ORIGINS-TEN DECADES OF THOUGHT ABOUT HUMAN
EVOLUTION
CAMBRIDGE, MASS, SCHENKMAN, 1969
018,

LEAKEY L S B
VERY EARLY EAST AFRICAN HOMINIDAE. AND THEIR ECOLOGICAL
SETTING.
IN F CLARK HOWELL AND FRANCOIS BOURLIERE (EDS.), AFRICAN
ECOLOGY AND HUMAN EVOLUTION, CHICAGO, ALDINE, 1966,
PP 448-457
018,

LEAKEY L S B
THE EVOLUTION OF MAN IN THE AFRICAN CONTINENT.
TARIKH 1 1966 PP 1-11
018,

LEAKEY L S B
    LEAKEY L S B
    MAN'S AFRICAN ORIGIN.
    ANNALS OF THE NEW YORK ACADEMY OF SCIENCES VOL 96 1962 PP
    495-503
    018,

    LEAKEY L S B
    OLDUVAI GORGE.
    LONDON, CAMBRIDGE UNIVERSITY PRESS, 1951
    018,

    LEAKEY L S B
    MAU MAU AND THE KIKUYU.
    LONDON, METHUEN, 1954
    055,117-06,

LEBEUF ANNIE
    LEBEUF ANNIE
    LES POPULATIONS DU CHAD.
    PARIS, PRESSES UNIVERSITAIRES DE FRANCE, 1959
    106-01,

LEBEUF JEAN PAUL
    LEBEUF JEAN PAUL
    RECENT RESEARCH ON MIGRATION IN WEST AFRICA.
    MIGRATION NEWS 7 1958 PP 13-17
    069,

    LEBEUF JEAN PAUL   MASSON-DEFOURRET A M
    LA CIVILIZATION DU CHAD.
    PARIS, PAYOT, 1950
    106-02,

LEBLANC MARIA
    LEBLANC MARIA
    ACCULTURATION OF ATTITUDE AND PERSONALITY AMONG KATANGESE
    WOMEN.
    JOURNAL OF SOCIAL PSYCHOLOGY 47 1958 PP 257-264
    041,108-03,

LEBON J H G
    LEBON J H G
    LAND USE IN SUDAN.
    MONOGRAPH 4, SIR DUDLEY STAMP (ED.) GEOGRAPHICAL
    PUBLICATIONS, BUDE, 1965
    070,134-08,

    LEBON J H G
    THE CONTROL AND UTILIZATION OF NILE WATERS--A PROBLEM OF
    POLITICAL GEOGRAPHY.
    REVIEW OF THE GEOGRAPHICAL INSTITUTE OF THE UNIVERSITY OF
    ISTANBUL 1960 PP 32-49
    078,134-09,140-09,

LECOQ RAYMOND
    LECOQ RAYMOND
    LES BAMILIKE (THE BAMILIKE).
    PARIS, PRESENCE AFRICAINE, 1953

104-01,

LEE J M
 LEE J M
 AFRICAN ARMIES AND CIVIL ORDER.
 NEW YORK, PRAEGER PUBLISHERS, 1969
 064,

 LEE J M
 PARLIAMENT IN REPUBLICAN GHANA.
 PARLIAMENTARY AFFAIRS 16 AUTUMN 1963 PP 376-395
 062,114-07,

LEE RICHARD B
 LEE RICHARD B   DEVORE IRVEN   EDS
 MAN THE HUNTER
 CHICAGO, ALDINE, 1968
 005, 009,

LEFEVER ERNEST W
 LEFEVER ERNEST W
 UNCERTAIN MANDATE-- POLITICS OF THE UN CONGO OPERATION.
 BALTIMORE, JOHNS HOPKINS UNIVERSITY PRESS, 1967
 079,081,108-09,

LEGUM COLIN
 LEGUM COLIN
 PAN-AFRICANISM A SHORT POLITICAL GUIDE.
 NEW YORK, PRAEGER, 1962
 077,079,

 LEGUM COLIN   ED
 AFRICA-- HANDBOOK TO A CONTINENT.
 NEW YORK, PRAEGER, 1966
 056,076,

 LEGUM COLIN   DRYSDALE JOHN
 AFRICA CONTEMPORARY RECORD.
 LONDON, AFRICA RESEARCH LIMITED, 1969
 002,062,080,081,087,

 LEGUM COLIN   DRYSDALE JOHN
 NIGERIAN CIVIL WAR.
 COLIN LEGUM AND JOHN DRYSDALE, AFRICA CONTEMPORARY RECORD,
 LONDON, AFRICA RESEARCH LIMITED, 1969, PP. 645-688
 065,128-06,

 LEGUM COLIN   LEGUM MARGARET
 THE BITTER CHOICE--EIGHT SOUTH AFRICANS RESISTANCE TO
 TYRANNY
 CLEVELAND AND NEW YORK, WORLD, 1968
 032, 089,

 LEGUM COLIN
 MODERN POLITICAL IDEAS.
 IN PETER J MCEWAN AND ROBERT B SUTCLIFFE (EDS), MODERN AFRICA,
 NEW YORK, THOMAS CROWELL, 1965, PP 239-263
 060,

 LEGUM COLIN

BANDUNG.
IN PAN-AFRICANISM, LONDON, PALL MALL PRESS, 1962
085,

LEGUM COLIN
 LEGUM COLIN   ED
 CONFRONTATION BETWEEN THE DEVELOPED AND DEVELOPING
 COUNTRIES.
 NEW YORK, INTERNATIONAL UNIVERSITY BOOKSELLERS, INC., 1969
 097,

 LEGUM COLIN
 PAN-AFRICANISM AND NATIONALISM CHP 30.
 IN JC ANENE AND GODFREY BROWN,AFRICA IN THE 19TH AND 20TH
 CENTURIES, LONDON, NELSON IUP,1966
 079,

 LEGUM COLIN
 THE CHANGING IDEAS OF PAN-AFRICANISM.
 AFRICAN FORUM I 2 1965 PP 50-61
 079,

 LEGUM COLIN
 JAPAN AND AFRICA, 1968.
 IN LEGUM AND DRYSDALE, AFRICA CONTEMPORARY RECORD,
 LONDON, AFRICA RESEARCH LIMITED, 1969, P. 43-45
 085,

 LEGUM COLIN
 CONGO DISASTER.
 HARMONDSWORTH, PENGUIN, 1961
 064,108-06,

 LEGUM COLIN
 KENYA'S LITTLE GUERRILLA WAR HEATS UP.
 AFRICA REPORT 12 APRIL 1967 P 39
 059,117-06,

 LEGUM COLIN
 BRITAIN'S YEAR IN AFRICA.
 IN LEGUM AND DRYSDALE, AFRICA CONTEMPORARY RECORD,
 LONDON, AFRICA RESEARCH LIMITED, 1969, P. 22-26
 082,

 LEGUM COLIN
 SOMALI LIBERATION SONGS.
 JOURNAL OF MODERN AFRICAN STUDIES, 1, 4, DEC. 1963
 133-07,

LEGUM MARGARET
 LEGUM COLIN   LEGUM MARGARET
 THE BITTER CHOICE--EIGHT SOUTH AFRICANS RESISTANCE TO
 TYRANNY
 CLEVELAND AND NEW YORK, WORLD,1968
 032, 089,

LEGVOLD ROBERT
 LEGVOLD ROBERT
 MOSCOW'S CHANGING VIEW OF AFRICA'S REVOLUTIONARY REGIMES.
 AFRICA REPORT, MARCH/APRIL, 1969, PP. 54-58

084,

LEHMANN D A
    TAYLOR JOHN   LEHMANN D A
    CHRISTIANS OF THE COPPERBELT-- THE GROWTH OF CHURCH IN
    NORTHERN RHODESIA.
    LONDON, SUDAN CHRISTIAN MISSION PRESS, 1961
    050,142-03,

LEIBENSTEIN HARVEY
    LEIBENSTEIN HARVEY
    ECONOMIC BACKWARDNESS AND ECONOMIC GROWTH.
    NEW YORK, JOHN WILEY, 1963
    073,

LEIGHTON A H
    LEIGHTON A H   ET-AL
    PSYCHIATRIC DISORDER AMONG THE YORUBA-- A REPORT FROM THE
    CORNELL ARO-MENTAL HEALTH RESEARCH PROJECT IN THE WESTERN
    REGION NIGERIA.
    ITHACA, CORNELL UNIVERSITY PRESS, 1963
    041,128-03,

LEIGHTON RICHARD M
    LEIGHTON RICHARD M SANDERS RALPH
    MILITARY CIVIC ACTION.
    IN LEWIS P FICKETT (ED), PROBLEMS OF THE DEVELOPING NATIONS,
    NEW YORK, CROWELL, 1966, PP 103-122
    064,

    LEIGHTON RICHARD M SANDERS RALPH
    AID'S PUBLIC SAFETY CIVIC ACTION AND COMMUNITY DEVELOPMENT
    PROGRAM.
    IN LEWIS P FICKETT (ED), PROBLEMS OF THE DEVELOPING NATIONS,
    NEW YORK, CROWELL, 1966, PP 116-122
    083,

LEIRIS MICHEL
    LEIRIS MICHEL   DELANGE JACQUELINE
    AFRICAN ART
    LONDON, THAMES AND HUDSON, 1968
    014,

LEITH-ROSS SYLVIA
    LEITH-ROSS SYLVIA
    AFRICAN WOMEN-- A STUDY OF THE IBO OF NIGERIA.
    LONDON, ROUTLEDGE AND KEGAN PAUL, 1963
    008,128-01,

LEM F H
    LEM F H
    SUDANESE SCULPTURE.
    PARIS, ARTS ET METIERS GRAPHIQUES, 1948
    014,

LEMARCHAND RENE
    LEMARCHAND RENE
    THE BASES OF NATIONALISM AMONG THE BAKONGO.
    AFRICA 31 OCTOBER 1961 PP 344-354
    055,108-06,

LEMARCHAND RENE
    LEMARCHAND RENE
    THE LIMITS OF SELF-DETERMINATION-- THE CASE OF THE KATANGA
    SECESSION.
    AMERICAN POLITICAL SCIENCE REVIEW 56 JUNE 1962 PP 404-416
    059,108-06,

    LEMARCHAND RENE
    POLITICAL AWAKENING IN THE BELGIAN CONGO.
    BERKELEY, UNIVERSITY OF CALIFORNIA PRESS, 1964
    055,108-07,

    LEMARCHAND RENE
    REVOLUTIONARY PHENOMENA IN STRATIFIED SOCIETIES--RWANDA AND
    ZANZIBAR.
    CIVILISATIONS, VOL XVIII, NO. 1, 1968, PP. 16-51
    057,129-06,136-06,

    LEMARCHAND RENE
    DAHOMEY--COUP WITHIN A COUP.
    AFRICA REPORT, JUNE, 1968, P. 46
    064,109-06,

    LEMARCHAND RENE
    RWANDA BURUNDI.
    LONDON, PALL MALL PRESS, 1970
    103-11, 129-11,

    LEMARCHAND RENE
    SOCIAL AND POLITICAL CHANGES IN BURUNDI.
    IN G.M. CARTER, ED, FIVE AFRICAN STATES--RESPONSES TO
    DIVERSITY, ITHACA, CORNELL UNIVERSITY PRESS, 1963
    103-07,

    LEMARCHAND RENE
    CONGO.
    IN COLEMAN, J.S. AND ROSBERG, C.G. (EDS), POLITICAL PARTIES
    AND NATIONAL INTEGRATION IN TROPICAL AFRICA, LOS ANGELES,
    UNIVERSITY OF CALIFORNIA PRESS, 1964
    108-06,

LEMELLE TILDEN
    LEMELLE TILDEN
    THE IDEOLOGY OF BLACKNESS AFRICAN-AMERICAN STYLE.
    AFRICA TODAY 14 DECEMBER 1967 PP 2-4
    094,

LERNER DANIEL
    LASSWELL HAROLD   LERNER DANIEL
    WORLD REVOLUTIONARY ELITES
    CAMBRIDGE, MASS, MIT PRESS, 1965
    044,

    LERNER DANIEL
    THE PASSING OF TRADITIONAL SOCIETY-- MODERNIZING THE MIDDLE
    EAST.
    NEW YORK, FREE PRESS, 1958
    037,

LERNER DANIEL
COMMUNICATION SYSTEMS AND SOCIAL SYSTEMS-- A STATISTICAL
EXPLORATION IN HISTORY AND POLICY.
BEHAVIORAL SCIENCE 4 OCTOBER 1957 PP 266-275
IN JASON L FINKLE AND RICHARD W GABLE, POLITICAL DEVELOPMENT
AND SOCIAL CHANGE, NEW YORK, JOHN WILEY, 1966
048,

LEROY JULES
LEROY JULES
ETHIOPIAN PAINTING--IN THE LATE MIDDLE AGES AND DURING THE
GONDAR DYNASTY.
NEW YORK, PRAEGER, 1967
014,110-02,

LESLIE J A K
LESLIE J A K
A SURVEY OF DAR ES SALAAM.
LONDON, OXFORD UNIVERSITY PRESS, 1963
136-05,

LEUZINGER ELSY
LEUZINGER ELSY
AFRICA-THE ART OF THE NEGRO PEOPLES
LONDON, METHUEN, 1960
014,

LEUZINGER ELSY
AFRICAN SCULPTURE, A DESCRIPTIVE CATALOGUE.
ZURICH, ATLANTIS RIETBERG MUSEUM, 1963
014,

LEVI-STRAUSS
LEVI-STRAUSS CLAUDE
STRUCTURAL ANTHROPOLOGY
NEW YORK, BASIC BOOKS, 1963, AND ANCHOR BOOKS, 1967
013,

LEVINE DONALD N
LEVINE DONALD N
ETHIOPIA--IDENTITY, AUTHORITY, AND REALISM.
LUCIAN W. PYE AND SIDNEY VERBA (EDS), POLITICAL CULTURE AND
POLITICAL DEVELOPMENT, PRINCETON, NEW JERSEY, PRINCETON
UNIVERSITY PRESS, 1965
061,110-07,

LEVINE DONALD N
WAX AND GOLD--TRADITION AND INNOVATION IN ETHIOPIAN CULTURE.
CHICAGO, UNIVERSITY OF CHICAGO PRESS, 1966
110-11,

LEVINE DONALD N
CLASS CONSCIOUSNESS AND CLASS SOLIDARITY IN THE NEW ETHIOPIA
ELITES.
IN LLOYD, THE NEW ELITES OF TROPICAL AFRICA, LONDON, OXFORD
UNIVERSITY PRESS, 1966, P. 212-327
110-04,

LEVINE ROBERT A
LEVINE ROBERT A

DREAMS AND DEEDS.
CHICAGO,UNIVERSITY OF CHICAGO PRESS,1966
038,041,098,128-03,

LEVINE ROBERT A
    LEVINE ROBERT A
    AFRICA.
    IN FRANCES K HSU ED., PSYCHOLOGICAL ANTHROPOLOGY, HOMEWOOD,
    ILLINOIS, DORSEY PRESS. 1961, PP 48-92
    039,099,100,

    LEVINE ROBERT A
    ANTI-EUROPEAN VIOLENCE IN AFRICA-- A COMPARATIVE ANALYSIS.
    JOURNAL OF CONFLICT RESOLUTION 3 DECEMBER 1959
    PP 420-429
    088,117-06,

    LEVINE ROBERT A
    THE INTERNALIZATION OF POLITICAL VALUES IN STATELESS
    SOCIETIES.
    HUMAN ORGANIZATION 19 1960 PP 51-58
    009,

    SAWYER JACK   LEVINE ROBERT A
    CULTURAL DIMENSIONS-- A FACTOR ANALYSIS OF THE WORLD ETHNO-
    GRAPHIC SAMPLE.
    AMERICAN ANTHROPOLOGIST VOL 68 NO 3 JUNE 1966 PP 708-731
    016,040,

    LEVINE ROBERT A   KLEIN N   OWEN C
    FATHER-CHILD RELATIONSHIPS AND CHANGING LIFE-STYLES IN
    IBADAN, NIGERIA.
    IN HORACE MINER (ED), THE CITY IN MODERN AFRICA, NEW YORK,
    PRAEGER, 1967
    040,128-03,

    LEVINE ROBERT A
    GUSII SEX OFFENCES-- A STUDY IN SOCIAL CONTROL.
    AMERICAN ANTHROPOLOGIST 61 1959 PP 965-990
    008,117-01,

    LEVINE ROBERT A
    WEALTH AND POWER IN GUSIILAND.
    IN PAUL BOHANNAN AND GEORGE DALTON (EDS.), MARKETS IN
    AFRICA, EVANSTON, NORTHWESTERN UNIVERSITY PRESS, 1962, PP
    520-536
    010,117-01,

    CAMPBELL DONALD T   LEVINE ROBERT A
    A PROPOSAL FOR COOPERATIVE CROSS-CULTURAL RESEARCH ON
    ETHNOCENTRISM.
    JOURNAL OF CONFLICT RESOLUTION 5 MARCH 1961 PP 82-108
    098,

    LEVINE ROBERT A
    SOCIALIZATION, SOCIAL STRUCTURE, AND INTERSOCIETAL IMAGES.
    IN HERMAN KELMAN ED, INTERNATIONAL BEHAVIOR-- A SOCIAL
    PSYCHOLOGICAL ANALYSIS, NEW YORK, HOLT, RINEHART AND
    WINSTON, 1965
    040,

LEVINE ROBERT A
    LEVINE ROBERT A
    ANTHROPOLOGY AND THE STUDY OF CONFLICT-- AN INTRODUCTION.
    JOURNAL OF CONFLICT RESOLUTION 5 1961 PP 3-15
    099,

    LEVINE ROBERT A
    ROLE OF FAMILY IN AUTHORITY SYSTEMS.
    BEHAVIORAL SCIENCE 5 1960 PP 291-296
    008,

LEVINE VICTOR T
    LEVINE VICTOR T
    POLITICAL LEADERSHIP IN AFRICA.
    PALO ALTO. THE HOOVER INSTITUTION ON WAR, REVOLUTION AND
    PEACE, STANFORD UNIVERSITY, 1967
    058,

    LEVINE VICTOR T
    INDEPENDENT AFRICA IN TROUBLE.
    TRANSACTION JULY-AUGUST 1967 PP 53-62
    064,

    LEVINE VICTOR T
    GENERATIONAL CONFLICT AND POLITICS IN AFRICA--A PARADIGM.
    CIVILISATIONS, VOL. XVIII, 1968, NO. 3, PP. 399-420
    091,

    LEVINE VICTOR T
    POLITICAL ELITE RECRUITMENT AND POLITICAL STRUCTURE IN
    FRENCH-SPEAKING AFRICA.
    CAHIERS D'ETUDES AFRICAINES, VOL. VIII, NO. 31, 1968,
    PP. 369-389
    043,

    LEVINE VICTOR T
    THE CAMEROONS FROM MANDATE TO INDEPENDENCE.
    BERKELEY, UNIVERSITY OF CALIFORNIA PRESS, 1964
    055,104-06,

    LEVINE VICTOR T
    CAMEROON.
    IN G.M. CARTER,ED,FIVE AFRICAN STATES-- RESPONSES TO
    DIVERSITY, ITHACA, CORNELL UNIVERSITY PRESS, 1963,
    104-07,

    LEVINE VICTOR T
    CAMEROON.
    IN J.S. COLEMAN AND C.G. ROSBERG EDS POLITICAL PARTIES AND
    NATIONAL INTEGRATION IN TROPICAL AFRICA, LOS ANGELES,
    UNIVERSITY OF CALIFORNIA PRESS, 1964
    104-07,

LEVTZION NEHEMIA
    LEVTZION NEHEMIA
    MUSLIMS AND CHIEFS IN WEST AFRICA.
    OXFORD, CLARENDON PRESS, 1968
    024,141-03,

LEVTZION NEHEMIA
COASTAL WEST AFRICA
IN KRITZECK AND LEWIS, PP 301-318
052.

LEVY MARION J
FALLERS LLOYD A   LEVY MARION J
THE FAMILY-- SOME COMPARATIVE CONSIDERATIONS.
IN PETER HAMMOND, ED, CULTURAL AND SOCIAL ANTHROPOLOGY,
NEW YORK, MACMILLAN CO, 1964, PP 163-166
008.

LEVY MARION J
MODERNIZATION AND THE STRUCTURE OF SOCIETIES-- A SETTING
FOR INTERNATIONAL AFFAIRS.
PRINCETON, NEW JERSEY, PRINCETON UNIVERSITY PRESS, 1966
037.

LEWENKOPF MARTIN
LEWENKOPF MARTIN
UGANDA
IN KRITZECK AND LEWIS, PP 214-226
139-03.

LEWIS ARTHUR
LEWIS ARTHUR
A REPORT ON THE INDUSTRIALIZATION OF THE GOLD COAST.
ACCRA, GOVERNMENT PRINTING DEPARTMENT, 1953
071.

LEWIS HERBERT S
LEWIS HERBERT S
A GALLA MONARCHY-- JIMMA ABBA JIFAR, ETHIOPIA, 1830-1932.
MADISON, UNIVERSITY OF WISCONSIN PRESS, 1965
009,110-02.

LEWIS HYLAN
BROWN WILLIAM O   LEWIS HYLAN
RACIAL SITUATIONS AND ISSUES IN AFRICA CHAPTER 6.
IN THE UNITED STATES AND AFRICA, BACKGROUND PAPERS OF THE
13TH ASSEMBLY, THE AMERICAN ASSEMBLY, COLUMBIA UNIVERSITY,
1958, PP 141-163
088.

LEWIS I M
LEWIS I M   ED
ISLAM IN TROPICAL AFRICA
LONDON, OXFORD UNIVERSITY PRESS, 1966
021,052.

LEWIS I M
THE CLASSIFICATION OF AFRICAN POLITICAL SYSTEMS.
RHODES-LIVINGSTONE JOURNAL 25 MARCH 1959 PP 59-69
009,133-06.

LEWIS I M
HISTORY AND SOCIAL ANTHROPOLOGY
LONDON, TAVISTOCK, 1968
036.

ANDRZEJEWSKI B W   LEWIS I M
SOMALI POETRY.
LONDON, OXFORD UNIVERSITY PRESS, 1964
012,133-01,

LEWIS I M
   LEWIS I M
   A PASTORAL DEMOCRACY.
   LONDON,OXFORD UNIVERSITY PRESS,1961
   009,133-01,

   LEWIS I M
   INTEGRATION IN THE SOMALI REPUBLIC CHAPTER 7.
   IN ARTHUR HAZLEWOOD, AFRICAN INTEGRATION AND DISINTEGRATION,
   LONDON, OXFORD UNIVERSITY PRESS, 1967, PP 251-284
   055,133-06,

   LEWIS I M
   LINEAGE CONTINUITY AND MODERN COMMERCE IN NORTHERN
   SOMALILAND.
   IN PAUL BOHANNAN AND GEORGE DALTON (EDS.),MARKETS IN
   AFRICA, EVANSTON, NORTHWESTERN UNIVERSITY PRESS, 1962, PP
   365-385
   038,133-03,

   LEWIS I M
   THE MODERN HISTORY OF SOMALILAND-- FROM NATION TO STATE.
   LONDON,WEIDENFELD AND NICOLSON,1965
   055,133-06,

   LEWIS I M
   PAN AFRICANISM AND PAN SOMALISM
   JOURNAL OF MODERN AFRICAN STUDIES 1 1963 PP 147-162
   059,077,133-09,

   LEWIS I M
   THE NORTHERN PASTORAL SOMALI OF THE HORN.
   IN JAMES L GIBBS JR (ED),PEOPLES OF AFRICA, NEW YORK, HOLT
   RINEHART AND WINSTON, 1965 PP. 319-360
   133-01,

   LEWIS I M
   CONFORMITY AND CONTRAST IN SOMALI ISLAM.
   IN LEWIS, ISLAM IN TROPICAL AFRICA, LONDON, OXFORD UNIVERSIT
   PRESS, 1966, P. 253-267
   133-03,

   LEWIS I M
   PEOPLES OF THE HORN OF AFRICA-SOMALI,AFAR,SANO
   LONDON,INTERNATIONAL AFRICAN INSTITUTE,1955
   133-01,

LEWIS MARTIN D
   LEWIS MARTIN D
   ONE HUNDRED MILLION FRENCHMEN-- THE ASSIMILATION THEORY IN
   FRENCH COLONIAL POLICY.
   COMPARATIVE STUDIES IN SOCIETY AND HISTORY 4 1962 PP 129-153
   035,

LEWIS W ARTHUR

LEWIS W ARTHUR
DEVELOPMENT PLANNING.
NEW YORK, HARPER AND ROW, 1966
071,072,

LEWIS W ARTHUR
    LEWIS W ARTHUR
    POLITICS IN WEST AFRICA.
    LONDON, GEORGE ALLEN AND UNWIN LTD, 1965
    061,

    LEWIS W ARTHUR
    EDUCATION FOR SCIENTIFIC PROFESSIONS IN THE POOR COUNTRIES.
    DAEDALUS 91 SPRING 1962 PP 310-318
    042,075,

LEWIS WILLIAM H
    KRITZECK JAMES   LEWIS WILLIAM H   EDS
    ISLAM IN AFRICA
    NEW YORK, VAN NOSTRAND-REINHOLD COMPANY, 1969
    021,052,

    LEWIS WILLIAM H
    ISLAM AND NATIONALISM IN AFRICA.
    IN TIBOR KEREKES (ED), THE ARAB MIDDLE EAST AND MUSLIM
    AFRICA, NEW YORK, PRAEGER, 1961, PP 83-84
    055,

    LEWIS WILLIAM H
    ISLAM--A RISING TIDE IN TROPICAL AFRICA.
    REVIEW OF POLITICS 19 OCTOBER 1957 PP 446-461
    052,

    LEWIS WILLIAM H
    URBAN CRUCIBLE--PARALLELS AND DIVERGENCES.
    AFRICA REPORT, MAY/JUNE 1969, PP. 62-65
    047,

    LEWIS WILLIAM H
    NATIONALISM AND MODERNISM
    IN KRITZECK AND LEWIS, PP 185-201
    054,

    LEWIS WILLIAM H
    FUNCTIONAL ELITES-AN EMERGENT POLITICAL FORCE
    IN NEW FORCES IN AFRICA, GEORGETOWN COLLOQUIUM ON AFRICA
    PAPERS, WASHINGTON PUBLIC AFFAIRS PRESS 1962 PP 114-128
    043,

    LEWIS WILLIAM H
    FEUDING AND SOCIAL CHANGE IN MOROCCO.
    JOURNAL OF CONFLICT RESOLUTION 5 1961 PP 43-54
    008,126-03,

LEYS COLIN
    LEYS COLIN
    POLITICIANS AND POLICIES-- AN ESSAY IN AXCHOLI
    UGANDA 1962-65.
    NAIROBI, KENYA, THE EAST AFRICAN PUBLISHING HOUSE, 1967
    061,139-07,

LEYS COLIN
    LEYS COLIN
    EUROPEAN POLITICS IN SOUTHERN RHODESIA.
    OXFORD,CLARENDON PRESS,1959
    087,145-06,

    LEYS COLIN   ED
    POLITICS AND CHANGE IN DEVELOPING COUNTRIES
    NEW YORK,CAMBRIDGE UNIVERSITY PRESS,1970
    076,

    LEYS COLIN   ROBSON PETER   EDS
    FEDERATION IN EAST AFRICA-- OPPORTUNITIES AND PROBLEMS.
    NAIROBI,OXFORD UNIVERSITY PRESS,1965
    078,

    LEYS COLIN
    TANGANYIKA--THE REALITIES OF INDEPENDENCE.
    INTERNATIONAL JOURNAL 17, 1962
    136-07,

LIBOIS JULES G
    LIBOIS JULES G
    KATANGA SECESSION.
    MADISON, UNIVERSITY OF WISCONSIN PRESS, 1966
    057,059,108-06,

LIBRARY
    LIBRARY OF CONGRESS
    AFRICAN MUSIC-A BRIEFLY ANNOTATED BIBLIOGRAPHY
    WASHINGTON,GENERAL REFERENCE AND BIBLIOGRAPHY DIVISION,
    AFRICAN SECTION,1964
    015,

    LIBRARY OF CONGRESS
    OFFICIAL PUBLICATIONS OF BRITISH EAST AFRICA, PART 3, KENYA
    AND ZANZIBAR.
    WASHINGTON, LIBRARY OF CONGRESS, 1962
    117-12,

    LIBRARY OF CONGRESS
    LIBERIA--A SELECTED LIST OF REFERENCES.
    WASHINGTON, LIBRARY OF CONGRESS, 1942
    119-12,

LIEBENOW J GUS
    LIEBENOW J GUS
    LIBERIA--THE EVOLUTION OF PRIVILEGE.
    ITHACA, CORNELL UNIVERSITY PRESS, 1969
    029,058,119-07,

    LIEBENOW J GUS
    COLONIAL RULE AND POLITICAL DEVELOPMENT IN TANZANIA-THE
    CASE OF THE MAKONDE
    EVANSTON,NORTHWESTERN UNIVERSITY PRESS,1970
    035,055,063,136-07,

    LIEBENOW J GUS
    LIBERIA.

IN G.M. CARTER, (ED), AFRICAN ONE-PARTY STATES, ITHACA,
CORNELL UNIVERSITY PRESS, 1962
119-07,

LIEBENOW J GUS
   LIEBENOW J GUS
   LIBERIA.
   IN COLEMAN, J.S. AND ROSBERG, C. G. (EDS), POLITICAL PARTIES
   AND NATIONAL INTEGRATION IN TROPICAL AFRICA, LOS ANGELES,
   UNIVERSITY OF CALIFORNIA PRESS, 1964
   119-06,

   LIEBENOW J GUS
   FEDERALISM IN RHODESIA AND NYASALAND.
   IN WILLIAM LIVINGSTON (ED), FEDERALISM IN THE COMMONWEALTH,
   LONDON, 1963
   122-07,

LIENHARDT GODFREY
   LIENHARDT GODFREY
   DIVINITY AND EXPERIENCE--THE RELIGION OF THE DINKA.
   LONDON, OXFORD UNIVERSITY PRESS, 1961
   013,134-01,

LIENHARDT PETER
   LIENHARDT PETER
   A CONTROVERSY OVER ISLAMIC CUSTOM IN KILWA KIVINJE, TANZANIA
   IN LEWIS, ISLAM IN TROPICAL AFRICA, LONDON, OXFORD UNIVERSITY
   PRESS, 1966, P. 374-386
   136-03,

LIESEGANG GERHARD
   LIESEGANG GERHARD
   DINGANES ATTACK ON LOURENCO MARQUES IN 1833
   JOURNAL OF AFRICAN HISTORY 10 1969 PP 565-580
   031,

LIJEMBE JOSEPH A
   LIJEMBE JOSEPH A   APOKO ANNA   MUTUKU NZIOKI J
   AN EAST AFRICAN CHILDHOOD--THREE VERSIONS.
   LONDON, OXFORD UNIVERSITY PRESS, 1967
   008,

LILLIAN O
   DOTSON FLOYD   LILLIAN O
   THE INDIAN MINORITY OF ZAMBIA, RHODESIA, AND MALAWI.
   NEW HAVEN, CONN. (YALE), MCGILL-QUEEN'S PRESS, 1969
   085,142-06,145-06,122-06,

LINCOLN ERIC C
   LINCOLN ERIC C
   THE BLACK MUSLIMS IN AMERICA.
   BOSTON, BEACON PRESS, 1961
   094,095,

LINDSAY KENNEDY
   LINDSAY KENNEDY
   HOW BIAFRA PAYS FOR THE WAR.
   VENTURE, MARCH 1969
   065,128-06,

LINTON NEVILLE
  LINTON NEVILLE
  NYERERE'S ROAD TO SOCIALISM
  CANADIAN JOURNAL OF AFRICAN STUDIES 2 1968 PP 1-6
  077,136-07,

LINTON RALPH
  LINTON RALPH
  NATIVISTIC MOVEMENTS.
  AMERICAN ANTHROPOLOGIST 45 APRIL 1943 PP 230-240
  051,

LIPSET SEYMOUR M
  LIPSET SEYMOUR M
  THE END OF IDEOLOGY CHAPTER 12.
  IN POLITICAL MAN, NEW YORK, DOUBLEDAY, 1960, PP 403-417
  060,

LIPSKY
  LIPSKY GEORGE ARTHUR
  ETHIOPIA--ITS PEOPLE, ITS SOCIETY, ITS CULTURE.
  NEW HAVEN, HRAF PRESS, 1962
  110-01,

LITTLE KENNETH
  LITTLE KENNETH
  WEST AFRICAN URBANIZATION-A STUDY OF VOLUNTARY ASSOCIATIONS
  IN SOCIAL CHANGE
  CAMBRIDGE, CAMBRIDGE UNIVERSITY PRESS, 1965
  046,

  LITTLE KENNETH
  THE ORGANIZATION OF VOLUNTARY ASSOCIATIONS IN WEST AFRICA.
  CIVILIZATIONS 9 1959 PP 283-300
  046,

  LITTLE KENNETH
  THE ORGANIZATION OF COMMUNAL FARMS IN THE GAMBIA.
  JOURNAL OF AFRICAN ADMINISTRATION 1 1949 PP 76-82
  070,113-08,

  LITTLE KENNETH
  RACE AND SOCIETY.
  PARIS, UNESCO, 1958
  088,

  LITTLE KENNETH
  ATTITUDES TOWARDS MARRIAGE AND THE FAMILY AMONG EDUCATED YOU
  SIERRA LEONEANS.
  IN LLOYD, THE NEW ELITES OF TROPICAL AFRICA, LONDON, OXFORD
  UNIVERSITY PRESS, 1966, P. 139-162
  131-04,

  LITTLE KENNETH
  THE MENDE OF SIERRA LEONE-A WEST AFRICAN PEOPLE IN
  TRANSITION
  LONDON, ROUTLEDGE AND KEGAN PAUL, 1951
  131-01,

LIVINGSTONE C
    LIVINGSTONE DAVID   LIVINGSTONE C
    NARRATIVE OF AN EXPEDITION TO THE ZAMBESI AND ITS
    TRIBUTARIES AND THE DISCOVERY OF THE LAKES SHIRWA AND
    NYASSA 1858-1865.
    LONDON, J MURRAY, 1965
    027,

LIVINGSTONE DAVID
    LIVINGSTONE DAVID
    MISSIONARY TRAVELS AND RESEARCHES IN SOUTH AFRICA.
    LONDON, J MURRAY, 1865
    027,

    LIVINGSTONE DAVID   LIVINGSTONE C
    NARRATIVE OF AN EXPEDITION TO THE ZAMBESI AND ITS
    TRIBUTARIES AND THE DISCOVERY OF THE LAKES SHIRWA AND
    NYASSA 1858-1865.
    LONDON, J MURRAY, 1965
    027,

    LIVINGSTONE DAVID   WALLER HORACE   EDS
    THE LAST JOURNALS OF DAVID LIVINGSTONE IN CENTRAL AFRICA.
    LONDON, J MURRAY, 1874, 2 VOLUMES
    027,

LLOYD ALAN
    LLOYD ALAN
    THE DRUMS OF KUMASI-- THE STORY OF THE ASHANTI WARS.
    LONDON, LONGMANS, 1964
    026,114-02,

LLOYD BARBARA B
    LLOYD BARBARA B
    EDUCATION AND FAMILY LIFE IN THE DEVELOPMENT OF CLASS
    IDENTIFICATION AMONG THE YORUBA.
    IN LLOYD, THE NEW ELITES OF TROPICAL AFRICA, LONDON, OXFORD
    UNIVERSITY PRESS, 1966, P. 163-183
    043,128-04,

LLOYD PETER C
    LLOYD PETER C   MABOGUNJE AKIN L   AWE B
    THE CITY OF IBADAN-- A SYMPOSIUM ON ITS STRUCTURE AND
    DEVELOPMENT.
    CAMBRIDGE, CAMBRIDGE UNIVERSITY PRESS, 1967
    026,045,128-05,

    LLOYD PETER C
    AFRICA IN SOCIAL CHANGE-- CHANGING TRADITIONAL SOCIETIES
    IN THE MODERN WORLD.
    BALTIMORE, PENGUIN, 1967
    001,038,053,

    LLOYD PETER C
    THE POLITICAL STRUCTURE OF AFRICAN KINGDOMS-- AN EXPLORATORY
    MODEL.
    IN POLITICAL SYSTEMS AND THE DISTRIBUTION OF POWER ED BY
    MICHAEL BANTON ASSOCIATION OF SOCIAL ANTHROPOLOGISTS
    MONOGRAPH NO 2 LONDON TAVISTOCK PUBLICATIONS LTD 1965
    PP 63-112

009,

LLOYD PETER C
    LLOYD PETER C
    TRADITIONAL RULERS.
    IN JAMES S COLEMAN AND CARL G ROSBERG JR. (EDS), POLITICAL
    PARTIES AND NATIONAL INTEGRATION IN TROPICAL AFRICA, BERKE-
    LY,UNIVERSITY OF CALIFORNIA PRESS,1964,PP 382-412
    009,

    LLOYD PETER C   ED
    THE NEW ELITES OF TROPICAL AFRICA
    LONDON,OXFORD UNIVERSITY PRESS,1966
    043,044,

    LLOYD PETER C
    TRIBALSIM IN NIGERIA.
    IN A A DUBB (ED), THE MULTI-TRIBAL SOCIETY, 16TH RHODES-
    LIVINGSTON INSTITUTE CONFERENCE PROCEEDINGS, 1962, LUSAKA
    PP 133-147
    057,128-06,

    LLOYD PETER C
    THE DEVELOPMENT OF POLITICAL PARTIES IN WESTERN NIGERIA.
    AMERICAN POLITICAL SCIENCE REVIEW 49 SEPTEMBER 1955
    PP 693-707
    062,128-07,

    LLOYD PETER C
    SOME MODERN DEVELOPMENTS IN YORUBA CUSTOMARY LAW.
    JOURNAL OF AFRICAN ADMINISTRATION 12 JANUARY 1960 PP 11-20
    066,128-03,

    LLOYD PETER C
    YORUBA MYTHS-- A SOCIOLOGIST≠S INTERPRETATION.
    ODU 2 1956 PP 20-28
    013,128-01,

    LLOYD PETER C
    SACRED KINGSHIP AND GOVERNMENT AMONG THE YORUBA.
    AFRICA 30 1960 PP 221-237
    009,128-01,

    LLOYD PETER C
    SOME COMMENTS ON THE ELECTIONS IN NIGERIA.
    JOURNAL OF AFRICAN ADMINISTRATION 4 1952 PP 82-92
    063,128-07,

    LLOYD PETER C
    CRAFT ORGANIZATIONS IN YORUBA TOWNS.
    AFRICA, VOL. XXIII, 1953
    010,128-01,

    LLOYD PETER C
    YORUBA LAND LAW.
    LONDON, OXFORD UNIVERSITY PRESS, 1962
    066,128-01,

    LLOYD PETER C
    THE YORUBA OF NIGERIA.

IN JAMES L GIBBS JR. (ED), PEOPLES OF AFRICA, NEW YORK, HOLT
RINEHART AND WINSTON, 1965, PP. 547-582
128-01,

LLOYD PETER C
    LLOYD PETER C
    CLASS CONSCIOUSNESS AMONG THE YORUBA.
    IN LLOYD, THE NEW ELITES OF TROPICAL AFRICA, LONDON, OXFORD
    UNIVERSITY PRESS, 1966, P. 328-341
    044,128-04,

LOCK MAX
    LOCK MAX
    A SURVEY AND PLAN OF THE CAPITAL TERRITORY FOR THE GOVERN-
    MENT OF NORTHERN NIGERIA.
    NEW YORK, PRAEGER, 1967
    092,128-05,

LOCKWOOD SHARON B
    LOCKWOOD SHARON B
    A GUIDE TO OFFICIAL PUBLICATIONS--NIGERIA.
    WASHINGTON, LIBRARY OF CONGRESS, 1966
    128-12,

LOEWENBERG GERHARD
    HESS ROBERT L   LOEWENBERG GERHARD
    THE ETHIOPIAN NO-PARTY STATE--A NOTE ON THE FUNCTIONS OF
    POLITICAL PARTIES IN DEVELOPING STATES.
    JASON L. FINKLE AND RICHARD W. GABLE (EDS), POLITICAL
    DEVELOPMENT AND SOCIAL CHANGE, JOHN WILEY AND SONS, INC.,
    NEW YORK, 1966, PP. 530-535
    061,110-07,

LOFCHIE MICHAEL
    LOFCHIE MICHAEL
    PARTY CONFLICT IN ZANZIBAR.
    JOURNAL OF MODERN AFRICAN STUDIES 1 1963 PP 185-207
    061,136-07,

    LOFCHIE MICHAEL
    ZANZIBAR-- BACKGROUND TO REVOLUTION.
    PRINCETON, NEW JERSEY, PRINCETON UNIVERSITY PRESS, 1965
    055,136-06,

LOGAN RAYFORD W
    LOGAN RAYFORD W
    THE HISTORICAL ASPECTS OF PAN-AFRICANISM 1900-1945.
    IN AMERICAN SOCIETY FOR AFRICAN CULTURE, PAN-AFRICANISM
    RECONSIDERED, BERKELEY, UNIVERSITY OF CALIFORNIA PRESS, 1962
    PP 37-52
    079,

    LOGAN RAYFORD W
    THE AFRICAN MANDATES IN WORLD POLITICS.
    WASHINGTON, PUBLIC AFFAIRS PRESS, 1948
    081,

    LOGAN RAYFORD W
    EDUCATION IN FORMER FRENCH WEST AND EQUATORIAL AFRICA AND
    MADAGASCAR.

JOURNAL OF NEGRO EDUCATION 30 1961 PP 277-285
042,

LOGAN RAYFORD W
  LOGAN RAYFORD W
  THE AMERICAN NEGRO'S VIEW OF AFRICA.
  IN AMSAC, AFRICA SEEN BY AMERICAN NEGROES, PARIS,
  PRESENCE AFRICAINE, 1958, PP 217-228
  094,

  LOGAN RAYFORD W
  THE HISTORICAL ASPECTS OF PAN-AFRICANISM-- A PERSONAL CHRON-
  ICLE.
  AFRICAN FORUM I 1 1965 PP 90-104
  030,079,

LOKEN ROBERT D
  LOKEN ROBERT D
  MANPOWER DEVELOPMENT IN AFRICA.
  NEW YORK, PRAEGER PUBLISHERS, 1969
  072,

LOMBARD J
  LOMBARD J
  COTONOU, VILLE AFRICAINE.
  ETUDES DAHOMEENES, 10, 1953
  109-05,

LONG NORMAN
  LONG NORMAN
  SOCIAL CHANGE AND THE INDIVIDUAL--A STUDY OF THE SOCIAL AND
  RELIGIOUS RESPONSES TO INNOVATION IN A ZAMBIAN RURAL
  COMMUNITY.
  NEW YORK, HUMANITIES PRESS, INC., 1968
  051,142-03,

LONG RICHARD A
  BERRIAN ALBERT H   LONG RICHARD A   EDS
  NEGRITUDE--ESSAYS AND STUDIES.
  HAMPTON, VIRGINIA, HAMPTON INSTITUTE PRESS, 1967
  060,

LONSDALE JOHN
  LONSDALE JOHN
  THE TANZANIAN EXPERIMENT
  AFRICAN AFFAIRS 67 1968 PP 330-344
  063,070,136-11,

LORIMER FRANK
  LORIMER FRANK   BRASS WILLIAM   VAN DE WALLE E
  DEMOGRAPHY.
  IN ROBERT A LYSTAD (ED), THE AFRICAN WORLD, NEW YORK,
  PRAEGER, 1966, PP 271-303
  069,074,

  LORIMER FRANK   KARP MARK   EDS
  POPULATION IN AFRICA.
  BOSTON, BOSTON UNIVERSITY PRESS, 1960
  069,074,

LORIN
    RAKOTO-RATSIMAMANGA LORIN CLAUDE-MARIE
    POETES MALGACHES DE LANGUE FRANCAISE.
    PARIS, PRESENCE AFRICAINE, 1956
    121-10,

LOUCHHEIM DONALD H
    LOUCHHEIM DONALD H
    THE MILITARY'S ECONOMIC LEGACY.
    AFRICA REPORT 11 MARCH 1966 P 18
    064,

LOUDON J B
    LOUDON J B
    PSYCHOGENIC DISORDER AND SOCIAL CONFLICT AMONG THE ZULU.
    IN MARVIN K OPLER (ED.), CULTURE AND MENTAL HEALTH, NEW YORK
    MACMILLAN, PP 351-369
    041,132-03,

LOUIS
    LOUIS WILLIAM ROGER
    RUANDA-URUNDI-- 1884-1919.
    OXFORD,CLARENDON PRESS,1963
    033,103-02,129-02,

LOUIS WILLIAM ROGER
    GIFFORD PROSSER   LOUIS WILLIAM ROGER
    BRITAIN AND GERMANY IN AFRICA--IMPERIAL RIVALRY AND COLONIAL
    RULE.
    NEW HAVEN, CONN. (YALE), MCGILL-QUEEN'S PRESS, 1969
    033,

LOW DAVID A
    LOW DAVID A
    THE NORTHERN INTERIOR 1840-1884
    IN OLIVER AND MATHEW,HISTORY OF EAST AFRICA, LONDON, OXFORD,
    1963 PP 297-351
    025,

    LOW DAVID A
    THE ADVENT OF POPULISM IN BUGANDA.
    COMPARATIVE STUDIES IN SOCIETY AND HISTORY 6 JULY 1964
    PP 424-444
    055,139-06,

    LOW DAVID A   PRATT R CRANFORD
    BUGANDA AND BRITISH OVERRULE 1900-1955.
    LONDON,OXFORD UNIVERSITY PRESS,1960
    035,139-02,

    LOW DAVID A
    POLITICAL PARTIES IN UGANDA 1949-1962.
    LONDON,1962
    055,139-07,

    LOW DAVID A
    UGANDA-- THE ESTABLISHMENT OF THE PROTECTORATE, 1894-1919.
    IN VINCENT HARLOW AND E M CHILVER (EDS),HISTORY OF EAST
    AFRICA VOL II,OXFORD,CLARENDON PRESS,1965,PP 57-122
    033,139-02,

LOW DAVID A
  LOW DAVID A
  BRITISH EAST AFRICA-- THE ESTABLISHMENT OF BRITISH RULE,
  1895-1912.
  IN VINCENT HARLOW AND E M CHILVER (EDS) HISTORY OF EAST
  AFRICA VOL II,OXFORD,CLARENDON PRESS,1965, PP 1-56
  033,

LOWENSTEIN STEVEN
  LOWENSTEIN STEVEN
  MATERIALS FOR THE STUDY OF THE PENAL LAW OF ETHIOPIA.
  EASTERN AFRICA, OXFORD UNIVERSITY PRESS, 1965
  067,110-06,

LOWENTHAL RICHARD
  LOWENTHAL RICHARD
  CHINA.
  IN Z BRZEZINSKI (ED), AFRICA AND THE COMMUNIST WORLD,
  STANFORD, CALIFORNIA, STANFORD UNIVERSITY PRESS, 1963,
  PP 142-203
  084,

LUCAS J OLUMIDE
  LUCAS J OLUMIDE
  THE RELIGION OF THE YORUBAS.
  LAGOS, C.M.S. BOOKSHOP, 1948
  038,

LUGARD FREDERICK D
  LUGARD FREDERICK D
  THE DUAL MANDATE IN BRITISH TROPICAL AFRICA.
  LONDON,CASS,1965
  035,

  LUGARD FREDERICK D
  THE WHITE MAN'S TASK IN TROPICAL AFRICA.
  IN PHILIP W QUIGG (ED.), AFRICA, NEW YORK, PRAEGER, 1964,
  PP 5-16
  035,

  LUGARD FREDERICK D
  THE RISE OF OUR EAST AFRICAN EMPIRE.
  LONDON,BLACKWOOD, 2 VOLS, 1893
  033,

  LUGARD FREDERICK D
  THE STORY OF THE UGANDA PROTECTORATE.
  LONDON,H MARSHALL,1901
  033,139-02,

LUKHERO M B
  LUKHERO M B
  THE SOCIAL CHARACTERISTICS OF AN EMERGENT ELITE IN HARARE.
  IN LLOYD, THE NEW ELITES OF TROPICAL AFRICA, LONDON, OXFORD
  UNIVERSITY PRESS, 1966, P. 126-138
  144-04,

LUMUMBA PATRICE
  LUMUMBA PATRICE

CONGO, MY COUNTRY.
NEW YORK, PRAEGER PUBLISHERS, 1962
060,108-04,

LUMUMBA PATRICE
LUMUMBA PATRICE
RESUME DE LA CONFERENCE DONEE LE 13 AVRIL 1958 AUX MEMBRES
DE LA FEDERATION DES BATETELA.
LEOPOLDVILLE, RONEOTYPE, 1958
108-04,

LUMUMBA PATRICE
LE CONGO, TERRE D'AVENIR EST-IL MENACE.
BRUXELLES, OFFICE DE PUBLICITE, 1961
108-04,

LUMUMBA PATRICE
LA PENSEE POLITIQUE DE PATRICE LUMUMBA--PREFACE DE JEAN-PAUL
SARTRE--TEXTES RECUEILLIS ET PRESENTES PAR JEAN VAN LIERDE.
PARIS, PRESENCE AFRICAINE, XLV, 1963
108-04,

LUMUMBA PATRICE
LA VERITE SUR LE CRIME ODIEUX DES COLONIALISTES.
MOSCOW. LES EDITIONS EN LANGUES ETRANGERES, 1961
108-04,

LUMUMBA PATRICE
PROPOS DE M PATRICE LUMUMBA, PREMIER MINISTRE DE LA
REPUBLIQUE DU CONGO.
BRUXELLES, COMMISSION DE COORDINATION, 1965
108-04,

LURY D A
ROBSON PETER   LURY D A   EDS
THE ECONOMIES OF AFRICA.
EVANSTON, NORTHWESTERN UNIVERSITY PRESS, 1969
073,

LUSIGNAN GUY DE
LUSIGNAN GUY DE
FRENCH-SPEAKING AFRICA SINCE INDEPENDENCE.
NEW YORK, PRAEGER PUBLISHERS, 1969
056,061,104-11,105-11,106-11,107-11,109-11,112-11,
115-11,116-11,123-11,137-11,141-11,

LUTHULI ALBERT
LUTHULI ALBERT
AFRICA AND FREEDOM CHAPTER 1.
IN AFRICA'S FREEDOM, NEW YORK, BARNES AND NOBLE,
1964, PP 9-23
079,089,132-04,

LY ABDOULAYE
LY ABDOULAYE
LA COMPAGNIE DU SENEGAL.
PARIS, PRESENCE AFRICAINE, 1958
130-08,

LY ABDOULAYE

UN NAVIRE DE COMMERCE SUR LA COTE SENEGAMBIENNE EN 1685.
DAKAR, IFAN, 1964
130-03,

LYE WILLIAM F
    LYE WILLIAM F
    THE DIFAQANE-THE MFECANE IN THE SOUTHERN SOTHO AREA 1822-24
    JOURNAL OF AFRICAN HISTORY 8 1967 PP 107-131
    031,118-02,132-02,

    LYE WILLIAM F
    THE NDEBELE KINGDOM SOUTH OF THE LIMPOPO RIVER.
    JOURNAL OF AFRICAN HISTORY, X, 1, 1969, PP. 87-104
    025,

LYNCH HOLLIS R
    LYNCH HOLLIS R
    PAN-NEGRO NATIONALISM IN THE NEW WORLD.
    IN JEFFREY BUTLER (ED) BOSTON UNIVERSITY PAPERS ON AFRICAN
    HISTORY VOLUME 2, BOSTON BOSTON UNIVERSITY PRESS 1966 PP
    147-180
    029,030,

    LYNCH HOLLIS R
    EDWARD WILMOT BLYDEN--PAN-NEGRO PATRIOT 1832-1912.
    LONDON, OXFORD UNIVERSITY PRESS, 1967
    029,030,119-02,

LYND STAUGHTON
    LYND STAUGHTON
    RETHINKING SLAVERY AND RECONSTRUCTION.
    JOURNAL OF NEGRO HISTORY 1 JULY 1965 PP 198-209
    030,

LYSTAD MARY H
    LYSTAD MARY H
    PAINTINGS OF GHANAIAN CHILDREN.
    AFRICA 30 1960 PP 238-242
    040,114-03,

    LYSTAD MARY H
    TRADITIONAL VALUES OF GHANAIAN CHILDREN.
    AMERICAN ANTHROPOLOGIST 42 1960 PP 454-464
    040,114-01,

LYSTAD ROBERT A
    LYSTAD ROBERT A   ED
    THE AFRICAN WORLD.
    NEW YORK, PRAEGER, 1965
    100,

    LYSTAD ROBERT A
    R AND D AT THE GRASS ROOTS.
    AFRICA REPORT, MAY 1968, P. 12
    075,

    APTER DAVID E   LYSTAD ROBERT A
    BUREAUCRACY, PARTY, AND CONSTITUTIONAL DEMOCRACY-- AN EXAM-
    INATION OF POLITICAL ROLE SYSTEMS IN GHANA.
    IN GWENDOLEN M CARTER AND WILLIAM O BROWN (EDS), TRANSITION

IN AFRICA-- STUDIES IN POLITICAL ADAPTATION, BOSTON, BOSTON
UNIVERSITY PRESS, 1958, PP 16-43
062,114-07,

LYSTAD ROBERT A
LYSTAD ROBERT A
MARRIAGE AND KINSHIP AMONG THE ASHANTI AND THE AGNI--
A STUDY OF DIFFERENTIAL ACCULTURATION CHAPTER 10.
IN WILLIAM BASCOM AND MELVILLE HERSKOVITS, CONTINUTY AND
CHANGE IN AFRICAN CULTURES, CHICAGO, UNIVERSITY OF CHICAGO
PRESS, 1962, PP 187-204
008,114-01,

M

MABOGUNJE AKIN L
LLOYD PETER C   MABOGUNJE AKIN L   AWE B
THE CITY OF IBADAN-- A SYMPOSIUM ON ITS STRUCTURE AND
DEVELOPMENT.
CAMBRIDGE, CAMBRIDGE UNIVERSITY PRESS, 1967
026,045,128-05,

MABOGUNJE AKIN L
URBANIZATION IN NIGERIA.
NEW YORK, AFRICANA PUBLISHING CORPORATION, 1969
045,047,128-05,

MABOGUNJE AKIN L
URBANIZATION IN WEST AFRICA.
INTERNATIONAL REVIEW OF MISSIONS 55 JULY 1966
045,

MABOGUNJE AKIN L
THE EVOLUTION OF RURAL SETTLEMENT IN EGBA DIVISION, NIGERIA.
JOURNAL OF TROPICAL GEOGRAPHY, SINGAPORE AND KUALA LUMPUR
13 DECEMBER 1959 PP 65-77
045,128-05,

MABOGUNJE AKIN L
THE GROWTH OF RESIDENTIAL DISTRICTS IN IBADAN.
GEOGRAPHICAL REVIEW JANUARY 1962 PP 56-77
046,128-05,

MABOGUNJE AKIN L
URBANIZATION IN NIGERIA-A CONSTRAINT ON ECONOMIC DEVELOPMENT
ECONOMIC DEVELOPMENT AND CULTURAL CHANGE 13 1965 PP 413-438
047,128-05,

MABOGUNJE AKIN L
YORUBA TOWNS.
IBADAN, IBADAN UNIVERSITY PRESS, 1962
128-05,

MACARTNEY W A J
MACARTNEY W A J
BOTSWANA GOES TO THE POLLS

AFRICA   REPORT DECEMBER 1969 PP 28-30
063,102-07,

MACKAY IAN K
   MACKAY IAN K
   BROADCASTING IN NIGERIA.
   IBADAN, IBADAN UNIVERSITY PRESS. 1964
   049,128-03,

MACKENZIE NORMAN
   MACKENZIE NORMAN
   A GUIDE TO THE SOCIAL SCIENCES.
   LONDON,WEIDENFELD AND NICOLSON,1966
   098,

MACKENZIE W J
   MACKENZIE W J   ROBINSON KENNETH
   FIVE ELECTIONS IN AFRICA.
   OXFORD,CLARENDON PRESS,1960
   063,

MACKINTOSH JOHN P
   MACKINTOSH JOHN P
   FEDERALISM IN NIGERIA.
   POLITICAL STUDIES 10 OCTOBER 1962 PP 223-247
   061,128-07,

   MACKINTOSH JOHN P
   ELECTORAL TRENDS AND THE TENDENCY TO A ONE PARTY
   SYSTEM IN NIGERIA.
   JOURNAL OF COMMONWEALTH POLITICAL STUDIES 1 NOVEMBER 1962
   PP 194-210
   063,128-07,

   MACKINTOSH JOHN P   ED
   NIGERIAN GOVERNMENT AND POLITICS.
   EVANSTON,NORTHWESTERN UNIVERSITY PRESS,1966
   061,128-07,

MADIERA KIETA
   MADIERA KIETA
   THE SINGLE PARTY IN AFRICA.
   PRESENCE AFRICAINE 30 FEBRUARY 1960 PP 3-24
   060,061,065,123-04,

MAESEN ALBERT
   MAESEN ALBERT
   UMBANGU, ART DU CONGO AU MUSEE ROYAL DU CONGO BELGE
   (UMBANGU, CONGO ART IN THE ROYAL MUSEUM OF THE BELGIAN
   CONGO).
   BRUXELLES,MUSEE ROYAL DE L'AFRIQUE CENTRALE,1960
   014,108-01,

MAGENAU MARY S
   MAGENAU MARY S
   A BIBLIOGRAPHY OF DEVELOPMENT PLANS IN AFRICA SOUTH OF THE
   SAHARA
   NEW HAVEN,YALE UNIVERSITY,ECONOMIC GROWTH CENTER LIBRARY,
   1966, 5P.
   072,

MAINI KRISHAN M
    MAINI KRISHAN M
    LAND LAW IN EAST AFRICA.
    EAST AFRICA, OXFORD UNIVERSITY PRESS, 1968
    066,

MAIR LUCY P
    MAIR LUCY P
    SOCIAL CHANGE IN AFRICA.
    INTERNATIONAL AFFAIRS 36 OCTOBER 1960 PP 447-456
    038,

    MAIR LUCY P
    MODERN DEVELOPMENTS IN AFRICAN LAND TENURE-- AN ASPECT
    OF CULTURE CHANGE.
    AFRICA 18 JULY 1948 PP 184-189
    070,

    MAIR LUCY P
    PRIMITIVE GOVERNMENT.
    BALTIMORE, PENGUIN 1962
    009,

    MAIR LUCY P
    THE GROWTH OF ECONOMIC INDIVIDUALISM IN AFRICAN SOCIETY.
    JOURNAL OF THE ROYAL AFRICAN SOCIETY 33 1934 PP 261-273
    074,

    MAIR LUCY P
    NATIVE POLICIES IN AFRICA.
    LONDON, G ROUTLEDGE, 1936
    035,

    MAIR LUCY P
    NATIVE ADMINISTRATION IN CENTRAL NYASALAND.
    LONDON, HIS MAJESTY'S STATIONERY OFFICE, 1952
    035,122-02,

    MAIR LUCY P
    THE NYASALAND ELECTIONS OF 1961.
    LONDON, ATHLONE PRESS, 1962
    063,122-07,

    MAIR LUCY P
    STUDIES IN APPLIED ANTHROPOLOGY.
    LONDON, THE ATHLONE PRESS, 1957
    010,

    MAIR LUCY P
    NEW NATIONS.
    LONDON, WEIDENFELD AND NICOLSON, 1963
    076,

    MAIR LUCY P
    WITCHCRAFT.
    NEW YORK, INTERNATIONAL UNIVERSITY BOOKSELLERS, INC., 1969
    013,

MAKINGS S M

MAKINGS S M
AGRICULTURAL PROBLEMS OF DEVELOPING AFRICAN COUNTRIES.
EASTERN AFRICA, OXFORD UNIVERSITY PRESS, 1967
070,

MALCOLM X
    MALCOLM X   EPPS ARCHIE EDITOR
    THE SPEECHES OF MALCOLM X AT HARVARD.
    NEW YORK, WILLIAM MORROW AND COMPANY, INC., 1968
    094,

MALINOWSKI B
    MALINOWSKI B
    THE DYNAMICS OF CULTURE CHANGE-- AN INQUIRY INTO
    RACE RELATIONS IN AFRICA.
    NEW HAVEN, YALE UNIVERSITY PRESS, 1945
    088,

    MALINOWSKI B
    MAGIC, SCIENCE AND RELIGION
    GARDEN CITY, DOUBLEDAY ANCHOR BOOKS, 1948
    013,

MALONGA JEAN
    MALONGA JEAN
    COEUR D'ARYENNE.
    PARIS, PRESENCE AFRICAINE, 1955
    107-10,

    MALONGA JEAN
    LA LEGENDE DE M PFOUMOU MA MAZONO.
    PARIS, PRESENCE AFRICAINE, 1954
    107-10,

MANGAT J S
    MANGAT J S
    A HISTORY OF THE ASIANS IN EAST AFRICA.
    LONDON, OXFORD UNIVERSITY PRESS, 1969
    085,

MANN H S
    MANN H S
    LAND TENURE IN CHORE.
    ADDIS ABABA, INSTITUTE OF ETHIOPIAN STUDIES, HAILE
    SELASSIE UNIVERSITY WITH OXFORD UNIVERSITY PRESS, 1965
    070,110-08,

MANNERS ROBERT
    DUFFY JAMES   MANNERS ROBERT   EDS
    AFRICA SPEAKS.
    PRINCETON, VAN NOSTRAND, 1961
    060,

MANNHEIM KARL
    MANNHEIM KARL
    IDEOLOGY AND UTOPIA CHAPTER 2.
    IN IDEOLOGY AND UTOPIA NEW YORK, HARCOURT BRACE AND
    WORLD, 1936, PP 49-96
    060,

MANNIX DANIEL
   MANNIX DANIEL   COWLEY MALCOLM
   BLACK CARGOES-- A HISTORY OF THE ATLANTIC SLAVE TRADE 1518-
   1865.
   NEW YORK, VIKING PRESS, 1962
   028,

MANNONI
   MANNONI DOMINIQUE O
   PROSPERO AND CALIBAN-- THE PSYCHOLOGY OF COLONIZATION.
   LONDON, METHUEN AND COMPANY, 1956 (NEW YORK, PRAEGER, 1964)
   035,041,088,121-03,

MANSERGH NICOLAS
   MANSERGH NICOLAS
   SOUTH AFRICA 1906-1961- THE PRICE OF MAGNANIMITY
   NEW YORK, PRAEGER, 1962
   032,

MANSFIELD PETER
   MANSFIELD PETER
   NASSER'S EGYPT.
   BALTIMORE, PENGUIN, 1966
   140-11,

MAQUET JACQUES J
   MAQUET JACQUES J
   PROBLEMES DES SCIENCES HUMAINES EN AFRIQUE CENTRALE,
   (PROBLEMS OF THE HUMAN SCIENCES IN CENTRAL AFRICA).
   INSTITUT DE RECHERCHE SCIENTIFIQUE D'AFRIQUE CENTRALE
   8TH RAPPORT 1955 PP 83-95
   099,

   MAQUET JACQUES J
   CONNAISSANCE DES RELIGIONS TRADITIONELLES (KNOWLEDGE OF
   TRADITIONAL RELIGIONS).
   IN RENCONTRES INTERNATIONALES DE BOUAKE, LES RELIGIONS
   AFRICAINES TRADITIONNELLES, PARIS, EDITIONS DU SEUIL, 1965,
   PP 57-74
   013,

   MAQUET JACQUES J
   THE PREMISE OF INEQUALITY IN RUANDA.
   LONDON, OXFORD UNIVERSITY PRESS, 1961
   057,129-01,

MARCUM JOHN A
   MARCUM JOHN A
   THE ANGOLAN REVOLUTION VOLUME 1- THE ANATOMY OF AN EXPLOSION
   CAMBRIDGE, MASS, MIT PRESS, 1969
   087,144-11,

   MARCUM JOHN A
   PAN-AFRICANISM OR FRAGMENTATION.
   IN WILLIAM H LEWIS, NEW FORCES IN AFRICA, GEORGETOWN
   COLLOQUIUM ON AFRICA, PAPERS, WASHINGTON, PUBLIC AFFAIRS
   PRESS, 1962, PP 25-41
   079,

   MARCUM JOHN A

THREE REVOLUTIONS.
AFRICA REPORT 12 NOVEMBER 1967 PP 8-22
064,

MARCUM JOHN A
   MARCUM JOHN A
   A MARTYR FOR MOZAMBIQUE.
   AFRICA REPORT, MARCH/APRIL, 1969, PP. 6-9
   087,144-06,

MARE W S
   MARE W S
   AFRICAN TRADE UNIONS.
   LONDON,LONGMANS,1949
   073,

MARIE-ANDRE SISTER
   MARIE-ANDRE SISTER
   TRIBAL LABOUR AND SOCIAL LEGISLATION IN FRENCH TROPICAL
   AFRICA.
   INTERNATIONAL LABOUR REVIEW 68 DECEMBER 1953 PP 493-508
   035,

MARINE GENE
   MARINE GENE
   THE BLACK PANTHERS
   NEW YORK,NEW AMERICAN LIBRARY-SIGNET BOOKS,1969
   095,

MARIOGHAE MICHAEL
   MARIOGHAE MICHAEL   FERGUSON JOHN
   NIGERIA UNDER THE CROSS.
   LONDON,THE HIGHWAY PRESS,1965
   050,128-03,

MARKOVITZ IRVING L
   MARKOVITZ IRVING L
   LEOPOLD SENGHOR AND THE POLITICS OF NEGRITUDE.
   NEW YORK, ATHENEUM, 1969   (LONDON, HEINEMANN
   EDUCATIONAL BOOKS)
   044,054,130-04,

   MARKOVITZ IRVING L   ED
   AFRICAN POLITICS AND SOCIETY
   NEW YORK,THE FREE PRESS,1970
   076,

MARRIS PETER
   MARRIS PETER
   FAMILY AND SOCIAL CHANGE IN AN AFRICAN CITY (LAGOS).
   EVANSTON, NORTHWESTERN UNIVERSITY PRESS, 1962
   128-05,

   MARRIS PETER
   MOTIVES AND METHODS--REFLECTIONS ON A STUDY IN LAGOS.
   IN THE CITY IN MODERN AFRICA, HORACE MINER (ED), NEW YORK,
   FREDERICK A. PRAEGER, 1967

MARSH WILLIAM W
   MARSH WILLIAM W

EAST GERMANY AND AFRICA.
AFRICA REPORT, MARCH/APRIL, 1969, PP. 59-64
084,

MARSHALL CHARLES B
MARSHALL CHARLES B
CRISIS OVER RHODESIA--A SKEPTICAL VIEW.
BALTIMORE SCHOOL OF ADVANCED INTERNATIONAL STUDIES, JOHNS
BALTIMORE, JOHNS HOPKINS PRESS, 1967
145-06,

MARTIN
EMERSON RUPERT   KILSON MARTIN L   EDS
THE POLITICAL AWAKENING OF AFRICA.
ENGLEWOOD CLIFFS, NJ, PRENTICE-HALL, 1965
060,

MARTIN B G
MARTIN B G
MUSLIM POLITICS AND RESISTANCE TO COLONIAL RULE.
IN JOURNAL OF AFRICAN HISTORY VOL 10 1969 P 471
034,

MARTIN B G
KANEM, BORNU, AND THE FAZZAN--NOTES ON THE POLITICAL HISTORY
OF A TRADE SOURCE.
JOURNAL OF AFRICAN HISTORY, X, 1, 1969, PP. 15-27
024,106-02,

MARTIN HUGH
JONES ARNOLD   MARTIN HUGH   MONROE ELIZABETH
A HISTORY OF ETHIOPIA
OXFORD, CLARENDON PRESS, 1955, SECOND EDITION
110-02,

MARTY PAUL
MARTY PAUL
ETUDES SUR L'ISLAM AU SENEGAL-- LES DOCTRINES ET LES
INSTITUTIONS (STUDIES ON ISLAM IN SENEGAL-- THE DOCTRINES
AND THE INSTITUTIONS).
COLLECTIONS DE LA REVUE DU MONDE, PARIS, MAISON ERNEST
LEROUX, 1917
021,130-03,

MARTY PAUL
ETUDES SUR L'ISLAM ET LES TRIBUS DU SOUDAN (STUDIES ON
ISLAM AND THE SUDANIC TRIBES).
PARIS, EDITIONS ERNEST LEROUX, 1920
021,123-03,

MARTY PAUL
LA REGION DE KAYES, LE PAYS BAMBARA, LE SAHEL DE NIORO VOL4
(THE KAYES REGION, BAMBARA COUNTRY, THE NIORO SAVANNAH).
IN ETUDES SUR L'ISLAM ET LES TRIBUS DU SOUDAN, PARIS,
EDITIONS ERNEST LEROUX, 1920
021,123-03,

MARTY PAUL
ETUDES SUR L'ISLAM ET LES TRIBUS MAURES-- LES BRAKNA
(STUDIES ON ISLAM AND THE MAURITANIAN TRIBES-- THE BRAKNA)

PARIS, EDITIONS ERNEST LEROUX, 1921
021,124-03,

MARTY PAUL
    MARTY PAUL
    L'ISLAM ET LES TRIBUS DANS LA COLONIE DU NIGER-- EXTRAIT
    DE LA REVUE DES ETUDES ISLAMIQUES (ISLAM AND THE TRIBES
    OF NIGER COLONY-- EXTRACT FROM THE REVIEW OF ISLAMIC
    STUDIES).
    PARIS, LIBRARIE ORIENTALISTE PAUL GEUTHNER, 1931
    021,127-03,

    MARTY PAUL
    ETUDES SUR L'ISLAM EN COTE D'IVOIRE (STUDIES ON ISLAM IN
    THE IVORY COAST).
    PARIS, EDITIONS ERNEST LEROUX, 1922
    021, 116-03,

    MARTY PAUL
    L'ISLAM EN GUINNEE-- FOUTA DJALLON (ISLAM IN GUINEA-- FOUTA
    DJALON).
    PARIS, EDITIONS ERNEST LEROUX, 1921
    021,115-03,

MARZOUK G A
    HANSEN B   MARZOUK G A
    DEVELOPMENT AND ECONOMIC POLICY IN THE UAR
    AMSTERDAM, NORTH HOLLAND PUBLISHING COMPANY, 1965
    073,140-08,

MASEFIELD G B
    MASEFIELD G B
    AGRICULTURAL CHANGE IN UGANDA, 1945-1960, CHAPTER 5.
    IN EDITH WHETHAM AND JEAN CURRIE (EDS.), READINGS IN THE
    APPLIED ECONOMICS OF AFRICA, LONDON, CAMBRIDGE UNIVERSITY
    PRESS, 1, 1967, PP 38-57
    070,139-08,

MASON MICHAEL
    MASON MICHAEL
    POPULATION DENSITY AND SLAVE RAIDING-THE CASE OF THE
    MIDDLE BELT OF NIGERIA
    JOURNAL OF AFRICAN HISTORY 10 1969 PP 551-564
    028,

MASON PHILIP
    MASON PHILIP
    THE BIRTH OF A DILEMMA-- THE CONQUEST AND SETTLEMENT OF
    RHODESIA.
    LONDON, OXFORD UNIVERSITY PRESS, 1958
    087,145-06,

MASSON-DEFOURRET A M
    LEBEUF JEAN PAUL   MASSON-DEFOURRET A M
    LA CIVILIZATION DU CHAD.
    PARIS, PAYOT, 1950
    106-02,

MATHEW GERVASE
    MATHEW GERVASE

THE EAST AFRICAN COAST UNTIL THE COMING OF THE PORTUGUESE.
IN ROLAND OLIVER AND GERVASE MATHEW (EDS), HISTORY OF EAST
AFRICA VOLUME ONE. OXFORD, CLARENDON PRESS, 1963. PP 94-128
023.

MATHEW GERVASE
OLIVER ROLAND   MATHEW GERVASE   EDS
HISTORY OF EAST AFRICA, VOLUME ONE.
OXFORD, CLARENDON PRESS, 1963
023,036.

MATHEW GERVASE
RECENT DISCOVERIES IN EAST AFRICAN ARCHAEOLOGY.
ANTIQUITY 27 1953 PP 212-218
023.

MATHEW GERVASE
THE CULTURE OF THE EAST AFRICAN COAST IN THE 17TH AND 18TH
CENTURIES IN THE LIGHT OF RECENT ARCHAEOLOGICAL STUDIES.
MAN 56 1956 PP 65-68
023.

MATTHEW DANIEL G
MATTHEW DANIEL G   COMP
A CURRENT BIBLIOGRAPHY ON ETHIOPIAN AFFIARS--A SELECT
BIBLIOGRAPHY FROM 1950-1964.
WASHINGTON. AFRICAN BIBLIOGRAPHIC CENTER, 1965
110-12.

MATTHEWS D G
MATTHEWS D G
A CURRENT BIBLIOGRAPHY ON SUDANESE AFFAIRS, 1960-64.
WASHINGTON, AFRICAN BIBLIOGRAPHIC CENTER, 1965
134-12.

MAUNY RAYMOND
MAUNY RAYMOND
THE QUESTION OF GHANA.
AFRICA 24 1954 PP 200-213
022.

MAUNY RAYMOND
TABLEAU GEOGRAPHIQUE DE L'OUEST AFRICAIN AU MOYEN AGE
D'APRES LES SOURCES ECRITES, LA TRADITION, ET L'ARCHEOLOGIE
(GEOGRAPHIC TABLEAU OF WEST AFRICA IN THE MIDDLE AGES BASED
ON WRITTEN SOURCES TRADITIONS AND ARCHEOLOGICAL FINDINGS.
DAKAR, INSTITUT FRANCAIS'D AFRIQUE NOIRE, MEMOIRES 61 1961
022.

MAUNY RAYMOND
UNE ROUTE PREHISTORIQUE A TRAVERS LE SAHARA OCCIDENTAL (A
PREHISTORIC ROUTE ACROSS THE WESTERN SAHARA).
BULLETIN DE L'INSTITUT FRANCAIS D'AFRIQUE NOIRE 19 1947
PP 341-357
022.

MAXWELL JOHN C
MAXWELL JOHN C
CONTINENTAL DRIFT AND A DYNAMIC EARTH
AMERICAN SCIENTIST 56 1968 PP 35-51

017,

MAY R S
   MAY R S
   DIRECT OVERSEAS INVESTMENT IN NIGERIA 1953-63 CHAPTER 8.
   IN EDITH WHETHAM AND JEAN CURRIE (EDS.), READINGS IN THE
   APPLIED ECONOMICS OF AFRICA, LONDON, CAMBRIDGE UNIVERSITY
   PRESS, 1, 1967, PP 72-92
   073,128-08,

MAYER PHILIP
   MAYER PHILIP
   TOWNSMEN OR TRIBESMEN-- CONSERVATISM AND THE PROCESS OF
   URBANIZATION IN A SOUTH AFRICAN CITY.
   CAPETOWN, OXFORD UNIVERSITY PRESS, 1961
   047,089,132-05,

   MAYER PHILIP
   THE TRIBAL ELITE AND THE TRANSKEIAN ELECTIONS OF 1963.
   IN LLOYD, THE NEW ELITES OF TROPICAL AFRICA, LONDON, OXFORD
   UNIVERSITY PRESS, 1966, P. 286-311
   132-07,

MAZERICK CARROLL F
   MAZERICK CARROLL F
   SOUTH WEST AFRICA AND THE UNITED NATIONS
   NEW YORK, UNIVERSITY PRESS OF KENTUCKY, 1968
   081,146-09,

MAZRUI ALI A
   MAZRUI ALI A
   THE UNITED NATIONS AND SOME AFRICAN POLITICAL ATTITUDES
   CHAPTER 12.
   IN ON HEROES AND UHURU-WORSHIP, LONDON, LONGMANS,
   1967, PP 183-208, ALSO INTERNATIONAL ORGANIZATION 18 1964
   PP 514-515
   081,

   MAZRUI ALI A
   TOWARDS A PAX AFRICANA-- A STUDY OF IDEOLOGY AND AMBITION.
   LONDON, WEIDENFELD AND NICOLSON, 1967
   CHICAGO, UNIVERSITY OF CHICAGO PRESS, 1967
   060,077,099,

   MAZRUI ALI A   ROTBERG ROBERT I   EDS
   THE TRADITIONS OF PROTEST IN BLACK AFRICA, 1886-1966.
   CAMBRIDGE, MASSACHUSETTS, HARVARD UNIVERSITY PRESS, 1970
   034,035,

   MAZRUI ALI A
   ON HEROES AND UHURU-WORSHIP
   LONDON, LONGMANS, 1967
   002,097,

   MAZRUI ALI A
   AFRICA AND THE THIRD WORLD CHAPTER 13
   IN ON HEROES AND UHURU-WORSHIP, LONDON, LONGMANS, 1967, 209-230
   085,

   MAZRUI ALI A

BORROWED THEORY AND ORIGINAL PRACTICE IN AFRICAN POLITICS.
IN HERBERT SPIRO ED, PATTERNS OF AFRICAN DEVELOPMENT,
ENGLEWOOD CLIFFS, NEW JERSEY, PRENTICE-HALL, 1967
060,

MAZRUI ALI A
    MAZRUI ALI A
    EXTERNAL EVENTS AND INTERNAL RACIAL TENSION CHAPTER 4.
    IN ON HEROES AND UHURU-WORSHIP, LONDON, LONGMANS,
    1967, PP 50-60
    088,

    MAZRUI ALI A
    AFRICA AND EGYPT'S FOUR CIRCLES CHAPTER 7.
    IN ON HEROES AND UHURU-WORSHIP, LONDON, LONGMANS,
    1967, PP 96-112
    086,140-09,

    MAZRUI ALI A
    EDMUND BURKE AND REFLECTIONS ON THE REVOLUTION IN THE CONGO.
    IN ON HEROES AND UHURU-WORSHIP, LONDON, LONGMANS, 1967
    064,108-06,

    MAZRUI ALI A
    ON HEROES AND UHURU-WORSHIP CHAPTER 2.
    IN ON HEROES AND UHURU-WORSHIP, LONDON, LONGMANS,
    1967, PP 19-34
    044,

    MAZRUI ALI A
    AFRICAN DOCTRINES OF NON-INTERVENTION CHAPTER 3.
    IN ON HEROES AND UHURU-WORSHIP, LONDON, LONGMANS,
    1967, PP 35-49
    081,

    MAZRUI ALI A
    POLITICAL COMMITMENT AND ECONOMIC INTEGRATION CHAPTER 5.
    IN ON HEROES AND UHURU-WORSHIP, LONDON, LONGMANS,
    1967, PP 63-72
    078,

    MAZRUI ALI A
    SOCIALISM AND SILENCE IN THE THIRD WORLD CHAPTER 10.
    IN ON HEROES AND UHURU-WORSHIP, LONDON, LONGMANS,
    1967, PP 146-156
    085,

    MAZRUI ALI A
    IS AFRICAN DEVELOPMENT PLANNABLE CHAPTER 9.
    IN ON HEROES AND UHURU-WORSHIP, LONDON, LONGMANS,
    1967, PP 137-145
    072,

    MAZRUI ALI A
    THE ANGLO-AFRICAN COMMONWEALTH.
    NEW YORK, PERGAMON, 1967
    082,

    MAZRUI ALI A
    POLITICAL SCIENCE AND THE DECLINE OF AFRICAN NATIONALISM.

IN CARTER, GWENDOLEN M. AND ANN PADEN (EDS), EXPANDING
HORIZONS IN AFRICAN STUDIES, EVANSTON, NORTHWESTERN
UNIVERSITY PRESS, 1969, PP. 147-156
004,100,

MAZRUI ALI A
  MAZRUI ALI A
  AFRICAN ATTITUDES TO THE EUROPEAN ECONOMIC COMMUNITY.
  LONDON, INTERNATIONAL AFFAIRS, VOL. 38, NO. 1, JANUARY,
  1963, PP. 24-35
  080,082,

  MAZRUI ALI A
  EUROPEAN EXPLORATION AND AFRICAS SELF DISCOVERY
  JOURNAL OF MODERN AFRICAN STUDIES 7 1969 PP 661-676
  027,038,100,

  MAZRUI ALI A
  ON THE CONCEPT OF 'WE ARE ALL AFRICANS?.
  AMERICAN POLITICAL SCIENCE REVIEW 57 MARCH 1963 PP 88-97
  079,

  MAZRUI ALI A
  HAS AFRICA'S INDEPENDENCE CHANGED THE WORLD CHAPTER 14.
  IN ON HEROES AND UHURU-WORSHIP,LONDON,LONGMANS
  1967 PP 231-244
  076,

  MAZRUI ALI A
  NKRUMAH-- THE LENINIST CZAR CHAPTER 8.
  IN ON HEROES AND UHURU-WORSHIP, LONDON, LONGMANS,
  1967, PP 113-134
  061,114-04,

  MAZRUI ALI A
  EXTERNAL EVENTS AND INTERNAL COMMUNAL TENSIONS.
  IN LAWRENCE SAGINI (ED),RACIAL AND COMMUNAL TENSIONS IN EAST
  AFRICA, NAIROBI,EAST AFRICAN PUBLISHING HOUSE,1966,PP 70-76
  088,

  MAZRUI ALI A
  ANTI-MILITARISM AND POLITICAL MILITANCY IN TANZANIA
  JOURNAL OF CONFLICT RESOLUTION 12 1968 PP269-284
  061,136-07,

  MAZRUI ALI A
  TANZANIA VERSUS EAST AFRICA CHAPTER 6.
  IN ON HEROES AND UHURU-WORSHIP, LONDON,LONGMANS
  1967 PP 73-95
  077,136-09,

  MAZRUI ALI A
  ISLAM, POLITICAL LEADERSHIP AND ECONOMIC RADICALISM IN
  AFRICA CHAPTER 11.
  IN ON HEROES AND UHURU-WORSHIP, LONDON, LONGMANS,
  1967, PP 157-179

MBEKI GOVAN
  MBEKI GOVAN
  SOUTH AFRICA- THE PEASANTS REVOLT

LONDON AND NEW YORK, PENGUIN, 1964
032,

MBITI JOHN S
MBITI JOHN S
AFRICAN RELIGIONS AND PHILOSOPHY.
NEW YORK, PRAEGER, 1969   (LONDON, HEINEMANN
EDUCATIONAL BOOKS)
013,

MBITI JOHN S
CONCEPTS OF GOD IN AFRICA.
NEW YORK, PRAEGER, 1970
013,

MBITI JOHN S
AKAMBA STORIES.
OXFORD, CLARENDON PRESS, 1966
012,

MBITI JOHN S
LA CONTRIBUTION PROTESTANTE A L'EXPRESSION CULTURELLE DE LA
PERSONNALITE AFRICAINE (THE PROTESTANT CONTRIBUTION TO
CULTURAL EXPRESSION OF THE AFRICAN PERSONALITY).
IN COLLOQUE SUR LES RELIGIONS, ABIDJAN, APRIL, 1961, PARIS
PRESENCE AFRICAINE, 1962, PP 137-146
039,050,

MBOYA TOM
MBOYA TOM
FREEDOM AND AFTER.
BOSTON, LITTLE, BROWN, AND COMPANY, 1963
044,060,117-04,

MBOYA TOM
EAST AFRICAN LABOUR POLICY AND FEDERATION.
IN COLIN LEYS AND P ROBSON (EDS), FEDERATION IN EAST AFRICA--
OPPORTUNITIES AND PROBLEMS, NAIROBI, OXFORD UNIVERSITY PRESS,
1965, PP 102-110
078,117-04,

MBOYA TOM
THE PARTY SYSTEM AND DEMOCRACY IN AFRICA.
IN PHILIP W QUIGG (ED.), AFRICA, NEW YORK, PRAEGER, 1964
PP 327-338
060,117-04,

MBOYA TOM
AFRICAN SOCIALISM CHAPTER 6.
IN AFRICA'S FREEDOM, NEW YORK, BARNES AND NOBLE, 1964,
PP 78-87
060,117-04,

MBOYA TOM
TENSIONS IN AFRICAN DEVELOPMENT CHAPTER 4.
IN AFRICA'S FREEDOM, NEW YORK, BARNES AND NOBLE, 1964,
PP 55-66
060,117-04,

MBOYA TOM

VISION IN AFRICA.
IN WILLIAM J HANNA (ED), INDEPENDENT BLACK AFRICA, CHICAGO,
RAND MCNALLY, 1964, PP 515-520
060,117-04,

MBOYA TOM
MBOYA TOM
THE AMERICAN NEGRO CANNOT LOOK TO AFRICA FOR AN ESCAPE.
THE NEW YORK TIMES MAGAZINE, JULY 13, 1969, SECTION 6, PP.
30-44
096,117-04,

MCCALL DANIEL F
MCCALL DANIEL F
AFRICA IN TIME-PERSPECTIVE--A DISCUSSION OF HISTORICAL
RECONSTRUCTION FROM UNWRITTEN SOURCES.
NEW YORK, OXFORD UNIVERSITY PRESS. 1969
036,

MCCALL DANIEL F   BENNETT NORMAN   BUTLER JEFFREY
EASTERN AFRICAN HISTORY
NEW YORK, PRAEGER, 1969
036,

MCCALL DANIEL F   BENNETT NORMAN   BUTLER JEFFREY
WESTERN AFRICAN HISTORY
NEW YORK, PRAEGER, 1969
036,

MCCALL DANIEL F
DYNAMICS OF URBANIZATION IN AFRICA.
ANNALS OF THE AMERICAN ACADEMY OF POLITICAL AND SOCIAL
SCIENCES NO 298 1955 PP 151-160 ALSO P R GOULD AFRICA-- CONT
INENT OF CHANGE WADSWORTH 1961 PP 183-195
045,

MCCALL DANIEL F
SLAVERY IN ASHANTI.
TRANS-ACTION, 1967
028,114-01,

MCCLELLAND DAVID
MCCLELLAND DAVID
THE ACHIEVEMENT MOTIVE IN ECONOMIC GROWTH CHAPTER 4.
IN JASON L FINKLE AND RICHARD W GABLE, POLITICAL
DEVELOPMENT AND SOCIAL CHANGE, NEW YORK, JOHN WILEY, 1966
037,

MCCLELLAND DAVID C
MCCLELLAND DAVID C
THE ACHIEVING SOCIETY.
PRINCETON, NEW JERSEY, VAN NOSTRAND, 1961
037,041,

MCDONELL G
MCDONELL G
THE DYNAMICS OF GEOGRAPHIC CHANGE--THE CASE OF KANO.
ANNALS OF THE ASSOCIATION OF AMERICAN GEOGRAPHERS
5J SEPTEMBER 1964 PP 355-371
046,128-05,

MCELRATH DENNIS
    GREER SCOTT   MCELRATH DENNIS   MINAR DAVID
    THE NEW URBANIZATION.
    NEW YORK, ST MARTINS PRESS, 1968
    046.

    MCELRATH DENNIS
    SOCIETAL SCALE AND SOCIAL DIFFERENTIATION--ACCRA, GHANA.
    THE NEW URBANIZATION. EDS. SCOTT GREER, ET AL., NEW YORK,
    ST. MARTINS PRESS, 1968
    037,114-05.

MCEWAN PETER J
    MCEWAN PETER J   ED
    TWENTIETH CENTURY AFRICA.
    LONDON, OXFORD UNIVERSITY PRESS, 1968
    002,076.

    MCEWAN PETER J   ED
    AFRICA FROM EARLY TIMES TO 1800.
    LONDON, OXFORD UNIVERSITY PRESS, 1968
    001,036.

    MCEWAN PETER J   SUTCLIFFE ROBERT B EDS
    MODERN AFRICA.
    NEW YORK, THOMAS CROWELL, 1965
    002,076,097.

MCKAY VERNON
    MCKAY VERNON
    THE AFRICAN OPERATIONS OF UNITED STATES GOVERNMENT AGENCIES.
    IN THE UNITED STATES AND AFRICA, BACKGROUND PAPERS OF THE
    13TH ASSEMBLY, THE AMERICAN ASSEMBLY, COLUMBIA UNIVERSITY,
    1958, PP 193-203 (APPENDIX)
    083.

    MCKAY VERNON
    EXTERNAL POLITICAL PRESSURES ON AFRICA TODAY CHAPTER 3.
    IN THE UNITED STATES AND AFRICA, BACKGROUND PAPERS OF THE
    13TH ASSEMBLY, THE AMERICAN ASSEMBLY, COLUMBIA UNIVERSITY,
    1958, PP 63-88
    083.

    MCKAY VERNON
    THE IMPACT OF ISLAM ON RELATIONS AMONG THE NEW AFRICAN
    STATES.
    IN J H PROCTOR (ED), ISLAM AND INTERNATIONAL RELATIONS, NEW
    YORK, PRAEGER, 1965, PP 158-191
    086.

    MCKAY VERNON
    AFRICAN DIPLOMACY-- STUDIES IN THE DETERMINANTS OF FOREIGN
    POLICY.
    NEW YORK, PRAEGER, 1966
    081.

    MCKAY VERNON
    AFRICA IN WORLD POLITICS.
    NEW YORK, HARPER AND ROW, 1963

081,083,084,085,

MCKELVEY JOHN J
MCKELVEY JOHN J
AGRICULTURAL RESEARCH.
IN ROBERT A LYSTAD (ED), THE AFRICAN WORLD, NEW YORK,
PRAEGER, 1966, PP 317-351
099,100,

MCKISSICK FLOYD
MCKISSICK FLOYD
THREE-FIFTHS A MAN
NEW YORK, MACMILLAN, 1969
095,

MCLOUGHLIN P F M
MCLOUGHLIN P F M
THE SUDAN S GEZIRA SCHEME-- AN ECONOMIC PROFILE.
SOCIAL AND ECONOMIC STUDIES 12 1963 PP 179-199
070,134-08,

MCLOUGHLIN P F M
THE SUDAN'S THREE TOWNS--A DEMOGRAPHIC AND ECONOMIC PROFILE
OF AN AFRICAN URBAN COMPLEX
ECONOMIC DEVELOPMENT AND CULTURAL CHANGE 12 1963 AND 1964,
PP 70-83, 158-173, 286-304
046,074,134-05,

MCLUHAN H MARSHALL
MCLUHAN H MARSHALL
THE GUTENBERG GALAXY.
TORONTO, UNIVERSITY OF TORONTO PRESS, 1962
037,043,

MCMASTER D N
MCMASTER D N
SPECULATIONS ON THE COMING OF THE BANANA TO UGANDA.
JOURNAL OF TROPICAL GEOGRAPHY, SINGAPORE, KUALA LUMPUR 16
OCTOBER 1962 PP 57-69
019,

MCNOWN JOHN S
MCNOWN JOHN S
ENGINEERING EDUCATION IN SUBSAHARAN AFRICA.
NEW YORK, PRAEGER, 1968
075,

MCNULTY MICHAEL
MCNULTY MICHAEL
URBAN STRUCTURE AND DEVELOPMENT-THE URBAN SYSTEM OF GHANA
JOURNAL OF THE DEVELOPING AREAS,3 1969 PP 159-176
047,048,114-05,

MCPHERSON JAMES M
MCPHERSON JAMES M
THE WORLD THE SLAVEHOLDERS MADE
NEW YORK, PANTHEON BOOKS, 1969
028,

MEAD DONALD C

MEAD DONALD C
ECONOMIC CO-OPERATION IN EAST AFRICA.
JOURNAL OF MODERN AFRICAN STUDIES, VOL. 7, NO. 2, 1969, PP.
277-287
078,

MEAD MARGARET
MEAD MARGARET   ED
SCIENCE AND THE CONCEPT OF RACE.
NEW YORK (COLUMBIA), MCGILL-QUEEN'S,1969
003,

MEADE JAMES E
MEADE JAMES E   ET AL
THE ECONOMIC AND SOCIAL STRUCTURE OF MAURITIUS
LONDON,METHUEN,1961,REPORT TO THE GOVERNOR OF MAURITIUS;
REPRINTED 1968

MEEK CHARLES K
MEEK CHARLES K
LAND LAW AND CUSTOM IN THE COLONIES.
LONDON,OXFORD UNIVERSITY PRESS,1949
010,066,070,

MEEK CHARLES K
LAND TENURE AND LAND ADMINISTRATION IN NIGERIA AND THE
CAMEROONS.
LONDON,HER MAJESTY'S STATIONERY OFFICE,1957
010,070,104-08,128-08,

MEILLASSOUX CLAUDE
MEILLASSOUX CLAUDE
URBANIZATION OF AN AFRICAN COMMUNITY--VOLUNTARY ASSOCIATIONS
IN BAMAKO.
SEATTLE, UNIVERSITY OF WASHINGTON PRESS, 1968
046,123-05,

MEINHOF CARL
MEINHOF CARL   TRANSLATED BY   WARMELO N J V
INTRODUCTION TO THE PHONOLOGY OF BANTU LANGUAGES.
BERLIN,DIETRICH REINER/ ERNST VOHSEN,1932
011,

MELSON ROBERT
MELSON ROBERT   WOLPE HOWARD   EDS
NIGERIA-MODERNIZATION AND THE POLITICS OF COMMUNALISM.
EAST LANSING, MICHIGAN STATE UNIVERSITY PRESS, 1970
006,065,128-03,

MELTZER MILTON
HUGHES LANGSTON   MELTZER MILTON
A PICTORIAL HISTORY OF THE NEGRO IN AMERICA.
NEW YORK,CROWN,1963
030,

MELTZER MILTON   ED
IN THEIR OWN WORDS-- A HISTORY OF THE AMERICAN NEGRO.
NEW YORK,CROWELL:1,1619-1865; 2,1865-1916; 3,1916-1966
030,

MEMMI ALBERT
    MEMMI ALBERT
    DOMINATED MAN.
    BOSTON, BEACON PRESS, 1969
    041,

MENDELSOHN JACK
    MENDELSOHN JACK
    GOD,ALLAH AND JU JU,RELIGION IN AFRICA TODAY
    NEW YORK,NELSON,1962
    013,

MENNEN WILLIAMS G
    MENNEN WILLIAMS G
    AFRICA FOR THE AFRICANS.
    GRAND RAPIDS, MICHIGAN, INTERNATIONAL UNIVERSITY BOOKSELLERS
        INC., 1969
    083,

MERCIER PAUL
    MERCIER PAUL
    PROBLEMS OF SOCIAL STRATIFICATION IN WEST AFRICA 1954.
    IN IMMANUEL WALLERSTEIN, SOCIAL CHANGE-- THE COLONIAL
    SITUATION, NEW YORK, WILEY, 1966 , PP 340-358
    044,

    MERCIER PAUL
    ON THE MEANING OF TRIBALISM IN BLACK AFRICA.
    IN PIERRE VAN DEN BERGHE (ED), AFRICA-- SOCIAL PROBLEMS OF
    CHANGE AND CONFLICT, SAN FRANCISCO,CHANDLER,1965,PP 483-501
    004,

    MERCIER PAUL
    EVOLUTION OF SENEGALESE ELITES
    INTERNATIONAL SOCIAL SCIENCE BULLETIN 8 1956 PP 441-451
    043,130-05,

    MERCIER PAUL
    AN EXPERIMENTAL INVESTIGATION INTO OCCUPATION AND SOCIAL
    CATEGORIES IN DAKAR.
    IN SOCIAL IMPLICATIONS OF INDUSTRIALIZATION AND URBANIZATION
    IN AFRICA SOUTH OF THE SAHARA, PARIS, UNESCO, 1956

    MERCIER PAUL
    LE GROUPMENT EUROPEAN DE DAKAR--ORIENTATION D'UNE ENQUETE.
    CAHIERS INTERNATIONAUX DE SOCIOLOGIE, 2, 19, 1955
    130-05,

    MERCIER PAUL
    ELITES ET FORCES POLITIQUES.
    IN LLOYD, THE NEW ELITES OF TROPICAL AFRICA, LONDON, OXFORD
    UNIVERSITY PRESS, 1966, P. 367-380
    044,

MERRIAM ALAN P
    MERRIAM ALAN P
    MUSIC AND THE DANCE.
    IN ROBERT A LYSTAD (ED), THE AFRICAN WORLD, NEW YORK,
    PRAEGER, 1966, CHP 17
    015,

MERRIAM ALAN P
   MERRIAM ALAN P
   AFRICAN MUSIC CHAPTER 4.
   IN WILLIAM BASCOM AND MELVILLE HERSKOVITS, CONTINUTY AND
   CHANGE IN AFRICAN CULTURES, CHICAGO, UNIVERSITY OF CHICAGO
   PRESS, 1962, PP 49-86
   015,

   MERRIAM ALAN P
   AFRICAN MUSIC ON LP-AN ANNOTATED   DISCOGRAPHY
   EVANSTON, NORTHWESTERN UNIVERSITY PRESS, 1970
   015,093,

   MERRIAM ALAN P
   THE CONCEPT OF CULTURE CLUSTERS APPLIED TO THE BELGIAN
   CONGO.
   SOUTHWESTERN JOURNAL OF ANTHROPOLOGY VOL 15 1959 PP 373-395
   004,108-01,

   MERRIAM ALAN P
   THE ANTHROPOLOGY OF MUSIC.
   EVANSTON, NORTHWESTERN UNIVERSITY PRESS, 1964
   015,

MERRITT RICHARD L
   MERRITT RICHARD L
   SYSTEMS AND THE DISINTEGRATION OF EMPIRES.
   YEARBOOK OF THE SOCIETY FOR GENERAL SYSTEMS RESEARCH 8 1963
   PP 91-103
   098,

MESSENGER JOHN C
   MESSENGER JOHN C
   REINTERPRETATIONS OF CHRISTIAN AND INDIGENOUS BELIEF IN A
   NIGERIAN NATIVIST CHURCH.
   AMERICAN ANTHROPOLOGIST 62 APRIL 1960 PP 268-278
   051,128-03,

   MESSENGER JOHN C
   RELIGIOUS ACCULTURATION AMONG THE ANANG IBIBIO CHAPTER 15.
   IN WILLIAM BASCOM AND MELVILLE HERSKOVITS, CONTINUITY AND
   CHANGE IN AFRICAN CULTURES, CHICAGO, UNIVERSITY OF CHICAGO
   PRESS, 1962, PP 279-299
   051,128-03,

MEYEROWITZ EVA L
   MEYEROWITZ EVA L
   THE AKAN OF GHANA-- THEIR ANCIENT BELIEFS.
   LONDON, FABER, 1958
   013,114-01,

MEZU S O
   MEZU S O   ED
   MTHE PHILOSOPHY OF PAN-AFRICANISM.
   WASHINGTON, GEORGETOWN UNIVERSITY PRESS, 1965
   079,

MFOULOU JEAN
   MFOULOU JEAN

SCIENCE ET PSEUDO-SCIENCE DES LANGUES AFRICAINES (SCIENCE
AND PSEUDO-SCIENCE OF AFRICAN LANGUAGES).
PRESENCE AFRICAINE, NO. 70, 2ND QUARTER, 1969, PP. 147-161
011,003,

MICAUD CHARLES A
   MICAUD CHARLES A
   TUNISIA--THE POLITICS OF MODERNIZATION.
   NEW YORK, PRAEGER, 1964
   138-07,

MIDDLETON CORAL
   MIDDLETON CORAL
   BECHUANALAND--A BIBLIOGRAPHY.
   CAPETOWN,UNIVERSITY OF CAPETOWN,SCHOOL OF LIBRARIANSHIP,1965
   102-12,

MIDDLETON JOHN
   COHEN RONALD   MIDDLETON JOHN   EDS
   COMPARATIVE POLITICAL SYSTEMS-- A READER IN POLITICAL
   ANTHROPOLOGY.
   NEW YORK,NATURAL HISTORY PRESS,1967
   009,

   COHEN RONALD   MIDDLETON JOHN   EDS
   FROM TRIBE TO NATION IN AFRICA.
   SAN FRANCISCO,CHANDLER,1970
   004,006,057,

   MIDDLETON JOHN   TAIT D   EDS
   TRIBES WITHOUT RULERS.
   LONDON,ROUTLEDGE AND KEGAN PAUL,1958
   009,

   MIDDLETON JOHN
   THE EFFECTS OF ECONOMIC DEVELOPMENT ON TRADITIONAL POLITICAL
   SYSTEMS IN AFRICA SOUTH OF THE SAHARA.
   THE HAGUE,MOUTON,1966
   053,073,

   BEATTIE J H M   MIDDLETON JOHN   EDS
   SPIRIT MEDIUMSHIP AND SOCIETY IN AFRICA
   NEW YORK,AFRICANA PUBLISHING CORPORATION,1969
   013,

   MIDDLETON JOHN
   KENYA-- CHANGES IN AFRICAN LIFE, 1912-1945.
   IN VINCENT HARLOW AND E M CHILVER (EDS),HISTORY OF EAST
   AFRICA VOL II,OXFORD,CLARENDON PRESS,1965, PP 333-394
   035,117-02,

   MIDDLETON JOHN   WINTER E H   EDS
   WITCHCRAFT AND SORCERY IN EAST AFRICA
   NEW YORK,PRAEGER,1963
   013,

   MIDDLETON JOHN   ED
   BLACK AFRICA- ITS PEOPLES AND THEIR CULTURES TODAY
   LONDON,MACMILLAN,1970
   004,016,053,

MIDDLETON JOHN
    MIDDLETON JOHN
    SOCIAL CHANGE AMONG THE LUGBARA OF UGANDA.
    CIVILIZATIONS 10 1960 PP 446-456
    038, 139-03,

    MIDDLETON JOHN
    LAND TENURE IN ZANZIBAR.
    LONDON, HER MAJESTY'S STATIONERY OFFICE, 1961
    070,136-08,

    MIDDLETON JOHN
    KENYA-- ADMINISTRATION AND CHANGES IN AFRICAN LIFE
    1912-45 CHAPTER 7.
    IN ROLAND OLIVER AND GERVASE MATHEW, HISTORY OF EAST
    AFRICA, 2, LONDON, OXFORD UNIVERSITY PRESS, 1965,
    PP 333-392
    035,117-03,

    MIDDLETON JOHN
    SLAVERY IN ZANZIBAR.
    TRANS-ACTION, 1967
    028,136-02,

    MIDDLETON JOHN
    LUGBARA RELIGION-RITUAL AND AUTHORITY AMONG AN EAST AFRICAN
    PEOPLE
    LONDON,OXFORD, FOR INTERNATIONAL AFRICAN INSTITUTE, 1960
    013,139-01,

    BOHANNAN PAUL   MIDDLETON JOHN   EDS
    MARRIAGE, FAMILY AND RESIDENCE.
    GARDEN CITY, NEW YORK, INTERNATIONAL UNIVERSITY BOOKSELLERS,
    INC., 1968
    008,

    MIDDLETON JOHN   ED
    MYTH AND COSMOS.
    GARDEN CITY, NEW YORK, THE NATURAL HISTORY PRESS, 1967
    012,013,099,

    MIDDLETON JOHN
    ZANZIBAR
    NEW YORK,OXFORD, 1965
    136-11,

    MIDDLETON JOHN   KERSHAW GREET
    THE KIKUYU AND KAMBA OF KENYA
    LONDON,INTERNATIONAL AFRICAN INSTITUTE, 1956
    117-01,

MIKESELL M W
    MIKESELL M W
    THE ROLE OF TRIBAL MARKETS IN MOROCCO--EXAMPLES FROM THE
    (NORTHERN ZONE).
    GEOGRAPHICAL REVIEW 48 OCTOBER 1958 PP 494-511
    010,126-01,

MILICENT ERNEST

MILICENT ERNEST
SENEGAL.
IN G.M. CARTER (ED), AFRICAN ONE-PARTY STATES, ITHACA,
CORNELL UNIVERSITY PRESS, 1962
130-07,

MILICENT ERNEST
    MILICENT ERNEST   SORDE MONIQUE
    LEOPOLD SEDAR SENGHOR ET LA NAISSANCE DE L'AFRIQUE MODERNE
    (LEOPOLD SEDAR SENGHOR AND THE BIRTH OF MODERN AFRICA).
    PARIS, INTERNATIONAL UNIVERSITY BOOKSELLERS, INC., 1969
    044,130-04,

MILLER ELIZABETH
    MILLER ELIZABETH
    THE NEGRO IN AMERICA, A BIBLIOGRAPHY.
    CAMBRIDGE,HARVARD UNIVERSITY PRESS,1968
    030,094,

MILLIKAN MAX F
    MILLIKAN MAX F   HAPGOOD DAVID
    NO EAST HARVEST-- THE DILEMMA OF AGRICULTURE IN UNDERDEVEL-
    OPED COUNTRIES.
    BOSTON,LITTLE,BROWN,1967
    070,

    MILLIKAN MAX F   BLACKMER DONALD   EDS
    RESISTANCE AND CONFLICT IN THE MODERNIZATION PROCESS CHP 3.
    IN EMERGING NATIONS, CENTER FOR INTERNATIONAL STUDIES, MIT,
    BOSTON,LITTLE,BROWN,1961;ALSO LEWIS P FICKETT,ED,PROBLEMS
    OF THE DEVELOPING NATIONS,NEW YORK,CROWELL,1966,PP 12-20
    037,

MILNER ALAN
    MILNER ALAN   ED
    AFRICAN LAW REPORTS, 2 VOLS, COMMERCIAL LAW SERIES 1966.
    DOBBS FERRY, NEW YORK, INTERNATIONAL UNIVERSITY BOOKSELLERS,
    INC.. 1969
    067,

MINAR DAVID
    GREER SCOTT   MCELRATH DENNIS   MINAR DAVID
    THE NEW URBANIZATION.
    NEW YORK,ST MARTINS PRESS,1968
    046,

MINER HORACE M
    MINER HORACE M   ED
    THE CITY IN MODERN AFRICA.
    NEW YORK,PRAEGER,1967
    047,

    MINER HORACE M
    THE PRIMITIVE CITY OF TIMBUCTOO
    GARDEN CITY,NEW JERSEY,DOUBLEDAY,1965
    045,123-05,

    MINER HORACE M
    CULTURE CHANGE UNDER PRESSURE-- A HAUSA CASE.
    HUMAN ORGANIZATION 19 FALL 1960 PP 164-167

041,128-03,

MIRACLE MARVIN P
    MIRACLE MARVIN P
    MAIZE IN TROPICAL AFRICA.
    MADISON, UNIVERSITY OF WISCONSIN PRESS, 1966
    069,

    MIRACLE MARVIN P
    AGRICULTURE IN THE CONGO BASIN--TRADITION AND CHANGE IN
    AFRICAN RURAL ECONOMIES.
    MADISON, UNIVERSITY OF WISCONSIN PRESS, 1967
    070,108-08,

MITCHELL
    HERSKOVITS MELVILLE J   HARWITZ MITCHELL EDS
    ECONOMIC TRANSITION IN AFRICA
    EVANSTON, NORTHWESTERN UNIVERSITY PRESS, 1964
    010,073,

MITCHELL J CLYDE
    MITCHELL J CLYDE
    TRIBALISM AND THE PLURAL SOCIETY.
    LONDON, OXFORD UNIVERSITY PRESS, 1960
    057,

    MITCHELL J CLYDE
    LABOUR MIGRATION AND THE TRIBE.
    IN PRUDENCE SMITH (ED.), AFRICA IN TRANSITION, LONDON,
    REINHARDT, 1956, PP 54-61
    038,

    MITCHELL J CLYDE
    THEORETICAL ORIENTATIONS IN AFRICAN URBAN STUDIES.
    IN MICHAEL BANTON (ED), THE SOCIAL ANTHROPOLOGY OF COMPLEX
    SOCIETIES, NEW YORK, PRAEGER, 1966
    045,

    MITCHELL J CLYDE
    WHITE-COLLAR WORKERS AND SUPERVISORS IN A PLURAL SOCIETY.
    CIVILIZATIONS 10 1960 PP 293-306
    088,

    MITCHELL J CLYDE
    AFRICAN TRIBES AND LANGUAGES OF THE FEDERATION OF RHODESIA
    AND NYASALAND.
    SALISBURY, FEDERAL GOVERNMENT PRINTERS, RHODESIA AND
    122-01,142-01,

    MITCHELL J CLYDE
    AFRICAN URBANIZATION IN NDOLA AND LUANSHYA.
    LUSAKA, RHODES-LIVINGSTONE INSTITUTE, 1954
    142-05,

MITCHELL N C
    MITCHELL N C
    YORUBA TOWNS.
    IN K M BARBOUR AND R M PROTHERO (EDS.), ESSAYS ON
    AFRICAN POPULATION, NEW YORK, PRAEGER, 1962, PP 279-301
    044,

MITCHELL ROBERT C
    MITCHELL ROBERT C   TURNER HAROLD
    A COMPREHENSIVE BIBLIOGRAPHY OF MODERN AFRICAN RELIGIOUS
    MOVEMENTS.
    EVANSTON, NORTHWESTERN UNIVERSITY PRESS, 1966
    051,

    MITCHELL ROBERT C   MORRISON DONALD G   PADEN JOHN N
    NATIONAL INTEGRATION AND STABILITY IN AFRICA.
    IN CARTER, GWENDOLEN M. AND ANN PADEN (EDS), EXPANDING
    HORIZONS IN AFRICAN STUDIES, EVANSTON, NORTHWESTERN
    UNIVERSITY PRESS, 1969, PP. 329-336
    100,

MITCHELL ROBERT E
    MITCHELL ROBERT E
    SURVEY MATERIALS COLLECTED IN THE DEVELOPING COUNTRIES--
    SAMPLING, MEASUREMENT, AND INTERVIEWING OBSTACLES TO INTRA-
    AND INTER-NATIONAL COMPARISONS.
    INTERNATIONAL SOCIAL SCIENCE JOURNAL 17 1965
    PP 665-685
    098,

MODISANE BLOKE
    MODISANE BLOKE
    BLAME ME ON HISTORY.
    LONDON, THAMES AND HUDSON, 1963
    090,132-10,

MOFFAT R L
    MOFFAT R L
    AFRICAN COURTS AND NATIVE CUSTOMARY LAW IN THE URBAN AREAS
    OF NORTHERN RHODESIA.
    JOURNAL OF AFRICAN ADMINISTRATION 9 APRIL 1957 PP 71-78
    066,142-03,

MOFFETT JOHN PERRY
    MOFFETT JOHN PERRY   ED
    HANDBOOK OF TANGANYIKA.
    DAR-ES-SALAAM, GOVERNMENT PRINTER (2ND EDITION), 1958
    136-11,

MOHAMADOU ELDRIDGE
    MOHAMADOU ELDRIDGE
    L'HISTOIRE DE TIBATI.
    YAOUNDE, EDITIONS ABBIA, 1965
    104-02,

    MOHAMADOU ELDRIDGE
    CONTES ET POEMES FOULBE DE LA BENOUE NORD-CAMEROUN.
    YAOUNDE, EDITIONS ABBIA-CLE, 1965
    104-01,

MOHAN JITENDRA
    MOHAN JITENDRA
    GHANA, THE CONGO AND THE UNITED NATIONS
    JOURNAL OF MODERN AFRICAN STUDIES 7 1969 PP 369-406
    079,081,

MOHOME PAULUS
   WEBSTER JOHN B   MOHOME PAULUS
   A BIBLIOGRAPHY ON LESOTHO.
   NEW YORK, SYRACUSE UNIVERSITY PROGRAM OF EASTERN AFRICAN
   STUDIES, 1968
   9, AUGUST, 1968

MONDLANE EDUARDO
   MONDLANE EDUARDO
   THE STRUGGLE FOR MOZAMBIQUE.
   BALTIMORE, PENGUIN BOOKS, 1969
   080,087,144-06,

MONOD THEODORE
   MONOD THEODORE   ED
   LES AFRO-AMERICAINES (THE AFRO-AMERICANS).
   DAKAR, MEMOIRES DE L'INSTITUTE FRANCAIS D'AFRIQUE NOIRE,27
   1953
   030,

MONROE ELIZABETH
   JONES ARNOLD   MARTIN HUGH   MONROE ELIZABETH
   A HISTORY OF ETHIOPIA
   OXFORD,CLARENDON PRESS,1955,SECOND EDITION
   110-02,

MONTEIL CHARLES
   MONTEIL CHARLES
   LES EMPIRES DU MALI (THE EMPIRES OF MALI).
   BULLETIN DU COMITE D'ETUDES HISTORIQUES ET SCIENTIFIQUES DE
   L'AFRIQUE OCCIDENTALE FRANCAISE 12 1929 PP 191-447
   022,123-02,

   MONTEIL CHARLES
   UNE CITE SOUDANAISE-- DJENNE METROPOLE DU DELTA CENTRAL
   DU NIGER (A SUDANESE CITY-- JENNE, METROPOLIS OF THE
   CENTRAL NIGER DELTA).
   SOCIETE D'EDITIONS DE GEOGRAPHIE MARITIME ET COLONIALE,PARIS,
   1932
   022,123-02,

MONTEIL VINCENT
   MONTEIL VINCENT
   MARABOUTS
   IN KRITZECK AND LEWIS,PP 88-109
   021,

   MONTEIL VINCENT
   UNE CONFRERIE MUSULMANE-- LES MOURIDES DU SENEGAL (A MUSLIM
   BROTHERHOOD-- THE MOURIDES OF SENEGAL).
   ARCHIVES DE SOCIOLOGIE DES RELIGIONS 14 JULY 1962 PP 77-102
   052,130-03,

   MONTEIL VINCENT
   LAT DIOR-- DAMAL DU KAYOR (1842-1886) ET L'ISLAMISATION DES
   WOLOFS (LAT DIOR-- DAMAL OF KAYOR (1842-1886) THE
   ISLAMIZATION OF THE WOLOF).
   ARCHIVES DE SOCIOLOGIE DES RELIGIONS 16 JULY 1963 PP 77-104
   052,130-03,

MONTEIL VINCENT
L'ISLAM NOIRE. (BLACK ISLAM).
PARIS, EDITIONS DU SEUIL, 1964
052,

MONTEIL VINCENT
    MONTEIL VINCENT
    LAT-DYOR, DAMEL DU KAYOR (1842-86) ET L≠ISLAMISATION DES
    WOLOFS DU SENEGAL.
    IN LEWIS, ISLAM IN TROPICAL AFRICA, LONDON, OXFORD UNIVERSIT
    PRESS, 1966, P. 342-349

MONTET PIERRE
    MONTET PIERRE
    ETERNAL EGYPT.
    NEW YORK, PRAEGER PUBLISHERS, 1969
    020,140-02,

MOORE CLEMENT H
    MOORE CLEMENT H
    MASS PARTY REGIMES IN AFRICA.
    IN HERBERT J SPIRO, ED., AFRICA THE PRIMACY OF POLITICS,
    NEW YORK, RANDOM HOUSE, 1966, PP 85-115
    061,

    MOORE CLEMENT H
    TUNISIA SINCE INDEPENDENCE.
    BERKELEY, UNIVERSITY OF CALIFORNIA PRESS, 1965
    138-11,

    MOORE CLEMENT H
    ONE-PARTYISM IN MAURITANIA.
    JOURNAL OF MODERN AFRICAN STUDIES 3 OCTOBER 1965 PP 409-420
    061,124-07,

    MOORE CLEMENT H
    THE NEO-DESTOUR PARTY OF TUNISIA-- A STRUCTURE FOR
    DEMOCRACY CHAPTER 15.
    IN JASON L FINKLE AND RICHARD W GABLE, POLITICAL
    DEVELOPMENT AND SOCIAL CHANGE, NEW YORK, JOHN WILEY, 1966
    061,138-07,

    MOORE CLEMENT H   HOCHSCHILD ARLIE R
    STUDENT UNIONS IN NORTH AFRICAN POLITICS.
    DAEDALUS, WINTER 1968, PP. 21-50
    063,138-07,

    MOORE CLEMENT H
    THE NEO-DESTOUR PARTY OF TUNISIA--A STRUCTURE FOR DEMOCRACY
    CHAPTER 15.
    IN JASON L. FINKLE AND RICHARD W GABLE, POLITICAL
    DEVELOPMENT AND SOCIAL CHANGE, NEW YORK, JOHN WILEY, 1966
    138-07,

MOORE GERALD
    MOORE GERALD   ED
    AFRICAN LITERATURE AND THE UNIVERSITIES.
    IBADAN, IBADAN UNIVERSITY PRESS, 1965
    090,

MOORE GERALD   BEIER ULLI   EDS
MODERN POETRY FROM AFRICA.
BALTIMORE,PENGUIN,1963
090,

MOORE WILBERT E
    MOORE WILBERT E
    THE ADAPTATION OF AFRICAN LABOR SYSTEMS TO SOCIAL CHANGE.
    IN M J HERSKOVITS AND M HARWITZ   (EDS.), ECONOMIC TRANSITION
    IN AFRICA. EVANSTON, NORTHWESTERN UNIVERSITY PRESS, 1964,
    PP 277-297
    073,

    MOORE WILBERT E   FELDMAN ARNOLD S
    LABOR COMMITMENT AND SOCIAL CHANGE IN DEVELOPING AREAS.
    NEW YORK,SOCIAL SCIENCE RESEARCH COUNCIL,1960
    073,

    MOORE WILBERT E
    SOCIAL CHANGE
    ENGLEWOOD CLIFFS,NEW JERSEY, PRENTICE-HALL,1963
    037,

MOREAU R L
    MOREAU R L
    LES MARABOUTS DE DORI (THE MARABOUS OF DORI).
    ARCHIVES DE SOCIOLOGIE DES RELIGIONS 17 JANUARY 1964
    PP 113-134
    052,123-03,

MOREL E D
    MOREL E D
    RED RUBBER-THE STORY OF THE RUBBER SLAVE TRADE FLOURISHING
    ON THE CONGO IN THE YEAR OF GRACE 1906
    LONDON,FISHER UNWIN,1906
    035,108-02,

MORGAN W T W
    MORGAN W T W
    THE 'WHITE HIGHLANDS' OF KENYA.
    GEOGRAPHICAL JOURNAL 129 JUNE 1963 PP 140-155
    035,117-02,

    MORGAN W T W   ED
    NAIROBI--CITY AND REGION
    NEW YORK, OXFORD UNIVERSITY PRESS, 1967
    117-05,

MORGENTHAU
    MORGENTHAU RUTH SCHACHTER
    FROM AOF FEDERATION TO SOVEREIGN NATIONS
    IN RUTH SCHACHTER MORGENTHAU POLITICAL PARTIES IN FRENCH-
    SPEAKING WEST AFRICA, OXFORD,CLARENDON PRESS,1964,PP 301-329
    078,

    MORGENTHAU RUTH SCHACHTER
    SINGLE-PARTY SYSTEMS IN WEST AFRICA.
    AMERICAN POLITICAL SCIENCE REVIEW 55 JUNE 1961 PP 294-307
    061,

MORGENTHAU RUTH SCHACHTER
POLITICAL PARTIES IN FRENCH-SPEAKING WEST AFRICA.
OXFORD, OXFORD UNIVERSITY PRESS, 1964
055,058,061,109-07,123-07,130-07,

MORGENTHAU HENRY
  MORGENTHAU HENRY
  GUIDES TO AFRICAN FILMS.
  AFRICA REPORT MAY 1968 PP 52-54
  093,

  MORGENTHAU HENRY
  ON FILMS AND FILMMAKERS
  AFRICA REPORT 14 MAY-JUNE 1969 PP 71-75
  049,093,

MORGENTHAU RUTH SCHA
  HODGKIN THOMAS   MORGENTHAU RUTH SCHACHTER
  MALI.
  IN COLEMAN, J.S. AND ROSBERG, C.G. (ED), POLITICAL PARTIES
  AND NATIONAL INTEGRATION IN TROPICAL AFRICA, LOS ANGELES,
  UNIVERSITY OF CALIFORNIA PRESS, 1964
  123-06,

MORISON DAVID
  MORISON DAVID
  THE U S S R AND AFRICA
  LONDON, OXFORD UNIVERSITY PRESS, 1964
  084,

  MORISON DAVID
   SOVIET UNION AND AFRICA, 1968
  IN LEGUM AND DRYSDALE, AFRICA CONTEMPORARY RECORD,
  LONDON, AFRICA RESEARCH LIMITED, 1969, P. 38-42
  084,

MORRILL R L
  TAAFFE E J   MORRILL R L   GOULD PETER
  TRANSPORT EXPANSION IN UNDERDEVELOPED COUNTRIES--A
  COMPARATIVE ANALYSIS.
  GEOGRAPHICAL REVIEW 53 OCTOBER 1963 PP 503-529
  048,

MORRIS ELIZABETH
  MORRIS ELIZABETH
  PORTUGAL'S YEAR IN AFRICA.
  IN LEGUM AND DRYSDALE, AFRICA CONTEMPORARY RECORD,
  LONDON, AFRICA RESEARCH LIMITED, 1969, P. 49-52
  087,

MORRIS CYNTHIA TAFT
  ADELMAN IRMA   MORRIS CYNTHIA TAFT
  SOCIETY, POLITICS, AND ECONOMIC DEVELOPMENT, A QUANTITATIVE
  APPROACH.
  BALTIMORE, JOHNS HOPKINS UNIVERSITY PRESS, 1967
  073,074,

  ADELMAN IRMA   DALTON GEORGE   MORRIS CYNTHIA TAFT
  SOCIETY, POLITICS, AND ECONOMIC DEVELOPMENT IN AFRICA.
  IN CARTER, GWENDOLEN M. AND ANN PADEN (EDS), EXPANDING

HORIZONS IN AFRICAN STUDIES, EVANSTON, NORTHWESTERN
UNIVERSITY PRESS, 1969, PP. 209-242
074,100,

MORRIS DONALD R
   MORRIS DONALD R
   THE WASHING OF THE SPEARS-A HISTORY OF THE RISE OF THE ZULU
   NATION UNDER THE SHAKA AND ITS FALL IN THE ZULU WAR OF 1879
   NEW YORK, SIMON AND SCHUSTER, 1965
   031,

MORRIS H S
   MORRIS H S
   THE INDIANS IN UGANDA
   CHICAGO, UNIVERSITY OF CHICAGO PRESS, 1968
   085,139-06,

   MORRIS H S
   SOME ASPECTS OF THE CONCEPT PLURAL SOCIETY.
   MAN VOL 2 NO 2 JUNE 1967 PP 169-184
   006,

MORRIS HENRY F
   MORRIS HENRY F
   THE HEROIC RECITATIONS OF THE BAHIMA OF ANKOLE.
   LONDON, OXFORD UNIVERSITY PRESS, 1964
   012,015,139-01,

MORRISON DONALD G
   MORRISON DONALD G   ET AL
   BLACK AFRICA- A HANDBOOK FOR COMPARATIVE ANALYSIS
   NEW YORK, FREE PRESS, 1970
   002,058,064,098,

   MITCHELL ROBERT C   MORRISON DONALD G   PADEN JOHN N
   NATIONAL INTEGRATION AND STABILITY IN AFRICA.
   IN CARTER, GWENDOLEN M. AND ANN PADEN (EDS), EXPANDING
   HORIZONS IN AFRICAN STUDIES, EVANSTON, NORTHWESTERN
   UNIVERSITY PRESS, 1969, PP. 329-336
   100,

MORROW JOHN H
   MORROW JOHN H
   FIRST AMERICAN AMBASSADOR TO GUINEA.
   NEW BRUNSWICK, NEW JERSEY, RUTGERS UNIVERSITY PRESS, 1968
   083,115-09,

MORTIMER EDWARD
   MORTIMER EDWARD
   FRANCE AND THE AFRICANS 1944-1960--A POLITICAL HISTORY.
   LONDON, INTERNATIONAL UNIVERSITY BOOKSELLERS, INC., 1969
   082,

MOSES LARRY
   MOSES LARRY
   KENYA, UGANDA, TANGANYIKA 1960-1964--A BIBLIOGRAPHY.
   WASHINGTON, DEPT. OF STATE, EXTERNAL RESEARCH STAFF, 1964
   117-12,139-12,

MOSLEY LEONARD

MOSLEY LEONARD
    HAILE SELASSIE-THE CONQUERING LION
    ENGLEWOOD CLIFFS,N.J.PRENTICE-HALL 1965
    110-04,

MOUME ETIA ISSAC
    MOUME ETIA ISSAC
    LES FABLES DE DOUALA CAMEROUN   EN LANGUE FRANCAISE ET DOUALA
    BERGERAC,IMP CASTANET, 1930
    104-01,

MOUMOUNI ABDOU
    MOUMOUNI ABDOU
    EDUCATION IN AFRICA.
    NEW YORK, PRAEGER, 1968
    042,

MOUNTJOY A B
    MOUNTJOY A B
    INDUSTRIALIZATION OF UNDERDEVELOPED COUNTRIES
    LONDON, HUTCHINSON, 1963; AND CHICAGO, ALDINE, 1967
    071,

MOURER HENRY
    MOURER HENRY
    ADMINISTRATIVE PROBLEMS OF URBANIZATION IN AFRICA--ADDITION-
    AL NOTE ON SENEGAL (DAKAR).
    ADDIS ABABA, WORKSHOP ON URBANIZATION IN AFRICA, 1962
    130-05,

MOWER J H
    MOWER J H
    THE REPUBLIC OF LIBERIA.
    THE JOURNAL OF NEGRO HISTORY XXXII 1947 PP 265-306
    029,119-02,

MOWLANA HAMID
    MOWLANA HAMID
    COMMUNICATIONS MEDIA IN AFRICA--A CRITIQUE IN RETROSPECT AND
    PROSPECT.
    IN CARTER, GWENDOLEN M. AND ANN PADEN (EDS), EXPANDING
    HORIZONS IN AFRICAN STUDIES, EVANSTON, NORTHWESTERN
    UNIVERSITY PRESS, 1969, PP. 259-274
    049,100,

MOXON JAMES
    MOXON JAMES
    VOLTA--MAN'S GREATEST LAKE.
    NEW YORK, PRAEGER PUBLISHERS, 1969
    075,114-08,

MPHAHLELE EZEKIEL
    MPHAHLELE EZEKIEL
    AFRICAN LITERATURE.
    IN LALAGE BOWN AND MICHAEL CROWDER (EDS.), PROCEEDINGS OF
    THE FIRST INTERNATIONAL CONGRESS OF AFRICANISTS, ACCRA,
    1962, LONDON, LONGMANS, 1964, PP 220-232
    090,132-10,

    MPHAHLELE EZEKIEL

DOWN SECOND AVENUE.
LONDON, FABER AND FABER, 1959
090,132-10,

MPHAHLELE EZEKIEL
MPHAHLELE EZEKIEL
CULTURAL TENSIONS IN A MIXED SOCIETY.
IN LAWRENCE SAGINI (ED), RACIAL AND COMMUNAL TENSIONS IN EAST
AFRICA, NAIROBI EAST AFRICAN PUBLISHING HOUSE, 1966, PP 123-
127
057,

MUENCH C Z
MUENCH C Z   MUENCH L H
PLANNING AND COUNTER-PLANNING IN NIGERIA--LAGOS AND IBADAN
JOURNAL OF THE AMERICAN INSTITUTE OF PLANNERS 34 1968
PP 374-381
092,

MUENCH L H
MUENCH C Z   MUENCH L H
PLANNING AND COUNTER-PLANNING IN NIGERIA--LAGOS AND IBADAN
JOURNAL OF THE AMERICAN INSTITUTE OF PLANNERS 34 1968
PP 374-381
092,

MUFFETT DAVID J M
MUFFETT DAVID J M
THE FAILURE OF ELITE-MASS COMMUNICATION--SOME PROBLEMS
CONFRONTING THE MILITARY REGIMES AND CIVIL SERVICES OF
NIGERIA.
THE SOUTH ATLANTIC QUARTERLY, VOL. LXVII, NO. 1, WINTER 1968
   PP. 125-140
058,128-06,

MUFFETT DAVID M J
MUFFETT DAVID M J
CONCERNING BRAVE CAPTAINS-- BEING A HISTORY OF THE BRITISH
OCCUPATION OF KANO AND SOKOTO AND OF THE LAST STAND OF THE
FULANI FORCES.
LONDON, A DEUTSCH, 1964
034,128-02,

MULAGO VINCENT
MULAGO VINCENT   THEUWS T
AUTOUR DU MOUVEMENT DE LA JAMAA.
LEOPOLDVILLE, CENTRE D'ETUDES PASTORALES, 1960
108-03,

MULAGO VINCENT
UN VISAGE AFRICAIN DU CHRISTIANISME, L'UNION VITALE BANTU
FACE A L'UNITE VITALE ECCLESIALE.
PARIS, PRESENCE AFRICAINE, 1965

MULFORD DAVID C
MULFORD DAVID C
THE NORTHERN RHODESIA GENERAL ELECTION 1962.
EASTERN AFRICA, OXFORD UNIVERSITY PRESS, 1964
063,142-07,

MULFORD DAVID C
ZAMBIA--THE POLITICS OF INDEPENDENCE 1957-1964.
OXFORD, OXFORD UNIVERSITY PRESS, 1967
142-07,

MULI M G
    WHITELEY W H   MULI M G
    PRACTICAL INTRODUCTION TO KAMBA.
    LONDON, OXFORD UNIVERSITY PRESS, 1962
    011,117-01,

MULLIN JOSEPH
    MULLIN JOSEPH
    THE CATHOLIC CHURCH IN MODERN AFRICA-- A PASTORAL THEOLOGY.
    LONDON CHAPMAN 1965
    050,

MULVEY MINA WHITE
    MULVEY MINA WHITE
    DIGGING UP ADAM-- THE STORY OF LSB LEAKEY.
    NEW YORK, MCKAY, 1969
    018,

MUNGEAM G H
    MUNGEAM G H
    BRITISH RULE IN KENYA 1895-1912
    OXFORD, CLARENDON PRESS, 1967
    035,117-02,

MUNGER EDWIN S
    MUNGER EDWIN S
    RELATIONAL PATTERNS OF KAMPALA, UGANDA.
    UNIVERSITY OF CHICAGO, DEPT OF GEOGRAPHY RESEARCH PAPERS,
    SEPTEMBER 1951 PP 1-178
    048,139-05,

    MUNGER EDWIN S
    JOHN VORSTER AND THE UNITED STATES
    AMERICAN UNIVERSITIES FIELD STAFF REPORTS 12 1968
    083,132-09,

    MUNGER EDWIN S
    BECHUANALAND PAN-AFRICANIST OUTPOST OR BANTU HOMELAND.
    LONDON, OXFORD UNIVERSITY PRESS, 1965
    102-09,

MUNRO DONALD
    PIETERSE COSMO   MUNRO DONALD   EDS
    PROTEST AND CONFLICT IN AFRICAN LITERATURE
    NEW YORK, AFRICANA PUBLISHING CORPORATION, 1969
    090,091,

MUNSTERBERGER W
    MUNSTERBERGER W   KISHNER I
    HASARDS OF CULTURE CLASH-- A REPORT ON THE HISTORY AND
    DYNAMICS OF A PSYCHOTIC EPISODE IN A WEST AFRICAN EXCHANGE
    STUDENT.
    IN W MUNSTERBERGER AND S AXERAD   EDS THE PSYCHO-
    ANALYTIC STUDY OF SOCIETY 4, NEW YORK, INTERNATIONAL
    UNIVERSITIES PRESS, PP 99-123

041,

MURDOCK G
 FAIR T J D   MURDOCK G   JONES H M
 DEVELOPMENT IN SWAZILAND-A REGIONAL ANALYSIS
 JOHANNESBURG,WITWATERSRAND UNIVERSITY PRESS,1969
 135-08,

MURDOCK GEORGE P
 MURDOCK GEORGE P
 AFRICA--ITS PEOPLES AND THEIR CULTURE HISTORY.
 NEW YORK,MCGRAW HILL,1959
 003,

 MURDOCK GEORGE P
 SOCIAL STRUCTURE.
 NEW YORK,   MACMILLAN CO. 1956
 004,008,

 MURDOCK GEORGE P
 ETHNOGRAPHIC ATLAS.
 PITTSBURGH,UNIVERSITY OF PITTSBURGH PRESS,1967
 003,

 MURDOCK GEORGE P
 STAPLE SUBSISTENCE CROPS OF AFRICA.
 THE GEOGRAPHICAL REVIEW AMERICAN GEOGRAPHICAL SOCIETY 50
 NO 3 OCTOBER 1960 PP 523-540
 010,069,

MURIUKI G
 MURIUKI G
 KIKUYU REACTION TO TRADERS AND BRITISH ADMINISTRATION 1850-
 1904
 IN OGOT, ED, HADITH 1,NAIROBI,EAST AFRICAN PUBLISHING HOUSE
 1967 PP 101-118
 034,

MURPHEY R
 MURPHEY R
 THE DECLINE OF NORTH AFRICA SINCE THE ROMAN OCCUPATION--
 CLIMATIC OR HUMAN.
 ANNALS OF THE ASSOCIATION OF AMERICAN GEOGRAPHERS 41
 JUNE 1951 PP 116-132
 020,

MURRAY PAULA
 RUBIN LESLIE   MURRAY PAULA
 THE CONSTITUTION AND GOVERNMENT OF GHANA.
 LONDON,SWEET AND MAXWELL,1961
 068,114-07,

MURRAY W A
 MURRAY W A
 ENGLISH IN THE SUDAN--TRENDS AND POLOTICS--RELATIONS WITH
 ARABIC.
 IN JOHN SPENCER (ED),LANGUAGE IN AFRICA, CAMBRIDGE,
 CAMBRIDGE UNIVERSITY PRESS, 1963
 134-06,

MUSEUM
    MUSEUM OF PRIMITIVE ART
    TRADITIONAL ART OF THE AFRICAN NATIONS.
    NEW YORK, UNIVERSITY PUBLISHERS, 1961
    014,

MUSEUM
    MUSEUM OF PRIMITIVE ART
    SCULPTURE FROM THREE AFRICAN TRIBES-- SENUFO, BAGA, DOGON.
    NEW YORK, UNIVERSITY PUBLISHERS, 1959
    014,

MUSTAFA SOPHIA
    MUSTAFA SOPHIA
    RACIAL AND COMMUNAL TENSIONS IN EAST AFRICA.
    IN LAWRENCE SAGINI (ED), RACIAL AND COMMUNAL TENSIONS IN EAST
    AFRICA, NAIROBI, EAST AFRICAN PUBLISHING HOUSE, 1966, PP 52-57
    057,

MUTESA II
    MUTESA II
    THE DESECRETION OF MY KINGDOM.
    LONDON, CONSTABLE, 1967
    054,064,139-04,

MUTUKU NZIOKI J
    LIJEMBE JOSEPH A   APOKO ANNA   MUTUKU NZIOKI J
    AN EAST AFRICAN CHILDHOOD--THREE VERSIONS.
    LONDON, OXFORD UNIVERSITY PRESS, 1967
    008,

MVENG ENGELBERT
    MVENG ENGELBERT
    HISTOIRE DU CAMEROUN.
    PARIS, PRESENCE AFRICAINE, 1963
    104-02,

    MVENG ENGELBERT
    L'ART D'AFRIQUE NOIRE. LITURGIE COSMIQUE ET LANGAGE
    RELIGEUX.
    PARIS, MAME, 1964
    104-01,

MWASE
    MWASE GEORGE SIMEON ROTBERG ROBERT   ED
    STRIKE A BLOW AND DIE.
    CAMBRIDGE, HARVARD UNIVERSITY PRESS, 1967
    034, 122-02,

MYINT H
    MYINT H
    THE ECONOMICS OF THE DEVELOPING COUNTRIES.
    NEW YORK, PRAEGER, 1964
    071,073,

MYRDAL GUNNAR
    MYRDAL GUNNAR
    RICH LANDS AND POOR.
    NEW YORK, HARPER, 1957 (ESP. CHAPTERS 1-3)
    037,071,073,

N

NADEL S F
    NADEL S F
    NUPE RELIGION.
    LONDON, ROUTLEDGE AND KEGAN PAUL LTD, 1954
    013,128-01,

    NADEL S F
    A FIELD EXPERIMENT IN RACIAL PSYCHOLOGY.
    BRITISH JOURNAL OF PSYCHOLOGY 28 1937 PP 195-211
    098,

    NADEL S F
    A BLACK BYZANTIUM, THE KINGDOM OF NUPE IN NIGERIA.
    OXFORD, OXFORD UNIVERSITY PRESS, 1942
    009,010,128-01,

    NADEL S F
    THE CONCEPT OF SOCIAL ELITES.
    PARIS, INTERNATIONAL SOCIAL SCIENCE BULLETIN A, SUMMER
    1956 PP 413-423
    040,

NADER CLAIRE
    NADER CLAIRE   ZAHLAN A B   EDS
    SCIENCE AND TECHNOLOGY IN DEVELOPING COUNTRIES
    NEW YORK, CAMBRIDGE UNIVERSITY PRESS, 1969
    075,

NAFZIGER E WAYNE
    NAFZIGER E WAYNE
    INTER-REGIONAL ECONOMIC RELATIONS IN THE NIGERIAN FOOTWEAR
    INDUSTRY.
    THE JOURNAL OF MODERN AFRICAN STUDIES, VOL 6, NO. 4, 1968,
    PP. 531-542
    057,128-06,

NAKASA N
    NAKASA N
    SOUTH AFRICAN IMPRESSION OF HARLEM.
    NEW YORK TIMES MAGAZINE FEBRUARY 7 1965 P 40
    096,

NAROLL RAOUL R
    NAROLL RAOUL R
    ON ETHNIC UNIT CLASSIFICATION.
    CURRENT ANTHROPOLOGY 5 OCTOBER 1964 PP 283-312
    005,

    NAROLL RAOUL R
    DATA QUALITY CONTROL-A NEW RESEARCH TECHNIQUE
    NEW YORK, THE FREE PRESS, 1962
    098,

NASH MANNING
   NASH MANNING
   SOME SOCIAL AND CULTURAL ASPECTS OF ECONOMIC DEVELOPMENT
   CHAPTER 8.
   IN JASON L FINKLE AND RICHARD W GABLE, POLITICAL
   DEVELOPMENT AND SOCIAL CHANGE, NEW YORK, JOHN WILEY, 1966
   074,

NASSER GAMAL ABDEL
   NASSER GAMAL ABDEL
   THE PHILOSOPHY OF THE REVOLUTION.
   BUFFALO, NEW YORK, SMITH, KEYNES AND MARSHALL PUBLISHERS,
   ENGLISH VERSION. 1959
   086,140-04,

NATHAN
   SHAMUYARIRA NATHAN M
   THE NATIONALIST MOVEMENT IN ZIMBABWE.
   AFRICAN FORUM 2 3 1967 PP 34-42
   087,145-06,

   SHAMUYARIRA NATHAN M
   CRISIS IN RHODESIA.
   LONDON, 1965
   087,145-06,

NATHAN MATHEW
   NATHAN MATHEW
   THE GOLD COAST AT THE END OF THE SEVENTEENTH CENTURY UNDER
   THE DANES AND THE DUTCH.
   JOURNAL OF THE AFRICAN SOCIETY IV 1904 PP 1-32
   027,114-02,

NDEGWA PHILIP
   NDEGWA PHILIP
   THE COMMON MARKET AND DEVELOPMENT IN EAST AFRICA.
   NAIROBI, THE EAST AFRICAN PUBLISHING HOUSE, 1965
   078,080,082,

   NDEGWA PHILIP
   THE COMMON MARKET AND DEVELOPMENT IN EAST AFRICA.
   KENYA, EAST AFRICAN PUBLISHING HOUSE, 1968
   078,

NDIAYE JEAN-PIERRE
   NDIAYE JEAN-PIERRE
   ELITES AFRICAINES ET CULTURE OCCIDENTALE--ASSIMILATION OU
   RESISTANCE (AFRICAN ELITES AND WESTERN CULTURE--
   ASSIMILATION OR RESISTANCE).
   PARIS, PRESENCE AFRICAINE, 1969
   043,

   NDIAYE JEAN-PIERRE
   ENQUETE SUR LES ETUDIANTS NOIRS EN FRANCE (STUDY OF BLACK
   STUDENTS IN FRANCE)
   PARIS, EDITIONS REALITES AFRICAINES, 1962
   043,096,

NDIAYE MASSATA
   NDIAYE MASSATA

LE SENEGAL A L'HEURE DE L'INDEPENDANCE.
DOULLENS, IMP. DESSAINT, 1962
130-07.

NEKAM ALEXANDER
  NEKAM ALEXANDER
  EXPERIENCES IN AFRICAN CUSTOMARY LAW.
  THIRD MELVILLE J. HERSKOVITS MEMORIAL LECTURE, FEB., 1966;
  13 PAGES
  066.

NELKIN DOROTHY
  NELKIN DOROTHY
  SOCIALIST SOURCES OF PAN-AFRICAN IDEOLOGY CHAPTER 4.
  IN WILLIAM FRIEDLAND AND CARL ROSBERG (EDS), AFRICAN
  SOCIALISM, STANFORD CALIFORNIA, STANFORD UNIVERSITY PRESS,
  1964, PP 63-79
  079,084,

  NELKIN DOROTHY
  THE ECONOMIC AND SOCIAL SETTING OF MILITARY TAKEOVERS IN
  AFRICA.
  JOURNAL OF ASIAN AND AFRICAN STUDIES, VOL. II, NOS. 3-4,
  JULY AND OCTOBER, 1967, PP. 230-244
  064.

NERES PHILIP
  NERES PHILIP
  FRENCH-SPEAKING WEST AFRICA, FROM COLONIAL STATUS TO
  INDEPENDENCE.
  LONDON, OXFORD UNIVERSITY PRESS, 1962
  055,056,

NETTING ROBERT
  NETTING ROBERT
  HILL FARMERS OF NIGERIA--CULTURAL ECOLOGY OF THE KOFYAR OF
  THE JOS PLATEAU.
  SEATTLE, UNIVERSITY OF WASHINGTON, 1968
  070,128-08,

NETTL J P
  NETTL J P
  POLITICAL MOBILIZATION.
  NEW YORK, BASIC BOOKS, 1967
  037,063,

NEUMARK S DANIEL
  NEUMARK S DANIEL
  THE CHARACTER AND POTENTIAL OF AFRICAN ECONOMIES CHAPTER 4.
  IN THE UNITED STATES AND AFRICA, BACKGROUND PAPERS OF THE
  13TH ASSEMBLY, THE AMERICAN ASSEMBLY, COLUMBIA UNIVERSITY,
  1958, PP 91-115
  073.

NEWBURY COLIN W
  NEWBURY COLIN W
  THE GOVERNMENT GENERAL AND POLITICAL CHANGE IN FRENCH WEST
  AFRICA.
  ST ANTHONY'S PAPERS 10, SOUTHERN ILLINOIS UNIVERSITY PRESS,
  1961, PP 41-59

035,

NEWBURY COLIN W
    NEWBURY COLIN W
    THE DEVELOPMENT OF FRENCH POLICY ON THE LOWER AND UPPER
    NIGER-- 1880-1898.
    JOURNAL OF MODERN HISTORY 31 1959 PP 146-155
    033,

    NEWBURY COLIN W
    THE FORMATION OF THE GOVERNMENT GENERAL OF FRENCH WEST
    AFRICA.
    JOURNAL OF AFRICAN HISTORY 1 1960 PP 111-128
    033,

    NEWBURY COLIN W   KANYA-FORSTNER A S
    FRENCH POLICY AND THE ORIGINS OF THE SCRAMBLE FOR WEST
    AFRICA.
    JOURNAL OF AFRICAN HISTORY, X,2, 1969, PP. 253-276
    033,

    NEWBURY COLIN W
    AN EARLY ENQUIRY INTO SLAVERY AND CAPTIVITY IN DAHOMEY.
    ZAIRE 14 1960 PP 53-67
    028,109-02,

NEWITT M D D
    NEWITT M D D
    THE PORTUGUESE ON THE ZAMBEZI--AN HISTORICAL INTERPRETATION
    OF THE PRAZO SYSTEM.
    JOURNAL OF AFRICAN HISTORY, X, 1, 1969, PP. 67-85
    027, 144-02,

NEWLYN W T
    NEWLYN W T
    MONEY IN AN AFRICAN CONTEXT.
    EASTERN AFRICA, OXFORD UNIVERSITY PRESS, 1967
    073,

NEWMAN PETER
    NEWMAN PETER
    THE ECONOMICS OF INTEGRATION IN EAST AFRICA.
    IN COLIN LEYS AND P ROBSON (EDS), FEDERATION IN EAST AFRICA--
    OPPORTUNITIES AND PROBLEMS, NAIROBI, OXFORD UNIVERSITY PRESS,
    1965, PP 56-71
    078,

NEWTON JOHN
    NEWTON JOHN
    THE JOURNAL OF A SLAVE TRADER 1750-1754.
    LONDON, EPWORTH PRESS, 1962 (BERNARD MARTIN AND MARK SPURRELL
    EDS.)
    028,

NGUGI JAMES
    NGUGI JAMES
    THE RIVER BETWEEN.
    IBADAN, HEINEMANN EDUCATIONAL BOOKS LTD, 1965
    090,117-10,

NGUGI JAMES
WEEP NOT, CHILD.
NEW YORK, MACMILLAN CO., 1969   (LONDON, HEINEMANN
EDUCATIONAL BOOKS)
090,117-10,

NGUGI JAMES
NGUGI JAMES
THE BLACK HERMIT.
NEW YORK, HUMANITIES PRESS INC., 1968   (LONDON, HEINEMANN
EDUCATIONAL BOOKS)
090,117-10,

NIANE DJIBRIL T
NIANE DJIBRIL T   SURET-CANALE J
HISTOIRE DE L'AFRIQUE OCCIDENTALE.
PARIS, PRESENCE AFRICAINE, 1962
115-02,

NIANE DJUBRIL T
NIANE DJUBRIL T
SUNDIATA--AN EPIC OF OLD MALI (TRANSLATED BY G D PICKETT)
LONDON, LONGMANS, 1965
022,123-02,

NIANE DJUBRIL T
RECHERCHES SUR L'EMPIRE DU MALI AU MOYEN AGE (RESEARCH
ON THE MALI EMPIRE IN THE MIDDLE AGES).
RECHERCHES AFRICAINES 2 1961 PP 31-51
022,123-02,

NICHOLS CHARLES H
NICHOLS CHARLES H
MANY THOUSAND GONE--THE EX-SLAVES' ACCOUNT OF THEIR BONDAGE
AND FREEDOM.
BLOOMINGTON, INDIANA UNIVERSITY PRESS, 1969
030,

NICOL DAVIDSON
NICOL DAVIDSON
POLITICS NATIONALISM AND UNIVERSITIES IN AFRICA.
AFRICAN AFFAIRS 62 JANUARY 1963 PP 20-28
042,

NICOL DAVIDSON
THE FORMATION OF A WEST AFRICAN INTELLECTUAL COMMUNITY
CHAPTER 3.
IN THE WEST AFRICAN INTELLECTUAL COMMUNITY SEMINAR,
IBADAN, IBADAN UNIVERSITY PRESS, 1962, PP 10-17
044,

NICOLAISEN
NICOLAISEN JOHANNES
ECOLOGY AND CULTURE OF THE PASTORAL TUAREG-- WITH SPECIAL
REFERENCE TO THE TUAREG OF AHAGGAR AND AIR.
COPENHAGEN THE NATIONAL MUSEUM OF COPENHAGEN
ETHNOGRAPHICAL SERIES 9 1963
010,127-01,

NICOLAISEN JOHANNES

STRUCTURES POLITIQUES ET SOCIALES DES TOUAREG DE L AIR ET
DE L'AHAGGAR. POLITICAL AND SOCIAL STRUCTURES OF THE TUAREG
ETUDES NIGERIENNES,7,NIAMEY,INSTITUT FRANCAIS D'AFRIQUE
NOIRE,1963
009,127-01,

NIELSEN WALDEMAR
    NIELSEN WALDEMAR
    THE GREAT POWERS AND AFRICA
    NEW YORK,PRAEGER,1969
    083, 097,

NIXON RAYMOND B
    NIXON RAYMOND B
    FACTORS RELATED TO FREEDOM IN NATIONAL PRESS SYSTEMS.
    JOURNALISM QUARTERLY 37 WINTER 1960 PP 13-28
    049,

    NIXON RAYMOND B
    FREEDOM IN THE WORLD'S PRESS-- A FRESH APPRAISAL OF NEW
    DATA.
    JOURNALISM QUARTERLY 42 WINTER 1965 PP 3-14, 118-119
    049,

NJAU ELIMO P
    NJAU ELIMO P
    AFRICAN ART.
    IN LALAGE BOWN AND MICHAEL CROWDER (EDS.), PROCEEDINGS OF
    THE FIRST INTERNATIONAL CONGRESS OF AFRICANISTS, ACCRA,
    1962, LONDON, LONGMANS, 1964, PP 235-242
    093,

NJOYA SULTAN
    NJOYA SULTAN
    HISTOIRE ET COUTUMES DES BAMUM.
    YAOUNDE,INSTITUT FRANCAIS D'AFRIQUE NOIRE,CENTRE   CAMEROON
    1952
    104-02,

NKETIA J H KWABENA
    NKETIA J H KWABENA
    UNITY AND DIVERSITY IN AFRICAN MUSIC-- A PROBLEM OF
    SYNTHESIS.
    IN LALAGE BOWN AND MICHAEL CROWDER (EDS.), PROCEEDINGS OF
    THE FIRST INTERNATIONAL CONGRESS OF AFRICANISTS, ACCRA,
    1962, LONDON, LONGMANS, 1964, PP 256-263
    015,

    NKETIA J H KWABENA
    THE LANGUAGE PROBLEM AND THE AFRICAN PERSONALITY.
    PRESENCE AFRICAINE, NO. 67, 3RD QUARTER, 1968, PP. 157-171
    049,

    NKETIA J H KWABENA
    DRUMS,DANCE AND SONG
    ATLANTIC MONTHLY 230 1959 PP 69-72
    015,

    NKETIA J H KWABENA
    ARTISTIC VALUES IN AFRICAN MUSIC

COMPOSER JOURNAL OF THE COMPOSERS GUILD OF GREAT BRITAIN
19 1966 PP16-19
015,093,

NKETIA J H KWABENA
NKETIA J H KWABENA
AFRICAN MUSIC IN GHANA
EVANSTON, NORTHWESTERN UNIVERSITY PRESS, 1963
015,

NKONGORI LAURENT
KAMANZI THOMAS   NKONGORI LAURENT
PROVERBES DU RWANDA.
TERVUREN, MUSEE ROYAL DU CONGO BELGE, 1957
129-01,

NKRUMAH KWAME
NKRUMAH KWAME
NEO-COLONIALISM, THE LAST STAGE OF IMPERIALISM.
NEW YORK, INTERNATIONAL PUBLISHERS, 1965
060,082,114-04,

NKRUMAH KWAME
DARK DAYS IN GHANA.
NEW YORK, INTERNATIONAL PUBLISHERS, 1968
064,114-04,

NKRUMAH KWAME
GHANA--THE AUTOBIOGRAPHY OF KWAME NKRUMAH.
NEW YORK, NELSON, 1957
044,114-04,

NKRUMAH KWAME
HANDBOOK OF REVOLUTIONARY WARFARE.
NEW YORK, INTERNATIONAL PUBLISHERS, INC., 1969
060,091,114-04,

NKRUMAH KWAME
NEO-COLONIALISM--THE LAST STAGE OF IMPERIALISM.
LONDON, HEINEMAN EDUCATIONAL BOOKS, 1965
096,114-04,

NKRUMAH KWAME
CONSCIENCISM-- PHILOSOPHY AND IDEOLOGY FOR DECOLONIZATION
AND DEVELOPMENT WITH PARTICULAR REFERENCE TO THE AFRICAN
REVOLUTION.
LONDON, HEINEMANN, 1964
013,060,114-04,

NKRUMAH KWAME
MOVEMENT FOR COLONIAL FREEDOM.
PHYLON 16 1955 PP 397-409
060,114-04,

NKRUMAH KWAME
CHALLENGE OF THE CONGO-- A CASE STUDY OF FOREIGN PRESSURES
IN AN INDEPENDENT STATE.
NEW YORK INTERNATIONAL PUBLISHERS 1967
060,114-04,

NKRUMAH KWAME
I SPEAK OF FREEDOM.
NEW YORK,PRAEGER,1961 (LONDON, HEINEMANN EDUCATIONAL BOOKS)
060,114-04,

NKRUMAH KWAME
    NKRUMAH KWAME
    AFRICAN PROSPECT.
    IN PHILIP W QUIGG (ED.), AFRICA, NEW YORK, PRAEGER, 1964,
    PP 272-282
    060,114-04,

    NKRUMAH KWAME
    GHANA--THE AUTOBIOGRAPHY OF KWAME NKRUMAH.
    NEW YORK, NELSON, 1957
    096,114-04,

NKUMBULA HARRY M
    BANDA HASTINGS K   NKUMBULA HARRY M
    FEDERATION IN CENTRAL AFRICA.
    LONDON,1951
    078,122-04,

NNOCHIRI ENYINNAYA
    NNOCHIRI ENYINNAYA
    PARASITIC DISEASE AND URBANIZATION IN A DEVELOPING
    COMMUNITY.
    LONDON, OXFORD MEDICAL PUBLICATIONS, 1968
    046,

NORMAN BENNETT
    GABEL CREIGHTON   NORMAN BENNETT   EDS
    RECONSTRUCTING AFRICAN CULTURE HISTORY.
    BROOKLINE,BOSTON UNIVERSITY PRESS,1967
    036,

NORMAN DANIEL
    NORMAN DANIEL
    THE SUDAN
    IN KRITZECK AND LEWIS,PP 202-213
    134-03,

NORREGARD GEORG
    NORREGARD GEORG
    DANISH SETTLEMENTS IN WEST AFRICA.
    BOSTON,BOSTON UNIVERSITY PRESS,1966
    027,

NORTH A C
    NORTH A C   ET-AL
    AFRICAN LAND TENURE DEVELOPMENTS IN KENYA AND UGANDA AND
    THEIR APPLICATION TO NORTHERN RHODESIA.
    JOURNAL OF AFRICAN ADMINISTRATION 13 OCTOBER 1961
    PP 211-219
    070,117-08,139-08,142-08,

NORTHCOTT
    NORTHCOTT WILLIAM C
    CHRISTIANITY IN AFRICA
    PHILADELPHIA,WESTMINSTER PRESS,1963

050,

NOTTINGHAM JOHN
    ROSBERG CARL G   NOTTINGHAM JOHN
    THE MYTH OF MAU-MAU-- NATIONALISM IN KENYA.
    NEW YORK, PRAEGER, 1966
    055,117-06,

    SANGER CLYDE   NOTTINGHAM JOHN
    THE KENYA GENERAL ELECTION OF 1963.
    JOURNAL OF MODERN AFRICAN STUDIES 2 1964 PP 1-40
    063,117-07,

NOVACCO N
    NOVACCO N   COMP
    ESSAI D'UNE BIBLIOGRAPHIE SUR LA COTE D'IVOIRE.
    PARIS, CENTRE DE DEVELOPPMENT DE L'ORGANISATION DE
    COOPERATION ET DE DEVELOPPMENT ECONOMIQUES, IV, 1964
    116-12,

NSOUGAN
    NSOUGAN AGBLEMAGNON
    MASSES ET ELITES EN AFRIQUE NOIRE - LE CAS DU TOGO.
    IN LLOYD, THE NEW ELITES OF TROPICAL AFRICA, LONDON, OXFORD
    UNIVERSITY PRESS, 1966, P. 118-125
    137-04,

NYARKO K A J
    NYARKO K A J
    THE DEVELOPMENT OF KUMASI.
    BULL. GHANA GEOG. ASSOC., 4, 1, 1959
    114-05,

NYE JOSEPH S
    NYE JOSEPH S
    PAN AFRICANISM AND EAST AFRICAN INTEGRATION.
    CAMBRIDGE, HARVARD UNIVERSITY PRESS, 1965
    077,

    NYE JOSEPH S
    PATTERNS AND CATALYSTS IN REGIONAL INTEGRATION.
    IN INTERNATIONAL REGIONALISM, ED BY J S NYE JR, BOSTON,
    LITTLE, BROWN, 1968, PP 333-349
    059,

    NYE JOSEPH S
    ECONOMIC INTEGRATION CHAPTER 5.
    IN PAN-AFRICANISM AND EAST AFRICAN INTEGRATION, CAMBRIDGE
    MASS, HARVARD UNIVERSTIY PRESS, 1965
    078,

    NYE JOSEPH S
    THE EXTENT AND VIABILITY OF EAST AFRICAN COOPERATION.
    IN COLIN LEYS AND P ROBSON (EDS), FEDERATION IN EAST AFRICA--
    OPPORTUNITIES AND PROBLEMS, NAIROBI, OXFORD UNIVERSITY PRESS,
    1965, PP 41-55
    078,

    NYE JOSEPH S
    SOCIAL INTEGRATION CHP 3.

IN PAN-AFRICANISM AND EAST AFRICAN INTEGRATION,CAMBRIDGE,
MASS,HARVARD UNIVERSITY PRESS,1965
058,

NYE JOSEPH S
    NYE JOSEPH S
    COMPARATIVE REGIONAL INTEGRATION--CONCEPT AND MEASUREMENT.
    INTERNATIONAL ORGANIZATION, VOL. XXII, NO. 4, 1968, PP. 855-
    880
    078,

    NYE JOSEPH S
    POLITICAL INTEGRATION CHAPTER 4.
    IN PAN-AFRICANISM AND EAST AFRICAN INTEGRATION, CAMBRIDGE,
    MASS, HARVARD UNIVERSITY PRESS, 1965
    057,059,

NYERERE JULIUS K
    NYERERE JULIUS K
    THE RELATIONSHIP BETWEEN THE CIVIL SERVICE, POLITICAL
    PARTIES AND MEMBERS OF LEGISLATIVE COUNCIL.
    INTERNATIONAL AFFAIRS 36 JANUARY 1960 PP 43-47
    062,136-04,

    NYERERE JULIUS K
    THE NATURE AND REQUIREMENTS OF AFRICAN UNITY.
    AFRICAN FORUM I 1 1965 PP 38-52
    079, 136-04,

    NYERERE JULIUS K
    WHY TANZANIA RECOGNIZED BIAFRA.
    AFRICA REPORT, JUNE 27, 1968
    065,136-09,

    NYERERE JULIUS K
    UJAMAA--ESSAYS ON SOCIALISM
    NEW YORK OXFORD UNIVERSITY PRESS 1969
    060,077,

    NYERERE JULIUS K
    UJAMAA-- THE BASIS OF AFRICAN SOCIALISM CHAPTER 5.
    IN AFRICA'S FREEDOM, NEW YORK, BARNES AND NOBLE, 1964,
    PP 67-77
    060, 136-04,

    NYERERE JULIUS K
    THE AFRICAN AND DEMOCRACY.
    IN WILLIAM J HANNA (ED), INDEPENDENT BLACK AFRICA, CHICAGO,
    RAND MCNALLY, 1964, PP 521-527
    060, 136-04,

    NYERERE JULIUS K
    TANGANYIKA TODAY-- THE NATIONALIST VIEW.
    INTERNATIONAL AFFAIRS 36 1960 PP43-47
    060,136-04,

    NYERERE JULIUS K
    INDEPENDENCE MEANS POWER.
    AFRICA REPORT, DECEMBER, 1968, P. 22
    087,136-04,

NYERERE JULIUS K
    NYERERE JULIUS K
    ESSAYS ON SOCIALISM.
    LONDON AND NEW YORK, INTERNATIONAL BOOKSELLERS, INC., 1969
    060,077,136-04,

    NYERERE JULIUS K
    FREEDOM AND UNITY--UHURU NA UMOJA.
    LONDON, OXFORD UNIVERSITY PRESS, 1967
    060,077,136-04,

NZEKWU M
    NZEKWU M
    LA CONTRIBUTION CATHOLIQUE (THE CATHOLIC CONTRIBUTION).
    IN COLLOQUE SUR LES RELIGIONS, ABIDJAN, APRIL, 1961, PARIS,
    PRESENCE AFRICAINE, 1962, PP 195-198
    050,

O

O'CONNELL JAMES
    COWAN L GRAY   O CONNELL JAMES   SCANLON DAVID G
    EDUCATION AND NATION-BUILDING IN AFRICA.
    NEW YORK, PRAEGER, 1965
    042,043,

O'CONNOR A M
    O CONNOR A M
    AN ECONOMIC GEOGRAPHY OF EAST AFRICA.
    NEW YORK, PRAEGER, 1966
    069,

    O CONNOR A M
    A WIDER EASTERN AFRICAN UNION--SOME GEOGRAPHICAL ASPECTS.
    THE JOURNAL OF MODERN AFRICAN STUDIES, VOL. 6, NO. 4, 1968,
    PP. 485-493
    078,

O'CONNOR M
    WOLSTENHOLME G   O CONNOR M   EDS
    MAN AND AFRICA
    LONDON, J AND A CHURCHILL, 1965
    075,

O'BRIEN CONNOR C
    O BRIEN CONNOR C
    TO KATANGA AND BACK--A U.N. CASE HISTORY.
    NEW YORK, SIMON AND SCHUSTER, 1962
    098,108-06,

O'CONNELL JAMES
    O CONNELL JAMES
    THE CHANGING ROLE OF THE STATE IN WEST AFRICA.
    NIGERIAN JOURNAL OF ECONOMIC AND SOCIAL STUDIES 3 NOVEMBER
    1961 PP1-21

061,

O'CONNELL JAMES
    O'CONNELL JAMES
    THE SCOPE OF THE TRAGEDY.
    AFRICA REPORT, FEB., 1968, P. 8
    065,128-06,

    O'CONNELL JAMES
    THE NORTHERN REGIONAL ELECTIONS, 1961, AN ANALYSIS.
    NIGERIAN JOURNAL OF ECONOMIC AND SOCIAL STUDIES 4 JULY
    JULY 1962
    063,128-07,

    O'CONNELL JAMES
    SENGHOR, NKRUMAH AND AZIKIWE-- UNITY AND DIVERSITY IN THE
    WEST AFRICAN STATES.
    NIGERIAN JOURNAL OF ECONOMIC AND SOCIAL STUDIES 5 MARCH
    1963 PP 77-93
    044,114-04,128-04,130-04,

    O'CONNELL JAMES
    POLITICAL INTEGRATION-- THE NIGERIAN CASE CHAPTER 5.
    IN ARTHUR HAZLEWOOD, AFRICAN INTEGRATION AND DISINTEGRATION,
    LONDON, OXFORD UNIVERSITY PRESS, 1967, P   129-184
    057,128-06,

OBICHERE BONIFACE
    OBICHERE BONIFACE
    AFRICAN HISTORY AND WESTERN CIVILIZATION.
    IN BLACK STUDIES IN THE UNIVERSITY, ARMSTEAD ROBINSON ET AL
    (EDS), NEW HAVEN, YALE UNIVERSITY PRESS, 1969, PP. 83-103
    096,099,

ODUHO JOSEPH
    ODUHO JOSEPH   DENG WILLIAM
    THE PROBLEM OF THE SOUTHERN SUDAN.
    LONDON, OXFORD UNIVERSITY PRESS, 1963
    134-06,

OGILVIE DONALD
    ROBINSON ARMSTEAD   FOSTER CRAIG   OGILVIE DONALD
    BLACK STUDIES IN THE UNIVERSITY--A SYMPOSIUM.
    NEW HAVEN, YALE UNIVERSITY PRESS, 1969
    002,094,095,

OGOT BETHWELL A
    OGOT BETHWELL A   KIERAN J A
    ZAMANI. A SURVEY OF EAST AFRICAN HISTORY
    NAIROBI, EAST AFRICAN PUBLISHING HOUSE, 1968
    ALSO AVAILABLE THROUGH NORTHWESTERN UNIVERSITY PRESS.
    001,036,

    OGOT BETHWELL A   ED
    HADITH 1.
    KENYA, EAST AFRICAN PUBLISHING HOUSE, 1968
    036,

    OGOT BETHWELL A
    HISTORY OF THE SOUTHERN LUO- VOLUME ONE,MIGRATION AND

SETTLEMENT
NAIROBI, EAST AFRICAN PUBLISHING HOUSE, 1967
025,

OGOT BETHWELL A
    OGOT BETHWELL A   WELBOURN F B
    A PLACE TO FEEL AT HOME--A STUDY OF TWO INDEPENDENT CHURCHES
    IN WESTERN KENYA.
    LONDON, OXFORD UNIVERSITY PRESS, 1966
    051,117-03,

    OGOT BETHWELL A
    KINGSHIP AND STATELESSNESS AMONG THE NILOTS
    IN VANSINA,ROGEN,MAUNY(EDS), THE HISTORIAN IN TROPICAL
    AFRICA, LONDON OXFORD UNIVERSITY PRESS 1964 PP 284-301
    009,025,

OJO G J AFOLABI
    OJO G J AFOLABI
    YORUBA PALACES
    LONDON, UNIVERSITY OF LONDON PRESS, 1966
    092,

    OJO G J AFOLABI
    YORUBA CULTURE- A GEOGRAPHICAL ANALYSIS
    IFE AND LONDON, UNIVERSITY OF LONDON PRESS, 1966
    026,

OJUKWU C ODUMEGWU
    OJUKWU C ODUMEGWU
    BIAFRA--SELECTED SPEECHES WITH JOURNAL OF EVENTS.
    NEW YORK, HARPER AND ROW, 1969
    065,128-06,

    OJUKWU C ODUMEGWU
    RANDOM THOUGHTS OF C ODUMEGWU OJUKWU, GENERAL OF THE
    PEOPLES ARMY, BIAFRA.
    NEW YORK, HARPER AND ROW, 1969
    065,128-06,

OKARA GABRIEL
    OKARA GABRIEL
    THE VOICE.
    NEW YORK, AFRICANA PUBLISHING CORPORATION, 1969 (LONDON,
    HEINEMAN EDUCATIONAL BOOKS)
    090,128-10,

OKEDIJI FRANCIS O
    OKEDIJI FRANCIS O
    SOME CORRELATES OF ETHNIC COHESIVENESS-- AFRICAN STUDENTS≠
    ADJUSTMENT IN TWO U S COMMUNITIES.
    NIGERIAN JOURNAL OF ECONIMIC AND SOCIAL STUDIES 7 NOVEMBER
    1965 PP 347-362
    096,

OKELLO JOHN
    OKELLO JOHN
    REVOLUTION IN ZANZIBAR.
    KENYA, EAST AFRICAN PUBLISHING HOUSE, 1967
    057,059,136-06,

OKIGBO CHRISTOPHER
   OKIGBO CHRISTOPHER
   LABYRINTHS WITH PATHS OF THUNDER .
   NEW YORK, AFRICANA PUBLISHING CORPORATION, 1970 (LONDON,
   HEINEMANN EDUCATIONAL BOOKS)
   090,128-10,

OKIGBO PIUS N C
   OKIGBO PIUS N C
   AFRICA AND THE COMMON MARKET.
   EVANSTON, NORTHWESTERN UNIVERSITY PRESS, 1967
   080,082,

   OKIGBO PIUS N C
   THE FISCAL SYSTEM AND THE GROWTH IN NATIONAL INCOME
   CHAPTER 26.
   IN EDITH WHETHAM AND JEAN CURRIE (EDS.), READINGS IN THE
   APPLIED ECONOMICS OF AFRICA, LONDON, CAMBRIDGE UNIVERSITY
   PRESS, 2, 1967, PP 126-140
   073,

   OKIGBO PIUS N C
   NIGERIAN NATIONAL ACCOUNTS 1950-7 CHAPTER 19.
   IN EDITH WHETHAM AND JEAN CURRIE (EDS.), READINGS IN THE
   APPLIED ECONOMICS OF AFRICA, LONDON, CAMBRIDGE UNIVERSITY
   PRESS, 2, 1967, PP 1-20
   073,128-08,

OKONDO PETER J
   OKONDO PETER J
   PROSPECTS OF FEDERALISM IN EAST AFRICA CHAPTER 2.
   IN DAVID P CURRIE, FEDERALISM AND THE NEW NATIONS OF AFRICA,
   CHICAGO, UNIVERSITY OF CHICAGO PRESS, 1964, PP 29-38
   078,

OKONJO C
   CALDWELL JOHN C   OKONJO C   EDS
   THE POPULATION OF TROPICAL AFRICA.
   LONDON, LONGMANS, 1968
   053,074,076,

OKOYE FELIX N C
   OKOYE FELIX N C
   DINGANE--A REAPPRAISAL.
   JOURNAL OF AFRICAN HISTORY, X, 2, 1969, PP. 221-235
   031,

OKUMU W A J
   OKUMU W A J
   RACIALISM AND TRIBALISM AS FACTORS IN NATIONAL AND INTER-
   NATIONAL TENSIONS.
   IN LAWRENCE SAGINI (ED), RACIAL AND COMMUNAL TENSIONS IN EAST
   AFRICA, NAIROBI EAST AFRICAN PUBLISHING HOUSE, 1966, PP 113-
   122
   057,

OLAKANPO O
   OLAKANPO O
   DISTRIBUTIVE TRADE-A CRITIQUE OF GOVERNMENT POLICY CHAPTER

17.
IN EDITH WHETHAM AND JEAN CURRIE (EDS.), READINGS IN THE
APPLIED ECONOMICS OF AFRICA, LONDON, CAMBRIDGE UNIVERSITY
PRESS, 1, 1967, PP 193-204
073,

OLATUNJI
    DIETZ BETTY W   OLATUNJI
    MUSICAL INSTRUMENTS OF AFRICA, THEIR NATURE, USE, AND
    PLACE IN THE LIFE OF A DEEPLY MUSICAL PEOPLE.
    NEW YORK, JOHN DAY, 1965
    015,

OLBRECHTS FRANS M
    OLBRECHTS FRANS M
    LES ARTS PLASTIQUES DU CONGO BELGE (SCULPTURE OF THE BELGIAN
    CONGO).
    BRUSSELS, EDITIONS ERASME, 1959
    014,

OLDFIELD RICHARD
    LAIRD MACGREGOR   OLDFIELD RICHARD
    NARRATIVE OF AN EXPEDITION INTO THE INTERIOR OF AFRICA BY
    THE RIVER NIGER IN THE STEAM VESSELS QUORRA AND ALBURKAH IN
    1832, 1833, AND 1834.
    LONDON, CASS, 1966
    027,

OLIVER ROLAND
    OLIVER ROLAND   FAGE JOHN D
    A SHORT HISTORY OF AFRICA.
    BALTIMORE, PENGUIN BOOKS, 1962
    001,036,

    OLIVER ROLAND   FAGE JOHN D
    THIRD CONFERENCE ON AFRICAN HISTORY AND ARCHAEOLOGY-- 1961.
    THE JOURNAL OF AFRICAN HISTORY VOL III NO 2 1962 (ENTIRE
    VOLUME)
    018,019,

    OLIVER ROLAND
    THE PROBLEM OF BANTU EXPANSION.
    THE JOURNAL OF AFRICAN HISTORY VII 3 1966 PP 361-366
    019,

    OLIVER ROLAND   MATHEW GERVASE   EDS
    HISTORY OF EAST AFRICA, VOLUME ONE.
    OXFORD, CLARENDON PRESS, 1963
    023,036,

    OLIVER ROLAND
    DISCERNIBLE DEVELOPMENTS IN THE INTERIOR C. 1500-1840.
    IN ROLAND OLIVER AND GERVASE MATHEW (EDS), HISTORY OF EAST
    AFRICA VOLUME ONE, OXFORD, CLARENDON PRESS, 1963, PP 169-211
    025,

    OLIVER ROLAND   ATMORE ANTHONY
    THE LAST YEARS OF COLONIAL RULE, 1940-1960.
    IN AFRICA SINCE 1800, CAMBRIDGE, CAMBRIDGE UNIVERSITY PRESS,
    1967, PP 213-222

056,

OLIVER ROLAND
    OLIVER ROLAND   ATMORE ANTHONY
    THE INTER-WAR PERIOD, 1918-1938
    IN AFRICA SINCE 1800, CAMBRIDGE, CAMBRIDGE UNIVERSITY PRESS,
    1967, PP 160-171
    035,

    OLIVER ROLAND   ATMORE ANTHONY
    COLONIAL RULE IN TROPICAL AFRICA-- SOCIAL AND RELIGIOUS
    DEVELOPMENTS.
    IN AFRICA SINCE 1800, CAMBRIDGE, CAMBRIDGE UNIVERSITY PRESS,
    1967, PP 141-159
    035,050,

    OLIVER ROLAND   ATMORE ANTHONY
    COLONIAL RULE IN TROPICAL AFRICA-- POLITICAL AND ECONOMIC
    DEVELOPMENTS, 1885-1914.
    IN AFRICA SINCE 1800, CAMBRIDGE, CAMBRIDGE UNIVERSITY PRESS,
    1967, PP 128-140
    033,

    OLIVER ROLAND   ATMORE ANTHONY
    THE PARTITION OF AFRICA ON THE GROUND, 1891-1901.
    IN AFRICA SINCE 1800, CAMBRIDGE, CAMBRIDGE UNIVERSITY PRESS,
    1967, PP 114-127
    033,

    OLIVER ROLAND   ATMORE ANTHONY
    THE PARTITION OF AFRICA ON PAPER, 1879-1891.
    IN AFRICA SINCE 1800, CAMBRIDGE, CAMBRIDGE UNIVERSITY PRESS,
    1967, PP 103-114
    033,

    OLIVER ROLAND   ATMORE ANTHONY
    WEST AFRICA BEFORE THE COLONIAL PERIOD, 1800-1875.
    IN AFRICA SINCE 1800, CAMBRIDGE, CAMBRIDGE UNIVERSITY PRESS,
    1967, PP 29-42
    026,

    OLIVER ROLAND
    REFLECTIONS ON THE SOURCES OF EVIDENCE FOR THE PRECOLONIAL
    HISTORY OF EAST AFRICA.
    HISTORIANS IN TROPICAL AFRICA SALISBURY S R UNIVERSITY
    COLLEGE OF RHODESIA AND NYASALAND 1962 PP 322-336
    099,

    OLIVER ROLAND
    BANTU GENESIS-AN INQUIRY INTO SOME PROBLEMS OF EARLY BANTU
    HISTORY
    AFRICAN AFFAIRS 65 1966 PP 245-258
    019,

    OLIVER ROLAND
    ANCIENT CAPITAL SITES OF ANKOLE.
    THE UGANDA JOURNAL 23 1959 PP 51-63
    025,139-02,

    OLIVER ROLAND

SOME FACTORS IN THE BRITISH OCCUPATION OF EAST AFRICA 1884-
1894.
THE UGANDA JOURNAL 15 1951 PP 49-64
033,

OLIVER ROLAND
   OLIVER ROLAND
   SIR HARRY JOHNSTON AND THE SCRAMBLE FOR AFRICA.
   LONDON, CHATTO AND WINDUS, 1957
   033,

   OLIVER ROLAND
   THE MISSIONARY FACTOR IN EAST AFRICA
   LONDON, LONGMANS, 1952
   050,

OLLENNU NII AMAA
   OLLENNU NII AMAA
   PRINCIPLES OF CUSTOMARY LAND LAW IN GHANA.
   LONDON, SWEET AND MAXWELL, 1962
   066,114-01,

OLORUNTIMEHIN B O
   OLORUNTIMEHIN B O
   RESISTANCE MOVEMENTS IN THE TUKULOR EMPIRE.
   CAHIERS D'ETUDES AFRICAINES, VOL. VIII, 1968, NO. 29,
   PP. 123-143
   034,123-02,

OLUSANYA G O
   OLUSANYA G O
   THE ROLE OF EX-SERVICEMEN IN NIGERIAN POLITICS.
   THE JOURNAL OF MODERN AFRICAN STUDIES, VOL. 6, NO. 2, 1968
   PP. 221-32
   063,128-07,

OLUWASANMI H A
   OLUWASANMI H A
   AGRICULTURE IN A DEVELOPING ECONOMY CHAPTER 18.
   IN EDITH WHETHAM AND JEAN CURRIE (EDS.), READINGS IN THE
   APPLIED ECONOMICS OF AFRICA, LONDON, CAMBRIDGE UNIVERSITY
   PRESS, 1, 1967, PP 205-216
   070,

   OLUWASANMI H A
   AGRICULTURE AND NIGERIAN ECONOMIC DEVELOPMENT.
   NIGERIA, OXFORD UNIVERSITY PRESS, 1966
   070,128-08,

OLYMPIO SYLVANUS
   OLYMPIO SYLVANUS
   AFRICAN PROBLEMS AND THE COLD WAR.
   IN PHILIP W QUIGG (ED.), AFRICA, NEW YORK, PRAEGER, 1964,
   PP 292-301
   081,137-04,

OMARI T PETER
   OMARI T PETER
   KWAME NKRUMAH--THE ANATOMY OF AN AFRICAN DICTATORSHIP.
   NEW YORK, AFRICANA PUBLISHING CORPORATION, 1970

061,114-07,

OMER-COOPER J D
  OMER-COOPER J D
  THE ZULU AFTERMATH-- A NINETEENTH-CENTURY REVOLUTION
  IN BANTU AFRICA.
  LONDON, LONGMANS, 1966
  032,034,132-02,

  OMER-COOPER J D   ET-AL
  NIGERIAN MARXISM AND SOCIAL PROGRESS.
  NIGERIAN JOURNAL OF ECONOMIC AND SOCIAL STUDIES 6 JULY
  1964 PP 133-198 SYMPOSIUM ON NIGERIA
  060,128-04,

OMINDE S H
  OMINDE S H
  LAND AND POPULATION MOVEMENTS IN KENYA
  EVANSTON,NORTHWESTERN UNIVERSITY PRESS,1968
  074,117-08,

ONITIRI H M A
  ONITIRI H M A
  TOWARDS A WEST AFRICAN ECONOMIC COMMUNITY.
  NIGERIAN JOURNAL OF ECONOMIC AND SOCIAL STUDIES 5 MARCH
  1963 PP 27-54
  078,

ONYEMELUKWE
  ONYEMELUKWE CLEMENT
  PROBLEMS OF INDUSTRIAL PLANNING AND MANAGEMENT IN NIGERIA.
  NEW YORK (COLUMBIA), MCGILL-QUEENS, 1969
  071,128-08,

ORAM N
  ORAM N
  TOWNS IN AFRICA.
  LONDON, OXFORD UNIVERSITY PRESS, 1965
  045,

ORD H W
  STEWART I G   ORD H W   EDS
  AFRICAN PRIMARY PRODUCTS AND INTERNATIONAL TRADE.
  EDINBURGH,UNIVERSITY PRESS,1965
  069,073,

ORDE M H
  ORDE M H
  DEVELOPMENT OF LOCAL GOVERNMENT IN RURAL AREAS IN THE
  GAMBIA.
  JOURNAL OF LOCAL ADMINISTRATIONS OVERSEAS, 4, 1, JAN., 1965

ORG FOR ECON COOP
  ORG FOR ECON COOP   ECON COOP AND DEVEL
  BIBLIOGRAPHY ON GUINEA.
  PARIS, O.E.C.D. DEVELOPMENT CENTRE, 1965
  115-12,

ORR CHARLES A
  ORR CHARLES A

TRADE UNIONISM IN COLONIAL AFRICA.
JOURNAL OF MODERN AFRICAN STUDIES 4 1966 PP 65-81
073,

OSER JACOB
   OSER JACOB
   PROMOTING ECONOMIC DEVELOPMENT-WITH ILLUSTRATIONS FROM KENYA
   EVANSTON, NORTHWESTERN UNIVERSITY PRESS, 1967
   072,117-08,

OSOGO JOHN
   OSOGO JOHN
   A HISTORY OF THE BALUYIA.
   LONDON, OXFORD UNIVERSITY PRESS, 1966
   117-01,

OTIENO N C
   OTIENO N C
   CURRENT PROBLEMS IN THE EDUCATION OF AN AFRICAN SCIENTIST
   AND THE ROLE SUCH A SCIENTIST COULD PLAY IN THE ECONOMIC
   AND SOCIAL DEVELOPMENT OF AFRICA.
   IN LALAGE BOWN AND MICHAEL CROWDER (EDS.), PROCEEDINGS OF
   THE FIRST INTERNATIONAL CONGRESS OF AFRICANISTS, ACCRA,
   1962, LONDON, LONGMANS, 1964, PP 309-317
   075,

OTTENBERG PHEOBE
   OTTENBERG SIMON   OTTENBERG PHEOBE
   SOCIAL GROUPINGS.
   IN PETER J MCEWAN AND ROBERT B SUTCLIFFE (EDS) MODERN AFRICA,
   NEW YORK, THOMAS CROWELL, 1965, PP 26-44
   003,

OTTENBERG PHOEBE
   OTTENBERG SIMON   OTTENBERG PHOEBE
   CULTURES AND SOCIETIES OF AFRICA.
   NEW YORK, RANDOM HOUSE, 1960
   003,012,016,

   OTTENBERG PHOEBE
   THE CHANGING ECONOMIC POSITION OF WOMEN AMONG THE AFIKPO
   IBO CHAPTER 11.
   IN WILLIAM BASCOM AND MELVILLE HERSKOVITS, CONTINUTY AND
   CHANGE IN AFRICAN CULTURES, CHICAGO, UNIVERSITY OF CHICAGO
   PRESS, 1962, PP 205-223
   038,128-03,

   OTTENBERG PHOEBE
   THE AFIKPO IBO OF EASTERN NIGERIA.
   IN JAMES L GIBBS JR. (ED) PEOPLES OF AFRICA, NEW YORK, HOLT
   RINEHART AND WINSTON, 1965, PP. 1-40
   128-01,

OTTENBERG SIMON
   OTTENBERG SIMON   OTTENBERG PHOEBE
   CULTURES AND SOCIETIES OF AFRICA.
   NEW YORK, RANDOM HOUSE, 1960
   003,012,016,

   OTTENBERG SIMON   OTTENBERG PHEOBE

SOCIAL GROUPINGS.
IN PETER J MCEWAN AND ROBERT B SUTCLIFFE (EDS), MODERN AFRICA,
NEW YORK, THOMAS CROWELL, 1965, PP 26-44
003,

OTTENBERG SIMON
    OTTENBERG SIMON
    IBO RECEPTIVITY TO CHANGE CHAPTER 7.
    IN WILLIAM BASCOM AND MELVILLE HERSKOVITS, CONTINUTY AND
    CHANGE IN AFRICAN CULTURES, CHICAGO, UNIVERSITY OF CHICAGO
    PRESS, 1962, PP 130-143
    038,128-03,

    OTTENBERG SIMON
    DOUBLE DESCENT IN AN AFRICAN SOCIETY--THE AFIKPO VILLIAGE-
    GROUP.
    SEATTLE, UNIVERSITY OF WASHINGTON PRESS, 1968
    008,128-01,

OUDES BRUCE J
    OUDES BRUCE J
    OCAM COMES OF AGE.
    AFRICA REPORT, FEBRUARY, 1968
    078,

OUDNEY WALTER
    DENHAM DIXON   CLAPPERTON HUGH   OUDNEY WALTER
    NARRATIVE OF TRAVELS AND DISCOVERIES IN NORTHERN AND CENTRAL
    AFRICA IN THE YEARS 1822, 1823 AND 1824.
    LONDON, CAMBRIDGE UNIVERSITY PRESS, 1966, 3 VOLUMES
    E W BOVILL, (ED.)
    027,099,

OWEN C
    LEVINE ROBERT A   KLEIN N   OWEN C
    FATHER-CHILD RELATIONSHIPS AND CHANGING LIFE-STYLES IN
    IBADAN, NIGERIA.
    IN HORACE MINER (ED), THE CITY IN MODERN AFRICA, NEW YORK,
    PRAEGER, 1967
    040,128-03,

OWEN D F
    OWEN D F   ED
    RESEARCH AND DEVELOPMENT IN EAST AFRICA.
    NAIROBI, EAST AFRICAN ACADEMY, EAST AFRICAN INSTITUTE PRESS
    LTD., 1966
    075,100,

OWEN WILFRED
    OWEN WILFRED
    STRATEGY FOR MOBILITY.
    WASHINGTON, THE BROOKINGS INSTITUTION, 1964
    048,

OWIREDU P A
    OWIREDU P A
    PROPOSALS FOR A NATIONAL LANGUAGE FOR GHANA.
    AFRICAN AFFAIRS 63 APRIL 1964 PP 142-145
    056,114-06,

OYONO FERDINAND
    OYONO FERDINAND   TRANSLATED BY   REED JOHN
    HOUSEBOY.
    LONDON, HEINEMANN EDUCATIONAL BOOKS LTD, 1966
    (NEW YORK, MACMILLAN, 1970)
    090,

OYONO FERDINAND
    OYONO FERDINAND
    LA VIEUX NEGRE ET LA MEDAILLE.
    PARIS, JULLIARD, 1956
    090,104-10,

    OYONO FERDINAND
    CHEMIN D'EUROPE.
    PARIS, JULLIARD, 1960
    104-10,

    OYONO FERDINAND
    ECRIVAIN CAMEROUNAIS. TEXTES COMMENTES PAR ROGER MERCIER ET
    M AND S BATTESTINI.
    PARIS, F NATHAN, 1964
    104-10,

P

PADELFORD NORMAN J
    PADELFORD NORMAN J EMERSON RUPERT   EDS
    AFRICA AND WORLD ORDER.
    NEW YORK, PRAEGER, 1963
    080,

    PADELFORD NORMAN J
    THE ORGANIZATION OF AFRICAN UNITY.
    INTERNATIONAL ORGANIZATION 18 SUMMER 1964 PP 521-542
    079,

PADEN ANN
    CARTER GWENDOLEN M PADEN ANN   EDS
    EXPANDING HORIZONS IN AFRICAN STUDIES.
    EVANSTON, NORTHWESTERN UNIVERSITY PRESS, 1969
    002,100,

PADEN JOHN N
    MITCHELL ROBERT C   MORRISON DONALD G   PADEN JOHN N
    NATIONAL INTEGRATION AND STABILITY IN AFRICA.
    IN CARTER, GWENDOLEN M. AND ANN PADEN (EDS), EXPANDING
    HORIZONS IN AFRICAN STUDIES, EVANSTON, NORTHWESTERN
    UNIVERSITY PRESS, 1969, PP. 329-336
    100,

    PADEN JOHN N
    URBAN PLURALISM, INTEGRATION, AND ADAPTATION OF COMMUNAL I-
    DENTITY IN KANO, NIGERIA.
    IN RONALD COHEN AND JOHN MIDDLETON (EDS), FROM TRIBE TO NA-
    TION IN AFRICA, SAN FRANCISCO, CHANDLER, 1970

006,128-05,

PADEN JOHN N
    PADEN JOHN N
    LANGUAGE PROBLEMS OF NATIONAL INTEGRATION IN NIGERIA-- THE
    SPECIAL POSITION OF HAUSA.
    IN JOSHUA A FISHMAN, CHARLES FERGUSON, AND JYOTIRINDRA DAS
    GUPTA (EDS), LANGUAGE PROBLEMS IN DEVELOPING NATIONS, NEW
    YORK, JOHN WILEY, 1968, P. 199-214
    057,128-06,

    PADEN JOHN N
    ASPECTS OF EMIRSHIP IN KANO
    IN MICHAEL CROWDER AND OBARO IKIME(EDS), WEST AFRICAN CHIEFS-
    THEIR CHANGING STATUS UNDER COLONIAL RULE AND INDEPENDENCE
    NEW YORK, AFRICANA PUBLISHING CORPORATION, 1970
    035,

    PADEN JOHN N
    COMMUNAL COMPETITION,CONFLICT AND VIOLENCE IN KANO
    IN ROBERT MELSON AND HOWARD WOLPE (EDS), NIGERIA-MODERNIZATION
    AND THE POLITICS OF COMMUNALISM,EAST LANSING,MICHIGAN STATE
    UNIVERSITY PRESS,1970
    065,

    PADEN JOHN N
    KANO HAUSA POETRY.
    KANO STUDIES 1 SEPTEMBER 1965 PP 33-39
    012,128-01,

PADMORE GEORGE
    PADMORE GEORGE
    PAN-AFRICANISM OR COMMUNISM.
    PARIS,DENNIS DOBSON,1960
    079,084,

    PADMORE GEORGE   ED
    HISTORY OF THE PAN-AFRICAN CONGRESS.
    LONDON,HAMMERSMITH,1963
    079,

    PADMORE GEORGE
    AFRICA-- BRITAIN S THIRD EMPIRE.
    LONDON,D DOBSON,1949
    060,

    PADMORE GEORGE
    THE GOLD COAST REVOLUTION-- THE STRUGGLE OF AN AFRICAN
    PEOPLE FROM SLAVERY TO FREEDOM.
    LONDON,D DOBSON,1953
    060,114-04,

PAEZ PERO
    PAEZ PERO
    THE GLORIOS VICTORIES OF AMDA SEYON, KING OF ETHIOPIA,
    TOGETHER WITH THE HISTORY OF THE EMPEROR ADN CEON OTHERWISE
    CALLED GABRA MAZCAL.
    LONDON, OXFORD UNIVERSITY PRESS, 1965
    012,110-02,

PALAU MARTI M
    PALAU MARTI M
    LE ROI-DIEU AU BENIN (THE GOD-KING OF BENIN).
    PARIS, BERGER-LEVRAULT, 1964
    026,128-01,

PALMER
    PALMER SIR HERBERT R
    SUDANESE MEMOIRS.
    LONDON, F. CASS, 1967
    099,128-02,

PANKHURST ESTELLE
    PANKHURST ESTELLE
    ETHIOPIA AND ERITREA-- LAST PHASE OF THE REUNION STRUGGLE
    1941-1952.
    WOODFORD GREEN, LALIBELA HOUSE, 1953
    059,110-06,

    PANKHURST ESTELLE
    ETHIOPIA--A CULTURAL HISTORY.
    ESSEX, LALEBELA HOUSE, 1955
    110-11,

PANKHURST RICHARD
    PANKHURST RICHARD
    ITALIAN SETTLEMENT POLICY IN ERITREA AND ITS REPERCUSSIONS,
    1889-1894.
    IN JEFFREY BUTLER (ED), BOSTON UNIVERSITY PAPERS IN AFRICAN
    HISTORY VOL I, BOSTON, BOSTON UNIVERSITY PRESS, 1964, PP 119-
    154
    033,110-02,

    PANKHURST RICHARD
    MENELIK AND THE FOUNDATION OF ADDIS ABABA.
    JOURNAL OF AFRICAN HISTORY 2 1961 PP 103-117
    045,110-05,

    PANKHURST RICHARD
    TRANSPORTATION AND COMMUNICATIONS IN ETHIOPIA 1835-1935.
    JOURNAL OF TRANSPORT HISTORY 5 1961 PP 69-88, 6 1962 PP166-
    181, 233-254
    048,110-08,

    PANKHURST RICHARD   ED
    THE ETHIOPIAN ROYAL CHRONICLES.
    LONDON, OXFORD UNIVERSITY PRESS, 1967
    012,110-02,

PANOFSKY HANS E
    PANOFSKY HANS E
    PAN-AFRICANISM-- A BIBLIOGRAPHIC NOTE ON ORGANIZATIONS.
    AFRICAN FORUM I 2 1965 PP 62-64
    079,

PARENTI MICHAEL
    PARENTI MICHAEL
    ETHNIC POLITICS AND THE PERSISTENCE OF ETHNIC IDENTIFICA-
    TION.
    AMERICAN POLITICAL SCIENCE REVIEW VOL LXI NO 3 SEPTEMBER

1967 PP 717-726
006,

PARK ANDREW E W
PARK ANDREW E W
THE SOURCES OF NIGERIAN LAW.
LAGOS, AFRICAN UNIVERSITIES PRESS, 1963
066,128-06,

PARK ROBERT E
PARK ROBERT E
REFLECTIONS ON COMMUNICATION AND CULTURE.
AMERICAN JOURNAL OF SOCIOLOGY 44 1939 PP 191-205
048,

PARKER   JOHN
PARKER   JOHN
EXPANDING GUERILLA WARFARE.
IN LEGUM AND DRYSDALE, AFRICA CONTEMPORARY RECORD,
087,

PARKIN DAVID J
PARKIN DAVID J
TYPES OF URBAN AFRICAN MARRIAGE IN KAMPALA.
AFRICA 36 JULY 1966 PP 269-285
047,139-05,

PARKIN DAVID J
NEIGHBORS AND NATIONALS IN AN AFRICAN CITY WARD.
BERKELEY, UNIVERSITY OF CALIFORNIA, 1969
046,139-05,

PARRINDER GEOFFREY
PARRINDER GEOFFREY
WEST AFRICAN PSYCHOLOGY.
LONDON, BUTTERWORTH PRESS, 1951
041,

PARRINDER GEOFFREY
RELIGION IN AFRICA.
NEW YORK, PRAEGER PUBLISHERS; AND BALTIMORE, PENGUIN, 1969
050,

PARRINDER GEOFFREY
INDIGENOUS CHURCHES IN NIGERIA.
WEST AFRICAN REVIEW 31 SEPTEMBER 1960 PP 87-93
LONDON, AFRICA RESEARCH LIMITED, 1969, P. 53-54
051,128-03,

PARRINDER GEOFFREY
RELIGION IN AN AFRICAN CITY.
LONDON, OXFORD UNIVERSITY PRESS, 1953
046,

PARSONS J J
PARSONS J J
THE MOORISH IMPRINT ON THE IBERIAN PENINSULA.
GEOGRAPHICAL REVIEW 52 JANUARY 1962 PP 120-122
021,

PARSONS ROBERT T
    PARSONS ROBERT T
    RELIGION IN AN AFRICAN SOCIETY.
    LEIDEN, E.J. BRILL. 1964
    013,

PARSONS TALCOTT
    PARSONS TALCOTT   CLARK KENNETH   EDS
    THE NEGRO AMERICAN.
    BOSTON, HOUGHTON MIFFLIN, DAEDALUS LIBRARY 7, 1966
    030,

PATON ALAN
    PATON ALAN
    CRY, THE BELOVED COUNTRY
    NEW YORK SCRIBNER 1948
    032,089,

    PATON ALAN
    THE LONG VIEW.
    NEW YORK, PRAEGER, 1968
    089,132-07,

PATTEN J W
    PATTEN J W
    ALTERNATIVE TO APARTHEID IN SOUTH AFRICA.
    IN PHILIP W QUIGG (ED.), AFRICA. NEW YORK, PRAEGER, 1964,
    PP 231-247
    089,132-06,

PATTERSON SHEILA
    PATTERSON SHEILA
    THE LAST TREK
    LONDON, ROUTLEDGE AND KEGAN PAUL, 1957
    032,

PAULME DENISE
    PAULME DENISE
    AFRICAN SCULPTURE.
    LONDON, ELEK BOOKS, 1962
    014,

    PAULME DENISE   ED
    WOMEN OF TROPICAL AFRICA.
    LONDON, ROUTLEDGE AND KEGAN PAUL, 1963
    008,

    PAULME DENISE
    STRUCTURES SOCIALES TRADITIONNELLES EN AFRIQUE NOIRE,
    (TRADITIONAL SOCIAL STRUCTURES OF BLACK AFRICA).
    CAHIERS D'ETUDES AFRICAINES 1 1960 PP 15-27
    008,

    PAULME DENISE
    QUE SAVONS-NOUS DES RELIGIONS AFRICAINES (WHAT DO WE KNOW
    ABOUT AFRICAN RELIGIONS).
    IN RENCONTRES INTERNATIONALES DE BOUAKE, LES RELIGIONS
    AFRICAINES TRADITIONNELLES, PARIS. EDITIONS DU SEUIL, 1965,
    PP 13-32
    013,

PAULOS TSADUA ABBA
  PAULOS TSADUA ABBA
  FETHA NEGAST--THE LAW OF THE KINGS.
  ADDIS ABABA, INTERNATIONAL UNIVERSITY BOOKSELLERS,INC., 1968
  066,110-01,

PAUVERT J C
  BALANDIER GEORGES   PAUVERT J C
  LES VILLAGES GABONAIS-- ASPECTS DEMOGRAPHIQUES, ECONOMIQUES
  SOCIOLOGIQUES, PROJETS DE MODERNISATION (GABON VILLAGES--
  DEMOGRAPHIC, ECONOMIC AND SOCIOLOGICAL ASPECTS, PROJECTS
  OF MODERNIZATION).
  BRAZZAVILLE,INSTITUT DES ETUDES CONTRFICAINES,1952
  070,112-03,

  PAUVERT J C
  URBANISATION ET PLANIFICATION DE L EDUCATION (URBANIZATION
  AND PLANNING OF EDUCATION).
  CIVILISATIONS, VOL. XVIII, 1967, PP. 30-44
  043,

PAYNE WILLIAM
  PAYNE WILLIAM
  AMERICAN PRESS COVERAGE OF AFRICA.
  AFRICA REPORT JANUARY 1966 PP 44-48
  083,

PEARSON J D
  PEARSON J D   JONES RUTH   EDS
  THE BIBLIOGRAPHY OF AFRICA-PROCEEDINGS AND PAPERS OF THE
  INTERNATIONAL CONFERENCE OF AFRICAN BIBLIOGRAPHY NAIROBI
  DECEMBER 1967
  NEW YORK,AFRICANA PUBLISHING CORPORATION,1969
  099,

PEASLEE AMOS
  PEASLEE AMOS
  CONSTITUTIONS OF NATIONS, VOLUME I, AFRICA.
  THE HAGUE,MARTINUS NIJHOFF, 1965
  067,068,

PECKHAM ROBERT
  PECKHAM ROBERT   RAGHEB ISIS   SOUTHALL AIDAN
  A BIBLIOGRAPHY ON ANTHROPOLOGY AND SOCIOLOGY IN UGANDA.
  NEW YORK, SYRACUSE UNIVERSITY PROGRAM OF EASTERN AFRICAN
  STUDIES, 1965
  139-12,

PEDRAZA G J W
  PEDRAZA G J W
  LAND CONSOLIDATION IN THE KIKUYU AREA OF KENYA CHAPTER 6.
  IN EDITH WHETHAM AND JEAN CURRIE (EDS.),READINGS IN THE
  APPLIED ECONOMICS OF AFRICA, LONDON, CAMBRIDGE UNIVERSITY
  PRESS, 1, 1967, PP 58-71
  070,117-08,

PEEL J D Y
  PEEL J D Y
  ALADURA--A RELIGIOUS MOVEMENT AMONG THE YORUBA.

LONDON, OXFORD UNIVERSITY PRESS, 1968
051,128-03,

PEISER G
   LAVROFF D G   PEISER G
   LES CONSTITUTIONS AFRICAINES (AFRICAN CONSTITUTIONS), VOL-
   UME ONE.
   PARIS,A PEDONE, 1961
   068,

PELISSIER RENE
   PELISSIER RENE
   SPANISH GUINEA-- AN INTRODUCTION.
   RACE 6 2 OCTOBER 1964 PP 117-128
   087, 111-01,

   PELISSIER RENE
   UNCERTAINTIES IN SPANISH GUINEA
   AFRICA REPORT MARCH 1968 PP 16-18
   111-07,

   WHEELER DOUGLAS L   PELISSIER RENE
   ANGOLA.
   LONDON, PALL MALL PRESS, 1970
   087,144-11,

PELLETIER R A
   PELLETIER R A
   MINERAL RESOURCES OF SOUTH-CENTRAL AFRICA.
   NEW YORK, OXFORD UNIVERSITY PRESS, 1965
   069,

PERHAM MARGERY
   PERHAM MARGERY
   COLONIAL SEQUENCE 1930-1949.
   LONDON,METHUEN AND CO,1967
   035,

   PERHAM MARGERY
   THE BRITISH PROBLEM IN AFRICA.
   IN PHILIP W QUIGG (ED.), AFRICA, NEW YORK, PRAEGER, 1964,
   PP 131-144
   035,

   PERHAM MARGERY
   THE PSYCHOLOGY OF AFRICAN NATIONALISM.
   IN WILLIAM J HANNA (ED), INDEPENDENT BLACK AFRICA, CHICAGO,
   RAND MCNALLY, 1964, PP 176-191
   054,

   PERHAM MARGERY
   THE COLONIAL RECKONING.
   NEW YORK, KNOPF, 1962
   056,

   PERHAM MARGERY
   THE KINGDOM OF AKSUM.
   IN P J M MCEWAN (ED), AFRICA FROM EARLY TIMES TO 1800, LONDON
   020,

PERHAM MARGERY   SIMMONS J
AFRICAN DISCOVERY
EVANSTON, NORTHWESTERN UNIVERSITY PRESS, 1963 (NEW EDITION)
027,

PERHAM MARGERY
    PERHAM MARGERY
    LUGARD-- THE YEARS OF ADVENTURE.
    LONDON, COLLINS, 1956
    035,

    PERHAM MARGERY
    LUGARD-- THE YEARS OF AUTHORITY.
    LONDON, COLLINS, 1960
    035,

    PERHAM MARGERY
    THE SYSTEM OF NATIVE ADMINISTRATION IN TANGANYIKA.
    AFRICA 2 1931 PP 302-312
    035,136-02,

    PERHAM MARGERY
    NATIVE ADMINISTRATION IN NIGERIA.
    LONDON, OXFORD UNIVERSITY PRESS, 1961
    035,128-02,

    PERHAM MARGERY   ED
    MINING, COMMERCE AND FINANCE IN NIGERIA.
    IN ECONOMICS OF A TROPICAL DEPENDENCY, VOL 2, LONDON, FABER
    1948
    073,128-08,

    PERHAM MARGERY   HUXLEY ELSPETH
    RACE AND POLITICS IN KENYA.
    LONDON, FABER, 1944
    035,117-06,

    PERHAM MARGERY
    THE GOVERNMENT OF ETHIOPIA.
    LONDON, FABER, 1948; 2D EDITION, EVANSTON, NORTHWESTERN
    UNIVERSITY PRESS, 1969
    110-07,

PERRAULT GILLES
    PERRAULT GILLES
    LES FANG DU PAYS YAOUNDE.
    LES CAHIERS D'OUTRE-MER OCTOBER-DECEMBER 1949
    104-01,

PERROT C
    PERROT C   SAUVALLE H
    REPUBLIQUE DU CONGO--BRAZZAVILLE--REPERTOIRE
    BIBLIOGRAPHIQUE.
    PARIS, BUREAU POUR LE DEVELOPMENT DE LA PRODUCTION AGRICOLE,
    1965
    107-12,

PESHKIN ALAN
    PESHKIN ALAN   COHEN RONALD
    THE VALUES OF MODERNIZATION

JOURNAL OF THE DEVELOPING AREAS 2 1967 PP 7-22
074,

PETEREC RICHARD J
    HANCE WILLIAM A   KOTSCHAP V   PETEREC RICHARD J
    SOURCE AREAS OF EXPORT PRODUCTION IN TROPICAL AFRICA.
    GEOGRAPHIC REVIEW 51 OCTOBER 1961 PP 487-499
    069,

    PETEREC RICHARD J
    DAKAR AND WEST AFRICAN ECONOMIC DEVELOPMENT.
    NEW YORK AND LONDON, COLUMBIA UNIVERSITY PRESS, 1967
    130-05,

PETERS E L
    PETERS E L
    SOME STRUCTURAL ASPECTS OF THE FEUDS AMONG THE CAMEL-HERDING
    BEDOUIN OF CYRENAICA.
    AFRICA 37 1967 PP 260-282
    009,120-01,

PETERSON JOHN
    PETERSON JOHN
    PROVINCE OF FREEDOM--A HISTORY OF SIERRA LEONE 1787-1870.
    EVANSTON, NORTHWESTERN UNIVERSITY PRESS, 1969
    029,131-02,

PFEFFER LEO
    PFEFFER LEO
    CHURCH, STATE AND FREEDOM.
    BOSTON, BEACON PRESS, 1967
    038,

PHILLIPS ARTHUR
    PHILLIPS ARTHUR
    SOME ASPECTS OF LEGAL DUALISM IN BRITISH COLONIAL
    TERRITORIES.
    CIVILISATIONS 3 SUMMER 1953 PP 189-197
    066,

PHILLIPS CLAUDE JR
    PHILLIPS CLAUDE JR
    THE DEVELOPMENT OF NIGERIAN FOREIGN POLICY.
    EVANSTON, ILLINOIS, NORTHWESTERN UNIVERSITY PRESS, 1964
    082,128-09,

PHILLIPS EARL
    PHILLIPS EARL
    THE EGBA AT ABEOKUTA--ACCULTURATION AND POLITICAL CHANGE,
    1830-1870.
    JOURNAL OF AFRICAN HISTORY, X, 1, 1969, PP. 117-131
    026,128-02,

PHILLIPS J F
    PHILLIPS J F
    AGRICULTURE AND ECOLOGY IN AFRICA ACTUAL AND POTENTIAL
    DEVELOPMENT SOUTH OF THE SAHARA.
    LONDON, FABER AND FABER, 1959
    069,

PHILLIPS J F
ECOLOGICAL INVESTIGATION IN SOUTH CENTRAL AND EAST AFRICA
OUTLINE OF A PROGRESSIVE SCHEME.
CAMBRIDGE JOURNAL OF ECOLOGY   19 NO 2 1931 PP 471-483
069,

PHILLIPS ULRICH B
    PHILLIPS ULRICH B
    THE SLAVE ECONOMY OF THE OLD SOUTH--SELECTED ESSAYS IN
    ECONOMIC AND SOCIAL HISTORY.
    BATON ROUGE, LOUISIANA STATE UNIVERSITY PRESS, 1968
    030,

PHILLIPSON D W
    PHILLIPSON D W
    THE CHANGE FROM HUNTING AND GATHERING TO PASTORALISM AND
    AGRICULTURE IN AFRICA.
    TARIKH,NEW YORK,HUMANITIES PRESS, 1 NO 3 1966 PP 33-44
    019,

PICTON J
    WILLETT FRANK   PICTON J
    ON THE IDENTIFICATION OF INDIVIDUAL CARVERS, A STUDY OF
    ANCESTOR SHRINE CARVINGS FROM OWO. NIGERIA.
    MAN 2 1967
    014,128-01,

PIETERSE COSMO
    PIETERSE COSMO   MUNRO DONALD   EDS
    PROTEST AND CONFLICT IN AFRICAN LITERATURE
    NEW YORK,AFRICANA PUBLISHING CORPORATION,1969
    090,091,

PIKE JOHN
    PIKE JOHN
    MALAWI.
    LONDON, PALL MALL PRESS, 1968
    122-11,

PIPER DONALD C
    PIPER DONALD C   COLE TAYLOR   EDS
    POST PRIMARY EDUCATION AND POLITICAL AND ECONOMIC
    DEVELOPMENT.
    DURHAM,NORTH CAROLINA,DUKE UNIVERSITY PRESS,1964
    042,

PITCHER G M
    PITCHER G M
    BIBLIOGRAPHY OF GHANA 1957-1959.
    KUMASI, KWAME NKRUMAH UNIVERSITY OF SCIENCE AND TECHNOLOGY,
    1960
    114-12,

PLACE J
    RICHARDS C   PLACE J   EDS
    EAST AFRICAN EXPLORERS
    LONDON,OXFORD UNIVERSITY PRESS,1960
    027,

PLASS MARGARET

PLASS MARGARET
AFRICAN MINIATURES-- THE GOLDWEIGHTS OF THE ASHANTI.
LONDON,LUND HUMPHRIES,1967;AND NEW YORK, PRAEGER 1967
014,

PLESSZ NICHOLAS G
  PLESSZ NICHOLAS G
  PROBLEMS AND PROSPECTS OF ECONOMIC INTEGRATION IN WEST
  AFRICA
  MONTREAL, MCGILL-QUEENS,1968
  078,

PLOTNICOV LEONARD
  PLOTNICOV LEONARD
  STRANGERS TO THE CITY-- URBAN MAN IN JOS, NIGERIA.
  PITTSBURGH,UNIVERSITY OF PITTSBURGH PRESS,1967
  046,128-05,

  TUDEN ARTHUR   PLOTNICOV LEONARD   EDS
  SOCIAL STRATIFICATION IN AFRICA
  NEW YORK,FREE PRESS,1970
  009,

POLANYI KARL
  POLANYI KARL   ROSTEIN ABRAHAM
  DAHOMEY AND THE SLAVE TRADE-ANALYSIS OF AN ARCHAIC ECONOMY
  SEATTLE,UNIVERSITY OF WASHINGTON PRESS,1966
  010,028,

  POLANYI KARL
  THE ECONOMY AS INSTITUTED PROCESS.
  IN K POLANYI, M ARENSBERG AND H W PEARSON (EDS),TRADE AND
  MARKET IN THE EARLY EMPIRES, GLENCOE,FREE PRESS, 1957; ALSO
  G DALTON (ED.),PRIMITIVE, ARCHAIC, AND MODERN ECONOMIES--
  ESSAYA OF KARL POLANYI, NEW YORK,DOUBLEDAY,1968
  010,

POLK WILLIAM R
  POLK WILLIAM R
  GENERATIONS CLASSES AND POLITICS.
  IN TIBOR KEREKES (ED),THE ARAB MIDDLE EAST AND MUSLIM
  AFRICA, NEW YORK,PRAEGER,1961,PP 105-120
  044,

POLOME EDGAR
  POLOME EDGAR
  CULTURAL LANGUAGES AND CONTACT VERNACULARS IN THE REPUBLIC
  OF THE CONGO.
  TEXAS STUDIES IN LITERATURE AND LANGUAGE, 1963
  108-01,

  POLOME EDGAR
  THE CHOICE OF OFFICIAL LANGUAGES IN THE DEMOCRATIC REPUBLIC
  OF THE CONGO.
  IN JOSHUA A. FISHMAN, CHARLES A. FERGUSON AND JYOTIRINDRA
  DAS GUPTA (EDS). LANGUAGE PROBLEMS OF DEVELOPING NATIONS,
  NEW YORK, JOHN WILEY AND SONS, INC., 1968
  108-06,

PONS VALDO

PONS VALDO
STANLEYVILLE-AN AFRICAN URBAN COMMUNITY UNDER BELGIAN
ADMINISTRATION
NEW YORK, OXFORD UNIVERSITY PRESS, 1969
046,108-05.

PONS VALDO
  PONS VALDO
  CHANGING SIGNIFICANCE OF ETHNIC AFFILIATIONS AND OF
  WESTERNIZATION IN THE AFRICA SETTLEMENT PATTERNS IN
  STANLEYVILLE.
  IN SOCIAL IMPLICATIONS OF INDUSTRIALIZATION AND URBANIZATION
  IN SOUTH OF THE SAHARA, PARIS, UNESCO, 1956
  108-05.

  PONS VALDO
  THE GROWTH OF STANLEYVILLE AND THE COMPOSITION OF ITS
  AFRICAN POPULATION.
  IN SOCIAL IMPLICATIONS OF INDUSTRIALIZATION AND URBANIZATION
  IN AFRICA SOUTH OF THE SAHARA, PARIS, UNESCO, 1956
  108-05.

PORGES LAURENCE
  PORGES LAURENCE
  ELEMENTS DE BIBLIOGRAPHIE SENEGALAISE, 1959-1963.
  DAKAR, ARCHIVES NATIONALES, CENTRE DE DOCUMENTATION, 1964
  130-12.

PORTER ARTHUR T
  PORTER ARTHUR T
  CREOLEDOM--A STUDY OF THE DEVELOPMENT OF FREETOWN SOCIETY.
  LONDON, OXFORD UNIVERSITY PRESS, 1963
  131-05.

PORTER DOROTHY B
  PORTER DOROTHY B
  A BIBIOGRAPHICAL CHECKLIST OF AMERICAN NEGRO WRITERS
  ABOUT AFRICA.
  IN AMSAC, AFRICA SEEN BY AMERICAN NEGROES, PARIS,
  PRESENCE AFRICAINE, 1958, PP 379-399
  094.

PORTER JAMES A
  PORTER JAMES A
  THE TRANSCULTURAL AFFINITIES OF AFRICAN NEGRO ART.
  IN AMSAC, AFRICA SEEN BY AMERICAN NEGROES, PARIS,
  PRESENCE AFRICAINE, 1958, PP 119-130
  030.

POSNANSKY MERRICK
  POSNANSKY MERRICK
  BANTU GENESIS--ARCHAEOLOGICAL REFLEXIONS.
  THE JOURNAL OF AFRICAN HISTORY VOL IX NO 1 1968 PP 1-12
  019.

  POSNANSKY MERRICK   ED
  PRELUDE TO EAST AFRICAN HISTORY.
  LONDON, OXFORD UNIVERSITY PRESS, 1966
  023.

POST KENNETH W J
    POST KENNETH W J
    THE NEW STATES OF WEST AFRICA
    BALTIMORE, PENGUIN BOOKS, REVISED EDITION, 1968
    076,

POST KENNETH W J
    POST KENNETH W J
    NATIONALIST MOVEMENTS IN WEST AFRICA CHP 20.
    IN JC ANENE AND GODFREY BROWN, AFRICA IN THE 19TH AND 20TH
    CENTURIES, LONDON, NELSON IUP, 1966
    055,

    POST KENNETH W J
    THE INDIVIDUAL AND THE COMMUNITY AND THE COMMUNITIES AND
    THE POLITICAL SYSTEM.
    IN WILLIAM J HANNA (ED), INDEPENDENT BLACK AFRICA, CHICAGO,
    RAND MCNALLY, 1964, PP 319-340
    063,

    POST KENNETH W J
    THE USE OF POWER.
    IN WILLIAM J HANNA (ED), INDEPENDENT BLACK AFRICA, CHICAGO,
    RAND MCNALLY, 1964, PP 444-453
    061,

    POST KENNETH W J
    NATIONALISM AND POLITICS IN NIGERIA-- A MARXIST APPROACH.
    NIGERIAN JOURNAL OF ECONOMIC AND SOCIAL STUDIES 6 JULY
    1964 PP 169-176
    054,128-06,

    POST KENNETH W J
    THE NIGERIAN FEDERAL ELECTION OF 1959--POLITICS AND
    ADMINISTRATION IN A DEVELOPING POLITICAL SYSTEM.
    LONDON, OXFORD UNIVERSITY PRESS (FOR NISER), 1963
    063,128-07,

POTEKHIN I I
    POTEKHIN I I
    FRONTIERS NATIONS AND GROUPINGS CHP 3.
    IN AFRICA'S FUTURE-- THE SOVIET VIEW, SUPPLEMENT TO MIZAN
    NEWSLETTER, 4 APRIL, 1961
    084,

    POTEKHIN I I
    THE FORMATION OF NATIONS IN AFRICA.
    MARXISM TODAY 2 1958 PP 308-314
    084,

    POTEKHIN I I
    PROBLEMS OF ECONOMIC INDEPENDENCE OF AFRICAN COUNTRIES.
    IN LALAGE BOWN AND MICHAEL CROWDER (EDS.), PROCEEDINGS OF
    THE FIRST INTERNATIONAL CONGRESS OF AFRICANISTS, ACCRA,
    1962, LONDON, LONGMANS, 1964, PP 171-183
    087,

    POTEKHIN I I
    AFRICAN PROBLEMS.
    TORONTO, PROGRESS BOOKS, 1969

084,

POVEY JOHN F
POVEY JOHN F
CANONS OF CRITICISM FOR NEO-AFRICAN LITERATURE.
IN PROCEEDINGS OF THE CONFERENCE ON AFRICAN LANGUAGES AND
LITERATURES, NORTHWESTERN UNIVERSITY, 1966, UNITED STATES
OFFICE OF EDUCATION, NO. OE-6-14-018, PP 73-90
090,

POVOLNY M
POVOLNY M
AFRICA IN SEARCH OF UNITY-- MODEL AND REALITY.
BACKGROUND 9 FEBRUARY 1966 PP 297-318
077,

POWDERMAKER H
POWDERMAKER H
NORTHERN RHODESIA, NOW ZAMBIA, PART 5.
IN STRANGER AND FRIEND, NEW YORK, W W NORTON,
1966, PP 235-306
099,142-03,

POWELL G B
ALMOND GABRIEL A   POWELL G B
COMPARATIVE POLITICS-- A DEVELOPMENTAL APPROACH.
BOSTON, LITTLE, BROWN AND COMPANY, 1966
098,

POWER PAUL
POWER PAUL
GANDHI IN SOUTH AFRICA
JOURNAL OF MODERN AFRICAN STUDIES 7 1969 PP 441-456
085,

POWNE MICHAEL
POWNE MICHAEL
ETHIOPIAN MUSIC--AN INTRODUCTION.
LONDON, OXFORD UNIVERSITY PRESS, 1968
015,110-01,

PRATT R CRANFORD
LOW DAVID A   PRATT R CRANFORD
BUGANDA AND BRITISH OVERRULE 1900-1955.
LONDON, OXFORD UNIVERSITY PRESS, 1960
035,139-02,

PRATT R CRANFORD
NATIONALISM IN UGANDA.
POLITICAL STUDIES JUNE 1961 PP 157-178
055,139-06,

PRATT R CRANFORD
MULTI-RACIALISM AND LOCAL GOVERNMENT IN TANGANYIKA.
RACE 2 1960 PP 33-49
088,136-06,

PRATT R CRANFORD
ADMINISTRATION AND POLITICS IN UGANDA, 1919-1945.
IN VINCENT HARLOW AND E M CHILVER (EDS), HISTORY OF EAST

AFRICA VOL II, OXFORD, CLARENDON PRESS, 1965, PP 476-542
035,139-02,

PRESCOTT J R V
    PRESCOTT J R V
    AFRICA'S MAJOR BOUNDARY PROBLEMS.
    AUSTRALIAN GEOGRAPHER 9 MARCH 1963 PP 3-12
    059,

    PRESCOTT J R V
    NIGERIA'S REGIONAL BOUNDARY PROBLEMS.
    GEOGRAPHICAL REVIEW 49 OCTOBER 1959 PP 485-505
    56,

    PRESCOTT J R V
    THE GEOGRAPHY OF FRONTIERS AND BOUNDARIES
    CHICAGO, ALDINE, 1965
    059,

PRESENCE AFRICAINE
    PRESENCE AFRICAINE   ED
    COLLOQUE SUR LES RELIGIONS. (COLLOQUIUM ON RELIGIONS).
    ABIDJAN 5/12 APRIL 1961 PARIS PRESENCE AFRICAINE 1962
    013,050,

    PRESENCE AFRICAINE
    L'ART NEGRE (NEGRO ART).
    PARIS, PRESENCE AFRICAINE, 1966, VOLS 10-11
    014,

PRESTAGE EDGAR
    PRESTAGE EDGAR
    THE ASHANTI QUESTION AND THE BRITISH-- EIGHTEENTH-CENTURY
    ORIGINS.
    THE JOURNAL OF AFRICAN HISTORY II 1961 PP 35-60
    033,114-32,
    033, 114-02,

PRICE J H
    PRICE J H
    THE EASTERN REGION OF NIGERIA CHAPTER 4.
    IN W J MACKENZIE AND KENNETH ROBINSON, FIVE ELECTIONS IN
    AFRICA, LONDON, OXFORD UNIVERSITY PRESS, 1960
    063,128-07,

PRICE THOMAS
    SHEPPERSON GEORGE   PRICE THOMAS
    INDEPENDENT AFRICAN-- JOHN CHILEMBWE AND THE ORIGINS SETTING
    AND SIGNIFICANCE OF THE NYASALAND RISING OF 1915.
    EDINBURGH, EDINBURGH UNIVERSITY PRESS, 1958
    034,122-02,

PRIESTLEY HERBERT
    PRIESTLEY HERBERT
    FRANCE OVERSEAS-- A STUDY OF MODERN IMPERIALISM.
    NEW YORK, APPLETON-CENTURY, 1938
    035,

PRIESTLEY MARGARET
    PRIESTLEY MARGARET

WEST AFRICAN TRADE AND COAST SOCIETY-A FAMILY STUDY
NEW YORK,OXFORD UNIVERSITY PRESS,1969
027,

PRIESTLEY MARGARET
PRIESTLEY MARGARET   WILKS IVOR
THE ASHANTI KINGS IN THE EIGHTEENTH CENTURY-- A REVISED
CHRONOLOGY.
THE JOURNAL OF AFRICAN HISTORY 1 1960 PP 83-92
026,114-02,

PRIESTLEY MARGARET
THE EMERGENCE OF AN ELITE - A CASE STUDY OF A WEST COAST FAM
IN LLOYD, THE NEW ELITES OF TROPICAL AFRICA, LONDON, OXFORD
UNIVERSITY PRESS, 1966, P. 87-103
114-04,

PRIMUS PEARL E
PRIMUS PEARL E
AFRICAN DANCE.
IN AMSAC, AFRICA SEEN BY AMERICAN NEGROES, PARIS,
PRESENCE AFRICAINE, 1958, PP 163-173
015,

PROCTOR J H
PROCTOR J H
THE HOUSE OF CHIEFS AND THE POLITICAL DEVELOPMENT OF
BOTSWANA
JOURNAL OF MODERN AFRICAN STUDIES 6 1968 PP 59-79
062, 102-07,

PROTHERO R MANSELL
BARBOUR K M   PROTHERO R MANSELL   EDS
ESSAYS ON AFRICAN POPULATION.
LONDON,ROUTLEDGE AND KEGAN PAUL,1961
069,074,

PROTHERO R MANSELL
PROTHERO R MANSELL
MIGRANTS AND MALARIA.
LONDON,LONGMANS,1965
069,075,

PROTHERO R MANSELL
HEINRICH BARTH AND THE WESTERN SUDAN.
THE GEOGRAPHICAL JOURNAL CXXIV 1958 PP 326-339
024,

PROTHERO R MANSELL
POPULATION MOVEMENT AND PROBLEMS OF MALARIA ERADICATION IN
AFRICA.
WORLD HEALTH ORGANIZATION BULLETIN 24 1961 PP 405-425
069,075,

PROTHERO R MANSELL ED
A GEOGRAPHY OF AFRICA--REGIONAL ESSAYS ON FUNDAMENTAL
CHARACTERISTICS, ISSUES AND PROBLEMS.
NEW YORK, PRAEGERS 1969
069,

PRUSSIN LABELLE
    PRUSSIN LABELLE
    THE ARCHITECTURE OF ISLAM IN WEST AFRICA.
    AFRICAN ARTS 1 2 WINTER 1968 PP 32-35, 70-74
    092,

PULLAN R A
    GROVE A T   PULLAN R A
    SOME ASPECTS OF THE PLEISTOCENE PALEOGEOGRAPHY OF THE
    CHAD BASIN.
    IN F CLARK HOWELL AND FRANCOIS BOURLIERE (EDS.), AFRICAN
    ECOLOGY AND HUMAN EVOLUTION, CHICAGO, ALDINE, 1966,
    PP 230-245
    018,

PYE LUCIAN W
    PYE LUCIAN W   ED
    COMMUNICATIONS AND POLITICAL DEVELOPMENT.
    PRINCETON, PRINCETON UNIVERSITY PRESS, 1963
    048,

    PYE LUCIAN W
    ASPECTS OF POLITICAL DEVELOPMENT.
    BOSTON, LITTLE, BROWN, 1966
    098,

    PYE LUCIAN W
    COMMUNICATIONS AND POLITICAL DEVELOPMENT CHAPTER 8.
    IN ASPECTS OF POLITICAL DEVELOPMENT, BOSTON, LITTLE, BROWN,
    1966, PP 153-171
    048,

    PYE LUCIAN W
    ARMIES IN THE PROCESS OF POLITICAL DEVELOPMENT.
    IN ASPECTS OF POLITICAL DEVELOPMENT, BOSTON, LITTLE, BROWN, 1966,
    PP 172-187; ALSO LEWIS P FICKETT, ED, PROBLEMS OF THE
    DEVELOPING NATIONS, NEW YORK, CROWELL, 1966, PP 85-102; ALSO
    L FINKLE AND R GABLE, POLITICAL DEVELOPMENT AND SOCIAL
    CHANGE, NEW YORK, JOHN WILEY, 1966
    064,

    PYE LUCIAN W
    COMMUNICATION PATTERNS AND THE PROBLEMS OF REPRESENATATIVE
    GOVERNMENT IN NON-WESTERN SOCIETIES.
    PUBLIC OPINION QUARTERLY 20 1956 PP 249-457
    048,

    PYE LUCIAN W
    THE NATURE OF TRANSITIONAL POLITICS CHAPTER 15.
    IN JASON L FINKLE AND RICHARD W GABLE, POLITICAL
    DEVELOPMENT AND SOCIAL CHANGE, NEW YORK, JOHN WILEY, 1966
    098,

    PYE LUCIAN W
    THE CONCEPT OF POLITICAL DEVELOPMENT CHAPTER 3.
    IN JASON L FINKLE AND RICHARD W GABLE, POLITICAL
    DEVELOPMENT AND SOCIAL CHANGE, NEW YORK, JOHN WILEY, 1966
    098,

    PYE LUCIAN W

THE NON-WESTERN POLITICAL PROCESS.
IN WILLIAM J HANNA (ED), INDEPENDENT BLACK AFRICA, CHICAGO,
RAND MCNALLY, 1964, PP 372-388
098,

Q

QUAISON-SACKEY
  QUAISON-SACKEY ALEX
  THE AFRICAN PERSONALITY CHAPTER 2.
  IN AFRICA UNBOUND, NEW YORK, PRAEGER, 1963,
  PP 35-58
  039,

  QUAISON-SACKEY ALEX
  AFRICAN UNITY CHAPTER 3.
  IN AFRICA UNBOUND, NEW YORK, PRAEGER, 1963, PP 59-99
  079,

  QUAISON-SACKEY ALEX
  AFRICA AND THE UNITED NATIONS-- OBSERVATIONS OF A GHANAIAN
  DIPLOMAT.
  ARICAN FORUM I 1 1965 PP 53-68
  081,114-09,

QUARLES BENJAMIN
  QUARLES BENJAMIN
  THE NEGRO IN THE MAKING OF AMERICA
  NEW YORK, MACMILLAN, 1969(REVISED EDITION)
  030,

QUIGG PHILIP W
  QUIGG PHILIP W   ED
  AFRICA-- A FOREIGN AFFAIRS READER.
  NEW YORK, PRAEGER, 1964
  081,

R

RABEMANANJARA
  RABEMANANJARA JACQUE
  AGAPES DES DIEUX--TRITRIVA, TRAGEIDE MALGACHE.
  PARIS, PRESENCE AFRICAINE, 1962
  121-10,

  RABEMANANJARA JACQUE
  ANTIDOTE, POEMES.
  PARIS, PRESENCE AFRICAINE, 1961
  121-10,

  RABEMANANJARA JACQUE
  ANTSA.

PARIS, PRESENCE AFRICAINE, 1962
121-10.

RABEMANANJARA
  RABEMANANJARA JACQUE
  LAMBA--POEME.
  PARIS, PRESENCE AFRICAINE, 1966 (2ND EDITION)
  121-10,

  RABEMANANJARA JACQUE
  LES BOUTRIERS DE L AURORE--TRAGEDIE EN 3 ACTES, 6 TABLEAUX.
  PARIS, PRESENCE AFRICAINE, 1957
  121-10,

  RABEMANANJARA JACQUE
  LES DIEUX MALGACHES, VERSION DESTINEE A LA SCENE.
  PARIS, HACHETTE, 1964 (2ND EDITION)
  121-10,

  RABEMANANJARA JACQUE
  NATIONALISME ET PROBLEMES MALGACHES.
  PARIS, PRESENCE AFRICAINE, 1958
  121-10,

  RABEMANANJARA JACQUE
  RITES MILLENAIRES.
  PARIS, SEGHERS, 1955
  121-10,

  RABEMANANJARA JACQUE
  TEMOIGNAGE MALGACHE ET COLONIALISME.
  PARIS, PRESENCE AFRICAINE, 1956
  121-10,

RACE RELATIONS
  INSTITUTE OF   RACE RELATIONS
  ANGOLA--A SYMPOSIUM--VIEWS OF A REVOLT.
  LONDON, OXFORD UNIVERSITY PRESS, 1962
  087,144-06,

RADCLIFFE-BROWN
  RADCLIFFE-BROWN A R FORDE C DARYLL   EDS
  AFRICAN SYSTEMS OF KINSHIP AND MARRIAGE.
  LONDON, OXFORD UNIVERSITY PRESS, 1950
  008,

  RADCLIFFE-BROWN A R
  ON THE CONCEPT OF FUNCTION IN SOCIAL SCIENCE.
  AMERICAN ANTHROPOLOGIST 37 JULY-SEPTEMBER 1935
  (BOBBS-MERRILL REPRINT S-227)
  098,

RADIN PAUL
  RADIN PAUL   SWEENEY JAMES J
  AFRICAN FOLKTALES AND SCULPTURE.
  PRINCETON, NEW JERSEY, PRINCETON UNIVERSITY PRESS, 1969
  012,014,

RADO E R
  RADO E R

MANPOWER EDUCATION AND ECONOMIC GROWTH
JOURNAL OF MODERN AFRICAN STUDIES 4 1966 PP 83-93
074,075,

RAGHEB ISIS
    KURIA LUCAS   RAGHEB ISIS   WEBSTER JOHN B
    A BIBLIOGRAPHY ON POLITICS AND GOVERNMENT IN UGANDA.
    COMPILED BY LUCAS KURIA, ISIS RAGHEB AND JOHN WEBSTER, NEW
    YORK, SYRACUSE UNIVERSITY PROGRAM OF EASTERN AFRICAN STUDIES
     1965
    139-12,

    PECKHAM ROBERT   RAGHEB ISIS   SOUTHALL AIDAN
    A BIBLIOGRAPHY ON ANTHROPOLOGY AND SOCIOLOGY IN UGANDA.
    NEW YORK, SYRACUSE UNIVERSITY PROGRAM OF EASTERN AFRICAN
    STUDIES, 1965
    139-12,

RAHAJASON
    RAHAJASON RAYMOND C
    ESSAI SUR LA LANGUE MALGACHE.
    TANANANRIVE, IMP. IARIVO, 1962
    121-01,

RAKE ALAN
    RAKE ALAN
    BLACK GUERRILLAS IN RHODESIA.
    AFRICAN REPORT, DECEMBER, 1968, P. 23
    087,145-06,

RAKOTO-RATSIMAMANGA
    RAKOTO-RATSIMAMANGA LORIN CLAUDE-MARIE
    POETES MALGACHES DE LANGUE FRANCAISE.
    PARIS, PRESENCE AFRICAINE, 1956
    121-10,

RAMANDRAIVONONA
    RAMANDRAIVONONA DESI
    LE MALGACHE, SA LANGUE ET SA RELIGION.
    PARIS, PRESENCE AFRICAINE, 1959
    121-01,

RAMIN JEAN CHARLES
    RAMIN JEAN CHARLES   KOUBETTI V   GUILHEM MARCEL
    HISTOIRE DU DAHOMEY.
    PARIS, L'AFRIQUE-LE MONDE, COURS MOYEN, LIGEL, 1964
    109-02,

RAMSARAN JOHN A
    RAMSARAN JOHN A
    MODERN AFRICAN WRITING IN ENGLISH.
    IN PROCEEDINGS OF THE CONFERENCE ON AFRICAN LANGUAGES AND
    LITERATURES, NORTHWESTERN UNIVERSITY, 1966, UNITED STATES
    OFFICE OF EDUCATION, NO. OE-6-14-018, PP 105-114
    090,

    RAMSARAN JOHN A
    BIBLIOGRAPHY OF AFRICAN LITERATURE.
    IBADAN,UNIVERSITY OF IBADAN PRESS,1965
    090,093,

RANAIVO GUY DE P
    RANAIVO GUY DE P
    BIOGRAPHIE ET HISTORIE SOCIALE DE MADAGASCAR.
    NIMES, IMP. MAUGER, 1954
    121-02,

RANDALL D
    RANDALL D
    FACTORS OF ECONOMIC DEVELOPMENT AND THE OKOVANGO DELTA.
    UNIVERSITY OF CHICAGO, DEPT OF GEOGRAPHY RESEARCH PAPERS,
    DECEMBER 1956, PP 1-282
    070,

RANGER TERENCE O
    RANGER TERENCE O   ED
    ASPECTS OF CENTRAL AFRICAN HISTORY.
    EVANSTON, NORTHWESTERN UNIVERSITY PRESS, 1968   (LONDON,
    HEINEMANN EDUCATIONAL BOOKS)
    025,036,

RANGER TERENCE O
    RANGER TERENCE O   ED
    EMERGING THEMES OF AFRICAN HISTORY.
    KENYA, EAST AFRICAN PUBLISHING HOUSE, 1965 (LONDON,
    HEINEMANN EDUCATIONAL BOOKS)
    036,

    RANGER TERENCE O
    CONNEXIONS BETWEEN PRIMARY RESISTANCE MOVEMENTS AND
    MODERN MASS NATIONALISM IN EAST AND CENTRAL AFRICA 2 PARTS
    JOURNAL OF AFRICAN HISTORY 9 1968 PP 437-453 AND 631-642
    034,055,

    RANGER TERENCE O
    REVOLT IN SOUTHERN RHODESIA, 1896-97--A STUDY IN AFRICAN
    RESISTANCE.
    EVANSTON, NORTHWESTERN UNIVERSITY PRESS, 1967 (LONDON,
    HEINEMANN EDUCATIONAL BOOKS)
    034, 145-02,

    RANGER TERENCE O
    THE ORGANIZATION OF THE REBELLIONS OF 1896 AND 1897.
    CONFERENCE OF THE HISTORY OF CENTRAL AFRICAN PEOPLES,
    LUSAKA, RHODES-LIVINGSTONE INSTITUTE, 1963
    034,

    RANGER TERENCE O
    REVOLT IN PORTUGUESE EAST AFRICA-- THE MAKOMBE RISING OF
    1917.
    ST ANTHONY'S PAPERS 15, 1963 PP 54-80, AFRICAN AFFAIRS 2
    034,

    RANGER TERENCE O
    TRADITIONAL AUTHORITIES AND THE RISE OF MODERN POLITICS IN
    SOUTHERN RHODESIA 1898-1930.
    CONFERENCE OF THE HISTORY OF CENTRAL AFRICAN PEOPLES, LUSAKA
    1963, RHODES-LIVINGSTONE INSTITUTE, 1963
    033, 145-02,

RAPONDA-WALKER
    RAPONDA-WALKER ANDRE
    CONTES GABONAIS--NOUVELLE EDITION REVUE ET AUGMENTEE--
    ACCOMPAGNEE DE 47 COMPOSITIONS ORIGINALES DE ROGER L
    SILLANS.
    PARIS, PRESENCE AFRICAINE, 1967
    112-10.

RAPONDA-WALKER
    RAPONDA-WALKER ANDRE
    NOTES D'HISTOIRE DU GABON.
    MONTPELLIER, IMPRIMERIE CHARITE, 1960
    112-02,

    RAPONDA-WALKER ANDRE   SILLANS ROGER
    RITES ET CROYANCES DES PEUPLES DU GABON, ESSAI SUR LES
    PRATIQUES RELIGIEUSES DE AUTREFOIS ET D'AUJORD'HUI.
    PARIS, PRESENCE AFRICAINE, 1962
    112-01,

RAPOPORT DAVID C
    RAPOPORT DAVID C
    COUP D'ETAT-- THE VIEW OF THE MEN FIRING PISTOLS.
    IN CARL J FRIEDRICH (ED.), REVOLUTION, NEW YORK,
    ATHERTON PRESS,1966
    064,

RATTRAY ROBERT S
    RATTRAY ROBERT S
    RELIGION AND ART IN ASHANTI.
    LONDON,OXFORD UNIVERSITY PRESS,1959
    013,114-01,

    RATTRAY ROBERT S
    ASHANTI LAW AND CONSTITUTION.
    OXFORD, CLARENDON PRESS, 1929
    026,066,099,114-01,

    RATTRAY ROBERT S
    AKAN-ASHANTI FOLK TALES.
    OXFORD, THE CLARENDON PRESS, 1930
    012,

    RATTRAY ROBERT S
    ASHANTI PROVERBS
    OXFORD,CLARENDON PRESS,1916
    012,

READ J S
    ALLOTT ANTHONY   READ J S
    THE LEGAL STATUS OF WOMEN IN AFRICA-- IN PRACTICE,
    PROCEDURE AND EVIDENCE IN THE NATIVE, AFRICAN, LOCAL
    OR CUSTOMARY COURTS.
    JOURNAL OF AFRICAN LAW 5 AUTUMN 1961 PP 125-138
    066,

READER D H
    READER D H
    A SURVEY OF CATEGORIES OF ECONOMIC ACTIVITIES AMONG THE
    PEOPLES OF AFRICA.

AFRICA (LONDON) 34 1964 PP 28-45
010,069,

REDDEN KENNETH R
REDDEN KENNETH R
THE LEGAL SYSTEM OF ETHIOPIA.
CHARLOTTESVILLE, VIRGINIA, THE MICHIE COMPANY, 1968
066,110-06,

REDDING SAUNDERS
REDDING SAUNDERS
THEY CAME IN CHAINS
PHILADELPHIA, J.B.LIPPINCOTT, 1950
030,094,

REDFIELD ROBERT
REDFIELD ROBERT   ET AL
ASPECTS OF PRIMITIVE ART.
NEW YORK, UNIVERSITY PUBLISHERS, 1959
014,

REDMAYNE ALISON
REDMAYNE ALISON
MKWAWA AND THE HEHE WARS
JOURNAL OF AFRICAN HISTORY 9 1968 PP 409-436
034,

REED JOHN
OYONO FERDINAND   TRANSLATED BY   REED JOHN
HOUSEBOY.
LONDON, HEINEMANN EDUCATIONAL BOOKS LTD, 1966
(NEW YORK, MACMILLAN, 1970)
090,

REEVES RICHARD A
REEVES RICHARD A
SHOOTING AT SHARPVILLE-THE AGONY OF SOUTH AFRICA
BOSTON HOUGHTON MIFFLIN 1961
032,

REHFISCH F
REHFISCH F
A STUDY OF SOME SOUTHERN MIGRANTS IN OMDURMAN.
SUDAN NOTES AND RECORDS, 43, 1962
134-05,

REHFISCH F
A UNRECORDED POPULATION COUNT OF OMDURMAN.
SUDAN NOTES, 46, 1965
134-05,

REINING CONRAD C
REINING CONRAD C
THE ZANDE SCHEME--AN ANTHROPOLOGICAL CASE STUDY OF ECONOMIC
DEVELOPMENT IN AFRICA.
EVANSTON, NORTHWESTERN UNIVERSITY PRESS, 1966
070,134-08,

REINSTEIN MAX
REINSTEIN MAX

LAW AND SOCIAL CHANGE IN AFRICA.
WASHINGTON UNIVERSITY LAW QUARTERLY 4 DECEMBER 1962
PP 443-453
066,

REPORT
    REPORT WORKING PARTY
    WHO CONTROLS INDUSTRY IN KENYA.
    KENYA, EAST AFRICAN PUBLISHING HOUSE, 1968
    071,117-08,

REPUBLIC OF KENYA
    REPUBLIC OF KENYA
    AFRICAN SOCIALISM AND ITS APPLICATION TO PLANNING IN KENYA
    NAIROBI, GOVERNMENT PRINTER,1965
    054,072,077,117-08,

REPUBLIQUE DU MALI
    REPUBLIQUE DU MALI
    COMPTES ECONOMIQUES DE LA REPUBLIQUE DU MALI 1959.
    MINISTERE DU PLAN ET DE LA COORDINATION, BAMAKO,
    GOVERNMENT PRINTER, 1962
    123-08,

RESNICK IDRIAN N
    RESNICK IDRIAN N   CLARKE JOHN HENRIK   ET AL
    DIALOG-THE FUTURE OF AFRICAN STUDIES AFTER MONTREAL
    AFRICA REPORT DECEMBER 1969 PP 22-27
    100,

    RESNICK IDRIAN N   ED
    TANZANIA--REVOLUTION BY EDUCATION.
    NEW YORK, HUMANITIES PRESS INC., 1968
    043,136-03,

REUTERS
    REUTERS NEWS AGENCY
    THE NEW AFRICANS--REUTERS GUIDE TO THE CONTEMPORARY HISTORY
    OF EMERGENT AFRICA AND ITS LEADERS.
    LONDON, PAUL HAMLYN, 1967
    044,

REX JOHN
    REX JOHN
    THE PLURAL SOCIETY IN SOCIOLOGICAL THEORY.
    BRITISH JOURNAL OF SOCIOLOGY VOL X NO 2 JUNE 1959 PP 114-124
    006,

REYNER ANTHONY S
    REYNER ANTHONY S
    CURRENT BOUNDARY PROBLEMS IN AFRICA.
    INSTITUTE OF AFRICAN AFFAIRS NO 15, DUQUESNE UNIVERSITY PRESS,
    1964
    059,

    REYNER ANTHONY S
    THE REPUBLIC OF THE CONGO-- DEVELOPMENT OF ITS INTERNATIONAL
    BOUNDARIES.
    PITTSBURGH, DUQUESNE UNIVERSITY PRESS, 1961, AFRICAN REPRINT
    SERIES, 9

059,108-06,

REYNER ANTHONY S
    REYNER ANTHONY S
    MOROCCO'S INTERNATIONAL BOUNDARIES--A FACTUAL BACKGROUND.
    JOURNAL OF MODERN AFRICAN STUDIES 1 SEPTEMBER 1963
    PP 313-326
    059,

RHEINSTEIN MAX
    RHEINSTEIN MAX
    PROBLEMS OF LAW IN THE NEW NATIONS OF AFRICA.
    IN CLIFFORD GEERTZ (ED),OLD SOCIETIES AND NEW NATIONS, NEW
    YORK,THE FREE PRESS,1963, PP 220-46
    067,

RICE BERKELEY
    RICE BERKELEY
    ENTER GAMBIA-- THE BIRTH OF AN IMPROBABLE NATION.
    BOSTON,HOUGHTON MIFFLIN,1967
    056,113-06,

RICHARDS AUDREY I
    RICHARDS AUDREY I
    EAST AFRICAN CHIEFS.
    LONDON,FABER AND FABER,1960
    009,

    RICHARDS AUDREY I
    MULTI-TRIBALISM IN AFRICAN URBAN AREAS.
    CIVILISATIONS 16 1966 PP 354-364
    046,

    RICHARDS AUDREY I
    AFRICAN SYSTEMS OF THOUGHT--AN ANGLO-FRENCH DIALOGUE.
    MAN, VOL. 2, NO. 2, JUNE, 1967, PP. 286-298
    013,

    RICHARDS AUDREY I   ED
    ECONOMIC DEVELOPMENT AND TRIBAL CHANGE-- A STUDY OF
    IMMIGRANT LABOUR IN BUGANDA.
    CAMBRIDGE,HEFFER,1956
    074,139-08,

    RICHARDS AUDREY I
    SOME EFFECTS OF THE INTRODUCTION OF INDIVIDUAL FREEHOLD
    INTO BUGANDA.
    IN D BIEBUYCK (ED), AFRICAN AGRARIAN SYSTEMS, LONDON,
    OXFORD UNIVERSITY PRESS, 1963, PP 267-280
    078,139-08,

    RICHARDS AUDREY I
    LAND, LABOUR AND DIET IN NORTHERN RHODESIA-- AN ECONOMIC
    STUDY OF THE BEMBA TRIBE.
    LONDON,ROUTLEDGE AND KEGAN PAUL,1939
    010,142-01,

    RICHARDS AUDREY I
    THE MULTICULTURAL STATES OF EAST AFRICA.
    MONTREAL, MCGILL-QUEENS, 1969

057,

RICHARDS C
RICHARDS C   PLACE J   EDS
EAST AFRICAN EXPLORERS
LONDON,OXFORD UNIVERSITY PRESS,1960
027,

RICHARDSON HENRY J
RICHARDSON HENRY J
MALAWI- BETWEEN BLACK AND WHITE AFRICA
AFRICA REPORT 15 FEBRUARY 1970 PP 18-21
088,122-09,

RICHARDSON I
RICHARDSON I
LINGUISTIC CHANGE IN AFRICA WITH SPECIAL REFERENCE TO THE
BEMBA-SPEAKING AREA OF NORTHERN RHODESIA.
COLLOQUE SUR LE MULTILINGUISME, BRAZZAVILLE, 1962
142-03,

RICHARDSON S S
RICHARDSON S S
SOCIAL LEGAL REFORM
IN KRITZECK AND LEWIS,PP 110-126
052,

RICHARDSON SAMUEL
KEAY ELLIOT A   RICHARDSON SAMUEL
THE NATIVE AND CUSTOMARY COURTS OF NIGERIA.
LONDON,SWEET AND MAXWELL,1966
066,128-03,

RICHELLE MARC
RICHELLE MARC
ASPECTS PSYCHOLOGIQUE DE L'ACCULTURATION (PSYCHOLOGICAL
ASPECTS OF ACCULTURATION).
ELISABETHVILLE KATANGA CENTRE D'ETUDE DES PROBLEMS SOCIAUX
INDIGENES VOL 6 1960
041,

RIDDELL J BARRY
RIDDELL J BARRY
THE SPATIAL DYNAMICS OF MODERNIZATION IN SIERRA LEONE
EVANSTON,NORTHWESTERN UNIVERSITY PRESS,1970
038,048,131-06,

RIEFF PHILIP
RIEFF PHILIP   ED
ON INTELLECTUALS.
NEW YORK, DOUBLEDAY AND CO., 1969
091,

RIGBY P J A
RIGBY P J A
CATTLE AND KINSHIP AMONG THE GOGO--A SEMIPASTORAL SOCIETY OF
CENTRAL TANZANIA.
ITHACA, CORNELL UNIVERSITY PRESS, 1969
008,136-01,

BETTISON DAVID G   RIGBY P J A
PATTERNS OF INCOME AND EXPENDITURE IN BLANTYRE-LIMBE,
NYASALAND.
LUSAKA, RHODES-LIVINGSTONE INSTITUTE, 1961
122-05,

RIGBY P J A
   RIGBY P J A
   SOCIOLOGICAL FACTORS IN THE CONTACT OF THE GOGO OF CENTRAL
   TANZANIA WITH ISLAM.
   IN LEWIS, ISLAM IN TROPICAL AFRICA, LONDON, OXFORD UNIVERSITY
   PRESS, 1966, P. 268-295
   136-03,

RIGGS FRED W
   RIGGS FRED W
   THE THEORY OF DEVELOPING POLITIES.
   WORLD POLITICS 16 OCTOBER 1963 PP 147-171
   037,098,

   RIGGS FRED W
   BUREAUCRATS AND POLITICAL DEVELOPMENT CHAPTER 12.
   IN JASON L FINKLE AND RICHARD W GABLE, POLITICAL
   DEVELOPMENT AND SOCIAL CHANGE, NEW YORK, JOHN WILEY, 1966
   062,

   RIGGS FRED W
   ADMINISTRATION IN DEVELOPING COUNTRIES-THE THEORY OF
   PRISMATIC SOCIETY
   BOSTON,HOUGHTON MIFFLIN,1964
   062,063,098,

RIGGS ROBERT E
   WEIGERT KATHLEEN M   RIGGS ROBERT E
   AFRICA AND UNITED NATIONS ELECTIONS--AN AGGREGATE DATA
   ANALYSIS.
   INTERNATIONAL ORGANIZATION, VOL. XXIII, NO. 1, WINTER, 1969,
   PP. 1-17
   081,

RIVE RICHARD
   RIVE RICHARD
   THE QUARTET.
   NEW YORK,CROWN PUBLISHERS,1963
   090,

   RIVE RICHARD
   EMERGENCY.
   NEW YORK, MACMILLAN CO., 1970
   090,

RIVKIN ARNOLD
   RIVKIN ARNOLD
   THE POLITICS OF NATION-BUILDING-- PROBLEMS AND
   PRECONDITIONS.
   JOURNAL OF INTERNATIONAL AFFIARS 16 PP 131-143
   073,

   RIVKIN ARNOLD
   AFRICA AND THE WEST-- ELEMENTS OF FREE-WORLD POLICY.

NEW YORK, FREDERICK A PRAEGER, 1962
082,083,

RIVKIN ARNOLD
RIVKIN ARNOLD
THE AFRICAN PRESENCE IN WORLD AFFAIRS.
NEW YORK, FREE PRESS, 1963, PP 67-94 PP 118-129
081,

RIVKIN ARNOLD   ED
NATIONS BY DESIGN-- INSTITUTION BUILDING IN AFRICA.
NEW YORK,   1969
057,

RIVKIN ARNOLD
AFRICA AND THE EUROPEAN COMMON MARKET.
DENVER, UNIVERSITY OF DENVER PRESS, 1966 PP 67
080,082,

RIVKIN ARNOLD
AFRICAN PROBLEMS OF TRADE AND AID.
CURRENT HISTORY 43 251 JULY 1962 PP 29-34
082,083,

RIVKIN ARNOLD
THE ROLE AND SCOPE OF INDUSTRIALIZATION IN DEVELOPMENT.
IN RONALD ROBINSON, ED, INDUSTRIALIZATION IN DEVELOPING
COUNTRIES, CAMBRIDGE, CAMBRIDGE UNIVERSITY PRESS, 1965, PP 54-
66
071,

RIVKIN ARNOLD
PRINCIPAL ELEMENTS OF U.S. POLICY TOWARDS UNDERDEVELOPED
COUNTRIES.
INTERNATIONAL AFFAIRS 37 4 OCTOBER 1961 PP 452-464
083,

ROACH PENELOPE
ROACH PENELOPE
POLITICAL SOCIALIZATION IN THE NEW NATIONS OF AFRICA.
NEW YORK, TEACHERS COLLEGE PRESS, COLUMBIA UNIVERSITY PRESS
1967
060,

ROBBINS WARREN
ROBBINS WARREN
AFRICAN ART IN AMERICAN COLLECTIONS.
NEW YORK, PRAEGER, ND
014,

ROBERT
MWASE GEORGE SIMEON ROTBERG ROBERT   ED
STRIKE A BLOW AND DIE.
CAMBRIDGE, HARVARD UNIVERSITY PRESS, 1967
034, 122-02,

ROBERT A
ROBERT A
A COMPARATIVE STUDY OF LEGISLATION AND CUSTOMARY LAW COURTS
IN THE FRENCH, BELGIAN AND PORTUGUESE TERRITORIES IN AFRICA

JOURNAL OF AFRICAN ADMINISTRATION 11 JULY 1959 PP 124-131
066,

ROBERTS A
  ROBERTS A   ED
  TANZANIA BEFORE 1900
  NAIROBI, EAST AFRICAN PUBLISHING HOUSE, 1968
  025,136-02,

ROBERTS B C
  ROBERTS B C
  LABOUR IN THE TROPICAL TERRITORIES OF THE COMMONWEALTH.
  DURHAM, NORTH CAROLINA, DUKE UNIVERSITY PRESS, 1964
  073,

ROBERTS STEPHEN H
  ROBERTS STEPHEN H
  HISTORY OF FRENCH COLONIAL POLICY 1870-1925.
  LONDON, CASS, 1963
  033,

ROBERTS-WRAY K
  ROBERTS-WRAY K
  THE ADAPTATION OF IMPORTED LAW IN AFRICA.
  JOURNAL OF AFRICAN LAW 4 SUMMER 1960 PP 66-78
  066,

ROBINSON ARMSTEAD
  ROBINSON ARMSTEAD   FOSTER CRAIG   OGILVIE DONALD
  BLACK STUDIES IN THE UNIVERSITY--A SYMPOSIUM.
  NEW HAVEN, YALE UNIVERSITY PRESS, 1969
  002,094,095,

ROBINSON ARTHUR E
  ROBINSON ARTHUR E
  THE ARAB DYNASTY OF DAR FOR (DARFUR),AD   1448-1874 OR
  AH 852-1201.
  JOURNAL OF THE AFRICAN SOCIETY 27 1927 PP 353-363;
  28 1928 PP 55-67, 274-280, 379-384; AND
  29 1929 PP 53-70, 164-180
  024,106-02,

ROBINSON E A G
  ROBINSON E A G   ED
  ECONOMIC DEVELOPMENT FOR AFRICA SOUTH OF THE SAHARA.
  NEW YORK, ST MARTIN'S PRESS, 1964
  073,

ROBINSON J T
  ROBINSON J T
  ADAPTIVE RADIATION IN THE AUSTRALOPITHECINES AND THE
  ORIGIN OF MAN.
  IN F CLARK HOWELL AND FRANCOIS BOURLIERE (EDS.), AFRICAN
  ECOLOGY AND HUMAN EVOLUTION, CHICAGO, ALDINE, 1966,
  PP 385-416
  018,

ROBINSON KENNETH
  MACKENZIE W J   ROBINSON KENNETH
  FIVE ELECTIONS IN AFRICA.

OXFORD, CLARENDON PRESS, 1960
063,

ROBINSON KENNETH
ROBINSON KENNETH
POLITICAL DEVELOPMENT IN FRENCH WEST AFRICA.
IN CALVIN STILLMAN (ED.), AFRICA IN THE MODERN WORLD, CHICAGO,
UNIVERSITY OF CHICAGO PRESS, 1955, PP 140-181
055,

ROBINSON KENNETH
CONSTITUTIONAL REFORM IN FRENCH TROPICAL AFRICA.
POLITICAL STUDIES 6 FEBRUARY 1958
068,

ROBINSON KENNETH
FRENCH AFRICA AND THE FRENCH UNION.
IN C G HAINES (ED), AFRICA TODAY, BALTIMORE, JOHNS HOPKINS
PRESS, 1955
082,

ROBINSON KENNETH
COLONIAL ISSUES AND POLICIES WITH SPECIAL REFERENCE TO
TROPICAL AFRICA.
ANNALS OF THE AMERICAN ACADEMY OF POLITICAL AND SOCIAL
SCIENCES MARCH 1955 PP 84-94
035,

ROBINSON KENNETH
THE DILEMMAS OF TRUSTEESHIP-- ASPECTS OF BRITISH COLONIAL
POLICY BETWEEN THE WARS.
LONDON, OXFORD UNIVERSITY PRESS, 1965
035,

ROBINSON KENNETH
SENEGAL--THE ELECTION TO THE TERRITORIAL ASSEMBLY MARCH
1957, CHAPTER 6.
IN W J MACKENZIE AND KENNETH ROBINSON, FIVE ELECTIONS IN
AFRICA, OXFORD, CLARENDON PRESS, 1960
063,130-07,

ROBINSON M E
ROBINSON M E
THE FOOD POTENTIAL OF AFRICA.
CHICAGO, FOOD AND CONTAINER INSTITUTE OF THE ARMED FORCES,
12 1960
069,075,

ROBINSON RONALD
ROBINSON RONALD   GALLAGHER JOHN
AFRICA AND THE VICTORIANS-- THE CLIMAX OF IMPERIALISM IN THE
DARK CONTINENT.
NEW YORK, ST MARTIN'S, 1961
033,

ROBSON PETER
ROBSON PETER
ECONOMIC INTEGRATION IN AFRICA
LONDON, GEORGE ALLEN AND UNWIN LTD, 1968; EVANSTON, NORTHWESTERN
071,078,

ROBSON PETER
    ROBSON PETER
    ECONOMIC INTEGRATION IN EQUATORIAL AFRICA CHAPTER 2.
    IN ARTHUR HAZLEWOOD, AFRICAN INTEGRATION AND DISINTEGRATION,
    LONDON, OXFORD UNIVERSITY PRESS, 1967, PP 27-69
    078,105-09,106-09,107-09,112-09,

    ROBSON PETER
    ECONOMIC INTEGRATION IN SOUTHERN AFRICA.
    THE JOURNAL OF MODERN AFRICAN STUDIES 5 4 DECEMBER 1967 PP
    469-490
    078,

    ROBSON PETER   LURY D A   EDS
    THE ECONOMIES OF AFRICA.
    EVANSTON, NORTHWESTERN UNIVERSITY PRESS, 1969
    073,

    ROBSON PETER
    PROBLEMS OF INTEGRATION BETWEEN SENEGAL AND
    GAMBIA CHAPTER 4.
    IN ARTHUR HAZLEWOOD, AFRICAN INTEGRATION AND DISINTEGRATION,
    LONDON, OXFORD UNIVERSITY PRESS, 1967, P   115-128
    078,113-09,130-09,

    ROBSON PETER
    THE PROBLEMS OF SENEGAMBIA.
    JOURNAL OF MODERN AFRICAN STUDIES 3 1965
    078,113-09,130-09,

    LEYS COLIN   ROBSON PETER   EDS
    FEDERATION IN EAST AFRICA-- OPPORTUNITIES AND PROBLEMS.
    NAIROBI, OXFORD UNIVERSITY PRESS, 1965
    078,

RODD FRANCIS
    RODD FRANCIS
    PEOPLE OF THE VEIL.
    LONDON, MACMILLAN, 1926
    127-01,

RODER W
    RODER W
    THE DIVISION OF LAND RESOURCES IN SOUTHERN RHODESIA.
    ANNALS OF THE ASSOCIATION OF AMERICAN GEOGRAPHERS 54 MARCH
    1964 PP 42-52
    087,145-06,

RODIER J
    RODIER J
    HYDROLOGY IN AFRICA.
    NEW YORK, UNESCO, 1953
    069,075,

    RODIER J
    THE BIBLIOGRAPHY OF AFRICAN HYDROLOGY.
    PARIS, UNESCO, 1963
    069,075,

RODNEY WALTER
   RODNEY WALTER
   WEST AFRICA AND THE ATLANTIC SLAVE-TRADE.
   NAIROBI, EAST AFRICAN PUBLISHING HOUSE, 1967
   028,

RODNEY WALTER
   RODNEY WALTER
   AFRICAN SLAVERY AND OTHER FORMS OF SOCIAL OPPRESSION ON THE
   UPPER GUINEA COAST IN THE CONTEXT OF THE AFRICAN SLAVE TRADE
   JOURNAL OF AFRICAN HISTORY 3 1966 PP 431-433
   028,

ROE ALAN R
   ROE ALAN R
   THE FUTURE OF THE COMPANY IN TANZANINA DEVELOPMENT.
   THE JOURNAL OF MODERN AFRICAN STUDIES, VOL. 7, NO. 1, 1969,
   PP. 47-67
   073,136-08,

ROGER
   LOUIS WILLIAM ROGER
   RUANDA-URUNDI-- 1884-1919.
   OXFORD, CLARENDON PRESS, 1963
   033,103-02,129-02,

   RAPONDA-WALKER ANDRE   SILLANS ROGER
   RITES ET CROYANCES DES PEUPLES DU GABON, ESSAI SUR LES
   PRATIQUES RELIGIEUSES DE AUTREFOIS ET D'AUJORD'HUI.
   PARIS, PRESENCE AFRICAINE, 1962
   112-01,

ROGERS CYRIL A
   ROGERS CYRIL A
   A STUDY OF RACE ATTITUDES IN NIGERIA.
   RHODES-LIVINGSTONE JOURNAL 26 1959 PP 51-64
   088,128-06,

   ROGERS CYRIL A   FRANTZ CHARLES
   RACIAL THEMES IN SOUTHERN RHODESIA-THE ATTITUDES OF THE
   WHITE POPULATION
   NEW HAVEN, YALE UNIVERSITY PRESS, 1962
   088,145-07,

ROGERS EVERETT M
   ROGERS EVERETT M
   MODERNIZATION AMONG PEASANTS--THE IMPACT OF COMMUNICATION.
   NEW YORK, HOLT, RINEHART AND WINSTON, INC., 1969
   048,

ROGIN MICHAEL
   ROTHCHILD DONALD S ROGIN MICHAEL
   UGANDA.
   IN CARTER, G.M. NATIONAL UNITY AND REGIONALISM IN EIGHT
   AFRICAN STATES, ITHACA, CORNELL UNIVERSITY PRESS, 1966
   139-09,

ROKKAN STEIN
   ROKKAN STEIN   ED
   COMPARATIVE RESEARCH ACROSS CULTURES AND NATIONS

PARIS, THE HAGUE, MOUTON, 1968
098,

ROSBERG
FRIEDLAND WILLIAM H ROSBERG CARL G   EDS
AFRICAN SOCIALISM.
LONDON, OXFORD UNIVERSITY PRESS, 1965
060,077,

ROSBERG CARL G
BENNETT GEORGE   ROSBERG CARL G
THE KENYATTA ELECTION-- KENYA 1960-1961.
LONDON, OXFORD UNIVERSITY PRESS, 1961
063,117-07,

COLEMAN JAMES S   ROSBERG CARL G   EDS
POLITICAL PARTIES AND NATIONAL INTEGRATION IN TROPICAL
AFRICA.
BERKELEY, CALIFORNIA, UNIVERSITY OF CALIFORNIA PRESS, 1964
002,061,

ROSBERG CARL G   NOTTINGHAM JOHN
THE MYTH OF MAU-MAU-- NATIONALISM IN KENYA.
NEW YORK, PRAEGER, 1966
055,117-06,

ROSBERG CARL G
THE FEDERATION OF RHODESIA AND NYASALAND-- PROBLEMS OF
DEMOCRATIC GOVERNMENT.
ANNALS OF THE AMERICAN ACADEMY OF POLITICAL AND SOCIAL
SCIENCES 306 1956 PP 98-105
078,

ROSCOE J
ROSCOE J
THE BAGANDA
LONDON, FRANK CASS, SECOND EDITION, 1965
025,139-01,

ROSENBERG MORRIS
LAZARSFELD PAUL F   ROSENBERG MORRIS   EDS
THE LANGUAGE OF SOCIAL RESEARCH.
NEW YORK, FREE PRESS, 1955
098,

ROSMAN ABRAHAM
ROSMAN ABRAHAM
SOCIAL STRUCTURE AND ACCULTURATION AMONG THE KANURI
OF BORNU PROVINCE, NORTHERN NIGERIA.
TRANSACTIONS OF THE NEW YORK ACADEMY OF SCIENCE 21 MAY
1958 PP 620-630
038,128-01,

ROSTEIN ABRAHAM
POLANYI KARL   ROSTEIN ABRAHAM
DAHOMEY AND THE SLAVE TRADE-ANALYSIS OF AN ARCHAIC ECONOMY
SEATTLE, UNIVERSITY OF WASHINGTON PRESS, 1966
010,028,

ROSTOW W W

ROSTOW W W
THE TAKE-OFF INTO SELF-SUSTAINED GROWTH CHAPTER 7.
IN JASON L FINKLE AND RICHARD W GABLE, POLITICAL
DEVELOPMENT AND SOCIAL CHANGE, NEW YORK, JOHN WILEY, 1966
072,

ROTBERG
MWASE GEORGE SIMEON ROTBERG ROBERT   ED
STRIKE A BLOW AND DIE.
CAMBRIDGE, HARVARD UNIVERSITY PRESS, 1967
034, 122-02,

ROTBERG ROBERT I
MAZRUI ALI A   ROTBERG ROBERT I   EDS
THE TRADITIONS OF PROTEST IN BLACK AFRICA, 1886-1966.
CAMBRIDGE,MASSACHUSETTS,HARVARD UNIVERSITY PRESS, 1970
034,035,

ROTBERG ROBERT I
THE ORIGINS OF NATIONALIST DISCONTENT IN EAST AND
CENTRAL AFRICA.
JOURNAL OF NEGRO HISTORY 48 1963 PP 130-141
055,

ROTBERG ROBERT I
A POLITICAL HISTORY OF TROPICAL AFRICA.
NEW YORK, HARCOURT BRACE AND WORLD, 1965
001,036,

ROTBERG ROBERT I
AFRICA IN ANCIENT TIMES CHAPTER 1.
IN A POLITICAL HISTORY OF TROPICAL AFRICA, NEW YORK,
HARCOURT, BRACE AND WORLD, 1965, PP 3-33
020,

ROTBERG ROBERT I
THE ERA OF EMPIRES AND CITY-STATES, 800-1500 CHAPTER 2.
IN A POLITICAL HISTORY OF TROPICAL AFRICA, NEW YORK,
HARCOURT, BRACE AND WORLD, 1965 PP 34-66
022,023,025,

ROTBERG ROBERT I
AFRICA AND THE FIRST WAVE OF EUROPEAN EXPANSION,
1400-1700 CHAPTER 3.
IN A POLITICAL HISTORY OF TROPICAL AFRICA, NEW YORK,
HARCOURT, BRACE AND WORLD, 1965 PP 67-94
027,

ROTBERG ROBERT I
KINGDOMS OF THE SAVANNAH AND FOREST, 1500-1800 CHAPTER 4.
IN A POLITICAL HISTORY OF TROPICAL AFRICA, NEW YORK,
HARCOURT, BRACE AND WORLD, 1965 PP 95-132
024,025,026,

ROTBERG ROBERT I
TROPICAL AFRICA AND THE WIDER WORLD-- COMMERCIAL CONNECTIONS
AND THE GROWTH OF THE SLAVE TRADE, 1600-1800 CHAPTER 5.
IN A POLITICAL HISTORY OF TROPICAL AFRICA, NEW YORK,
HARCOURT, BRACE AND WORLD, 1965, PP 133-164
028,

ROTBERG ROBERT I
    ROTBERG ROBERT I
    POLITICAL CHANGE IN THE INTERIOR, 1800-1880 CHAPTER 6.
    IN A POLITICAL HISTORY OF TROPICAL AFRICA, NEW YORK,
    HARCOURT, BRACE AND WORLD, 1965, PP 165-189
    033,

    ROTBERG ROBERT I
    THE INTERACTION OF AFRICA AND EUROPE, 1788-1884 CHAPTER 7.
    IN A POLITICAL HISTORY OF TROPICAL AFRICA, NEW YORK,
    HARCOURT, BRACE AND WORLD, 1965, PP 190-243
    033,

    ROTBERG ROBERT I
    THE PERIOD OF THE EUROPEAN PARTITION, 1885-1902 CHAPTER 8.
    IN A POLITICAL HISTORY OF TROPICAL AFRICA, NEW YORK,
    HARCOURT, BRACE AND WORLD, 1965, PP 244-285
    033,

    ROTBERG ROBERT I
    THE CONSOLIDATION OF THE COLONIAL INITIATIVE, 1891-1918
    CHAPTER 9.
    IN A POLITICAL HISTORY OF TROPICAL AFRICA, NEW YORK,
    HARCOURT, BRACE AND WORLD, 1965, PP 286-314
    034,

    ROTBERG ROBERT I
    THE ADMINISTRATIVE INTERLUDE, 1919-1939 CHAPTER 10.
    IN A POLITICAL HISTORY OF TROPICAL AFRICA, NEW YORK,
    HARCOURT, BRACE AND WORLD, 1965, PP 315-347
    035,

    ROTBERG ROBERT I
    THE TRIUMPH OF NATIONALISM, 1940-1965 CHAPTER 11.
    IN A POLITICAL HISTORY OF TROPICAL AFRICA, NEW YORK,
    HARCOURT, BRACE AND WORLD, 1965, PP 348-372
    055,

    ROTBERG ROBERT I
    CHRISTIAN MISSIONARIES AND THE CREATION OF NORTHERN
    RHODESIA, 1800-1924.
    PRINCETON, PRINCETON UNIVERSITY PRESS, 1965
    050,142-03,

    ROTBERG ROBERT I
    PLYMOUTH BRETHREN AND THE OCCUPATION OF KATANGA 1886-1907.
    JOURNAL OF AFRICAN HISTORY 5 1964 PP 285-297
    050,108-03,

    ROTBERG ROBERT I
    THE FEDERATION MOVEMENT IN BRITISH EAST AND CENTRAL AFRICA
    1889-1953.
    JOURNAL OF COMMONWEALTH POLITICAL STUDIES 2 1964 PP 141-160
    035,

    ROTBERG ROBERT I
    THE RISE OF NATIONALISM IN CENTRAL AFRICA-- THE MAKING
    OF MALAWI AND ZAMBIA, 1873-1964.
    CAMBRIDGE, HARVARD UNIVERSITY PRESS, 1966

055,122-06,142-06,

ROTBERG ROBERT I
    ROTBERG ROBERT I
    MISSIONARIES AS CHIEFS AND ENTREPRENEURS-- NORTHER RHODESIA,
    1887-1924.
    IN JEFFREY BUTLER (ED), BOSTON UNIVERSITY PAPERS IN AFRICAN
    HISTORY VOL I, BOSTON, BOSTON UNIVERSITY PRESS,1964, PP 195-
    216
    041,142-03,

    ROTBERG ROBERT I
    THE RISE OF AFRICAN NATIONALISM-- THE CASE OF EAST AND
    CENTRAL AFRICA.
    WORLD POLITICS OCTOBER 1962 P 75
    055,

ROTHCHILD DONALD S
    ROTHCHILD DONALD S
    THE POLITICS OF AFRICAN SEPARATISM.
    IN WILLIAM J HANNA (ED), INDEPENDENT BLACK AFRICA, CHICAGO,
    RAND MCNALLY, 1964, PP 595-606
    064,

    ROTHCHILD DONALD S
    SAFE GUARDING NIGERIAN MINORITIES.
    INSTITUTE OF AFRICAN AFFAIRS PUBLICATION,PHILADELPHIA,
    UNIVERSITY OF PENSYLVANIA,1964
    057,128-06,

    ROTHCHILD DONALD S   ED
    POLITICS OF INTEGRATION-AN EAST AFRICAN DOCUMENTARY
    NAIROBI,EAST AFRICAN PUBLISHING HOUSE, 1968
    078,

    ROTHCHILD DONALD S
    ETHNIC INEQUALITIES IN KENYA
    JOURNAL OF MODERN AFRICAN STUDIES 7 1969 PP 689-711
    057,117-03,

    ROTHCHILD DONALD S   ROGIN MICHAEL
    UGANDA.
    IN CARTER, G.M.,NATIONAL UNITY AND REGIONALISM IN EIGHT
    AFRICAN STATES, ITHACA. CORNELL UNIVERSITY PRESS, 1966
    139-09,

ROUCH JEAN
    ROUCH JEAN
    SONGHAY.
    IN P J M MCEWAN (ED), AFRICA FROM EARLY TIMES TO 1800, LONDON,
    OXFORD UNIVERSITY PRESS ,1968, PP 59-89
    022,123-02,

    ROUCH JEAN
    THE AWAKENING AFRICAN CINEMA.
    THE UNESCO COURIER MARCH 1962
    093,

    ROUCH JEAN
    SECOND GENERATION MIGRANTS IN GHANA AND THE IVORY COAST.

IN AIDAN SOUTHALL (ED.), SOCIAL CHANGE IN MODERN AFRICA.
LONDON, OXFORD UNIVERSITY PRESS, 1961
046,114-03,116-03,

ROUCH JEAN
  ROUCH JEAN
  LA RELIGION ET LA MAGIE SONGHAY (RELIGION AND MAGIC OF
  SONGHAY).
  PARIS, PRESSES UNIVERSITAIRES DE FRANCE, 1960
  013,127-01,

  ROUCH JEAN
  PROBLEMES RELATIFS A L'ETUDE DES MIGRATIONS
  TRADITIONNELLES ET DES MIGRATIONS ACTUELLES EN AFRIQUE
  OCCIDENTALE (PROBLEMS RELATIVE TO THE STUDY OF
  TRADITIONAL AND PRESENT DAY MIGRATIONS IN WEST AFRICA).
  BULLETIN DE L'INSTITUT FRANCAIS D'AFRIQUE NOIRE 22
  1960 PP 369-378
  099,

  ROUCH JEAN
  MIGRATION AU GOLD COAST (MIGRATION TO THE GOLD COAST).
  JOURNAL DE LA SOCIETE DES AFRICANISTES 26 1956 PP 33-196
  045,114-05,

  ROUCH JEAN
  CONTRIBUTION A L HISTOIRE DES SONGHAY (A CONTRIBUTION TO
  THE HISTORY OF SONGHAI).
  DAKAR,INSTITUT FRANCAIS D'AFRIQUE NOIRE,MEMOIRE 29,1953
  022,123-02,

ROUGET GILBERT
  ROUGET GILBERT
  AFRICAN TRADITIONAL NON-PROSE FORMS-- RECITING, DECLAIMING,
  SINGING, AND STROPHIC STRUCTURE.
  IN PROCEEDINGS OF THE CONFERENCE ON AFRICAN LANGUAGES
  AND LITERATURES, NORTHWESTERN UNIVERSITY, 1966, UNITED
  STATES OFFICE OF EDUCATION, NO. OF-6-14-018, PP 45-58
  012,

ROUNDTABLE
  ROUNDTABLE INTERVIEW
  SOME ASSUMPTIONS REEXAMINED.
  AFRICA REPORT, FEB., 1968, P. 20
  065,

ROUX EDWARD
  ROUX EDWARD
  TIME LONGER THAN ROPE--A HISTORY OF THE BLACK MAN≠S STRUGGLE
  FOR FREEDOM IN SOUTH AFRICA.
  MADISON, WISCONSIN, UNIVERSITY OF WISCONSIN PRESS, 1966
  032,132-07,

ROYAL
  EAST AFRICA ROYAL COMMISSION
  EAST AFRICA ROYAL COMMISSION 1953-1955 REPORT.
  LONDON,HER MAJESTY'S STATIONERY OFFICE,COMMAND PAPER NO 9475,
  REPRINT 482,1961
  035,045,

ROYAL INSTITUTE OF INTERNATIONAL AFFAIRS
NIGERIA--THE POLITICAL AND ECONOMIC BACKROUND.
LONDON, OXFORD UNIVERSITY PRESS, 1960
128-07,

RUBIN LESLIE
    RUBIN LESLIE   MURRAY PAULA
    THE CONSTITUTION AND GOVERNMENT OF GHANA.
    LONDON, SWEET AND MAXWELL, 1961
    068,114-07,

RUBIN N
    WARREN M W   RUBIN N
    DAMS IN AFRICA-AN INTERDISCIPLINARY STUDY OF MAN-MADE LAKES
    IN AFRICA
    LONDON, FRANK CASS, 1968
    075,

RUBIN NEVILLE
    RUBIN NEVILLE   COTRAN EUGENE   EDS
    READINGS IN AFRICAN LAW--VOLS 1 AND 2.
    NEW YORK, INTERNATIONAL UNIVERSITY BOOKSELLERS, INC., 1970
    067,

    RUBIN NEVILLE   COTRAN EUGENE   EDS
    AN ANNUAL SURVEY OF AFRICAN LAW, VOL 1.
    NEW YORK, INTERNATIONAL UNIVERSITY BOOKSELLERS, INC., 1970
    067,

RUBIN VERA
    RUBIN VERA   ED
    PLANTATION SYSTEMS OF THE NEW WORLD.
    WASHINGTON, 1959
    028,

RUDIN HARRY R
    RUDIN HARRY R
    GERMANS IN THE CAMEROONS 1884-1914-- A STUDY IN MODERN
    IMPERIALISM.
    LONDON, 1938
    033,

RUDOFSY BERNARD
    RUDOFSY BERNARD
    ARCHITECTURE WITHOUT ARCHITECTS.
    MUSEUM OF MODERN ART, NEW YORK, DOUBLEDAY, 1965
    092,

RUMMEL R J
    RUMMEL R J
    DIMENSIONS OF CONFLICT BEHAVIOR WITHIN NATIONS, 1946-59.
    JOURNAL OF CONFLICT RESOLUTION 10 1966 PP 65-73
    064,

RUPERT
    EMERSON RUPERT   KILSON MARTIN L   EDS
    THE POLITICAL AWAKENING OF AFRICA.
    ENGLEWOOD CLIFFS, NJ, PRENTICE-HALL, 1965
    060,

RUSSELL
    HOWE RUSSELL WARREN
    BLACK AFRICA-- AFRICA SOUTH OF THE SAHARA FROM PRE-
    HISTORY TO INDEPENDENCE.
    CHICAGO,WALKER,1967
    036,076,

RUSSELL G H
    RUSSELL G H   ED
    THE NATURAL RESOURCES OF EAST AFRICA.
    NAIROBI,D A HAWKINS LTD,1962
    069,

RUSSETT BRUCE M
    RUSSETT BRUCE M
    INTERNATIONAL REGIONS AND THE INTERNATIONAL SYSTEM
    CHICAGO,RAND MCNALLY,1967
    078,

RUTHENBERG HANS
    RUTHENBERG HANS
    AGRICULTURAL DEVELOPMENT IN TANGANYIKA.
    BERLIN,SPRINGER-VERLAG,1964
    070,136-08,

RUXTON
    KHALIL SIDI   TRANS BY   RUXTON
    MALIKI LAW
    LONDON, LUZAC AND CO., 1916
    021,066,

RYCKMANS PIERRE
    RYCKMANS PIERRE
    BELGIAN COLONIALISM .
    IN PHILIP Q QUIGG (ED), AFRICA, NEW YORK, PRAEGER, 1964,
    PP 71-83 ALSO FOREIGN AFFAIRS 34 1955 PP 89-101
    035,108-02,

RYDER A F C
    RYDER A F C
    THE RE-ESTABLISHMENT OF PORTUGUESE FACTORIES ON THE COSTA
    DA MINA TO THE MID-EIGHTEENTH CENTURY.
    JOURNAL OF THE HISTORICAL SOCIETY OF NIGERIA I 1958 PP 157-
    183
    027,

    RYDER A F C
    AN EARLY PORTUGUESE TRADING VOYAGE TO THE FORCADOS RIVER.
    JOURNAL OF THE HISTORICAL SOCIETY OF NIGERIA I 1959 PP 294
    -321
    027,

    RYDER A F C
    MISSIONARY ACTIVITY IN THE KINGDOM OF WARRI TO THE EARLY
    NINETEENTH CENTURY.
    JOURNAL OF THE HISTORICAL SOCIETY OF NIGERIA 22 1960 PP 2-
    27
    027,128-02,

S

SAADALLAH BELKACEM
  SAADALLAH BELKACEM
  THE RISE OF THE ALGERIAN ELITE, 1900-24.
  THE JOURNAL OF MODERN AFRICAN STUDIES 5 MAY 1967 PP 69-77
  044,101-04,

SACKS B
  SACKS B
  SOUTH AFRICA,AN IMPERIAL DILEMMA- NON-EUROPEANS AND THE
  BRITISH NATION 1902-1914
  ALBUQUERQUE,UNIVERSITY OF NEW MEXICO PRESS,1967
  032,

SADIE J L
  SADIE J L
  THE SOCIAL ANTHROPOLOGY OF ECONOMIC DEVELOPMENT.
  ECONOMIC JOURNAL 70 JUNE 1960 PP 294-303
  074,

SAFRAN N
  SAFRAN N
  EGYPT IN SEARCH OF POLITICAL COMMUNITY.
  CAMBRIDGE, HARVARD UNIVERSITY PRESS, 1961
  140-06,

SAGINI LAWRENCE
  SAGINI LAWRENCE
  SOME THOUGHTS ON RACIAL AND COMMUNAL TENSIONS IN EAST
  AFRICA.
  IN LAWRENCE SAGINI (ED),RACIAL AND COMMUNAL TENSIONS IN EAST
  AFRICA, NAIROBI,EAST AFRICAN PUBLISHING HOUSE,1966
  057,

SAHLINS MARSHALL D
  SAHLINS MARSHALL D
  TRIBESMEN.
  ENGLEWOOD CLIFFS, NEW JERSEY,PRENTICE-HALL,1968
  005,006,010,

  SAHLINS MARSHALL D
  THE SEGMENTARY   LINEAGE--AN ORGANIZATION OF PREDATORY
  EXPANSION.
  AMERICAN ANTHROPOLOGIST, VOL. 63, 1961, PP. 322-345
  005,

  SAHLINS MARSHALL D SERVICE ELMAN R   EDS
  EVOLUTION AND CULTURE.
  ANN ARBOR, UNIVERSITY OF MICHIGAN. 1960
  005,

SAID ABDUL A
  SAID ABDUL A
  THE AFRICAN PHENOMENON.
  BOSTON,ALLYN AND BACON INC,1968
  097,

SAID BEWSHIR M
    SAID BEWSHIR M
    THE SUDAN--CROSSROADS OF AFRICA.
    LONDON, BODLEY HEAD, 1967
    134-11,

SALACUSE JESWALD W
    SALACUSE JESWALD W
    DEVELOPMENTS IN AFRICAN LAW.
    AFRICAN REPORT, MARCH, 1968, P. 39
    067,

    SALACUSE JESWALD W
    EXPLORING AFRICAN LAW.
    AFRICA REPORT, MAY/JUNE, 1969, PP. 60-61
    067,

    SALACUSE JESWALD W
    AN INTRODUCTION TO LAW IN FRENCH-SPEAKING AFRICA--VOL I--
    AFRICA SOUTH OF THE SAHARA.
    CHARLOTTESVILLE, VIRGINIA, THE MICHE CO., 1969
    066,

SALZBERG JOHN
    ELLIS WILLIAM W   SALZBERG JOHN
    AFRICA AND THE U N-- A STATISTICAL NOTE.
    AMERICAN BEHAVIORAL SCIENTIST 8 APRIL 1965 PP 30-32
    081,

SAMARIN WILLIAM J
    SAMARIN WILLIAM J
    UNE LINGUA CENTRAFRICAINE.
    COLLOQUE SUR LE MULTILINGUISME, BRAZZAVILLE, 1962
    105-01,

SAMUELS MICHAEL A
    ABSHIRE DAVID M   SAMUELS MICHAEL A   EDS
    PORTUGUESE AFRICA--A HANDBOOK.
    NEW YORK, PRAEGER PUBLISHERS, 1969
    087,144-11,

SANDERS EDITH R
    SANDERS EDITH R
    THE HAMITIC HYPOTHESIS ITS ORIGINS AND FUNCTIONS IN TIME
    PERSPECTIVE.
    IN JOURNAL OF AFRICAN HISTORY VOL 10 1969 P 521
    003,

SANDERS P B
    SANDERS P B
    SEKONYELA AND MOSHESHWE-FAILURE AND SUCCESS IN THE AFTERMATH
    OF THE DIFAGANE
    JOURNAL OF AFRICAN HISTORY 10 1969 PP 439-456
    031,

SANDERS RALPH
    LEIGHTON RICHARD M SANDERS RALPH
    MILITARY CIVIC ACTION.
    IN LEWIS P FICKETT (ED), PROBLEMS OF THE DEVELOPING NATIONS,

NEW YORK, CROWELL, 1966, PP 103-122
064,

SANDERS RALPH
LEIGHTON RICHARD M   SANDERS RALPH
AID'S PUBLIC SAFETY CIVIC ACTION AND COMMUNITY DEVELOPMENT
PROGRAM.
IN LEWIS P FICKETT. (ED), PROBLEMS OF THE DEVELOPING NATIONS,
NEW YORK, CROWELL, 1966, PP 116-122
083,

SANDERSON G N
SANDERSON G N
THE FOREIGN POLICY OF THE NEGUS MENELIK, 1896-1898.
JOURNAL OF AFRICAN HISTORY 5 1964 PP 87-98
034,110-02,

SANDS WILLIAM
SANDS WILLIAM
PROSPECTS FOR A UNITED MAGHRIB
IN TIBOR KEREKES (ED), THE ARAB MIDDLE EAST AND MUSLIM
AFRICA, NEW YORK PRAEGER 1961
078,101-09,120-09,126-09,138-09,

SANGER CLYDE
SANGER CLYDE   NOTTINGHAM JOHN
THE KENYA GENERAL ELECTION OF 1963.
JOURNAL OF MODERN AFRICAN STUDIES 2 1964 PP 1-40
063,117-07,

SARBAH JOHN MENSAH
SARBAH JOHN MENSAH
FANTI NATIONAL CONSTITUTION.
NEW YORK, HUMANITIES PRESS INC., 1968
066,114-01,

SARBAH JOHN MENSAH
FANTI CUSTOMARY LAWS.
NEW YORK, HUMANITIES PRESS INC., 1968
066,114-01,

SASNETT MARTENA
SASNETT MARTENA   SEPMEYER INEZ
EDUCATIONAL SYSTEMS OF AFRICA.
BERKELY, UNIVERSITY OF CALIFORNIA PRESS, 1966
042,

SASTRE L'ABBE
SASTRE L'ABBE
CONTRIBUTION DE L'EGLISE CATHOLIQUE A L'EXPRESSION
CULTURELLE DE LA PERSONNALITE AFRICAINE (CONTRIBUTION OF
THE CATHOLIC CHURCH TO THE CULTURAL EXPRESSION OF THE
AFRICAN PERSONALITY).
IN COLLOQUE SUR LES RELIGIONS, ABIDJAN, APRIL, 1961, PARIS,
PRESENCE AFRICAINE, 1962, PP 183-194
039,050,

SAUL JOHN S
ARRIGHI GIOVANNI   SAUL JOHN S
SOCIALISM AND ECONOMIC DEVELOPMENT IN TROPICAL AFRICA.

THE JOURNAL OF MODERN AFRICAN STUDIES, VOL. 6, NO. 2, 1968,
PP. 141-69
073,

SAUVALLE H
    PERROT C   SAUVALLE H
    REPUBLIQUE DU CONGO--BRAZZAVILLE--REPERTOIRE
    BIBLIOGRAPHIQUE.
    PARIS, BUREAU POUR LE DEVELOPMENT DE LA PRODUCTION AGRICOLE,
    1965
    107-12,

SAWYER HARRY
    HARRIS W T   SAWYER HARRY
    THE SPRINGS OF MENDE BELIEF AND CONDUCT.
    FREETOWN, SIERRA LEONE UNIVERSITY PRESS, 1968
    013,131-01,

SAWYER JACK
    SAWYER JACK   LEVINE ROBERT A
    CULTURAL DIMENSIONS-- A FACTOR ANALYSIS OF THE WORLD ETHNO-
    GRAPHIC SAMPLE.
    AMERICAN ANTHROPOLOGIST VOL 68 NO 3 JUNE 1966 PP 708-731
    016,040,

SAWYERR G F A
    SAWYERR G F A   ED
    EAST AFRICAN LAW AND SOCIAL CUSTOM.
    KENYA, EAST AFRICAN PUBLISHING HOUSE, 1967
    067,

    SAWYERR G F A   ED
    EAST AFRICAN LAW AND SOCIAL CHANGE.
    NAIROBI, EAST AFRICAN PUBLISHING HOUSE, 1967
    MIMEO FORM OF SEMINAR ON LAW AND SOCIAL CHANGE IN EAST
    AFRICA, APRIL 1966
    066,

SAYLOR
    SAYLOR RALPH GERALD
    THE ECONOMIC SYSTEM OF SIERRA LEONE.
    DURHAM, DUKE UNIVERSITY PRESS, 1967
    131-08,

SCALAPINO ROBERT A
    SCALAPINO ROBERT A
    SINO-SOVIET COMPETITION IN AFRICA.
    FOREIGN AFFAIRS 42 4 JULY 1964 PP 640-654
    084,

SCANLON DAVID G
    COWAN L GRAY   O'CONNELL JAMES   SCANLON DAVID G
    EDUCATION AND NATION-BUILDING IN AFRICA.
    NEW YORK, PRAEGER, 1965
    042,043,

    SCANLON DAVID G   ED
    CHURCH, STATE AND EDUCATION IN AFRICA.
    NEW YORK, TEACHERS COLLEGE PRESS, COLUMBIA UNIVERSITY, 1966
    042,

SCANLON DAVID G
   SCANLON DAVID G
   EDUCATION.
   IN ROBERT A LYSTAD (ED), THE AFRICAN WORLD, NEW YORK,
   PRAEGER, 1966, PP 199-220
   100,

   SCANLON DAVID G   ED
   TRADITIONS OF AFRICAN EDUCATION.
   NEW YORK, COLUMBIA UNIVERSITY, 1964
   042,

SCARRITT JAMES R
   SCARRITT JAMES R
   THE IMPACT OF NATIONALISM.
   IN POLITICAL CHANGE IN A TRADITIONAL AFRICAN CLAN-- A
   STRUCTURAL-FUNCTIONAL ANALYSIS OF THE NSITS OF NIGERIA
   DENVER, MONOGRAPH SERIES IN WORLD AFFAIRS 3 1964-5, UNIVERSITY
   OF DENVER
   038,128-03,

SCHACHT JOSEPH
   SCHACHT JOSEPH
   ISLAM IN NORTHERN NIGERIA.
   STUDIA ISLAMICA 8 SUMMER 1957 PP 123-146
   052,128-03,

   SCHACHT JOSEPH
   ISLAMIC LAW IN CONTEMPORARY STATES.
   AMERICAN JOURNAL OF COMPARATIVE LAW 8 1959 PP 133-147
   066,

   SCHACHT JOSEPH
   INTRODUCTION TO ISLAMIC LAW.
   OXFORD, CLARENDON PRESS, 1964
   066,

SCHAEFFNER ANDRE
   SCHAEFFNER ANDRE
   LA MUSIQUE D'AFRIQUE NOIRE
   IN NORBERT DUFOURQ LA MUSIQUE DES ORIGINES A NOS JOURS
   PARIS, LAROUSSE, 1946, PP 460-465
   015,

SCHAPERA ISAAC
   SCHAPERA ISAAC
   GOVERNMENT AND POLITICS IN TRIBAL SOCIETIES.
   LONDON, WATTS, 1956
   009,

   SCHAPERA ISAAC
   MIGRANT LABOUR AND TRIBAL LIFE-- A STUDY OF CONDITIONS
   IN THE BECHUANALAND PROTECTORATE.
   LONDON, OXFORD UNIVERSITY.PRESS, 1947
   038,102-03,

   SCHAPERA ISAAC
   SOME PROBLEMS OF ANTHROPOLIGICAL RESEARCH IN KENYA COLONY.
   LONDON, INTERNATIONAL AFRICAN INSTITUTE, 1949

099,117-01,

SCHAPERA ISAAC
     SCHAPERA ISAAC   ED
     PRAISE POEMS OF TSWANA CHIEFS.
     OXFORD,CLARENDON PRESS, 1965
     012,102-01,

     SCHAPERA ISAAC
     ECONOMIC CHANGES IN SOUTH AFRICAN NATIVE LIFE.
     AFRICA,1928;ALSO G DALTON (ED.),TRIBAL AND PEASANT SOCIETIES,
     DOUBLEDAY, 1967
     010,132-03,

     SCHAPERA ISAAC   GOODWIN A J H
     WORK AND WEALTH.
     IN I SCHAPERA (ED.), THE BANTU-SPEAKING TRIBES OF SOUTH
     AFRICA, LONDON, ROUTLEDGE, 1937
     010,

     SCHAPERA ISAAC   ED
     THE BANTU-SPEAKING TRIBES OF SOUTH AFRICA.
     LONDON, ROUTLEDGE AND KEGAN PAUL, 1937
     132-01,

     SCHAPERA ISAAC
     A HANDBOOK OF TSWANA LAW AND CUSTOM
     NEW YORK,OXFORD UNIVERSITY PRESS,1955
     102-01,

     SCHAPERA ISAAC
     MARRIED LIFE IN AN AFRICAN TRIBE
     EVANSTON,NORTHWESTERN UNIVERSITY PRESS, 1966
     102-01,

     SCHAPERA ISAAC
     THE TSWANA
     LONDON,INTERNATIONAL AFRICAN INSTITUTE,1953
     102-01,

SCHATTEN F
     SCHATTEN F
     COMMUNISM IN AFRICA.
     LONDON, ALLEN AND UNWIN, 1966.
     084,

SCHATZ SAYER P
     SCHATZ SAYER P
     GOVERNMENT LENDING TO AFRICAN BUSINESSMEN--INEPT INCENTIVES.
     THE JOURNAL OF MODERN AFRICAN STUDIES, VOL. 6, NO. 4, 1968,
     PP. 519-29
     073,

     SCHATZ SAYER P
     THE CAPITAL SHORTAGE ILLUSION-- GOVERNMENT LENDING IN
     NIGERIA CHAPTER 9.
     IN EDITH WHETHAM AND JEAN CURRIE. (EDS.), READINGS IN THE
     APPLIED ECONOMICS OF AFRICA, LONDON, CAMBRIDGE UNIVERSITY
     PRESS, 1, 1967, PP 93-101
     073, 128-08,

SCHILDKNECHT FRANK
    SCHILDKNECHT FRANK
    TANZANIA
    IN KRITZECK AND LEWIS, PP 227-242
    136-03,

SCHILLER A ARTHUR
    SCHILLER A ARTHUR
    LAW CHAPTER 6.
    IN ROBERT A LYSTAD (ED), THE AFRICAN WORLD, NEW YORK,
    PRAEGER, 1966, PP 166-198
    066,

SCHLEGEL A
    COHEN RONALD   SCHLEGEL A
    THE TRIBE AS A SOCIO-POLITICAL UNIT-- A CROSS CULTURAL
    EXAMINATION.
    IN HELM (ED), ESSAYS ON THE PROBLEM OF TRIBE, AMERICAN
    ETHNOLOGICAL SOCIETY, 1968, PP 120-149
    005,

SCHLIPPE P
    SCHLIPPE P
    SHIFTING CULTIVATION IN AFRICA.
    LONDON, ROUTLEDGE AND KEGAN PAUL, 1956
    069, 134-08,

SCHMITTER
    SCHMITTER PHILIPPE C
    FURTHER NOTES ON OPERATIONALIZING SOME VARIABLES RELATED TO
    REGIONAL INTEGRATION.
    INTERNATIONAL ORGANIZATION, SPRING, 1969, VOL. XXIII, NO. 2,
    PP. 327-336
    078,

    SCHMITTER PHILIPPE C
    THREE NEO-FUNCTIONAL HYPOTHESES ABOUT INTERNATIONAL
    INTEGRATION.
    INTERNATIONAL ORGANIZATION, VOL. XXIII, NO. 1, 1969, PP. 161
    -166
    078,

SCHNAPPER BERNARD
    SCHNAPPER BERNARD
    LA POLITIQUE ET LE COMMERCE FRANCAIS DANS LE GOLFE DE
    GUINEE DE 1838 A 1871 (POLITICS AND FRENCH COMMERCE IN THE
    GULF OF GUINEA FROM 1836-1871).
    PARIS, MOURON, 1961
    033,

SCHNEIDER HAROLD K
    SCHNEIDER HAROLD K
    A FORMALIST VIEW OF AFRICAN ECONOMIC ANTHROPOLOGY.
    IN CARTER, GWENDOLEN M. AND ANN PADEN (EDS), EXPANDING
    HORIZONS IN AFRICAN STUDIES, EVANSTON, NORTHWESTERN
    UNIVERSITY PRESS, 1969, PP. 243-255
    010, 100,

    SCHNEIDER HAROLD K

PAKOT RESISTANCE TO CHANGE CHAPTER 8.
IN WILLIAM BASCOM AND MELVILLE HERSKOVITS, CONTINUTY AND
CHANGE IN AFRICAN CULTURES, CHICAGO, UNIVERSITY OF CHICAGO
PRESS, 1962, PP 144-167
038,

SCHRAMM WILBUR
   SCHRAMM WILBUR
   THE ROLE OF INFORMATION IN NATIONAL DEVELOPMENT (ABRIDGED
   VERSION OF MASS MEDIA AND NATIONAL DEVELOPMENT)
   PARIS,UNESCO,1964
   049,

SCHREINER O D
   SCHREINER O D
   POLITICAL POWER IN SOUTH AFRICA.
   IN PETER J MCEWAN AND ROBERT B SUTCLIFFE (EDS) MODERN AFRICA
   NEW YORK THOMAS CROWELL 1965 PP 229-238
   089,132-06,

SCHWAB WILLIAM B
   SCHWAB WILLIAM B
   THE GROWTH AND CONFLICTS OF RELIGION IN A MODERN YORUBA
   COMMUNITY.
   ZAIRE 6 8 OCTOBER 1952 PP 829-35
   089,128-03,

   SCHWAB WILLIAM B
   OSHOGBO- AN URBAN COMMUNITY CHAPTER 6.
   IN HILDA KUPER (ED), URBANIZATION AND MIGRATION IN WEST
   AFRICA,BERKELEY,UNIVERSITY OF CALIFORNIA PRESS,1965
   045,

   SCHWAB WILLIAM B
   SOCIAL SURVEY OF LAGOS.
   AMERICAN ANTHROPOLOGIST, VOL.66, 2, APRIL, 1964
   128-05,

SCHWARTZ
   SCHWARTZ FREDERICK A
   NIGERIA--THE TRIBES, THE NATION OT THE RACE,THE POLITICS OF
   INDEPENDENCE.
   CAMBRIDGE, MASSACHUSETTS, INSTITUTE OF TECHNOLOGY PRESS,
   1965
   065,128-06,

SCHWARZ WALTER
   SCHWARZ WALTER
   FOREIGN POWERS AND THE NIGERIAN WAR
   AFRICA REPORT 15 FEBRUARY 1970 PP 12-14
   065,

   SCHWARZ WALTER
   NIGERIA.
   LONDON, PALL MALL PRESS, 1968
   128-11,

SCOTCH NORMAN A
   SCOTCH NORMAN A
   A PRELIMINARY REPORT ON THE RELATION OF SOCIOCULTURAL

FACTORS TO HYPERTENSION AMONG THE ZULU.
ANNALS OF THE NEW YORK ACADEMY OF SCIENCES 134 1960
PP 1000-1009
041,132-03,

SCOTT
    FORDE C DARYLL   SCOTT R
    THE NATIVE ECONOMIES OF NIGERIA.
    LONDON, FABER, 1946
    010,128-01,

SCOTT D J
    SCOTT D J
    THE SIERRE LEONE ELECTION MAY, 1957 CHAPTER 5.
    IN W J MACKENZIE AND KENNETH ROBINSON, FIVE ELECTIONS IN
    AFRICA, LONDON, OXFORD UNIVERSITY PRESS, 1960
    063,131-07,

SCUDDER T
    SCUDDER T
    THE ECOLOGY OF THE GWEMBE TONGA.
    MANCHESTER, MANCHESTER UNIVERSITY PRESS, 1962
    010,142-01,

SEDDON D
    SEDDON D
    THE ORIGINS AND DEVELOPMENT OF AGRICULTURE IN EAST AND
    SOUTHERN AFRICA
    CURRENT ANTHROPOLOGY 9 1968 PP 489-509
    019,

SEERS DUDLEY
    SEERS DUDLEY
    THE ROLE OF INDUSTRY IN DEVELOPMENT-SOME FALLACIES
    JOURNAL OF MODERN AFRICAN STUDIES 1 1963 PP 461-465
    071,

    SEERS DUDLEY
    INTERNATIONAL AID-THE NEXT STEPS
    JOURNAL OF MODERN AFRICAN STUDIES 2 1964 PP 471-489
    073,080,

SEGAL AARON
    SEGAL AARON
    ISRAEL IN AFRICA.
    AFRICA REPORT 8 4 APRIL 1963 PP 19-21
    086,

    SEGAL AARON
    THE INTEGRATION OF DEVELOPING COUNTRIES--SOME THOUGHTS ON
    EAST AFRICA AND CENTRAL AMERICA.
    JOURNAL OF COMMON MARKET STUDIES, VOL. V, NO. 3, MARCH 1967,
    PP. 252-282
    078,

SEGAL RONALD
    SEGAL RONALD
    POLITICAL AFRICA--A WHO≠S WHO OF PERSONALITIES AND PARTIES.
    NEW YORK, PRAEGER, 1961
    044,

SEGAL RONALD
   SEGAL RONALD   FIRST RUTH   EDS
   SOUTH-WEST AFRICA- TRAVESTY OF TRUST
   LONDON,OXFORD UNIVERSITY PRESS,1967, INTERNATIONAL CONFERENCE
   ON SOUTH-WEST AFRICA,OXFORD 1966
   081,146-07,146-11,

SEGALL MARSHALL H
   SEGALL MARSHALL H
   THE GROWTH OF PSYCHOLOGY IN AFRICAN STUDIES.
   IN CARTER, GWENDOLEN M. AND ANN PADEN (EDS), EXPANDING
   HORIZONS IN AFRICAN STUDIES, EVANSTON, NORTHWESTERN
   UNIVERSITY PRESS, 1969, PP. 47-65
   039,098,100,

   SEGALL MARSHALL H   CAMPBELL DONALD T   HERSKOVITS MELVILLE
   THE INFLUENCE OF CULTURE ON VISUAL PERCEPTION
   INDIANAPOLIS,BOBBS-MERRILL,1966
   040,

   SEGALL MARSHALL H   EVANS J L
   LEARNING TO CLASSIFY BY COLOR AND FUNCTION-A STUDY IN
   CONCEPT FORMATION BY GANDA CHILDREN
   JOURNAL OF SOCIAL PSYCHOLOGY 77 1969 PP 35-53
   040,

SEGY LADISLAS
   SEGY LADISLAS
   AFRICAN SCULPTURE SPEAKS.
   NEW YORK, INTERNATIONAL UNIVERSITY BOOKSELLERS, INC., 1969
   014,

SEID JOSEPH BRAHIM
   SEID JOSEPH BRAHIM
   UN ENFANT DU TCAD--RECIT.
   PARIS, ED. SAGEREP, 1967
   106-10,

SEIDMAN ANN
   GREEN REGINALD H   SEIDMAN ANN
   UNITY OR POVERTY THE ECONOMICS OF PAN-AFRICANISM.
   BALTIMORE,PENGUIN,1968
   071,079,

SEIDMAN ROBERT B
   SEIDMAN ROBERT B
   A SOURCEBOOK OF THE CRIMINAL LAW OF AFRICA.
   LONDON,SWEET AND MAXWELL,1966
   066,

SELIGMAN CHARLES G
   SELIGMAN CHARLES G
   RACES OF AFRICA.
   LONDON, OXFORD UNIVERSITY PRESS, 1957
   020,

SELIGMAN LESTER G
   SELIGMAN LESTER G
   ELITE RECRUITMENT AND POLITICAL DEVELOPMENT CHAPTER 10.

IN JASON L FINKLE AND RICHARD W GABLE, POLITICAL
DEVELOPMENT AND SOCIAL CHANGE, NEW YORK, JOHN WILEY, 1966
043,

SEMBENE OUSMANE
SEMBENE OUSMANE
GOD'S BITS OF WOOD TRANS BY FRANCIS PRICE
LONDON, HEINEMANN EDUCATIONAL BOOKS, 1970 (ORIGINALLY
LES BOUTS DE DIEU. PARIS, LE LIVRE CONTEMPORAIN, 1960)
130-10,

SEMBENE OUSMANE
LE DOCKER NOIR.
PARIS, NOUVELLES EDITIONS DEBRESSE, 1956
130-10,

SEMBENE OUSMANE
L'HARMATTAN.
PARIS, PRESENCE AFRICAINE, 1964
130-10,

SEMBENE OUSMANE
O PAYS, MON BEAU PEUPLE.
PARIS, AMIOT-DUMONT, 1957
130-10.

SEMBENE OUSMANE
VOLTAIQUES, NOUVELLES.
PARIS, PRESENCE AFRICAINE, 1962
130-10,

SENGHOR LEOPOLD S
SENGHOR LEOPOLD S
SELECTED POEMS.
NEW YORK ATHENEUM 1966
090,130-10,

SENGHOR LEOPOLD S
THE PSYCHOLOGY OF THE AFRICAN NEGRO.
IN ALBERT BERRIAN AND RICHARD LONG (EDS), NEGRITUDE--
ESSAYS AND STUDIES, HAMPTON, VIRGINIA, HAMPTON INSTITUTE
PRESS, 1967, PP 48-55
039,

SENGHOR LEOPOLD S
ON AFRICAN SOCIALISM.
NEW YORK, PRAEGER, 1964
013,054,060,130-04,

SENGHOR LEOPOLD S
WEST AFRICA IN EVOLUTION.
FOREIGN AFFAIRS 39 1960-61 PP 240-246, ALSO PHILIP W QUIGG,
ED, AFRICA, NEW YORK, PRAEGER, 1964, PP 283-291
060,130-04,

SENGHOR LEOPOLD S
LES FONDEMENTS DE L'AFRICANITE OU NEGRITUDE ET ARABITE.
PARIS, PRESENCE AFRICAINE, 1967
091,130-04,

SENGHOR LEOPOLD S
PIERRE TEILHARD DE CHARDIN ET LA POLITIQUE AFRICAINE (PIERRE
TEILHARD DE CHARDIN AND AFRICAN POLITICS).
PARIS, EDITIONS DU SEUEL, 1962
060,

SENGHOR LEOPOLD S
   SENGHOR LEOPOLD S
   CHANTS D'OMBRE, SUIVIS DE HOSTIES NOIRES.
   PARIS, SEUIL, 1956 (2ND EDITION)
   130-04,

   SENGHOR LEOPOLD S
   CONGRES CONSTITUTIF DU P F A (PARTI DE LA FEDERATION
   AFRICAINE), DAKAR, 1-3, JUILLET 1959--RAPPORT SUR LA
   DOCTRINE ET LE PROGRAMME DU PARTI.
   PARIS, PRESENCE AFRICAINE, 1959
   130-04,

   SENGHOR LEOPOLD S
   ETHIOPIQUES.
   PARIS, SEUIL, 1956
   130-04,

   SENGHOR LEOPOLD S
   A AFRIQUE A L' O.N.U.--ALLOCUTION DU PRESIDENT DE LA
   REPUBLIQUE DU SENEGAL A LA XVIEME SESSION DE L ASSEMBLEE
   GENERALE DES NATIONS UNIES TENUE LE 31 OCTOBRE 1961.
   PARIS, PRESENCE AFRICAINE, 1961
   130-04,

   SENGHOR LEOPOLD S
   LIBERTE--NEGRITUDE ET HUMANISME.
   PARIS, SEUIL, 1964
   130-04,

   SENGHOR LEOPOLD S
   NATION ET VOIE AFRICAINE DU SOCIALISME.
   PARIS, PRESENCE AFRICAINE, 1961
   130-04,

   SENGHOR LEOPOLD S
   NOCTURNES. TRANS BY CLIVE WAKE AND JOHN REED
   LONDON, HEINEMANN EDUCATIONAL BOOKS, 1970 (ORIGINALLY
   NOCTURNES. PARIS, SEUIL, 1961)
   130-04,

   SENGHOR LEOPOLD S
   PIERRE TEILHARD DE CHARDIN ET LA POLITIQUE AFRICAINE.
   PARIS, SEUIL, 1962
   130-04,

   SENGHOR LEOPOLD S
   POETE SENEGALAIS--TEXTES COMMENTES PAR ROGER MERCIER ET M ET
   S BATTESTINI.
   PARIS, F. NATHAN, 1964
   130-04,

   SENGHOR LEOPOLD S
   CHANTS POUR NAET.

PARIS, SEGHERS, 1949
130-04,

SEPMEYER INEZ
SASNETT MARTENA   SEPMEYER INEZ
EDUCATIONAL SYSTEMS OF AFRICA.
BERKELY,UNIVERSITY OF CALIFORNIA PRESS,1966
042,

SERVICE ELMAN R
SAHLINS MARSHALL D SERVICE ELMAN R   EDS
EVOLUTION AND CULTURE.
ANN ARBOR, UNIVERSITY OF MICHIGAN, 1960
005,

SERVICE ELMAN R
PRIMITIVE SOCIAL ORGANIZATION.
NEW YORK,RANDOM HOUSE,1962
005,009,

SHAFFER N M
FAIR T J D   SHAFFER N M
POPULATION PATTERNS AND POLICIES IN SOUTH AFRICA, 1951-1960
ECONOMIC GEOGRAPHY, 40 JULY 1964 PP 261-274
089,132-06,

SHAMUYARIRA
SHAMUYARIRA NATHAN M
THE NATIONALIST MOVEMENT IN ZIMBABWE.
AFRICAN FORUM 2 3 1967 PP 34-42
087,145-06,

SHAMUYARIRA NATHAN M
CRISIS IN RHODESIA.
LONDON,1965
087,145-06,

SHANTZ H L
SHANTZ H L
AGRICULTURAL REGIONS OF AFRICA.
ECONOMIC GEOGRAPHY 16 1940 PP 1-47 AND 341-389, 17 1941 PP
217-249, 18 1942 PP 229-246, 19 1943 PP 77-109
069,

SHARMA B S
SHARMA B S
THE SUDAN.
THE POLITICS OF DEMILITARISATION, UNIVERSITY OF LONDON
APRIL-MAY 1966 PP 32-40
INSTITUTE OF COMMONWEALTH STUDIES
064,134-06,

SHAW C T
SHAW C T
NIGERIA'S PAST UNEARTHED.
WEST AFRICAN REVIEW DECEMBER 1960 PP 30-37
026,128-02,

SHAW C T
IGBO-UKWU-AN ACCOUNT OF ARCHEOLOGICAL DISCOVERIES IN

EASTERN NIGERIA
LONDON, FABER AND FABER; AND EVANSTON, NORTHWESTERN UNIVERSITY
PRESS, 1970
020,026,128-02,

SHELTON AUSTIN J
SHELTON AUSTIN J   ED
THE AFRICAN ASSERTION-- A CRITICAL ANTHOLOGY OF
AFRICAN LITERATURE.
NEW YORK, ODYSSEY PRESS, 1968
090,

SHELTON AUSTIN J
THE CYCLIC PRINCIPLE OF AFRICAN PERSONALITY.
IN ALBERT BERRIAN AND RICHARD LONG (EDS), NEGRITUDE--
ESSAYS AND STUDIES, HAMPTON, VIRGINIA, HAMPTON INSTITUTE
PRESS, 1967, PP 63-68
039,

SHEPHERD GEORGE W
SHEPHERD GEORGE W
UNITED STATES AND NON-ALIGNED AFRICA.
DENVER, INTERNATIONAL UNIVERSITY BOOKSELLERS, INC., 1969
083,

SHEPPERSON GEORGE
SHEPPERSON GEORGE
ETHIOPIANISM AND AFRICAN NATIONALISM.
PHYLON 14 1953 PP 9-18
050,051,

SHEPPERSON GEORGE
PAN-AFRICANISM-- SOME HISTORICAL NOTES.
PHYLON 23 WINTER 1962 PP 346-358
079,

SHEPPERSON GEORGE
NOTES ON NEGRO AMERICAN INFLUENCES ON THE EMERGENCE OF
AFRICAN NATIONALISM.
IN WILLIAM J HANNA (ED), INDEPENDENT BLACK AFRICA, CHICAGO,
RAND MCNALLY, 1964, PP 192-207
094,

SHEPPERSON GEORGE
THE POLITICS OF AFRICAN CHURCH SEPARATIST MOVEMENTS IN
BRITISH CENTRAL AFRICA 1892-1916.
AFRICA 24 1954 PP 233-245
051,

SHEPPERSON GEORGE
THE LITERATURE OF BRITISH CENTRAL AFRICA.
RHODES-LIVINGSTONE JOURNAL 23 1958 PP 12-46
090,122-10,142-10,145-10,

SHEPPERSON GEORGE
NYASALAND AND THE MILLENIUM.
IN SYLVIA L THRUPP (ED), MILLENNIAL DREAMS IN ACTION,
THE HAGUE, MOUTON, 1962, PP 144-159
051,122-03,

SHEPPERSON GEORGE   PRICE THOMAS
INDEPENDENT AFRICAN-- JOHN CHILEMBWE AND THE ORIGINS SETTING
AND SIGNIFICANCE OF THE NYASALAND RISING OF 1915.
EDINBURGH,EDINBURGH UNIVERSITY PRESS,1958
034,122-02,

SHEPPERSON GEORGE
    SHEPPERSON GEORGE
    EXTERNAL FACTORS IN THE DEVELOPMENT OF AFRICAN NATIONALISM
    WITH PARTICULAR REFERENCE TO BRITISH CENTRAL AFRICA.
    SALISBURY, S R, HISTORIANS IN TROPICAL AFRICA, UNIVERSITY
    OF RHODESIA AND NYASALAND, 1962, PP 144-159
    055,

    SHEPPERSON GEORGE
    THE JUMBE OF KOTA KOTA AND SOME ASPECTS OF THE HISTORY OF
    ISLAM IN BRITISH CENTRAL AFRICA.
    IN LEWIS, ISLAM IN TROPICAL AFRICA, LONDON, OXFORD UNIVERSITY
    PRESS, 1966, P. 193-207
    122-03,

SHERRILL ROBERT
    SHERRILL ROBERT
    BIRTH OF A BLACK NATION.
    ESQUIRE, JANUARY, 1969, VOL. LXXI, NO. 1, PP. 70-77
    095,

SHERWOOD HENRY N
    SHERWOOD HENRY N
    THE FORMATION OF THE AMERICAN COLONIZATION SOCIETY.
    THE JOURNAL OF NEGRO HISTORY II 1917 PP 209-228
    029,

SHIBUTANI TAMOTSU
    SHIBUTANI TAMOTSU   KWAN KIAN
    ETHNIC STRATIFICATION-- A COMPARATIVE APPROACH.
    NEW YORK,MACMILLAN COMPANY,1965
    004,057,

SHILS EDWARD
    SHILS EDWARD
    POLITICAL DEVELOPMENT IN THE NEW STATES.
    S'GRAVENHAGE,MOUTON,1962;ALSO COMPARATIVE STUDIES IN
    SOCIETY AND HISTORY 2 APRIL 1960 PP 265-292 AND JULY 1960
    PP 379-411
    061,

    SHILS EDWARD
    THE CONCENTRATION AND DISPERSION OF CHARISMA-- THEIR
    BEARING ON ECONOMIC POLICY IN UNDERDEVELOPED COUNTRIES.
    WORLD POLITICS 11 OCT 1958 PP 1-19;ALSO WILLIAM J HANNA,ED,
    INDEPENDENT BLACK AFRICA,CHICAGO,RAND MCNALLY,1964,PP
    389-406
    072,

    SHILS EDWARD
    INTELLECTUALS, PUBLIC OPINION AND ECONOMIC DEVELOPMENT.
    WORLD POLITICS 10 JAN 1958 PP 232-255;ALSO WILLIAM J HANNA,
    ED,INDEPENDENT BLACK AFRICA,CHICAGO,RAND MCNALLY,1964,PP
    472-494

091,

SHILS EDWARD
   SHILS EDWARD
   ALTERNATIVE COURSES OF POLITICAL DEVELOPMENT CHAPTER 13.
   IN JASON L FINKLE AND RICHARD W GABLE, POLITICAL
   DEVELOPMENT AND SOCIAL CHANGE, NEW YORK, JOHN WILEY, 1966
   061,

   SHILS EDWARD
   THE INTELLECTUALS IN THE POLITICAL DEVELOPMENT OF NEW
   STATES.
   WORLD POLITICS 12 APRIL 1960 PP 329-368
   044,

SHINAR P
   SHINAR P
   NOTE ON THE SOCIO-ECONOMIC AND CULTURAL ROLE OF SUFI
   BROTHERHOODS AND MARABUTISM IN THE MODERN MAGHRIB.
   IN LALAGE BOWN AND MICHAEL CROWDER (EDS.), PROCEEDINGS OF
   THE FIRST INTERNATIONAL CONGRESS OF AFRICANISTS, ACCRA,
   1962, LONDON, LONGMANS, 1964, PP 272-285
   046,

SHINGLER JOHN
   SINGLETON F SETH   SHINGLER JOHN
   AFRICA IN PERSPECTIVE.
   NEW YORK, HAYDEN BOOK COMPANY, 1967
   036,

SHINNIE M
   SHINNIE P L   SHINNIE M
   NEW LIGHT ON MEDIEVAL NUBIA
   JOURNAL OF AFRICAN HISTORY 6 1965 PP 263-273
   020,

SHINNIE P L
   SHINNIE P L
   MEROE, A CIVILIZATION OF THE SUDAN.
   LONDON, THAMES AND HUDSON, 1967
   020,134-02,

   SHINNIE P L   SHINNIE M
   NEW LIGHT ON MEDIEVAL NUBIA
   JOURNAL OF AFRICAN HISTORY 6 1965 PP 263-273
   020,

   BIVAR A D H   SHINNIE P L
   OLD KANURI CAPITALS.
   JOURNAL OF AFRICAN HISTORY 3 1962 PP 1-10
   024,128-02,

SIEBER ROY
   SIEBER ROY
   THE VISUAL ARTS.
   IN ROBERT A LYSTAD (ED), THE AFRICAN WORLD, NEW YORK,
   PRAEGER, 1966, PP 442-451
   014,093,

   SIEBER ROY

SCULPTURE OF NORTHERN NIGERIA.
NEW YORK, MUSEUM OF PRIMITIVE ART, 1961
014,128-01,

SIEBER ROY
    SIEBER ROY
    THE ARTS AND THEIR CHANGING SOCIAL FUNCTION.
    ANNALS OF THE NEW YORK ACADEMY OF SCIENCES
    46 1962 PP 653-658
    014,

SIGMUND PAUL
    SIGMUND PAUL
    THE IDEOLOGIES OF THE DEVELOPING NATIONS.
    NEW YORK, PRAEGER, 1963
    060,

SILBERMANN CHARLES
    SILBERMANN CHARLES
    CRISIS IN BLACK AND WHITE.
    NEW YORK, RANDOM HOUSE, 1964
    095,

SILLANS
    RAPONDA-WALKER ANDRE   SILLANS ROGER
    RITES ET CROYANCES DES PEUPLES DU GABON, ESSAI SUR LES
    PRATIQUES RELIGIEUSES DE AUTREFOIS ET D AUJORD HUI.
    PARIS, PRESENCE AFRICAINE, 1962
    112-01,

SIMMONS J
    PERHAM MARGERY   SIMMONS J
    AFRICAN DISCOVERY
    EVANSTON, NORTHWESTERN UNIVERSITY PRESS, 1963 (NEW EDITION)
    027,

SIMMS RUTH P
    SIMMS RUTH P
    URBANIZATION IN WEST AFRICA-- A REVIEW OF CURRENT
    LITERATURE.
    EVANSTON, NORTHWESTERN UNIVERSITY PRESS, 1965
    046,

SIMONS H J
    SIMONS H J   SIMONS R E
    CLASS AND COLOR IN SOUTH AFRICA 1850-1950
    BALTIMORE, PENGUIN, 1969
    032,089,

SIMONS R E
    SIMONS H J   SIMONS R E
    CLASS AND COLOR IN SOUTH AFRICA 1850-1950
    BALTIMORE, PENGUIN, 1969
    032,089,

SIMOONS
    SIMOONS FREDERICK J
    NORTHWEST ETHIOPIA, PEOPLES AND ECONOMY
    MADISON, UNIVERSITY OF WISCONSIN PRESS, 1960
    110-01,

SIMPSON MORAG C
    KHIDER MAHASSIN   SIMPSON MORAG C
    CO-OPERATIVES AND AGRICULTURAL DEVELOPMENT IN THE SUDAN.
    THE JOURNAL OF MODERN AFRICAN STUDIES, VOL. 6, NO. 4, 1968,
    PP. 509-18
    070,134-08,

SINAI I ROBERT
    SINAI I ROBERT
    THE CHALLENGE OF MODERNIZATION-- THE WEST≠S IMPACT ON THE
    NON-WESTERN WORLD.
    LONDON, CHATTO AND WINDUS, 1964
    037,

SINGER HANS
    SINGER HANS
    INTERNATIONAL ECONOMIC DEVELOPMENT, GROWTH AND CHANGE.
    NEW YORK, MCGRAW-HILL, 1964
    073,

SINGH J
    SINGH J   ED
    AFRICAN FILM
    NAIROBI, DRUM PUBLICATIONS, 1968
    049,093,

SINGLETON F SETH
    SINGLETON F SETH   SHINGLER JOHN
    AFRICA IN PERSPECTIVE.
    NEW YORK, HAYDEN BOOK COMPANY, 1967
    036,

SISSOKO FILY-DABO
    SISSOKO FILY-DABO
    COUPS DE SAGAIE, CONTROVERSES SUR L'UNION FRANCAISE.
    PARIS, ED. DE LA TOUR DU GUET, 1957
    123-10,

    SISSOKO FILY-DABO
    CRAYONS ET PORTRAITS.
    MULHOUSE, IMP. UNION, 1953
    123-10,

    SISSOKO FILY-DABO
    HARMAKHIS--POEMES DU TERROIR AFRICAIN.
    PARIS, ED. DE LA TOUR DU GUET, 1955
    123-10,

    SISSOKO FILY-DABO
    LA PASSION DE DJIME.
    PARIS, ED. DE LA TOUR DU GUET. 1956
    123-10,

    SISSOKO FILY-DABO
    LA SAVANE ROUGE.
    AVIGNON, LES PRESSES UNIVERSELLES, 1962
    123-10,

    SISSOKO FILY-DABO

POEMES DE L'AFRIQUE NOIRE FEUX DE BROUSSE HARMAKHIS--FLEURS
ET CHARDONS.
PARIS, DEBRESSE, 1963
123-10,

SISSOKO FILY-DABO
   SISSOKO FILY-DABO
   SAGESSE NOIRE, SENTENCES ET PROVERBES MALINKES.
   PARIS, ED. DE LA TOUR DU GUET, 1955, SVIII
   123-10,

SITHOLE NDABANINGI
   SITHOLE NDABANINGI
   AFRICAN NATIONALISM.
   LONDON, OXFORD UNIVERSITY PRESS, 1968
   054,091,145-04,

SJOBERG GIDEON
   SJOBERG GIDEON
   FOLK AND FEUDAL SOCIETIES CHAPTER 2.
   IN JASON L FINKLE AND RICHARD W GABLE, POLITICAL
   DEVELOPMENT AND SOCIAL CHANGE, NEW YORK, JOHN WILEY, 1966
   045,

   SJOBERG GIDEON
   THE PREINDUSTRIAL CITY PAST AND PRESENT.
   GLENCOE, ILLINOIS, GLENCOE FREE PRESS, 1960
   045,

SKALNIKOVA O
   SKALNIKOVA O
   ETHNOGRAPHICAL RESEARCH INTO THE PRESENT CHANGES IN THE
   MODE OF LIFE OF URBAN POPULATION IN AFRICA.
   IN LALAGE BOWN AND MICHAEL CROWDER (EDS.), PROCEEDINGS OF
   THE FIRST INTERNATIONAL CONGRESS OF AFRICANISTS, ACCRA,
   1962, LONDON, LONGMANS, 1964, PP 286-297
   046,

SKINNER ELLIOTT P
   SKINNER ELLIOTT P
   STRANGERS IN WEST AFRICAN SOCIETIES.
   AFRICA (LONDON) 33 1963 PP 307-320
   046,

   SKINNER ELLIOTT P
   GROUP DYNAMICS IN THE POLITICS OF CHANGING SOCIETIES-- THE
   PROBLEM OF TRIBAL POLITICS IN AFRICA.
   IN JUNE HELM (ED), ESSAYS ON THE PROBLEM OF TRIBE, AMERICAN
   ETHNOLOGICAL SOCIETY, 1968, PP 170-185
   004,005,006,007,

   SKINNER ELLIOTT P
   CHRISTIANITY AND ISLAM AMONG THE MOSSI.
   AMERICAN ANTHROPOLOGIST 60 DECEMBER 1958 PP 1102-1119
   050,052,141-03,

   SKINNER ELLIOTT P
   INTERGENERATIONAL CONFLICT AMONG THE MOSSI-- FATHER
   AND SON.
   JOURNAL OF CONFLICT RESOLUTION 5 1961 PP 55-60

043,141-03,

SKINNER ELLIOTT P
    SKINNER ELLIOTT P
    LABOUR MIGRATION AND ITS RELATIONSHIP TO SOCIOCULTURAL
    CHANGE IN MOSSI SOCIETY.
    AFRICA (LONDON) 30 1960 PP 375-401
    038,141-03,

    SKINNER ELLIOTT P
    TRADITIONAL AND MODERN PATTERNS OF SUCCESSION TO POLITICAL
    OFFICE AMONG THE MOSSI OF THE VOLTAIC REPUBLIC.
    JOURNAL OF HUMAN RELATIONS 8 1960 PP 394-406
    009,141-01,

    SKINNER ELLIOTT P
    THE MOSSI OF THE UPPER VOLTA-- THE POLITICAL DEVELOPMENT OF
    A SUDANESE PEOPLE.
    STANFORD, STANFORD UNIVERSITY PRESS, 1964
    061,141-07,

    SKINNER ELLIOTT P
    ISLAM IN MOSSI SOCIETY.
    IN LEWIS, ISLAM IN TROPICAL AFRICA, LONDON, OXFORD UNIVERSIT
    PRESS, 1966, P. 350-373
    141-03,

SKINNER NEIL
    SKINNER NEIL
    HAUSA READINGS--SELECTIONS FROM EDGAR≠S TATSUNIYOYI.
    MADISON, UNIVERSITY OF WISCONSIN PRESS, 1968
    012,128-01,

    SKINNER NEIL   TRANS AND ED
    HAUSA TALES AND TRADITIONS.
    NEW YORK, AFRICANA PUBLISHING CORPORATION, 1969
    012,128-01,

    SKINNER NEIL   TRANS   ED
    HAUSA TALES AND TRADITIONS-AN ENGLISH TRANSLATION OF EDGAR≠S
    TATSUNIYOYI NA HAUSA 3 VOLUMES
    NEW YORK, AFRICANA PUBLISHING CORPORATION, 1969
    012,

SKLAR RICHARD L
    SKLAR RICHARD L
    POLITICAL SCIENCE AND NATIONAL INTEGRATION- A RADICAL
    APPROACH.
    JOURNAL OF MODERN AFRICAN STUDIES 5 MAY 1967 PP 1-11
    058,

    SKLAR RICHARD L
    NIGERIAN POLITICS--THE ORDEAL OF CHIEF AWOLOWO, 1960-65.
    GWENDOLEN M. CARTER (ED), POLOTICS IN AFRICA--7 CASES, NEW
    YORK, HARCOURT, BRACE AND WORLD INC., 1966, PP. 119-166
    065,128-07,

    SKLAR RICHARD L
    CONTRADICTIONS IN THE NIGERIAN POLOTICAL SYSTEM.
    THE JOURNAL OF MODERN AFRICAN STUDIES, VOL. 3, NO. 2, 1965,

PP. 201-13
065,128-06,

SKLAR RICHARD L
    SKLAR RICHARD L
    DIALOG-THE UNITED STATES AND THE BIAFRAN WAR
    AFRICA REPORT NOVEMBER 1969 PP 22-23
    065,

    SKLAR RICHARD L
    THE CONTRIBUTION OF TRIBALISM TO NATIONALISM IN WESTERN
    NIGERIA.
    IN IMMANUEL WALLERSTEIN, SOCIAL CHANGE, THE COLONIAL
    SITUATION, NEW YORK, JOHN WILEY AND SONS, 1966, PP 290-300
    057,128-06,

    SKLAR RICHARD L
    NIGERIAN POLITICAL PARTIES-- POWER IN AN EMERGENT AFRICAN
    NATION.
    PRINCETON, NEW JERSEY, PRINCETON UNIVERSITY PRESS, 1963
    061, 128-07,

    WHITAKER C S   SKLAR RICHARD L
    NIGERIA.
    IN G.M. CARTER (ED), NATIONAL UNITY AND REGIONALISM IN EIGHT
    AFRICAN STATES. ITHACA, CORNELL UNIVERSITY PRESS, 1966
    065,128-06,

SKOROV GEORGE
    SKOROV GEORGE
    INTEGRATION OF EDUCATIONAL AND ECONOMIC PLANNING IN
    TANZANIA.
    PARIS, UNESCO, 1967
    072,136-08,

SKURNIK W A E
    SKURNIK W A E
    AFRICAN POLITICAL THOUGHT--LUMUMBA, NKRUMAH, AND TOURE.
    DENVER, COLORADO, INTERNATIONAL UNIVERSITY BOOKSELLERS, INC.
     1968
    060,108-04,114-04,115-04,

    SKURNIK W A E
    THE MILITARY AND POLITICS. DAHOMEY AND UPPER VOLTA.
    IN CLAUDE WELCH (ED), SOLDIER AND STATE IN AFRICA, EVANSTON,
    NORTHWESTERN UNIVERSITY PRESS, 1970
    064,

SLADE RUTH
    SLADE RUTH
    ENGLISH SPEAKING MISSIONS IN THE CONGO INDEPENDENT STATE--
    1878-1908.
    BRUXELLES, ACADEMIE ROYALE DES SCIENCES COLONIALES 1959
    050,108-03,

    SLADE RUTH
    KING LEOPOLD'S CONGO.
    LONDON, OXFORD UNIVERSITY PRESS, 1962
    035,108-02,

SMET G
   SMET G
   COMMERCE, MARCHE ET SPECULATION CHEZ LES BARUNDI, COMMERCE
   MARKETING AND SPECULATION AMONG THE BARUNDI,.
   REVUE DE L' INSTITUT DE SOCIOLOGIE SOLVAY 18 1938 PP 53-57
   010,129-01,

SMITH
   BOWEN ELENORE SMITH
   RETURN TO LAUGHTER
   GARDEN CITY, NEW YORK, DOUBLEDAY AND COMPANY, 1964
   098,

SMITH ALISON
   SMITH ALISON
   THE SOUTHERN SECTION OF THE INTERIOR, 1840-84.
   IN ROLAND OLIVER AND GERVASE MATHEW (EDS), HISTORY OF EAST
   AFRICA VOLUME ONE, OXFORD, CLARENDON PRESS, 1963, PP 253-96
   025,

SMITH BRUCE L
   SMITH BRUCE L
   COMMUNICATIONS RESEARCH ON NON-INDUSTRIAL COUNTRIES.
   PUBLIC OPINION QUARTERLY 16 WINTER 1952-1953 PP 527-538
   048,

SMITH E W
   SMITH E W
   AFRICAN IDEAS OF GOD.
   IN PETER J MCEWAN AND ROBERT B SUTCLIFFE (EDS), MODERN AFRICA,
   NEW YORK, THOMAS CROWELL, 1965, PP 6L74
   013,
   012,

   SMITH E W
   AFRICAN IDEAS OF GOD
   LONDON, EDINBURGH HOUSE PRESS, 1950
   012,013,

SMITH EDWIN W
   SMITH EDWIN W
   GREAT LION OF BECHUANALAND
   LONDON, INDEPENDENT PRESS, 1957
   031,102-02,

SMITH ELSON D
   ANSCHEL KURT R   BRANNON RUSSELL H   SMITH ELSON D
   AGRICULTURAL COOPERATIVES AND MARKETS IN DEVELOPING
   COUNTRIES.
   NEW YORK, PRAEGER PUBLISHERS, 1969
   070,

SMITH H F C
   SMITH H F C
   THE ISLAMIC REVOLUTIONS OF THE 19TH CENTURY.
   JOURNAL OF THE HISTORICAL SOCIETY OF NIGERIA 2 DECEMBER
   1961 PP 169-185
   024,

SMITH HADLEY E

SMITH HADLEY E   ED
READINGS ON ECONOMIC DEVELOPMENT AND ADMINISTRATION IN
TANZANIA.
EASTERN AFRICA, OXFORD UNIVERSITY PRESS, 1966
073,136-08,

SMITH HADLEY E
    SMITH HADLEY E   ED
    AGRICULTURAL DEVELOPMENT IN TANZANIA.
    LONDON,OXFORD UNIVERSITY PRESS,1965
    INSTITUTE OF PUBLIC ADMINISTRATION DAR-ES-SALAAM STUDY 2
    070,136-08,

SMITH K W
    SMITH K W
    THE FALL OF THE BAPEDI OF THE NORTH-EASTERN TRANSVAAL.
    JOURNAL OF AFRICAN HISTORY, X, 1, 1969, PP. 237-252.
    031,132-02,

SMITH M G
    KUPER LEO   SMITH M G   EDS
    PLURALISM IN AFRICA.
    BERKELEY AND LOS ANGELES, UNIVERSITY OF CALIFORNIA PRESS,
    1969
    006,007,016,057,

    SMITH M G
    GOVERNMENT IN ZAZZAU, 1800-1950.
    LONDON,OXFORD UNIVERSITY PRESS,1960
    024,128-01,

    SMITH M G
    SOCIAL AND CULTURAL PLURALISM.
    ANNALS OF THE NEW YORK ACADEMY OF SCIENCES 83 JANUARY 1960
    006,

    SMITH M G
    THE HAUSA--MARKETS IN A PEASANT ECONOMY.
    IN BOHANNAN AND DALTON (EDS), MARKETS IN AFRICA, DOUBLEDAY,
    1965.
    010,128-01,

    SMITH M G
    THE JIHAD OF SHEHU DAN FODIO - SOME PROBLEMS.
    IN LEWIS, ISLAM IN TROPICAL AFRICA, LONDON, OXFORD UNIVERSIT
    PRESS, 1966, P. 408-424
    024,

    SMITH M G
    CO-OPERATION IN HAUSA SOCIETY.
    INFORMATION VOL 11 1957 PP 2-20
    009,128-01,

    SMITH M G
    PRE-INDUSTRIAL STRATIFICATION SYSTEMS.
    IN NEIL J. SMELSER AND SEYMOUR LIPSET,EDS, SOCIAL
    STRUCTURE AND MOBILITY IN ECONOMIC DEVELOPMENT, CHICAGO,
    ALDINE PUBLISHING CO, 1966, PP 141-176
    098,

SMITH M G
THE HAUSA OF NORTHERN NIGERIA.
IN JAMES L GIBBS JR. (ED), PEOPLES OF AFRICA, NEW YORK, HOLT,
RINEHART AND WINSTON, 1965, PP. 119-156
128-01,

SMITH MARIAN W
   SMITH MARIAN W   ED
   THE ARTIST IN TRIBAL SOCIETY. PROCEEDINGS HELD AT THE
   ROYAL ANTHROPOLOGICAL INSTITUTE SYMPOSIUM ON THE ARTIST
   IN TRIBAL SOCIETY.
   NEW YORK, FREE PRESS, AND LONDON, ROUTLEDGE AND KEGAN PAUL,
   1961
   014,

SMITH MARY
   SMITH MARY
   BABA OF KARO--A WOMAN OF THE MOSLEM HAUSA.
   NEW YORK, PRAEGER, 1964
   008,128-01,

SMITH NOEL
   SMITH NOEL
   THE PRESBYTERIAN CHURCH OF GHANA 1835-1960--A YOUNGER CHURCH
   IN A CHANGING SOCIETY.
   GHANA, GHANA UNIVERSITIES PRESS, 1966
   050,114-03,

SMITH ROBERT
   AJAYI J F ADE   SMITH ROBERT
   YORUBA WARFARE IN THE 19TH CENTURY.
   CAMBRIDGE, ENGLAND, CAMBRIDGE UNIVERSITY PRESS, 1964
   026,128-02,

   SMITH ROBERT
   KINGDOMS OF THE YORUBA
   LONDON, METHUEN, 1969
   026,128-01,

SMOCK
   SMOCK AUDREY CHAPMAN
   THE N.C.N.C. AND ETHNIC UNIONS IN BIAFRA.
   THE JOURNAL OF MODERN AFRICAN STUDIES, 7, 1, 1969
   007,128-07,

SMOCK AUDREY
   SMOCK AUDREY   SMOCK DAVID
   ETHNICITY AND ATTITUDES TOWARD DEVELOPMENT IN EASTERN
   NIGERIA
   JOURNAL OF THE DEVELOPING AREAS 3 1969 PP 499-512
   074,

SMOCK DAVID
   SMOCK AUDREY   SMOCK DAVID
   ETHNICITY AND ATTITUDES TOWARD DEVELOPMENT IN EASTERN
   NIGERIA
   JOURNAL OF THE DEVELOPING AREAS 3 1969 PP 499-512
   074,

SMYKE RAYMOND

SMYKE RAYMOND
CHRISTIANITY IN AFRICA.
AFRICA REPORT, MAY 8, 1968
050,

SMYTHE HUGH H
    SMYTHE HUGH H   SMYTHE MABEL M
    BLACK AFRICA'S NEW POWER ELITE.
    SOUTH ATLANTIC QUARTERLY 59 WINTER 1960 PP 13-23
    044,

    SMYTHE HUGH H   SMYTHE MABEL M
    AFRICA'S NEW CLASS.
    QUEEN'S QUARTERLY 47 SUMMER 1960 PP 225-231
    044,

    SMYTHE HUGH H
    AFRICAN ELITE IN NIGERIA.
    IN AMSAC, AFRICA SEEN BY AMERICAN NEGROES, PARIS,
    PRESENCE AFRICAINE, 1958, PP 71-82
    044,128-04,

    SMYTHE HUGH H
    URBANIZATION IN NIGERIA.
    ANTHROPOLOGICAL QUARTERLY 33 JULY 1960 PP 143-148
    046,

SMYTHE MABEL M
    SMYTHE HUGH H   SMYTHE MABEL M
    BLACK AFRICA'S NEW POWER ELITE.
    SOUTH ATLANTIC QUARTERLY 59 WINTER 1960 PP 13-23
    044,

    SMYTHE HUGH H   SMYTHE MABEL M
    AFRICA'S NEW CLASS.
    QUEEN'S QUARTERLY 47 SUMMER 1960 PP 225-231
    044,

SNELL G S
    SNELL G S
    NANDI CUSTOMARY LAW.
    LONDON,MACMILLAN,1954
    066,

SNOW PETER G
    SNOW PETER G
    A SCALOGRAM ANALYSIS OF POLITICAL DEVELOPMENT.
    AMERICAN BEHAVIORAL SCIENTIST 9 MARCH 1966 PP 33-36
    098,

SNOWDEN
    SNOWDEN FRANCK M JR
    BLACKS IN ANTIQUITY--ETHIOPIANS IN THE GRECO-ROMAN
    EXPERIENCE.
    CAMBRIDGE, HARVARD UNIVERSITY PRESS, 1969
    020,027,

SNYDER EMILE
    SNYDER EMILE
    THE TEACHING OF MODERN AFRICAN LITERATURE WRITTEN IN A

WESTERN LANGUAGE.
IN PROCEEDINGS OF THE CONFERENCE ON AFRICAN LANGUAGES AND
LITERATURES, NORTHWESTERN UNIVERSITY, 1966, UNITED STATES
OFFICE OF EDUCATION NO. OE-6-14-018, PP 92-102
090,

SNYDER FRANCIS G
    SNYDER FRANCIS G
    POLITICAL IDEOLOGY AND PERCEPTIONS.
    IN ONE-PARTY GOVERNMENT IN MALI--TRANSITION TOWARD CONTROL
    NEW HAVEN, YALE UNIVERSITY PRESS, 1965
    060,

    SNYDER FRANCIS G
    THE POLITICAL THOUGHT OF MODIBO KEITA.
    JOURNAL OF MODERN AFRICAN STUDIES 5 MAY 1967 PP 79-106
    054,123-04,

    SNYDER FRANCIS G
    ONE-PARTY GOVERNMENT IN MALI-- TRANSITION TOWARD CONTROL.
    NEW HAVEN, YALE UNIVERSITY PRESS, 1965
    061,123-07,

    SNYDER FRANCIS G
    AN ERA ENDS IN MALI.
    AFRICA REPORT, MARCH/APRIL, 1969, PP. 16-53
    064,123-06,

SOCIETY OF AFRICAN
    SOCIETY OF AFRICAN CULTURE-PARIS
    COLLOQUIUM ON NEGRO ART.
    PARIS, PRESENCE AFRICAINE, 1968
    093,

SOFER CYRIL
    SOFER CYRIL   SOFER RHONA
    JINJA TRANSFORMED--A SOCIAL SURVEY OF A MULTI-RACIAL
    TOWNSHIP.
    EAST AFRICAN STUDIES NO. 4, KAMPALA, EAST AFRICAN INSTITUTE
    OF SOCIAL RESEARCH, 1955
    139-05,

    SOFER CYRIL   SOFER RHONA
    RECENT POPULATION GROWTH IN JINJA.
    UGANDA JOURNAL, 17, 1, 1953
    139-05,

SOFER RHONA
    SOFER CYRIL   SOFER RHONA
    JINJA TRANSFORMED--A SOCIAL SURVEY OF A MULTI-RACIAL
    TOWNSHIP.
    EAST AFRICAN STUDIES NO. 4, KAMPALA, EAST AFRICAN INSTITUTE
    OF SOCIAL RESEARCH, 1955
    139-05,

    SOFER CYRIL   SOFER RHONA
    RECENT POPULATION GROWTH IN JINJA.
    UGANDA JOURNAL, 17, 1, 1953
    139-05,

SOJA EDWARD
    SOJA EDWARD
    COMMUNICATIONS AND TERRITORIAL INTEGRATION IN EAST AFRICA-
    AN INTRODUCTION TO TRANSACTION FLOW ANALYSIS
    EAST LAKES GEOGRAPHER 4 1968 PP 39-57
    048,059,077,

SOJA EDWARD W
    SOJA EDWARD W
    TRANSACTION FLOWS AND NATIONAL UNITY--THE NIGERIAN CASE.
    IN CARTER, GWENDOLEN M. AND ANN PADEN (EDS) EXPANDING
    HORIZONS IN AFRICAN STUDIES, EVANSTON, NORTHWESTERN
    UNIVERSITY PRESS, 1969, PP. 321-328
    100,128-06,

    SOJA EDWARD W
    THE GEOGRAPHY OF MODERNIZATION IN KENYA.
    SYRACUSE, SYRACUSE UNIVERSITY PRESS, 1968
    038,047,048,117-03,

    SOJA EDWARD W
    RURAL-URBAN INTERACTION
    CANADIAN JOURNAL OF AFRICAN STUDIES 1 1969 PP 284-290
    047,

    SOJA EDWARD W
    SPECIAL GEOGRAPHY ISSUE
    AFRICAN URBAN NOTES 2 MAY 1967
    047,048,

SOLOMON LAURENCE
    SOLOMON LAURENCE
    THE ECONOMIC BACKGROUND TO THE REVIVAL OF AFRIKANER NATION-
    ALISM.
    IN JEFFREY BUTLER (ED), BOSTON UNIVERSITY PAPERS IN AFRICAN
    HISTORY VOL I, BOSTON, BOSTON UNIVERSITY PRESS,1964, PP 217-
    242
    089,132-06,

SOLOMON MARVIN D
    SOLOMON MARVIN D   D AZEVEDO   COMPS
    A GENERAL BIBLIOGRAPHY OF THE REPUBLIC OF LIBERIA.
    EVANSTON, NORTHWESTERN UNIVERSITY PRESS, 1962
    119-12,

SOMMER JOHN W
    SOMMER JOHN W
    BIBLIOGRAPHY OF AFRICAN GEOGRAPHY 1940-1964
    HANOVER, GEOGRAPHY PUBLICATIONS AT DARTMOUTH, NUMBER 3, 1965
    069,

SONNE CHRISTIAN R
    ERLICH ALEXANDER   SONNE CHRISTIAN R
    THE SOVIET UNION-- ECONOMIC ACTIVITY.
    IN Z BRZEZINSKI (ED), AFRICA AND THE COMMUNIST WORLD,
    STANFORD, CALIFORNIA, STANFORD UNIVERSITY PRESS, 1963,
    PP 49-83
    084,

SORDE MONIQUE

MILICENT ERNEST   SORDE MONIQUE
LEOPOLD SEDAR SENGHOR ET LA NAISSANCE DE L'AFRIQUE MODERNE
(LEOPOLD SEDAR SENGHOR AND THE BIRTH OF MODERN AFRICA).
PARIS, INTERNATIONAL UNIVERSITY BOOKSELLERS, INC., 1969
044,130-04,

SOUTHALL AIDAN
    SOUTHALL AIDAN   ED
    SOCIAL CHANGES IN MODERN AFRICA
    LONDON, OXFORD UNIVERSITY PRESS, 1961
    038,

    SOUTHALL AIDAN
    ALUR SOCIETY-- A STUDY IN PROCESSES AND TYPES OF
    DOMINATIONS.
    CAMBRIDGE, HEFFER, 1956
    009,

    PECKHAM ROBERT   RAGHEB ISIS   SOUTHALL AIDAN
    A BIBLIOGRAPHY ON ANTHROPOLOGY AND SOCIOLOGY IN UGANDA.
    NEW YORK, SYRACUSE UNIVERSITY PROGRAM OF EASTERN AFRICAN
    STUDIES, 1965
    139-12,

    SOUTHALL AIDAN
    A CRITIQUE OF THE TYPOLOGY OF STATES AND POLITICAL SYSTEMS.
    IN POLITICAL SYSTEMS AND THE DISTRIBUTION OF POWER, MICHAEL
    BANTON, ED, ASSOCIATION OF SOCIAL ANTHROPOLOGISTS MONOGRAPH
    NO 2, LONDON, TAVISTOCK PUBLICATIONS LTD, 1965, PP 113-140
    009,

    SOUTHALL AIDAN
    DETERMINANTS OF THE SOCIAL STRUCTURE OF AFRICAN URBAN
    POPULATIONS, WITH SPECIAL REFERENCE TO KAMPALA, (UGANDA)
    (1956).
    IN IMMANUEL WALLERSTEIN, SOCIAL CHANGE-- THE COLONIAL
    SITUATION, NEW YORK, WILEY, 1966, PP 321-339
    046,139-05,

    SOUTHALL AIDAN
    KAMPALA-MENGO.
    IN THE CITY IN MODERN AFRICA, HORACE MINER (ED), PRAEGER,
    1967
    139-05,

    SOUTHALL AIDAN
    SOME PROBLEMS OF STATISTICAL ANALYSIS IN COMMUNITY STUDIES,
    ILLUSTRATED FROM KAMPALA, UGANDA.
    IN SOCIAL IMPLICATIONS OF INDUSTRIALIZATION AND URBANIZATION
    IN AFRICA SOUTH OF THE SAHARA, PARIS, UNESCO, 1956
    139-05,

    SOUTHALL AIDAN
    TOWNSMEN IN THE MAKING--KAMPALA AND ITS SUBURBS.
    EAST AFRICAN STUDIES NO. 9, KAMPALA, EAST AFRICAN INSTITUTE
    OF SOCIAL RESEARCH, 1957
    139-05,

    SOUTHALL AIDAN
    THE CONCEPT OF ELITES AND THEIR FORMATION IN UGANDA.

IN LLOYD, THE NEW ELITES OF TROPICAL AFRICA, LONDON, OXFORD
UNIVERSITY PRESS, 1966, P. 342-366
044,139-04,

SOUTHWALD MARTIN
   SOUTHWALD MARTIN
   THE GANDA OF UGANDA.
   IN JAMES L. GIBBS JR. (ED), PEOPLES OF AFRICA, NEW YORK,
   HOLT, RINEHART AND WINSTON, 1965, PP. 81-118
   139-01,

SOW ALFA IBRAHIM
   SOW ALFA IBRAHIM
   CHRONIQUES ET RECITS DU FOUTA DJALON (CHRONICLES AND
   RECITATIONS OF FUTA JALLON).
   PARIS, KLINCKSIECK, NEW YORK, INTERNATIONAL UNIVERSITY BOOK-
   SELLERS, 1968
   012,115-01,

   SOW ALFA IBRAHIM
   LA FEMME, LA VACHE, LA FOI--ECRIVAINS ET POETES DU FOUTA-
   DJALON.
   PARIS, JULLIARD, 1966
   115-01,

SOWANDE FELA
   SOWANDE FELA
   OYIGIYIGI-INTRODUCTION,THEME AND VARIATIONS ON A YORUBA FOLK
   THEME FOR ORGAN
   NEW YORK,RICORDI,1958
   015,093,

SOYINKA WOLE
   SOYINKA WOLE
   THE SWAMP DWELLERS.
   IN FIVE PLAYS,LONDON,OXFORD UNIVERSITY PRESS,1964
   090,128-10,

   SOYINKA WOLE
   DANCE OF THE FORESTS.
   LONDON,OXFORD UNIVERSITY PRESS,1963
   013,090,

   SOYINKA WOLE
   KONGI S HARVEST.
   LONDON,OXFORD UNIVERSITY PRESS,1967
   090,128-10,

   SOYINKA WOLE
   THREE PLAYS.
   IBADAN, MBARI PUBLISHERS, 1963
   090,128-10,

   SOYINKA WOLE
   THE INTERPRETERS.
   LONDON, HEINEMANN EDUCATIONAL BOOKS 1965
   090,128-10,

   SOYINKA WOLE   FAGUNWA D O
   THE FOREST OF A THOUSAND DAEMONS.

NEW YORK, HUMANITIES PRESS, INC., 1968
090,128-10,

SPARK
    SPARK
    SOME ESSENTIAL FEATURES OF NKRUMAISM.
    NEW YORK, INTERNATIONAL PUBLISHERS, 1965
    THE SPARK-JOURNAL OF THE CONVENTION PEOPLE'S PARTY, GHANA
    BY THE EDITORS
    060,114-04,

    SPARK
    SOME ESSENTIAL FEATURES OF NKRUMAISM.
    NEW YORK, INTERNATIONAL PUBLISHERS, 1965
    060,

SPEKE J H
    SPEKE J H
    JOURNAL OF DISCOVERY OF THE SOURCE OF THE NILE.
    LONDON, WILLIAM BLACKWOOD AND SONS, 1863
    027,

SPENCE JOHN EDWARD
    SPENCE JOHN EDWARD
    LESOTHO--THE POLITICS OF DEPENDENCE.
    LONDON, OXFORD UNIVERSITY PRESS, 1968
    118-09,

SPENCER JOHN
    SPENCER JOHN
    AFRICA AT THE U N-- SOME OBSERVATIONS.
    IN WILLIAM J HANNA (ED), INDEPENDENT BLACK AFRICA, CHICAGO,
    RAND MCNALLY, 1964, PP 542-544
    081,

    SPENCER JOHN   ED
    LANGUAGE IN AFRICA.
    LONDON, CAMBRIDGE UNIVERSITY PRESS, 1963
    011,049,

SPENGLER J J
    SPENGLER J J
    ECONOMIC DEVELOPMENT -- POLITICAL PRECONDITIONS AND
    POLITICAL CONSEQUENCES CHAPTER 7.
    IN JASON L FINKLE AND RICHARD W GABLE, POLITICAL
    DEVELOPMENT AND SOCIAL CHANGE, NEW YORK, JOHN WILEY, 1966
    074,

SPIRO HERBERT J
    SPIRO HERBERT J
    THE PRIMACY OF POLITICAL DEVELOPMENT.
    IN AFRICA THE PRIMACY OF POLITICS,
    NEW YORK, RANDOM HOUSE, 1966, PP 150-169
    061,

    SPIRO HERBERT J
    NEW CONSTITUTIONAL FORMS IN AFRICA.
    WORLD POLITICS 8 1 OCTOBER 1960 PP 69 FF
    068,

SPIRO HERBERT J   ED
AFRICA, THE PRIMACY OF POLITICS.
NEW YORK, RANDOM HOUSE, 1966
061,

SPIRO HERBERT J
    SPIRO HERBERT J   ED
    PATTERNS OF AFRICAN DEVELOPMENT-- FIVE COMPARISONS.
    ENGLEWOOD CLIFFS, NEW JERSEY, PRENTICE-HALL (SPECTRUM), 1967
    061,

    SPIRO HERBERT J
    THE FEDERATION OF RHODESIA AND NYASALAND.
    IN THOMAS FRANCK (ED), WHY FEDERATIONS FAIL, NEW YORK, NEW
    YORK UNIVERSITY PRESS, 1968, PP. 37-90
    078,122-06,145-06,

    SPIRO HERBERT J
    RHODESIA AND NYASALAND.
    IN G.M. CARTER (ED) FIVE AFRICAN STATES--RESPONSES TO
    DIVERSITY, ITHACA, CORNELL UNIVERSITY PRESS, 1963
    122-07,

STABLER ERNEST
    STABLER ERNEST
    EDUCATION SINCE UHURU-- THE SCHOOLS OF KENYA.
    MIDDLETOWN CONN WESLEYAN UNIVERSITY PRESS 1969
    042,117-04,

STAMP L D
    STAMP L D
    AFRICA-A STUDY IN TROPICAL DEVELOPMENT.
    NEW YORK, JOHN WILEY AND SONS, 1953
    069,

STAMPP KENNETH
    STAMPP KENNETH
    THE PECULIAR INSTITUTION.
    NEW YORK, ALFRED A KNOPF, 1956
    028,030,

STANDENRAUS P J
    STANDENRAUS P J
    THE AFRICAN COLONIZATION MOVEMENT 1816-1865.
    NEW YORK, COLUMBIA UNIVERSITY PRESS, 1961
    029,

STANLEY H M
    STANLEY H M
    THROUGH THE DARK CONTINENT.
    LONDON, 1878, TWO VOLUMES
    027,

STARK RODNEY
    GLOCK CHARLES Y   STARK RODNEY
    RELIGION AND SOCIETY IN TENSION.
    CHICAGO, RAND MCNALLY, 1965
    013,

STARR ISADORE

FRANKLIN JOHN H   STARR ISADORE
THE NEGRO IN TWENTIETH CENTURY AMERICA.
NEW YORK, VINTAGE BOOKS, 1967
030.

STAUDENRAUS P J
   STAUDENRAUS P J
   THE AFRICAN COLONIZATION MOVEMENT.1816-1865
   NEW YORK, COLUMBIA UNIVERSITY PRESS, 1961
   029,119-02.

STEEL RONALD
   STEEL RONALD
   LETTER FROM OAKLAND. THE PANTHERS.
   THE NEW YORK REVIEW OF BOOKS,VOL XIII, NO. 4, SEPTEMBER 11,
   1969, PP. 14-25
   095.

STEEL R W
   STEEL R W
   LAND AND POPULATION IN BRITISH TROPICAL AFRICA.
   GEOGRAPHY, JOURNAL OF THE GEOGRAPHICAL ASSOCIATION
   SHEFFIELD 40 1955 PP 1-17
   069.

STEINBERG E B
   HAEFELE E T   STEINBERG E B
   GOVERNMENT CONTROLS ON TRANSPORT-AN AFRICAN CASE (ZAMBIA)
   WASHINGTON, BROOKINGS INSTITUTE, 1965
   048,142-08.

STENNING DERRICK J
   STENNING DERRICK J
   CATTLE VALUES AND ISLAMIC VALUES IN A PASTORAL POPULATION.
   IN LEWIS, ISLAM IN TROPICAL AFRICA, LONDON, OXFORD UNIVERSIT
   PRESS, 1966, P. 387-400
   013.

   STENNING DERRICK J
   THE PASTORAL FULANI OF NORTHERN NIGERIA.
   IN JAMES L. GIBBS (ED). PEOPLES OF AFRICA, NEW YORK, HOLT
   RINEHART AND WINSTON, 1965 PP. 361-402
   128-01.

   STENNING DERRICK J
   SAVANNAH NOMADS--A STUDY OF THE WODAABE PASTORAL FULANI OF
   WESTERN BORNU PROVINCE NORTHERN REGION NIGERIA.
   LONDON, OXFORD UNIVERSITY PRESS, 1959
   128-01.

STEVENS RICHARD P
   STEVENS RICHARD P
   LESOTHO BOTSWANA AND SWAZILAND.
   LONDON, PALL MALL PRESS, 1967
   102-11, 118-11, 135-11.

STEVENSON R C
   STEVENSON R C
   SOME ASPECTS OF THE SPREAD OF ISLAM IN THE NUBA MOUNTAINS.
   IN LEWIS, ISLAM IN TROPICAL AFRICA, LONDON, OXFORD UNIVERSIT

PRESS, 1966, P. 208-232
134-03,

STEVENSON ROBERT F
STEVENSON ROBERT F
POPULATION AND POLITICAL SYSTEMS IN TROPICAL AFRICA.
NEW YORK, COLUMBIA UNIVERSITY PRESS, 1968
009,

STEWART I G
STEWART I G   ORD H W   EDS
AFRICAN PRIMARY PRODUCTS AND INTERNATIONAL TRADE.
EDINBURGH, UNIVERSITY PRESS, 1965
069, 073,

STOKES E
STOKES E   BROWN RICHARD   EDS
THE ZAMBESIAN PAST-STUDIES IN CENTRAL AFRICAN HISTORY
MANCHESTER, MANCHESTER UNIVERSITY PRESS, 1966
025, 122-02, 142-02, 145-02,

STOKKE
STOKKE BAARD RICHARD
SOVIET AND EASTERN EUROPEAN TRADE AND AID IN AFRICA.
NEW YORK, PRAEGER, 1967
084,

STOLPER W
STOLPER W
PLANNING WITHOUT FACTS.
CAMBRIDGE, HARVARD UNIVERSITY PRESS, 1966
072, 128-08,

STRANDES J
STRANDES J
THE PORTUGESE PERIOD IN EAST AFRICA
TRANSACTIONS OF THE KENYA HISTORICAL SOCIETY VOLUME 11
NAIROBI, EAST AFRICAN LITERATURE BUREAU, 1961
027,

STRICKLAND J T
DADZIE E W   STRICKLAND J T
DIRECTORY OF ARCHIVES, LIBRARIES AND SCHOOLS OF
LIBRARIANSHIP IN AFRICA.
UNESCO , 1965
098, 099,

STUART JAMES
STUART JAMES   ED
IZIBONGO, ZULU PRAISE-POEMS.
OXFORD, CLARENDON PRESS, 1968
012, 132-01,

STUCKEY STERLING
STUCKEY STERLING
AFRICAN AND AFRO-AMERICAN RELATIONSHIPS--RESEARCH POSSIBIL-
ITIES.
IN CARTER, GWENDOLEN M. AND ANN PADEN (EDS), EXPANDING
HORIZONS IN AFRICAN STUDIES, EVANSTON, NORTHWESTERN
UNIVERSITY PRESS, 1969, PP. 291-302

030,094,100,

STULTZ NEWELL M
    CARTER GWENDOLEN M   KARIS THOMAS   STULTZ NEWELL M
    SOUTH AFRICA'S TRANSKEI-- THE POLITICS OF DOMESTIC COLONIAL-
    IALISM.
    EVANSTON, NORTHWESTERN UNIVERSITY PRESS, 1967 (LONDON,
    HEINEMANN EDUCATIONAL BOOKS)
    089,132-06,

    STULTZ NEWELL M
    THE POLITICS OF SECURITY-SOUTH AFRICA UNDER VERWOERD 1961-6
    JOURNAL OF MODERN AFRICAN STUDIES 7 1969 PP 3-20
    089,132-07,

SULLIVAN CAPT G L
    SULLIVAN CAPT G L
    DHOW CHASING IN ZANZIBAR WATERS (1873).
    NEW YORK, HUMANITIES PRESS, INC., 1967 (NEW INTRODUCTION)
    028,136-02,

SULLIVAN WALTER
    SULLIVAN WALTER
    A FORCE THAT PUSHES CONTINENTS APART.
    NEW YORK TIMES, JULY 9, 1967
    017,

SUMMERS ROGER
    SUMMERS ROGER
    ZIMBABWE-- A RHODESIAN MYSTERY.
    CAPE TOWN, THOMAS NELSON AND SONS, 1963
    025,145-02,

SUNDIATA I K
    SUNDIATA I K
    THE MORES OF EXPANSION--1837-1914.
    PRESENCE AFRICAINE, 2ND QUARTER, 1969, NO. 70, P. 46-65
    033,

SUNDKLER BENGT
    SUNDKLER BENGT
    BANTU PROPHETS IN SOUTH AFRICA.
    LONDON, OXFORD UNIVERSITY PRESS (2ND ED), 1961
    051,132-03,

SURET-CANALE J
    NIANE DJIBRIL T   SURET-CANALE J
    HISTOIRE DE L'AFRIQUE OCCIDENTALE.
    PARIS, PRESENCE AFRICAINE, 1962
    115-02,

SUTCLIFFE ROBERT B
    MCEWAN PETER J   SUTCLIFFE ROBERT B   EDS
    MODERN AFRICA.
    NEW YORK THOMAS CROWELL 1965
    002,076,097,

SUTTON FRANCIS X
    SUTTON FRANCIS X
    AUTHORITY AND AUTHORITARIANISM IN THE NEW AFRICA.

IN WILLIAM J HANNA (ED), INDEPENDENT BLACK AFRICA, CHICAGO,
RAND MCNALLY, 1964, PP 407-418
061,

SUTTON FRANCIS X
    SUTTON FRANCIS X
    ANALIZING SOCIAL SYSTEMS CHAPTER 1.
    IN JASON L FINKLE AND RICHARD W GABLE, POLITICAL
    DEVELOPMENT AND SOCIAL CHANGE, NEW YORK, JOHN WILEY, 1966
    098,

SUTTON J E G
    SUTTON J E G
    THE EAST AFRICAN COAST-- AN HISTORICAL AND ARCHAEOLOGICAL
    REVIEW.
    NAIROBI, EAST AFRICAN PUBLISHING HOUSE, 1966
    023,

SVANIDZE I A
    SVANIDZE I A
    THE AFRICAN STRUGGLE FOR AGRICULTURAL PRODUCTIVITY.
    THE JOURNAL OF MODERN AFRICAN STUDIES, VOL. 6,1968, PP. 311-
    328
    070,

SWARTZ MARC
    SWARTZ MARC   TURNER VICTOR W   TUDEN ARTHUR
    POLITICAL ANTHROPOLOGY
    CHICAGO,ALDINE, 1966
    009,

    SWARTZ MARC   ED
    LOCAL-LEVEL POLITICS
    CHICAGO, ALDINE, 1968
    009,047,

SWEEN JOYCE
    CLIGNET REMI   SWEEN JOYCE
    SOCIAL CHANGE AND TYPE OF MARRIAGE.
    AMERICAN JOURNAL OF SOCIOLOGY, VOL. 74, NO. 1, JULY 1969,
    PP. 123-145
    046,

SWEENEY JAMES J
    RADIN PAUL   SWEENEY JAMES J
    AFRICAN FOLKTALES AND SCULPTURE.
    PRINCETON, NEW JERSEY, PRINCETON UNIVERSITY PRESS, 1969
    012,014,

SY CHEIKH TIDIANE
    SY CHEIKH TIDIANE
    LA CONFRERIE SENEGALAISE DES MOURIDES (THE SENEGAL
    BROTHERHOOD OF MOURIDES).
    PARIS, PRESENCE AFRICAINE, 1969
    052,130-03,

SYAD WILLIAM
    SYAD WILLIAM
    SHAMSINE, POEMES--PREFACE BY LEOPOLD SEDAR SENGHOR.
    PARIS, PRESENCE AFRICAINE, 1959

133-10,

SYMMONS-SYMONOLEWICZ
   SYMMONS-SYMONOLEWICZ K
   NATIONALISM MOVEMENTS-- AN ATTEMPT AT A COMPARATIVE
   TYPOLOGY.
   COMPARATIVE STUDIES IN SOCIETY AND HISTORY 7 JANUARY 1965
   PP 221-230
   054,

SZENTES TAMAS
   SZENTES TAMAS
   ECONOMIC AND SOCIAL DISINTEGRATION AND SOME QUESTIONS OF
   SELF-HELP IN THE DEVELOPING COUNTRIES.
   BUDAPEST, STUDIES ON DEVELOPING COUNTRIES SERIES, 1967, 23P.
   058,

SZWED JOHN F
   WHITTEN NORMAN E   SZWED JOHN F   EDS
   AFRO-AMERICAN ANTHROPOLOGY
   NEW YORK,THE FREE PRESS,1970
   030,

T

TAAFFE E J
   TAAFFE E J   MORRILL R L   GOULD PETER
   TRANSPORT EXPANSION IN UNDERDEVELOPED COUNTRIES--A
   COMPARATIVE ANALYSIS.
   GEOGRAPHICAL REVIEW 53 OCTOBER 1963 PP 503-529
   048,

TAIT D
   MIDDLETON JOHN   TAIT D   EDS
   TRIBES WITHOUT RULERS.
   LONDON,ROUTLEDGE AND   KEGAN PAUL,1958
   009,

TAIWO ODELELE
   TAIWO ODELELE
   INTRODUCTION TO WEST AFRICAN LITERATURE.
   LONDON,NELSON,1967
   090,

TALBOT PERCY A
   TALBOT PERCY A
   THE PEOPLES OF SOUTHERN NIGERIA.
   LONDON, CASS, 1966
   128-01,

TALMON JACOB L
   TALMON JACOB L
   MESSIANIC NATIONALISM PT 2.
   IN POLITICAL MESSIANISM, NEW YORK. PRAEGER, 1960
   054,

TAMUNO TEKENA N
  TAMUNO TEKENA N
  NIGERIA AND ELECTIVE REPRESENTATION 1923-1947.
  LONDON, HEINEMANN, 1966
  056,063,128-07,

TANGRI SHANTI
  TANGRI SHANTI
  URBANIZATION, POLITICAL STABILITY AND ECONOMIC GROWTH
  CHAPTER 9.
  IN JASON L FINKLE AND RICHARD W GABLE, POLITICAL
  DEVELOPMENT AND SOCIAL CHANGE, NEW YORK, JOHN WILEY, 1966
  047,074,

TANNENBAUM FRANK
  TANNENBAUM FRANK
  SLAVE AND CITIZEN THE NEGRO IN THE AMERICAS.
  NEW YORK, ALFRED A KNOPF, 1947
  030,

TANZANIA
  TANZANIA AFRICAN NATIONAL UNION
  THE ARUSHA DECLARATION AND TANU S POLICY ON SOCIALISM AND
  SELF-RELIANCE.
  DAR ES-SALAAM, GOVERNMENT PRINTER, 1967
  058,060,070,073,136-04,

  GOVERNMENT OF TANZANIA
  REPORT OF THE PRESIDENTIAL COMMISSION ON THE ESTABLISHMENT
  OF A DEMOCRATIC ONE-PARTY STATE.
  DAR ES SALAAM, 1965
  061,136-04,

TAPIERO NORBERT
  TAPIERO NORBERT
  EVOLVING SOCIAL PATTERNS
  IN KRITZECK AND LEWIS, PP 54-87
  021,

TARDITS M CLAUDE
  TARDITS M CLAUDE
  THE NOTION OF THE ELITE AND THE URBAN SOCIAL SURVEY
  IN AFRICA.
  INTERNATIONAL SOCIAL SCIENCE BULLETIN 8 1956 PP 492-495
  043,

  TARDITS M CLAUDE
  PARENTE ET CLASSE SOCIALE A PORTO-NOVO, DAHOMEY.
  IN LLOYD, THE NEW ELITES OF TROPICAL AFRICA, LONDON, OXFORD
  UNIVERSITY PRESS, 1966, P. 184-198
  109-04,

TATHAM M A
  BROOKFIELD H C   TATHAM M A
  THE DISTRIBUTION OF RACIAL GROUPS IN DURBAN--THE BACKGROUND
  OF APARTHEID IN A SOUTH AFRICAN CITY.
  GEOGRAPHICAL REVIEW 47 JANUARY 1957 PP 44-65
  089,132-05,

TAYLOR

TAYLOR JAMES C   1
THE POLITICAL DEVELOPMENT OF TANGANYIKA.
LONDON, OXFORD UNIVERSITY PRESS; AND STANFORD, STANFORD
UNIVERSITY PRESS, 1963
136-07.

TAYLOR A
    TAYLOR A   ED
    EDUCATIONAL AND OCCUPATIONAL SELECTION IN WEST AFRICA.
    LONDON, OXFORD UNIVERSITY PRESS, 1962
    043.

TAYLOR F W
    TAYLOR F W
    A PRACTICAL HAUSA GRAMMAR.
    LONDON, OXFORD UNIVERSITY PRESS, 1959
    011,128-01.

TAYLOR J V
    TAYLOR J V
    CHRISTIANITY AND POLITICS IN AFRICA
    LONDON, PENGUIN BOOKS, 1957
    050.

TAYLOR JOHN
    TAYLOR JOHN   LEHMANN D A
    CHRISTIANS OF THE COPPERBELT-- THE GROWTH OF CHURCH IN
    NORTHERN RHODESIA.
    LONDON, SUDAN CHRISTIAN MISSION PRESS, 1961
    050,142-03.

TAYLOR MILTON
    TAYLOR MILTON   ED
    TAXATION FOR AFRICAN ECONOMIC DEVELOPMENT.
    NEW YORK, AFRICANA PUBLISHING CORPORATION, 1970
    073.

TCHICAYA
    TCHICAYA U TAM'SI G
    EPITOME--PREFACE DE L S SENGHOR.
    HONFLEU, PIERRE JEAN OSWALD, NOUVELLE EDITION. 1968
    107-10.

    TCHICAYA U TAM'SI G
    FEU DE BROUSSE.
    PARIS, CARACTERES, 1956 NEW EDITION BY PIERRE JEAN OSWALD
    107-10.

    TCHICAYA U TAM'SI G
    LE MAUVIS SANG.
    PARIS, CARACTERES, 1956 NEW EDITION BY PIERRE JEAN OSWALD

    107-10.

    TCHICAYA U TAM'SI G
    LE VENTRE.
    PARIS, PRESENCE AFRICAINE, 1964
    107-10.

    TCHICAYA U TAM'SI G

EPITOME.
TUNIS, SOCIETE NATIONALE D'EDITION ET DE DIFFUSION, 1962
HONFLEU, PIERRE JEAN OSWALD, NEW EDITION, 1968
107-10,

TCHICAYA
TCHICAYA U TAM'SI G
A TRICHE COEUR.
PARIS, ED. HAUTE-FEUILLE, 1958; NEW EDITION IN 1968 BY
PIERRE JEAN OSWALD
107-10,

TCHICAYA U TAM'SI G
L'ARC MUSICAL.
HONFLEUR, PIERRE JEAN OSWALD, FORTHCOMING
107-10,

TCHICAYA U TAM'SI G
TRESOR AFRICAIN (ANTHOLOGIE DE LEGENDES AFRICAINES).
PARIS, SEGHERS, FORTHCOMING
107-10,

TELLI DIALLO
TELLI DIALLO
THE ORGANIZATION OF AFRICAN UNITY IN HISTORICAL PERSPEC-
TIVES.
AFRICAN FORUM I 2 1965 PP 7-27
079,080,

TEMPELS RES PLACID
TEMPELS RES PLACID   TRANSLATED BY   KING COLIN
LA PHILOSOPHIE BANTOUE (BANTU PHILOSOPHY).
PARIS, PRESENCE AFRICAINE, 2ND ED., 1961
013,

TEMPELS REV PLACID
TEMPELS REV PLACID
L'HOMME BANTOU ET LE CHRIST (THE BANTU MAN AND CHRIST).
IN COLLOQUE SUR LES RELIGIONS, ABIDJAN, APRIL, 1961, PARIS,
PRESENCE AFRICAINE, 1962, PP 219-224
050,

TEMPLE P H
TEMPLE P H
KAMPALA--INFLUENCES UPON ITS GROWTH AND DEVELOPMENT.
EAST AFRICAN, INSTITUTE OF SOCIAL RESEARCH CONFERENCE PAPER,
JUNE, 1963
139-05,

TEMU A J
KIMAMBO ISARIA N   TEMU A J   EDS
A HISTORY OF TANZANIA
NAIROBI, EAST AFRICAN PUBLISHING HOUSE, 1969
136-02,

TERRASSE H
TERRASSE H
LA MASQUEE AL-QUARADUIYIR A FES (THE QUADIRIYYA MOSQUE AT
FEZ).
PARIS, KLINCKSIECK, 1969

092,126-01,

TEVOEDJRE ALBERT
    TEVOEDJRE ALBERT
    CONTRIBUTION A UNE SYNTHESE SUR LE PROBLEME DE LA FORMATION
    DES CADRES AFRICAINS EN VUE DE LA CROISSANCE ECONOMIQUE.
    PARIS. DILOUTREMER, 1965
    109-04,

    TEVOEDJRE ALBERT
    L'AFRIQUE REVOLTEE.
    PARIS, PRESENCE AFRICAINE, 1958
    109-04,

THABIT T H
    THABIT T H
    INTERNATIONAL RELATIONS OF THE SUDAN IN NAPATAN TIMES.
    SUDAN NOTES AND RECORDS 40 1959 PP 19-22
    020,

THEOBALD A B
    THEOBALD A B
    THE MAHDIYA-- A HISTORY OF THE ANGLO-EGYPTIAN SUDAN 1881-
    1899.
    LONDON,LONGMANS,1951
    034,052,134-02,

THEODORSON GEORGE
    THEODORSON GEORGE
    ACCEPTANCE OF INDUSTRIALIZATION AND ITS ATTENDANT
    CONSEQUENCES FOR THE SOCIAL PATTERNS OF NON-WESTERN
    SOCIETIES CHAPTER 9.
    IN JASON L FINKLE AND RICHARD W GABLE, POLITICAL
    DEVELOPMENT AND SOCIAL CHANGE, NEW YORK, JOHN WILEY, 1966
    071,

THEROUX PAUL
    THEROUX PAUL
    HATING THE ASIANS
    TRANSITION 7 1967 PP 46-51
    085,

THEUWS T
    MULAGO VINCENT   THEUWS T
    AUTOUR DU MOUVEMENT DE LA JAMAA.
    LEOPOLDVILLE, CENTRE D'ETUDES PASTORALES, 1960
    108-03,

THIAM DOUDOU
    THIAM DOUDOU
    THE FOREIGN POLICY OF AFRICAN STATES.
    NEW YORK, PRAEGER, 1965
    081,130-09,

    THIAM DOUDOU
    LE NATIONALISME (NATIONALISM) CHP 1.
    IN LA POLITIQUE ETRANGER DES ETATS AFRICAINES, PRESSES
    UNIVERSITAIRES DE FRANCE, PARIS, 1963
    054,

THIAM DOUDOU
LA PORTEE DE LA CITOYENNETE FRANCAISE DANS LES TERRITOIRES
OUTRE-MER.
PARIS, ED. AFRICAINES, 1953
130-04,

THOMAS B E
    THOMAS B E
    MODERN TRANS-SAHARAN ROUTES.
    GEOGRAPHICAL REVIEW 42 APRIL 1952 PP 267-282
    048,

    THOMAS B E
    RAILWAYS AND PORTS IN FRENCH WEST AFRICA.
    ECONOMIC GEOGRAPHY 33 NO 1 JANUARY 1957 PP 1-15
    048,

    THOMAS B E
    TRANSPORTATION AND PHYSICAL GEOGRAPHY IN WEST AFRICA.
    LOS ANGELES,NATIONAL ACADEMY OF SCIENCES,NATIONAL RESEARCH
    COUNCIL,1960
    048,

    THOMAS B E
    THE LOCATION AND NATURE OF WEST AFRICAN CITIES CHAPTER 2.
    IN HILDA KUPER (ED),URBANIZATION AND MIGRATION IN WEST
    AFRICA,BERKELEY,UNIVERSITY OF CALIFORNIA PRESS,1965
    045,

    THOMAS B E
    TRADE ROUTES OF ALGERIA AND THE SAHARA.
    BERKELEY,UNIVERSITY OF CALIFORNIA PRESS,1957
    048,101-08,

    THOMAS B E
    GEOGRAPHY.
    IN ROBERT A LYSTAD (ED), THE AFRICAN WORLD, NEW YORK,
    PRAEGER, 1966, PP 245-270
    100,

THOMAS L V
    THOMAS L V
    THE PRINCIPAL THEMES OF NEGRITUDE.
    IN ALBERT BERRIAN AND RICHARD LONG (EDS), NEGRITUDE--
    ESSAYS AND STUDIES, HAMPTON, VIRGINIA, HAMPTON INSTITUTE
    PRESS, 1967, PP 39-47
    090,

    THOMAS L V
    THE STUDY OF DEATH IN NEGRO AFRICA.
    IN LALAGE BOWN AND MICHAEL CROWDER (EDS.), PROCEEDINGS OF
    THE FIRST INTERNATIONAL CONGRESS OF AFRICANISTS, ACCRA,
    1962, LONDON, LONGMANS, 1964, PP 146-168
    013,

    THOMAS L V
    ETAT ACTUEL ET AVENIR DE L'ANIMISME (THE ACTUAL STATE AND
    FUTURE OF ANIMISM).
    IN COLLOQUE SUR LES RELIGIONS, ABIDJAN, 5-12 APRIL, 1961,
    PARIS PRESENCE AFRICAINE, 1962, PP 59-70

013,

THOMPSON B W
    THOMPSON B W
    CLIMATE OF AFRICA.
    OXFORD, OXFORD UNIVERSITY PRESS, 1965
    069,

THOMPSON LEONARD
    WILSON MONICA   THOMPSON LEONARD   EDS
    THE OXFORD HISTORY OF SOUTH AFRICA. VOL I — SOUTH AFRICA
    TO 1870
    LONDON, OXFORD UNIVERSITY PRESS, 1970
    031,032,132-02,

    THOMPSON LEONARD   ED
    AFRICAN SOCIETIES IN SOUTHERN AFRICA.
    NEW YORK, OXFORD UNIVERSITY PRESS, 1970
    031,132-01,

    THOMPSON LEONARD
    THE UNIFICATION OF SOUTH AFRICA 1902-1910
    OXFORD, CLARENDON PRESS, 1960
    032,

THOMPSON V BAKPETU
    THOMPSON V BAKPETU
    AFRICA AND UNITY--THE EVOLUTION OF PAN-AFRICANISM.
    LONDON, INTERNATIONAL UNIVERSITY BOOKSELLERS, INC., 1969
    079,

THOMPSON VIRGINIA
    ALBINO RONALD C   THOMPSON VIRGINIA
    THE EFFECTS OF SUDDEN WEANING ON ZULU CHILDREN.
    BRITISH JOURNAL OF MEDICAL PSYCHOLOGY 29 1956 PP 177-210
    040,

    THOMPSON VIRGINIA   ADLOFF RICHARD
    DJIBOUTI AND THE HORN OF AFRICA.
    STANFORD, STANFORD UNIVERSITY PRESS, 1968
    087,133-09,143-11,

    THOMPSON VIRGINIA   ADLOFF RICHARD
    THE EMERGING STATES OF FRENCH EQUATORIAL AFRICA.
    STANFORD, STANFORD UNIVERSITY PRESS, 1960
    105-11,107-11,112-11,106-11,

    THOMPSON VIRGINIA   ADLOFF RICHARD
    CHAD.
    IN V. THOMPSON AND R. ADLOFF, THE EMERGING STATES OF FRENCH
    EQUATORIAL AFRICA, STANFORD, STANFORD UNIVERSITY PRESS, 1960
    106-11,

    THOMPSON VIRGINIA   ADLOFF RICHARD
    CONGO-BRAZZAVILLE.
    IN V. THOMPSON AND R. ADLOFF, THE EMERGING STATES OF FRENCH
    EQUATORIAL AFRICA, STANFORD, STANFORD UNIVERSITY PRESS, 1960
    107-11,

    THOMPSON VIRGINIA

DAHOMEY.
IN G.M. CARTER (ED), FIVE AFRICAN STATES--RESPONSES TO
DIVERSITY, ITHACA, CORNELL UNIVERSITY PRESS, 1963
109-07,

THOMPSON VIRGINIA
THOMPSON VIRGINIA
IVORY COAST.
IN G. M. CARTER (ED), AFRICAN ONE-PARTY STATES, ITHACA,
CORNELL UNIVERSITY PRESS, 1962
116-07,

THOMPSON VIRGINIA   ADLOFF RICHARD
THE MALAGASY REPUBLIC--MADAGASCAR TODAY.
STANFORD, STANFORD UNIVERSITY PRESS, 1965
121-11,

THOMPSON VIRGINIA
NIGER.
IN G.M. CARTER (ED), NATIONAL UNITY AND REGIONALISM IN EIGHT
AFRICAN STATES, ITHACA, CORNELL UNIVERSITY PRESS, 1966
127-06,

THOMPSON W SCOTT
THOMPSON W SCOTT
GHANA'S FOREIGN POLICY,1957-1966- DIPLOMACY,IDEOLOGY AND THE
NEW STATE
PRINCETON,PRINCETON UNIVERSITY PRESS,1969
060,082,083,084,085,114-09,

TIDJANI A S
TIDJANI A S
NOTES SUR LE MARIAGE AU DAHOMEY.
PORTO-NOVO, IFAN-DAHOMEY, 1951
109-01,

TIMOTHY BANKHOLE
TIMOTHY BANKHOLE
KWAME NKRUMAH-- HIS RISE TO POWER.
LONDON, ALLEN AND UNWIN, 1963
060,114-03,

TITMUSS RICHARD M
TITMUSS RICHARD M   ABEL-SMITH B
SOCIAL AND POPULATION GROWTH IN MAURITIUS
LONDON,METHUEN,1961,REPORT TO THE GOVERNMENT OF MAURITIUS,
REPRINTED 1968
125-03,

TODD H M
TODD H M
AFRICAN MISSION-A HISTORICAL STUDY OF THE SOCIETY OF AFRICAN
MISSIONS
LONDON,BURNS AND GATES,1962
050,

TOE SYLVAIN
TOE SYLVAIN   GUILHEM MARCEL
HAUTE-VOLTA--RECITS HISTORIQUES--COURS ELEMENTAIRE.
PARIS, LIGEL, 1964

141-02,

TOE SYLVAIN
    TOE SYLVAIN   GUILHEM MARCEL   HEBERT JEAN
    HISTOIRE DE LA HAUTE-VOLTA.
    PARIS, L'AFRIQUE-LE MONDE, COURS MOYEN, LIGEL, 1964
    141-02,

TORDOFF WILLIAM
    TORDOFF WILLIAM
    THE ASHANTI CONFEDERACY.
    JOURNAL OF AFRICAN HISTORY 3 1962 PP 399-417
    026,114-02,

    TORDOFF WILLIAM
    THE EXILE AND THE REPATRIATION OF NANA PREMPEH 1 OF ASHANTI
    1896-1924.
    TRANSACTIONS OF THE HISTORICAL SOCIETY OF GHANA 4 1960
    PP 33-58
    026,114-02,

    TORDOFF WILLIAM
    ASHANTI UNDER THE PREMPEHS, 1888-1935.
    LONDON, OXFORD UNIVERSITY PRESS, 1965
    026,114-02,

TOSCANO JAMES V
    JACOB PHILIP E   TOSCANO JAMES V
    THE INTEGRATION OF POLITICAL COMMUNITIES.
    PHILADELPHIA, LIPPINCOTT, 1964
    048,057,

TOUPET CHARLES
    TOUPET CHARLES
    ORIENTATION BIBLIOGRAPHIQUE SUR LA MAURITANIE.
    DAKAR, INSTITUT FRANCAISE D'AFRIQUE NOIRE, 1958
    124-12,

TOURE SEKOU
    TOURE SEKOU
    AFRICA'S FUTURE AND THE WORLD.
    IN PHILIP W QUIGG (ED.), AFRICA, NEW YORK, PRAEGER, 1964
    PP 314-326
    060,115-04,

    TOURE SEKOU
    EXPERIENCE GUINEENNE ET UNITE AFRICAINE (GUINEAN EXPERIENCE
    AND AFRICAN UNITY).
    PARIS, PRESENCE AFRICAINE, 1959
    057,115-09,

    TOURE SEKOU
    CONGRES DE L'UNION GENERALE DES TRAVAILLEURS D'AFRIQUE NOIRE
    (UGTAN), CONAKRY, 15-18 JANVIER 1959--RAPPORT OF D ORIENTA-
    TION ET DE DOCTRINE.
    PARIS, PRESENCE AFRICAINE, 1959

    TOURE SEKOU
    GUINEE, PRELUDE A L INDEPENDANCE.
    PARIS, PRESENCE AFRICAINE, 1959

115-04,

TOURE SEKOU
    TOURE SEKOU
    L'AFRIQUE ET LA REVOLUTION.
    PARIS, PRESENCE AFRICAINE, 1966
    115-04,

    TOURE SEKOU
    LA GUINEE ET L EMANCIPATION AFRICAINE--L ACTION POLITIQUE DU
    PARTI DEMOCRATIQUE DE GUINEE.
    PARIS, PRESENCE AFRICAINE, 1959
    115-04,

    TOURE SEKOU
    LA REVOLUTION GUINEENNE ET LE PROGRES SOCIAL.
    CONAKRY, IMP. PATRICE LUMUMBA, 1963
    115-04,

    TOURE SEKOU
    POEMES MILITANTS, PARTI DEMOCRATIQUE DE GUINEE.
    CONAKRY, IMP. PATRICE LUMUMBA, 1964
    115-04,

    TOURE SEKOU
    REPUBLIQUE DE GUINEE--LA LUTTE DU PARTI DEMOCRATIQUE DE
    GUINEE POUR L EMANCIPATION AFRICAINE.
    CONAKRY, IMP. PATRICE LUMUMBA, 1959
    115-04,

TOUSSAINT AUGUSTE
    BARNWELL PATRICK J   TOUSSAINT AUGUSTE
    A SHORT HISTORY OF MAURITIUS
    NEW YORK AND LONDON, LONGMANS, GREEN, FOR THE GOVERNMENT OF
    MAURITIUS, 1949
    125-02,

TOUVAL SAADIA
    TOUVAL SAADIA
    TREATIES BORDERS AND THE PARTITION OF AFRICA.
    JOURNAL OF AFRICAN HISTORY 7 1966 PP 279-294
    033,059,

    TOUVAL SAADIA
    SOMALI NATIONALISM-- INTERNATIONAL POLITICS AND THE DRIVE
    FOR UNITY IN THE HORN OF AFRICA.
    CAMBRIDGE, MASS, HARVARD UNIVERSITY PRESS, 1963
    054,055,133-09,

TOWNSEND
    TOWNSEND E REGINALD ED
    THE OFFICIAL PAPERS OF WILLIAM V S TUBMAN, PRESIDENT OF THE
    REPUBLIC OF LIBERIA.
    NEW YORK, HUMANITIES PRESS INC., 1968
    060,119-04,

TRACEY H
    TRACEY H
    THE DEVELOPMENT OF MUSIC IN EAST AFRICA
    TANGANYIKA NOTES AND RECORDS 63 1964 PP 213-221

015,

TRACHTMAN LESTER N
      TRACHTMAN LESTER N
      THE LABOR MOVEMENT OF GHANA-- A STUDY IN POLITICAL
      UNIONISM.
      ECONOMIC DEVELOPMENT AND CULTURAL CHANGE 10 1962 PP 183-200
      073,114-08,

TRAORE ANDRE
      TRAORE ANDRE   GUILHEM MARCEL
      MALI--RECITS HISTORIQUES--3EME ET 4EME ANNEES DU CYCLE
      FONDAMENTAL.
      PARIS, LIGEL, 1964
      123-02,

TRAORE B
      TRAORE B
      LE THEATRE NEGRO-AFRICAINE ET SES FONCTIONS SOCIALES (BLACK
      AFRICAN THEATER AND ITS SOCIAL FUNCTIONS).
      PARIS, PRESENCE AFRICAINE, 1958
      093,

TRAPIDO STANLEY
      TRAPIDO STANLEY
      AFRICAN DIVISIONAL POLITICS IN THE CAPE COLONY,1884 TO 1910
      JOURNAL OF AFRICAN HISTORY 9 1968 PP 79-98
      032,

TRAUTMANN RENE
      TRAUTMANN RENE
      LA LITTERATURE POPULAIRE A LA COTE DES ESCLAVES-- CONTES,
      PROVERBS, DEVINETTES (POPULAR LITERATURE OF THE SLAVE COAST
      -- TALES, PROVERBS, RIDDLES).
      PARIS, INSTITUT D'ETHNOLOGIE, TRAVEAUX ET MEMOIRES 4, 1927
      012,

TRAVELE MOUSSA
      TRAVELE MOUSSA
      PETIT MANUEL FRANCAIS-BAMBARA.
      PARIS, LIBRAIRIE ORIENTALISTE PAUL GEUTHNER, 1955
      123-01,

TREVALLION B A W
      TREVALLION B A W
      METROPOLITAN KANO-- REPORT ON THE TWENTY YEAR DEVELOPMENT
      PLAN 1963-1983.
      OXFORD, PERGAMON PRESS, 1966
      092,128-05,

TREVASKIS G K N
      TREVASKIS G K N
      ERITREA-A COLONY IN TRANSITION 1941-1952
      LONDON,OXFORD,FOR ROYAL INSTITUTE OF INTERNATIONAL
      AFFAIRS,1960
      110-07,

TREWARTHA G T
      TREWARTHA G T   ZELINSKY W
      POPULATION PATTERNS IN TROPICAL AFRICA.

ANNALS OF THE ASSOCIATION OF AMERICAN GEOGRAPHERS WASHINGTON
VOL 44 JUNE 1954 PP 135-193
069,074,

TRIMINGHAM J S
    TRIMINGHAM J S
    ISLAM IN WEST AFRICA.
    OXFORD, OXFORD UNIVERSITY PRESS, 1959
    021,

    TRIMINGHAM J S
    THE INFLUENCE OF ISLAM UPON AFRICA.
    LONDON, LONGMANS, GREEN AND CO. LTD., 1968
    021,052,

    TRIMINGHAM J S
    ISLAM IN EAST AFRICA.
    OXFORD, CLARENDON PRESS, 1964
    021,

    TRIMINGHAM J S
    A HISTORY OF ISLAM IN WEST AFRICA.
    OXFORD, CLARENDON PRESS, 1962
    021,

    TRIMINGHAM J S
    THE PHASES OF ISLAMIC EXOANSION AND ISLAMIC CULTURE ZONES
    IN AFRICA.
    IN LEWIS, ISLAM IN TROPICAL AFRICA, LONDON, OXFORD UNIVERSITY
    PRESS, 1966, P. 127-143
    021,

    TRIMINGHAM J S
    THE EXPANSION OF ISLAM
    IN KRITZECK AND LEWIS, PP 13-34
    021,

    TRIMINGHAM J S
    ISLAM IN THE SUDAN.
    LONDON, FRANK CASS LTD, 1965
    021,134-03,

TROWELL MARGARET
    TROWELL MARGARET
    AFRICAN DESIGN.
    LONDON, FABER AND FABER, 1960; ALSO 1965, 2ND EDITION
    014,

    TROWELL MARGARET
    CLASSICAL AFRICAN SCULPTURE.
    NEW YORK, PRAEGER, 1964, 2ND. EDITION
    014,

    TROWELL MARGARET   WACHSMANN KLAUS
    TRIBAL CRAFTS OF UGANDA
    LONDON, OXFORD UNIVERSITY PRESS, 1953
    014,139-01,

TSHOMBE MOISE
    TSHOMBE MOISE

BILAN DE DEUX ANS D'INDEPENDANCE--RAPPORT SUR LES
REALISATIONS DE GOUVERNEMENT KATANGAIS DE 1960-1962--
DISCOURS PRONONCE A L'ASSEMBLEE NATIONALE, LE 7 SEPTEMBRE
1962.
ELISABETHVILLE, SECRETARIAT D'ETAT A L'INFORMATION, SERVICE
DE EDUCATION DE LA MASSE, 1962
108-04,

TSHOMBE MOISE
    TSHOMBE MOISE
    QUINZE MOIS DE GOVERNEMENT DE CONGO.
    PARIS, ED. DE LA TABLE RONDE, 1966
    108-04,

TUBIANA MARIE-JOSE
    TUBIANA MARIE-JOSE
    CONTES ZAGHAWA--TRENTE-SEPT CONTES ET DEUX LEGENDES
    RECUEILLIS AU TCHAD--PREFACE DE MICHEL LEIRS--OUVRAGE PUBLIE
    AVEC LE CONCOURS DU CENTRE NATIONAL DE LA RECHERCHE
    SCIENTIFIQUE.
    PARIS, LES QUATRE-JEUDIS, 1962
    106-01,

TUCKER A N
    TUCKER A N
    PHILOLOGY AND AFRICA.
    BULLETIN OF THE SCHOOL OF ORIENTAL AND AFRICAN STUDIES   20
    1957
    011,

TUCKER MARTIN
    TUCKER MARTIN
    AFRICA IN MODERN LITERATURE-- A SURVEY OF CONTEMPORARY
    WRITING IN ENGLISH.
    NEW YORK, F UNGAR PUBLISHING COMPANY, 1967
    090,

TUDEN ARTHUR
    TUDEN ARTHUR   PLOTNICOV LEONARD   EDS
    SOCIAL STRATIFICATION IN AFRICA
    NEW YORK, FREE PRESS, 1970
    009,

    SWARTZ MARC   TURNER VICTOR W   TUDEN ARTHUR
    POLITICAL ANTHROPOLOGY
    CHICAGO, ALDINE, 1966
    009,

    TUDEN ARTHUR
    ILA SLAVERY (ZAMBIA).
    TRANS-ACTION, 1967
    028,142-01,

TURNBULL COLIN M
    TURNBULL COLIN M
    TRIBALISM AND SOCIAL EVOLUTION IN AFRICA.
    THE ANNALS OF THE AMERICAN ACADEMY OF POLITICAL AND SOCIAL
    SCIENCE VOL 354 JULY 1964 PP 22-31
    006,013,

TURNBULL COLIN M
THE LONELY AFRICAN.
NEW YORK, DOUBLEDAY, 1963
040,

TURNBULL COLIN M
TURNBULL COLIN M
THE FOREST PEOPLE
NEW YORK, SIMON AND SCHUSTER, 1961
108-01,

TURNBULL COLIN M
WAYWARD SERVANTS,THE TWO WORLDS OF THE AFRICAN PYGMIES
NEW YORK, NATIONAL HISTORY PRESS, DIST. BY DOUBLEDAY, 1965.
108-01,

TURNER H W
TURNER H W
A TYPOLOGY FOR AFRICAN RELIGIOUS MOVEMENTS
JOURNAL OF RELIGION IN AFRICA 1 1964 PP 1-34
051,

TURNER HAROLD
MITCHELL ROBERT C   TURNER HAROLD
A COMPREHENSIVE BIBLIOGRAPHY OF MODERN AFRICAN RELIGIOUS
MOVEMENTS.
EVANSTON, NORTHWESTERN UNIVERSITY PRESS, 1966
051,

TURNER HAROLD
AFRICAN INDEPENDENT CHURCH-- THE LIFE AND FAITH OF THE
CHURCH OF THE LORD (ALADURA).
LONDON, OXFORD UNIVERSITY PRESS, 1967
051,128-03,

TURNER JOHN E
HOLT ROBERT T   TURNER JOHN E
THE POLITICAL BASIS OF ECONOMIC DEVELOPMENT.
PRINCETON, VAN NOSTRAND, 1966
074,

TURNER LORENZO
TURNER LORENZO
AFRICANISMS IN THE GULLAH DIALECT
NEW YORK, ARNO PRESS, 1969; ORIGINALLY PUBLISHED IN 1949
030,

TURNER LORENZO D
TURNER LORENZO D
AFRICAN SURVIVALS IN THE NEW WORLD WITH SPECIAL EMPHASIS ON
THE ARTS.
IN AMSAC, AFRICA SEEN BY AMERICAN NEGROES, PARIS,
PRESENCE AFRICAINE, 1958, PP 101-116
030,

TURNER VICTOR W
SWARTZ MARC   TURNER VICTOR W   TUDEN ARTHUR
POLITICAL ANTHROPOLOGY
CHICAGO, ALDINE, 1966
009,

TURNER VICTOR W
   TURNER VICTOR W
   THE FOREST OF SYMBOLS--ASPECTS OF NDEMBU RITUAL.
   ITHACA, CORNELL UNIVERSITY PRESS, 1969
   013,

   TURNER VICTOR W
   THE DRUMS OF AFFLICTION.
   LONDON, OXFORD UNIVERSITY PRESS, 1968
   013,

TUTUOLA AMOS
   TUTUOLA AMOS
   THE PALM-WINE DRINKARD.
   NEW YORK, GROVE PRESS INC, 1953
   090,128-10,

   TUTUOLA AMOS
   SIMBI AND THE SATYR OF THE DARK JUNGLE
   LONDON, FABER AND FABER, 1955
   090,

   TUTUOLA AMOS
   MY LIFE IN BUSH OF GHOSTS
   LONDON, FABER AND FABER, 1954
   090,

   TUTUOLA AMOS
   FEATHER WOMEN OF JUNGLE
   LONDON, FABER AND FABER, 1962
   090,

   TUTUOLA AMOS
   THE BRAVE AFRICAN HUNTRESS
   LONDON, FABER AND FABER, 1958
   090,

   TUTUOLA AMOS
   AJAIYI THIS INHERITED POVERTY
   LONDON, FABER AND FABER, 1967
   090,

TWINING WILLIAM
   TWINING WILLIAM
   THE RESTATEMENT OF AFRICAN CUSTOMARY LAW-- A COMMENT.
   JOURNAL OF MODERN AFRICAN STUDIES 1 JUNE 1963 PP 221-228
   066,

TWITCHETT K J
   TWITCHETT K J
   COLONIALISM-- AN ATTEMPT AT UNDERSTANDING IMPERIAL,
   COLONIAL AND NEO-COLONIAL RELATIONSHIPS.
   POPULATION STUDIES 13 OCTOBER 1965 PP 300-323
   087,

U

UCHENDU VICTOR C
UCHENDU VICTOR C
PRIORITY ISSUES FOR SOCIAL ANTHROPOLOGICAL RESEARCH IN
AFRICA IN THE NEXT TWO DECADES.
IN CARTER, GWENDOLEN M. AND ANN PADEN (EDS), EXPANDING
HORIZONS IN AFRICAN STUDIES, EVANSTON, NORTHWESTERN
UNIVERSITY PRESS, 1969, PP. 3-23
016,100,

UCHENDU VICTOR C
SLAVERY IN SOUTHEAST NIGERIA.
TRANS-ACTION, 1967
028,128-01,

UGOH S U
UGOH S U
THE NIGERIAN CEMENT INDUSTRY CHAPTER 10.
IN EDITH WHETHAM AND JEAN CURRIE (EDS.), READINGS IN THE
APPLIED ECONOMICS OF AFRICA, LONDON, CAMBRIDGE UNIVERSITY
PRESS, 1, 1967, PP 102-113
071,128-08,

UKWU U I
HODDER B W   UKWU U I
MARKETS IN WEST AFRICA
IBADAN UNIVERSITY PRESS, 1969
010,

ULLENDORFF EDWARD
ULLENDORFF EDWARD
ETHIOPIA AND THE BIBLE.
LONDON, OXFORD UNIVERSITY PRESS, 1968
050,110-02,

UMEASIEGBU
UMEASIEGBU REMS NNA
THE WAY WE LIVED--IBO CUSTOMS AND STORIES.
NEW YORK, HUMANITIES PRESS INC., 1969 (LONDON, HEINEMANN
EDUCATIONAL BOOKS)
012,128-01,

UNDERWOOD LEON
UNDERWOOD LEON
MASKS OF WEST AFRICA.
LONDON, A TIRANTI, 1948
014,

UNDERWOOD LEON
BRONZES OF WEST AFRICA.
LONDON, A TIRANTI, 1949
014,

UNDERWOOD LEON
FIGURES IN WOOD IN WEST AFRICA
LONDON, A TARANTE, 1947

014,

UNESCO
    UNESCO
    WORLD COMMUNICATIONS-PRESS,RADIO,TELEVISION,FILM
    PARIS,UNESCO,1966
    049,

    UNESCO
    SOCIAL IMPLICATIONS OF INDUSTRIALIZATION AND URBANIZATION
    IN AFRICA SOUTH OF THE SAHARA.
    PARIS,UNESCO,1956
    047,071,074,

    UNESCO
    DEVELOPING INFORMATION MEDIA IN AFRICA.
    UNESCO, REPORTS AND PAPERS ON MASS COMMUNICATION NO. 37
    049,

    UNESCO
    THE DEVELOPMENT OF HIGHER EDUCATION IN AFRICA-- REPORT OF
    THE CONFERENCE. TANANARIVE, SEPTEMBER 1962.
    PARIS,UNESCO,1963
    042,

    UNESCO
    A REVIEW OF THE NATURAL RESOURCES OF THE AFRICAN CONTINENT.
    NEW YORK, COLUMBIA   UNIVERSITY PRESS, 1969
    069,

    UNESCO
    VERNACULAR LANGUAGES IN EDUCATION.
    UNESCO,1953
    042,

UNITED NATIONS
    UNITED NATIONS
    INDUSTRIAL GROWTH IN AFRICA.
    NEW YORK, ECONOMIC COMMISSION FOR AFRICA 1963
    E/CN-14/INR/1REV.1/
    071,

    UNITED NATIONS
    AFRICAN AGRICULTURAL DEVELOPMENT.
    NEW YORK,1966 E/CN 141/342
    070,

    UNITED NATIONS
    INDUSTRIAL DEVELOPMENT IN AFRICA
    NEW YORK,UNITED NATIONS,1967
    071,104-08,110-08,117-08,127-08,134-08,140-08,142-08,

    UNITED NATIONS
    REPORT OF THE UNITED NATIONS CONFERENCE ON TRADE
    AND DEVELOPMENT.
    IN LEWIS P FICKETT   (ED),PROBLEMS OF THE DEVELOPING NATIONS,
    NEW YORK, CROWELL. 1966 PP 64-83
    073,

    UNITED NATIONS   FAO

REPORT ON THE POSSIBILITIES OF AFRICAN RURAL DEVELOPMENT
IN RELATION TO ECONOMIC AND SOCIAL GROWTH.
ROMA,FAO,1961
070,

UNITED NATIONS
UNITED NATIONS
ENLARGEMENT OF THE EXCHANGE ECONOMY IN TROPICAL AFRICA.
NEW YORK,UN DEPARTMENT OF ECONOMIC AFFAIRS (E/2557 ST/ECA/23
1954. II.C.4)
073,

UNITED NATIONS
MILITARY AND POLICE FORCES IN THE REPUBLIC OF SOUTH AFRICA.
ST/PSCA/SER. A/3A/AC. 115/S. 203-204, 1967, 15 PAGES
089,132-06,

URVOY YVES
URVOY YVES
HISTOIRE DE L'EMPIRE DU BORNU (HISTORY OF THE EMPIRE OF
BORNU).
PARIS,LAROSE,1949 (IFAN MEMOIRES 7)
024,128-02,

URVOY YVES
HISTOIRE DES POPULATIONS DU SOUDAN CENTRAL--COLONIE DU
NIGER.
PARIS, LAROSE, 1936
127-02,

USSR ACAD SCIENCES
USSR ACAD SCIENCES INSTITUTE OF AFRICA
A HISTORY OF AFRICA 1914-1967
MOSCOW,NAUKA PUBLISHING HOUSE CENTRAL DEPARTMENT OF ORIENTAL
LITERATURE 1968
036,

UWECHUE RAPH
UWECHUE RAPH
REFLECTIONS ON THE NIGERIAN CIVIL WAR-A CALL FOR REALISM
NEW YORK,AFRICANA PUBLISHING CORPORATION,1970
065,

V

VAEREN-AGUESSY
VAN DER VAEREN-AGUESSY D
LES FEMMES COMMERCANTES AU DETAIL SUR LES MARCHES DAKAROIS.
IN LLOYD, THE NEW ELITES OF TROPICAL AFRICA, LONDON, OXFORD
UNIVERSITY PRESS, 1966, P. 244-255
046,130-05,

VAN
VAN DER VAEREN-AGUESSY D
LES FEMMES COMMERCANTES AU DETAIL SUR LES MARCHES DAKAROIS.
IN LLOYD, THE NEW ELITES OF TROPICAL AFRICA, LONDON, OXFORD

UNIVERSITY PRESS, 1966, P. 244-255
046,130-05.

VAN ARKADIE B
VAN ARKADIE B
IMPORT SUBSTITUTION AND EXPORT PROMOTION AS AIDS TO
INDUSTRIALIZATION IN EAST AFRICA CHAPTER 28.
IN EDITH WHETHAM AND JEAN CURRIE (EDS.), READINGS IN THE
APPLIED ECONOMICS OF AFRICA, LONDON, CAMBRIDGE UNIVERSITY
PRESS, 2, 1967, PP 149-162
071.

VAN BILSEN A A A J
VAN BILSEN A A A J
SOME ASPECTS OF THE CONGO PROBLEM.
INTERNATIONAL AFFAIRS 38 1962 PP 41-51
079.

VAN DE WALLE E
LORIMER FRANK   BRASS WILLIAM   VAN DE WALLE E
DEMOGRAPHY.
IN ROBERT A LYSTAD (ED), THE AFRICAN WORLD, NEW YORK,
PRAEGER, 1966, PP 271-303
069,074.

VAN DE WALLE E
FACTEURS ET INDICES DE STABILISATION ET D'URBANIZATION A
A USUMBURA RUANDA-URUNDI.
RECHERCHES ECONOMIQUE DE LOUVAIN 27 2 1961
103-05.

VAN DEN BERGHE P
VAN DEN BERGHE P
RACE AND RACISM-- A COMPARATIVE PERSPECTIVE.
NEW YORK JOHN WILEY 1967
030,088,132-06.

VAN DEN BERGHE P
AFRICA-- SOCIAL PROBLEMS OF CHANGE AND CONFLICT.
SAN FRANCISCO, CHANDLER, 1965
038,053.

VAN DEN BERGHE P
THE ROLE OF THE ARMY IN CONTEMPORARY AFRICA.
AFRICA REPORT 10 MARCH 1965 PP 12-17
064.

VAN DEN BERGHE P
SOUTH AFRICA- A STUDY OF CONFLICT
MIDDLETOWN, CONNECTICUT, WESLEYAN UNIVERSITY PRESS, 1965
032,089.

VAN DEN BERGHE P
THE MILITARY AND POLITICAL CHANGE IN AFRICA
IN CLAUDE WELCH (ED), SOLDIER AND STATE IN AFRICA, EVANSTON,
NORTHWESTERN UNIVERSITY PRESS, 1970
064.

VAN DER KOLFT G H
VAN DER KOLFT G H

THE SOCIAL ASPECTS OF THE GEZIRA SCHEME IN THE SUDAN.
AMSTERDAM, TROPENINSTITUUT, 1953
070,134-08,

VAN DER LAAN H L
    VAN DER LAAN H L
    THE SIERRA LEONE DIAMONDS.
    FREETOWN, UNIVERSITY OF SIERRA LEONE, 1965
    069,131-08,

VAN DER PLAS C O
    VAN DER PLAS C O
    REPORT OF A SOCIO-ECONOMIC SURVEY OF BATHURST AND KOMBO ST
    MARY IN THE GAMBIA.
    NEW YORK, UNITED NATIONS, 1956
    113-05,

VAN DER POST L
    VAN DER POST L
    THE HEART OF THE HUNTER
    NEW YORK, MORROW, 1961
    102-01,

VAN DONGEN I S
    VAN DONGEN I S
    ROAD VERSUS RAIL IN AFRICA.
    GEOGRAPHICAL REVIEW 52 1962 PP 296-298
    048,

    HANCE WILLIAM A   VAN DONGEN I S
    DAR ES SALAAM, THE PORT AND ITS TRIBUTARY.
    ANNALS OF THE ASSOCIATION OF AMERICAN GEOGRAPHERS
    48 DECEMBER 1958 PP 419-435
    048,136-08,

    HANCE WILLIAM A   VAN DONGEN I S
    LOURENCO MARQUES IN DELAGOA BAY.
    ECONOMIC GEOGRAPHY 33 JULY 1957 PP 238-256
    048,144-05,

    HANCE WILLIAM A   VAN DONGEN I S
    THE PORT OF LOBITO AND THE BENGUELA RAILWAY.
    GEOGRAPHICAL REVIEW 46 OCTOBER 1956 PP 460-487
    048,

    HANCE WILLIAM A   VAN DONGEN I S
    MATADI, FOCUS OF BELGIAN AFRICAN TRANSPORT.
    ANNALS OF THE ASSOCIATION OF AMERICAN GEOGRAPHERS 48
    MARCH 1958 PP 41-72
    48 MARCH 1958 PP 41-72
    048,

    VAN DONGEN I S
    THE BRITISH EAST AFRICA TRANSPORT COMPLEX.
    UNIVERSITY OF CHICAGO, DEPARTMENT OF GEOGRAPHY PAPER 38,
    1954
    048,

    VAN DONGEN I S
    NACALA--NEWEST MOZAMBIQUE GATEWAY TO INTERIOR AFRICA.

TIJDSCRIFT VOOR ECONOMISHE EN SOCIALE GEOGRAFIE AMSTERDAM
48STE JAARGANANG MARCH 1959 PP 65-73
048,

VAN HOEY LEO F
   VAN HOEY LEO F
   THE COERCIVE PROCESS OF URBANIZATION--THE CASE OF NIGER.
   IN THE NEW URBANIZATION, ED. SCOTT GREER, ET AL., NEW YORK,
   SAINT MARTINS PRESS, 1968
   127-05,

VAN LANGENHOVE F
   VAN LANGENHOVE F
   FACTORS OF DECOLONIZATION.
   IN WILLIAM J HANNA (ED), INDEPENDENT BLACK AFRICA, CHICAGO,
   RAND MCNALLY, 1964, PP 150-175
   056,

VAN LIERDE JEAN
   VAN LIERDE JEAN
   LA PENSEE POLITIQUE DE PATRICE LUMUMBA.   (THE POLITICAL
   THOUGHT OF PATRICE LUMUMBA).
   PARIS, PRESENCE AFRICAINE, 1963
   060,108-04,

VAN VELSEN J
   VAN VELSEN J
   LABOUR MIGRATION AS A POSITIVE FACTOR IN THE CONTINUITY
   OF TONGA TRIBAL SOCIETY.
   ECONOMIC DEVELOPMENT AND CULTURAL CHANGE 8 1960 PP 265-278
   038,142-03,

   VAN VELSEN J
   THE ESTABLISHMENT OF THE ADMINISTRATION IN TONGALAND.
   SALISBURY, HISTORIANS IN TROPICAL AFRICA, UNIVERSITY
   COLLEGE OF RHODESIA AND NYASALAND, 1962, PP 177-196
   035,142-02,

   KUPER HILDA   HUGHES A J B   VAN VELSEN J
   THE SHONA AND NDEBELE OF SOUTHERN RHODESIA
   LONDON, INTERNATIONAL AFRICAN INSTITUTE, 1954
   145-01,

VANNE MORRIS-GOODALL
   LEAKEY L S B   VANNE MORRIS-GOODALL
   UNVEILING MAN?S ORIGINS-TEN DECADES OF THOUGHT ABOUT HUMAN
   EVOLUTION
   CAMBRIDGE, MASS, SCHENKMAN, 1969
   018,

VANSINA JAN
   VANSINA JAN
   ORAL TRADITION, A STUDY OF HISTORICAL METHODOLOGY.
   CHICAGO, ALDINE, 1961
   012,090,

   VANSINA JAN
   KINGDOMS OF THE SAVANNA.
   MADISON, UNIVERSITY OF WISCONSIN, 1968
   025,108-02,

VANSINA JAN
  VANSINA JAN
  INTRODUCTION A L'ETHNOGRAPHE DU CONGO.
  BRUXELLES, EDITIONS UNIVERSITAIRES DU CONGO, NO. 1, 1966
  003,108-01,

  COHEN RONALD   VANSINA JAN   ZOLBERG ARISTIDE R
  ORAL HISTORY IN AFRICA.
  EVANSTON ILLINOIS, NORTHWESTERN UNIVERSITY, PROGRAM OF
  AFRICAN STUDIES, REPRINT SERIES, 2, NO.1 SEPTEMBER 1965
  012,099,

  CURTIN PHILIP D   VANSINA JAN
  SOURCES OF THE 19TH CENTURY ATLANTIC SLAVE TRADE.
  JOURNAL OF AFRICAN HISTORY 5 1964 PP 185-208
  028,

  VANSINA JAN
  LONG-DISTANCE TRADE-ROUTE IN CENTRAL AFRICA.
  JOURNAL OF AFRICAN HISTORY 3 1962 PP 375-390
  025,

  VANSINA JAN
  A COMPARISON OF AFRICAN KINGDOMS.
  AFRICA 32 1962 PP 324-335
  009,

  VANSINA JAN   ET AL   EDS
  THE HISTORIAN IN TROPICAL AFRICA.
  LONDON, OXFORD UNIVERSITY PRESS, 1964
  036,099,

  VANSINA JAN
  L'EVOLUTION DU ROYAUME RWANDA DES ORIGINES A 1900   (EV-
  OLUTION OF THE KINGDOM OF RWANDA FROM ITS ORIGINS TO 1900.
  BRUXELLES ACADEMIE ROYALE DE SCIENCES D'OUTRE MER 1962
  025,129-02,

  VANSINA JAN
  LA FONDATION DU ROYAUME DE KASANJE (THE FOUNDATION OF THE
  KINGDOM OF KASANJE) .
  AEQUATORIA 25 1962 PP 45-62
  025,

  VANSINA JAN
  THE FUNCTIONS OF ORAL TRADITIONS AND THEIR INFLUENCE ON THE
  HISTORICAL CONTENT OF THESE SOURCES.
  SALISBURY, SOUTHERN RHODESIA,HISTORIANS IN TROPICAL AFRICA,
  UNIVERSITY COLLEGE OF RHODESIA AND NYASALAND, 1962
  PP 119-126
  098,

  VANSINA JAN
  NOTES SUR L'ORIGINE DU ROYAUME DE KONGO (NOTES ON THE
  ORIGIN OF THE KINGDOM OF KONGO).
  JOURNAL OF AFRICAN HISTORY 4 1963 PP 33-38
  025,108-02,

VARMA S N

VARMA S N
NATIONAL UNITY AND POLITICAL STABILITY IN NIGERIA.
INTERNATIONAL STUDIES 4 JANUARY 1963 PP 265-280
057,

VATIKIOTIS P J
VATIKIOTIS P J
THE MODERN HISTORY OF EGYPT
LONDON, WEIDENFELD AND NICOLSON, 1969
140-11,

VENNETIER PIERRE
VENNETIER PIERRE
L'URBANISATION ET SES CONSEQUENCES AU CONGO (BRAZZAVILLE).
IN LES CAHIERS D'OUTRE MER, 16, 63, JULY-SEPT., 1963
107-05,

VERGER PIERRE
VERGER PIERRE
LES RELIGIONS TRADITIONNELLES AFRICAINES, SONT ELLES
COMPATABLE AVEC LES FORMES ACTUELLES DE L'EXISTENCE
(TRADITIONAL AFRICAN RELIGIONS, ARE THEY COMPATABLE WITH
ACTUAL FORMS OF DAILY LIFE).
IN RENCONTRES INTERNATIONALES DE BOUAKE, LES RELIGIONS
AFRICAINES TRADITIONELLES, PARIS,   EDITIONS DU SEUIL,
1965, PP 97-118
013,

VERHAEGEN BENOIT
VERHAEGEN BENOIT
REBELLIONS AU CONGO. REBELLIONS OF THE CONGO.
BRUSSELS CENTRE DE RECHERCHE ET D'INFORMATION SOCIO-
POLITIQUES 1 1966
064,108-06,

VERHELST THIERRY
VERHELST THIERRY
SAFEGUARDING AFRICAN CUSTOMARY LAW--JUDICIAL AND LEGISLATIVE
PROCESSES FOR ITS ADAPTATION AND INTEGRATION.
AFRICA. OCCASIONAL PAPER NO. 7, 1968, 32 PAGES
066,

VILAKAZI ABSOLOM L
VILAKAZI ABSOLOM L
SOCIAL RESEARCH AND PROBLEMS OF AFRICAN ECONOMIC AND SOCIAL
DEVELOPMENT.
IN LALAGE BOWN AND MICHAEL CROWDER (EDS.), PROCEEDINGS OF
THE FIRST INTERNATIONAL CONGRESS OF AFRICANISTS, ACCRA,
1962, LONDON, LONGMANS, 1964, PP 184-189
074,

VILLIEN-ROSSI
VILLIEN-ROSSI MARIE
BAMAKO, CAPITALE DU MALI.
BULLETIN IFAN, 28, B, 1-2, JAN.-APR., 1966)
123-05,

VOEGELIN C F
VOEGELIN C F   VOEGELIN F M
LANGUAGES OF THE WORLD--AFRICA FACSIMILE ONE

ANTHROPOLOGICAL LINGUISTICS, VOL. 6, NO. 5, MAY, 1964, PP.
1-339
011,

VOEGELIN F M
    VOEGELIN C F   VOEGELIN F M
    LANGUAGES OF THE WORLD--AFRICA FACSIMILE ONE
    ANTHROPOLOGICAL LINGUISTICS, VOL. 6, NO. 5, MAY, 1964, PP.
    1-339
    011,

VON
    VON HORNBOSTEL ERICH
    AFRICAN NEGRO MUSIC
    AFRICA 1 1928 PP 30-62
    015,

VON DER MEHDEN FRED
    ANDERSON CHARLES   VON DER MEHDEN FRED YOUNG CRAWFORD
    ISSUES OF POLITICAL DEVELOPMENT.
    ENGLEWOOD CLIFFS,N J,PRENTICE-HALL,1967
    002,

VON DER MUHLL G
    KOPF DAVID   VON DER MUHLL G
    POLITICAL SOCIALIZATION IN KENYA AND TANZANIA.
    JOURNAL OF MODERN AFRICAN STUDIES 5 MAY 1967 PP 13-51
    043,117-03,136-03,

VON GRUNEBAUM G
    VON GRUNEBAUM G
    PROBLEMS OF MUSLIM NATIONALISM CHP 9.
    IN MODERN ISLAM-- THE SEARCH FOR CULTURAL IDENTITY,BERKELEY
    UNIVERSITY OF CALIFORNIA PRESS, CHP 9, 1962
    054,

VON SYDOW ECKART
    VON SYDOW ECKART
    AFRIKANISCHE PLASTIK (AFRICAN SCULPTURE).
    BERLIN,MANN VERLAG,1954
    014,

VOORHOEVE J
    VOORHOEVE J
    CREOLE LANGUAGES AND COMMUNICATION.
    COLLOQUE SUR LE MULTILINGUISME, BRAZZAVILLE, 1962
    131-03,

W

WACHSMANN KLAUS
    WACHSMANN KLAUS
    ETHNOMUSICOLOGY IN AFRICAN STUDIES--THE NEXT TWENTY YEARS.
    IN CARTER, GWENDOLEN M. AND ANN PADEN (EDS) EXPANDING
    HORIZONS IN AFRICAN STUDIES, EVANSTON, NORTHWESTERN
    UNIVERSITY PRESS, 1969, PP. 131-142

015,100,

WACHSMANN KLAUS
    WACHSMANN KLAUS
    INTERNATIONAL CATALOGUE OF PUBLISHED RECORDS OF FOLK MUSIC
    LONDON, INTERNATIONAL FOLK MUSIC COUNCIL, 1960
    015,

    TROWELL MARGARET   WACHSMANN KLAUS
    TRIBAL CRAFTS OF UGANDA
    LONDON, OXFORD UNIVERSITY PRESS, 1953
    014,139-01,

WAHL NICHOLAS
    WAHL NICHOLAS
    THE FRENCH CONSTITUTION OF 1958--2, THE INITIAL DRAFT AND
    ITS ORIGINS.
    THE AMERICAN POLITICAL SCIENCE REVIEW 53 JUNE 1959 PP 358-82
    B-M REPRINT PS-361
    061,

WAINHOUSE DAVID W
    WAINHOUSE DAVID W
    REMNANTS OF EMPIRE-- THE UNITED NATIONS AND THE END OF
    COLONIALISM.
    NEW YORK, HARPER AND ROW, 1964
    081,087,

WALKER AUDREY A
    WALKER AUDREY A   ED
    THE RHODESIAS AND NYASALAND--A GUIDE TO OFFICIAL PUBLICA-
    TIONS.
    WASHINGTON, U.S. GOVERNMENT PRINTING OFFICE, 1965
    122-12,142-12,

    WALKER AUDREY A   ET COMP
    THE RHODESIAS AND NYASALAND--A GUIDE TO OFFICIAL PUBLICA-
    TIONS.
    WASHINGTON, U.S. GOVERNMENT PRINTING OFFICE, 1965
    142-12,

WALKER BARBARA K
    WALKER BARBARA K   WALKER WARREN S   EDS
    NIGERIAN FOLK TALES.
    NEW BRUNSWICK, RUTGERS UNIVERSITY PRESS, 1961
    012,

WALKER ERIC
    WALKER ERIC
    THE GREAT TREK
    LONDON, ADAM AND CHARLES BLACK, 1948
    032,

    WALKER ERIC
    A HISTORY OF SOUTHERN AFRICA.
    LONDON, LONGMANS, 1957
    031,132-02,

WALKER WARREN S
    WALKER BARBARA K   WALKER WARREN S   EDS

NIGERIAN FOLK TALES.
NEW BRUNSWICK,RUTGERS UNIVERSITY PRESS,1961
012,

WALLACE ANTHONY F
    WALLACE ANTHONY F
    REVITALIZATION MOVEMENTS.
    AMERICAN ANTHROPOLOGIST 58 APRIL 1956
    051,

    WALLACE ANTHONY F
    RELIGION-AN ANTHROPOLOGICAL VIEW
    NEW YORK,RANDOM HOUSE,1966
    013,

WALLER HORACE
    LIVINGSTONE DAVID   WALLER HORACE   EDS
    THE LAST JOURNALS OF DAVID LIVINGSTONE IN CENTRAL AFRICA.
    LONDON,J MURRAY,1874,2 VOLUMES
    027,

WALLERSTEIN I M
    WALLERSTEIN I M
    THE POLITICS OF INDEPENDENCE.
    NEW YORK,VINTAGE,1961
    056,076,

    WALLERSTEIN I M
    AFRICA-- THE POLITICS OF UNITY.
    NEW YORK,RANDOM HOUSE,1967
    002,079,080,097,

    WALLERSTEIN I M   ED
    SOCIAL CHANGE, THE COLONIAL SITUATION.
    NEW YORK,JOHN WILEY,1966
    037,038,053,

    WALLERSTEIN I M
    ETHNICITY AND NATIONAL INTEGRATION IN WEST AFRICA
    CAHIERS D'ETUDES AFRICAINES 3 OCTOBER 1960 PP 129-139
    004,007,057,

    WALLERSTEIN I M
    VOLUNTARY ASSOCIATIONS.
    IN JAMES S COLEMAN AND CARL ROSBERG (EDS),POLITICAL
    PARTIES AND NATIONAL INTEGRATION IN TROPICAL AFRICA,
    BERKELEY,UNIVERSITY OF CALIFORNIA PRESS,1964,PP 318-339
    046,

    WALLERSTEIN I M
    THE DECLINE OF THE PARTY IN SINGLE-PARTY AFRICAN STATES.
    IN J LAPALOMBARA AND M WEINER, POLITICAL PARTIES AND
    POLITICAL DEVELOPMENT, PRINCETON, PRINCETON UNIVERSITY
    PRESS, 1966, PP 201-216
    061,

    WALLERSTEIN I M
    PAN-AFRICANISM AS PROTEST.
    IN MORTON A KAPLAN, THE REVOLUTION IN WORLD POLITICS,
    NEW YORK, JOHN WILEY, 1962, PP 137-151

079,

WALLERSTEIN I M
    WALLERSTEIN I M
    LARGER UNITIES-- PAN-AFRICANISM AND REGIONAL FEDERATIONS.
    IN PETER J MCEWAN AND ROBERT B SUTCLIFFE (EDS),MODERN AFRICA,
    NEW YORK,THOMAS CROWELL,1965,PP 217-228
    079,

    WALLERSTEIN I M
    FROM NIXON- IS AMERICAS OUTMODED POLICY TOWARDS A
    CHANGING AFRICA ABOUT TO CROSS A NEW FRONTIER
    AFRICA REPORT NOVEMBER 1969 PP 28-30
    083,

    WALLERSTEIN I M
    THE POLITICAL IDEOLOGY OF THE PDG.
    PRESENCE AFRICAINE 12 JANUARY 1962 PP 30-41
    060,115-04,

WALSH ANNMARIE H
    WILLIAMS BABATUNDE WALSH ANNMARIE H
    URBAN GOVERNMENT FOR METROPOLITAN LAGOS.
    NEW YORK, PRAEGER, 1967
    128-05,

WALSHE A P
    WALSHE A P
    THE ORIGIN OF AFRICAN POLITICAL CONSCIOUSNESS IN SOUTH
    AFRICA
    JOURNAL OF MODERN AFRICAN STUDIES 7 1969 PP 583-610
    032,089,

WARD W E F
    WARD W E F
    THE ROYAL NAVY AND THE SLAVERS.
    NEW YORK, INTERNATIONAL UNIVERSITY BOOKSELLERS, INC., 1969
    030,

    WARD W E F
    A HISTORY OF GHANA.
    LONDON, ALLEN AND UNWIN, 1966
    114-02,

WARMELO N J V
    MEINHOF CARL   TRANSLATED BY   WARMELO N J V
    INTRODUCTION TO THE PHONOLOGY OF BANTU LANGUAGES.
    BERLIN,DIETRICH REINER/ ERNST VOHSEN,1932
    011,

WARMINGTON W A
    ARDENER EDWIN   ARDENER S   WARMINGTON W A
    PLANTATION AND VILLAGE IN THE CAMEROONS.
    LONDON,OXFORD UNIVERSITY PRESS,1960
    047,104-01,

    WARMINGTON W A
    A WEST AFRICAN TRADE UNION.
    LONDON,OXFORD UNIVERSITY PRESS,1960
    A CASE STUDY OF THE CAMEROONS DEVELOPMENT CORPORATION

WORKERS' UNIONS AND ITS RELATIONS WITH THE EMPLOYERS
073,104-08,

WARMINGTON W A
WELLS F A   WARMINGTON W A
STUDIES IN INDUSTRIALIZATION--NIGERIA AND THE CAMEROONS.
LONDON, OXFORD UNIVERSITY PRESS, 1962
071,104-08,128-08,

WARREN
HOWE RUSSELL WARREN
BLACK AFRICA-- AFRICA SOUTH OF THE SAHARA FROM PRE-
HISTORY TO INDEPENDENCE.
CHICAGO, WALKER, 1967
036,076,

WARREN A
GROVE A T   WARREN A
QUATERNARY LANDFORMS AND THE CLIMATE ON THE SOUTH SIDE OF
THE SAHARA
GEOGRAPHICAL JOURNAL 134 1968 PP 194-208
017,

WARREN M W
WARREN M W   RUBIN N
DAMS IN AFRICA-AN INTERDISCIPLINARY STUDY OF MAN-MADE LAKES
IN AFRICA
LONDON, FRANK CASS, 1968
075,

WARREN ROBERT PENN
WARREN ROBERT PENN
WHO SPEAKS FOR THE NEGRO.
NEW YORK, HARCOURT, BRACE AND WORLD, 1965
094,

WASHBURN S L
DEVORE IRVEN   WASHBURN S L
BABOON ECOLOGY AND HUMAN EVOLUTION.
IN F CLARK HOWELL AND FRANCOIS BOURLIERE (EDS.), AFRICAN
ECOLOGY AND HUMAN EVOLUTION, CHICAGO, ALDINE, 1966,
PP 335-367
018,

WASHBURN S L
THE STUDY OF RACE
AMERICAN ANTHROPOLOGIST 65 1963 PP 521-531
018,

WASSERMAN B
WASSERMAN B
THE ASHANTI WAR OF 1900-A STUDY OF CULTURAL CONFLICT
AFRICA 31 1961 PP 167-179
034,

WASSING R S
WASSING R S
AFRICAN ART--ITS BACKGROUND AND TRADITIONS
NEW YORK, HARRY N ABRAMS, 1968
014,

WASTBERG PER
    WASTBERG PER   ED
    THE WRITER IN MODERN AFRICA-AFRICAN-SCANDANAVIAN WRITER≠S
    CONFERENCE,STOCKHOLM 1967
    NEW YORK,AFRICANA PUBLISHING CORPORATION AND SCANDANAVIAN
    INSTITUTE OF AFRICAN STUDIES,1969
    090,

WATERMAN RICHARD A
    WATERMAN RICHARD A
    AFRICAN INFLUENCE ON THE MUSIC OF THE AMERICAS
    IN SOL TAX,ED ,ACCULTURATION IN THE AMERICAS,CHICAGO,
    UNIVERSITY OF CHICAGO PRESS,1952
    015,030,

WATSON WILLIAM
    WATSON WILLIAM
    TRIBAL COHESION IN A MONEY ECONOMY.
    MANCHESTER,UNIVERSITY OF MANCHESTER PRESS,1958
    010,

WATT W M
    WATT W M   ED
    RELIGION IN AFRICA
    EDINBURGH,CENTRE OF AFRICAN STUDIES,UNIVERSITY OF EDINBURGH,
    1964
    050,

WATTERS R F
    WATTERS R F
    THE NATURE OF SHIFTING CULTIVATION--A REVIEW OF RECENT
    RESEARCH.
    PACIFIC VIEWPOINT 1 MARCH 1960 PP 59-99
    010,070,

WAUTHIER CLAUDE
    WAUTHIER CLAUDE
    THE LITERATURE AND THOUGHT OF MODERN AFRICA.
    LONDON, PALL MALL, 1966 (NEW YORK, PRAEGER, 1967)
    090,091,

WAYLAND E J
    WAYLAND E J
    THE AFRICAN BULGE
    GEOGRAPHICAL JOURNAL 75 1930 PP 381-383
    017,

WEBER MAX
    WEBER MAX
    THE SOCIOLOGY OF RELIGION.
    BOSTON, BEACON PRESS, 1963
    013,

WEBSTER J B
    AJAYI J F ADE   WEBSTER J B
    THE EMERGENCE OF A NEW ELITE IN AFRICA
    IN CHAPTER 9 IN J C ANENE AND GODFREY BROWN,AFRICA IN THE
    NINETEENTH AND TWENTIETH CENTURIES,LONDON,NELSON,AND IBADAN
    UNIVERSITY PRESS,1966

044,

WEBSTER J B
    WEBSTER J B
    THE AFRICAN CHURCHES AMONG THE YORUBA   1888-1922.
    OXFORD, CLARENDON PRESS, 1964
    051,128-03,

WEBSTER JOHN B
    BROWN EDWARD E   WEBSTER JOHN B
    A BIBLIOGRAPHY ON POLITICS AND GOVERNMENT IN KENYA.
    NEW YORK, SYRACUSE UNIVERSITY PROGRAM OF EASTERN AFRICAN
    STUDIES, 1965
    117-12,

    KURIA LUCAS   WEBSTER JOHN B
    A BIBLIOGRAPHY ON ANTHROPOLOGY AND SOCIOLOGY IN TANZANIA AND
    EAST AFRICA.
    NEW YORK, SYRACUSE UNIVERSITY PROGRAM OF EASTERN AFRICAN
    STUDIES, 1966
    136-12,

    KURIA LUCAS   RAGHEB ISIS   WEBSTER JOHN B
    A BIBLIOGRAPHY ON POLITICS AND GOVERNMENT IN UGANDA.
    COMPILED BY LUCAS KURIA, ISIS RAGHEB AND JOHN WEBSTER, NEW
    YORK, SYRACUSE UNIVERSITY PROGRAM OF EASTERN AFRICAN STUDIES
      1965
    139-12,

    WEBSTER JOHN B   ET AL
    A SUPPLEMENT TO A BIBLIOGRAPHY ON BECHUANALAND.
    SYRACUSE, NEW YORK, MAXWELL SCHOOL OF PUBLIC AFFAIRS, PRO-
    GRAM OF EASTERN AFRICAN STUDIES, AUGUST 12, 1968
    102-12,

    WEBSTER JOHN B
    THE CONSTITUTIONS OF BURUNDI MALAGASY AND RWANDA.
    SYRACUSE, NEW YORK, MAXWELL GRADUATE SCHOOL OF PUBLIC AFFAIRS,
    THE PROGRAM OF EASTERN STUDIES, NO. 3, FEB., 1964
    066,103-07,121-07,129-07,

    WEBSTER JOHN B
    THE POLITICAL DEVELOPMENT OF RWANDA AND BURUNDI.
    SYRACUSE,NEW YORK,MAXWELL GRADUATE SCHOOL OF PUBLIC AFFAIRS
    PROGRAM OF EASTERN AFRICAN STUDIES, NO. 16, JUNE, 1966
    103-07,129-07,

    WEBSTER JOHN B
    A BIBLIOGRAPHY ON KENYA.
    NEW YORK, SYRACUSE UNIVERSITY PROGRAM OF EASTERN AFRICAN
    STUDIES, 1967
    117-12,

    WEBSTER JOHN B   MOHOME PAULUS
    A BIBLIOGRAPHY ON LESOTHO.
    NEW YORK, SYRACUSE UNIVERSITY PROGRAM OF EASTERN AFRICAN
    STUDIES, 1968
    9, AUGUST, 1968

WEEKS GEORGE

WEEKS GEORGE
   THE ARMIES OF AFRICA.
   AFRICA REPORT 9 JANUARY 1964 PP 4-21
   064,

WEGENER ALFRED
   WEGENER ALFRED
   THE ORIGIN OF CONTINENTS AND OCEANS(TRANS BY JOHN BIRAM)
   NEW YORK, DOVER, 1966 (ORIGINALLY PUBLISHED IN GERMAN IN 1929)
   017,

WEIGERT KATHLEEN M
   WEIGERT KATHLEEN M   RIGGS ROBERT E
   AFRICA AND UNITED NATIONS ELECTIONS--AN AGGREGATE DATA
   ANALYSIS.
   INTERNATIONAL ORGANIZATION, VOL. XXIII, NO. 1, WINTER, 1969,
   PP. 1-17
   081,

WEILER HANS N
   WEILER HANS N
   ERZIEHUNGSWESEN AND POLITIK IN NIGERIA, EDUCATION AND
   POLITICS IN NIGERIA (BILINGUAL EDITION)
   FREIBURG IM BREISGAU, VERLAG ROMBACH, 1964
   042,043,128-03,

WEINER MYRON
   WEINER MYRON
   POLITICAL MODERNIZATION AND EVOLUTIONARY THEORY.
   IN HR BARRINGER, GI BLANKSTEN, RW MACK, SOCIAL CHANGE IN
   DEVELOPING AREAS, CAMBRIDGE, MASS, SCHENKMAN, 1965,
   PP 102-111
   037,

   WEINER MYRON   LAPALOMBARA JOSEPH   EDS
   POLITICAL PARTIES AND POLITICAL DEVELOPMENT.
   PRINCETON, PRINCETON UNIVERSITY PRESS 1966
   061,

   WEINER MYRON
   POLITICAL INTEGRATION AND POLITICAL DEVELOPMENT CHAPTER 15.
   IN JASON L FINKLE AND RICHARD W GABLE, POLITICAL
   DEVELOPMENT AND SOCIAL CHANGE, NEW YORK, JOHN WILEY, 1966
   057,

   WEINER MYRON
   URBANIZATION AND POLITICAL PROTEST.
   CIVILISATIONS, VOL. XVII, 1967, PP. 44-53
   047,

   WEINER MYRON   ED
   MODERNIZATION-THE DYNAMICS OF GROWTH
   NEW YORK, BASIC BOOKS, 1966
   037,

WEINSTEIN BRIAN
   WEINSTEIN BRIAN
   THE FRENCH COMMUNITY-- DOES IT EXIST .
   CURRENT HISTORY 50 296 APRIL 1966 PP 214-220
   082,

WEINSTEIN BRIAN
    WEINSTEIN BRIAN
    GABON--NATION-BUILDING ON THE OGOOUE.
    CAMBRIDGE, MASSACHUSETTS INSTITUTE OF TECHNOLOGY PRESS, 1966
    048,057,112-06,

    WEINSTEIN BRIAN
    GABON--A BIBLIOGRAPHIC ESSAY.
    AFRICANA NEWSLETTER, VOL. 1, NOV. 4, 1963
    112-12,

WEISS CHARLES JR
    WEISS CHARLES JR
    A BIOPHYSICIST LOOKS AT SCIENCE IN AFRICA.
    AFRICA REPORT, JANUARY 1968, P. 13
    075,

WEISS HERBERT
    WEISS HERBERT
    POLITICAL PROTEST IN THE CONGO--THE PARTI SOLIDAIRE AFRICAIN
    DURING THE INDEPENDENCE STRUGGLE.
    PRINCETON, PRINCETON UNIVERSITY PRESS, 1967
    061,108-07,

WELBOURN F B
    WELBOURN F B
    EAST AFRICAN REBELS-- A STUDY OF SOME INDEPENDENT CHURCHES.
    LONDON,SUDAN CHRISTIAN MISSION PRESS,1961
    051,

    OGOT BETHWELL A   WELBOURN F B
    A PLACE TO FEEL AT HOME--A STUDY OF TWO INDEPENDENT CHURCHES
    IN WESTERN KENYA.
    LONDON, OXFORD UNIVERSITY PRESS, 1966
    051,117-03,

WELCH CLAUDE E
    WELCH CLAUDE E
    SOLDIER AND STATE IN AFRICA.
    EVANSTON, NORTHWESTERN UNIVERSITY PRESS, 1970
    064,

    WELCH CLAUDE E
    SOLDIER AND STATE IN AFRICA.
    JOURNAL OF MODERN AFRICAN STUDIES 5 NOVEMBER 1967 PP 305-322
    064,

    WELCH CLAUDE E   ED
    POLITICAL MODERNIZATION-- A READER IN COMPARATIVE POLITICAL
    CHANGE.
    BELMONT, CALIFORNIA,WADSWORTH PUBLISHING COMPANY,1967
    076,

    WELCH CLAUDE E
    DREAM OF UNITY-PAN-AFRICANISM AND POLITICAL UNIFICATION IN
    WEST AFRICA
    ITHACA,CORNELL UNIVERSITY PRESS,1966
    054,059,079,

WELLINGTON J H
   WELLINGTON J H
   SOUTH WEST AFRICA AND ITS HUMAN ISSUES.
   LONDON AND NEW YORK, OXFORD UNIVERSITY PRESS, 1967
   081,

WELLS F A
   WELLS F A   WARMINGTON W A
   STUDIES IN INDUSTRIALIZATION--NIGERIA AND THE CAMEROONS.
   LONDON, OXFORD UNIVERSITY PRESS, 1962
   071,104-08,128-08,

WELSCH ERWIN K
   WELSCH ERWIN K
   THE NEGRO IN THE UNITED STATES A RESEARCH GUIDE.
   BLOOMINGTON, INDIANA UNIVERSITY PRESS, 1965
   030,

WENDORF FRED
   WENDORF FRED   ED
   THE PREHISTORY OF NUBIA.
   DALLAS, SMU, 1968
   020,

WERE GIDEON S
   WERE GIDEON S
   A HISTORY OF THE ABALUYIA OF WESTERN KENYA.
   KENYA, EAST AFRICAN PUBLISHING HOUSE, 1967
   117-01,

WESCOTT R W
   WESCOTT R W
   ANCIENT EGYPT AND MODERN AFRICA
   JOURNAL OF AFRICAN HISTORY 2 1961 PP 311-321
   020,

WESLEY CHARLES H
   WESLEY CHARLES H
   THE STRUGGLE FOR THE RECOGNITION OF HAITI AND LIBERIA AS
   INDEPENDENT REPUBLICS.
   THE JOURNAL OF NEGRO HISTORY II 1917 PP 369-383
   029,119-02,

WEST ROBERT L
   WEST ROBERT L
   LOOKING AT AFRICAN DEVELOPMENT--AN ANNOTATED OVERVIEW.
   AFRICAN REPORT, MAY, 1968, P. 58
   073,

WESTERMANN D
   WESTERMANN D   BRYAN M A
   LANGUAGES OF WEST AFRICA.
   LONDON, OXFORD UNIVERSITY PRESS, 1952
   011,

   WESTERMANN D
   AFRICA AND CHRISTIANITY.
   LONDON, OXFORD UNIVERSITY PRESS, 1937
   050,

BAUMANN H   WESTERMANN D
LES PEUPLES LES CIVILISATIONS DE L'AFRIQUE NOIRE (THE
PEOPLES AND THE CIVILIZATIONS OF BLACK AFRICA).
PARIS, PAYOT, 1962
003,

WESTERMANN D
    WESTERMANN D
    DIE WESTLICHEN SUDANSPRACHEN (THE LANGUAGES OF THE WESTERN
    SUDAN).
    BERLIN, IN KOMMISSION BEI W. DE GRUYTER AND CO, 1927
    011,

    WESTERMANN D
    DIE SUDANSPRACHEN (LANGUAGES OF THE SUDAN).
    HAMBURG, L FRIEDERICSEN AND CO, 1911
    011,

WHARTON CLIFTON R
    WHARTON CLIFTON R   ED
    SUBSISTENCE AGRICULTURE AND ECONOMIC DEVELOPMENT
    CHICAGO, ALDINE, 1969
    010,070,

WHEARE JOAN
    WHEARE JOAN
    THE NIGERIAN LEGISLATIVE COUNCIL.
    LONDON, FABER, 1950
    061,128-07,

WHEATLEY PAUL
    WHEATLEY PAUL
    THE LAND OF ZANJ-- EXEGETICAL NOTES ON CHINESE KNOWLEDGE OF
    EAST AFRICA PRIOR TO AD 1500.
    IN ROBERT W STEEL AND R MANSELL PROTHERO (EDS), GEOGRAPHERS
    AND THE TROPICS-- LIVERPOOL ESSAYS, LONDON, LONGMANS,
    1964, PP 139-188
    023,

WHEELER DOUGLAS L
    WHEELER DOUGLAS L   PELISSIER RENE
    ANGOLA.
    LONDON, PALL MALL PRESS, 1970
    087,144-11,

WHEELER ROBERT E
    WHEELER ROBERT E
    ARCHAEOLOGY FROM THE EARTH.
    LONDON, OXFORD UNIVERSITY PRESS, 1954
    018,

WHEN PERCY
    WHEN PERCY
    THE AFRICAN HUSBANDMAN.
    IN R FIRTH THEMES IN ECONOMIC ANTHROPOLOGY, LONDON,
    TAVISTOCK, 1967
    010,070,

WHETHAM EDITH H
    WHETHAM EDITH H   CURRIE JEAN I   EDS

READINGS IN THE APPLIED ECONOMICS OF AFRICA.
LONDON, CAMBRIDGE UNIVERSITY PRESS, 1, 1967
073,

WHETHAM EDITH H
   WHETHAM EDITH H   CURRIE JEAN I   EDS
   READINGS IN THE APPLIED ECONOMICS OF AFRICA.
   LONDON, CAMBRIDGE UNIVERSITY PRESS, 2, 1967,
   073,128-08,

   WHETHAM EDITH H   CURRIE JEAN I
   THE ECONOMICS OF AFRICAN COUNTRIES.
   LONDON AND NEW YORK, INTERNATIONAL UNIVERSITY BOOKSELLERS,
   INC., 1969
   073,

WHITAKER C S
   WHITAKER C S
   A DYSRHYTHMIC PROCESS OF POLITICAL CHANGE.
   WORLD POLITICS, XIX, NO. 2, JANUARY 1967, PP. 190-217
   065,

   WHITAKER C S
   THE POLITICS OF TRADITION-CONTINUITY AND CHANGE IN NORTHERN
   NIGERIA
   PRINCETON,NEW JERSEY,PRINCETON UNIVERSITY PRESS, 1970
   061,128-07,

   WHITAKER C S   SKLAR RICHARD L
   NIGERIA.
   IN G.M. CARTER (ED),NATIONAL UNITY AND REGIONALISM IN EIGHT
   AFRICAN STATES. ITHACA, CORNELL UNIVERSITY PRESS, 1966
   065,128-06,

   WHITAKER C S
   NIGERIA.
   IN COLEMAN S. AND ROSBERG, C.G. (EDS),POLITICAL PARTIES AND
   NATIONAL INTEGRATION IN TROPICAL AFRICA, LOS ANGELES,
   UNIVERSITY OF CALIFORNIA PRESS, 1964

WHITAKER PHILIP
   WHITAKER PHILIP
   THE WESTERN REGION OF NIGERIA CHAPTER 3.
   IN W J MACKENZIE AND KENNETH ROBINSON, FIVE ELECTIONS IN
   AFRICA, LONDON, OXFORD UNIVERSITY PRESS, 1960
   063,

WHITE C M N
   WHITE C M N
   THE ETHNO-HISTORY OF THE UPPER ZAMBEZI.
   AFRICAN STUDIES 21 1962 PP 10-27
   025,

   WHITE C M N
   SOME PROBLEMS OF THE CLASSIFICATION OF TRIBAL STRUCTURES.
   IN R J APTHORPE,ED., FROM TRIBAL RULE TO MODERN GOVERNMENT,
   LUSAKA, RHODES-LIVINGSTONE INSTITUTE, 1959, PP 181-186
   009,

WHITELEY W H

WHITELEY W H
SWAHILI—THE RISE OF A NATIONAL LANGUAGE
NEW YORK, BARNES AND NOBLE, 1969
023,049,

WHITELEY W H
    WHITELEY W H   MULI M G
    PRACTICAL INTRODUCTION TO KAMBA.
    LONDON, OXFORD UNIVERSITY PRESS, 1962
    011,117-01,

WHITEMAN K
    WHITEMAN K
    FRANCE'S YEAR IN AFRICA.
    IN LEGUM AND DRYSDALE, 1969, P. 27-31
    082,

WHITHAM DAVID
    AMARTEIFIO G W   BUTCHER D A P   WHITHAM DAVID
    TEMA MANHEAN--A STUDY OF RESETTLEMENT.
    GHANA, GHANA UNIVERSITIES PRESS, 1966
    092,114-05,

WHITTEN NORMAN E
    WHITTEN NORMAN E   SZWED JOHN F   EDS
    AFRO-AMERICAN ANTHROPOLOGY
    NEW YORK, THE FREE PRESS, 1970
    030,

WHITTLESEY DERWENT
    WHITTLESEY DERWENT
    BRITISH AND FRENCH COLONIAL TECHNIQUE IN WEST AFRICA.
    IN PHILIP W QUIGG (ED.), AFRICA, NEW YORK, PRAEGER, 1964
    PP 57-70
    035,

    WHITTLESEY DERWENT
    KANO A SUDANESE METROPOLIS.
    GEOGRAPHICAL REVIEW 27 APRIL 1937 PP 177-200
    045,

WICKERT FREDERIC R
    WICKERT FREDERIC R   ED
    READINGS IN AFRICAN PSYCHOLOGY FROM FRENCH LANGUAGE SOURCES.
    EAST LANSING, MICHIGAN STATE UNIVERSITY PRESS, 1967
    039,040,098,

WIDSTRAND CARL
    WIDSTRAND CARL   ED
    AFRICAN BOUNDARY PROBLEMS
    UPPSALA, THE SCANDANAVIAN INSTITUTE OF AFRICAN STUDIES; AND NEW
    YORK, AFRICANA PUBLISHING CORPORATION, 1969
    059,078,080,

WIEDNER DONALD
    WIEDNER DONALD
    A HISTORY OF AFRICA SOUTH OF THE SAHARA.
    NEW YORK, RANDOM HOUSE, 1962
    036,

WILKS IVOR
    WILKS IVOR
    ASHANTI GOVERNMENT, IN DARYLL FORDE AND P M KABERRY (EDS)
    WEST AFRICAN KINGDOMS IN THE NINETEENTH CENTURY.
    LONDON, OXFORD UNIVERSITY PRESS, 1967
    026,038,114-01,

WILKS IVOR
    PRIESTLEY MARGARET WILKS IVOR
    THE ASHANTI KINGS IN THE EIGHTEENTH CENTURY-- A REVISED
    CHRONOLOGY.
    THE JOURNAL OF AFRICAN HISTORY 1 1960 PP 83-92
    026,114-02,

    WILKS IVOR
    THE RISE OF THE AKWAMU EMPIRE 1650-1710.
    TRANSACTIONS OF THE HISTORICAL SOCIETY OF GHANA 3 1957
    PP 99-136
    026,114-02,

    WILKS IVOR
    AKAMU AND OTUBLOHUM-- AN EIGHTEENTH CENTURY AKAN
    MARRIAGE ARRANGEMENT.
    AFRICA 29 1959 PP 391-404
    026,114-01,

    WILKS IVOR
    A NOTE ON THE TRADITIONAL HISTORY OF MAMPONG.
    TRANSACTIONS OF THE HISTORICAL SOCIETY OF GHANA 4 1960
    PP 26-29
    026,114-02,

    WILKS IVOR
    THE NORTHERN FACTOR IN ASHANTI HISTORY.
    LEGON, INSTITUTE OF AFRICAN STUDIES, UNIVERSITY COLLEGE OF
    GHANA, 1961
    026,114-02,

    WILKS IVOR
    THE POSITION OF MUSLIMS IN METROPOLITAN ASHANTI IN THE EARLY
    NINETEENTH CENTURY.
    IN LEWIS, ISLAM IN TROPICAL AFRICA, LONDON, OXFORD UNIVERSITY
    PRESS, 1966, P. 318-341
    114-03,

WILLAME
    WILLAME JEAN-CLAUDE
    MILITARY INTERVENTION IN THE CONGO.
    AFRICA REPORT 11 NOVEMBER 1966 PP 41-45
    064,108-06,

    WILLAME JEAN-CLAUDE
    CONGO-KINSHASA- GENERAL MOBUTU AND TWO POLITICAL
    GENERATIONS.
    IN CLAUDE WELCH (ED), SOLDIER AND STATE IN AFRICA, EVANSTON,
    NORTHWESTERN UNIVERSITY PRESS, 1970
    064,

WILLETT FRANK
    WILLETT FRANK

IFE IN THE HISTORY OF WEST AFRICAN SCULPTURE.
NEW YORK MCGRAW HILL 1967
014,128-01,

WILLETT FRANK
    WILLETT FRANK
    ARCHAEOLOGY IN AFRICA.
    IN CARTER, GWENDOLEN M. AND ANN PADEN (EDS), EXPANDING
    HORIZONS IN AFRICAN STUDIES, EVANSTON, NORTHWESTERN
    UNIVERSITY PRESS, 1969, PP. 91-110
    036,100,

    WILLETT FRANK
    INVESTIGATIONS AT OLD OYO. 1956-1957-- AN INTERIM REPORT.
    JOURNAL OF THE HISTORICAL SOCIETY OF NIGERIA 2 1960 PP 57-77
    026,128-02,

    WILLETT FRANK
    IFE AND ITS ARCHAEOLOGY.
    THE JOURNAL OF AFRICAN HISTORY 1 1960 PP 231-248
    014,020,026,128-01,

    WILLETT FRANK   PICTON J
    ON THE IDENTIFICATION OF INDIVIDUAL CARVERS, A STUDY OF
    ANCESTOR SHRINE CARVINGS FROM OWO. NIGERIA.
    MAN 2·1967
    014,128-01,

WILLIAMS
    WILLIAMS GEOFFREY J
    A BIBLIOGRAPHY OF SIERRA LEONE
    NEW YORK, AFRICANA PUBLISHING CORPORATION, 1969
    131-12,

WILLIAMS BABATUNDE
    WILLIAMS BABATUNDE   WALSH ANNMARIE H
    URBAN GOVERNMENT FOR METROPOLITAN LAGOS.
    NEW YORK, PRAEGER, 1967
    128-05,

WILLIAMS E
    WILLIAMS E
    CAPITALISM AND SLAVERY
    CHAPEL HILL, UNIVERSITY OF NORTH CAROLINA PRESS, 1944
    028,

WILLIAMS G MENNEN
    WILLIAMS G MENNEN
    DIPLOMATIC RAPPORT BETWEEN AFRICA AND THE UNITED STATES.
    ANNALS OF THE AMERICAN ACADEMY OF POLITICAL AND SOCIAL SCI-
    ENCE 354 JULY 1964 PP 54-64
    083,

WILLIAMS J W
    WILLIAMS J W
    THE ECONOMY OF GHANA CHAPTER 6.
    IN CALVIN B HOOVER, ECONOMIC SYSTEMS OF THE COMMONWEALTH,
    DURHAM, DUKE UNIVERSITY PRESS, 1962, PP 238-261
    073,114-08,

WILLIAMS P
  WILLIAMS P
  THE COST AND FINANCE OF EDUCATION CHAPTER 27.
  IN EDITH WHETHAM AND JEAN CURRIE (EDS.), READINGS IN THE
  APPLIED ECONOMICS OF AFRICA, LONDON, CAMBRIDGE UNIVERSITY
  PRESS, 2, 1967, PP 141-148
  074,

WILLIAMS S
  WILLIAMS S
  START-UP OF A TEXTILE INDUSTRY CHAPTER 11.
  IN EDITH WHETHAM AND JEAN CURRIE (EDS.), READINGS IN THE
  APPLIED ECONOMICS OF AFRICA, LONDON, CAMBRIDGE UNIVERSITY
  PRESS, 1, 1967, PP 114-125
  071,

WILLIAMSON
  WILLIAMSON SIDNEY G
  AKAN RELIGION AND THE CHRISTIAN FAITH.
  GHANA, GHANA UNIVERSITIES PRESS, 1965
  050,114-03,

WILLIS JOHN R
  WILLIS JOHN R   ED
  STUDIES ON THE HISTORY OF ISLAM IN WEST AFRICA,(3 VOLS)
  I--THE CULTIVATORS OF ISLAM
  II--THE EVOLUTION OF ISLAMIC INSTITUTIONS
  III--THE GROWTH OF ARABIC LITERATURE.
  NEW YORK, INTERNATIONAL UNIVERSITY BOOKSELLERS (FORTHCOMING)
  021,

  WILLIS JOHN R
  JIHAD FI SABIL ALLAH-ITS DOCTRINAL BASIS IN ISLAM AND SOME
  ASPECTS OF ITS EVOLUTION IN NINETEENTH CENTURY WEST AFRICA
  JOURNAL OF AFRICAN HISTORY 8 1967 PP 383-394
  021,

WILLIS R G
  WILLIS R G
  THE FIPA AND RELATED PEOPLES OF SOUTH-WEST TANZANIA AND
  NORTH-EAST ZAMBIA
  LONDON,INTERNATIONAL AFRICAN INSTITUTE,1966
  136-01,

WILSON GODFREY
  WILSON GODFREY   WILSON MONICA
  THE ANALYSIS OF SOCIAL CHANGE-BASED ON OBSERVATIONS IN
  CENTRAL AFRICA
  CAMBRIDGE,CAMBRIDGE UNIVERSITY PRESS,F145,NEW EDITION,1968
  037,038,048,

  WILSON GODFREY
  THE NYAKYUSA OF SOUTH-WESTERN TANGANYIKA.
  IN E. COLSON AND M. GLICKMAN (EDS), SEVEN TRIBES OF BRITISH
  CENTRAL AFRICA, MANCHESTER, UNIVERSITY OF MANCHESTER PRESS,
  1951, PP. 253-291
  136-01,

WILSON GORDON
  WILSON GORDON

MOMBASA--A MODERN COLONIAL MUNICIPALITY.
IN A.W. SOUTHALL (ED),SOCIAL CHANGE IN MODERN AFRICA,
LONDON, OXFORD UNIVERSITY PRESS, 1961
117-05,

WILSON J TUZO
    WILSON J TUZO
    CONTINENTAL DRIFT.
    SCIENTIFIC AMERICAN 208 NO 4 APRIL 1963 PP 86-100
    017,

WILSON MONICA
    WILSON GODFREY   WILSON MONICA
    THE ANALYSIS OF SOCIAL CHANGE-BASED ON OBSERVATIONS IN
    CENTRAL AFRICA
    CAMBRIDGE,CAMBRIDGE UNIVERSITY PRESS,F145,NEW EDITION,1968
    037,038,048,

    WILSON MONICA   THOMPSON LEONARD   EDS
    THE OXFORD HISTORY OF SOUTH AFRICA. VOL I   SOUTH AFRICA
    TO 1870
    LONDON, OXFORD UNIVERSITY PRESS, 1970
    031,032,132-02,

    WILSON MONICA
    GOOD COMPANY-A STUDY OF NYAKYUSU AGE VILLAGES
    LONDON,OXFORD UNIVERSITY PRESS,1951
    009,136-01.

WINANS EDGAR V
    WINANS EDGAR V
    SHAMBALA-THE CONSTITUTION OF A TRADITIONAL STATE
    BERKELEY,UNIVERSITY OF CALIFORNIA PRESS,1962
    136-01,

WINDER R BAYLEY
    WINDER R BAYLEY
    THE LEBANESE IN WEST AFRICA.
    COMPARATIVE STUDIES IN SOCIETY AND HISTORY 4 APRIL 1962
    PP 296-333
    046,

    WINDER R BAYLEY
    THE LEBANESE IN WEST AFRICA.
    IMMIGRANTS AND ASSOCIATIONS, FALLERS, L.A. (ED.), 1967,
    PP. 103-154
    086,

WINGARD PETER
    WINGARD PETER
    PROBLEMS OF THE MEDIA OF INSTRUCTION IN SOME UGANDA SCHOOL
    CLASSES--A PRELIMINARY SURVEY.
    IN JOHN SPENCER (ED),LANGUAGE IN AFRICA, PAPERS OF THE
    LEVERHULME CONFERENCE ON UNIVERSITIES AND THE LANGUAGE
    PROBLEMS OF TROPICAL AFRICA, CAMBRIDGE, CAMBRIDGE UNIVERSITY
    PRESS, 1963
    139-03,

WINGERT PAUL S
    WINGERT PAUL S

THE SCULPTURE OF NEGRO AFRICA.
NEW YORK, COLUMBIA UNIVERSITY PRESS, 1950
014,

WINGERT PAUL S
   WINGERT PAUL S
   PRIMITIVE ART-- ITS TRADITIONS AND STYLES.
   NEW YORK, OXFORD UNIVERSITY PRESS, 1962
   014,

WINSTON F D D
   WINSTON F D D
   GREENBERG'S CLASSIFICATION OF AFRICAN LANGUAGES.
   AFRICAN LANGUAGE STUDIES 7 PP 160-170 1966
   011,

WINTER E H
   MIDDLETON JOHN   WINTER E H   EDS
   WITCHCRAFT AND SORCERY IN EAST AFRICA
   NEW YORK, PRAEGER, 1963
   013,

WISEMAN HERBERT V
   WISEMAN HERBERT V
   POLITICAL SYSTEMS--SOME SOCIOLOGICAL APPROACHES.
   NEW YORK, PRAEGER. 1966
   009,061,

WISHLADE R L
   WISHLADE R L
   SECTARIANISM IN SOUTHERN NYASALAND.
   LONDON, OXFORD UNIVERSITY PRESS, 1965
   051,122-03,

WITHERELL JULIAN T
   WITHERELL JULIAN T
   OFFICIAL PUBLICATIONS OF THE FRENCH EQUATORIAL AFRICA,
   FRENCH CAMEROUNS AND TOGO, 1949-1958.
   WASHINGTON, LIBRARY OF CONGRESS, AFRICAN SECTION, 1964
   104-12,105-12,106-12,107-12,112-12,137-12,

WITTHUHN BURTON O
   WITTHUHN BURTON O
   THE SPATIAL INTEGRATION OF UGANDA AS EVIDENCED BY THE
   DIFFUSION OF POSTAL AGENCIES-1900-1965
   EAST LAKES GEOGRAPHER 4 1968 PP 5-20
   048,

WOLFF HANS
   WOLFF HANS
   INTELLIGIBILITY AND INTER-ETHNIC ATTITUDES.
   ANTHROPOLOGICAL LINGUISTICS MARCH 1959
   007,

   WOLFF HANS
   LANGUAGE, ETHNIC IDENTITY, AND SOCIAL CHANGE IN SOUTHERN
   NIGERIA.
   ANTHROPOLOGICAL LINGUISTICS JANUARY 1967
   006,128-03,

WOLPE HOWARD
    MELSON ROBERT   WOLPE HOWARD   EDS
    NIGERIA-MODERNIZATION AND THE POLITICS OF COMMUNALISM.
    EAST LANSING, MICHIGAN STATE UNIVERSITY PRESS, 1970
    006,065,128-03,

WOLSTENHOLME G
    WOLSTENHOLME G   O CONNOR M   EDS
    MAN AND AFRICA
    LONDON, J AND A CHURCHILL, 1965
    075,

WOOD DONALD S
    WOOD DONALD S
    THE PATTERN OF SETTLEMENT AND DEVELOPMENT IN LIBERIA.
    JOURNAL OF GEOGRAPHY, VOL. 62, 9, DECEMBER, 1963
    119-05,

WOOD ERIC W
    WOOD ERIC W
    THE IMPLICATIONS OF MIGRANT LABOUR FOR URBAN SOCIAL SYSTEMS
    IN AFRICA.
    CAHIERS D'ETUDES AFRICAINES, VOL. VIII, 29, 1968, PP. 5-31
    047,

WOOLF LEONARD
    WOOLF LEONARD
    EMPIRE AND COMMERCE IN AFRICA-A STUDY IN ECONOMIC
    IMPERIALISM
    LONDON, ALLEN UNWIN, 1968
    033,

WORTHINGTON E B
    WORTHINGTON E B
    SCIENCE IN THE DEVELOPMENT OF AFRICA.
    LONDON, COMMISSION FOR TECHNICAL COOPERATION IN AFRICA SOUTH
    OF THE SAHARA, 1958
    073,075,

WRIGHT JOHN
    WRIGHT JOHN
    LIBYA.
    NEW YORK, PRAEGER, 1969
    120-11,

WRIGHT RICHARD
    WRIGHT RICHARD
    BLACK POWER.
    NEW YORK, HARPER, 1954
    094,

WRIGHT STEPHEN G
    WRIGHT STEPHEN G
    A BIBLIOGRAPHY OF PRE-1963 PRINTED MATERIAL PRODUCED IN
    ETHIOPIA.
    ADDIS ABABA, INSTITUTE OF ETHIOPIAN STUDIES, HAILE SELASSIE
    I UNIVERSITY, 1964
    110-12,

WRIGLEY C.C.

WRIGLEY C.C.
SPECULATIONS ON THE ECONOMIC PREHISTORY OF AFRICA.
JOURNAL OF AFRICAN HISTORY 2 1960 PP 189-203
019,

WYNDHAM H A
WYNDHAM H A
THE ATLANTIC AND EMANCIPATION
LONDON, OXFORD UNIVERSITY PRESS, 1937
029,

WYNDHAM H A
THE ATLANTIC AND SLAVERY
LONDON, OXFORD UNIVERSITY PRESS, 1935
028,

X

X MALCOLM
X MALCOLM
THE AUTOBIOGRAPHY OF MALCOLM X.
NEW YORK, GROVE PRESS, 1965
094,095,

Y

YESUFU T M
YESUFU T M
THE SHORTAGE OF SKILLED LABOUR CHAPTER 12.

IN EDITH WHETHAM AND JEAN CURRIE (EDS.), READINGS IN THE
APPLIED ECONOMICS OF AFRICA, LONDON, CAMBRIDGE UNIVERSITY
PRESS, 1, 1967, PP 126-132
073,

YESUFU T M
YESUFU T M
AN INTRODUCTION TO INDUSTRIAL RELATIONS IN NIGERIA.
LONDON, OXFORD UNIVERSITY PRESS, 1962
071,128-08,

YOUNG CRAWFORD
ANDERSON CHARLES   VON DER MEHDEN FRED YOUNG CRAWFORD
ISSUES OF POLITICAL DEVELOPMENT.
ENGLEWOOD CLIFFS, N J, PRENTICE-HALL, 1967
002,

YOUNG CRAWFORD
POLITICS IN THE CONGO--DECOLONIZATION AND INDEPENDENCE.
PRINCETON, NEW JERSEY, PRINCETON UNIVERSITY PRESS, 1965
054,061,081,108-07,

YOUNG CRAWFORD
THE OBOTE REVOLUTION.
AFRICA REPORT 11 JUNE 1966 PP 8-14
064,139-06,

YOUNG CRAWFORD
THE CONGO REBELLION.
AFRICA REPORT 10 APRIL 1965 PP 6-11
064,081,108-06,

YOUNG ROLAND A
    YOUNG ROLAND A
    POLITICAL RESEARCH IN THE NEW AFRICAN NATIONS.
    THE AMERICAN BEHAVIORAL SCIENTIST APRIL 1962 PP 3-5
    100,

    YOUNG ROLAND A   FOSBROOKE H
    SMOKE IN THE HILLS-- POLITICAL TENSION IN THE MOROGORO
    DISTRICT OF TANGANYIKA.
    EVANSTON,ILLINOIS,NORTHWESTERN UNIVERSITY PRESS,1960
    (LAND AND POLITICS AMONG THE LUGURU OF TANGANYIKA,LONDON,
    ROUTLEDGE AND KEGAN PAUL,1960)
    067,136-03,

YUDELMAN M
    YUDELMAN M
    AFRICANS ON THE LAND-- ECONOMIC PROBLEMS OF AFRICAN
    AGRICULTURAL DEVELOPMENT IN SOUTHERN CENTRAL AND EAST
    AFRICA.
    CAMBRIDGE,HARVARD UNIVERSITY PRESS,1964
    070,

    YUDELMAN M
    SOME ASPECTS OF AFRICAN AGRICULTURAL DEVELOPMENT.
    IN E A G ROBINSON (ED.),ECONOMIC DEVELOPMENT FOR AFRICA
    SOUTH OF THE SAHARA, 1964.
    010,070,

Z

ZAHAN DOMINIQUE
ZAHAN DOMINIQUE
PROBLEMS SOCIAUX POSES PAR LA TRANSPLANTATION DES MOSSI SUR
LES TERRES IRRIGUEES DE L'OFFICE DU NIGER (SOCIAL PROBLEMS
POSED BY THE SHIFTING OF THE MOSSI TO THE IRRIGATED LANDS
OF THE NIGER OFFICE).
IN D BIEBUYCK (ED), AFRICAN AGRARIAN SYSTEMS, LONDON,
OXFORD UNIVERSITY PRESS, 1963, PP 392-403
070,

ZAHLAN A B
NADER CLAIRE   ZAHLAN A B   EDS
SCIENCE AND TECHNOLOGY IN DEVELOPING COUNTRIES
NEW YORK, CAMBRIDGE UNIVERSITY PRESS, 1969
075,

ZAKE S JOSHUA L
ZAKE S JOSHUA L
REVISION AND UNIFICATION OF AFRICAN LEGAL SYSTEMS--THE
UGANDA EXPERIENCE.
IN CARTER, GWENDOLEN M. AND ANN PADEN (EDS), EXPANDING
HORIZONS IN AFRICAN STUDIES, EVANSTON, NORTHWESTERN
UNIVERSITY PRESS, 1969, PP. 157-168
066, 100, 139-06,

ZARTMAN I WILLIAM
ZARTMAN I WILLIAM
INTERNATIONAL RELATIONS IN THE NEW AFRICA.
NEW JERSEY, PRENTICE-HALL, 1966
059,078,080,

ZARTMAN I WILLIAM
THE EEC S NEW DEAL WITH AFRICA
AFRICA REPORT 15 FEBRUARY 1970 PP 28-31
082,

ZARTMAN I WILLIAM
THE POLITICS OF BOUNDARIES IN NORTH AND WEST AFRICA.
JOURNAL OF MODERN AFRICAN STUDIES 8 AUGUST PP 155-173
059,

ZARTMAN I WILLIAM
GUINEA-- THE QUIET WAR GOES ON.
AFRICA REPORT 12 NOVEMBER 1967 PP 67-72
087,115-09,

ZARTMAN I WILLIAM
THE ALGERIAN ARMY IN POLITICS.
IN CLAUDE WELCH (ED), SOLDIER AND STATE IN AFRICA, EVANSTON,
NORTHWESTERN UNIVERSITY PRESS, 1970
064,

ZAVALLONI MARISA
KLINEBERG OTTO   ZAVALLONI MARISA
NATIONALISM AND TRIBALISM AMONG AFRICAN STUDENTS.

NEW YORK, HUMANITIES PRESS INC., 1969
096,

ZELINSKY W
    TREWARTHA G T   ZELINSKY W
    POPULATION PATTERNS IN TROPICAL AFRICA.
    ANNALS OF THE ASSOCIATION OF AMERICAN GEOGRAPHERS WASHINGTON
    VOL 44 JUNE 1954 PP 135-193
    069,074,

ZELL HANS M
    ZELL HANS M   ED
    THE LITERATURE OF AFRICA.
    NEW YORK, AFRICANA PUBLISHING CORPORATION, 1970
    090,

ZIVS S L
    ZIVS S L
    PROBLEMS OF THE ESTABLISHMENT OF NATIONAL LEGAL SYSTEMS IN
    AFRICAN COUNTRIES.
    II INTERNATIONAL CONGRESS OF AFRICANISTS, PAPERS PRESENTED
    BY THE USSR DELEGATION, DAKAR, 10 PAGES
    067,

ZOLBERG ARISTIDE R
    ZOLBERG ARISTIDE R
    CREATING POLITICAL ORDER-- THE PARTY STATES OF WEST AFRICA.
    NEW YORK, RAND-MCNALLY, 1966
    060,061,

    ZOLBERG ARISTIDE R
    PATTERNS OF NATIONAL INTEGRATION.
    THE JOURNAL OF MODERN AFRICAN STUDIES, 5, 4, 1967, PP 449-67
    055,058,116-06,123-06,

    COHEN RONALD   VANSINA JAN   ZOLBERG ARISTIDE R
    ORAL HISTORY IN AFRICA.
    EVANSTON,ILLINOIS, NORTHWESTERN UNIVERSITY, PROGRAM OF
    AFRICAN STUDIES. REPRINT SERIES, 2, NO.1 SEPTEMBER 1965
    012,099,

    ZOLBERG ARISTIDE R
    MILITARY INTERVENTION IN THE NEW STATES OF TROPICAL AFRICA--
    ELEMENTS OF COMPARATIVE ANALYSIS.
    HENRY BIENEN (ED), THE MILITARY INTERVENES, NEW YORK, THE
    RUSSELL SAGE FOUNDATION, 1968
    064,

    ZOLBERG ARISTIDE R
    THE STRUCTURE OF POLITICAL CONFLICT IN THE NEW STATES OF
    TROPICAL AFRICA.
    THE AMERICAN POLITICAL SCIENCE REVIEW, VOL. 62, NO. 1, MARCH
    1968, PP. 70-87
    064,

    ZOLBERG ARISTIDE R
    MASS PARTIES AND NATIONAL INTEGRATION--THE CASE OF IVORY
    COAST.
    JOURNAL OF POLITICS 25 FEBRUARY 1963 PP 36-48
    057,116-06,

ZOLBERG ARISTIDE R
    ZOLBERG ARISTIDE R
    ONE PARTY GOVERNMENT IN THE IVORY COAST.
    PRINCETON, PRINCETON UNIVERSITY PRESS, 1964 (AND 1969)
    058,061,116-06.

DATE DUE

7/6			
DEC 3 1972			